PACIFIC
NORTHWEST
HIKING

PACIFIC NORTHWEST HIKING

The Complete Guide to More Than 1,000 Hikes in Washington and Oregon

FOURTH EDITION

Ron C. Judd & Dan A. Nelson

AVALON
TRAVEL

FOGHORN OUTDOORS:
PACIFIC NORTHWEST HIKING
The Complete Guide to
More Than 1,000 Hikes in
Washington and Oregon

4th Edition

Ron C. Judd & Dan A. Nelson

Published by
Avalon Travel Publishing
1400 65th Street, Suite 250
Emeryville, CA 94608, USA
Avalon Travel Publishing is a
division of Avalon Publishing Group, Inc.

Please send all comments, corrections,
additions, amendments, and critiques to:

ⒻOGHORN OUTDOORS®
PACIFIC NORTHWEST HIKING
AVALON TRAVEL PUBLISHING
1400 65th STREET, SUITE 250
EMERYVILLE, CA 94608, USA
email: atpfeedback@avalonpub.com
website: www.foghorn.com

Printing History
1st edition—1995
4th edition—May 2002
5 4 3 2

ISBN: 1-56691-380-2
ISSN: 1538-2729

Editor: Marisa Solís
Series Manager: Marisa Solís
Copy Editor: Valerie Sellers Blanton
Proofreader: Julie Leigh
Graphics Coordinator: Melissa Sherowski
Production Coordinator: Darren Alessi
Cover Designer: Jacob Goolkasian
Map Editors: Olivia Solís
Cartographers: CHK America, Kat Kalamaras, Suzanne Service, Mike Morgenfeld
Indexer: Vera Gross

Front cover photo: © Stuart Westmorland

Distributed by Publishers Group West
Printed in the United States by Arvato Services

Contents

Washington

Oregon

Our Commitment

We are committed to making *Foghorn Outdoors: Pacific Northwest Hiking* the most accurate, thorough, and enjoyable hiking guide to the Oregon and Washington. With this fourth edition you can rest assured that every hiking trail in this book has been carefully reviewed and accompanied by the most up-to-date information. But as current as we strive to make this book, be aware that with the passing of time some of the fees listed herein may have changed, and that a change in season or weather patterns may have had ill effects on a trail. With that in mind, or if you have a specific need or concern, it's best to call the location ahead of time.

If you would like to comment on the book, whether it's to suggest a trail we overlooked, or to let us know about any noteworthy experience—good or bad—that occurred while using *Foghorn Outdoors: Pacific Northwest Hiking* as your guide, we would appreciate hearing from you. Please address correspondence to:

Foghorn Outdoors: Pacific Northwest Hiking, 4th edition
Avalon Travel Publishing
1400 65th Street, Suite 250
Emeryville, CA 94608
U.S.A

email: atpfeedback@avalonpub.com

If you send us an email, please put "Pacific Northwest Hiking" in the subject line. Thanks.

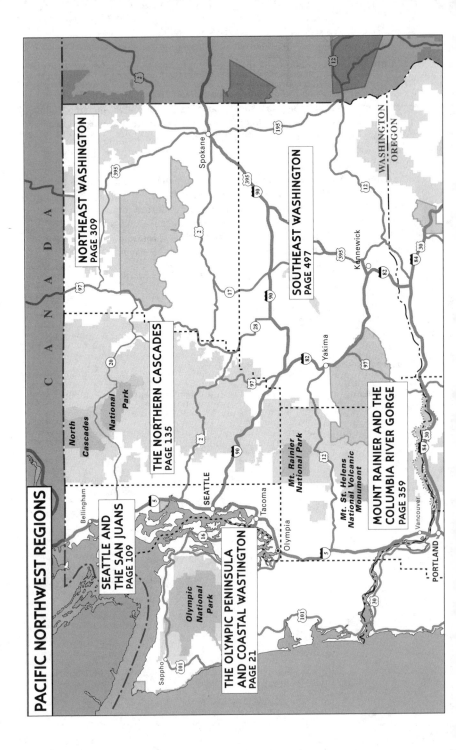

PACIFIC NORTHWEST REGIONS

CANADA

SEATTLE AND THE SAN JUANS
PAGE 109

THE OLYMPIC PENINSULA AND COASTAL WASHINGTON
PAGE 21

THE NORTHERN CASCADES
PAGE 135

NORTHEAST WASHINGTON
PAGE 309

SOUTHEAST WASHINGTON
PAGE 497

MOUNT RAINIER AND THE COLUMBIA RIVER GORGE
PAGE 359

North Cascades National Park

Olympic National Park

Mt. Rainier National Park

Mt. St. Helens National Volcanic Monument

WASHINGTON
OREGON

Bellingham

Sappho

SEATTLE

Tacoma

Olympia

Vancouver

PORTLAND

Spokane

Kennewick

Yakima

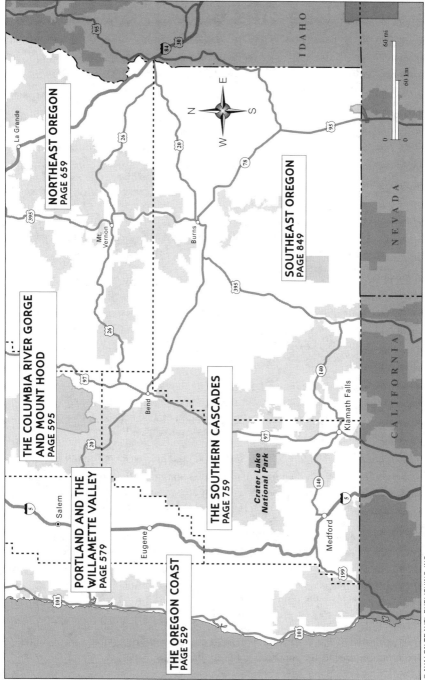

THE COLUMBIA RIVER GORGE AND MOUNT HOOD
PAGE 595

NORTHEAST OREGON
PAGE 659

PORTLAND AND THE WILLAMETTE VALLEY
PAGE 579

SOUTHEAST OREGON
PAGE 849

THE SOUTHERN CASCADES
PAGE 759

THE OREGON COAST
PAGE 529

Crater Lake National Park

IDAHO

NEVADA

CALIFORNIA

La Grande

Mt. Vernon

Burns

Bend

Salem

Eugene

Klamath Falls

Medford

N E W S

0   60 mi

0   60 km

© AVALON TRAVEL PUBLISHING, INC.

How to Use This Book

Foghorn Outdoors: Pacific Northwest Hiking is divided into two primary sections: Washington and Oregon. These sections are further broken down into 12 chapters based on regional boundaries. Each chapter begins with a map of the area, which is further broken down into grid maps. These grid maps show the location of all the hikes in that chapter.

Despite the vast number of hikes featured in this guide, it's not difficult to navigate this book. In fact, it can be done easily in two ways:

1. If you know the name of the specific trail you want to hike, or the name of the surrounding geographical area or nearby feature (town, national or state park, or forest, mountain, lake, river, etc.), look it up in the index beginning on page 870 and turn to the corresponding page.

2. If you know the general area you want to visit, you can determine what chapter covers that territory by turning to one of the state maps. Then turn to the chapter map at the beginning of the chapter you're interested in. Each chapter map is broken down into grid maps, which show by number all the hikes in that chapter. You can then determine which trails are in or near your destination by their corresponding numbers. At the end of the map set will be a chapter table of contents listing each hike in the chapter by map number and the page that it's profiled on. Then turn to the corresponding page for the hike you're interested in.

Trail Names, Distances, and Times

Each trail in this book has a number (that corresponds to a chapter map), name, mileage information, and the approximate amount of time needed to complete the hike. The trail's number allows you to find it's approximate location on the corresponding chapter map. The name is either the actual name of the trail (as listed on signposts and maps) or a name we've given to a series of trails or a loop trail. In these cases, the trail name is taken from the major destination or focal point of the hike. Most mileage listings are precise, though a few are very good estimates. All mileages and approximate times refer to round-trip travel unless specifically noted as one-way. In the case of one-way hikes, a car shuttle is advised. The estimated time is based on how long we feel an average adult in moderate physical condition would take to complete the hike. Actual times can vary widely, especially on longer hikes.

About the Ratings

Every hike in this book has been rated on a scale of **1** to **5** for difficulty, and on a scale of **1** to **10** for overall appeal.

The difficulty rating is based on the steepness of the trail and how difficult it is to traverse it. A flat, open, clearly marked trail is rated **1**, while a cross-country scramble with huge elevation gains is rated **5**.

The overall rating is based largely on scenic beauty, but it also takes into account how crowded the trail is and whether or not you'll hear the noise of nearby civilization.

User Groups
We have designated a list of user groups for each trail, including hikers, mountain bikers, horseback riders, and dogs. Under this category we have also attempted to list as much information about wheelchair facilities and access as possible. Since definitions of wheelchair accessibility and facilities vary, please call the contact number to ensure that your particular needs will be met. In addition, call ahead for any leash restrictions if hiking with your dog.

Hiking the Pacific Crest Trail (PCT)
In addition to describing over 1,000 individual out-and-back or loop hikes, this book features the entire Pacific Crest Trail (PCT) in Oregon and Washington. The PCT is split into 16 sections throughout *Foghorn Outdoors: Pacific Northwest Hiking*. The 16 PCT sections are arranged in chapters according to the location of their major trailheads.

Because the PCT is usually hiked from south to north, you will find that the PCT numbering system follows this direction. In each chapter in which the PCT appears, the segments are grouped together at the end of the chapter, so you can plan to hike individual segments or if you've very ambitious, the entire length of both states.

Maps
The Outdoor Recreation Information Center is an excellent source of maps and is listed as a contact in either the "Maps" or "Contact" fields in many trail listings in this book.

For every trail in *Foghorn Outdoors: Pacific Northwest Hiking*, we provide the names of the U.S.G.S. (United States Geologic Survey) topographic maps that feature the trail. These maps are sold by major sporting goods stores, outdoor retailers, and the U.S.G.S. To order maps from the U.S.G.S. or to request a catalog of their maps, write to:

United States Geologic Survey
Western Distribution Branch
Box 25286, Federal Center
Denver, CO 80225

The Department of Natural Resources in Washington is also a good source for U.S.G.S. and other maps. For more information call 360/902-1234 or write to:

The Department of Natural Resources
P.O. Box 47031
Olympia, WA 98504-7031

INTRODUCTION

Introduction

Dazed and confused?

It's easy to get that way if you're a hiker in Washington and Oregon, where just about every road leads in time to a trail, which in turn leads to another—which typically leads somewhere magnificent.

Back in the Good Old Days—for our purposes from the mid-1990s on back—the main source of confusion was the very plethora of trails: there is, quite simply, so much good hiking to be done in the Northwest that many people can, and do, spend lifetimes in a vain pursuit of tasting it all.

Alas, new layers of confusion have been added in recent years: hiking permits. Love 'em or loathe 'em, they're now a fact of life for every Northwest hiker. Increasingly, the number of overnight visitors is limited in the Northwest's more pristine backcountry areas, including Washington's Alpine Lakes Wilderness and Oregon's Mount Hood and Mount Jefferson Wildernesses, and Mount Rainier and Olympic National Parks. That often means permits that must be reserved in advance.

And since 1997, Northwest hikers have been faced with a new layer of user fees: parking permits required to park at the vast majority of U.S. Forest Service trailheads. Today, the latest incarnation of this "demonstration" project, the Northwest Forest Pass, is required to park at most trailheads in nearly all of the Northwest's most popular national forests: Washington's Mount Baker-Snoqualmie, Olympic, Wenatchee, Okanogan, and Gifford Pinchot and Oregon's Deschutes, Mount Hood, Rogue River, Siskiyou, Siuslaw, Umatilla, Wallowa-Whitman, and Willamette National Forests. And don't forget the Columbia River Gorge National Scenic Area, one jurisdiction straddling the border.

Government officials insist the passes, which cost $5 per day or $30 per season, are necessary to cut into the backlog of trail maintenance over the 20,000 miles of trails in the Forest Service's Pacific Northwest Region. At least 80 percent of revenue from the passes is supposed to remain in the forest district that sold it, rather than slip into a federal general fund. But opposition to the passes seems to have increased since 2000, when the feds raised the price of an annual pass, and more details about the money's actual use have trickled out. While it's clear these user fees have provided many needed improvements to recreation lands, critics point out that most of the money collected from hikers has financed capital projects—restrooms, visitor centers, roads, etc.—that are more commonly used by non-hiking National Forest visitors. Furthermore, it's been difficult to get a handle on exactly how much of this user-fee money is spent on policing of the permits themselves. Some frequent forest visitors—we among them—continue to wonder if a strictly voluntary fee program might be more effective, and perhaps even more profitable.

Meanwhile, the debate rages on in Congress, with some representatives seeking to make the user fees permanent, others trying to ditch them altogether. In recent years, more organized hiking and wilderness-advocacy groups have gone on the record opposing trailhead parking fees, often citing public confusion about which passes are required where. It's a point well taken: In spite of year-2000 changes designed to "simplify" user fees, Washington hikers still need separate permits to backpack in Olympic National Park, Mount Rainier National Park, Mount St. Helens National Volcanic Monument, and their local national forest of choice. To further confuse the issue, North Cascades National Park in 2000 began requiring Northwest Forest Passes for some of its trails—the first such mixing of these jurisdictions. Clearly, someone needs to lock the bureaucrats from the Forest Service and National Park Service together in an outhouse and leave them there until they come up with a common fee system for all national recreation lands.

In the meantime, we're here to help, in the form of the fourth edition of *Foghorn Outdoors: Pacific Northwest Hiking,* which contains the most up-to-date permit information available. (When we compiled the first version of this guide in 1995, the permit system was a no-brainer. Ninety percent of the more than 1,000 trails in this guide said simply, "no permits required." Don't expect that in this edition. Many entries detail not one but two or more separate permits needed to hike a trail where all you used to need were boots and a canteen.)

Detailed permit information is far from the only change in this new guide, however. In response to reader feedback, we've added even more new trails, many geared specifically for families with children or other hikers who wish to sample the outdoors in urban/suburban areas without venturing too far. And we've weeded out those that have gone by the wayside, usually due to flood or fire. To help you keep up with rampant Forest Service consolidations (two or more ranger districts that have been combined into single offices in many areas), we've also updated the more than 1,000 contact addresses and telephone numbers in this guide. Add to that a completely revised and improved mapping system (see the How to Use This Book section for more on that), as well as updated and more in-depth trail-notes information such as trail elevations, new hazards, and seasonal tips, and you've got an all-new, highly improved hiking guide in your hands.

We're proud of the success this guide—which has become one of the most commonly sought, dog-eared reference books in the library at REI and in many hikers' homes—has enjoyed in its first seven years. As we said in the introduction to the first edition, "We sought to create a single hiking guide like no other book available—one that provides crucial, well-organized, easily accessible information for not only all the Northwest's tried and true hiking classics, but also for the hundreds of other trails that even the most avid Northwest hiker might have overlooked." We consider that goal solidly met. But we think this new version is a full notch above.

It remains, of course, a work in progress. We can't be on every trail in this book at once, so we count on the eyes, ears, and blisters of fellow hikers to keep us informed of trail developments. Feel free to drop us a line or two at Foghorn

Outdoors: Pacific Northwest Hiking, 4th edition, Avalon Travel Publishing, 5855 Beaudry Street, Emeryville, CA 94608.

A word on the organization of *Foghorn Outdoors: Pacific Northwest Hiking*: Ron, a native of the we(s)t side of the Cascades, compiled the majority of the hikes from the Pacific Coast to just east of the Cascade crest. Dan, a native dry-sider, compiled most of the hikes in the central and eastern portions of both states, as well as all of southern Oregon.

And finally, a renewed request: Even with the addition of new permit money, most Northwest land-management agencies still rely—in many cases exclusively—on volunteer labor to keep trails up to snuff. Do your part by picking up a shovel and pitching in. All of these trails are a gift from our hiking forefathers and a responsibility to maintain for the next generation. And there's an added bonus: Volunteer for two trail-work parties, and you can earn a free Northwest Forest Pass. You can sign up and find more information on this at Washington Trails Association's excellent website: www.wta.org.

Parting advice as we lace up the boots and head out: Spend a few minutes familiarizing yourself with the use of this guide. Then spend a few decades wandering its trails. You never know where they might lead.

—Ron C. Judd and Dan A. Nelson, March 2002

Best Hikes in Oregon and Washington

Can't decide where to hike this weekend? Here are our picks for 10 great hikes in several categories:

Waterfall Trails

1. **Oneonta/Horsetail Falls,** The Columbia River Gorge and Mount Hood, page 608
2. **Multnomah Falls,** The Columbia River Gorge and Mount Hood, page 607
3. **Spray Park,** Mount Rainier and the Columbia River Gorge, page 391
4. **Kentucky Falls,** Oregon Coast, page 555
5. **Stuart Falls,** The Southern Cascades, page 825
6. **Comet Falls,** Mount Rainier and the Columbia River Gorge, page 412
7. **Palouse Falls,** Southeast Washington, page 508
8. **Ramona Falls,** The Columbia River Gorge and Mount Hood, page 621
9. **Boulder River,** The Northern Cascades, page 181
10. **Sol Duc Falls,** The Olympic Peninsula and Coastal Washington, page 50

Beginner Backpacking Routes

1. **Hoh River Trail,** The Olympic Peninsula and Coastal Washington, page 43
2. **Packwood Lake,** Mount Rainier and the Columbia River Gorge, page 432
3. **Eagle Lake,** The Northern Cascades, page 238
4. **Dutch Miller Gap,** The Northern Cascades, page 271
5. **Royal Basin,** The Olympic Peninsula and Coastal Washington, page 61
6. **Waldo Lake Loop,** The Southern Cascades, page 803
7. **Dumbbell Lake Loop,** Mount Rainier and the Columbia River Gorge, page 428
8. **Cape Alava/Sand Point,** The Olympic Peninsula and Coastal Washington, page 33
9. **Halliday,** Northeast Washington, page 339
10. **Slick Ear,** Southeast Washington, page 521

Day Hikes with Children

1. **Hurricane Hill Trail,** The Olympic Peninsula and Coastal Washington, page 56
2. **Bridal Veil Falls,** The Columbia River Gorge and Mount Hood, page 605
3. **Mount Fremont Lookout,** Mount Rainier and the Columbia River Gorge, page 394
4. **Naches Peak,** Mount Rainier and the Columbia River Gorge, page 401
5. **Heather Lake,** The Northern Cascades, page 193
6. **Mount Scott,** The Southern Cascades, page 817
7. **Staircase Rapids,** The Olympic Peninsula and Coastal Washington, page 88
8. **Umtanum Creek,** Southeast Washington, page 503
9. **Lakes Lookout,** Northeast Oregon, page 724
10. **Coldwater Lake,** Mount Rainier and the Columbia River Gorge, page 369

Lake Hikes

1. **Enchantment Basin**, The Northern Cascades, page 300
2. **Wizard Island**, The Southern Cascades, page 817
3. **High Divide Loop/Seven Lakes Basin**, The Olympic Peninsula and Coastal Washington, page 51
4. **Lakes Basin**, Northeast Oregon, page 693
5. **Sky Lakes**, The Southern Cascades, page 831
6. **Shoe Lake**, Mount Rainier and the Columbia River Gorge, page 434
7. **Patjen Lakes Loop**, The Southern Cascades, page 776
8. **Goat Ridge**, Mount Rainier and the Columbia River Gorge, page 443
9. **Lyman Lakes**, The Northern Cascades, page 231
10. **Domke Lake**, The Northern Cascades, page 232

Day Hikes

1. **Indian Heaven**, Mount Rainier and Columbia River Gorge, page 472
2. **Phantom Bridge**, The Columbia River Gorge and Mount Hood, page 644
3. **Rock Lakes Loop**, The Columbia River Gorge and Mount Hood, page 639
4. **John Day Fossil Beds**, Northeast Oregon, page 705
5. **Cutthroat Pass**, Northeast Oregon, page 215
6. **Dungeness Spit**, The Olympic Peninsula and Coastal Washington, page 41
7. **Sucker Creek Fern Forest**, Oregon Coast, page 557
8. **Oregon Butte**, Southeast Washington, page 516
9. **Sutton Creek Sand Dunes**, Oregon Coast, page 551
10. **Flume Creek**, Northeast Washington, page 339

Backpacking Hikes

1. **Echo Lake**, Northeast Oregon, page 692
2. **Domke Mountain/Domke Lake**, Northern Cascades, page 232
3. **Hanging Rock**, Oregon Coast, page 566
4. **Waldo Lake Loop**, Southern Cascades, page 803
5. **Fourth of July Ridge**, Northeast Washington, page 317
6. **Highline**, Mount Rainier and the Columbia River Gorge, page 462
7. **Packwood Lake**, Mount Rainier and the Columbia River Gorge, page 432
8. **Dutch Flat**, Northeast Oregon, page 729
9. **Grizzley Bear**, Southeast Washington, page 517
10. **Windy Gap**, Mount Rainier and the Columbia River Gorge, page 387

Extended Backpacking Hikes

1. **Wonderland Trail**, Mount Rainier and Columbia River Gorge, page 421
2. **Loowit**, Mount Rainier and the Columbia River Gorge, page 379
3. **Willamette Pass to McKenzie Pass**, The Southern Cascades, page 842
4. **Middle Bear Valley**, Northeast Oregon, page 686
5. **Snake River**, Northeast Oregon, page 701
6. **Third Beach**, The Olympic Peninsula and Washington Coast, page 42

7. **Shedroof Divide**, Northeast Washington, page 347
8. **Hoh River Valley**, The Olympic Peninsula and Washington Coast, page 48
9. **Potato Hill to White Pass**, Mount Rainier and the Columbia River Gorge, page 489
10. **Chilliwack River**, Northern Cascades, page 155

Hikes for Wildlife Viewing

1. **Summerland/Panhandle Gap**, Mount Rainier and the Columbia River Gorge, page 398
2. **Umtanum Creek**, Southeast Washington, page 503
3. **Poker Jim Ridge**, Southeast Oregon, page 867
4. **Hawkins Pass**, Northeast Oregon, page 694
5. **Rattlesnake**, Southeast Washington page 509
6. **Slate Creek**, Northeast Washington, page 340
7. **Juniper Dunes**, Southeast Washington, page 507
8. **Hannegan Pass**, Northern Cascades, page 152
9. **Metolius River**, The Columbia River Gorge and Mount Hood, page 654
10. **Johnson Butte**, The Oregon Coast, page 561

Hikes for Wildflower Viewing

1. **Skyline Loop**, Mount Rainier and the Columbia River Gorge, page 417
2. **Cunningham Cove**, Northeast Oregon, page 723
3. **Rainy Lake Nature Trail**, Northern Cascades, page 213
4. **Lemei**, Mount Rainier and the Columbia River Gorge, page 474
5. **Heather Park/Mount Angeles**, The Olympic Peninsula and Coastal Washington, page 39
6. **Dark Meadow**, Mount Rainier and the Columbia River Gorge, page 458
7. **Paddy Go Easy Pass**, Northern Cascades, page 272
8. **Granite Mountain**, Northern Cascades, page 251
9. **Longs Pass/Ingalls Lake/Esmeralda Basin**, Northern Cascades, page 301
10. **Canyon Creek Meadows Loop**, Southern Cascades, page 774

Hikes with Dogs

1. **Dog Mountain**, Mount Rainier and the Columbia River Gorge, page 487
2. **Larch Mountain**, The Columbia River Gorge and Mount Hood, page 606
3. **East Fork Wallowa**, Northeast Oregon, page 693
4. **Poodle Dog Pass**, Northern Cascades, page 254
5. **Fall Creek**, Oregon Coast, page 569
6. **Mount Rose**, The Olympic Peninsula and Coastal Washington, page 92
7. **Blue Lake**, Northern Cascades page 214
8. **Clackamas River**, The Columbia River Gorge and Mount Hood, page 610
9. **Tucannon River**, Southeast Washington, page 518
10. **Chucksney Mountain Loop**, Southern Cascades, page 789

Hiking Tips

General Trail Etiquette

Most hikers seek a sense of quiet solitude for themselves, or for their group, when they start up a trail. Yet trails in Oregon and Washington are used by more hikers each year. To ensure that we preserve the serene experience we seek, we each must work to preserve the tranquility of wild lands.

When you encounter other trail users, common sense and simple courtesy must be observed. That's the golden rule of hiking. Regardless of who you encounter—other hikers, horse riders, mountain bikers, trail runners, or hunters—be polite, be courteous, and be considerate.

There are a few specific ways you can achieve these traits. When hikers meet other hikers, the group heading uphill has the right-of-way. Why? Because on steep ascents, hikers may be watching their feet to make sure they don't stumble, so they may not notice the approach of descending hikers until they are face-to-face. Also, descending hikers can break their stride and step off the trail more easily than climbing hikers who have established a steady, hill-climbing plod.

When meeting people employing other forms of trail recreation, hikers generally should yield because they are the most mobile and flexible users of trail. For instance, when encountering a mountain biker, a hiker can simply step off in the brush, but the biker would have to toss his bike into the brambles, then dig it back out after the hiker had passed. Likewise, horse riders would actually put themselves and hikers at risk if they had to move their mounts off a steep trail, whereas the hiker can easily scurry off the trail.

In addition to simply yielding to horses, hikers must give the mounted trail user special consideration. When yielding, try to stay below the eye level of the horse so as not to spook it, which could cause the horse to rear up and throw its rider, or it may simply side-step in fright and tumble off the trail. Do this by moving to the downhill side of the trail when possible. If you have to move uphill from the trail, do so but crouch down as the horse passes so you don't tower over it. Stay in clear view and talk in a normal voice to the riders. This calms the horses. Do not stand behind trees or brush if you can avoid it, as this could make you invisible to the animals until they get close, and then your sudden appearance could startle them.

Unless you plan to go cross-country hiking, you should stay on trails and practice minimum impact. You should never cut switchbacks (i.e., drop down across the neck of the switchback), as this promotes erosion and could destroy the trail. In fact, avoid any type of shortcut. If your final destination is off-trail, leave the trail in as direct a manner as possible—don't parallel the trail for any distance. Move straight away from the trail until it is well out of sight.

Since many trails are closed to certain types of use, including hiking with dogs or riding horses, you must know and obey the local rules and regulations. Further, even if a trail is open to dogs, pets should be kept on a leash at all times.

Even a well-behaved dog can get excited and give chase when it sees wildlife. And you must avoid disturbing wildlife—observe animals from a distance. In fact, it's not just animals that should remain undisturbed: Leave all natural features as you found them for others to enjoy.

When in doubt about what to do to be a good trail steward and trail user, just remember: exercise common sense and courtesy toward others—both those you see and those who will come after you.

Minimize Wildlife Encounters

If you hike in Washington or Oregon, you'll be hiking in cougar and bear country—virtually every trail in the state pierces predator habitat. Black bears, which outnumber cougars 10 to 1 in the Northwest, can be found in any forested area of the region, and cougars can be found anywhere deer can be found—that is, everywhere.

There are other predators prowling the backcountry, but these two are the biggest and most likely to cause concern when hikers encounter them. However, an encounter with a cougar or bear doesn't have to be a negative experience. These critters rarely attack or even threaten humans, and in most of the attacks that have occurred, the human could have prevented the confrontation with a little forethought and understanding of the animal.

You can minimize the odds of an encounter with aggressive predators by making sure you don't surprise them. To do this, you should:

- Hike in a group and hike only during daylight hours. Talking or singing as you hike is also a good idea. If bears or any other creatures hear you coming, they will usually avoid you. Make noises that will identify you as a human—talk, sing, rattle pebbles in a tin can—especially when hiking near a river or stream, which can mask more subtle sounds that might normally alert a bear to your presence.
- Leave perfume, cologne, hair spray, scented soaps, and any other strong-scented items at home. Using scented sprays and body lotions makes you smell like a big, tasty treat.
- Keep dogs on a leash and under control. Many bear encounters have resulted from unleashed dogs chasing a bear: the bear gets angry and turns on the dog, the dog gets scared and runs for help (i.e., back to its owner), and the bear follows right back into the dog owner's lap.
- Be aware of your environment, and know how to identify "bear signs." Overturned rocks and torn-up deadwood logs often are the result of a bear searching for grubs. Berry bushes that are stripped of berries, with leaves, branches, and berries littering the ground under the bushes, show where a bear has fed. Tracks and scat are the most common signs of a bear's recent presence.
- Stay away from abundant food sources and dead animals. Black bears are opportunistic and will scavenge food. A bear that finds a dead deer will hang around until the meat is gone, and it will defend that food against any perceived threat.

- Never eat or cook in your tent. The spilled food or even food odors can permeate the nylon material, essentially making your tent smell, at least to a bear, like dinner.
- Never clean fish within 100 feet of camp.
- Always store all your food and other scented items in their own stuff sacks when preparing to hang them (i.e., don't use your sleeping bag's stuff sack or the food odors can be transferred to the sack and then to the sleeping bag, making the bear think you are a big, smelly meat roll).
- Always suspend your food bags at least 12 feet in the air and 8 to 10 feet from the nearest tree trunk. In some popular backcountry camps, land managers provide wires, complete with pulleys, to help you do this, but you'll have to learn how to string your own rope to achieve these heights, too.

Dealing with Black Bears

Although there is a small, remnant population of grizzly bears in the extreme northern forests of Washington (approximately 20 bears in the Pasayten Wilderness Area), hikers are unlikely to ever see them. So, when hikers encounter a bear in Washington or Oregon, it will most likely be a black bear.

The most important thing to remember is to respect a bear's need for personal space. If you see a bear in the distance, make a wide detour around it, or if that's not possible (e.g., if the trail leads close to the bear) leave the area.

If you encounter a bear at close range, remain calm. Do not run, as this may trigger a predator/prey reaction from the bear. Talk to the bear in a low, calm manner to help identify yourself as human. Don't stare directly at the bear—the bear may interpret this as a direct threat or challenge. Watch the animal without making direct eye-to-eye contact. Hold your arms out from your body. If you are wearing a jacket, hold open the front so you appear to be as big as possible. Then, slowly move upwind of the bear if you can do so without crowding it. The bear's strongest sense is its sense of smell, and if it can sniff you and identify you as human, it may retreat.

Bear Surprise

If you aren't heeding signs of bear activity (fresh scat or tracks, or berries stripped from bushes), you might round a corner and surprise a bear—and yourself. It's still not too late to exercise good judgment and stay safe.

If a surprised bear charges from close range, the best thing to do is to lie down and play dead. The bear will generally leave you once the perceived threat is neutralized. However, if the bear charges from a distance, you should fight back. A bear in this situation is behaving in a predatory manner (as opposed to the defensive reaction of a bear that has merely been surprised) and is looking at you as food. Kick, stab, and punch at the bear. If it knows you will fight back, it may leave you and search for easier prey.

Your safety also depends upon knowing how to interpret bear actions. A nervous bear will often rumble in its chest, clack its teeth, and "pop" its jaw. It may paw the ground and swing its head violently side to side. If the bear does this, watch it closely without staring directly at it. Continue to speak low and calmly. A bear may bluff-charge (run at you but stop well before reaching you) to try and intimidate you. Resist the urge to run from this charge, because you will not be able to outrun the bear; they can attain speeds up to 35 miles per hour through log-strewn forests.

Another precautionary tactic is to carry a 12-ounce (or larger) can of pepper spray bear deterrent, such as Counter Assault. The spray—a high concentration of oils from hot peppers—should fire out at least 20 or 30 feet in a broad mist. Don't use the spray unless a bear is actually charging and is in range of the spray, and be conscious of the direction the wind is blowing so the spray does not get in your own eyes.

Dealing with Cougars

The essential thing to remember about cougars is that they rely on prey that can't or won't fight back. If you see a cat, *do not run!* Running may trigger a cougar's attack instinct. Instead, stand up and face the animal. Virtually every recorded cougar attack on humans has been a predator/prey attack. If you appear as another aggressive predator, rather than as prey, the cougar will back down.

Try to appear large—wave your arms or a jacket over your head. The idea is to make the cougar think you are the bigger, meaner beast. Maintain eye contact with the animal. The cougar will interpret this as a show of dominance on your part. Do not approach the animal. Back away slowly if you can safely do so. If hiking with children, pick them up or keep them close to your side.

Cougars tend to be more aggressive toward women, teens, and children—that is, people with smaller body frames. These hikers should take extra precautions while on trails.

If the above tactics do not ward off the cougar and the animal begins to display aggressive behavior, follow this advice:

- Do not turn your back or take your eyes off the cougar
- Remain standing
- Shout loudly
- Fight back aggressively

You should also try to throw things at the cougar, provided you don't have to bend over to pick them up. If you have a water bottle on your belt, chuck it at the cat. Throw your camera, wave your hiking stick, and if the cat gets close enough, whack it hard with your hiking staff (I know of two cases in which women delivered good, hard whacks across the nose of aggressive-acting cougars, and the cats immediately turned tail and ran away).

Remember, above all else, cougars are curious animals. They may appear threatening when they are only being inquisitive. By making the cougar think you are a bigger, meaner critter than it is, you will be able to avoid an attack. Big cats in the wild realize that there is enough easy prey that they don't have to mess with something that will fight back.

Low-Impact Hiking and Camping

In days gone by, wilderness travelers did as they pleased when hiking through the backcountry. Young, fragrant pine boughs were cut and stacked to create soft bedding, trenches were dug around tents to channel rainwater away from the shelter, and fires were lit to brighten the night and warm the camp. As more and more people took to the hills, those actions began to leave large, noticeable scars on the land.

Today, however, with millions of hikers flocking to the backcountry, such intrusive actions as those practiced in the past would leave the wilderness blighted for decades to come. To ensure we don't destroy the essence of the wild country we all enjoy visiting, hikers today are encouraged to employ the Leave No Trace (LNT) camping principles.

In short, these principles and practices are built around the idea that human visitors to the backcountry should "leave only footprints, take only pictures." In fact, done right, even the footprints will be minimized.

One of the first and most important LNT practices involves fire. Everyone loves a campfire. The acrid, sweet smoke wafts upward, stirring memories of childhood camping, roasting marshmallows, and sizzling hot dogs on sticks. But campfires have no place in the backcountry. If everyone who entered the wilderness were to build a fire, campsites would be filled with charcoal and forests would soon be picked clean of dead wood, leaving hordes of small critters with nowhere to scrounge for food (the insects that eat the dead wood provide meals for an army of birds and animals). Fires should be left to the car campgrounds where structured fire pits and supplies of firewood are readily avail-

Leave Only Footprints, Take Only Pictures

The importance of the Leave No Trace ethic cannot be understated. In fact, a national nonprofit organization was created solely for the purpose of developing and promoting the best no-impact practices for the wilderness areas of this country. Leave No Trace, a 501(c)3 nonprofit organization, works with the U.S. Forest Service, National Park Service, Bureau of Land Management, and other nonprofits to educate and inform backcountry visitors on these basic LNT Principles:

1. Plan ahead and prepare
2. Travel and camp on durable surfaces
3. Dispose of waste properly
4. Leave what you find
5. Minimize campfire impacts
6. Respect wildlife
7. Be considerate of other visitors

For more on Leave No Trace, visit its website: www.lnt.org.

able. Backcountry campers should stick to small pack stoves, even when regulations technically allow campfires.

To protect the wilderness water resources, hikers must camp at least 100 feet away from lake shores and stream banks. This not only lets other hikers—and animals—get to the water without having to bypass you, but it helps keep the water clean.

Perhaps the least talked about but most important Leave No Trace principle focuses on the business of taking care of personal business. The first rule of backcountry bathroom etiquette says that if an outhouse exists, use it. This seems obvious, but all too often folks choose to use the woods rather than the rickety wooden structures provided by the land manager. It may be easier on your nose to head off into the woods, but this disperses human waste around camping and hiking areas. Privies, on the other hand, keep the waste concentrated in a single site, minimizing contamination of area waters. The outhouses get even higher environmental marks if they feature holding tanks that can be airlifted out.

When privies aren't provided, the key factor to consider is location. You'll want to choose a site at least 200 to 300 feet from water, campsites, and trails. A location well out of sight of trails and viewpoints will give you privacy and reduce the odds of other hikers stumbling upon the site after you leave. Once you pick your place, start digging. The idea is to bury your waste. You need to dig down through the organic duff into the mineral soil below—a hole six to eight inches deep is usually adequate. When you've taken care of business, refill the hole and camouflage it with rocks and sticks—this helps prevent other humans or animals from digging in the same location before decomposition has done its job.

Volunteers and Trail Building

As congressional budget allocations diminished throughout the 1980s and early 1990s, a nonprofit hikers organization stepped in to pick up some of the slack. Washington Trails Association (WTA), tired of watching backcountry trails fall into disarray and at times disappear due to lack of maintenance, created a volunteer trail maintenance program to ensure that not another mile is lost to neglect. In less than a decade, the program grew from 250 volunteer hours a year to nearly 50,000 hours of volunteer trail maintenance time coordinated each year. More than 1,500 volunteers each year help maintain trails from the Columbia River Gorge to the Canadian Border, from the Quinault rainforests to dry ridges of the Teanaway country. WTA teams have built sections of the world-renowned 94-mile Wonderland Trail that encircles Mount Rainier. They've also maintained largely unknown but still spectacular trails, such as the Tinkham Mountain Loop near Snoqualmie Pass.

Washington Trails' volunteer trail maintenance program is now responsible for much of the routine maintenance on hiking trails in Washington. They work on trails governed by federal, state, and county agencies, and a few on private lands (when the trails are open and accessible to the public).

So what can volunteers expect when they join a work party? Here's a basic outline from WTA:

On the average summer weekend there are as many as five different work parties going on each day. Work parties start at 8:30 A.M. and end at or before 3:30 P.M. There are at least two work parties a week all winter long. Projects take place anywhere from the Olympic Peninsula to the Wenatchee National Forest and from the Oregon border to the North Cascades National Park. No experience is necessary to participate, and WTA representatives say you're guaranteed to have a good time.

Depending on the amount of time volunteers have available, there are several options for trail projects. **Front Country** parties are best if you require a short drive, or if you're new to trail work; try joining on the trail in places like Tiger Mountain or Wallace falls. **Backcountry** trails need the most work. Join a work party for a day on a Forest Service trail and earn a free one-day Northwest Forest Pass. **Weekend** projects entail two days of trail work with a potluck barbecue Saturday night. You can work both days or work one and hike on the other. **Weeklong** projects are like "backcountry vacations," enjoyable to both core trail volunteers and first-timers. Choose from car camping or backpacking in.

WASHINGTON
THE OLYMPIC PENINSULA
AND COASTAL WASHINGTON

Washington Regions

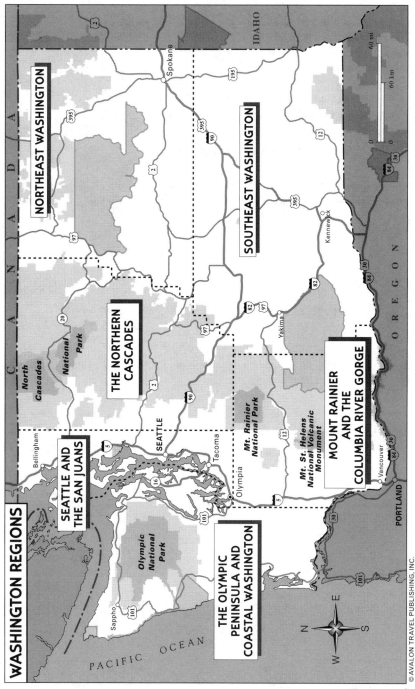

WASHINGTON REGIONS

NORTHEAST WASHINGTON

SOUTHEAST WASHINGTON

THE NORTHERN CASCADES

MOUNT RAINIER AND THE COLUMBIA RIVER GORGE

SEATTLE AND THE SAN JUANS

THE OLYMPIC PENINSULA AND COASTAL WASHINGTON

North Cascades National Park

Mt. Rainier National Park

Mt. St. Helens National Volcanic Monument

Olympic National Park

CANADA

IDAHO

OREGON

PACIFIC OCEAN

Spokane

Bellingham

SEATTLE

Tacoma

Olympia

Sappho

Yakima

Kennewick

Vancouver

PORTLAND

© AVALON TRAVEL PUBLISHING, INC.

N E S W

60 mi

60 km

The Olympic Peninsula and Coastal Washington

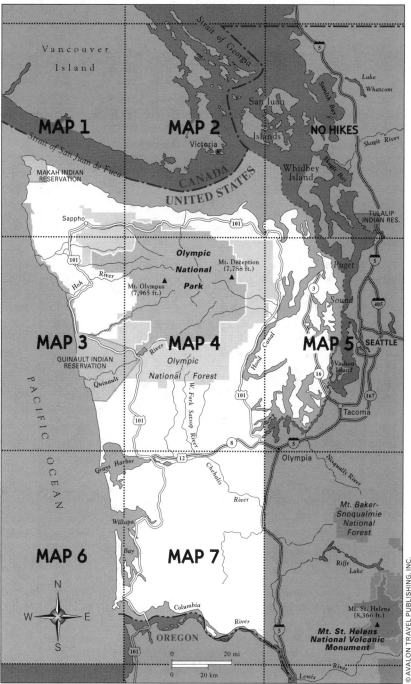

MAP 1

MAP 2

NO HIKES

Vancouver
Island

Strait of San Juan de Fuca

MAKAH INDIAN
RESERVATION

Sappho

Lake
Whatcom

San Juan

Islands

Victoria

Skagit River

Whidbey
Island

CANADA

UNITED STATES

TULALIP
INDIAN RES.

101

Hoh

River

Olympic

National

Park

Mt. Olympus
(7,965 ft.)

Mt. Deception
(7,788 ft.)

Puget

101

MAP 3

QUINAULT INDIAN
RESERVATION

Quinault

River

MAP 4

Olympic

National Forest

W. Fork Satsop River

Hood Canal

Sound

MAP 5

SEATTLE

Vashon
Island

405

101

101

Grays Harbor

12

Chehalis

8

River

Tacoma

167

16

Olympia

Nisqually River

PACIFIC OCEAN

Willapa

Bay

MAP 6

MAP 7

Columbia

River

OREGON

N

W   E

S

Mt. Baker-
Snoqualmie
National
Forest

Riffe
Lake

Mt. St. Helens
(8,366 ft.)

Mt. St. Helens
National Volcanic
Monument

101

0   20 mi

0   20 km

Lewis   River

© AVALON TRAVEL PUBLISHING, INC.

The Olympic Peninsula and Coastal Washington 21

Map 1

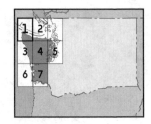

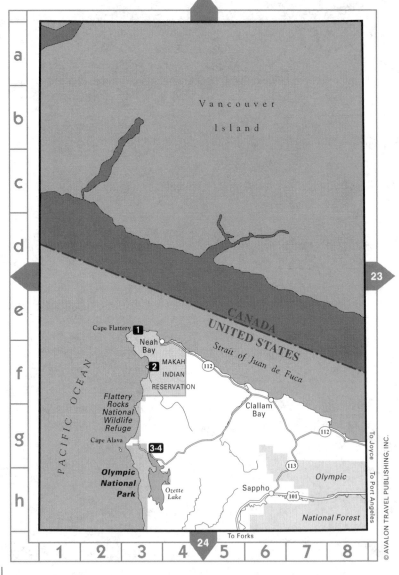

Map 2

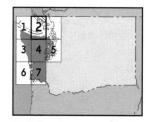

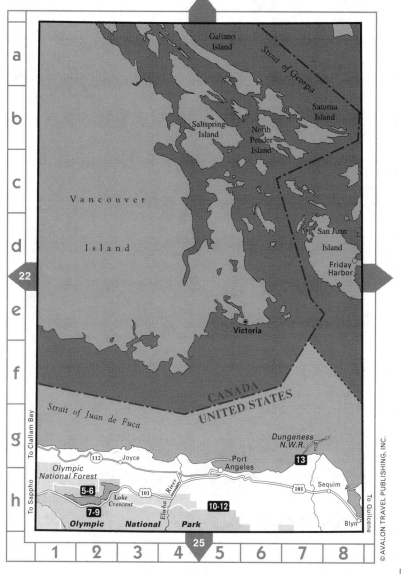

© AVALON TRAVEL PUBLISHING, INC.

Map 3

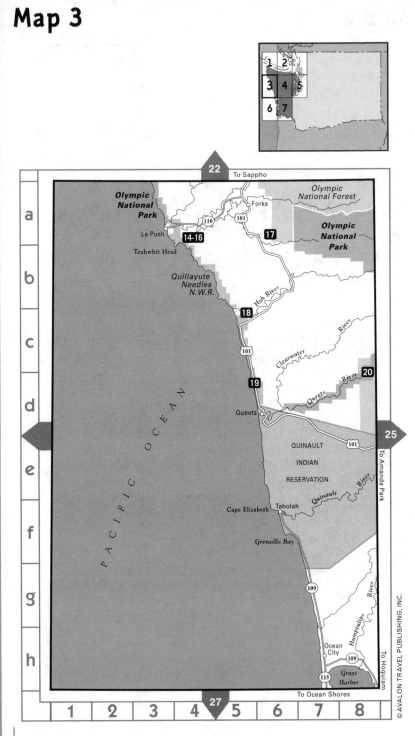

Map 4

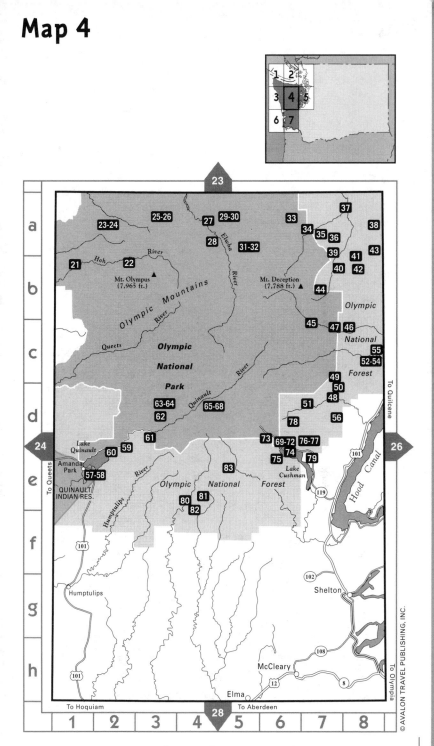

Map 5

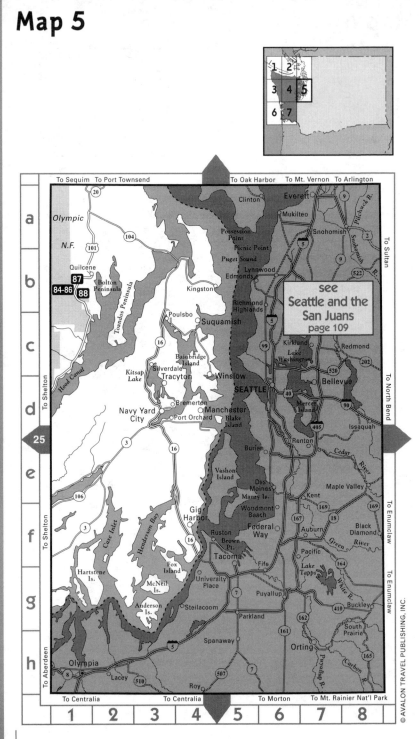

To Sequim   To Port Townsend

To Oak Harbor   To Mt. Vernon   To Arlington

a

Olympic

N.F.

20

104

101

Quilcene

87

84-86   88

Bolton Peninsula

Toandos Peninsula

Clinton

Everett

9

Mukilteo

Possession Point

Picnic Point

Puget Sound

Snohomish

Pilchuck R.

Snohomish R.

2

To Sultan

Lynnwood

Edmonds

5

9

522

b

Kingston

Richmond Highlands

see
**Seattle and the
San Juans**
page 109

To Shelton

Hood Canal

Poulsbo

Suquamish

Kitsap Lake

Bainbridge Island

Silverdale

99

Kirkland

Lake Washington

Redmond

202

c

16

Tracyton

Winslow

520

Bellevue

To North Bend

SEATTLE

40

Mercer Island

90

Bremerton

Manchester

Navy Yard City

Port Orchard

Blake Island

405

Issaquah

d

25

3

16

Renton

Burien

Cedar River

106

Vashon Island

Des Moines

Maury Is.

Maple Valley

e

To Shelton

Case Inlet

Henderson Bay

3

Kent

169

169

To Enumclaw

Woodmont Beach

Federal Way

167

18

Black Diamond

f

Gig Harbor

16

Ruston

Brown Pt.

Auburn

Green River

To Enumclaw

Hartstene Is.

Fox Island

Tacoma

Fife

Pacific

Lake Tapps

164

McNeil Is.

University Place

7

Puyallup

White R.

410

Buckley

g

Anderson Is.

Steilacoom

Parkland

162

South Prairie

165

5

Spanaway

161

Orting

Carbon

h

To Aberdeen

Olympia

8

Lacey

510

Roy

507

7

Puyallup R.

To Mt. Rainier Nat'l Park

To Centralia

To Centralia

To Morton

1   2   3   4   5   6   7   8

© AVALON TRAVEL PUBLISHING, INC.

Map 6

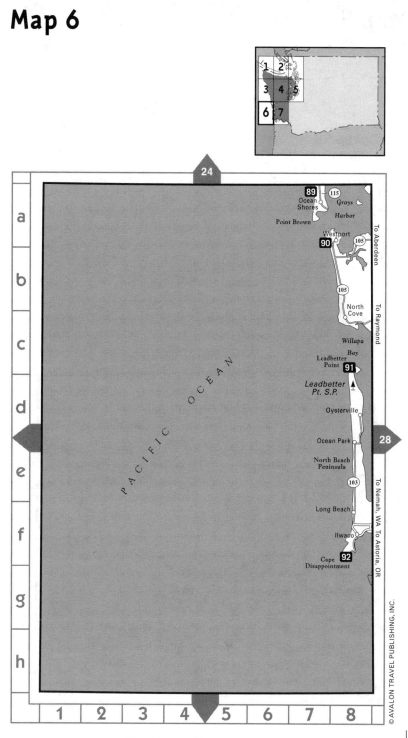

89 Ocean Shores
115 Grays Harbor
Point Brown
Westport
90
105
To Aberdeen
105
North Cove
To Raymond
Willapa Bay
Leadbetter Point
91
Leadbetter Pt. S.P.
Oysterville
Ocean Park
North Beach Peninsula
103
Long Beach
Ilwaco
Cape Disappointment
92
To Nemah, WA To Astoria, OR

PACIFIC OCEAN

24

28

Map 7

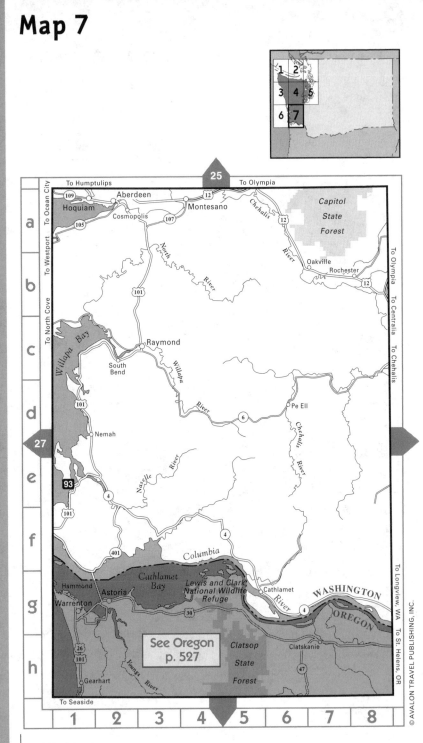

To Ocean City
To Humptulips
To Olympia

a 109 Hoquiam Aberdeen
105 Cosmopolis 107 Montesano 12
Chehalis

Capitol
State
Forest

To Westport

b 101
North River
River
Oakville
Rochester
12

To Olympia
To Centralia
To Chehalis

To North Cove

c Willapa Bay
Raymond
South Bend
Willapa

d 101
River
6
Pe Ell
Chehalis River

27

Nemah

e 93
101
4
Naselle River

f 401
4
Columbia

g Hammond
Warrenton
Astoria
Cathlamet Bay
Lewis and Clark National Wildlife Refuge
Cathlamet
WASHINGTON
OREGON
To Longview, WA
To St. Helens, OR

30

h 26
101
See Oregon p. 527
Clatsop State Forest
Clatskanie
47

Gearhart
Lewis River

To Seaside

1 2 3 4 5 6 7 8

© AVALON TRAVEL PUBLISHING, INC.

The Olympic Peninsula and Coastal Washington

(CONTINUED ON NEXT PAGE)

◼ Cape Flattery
1.0 mi/0.5 hr

The short, well-traveled Cape Flattery Trail leads to the westernmost tip of the contiguous United States; it's obscure and out-of-the-way but well worth the search. The path leads through windblown forest, across planking over a swamp, and down rocky shoulders before opening onto the top of smooth, 1,200-foot cliffs (located directly above one of the most tumultuous displays of surf you'll ever see). Below this spectacular headland the surf is alternately frothy white and deep, rich aqua, like an otherworldly dishwasher with the door open.

The craggy cliffs of Tatoosh Island, a former Makah tribe whaling camp most recently occupied by a Coast Guard lighthouse crew, are located half a mile off the coast. The light, constructed in 1857, is in a stunning—and scary—location. Try to imagine being stationed here. Early light-keepers reportedly sought hasty changes of assignments after bouts with storms, ghosts, and other frightening encounters before the light was finally automated. Staring across this roiling sea, it's easy to imagine being marooned on the island with nothing but the constant swirl of wind and sea spray to keep you company. Well, almost nothing: sea life is abundant here, and (during migration periods from March through April and from November through December) this is possibly the best vantage point on the Northwest coast for observing gray whales, which cruise just off the cliffs. In 2000, the local Makah tribe followed through with its plans to renew hunting of gray whales from cedar canoes, taking a gray whale off the coast. However you might feel about that, this is a good place to watch for the activity. Birdwatchers are happy here year-round: seabirds in this area are thicker than traffic on I-5—239 individual species have been identified in the surrounding Olympic Coast National Marine Sanctuary. You'll be glad you packed your binoculars.

Use extreme caution near the cliffs. Although trail improvements have been made to the trail near the bluff overlook, the cliffs are still precipitous, and it's still dangerous. Keep small children in your clutches here. Also, the access road has been known to wash out. Call the contact number before you make the long drive.

Location: On the extreme northwestern tip of Washington; see The Olympic Peninsula and Coastal Washington Map 1, grid e3.

User Groups: Hikers only. No dogs, horses, or mountain bikes are allowed. No wheelchair facilities.

Permits: No permits are required. Parking and access are free.

Maps: Green Trails, Inc.'s excellent topographic map of the region is available for $3.99 at outdoor retail outlets. Ask for map number 98S, Cape Flattery. Ask for a USGS topographic map of the Cape Flattery area.

Directions: From Port Angeles follow U.S. 101 five miles west to Highway 112. Veer right and follow Highway 112 about 60 miles, through Sekiu to the village of Neah Bay. Follow the main (only) highway through town and drive three miles west on Arrowhead Road, keeping right as the road forks and the left fork crosses a bridge over the Waatch River (follow signs for Cape Flattery Resort). The road, which becomes Cape Loop Road, continues for several miles past an old Air Force station to the marked trailhead on the left; you can park alongside the road.

Contact: Outdoor Recreation Information Center, Seattle REI, 222 Yale Avenue North, Seattle, WA 98109; 206/470-4060.

2 Shi Shi Beach/Point of the Arches

7.0 mi/5.0 hrs

Since adding the Shi Shi Beach area to Olympic National Park in 1976, park officials have sought to establish an easily accessible public trailhead. They haven't as of yet, which is just fine with persistent hikers who find the Shi Shi Beach Trail and make their way to one of the most spectacular seascapes in the United States. The trail, actually the remnant of the old Sooes Beach Road, winds two miles through mostly level brush to a steep access trail to Shi Shi, with trails leading down to Anderson Point and Portage Head. Local landowners, however, recently ruled the route off-limits for national park trail-building; the Makahs plan to construct a new path of their own from road's end to Shi Shi Beach. When finished, it should be about two miles long and about an hour's hike from the parking area. Meanwhile, local residents have turned the trail into a cottage industry, collecting parking fees from hikers. And the Makah Tribal Council says it has no intention to cite hikers walking to Shi Shi Beach. (Olympic National Park's "official" access to Shi Shi, meanwhile, is the southern route, a tricky, sometimes hazardous hike north from the Cape Alava area; see hike Cape Alava/Sand Point Loop in this chapter for trailhead information.)

Given all that, getting from your car to the beach requires a little route-finding and a lot of diligence. But it's more than worth it once you get there. This is one of the Northwest's most beautiful ocean beaches, and it offers outstanding exploration potential. At low tide, it's possible to scramble north over the rocks near Portage Head and explore the remains of the General M.C. Meigs, a World War II–era troopship that broke up here in the early 1970s. From south of the beach/trail junction,

it's a 0.9-mile beach walk to magnificent Point of the Arches, a series of pyramidal sea stacks (offshore rock formations) that juts into the Pacific like a gargantuan fossilized spine. Good campsites are available all along the beach and are likely to be very crowded in summer months. Water is available at Petroleum Creek (if you don't filter your water from this one, you never will) and other small streams. To continue south on Olympic National Park's coastal strip, see Cape Alava (below).

Observant hikers with an eye on the news in recent years will note that there's even more intrigue here than meets the eye: A group of "entrepreneurs" has claimed it has a legal right, through an antiquated mining claim, to "mine" the sands of Shi Shi Beach for gold. The Park Service says it won't happen. The claimholders say they want something in return for forgoing their mining adventure. Stay tuned.

Location: On the northwest coast of the Olympic Peninsula, on a beach strip of Olympic National Park; see The Olympic Peninsula and Coastal Washington Map 1, grid f3.

User Groups: Hikers only. No dogs, horses, or mountain bikes are allowed. No wheelchair access.

Permits: Day-hiking permits are not required. Wilderness camping permits, available at major trailheads and at all Olympic National Park visitor centers and ranger stations, are required for all overnight stays in undeveloped park areas. The permit fee is $5 per party (up to 12), plus an additional $2 per person per night, with a cap of $100 for trips of up to 14 nights with a party of 7–12 people. There is no nightly charge for youths 16 years of age and under. Parking and access via this (northern) route to Shi Shi Beach are on private land, and some Makah landowners charge parking fees.

Maps: To obtain a free Olympic National Park map, contact the Outdoor Recreation Information Center at 206/470-4060. Green Trails, Inc.'s excellent topographic map of the region is available for $3.99 at outdoor retail outlets. Ask for map number 98S, Cape Flattery. Ask for a USGS topographic map of the Makah Bay area.

Directions: Plans to build a new Shi Shi Beach Trail always seem to be underway, but construction still hasn't taken place. Call the Makah Tribal Council at 360/645-2201 for updated trailhead information.

To reach the old trailhead (not recognized as an official trail by Olympic National Park) from Port Angeles, follow U.S. 101 west five miles to Highway 112. Veer right and follow Highway 112 for about 60 miles, through Sekiu to the village of Neah Bay. At the end of the town's main street, turn west on Arrowhead Road and follow signs to the fish hatchery and air force base. After almost three miles, turn left on Hobuck Beach Road and cross the Waatch River. (At all intersections with private logging roads, watch for signs pointing to Sooes Beach or the Makah Salmon Hatchery.) Hobuck Beach Road becomes Sooes Beach Road as it crosses the Sooes River. A short distance beyond here, the road approaches a group of homes on Mukkaw Bay. Park on the shoulder near the homes and walk up the decaying road to the trailhead, where signs warn of car vandalism. (Or drop off your pack at the trailhead and return to park.) Most visitors ask for landowners' permission to park near the homes. We recommend paying a parking fee to one of the local landowners—you may be able to park free farther down the road, but your unattended car could be looted.

Contact: Outdoor Recreation Information Center, Seattle REI, 222 Yale Ave North, Seattle, WA 98109; 206/470-4060; Olympic National Park, Wilderness Information Center, 360/565-3100.

3 Cape Alava/Sand Point Loop
9.1 mi/7.0 hrs

The spectacular, triangular Cape Alava/Sand Point Loop showcases the unique elements that make the northwestern Olympic coast a national treasure. Accessible year-round, these trails leave the Lake Ozette area and wind along cedar-plank boardwalks through marshy coastal forest and grassland literally teeming with wildlife. Both trails empty onto a three-mile stretch of wilderness beach that forms the triangle's third leg. Whichever trail you choose, beware of the wood planks, which (when wet) can be slipperier than the underside of a banana slug. This is one of the few trails in Washington better suited to sneakers than Vibram lugs.

Coming upon the Pacific via the Cape Alava Trail is particularly memorable. The path crosses Ahlstrom's Prairie, the site of a Swedish homesteader's cabin, before passing through waist-deep sword ferns and out to the frothing Pacific. You might find the beach area here at the westernmost point in the contiguous United States a good place to camp. You'd hardly be the first. Nearby is the site of an archaeological dig of an ancient Makah village; artifacts and remains (nearly 1,000 years old) of tribal longhouses were excavated here and placed on display in the Makah Tribal Museum in Neah Bay. Wedding Rock, where ancient petroglyphs are visible on several rocks close to the high-tide line, is one mile south down the beach. This site is considered something of a holy area by a full range of visitors, including New Age types and various members of other religious sects.

Two miles farther south, the Sand Point Trail leads three easy miles back to Ozette. Permit reservations for overnight use are a must here, because the beach is

Coastal Beach Hikes and Backpacking Trips

If you're an overnight beach hiker, do yourself a favor and be prepared. Olympic Peninsula ocean shorelines aren't Huntington Beach. They're wild, often dangerous places where weather can turn bad in an instant and stay bad for a month. Wind-resistant, sturdy gear is a must, and it's a good idea to bring extra food and supplies. Always consult tide tables and park rangers before setting out on a long-distance beach trip. Contact the Outdoor Recreation Information Center (Seattle REI, 222 Yale Avenue North, Seattle, WA 98109; 206/470-4060) and request a copy of the *Olympic Coastal Strip* brochure and a tide table.

The region's high cliffs and quickly shifting tides can easily trap a hiker in an isolated inlet, with disastrous results. Navigating them often requires scaling rock or sand faces on rope ladders, which may or may not be in good repair. Also note that all along the Olympic Coast, backpackers' food caches are the frequent targets of voracious raccoons and crows. Raccoons in this area have been known to hop on backpackers' backs, take swan dives into hot skillets, and chew through layers of tent material to hit pay dirt. Watch your back! Olympic National Park requires that all food carried on overnight coastal hikes be carried in raccoon-proof plastic containers, which are available for rent at local vendors. Call the park's Wilderness Information Center, 360/565-3100, for details.

generally overrun by visitors on summer weekends. To continue south on Olympic National Park's coastal beach strip, see Sand Point to Rialto Beach (below).

For beach hiking and backpacking precautions and recommendations, see Shi Shi Beach/Point of the Arches (above).

Location: On Washington's extreme northwest coast on a coastal strip of Olympic National Park; see The Olympic Peninsula and Coastal Washington Map 1, grid g3.

User Groups: Hikers only. No dogs, horses, or mountain bikes are allowed. No wheelchair facilities.

Permits: Day-hiking permits are not required. Wilderness camping permits, available at major trailheads and at all Olympic National Park visitor centers and ranger stations, are required for all overnight stays in undeveloped park areas. The permit fee is $5 per party (up to 12), plus an additional $2 per person per night, with a cap of $100 for trips of up to 14 nights with a party of

7–12 people. There is no nightly charge for youths 16 years of age and under. Because of overuse in this area, a maximum of 300 overnight permits are issued per day from May 1 through September 30 (note that the permit season formerly ran only from Memorial Day to Labor Day). Call Olympic National Park's Wilderness Information Center at 360/565-3100 for information and reservations. A $1 per car parking fee is collected at the Ozette trailhead.

Maps: To obtain a free Olympic National Park map, contact the Outdoor Recreation Information Center, Seattle REI, 222 Yale Avenue North, Seattle, WA 98109; 206/470-4060. Green Trails, Inc.'s excellent topographic map of the region is available for $3.99 at outdoor retail outlets. Ask for map number 130S, Lake Ozette. Ask for a USGS topographic map of the Ozette area.

Directions: From Port Angeles take U.S. 101 west five miles to Highway 112. Follow Highway 112 west for 32 miles to Hoko-Ozette

Road, just past Sekiu. Turn left (south) on Hoko-Ozette Road and drive about 20 miles to its end at the Ozette Ranger Station.

Contact: Olympic National Park, 600 East Park Avenue, Port Angeles, WA 98362; 360/565-3100.

▟ North Olympic Coast: Sand Point to Rialto Beach

17.2 mi one way/
2.0–3.0 days

Often called the Shipwreck Coast, this stretch of wild Olympic Peninsula beach lives up to its romantic billing. Along the way, campsites are set next to memorials that mark the sinking of ships on this rugged, storm-wracked coastal strip. The 17.2-mile (one-way) jaunt can be hiked from the north or south, beginning on the beach at the end of the Sand Point Trail (see hike above), or at Rialto Beach near Mora Campground, just across the Quillayute River from the fishing village of La Push. Either way you go, this is a trip into the wild, wondrous past. Other than the aforementioned shipwreck memorials, an abandoned mine, and a decaying lookout site, few signs of modern life are visible anywhere.

As with other coastal hikes, be sure to consult a tide guide. Some headlands along the way are passable only at low tide, and several headlands are passable only at rare, extremely low tides; otherwise, they must be circumnavigated, which usually involves climbing and bushwhacking. Most of the route is on wet, flat sand, and the going is pleasurable when weather cooperates (which isn't as often as you'd like). Take your time and enjoy the walk, with little elevation gain, except for occasional headland crossings. Wildlife viewing is excellent, and off-season hikers find plenty of privacy. This coastal stretch is commonly referred to as

Olympic National Park's North Coast Beach Travelway. To continue south from La Push along the Olympic coastal strip, see Third Beach to Hoh River (in this chapter).

Yellow Banks headlands can be rounded only at or near low tide. Fires are not allowed between the headlands north of Yellow Banks and the headlands at Wedding Rocks near Sand Point. In all other areas gather firewood from the beach only. For beach hiking and backpacking precautions and recommendations see Shi Shi Beach/Point of the Arches (in this chapter).

Location: On Washington's Pacific coast between Lake Ozette and La Push, on a coastal strip of Olympic National Park; see The Olympic Peninsula and Coastal Washington Map 1, grid g3.

User Groups: Hikers only. No dogs, horses, or mountain bikes are allowed. No wheelchair facilities.

Permits: Day-hiking permits are not required. Wilderness camping permits, available at major trailheads and at all Olympic National Park visitor centers and ranger stations, are required for all overnight stays in undeveloped park areas. The permit fee is $5 per party (up to 12), plus an additional $2 per person per night, with a cap of $100 for trips of up to 14 nights with a party of 7–12 people. There is no nightly charge for youths 16 years of age and under. Parking and access are free.

Maps: For a free Olympic National Park map, contact the Outdoor Recreation Information Center, Seattle REI, 222 Yale Avenue North, Seattle, WA 98109; 206/470-4060. Green Trails, Inc.'s excellent topographic map of the region is available for $3.99 at outdoor retail outlets. Ask for map number 130S, Ozette. Ask for a USGS topographic map of the Allens Bay and La Push areas.

Directions: From Port Angeles take U.S. 101 about five miles west to Highway 112.

Follow Highway 112 west for about 32 miles and then turn left on Ozette Lake Road, just beyond Sekiu. Follow Ozette Lake Road about 20 miles to its end at the Ozette Ranger Station.

Contact: Olympic National Park, 600 East Park Avenue, Port Angeles, WA 98362; 360/565-3100.

⑤ Pyramid Mountain
7.0 mi/4.0 hrs

A thigh-burner both ways, this trail consists of 2,600 feet of switchbacks that stand between you and a sterling view at Pyramid's summit (3,100 feet). After a brief detour through second-growth trees, the trail climbs quickly into pristine, old-growth coniferous forest interlaced occasionally with madronas, which a good friend insists are alien creatures from another galaxy. The trail climbs quickly to an opening featuring views of Lake Crescent, before running head-on into a saddle marred by a recovering clear-cut. This saddle, about 1.75 miles in, marks the border between Olympic National Forest and Olympic National Park. You have three guesses as to which side of the fence you're on. The trail then switches back sharply up Pyramid's north shoulder, and, after about three miles, opens onto a rocky ridge with excellent views all around. Just ahead is the World War II–vintage summit lookout, which once stood guard against Japanese invasions but today just keeps a lonely, watchful eye on Lake Crescent. Take a good look at Mount Storm King to the south and plot your route for another day's hike—as soon as your thighs have recovered.

Location: On the north shore of Lake Crescent, near the northern boundary of Olympic National Park; see The Olympic Peninsula and Coastal Washington Map 2, grid; see The Olympic Peninsula and Coastal Washington Map 2, grid h2.

User Groups: Hikers only. No dogs, horses, or mountain bikes are allowed. No wheelchair facilities.

Permits: No day-use permits are required. Parking and access are free.

Maps: For a free Olympic National Park map, contact the Outdoor Recreation Information Center, Seattle REI, 222 Yale Avenue North, Seattle, WA 98109; 206/470-4060. Green Trails, Inc.'s excellent topographic map of the region is available for $3.99 at outdoor retail outlets. Ask for map number 101, Lake Crescent. Ask for a USGS topographic map of the Lake Crescent area.

Directions: From Port Angeles follow U.S. 101 about 27 miles southwest to North Shore Road at Fairholm Campground. Turn right and follow North Shore Road/Camp David Jr. Road 3.2 miles to the trailhead parking lot. The trailhead is one-quarter mile back up the road, opposite the lake.

Contact: Olympic National Park, 600 East Park Avenue, Port Angeles, WA 98362; 360/565-3100.

⑥ Spruce Railroad
8.0 mi/3.0 hrs

The Spruce Railroad Trail is without a doubt the flattest trail in the Olympic region and arguably one of the best appetizers for the Olympic Peninsula's scrumptious, glacier-carved smorgasbord. There's a reason for the flatness: this trail was a railroad grade built between Port Angeles and the western Olympic Peninsula during World War I. Spruce Railroad's loss of a grade is Olympic hikers' gain. The trail skirts magnificent Lake Crescent, which stirs the imagination; this lake is a deep, glacier-carved, aqua jewel with ice-cold water. For centuries Crescent was a mystical place for native peoples, and a lakeside walk on a quiet winter day reveals that it has lost little of its magic.

The grade skirts Lake Crescent's north shore, offering occasional views of the rustic Lake Crescent Lodge and the often mist-shrouded Mount Storm King. You pass by two abandoned railroad tunnels (look at them, but don't go in; they're prone to deadly collapses) and a bridge over a picturesque cove at Devil's Point. This trail is a good winter or early spring hike in Olympic National Park because it's rarely snow-covered during those times. It's also an excellent day trip from nearby Fairholm Campground. Mountain bikers: Get your licks in here. As of this writing, Spruce Railroad is the only nonpaved Olympic National Park trail open to two-wheelers. Peninsula cyclists, in fact, often choose this route as a detour around the narrow, winding stretch of U.S. 101 on the other side of Lake Crescent.

And one last piece of advice: Watch for ticks and poison oak along this trail.

Location: On the north shore of Lake Crescent, near the northern boundary of Olympic National Park; see The Olympic Peninsula and Coastal Washington Map 2, grid h2.

User Groups: Hikers, horses, and mountain bikes. Wheelchair access is possible, but difficult due to narrow bridges and occasional fallen trees—bring an attendant. No dogs are allowed.

Permits: No permits are required. Parking and access are free.

Maps: For a free Olympic National Park map, contact the Outdoor Recreation Information Center, Seattle REI, 222 Yale Avenue North, Seattle, WA 98109; 206/470-4060. Green Trails, Inc.'s excellent topographic map of the region is available for $3.99 at outdoor retail outlets. Ask for map number 101, Lake Crescent. Ask for a USGS topographic map of the Lake Crescent area.

Directions: From Port Angeles take U.S. 101 about 27 miles southwest to North Shore Road/Camp David Jr. Road at Fairholm

Campground. Turn right on North Shore Road and follow it to the trailhead at road's end, a distance of about four miles.

Contact: Olympic National Park, 600 East Park Avenue, Port Angeles, WA 98362; 360/565-3100.

◼ Moments in Time Nature Trail
1 mi loop/1.0 hrs

This new trail near Lake Crescent, the most magnificent body of water in Olympic National Park, if not all of Washington, provides a short, easy lesson in geography and topography for first-time visitors to the Olympic Peninsula. The trail winds through some splendid old-growth forest along the lakeshore, passing some early homestead sites. Visitors, especially those with children, might enjoy walking this trail in conjunction with the Marymere Falls Trail (hike number 13), a slightly longer hike located across U.S. 101 from this path. The elevation gain on the Moments in Time Trail is negligible.

The loop trail itself is about a half mile. Combining it with the short walk to and from the ranger station parking lot makes a hike of about one mile round-trip.

Location: On the south shore of Lake Crescent, near the northern boundary of Olympic National Park; see The Olympic Peninsula and Coastal Washington Map 2, grid h2.

User Groups: Hikers and wheelchairs. No dogs, horses, or mountain bikes are allowed.

Permits: No day-use permits are required. Parking and access are free.

Maps: For a free Olympic National Park map, contact the Outdoor Recreation Information Center, Seattle REI, 222 Yale Ave North, Seattle, WA 98109; 206/470-4060. Green Trails, Inc.'s excellent topographic map of the region is available for $3.99 at outdoor retail outlets. Ask for map number 101, Lake Crescent. Ask for a USGS topographic map of the Lake Crescent area.

Directions: From Port Angeles follow U.S. 101 18.5 miles southwest to the Storm King Ranger Station. Parking is available at the ranger station. Walk the 0.3-mile connecting path from the ranger station parking lot to the trailhead, located between Olympic Park Institute and the Lake Crescent Lodge.

Contact: Olympic National Park, 600 East Park Avenue, Port Angeles, WA 98362; 360/565-3100.

8 Marymere Falls
2.0 mi/1.0 hr

Many Northwest tykes make their first venture into Olympic's majestic forests along this self-guided nature trail. The smooth, wide path to Marymere Falls remains one of the Olympic Peninsula's most traveled and popular walkways, and it is especially popular among seniors and parents with small children. Follow the Barnes Creek Trail from the parking lot for 0.7 mile through broad maples and conifers to the Marymere Falls Trail turnoff. From this point, the trail crosses Barnes and Falls Creeks before climbing to vantage points near the falls. It's a most memorable sight. The moss-covered, stony face of the falls juts 100 feet into the air, with Falls Creek cascading across a brilliant green, mossy backdrop. On warm summer days here, cameras whir so persistently that you'd almost swear Madonna (and child) had just been spotted behind a massive Douglas fir. Marymere Falls is one of the more memorable spots within easy walking distance of U.S. 101 in Olympic National Park.

Location: On the south shore of Lake Crescent, near the northern boundary of Olympic National Park; see The Olympic Peninsula and Coastal Washington Map 2, grid h2.

User Groups: Hikers and wheelchairs. The gravel trail is barrier-free for the first mile. No dogs, horses, or mountain bikes are allowed.

Permits: No day-use permits are required. Parking and access are free.

Maps: For a free Olympic National Park map, contact the Outdoor Recreation Information Center, Seattle REI, 222 Yale Ave North, Seattle, WA 98109; 206/470-4060. Green Trails, Inc.'s excellent topographic map of the region is available for $3.99 at outdoor retail outlets. Ask for map number 101, Lake Crescent. Ask for a USGS topographic map of the Lake Crescent area.

Directions: From Port Angeles follow U.S. 101 18.5 miles southwest to the Storm King Ranger Station. Parking is available at the ranger station.

Contact: Olympic National Park, 600 East Park Avenue, Port Angeles, WA 98362; 360/565-3100.

9 Mount Storm King
6.2 mi/4.0 hrs

Like the Marymere Falls Trail (hike number 8), this path begins on the Barnes Creek Trail near the Storm King Ranger Station. Watch for the Mount Storm King sign, located one-third mile from the trailhead. Follow the switchbacks upward through Douglas fir; along the way, you catch glimpses of Lake Crescent and nearby peaks. After about three miles, hikers come to a ridge top and a sign warning of the dangers of proceeding further. The sign is correct. We remember slipping on the scree here years ago and nearly plummeting straight down the rocky face. Experienced hikers and climbers, however, can and often do venture farther, to the trail's end at 4,200 feet. The view of the surrounding peaks and Lake Crescent almost makes the harrowing final steps worthwhile. Almost.

Location: On the north shore of Lake Crescent, near the northern boundary of Olympic National Park; see The Olympic Peninsula and Coastal Washington Map 2, grid h2.

User Groups: Hikers only. No dogs, horses, or mountain bikes are allowed. No wheelchair facilities.

Permits: No day-use permits are required. Parking and access are free.

Maps: For a free Olympic National Park map, contact the Outdoor Recreation Information Center, Seattle REI, 222 Yale Ave North, Seattle, WA 98109; 206/470-4060. Green Trails, Inc.'s excellent topographic map of the region is available for $3.99 at outdoor retail outlets. Ask for map number 101, Lake Crescent. Ask for a USGS topographic map of the Lake Crescent area.

Directions: From Port Angeles follow U.S. 101 18.5 miles south to the Storm King Ranger Station, where parking is available.

Contact: Olympic National Park, 600 East Park Avenue, Port Angeles, WA 98362; 360/565-3100.

🔟 Heart of the Forest Loop
2.0 mi/1.0 hr

"Daaaad, let's DO something." You've all heard it. Well, here's a way to stop the chanting. This short, pleasant forested path inside the popular Heart O' the Hills Campground is a great place to work those inevitable campground-boredom jitters out of the kids. (Day visitors to the park will probably find other nearby trails, such as those atop Hurricane Ridge, more rewarding.) The easy walk winds through the thick, lowland forest typical of the north Olympics, and interpretive signs provide breathers and educational information. Wildlife, such as black-tailed deer and raccoons, is a common sight along the trail. This is the easiest hiking trail within walking distance of Heart O' the Hills. For a more

thorough, uphill workout, check out the Heather Park/Mount Angeles/Lake Angeles trail network across the highway (see hikes below).

Location: At Heart O' the Hills Campground near the northern boundary of Olympic National Park; see The Olympic Peninsula and Coastal Washington Map 2, grid h5.

User Groups: Hikers only. No dogs, horses, or mountain bikes are allowed. No wheelchair facilities.

Permits: Day-hiking permits are not required. A $10 per car entrance fee is collected at the Heart O' the Hills entrance station. Parking is free.

Maps: For a free Olympic National Park map, contact the Outdoor Recreation Information Center, Seattle REI, 222 Yale Avenue North, Seattle, WA 98109; 206/470-4060. Green Trails, Inc.'s excellent topographic map of the region is available for $3.99 at outdoor retail outlets. Ask for map number 135, Mount Angeles. Ask for a USGS topographic map of the Mount Angeles area.

Directions: From U.S. 101 in Port Angeles, follow Hurricane Ridge Road five miles south to the Heart O' the Hills Entrance Station. A short distance beyond the entrance station, turn left into the campground. The trailhead is in camping Loop E.

Contact: Olympic National Park, 600 East Park Avenue, Port Angeles, WA 98362; 360/565-3100.

🔟🔟 Heather Park/Mount Angeles
12.4 mi/8.0 hrs

Heather Park/Mount Angeles is one of two well-traveled trails that lead from the vicinity of the popular Heart O' the Hills Campground into the alpine country near Hurricane Ridge. Actually, the trail ascends 10 miles to the Hurricane Ridge Visitor Center, but most day hikers prefer to turn back at Mount Angeles (6.2 miles) or make a 12.4-mile loop return via the Klahhane Ridge Trail, which skirts Lake Angeles (see hike below). The upper 2.7 miles, from Mount Angeles to Hurricane Ridge, are best walked as a day hike from the Hurricane Ridge parking area (see hike in this chapter). From its starting point near Heart O' the Hills, the trail climbs slowly through deep forest. After 2.2 miles you see the hulking figure of Halfway Rock, a glacial oddity that tauntingly reminds hikers they're only halfway to Heather Park. At about four miles, the trail breaks into the open, rocky meadows of Heather Park, where good campsites are available. Note: There is no water, so pack in your own.

Heather Park is a wonderful world of broken rock, fragile wildflowers, and spectacular views of the Strait of Juan de Fuca to the north. Separate side trails lead to Mount Angeles' First Peak (5,700 feet) and Second Peak (6,100 feet). Beyond, the trail leads through a magnificent (and ankle-twisting) jungle of decaying rock and a narrow notch between Second and Third Peaks, before reaching Victor Pass, where it intersects the Klahhane Ridge Trail. Choose your torture: from here, it's 6.2 steep, toe-jamming miles and 4,000 vertical feet back to the parking lot via either route. The trail usually is snow-free from July through October.

Location: In the northern interior of Olympic National Park; see The Olympic Peninsula and Coastal Washington Map 2, grid h5.

User Groups: Hikers only. No dogs, horses, or mountain bikes are allowed. No wheelchair facilities.

Permits: Day-hiking permits are not required. Wilderness camping permits, available at major trailheads and at all Olympic National Park visitor centers and ranger stations, are required for all overnight stays in undeveloped park areas. The permit fee is $5 per party (up to 12), plus an additional $2 per person per night, with a cap of $100 for trips of up to 14 nights with a party of 7–12 people. There is no nightly charge for youths 16 years of age and under. Parking and access are free.

Maps: For a free Olympic National Park map, contact the Outdoor Recreation Information Center, Seattle REI, 222 Yale Avenue North, Seattle, WA 98109; 206/470-4060. Green Trails, Inc.'s excellent topographic map of the region is available for $3.99 at outdoor retail outlets. Ask for map number 135, Mount Angeles. Ask for a USGS topographic map of the Mount Angeles area.

Directions: From U.S. 101 in Port Angeles, follow Hurricane Ridge Road five miles south to the Heart O' the Hills entrance station. Turn right where the sign indicates trailhead parking.

Contact: Olympic National Park, 600 East Park Avenue, Port Angeles, WA 98362; 360/565-3100.

12 Klahhane Ridge (Lake Angeles)
12.4 mi/8.0 hrs

A western companion to the Mount Angeles Trail, this trek takes a more scenic—and direct—route to the rocky alpine slopes of Mount Angeles and Klahhane Ridge. The trail begins in dark, second-growth fir forest, but it breaks brilliantly (after 3.7 miles) into the open at Lake Angeles, a deep turquoise teardrop; a waterfall drips from the incredibly steep, rocky cliff at the lake's southern end. You find eastern brook trout here, as well as a few scattered campsites. The route is likely to be crowded with tourists, especially on weekends. Beyond the lake, however, the trail gets vertical, and the gapers get discouraged. The path climbs at a breathtaking pace up the rocky slopes of Ennis Ridge before flattening out atop Klahhane Ridge, about two miles beyond Lake Angeles. From here on, trodding the narrow trail is like walking a tightrope along the narrow ridge, with the Olympics pulling from the south and the Strait of Juan de Fuca from the north. The turnaround point is located at the trail's junction with the Heather Park Trail (see hike in this chapter). Until recent years, this area was a prime habitat for mountain goats, which flocked to salt licks left by park rangers. A relocation program, however, has stripped the ridge of nearly all of its friendly ghost-white companions. The trail is usually snow-free from July through October.

Location: In the northern interior of Olympic National Park; see The Olympic Peninsula and Coastal Washington Map 2, grid h5.

User Groups: Hikers only. No dogs, horses, or mountain bikes are allowed. No wheelchair facilities.

Permits: Day-hiking permits are not required. Wilderness camping permits, available at major trailheads and at all Olympic National Park visitor centers and ranger stations, are required for all overnight stays in undeveloped park areas. The permit fee is $5 per party (up to 12), plus an additional $2 per person per night, with a cap of $100 for trips of up to 14 nights with a party of 7–12 people. There is no nightly charge for youths 16 years of age and under. Parking and access are free.

Maps: For a free Olympic National Park map, contact the Outdoor Recreation Information Center, Seattle REI, 222 Yale Avenue North, Seattle, WA 98109; 206/470-4060. Green Trails, Inc.'s excellent topographic map of the region is available for $3.99 at outdoor retail outlets. Ask for map number 135, Mount Angeles. Ask for a USGS topographic map of the Mount Angeles area.

Directions: From U.S. 101 in Port Angeles, follow Hurricane Ridge Road 5.2 miles south to the Heart O' the Hills entrance station. Turn right where the sign indicates trailhead parking.

Contact: Olympic National Park, 600 East Park Avenue, Port Angeles, WA 98362; 360/565-3100.

13 Dungeness Spit
9.0 mi/6.0 hrs

For most Olympic Peninsula visitors, the Dungeness Wildlife Refuge is little more than a curious, brown road sign on U.S. 101 between Sequim and Port Angeles. Drive right by, though, and you're skipping one of the state's best-kept natural secrets. The Dungeness Spit, a 5.5-mile (and growing) curved sand finger formed by the Dungeness River, is a saltwater beach walk extraordinaire. It's also the longest natural sand spit in the world, according to the U.S. Fish and Wildlife Service. Hidden from view by massive, sandy cliffs separating Clallam County's rural farmlands from the Strait of Juan de Fuca, the spit is cut off from civilization on all sides; walking its sandy stretches far into the strait, you get the sensation that you're literally walking away from the mainland to your own private marine observatory. Biologists say more than 250 species of birds and 41 species of land mammals have been recorded on the refuge, as well as eight species of marine mammals. As many as 30,000 waterfowl stop briefly in the Dungeness area each fall on their journey south for the winter and again when they head north in the spring. An additional 15,000 waterfowl winter in the area. As many as 600 harbor seals have been seen hauling out to rest and give birth near the end of the spit.

The refuge is open from sunrise to sunset daily. A 0.4-mile entrance trail leads to a viewpoint on the bluff and then down to the beach, where sand-walking commences. You can walk the spit from either side, but be sure to consult a tide table before you leave. Walking on the north (seaward) side can be tricky during foul weather or high winds. Whichever way you go, the scenery is grand. On the outside, peer across the strait to Vancouver Island and northeast to Mount Baker. On the inside, watch waterfowl relax in the protected waters and windsurfers jet across the water from a launching spot at Cline Spit. Five miles up the spit is the New Dungeness Lighthouse, a fixture on the beach since 1857. Ask the friendly lighthouse keeper for a tour. The spit is closed beyond this point, as is the adjoining Graveyard Spit. On the way back, apply the knowledge you've probably learned about walking close to the water, where traction is much better on the firmer sand. Bring your binoculars. Managers say the refuge is visited by nearly every waterfowl species that winters in western Washington. Harlequin seals also are commonly seen here. The spit's strait side is open to saltwater fishing all year.

Location: In the Dungeness National Wildlife Refuge at the Dungeness River mouth, near Sequim on the Strait of Juan de Fuca; see The Olympic Peninsula and Coastal Washington Map 2, grid g7.

User Groups: Hikers and horses (with restrictions)only. Horseback riding is allowed daily October 1 to May 14 and on weekdays May 15 to September 30 on the designated horse trail through the uplands and the beach west of Dungeness Spit base. Reservations are required; call 360/457-8451. No dogs or mountain bikes are allowed. No wheelchair facilities.

Permits: A $3-per-family fee box is located at the trailhead. Funds support refuge maintenance and interpretive programs. Parking and access are free.

Maps: For a Dungeness National Wildlife Refuge brochure, contact the Nisqually National Wildlife Refuge at 360/753-9467. Ask for a USGS topographic map of the Dungeness area.

Directions: From Sequim drive 4.5 miles west on U.S. 101 and turn right (north) on Kitchen Dick Road. At 3.5 miles, enter the Dungeness Recreation Area on the left. Follow the road one mile beyond the entrance station and campground to the refuge parking lot at the road's end.

Contact: Nisqually National Wildlife Refuge, 100 Brown Farm Road, Olympia, WA 98516; 360/753-9467. The U.S. Fish and Wildlife Service Washington Maritime Refuge Complex, which is not always staffed, may be reached at 33 South Barr Road, Port Angeles, WA 98362-9202; 360/457-8451.

14 Third Beach
2.8 mi/1.5 hrs

This short, relatively easy hike to Third Beach, south of the native fishing village at La Push, is well worth the time spent detouring from a long drive up or down U.S. 101. The mostly flat path winds through storm-wracked lowland forest before opening onto Third Beach, one of the most scenic on Olympic National Park's 57-mile coastal strip. The beach here is usually piled with driftwood. And a series of scenic sea stacks (offshore rock formations) looming from the ocean just offshore make a grand photo opportunity. The trail is open all year, but exercise caution during winter months when storms pound the ocean coast. For longer, multiday hikes south from this point, see Third Beach to Hoh River, below.

Location: On a coastal strip of Olympic National Park, south of La Push; see The

Olympic Peninsula and Coastal Washington Map 3, grid a4.

User Groups: Hikers only. No dogs, horses, or mountain bikes are allowed. No wheelchair facilities.

Permits: Day-hiking permits are not required. Parking and access are free.

Maps: For a free Olympic National Park map, contact the Outdoor Recreation Information Center, Seattle REI, 222 Yale Avenue North, Seattle, WA 98109; 206/470-4060. Green Trails, Inc.'s excellent topographic map of the region is available for $3.99 at outdoor retail outlets. Ask for map number 163S, La Push. Ask for a USGS topographic map of the Toleak Point and Hoh Head areas.

Directions: From U.S. 101 about one mile north of Forks, turn west on Highway 110. Continue left on Highway 110 at the Quillayute Road Junction, at about three miles. At eight miles, stay left at the Y, where La Push Road splits. The Third Beach parking area is three miles beyond the Y.

Contact: Olympic National Park, 600 East Park Avenue, Port Angeles, WA 98362; 360/565-3100.

ⓕ Central Olympic Coast: Third Beach to Hoh River

17.7 mi one way/
3.0–4.0 days

The Third Beach to Hoh River trek, the southern leg of the Olympic coast beach walk (it's also known as the South Coast Beach Travelway), is more rugged and less traveled than its northern counterparts. It requires a bit more ambitious headland bushwhacking, occasionally on old roads built by oil companies that had large (and, we're grateful to say, overly optimistic) plans for oil extraction here. The path has a way of weeding out the ill equipped. It's not a trek for weenies or beach-walking wannabes. Not far down the beach, the daunting specter of the long, steep sand ladders (constructed of cables and wood spars) at Taylor Point are enough to send the easily spooked back toward the car. Farther along, the 17.7-mile (one-way) hike passes many old shipwreck sites, magnificent sea stacks (offshore rock formations), and abundant coastal wildlife. A highlight is Toleak Point, a sheltered, wildlife-rich campsite about 5.5 miles down the beach. Long ago this site was used as a camp for the Quileute people, and today by weary backpackers who wonder how far it is to Oil City (the journey's end).

This hike is a rewarding one for the fit, but it's not recommended for rookie beach hikers less than skilled with a tide table. The payoffs are many, however. Wildlife is plentiful along this route, which is part of the Olympic Coast National Marine Sanctuary. To continue north along the coast, via the North Coast Beach Travelway, see hike North Olympic Coast in this chapter.

For general beach hiking recommendations, see Shi Shi Beach/Point of the Arches (see hike in this chapter). Although this trail section is advertised as hikable year-round, it can be quite dangerous in the winter when storms and high tides push waves not only to the heads of most beaches, but often into established campsites in forested areas near the beach. Beach camping is not recommended. Also note that in recent years swollen streams such as Goodman and Falls Creeks have been unfordable during storms and high tides. This, coupled with large numbers of downed trees, have made some trail portions extremely difficult to negotiate, especially for backpackers, during winter months.

Location: On a coastal strip of Olympic National Park, between La Push and the mouth of the Hoh River; see The

Olympic Peninsula and Coastal Washington Map 3, grid a4.

User Groups: Hikers only. No dogs, horses, or mountain bikes are allowed. No wheelchair facilities.

Permits: Day-hiking permits are not required. Wilderness camping permits, available at major trailheads and at all Olympic National Park visitor centers and ranger stations, are required for all overnight stays in undeveloped park areas. The permit fee is $5 per party (up to 12), plus an additional $2 per person per night, with a cap of $100 for trips of up to 14 nights with a party of 7–12 people. There is no nightly charge for youths 16 years of age and under. Parking and access are free.

Maps: For a free Olympic National Park map, contact the Outdoor Recreation Information Center, Seattle REI, 222 Yale Avenue North, Seattle, WA 98109; 206/470-4060. Green Trails, Inc.'s excellent topographic map of the region is available for $3.99 at outdoor retail outlets. Ask for map number 163S, La Push. Ask for a USGS topographic map of the Toleak Point and Hoh Head areas.

Directions: From U.S. 101 about a mile north of Forks, turn west on Highway 110. Continue left on Highway 110 at the Quillayute Road Junction, at about three miles. At eight miles, stay left at the Y, where La Push Road splits. The Third Beach parking area is three miles beyond the Y. To leave a shuttle car at the end of the trail, continue about 17 miles south of Forks to Oil City Road. Turn west and proceed about three miles to the Oil City Trailhead.

Contact: Olympic National Park, 600 East Park Avenue, Port Angeles, WA 98362; 360/565-3100.

🔢 Second Beach
1.5 mi/1.0 hrs

Another easy, friendly day hike to a highly scenic beach south of La Push, Second Beach often is hiked in conjunction with the nearby and slightly more strenuous Third Beach Trail (see hike in this chapter). Combined, they're a great way to spend a full day on Olympic National Park's 57-mile coastal strip, home to some of the most wild, unspoiled ocean beaches in the lower 48 states. Second Beach makes a great day trip for campers who've set up base at Mora Campground, near Rialto Beach. The trail is open all year, although winter visitors should pay heed to high tides, which often toss house-sized driftwood logs around like Styrofoam on this beach.

Location: On a coastal strip of Olympic National Park, south of La Push; see The Olympic Peninsula and Coastal Washington Map 3, grid a4.

User Groups: Hikers only. No dogs, horses, or mountain bikes are allowed. No wheelchair facilities.

Permits: Day-hiking permits are not required. Parking and access are free.

Maps: For a free Olympic National Park map, contact the Outdoor Recreation Information Center, Seattle REI, 222 Yale Avenue North, Seattle, WA 98109; 206/470-4060. Green Trails, Inc.'s excellent topographic map of the region is available for $3.99 at outdoor retail outlets. Ask for map number 163S, La Push. Ask for a USGS topographic map of the Toleak Point and Hoh Head areas.

Directions: From U.S. 101 about one mile north of Forks, turn west on Highway 110. Continue left on Highway 110 at the Quillayute Road Junction, at about three miles. At eight miles, stay left at the Y, where La Push Road splits. The Second Beach parking area is about 4.5 miles beyond the Y.

Contact: Olympic National Park, 600 East Park Avenue, Port Angeles, WA 98362; 360/565-3100.

17 Bogachiel River

12.2 mi/1.0-2.0 days

Although it's a damp, occasionally dark river-side walk, this hike along the Bogachiel River is one of our favorite alternatives to the over-crowded rainforest of the Hoh River Valley, farther south. The Bogachiel—twin sister in appearance, size, and beauty to the Hoh—begins as snowmelt on High Divide, one of the interior Olympics' more spectacular vis-tas. The trail skirting its lower flanks is a sublime walk into the primordial past, with massive Douglas fir, spruce, western red cedar, and bigleaf maple providing a con-stant, soothing shield from the real world. The largest silver fir in the world is located on the river's south banks, about 2.5 miles beyond the former Bogachiel Shelter site.

This is a grand hike in the fall and early win-ter, when backpackers can take advantage of the private campsites on the river; these spots are generally only disturbed by ex-tremely polite Roosevelt elk. The route is mostly flat, but thanks to numerous streams that gush across the path, it can be very chal-lenging in the spring or during particularly rainy periods. (Any time of year can be soggy here—the area's pelted by up to 200 inches of rain a year.) You find good campsites at the old Bogachiel Shelter (6.1 miles—our rec-ommended turnaround point) and Flapjack Camp (8.25 miles). From Flapjack Camp, the trail continues on as a little-used access to Deer Lake (26 miles) and High Divide (31 miles). Watch out for monster banana slugs.

In recent years, dozens of large trees have fallen across the trail between the park boundary and Mosquito Creek. All are pass-able with some scrambling. But always be prepared to scramble over obstacles on this rarely maintained trail.

Location: On the western edge of Olympic National Park, south of the town of Forks; see The Olympic Peninsula and Coastal Washington Map 3, grid a6.

User Groups: Hikers only. No dogs, horses, or mountain bikes are allowed. No wheel-chair facilities.

Permits: Day-hiking permits are not required. Wilderness camping permits, available at major trailheads and at all Olympic National Park visitor centers and ranger stations, are required for all overnight stays in undevel-oped park areas. The permit fee is $5 per party (up to 12), plus an additional $2 per per-son per night, with a cap of $100 for trips of up to 14 nights with a party of 7–12 people. There is no nightly charge for youths 16 years of age and under. Parking and access are free.

Maps: To obtain a free Olympic National Park map, contact the Outdoor Recreation Infor-mation Center, Seattle REI, 222 Yale Avenue North, Seattle, WA 98109; 206/470-4060. Green Trails, Inc.'s excellent topographic map of the region is available for $3.99 at outdoor retail outlets. Ask for map number 132, Spruce Mountain. Ask the USGS for topographic maps of the Reade Hill and Indian Pass areas.

Directions: From the town of Forks, drive five miles south on U.S. 101 to Bogachiel State Park. Undie Road/Forest Service Road 2932 is directly across from the park. Turn left on Undie Road and follow it 5.5 miles to the gate and trailhead parking lot. Note: This road often is closed by washouts in winter months.

Contact: Olympic National Park, 600 East Park Avenue, Port Angeles, WA 98362; 360/565-3100.

18 South Olympic Coast: Hoh River to Queets River

14.7 mi one way/2.0 days

The Hoh River to Queets River Coastal Route—the south-ernmost stretch of Olympic's famous undeveloped coastal beach—is much less wild than its northern counterparts. Beach camping is prohibited along this route, so day hikers should plan to hike between any of the nine coastal trailheads north and south of Kalaloch Campground, Lodge, and Information Station. Alternatively, choose one trailhead and make a round-trip hike up or down the beach. Better yet, go nuts and hike the entire 14.7 miles, dodging high tides along the way. Whichever route you choose, the going here is easy, pleasant, and memorable. Beaches are wide, flat, and smooth, and you're rarely more than three miles away from a trailhead with a short access trail leading back to U.S. 101. For beach backpacking recommendations and precautions, see the text for Shi Shi Beach. One bonus to hiking the southern coastal beach is the opportunity for surf fishing. See trail notes for the hike following.

Location: On a coastal strip of Olympic National Park, between the Hoh and Queets Rivers; see The Olympic Peninsula and Coastal Washington Map 3, grid c5.

User Groups: Hikers only. No dogs, horses, or mountain bikes are allowed. No wheelchair facilities.

Permits: Day-hiking permits are not required. Wilderness camping permits, available at major trailheads and at all Olympic National Park visitor centers and ranger stations, are required for all overnight stays in undeveloped park areas. The permit fee is $5 per party (up to 12), plus an additional $2 per person per night, with a cap of $100 for trips of up to 14 nights with a party of 7–12 people. There is no nightly charge for youths 16 years of age and under. Parking and access are free.

Maps: For a free Olympic National Park map, contact the Outdoor Recreation Information Center, Seattle REI, 222 Yale Avenue North, Seattle, WA 98109; 206/470-4060. Green Trails, Inc.'s excellent topographic map of the region is available for $3.99 at outdoor retail outlets. Ask for map number 163S, La Push. Ask the USGS for topographic maps of the Destruction Island and Queets areas.

Directions: From Port Angeles, drive about 50 miles south on U.S. 101 to Forks. Proceed about 20 miles south on U.S. 101 to the Ruby Beach parking lot on the right side of the road.

Contact: Olympic National Park, 600 East Park Avenue, Port Angeles, WA 98362; 360/565-3100.

🔢 Kalaloch Area Beaches
0.5–1.5 mi/0.25–1.0 hr 🥾 🔟

Call it a double bonus. Campers lucky enough to snare a beachfront site at Kalaloch Campground, one of the most spectacular in the Northwest, have the ocean literally at their feet. But less-lucky campers can get into the saltwater—on beaches even more beautiful than the one at the campground—by hiking one of the half dozen beach trails immediately to the north and south. The well-signed trailheads, from north to south along U.S. 101, are Ruby Beach, about 7.2 miles north of the campground and beach trails discussed earlier in this chapter.

Each of these paths follows a stream drainage a short distance through this area's storm-blasted spruce forest to a unique beach area. Some beaches are quite rocky and rugged, others sprawling, smooth sand. And there's much more to do here than merely stare across the Pacific. The waters near Ruby Beach and Beach Four and Beach Six offer Washington's best coastal surf perch and skate fishing, and at times, smelt dipping. Also, consider that, with the help of a trailhead-dropoff, each of these beaches can be hiked all the way back to Kalaloch Campground. A day-long beach hike along this stretch is one of the Olympic Peninsula's most enduring pleasures. Expect large crowds in the summer and damp, drizzly weather all year long—except for a few choice summer days when the winds cooperate and blow it all away.

Don't forget your Moby scope. The Destruction Island overlook, midway in this stretch of grand hikes, is a great place to watch for migrating gray whales at peak periods in March/April and November/December.

Location: On a coastal strip of Olympic National Park, immediately north and south of Kalaloch Campground; see The Olympic Peninsula and Coastal Washington Map 3, grid d6.

User Groups: Hikers only. No dogs, horses, or mountain bikes are allowed. No wheelchair facilities.

Permits: Day-hiking permits are not required. Parking and access are free.

Maps: For a free Olympic National Park map, contact the Outdoor Recreation Information Center, Seattle REI, 222 Yale Avenue North, Seattle, WA 98109; 206/470-4060. Green Trails, Inc.'s excellent topographic map of the region is available for $3.99 at outdoor retail outlets. Ask for map number 163S, La Push. Ask the USGS for topographic maps of the Destruction Island and Queets areas.

Directions: From Kalaloch Campground drive north or south on U.S. 101 and watch for trail signs on the west side of the highway.

Contact: Olympic National Park, 600 East Park Avenue, Port Angeles, WA 98362; 360/565-3100.

20 Queets River
31.0 mi/4.0 days

You might call the Queets River Valley the locals' rainforest. The long, gradual valley ascent offers privacy not often found on other western Olympic drainage hikes. The reason? You have to ford the river not once, but several times. Getting across the often-raging Queets is a dilemma you initially face less than 50 yards from the car. The river can be waded in late summer or fall (or other times of the year when it's unseasonably dry), but use caution—if not a rope and multiple partners—to avoid a wet demise. If you're alone or with only one other partner, your best defense is a stout stick, which can be used to brace yourself against the current and poke for deep spots. Tip: It's usually easier to first ford the smaller Sams River, which enters from the right, and then cross the Queets a bit farther upstream.

Once across the river, take your time going through the cool, lush river valley shaded by the magnificent old-growth canopy. Watch for Roosevelt elk here, particularly during the fall rut (or mating season) when mature bulls will bugle and snort and pretend to menace hikers, cows, bushes, shrubs, or anything else they deem inferior, which is pretty much everything. At approximately 2.5 miles, whip out the camera for a Kodak moment at the base of the largest Douglas fir on the planet, which lies a short distance up the trail. (Hint: It's way bigger than a breadbox.) At five miles, good campsites are found at Spruce Bottom, where several fishing holes are the stuff of legend among steelhead anglers. The trail then jumps up and down along the river and winds through massive trees to its end at Pelton Creek (elevation 800 feet), where camping is available.

Location: In the Queets River drainage in the southwestern corner of Olympic National Park; see The Olympic Peninsula and Coastal Washington Map 3, grid d8.

User Groups: Hikers and horses. No dogs or mountain bikes are allowed. No wheelchair facilities.

Permits: Day-hiking permits are not required. Wilderness camping permits, available at major trailheads and at all Olympic

National Park visitor centers and ranger stations, are required for all overnight stays in undeveloped park areas. The permit fee is $5 per party (up to 12), plus an additional $2 per person per night, with a cap of $100 for trips of up to 14 nights with a party of 7–12 people. There is no nightly charge for youths 16 years of age and under. Parking and access are free.

Maps: For a free Olympic National Park map, contact the Outdoor Recreation Information Center, Seattle REI, 222 Yale Avenue North, Seattle, WA 98109; 206/470-4060. Green Trails, Inc.'s excellent topographic map of the region is available for $3.99 at various outdoor retail outlets. Ask for map number 165, Kloochman Rock. Ask for a USGS topographic map of the Kloochman Rock area.

Directions: From Queets drive seven miles south on U.S. 101. Turn left (east) on Queets River Road and drive 14 rough, gravel miles to a parking area near Queets River Campground at the road's end.

Contact: Olympic National Park, 600 East Park Avenue, Port Angeles, WA 98362; 360/565-3100.

21 Hoh River Valley
up to 35.0 mi/3.0 days   2 10

Whether you're strolling several hundred yards into the velvety green drapery of the Hoh's ethereal rainforest or trekking 17 miles to the icy shoulders of Mount Olympus, the Hoh River Trail is a magical experience you won't soon forget. Don't let the hefty mileage fool you: The first 13 miles of this trail are flat, easy walking through Hoh River Valley bottomlands. Day hikers can venture in as far as they please and pause for lunch beneath the canopy of almost ridiculously massive old-growth western red cedar, Douglas fir, bigleaf maple, and Sitka spruce, all of which are draped with long, flowing beards of pea green moss. If you hike here in late autumn, you're likely to see ghostly figures emerging and disappearing in the forest's murky fog. The Olympic Peninsula's largest herds of Roosevelt elk live here, roaming in large, silent clans.

Several miles up the trail, the leafy underbrush beneath the old-growth canopy gives way to rolling, tall grass meadows that stretch to the river. These river flats, particularly at established sites such as Happy Four Camp (5.75 miles) and the Olympus Guard Station (9.0 miles), make outstanding lunch stops or campsites. Beyond the guard station, the trail passes a junction with the Hoh Lake Trail (which accesses the High Divide hike). It then ascends at a breathtaking pace to Glacier Meadows (17.5 miles). Here, alongside a rocky moraine of the Blue Glacier, you find excellent campsites and unforgettable scenery. An open meadow, flooded in early summer with brilliant wildflowers, leads to the heavily crevassed Blue Glacier. It is the largest ice formation on Mount Olympus, the Olympic Peninsula's highest peak at 7,965 feet. Side trails lead in several directions to equally impressive overlooks. This is the primary climber's access route to Olympus; it is best scaled before July, when crevasses melt out and glacier travel turns deadly.

Location: In the interior lowland rainforest of Olympic National Park; see The Olympic Peninsula and Coastal Washington Map 4, grid b1.

User Groups: Hikers only. Wheelchair access to a paved, quarter-mile-loop nature trail near the Hoh Visitor Center is available. No dogs, horses, or mountain bikes are allowed.

Permits: Day-hiking permits are not required. Wilderness camping permits, available at major trailheads and at all Olympic National Park visitor centers and ranger stations, are required for all overnight stays in undeveloped park areas. The permit fee is $5 per party (up to 12), plus an additional $2 per person per night, with a cap of $100 for trips of up to 14 nights with a party of 7–12 people. There is no nightly charge for youths 16 years of age and under. The Hoh River Valley is a limited-quota backcountry area between May 1 and September 30. Campsite reservations (no more than 30 days prior) are suggested. Contact the Park's Wilderness Information Center, 360/565-3100, for details. A $10-per-car access permit, good for seven days at any park entrance, is collected on Hoh River Road from June through September. Parking is free.

Maps: For a free Olympic National Park map, contact the Outdoor Recreation Information Center, Seattle REI, 222 Yale Avenue North, Seattle, WA 98109; 206/470-4060. Green Trails, Inc.'s excellent topographic maps of the region are available for $3.99 each at outdoor retail outlets. Ask for map numbers 133 and 134, Mount Tom and Mount Olympus. Ask the USGS for topographic maps of the Owl Mountain, Mount Tom, and Mount Olympus areas.

Directions: From Forks follow U.S. 101 south for 15 miles and then turn left (east) on Hoh River Road. Follow the road 18 miles to ample parking at the Hoh Ranger Station and Visitor Center. The trailhead is adjacent to the ranger station.

Contact: Olympic National Park, 600 East Park Avenue, Port Angeles, WA 98362; 360/565-3100.

22 Hoh Lake
29.0 mi/2.0–3.0 days

The Hoh Lake Trail, which begins just east of the Olympus Guard Station on the Hoh River Trail, is a pleasant day trip for Hoh River hikers who've pitched a camp at the nine-mile mark. It's also an alternate route

to High Divide (see Loop hike in this chapter), and a connecting leg for backpackers crossing from the Hoh to Soleduck River drainages. The trail begins near a grassy flat along the Hoh. This path switches back very steeply through tree stumps that stand as charred reminders of a 1978 forest fire that consumed a thousand acres of prime greenery. Here, the underbrush is thick, the trail is narrow, and the campsites are few. Above the burn, the trail levels out somewhat, passing through a series of small meadows (including one good campsite at C. B. Flats) before opening to Hoh Lake, a pristine, aqua jewel set 5.25 miles above the Hoh River Trail.

Fishing is good here in the fall, when water thaws and warms enough to awake sleeping rainbow and eastern brook trout. Campsites are scarce, the area has been revegetated, and visitors should stay in established sites only. The trail skirts Hoh Lake to the east and climbs steadily about 1.2 miles to High Divide, where it intersects with the High Divide Trail just below the Bogachiel Peak summit. Views from here of the interior Olympics are outstanding. Caution: Upper trail stretches are snowbound until mid- to late summer. Don't venture toward High Divide without an ice ax and the ability to use it.

Location: In the interior lowland rainforest of Olympic National Park; see The Olympic Peninsula and Coastal Washington Map 4, grid b2.

User Groups: Hikers and horses. No dogs or mountain bikes are allowed. No wheelchair facilities.

Permits: Day-hiking permits are not required. Wilderness camping permits, available at major trailheads and at all Olympic National Park visitor centers and ranger stations, are required for all overnight stays in undeveloped park areas. The permit fee is $5 per party (up to 12), plus an additional $2 per person per night, with a cap of $100 for trips of up to 14 nights with a party of 7–12 people. There is no nightly charge for youths 16 years of age and under. The Hoh River Valley is a limited-quota backcountry area from May 1 to September 30. Campsite reservations (no more than 30 days prior) are suggested. Contact the Park's Wilderness Information Center, 360/565-3100, for current information. A $10-per-car access permit, good for seven days at any park entrance, is collected on Hoh River Road from June through September. Parking is free.

Maps: To obtain a free Olympic National Park map, contact the Outdoor Recreation Information Center, Seattle REI, 222 Yale Avenue North, Seattle, WA 98109; 206/470-4060. Green Trails, Inc.'s excellent topographic map of the region is available for $3.99 at outdoor retail outlets. Ask for map number 133, Mount Tom. Ask the USGS for topographic maps of the Mount Tom and Bogachiel Peak areas.

Directions: From Forks follow U.S. 101 south for 15 miles and then turn left on Hoh River Road. Follow the road 18 miles to ample parking at the Hoh Ranger Station and Visitor Center. The trailhead is adjacent to the ranger station. Hike 9.2 miles up the Hoh River Trail to the Hoh Lake Trailhead, which is on the left (north).

Contact: Olympic National Park, 600 East Park Avenue, Port Angeles, WA 98362; 360/565-3100.

23 Sol Duc Falls/Lover's Lane
1.6–6.0 mi/1.0–3.0 hrs

This is the perfect half-day trip for people camped at Sol Duc Campground or taking it easy at Sol Duc Hot Springs Resort. Shut-terbugs, take note: it's also the path to one of the most scenic waterfalls in the Olympics. From the trailhead at the end of Sol Duc Road, the path climbs gently but steadily about 0.8 miles to the falls, a low, thundering cascade. The trail crosses the river on a bridge below the falls. This is a good turnaround spot for many. But for a longer hike, continue on the well-signed, occasionally rocky Lover's Lane Trail, which leads back along the other side of the river to an exit in Sol Duc Campground. This trail usually is passable all year, although deadfalls may make travel difficult during the winter. Backpackers seeking a longer route in the same area can continue up the Sol Duc River Trail to Deer Lake, Seven Lakes Basin, and beyond to High Divide (see hike below).

Location: In the interior of Olympic National Park; see The Olympic Peninsula and Coastal Washington Map 4, grid a2.

User Groups: Hikers only. No dogs, horses, or mountain bikes are allowed. No wheelchair facilities.

Permits: Day-hiking permits are not required. A $10-per-car access permit, good for seven days at any park entrance, is collected on Sol Duc Hot Springs Road from June through September. Parking is free.

Maps: To obtain a free Olympic National Park map, contact the Outdoor Recreation Information Center, Seattle REI, 222 Yale Avenue North, Seattle, WA 98109; 206/470-4060. Green Trails, Inc.'s excellent topographic maps of the region are available for $3.99 each at outdoor retail outlets. Ask for map numbers 133 and 134, Mount Tom and Mount Olympus. Ask the USGS for topographic maps of the Bogachiel Peak and Mount Carrie areas.

Directions: From Port Angeles follow U.S. 101 south for 27 miles to Sol Duc Hot Springs

Road. Follow the road east about 14 miles to its end at the trailhead parking lot.

Contact: Olympic National Park, 600 East Park Avenue, Port Angeles, WA 98362; 360/565-3100.

②④ High Divide Loop/Seven Lakes Basin
18.5 mi/2.0–3.0 days

The High Divide Loop, which begins on the Soleduck River and climbs to one of the most spectacular alpine vistas in the Northwest, is the classic Olympic Peninsula forest-to-alpine trek. Our favorite route is counterclockwise: it climbs the cool, occasionally steep, wooded trail past Sol Duc Falls and ascends sharply along Canyon Creek to picturesque Deer Lake, which is an excellent first-night campsite. From here it's onward and upward to a trail wandering north into Seven Lakes Basin, which offers lovely—and extremely over-used—campsites. You need to reserve a camping permit to pitch the tent here. To access the wildflower-dotted shoulders of Bogachiel Peak (7.8 miles, 5,474 feet), stay straight at the junction. Here, the trail intersects with the Hoh Lake Trail, which drops sharply to the Hoh River Valley (see hike in this chapter).

If it's early in the year and enough snow lingers here to provide water, camping atop Bogachiel Peak can be a mesmerizing experience. The view is unobstructed in every direction. You never forget the magenta Pacific sunsets to the west and the magical view of the broad, tree-lined Hoh River Valley and ice-capped Mount Olympus to the south. From Bogachiel Peak the trail drops 2.1 miles to Heart Lake, with more good campsites, before intersecting with the Appleton Pass Trail at 14 miles. From here it's

4.9 miles back down through the Sol Duc Valley forest.

This loop is largely impassable until mid-summer. Snow lingers on High Divide well into July, which can make travel extremely hazardous. Call ahead to find out the trail conditions if you plan to hike before July.

Location: In the interior of Olympic National Park; see The Olympic Peninsula and Coastal Washington Map 4, grid a2.

User Groups: Hikers only. No dogs, horses, or mountain bikes are allowed. No wheelchair facilities.

Permits: Day-hiking permits are not required. Wilderness camping permits, available at major trailheads and at all Olympic National Park visitor centers and ranger stations, are required for all overnight stays in undeveloped park areas. The permit fee is $5 per party (up to 12), plus an additional $2 per person per night, with a cap of $100 for trips of up to 14 nights with a party of 7–12 people. There is no nightly charge for youths 16 years of age and under. The Seven Lakes Basin area is a limited-quota backcountry area from May 1 to September 30. Campsite reservations (no more than 30 days prior) are suggested. Contact the Park's Wilderness Information Center, 360/565-3100, for current information. A $10-per-car access permit, good for seven days at any park entrance, is collected on Sol Duc Hot Springs Road from June through September. Parking is free.

Maps: To obtain a free Olympic National Park map, contact the Outdoor Recreation Information Center, Seattle REI, 222 Yale Avenue North, Seattle, WA 98109; 206/470-4060. Green Trails, Inc.'s excellent topographic maps of the region are available for $3.99 each at outdoor retail outlets. Ask for map numbers 133 and 134, Mount Tom and Mount Olympus. Ask the USGS for topographic maps of the Bogachiel Peak and Mount Carrie areas.

Directions: From Port Angeles follow U.S. 101 south for 27 miles to Sol Duc Hot Springs Road. Follow the road east about 14 miles to its end at the trailhead parking lot.

Contact: Olympic National Park, 600 East Park Avenue, Port Angeles, WA 98362; 360/565-3100.

25 Appleton Pass
15.2 mi/9.0 hrs

This relatively steep, brisk ascent to sweet-smelling Olympic alpine country is one of the most crowded trails in Olympic National Park. Beginning above Lake Mills, which was created by the upper dam (perhaps short-lived—it might be removed if obstructionist officials such as U.S. Senator Slade Gorton ever see the light) on the Elwha River, the first 2.4 miles consist of decaying black-topped road. The park closed Upper Elwha Road here years ago to prevent fans of the primitive Olympic Hot Springs, which lie above Boulder Creek at the road's end, from making permanent camps at Boulder Creek Campground. Nice try. Appleton Pass hikers see dozens of resilient hot-springers trucking up the road. These persistent individuals ride mountain bikes, push wheelbarrows, or just walk to their favorite pool, where many of them blatantly violate the park's no-nudity hot-springs policy. Cover your eyes!

From Boulder Creek Campground near the hot springs, the trail climbs through forest past the Boulder Lake Trail (see hike below). Continue straight for Appleton Pass. After crossing Boulder Creek, the real wind-sucking begins as the trail climbs rapidly to the Olympic high country. Between the six- and seven-mile points, snowfields are likely to linger well into summer. When the snow retreats, brilliant displays of alpine wildflowers advance. The trail climbs steeply to 5,100 feet and then drops slightly to Appleton

Pass. If you're up for a little more activity, follow the side trail about one mile east of nearby Oyster Lake to an overlook, where the view of Mount Carrie and the Bailey Range sends a tingle up your weary back. Appleton Pass is also accessible from the west via the Soleduck River Trail, which (from this point) drops 7.3 miles to Sol Duc Hot Springs Resort (see hike High Divide Loop, this chapter). The elevation gain from the Elwha side is 2,400 feet. The trail is usually snow-free by early July.

Bear-resistant food containers are recommended in this area. Contact Olympic National Park at the number above for rental information.

Location: In the northern interior of Olympic National Park, between the Elwha and Soleduck River drainages; see The Olympic Peninsula and Coastal Washington Map 4, grid a3.

User Groups: Hikers and horses. No dogs or mountain bikes are allowed. No wheelchair facilities.

Permits: Day-hiking permits are not required. Wilderness camping permits, available at major trailheads and at all Olympic National Park visitor centers and ranger stations, are required for all overnight stays in undeveloped park areas. The permit fee is $5 per party (up to 12), plus an additional $2 per person per night, with a cap of $100 for trips of up to 14 nights with a party of 7–12 people. There is no nightly charge for youths 16 years of age and under. A $10-per-car access permit, good for seven days at any park entrance, is required. The fee is collected at the Elwha River entrance station from June through September. Parking is free.

Maps: For a free Olympic National Park map, contact the Outdoor Recreation Information Center, Seattle REI, 222 Yale Avenue North, Seattle, WA 98109; 206/470-4060. Green Trails, Inc.'s excellent topographic map of the region is available for $3.99 at outdoor retail outlets. Ask for map number 134, Mount Olympus. Ask for a USGS topographic map of the Mount Carrie area.

Directions: From Port Angeles take U.S. 101 8.5 miles west to Elwha River Road. Follow the road south about 10 miles to its end at a National Park Service gate. Parking is available on the road's east shoulder. The trail (which is a road at first) begins at the gate.

Contact: Olympic National Park, 600 East Park Avenue, Port Angeles, WA 98362; 360/565-3100.

26 Boulder Lake
11.6 mi/6.0 hrs

Boulder Lake is a favorite weekend day-hiking or backpacking escape for many Seattle-area smog breathers, especially harried outdoor writers seeking a break from deadlines and credit-card statements. The Boulder Lake Trail is accessible via a 2.4-mile walk on Upper Elwha Road and a half-mile trek along the Appleton Pass Trail (see hike this chapter). The trail diverges from Appleton Trail to the right, climbs slowly above Boulder Creek Canyon, and then intersects the Happy Lake Ridge Trail just before opening to Boulder Lake (at 5.8 miles). The lake is an alpine jewel, at its best in early summer when snow covers the ground from the top of nearby Boulder Peak (elevation 5,600 feet) to the lake's northern shore. The clear, ice-cold water is inhabited by many eastern brook and, allegedly, rainbow trout. With a hook, line, frying pan, can of almonds, Swiss Army knife, and a dose of ingenuity, you can cook up a fine brook trout amandine dinner on the shores of the lake; many good campsites are also available here. Aggressive hikers will enjoy a day trip to the Boulder Peak summit, which can be reached by ascending the right shoulder or, for those trained in snow travel, head-

ing straight up snowfields on the southern face. Views from the top are stupendous in all directions. The trip out is pleasant and fast, although the 2.4-mile trudge down the paved road will seem to have grown by four miles since you hiked in. Total elevation gain is 1,950 feet. The trail is usually snow free by mid-June.

Black bears are frequent visitors to this area, particularly in early summer. Use the bear wires near the lake to hang food out of reach.

Location: In the northern interior of Olympic National Park, southwest of Port Angeles; see The Olympic Peninsula and Coastal Washington Map 4, grid a3.

User Groups: Hikers only. No dogs, horses, or mountain bikes are allowed. No wheelchair facilities.

Permits: Day-hiking permits are not required. Wilderness camping permits, available at major trailheads and at all Olympic National Park visitor centers and ranger stations, are required for all overnight stays in undeveloped park areas. The permit fee is $5 per party (up to 12), plus an additional $2 per person per night, with a cap of $100 for trips of up to 14 nights with a party of 7–12 people. There is no nightly charge for youths 16 years of age and under. A $10-per-car access permit, good for seven days at any park entrance, is required. The fee is collected at the Elwha River entrance station from June through September. Parking is free.

Maps: For a free Olympic National Park map, contact the Outdoor Recreation Information Center, Seattle REI, 222 Yale Avenue North, Seattle, WA 98109; 206/470-4060. Green Trails, Inc.'s excellent topographic map of the region is available for $3.99 at outdoor retail outlets. Ask for map number 134, Mount Olympus. Ask for a USGS topographic map of the Mount Carrie area.

Directions: From Port Angeles take U.S. 101 8.5 miles

west to Elwha River Road. Follow the road about 10 miles to its end at a National Park Service gate. Parking is available on the road's east shoulder. The trail (it's a road at first) begins at the gate.

Contact: Olympic National Park, 600 East Park Avenue, Port Angeles, WA 98362; 360/565-3100.

27 Elwha River
4.0 mi–45.6 mi one way/
2.0 hrs–7.0 days

Take a stroll through history. The 1889 Press Expedition took this spectacular north/south crossing of the Olympic range; it was the first major recorded incursion into the Olympics' interior. If you can arrange transportation between the beginning (Whiskey Bend Trailhead) and the end (North Fork Quinault Campground, a long drive south on U.S. 101) of this Elwha River hike, which follows the aqua-green Elwha River to Low Divide and then descends along the North Fork Quinault River, it can be an excellent week-long backpacking trip. It's also a superb, 56.8-mile round-trip for backpackers who follow the Elwha to its trickling beginnings near Low Divide, then retrace their steps out.

The Elwha/Quinault crossing is a magical blend of moist river-valley lowlands, gently ascending slopes and occasional thigh-frying climbs to slushy snowfields, such as the high point at Low Divide (elevation 3,650 feet, or 2,450 feet above Whiskey Bend Trailhead). Water is normally plentiful on the trail, and several backcountry shelters are available if hikers need to wait out a gullywasher. The shelters also serve as primary campsites; many backpackers sleep at Elkhorn (11.5 miles), Hayes River (17 miles), and Low Divide (29.5 miles). Average backpackers should allow seven days for the full crossing. Aggressive, experienced day hikers sometimes make this 46-mile, mountain-range crossing in a single, 18-hour day during the long daylight hours of June and July. Expect fairly heavy traffic in the summer. Day hikers can get a good feel for the trail by hiking its first portion and a connecting side path, which combine for a 4.3-mile loop that includes stops at Krause Bottom, Goblin's Gate, Humes Ranch, and Michael's Cabin—all early homesteaders' sites.

Black bears are frequent visitors to this area, particularly in early summer. The use of bear-resistant food containers (call Olympic National Park at the number below for rental information) or bear wires is recommended. Cougars also have been encountered on the trail in recent years.

Location: In Olympic National Park from Whiskey Bend (southwest of Port Angeles) to the North Fork Quinault Ranger Station; see The Olympic Peninsula and Coastal Washington Map 4, grid a4.

User Groups: Hikers and horses. No dogs or mountain bikes are allowed. No wheelchair facilities.

Permits: Day-hiking permits are not required. Wilderness camping permits, available at major trailheads and at all Olympic National Park visitor centers and ranger stations, are required for all overnight stays in undeveloped park areas. The permit fee is $5 per party (up to 12), plus an additional $2 per person per night, with a cap of $100 for trips of up to 14 nights with a party of 7–12 people. There is no nightly charge for youths 16 years of age and under. A $10-per-car access permit, good for seven days at any park entrance, is collected at the Elwha River entrance station from June through September. Parking is free.

Maps: To obtain a free Olympic National Park map, contact the Outdoor Recreation Information Center, Seattle REI, 222 Yale Avenue North, Seattle, WA 98109; 206/470-4060. Green Trails, Inc.'s excellent topographic maps of the region are available for $3.99 each at outdoor retail outlets. Ask for map numbers 134, 135, 166, and 167: Mount Olympus, Mount Angeles, Mount Christie, and Mount Steel. Ask the USGS for topographic maps of the Hurricane Hill, Mount Angeles, McCartney Peak, Chimney Peak, Mount Christie, Bunch Lake, and Lake Quinault East areas.

Directions: From Port Angeles take U.S. 101 8.5 miles west to Elwha River Road. Turn left (south) and follow the road four miles to the Elwha Ranger Station. Just past the station, turn left on Whiskey Bend Road. Follow the gravel road 4.3 miles to the parking lot at the end. To leave a shuttle car at the south end of the trail, drive about 45 miles north from Hoquiam on U.S. 101 to North Shore Road. Turn east on North Shore Road and drive about 17 miles to the North Fork Trailhead.

Contact: Olympic National Park, 600 East Park Avenue, Port Angeles, WA 98362; 360/565-3100.

28 Lillian River
14.5 mi/8.0 hrs

For hikers who want a day-long trip to the Elwha River Valley, the Lillian River Trail is a great day hike that leads to one of Olympic Park's more unique subclimates. Turn left (east) off the Elwha Trail after about four miles and walk up the Lillian River, which flows from Lake Lillian. You pass an unusual rain shadow area filled with madronas and other dry trees and bushes before dropping into more familiar, mossy rainforest. You climb moderately upward beneath Lost Cabin Mountain and then drop gradually into

a canyon containing the Lillian River. It's mostly a river walk, but along the way you get occasional glimpses of the Bailey Range to the southwest, which blocks out most of the blustery, wet weather that buffets other nearby Olympic areas. Good campsites are found at the trail's end, near the river gorge. If you're day hiking, knock down your lunch here and tighten your laces for the long but relaxing trip back.

Location: South of Hurricane Ridge in Olympic National Park; see The Olympic Peninsula and Coastal Washington Map 4, grid a4.

User Groups: Hikers only. No dogs, horses, or mountain bikes are allowed. No wheelchair facilities.

Permits: Day-hiking permits are not required. Wilderness camping permits, available at major trailheads and at all Olympic National Park visitor centers and ranger stations, are required for all overnight stays in undeveloped park areas. The permit fee is $5 per party (up to 12), plus an additional $2 per person per night, with a cap of $100 for trips of up to 14 nights with a party of 7–12 people. There is no nightly charge for youths 16 years of age and under. A $10-per-car access permit, good for seven days at any park entrance, is collected at the Elwha River entrance station from June through September. Parking is free.

Maps: For a free Olympic National Park map, contact the Outdoor Recreation Information Center, Seattle REI, 222 Yale Avenue North, Seattle, WA 98109; 206/470-4060. Green Trails, Inc.'s excellent topographic maps of the region are available for $3.99 each at outdoor retail outlets. Ask for map numbers 134 and 135, Mount Olympus and Mount Angeles. Ask the USGS for topographic maps of the Hurricane Hill and Mount Angeles areas.

Directions: From Port Angeles take U.S. 101 8.5 miles west to Elwha River Road. Turn left and follow the road four miles to the Elwha Ranger Station. Just past the station, turn left on Whiskey Bend Road. Follow the gravel road 4.3 miles to the parking lot at the end. Hike the Elwha River Trail four miles to the Lillian River Trailhead.

Contact: Olympic National Park, 600 East Park Avenue, Port Angeles, WA 98362; 360/565-3100.

29 Hurricane Ridge to Klahhane Ridge
7.0 mi/4.0 hrs

Beware baby strollers with bad brakes: this is one of the most accessible, thus most used, alpine trails on the Olympic Peninsula. From the Hurricane Ridge area, it climbs sharply to Sunrise Ridge and passes beneath the stony eyebrows of Mount Angeles. Early in the year, watch for climbers; they will probably cross your path while ascending the steep Switchback Trail, which leaves Hurricane Ridge Road several miles below the summit. At 3.5 miles, you arrive on Klahhane Ridge and collide with the trail down to Lake Angeles and Heart O' the Hills (see hike in this chapter). This is your turnaround point. Pause to enjoy the dual saltwater and alpine views. This hike is best done in late spring, when most snowfields have given way to Impressionist-painting meadows of brilliant wildflowers.

Location: In the northern interior of Olympic National Park, near Hurricane Ridge; see The Olympic Peninsula and Coastal Washington Map 4, grid a5.

User Groups: Hikers only. No dogs, horses, or mountain bikes are allowed. No wheelchair facilities.

Permits: No day-use permits are required. A $10-per-car access permit, good for seven days at any park entrance, is collected at the

Heart O' the Hills entrance station on Hurricane Ridge Road from June through September. Parking is free.

Maps: For a free Olympic National Park map, contact the Outdoor Recreation Information Center, Seattle REI, 222 Yale Avenue North, Seattle, WA 98109; 206/470-4060. Green Trails, Inc.'s excellent topographic map of the region is available for $3.99 at outdoor retail outlets. Ask for map number 135, Mount Angeles. Ask for a USGS topographic map of the Mount Angeles area.

Directions: From U.S. 101 in Port Angeles, turn south on Hurricane Ridge Road and drive 18 miles to the large parking lot at Hurricane Ridge Lodge. Look for the trailhead sign for Lake Angeles: Klahhane Ridge at the east end. Note: Hurricane Ridge Road is closed during heavy winter snow and is sometimes plowed and opened by national park crews only on weekends. Call the park at 360/565-3131 for current road conditions.

Contact: Olympic National Park, 600 East Park Avenue, Port Angeles, WA 98362; 360/565-3100.

30 Hurricane Hill
3.0 mi/2.0 hrs

RV-bound park visitors often find that this route—a broad, easy hike on a long-abandoned roadway—is their only entry into Olympic National Park's alpine wilderness. And what a grand entry it is. The trail begins at 5,000 feet, and on spring days brilliant wildflowers can be found right near the parking lot. Go higher and it only gets better. The climb is slow but steady, with magnificent views of the interior Olympics and the valley carved by the mighty Elwha River. Eventually the trail leaves rocky ridge slopes and opens into a series of splendid meadows. The views from the summit, the site of an old lookout, are unforgettable. This may be the grandest lunch spot in the entire Northwest, with wildflowers at your feet; Olympic's grandest peaks seemingly within arm's reach; and the sweet, pungent smell of alpine air all around. If that's not enough, the Strait of Juan de Fuca, Vancouver Island, and the city of Victoria often are visible to the north.

Locals prefer this hike in the spring, when snowfields still linger and help to chill drinks and sunburned faces. Winter visits on cross-country skis are also a rare treat, although the weather (as the hill's name indicates) can be frightful. Until the mid-1980s, this trail was a great place to get up close and personal with a wild mountain goat. But park rangers, saying the goats aren't native to the park and therefore must go, began relocating them to other states. Today, the only white creature you're likely to see on Hurricane Hill is a park scientist in a lab coat.

Location: In the northern interior of Olympic National Park, near Port Angeles; see The Olympic Peninsula and Coastal Washington Map 4, grid a5.

User Groups: Hikers only. No dogs, horses, or mountain bikes are allowed. The trail is paved and barrier-free for the first half mile.

Permits: No day-use permits are required. A $10-per-car access permit, good for seven days at any park entrance, is required. The fee is collected at the Heart O' the Hills entrance station from June through September.

Maps: For a free Olympic National Park map, contact the Outdoor Recreation Information Center, Seattle REI, 222 Yale Avenue North, Seattle, WA 98109; 206/470-4060. Green Trails, Inc.'s excellent topographic map of the region is available for $3.99 at outdoor retail outlets. Ask for map number 134, Mount

Olympus. Ask for a USGS topographic map of the Hurricane Ridge area.

Directions: From U.S. 101 in Port Angeles, follow Hurricane Ridge Road 18.6 miles south to the trailhead parking lot at road's end. Note: Hurricane Ridge Road is closed during heavy winter snows and is sometimes plowed and opened by national park crews only on weekends. Call the park at 360/565-3131 for current road conditions.

Contact: Olympic National Park, 600 East Park Avenue, Port Angeles, WA 98362; 360/565-3100.

31 Grand Ridge
15.0 mi/8.0 hrs

The highest trail in the Olympics, this high-altitude ridge walk can be made in either direction, with trailheads accessible via Obstruction Point Road to the west or Deer Park Road to the east. That's hardly a coincidence: Originally the trail was supposed to link the Hurricane Ridge area with Deer Park, a mountaintop viewpoint with truly breathtaking views of the Strait of Juan de Fuca, Vancouver Island, northern Puget Sound, and even ice-capped Mount Baker. Somewhere along the line, road crews gave up. Good for them. The trail is a grand walkway in either direction and, for strong hikers, an excellent 15-mile round-trip day hike.

Most hikers prefer to begin at the western trailhead—probably just because they're arriving from the Seattle area. The trail is mostly above timberline in tundra-like terrain, with outstanding views. At one point, the path tops 6,500 feet, making it the highest maintained trail in the park. Yet the total elevation gain is only about 1,100 feet from start to finish. Note: Carry plenty of water because little or none is available on the route. And be mindful of inclement weather; much of the trail is very exposed.

Location: In the northern interior of Olympic National Park, near Hurricane Ridge; see The Olympic Peninsula and Coastal Washington Map 4, grid a5.

User Groups: Hikers only. No dogs, horses, or mountain bikes are allowed. No wheelchair facilities.

Permits: Day-hiking permits are not required. Wilderness camping permits, available at major trailheads and at all Olympic National Park visitor centers and ranger stations, are required for all overnight stays in undeveloped park areas. The permit fee is $5 per party (up to 12), plus an additional $2 per person per night, with a cap of $100 for trips of up to 14 nights with a party of 7–12 people. There is no nightly charge for youths 16 years of age and under. Parking and access are free.

Maps: For a free Olympic National Park map, contact the Outdoor Recreation Information Center, Seattle REI, 222 Yale Avenue North, Seattle, WA 98109; 206/470-4060. Green Trails, Inc.'s excellent topographic map of the region is available for $3.99 at various outdoor retail outlets. Ask for map number 135, Mount Angeles. Ask for a USGS topographic map of the Maiden Peak area.

Directions: From Port Angeles, drive three miles east on U.S. 101 and turn south on Deer Park Road, which opens in midsummer, closes in winter, and turns to gravel after five miles. Turn right into the trailhead parking lot after 16 miles.

Contact: Olympic National Park, 600 East Park Avenue, Port Angeles, WA 98362; 360/565-3100.

32 Grand Valley/Grand Pass
16.0 mi/1.0–2.0 days   3   9

Grand Valley is unique because of its altitude. Unlike most Olympic hikes, which begin with extended tromps through dark forests, this one is in the high country from eager start to weary finish. You begin high (6,200 feet) and actually drop about 1,700 feet down into Grand Valley, leaving the hardest huffing for the return trip. In between, the valley is a marvelous melding of alpine peaks, gentle, marmot-inhabited slopes, and a charm-bracelet string of three crystal-clear lakes. The route climbs gradually for one mile, heading south, and then drops over Lillian Ridge, with excellent views of the Elwha River drainage and Mount Olympus. At 3.5 miles, the trail forks, and the left route drops to Grand Lake. Stay right and continue on for the good stuff. It's a half mile farther to Moose Lake (the origin of its name is unknown, since there are no moose in the Olympics) and another half mile to Gladys Lake, which lies like a jewel at the head of the valley. Both lakes offer superb, even private campsites—but please stick to designated ones, as overuse is taking a toll on the area. Watch the daily games of marmot tag in the meadows and try to scare away the deer, which will stick their heads right in your tent.

With camp established, hop back onto the trail and climb to Grand Pass (elevation 6,400 feet) and a sweeping view of Olympic peaks, including Mount Olympus. On the way out, some prefer to turn right at the trail fork to Grand Lake, which drops nearly 2,000 additional feet to Grand Creek before climbing back to Obstruction Point via Badger Valley. Our advice: Forget it unless you enjoy lugging a full pack up an in-your-face-steep trail for no apparent reason. One good reason might be weather. Exiting via the Lillian Ridge entry route can be a harrowing experience in cold, windy weather, and we've been caught in snow here on the Fourth of July. It wreaked absolute havoc with our fried-chicken and potato-salad picnic lunch.

Location: In the northern interior of Olympic National Park, west of Port Angeles near Hurricane Ridge; see The Olympic Peninsula and Coastal Washington Map 4, grid a5.

User Groups: Hikers only. No dogs, horses, or mountain bikes are allowed. No wheelchair facilities.

Permits: Day-hiking permits are not required. Wilderness camping permits, available at major trailheads and at all Olympic National Park visitor centers and ranger stations, are required for all overnight stays in undeveloped park areas. The permit fee is $5 per party (up to 12), plus an additional $2 per person per night, with a cap of $100 for trips of up to 14 nights with a party of 7–12 people. There is no nightly charge for youths 16 years of age and under. Grand Valley is a limited-permit backcountry area between May 1 and September 30. Campsite reservations (no more than 30 days prior) are suggested. Call the park's Wilderness Information Center, 360/565-3100, for current information. A $10-per-car access permit, good for seven days at any park entrance, is collected at the Heart O' the Hills entrance station on Hurricane Ridge Road from June through September. Parking is free.

Maps: For a free Olympic National Park map, contact the Outdoor Recreation Information Center, Seattle REI, 222 Yale Avenue North, Seattle, WA 98109; 206/470-4060. Green Trails, Inc.'s excellent topographic map of the region is available for $3.99 at various outdoor retail outlets. Ask for map number 135, Mount Angeles. Ask for a USGS topographic map of the Maiden Peak area.

Directions: From Port Angeles follow Hurricane Ridge Road south for 17.3 miles to Obstruction Point Road, a gravel road that turns sharply downhill to the left. Follow Obstruction Point Road 7.8 miles to the trailhead parking lot at the road's end. Note: Hurricane Ridge Road is closed during heavy winter snows and is sometimes plowed and opened by national park crews only on weekends. Call the park at 360/565-3131 for current road conditions. Obstruction Point Road usually does not open until early July.

Contact: Olympic National Park, 600 East Park Avenue, Port Angeles, WA 98362; 360/565-3100.

33 Deer Ridge to Deer Park
10.0 mi/6.0 hrs

This is the direct route to Deer Park and its expansive views of northern Puget Sound. Very direct. The trail gains 3,000 feet in just under five miles, making it a good break-in-your-boots route. From Slab Camp, the trail parallels the road for a time and then breaks out on Deer Ridge at View Rock (1.5 miles), where, guess what, the views are grand. If they give you a taste for more, proceed up the ridge to the national park boundary (3.5 miles). You pass through twisted, gray pine trees that appear older than time, eventually crossing a meadow and topping out at Deer Park, which also is reachable by a gravel road from the north in the summer months. Views of the Juan de Fuca Strait, Puget Sound, and the surrounding Olympic Range peaks take your breath away—whatever breath you have left, that is.

Location: In Olympic National Forest near the northeastern corner of Olympic National Park; see The Olympic Peninsula and Coastal Washington Map 4, grid a6.

User Groups: Hikers only. No dogs, horses, or mountain bikes are allowed. No wheelchair facilities.

Permits: A federal Northwest Forest Pass, $5 per day or $30 annually, is required to park at the trailhead. Passes are available from ranger stations and many private vendors, online at website: www.wta.org, or by calling 800/270-7504.

Maps: For a map of Olympic National Forest and Olympic National Park, contact the Outdoor Recreation Information Center, Seattle REI, 222 Yale Avenue North, Seattle, WA 98109; 206/470-4060. Green Trails, Inc.'s excellent topographic map of the region is available for $3.99 at outdoor retail outlets; ask for map number 135, Mount Angeles. Ask for a USGS topographic map of the Tyler Peak area.

Directions: From Sequim, follow U.S. 101 west for 2.5 miles to Taylor Cutoff Road. Turn left and follow the road to its intersection with Forest Service Road 2870. Head straight on Forest Service Road 2870 to Forest Service Road 2875. Turn right and follow this road to the parking area at Slab Camp, near the northern border of the Buckhorn Wilderness.

Contact: Olympic National Forest, Hood Canal Ranger District's Quilcene office, 295142 Highway 101 South, P.O. Box 280, Quilcene, WA 98376; 360/765-2200.

34 Cameron Creek/Lost Pass
24.0 mi one way/
3.0–4.0 days

Whether your destination is Grand Pass near Hurricane Ridge, the Dosewallips River Trail via Lost Pass, or somewhere in between, Cameron Creek is a trail that tries your patience, not to mention your legs. It offers a bit of nearly everything the high Olympics have to offer. From the point where it splits from the Lower Gray Wolf River Trail (10.2 miles in; see hike in this chapter), this path follows Cameron Creek to many good fishing holes, where an occasional large rainbow trout can be caught for dinner. (No fishing license is required within Olympic National Park; check with rangers for regulations.)

Higher up, you pass through a series of meadows before reaching a junction with the Grand Pass Trail (17.5 miles), which leads north to Grand Pass, Grand Valley, and Obstruction Point Road. The main path swings south here, traveling up and along a ridge top to Cameron Basin, which offers excellent campsites. Leave your stuff here and hike up another 1,000 feet to Cameron Pass (elevation 6,450 feet, 21 miles). Plan to spend at least an hour soaking up the view. It's one of those places you try to sear permanently into your brain for retrieval in stressful times. You can turn around here for a 42-mile hike round-trip, but if you have the time and gumption, we highly recommend crossing over Lost Pass and down to the Dosewallips River Trail. From here, it's about 12.5 miles east to the Dosewallips Trailhead or about 15.5 miles northeast back to the Lower Gray Wolf River Trail via the Upper Gray Wolf River Trail. Loop hikers find that the latter route, including the Lower Gray Wolf, Cameron Creek, Dosewallips, and Upper Gray Wolf, is an awesome, six-to eight-day, 50-mile Olympic backcountry trip.

Ask rangers about snow conditions before embarking. The crossing at Cameron Pass can be icy and hazardous at times. Always carry an ice ax if snow is present on the trail.

Location: In the northeast corner of Olympic National Park; see The Olympic Peninsula and Coastal Washington Map 4, grid a7.

User Groups: Hikers only. No dogs, horses, or mountain bikes are allowed. No wheelchair facilities.

Permits: Day-hiking permits are not required. Wilderness camping permits, available at major trailheads and at all Olympic National Park visitor centers and ranger stations, are required for all overnight stays in undeveloped park areas. The permit fee is $5 per party (up to 12), plus an additional $2 per person per night, with a cap of $100 for trips of up to 14 nights with a party of 7–12 people. There is no nightly charge for youths 16 years of age and under. Parking and access are free.

Maps: For a map of Olympic National Forest and Olympic National Park, contact the Outdoor Recreation Information Center, Seattle REI, 222 Yale Avenue North, Seattle, WA 98109; 206/470-4060. Green Trails, Inc.'s excellent topographic maps of the region are available for $3.99 each at outdoor retail outlets; ask for map numbers 135 and 136, Mount Angeles and Tyler Peak. Ask the USGS for topographic maps of the Tyler Peak, Maiden Peak, and Wellesley Peak areas.

Directions: From Sequim drive 2.5 miles west on U.S. 101 to Taylor Cutoff Road. Continue 2.5 miles and turn right onto Lost Mountain Road. Proceed to the intersection with Forest Service Road 2870. Veer left and follow Forest Service Road 2870 to the Gray Wolf River Trailhead on the west side of the bridge, where ample parking is available. Hike the Lower Gray Wolf River Trail for 10.2 miles to the Cameron Creek Trailhead.

Contact: Olympic National Park, 600 East Park Avenue, Port Angeles, WA 98362; 360/565-3100.

35 Royal Basin
14.0 mi/1.0–2.0 days

The last time we visited here, we were so anxious to get back into the Olympic alpine country after a long, wet winter that we jumped the gun. Trust us: The last two miles of the Royal Basin Trail are an experience you'll never forget if you're sinking up to your bumpers in deep, sloppy snow with every step. Waiting until late June might be a good idea. But we kept going because we knew what lay ahead. This is an exceptional overnight hike. It's just the right distance, with just the right amount of vertical (2,800

feet) and just the right amount of can't-miss alpine splendor. Royal Basin is royal indeed, surrounded on three sides by jutting rocky walls that keep the annoying world out and the soothing world of deer, marmots, black bears, and wildflowers in. Early in the summer, it's a very short walk up the head of the basin to lingering snowfields, which provide prime mixing materials for snow margaritas. You also find a small lake that offers marginal fishing opportunities. Don't camp too close to it. You'll only muck it up. Note that this area now falls under Olympic National Park's backcountry quota system. Advance reservations aren't required, but they're a good idea: Only half of the available sites are available first-come, first-served.

Location: In the Dungeness River drainage in northeastern Olympic National Park; see The Olympic Peninsula and Coastal Washington Map 4, grid a7.

User Groups: Hikers only. No dogs, horses, or mountain bikes are allowed. No wheelchair facilities.

Permits: Day-hiking permits are not required. Wilderness camping permits, available at major trailheads and at all Olympic National Park visitor centers and ranger stations, are required for all overnight stays in undeveloped park areas. The permit fee is $5 per party (up to 12), plus an additional $2 per person per night, with a cap of $100 for trips of up to 14 nights with a party of 7–12 people. There is no nightly charge for youths 16 years of age and under. Royal Basin is an overnight quota area from May 1 to September 30. Campsite reservations are suggested. Call the parks' Wilderness Information Center, 360/565-3100, for current information. Parking and access are free.

Maps: For a map of Olympic National Forest and Olympic National Park, contact the Outdoor Recreation Information Center,

Seattle REI, 222 Yale Avenue North, Seattle, WA 98109; 206/470-4060. Green Trails, Inc.'s excellent topographic map of the region is available for $3.99 at outdoor retail outlets; ask for map number 136, Tyler Peak. Ask for a USGS topographic map of the Tyler Peak area.

Directions: From U.S. 101 at Sequim Bay State Park, head two miles north to Palo Alto Road and turn left (southwest). Continue on Palo Alto Road as it turns into Forest Service Road 28. Follow Forest Service Road 28 just over a mile to Forest Service Road 2860. Veer right and follow the Forest Service road for 11 miles to the large trailhead parking lot on the right, where the road crosses the Dungeness River. Hike on the Dungeness Trail one mile to the Royal Basin Trailhead, on the right.

Contact: Olympic National Park, 600 East Park Avenue, Port Angeles, WA 98362; 360/565-3100.

36 Gold Creek
12.4 mi/7.0 hrs

On a spring afternoon, this is a good woodlands hike. Start at the bottom of what once was the Tubal Cain Mine Trail (another trail bisected by Forest Service road construction), climb past Gold Creek Shelter at a quarter mile (elevation 1,210 feet), where good campsites are found, and continue to open, high country. The remainder of the trail climbs moderately and parallels the Dungeness River, offering views of the Dungeness Valley that are occasionally quite good. In all, you gain about 2,000 vertical feet. In spring, expect to see lots of wild rhododendrons. The trail ends at Forest Service Road 2860, near the trailhead for the Tubal Cain Mine Trail. You can make it a 6.2-mile shuttle hike by arranging for pickup there. (See directions to the Tubal Cain Mine Trail, in this chapter). This also is one of the eastern Olympics' best mountain bike routes.

Location: In the Dungeness River drainage of Olympic National Forest; see The Olympic Peninsula and Coastal Washington Map 4, grid a7.

User Groups: Hikers, dogs, horses, and mountain bikes. No wheelchair facilities.

Permits: A federal Northwest Forest Pass, $5 per day or $30 annually, is required to park at the trailhead. Passes are available from ranger stations and many private vendors, online at website: www.wta.org, or by calling 800/270-7504.

Maps: For a map of Olympic National Forest and Olympic National Park, contact the Outdoor Recreation Information Center, Seattle REI, 222 Yale Avenue North, Seattle, WA 98109; 206/470-4060. Green Trails, Inc.'s excellent topographic map of the region is available for $3.99 at outdoor retail outlets; ask for map number 136, Tyler Peak. Ask for a USGS topographic map of the Tyler Peak area.

Directions: From U.S. 101 at Sequim Bay State Park, head two miles north to Palo Alto Road and turn left (southwest). Continue on Palo Alto Road as it turns into Forest Service Road 28. Follow Forest Service Road 28 just over a mile to Forest Service Road 2860. Turn right and drive three miles, one mile south of East Crossing Campground, to the trailhead parking lot on the left, just before the Dungeness River Bridge.

Contact: Olympic National Forest, Hood Canal Ranger District, Quilcene office, 295142 Highway 101 South, P.O. Box 280, Quilcene, WA 98376; 360/765-2200.

37 Gray Wolf Pass via the Gray Wolf River
38.6 mi/4.0–5.0 days

There are few river valleys left on the east side of the Olympics where it's easy to forget that large clusters of humans are anywhere within a thousand miles. This is one of those last, best places. The Gray Wolf, a pure, crystal river running from the Olympic alpine country to the Dungeness River and, ultimately, the Strait of Juan de Fuca, is now fully protected, with the upper reaches in Olympic National Park and its lower stretches within Olympic National Forest's Buckhorn Wilderness. Many single- or multiday hikes can be planned along its route, and other lengthy treks are made possible by connecting trails to the nearby Dungeness and Dosewallips trail networks. Still, a hike that sticks to the Gray Wolf from its lowland origins to Gray Wolf Pass is especially rewarding. People who find themselves transfixed by clear, bubbling mountain water will fall in love with the Gray Wolf, which rushes through rapids, collects in pools, and drops through canyons along the route.

An abundance of good, lower-river campsites make this an excellent trail to hike at a relaxed pace. Depending on your speed and strength, you can camp at either Twomile Camp, Cliff Camp, Camp Tony, or Slide Camp, all of which are spaced at roughly two-mile intervals over the trail's first 8.8 miles. At the intersection with the Cameron Pass Trail just beyond the national park border (9.8 miles), the path turns south and follows the Upper Gray Wolf until it becomes a mere stream gurgling through Gray Wolf Basin, a magical alpine valley with outstanding views. They get even better as the trail leaves the meadow and its dancing wildflowers and climbs steeply through loose rock to Gray Wolf Pass, elevation 6,150 feet. Those who brave the wind and camp on the flats here are rewarded with one of the most memorable vistas in the Olympics. While Gray Wolf Pass is our recommended turnaround point (at 19.3 miles), the trail continues down to the Dosewallips River (see hike in this chapter), which lies due south.

Location: In the northeastern corner of Olympic National Park; see The Olympic Peninsula and Coastal Washington Map 4, grid a8.

User Groups: Hikers and horses. No dogs or mountain bikes are allowed. No wheelchair facilities.

Permits: A federal Northwest Forest Pass, $5 per day or $30 annually, is required to park at the trailhead. Passes are available from ranger stations and many private vendors, online at website: www.wta.org, or by calling 800/270-7504. In addition, because the trail enters Olympic National Park, wilderness camping permits also are required. They're available at major trailheads and at all Olympic National Park visitor centers and ranger stations. The permit fee is $5 per party (up to 12), plus an additional $2 per person per night, with a cap of $100 for trips of up to 14 nights with a party of 7–12 people. There is no nightly charge for youths 16 years of age and under.

Maps: For a map of Olympic National Forest and Olympic National Park, contact the Outdoor Recreation Information Center, Seattle REI, 222 Yale Avenue North, Seattle, WA 98109; 206/470-4060. Green Trails, Inc.'s excellent topographic maps of the region are available for $3.99 each at outdoor retail outlets; ask for map numbers 135 and 136, Mount Angeles and Tyler Peak. Ask the USGS for topographic maps of the Tyler Peak, Maiden Peak, and Wellesley Peak areas.

Directions: From Sequim drive 2.5 miles west on U.S. 101 to Taylor Cutoff Road and turn left (south). Turn right onto Lost Mountain Road after about 2.5 miles. Proceed to the intersection with Forest Service Road 2870. Veer left and follow Forest Service Road 2870 to the trailhead on the west side of the bridge, where ample parking is available.

Contact: Olympic National Park, 600 East Park Avenue, Port Angeles, WA 98362; 360/565-3100; Olympic National Forest,

Hood Canal Ranger District, Quilcene office, 295142 Highway 101 South, P.O. Box 280, Quilcene, WA 98376; 360/765-2200.

38 Mount Zion
3.6 mi/3.0 hrs

As children, a bunch of us were herded up the Mount Zion Trail early one August morning on an outing for a church camp at Discovery Bay. Most of us found it to be the most harrowing forced march we had ever endured, at least up to that point. Many years later, the trail seems much shorter, not quite so steep, and vastly more rewarding. This is an excellent day hike for Seattle-area residents who want a taste of the eastern Olympic high country without committing to a full-day or overnight trek. Like Mount Townsend to the south, Zion provides a grand floral display of blooming wild rhododendrons in June. The trail is smooth and well maintained, but fairly steep. From the summit, enjoy the awesome western views of Puget Sound, Mount Rainier, and Seattle. You also find remnants of an old lookout station and a delightful mountaintop spring. They're good enough to stick in your memory for decades.

Although this trail is technically open to mountain bikes, it's quite steep in places, and several drainage channels make cycle passage difficult.

Location: In the Hood Canal Ranger District of Olympic National Forest, west of Hood Canal; see The Olympic Peninsula and Coastal Washington Map 4, grid a8.

User Groups: Hikers, dogs, mountain bikes, and horses. No wheelchair facilities.

Permits: A federal Northwest Forest Pass, $5 per day or $30 annually, is required to park at the trailhead. Passes are available from ranger stations and many private vendors,

online at website: www.wta.org, or by calling 800/270-7504.

Maps: For a map of Olympic National Forest and Olympic National Park, contact the Outdoor Recreation Information Center, Seattle REI, 222 Yale Avenue North, Seattle, WA 98109; 206/470-4060. Green Trails, Inc.'s excellent topographic map of the region is available for $3.99 at outdoor retail outlets; ask for map number 136, Tyler Peak. Ask for a USGS topographic map of the Mount Zion area.

Directions: From Quilcene, drive two miles north on U.S. 101 to Lords Lake Loop Road. Turn left (west) and follow the road 3.4 miles to Forest Service Road 28. Turn left and follow Forest Service Road 28; stay right at the three-way fork. The road becomes Forest Service Road 2810 at Bon Jon Pass. Continue two miles on Forest Service Road 2810 to the trailhead.

Contact: Olympic National Forest, Hood Canal Ranger District, Quilcene office, 295142 Highway 101 South, P.O. Box 280, Quilcene, WA 98376; 360/765-2200.

39 Upper Dungeness
12.8 mi/7.0 hrs

On many a wet, windy autumn evening, Northwest backpackers convene teleconferences to discuss the weekend's weather-dependent plans. More often than not the final word is thus: "If it rains, we go up the Dungeness." There's more than whimsy behind that notion. The Dungeness River Valley, a deep-cut groove between the Gray Wolf and Quilcene drainages, is smack in the armpit of the Olympic rain shadow. Because the interior Olympics shield it from prevailing storm patterns (squalls from the southwest), it receives dramatically less rain than most of the Olympic Peninsula. This phenomenon draws flocks of retired folks to nearby Sequim. It also draws herds of hikers, who hope to escape the squishy-boot blues by fleeing up the Dungeness.

Sun or not, it's a grand hike. The route follows the river, which is refreshingly clear year-round. Good campsites are found at Camp Handy (3.2 miles) and at the Boulder Shelter site, near the intersection with the Constance Pass and Marmot Pass/Big Quilcene Trails (6.4 miles). This is an outstanding fall hike, but be careful: Cougars have been on the prowl here lately. Not too long ago, a small boy was attacked on the banks of the river and escaped, thankfully, with only minor cuts.

Location: In the Dungeness River drainage of Olympic National Forest; see The Olympic Peninsula and Coastal Washington Map 4, grid a7.

User Groups: Hikers, horses, and leashed dogs. No mountain bikes are allowed. No wheelchair facilities.

Permits: A federal Northwest Forest Pass, $5 per day or $30 annually, is required to park at the trailhead. Passes are available from ranger stations and many private vendors, online at website: www.wta.org, or by calling 800/270-7504.

Maps: For a map of Olympic National Forest and Olympic National Park, contact the Outdoor Recreation Information Center, Seattle REI, 222 Yale Avenue North, Seattle, WA 98109; 206/470-4060. Green Trails, Inc.'s excellent topographic map of the region is available for $3.99 at outdoor retail outlets; ask for map number 136, Tyler Peak. Ask for a USGS topographic map of the Tyler Peak area.

Directions: From U.S. 101 at Sequim Bay State Park, head two miles north to Palo Alto Road and turn left (southwest). Continue on Palo Alto Road as it turns into Forest Service Road 28. Follow Forest Service Road 28 just over a mile to Forest Service Road 2860.

Veer right and follow this road for 11 miles to the large trailhead parking lot on the right, where the road crosses the Dungeness River.

Contact: Olympic National Forest, Hood Canal Ranger District, Quilcene office, 295142 Highway 101 South, P.O. Box 280, Quilcene, WA 98376; 360/765-2200.

40 Tubal Cain Mine
17.2 mi/2.0 days

High Olympic alpine scenery and Northwest mining history enrich this hike. It's an unusual combination, but one well worth the 17-mile trudge into the high country. The Tubal Cain Mine Trail starts high, at 3,300 feet, and ends much higher at the Marmot Pass junction with the Big Quilcene Trail at 6,100 feet. Along the way, the trail traverses second-growth forest filled with wild rhododendrons that bloom in early summer. It then climbs through thicker forest to the Tubal Cain Mine, where remains of a copper and magnesium mine that was abandoned in 1911 remain for curious hikers. You want to avoid the mine shaft itself, which goes some 2,800 feet into Iron Mountain. It would be unsafe, even if you were near a hospital (the closest hospital is in Port Angeles). Above Tubal Cain, you get into some luscious alpine meadows at about mile four, passing a way trail to Buckhorn Lake at about 5.5 miles. From here the trail gets rockier as it climbs to Buckhorn Pass (seven miles, elevation 5,900 feet) and its end at Marmot Pass (8.6 miles, elevation 6,000 feet).

Water is scarce along this route in late summer, so make sure you carry enough.

Location: Northwest of Quilcene in the Buckhorn Wilderness, on the eastern slopes of the Olympic Mountains; see The Olympic Peninsula and Coastal Washington Map 4, grid b7.

User Groups: Hikers, dogs, and horses. No mountain bikes are allowed. No wheelchair facilities.

Permits: A federal Northwest Forest Pass, $5 per day or $30 annually, is required to park at the trailhead. Passes are available from ranger stations and many private vendors, online at website: www.wta.org, or by calling 800/270-7504.

Maps: For a map of Olympic National Forest and Olympic National Park, contact the Outdoor Recreation Information Center, Seattle REI, 222 Yale Avenue North, Seattle, WA 98109; 206/470-4060. Green Trails, Inc.'s excellent topographic map of the region is available for $3.99 at outdoor retail outlets; ask for map number 136, Tyler Peak. Ask for a USGS topographic map of the Tyler Peak area.

Directions: From U.S. 101 at Sequim Bay State Park, head two miles north to Palo Alto Road and turn left (southwest). Continue on Palo Alto Road as it turns into Forest Service Road 28. Follow Forest Service Road 28 just over a mile to Forest Service Road 2860. Veer right and drive 15 miles on Forest Service Road 2860, about four miles past the Dungeness Trailhead, to the Tubal Cain Mine Trailhead near the Silver Creek Shelter.

Contact: Olympic National Forest, Hood Canal Ranger District, Quilcene office, 295142 Highway 101 South, P.O. Box 280, Quilcene, WA 98376; 360/765-2200.

41 Silver Lakes
13.0 mi/1.0–2.0 days

Here's the perfect way to spend a night in the Buckhorn Wilderness and be within striking distance of magnificent alpine views the next morning. From its beginnings just beyond Camp Windy on the Mount Townsend Trail, the Silver Lakes Trail drops quickly off a ridge and into the forest, switching back between firs and meadows before opening to the two Silver Lakes, which lie in a glacial cirque 2.5 miles south of the Mount Townsend Trail (see below). In midsummer, both lakes are popular with skinny-dippers and trout anglers (the lakes are stocked with trout), both of whom take advantage of Volkswagen-sized rocks that have tumbled from nearby peaks to the lakeshore. The smaller lake, which is typically somewhat more private, is down a side trail about a quarter mile below the first lake. From your campsite here (make it at least 100 feet from the water), it's a seven-mile round-trip day hike to the top of Mount Townsend. Be sure to pack bug juice.

Location: In the Little Quilcene River drainage of Olympic National Forest, west of Hood Canal; see The Olympic Peninsula and Coastal Washington Map 4, grid a.

User Groups: Hikers, dogs, and horses. No mountain bikes are allowed. No wheelchair facilities.

Permits: A federal Northwest Forest Pass, $5 per day or $30 annually, is required to park at the trailhead. Passes are available from ranger stations and many private vendors, online at website: www.wta.org, or by calling 800/270-7504.

Maps: For a map of Olympic National Forest and Olympic National Park, contact the Outdoor Recreation Information Center, Seattle REI, 222 Yale Avenue North, Seattle, WA 98109; 206/470-4060. Green Trails, Inc.'s excellent topographic map of the region is available for $3.99 at outdoor retail outlets; ask for map number 136, Tyler Peak. Ask for a USGS topographic map of the Tyler Peak area.

Directions: From Quilcene, drive one mile south on U.S. 101 and turn right (west) on Penny Creek Road. After 1.5 miles, turn right on Big Quilcene River Road, which becomes Forest Service Road 27 at the forest boundary. Continue 13.5 miles to Forest Service

Road 2760 and turn left (west). The Mount Townsend Trailhead is three-quarters of a mile up the road on the right. Hike four miles up the Mount Townsend Trail to the Silver Lakes Trailhead on the left.

Contact: Olympic National Forest, Hood Canal Ranger District, Quilcene office, 295142 Highway 101 South, P.O. Box 280, Quilcene, WA 98376; 360/765-2200.

42 Mount Townsend
11.0 mi/6.5 hrs

Hike this trail in spring or early summer and bring your camera. The wildflowers on the way up, including what may be the Northwest's grandest display of wild rhododendrons, will be out in full force. And views from the top of this 6,280-foot peak are among the best in the Olympics. June is a grand time to be here, but wildflowers in the alpine meadows bloom in shifts all the way through September. From the trailhead at 2,850 feet, the trail climbs steadily along Townsend Creek. You find good campsites at 3.5 miles at Camp Windy, near Windy Lake. One-half mile beyond here, the trail splits. The left fork connects to the Silver Lakes Trail (see hike in this chapter).

Stay to the right to reach the summit. It's a fairly steep climb to Townsend's long, north-south ridge, where the trail connects with the Little Quilcene Trail (5.5 miles). Still, the views are so inspiring all along the top that you'll likely want to sit down and pen a line or two of poetry. You can gaze over Hood Canal and Puget Sound to the Cascades, straining to see the little poof of brown smog (yes, smog) over downtown Seattle. And in every other direction, peaks too numerous to mention are in full, glorious display.

Location: In the Little Quilcene River drainage of Olympic National Forest, west of Hood Canal; see The Olympic Peninsula and Coastal Washington Map 4, grid b8.

User Groups: Hikers, dogs, and horses. No mountain bikes are allowed. No wheelchair facilities.

Permits: A federal Northwest Forest Pass, $5 per day or $30 annually, is required to park at the trailhead. Passes are available from ranger stations and many private vendors, online at website: www.wta.org, or by calling 800/270-7504.

Maps: For a map of Olympic National Forest and Olympic National Park, contact the Outdoor Recreation Information Center, Seattle REI, 222 Yale Avenue North, Seattle, WA 98109; 206/470-4060. Green Trails, Inc.'s excellent topographic map of the region is available for $3.99 at outdoor retail outlets; ask for map number 136, Tyler Peak. Ask for a USGS topographic map of the Tyler Peak area.

Directions: From Quilcene, drive one mile south on U.S. 101 and turn right (west) on Penny Creek Road. After 1.5 miles, turn right on Big Quilcene River Road, which becomes Forest Service Road 27 at the forest. Continue 13.5 miles to Forest Service Road 2760. The trailhead is on the right, 0.7 mile down Forest Service Road 2760.

Contact: Olympic National Forest, Hood Canal Ranger District, Quilcene office, 295142 Highway 101 South, P.O. Box 280, Quilcene, WA 98376; 360/765-2200.

43 Little Quilcene/Dirty Face
8.2 mi/5.0 hrs

In the spring, when wildflowers and wild rhododendrons bloom in abundance in the eastern Olympic foothills, this is an excellent hike. Less than a mile up the trail, you cross a stream at what used to be Last Water Camp. Heed the name; it really is the last water. The climb is steady to Little River Summit, about one mile up the trail. Farther up, the trail gets worse (steeper, more rutted) and the views get better (the Strait of Juan de Fuca, Puget Sound, and mighty Mount Baker often are visible).

At the top (elevation approximately 5,300 feet, two miles), the trail intersects the Mount Townsend Trail (see above). You can turn south and hike the 1.2 miles to the summit and more grand views, or continue straight, down the other side of Dirty Face Ridge to the trail's inglorious end at Forest Service Road 2860, at 4.1 miles. The latter is not highly recommended. The grade is so steep (35 to 40 percent) that your toes will never forgive you. If you must try it, however, make it a shuttle hike.

Location: In the Hood Canal Ranger District of Olympic National Forest; see The Olympic Peninsula and Coastal Washington Map 4, grid a8.

User Groups: Hikers, dogs, horses, and mountain bikes. No wheelchair facilities.

Permits: A federal Northwest Forest Pass, $5 per day or $30 annually, is required to park at the trailhead. Passes are available from ranger stations and many private vendors, online at website: www.wta.org, or by calling 800/270-7504.

Maps: For a map of Olympic National Forest and Olympic National Park, contact the Outdoor Recreation Information Center, Seattle REI, 222 Yale Avenue North, Seattle, WA 98109; 206/470-4060. Green Trails, Inc.'s excellent topographic map of the region is available for $3.99 at outdoor retail outlets; ask for map number 136, Tyler Peak. Ask for a USGS topographic map of the Tyler Peak area.

Directions: From Quilcene, drive two miles north on U.S. 101 to Lords Lake Loop Road. Turn left (west) and drive 3.4 miles to Forest Service Road 28. Turn left and continue over Bon Jon Pass to the intersection with Forest Service Road 2820. Turn left and drive approximately four miles to the trailhead, on the right.

Contact: Olympic National Forest, Hood Canal Ranger District, Quilcene office, 295142 Highway 101 South, P.O. Box 280, Quilcene, WA 98376; 360/765-2200.

44 Constance Pass
11.1 mi one way/7.0 hrs 🥾 🥾

Two popular river trails, the Dosewallips to the south and the Dungeness to the north, are connected by this ridgetop route. From the Main Fork Dosewallips Trail, the route climbs moderately through forested terrain, becoming a smooth, relatively flat path after Constance Pass (about 7.5 miles from the Dosewallips Trailhead). The trail, which offers fine views, abundant water, and wonderful fields of wildflowers in season, skirts Mount Constance and ends 3.4 miles later at Boulder Shelter in Olympic National Forest, where it intersects with the Upper Big Quilcene Trail and the Upper Dungeness Trail (see hikes in this chapter).

Location: Between the Dosewallips and Dungeness River drainages in northeast Olympic National Park; see The Olympic Peninsula and Coastal Washington Map 4, grid b7.

User Groups: Hikers only. No dogs, horses, or mountain bikes are allowed. No wheelchair facilities.

Permits: Day-hiking permits are not required. Wilderness camping permits, available at major trailheads and at all Olympic National Park visitor centers and ranger stations, are required for all overnight stays in undeveloped park areas. The permit fee is $5 per party (up to 12), plus an additional $2 per person per night, with a cap of $100 for trips of up to 14 nights with a party of 7–12 people. There is no nightly charge for youths 16 years of age and under. Parking and access to the park are free.

Maps: For a map of Olympic National Forest and Olympic National Park, contact the Outdoor Recreation Information Center, Seattle REI, 222 Yale Avenue North, Seattle, WA 98109; 206/470-4060. Green Trails, Inc.'s excellent topographic maps of the region are available for $3.99 each at outdoor retail outlets; ask for map numbers 136 and 168, Tyler Peak and the Brothers. Ask the USGS for topographic maps of the Mount Deception and the Brothers areas.

Directions: From Hoodsport, travel 26 miles north on U.S. 101 to Brinnon. Turn west on Dosewallips Road (which is gravel, occasionally narrow and/or rough) and follow it 16 miles to the trailhead near the Dosewallips Campground and Summer Ranger Station. Note: In winter months, the road closes at the national park boundary, approximately two miles east of the Dosewallips Campground. Hike 2.5 miles up the Main Fork Dosewallips Trail to the Constance Pass Trailhead.

Contact: Olympic National Park/National Forest Information Center, 150 North Lake Cushman Road, P.O. Box 68, Hoodsport, WA 98548; 360/877-5254.

45 West Fork Dosewallips (Anderson Pass)
21.0 mi/2.0–3.0 days

For many years this has been one of our favorite weekend getaways. Unfortunately, Olympic National Park's inability to keep a functioning High Dose Bridge has left the more spectacular, upper portions of this route off limits in recent years. At press time, the suspension bridge—closed several years ago for a costly replacement—was closed yet again after being destroyed "by a heavy snowfall." So call for information before you head this way. With the bridge out, the upper

trail has fallen into extreme disrepair and may take several years to get back in shape, even after the bridge is replaced. If and when that happens, however, this is a grand east-slope Olympics hike. The trail climbs to excellent campsites at Diamond Meadow (6.8 miles) and Honeymoon Meadows (8.8 miles). The latter, reached by a final thigh-burning, half-mile scramble, has particularly impressive views of Mount Anderson, one of the Olympics' more awesome peaks. If the weather is bad, stop here, relax, and drink camp-brewed coffee. If it's good, consider a day hike higher up.

The trail switches back to a campsite at 10 miles named Camp Siberia because of the winds that sweep off the Anderson Glacier. From here, it's a half mile to Anderson Pass (elevation 4,400 feet), where the trail descends to its junction with the East Fork Quinault Trail (see hike in this chapter). But the truly spectacular views lie up and to the north. From Camp Siberia, the Anderson Glacier Way Trail, a climber's access route, leads about 0.75 miles and 500 feet up, offering sweeping views of the glacier, the peak and the entire eastern Olympics. The trail is a major thoroughfare for long-distance hikers bound for the Enchanted or North Fork Skokomish Valleys.

Be prepared for nasty weather here any time of the year, particularly in the exposed upper portions. That means snow. Also, be aware that the black bear population in the Honeymoon Meadows area is quite healthy, so hang your food.

Location: In the Dosewallips River drainage in eastern Olympic National Park; see The Olympic Peninsula and Coastal Washington Map 4, grid c7.

User Groups: Hikers only. No dogs, horses, or mountain bikes are allowed. No wheelchair facilities.

Permits: Day-hiking permits are not required. Wilderness camping permits, available at major trailheads and at all Olympic National Park visitor centers and ranger stations, are required for all overnight stays in undeveloped park areas. The permit fee is $5 per party (up to 12), plus an additional $2 per person per night, with a cap of $100 for trips of up to 14 nights with a party of 7–12 people. There is no nightly charge for youths 16 years of age and under. Parking and access are free.

Maps: For a map of Olympic National Park and Olympic National Forest, contact the Outdoor Recreation Information Center, Seattle REI, 222 Yale Avenue North, Seattle, WA 98109; 206/470-4060. Green Trails, Inc.'s excellent topographic maps of the region are available for $3.99 each at outdoor retail outlets; ask for map numbers 167 and 168, Mount Steel and the Brothers. Ask the USGS for topographic maps of the Brothers and Mount Steel areas.

Directions: From Hoodsport drive 26 miles north on U.S. 101 to Brinnon. Turn west on Dosewallips Road (gravel, occasionally narrow and/or rough) and follow it 16 miles to the trailhead near the Dosewallips Campground and Summer Ranger Station. Hike the Dosewallips Trail 1.5 miles to the West Fork Dosewallips Trailhead. Note: In winter months, the road closes at the national park border, approximately two miles east of the Dosewallips Campground.

Contact: Olympic National Park/National Forest Information Center, 150 North Lake Cushman Road, P.O. Box 68, Hoodsport, WA 98548; 360/877-5254.

46 Main Fork Dosewallips (Hayden Pass)

30.8 mi/3.0–4.0 days 🥾3 👢8

Bring a friend to rub your neck, because you'll be doing lots of craning on this hike.

The Dosewallips Valley, which lies smack dab in the center of the eastern Olympics, winds through some of the region's highest and most majestic peaks. It's a favorite route for many Olympic hikers who favor extended walks through the little-traveled central portion of the park. The trail climbs gradually 1.5 miles up the Dosewallips to Dose Forks and then swerves right (north), following the river's main fork. Good campsites are numerous on the trail's middle stretch, particularly at Deception Creek (about 8.5 miles). Continue to a junction at about nine miles with the Upper Gray Wolf Trail (see hike in this chapter), which leads north to the Dungeness area. More good campsites are found at Bear Camp (11.5 miles). Views become more expansive and the route gets steeper as you climb past Wellesley Peak. At 12.7 miles, you meet the Lost Pass/Cameron Pass Trail, which leads north to a side trail to Grand Pass (see hike in this chapter). Views are excellent throughout this upper section, particularly at Dose Meadows (12.9 miles), where jutting peaks are framed by wildflowers and robust streams. Beyond the meadows, the route climbs another 2.5 miles to Hayden Pass, elevation 5,847 feet. Turn around here or continue straight and down 8.4 miles west to the Hayes River Ranger Station on the Elwha River Trail (see hike in this chapter).

Location: In the Dosewallips River drainage in eastern Olympic National Park; see The Olympic Peninsula and Coastal Washington Map 4, grid c8.

User Groups: Hikers only. No dogs, horses, or mountain bikes are allowed. No wheelchair facilities.

Permits: Day-hiking permits are not required. Wilderness camping permits, available at major trailheads and at all Olympic National Park visitor centers and ranger stations, are required for all overnight stays in undeveloped park areas. The permit fee is $5 per party (up to 12), plus an additional $2 per person per night, with a cap of $100 for trips of up to 14 nights with a party of 7–12 people. There is no nightly charge for youths 16 years of age and under. Parking and access to the park are free.

Maps: For a map of Olympic National Forest and Olympic National Park, contact the Outdoor Recreation Information Center, Seattle REI, 222 Yale Avenue North, Seattle, WA 98109; 206/470-4060. Green Trails, Inc.'s excellent topographic maps of the region are available for $3.99 each at outdoor retail outlets; ask for map numbers 135, 136, and 168, Mount Angeles, Tyler Peak, and the Brothers. Ask the USGS for topographic maps of the Brothers, Mount Steel, and Wellesley Peak areas.

Directions: From Hoodsport travel 26 miles north on U.S. 101 to Brinnon. Turn west on Dosewallips Road (which is gravel, occasionally narrow and/or rough) and follow it 16 miles to the trailhead near the Dosewallips Campground and Summer Ranger Station. Note: In winter months, the road closes at the national park boundary, approximately two miles east of Dosewallips Campground.

Contact: Olympic National Park/National Forest Information Center, 150 North Lake Cushman Road, P.O. Box 68, Hoodsport, WA 98548; 360/877-5254.

⁴⁷ Lake Constance
4.0 mi/6.0 hrs

Someday, someone will invent a cure for the affliction known as Thighus Fryus, which strikes gung-ho hikers with more lower-body muscles than common sense. If and when they do, they'll make a mint selling it at the exit to the Lake Constance Trail, one of the steeper, more punishing routes in the Northwest. The trail begins near the national park boundary and goes up—way up—for two miles, gaining 3,400 feet. Don't be fooled into thinking you can meander up a long string of switchbacks. This trail has few; more often than not, you risk sucking in gravel when you stop to gasp and find the next few feet of the trail rising up to meet your nose. Amazingly, this trail still receives heavy use, enough to prompt limits of 20 campers per day at the lake. Except for the high level of (ab)use, it is a magnificent site. We highly recommend the side trail around the head of the lake farther up the mountain, where memorable views and rock formations await.

Location: In the Dosewallips River Valley in eastern Olympic National Park; see The Olympic Peninsula and Coastal Washington Map 4, grid c7.

User Groups: Hikers only. No dogs, horses, or mountain bikes are allowed. No wheelchair facilities.

Permits: Day-hiking permits are not required. Wilderness camping permits, available at major trailheads and at all Olympic National Park visitor centers and ranger stations, are required for all overnight stays in undeveloped park areas. The permit fee is $5 per party (up to 12), plus an additional $2 per person per night, with a cap of $100 for trips of up to 14 nights with a party of 7–12 people. There is no nightly charge for youths 16 years of age and under. Note: Lake Constance is a limited-permit backcountry area. Overnight stays at Lake Constance are limited to 20 people per day from May 1 to September 30. Campsite reservations (no more than 30 days prior) are suggested. Call the park's Wilderness Information Center, 360/565-3100, for current information. Parking and access to the park are free.

Maps: For a map of Olympic National Forest and Olympic National Park, contact the

Outdoor Recreation Information Center, Seattle REI, 222 Yale Avenue North, Seattle, WA 98109; 206/470-4060. Green Trails, Inc.'s excellent topographic maps of the region are available for $3.99 each at outdoor retail outlets; ask for map numbers 136 and 168, Tyler Peak and the Brothers. Ask the USGS for topographic maps of the Mount Deception and the Brothers areas.

Directions: From Hoodsport drive 26 miles north on U.S. 101 to Brinnon. Turn west on Dosewallips Road (which is gravel, occasionally narrow and/or rough) and follow it 14.2 miles to the trailhead on the right, just inside the national park boundary.

Contact: Olympic National Park/National Forest Information Center, 150 North Lake Cushman Road, P.O. Box 68, Hoodsport, WA 98548; 360/877-5254.

48 Lena Lake
7.0 mi/3.5 hrs

It's an easy stroll. It's an easy, scenic stroll. It's a crowded, easy, scenic stroll. This route, probably the most crowded on the Olympic Peninsula, continues to draw scores of Seattle-area visitors, who are attracted to the easy grade and, compared to other Olympic National Forest trails, relatively easy auto access. The trail climbs 1,200 feet through a mix of old- and second-growth forest to a junction with the Upper Lena Lake Trail (see hike below) at 2.8 miles. It then drops another quarter mile down to Lena Lake, which offers good fishing for eastern brook and rainbow trout as the water warms. The trail ends at its junction with the Brothers Trail (see hike in this chapter).

Massive revegetation projects have been undertaken at Lena, one of the more abused backcountry areas on the Olympic Peninsula. Campers are asked to heed the No Camping signs and stay in one of the 29 designated campsites. Backcountry rules are strictly enforced. Yes, rangers do write tickets for out-of-bounds camping.

Location: In the Hood Canal Ranger District of Olympic National Forest, near the eastern border of Olympic National Park; see The Olympic Peninsula and Coastal Washington Map 4, grid d7.

User Groups: Hikers, dogs, and mountain bikes. No horses are allowed. No wheelchair facilities.

Permits: A federal Northwest Forest Pass, $5 per day or $30 annually, is required to park at the trailhead. Passes are available from ranger stations and many private vendors, online at website: www.wta.org, or by calling 800/270-7504.

Maps: For a map of Olympic National Forest, contact the Outdoor Recreation Information Center, Seattle REI, 222 Yale Avenue North, Seattle, WA 98109; 206/470-4060. Green Trails, Inc.'s excellent topographic map of the region is available for $3.99 at outdoor retail outlets; ask for map number 168, The Brothers. Ask for a USGS topographic map of the Mount Washington area.

Directions: From Hoodsport travel 13 miles north on U.S. 101 to Forest Service Road 25. Turn west and follow the road for eight miles to the trailhead, which has parking on both sides of the road.

Contact: Olympic National Park/National Forest Information Center, 150 North Lake Cushman Road, P.O. Box 68, Hoodsport, WA 98548; 360/877-5254.

49 Upper Lena Lake
14.0 mi/2.0 days

An extension of the Lena Lake Trail (see above), this trail resembles its little sister only in name. It's much steeper, climbing 2,800 feet in just over four miles from Lower Lena. The crowds should be thinned out by the time you reach the upper lake, but they never thin out too much. Like Lower Lena Lake, this site, too, has undergone fairly major revegetation work. Come here early in the summer and you see why all that planting pays off. Wildflower displays are sublime in the meadows around Upper Lena. So are the views on the way up. The lake itself is nestled in front of Mount Bretherton. In spite of heavy use, this is a memorable hike if you hit it off season, preferably during the week, when you might even be able to find a bit of solitude not far from the lake. The trail may well be at its very best in October, when thousands of bigleaf and vine maples bloom in a red and yellow crescendo. For backpackers, good off-trail day trips include Mount Lena, Scout Lake, and Milk Lake.

Location: In the Hood Canal Ranger District of Olympic National Forest, near the eastern border of Olympic National Park; see The Olympic Peninsula and Coastal Washington Map 4, grid c7.

User Groups: Hikers only. No dogs, horses, or mountain bikes are allowed. No wheelchair facilities.

Permits: A federal Northwest Forest Pass, $5 per day or $30 annually, is required to park at the trailhead. Passes are available from ranger stations and many private vendors, online at website: www.wta.org, or by calling 800/270-7504.

Maps: For a map of Olympic National Forest and Olympic National Park, contact the Outdoor Recreation Information Center, Seattle REI, 222 Yale Avenue North, Seattle, WA 98109; 206/470-4060. Green Trails, Inc.'s excellent topographic map of the region is available for $3.99 at outdoor retail outlets; ask for map number 168, The Brothers. Ask for a USGS topographic map of the Mount Washington area.

Directions: From Hoodsport travel 13 miles north on U.S. 101 to Forest Service Road 25.

Turn west and follow the road eight miles to the trailhead, which has parking. The trailhead is 2.8 miles up the Lena Lake Trail, a popular first-night destination.

Contact: Olympic National Park/National Forest Information Center, 150 North Lake Cushman Road, P.O. Box 68, Hoodsport, WA 98548; 360/877-5254.

50 The Brothers
12.0 mi/1.0–2.0 days

No matter where you travel in the greater Puget Sound region, the Brothers call out to you. Among the eastern Olympics' most prominent peaks, they are regional landmarks—dual sentinels connected in the center by a knife-edge ridge and sheer upper spires—that hold snow well into August. That makes it all the more exciting to climb to the top (or at least close to it)—knowing that, for the rest of your life, you are able to stare across Elliott Bay from Seattle and mutter, "Been there." The Brothers is not a simple climb, however, and summit attempts should be left to experienced climbers. Mountain rescue people spend more than their fair share of time up here. Still, just about anyone can hike the three miles from Lower Lena Lake, a popular first-night campsite, to the end of the maintained trail high on the shoulders of the 6,866-foot peak.

The Brothers Trail travels 1,300 feet up from the north end of Lower Lena Lake, through the rugged East Fork Lena Creek Canyon to a base camp at 3,100 feet. The most common route for the challenging ascent is a chute to the top of the south peak (Mount Edward). You're likely to run into mountaineering students here, perhaps from the noted climbing class at Olympic College in Bremerton. Whether you're a climber or not, the Brothers is a delicious dessert for a three- or four-day backpacking feast that includes the two Lena Lakes (see above). It's a superb hike in September, when crowds die down and the air above 5,000 feet stays crisper than a Methow Valley apple all day long. Incidentally, the peaks are named for brothers Edward and Arthur Fauntleroy, whose sisters' names, Ellinor and Constance, also grace prominent Olympic mountains.

Don't forget to pack a stove if you plan on heating food or water; campfires are not allowed above 3,500 feet.

Location: In the Brothers Wilderness on the border between Olympic National Forest and Olympic National Park; see The Olympic Peninsula and Coastal Washington Map 4, grid d7.

User Groups: Hikers, climbers, and dogs. No horses or mountain bikes are allowed. No wheelchair facilities.

Permits: A federal Northwest Forest Pass, $5 per day or $30 annually, is required to park at the trailhead. Passes are available from ranger stations and many private vendors, online at website: www.wta.org, or by calling 800/270-7504.

Maps: For maps of Olympic National Forest and Olympic National Park, contact the Outdoor Recreation Information Center, Seattle REI, 222 Yale Avenue North, Seattle, WA 98109; 206/470-4060. Green Trails, Inc.'s excellent topographic map of the region is available for $3.99 at outdoor retail outlets; ask for map number 168, The Brothers. Ask for a USGS topographic map of the Brothers area.

Directions: From Hoodsport travel 13 miles north on U.S. 101 to Forest Service Road 25 (follow the signs to the Hamma Hamma Recreation Area). Turn west and drive eight miles to the Lena Lake Trailhead. Follow the Lena Lake Trail for 3.2 miles to the beginning of the Brothers Trail at the inlet of the East Fork of Lena Creek.

Contact: Olympic National Park/National Forest Information Center, 150 North Lake Cushman Road, P.O. Box 68, Hoodsport, WA 98548; 360/877-5254.

51 Putvin
7.4 mi/8.0 hrs

Several years ago, an acquaintance asked if we'd ever hiked the Putvin Trail. Two days after doing it himself, he remained in great pain. It was, he said, the steepest, most miserable trail he'd ever encountered in the Olympics. Not wanting an opportunity like that to slip away, we tried it ourselves. He was right. Putvin is a killer. It rises 3,350 feet in 3.8 miles and is covered with more loose rock than an industrial gravel pit. After all the twisting, turning, ankle spraining, and cursing you can endure as you hike along Whitehorse Creek, you arrive at Lake of the Angels, just inside Olympic National Park. It's a pretty spot but really only a starting place. From here, a number of side trails fan out toward Mount Skokomish, Mount Stone, and who knows where else. We don't, because we were saving what was left of our legs for the return trudge. One humorous side note: We were wise enough not to repeat our hike up this trail, but our acquaintance recently returned for Round Two. He reports the trail, amazingly, is winning many converts and has been crowded on recent summer days. Gluttons!

If you plan to camp overnight, don't forget to pack a stove; campfires are not allowed above 3,500 feet.

Location: In the Mount Skokomish Wilderness within the Hamma Hamma River drainage of Olympic National Forest; see The Olympic Peninsula and Coastal Washington Map 4, grid d7.

User Groups: Hikers and dogs. No horses or mountain bikes. No wheelchair facilities.

Permits: A federal Northwest Forest Pass, $5 per day or $30 annually, is required to park at the trailhead. Passes are available from ranger stations and many private vendors, online at website: www.wta.org, or by calling 800/270-7504. Backpackers who plan to spend the night in Olympic National Park also will need wilderness camping permits, available at major trailheads and at all Olympic National Park visitor centers and ranger stations. The permit fee is $5 per party (up to 12), plus an additional $2 per person per night, with a cap of $100 for trips of up to 14 nights with a party of 7–12 people. There is no nightly charge for youths 16 years of age and under.

Maps: For a map of Olympic National Forest and Olympic National Park, contact the Outdoor Recreation Information Center, Seattle REI, 222 Yale Avenue North, Seattle, WA 98109; 206/470-4060. Green Trails, Inc.'s excellent topographic maps of the region are available for $3.99 each at outdoor retail outlets; ask for map numbers 167 and 168, Mount Steel and The Brothers. Ask for a USGS topographic map of the Mount Washington area.

Directions: From Hoodsport travel 13 miles north on U.S. 101 to Forest Service Road 25 (follow the signs to the Hamma Hamma Recreation Area). Follow the road 12 miles to the trailhead, just past the Boulder Creek Bridge.

Contact: Olympic National Park/National Forest Information Center, 150 North Lake Cushman Road, P.O. Box 68, Hoodsport, WA 98548; 360/877-5254.

52 Duckabush River
10.0 mi/7.0 hrs

The lovely Duckabush Valley is home to one of the longer, straighter, more direct crossings of the Olympics. Although many day hikers and backpackers venture only five miles up the river's cool, clean banks, the Duckabush River Trail continues 23 miles into Olympic National Park, where it connects with the see-it-to-believe-it, high-alpine paradise of the Hart Lake/Marmot Lake/LaCrosse Basin area. From there, one can venture via one of two routes to the O'Neil Pass Trail (see hike in this chapter), which ultimately links the Duckabush to the Enchanted Valley and the East Fork Quinault River Trail.

Extended cross-Olympic backpacking trips via this route or the roughly parallel Dosewallips-to-Quinault route can be unforgettable and well worth the time required to plan and undertake them. For those with less time on their hands, though, the Duckabush River Trail itself is a grand day hike or overnight backpacking trip. The first 2.5 miles are easy; then you have to work a bit to get over the 400-foot "Little Hump." Just beyond it is the more ominous, 1,000-foot "Big Hump." But it's worth all the grunting and moaning. By now, the trail has entered some of the more inspiring old-growth river-bottom forest you'll ever see. Just beyond the Big Hump, excellent campsites await along the river. Stick your feet in the water. You've earned it.

At 15.4 miles, hikers will encounter the LaCrosse Pass Trail, which leads 6.4 miles north to the West Fork Dosewallips Trail near Mount Anderson. This allows a spectacular, 31-mile loop combining both river valleys and a memorable alpine crossing. It's a great weeklong backpacking trip.

Location: In the Duckabush River drainage of Olympic National Park and Olympic National Forest; see The Olympic Peninsula and Coastal Washington Map 4, grid c8.

User Groups: Hikers and horses. No mountain bikes are allowed. No dogs are allowed inside the national park boundary. No wheelchair facilities.

Permits: A federal Northwest Forest Pass, $5 per day

or $30 annually, is required to park at the trail-head. Passes are available from ranger stations and many private vendors, online at website: www.wta.org, or by calling 800/270-7504. In addition, backpackers staying within Olympic National Park will need wilderness camping permits, available at major trailheads and at all Olympic National Park visitor centers and ranger stations. The permit fee is $5 per party (up to 12), plus an additional $2 per person per night, with a cap of $100 for trips of up to 14 nights with a party of 7–12 people. There is no nightly charge for youths 16 years of age and under.

Maps: For a map of Olympic National Forest and Olympic National Park, contact the Outdoor Recreation Information Center, Seattle REI, 222 Yale Avenue North, Seattle, WA 98109; 206/470-4060. Green Trails, Inc.'s excellent topographic maps of the region are available for $3.99 each at outdoor retail outlets; ask for map numbers 167 and 168, Mount Steel and The Brothers. Ask the USGS for topographic maps of the Mount Steel, the Brothers, and Mount Washington areas.

Directions: From Hoodsport drive 22 miles north on U.S. 101 to Forest Service Road 2510 (follow the signs to the Duckabush Recreation Area). Turn west and follow the road for six miles to Forest Service Road 2510-060, where you find the trailhead and a horse-unloading area.

Contact: Olympic National Park/National Forest Information Center, 150 North Lake Cushman Road, P.O. Box 68, Hoodsport, WA 98548; 360/877-5254.

53 Interrorem Interpretive Trail
0.5 mi/0. 5 hr

Bring the kids and the camera on this interpretive nature walk. Many a "Little Johnny and Suzy by the big, big Douglas fir stump" snap-shots are taken on this short loop trail, which juts off the Ranger Hole Trail (see hike below). It's a great place to bring a picnic lunch (good eating spots are found at the trailhead), watch for deer, and amble about in some of the freshest air in the West. You are in second-growth forest, but it's old second-growth forest. The large, ghostly stumps of old-growth trees now are rich food for one of the region's more bustling crops of sword ferns and other forest shrubbery. Warning: This trail will make you and your family want to put many more miles on those new boots in the Olympic forests. That's exactly what it was designed to do.

Location: In the Duckabush River drainage of Olympic National Forest, west of Hood Canal; see The Olympic Peninsula and Coastal Washington Map 4, grid c8.

User Groups: Hikers, dogs, and mountain bikes. No horses are allowed. No wheelchair facilities.

Permits: A federal Northwest Forest Pass, $5 per day or $30 annually, is required to park at the trailhead. Passes are available from ranger stations and many private vendors, online at website: www.wta.org, or by calling 800/270-7504.

Maps: For a map of Olympic National Forest and Olympic National Park, contact the Outdoor Recreation Information Center, Seattle REI, 222 Yale Avenue North, Seattle, WA 98109; 206/470-4060. Ask for a USGS topographic map of The Brothers area.

Directions: From Hoodsport, drive 22 miles north on U.S. 101 to Forest Service Road 2510 (follow the signs to the Duckabush Recreation Area). Turn west and drive four miles to the end of the pavement. The Interrorem Guard Station and the trailhead are on the left.

Contact: Olympic National Park/National Forest Information Center, 150 North Lake Cushman Road, P.O. Box 68, Hoodsport, WA 98548; 360/877-5254.

54 Ranger Hole
1.6 mi/1.0 hr

The "Ranger Hole" for which this trail is named is a Duckabush River fishing hole that dates to the early 1900s, when a ranger lived full-time in the Interrorem Guard Station. Consider this: That was way, way before Tuna Helper, and rangers had to rely on local trout for a hot, fresh meal on lonely evenings along the Duckabush. To find them, they bounded down a side trail to the river, which since has become a popular, maintained trail for thousands of visitors in all seasons.

On your way to the river, you pass unusually rotund second-growth Douglas fir. You also find large maples, a delight in autumn, and many wild birds and small critters. At the river, the deep, aqua waters of Ranger Hole are mesmerizing. The pool lies just below moving white water, which supplies a burst of bubbles. You might figure it's a good place to find fish, and you might be wrong. Although locals once pulled large trout and massive steelhead from these waters, fishing in the hole isn't what it used to be. Try your luck, anyway. You're not likely to find a more beautiful spot to wet a line. If you do get lucky, consider releasing your catch. The river needs all the help it can get repopulating its waters. This is a great family hike after a picnic near the guard station. Use caution on the lower portion, near the river. It can be slippery.

In case the water looks inviting, note that the Duckabush River is not floatable. Stay out of the river, which has dangerous currents.

Location: In the Duckabush River drainage in the Hood Canal Ranger District of Olympic National Forest; see The Olympic Peninsula and Coastal Washington Map 4, grid c8.

User Groups: Hikers, dogs, horses, and mountain bikes. No wheelchair facilities.

Permits: A federal Northwest Forest Pass, $5 per day or $30 annually, is required to park at the trailhead. Passes are available from ranger stations and many private vendors, online at website: www.wta.org, or by calling 800/270-7504.

Maps: For a map of Olympic National Forest and Olympic National Park, contact the Outdoor Recreation Information Center, Seattle REI, 222 Yale Avenue North, Seattle, WA 98109; 206/470-4060. Ask for a USGS topographic map of the Mount Jupiter area.

Directions: From Hoodsport, drive 22 miles north on U.S. 101 and turn west on Forest Service Road 2510 (follow the signs to the Duckabush Recreation Area). Drive four miles to the end of the pavement. The trailhead is near the Interrorem Guard Station and is on the left side of the road; there is a parking lot and picnic area.

Contact: Olympic National Park/National Forest Information Center, 150 North Lake Cushman Road, P.O. Box 68, Hoodsport, WA 98548; 360/877-5254.

55 Jupiter Ridge/Jupiter Lakes
19.4 mi/2.0 days

This trail is rough going. In fact, just finding it can be rough going. The Mount Jupiter Road is in shabby condition under any circumstances, and the logging activity that takes place in the region can make it downright tough to follow at certain times. What's worse, a gate near Forest Service Road 2610-011 adds a 2.5-mile slog up a logging road to the beginning and end of each trek onto Mount Jupiter. But we wanted to include this trail in this book because, for the diligent, it makes an excellent two- or three-day trek that often rewards visitors with something that's hard to come by these days—solitude.

The trail, once you get on it, isn't difficult to follow as it straddles the ridge separating the Duckabush and Dosewallips River Valleys. At six miles, you find an excellent clearing with views of the Duckabush River and the Brothers peaks—a good turnaround spot for day hikers. At eight miles, the increasingly difficult trail enters the Brothers Wilderness. You'll soon see a series of side trails leading down to Jupiter Lakes, which lie 900 feet below and offer good camping and fishing opportunities. Ahead, up a steep, rocky pitch, is the summit, the site of an old lookout cabin. Views of Seattle, Mount Rainier, Mount Adams, and Mount St. Helens are outstanding from here and the trail on the way out.

Location: In the Duckabush River drainage in the Hood Canal Ranger District of Olympic National Forest; see The Olympic Peninsula and Coastal Washington Map 4, grid c8.

User Groups: Hikers, dogs, and horses. No mountain bikes are allowed. No wheelchair facilities.

Permits: A federal Northwest Forest Pass, $5 per day or $30 annually, is required to park at the trailhead. Passes are available from ranger stations and many private vendors, online at website: www.wta.org, or by calling 800/270-7504.

Maps: For a map of Olympic National Forest and Olympic National Park, contact the Outdoor Recreation Information Center, Seattle REI, 222 Yale Avenue North, Seattle, WA 98109; 206/470-4060. Ask for a USGS topographic map of the Mount Jupiter area.

Directions: From Hoodsport drive approximately 22.5 miles north on U.S. 101 and then turn west on Mount Jupiter Road/Forest Service Road 2610-010, just beyond Duckabush Recreation Area Road. Follow the road for 2.5 miles and veer left onto Forest Service Road 2610-011. The road is gated just north of this intersection. Park at the gate and walk 2.5 miles to the trailhead, on the left.

Contact: Olympic National Park/National Forest Information Center, 150 North Lake Cushman Road, P.O. Box 68, Hoodsport, WA 98548; 360/877-5254.

56 Elk Lake
3.0 mi/1.0 hr

You won't want to memorialize this hike with 500 rolls of Fuji Velvia color film. But it is a good, quick sampling of the east-slope Olympic ecosystem, not to mention a decent starter backpack trip for kids and a pleasant day trip for bird-watchers. The Forest Service's myriad roads have created a truncated trail system here, with two trails at the main trailhead. The left fork takes you along the south shore to Cedar Creek and several good campsites before ending at just over one-half mile, thanks to construction of the Forest Service road on which you drove in. The right fork crosses Jefferson Creek, and then follows the creek drainage for about 1.5 miles before dead-ending on another Forest Service road. Walk either or both forks for a relaxing, quick day trip with the kids.

Location: In the Hamma Hamma River drainage of Olympic National Forest; see The Olympic Peninsula and Coastal Washington Map 4, grid d7.

User Groups: Hikers, dogs, horses, and mountain bikes. No wheelchair facilities.

Permits: A federal Northwest Forest Pass, $5 per day or $30 annually, is required to park at the trailhead. Passes are available from ranger stations and many private vendors, online at website: www.wta.org, or by calling 800/270-7504.

Maps: For a map of Olympic National Forest and Olympic National Park, contact the Outdoor Recreation Information Center, Seattle REI, 222 Yale Avenue North, Seattle, WA 98109; 206/470-4060. Green Trails, Inc.'s excellent topographic map of the region is available for $3.99 at outdoor retail outlets; ask for map number 168, The Brothers. Ask for a USGS topographic map of the Mount Washington area.

Directions: From Hoodsport drive 10 miles north on U.S. 101 to Jorsted Creek Road/Forest Service Road 24. Turn west and drive 1.25 miles to Forest Service Road 2480. Veer right onto Forest Service Road 2480, continue for 5.5 miles, then veer left on Forest Service Road 2401, and continue 2.5 miles. The trailhead is on the right, at the end of a short spur road.

Contact: Olympic National Park/National Forest Information Center, 150 North Lake Cushman Road, P.O. Box 68, Hoodsport, WA 98548; 360/877-5254.

57 Lake Quinault Loop
4.0 mi/3.0 hrs

Here's a hidden Olympic Peninsula gem. This quiet, majestic nature hike through the somber Quinault Rainforest is one of the most easily accessible, enjoyable Forest Service trails in Washington. It's also impeccably maintained, with an even, smooth grade, which makes this an excellent educational hike for seniors or parents with small children. The loop passes along the shores of the deep-turquoise Lake Quinault (watch for loons swimming just offshore) and winds by historic Lake Quinault Lodge, Willaby and Falls Creek Campgrounds, and other lakeside attractions. The trail then winds into the memorable Big Tree Grove, one of the most impressive stands of gargantuan, 500-year-old Douglas fir remaining on the West Coast. It is here that the trail excels, even when, as is often the case, gray clouds linger overhead and misty rain runs down your back. The trail rises and falls gently through magnificent, massive rainforest, supplemented by excellent interpretive displays.

One unique feature is a cedar swamp near the trail's high point. The path climbs onto cedar planking and crosses a marsh dotted with ghostly white cedar snags that stand like silent sentries. If time is short, you can hike the trail's most impressive portion, the Big Tree Grove, in a mile-long loop from the Rainforest Nature Trail parking lot. This trail is open all year. It's even a memorable walk on those rare occasions when snow blankets the lower Quinault Valley. The elevation gain is minimal.

Location: On the south shore of Lake Quinault, in Olympic National Forest; see The Olympic Peninsula and Coastal Washington Map 4, grid e1.

User Groups: Hikers and dogs. No horses or mountain bikes are allowed. No wheelchair facilities.

Permits: A federal Northwest Forest Pass, $5 per day or $30 annually, is required to park at the trailhead. Passes are available from ranger stations and many private vendors, online at website: www.wta.org, or by calling 800/270-7504.

Maps: For a map of Olympic National Forest, contact the Outdoor Recreation Information Center, Seattle REI, 222 Yale Avenue North, Seattle, WA 98109; 206/470-4060. Green Trails, Inc.'s excellent topographic map of the region is available for $3.99 at outdoor retail outlets. Ask for map number 197, Quinault Lake. Ask for a USGS topographic map of the Lake Quinault East area.

Directions: From Hoquiam drive 43 miles north on U.S. 101 to Lake Quinault's South Shore Road. Turn right and follow South Shore Road 1.5 miles to the parking lot on the south side of the road. Other trailheads are found at Lake Quinault Lodge, Willaby Campground, Quinault Ranger Station and Falls Creek Campground.

Contact: Olympic National Forest, Pacific Ranger District, Quinault office, 353

South Shore Road, P.O. Box 9, Quinault, WA 98575; 360/288-2525.

58 Willaby Creek
3.4 mi/3.0 hrs

The Willaby Creek Trail allows hikers to extend the Lake Quinault Loop Trail (see above) into a longer day hike. This path leaves the impeccably maintained Lake Quinault Loop and follows Willaby Creek upward at a moderate pace, crossing the Quinault Research Area. The first mile is relatively flat, with excellent old-growth hemlock, fir, and spruce all around. After crossing the creek, the trail climbs swiftly to one of the more massive western red cedar trees you'll ever find. Photograph your dog in front of the tree, and she'll look like a flyspeck when the prints come back.

Location: In the Quinault River drainage of Olympic National Forest, near its southwestern boundary with Olympic National Park; see The Olympic Peninsula and Coastal Washington Map 4, grid e1.

User Groups: Hikers and dogs. No horses or mountain bikes are allowed. No wheelchair facilities.

Permits: A federal Northwest Forest Pass, $5 per day or $30 annually, is required to park at the trailhead. Passes are available from ranger stations and many private vendors, online at website: www.wta.org, or by calling 800/270-7504.

Maps: For a map of Olympic National Forest, contact the Outdoor Recreation Information Center, Seattle REI, 222 Yale Avenue North, Seattle, WA 98109; 206/470-4060. Green Trails, Inc.'s excellent topographic map of the region is available for $3.99 at outdoor retail outlets. Ask for map number 197, Quinault Lake. Ask for a USGS topographic map of the Lake Quinault East area.

Directions: From Hoquiam, drive 43 miles north on U.S. 101 to Lake Quinault's South Shore Road. Turn right and follow South Shore Road 1.5 miles east to the large Rainforest Nature Trail parking lot, which is on the right near Willaby Campground. The trailhead is about a mile up the Quinault Loop Trail.

Contact: Olympic National Forest, Pacific Ranger District, Quinault office, 353 South Shore Road, P.O. Box 9, Quinault, WA 98575; 360/288-2525.

59 Colonel Bob Mountain
14.6 mi/2.0 days

Ouch. This is a tough, often steep hike from rainforest lowlands to a 4,500-foot peak with magnificent views. It begins in damp, coniferous forest and switches back sharply to an old Civilian Conservation Corps (CCC) shelter at the four-mile point. The trail continues up steeply, then drops steeply (do we detect a trend?), and then climbs again before intersecting with the Pete's Creek Trail. On the trail's alpine upper stretches, the going gets steep and rough, and route-finding can be difficult. Unless you're familiar with the area, avoid this trail in the early summer, when snow lingers at high elevations. The last stretch climbs a near-vertical rock face. Watch your footing. The view from the 4,500-foot summit is outstanding. Overnighters take note: good campsites are located at Mulkey Shelter (four miles), Moonshine Flats (6.5 miles), and several other creekside locations.

Location: In Olympic National Forest near the southwestern border of Olympic National Park; see The Olympic Peninsula and Coastal Washington Map 4, grid d2.

User Groups: Hikers, dogs, and horses. No mountain bikes are allowed. No wheelchair facilities.

Permits: A federal Northwest Forest Pass, $5 per day or $30 annually, is required to park

at the trailhead. Passes are available from ranger stations and many private vendors, online at website: www.wta.org, or by calling 800/270-7504.

Maps: For a map of Olympic National Forest, contact the Outdoor Recreation Information Center, Seattle REI, 222 Yale Avenue North, Seattle, WA 98109; 206/470-4060. Green Trails, Inc.'s excellent topographic maps of the region are available for $3.99 at outdoor retail outlets. Ask for map numbers 197 and 198, Quinault Lake and Grisdale. Ask the USGS for topographic maps of the Lake Quinault East and Colonel Bob areas.

Directions: From Hoquiam drive 43 miles north on U.S. 101 to Lake Quinault's South Shore Road. Turn right and follow the road six miles to the trailhead parking area, which is just off the road to the right.

Contact: Olympic National Forest, Pacific Ranger District, Quinault office, 353 South Shore Road, P.O. Box 9, Quinault, WA 98575; 360/288-2525.

60 Maple Glade Rainforest
0.5 mi/0.5 hr

A quick tour of a typical Quinault deciduous rainforest, this interpretive trail never takes you more than 30 minutes from your car. The interpretive trail, which has a flat, smooth grade, offers exhibits on rainforest development and wildlife. Along the way, you pass through a diverse mix of oversized, leafy trees, an open meadow, and a very peaceful abandoned beaver pond. Take your time and take the kids, because this is an enjoyable cruiser. Also, keep your eyes peeled for ghostly figures in the woods. The Lower Quinault's healthy Roosevelt elk herd is often seen in the woods near this trail or in the meadow area a short distance down the road to the east.

Location: In the Quinault River drainage of Olympic National Park; see The Olympic

Peninsula and Coastal Washington Map 4, grid e2.

User Groups: Hikers only. No dogs, horses, or mountain bikes are allowed. No wheelchair facilities.

Permits: No permits are required. Parking and access are free.

Maps: For a free map of Olympic National Park, contact the Outdoor Recreation Information Center, Seattle REI, 222 Yale Avenue North, Seattle, WA 98109; 206/470-4060. Green Trails, Inc.'s excellent topographic map of the region is available for $3.99 at various outdoor retail outlets. Ask for map number 165, Kloochman Rock. Ask for a USGS topographic map of the Finley Creek area.

Directions: From Hoquiam drive about 45 miles north on U.S. 101 to Lake Quinault's North Shore Road. Turn right and drive 8.2 miles east to the Olympic National Park Visitor Center.

Contact: Olympic National Park, 600 East Park Avenue, Port Angeles, WA 98362; 360/565-3100.

61 Fletcher Canyon
2.0 mi/2.0 hrs

The short Fletcher Canyon rainforest trail is only maintained for a mile, but it whips you through some of the old-growth forest for which this region is famous. The trail passes a plethora of fallen trees—apparently windblown—before climbing steeply into the forest for about a mile. At the end of the maintained trail, the path meanders to Fletcher Creek (where you find campsites) and into Fletcher Canyon, about another mile. Watch for elk here.

Location: In the Quinault River drainage of Olympic National Park; see The Olympic Peninsula and Coastal Washington Map 4, grid d3.

User Groups: Hikers, dogs, and horses. No mountain bikes are allowed. No wheelchair facilities.

Permits: A federal Northwest Forest Pass, $5 per day or $30 annually, is required to park at the trailhead. Passes are available from ranger stations and many private vendors, online at website: www.wta.org, or by calling 800/270-7504.

Maps: For a map of Olympic National Forest, contact the Outdoor Recreation Information Center, Seattle REI, 222 Yale Avenue North, Seattle, WA 98109; 206/470-4060. Green Trails, Inc.'s excellent topographic map of the region is available for $3.99 at outdoor retail outlets. Ask for map number 197, Quinault Lake. Ask for a USGS topographic map of the Lake Quinault East area.

Directions: From Hoquiam drive 43 miles north on U.S. 101 to Lake Quinault's South Shore Road. Turn right and drive 12 miles to the trailhead on the right.

Contact: Olympic National Park, 600 East Park Avenue, Port Angeles, WA 98362; 360/565-3100.

62 Three Lakes/Irely Lake
8.0–14.0 mi/5.0–8.0 hrs 🥾 🎒

Whether it's the first or last leg on the Skyline Loop (see next hike), an overnight backpack destination, or just an ambitious day hike, the Three Lakes Trail is a wondrous sampling of the Olympic's spectacular old-growth forest, free-roaming wildlife, and hard-to-find solitude. The trail begins a half mile south of the North Fork Quinault Trail and climbs through sponge-moist rainforest to Irely Lake (which offers osprey sightings and good fishing at times, we're told). Farther up the steadily climbing route, you cross Big Creek and pass through stands of western red cedar that are wider than your dining room. Stop at about four miles to

see the largest-known yellow (Alaska) cedar on the planet. Bring the wide-angle lens: this baby is 12 feet in diameter at the base.

The trail intersects with the Skyline Trail at 6.5 miles, in a meadow area with abundant wildflowers, good campsites, and—you guessed it—three small lakes. Special tip for fruit hounds: Wild huckleberries are very, very abundant here in late summer. Bring a pie-crust mix for that backpacker's oven. From the meadow, it's a quick half mile to the Three Lakes Shelter site, near the Quinault-Queets divide.

Weekend backpackers or gung-ho day hikers might consider using the Three Lakes Trail for a loop that climbs seven miles to the Skyline Trail, 2.8 miles to the Elip Creek Trail, 5.1 miles east to the North Fork Quinault Trail, and then 6.5 miles back to the North Fork Road.

Location: In the North Fork Quinault River drainage of southwest Olympic National Park; see The Olympic Peninsula and Coastal Washington Map 4, grid d3.

User Groups: Hikers and horses. No dogs or mountain bikes are allowed. No wheelchair facilities.

Permits: Day-hiking permits are not required. Wilderness camping permits, available at major trailheads and at all Olympic National Park visitor centers and ranger stations, are required for all overnight stays in undeveloped park areas. The permit fee is $5 per party (up to 12), plus an additional $2 per person per night, with a cap of $100 for trips of up to 14 nights with a party of 7–12 people. There is no nightly charge for youths 16 years of age and under. Parking and access are free.

Maps: For a free map of Olympic National Park, contact the Outdoor Recreation Information Center, Seattle REI, 222 Yale Avenue North, Seattle, WA 98109; 206/470-4060. Green Trails, Inc.'s excellent topographic map of the region is available for $3.99 at outdoor retail outlets. Ask for map number 166, Mount Christie. Ask for a USGS topographic map of the Bunch Lake area.

Directions: From Hoquiam drive about 45 miles north on U.S. 101 to Lake Quinault's North Shore Road. Turn right (east) and drive 16.5 miles to the trailhead on the left, just west of North Fork Campground. Note: If North Shore Road is closed for construction (washouts are common), the trailhead is accessible via South Shore Road.

Contact: Olympic National Park, 600 East Park Avenue, Port Angeles, WA 98362; 360/565-3100.

63 North Fork Quinault
30.4 mi/3.0–4.0 days

The North Fork Quinault Trail—which runs from the Lake Quinault area to Low Divide, near the headwaters of the Elwha River—is the tail end of a trans-Olympics crossing described earlier in this chapter. But it's also an excellent 30.5-mile round-trip hike from Lake Quinault, or for more experienced route-finders, the center leg on the 47-mile Skyline Loop (see previous and next hikes). The trail is easy going for the first dozen miles, as it gradually follows the North Fork Quinault River toward its birthplace near Mount Seattle. Campsites are found at Wolf Bar (2.5 miles), Halfway House (5.3 miles), and in a gorge near Elip Creek (6.5 miles). The trail then climbs, steeply near the end, to Low Divide (at 3,600 feet), where snow can hang tough until midsummer. Good campsites are found in the general Divide vicinity, which includes Mary and Margaret Lakes; both of these spots offer trout fishing. The area is generally quite crowded. A ranger station and campground operate here during the summer. Good side trips are available to nearby Mount Christie and Mount Seattle.

Location: In the North Fork Quinault River drainage of southwest Olympic National Park; see The Olympic Peninsula and Coastal Washington Map 4, grid d3.

User Groups: Hikers and horses. No dogs or mountain bikes are allowed. No wheelchair facilities.

Permits: Day-hiking permits are not required. Wilderness camping permits, available at major trailheads and at all Olympic National Park visitor centers and ranger stations, are required for all overnight stays in undeveloped park areas. The permit fee is $5 per party (up to 12), plus an additional $2 per person per night, with a cap of $100 for trips of up to 14 nights with a party of 7–12 people. There is no nightly charge for youths 16 years of age and under. Parking and access are free.

Maps: For a free map of Olympic National Park, contact the Outdoor Recreation Information Center, Seattle REI, 222 Yale Avenue North, Seattle, WA 98109; 206/470-4060. Green Trails, Inc.'s excellent topographic map of the region is available for $3.99 at outdoor retail outlets. Ask for map number 166, Mount Christie. Ask the USGS for topographic maps of the Bunch Lake, Kimta Peak, and Mount Christie areas.

Directions: From Hoquiam drive about 45 miles on U.S. 101 to North Shore Road. Turn right (east) on North Shore Road and drive 17 miles to the North Fork Trailhead, Campground, and Summer Ranger Station. Note: If North Shore Road is closed for construction (washouts are common), the trailhead is accessible via South Shore Road.

Contact: Olympic National Park, 600 East Park Avenue, Port Angeles, WA 98362; 360/565-3100.

64 Skyline Trail
21.0 mi one way/3.0 days 🥾 ⛺8

For experienced backcountry route-finders only, this is the 21-mile (one-way) connecting leg of the 47-mile Skyline Loop. It follows sharp, difficult ridgelines, connecting the North Fork Quinault Trail with the Three Lakes Trail (see two previous hikes). From Low Divide, the route (it's difficult to call some sections of this cairn-marked path a trail) straddles a ridgeline dividing the Queets and Quinault River Valleys.

The first seven miles to Lake Beauty are manageable, and good campsites are found at the lake. The next half dozen miles can be torturous. The trail is difficult to follow, especially in bad weather, when visibility is limited. The trail becomes more moderate for the last eight miles but can never be considered easy. You are fully exposed to the elements much of the time, because most of this route is above tree line. Still, for the experienced navigator—or for the novice lucky enough to hook up with a route veteran—the experience is unforgettable. Views are outstanding, and you are exposed to what may be the greatest concentrations of wildlife in Olympic National Park. Heavy snow makes passage dangerous before mid-August. The best trips are usually undertaken in September. Ask rangers for trail conditions and weather forecasts before you depart.

Location: In the North Fork Quinault River drainage in southwest Olympic National Park; see The Olympic Peninsula and Coastal Washington Map 4, grid d3.

User Groups: Hikers and horses. No dogs or mountain bikes are allowed. No wheelchair facilities.

Permits: Day-hiking permits are not required. Wilderness camping permits, available at major trailheads and at all Olympic National Park visitor centers and ranger stations, are required for all overnight stays in undeveloped park areas. The permit fee is $5 per party (up to 12), plus an additional $2 per person per night, with a cap of $100 for trips of up to 14 nights with a party of 7–12 people. There is no nightly charge for youths 16 years of age and under. Parking and access are free.

Maps: For a free map of Olympic National Park, contact the Outdoor Recreation Information Center, Seattle REI, 222 Yale Avenue North, Seattle, WA 98109; 206/470-4060. Green Trails, Inc.'s excellent topographic map of the region is available for $3.99 at outdoor retail outlets. Ask for map number 166, Mount Christie. Ask the USGS for topographic maps of the Bunch Lake, Kimta Peak, and Mount Christie areas.

Directions: From Hoquiam follow U.S. 101 north for 45 miles to Lake Quinault's North Shore Road. Turn east and drive 17 miles (the pavement ends after about seven miles) to the North Fork Trailhead, Campground, and Summer Ranger Station. Hike 16 miles to Low Divide, where the Skyline Trailhead exits to the east. Note: If North Shore Road is closed for construction (washouts are common), the trailhead can be reached via the South Shore Road.

Contact: Olympic National Park, 600 East Park Avenue, Port Angeles, WA 98362; 360/565-3100.

65 Enchanted Valley (East Fork Quinault)
26.2 mi/3.0 days 🥾 ⛺10

This area is so special that you'd like to hike it once, shrink-wrap it, and store it away, to preserve the look and feel of wild, unspoiled alpine country for future generations. The route begins on an abandoned roadway on the East Fork Quinault, winds through spectacular old-growth forest, and crosses a picturesque river canyon at Pony Bridge three miles up the trail. It rises and falls gently for the next eight miles, crosses numerous streams with excellent campsites, and then enters Enchanted Valley via a suspension bridge.

As you approach the three-story, log-hewn Enchanted Valley Chalet, the valley view is overwhelming. The flat valley bottom sits in a glacial cirque, surrounded by steep, rocky, often snow-covered mountain walls. Early in the summer, melting snow creates a delightful chorus of waterfalls down the wall's many faces. You're likely to spot deer, elk, black bear, and any number of other wild creatures who love the valley as much as its many backpack-toting visitors. Good campsites abound; treat them with care. Beyond the chalet, the trail continues 4.9 miles east to Anderson Pass, which connects 1.5 miles later with the West Fork Dosewallips Trail (see hike in this chapter). Many long-distance hikers arrange for transportation at both ends, allowing a spectacular, 37-mile east/west crossing of the Olympics.

Location: In the Quinault River drainage in southern Olympic National Park; see The Olympic Peninsula and Coastal Washington Map 4, grid d4.

User Groups: Hikers only. No dogs, horses, or mountain bikes are allowed. No wheelchair facilities.

Permits: Day-hiking permits are not required. Wilderness camping permits, available at major trailheads and at all Olympic National Park visitor centers and ranger stations, are required for all overnight stays in undeveloped park areas. The permit fee is $5 per party (up to 12), plus an additional $2 per person per night, with a cap of $100 for trips of up to 14 nights with a party of 7–12 people. There is no nightly charge for youths 16 years of age and under. Parking and access are free.

Maps: For a free Olympic National Park map, contact the Outdoor Recreation Information Center, Seattle REI, 222 Yale Avenue North, Seattle, WA 98109; 206/470-4060. Green Trails, Inc.'s excellent topographic maps of the region are available for $3.99 each at various outdoor retail outlets. Ask for map numbers 166 and 167, Mount Christie and Mount Steel. Ask the USGS for topographic maps of the Mount Hoquiam, Mount Olson, Chimney Peak, and Mount Steel areas.

Directions: From Hoquiam drive 43 miles north on U.S. 101 to Lake Quinault's South Shore Road. Turn right (east) and follow the road 19.2 miles to the parking lot at Graves Creek Campground and Ranger Station.

Contact: Olympic National Park, 600 East Park Avenue, Port Angeles, WA 98362; 360/565-3100.

66 Graves Creek Nature Loop
1.0 mi/0.5 hr

If you don't have the time or inclination to head up the East Fork or North Fork Quinault Trails, both of which offer full-course immersion into the Quinault Valley's temperate rainforest, the Graves Creek Nature Loop is a good first course. From a trailhead right in the campground, the path winds about a mile through the thick, moss-draped forest of fir, hemlock, and alder. Wildlife abounds here. Keep your eyes peeled for black-tailed deer, Roosevelt elk, black bears, raccoons, and other critters. An alternative day hike in this area is the first portion of the East Fork Quinault/Enchanted Valley trail (see hike above).

Location: In the Quinault River drainage in southern Olympic National Park; see The Olympic Peninsula and Coastal Washington Map 4, grid d4.

User Groups: Hikers only. No dogs, horses, or mountain bikes are allowed. No wheelchair facilities.

Permits: Day-hiking permits are not required. Parking and access are free.

Maps: For a free Olympic National Park map, contact the Outdoor Recreation Information Center, Seattle REI, 222 Yale Avenue North, Seattle, WA 98109; 206/470-4060. Green Trails, Inc.'s excellent topographic maps of the region are available for $3.99 each at various outdoor retail outlets. Ask for map numbers 166 and 167, Mount Christie and Mount Steel. Ask the USGS for topographic maps of the Mount Hoquiam, Mount Olson, Chimney Peak, and Mount Steel areas.

Directions: From Hoquiam drive 43 miles north on U.S. 101 to Lake Quinault's South Shore Road. Turn right (east) and follow the road 19.2 miles to the parking lot at Graves Creek Campground and Ranger Station.

Contact: Olympic National Park, 600 East Park Avenue, Port Angeles, WA 98362; 360/565-3100.

67 Graves Creek to Six Ridge Pass
18.0 mi/2.0 days

Hang a right and avoid the crowds. Those are the watchwords of some East Fork Quinault hikers who find the splendid Enchanted Valley too crowded for their tastes. The Graves Creek Trail, which leaves the Enchanted Valley Trail shortly after it begins, climbs steadily up the creek drainage to a sometimes difficult stream crossing at optimistically named Success Creek, at 3.5 miles. At five miles, the trail enters Graves Creek Basin, which is a prime grazing spot for elk and blooming spot for wildflowers. Good campsites are found here.

The trail intersects the Wynoochee Pass Trail at about six miles and the Upper South Fork Skokomish Trail (see hikes in this chapter) at just beyond seven miles. Sundown Lake (at 7.5 miles) offers shelter and good campsites in a lovely alpine setting. The trail beyond, a steep 1.5-mile climb to Six Ridge Pass (elevation 4,650 feet) offers breathtaking views of Mount Olympus, Mount Rainier, Six Ridge, and Three Sisters. It's an enjoyable side trip after camping near Sundown Lake.

Location: In the Quinault River drainage in southern Olympic National Park; see The Olympic Peninsula and Coastal Washington Map 4, grid d4.

User Groups: Hikers only. No dogs, horses, or mountain bikes are allowed. No wheelchair facilities.

Permits: Day-hiking permits are not required. Wilderness camping permits, available at major trailheads and at all Olympic National Park visitor centers and ranger stations, are required for all overnight stays in undeveloped park areas. The permit fee is $5 per party (up to 12), plus an additional $2 per person per night, with a cap of $100 for trips of up to 14 nights with a party of 7–12 people. There is no nightly charge for youths 16 years of age and under. Parking and access are free.

Maps: For a free Olympic National Park map, contact the Outdoor Recreation Information Center, Seattle REI, 222 Yale Avenue North, Seattle, WA 98109; 206/470-4060. Green Trails, Inc.'s excellent topographic map of the region is available for $3.99 at outdoor retail outlets. Ask for map number 166, Mount Christie. Ask for a USGS topographic map of the Mount Hoquiam area.

Directions: From Hoquiam follow U.S. 101 north for 43 miles to Lake Quinault's South Shore Road. Turn right and follow the road 19.2 miles east to the parking lot at Graves Creek Campground and Ranger Station.

Contact: Olympic National Park, 600 East Park Avenue, Port Angeles, WA 98362; 360/565-3100.

68 O'Neil Pass/Lake LaCrosse
52.0 mi/6.0–7.0 days

O'Neil Pass, a spectacular alpine destination, is accessible by several routes in the southern portion of Olympic National Park, including the east-slope Olympics' West Fork Dosewallips and Duckabush River Trails (see hikes in this chapter). Olympic mountaineering veterans consider a cross-Olympics hike combining the East Fork Quinault, O'Neil Pass, and the Duckabush River, or West Fork Dosewallips Trails a rite of passage. But for those seeking the biggest bang for their vacation buck, the trip up the East Fork Quinault Trail via Enchanted Valley (see hike in this chapter) might be the most rewarding route.

Enchanted Valley (13.2 miles) is a good first- or second-night stop and staging point for the climb to come. O'Neil Pass Trail leaves the Enchanted Valley Trail three miles beyond the Enchanted Valley Chalet and two miles beyond Anderson Pass. It climbs to scenic White Creek Meadow, where the last good campsites for some time are found. At about six miles, the path opens into a majestic basin where elk are frequently seen and snow lingers late into the summer.

From O'Neil Pass, named for an early exploration party, the views are mind-altering. Below lies Enchanted Valley, the entire Quinault River drainage, massive stone-faced peaks too numerous to count, and on a clear day, the Pacific Ocean. Ahead, down a side trail, are great campsites at Marmot Lake and a path leading up to Hart and LaCrosse Lakes (the final destination), at 26 miles. Back on the main path, those who hike this route one way to the east can walk 3.4 miles on the

Upper Duckabush River Trail to the Upper Duckabush Camp and an eventual exit on the Duckabush River Trail. The O'Neil Pass region is about as removed from civilization as one can get in the Olympics without venturing off trail. Choose your week carefully, however: Weather on O'Neil Pass can turn nasty in the blink of an eye.

Few good campsites are found on the way up to O'Neil Pass. Plan on making it to the upper chain of lakes in one day.

Location: In the southern portion of Olympic National Park, from Graves Creek to Lake LaCrosse via the Quinault River and O'Neil Pass; see The Olympic Peninsula and Coastal Washington Map 4, grid d4.

User Groups: Hikers only. No dogs, horses, or mountain bikes are allowed. No wheelchair facilities.

Permits: Day-hiking permits are not required. Wilderness camping permits, available at major trailheads and at all Olympic National Park visitor centers and ranger stations, are required for all overnight stays in undeveloped park areas. The permit fee is $5 per party (up to 12), plus an additional $2 per person per night, with a cap of $100 for trips of up to 14 nights with a party of 7–12 people. There is no nightly charge for youths 16 years of age and under. Parking and access are free.

Maps: For a free Olympic National Park map, contact the Outdoor Recreation Information Center, Seattle REI, 222 Yale Avenue North, Seattle, WA 98109; 206/470-4060. Green Trails, Inc.'s excellent topographic maps of the region are available for $3.99 at outdoor retail outlets. Ask for map numbers 166 and 167, Mount Christie and Mount Steel. Ask for a USGS topographic map of the Mount Steel area.

Directions: From Hoquiam follow U.S. 101 north for 43 miles to Lake Quinault's

South Shore Road. Turn right and follow the road 19 miles to the parking lot at Graves Creek Campground and Ranger Station. Note: Washouts are common here; call before you set out.

Contact: Olympic National Park, 600 East Park Avenue, Port Angeles, WA 98362; 360/565-3100.

69 Staircase Rapids
2.0 mi/1.0 hrs

On a hot day, head here. That's the advice we often follow when the weather gets too sultry for sitting, let alone walking. The Staircase Rapids Trail, one of many day hikes within short distance of prime campgrounds around cold, clear Lake Cushman, is usually crowded but always delightful. From the Staircase Ranger Station, the path follows the North Fork Skokomish River up through a lush, cool playland filled with larger-than-life cedar trees, water so clear you can't see it when it stands still, and of course, the Staircase Rapids themselves. (Park officials say the rapids were named after the trail, which the O'Neil Expedition of 1890 recalled was composed of a series of cedar-root stair steps.) Just beyond the rapids, the trail forks to the right, crossing the river and returning to the parking lot via a path on the other side. Returning via the bridge makes for a pleasant, two-mile loop. Or continue straight and away from the river along O'Neil's route for another 1.5 miles to a dead end in the forest, at 3.2 miles. This trail is accessible most of the year.

Location: In the North Fork Skokomish River drainage in the extreme southeastern corner of Olympic National Park; see The Olympic Peninsula and Coastal Washington Map 4, grid d6.

User Groups: Hikers and horses. No dogs or mountain bikes are allowed. No wheelchair facilities.

Permits: Day-hiking permits are not required. Parking and access are free.

Maps: For a map of Olympic National Park, contact the Outdoor Recreation Information Center, Seattle REI, 222 Yale Avenue North, Seattle, WA 98109; 206/470-4060. Green Trails, Inc.'s excellent topographic map of the region is available for $3.99 at outdoor retail outlets; ask for map number 167, Mount Steel. Ask for a USGS topographic map of the Mount Skokomish area.

Directions: From U.S. 101 near Hoodsport, turn west on Lake Cushman Road/Highway 119 and proceed 18 miles west to the trailhead at the end of the road, near the Staircase Ranger Station.

Contact: Olympic National Park, Staircase Ranger Station, P.O. Box 186, Hoodsport, WA 98548; 360/877-5569; Olympic National Park/National Forest Information Center, 150 North Lake Cushman Road, P.O. Box 68, Hoodsport, WA 98548; 360/877-5254.

70 North Fork Skokomish River
15.5 mi one way/2.0 days

A long and gentle route between the Skokomish and Duckabush River drainages on the Olympics' southeastern slopes, this trail is a popular one-way walk for backpackers and one-way ride for horse packers. Because the elevation is fairly low (about 1,700 feet at the high point), the trail is snow-free much of the year. From the Staircase Ranger Station, the first four miles follow a roadway the Park Service abandoned long ago. It then gradually climbs to Nine Stream and First Divide (elevation 4,688 feet, 13 miles), near the Skokomish headwaters. The highlight is a prime camping site at Home Sweet Home—it's set between Mount Hopper and Mount Steel, which are surrounded by wildflowers in season.

Along the way, you pass many a tempting trout-fishing hole (the Skoke is one of the Olympic Peninsula's more noted trout streams), good campsites, plenty of water, outstanding mountain views, and some of the Olympics' grander meadows of lupine and avalanche lilies. You also get a dose of interesting history (abandoned mine sites). For backpackers, plenty of side trails lead to good day-trip peaks such as Mount Steel and Mount Stone. The trail ultimately drops into the Duckabush River drainage, connecting with the Duckabush Trail. From here, you can venture four miles up and west toward Lake LaCrosse, O'Neil Pass and Enchanted Valley (see hikes in this chapter), or east, 17 miles down the Duckabush to a trailhead at Little Hump. Many backpackers, however, turn around at Home Sweet Home (13.5 miles) or the aptly named Camp Pleasant, about seven miles in.

Location: In the North Fork Skokomish and Duckabush River drainages of Olympic National Park; see The Olympic Peninsula and Coastal Washington Map 4, grid d6.

User Groups: Hikers and horses only. No dogs or mountain bikes are allowed. No wheelchair facilities.

Permits: Day-hiking permits are not required. Wilderness camping permits, available at major trailheads and at all Olympic National Park visitor centers and ranger stations, are required for all overnight stays in undeveloped park areas. The permit fee is $5 per party (up to 12), plus an additional $2 per person per night, with a cap of $100 for trips of up to 14 nights with a party of 7–12 people. There is no nightly charge for youths 16 years of age and under. Parking and access to the park are free.

Maps: For a map of Olympic National Park, contact the Outdoor Recreation Information Center, Seattle REI, 222 Yale Avenue North, Seattle, WA 98109; 206/470-4060. Green Trails, Inc.'s excellent topographic map of the region is available for $3.99 at various outdoor retail outlets; ask for map number 167, Mount Steel. Ask the USGS for topographic maps of the Mount Skokomish and Mount Steel areas.

Directions: From U.S. 101 near Hoodsport, turn west on Lake Cushman Road/Highway 119 and proceed 18 miles west to the trailhead at the end of the road, near the Staircase Ranger Station.

Contact: Olympic National Park, Staircase Ranger Station, P.O. Box 186, Hoodsport, WA 98548; 360/877-5569.

71 Wagonwheel Lake
5.8 mi/4.0 hrs

These are the climbs that try men's soles. Women's, too. Anyone who sets Vibramed-foot to the Wagonwheel Lake Trail will be feeling it the next day, whether they're aerobically challenged loafers or supercharged trail runners. The trail gains 3,200 feet in less than three miles, in one of the more demanding climbs in the Olympics. To make things even more demanding, no water is available until you're near the top. Still interested? The path winds through some cool, memorable forest and a couple of interesting, aborted mining sites before opening onto Wagonwheel Lake, a tarn below Copper Mountain, 5,425 feet. Try your luck casting for cutthroat trout, which Washington State stocks in the lake. Pay quiet homage to the brave souls who haul the fingerlings up here.

Location: In the North Fork Skokomish River drainage in the extreme southeastern corner of Olympic National Park; see The Olympic Peninsula and Coastal Washington Map 4, grid d6.

User Groups: Hikers only. No dogs, horses, or mountain bikes are allowed. No wheelchair facilities.

Permits: Day-hiking permits are not required. Wilderness camping permits, available at major trailheads and at all Olympic National Park visitor centers and ranger stations, are required for all overnight stays in undeveloped park areas. The permit fee is $5 per party (up to 12), plus an additional $2 per person per night, with a cap of $100 for trips of up to 14 nights with a party of 7–12 people. There is no nightly charge for youths 16 years of age and under. Parking and access to the park are free.

Maps: For a map of Olympic National Park, contact the Outdoor Recreation Information Center, Seattle REI, 222 Yale Avenue North, Seattle, WA 98109; 206/470-4060. Green Trails, Inc.'s excellent topographic map of the region is available for $3.99 at outdoor retail outlets; ask for map number 167, Mount Steel. Ask for a USGS topographic map of the Mount Skokomish area.

Directions: From U.S. 101 at Hoodsport, turn west on Lake Cushman Road/Highway 119 and proceed 18 miles west to the trailhead at the end of the road, near the Staircase Ranger Station.

Contact: Olympic National Park, Staircase Ranger Station, P.O. Box 186, Hoodsport, WA 98548; 360/877-5569. Olympic National Park/National Forest Information Center, 150 North Lake Cushman Road, P.O. Box 68, Hoodsport, WA 98548; 360/877-5254.

72 Flapjack Lakes
16.2 mi/1.0–2.0 days

It's only 4.3 miles to Flapjack Lakes from the trail's starting point on the North Fork Skokomish River Trail (see hike in this chapter). But add the 3.8 miles up the Skokomish to the trailhead, and this becomes a seriously long day hike or overnight backpacking trip. It's also a very popular one. Don't expect to find much solitude, unless you plan to hoof it off trail from Flapjack Lakes to nearby Black and White Lakes or Smith Lake. The Flapjacks are nestled beneath the Olympics' small Sawtooth Range, a fascinating string of razor-sharp peaks that provide the most challenging rock climbing in the Olympics. Both lakes offer fishing for eastern brook and rainbow trout. (No licenses are required.) Beyond the lakes, the trail continues about three-quarters of a mile to Gladys Divide (elevation 5,000 feet), which splits the Hamma Hamma and Skokomish River drainages and provides awesome views to winded day hikers.

Because of extreme overuse, there is a limit of 30 campers per day at Flapjack Lakes in the summer; permits are required. Call to reserve one in advance or you're not likely to get a spot. Once you're in, be nice. Many volunteer hours have been spent revegetating this loved-to-death Olympics destination. Don't be a pig. Camp in established sites only and pack out all garbage. Do all that and the Flapjacks will take care of the rest.

Location: In the North Fork Skokomish River drainage of Olympic National Park; see The Olympic Peninsula and Coastal Washington Map 4, grid d6.

User Groups: Hikers and horses. No dogs or mountain bikes are allowed. No wheelchair facilities.

Permits: Day-hiking permits are not required. Wilderness camping permits, available at major trailheads and at all Olympic National Park visitor centers and ranger stations, are required for all overnight stays in undeveloped park areas. The permit fee is $5 per party (up to 12), plus an additional $2 per person per night, with a cap of $100 for trips of up to 14 nights with a party of 7–12 people. There is no nightly charge for youths 16 years of age and under. Note: Flapjack Lakes is a limited-permit backcountry area; overnight permits are limited to 30 per day between May 1 and September 30. Campsite reservations (no more than 30 days prior) are suggested. Contact the park's Wilderness Information Center, 360/565-3100, for current information. Parking and access to the park are free.

Maps: For a map of Olympic National Park, contact the Outdoor Recreation Information Center, Seattle REI, 222 Yale Avenue North, Seattle, WA 98109; 206/470-4060. Green Trails, Inc.'s excellent topographic map of the region is available for $3.99 at outdoor retail outlets; ask for map number 167, Mount Steel. Ask for a USGS topographic map of the Mount Skokomish area.

Directions: From U.S. 101 at Hoodsport, turn west on Lake Cushman Road/Highway 119 and proceed 18 miles west to the trailhead at the end of the road, near the Staircase Ranger Station. The Flapjack Lakes Trail begins 3.8 miles up the North Fork Skokomish River Trail (see hike in this chapter).

Contact: Olympic National Park, Staircase Ranger Station, P.O. Box 186, Hoodsport, WA 98548; 360/877-5569.

☑3 Six Ridge to Sundown Pass
16.4 mi one way/1.0 day 🥾 ◀8

The faint of heart should stay away. But those of you who eat scree for breakfast can strap on a pair of sturdy high ones and give this challenging one-way traverse between the North and South Forks of the Skokomish River a shot. The route begins 5.6 miles up the North Fork Skokomish River Trail (see hike in this chapter) and follows Six Ridge west to Six Ridge Pass and ultimately Sundown Lake and Sundown Pass, where it links with the Graves Creek and Upper South Fork Skokomish trail system (see hikes in this chapter). Finding your way can be difficult,

if not downright nasty. The trail is not recommended for anyone inexperienced at route-finding. Still, the views throughout are rewarding, and solitude is easier to come by here than at most other eastern Olympics destinations.

Location: In the Skokomish River drainage near the southeastern corner of Olympic National Park; see The Olympic Peninsula and Coastal Washington Map 4, grid d6.

User Groups: Hikers only. No dogs, horses, or mountain bikes are allowed. No wheelchair facilities.

Permits: Day-hiking permits are not required. Wilderness camping permits, available at major trailheads and at all Olympic National Park visitor centers and ranger stations, are required for all overnight stays in undeveloped park areas. The permit fee is $5 per party (up to 12), plus an additional $2 per person per night, with a cap of $100 for trips of up to 14 nights with a party of 7–12 people. There is no nightly charge for youths 16 years of age and under. Parking and access to the park are free.

Maps: For a map of Olympic National Park, contact the Outdoor Recreation Information Center, Seattle REI, 222 Yale Avenue North, Seattle, WA 98109; 206/470-4060. Green Trails, Inc.'s excellent topographic map of the region is available for $3.99 at various outdoor retail outlets; ask for map number 167, Mount Steel. Ask the USGS for topographic maps of the Mount Skokomish, Mount Olson, and Mount Tebo areas.

Directions: From U.S. 101 near Hoodsport, turn west on Lake Cushman Road/Highway 119 and proceed 18 miles west to the trailhead at the end of the road, near the Staircase Ranger Station. The Six Ridge Trail begins 5.6 miles up the North Fork Skokomish River Trail.

Contact: Olympic National Park/National Forest Information Center, 150 North

Lake Cushman Road, P.O. Box 68, Hoodsport, WA 98548; 360/877-5254.

74 Mount Rose
5.9 mi/6.8 hrs

Eat your new, improved Wheaties before you lace up your boots for this one. The Mount Rose Trail, a 3,500-vertical-foot, ultra-steep access trail for a 4,300-foot peak, is all up, up, up, with tricky route-finding at the top adding to the fun, especially in foggy weather. The maintained trail ends at about 2.8 miles, giving way to a .75-mile side trail that scrambles up to the tiny, rocky summit. Views—straight down!—of Lake Cushman and the surrounding Hood Canal region are grand.

Location: In the Hood Canal Ranger District of Olympic National Forest, north of Lake Cushman; see The Olympic Peninsula and Coastal Washington Map 4, grid e6.

User Groups: Hikers and dogs. No horses or mountain bikes are allowed. No wheelchair facilities.

Permits: No permits are required. Parking and access are free.

Maps: For a map of Olympic National Forest, contact the Outdoor Recreation Information Center, Seattle REI, 222 Yale Avenue North, Seattle, WA 98109; 206/470-4060. Green Trails, Inc.'s excellent topographic map of the region is available for $3.99 at outdoor retail outlets; ask for map number 167, Mount Steel. Ask for a USGS topographic map of the Mount Skokomish area.

Directions: From U.S. 101 near Hoodsport, turn west on Lake Cushman Road. After nine miles, turn left on Jorsted Creek Road/Forest Service Road 24 and drive approximately three miles to the trailhead on the right.

Contact: Olympic National Park/National Forest Information Center, 150 North Lake Cushman Road, P.O. Box 68, Hoodsport, WA 98548; 360/877-5254.

75 Dry Creek
14.5 mi/2.0 days

This is one of many good day hikes within a short reach of prime camping grounds on Lake Cushman, a deep, clear reservoir formed when Tacoma City Light dammed the Skokomish River. The trail, which begins near a klatch of summer cabins, skirts the lakeshore and then climbs to a lookout over Mount Rose. It then rises sharply up what's left of an old logging road to a stand of old-growth timber. The climb is steady from here—switchback city. Your lungs remind you that you are, indeed, climbing 2,450 feet along the way. But good views (thanks, alas, to clear-cutting) await as the trail opens onto Prospect Ridge (5.5 miles), which the trail follows to the pass between the ridge and Dry Mountain. From this 3,200-foot high point, the path drops to an unremarkable end on another logging road. Skip the pain of a return trip and turn back at the pass.

Location: In the North Fork Skokomish River drainage near Lake Cushman on the southeastern Olympic Peninsula; see The Olympic Peninsula and Coastal Washington Map 4, grid e6.

User Groups: Hikers, dogs, mountain bikes, and horses. No wheelchair facilities.

Permits: A federal Northwest Forest Pass, $5 per day or $30 annually, is required to park at the trailhead. Passes are available from ranger stations and many private vendors, online at website: www.wta.org, or by calling 800/270-7504.

Maps: For a map of Olympic National Forest, contact the Outdoor Recreation Information Center, Seattle REI, 222 Yale Avenue North, Seattle, WA 98109; 206/470-4060. Green Trails, Inc.'s excellent topographic map of the region is available for $3.99 at outdoor retail outlets; ask for map number 199, Mount Tebo.

Ask the USGS for topographic maps of the Lightning Peak and Mount Tebo areas.

Directions: From U.S. 101 near Hoodsport, turn west on Lake Cushman Road. After nine miles, turn left on Jorsted Creek Road/Forest Service Road 24. Follow the road six miles to Forest Service Road 2451 at the end of Lake Cushman. Turn left over the North Fork Skokomish River. The trailhead is on the left, across from the lake.

Contact: Olympic National Park/National Forest Information Center, 150 North Lake Cushman Road, P.O. Box 68, Hoodsport, WA 98548; 360/877-5254.

76 Mount Ellinor
6.2 mi/6.0 hrs

The short, steep Mount Ellinor ascent is one of our favorite hikes for early spring, when the upper slopes are still blanketed with snow but the treed trail below is melted out. At that time of year, snow blocks access to the upper trailhead. That's just as well: even though it's 1.6 miles longer, the lower 6.2-mile route is the better one. It starts in a cool, moist forest canopy before opening onto Ellinor's lower slopes. Here, at about 2.5 miles, you find Chute Flats, which is a pleasant meadow in summer and a snow-climb staging point in spring. There are two summit routes. The winter route is a straight-ahead scramble up a narrow avalanche chute on the mountain's face. The summer route follows Ellinor's southern ridge, allowing a more moderate ascent. Trail managers urge use of the latter when no snow is present in the chute, as climbing the chute in summer can cause serious erosion and plant damage. If that doesn't dissuade you, the loose rock should. From the top (elevation 5,944 feet), the views of Lake Cushman, Mount Adams, Mount Rainier, Seattle, and even Mount St. He-

lens are among the best in the Puget Sound region.

Location: In the Hood Canal Ranger District of Olympic National Forest, north of Lake Cushman; see The Olympic Peninsula and Coastal Washington Map 4, grid d6.

User Groups: Hikers and dogs. No horses or mountain bikes are allowed. No wheelchair facilities.

Permits: A federal Northwest Forest Pass, $5 per day or $30 annually, is required to park at the trailhead. Passes are available from ranger stations and many private vendors, online at website: www.wta.org, or by calling 800/270-7504.

Maps: For a map of Olympic National Forest, contact the Outdoor Recreation Information Center, Seattle REI, 222 Yale Avenue North, Seattle, WA 98109; 206/470-4060. Green Trails, Inc.'s excellent topographic map of the region is available for $3.99 at outdoor retail outlets; ask for map number 167, Mount Steel. Ask for a USGS topographic map of the Mount Washington area.

Directions: From U.S. 101 near Hoodsport, turn west on Lake Cushman Road/Highway 119. After nine miles, turn right on Jorsted Creek Road/Forest Service Road 24. Follow the road 1.6 miles and veer right onto Big Creek Road/Forest Service Road 2419. There are two trailheads: travel 4.9 miles to the lower one or 7.5 miles to the upper one, off Spur Road 014.

Contact: Olympic National Park/National Forest Information Center, 150 North Lake Cushman Road, P.O. Box 68, Hoodsport, WA 98548; 360/877-5254.

77 Mount Washington
4.0 mi/3.0 hrs

This easy, well-maintained trail travels just over 1.5 miles to the launching point for climbs of Mount Washington. It starts high (at about 3,000 feet) and, if you make the climb, ends very high at 6,255 feet. Should you attempt the tempting climb to the summit? It depends completely on your experience level. For trained mountaineers, it's not at all difficult. For rookies, it could be deadly. Be conservative. If you have doubts, don't go. Needless to say, this trail's easy grade, good condition, and superb mountain views, whether from the Mount Washington base or its summit, make this a wildly popular trail in the summer months.

Location: In the Hood Canal Ranger District of Olympic National Forest, northeast of Lake Cushman; see The Olympic Peninsula and Coastal Washington Map 4, grid d7.

User Groups: Hikers and dogs. No horses or mountain bikes are allowed. No wheelchair facilities.

Permits: A federal Northwest Forest Pass, $5 per day or $30 annually, is required to park at the trailhead. Passes are available from ranger stations and many private vendors, online at website: www.wta.org, or by calling 800/270-7504.

Maps: For a map of Olympic National Forest, contact the Outdoor Recreation Information Center, Seattle REI, 222 Yale Avenue North, Seattle, WA 98109; 206/470-4060. Green Trails, Inc.'s excellent topographic map of the region is available for $3.99 at outdoor retail outlets; ask for map number 168, the Brothers. Ask for a USGS topographic map of the Mount Washington area.

Directions: From U.S. 101 near Hoodsport, turn west on Lake Cushman Road/Highway 119. After nine miles, turn right on Jorsted Creek Road/Forest Service Road 24. Follow the road for 1.6 miles to Big Creek Road/Forest Service Road 2419. Turn left and drive seven miles to the trailhead.

Contact: Olympic National Park/National Forest Information Center, 150 North Lake Cushman Road, P.O. Box 68, Hoodsport, WA 98548; 360/877-5254.

78 Mildred Lakes
11.0 mi/8.0 hrs

Strap up your stiff boots for this one. Over the years climbers and anglers have beaten this path, which receives little, if any, attention from trail crews. Plan to spend far more time than usual traveling the 4.5 miles to the first lake. The trail is often difficult to follow, and even when it's plainly identified, it meanders over countless deadfalls, rock slides, and other obstacles. But the payoff is worthwhile: three alpine lakes offering a frontal view of the Olympics' impressive Sawtooth Range, which is more frequently viewed from the back, at Flapjack Lakes (see hike in this chapter). You find good campsites, excellent views, and fair fishing at all three lakes. The trip up the side trail from the upper lake to an overlook on Mount Lincoln is worth the walk. This is about as far removed from civilization—and civilized hikers—as one is likely to get on a day trip in Olympic National Forest. Just don't forget extra moleskin.

If you plan to camp overnight, don't forget to pack a stove; campfires are not allowed above 3,500 feet.

Location: In the Hamma Hamma River drainage of the Mount Skokomish Wilderness, in Olympic National Forest; see The Olympic Peninsula and Coastal Washington Map 4, grid d6.

User Groups: Hikers and leashed dogs. No horses or mountain bikes are allowed. No wheelchair facilities.

Permits: A federal Northwest Forest Pass, $5 per day or $30 annually, is required to park at the trailhead. Passes are available from ranger stations and many private vendors, online at website: www.wta.org, or by calling 800/270-7504.

Maps: For a map of Olympic National Forest and Olympic National Park, contact the Outdoor Recreation Information Center, Seattle REI, 222 Yale Avenue North, Seattle, WA 98109; 206/470-4060. Green Trails, Inc.'s excellent topographic map of the region is available for $3.99 at outdoor retail outlets; ask for map number 167, Mount Steel. Ask for a USGS topographic map of the Mount Skokomish area.

Directions: From Hoodsport drive 13 miles north on U.S. 101 to Forest Service Road 25 (follow the signs for the Hamma Hamma Recreation Area). Follow the road 13 miles to the trailhead at the end of the road. Parking is found on either side of the concrete bridge spanning the Hamma Hamma River.

Contact: Olympic National Park/National Forest Information Center, 150 North Lake Cushman Road, P.O. Box 68, Hoodsport, WA 98548; 360/877-5254.

79 Big Creek Campground Loop
1.1 mi/0.5 hr

Lace up your jogging shoes for this pleasant stroll through the lowland forest at Big Creek. The trail crosses the creek twice, and the two bridges have been known to wash out, requiring a stream ford to complete the loop. This is an easy walk, making it an excellent choice in the spring, summer, or fall for parents with children.

Note: A new, family-friendly loop trail is under construction here, adding as much as 4.0 miles to this loop.

Location: In the Skokomish River Valley north of Lake Cushman in Olympic National Forest; see The Olympic Peninsula and Coastal Washington Map 4, grid e7.

User Groups: Hikers, dogs, and mountain bikes. No horses are allowed. No wheelchair facilities.

Permits: A federal Northwest Forest Pass, $5 per day or $30 annually, is required to park at the trailhead. Passes are available from ranger stations and many private vendors, online at website: www.wta.org, or by calling 800/270-7504.

Maps: For a map of Olympic National Forest, contact the Outdoor Recreation Information Center, Seattle REI, 222 Yale Avenue North, Seattle, WA 98109; 206/470-4060. Green Trails, Inc.'s excellent topographic map of the region is available for $3.99 at outdoor retail outlets; ask for map number 168, the Brothers. Ask for a USGS topographic map of the Mount Washington area.

Directions: From U.S. 101 near Hoodsport, turn west on Lake Cushman Road. Proceed nine miles to Jorsted Creek Road/Forest Service Road 24. Turn left and drive 100 feet. Big Creek Campground is on the right. The trailhead is just 200 feet beyond the gate on the main campground road.

Contact: Olympic National Park/National Forest Information Center, 150 North Lake Cushman Road, P.O. Box 68, Hoodsport, WA 98548; 360/877-5254.

80 Wynoochee Lake Shore Loop
12.0 mi/6.0 hrs

The haphazardly maintained Wynoochee Lake Shore Loop skirts the scenic shores of Wynoochee Lake, which was created by the construction of Wynoochee Dam. The trail starts at Coho, a Forest Service campground and boat launch, and then winds through spindly second growth, which—along with the many massive stumps—is a depressing reminder of the incredible old-growth forest that once existed here. Aside from a possible encounter with the occasional fallen tree early in the season, it's an easy walk, climbing and dropping only 100 feet or so to cross ravines and creeks. The only slightly harrowing experience is a surprise fording of the Wynoochee River at the halfway point, six miles. It can be a chilly, knee-deep experience when water flows are high. After skirting the lake's east shore, the trail crosses the top of the dam and returns you (safe, sound, and only slightly sore) to Coho Campground. Caution: Don't expect peaceful serenity here. This lake, like many others in Washington under Forest Service supervision, has been taken over by personal watercraft in recent years. And the path hasn't been well maintained; deadfalls and thick brush are a problem.

Location: On Wynoochee Lake in the Hood Canal Ranger District of Olympic National Forest; see The Olympic Peninsula and Coastal Washington Map 4, grid e4.

User Groups: Hikers, dogs, and mountain bikes. No horses are allowed. No wheelchair facilities.

Permits: A federal Northwest Forest Pass, $5 per day or $30 annually, is required to park at the trailhead. Passes are available from ranger stations and many private vendors, online at website: www.wta.org, or by calling 800/270-7504.

Maps: For a map of Olympic National Forest, contact the Outdoor Recreation Information Center, Seattle REI, 222 Yale Avenue North, Seattle, WA 98109; 206/470-4060. Green Trails, Inc.'s excellent topographic map of the region is available for $3.99 at various outdoor retail outlets. Ask for map number 198, Grisdale. Ask for a USGS topographic map of the Wynoochee Lake area.

Directions: From Montesano take U.S. 12 one mile west and turn right on Wynoochee Valley Road/Forest Service Road 22. Continue 33.5 miles to the three-way intersection; turn left, remaining on Forest Service Road 22; then turn right in 0.3 mile on Forest Service Road 2294. The trailhead is near Coho Campground, 1.3 miles up Forest Service Road 2294.

Contact: Olympic National Forest, Pacific Ranger District, Quinault office, 353 South Shore Road, P.O. Box 9, Quinault, WA 98575; 360/288-2525.

81 Wynoochee Pass
4.4 mi/4.0 hrs

The construction of Wynoochee Dam, which sent much of the old, extensive Wynoochee Valley Trail straight to Davy Jones' locker, made this trail tough to find. What remains of this path begins in old-growth forest, quickly crosses into Olympic National Park (0.2 mile), and climbs 1,100 feet to Wynoochee Pass, with small meadows and pleasant views. After another 1.2 miles, the trail intersects with Olympic National Park's Graves Creek Trail (see hike in this chapter), which serves as the turnaround point.

Location: On the southern boundary of Olympic National Park and Olympic National Forest; see The Olympic Peninsula and Coastal Washington Map 4, grid e4.

User Groups: Hikers only. No dogs, horses, or mountain bikes are allowed. No wheelchair facilities.

Permits: Day-hiking permits are not required. Because the trailhead is located on national forest land, a federal Northwest Forest Pass, $5 per day or $30 annually, is required to park at the trailhead. Passes are available from ranger stations and many private vendors, online at website: www.wta.org, or by calling 800/270-7504.

Maps: For a map of Olympic National Park, contact the Outdoor Recreation Information Center, Seattle REI, 222 Yale Avenue North, Seattle, WA 98109; 206/470-4060. Green Trails, Inc.'s excellent topographic map of the region is available for $3.99 at outdoor retail outlets. Ask for map number 198, Grisdale.

Ask for a USGS topographic map of the Mount Hoquiam area.

Directions: From Montesano, take U.S. 12 one mile west and turn right on Wynoochee Valley Road/Forest Service Road 22. Continue 33.5 miles to a three-way intersection and stay straight as the road becomes Forest Service Road 2270. After approximately 11 miles, turn right on Forest Service Road 874. Continue 1.8 miles to the trailhead at road's end.

Contact: Olympic National Forest, Quinault Ranger District, 353 South Shore Road, P.O. Box 9, Quinault, WA 98575; 360/288-2525.

82 Spoon Creek Falls
0.6 mi/1.0 hr

This is a pleasant, short trek to a good dunking pool, either on the way home from hiking the Wynoochee Pass Trail or the Wynoochee Lake Shore Loop (see hikes in this chapter). It's also a good one for parents of young hike tykes. The trail drops quickly to the base of the falls, which has a deep pool for those who can stand cold water and the occasional wayward leech.

Location: Southeast of Wynoochee Lake in the Hood Canal Ranger District of Olympic National Forest; see The Olympic Peninsula and Coastal Washington Map 4, grid e4.

User Groups: Hikers and dogs. No horses or mountain bikes are allowed. No wheelchair facilities.

Permits: A federal Northwest Forest Pass, $5 per day or $30 annually, is required to park at the trailhead. Passes are available from ranger stations and many private vendors, online at website: www.wta.org, or by calling 800/270-7504.

Maps: For a map of Olympic National Forest and Olympic National Park, contact the Outdoor Recreation Information Center, Seattle REI, 222 Yale Avenue North, Seattle, WA

98109; 206/470-4060. Green Trails, Inc.'s excellent topographic map of the region is available for $3.99 at outdoor retail outlets. Ask for map number 198, Grisdale. Ask for a USGS topographic map of the Grisdale area.

Directions: From Montesano take U.S. 12 one mile west and turn right on Wynoochee Valley Road/Forest Service Road 22. Follow Road 22 for approximately 33.5 miles. Turn right on Road 23. The trailhead and small parking area are three miles ahead, just past Spoon Creek.

Contact: Olympic National Forest, Quinault Ranger District, 353 South Shore Road, P.O. Box 9, Quinault, WA 98575; 360/288-2525.

83 Upper South Fork Skokomish
17.2 mi/1.0–2.0 days

Open year-round for city dwellers in search of a quick nature fix, this Skokomish Recreation Area trail starts out deceptively easy. You stroll beneath old-growth forest for about two miles, actually losing altitude as you drop toward a stream crossing. But at about two miles, you cross an old avalanche-scarred area, and the trail gets more serious, rising swiftly to the Olympic National Park boundary at 4.8 miles. From here the trail deteriorates; it is not well maintained by the park. Defy it and plunge ahead. The path is negotiable, even though following it means splashing through a number of streams and marshy areas. The last mile to Sundown Pass (seven miles in) will make the sweat roll, but you are rewarded with a fine view of the interior Olympics. Just beyond here, the trail comes to a T. Hang a left and you connect with the Graves Creek Trail, which leads to the East Fork Quinault Trailhead (see hikes in this chapter). You can also go right to reach Sundown Lake in about one-third mile, or continue beyond to Six Ridge Trail, the rugged, ridgetop route to the North Fork Skokomish River Trail (see hike in this chapter).

Location: In Olympic National Forest near its southeastern boundary with Olympic National Park; see The Olympic Peninsula and Coastal Washington Map 4, grid e5.

User Groups: Hikers, horses, and mountain bikes (which are allowed to the Olympic National Park boundary). No dogs are allowed. No wheelchair facilities.

Permits: Day-hiking permits are not required. Wilderness camping permits, available at major trailheads and at all Olympic National Park visitor centers and ranger stations, are required for all overnight stays in undeveloped park areas. The permit fee is $5 per party (up to 12), plus an additional $2 per person per night, with a cap of $100 for trips of up to 14 nights with a party of 7–12 people. There is no nightly charge for youths 16 years of age and under. In addition, U.S. Forest Service Region 6 Trail Park Passes are required to park at this trailhead. The window decal passes are available for $3 per day or $25 annually. The annual pass is valid at Forest Service trailheads throughout Washington and Oregon. Contact the Quinault Ranger District at 360/288-2525.

Maps: For a map of Olympic National Forest and Olympic National Park, contact the Outdoor Recreation Information Center, Seattle REI, 222 Yale Avenue North, Seattle, WA 98109; 206/470-4060. Green Trails, Inc.'s excellent topographic maps of the region are available for $3.99 each at outdoor retail outlets. Ask for map numbers 167 and 199, Mount Steel and Mount Tebo. Ask for a USGS topographic map of the Mount Steel area.

Directions: From Shelton drive six miles north on U.S. 101 to Valley Road. Turn west and proceed approximately five miles to Forest Service Road 23. Turn right and drive 15

miles to the junction with Forest Service Road 2361. Turn right and continue four miles to the end of the road and the trailhead, which has a small parking area. Note: A wildlife gate at the entrance to Road 2361 is closed from October through April.

Contact: Olympic National Forest, Pacific Ranger District, Quinault office, 353 South Shore Road, P.O. Box 9, Quinault, WA 98575; 360/288-2525.

84 Upper Big Quilcene (Marmot Pass)
10.5 mi/8.0 hrs

This river-valley ascent to Marmot Pass begins in an old-growth fir forest that's dotted with wonderful blobs of pink early in the summer, when wild rhododendrons are in full bloom. The trail then climbs into alpine meadows and boulder fields, crossing avalanche chutes before opening onto Camp Mystery (4.5 miles). You'll see it's no mystery that many hikers choose to camp here, where good shelter, water, and views await.

The trail then climbs through alpine country to Marmot Pass (elevation 6,000 feet, 5.25 miles), where it intersects the Tubal Cain Mine Trail (see hike in this chapter), which leads 8.8 miles north. You won't soon forget the views from here, which include many of the interior Olympic peaks and even Puget Sound and part of the Cascade Range to the east. Nor will you forget the weather. Whenever we've visited, the wind has always been humming along. Beyond Marmot Pass, the trail drops to connect with the Upper Dungeness Trail near the Olympic National Park border (see hike in this chapter). Warning: Water is scarce to nonexistent beyond Camp Mystery.

If you plan to camp overnight, don't forget to pack a stove; campfires are not allowed above 3,500 feet.

Location: West of Hood Canal in the Buckhorn Wilderness on the eastern slope of the Olympic Mountains; see The Olympic Peninsula and Coastal Washington Map 5, grid b1.

User Groups: Hikers, dogs, and horses. No mountain bikes are allowed. No wheelchair facilities.

Permits: A federal Northwest Forest Pass, $5 per day or $30 annually, is required to park at the trailhead. Passes are available from ranger stations and many private vendors, online at website: www.wta.org, or by calling 800/270-7504.

Maps: For a map of Olympic National Forest and Olympic National Park, contact the Outdoor Recreation Information Center, Seattle REI, 222 Yale Avenue North, Seattle, WA 98109; 206/470-4060. Green Trails, Inc.'s excellent topographic map of the region is available for $3.99 at outdoor retail outlets; ask for map number 136, Tyler Peak. Ask the USGS for topographic maps of the Mount Jupiter and the Brothers areas.

Directions: From Quilcene follow U.S. 101 south one mile to Penny Creek Road. Turn right. Continue to Forest Service Road 27 and drive approximately 11 miles, turning left on Forest Service Road 2750. The trailhead is five miles ahead, where the Lower Big Quilcene Trail meets the road at Ten Mile Shelter.

Contact: Olympic National Forest, Hood Canal Ranger District, Quilcene office, 295142 Highway 101 South, P.O. Box 280, Quilcene, WA 98376; 360/765-2200.

85 Tunnel Creek
7.3 mi. one way/1.0 day

A popular choice among high-lakes trout anglers, this trail is a good one-way jaunt for people with two cars or some helpful friends who'll agree to pick them up at the far end. (Like many trails in logging-road-bisected Olympic National Park, this one has roads at either end.) The trail begins on the South Fork of Tunnel Creek, meandering 2.8 miles to the Tunnel Creek Shelter site, where the real fun begins. From here, the trail gets steep and narrow on the way to Karnes and Harrison Lakes, at 4,900 feet, where camping is only so-so, but fishing can be quite good. (State fishing licenses are required in the national forest.) Just when you think the trail maxes out on painful steepness, it climbs again, leading to outstanding views of Mount Constance and the Brothers. Then it plunges down at a toenail-jamming pace to the Dosewallips River and, ultimately, a trailhead that lies about 1.5 miles east of Elkhorn Campground on Dosewallips River Road.

Location: In the Hood Canal Ranger District of Olympic National Forest; see The Olympic Peninsula and Coastal Washington Map 5, grid b1.

User Groups: Hikers only. Horses are allowed on the lower trail but not recommended. No dogs or mountain bikes are allowed. No wheelchair facilities.

Permits: A federal Northwest Forest Pass, $5 per day or $30 annually, is required to park at the trailhead. Passes are available from ranger stations and many private vendors, online at website: www.wta.org, or by calling 800/270-7504.

Maps: For a map of Olympic National Forest and Olympic National Park, contact the Outdoor Recreation Information Center, Seattle REI, 222 Yale Avenue North, Seattle, WA 98109; 206/470-4060. Green Trails, Inc.'s excellent topographic map of the region is available for $3.99 at outdoor retail outlets; ask for map number 136, Tyler Peak. Ask for a USGS topographic map of the Tyler Peak area.

Directions: From Quilcene follow U.S. 101 one mile south to Penny Creek Road.

Turn right (west) and continue to Forest Service Road 27. Continue on this road, bearing left onto Forest Service Road 2740. Travel 6.6 miles to the trailhead, near the Tunnel Creek crossing.

Contact: Olympic National Forest, Hood Canal Ranger District, Quilcene office, 295142 Highway 101 South, P.O. Box 280, Quilcene, WA 98376; 360/765-2200.

86 Lower Big Quilcene
12.0 mi/8.0 hrs

Mountain bikers, this one's for you. The lower-elevation leftover portion of what once was a grander Quilcene Trail, this trail is a relatively flat, easy grade, making it one of the region's more popular venues for the two-wheeled set, not to mention equestrians. In fact, the Forest Service steers mountain bikers and horse riders this way. By combining the two trailheads and connecting road, you can ride a loop of about 18 miles. The trail begins at old Big Quilcene Campground and climbs gradually up the river valley to Ten Mile Shelter, where the Upper Big Quilcene Trail begins (see hike in this chapter). Cyclists who don't like the uphill grind might try riding it backward, from the Ten Mile Shelter to the lower trailhead. Horse and pet owners take note: This trail also is popular with dirt bikers and owners of off-road vehicles. That's a shame, given that the central portion of the trail is a sublime walk through old-growth forest, with the river rushing through a gorge below.

Location: In the Big Quilcene River drainage of Olympic National Forest; see The Olympic Peninsula and Coastal Washington Map 5, grid b1.

User Groups: Hikers, dogs, horses, and mountain bikes. No wheelchair facilities.

Permits: A federal Northwest Forest Pass, $5 per day or $30 annually, is required to park at the trailhead. Passes are available from ranger stations and many private vendors, online at website: www.wta.org, or by calling 800/270-7504.

Maps: For a map of Olympic National Forest and Olympic National Park, contact the Outdoor Recreation Information Center, Seattle REI, 222 Yale Avenue North, Seattle, WA 98109; 206/470-4060. Green Trails, Inc.'s excellent topographic map of the region is available for $3.99 at outdoor retail outlets; ask for map number 136, Tyler Peak. Ask for a USGS topographic map of the Mount Walker area.

Directions: From Quilcene follow U.S. 101 one mile south and turn right (west) on Penny Creek Road. Follow Penny Creek Road to Forest Service Road 27. Continue five miles to the intersection with Forest Service Road 2700-080. Turn left on Forest Service Road 2700-080. The trailhead is on the left at the old Big Quilcene Campground.

Contact: Olympic National Forest, Hood Canal Ranger District, Quilcene office, 295142 Highway 101 South, P.O. Box 280, Quilcene, WA 98376; 360/765-2200.

87 Rainbow Canyon
1.0 mi/0.5 hr

Auto commuters making the long, slow, windy trip around the west side of Hood Canal find this nature trail is a pleasant, short leg-stretcher. The trailhead is in Rainbow Campground, just off U.S. 101, near Walker Pass. You stroll through a mixed forest that's particularly pretty in the fall, when the path is carpeted by red and yellow leaves. Take in a lungful of sweetly pungent, crisp air. The trail drops slightly to Rainbow Canyon, where the Big Quilcene receives an extra boost from a waterfall. The trail ends at the river, 160 feet below the trailhead.

Location: In the Big Quilcene River drainage of Olympic National Forest, west of Hood Canal; see The Olympic Peninsula and Coastal Washington Map 5, grid b1.

User Groups: Hikers and dogs only. No horses or mountain bikes are allowed. No wheelchair facilities.

Permits: No permits are required. Parking and access are free.

Maps: For a map of Olympic National Forest and Olympic National Park, contact the Outdoor Recreation Information Center, Seattle REI, 222 Yale Avenue North, Seattle, WA 98109; 206/470-4060. Ask for a USGS topographic map of the Mount Walker area.

Directions: From Quilcene follow U.S. 101 five miles south. The trailhead is in the Rainbow Campground/Picnic Area.

Contact: Olympic National Forest, Hood Canal Ranger District, Quilcene office, 295142 Highway 101 South, P.O. Box 280, Quilcene, WA 98376; 360/765-2200.

88 Mount Walker
4.0 mi/3.0 hrs

This is a favorite Hood Canal-area hike in the off-season. The fall colors are lovely, and the route is snow-free virtually all year. You can drive two miles up the road to the same viewpoint where this trail concludes, atop Mount Walker. But it's worth the walk, a steep, brisk hike that climbs through Douglas fir and, in early summer, wild rhododendrons. The route tops out at 2,730 feet on the mountain's North Knoll, with very pleasing views of the eastern Olympics. The elevation gain is a hefty 2,204 feet. If you're smart, you'll have someone drop you off at the top!

Location: In the Big Quilcene River drainage of Olympic National Forest, west of Hood Canal; see The Olympic Peninsula and Coastal Washington Map 5, grid b1.

User Groups: Hikers, dogs, and horses. No mountain bikes are allowed. No wheelchair facilities.

Permits: No permits are required. Parking and access are free.

Maps: For a map of Olympic National Forest and Olympic National Park, contact the Outdoor Recreation Information Center, Seattle REI, 222 Yale Avenue North, Seattle, WA 98109; 206/470-4060. Ask for a USGS topographic map of the Mount Walker area.

Directions: From Quilcene follow U.S. 101 south for 5.5 miles. Turn left (east) on Forest Service Road 2730. The trailhead is a quarter mile up the road, which continues to the summit viewpoint on Mount Walker.

Contact: Olympic National Forest, Hood Canal Ranger District, Quilcene office, 295142 Highway 101 South, P.O. Box 280, Quilcene, WA 98376; 360/765-2200.

89 Grays Harbor North Ocean Beaches
1.0 mi–10.0 mi/
0.5 hrs–5.0 hrs

Most upland areas above the broad, flat beach north of Grays Harbor are private property, dotted with summer cabins and vacation homes. But it's a fairly well-kept secret that much of the 22 miles of beach between Moclips and Ocean Shores is wide open to the public and makes for grand, year-round beachcombing and day hiking. The strip, collectively known as the North Beach Seashore Conservation Area, can be reached via numerous trailheads (which are actually access roads) all along Highway 109. The northern region near Moclips is the most scenic, although public access to the area is somewhat limited. Major public entrance points along the strip include Pacific Beach, Ocean City, and Griffiths-Priday State Parks, all north of

Ocean Shores along Highway 109. The latter, at the mouth of the Copalis River, has picnic facilities and restrooms and is a noted nesting ground for the endangered snowy plover.

The beach here is far from the most scenic in the state—it's fairly nondescript, with few headlands or other natural features. But it is ocean beach, and the closest seashore hiking to the Puget Sound area. From any of the beach accesses here, it's possible to take a relaxing stroll of half a mile or 10 miles, all year-round. Unfortunately, the state of Washington (in its infinite lack of wisdom) allows automobiles to drive on some beach stretches for much of the year. Use caution when hiking in the area and then write your legislator to complain about this policy.

When this book went to press, Washington State Parks were considering implementing a day-use parking fee; call the contact number for current information.

Location: 22 miles of ocean beach north of Point Brown, in the Ocean Shores area; see The Olympic Peninsula and Coastal Washington Map 6, grid a7.

User Groups: Hikers, dogs, horses, and mountain bikes. No wheelchair facilities.

Permits: No permits are required. Parking and access are free.

Maps: For a Washington State Parks brochure, contact Washington State Parks at 800/233-0321. Ask for USGS topographic maps of the Moclips, Copalis Beach, and Point Brown areas.

Directions: From Seattle take I-5 south to Olympia. Follow Highway 8 and U.S. 12 west to Aberdeen and cross the bridge into Hoquiam. From Hoquiam follow Highway 109 (signs indicate Ocean Shores) about 30 miles to trailheads at Ocean Shores, Ocean City, or Copalis.

Contact: Washington State Parks and Recreation Commission, Public Affairs Office, P.O. Box 42650, Olympia, WA 98504-2650; 800/233-0321.

90 Grays Harbor South Ocean Beaches
2.0 mi–10.0 mi/
1.0 hr–5.0 hrs

The 19 miles of beach stretching south from the tiny fishing burg of Westport are mostly open to the public, and excellent access is available at three pleasant state parks (Westhaven, Twin Harbors, and Grayland Beach) along Highway 105. The beach strip, known as the South Beach Seashore Conservation Area, is managed by the state; the most direct access to it is found at Westhaven. The parking lot at Westhaven is literally on the beach—so close, in fact, that parts of it have washed away in recent years, leaving state parks crews struggling to shore it up.

From this day-use park, which is popular with surfers and jetty anglers, you can stroll south on the beach all the way to Grayland if you're so inclined—a distance of about 15 miles. Most people prefer to stroll a few miles south and return. A new trail here eliminates the need to get your feet sandy. The Westport Nature Trail stretches south from Westhaven to Ocean Avenue, site of the historic Westport Lighthouse. The concrete path is about a mile one-way and is open to in-line skaters and cyclists.

Westhaven beach access is preferable to the more southern entrance points for yet another reason: amazingly, it's legal to drive cars on many stretches of this beach, and the Twin Harbors and Grayland Beach State Parks both provide ready automobile access. There's no place to drive onto the beach at Westhaven, so beachcombers who don't want to dodge traffic prefer hiking here.

When this book went to press, Washington State Parks were considering implementing a day-use parking fee; call the contact number for current information.

Location: 19 miles of ocean beach south of Westport; see The Olympic Peninsula and Coastal Washington Map 6, grid b7.

User Groups: Hikers, dogs, horses, and mountain bikes. Limited wheelchair access.

Permits: No permits are required. Parking and access are free.

Maps: For a Washington State Parks brochure, contact Washington State Parks at 800/233-0321. Ask the USGS for topographic maps of the Westport, Grayland, and North Cove areas.

Directions: From Seattle take I-5 south to Olympia. Follow Highway 8 and U.S. 12 west to Aberdeen. From Aberdeen (following signs to Westport) take Highway 105 about 25 miles west to Twin Harbors State Park. Other popular beach access points are located at Westhaven State Park near Westport and Grayland Beach State Park near Grayland.

Contact: Washington State Parks and Recreation Commission, Public Affairs Office, P.O. Box 42650, Olympia, WA 98504-2650; 800/233-0321.

91 Leadbetter Point
4.0 mi/2.0 hrs

Do your kids a favor. Next time you're in the tourist-trap town of Long Beach spending far too much money on cheesy souvenirs, take a quick drive north to Leadbetter Point and show them the natural environment that truly makes the Long Beach Peninsula special. From Leadbetter's small parking lot, a variety of trails lace through upland tidal dunes and grass to Leadbetter Point, the northern tip of the peninsula. You see the quiet, protected waters of Willapa Bay to the east and the roiling Pacific to the west. The area is rich with wildlife, with a mix of freshwater- and saltwater-habitat birds and mammals. This is a major stopover for migrating waterfowl during the spring and fall. More than 200 bird species have been spotted here, so bring the binoculars.

Location: At the north tip of Long Beach Peninsula; see The Olympic Peninsula and Coastal Washington Map 6, grid c8.

User Groups: Hikers and leashed dogs. No horses or mountain bikes are allowed. No wheelchair facilities.

Permits: No permits are required. Parking and access are free.

Maps: For a Willapa National Wildlife Refuge brochure, contact the refuge headquarters at 360/484-3482. Ask for a USGS topographic map of the North Cove area.

Directions: From Seattle take I-5 south to Olympia. Turn west on U.S. 12 and drive to Aberdeen; then take U.S. 101 south to Long Beach. Turn right (north) on Highway 103 and follow signs north to Leadbetter Point.

From Portland drive north on I-5 to Highway 4 at Kelso. Follow Highway 4 west to U.S. 101. Turn south on U.S. 101 and proceed to Long Beach. Turn right (north) on Highway 103 and follow signs north to Leadbetter Point.

Contact: Willapa National Wildlife Refuge, 3888 SR 101, Ilwaco, WA 98624; 360/484-3482.

92 Fort Canby State Park
1.5–5.0 mi/0.75–2.5 hrs

Fort Canby is on a shortlist of our absolute favorite Washington state parks. Unfortunately, the same thing can be said by at least several hundred thousand other Northwest residents who flock here to enjoy some of the best coastal camping in the state.

But the true beauty of Fort Canby is the space it offers outside the campground area; this expanse makes the park a prime day-hiking destination for both Portland- and Seattle-area residents.

The park consists of almost 1,900 acres of saltwater and Columbia River shoreline, rocky uplands, mossy forest, and a swamp or two. The foremost attraction here is 43,000 feet of shoreline. You can walk south from the main camping area to the jetty, which divides the Pacific from the mighty Columbia River. Lewis and Clark first touched the Pacific at this spot, and (if you squint a bit and ignore the kite-flyers nearby) you can almost imagine how they must have felt. Look behind you for a view of the Cape Disappointment Light-house. To the north, toward the towering bluff topped by the majestic North Head Light-house, another excellent beach walk beckons. You can reach the cliffs in about a mile, and side trails—for the very adventurous—lead across the face up to the lighthouse.

Other trails within this park's immense boundaries include a three-quarter-mile path from the Waikiki Beach day-use area to the Lewis and Clark Interpretive Center, on the bluff near Cape Disappointment Lighthouse; and a 1.5-mile nature trail loop through old-growth coastal forest, near Lake O'Neil. If the beach is too windy for your taste, try hiking the short trail to the old gun emplacement on McKenzie Head, near Lake O'Neil, or a 3.5-mile round-trip upland trail to the North Beach Lighthouse, which also can be reached via a shorter trail from the main highway. Across Highway 100 from the park entrance, one path leads one-third mile to the Cape Disappointment Lighthouse, and a 1.5-mile loop follows the Columbia River. The latter is a nature trail known as the Coastal Forest Trail. All things considered, we can't think of a better destination to pitch a tent and gradually wear down the kids.

When this book went to press, Washington State Parks were considering implementing a day-use parking fee; call the contact number for current information.

Location: Southwest of Ilwaco on Washing-ton's southwestern coast; see The Olympic Peninsula and Coastal Washington Map 6, grid f8.

User Groups: Hikers and leashed dogs. No horses or mountain bikes are allowed. No wheelchair facilities.

Permits: No permits are required. Parking and access are free.

Maps: For a state parks brochure, contact Washington State Parks at 800/233-0321. Ask for a USGS topographic map of the Cape Disappointment area.

Directions: From Seattle, drive south on I-5 to Olympia. In Olympia turn west on U.S. 12 to Aberdeen. In Aberdeen take U.S. 101 south to Ilwaco. At First Street in Ilwaco, turn west and drive 3.5 miles to the park entrance.

From Portland, take I-5 north to Highway 4 at Kelso. Drive west on Highway 4 to U.S. 101. Turn south on U.S. 101 and proceed to Ilwaco. Follow signs to the park.

Contact: Fort Canby State Park, Box 488, Ilwaco, WA 98624; 360/642-3078; Washington State Parks and Recreation Commission, Public Affairs Office, P.O. Box 42650, Olympia, WA 98504-2650; 800/233-0321.

93 Long Island
5.0 mi/1.0 day

BYOB (bring your own boat). Long Island's fascinating, wildlife-rich trail system is one of few in the Northwest that require you to bring your own water transportation. It's needed to cross a very short (about 10 paddle strokes) passage between the Willapa Na-tional Wildlife Refuge Headquarters along U.S. 101 and the southern tip of the largest estuarine island on the Pacific Coast. This passage makes 5,000-acre Long Island a favorite haunt of Northwest canoeists and kayakers, who use its five primitive campgrounds as a base for waterborne exploration of the marshy tidal area in Willapa Bay.

A five-mile network of trails, some of them old logging roads, rings the island and connects four of the five campgrounds. If you're looking for a day trip, cross the waterway at the main parking lot to a trail that leads 2.5 miles northwest toward a grove of magnificent old-growth cedars; these trees are believed to be the last of their kind on the Pacific Coast. It's difficult to reach the 274-acre cedar grove with machinery, so it was spared from the logging that ended here in the 1980s. Scientists say the old cedars represent a rare terminal forest, one that has managed to reach full maturity without interference. Protected as it is from wind and fire damage, the forest is believed to be just as it was as long as 4,000 years ago. A walk from the island's south tip to the grove and back is an excellent day trip, and, when the tides are right, the surrounding bay is an ideal place to introduce newcomers to canoeing or sea kayaking.

Be sure to consult a tide table before canoeing or kayaking to Long Island. The plentiful water that carried you in might turn into a massive mud pie by the time you're ready to leave.

Location: In Willapa National Wildlife Refuge near the mouth of the Naselle River; see The Olympic Peninsula and Coastal Washington Map 7, grid e1.

User Groups: Hikers and leashed dogs. No horses or mountain bikes. No wheelchair access.

Permits: No permits are required. Parking and access are free.

Maps: For a free Long Island map and brochure, contact the Willapa National Wildlife Refuge at 360/484-3482. Ask for a USGS topographic map of the Long Island area.

Directions: From Seattle take I-5 south to Olympia. In Olympia turn west on U.S. 12 and drive to Aberdeen. Turn south on U.S. 101 near Cosmopolis. Proceed on U.S. 101 toward Long Beach and find the Long Island parking lot for the Willapa National Wildlife Refuge on the left (south) side of the highway, approximately 60 miles south of Cosmopolis.

From Portland drive north on I-5 to Highway 4 at Kelso. Turn west on Highway 4 and continue to U.S. 101. Turn south on U.S. 101 and find the Willapa National Wildlife Refuge Headquarters on the left (south) side of the highway.

Contact: Willapa National Wildlife Refuge, 3888 SR 101, Ilwaco, WA 98624; 360/484-3482.

SEATTLE AND THE SAN JUANS

Seattle and the San Juans

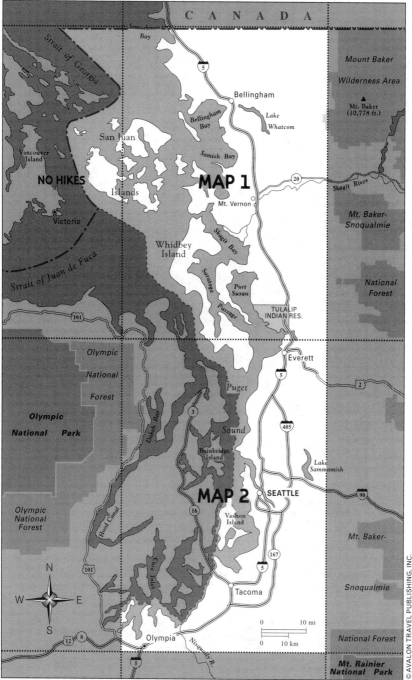

Map 1

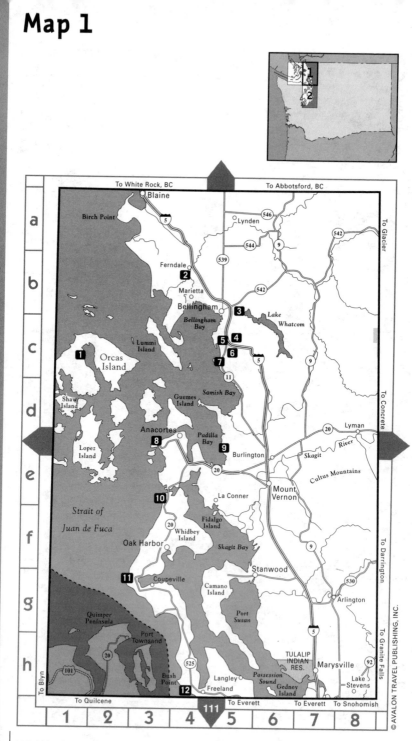

Map 2

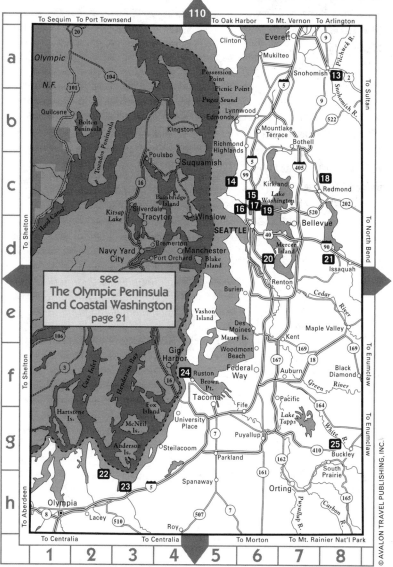

Seattle and the San Juans

1 Mountain Lake to Mount Constitution

7.0 mi/4.0 hrs

Many state parks employees consider Moran the true jewel of one of the nation's most scenic park systems. You get no argument from us. The park combines the tranquil beauty of San Juan Island shorelines with several lakes and airplane-like views from the top of Mount Constitution. And you have nearly 30 miles of hiking trails from which to choose. The route we suggest—a path from Mountain Lake up to Mount Constitution's stone observation tower—includes everything but the saltwater shoreline.

Pack a lunch and hit the trail, which climbs quickly above Mountain Lake, to Twin Lakes (1.5 miles). You can walk around one lake or both, then proceed west toward the mountain summit. Here, several inviting picnic tables await. The view is truly amazing. At your feet are Lummi, Sucia, and Matia Islands (the latter two are designated state parks), the city of Bellingham, and on the horizon, Mount Baker. In the distance, the Cascade Range reaches far into British Columbia. Plan to leave yourself at least an hour to take all this in. The route back is mostly downhill and speedy. For that reason, many people prefer to make the hike a one-way, 3.5-mile shuttle hike, from the summit to Mountain Lake.

For an alternate, shorter hike to the same place, you can park at the Little Summit Trailhead on Summit Road (about a half mile beyond the Mountain Lake turnoff) and hike 5.2 miles to the summit.

When this book went to press, Washington State Parks were considering implementing a day-use parking fee; call the contact number for current information.

Location: In Moran State Park on Orcas Island in the San Juan Archipelago; see Seattle and the San Juans Map 1, grid c1.

User Groups: Hikers, dogs, and mountain bikes. (For bike trails see the Moran State Park ranger.) No horses are allowed. No wheelchair facilities.

Permits: No permits are required. Parking and access are free.

Maps: For a state parks map and brochure, contact Washington State Parks at 800/233-0321. Ask the USGS for a topographic map of the Eastsound area.

Directions: From Seattle drive 64 miles north on I-5 to Mount Vernon. Take Exit 230 and turn left (west) under the freeway. Traveling on Highways 20 and 237, follow the signs for about 14 miles northwest to Anacortes. From Anacortes, follow the signs three miles west to the Washington State Ferry Terminal, where you catch the ferry to Orcas Island. On the island take Olga Road 13 miles through Eastsound to Moran State Park's arched entry. Inside the park, follow Mount Constitution Road to the Mountain Lake turnoff. Turn right and park at the trailhead near Mountain Lake Campground.

Contact: Moran State Park, Highway 22, Eastsound, WA 98245; 360/376-2326; Washington State Parks and Recreation Commission, Public Affairs Office, P.O. Box 42650, Olympia, WA 98504-2650; 800/233-0321.

2 Tennant Lake Wildlife Area/Hovander Homestead Park

0.5–2.0 mi/1.0 hrs

Bird-watchers, wheelchair users, and kids of all ages will love the flat, easy trails around Tennant Lake Wildlife Area—a marshy, water lily–festooned lake—and Hovander Homestead Farm, an intact, 1900s homestead still stocked with draft horses, cattle, pigs, ducks, chickens, and other farm animals. The land settled and farmed by the Hovanders, a pioneer Swedish family, today is a grand place for a Sunday walk. Start at either the Wildlife Area or Homestead Park parking lots, but make time to see both. You can walk all the developed trails in the complex in a couple hours. If you're pressed for time, park at the Wildlife Area interpretive center (summer hours for the center, staffed by a naturalist, are Thursday through Sunday, noon to 5 P.M.) and begin your visit by strolling the award-winning fragrance garden, a series of raised flower beds containing fragrant plants. It's all barrier-free, and a delightful stop for sighted and non-sighted visitors. The fragrance garden is particularly beautiful in early summer, when many of the herbs and flowers are in full bloom. From here, walk a short distance to the 50-foot Tennant Lake viewing tower (worth a stop for the view of Mount Baker; wheelchair users can take in the view from the top via a closed-circuit camera viewing screen at the bottom) then head out on the Boardwalk Loop Trail, which forks at about one-third mile. Take the left fork a short distance to the best viewpoint of Tennant Lake. Take the right fork for a meandering boardwalk-loop stroll of about a mile through this lush, sprawling wetland. Bring binoculars and count bird species. Back at the parking lot, take the time to walk the half-mile path to Hovander Park. For an extended hike, follow the Wildlife Area's River Dike Access Trail, which leads about two miles to a dike along the Nooksack River.

Location: In Whatcom County, south of Ferndale; see Seattle and the San Juans Map 1, grid b4.

User Groups: Hikers only. No dogs, horses, or mountain bikes are allowed. Most of the trails in Hovander Homestead Park are barrier-free. The trail around Tennant Lake is on a four-foot-wide boardwalk and could be navigable with assistance.

Permits: No permits are required. Parking and access are free.

Maps: For a park brochure, contact Whatcom County Parks at the address below. The USGS topographic map is Ferndale.

Directions: From I-90 at Bellingham, drive five miles north to Exit 262, Ferndale. Proceed one-half mile west to Hovander Road. Turn left (south) and in a short distance fork right on Neilsen Road. Follow signs about a half mile to the dual entrances for Tennant Lake and Hovander Homestead Parks (proceed straight at the junction for Tennant Lake; turn right to park at Hovander Homestead Park, which is connected by a half-mile path).

Contact: Whatcom County Parks and Recreation; 3373 Mount Baker Highway, Bellingham, WA 98226; 360/733-2900.

3 Whatcom Falls Park
0.5–2.0 mi/0.5–1.5 hrs 🥾 ⚐

In June 1999, the Whatcom Creek Gorge, a longtime favorite cool, forested retreat in Bellingham's urban core, became the sight of something no one ever imagined: a conflagration, the result of a firestorm erupting from a massive spill of gasoline from a pipeline running through this pleasant, 200-acre city park. The gasoline filled Whatcom Creek for several miles downstream and accidentally ignited, creating a firestorm visible for miles. Three young people in or on the creek were killed, and everything within about 50 yards on either side of the stream was burnt to a crisp. This man-made disaster has left an ugly scar along Whatcom Creek—one that's worth viewing to mull the destructive carelessness of man, and the amazing resiliency of nature. At this writing, two years after the explosion, life is returning to the water and surrounding ecosystem of Whatcom Creek. Thanks to an aggressive, ongoing reforestation project largely manned by volunteers, Whatcom Falls remains a still-pleasant, shady, mostly green and highly instructive place for an afternoon stroll. But the tall, burnt trees still stand as a sober reminder of what was.

From the main parking area in the center of the park, follow the path a short distance downhill to an old WPA-constructed stone bridge over Whatcom Falls. Cross the bridge, and on the other side, choose a trail fork to hike along the north side of Whatcom Creek Gorge, where the creek drops about 300 feet in only a few miles on its way from Lake Whatcom to Bellingham Bay. After the fire, the trail system here remains in flux, with many north-side trails remaining closed for restoration. For now, after crossing the bridge take the right trail fork and follow the obvious path along the southside for about a half mile to a recently constructed overlook of the blast zone. Return the way you came or by continuing the loop downhill to Bay View Cemetery and Woburn Street, then follow the path back along Lakeway Drive to the starting point. To extend your hike by about a mile, park at Bloedel-Donovan Park on Lake Whatcom and follow the old railroad grade across Electric Avenue to the Whatcom Falls trail system.

Location: Near Lake Whatcom on the east side of Bellingham, Seattle and the San Juans Map 1, grid b5.

User Groups: Hikers, horses, dogs, and mountain bikes. No wheelchair facilities.

Permits: No permits are required. Parking and access are free.

Maps: For a parks brochure, contact Bellingham Parks and Recreation Department at the address below. Ask the USGS for a topographic map of Bellingham South.

Directions: From Seattle, drive approximately 90 miles north on I-5 to Bellingham exit 253, Lakeway Drive. Turn east on Lakeway Drive and proceed 1.5 miles to Kenoyer Drive. Turn left and continue 0.4 mile to the parking area. Follow the sound of the waterfall to the trailhead on the west side of the parking lot.

Contact: Bellingham Parks and Recreation Department, 3424 Meridian Street, Bellingham, WA 98225; 360/676-6985.

4 Lake Padden
2.6 mi/1.0 hrs

Discover the secret that thousands of Bellingham residents already know: A daily stroll around Lake Padden is good for the soul and good for the soles. The delightfully quiet lake (no gas motors allowed) is completely ringed by a trail, much of which is an old roadway turned wide, well-stamped path. Start at the east or west park entrance and set out in either direction on the loop, which runs 2.6 miles around the lake, climbing a couple short hills along the way. The path on the south side of the lake runs through deep, second-growth forest of western red cedar, Douglas fir, spruce, and alder. The north side is more exposed to sunlight. In summer months, you'll be joined by anglers headed for the lake's excellent bank-fishing spots. All year long, you'll be joined by local residents taking advantage of an exercise path that qualifies as a city treasure. It's a very pleasant walk in a very pleasant place, well worthy of one stop or a thousand. If you're up for more of the same, see the park map at either entrance for connecting fire-road loops of up to six miles (many of these trails through hills above the lake are favored by mountain bikers and horse riders).

Location: In the southeast city limits of Bellingham; see Seattle and the San Juans Map 1, grid c5.

User Groups: Hikers, horses, dogs, and mountain bikes. The path is mostly wide gravel, much of which is firm and level enough for wheelchairs with assistance.

Permits: No permits are required. Parking and access are free.

Maps: For a park brochure, contact Bellingham Parks and Recreation Department at the address below. Ask the USGS for a topographic map of Bellingham South.

Directions: From I-5 at Bellingham, take Exit 252, Samish Way. Proceed southeast on Samish Way for approximately 2 miles to Lake Padden Park, on the right side of the road. Parking areas are located at both the east and west ends of the lake.

Contact: Bellingham Parks and Recreation Department, 3424 Meridian Street, Bellingham, WA 98225; 360/676-6985.

5 Interurban Trail
7.0 mi/2.0 hrs

This former route of the old interurban electric trolley between Bellingham and Mount Vernon parallels famed Chuckanut Drive, providing foot, wheel, and hoof access between the splendid city and state parks in the forested, rocky-shored southern reaches of Bellingham. To ride the entire length, park at the trailhead on Fairhaven Parkway and proceed south, through Fairhaven Park, and into dark, hilly Arroyo Park. The trail immediately south of Old Samish Highway in Arroyo Park is the Interurban's steep section. Walkers or cyclists who wish to avoid it are best served by traveling west on Old Samish Highway and proceeding north on Chuckanut Drive to the North Chuckanut Trailhead at California Street, where the path can be rejoined. But the entire trail is open to bikes and horses, and the Arroyo Park section is one of the most interesting stretches for hikers. The trail's southern terminus is at Larrabee State Park, near the Fragrance Lake Trailhead (see hike in this chapter). Other side trails leading

from the Interurban include a short, steep path down to Teddy Bear Cove, a popular (and sometimes nude) bathing beach on Samish Bay, just south of the city limits, and the Larrabee/Post Point Trail, a half-mile path that connects the Interurban at 10th and Donovan to the Padden Lagoon and the south shore of Marine Park. One popular option: Park at Fairhaven or Arroyo Park, mountain bike south to Larrabee, then climb the scenic Fragrance Lake Trail on foot.

Location: From south Bellingham to Larrabee State Park on Chuckanut Drive; see Seattle and the San Juans Map 1, grid c5.

User Groups: Hikers, horses, dogs, and mountain bikes. No wheelchair facilities.

Permits: No permits are required. Parking and access are free.

Maps: For a Bellingham trail brochure, contact the Bellingham Parks and Recreation Department at the address below. The USGS topographic map is Bellingham South.

Directions: The Interurban Trail is accessible from trailheads in Bellingham on Fairhaven Parkway near 24th Street; at 10th Street and Donovan Avenue; in Fairhaven and Arroyo city parks; and along Chuckanut Drive at the North Chuckanut Trailhead (California Street and Chuckanut Drive) and near the main entrance to Larrabee State Park, seven miles south of Bellingham.

Contact: Bellingham Parks and Recreation Department, 3424 Meridian Street, Bellingham, WA 98225; 360/676-6985.

6 Pine and Cedar Lakes
4.0–6.0 mi/2.0–4.0 hrs

The two subalpine lakes (at about 1,600 feet) are only part of the attraction on this popular, fairly steep day hike up Chuckanut Mountain, on Whatcom County Parks property south of Bellingham. The trail, a steep, old road for the first mile or so, finally levels out before you meet a spur trail leading to Cedar Lake. Keep straight for Pine Lake or go down and left to Cedar Lake, which is ringed by a trail. Several unmarked spur trails lead a short distance to viewpoints of Bellingham and the San Juan Islands. Back on the main trail, proceed about a half mile to picturesque Pine Lake, which has four designated campsites. Stronger hikers can make a longer walk by taking the Hemlock Trail, which exits west below the Cedar Lake Spur and leads about 3.5 miles down and north to Arroyo Park, near the Chuckanut Drive/Old Samish Highway junction. Total elevation gain via the main trail is about 1,280 feet to Cedar Lake (four-mile round trip) and 1,575 feet to Pine Lake (4.5-mile round-trip).

Location: On Chuckanut Mountain south of Bellingham; see Seattle and the San Juans Map 1, grid c5.

User Groups: Hikers, horses, dogs, and mountain bikes. No wheelchair facilities.

Permits: No permits are required. Parking and access are free.

Maps: For a Chuckanut Mountain map and brochure, contact the Washington Department of Natural Resources at the address below. Ask the USGS for a topographic map of Bellingham South.

Directions: From Seattle drive 65 miles north on I-5 past Mount Vernon to Exit 231/Chuckanut Drive. Turn left (west) under the freeway and drive about 18 miles north on Chuckanut Drive, continuing beyond Larrabee State Park to the city limits of Bellingham. Turn right (east) on Old Samish Highway and proceed 1.9 miles to the signed trailhead parking area on the right (south) side of the road.

Contact: Washington Department of Natural Resources, Northwest Region, 919 North Township Street, Sedro-Woolley, WA 98284; 360/856-5700. Alternate contact: Whatcom County Parks and Recreation, 3373 Mount

Baker Highway, Bellingham, WA 98226; 360/733-2900.

◨ Larrabee State Park
1.4–8.0 mi/0.5–5.0 hrs

Washington's oldest state park (1915) is also one of its grandest for hikers. Larrabee State Park's 2,500 acres offer a bit of the best of everything about western Washington: camping, hiking, picnicking, and grand sunsets over the close-enough-to-touch San Juan Islands. Connecting the far reaches of this 2,500-acre park are eight miles of hiking trails, which lead to the seashore at Wildcat Cove and Clayton Beach and to the mountainous climes of Fragrance Lake, Lost Lake, the top of Chuckanut Mountain, and some creepy bat caves (yes, real bats) that you might stumble upon all by yourself. The entire west side of Chuckanut Mountain (technically, the only place in the state where the Cascades reach down and touch the saltwater) is a play area begging to be explored. A large forest fire in the 1960s cleared much of the greenery, leaving behind fascinating geologic formations and heart-stopping vistas. Plans call for further linking of this area with the Blanchard Mountain trail system to the south.

For a first taste—or whiff, as the case may be—of the park's upland areas, follow the Fragrance Lake Trail from the main trailhead. The moderate grade climbs about a mile up the hill, with a short (.25-mile) spur trail leading to a fine viewpoint of Georgia Strait. The main path leads just under a mile farther, with a steepening pace, to Fragrance Lake, which is circled by a short path. To sample the seashore, park at the Clayton Beach parking area south of Larrabee's main entrance, cross Chuckanut Drive, and follow the path 0.7 miles down to a lovely gravel beach on Samish Bay. (If the tide is out, you can walk the beach north back to Larrabee State Park proper.) Sunsets from the beach here are glorious, but use caution on the trail, which has decayed in recent years and is very slippery in spots where it crosses large spans of smooth sandstone. New Washington State Parks facilities including a redesigned trail, pedestrian overpass, and restrooms are planned for Clayton Beach, budgets allowing.

When this book went to press, Washington State Parks were considering implementing a day-use parking fee; call the contact number for current information.

Location: South of Bellingham; see Seattle and the San Juans Map 1, grid c5.

User Groups: Hikers and leashed dogs only on the Fragrance Lake Trail from the main (Larrabee State Park) trailhead. Horses and mountain bikes are allowed on the trail from an alternate trailhead off Cleator Road. No wheelchair facilities.

Permits: No permits are required. Parking and access are free.

Maps: For a state parks map and brochure, contact Washington State Parks at 800/233-0321. For a Chuckanut Mountain Trail Map, contact the Washington Department of Natural Resources, Northwest Region, 919 North Township Street, Sedro-Woolley, WA 98284; 360/856-5700. The USGS topographic map is Bellingham South.

Directions: From Seattle, drive 65 miles north on I-5 past Mount Vernon to Exit 231, Chuckanut Drive. Turn left (west) under the freeway and drive about 12 miles north to the main entrance of Larrabee State Park, seven miles south of Bellingham on the left (west) side of the road. Trailheads are found at the main entrance; the trailhead for the Fragrance Lake/Interurban Trail is on the east side of Chuckanut Drive, immediately north of the park gate. The well-signed trailhead for Clayton Beach is 0.25 miles south of

Larrabee State Park's main entrance on the east side of Chuckanut Drive.

Contact: Larrabee State Park, 245 Chuckanut Drive, Bellingham, WA 98226; 360/676-2093. Washington State Parks and Recreation Commission, P.O. Box 42650, Olympia, WA 98504; 800/233-0321.

◘ Washington Park Loop
3.0 mi/2.5 hrs

Here's your chance to impress friends from out of town. Drive north of Seattle to Anacortes, past the angry throng of tourists waiting in a four-hour line to escape civilization on the San Juan Islands. Five minutes past that spectacle, pull off in Washington Park, unload your lunch, and set out to enjoy the very seaside tranquility all those would-be ferry passengers are seeking. This truly is one of the state's better-kept secrets, probably because 220-acre Washington Park, which covers all of Fidalgo Head, is a city park in a small town and is rarely advertised.

Fidalgo Head, a rocky peninsula whose crown is capped by forest, is almost completely surrounded by saltwater. Motorists and smooth-track cyclists can enjoy the many seaside views on a road that loops around the park. Hikers and mountain bikers can enjoy the same scenery—only more close up—on a loop trail that runs nearly parallel to the road. At times it's necessary to walk on the road to reach connecting trails, but it's a one-way path with many speed bumps, so traffic isn't a hazard. Along the way, you enjoy spectacular views of the San Juans, ferries carrying harried island visitors, fishing vessels, and oil tankers bound for refineries east of Anacortes. It's never boring, always pleasant, and rarely crowded. You'll want to take your time here. It's a marvelous diversion from city life any time of year.

Note: Given its relatively humble size, the city of Anacortes manages an unusually large number of excellent, very scenic hiking trails, including the Mount Erie Viewpoint, Heart Lake, and Cranberry Lakes Trails. For information and updated maps, contact the City of Anacortes Parks and Recreation Department at the address below.

Location: Northwest of Anacortes; see Seattle and the San Juans Map 1, grid d3.

User Groups: Hikers, dogs, and mountain bikes. No horses are allowed. No wheelchair facilities.

Permits: No permits are required. Parking and access are free.

Maps: Ask the USGS for a topographic map of the Anacortes North area.

Directions: From Seattle drive 64 miles north on I-5 to Mount Vernon. Take Exit 230/Anacortes/Burlington and turn left (west) under the freeway. Traveling on Highways 20 and 237, follow the signs for about 14 miles northwest to Anacortes. In downtown Anacortes, turn left where the signs indicate the Washington State Ferry Terminal. Drive approximately three miles west, continuing straight on Sunset where the road veers right to the ferry terminal. The road ends at Washington Park, where ample parking is available near the boat launch.

Contact: City of Anacortes Parks and Recreation Department, P.O. Box 547, Anacortes, WA 98221; 360/293-1918 or fax 360/293-1928.

⑨ Padilla Bay National Marine Estuary

5.5 mi/2.0 hrs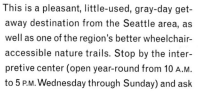

This is a pleasant, little-used, gray-day getaway destination from the Seattle area, as well as one of the region's better wheelchair-accessible nature trails. Stop by the interpretive center (open year-round from 10 A.M. to 5 P.M. Wednesday through Sunday) and ask the staff to show you where to look for the reserve's many waterfowl. You have your choice of three trails: the 0.8-mile upland trail through a meadow and forest, the short stroll to a viewing deck, or the 2.25-mile shore trail, which is reached by driving 3.3 miles south of the interpretive center on Bayview-Edison Road. (Handicapped parking is at the south trailhead.) The shore trail skirts the top of a dike, offering excellent views of a massive tidal mudflat, the likely home of any of a variety of shorebirds, including great blue herons, which are commonly seen. All three trails are barrier-free. From the observation platform at the interpretive center, a spiral staircase leads to the beach. It's open from April to October and closed in the winter to foster stopovers by migratory waterfowl.

Wheelchair hikers must stop at the interpretive center and check out a key for access to the shore trail. The shore trail is open to hunters from October to January.

Location: East of Anacortes; see Seattle and the San Juans Map 1, grid e5.

User Groups: Hikers, leashed dogs, and mountain bikes. The shore trail is fully wheelchair accessible. No horses are allowed.

Permits: No permits are required. Parking and access are free.

Maps: For a descriptive brochure contact the Padilla Bay National Estuarine Research Reserve at 360/428-1558. Ask the USGS for topographic maps of the Anacortes South and LaConner areas.

Directions: From Seattle drive 64 miles north on I-5 to Exit 230/Anacortes/Burlington. Drive west on Highway 20 for about six miles to the stoplight at Bayview-Edison Road (the Farm House Inn Restaurant is on your left). Turn right (north) and drive about five miles, past Bay View State Park. The Breazeale Interpretive Center is on the right, a quarter mile past the state park.

Contact: Padilla Bay National Estuarine Research Reserve, 10441 Bayview-Edison Road, Mount Vernon, WA 98273; 360/428-1558.

10 Deception Pass State Park
1.0–12.0 mi/
1.0 hr–1.0 day

Every year, we Northwest natives ponder a visit to Deception Pass State Park and pause to consider the crowds, which often are greater than the masses of people attending a Seattle Seahawks game. And every year, we reach the same conclusion: Deception Pass is worth a visit, crowded or not. Even with the more than two million visitors who come each year to the lovely campground, pristine beaches, and soothing woodlands, it's easy to get lost in your thoughts—not to mention the woods—at Deception Pass. No other spot in the Northwest, and perhaps the nation, offers a more pleasant combination of marine, forest, and mountain environments.

Excellent day hikes on the park's 18 miles of trails and beaches are too numerous to mention them all here, but there are a few favorites. Try the beach walk from the West Point parking area to the foot of the Deception Pass Bridge. Return via the upland forested trail, which offers sublime views of Fidalgo's rocky face and the often-frightening tidal-flush currents through Deception Pass. It's a two-mile round-trip hike. When you're finished, explore the upper woodlands of the same area, strolling beneath massive Douglas firs and smooth, twisted trunks of giant madronas. Walk across the impressive bridge to the east side and try trails from Bowman Bay to Rosario Head or Reservation Head. Both are round-trips of about two miles and offer high cliff-top views that qualify as the most memorable on northern Puget Sound. And

that's just the beginning. Explore for yourself and take your time; this area is prime for exploration year-round, and you're sure to return.

Each year the dangerous, high cliffs around Deception Pass, especially on Canoe Island in the center of the channel, draw fools who end up requiring rescue, or memorial, services. If you know what's good for you, stay on maintained trails.

When this book went to press, Washington State Parks were considering implementing a day-use parking fee; call the contact number for current information.

Location: On the northeastern tip of Whidbey Island, west of Mount Vernon; see Seattle and the San Juans Map 1, grid e3.

User Groups: Hikers, leashed dogs, and mountain bikes. (For open cycling trails, see the Deception Pass State Park ranger.) No horses are allowed. The park has some wheelchair facilities, including the 0.8-mile Deception Pass Sand Dune Trail.

Permits: No permits are required. Parking and access are free.

Maps: Ask the USGS for a topographic map of the Deception Pass area.

Directions: From Seattle drive 64 miles north on I-5 to Exit 230/Anacortes/Burlington. Turn west on Highway 20 and drive about 12 miles to the Whidbey Island junction. Proceed about six miles south on Highway 20 to the park, which lies on both the Whidbey Island and Fidalgo Island sides of the Deception Pass Bridge. Main trailheads are found at Bowman Bay on the Fidalgo Island (north) side and at West Point near Cranberry Lake on the Whidbey Island (south) side.

Contact: Deception Pass State Park, 5175 North Highway 20, Oak Harbor, WA 98277; 360/675-2417; Washington State Parks and Recreation Commission, P.O. Box 42650, Olympia, WA 98504; 800/233-0321.

⓫ Fort Ebey State Park
6.0 mi/3.0 hrs

When Deception Pass is just too crowded, this Whidbey Island park is the perfect casual day hike destination. Fort Ebey State Park has a substantial—and developing—trail system that includes some excellent beach walks north to Joseph Whidbey State Park. But most people come to stroll the Bluff Trail, which leads three miles on either side of Point Partridge, past gun emplacements that are holdovers from the fort's World War II active-duty days. Views are excellent all along the mostly flat path. This is a great walk for a spring or fall day, when the mountains are snowed in and the body is winding up for, or down from, the vigorous summer hiking season. Bring a raincoat; even if it's not raining, it helps cut the almost constant breeze.

When this book went to press, Washington State Parks were considering implementing a day-use parking fee; call the contact number for current information.

Location: On the west side of central Whidbey Island, southwest of Oak Harbor; see Seattle and the San Juans Map 1, grid g2.

User Groups: Hikers and leashed dogs. No horses or mountain bikes are allowed. No wheelchair facilities.

Permits: No permits are required. Parking and access are free.

Maps: Ask the USGS for a topographic map of the Port Townsend North area.

Directions: From Oak Harbor take Highway 20 south to Libby Road. Drive one mile west, turn left on Valley Drive, and continue to the Fort Ebey State Park entrance. Inside the gate, turn right at the T and follow signs to trailhead parking near the bluff.

Contact: Fort Ebey State Park, 395 North Fort Ebey Road, Coupeville, WA 98239; 360/678-4636; Washington State Parks and Recreation Commission, P.O. Box 42650, Olympia, WA 98504; 800/233-0321.

⓬ South Whidbey State Park
1.0–3.0 mi/1.0–3.0 hrs

South Whidbey, a campground and day-use area tucked away on Admiralty Inlet between Bush and Lagoon Points, is a pleasant off-season destination. In winter, the park is gated at the main road, but hikers can cycle to the spot and proceed around the gate or park outside and walk in. A favorite destination is an unnamed trail leading from the picnic area and dropping a half mile to the gravel beach below. From here, the walking is fine in both directions and crowds are minimal. The sun seems to linger here long beyond its regular schedule on cold, clear winter days. Other excellent park hikes include a one-mile nature trail loop on the bluff above the beach and, on the opposite side of the highway, the Wilbert Trail, which winds 1.5 miles through some rare, magnificent old-growth forest and back to the highway a quarter mile from the park gate.

When this book went to press, Washington State Parks were considering implementing a day-use parking fee; call the contact number for current information.

Location: Southwest of Greenbank on Whidbey Island; see Seattle and the San Juans Map 1, grid h4.

User Groups: Hikers and leashed dogs. No horses or mountain bikes are allowed. No wheelchair facilities.

Permits: No permits are required. Parking and access are free.

Maps: Ask the USGS for a topographic map of the Freeland area.

Directions: From Mukilteo (about 25 miles north of Seattle) take the Washington State Ferry to Clinton on south Whidbey

Island. Drive north on Highway 525 to Bush Point Road. Turn left (west) and follow the road (it becomes Smugglers Cove Road) six miles to the state park entrance on the left. **Contact:** South Whidbey State Park, 4128 South Smugglers Cove Road, Freeland, WA 98249; 360/331-4559; Washington State Parks and Recreation Commission, P.O. Box 42650, Olympia, WA 98504; 800/233-0321.

13 Snohomish Centennial Trail
14.0 mi/5.0 hrs

For a prime example of a government agency getting the very most out of what it has, stop here. The Centennial Trail may not look like much on a map, but a day spent horseback riding, mountain biking, or just strolling on the paved trail always seems like a productive one. At the moment, the route is seven miles long, connecting Snohomish to Lake Stevens. But the former route of the Seattle, Lake Shore, and Eastern Railway (the Burke-Gilman Trail in Seattle, featured in this chapter, uses part of the same route) is someday is expected to link King and Skagit Counties through Snohomish County farmlands. About 17 miles of the right-of-way already has been acquired; the trail could grow to 44 miles upon completion. From the major trailhead near Snohomish, travel near the Pilchuck River through rural farm country. (Be sure to visit before the area gets swallowed up by creeping suburbia.) You get more than a few whiffs of fresh cow pies, which somehow seems good for a smog-congested soul. The trail is completely barrier free and accessible from various points, including downtown Snohomish. You get occasional good views of Mount Pilchuck and other western Cascade Range peaks. A short distance up the trail from Snohomish, pull off at Machias and check out the nicely restored railroad depot.

Location: Linking the towns of Snohomish and Lake Stevens; see Seattle and the San Juans Map 2, grid a8.
User Groups: Hikers, leashed dogs, horses, and mountain bikes. Fully wheelchair accessible.
Permits: No permits are required. Parking and access are free.
Maps: For a Centennial Trail map contact the Snohomish County Parks Department at 425 388-6600. Ask the USGS for a topographic map of the Snohomish area.
Directions: From Seattle drive 28 miles north on I-5 to Exit 194. Drive east on U.S. 2 to Snohomish. The trail begins at the intersection of Maple Street and Pine Avenue. For additional parking, turn east on Maple Street and drive 1.5 miles to a large parking area on the right. Another trailhead is located farther northeast on the trail, near the town of Machias.
Contact: Snohomish County Parks and Recreation Department, 9623 32nd St. SE, Everett, WA 98205; 425/388-6600.

14 Carkeek Park
2.0–4.0 mi/1.0–2.0 hrs

In many respects, Carkeek is like a little sister to Seattle's other grand waterfront upland park, Discovery. Smaller, at 193 acres, it is also less known and usually less crowded. A variety of hiking trails awaits. The most easily followed route is the Piper's Creek Trail, which begins at the saltwater beach near the lower parking lot and climbs up along Piper's Creek. It parallels the park entrance road before splitting north to a dead end up Venema Creek or south to several other trails, most of which loop back down to the main trail.

Views of Puget Sound and the Olympic Mountains are excellent throughout the park. Even when clouds settle over Seattle for the winter, however, Carkeek remains a good hiking destination for yet another reason: salmon. You can't catch them, but you're welcome to watch them spawn. A run of chum salmon, planted in Piper's Creek by community volunteers, is growing larger each year, and the Piper's Creek Trail offers several prime spawning vantage points, often marked by volunteers more than happy to pass on their fish-spawning knowledge. The run usually arrives in October or November. Remember: Don't approach the stream or allow animals off leash while the fish are spawning.

Location: On Puget Sound in north Seattle; see Seattle and the San Juans Map 2, grid c5.

User Groups: Hikers and leashed dogs. No horses or mountain bikes are allowed. No wheelchair facilities.

Permits: No permits are required. Parking and access are free.

Maps: Ask the USGS for topographic maps of the Shilshole Bay and Seattle North areas.

Directions: From downtown Seattle drive north on Elliott Avenue West, which becomes 15th Avenue West. Drive over the Ballard Bridge, through the Crown Hill neighborhood. The road veers right (east) as it becomes Holman Road Northwest/Northwest 101st Street. Turn left (north) at the stoplight at the intersection with Third Avenue Northwest. Take Third Avenue to Northwest 110th Street. Turn left (west) and veer sharply right as the street becomes Northwest Carkeek Park Road. Turn left into the park entrance and drive a half mile to one of two parking lots, both of which have access to hiking trails.

Contact: Seattle Parks Department Recreation Information Office, 5201 Greenlake Way North, Seattle, WA 98103; 206/684-4075.

15 Green Lake
2.8 mi/1.0 hr

If you're looking for solitude, go elsewhere. But if sheer numbers are your thing, this is the mother of all Northwest trails. The Green Lake Trail, paved on the inside (near the lake) and gravel on the outer rim, is the jogging/power-walking/in-line skating/baby-carriage-pushing/skateboarding/cycling/sailboarding/lounging/even trout-fishing capital of Seattle. It's an institution unto itself, and the more than two million annual patrons, ranging from genteel to buffed, make it one of the most-used public parks in the nation. Still, it somehow seems to maintain a special charm. Much credit must go to the Seattle Parks Department, which has been wise enough to adopt a minimalist approach to Green Lake.

The park is a path, a lake, a cornucopia of trees, and little else. Its main function is to get people outdoors and circulating around a 2.8-mile oval (3.2 miles for the outer gravel ring), sucking in fresh air. And it does that quite nicely, thank you. The Green Lake Trail, which received substantial and long overdue widening and repaving in 1987 and 1988, is accessible from city streets all around the lake. Start wherever you can find parking, heed the directional signs and take off. It's likely to be crowded, and newcomers who fail to heed Green Lake etiquette (walkers go clockwise, wheeled people counterclockwise, no sudden stops, use voice or bell warnings to pass) are likely to feel the wrath of the regulars. Some of us have stopped going to Green Lake in the summer because the crowds are so great. But in the fall and winter, there's nothing like an hour-long stroll around Green Lake to take your mind off Christmas shopping or Thanksgiving Day family politics. Whether you're there for exercise, bird-watching, nature photography, or the most popular sport of all, people watching, Green Lake seldom disappoints. (Watch for the guy on the mountain bike with the cat riding on his head, and his pal, the Marathon Man, who skirts the lake year-round in a Speedo.)

Don't leave valuables—or expensive car stereos, for that matter—in your car at the main Green Lake parking lot. It's a haven for thieves.

Location: In the heart of north Seattle, west of I-5; see Seattle and the San Juans Map 2, grid c6.

User Groups: Hikers, leashed dogs, and mountain bikes. Fully wheelchair accessible. No horses are allowed.

Permits: No permits are required. Parking and access are free.

Maps: Ask the USGS for a topographic map of the Seattle North area.

Directions: From Seattle drive five miles north on I-5. Take Exit 170 and drive just under a half mile west on Ravenna Boulevard to East Greenlake Drive North. Turn right at the five-way stop sign and drive 0.1 mile to the first stoplight, at Lawton Street. Turn left into the main parking lot, adjacent to the paved Green Lake Trail. If the lot is full, exit the way you came and park along East Greenlake Drive.

Contact: Seattle Parks Department Recreation Information Office, 5201 Greenlake Way North, Seattle, WA 98103; 206/684-4075.

16 Discovery Park Nature Loop
2.8 mi/2.0 hrs

Few cities in the country offer wild parks that rival Seattle's, and Discovery is the crown jewel in that impressive array. In fact, once you're inside the 535-acre, tree-walled park, it's easy to forget that one of Seattle's largest and swankiest neighborhoods is less than a mile away. The park, which essentially surrounds the Fort Lawton military installation, has three main entrances and an extensive trail network, ranging from bluff-top strolls to sandy beach walks. It's easy to get lost

among the joggers, picnickers, dog walkers, and other park users.

One good introduction to the park and its ecosystem is a 2.8-mile loop from the visitor center, above North and South Beaches, and back. You pass through an interesting forest composed of old-growth broad-leaved trees and second-growth conifers, occasionally stopping at overlooks with excellent views of Puget Sound below. Side trails lead to the beach, where walking has been disturbed by construction of a massive West Point sewage treatment plant. Keep your eyes peeled for wildlife. Sea lions, seals, and even porpoises and orcas are occasionally spotted off West Point, and at least one pair of nesting bald eagles calls the park home. The park is a pleasant place to visit all year long but is perhaps most enjoyable in autumn, when the kids are back in school and all those tourists are back where they belong.

Location: On Puget Sound and Magnolia Bluff in Seattle; see Seattle and the San Juans Map 2, grid c6.

User Groups: Hikers and leashed dogs. No horses or mountain bikes are allowed. No wheelchair facilities.

Permits: No permits are required. Parking and access are free.

Maps: Ask the USGS for a topographic map of the Shilshole Bay area.

Directions: From downtown Seattle drive north on 15th Avenue West to the Dravus Street exit. Drive west on Dravus Street for about one-half mile to the stop sign at 20th Avenue West. Turn right, follow the signs to the park entrance, and then turn left into the visitor center parking lot.

Contact: Seattle Parks Department Recreation Information Office, 5201 Greenlake Way North, Seattle, WA 98103; 206/684-4075.

⓲ Burke-Gilman/Sammamish River

28.0 mi/1.0 hr–1.0 day

Look up "prototype rails-to-trails project" in the encyclopedia and there should be a picture of cyclists on the Burke-Gilman Trail. The Burke, as it is popularly known, stretches from north Seattle's Fremont neighborhood 14 miles northeast around Lake Union, through the University of Washington, to Lake Washington and Kenmore. Here amid the bustling traffic of Lake City Way, it connects to the Sammamish River Trail, which follows the Sammamish Slough for 14 miles to the spacious open fields of Marymoor Park, King County's grandest playground.

Despite a strong mixed-use sermon preached by the various government agencies that cooperate to manage the trail, it's more geared to cyclists than walkers. This is not by design but by necessity. Because it's one of the best all-flat cycle tracks close to a major city in the United States, it now attracts so many cyclists that walking it can be troublesome. Don't misunderstand: The vast majority of cyclists are very polite. It's just that with so many smiling faces whizzing by, pedestrians usually find themselves wishing that they, too, were on cycles. The most popular starting points are at Marymoor Park for Eastsiders and at the parking lot at Gas Works Park for city dwellers. The trail winds along a mostly brushy course to Kenmore, offering occasional views of Lake Washington. It becomes more scenic thereafter, breaking out into the open fields of the Sammamish Valley, past cow pastures and high-tech office facilities. Thanks to land acquisitions, this trail keeps expanding incrementally every year, gradually creeping both west and east. Ultimately, we hope it will form an unbroken link from Puget Sound to the crest of Snoqualmie Pass and beyond.

Location: Between the north end of Lake Union in Seattle and Marymoor Park in Redmond; see Seattle and the San Juans Map 2, grid c6.

User Groups: Hikers, dogs, and mountain bikes. Wheelchair accessible. No horses are allowed.

Permits: No permits are required. Parking and access are free.

Maps: Ask the USGS for topographic maps of the Seattle North and Kirkland areas.

Directions: The trail is accessible at dozens of points along Lake Union, the University of Washington, Sand Point, Kenmore, and Redmond. Most people start at the trail's east end at Marymoor Park or at Gas Works Park on north Lake Union in Seattle.

To the Marymoor Park Trailhead: From Seattle take I-5 north to Exit 168, following Highway 520 and crossing the Evergreen Point Floating Bridge. Drive approximately 10 miles east to the West Lake Sammamish Parkway exit. Turn right on the parkway. Just ahead, the park entrance is plainly visible on the left side of the road.

To the Gas Works Park Trailhead: From downtown Seattle drive north on Westlake Boulevard. Turn right on Fremont Avenue North and cross the Fremont Bridge. At the stoplight on the other side, turn right on North 34th Street. At the intersection with Stone Way North, turn right on North Northlake Way and then drive a quarter mile to the park entrance on the right.

Contact: Seattle Parks Department Recreation Information Office, 5201 Greenlake Way North, Seattle, WA 98103; 206/684-4075.

⓳ Bridle Trails State Park Loop

4.0 mi/1.5 hrs

Horse lovers, this one's for you. Everyone else, it's for you, too, if you don't mind an occasional muddy spot and a horse puck or two lying in your path. Bridle Trails, a wonderful suburban state park established by horse enthusiasts, is an excellent getaway for both hikers and equestrians. A network of nearly 50 miles of trails (most without directional signs) leads throughout the forested, 480-acre park. To make things even more confusing, many lead outside the park to private stables and homes. It's easy to get lost, but only temporarily. Eventually, you find your way back to one of the park's major routes.

Some friends of ours enjoy stopping by the park once a year, wandering blindly in an attempt to get lost, then seeing how long it takes to extricate themselves. Even though most of the horse riders who frequent the park are friendly and helpful, we can't say we recommend the get-lost approach. Instead, first-timers should consider walking the park's broad, four-mile-long perimeter loop. It departs from the south end of the parking lot and loops counterclockwise around the park. You emerge by park headquarters and then walk the final half mile south back to the car.

On these trails, as on all hiker/horse trails, horses have the right-of-way. Step off the path and allow them to pass. It's easier for you than for a hoofed animal to get out of the way. As our friend Marlene likes to say of trail hiking and freeway driving alike, "Tonnage rules!"

When this book went to press, Washington State Parks were considering implementing a day-use parking fee; call the contact number for current information.

Location: Adjacent to I-405 between Kirkland, Bellevue, and Renton; see Seattle and the San Juans Map 2, grid c8.

User Groups: Hikers, leashed dogs, and horses. No mountain bikes are allowed. No wheelchair facilities.

Permits: No permits are required. Parking and access are free.

Maps: For a Bridle Trails State Park brochure, contact Washington State Parks at 800/233-0321. Ask the USGS for a topographic map of the Kirkland area.

Directions: From the Seattle area take I-90 or Highway 520 east to I-405. Drive north to Exit 17 and then turn right (east) on Northeast 60th Street. Take an immediate right on 116th Avenue Northeast and drive south to the park entrance, on the left side of the road.

Contact: Lake Sammamish State Park, 20606 Southeast 56th Street, Issaquah, WA 98027; 425/455-7010; Washington State Parks and Recreation Commission, P.O. Box 42650, Olympia, WA 98504; 800/233-0321.

19 Washington Park Arboretum Waterfront
1.0 mi/1.0 hr

Odds are this is as close as you can get to a natural marshland environment without getting your feet wet. The Waterfront Trail, which is highly visible to auto commuters passing the University of Washington on the Evergreen Point Floating Bridge, follows a planked, floating boardwalk along the Montlake Cut (home of the city's annual boat parade and numerous crew races) to Marsh and Foster Islands. On both sides of the trail, aquatic flora and fauna are on display, most corresponding to numbers on the park's free interpretive brochure (available at the Museum of History and Industry).

Needless to say, the waterborne nature of this nature trail makes it an ideal way to introduce the wonders of the outdoors to children. In spring and summer, the water is nearly covered in places by stunning green water lilies, and ducks and other fowl cavort here by the hundreds in winter. Watch for red-winged blackbirds in the cattails and great blue herons wading the shallows. If you're lucky, you might even spot a beaver fleeing a canoeist from the rental facility at the university, across Montlake Cut. The trail ends on Foster Island, at a second, eastern trailhead, which is accessible by continuing south on Lake Washington Boulevard and turning left (west) on Foster Island Road. But the path is so short—and so entertaining—that your kids will likely drag you right back the way you came.

Location: Southeast of the University of Washington in Seattle; see Seattle and the San Juans Map 2, grid c6.

User Groups: Hikers and dogs. Some wheelchair facilities. No horses or mountain bikes are allowed.

Permits: No permits are required. Parking and access are free.

Maps: Ask the USGS for a topographic map of the Seattle North area.

Directions: From downtown Seattle, take I-5 north for two miles to Highway 520. Drive east on Highway 520 to the Montlake Boulevard exit. At the stoplight go straight onto East Lake Washington Drive. After approximately 100 yards, turn left on Park Drive, heading over the overpass to the Museum of History and Industry parking lot. Look for the Waterfront Trail interpretive sign in the lot's northwest corner.

Contact: Seattle Parks Department Recreation Information Office, 5201 Greenlake Way North, Seattle, WA 98103; 206/684-4075. You can pick up a free interpretive brochure for the Waterfront Trail at the Museum of History and Industry or at the Washington Park Arboretum headquarters on Lake Washington Boulevard.

20 Seward Park Loop
1.75 mi/1.0 hr

Seward Park, which sits on Bailey Peninsula in Lake Washington near a cozy residential neighborhood, isn't exactly wild. Still, it does offer a 280-acre natural escape composed of three miles of natural shoreline, a deep, primeval forest, and a few hills steep enough to get your blood moving. From the parking area, hike uphill through the forest of Douglas fir, passing an occasional large western red cedar or broad-leaf maple, to the hillcrest, about a half mile. Enjoy the forest here; it's probably the largest stand of uncut timber remaining in the city limits. The path then drops over the other side, with myriad side trails branching off to other park locations. Follow the trail to its outlet on Park Loop Road and walk the beach or road about a mile back to the trailhead. For cyclists and other fresh-air lovers looking for a flat path, the 2.75-mile loop along the shore is pleasant, particularly in the spring or fall, before the teenagers cruising in their cars awake from hibernation.

Location: On the shores of Lake Washington in southeast Seattle; see Seattle and the San Juans Map 2, grid d6.

User Groups: Hikers and dogs. No horses or mountain bikes are allowed. No wheelchair facilities.

Permits: No permits are required. Parking and access are free.

Maps: Ask the USGS for a topographic map of the Seattle South area.

Directions: The park is accessible via various routes in south Seattle. For the most direct route from downtown, drive south on Rainier Boulevard, turn left on Genesee Street, and continue to Lake Washington and the park entrance. For the most scenic approach, take I-5 north for two miles from downtown Seattle to Exit 168. Follow Highway 520 east to the Montlake Boulevard exit. At the stoplight go straight onto East Lake Washington Boulevard and follow its winding path to the park entrance. Once inside, turn left and drive one mile to the parking lot on the left.

Contact: Seattle Parks Department Recreation Information Office, 5201 Greenlake Way North, Seattle, WA 98103; 206/684-4075.

21 Cougar Mountain Regional Wildland Park
5.0–10.0 mi/2.0–4.0 hrs

Yes, Virginia, there are cougars. Cougar Mountain Regional Wildland Park, bordered by Lake Washington, Bellevue, Issaquah, and Renton, is a mishmash of roads, trails, abandoned Army missile silos, abandoned landfills, and, somehow, plenty of wildlife. Cougars really do live here—and bears, too. Plenty of other creatures are likely to stumble across the trail without warning, as well. That's what makes this park unique: Not only is it King County's largest park, it's undoubtedly one of the largest wildland parks in an urban area in the United States. Where else can wild animals roam within a five-minute walk of a major shopping center and one of the world's largest concrete-monster freeways, I-90? The mountain's trail system is ever-changing (growing, thankfully), and the best way to discover what's here is to grab a friend, pack a lunch, and head out from Radar Park or one of the other trailheads at West Fork Tibbetts Creek or Lakemont Gorge. You can find high-country views that just might shock you.

Location: Near Issaquah south of I-90; see Seattle and the San Juans Map 2, grid d8.

User Groups: Hikers, dogs, and horses. No mountain bikes are allowed. No wheelchair facilities.

Permits: No permits are required. Parking and access are free.

Maps: For a Cougar Mountain Regional Wildland Park trail map, contact the Issaquah Alps Trail Club at 206/328-0480. Ask the USGS for topographic maps of the Issaquah and Fall City areas.

Directions: From Seattle drive east on I-90 to Exit 11A/150th Avenue Southeast. Turn right at the stop sign and drive to Southeast Newport Way. Turn left and proceed to 164th Avenue Southeast. Turn right. After about a mile, the road becomes Southeast 60th Street. Continue to Cougar Mountain Drive and turn right. Head to the gate or the parking area beyond it at Radar Park.

Contact: Issaquah Alps Trails Club, P.O. Box 351, Issaquah, WA 98022; 206/328-0480.

22 Tolmie State Park Loop
2.5 mi/1.5 hrs

No matter where you walk in this relatively little-known waterfront state park, the saltwater breeze helps blow away big-city angst. Tolmie State Park, which consists of 106 saltwater shoreline acres on Nisqually Reach, has a delightful saltwater marsh, beach, and twin picnic areas matched by an excellent loop trail that begins at the main parking area near the lower picnic area. The trail rises and falls gently through a typical Puget Sound mixed forest, with planking over several very marshy spots. At the end of the loop, continue walking down the spur trail to the beach, which sports prime-time views of McNeil and Anderson Islands. Watch the tank creatures emerge from the depths: a popular underwater park is located just offshore.

When this book went to press, Washington State Parks were considering implementing a day-use parking fee; call the contact number for current information.

Location: Northeast of Olympia on Nisqually Reach in South Puget Sound; see Seattle and the San Juans Map 2, grid h2.

User Groups: Hikers and leashed dogs. No horses or mountain bikes are allowed. No wheelchair facilities.

Permits: No permits are required. Parking and access are free.

Maps: For a Washington State Parks brochure, contact Washington State Parks at 800/233-0321. Ask the USGS for a topographic map of the Lacey area.

Directions: From I-5 north of Olympia, take Exit 111/Yelm/Marvin Road/Highway 510. Drive north on Marvin Road for 3.8 miles to 56th Avenue Northeast. Turn east onto 56th Avenue Northeast and proceed a half mile to Hill Road Northeast. Turn north onto Hill Road Northeast and follow signs about a half mile to the park entrance.

Contact: Washington State Parks and Recreation Commission, Public Affairs Office, P.O. Box 42650, Olympia, WA 98504-2650; 800/233-0321.

23 Nisqually National Wildlife Refuge Loop
5.5 mi/3.0 hrs

When old bird-watchers finally hang up their binoculars and move on to the next realm, they often wind up here: Nisqually Refuge is a birder's heaven. The 2,818-acre refuge, a former farm that most Northwesterners pass on I-5 without noticing, was established in 1974 to preserve one of the last, finest undisturbed estuaries on Puget Sound. It's a major mid-trip stopover for migratory mallards, teal, widgeon, Canada geese, and a slew of other birds; other spectacular Northwest species, including the red-tailed hawk and great blue heron, are frequently seen here year-round.

The refuge is wonderfully simple: A flat, 5.5-mile loop, the Brown Farm Dike Trail leads all the way around the perimeter on a dike (A portion of the trail is closed during winter hunting season; call for updates). The trail is wide and easy but difficult to stay on. You'll probably be lured off to the marshy inner refuge on one of many side trails—these paths lead through the marshes to photo blinds and other bird-viewing spots. On the loop's outer edge, a two-story viewing stand provides excellent views of the vast, unspoiled saltwater tidal flats and any number of seagoing birds. The southern leg of the square loop skirts the Nisqually River. While this is a pleasant walk all year long, many bird-watchers flock here in the winter and spring, when the migratory-bird highway nears gridlock. In the summer, much of the inner marsh area is obscured by blackberry vines (bearing oodles of fresh berries) and leaves. In the winter, views throughout the refuge are excellent. Bring binoculars, camera, big lens, water (there isn't any on the trail), and in the summer, a hat.

The Nisqually National Wildlife Refuge, visited by about 70,000 people a year, is open from dawn to dusk year-round. A new visitor center is open 9 A.M. to 4 P.M., Wednesday to Sunday. If time is short, consider the refuge's one-mile and half-mile nature-trail loops. The perimeter loop is fully accessible to wheelchairs but can be quite muddy. The trail leading to the Twin Barns is a boardwalk accessed by ramps, with a gradient of 6–20 percent. Wheelchair users might need assistance.

Location: In the Nisqually River Delta north of Olympia; see Seattle and the San Juans Map 2, grid h3.

User Groups: Hikers only. Much of the refuge trail system is a flat grade and accessible to wheelchairs. No dogs, horses, or mountain bikes are allowed.

Permits: No permits are required. A $3-per-family access fee is collected at a donation station at the main trail entrance. Parking is free.

Maps: For a free brochure and map, contact the Nisqually National Wildlife Refuge at 360/753-9467.

Ask the USGS for a topographic map of the Nisqually area.

Directions: From Seattle or Portland drive on I-5 to Exit 114/Nisqually, 56 miles south of Seattle. Turn west under the freeway and drive one-quarter mile north on Brown Farm Road to the wildlife-refuge parking lot, where the main trailhead is in view.

Contact: Nisqually National Wildlife Refuge, 100 Brown Farm Road, Olympia, WA 98516; 360/753-9467.

24 Point Defiance Park Loop
7.5 mi/4.0 hrs

Often called the nation's best by proud Tacomans, this city park has it all: a zoo, aquarium, miles of saltwater beach, magnificent high-bluff views in all directions, floral gardens, historic fort, children's attractions, and hundreds of picnic land acres. Take your pick. In the midst of it all, you find a fine network of trails that extends nearly 50 miles, if you walk it all. You won't and probably couldn't if you wanted to. They're not all signed, and you'd be bound to miss one here and there. Still, it's easy to navigate in Defiance and always rewarding. A segmented loop that runs along the bluff top—making a circle of nearly eight miles through open fields, magnificent old-growth forest and massive madronas—is a good introductory tour. The loop includes a stop at historic Fort Nisqually, an 1833 Hudson's Bay settlement that marked the first major European incursion into Puget Sound. A stop at the park's zoo and aquarium is well worth your time. Other trails lead to the saltwater beach below the bluffs, which (at low to medium tides) can be hiked in its entirety. For a leisurely Sunday afternoon, Point Defiance is tough to beat, especially for parents with children.

Location: On Commencement Bay near the Tacoma Narrows Bridge; see Seattle and the San Juans Map 2, grid f4.

User Groups: Hikers, leashed dogs, and mountain bikes (consult rangers for open trails). Some wheelchair facilities are available. Horses are not allowed.

Permits: No permits are required. Parking and access are free.

Maps: For a free Tacoma City Parks brochure, contact the Metropolitan Parks District of Tacoma at 253/305-1000. Ask the USGS for a topographic map of the Gig Harbor area.

Directions: From Seattle drive 34 miles south on I-5 to Exit 132/Bremerton/Gig Harbor. Turn right onto Highway 16 and drive west to Pearl Street. Exit to the right and follow signs to the park.

Contact: Metropolitan Parks District of Tacoma, 4702 South 19th Street, Tacoma, WA 98405; 253/305-1000.

25 Green River at Flaming Geyser State Park
0.5–10.0 mi/0.5–5.0 hrs

First, let's dispense with the flaming geyser. It's hardly a Yellowstone thing, although it used to be. The park's geyser is a flame that burns the remnants of a methane-gas pocket, which is located some 1,000 feet below the surface. The gas was discovered by early-1900s coal miners, who drilled a test hole here and struck gas and salt water all at once. Next thing they knew, they had giant gushes of water and flames 25 feet high blasting from their test hole, which made for excellent dinner conversation, if not coal profits. Over the years, the flame dwindled and is now something you can approximate at home on your portable gas-powered Weber. Anyway, you're not really here for this lackluster spectacle.

The park built around Flaming Geyser and its mud-sputtering cousin, Bubbling Geyser, is a prime wildlife habitat and hiker hangout on the Green River banks. About 10 miles' worth of paths skirt the park, and most of its 34,000 feet of river shoreline is walkable. If you only have time to take one hike, try the longest trail; it leads from near the park entrance up a hillside to Bubbling Geyser. Several other trails skirt both banks of the Green River, where sharp eyes can detect trout, salmon, steelhead, deer, bears, and more species of birds than you'll ever be able to identify. It's a grand place to bring a lunch and spend an entire afternoon meandering, just like the river.

When this book went to press, Washington State Parks were considering implementing a day-use parking fee; call the contact number for current information.

Location: On the Green River south of Black Diamond; see Seattle and the San Juans Map 2, grid g8.

User Groups: Hikers and leashed dogs. No horses or mountain bikes are allowed. No wheelchair facilities.

Permits: No permits are required. Parking and access are free.

Maps: For a Washington State Parks brochure, contact Washington State Parks at 800/233-0321. Ask the USGS for a topographic map of the Black Diamond area.

Directions: From Highway 169 between Black Diamond and Enumclaw, turn west onto Southeast Green Valley Road and proceed 2.7 miles to Flaming Geyser Road/228th Place Southeast. Turn south and cross the bridge over the Green River to the park entrance.

Contact: Washington State Parks and Recreation Commission, Public Affairs Office, P.O. Box 42650, Olympia, WA 98504-2650; 800/233-0321.

THE NORTHERN CASCADES

The Northern Cascades

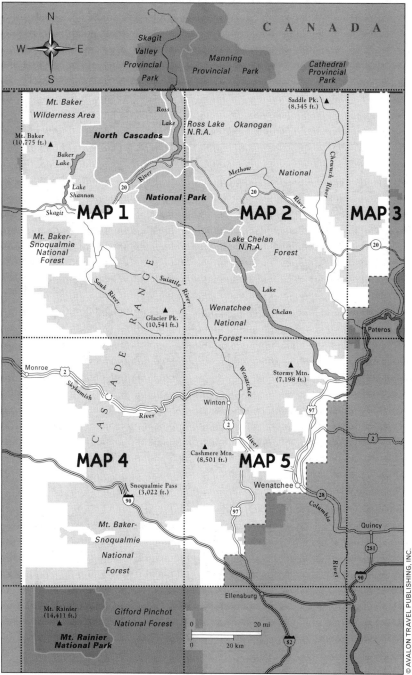

Map 1

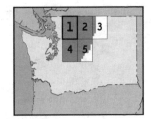

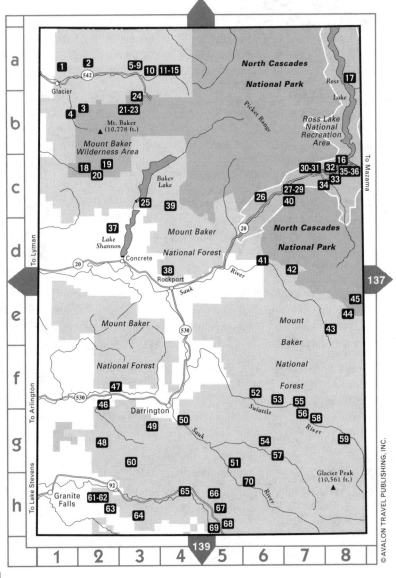

Map 2

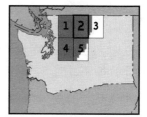

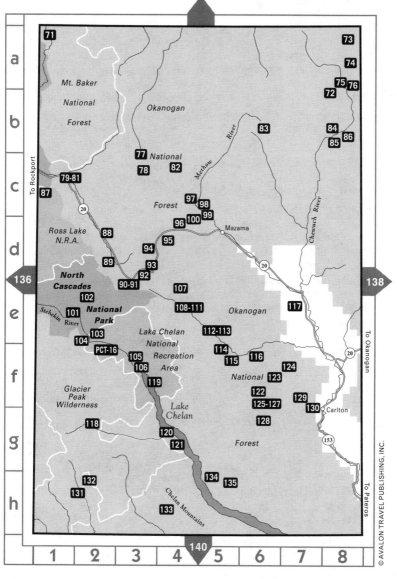

© AVALON TRAVEL PUBLISHING, INC.

Map 3

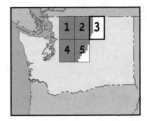

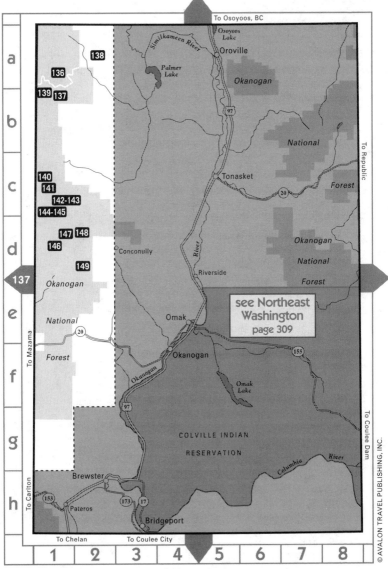

Map 4

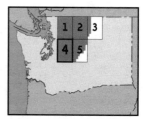

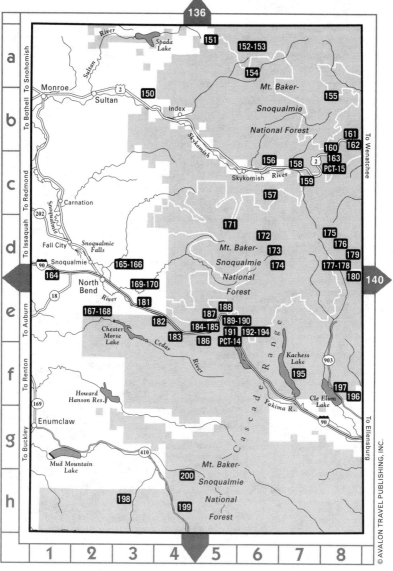

Map 5

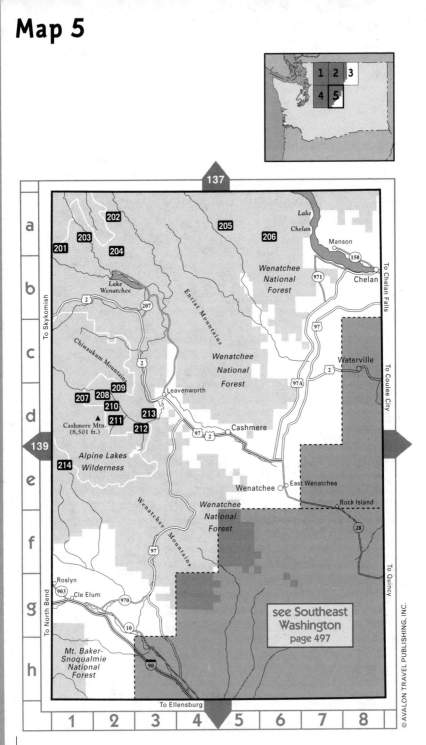

© AVALON TRAVEL PUBLISHING, INC.

The Northern Cascades

(CONTINUED ON NEXT PAGE)

(CONTINUED ON NEXT PAGE)

The Northern Cascades 143

■ Church Mountain
8.4 mi/6.0 hrs

Be prepared to sweat. Church Mountain, a high perch above the North Fork Nooksack River, gets those glands working in no time. It rises steeply (as in stop every five minutes and rest), first up an old logging road, then through luscious old-growth forest bisected by about twice as many steep switchbacks as you would have sworn you could hike in a single outing. About halfway up, the scenery switches to meadows sporting fine displays of lupine, heather, and other colorful flora.

The view from the 6,315-foot summit is one of those that you start to photograph, then stop, realizing that no single shutter frame could ever do justice to the scene. You see north into Canada, south to Mount Rainier, east to Mount Shuksan and Mount Baker, and straight down the entire Nooksack Valley. You might want to pack your pockets with rocks before striking out for the final 100 yards to the lookout station—it's breezier than a wind tunnel down at Boeing. The total elevation gain is about 3,700 feet.

Location: In the North Fork Nooksack River drainage, east of Bellingham near Mount Baker; see Northern Cascades Map 1, grid a1.

User Groups: Hikers and dogs. No horses or mountain bikes are allowed. No wheelchair facilities.

Permits: A federal Northwest Forest Pass, $5 per day or $30 annually, is required to park at the trailhead. Passes are available from ranger stations and many private vendors, online at website: www.wta.org, or by calling 800/270-7504.

Maps: For a map of Mount Baker-Snoqualmie National Forest, contact the Outdoor Recreation Information Center, Seattle REI, 222 Yale Avenue North, Seattle, WA 98109; 206/470-4060. Green Trails, Inc.'s excellent topographic map of the region is available for $3.99 at outdoor retail outlets; ask for map number 13, Mount Baker. Ask the USGS for a topographic map of the Bearpaw Mountain area.

Directions: From Seattle drive approximately 90 miles north on I-5 to Bellingham and take Exit 255/Mount Baker. Drive 31 miles east on Highway 542/Mount Baker Highway to the town of Glacier and continue another 5.2 miles to East Church Road/Forest Service Road 3040. Turn left (north) and drive 2.5 miles to the trailhead at the road's end.

Contact: Mount Baker-Snoqualmie National Forest, Glacier Public Service Center, 1094 Mount Baker Highway, Glacier, WA 98244; 360/599-2714.

■ Excelsior Pass
6.0 mi/4.0 hrs

Blueberries and blue skies. You take home ample memories of both after an early autumn hike to Excelsior Pass, a high alpine lookout due north of Mount Baker. After the long drive up the dirt road to the trailhead, the path is a relief. It winds just under a mile and about 500 feet in elevation through fir forest to Damfino Lakes (elevation 4,600 feet), which are quite small and not much for camping. But they do happen to be surrounded by one of the more productive wild blueberry patches in the region. Enjoy, but remember: blueberry stains and light-colored windshirts are not a match made in heaven.

Beyond, more meadows and switchbacks await. Before you know it, you're 700 feet higher at Excelsior Pass (5,300 feet), from which you can see just about forever. The view of Mount Baker is especially memorable. Go back the way you came or, if you can arrange a car shuttle, take Trail 670 straight down to Mount Baker Highway 4.2

miles away or continue five miles east along Excelsior Ridge to Welcome Pass and down to Forest Service Road 3060. Don't forget to lace up your boots again before setting off. Either way you go, you drop like a rock. The total elevation gain to the pass is about 1,150 feet. During our last visit, the trail was in poor shape near the top.

Location: In the North Fork Nooksack River drainage, east of Bellingham near Mount Baker; see Northern Cascades Map 1, grid a2.

User Groups: Hikers, dogs, and horses. No mountain bikes are allowed. No wheelchair facilities.

Permits: A federal Northwest Forest Pass, $5 per day or $30 annually, is required to park at the trailhead. Passes are available from ranger stations and many private vendors, online at website: www.wta.org, or by calling 800/270-7504.

Maps: For a map of Mount Baker-Snoqualmie National Forest, contact the Outdoor Recreation Information Center, Seattle REI, 222 Yale Avenue North, Seattle, WA 98109; 206/470-4060. Green Trails, Inc.'s excellent topographic map of the region is available for $3.99 at outdoor retail outlets; ask for map number 13, Mount Baker. Ask the USGS for a topographic map of the Bearpaw Mountain area.

Directions: From Seattle drive approximately 90 miles north on I-5 to Bellingham and take Exit 255/Mount Baker. Drive 31 miles east on Highway 542/Mount Baker Highway to the town of Glacier and then another two miles beyond the Glacier Public Service Center to Canyon Creek Road/Forest Service Road 31. Turn left (north) and drive 15.6 miles to the trailhead.

Contact: Mount Baker-Snoqualmie National Forest, Glacier Public Service Center, 1094 Mount Baker Highway, Glacier, WA 98244; 360/599-2714.

🔟 Heliotrope Ridge
6.5 mi/4.5 hrs

One of the most popular routes in the Mount Baker area, the Heliotrope Ridge Trail does double duty. Not only does it shuttle in the hordes of climbers who are heading for the summit, it also lures legions of day hikers who come for the unsurpassed views of the peak, the surrounding region, and especially the Coleman Glacier. The trail puts you literally in touch with the massive ice tongue, which you should not tread upon in late summer, when it is heavily crevassed.

The route up is very pleasant, cool even in summer as you climb through the forest to open meadows. In early summer, those meadows are laced with bustling streams. Some of them can be difficult to cross in warm weather, particularly later in the day. Be prepared for water up to your knees or higher; a hiking staff is helpful. Or wait until mid- to late autumn, when the snow is all water milling around in Bellingham Bay. In an average year, this trail isn't easily passable until early August. The total elevation gain is 1,900 feet.

The Heliotrope Ridge Trail doubles as a cross-country and telemark ski access point to Mount Baker in the winter and early spring.

Location: In the North Fork Nooksack River drainage, east of Bellingham near Mount Baker; see Northern Cascades Map 1, grid b2.

User Groups: Hikers and dogs. No horses or mountain bikes are allowed. No wheelchair facilities.

Permits: A federal Northwest Forest Pass, $5 per day or $30 annually, is required to park at the trailhead. Passes are available from ranger stations and many private vendors, online at website: www.wta.org, or by calling 800/270-7504.

Maps: For a map of Mount Baker-Snoqualmie National Forest, contact the Outdoor Recreation Information Center, Seattle REI, 222 Yale Avenue North, Seattle, WA 98109; 206/470-4060. Green Trails, Inc.'s excellent topographic map of the region is available for $3.99 at outdoor retail outlets; ask for map number 13, Mount Baker. Ask the USGS for a topographic map of the Mount Baker area.

Directions: From the Seattle area, drive approximately 90 miles north on I-5 to Bellingham and then take Exit 255/Mount Baker. Drive 31 miles east on Highway 542/Mount Baker Highway to the town of Glacier and another mile past that to Glacier Creek Road/Forest Service Road 39. Turn right (south) on Glacier Creek Road and drive eight miles to the expansive trailhead parking lot.

Contact: Mount Baker-Snoqualmie National Forest, Glacier Public Service Center, 1094 Mount Baker Highway, Glacier, WA 98244; 360/599-2714.

4 Skyline Divide
6.0 mi/4.0 hrs

Not many places in the United States offer an alpine meadow vista as spectacular as the one from Skyline Divide—especially one within a three-mile walk from the car. The trail climbs quite steadily through a forest of hemlock and fir (one brief flat spot lasts only about 10 strides); it is interrupted twice by small meadows that are wildflower-wealthy in summer. Just beyond mile two, the trail breaks out onto a ridge. All that stands between you and magnificent Mount Baker are miles of sprawling white, purple, and green. The wildflowers are as glorious as the mountain itself—any novice with a disposable camera can take his or her own July photo for a personal nature calendar.

The views are even better about a mile up the ridge, atop a knoll at 6,215 feet. Mount Baker is on display, close enough to watch steam drifting lazily from the summit crater. Most people stop here, but the adventurous can continue up the ridge to explore Chowder Basin. This hike is at its best in August. Before that, snow lingers on the ridge. But there's a price to be paid for all that unbridled wildflower viewing: flies can be horrendous in midsummer. You start out dabbing bug juice daintily behind your ears, but by the time you reach the knoll, you are slathering it on like suntan lotion. The total elevation gain is about 2,000 feet.

Be sure to carry plenty of water. Once the snow melts on the ridge, no water is available. Equestrians should note that the trail is open for stock use only from August 1 to November 1.

Location: In the North Fork Nooksack River drainage, east of Bellingham near Mount Baker; see Northern Cascades Map 1, grid b1.

User Groups: Hikers and dogs. Horses are permitted August 1 through November 1 only. No mountain bikes are allowed. No wheelchair facilities.

Permits: A federal Northwest Forest Pass, $5 per day or $30 annually, is required to park at the trailhead. Passes are available from ranger stations and many private vendors, online at website: www.wta.org, or by calling 800/270-7504.

Maps: For a map of Mount Baker-Snoqualmie National Forest, contact the Outdoor Recreation Information Center, Seattle REI, 222 Yale Avenue North, Seattle, WA 98109; 206/470-4060. Green Trails, Inc.'s excellent topographic map of the region is available for $3.99 at outdoor retail outlets; ask for map number 13, Mount Baker. Ask the USGS for a topographic map of the Mount Baker area.

Directions: From Seattle drive approximately 90 miles north on I-5 to Bellingham and take Exit 255/Mount Baker. Drive 31 miles east on Highway 542/Mount Baker Highway to the town of Glacier and another mile to Glacier Creek Road/Forest Service Road 39. Turn right (south) and take an immediate left on Dead-horse Road/Forest Service Road 37. Drive 13 occasionally steep, narrow miles to the trailhead, which has parking for about two dozen vehicles.

Contact: Mount Baker-Snoqualmie National Forest, Glacier Public Service Center, 1094 Mount Baker Highway, Glacier, WA 98244; 360/599-2714.

5 Yellow Aster Butte
7.0 mi/8.0 hrs

Yellow Aster Butte, named for the flowers that proliferate in this alpine valley in midsummer, is an especially endearing place in late fall, particularly October, when the local underbrush puts on a color show you won't soon forget. Come prepared, for nights are cold in the fall. Quite cold. (This is the perfect trail to test that new down sleeping bag.) For the equipped, a late autumn hike offers a rare slice of solitude in one of the Nooksack Valley's loveliest spots.

The old path, which went straight up the mountain at a miner's pace, has been replaced by a somewhat gentler trail grade in recent years. Unlike the old trail, also known as the Keep Kool Trail, the new one does not include wayside campsites. Whichever path you take, you eventually cross a series of tarns, one above the other, all the way to the top of Yellow Aster Butte, elevation 6,145 feet (the final 500 feet or so require a difficult scramble; use extreme caution). Above and to the north is 7,451-foot Tomyhoi Peak, while to the south the peaks of Mounts Baker, Shuksan, and Cascade extend as far as the eye can see. The total

elevation gain to the first tarn (a popular turnaround spot, 3.5 miles from the trailhead) is about 2,100 feet; it's 3,200 feet to the summit.

Location: In the North Fork Nooksack River drainage north of Mount Baker; see Northern Cascades Map 1, grid a3.

User Groups: Hikers and dogs. No horses or mountain bikes. No wheelchair facilities.

Permits: A federal Northwest Forest Pass, $5 per day or $30 annually, is required to park at the trailhead. Passes are available from ranger stations and many private vendors, online at website: www.wta.org, or by calling 800/270-7504.

Maps: For a map of Mount Baker-Snoqualmie National Forest, contact the Outdoor Recreation Information Center, Seattle REI, 222 Yale Avenue North, Seattle, WA 98109; 206/470-4060. Green Trails, Inc.'s excellent topographic map of the region is available for $3.99 at outdoor retail outlets; ask for map number 14, Mount Shuksan. Ask the USGS for a topographic map of the Mount Larrabee area.

Directions: From Seattle drive 90 miles north on I-5 to Bellingham and Exit 255/Mount Baker Highway. Drive 31 miles east on Mount Baker Highway to the town of Glacier and another 13.5 miles to the Department of Transportation sheds. Just beyond them, turn left on Forest Service Road 3065 (follow the signs to the Tomyhoi Trail/Twin Lakes). Follow the road approximately 2.2 miles, then veer left at the trail sign, and proceed about a quarter mile to the trailhead, marked Trail 699.

Contact: Mount Baker-Snoqualmie National Forest, Glacier Public Service Center, 1094 Mount Baker Highway, Glacier, WA 98244; 360/599-2714.

6 Tomyhoi Lake
10.0 mi/6.0–8.0 hrs

On the first two miles of this classic up-and-downer, you puff your way toward 5,400-foot

Gold Run Pass. Stop on the pass and enjoy the wildflowers (in early summer), or plod on for the final three miles to deep, clear, mile-long Tomyhoi Lake, where camping is excellent (although it's snow-laden until late summer). The only problem is if you're backpacking into Tomyhoi, you lose almost all the elevation that you gained on the way in and have to regain it on the way out. But your thighs will be the better for it. Tomyhoi Lake is only about two miles from the Canadian border. Watch for snowboarders sneaking in the back way to the Mount Baker Ski Area.

Location: In the North Fork Nooksack River drainage north of Mount Baker; see Northern Cascades Map 1, grid a3.

User Groups: Hikers and dogs. No horses or mountain bikes. No wheelchair facilities.

Permits: A federal Northwest Forest Pass, $5 per day or $30 annually, is required to park at the trailhead. Passes are available from ranger stations and many private vendors, online at website: www.wta.org, or by calling 800/270-7504.

Maps: For a map of Mount Baker-Snoqualmie National Forest, contact the Outdoor Recreation Information Center, Seattle REI, 222 Yale Avenue North, Seattle, WA 98109; 206/470-4060. Green Trails, Inc.'s excellent topographic map of the region is available for $3.99 at outdoor retail outlets; ask for map number 14, Mount Shuksan. Ask the USGS for a topographic map of the Mount Larrabee area.

Directions: From Seattle drive 90 miles north on I-5 to Bellingham and Exit 255/Mount Baker Highway. Drive 31 miles east on Mount Baker Highway to the town of Glacier and another 13.5 miles to the Department of Transportation sheds. Just beyond them turn left on Forest Service Road 3065 (follow the signs to the Tomyhoi Trail/Twin Lakes). Follow the road 4.5 miles to the trailhead on the left.

Contact: Mount Baker-Snoqualmie National Forest, Glacier Public Service Center, 1094 Mount Baker Highway, Glacier, WA 98244; 360/599-2714.

7 Winchester Mountain
4.0 mi/2.5 hrs

Very popular for summer day hikes, this trail is a good choice for people with children or dogs—not too far, not too steep, with a big payoff at the top. Views throughout this walk, in fact, are by far the grandest per ounce of sweat of any trail in this region. The trail climbs 1,300 feet, past some snowfields that typically linger well into August (be prepared to wield your ice ax or walk below them), through meadows to the summit lookout on Winchester Mountain. At the summit, you get amazing views in all directions, particularly south to Baker and Shuksan and north into British Columbia. For those who are more adventurous and seek solitude, it's possible to find a cross-country route from here to High Pass (see hike below).

This trail lies smack in the middle of sporadic but persistent mining activity. Watch for trucks and other annoyances on the roads.

Location: Northeast of Mount Baker near the Canadian border; see Northern Cascades Map 1, grid a3.

User Groups: Hikers and dogs. No horses or mountain bikes are allowed. No wheelchair facilities.

Permits: A federal Northwest Forest Pass, $5 per day or $30 annually, is required to park at the trailhead. Passes are available from ranger stations and many private vendors, online at website: www.wta.org, or by calling 800/270-7504.

Maps: For a map of Mount Baker-Snoqualmie National Forest, contact the Outdoor

Recreation Information Center, Seattle REI, 222 Yale Avenue North, Seattle, WA 98109; 206/470-4060. Green Trails, Inc.'s excellent topographic map of the region is available for $3.99 at outdoor retail outlets; ask for map number 14, Mount Shuksan. Ask the USGS for a topographic map of the Mount Larrabee area.

Directions: From Seattle drive 90 miles north on I-5 to Bellingham and Exit 255/Mount Baker Highway. Drive 31 miles east on Mount Baker Highway to the town of Glacier and another 13.5 miles to the Department of Transportation sheds. Just beyond them, turn left on Forest Service Road 3065 (follow the signs to the Tomyhoi Trail/Twin Lakes). Follow the road seven miles to the trailhead at Twin Lakes. Note: Four-wheel drive might be necessary to negotiate the last two miles of this steep, narrow, rutted road. Many hikers park at the Tomyhoi Lake Trailhead (see hike in this chapter) and walk the final two miles.

Contact: Mount Baker-Snoqualmie National Forest, Glacier Public Service Center, 1094 Mount Baker Highway, Glacier, WA 98244; 360/599-2714.

8 High Pass
6.0 mi/4.0 hrs

The first half mile of this relatively flat, pleasant walk is on the Winchester Mountain Trail (see hike above). Where that trail meets the High Pass Trail, take the right fork and ascend 500 feet over four miles, first to Low Pass, then to High Pass (elevation 5,900 feet). Views are outstanding here, but the real adventure awaits off trail. From High Pass numerous side trails lead upward and onward toward Mount Larrabee. An old miners' trail runs to Gargett Mine, where plenty of mining equipment lies as a rusting memorial to the mixed use (recreational and industrial) of national forestland. Higher and to the east, the fabulous Pleiades, a series of razor-sharp peaks forming a dinosaur-spine barrier between the United States and Canada, pose for your photos. The total elevation gain is about 1,450 feet.

Location: Northeast of Mount Baker near the Canadian border; see Northern Cascades Map 1, grid a3.

User Groups: Hikers and dogs. No horses or mountain bikes are allowed. No wheelchair facilities.

Permits: A federal Northwest Forest Pass, $5 per day or $30 annually, is required to park at the trailhead. Passes are available from ranger stations and many private vendors, online at website: www.wta.org, or by calling 800/270-7504.

Maps: For a map of Mount Baker-Snoqualmie National Forest, contact the Outdoor Recreation Information Center, Seattle REI, 222 Yale Avenue North, Seattle, WA 98109; 206/470-4060. Green Trails, Inc.'s excellent topographic map of the region is available for $3.99 at outdoor retail outlets; ask for map number 14, Mount Shuksan. Ask the USGS for a topographic map of the Mount Larrabee area.

Directions: From Seattle drive 90 miles north on I-5 to Bellingham and Exit 255/Mount Baker Highway. Drive 31 miles east on Mount Baker Highway to the town of Glacier and another 13.5 miles to the Department of Transportation sheds. Just beyond them, turn left on Forest Service Road 3065 (follow the signs to the Tomyhoi Trail/Twin Lakes). Follow the road seven miles to the trailhead at Twin Lakes. Note: Four-wheel drive might be necessary to negotiate the last two miles of this steep, narrow, rutted road. Many hikers park at the Tomyhoi Lake Trailhead (see hike in this chapter) and walk the final two miles.

Contact: Mount Baker-Snoqualmie National Forest, Glacier Public Service Center, 1094

Mount Baker Highway, Glacier, WA 98244; 360/599-2714.

9 Silesia Creek
12.0 mi/6.0 hrs

As Reagan-era college students in the early 1980s, many of us underwent political awakening just as registration for the military draft was reinstated. Some of us were busy making alternate plans in the event of an actual draft. For some people we knew, those fantasy-world plans actually involved the Silesia Creek Trail. On a map, it seemed like the perfect draft-dodger's alley: a 90-minute drive up Mount Baker Highway, a six-mile stroll (downhill, yet!) along Silesia Creek to the end of the trail, and just two more miles to the Canadian border. Needless to say, the draft never came—and we never did make it all the way down the Silesia Creek Trail. The trail, at least the U.S. portion, is a pleasant walk through lowland forest, a place where you might actually find some summertime solitude along the stream. You pass between the Skagit Range and the Mount Larrabee/ American Border Peak massif, losing some 2,800 feet in the process. It's as close to British Columbia as you can get without being asked if you're transporting any fruit. Note: This trail has been extremely brushy in recent years. Be prepared to do some bushwhacking if trail crews haven't passed through before your visit.

Location: Northeast of Mount Baker near the Canadian border; see map Northern Cascades Map 1, grid a3.

User Groups: Hikers, dogs, and horses (horses are permitted after August 1 until the trail closes to snow). No mountain bikes are allowed. No wheelchair facilities.

Permits: A federal Northwest Forest Pass, $5 per day or $30 annually, is required to park at the trailhead. Passes are available from ranger stations and many private vendors, online at website: www.wta.org, or by calling 800/270-7504.

Maps: For a map of Mount Baker-Snoqualmie National Forest, contact the Outdoor Recreation Information Center, Seattle REI, 222 Yale Avenue North, Seattle, WA 98109; 206/470-4060. Green Trails, Inc.'s excellent topographic map of the region is available for $3.99 at outdoor retail outlets; ask for map number 14, Mount Shuksan. Ask the USGS for a topographic map of the Mount Sefrit area.

Directions: From Seattle drive 90 miles north on I-5 to Bellingham and Exit 255/Mount Baker Highway. Drive 31 miles east on Mount Baker Highway to the town of Glacier and another 13.5 miles to the Department of Transportation sheds. Just beyond them, turn left on Forest Service Road 3065 (follow the signs to the Tomyhoi Trail/Twin Lakes). Follow the road seven miles to the trailhead at Twin Lakes. The Silesia Creek Trailhead is a half mile beyond the gate on Forest Service Road 3065. Note: Four-wheel drive might be necessary to negotiate the last 2.5 miles of this steep, narrow, rutted road. Many hikers park at the Tomyhoi Lake Trailhead (see hike in this chapter) and walk the final 2.5 miles.

Contact: Mount Baker-Snoqualmie National Forest, Glacier Public Service Center, 1094 Mount Baker Highway, Glacier, WA 98244; 360/599-2714.

10 Goat Mountain
8.0 mi/6.0 hrs

Goat Mountain has two peaks, one 6,721 feet high, the other 6,891 feet. Both are noble goals, but which one to aim for? The Goat Mountain Trail is a great compromise, heading right between the twin icy peaks, beyond a former lookout site to a knoll with a to-die-for view of the Upper Nooksack Valley and more craggy, ice-covered peaks than you can count. The steep trail begins by climbing straight up (with a few switchbacks) to open meadows of heather and then up and around to a knoll where a lookout cabin once was located. This is as good a lunch spot as you're likely to find in your lifetime, so bring a meal and enjoy it here. Stare straight across the valley into the ice-bearded north face of Mount Shuksan, one of Washington's most inspiring peaks. From here, the trail continues another two miles or so up the mountain, between the twin summits. Plenty of good routes await off-trail scramblers who enjoy climbing (and camping) above the timberline. The total elevation gain to the pass is about 1,500 feet; it's more than double that if you're headed all the way to the summit (an eight-mile round-trip.)

Location: Northeast of Mount Baker in the North Fork Nooksack River drainage; see Northern Cascades Map 1, grid a3.

User Groups: Hikers, dogs, and horses. No mountain bikes are allowed. No wheelchair facilities.

Permits: A federal Northwest Forest Pass, $5 per day or $30 annually, is required to park at the trailhead. Passes are available from ranger stations and many private vendors, online at website: www.wta.org, or by calling 800/270-7504.

Maps: For a map of Mount Baker-Snoqualmie National Forest, contact the Outdoor Recreation Information Center, Seattle REI, 222 Yale Avenue North, Seattle, WA 98109; 206/470-4060. Green Trails, Inc.'s excellent topographic map of the region is available for $3.99 at outdoor retail outlets; ask for map number 14, Mount Shuksan. Ask the USGS for a topographic map of the Mount Larrabee area.

Directions: From Seattle drive 90 miles north on I-5 to Bellingham and Exit 255/Mount Baker Highway. Drive 31 miles east on Mount Baker Highway to the town of Glacier and another 13 miles to Forest Service Road 32. Turn left (north), stay left at the fork in 1.3 miles, and drive a total of 2.5 miles to the trailhead on the left.

Contact: Mount Baker-Snoqualmie National Forest, Glacier Public Service Center, 1094 Mount Baker Highway, Glacier, WA 98244; 360/599-2714.

11 Hannegan Pass
10.0 mi/8.0 hrs

For many a backpacker, this is the preferred entrance to North Cascades National Park and all its wonders. The trail follows Ruth Creek beneath the shadow of icy Mount Sefrit, Nooksack Ridge, and ultimately Ruth Mountain, which guards the northwestern boundary of the national park. Along the way, you gaze up at myriad avalanche chutes and wonder what it must be like to be here in the winter, when snowfalls as deep as you'll find in the Lower 48 create massive avalanches down both sides of this valley.

Good campsites are found at 3.7 miles and again at Boundary Camp, the turnaround point at five miles (about one mile, plus 650 vertical feet, beyond and below the pass). Both spots have designated campsites; please use them. No camping is available at Hannegan Pass (elevation 5,100 feet, four miles) itself, but a good side trail leads north through meadows along Hannegan Ridge to the unforgettable Hannegan Peak summit (elevation 6,138 feet).

This is a special trail that predictably attracts many backpackers in the summer. Be polite and smile; there are more than enough views to go around. The trail officially ends at

Boundary Camp (five miles), where it joins with the Copper Mountain and Chilliwack Ridge Trails in North Cascades National Park. The total elevation gain is 1,975 feet.

Location: Northeast of Mount Baker in the North Fork Nooksack River drainage; see Northern Cascades Map 1, grid a4.

User Groups: Hikers and horses (horses are permitted after August 15 until the trail closes to snow). No dogs or mountain bikes are allowed. No wheelchair facilities.

Permits: A federal Northwest Forest Pass, $5 per day or $30 annually, is required to park at the trailhead. Passes are available from ranger stations and many private vendors, online at website: www.wta.org, or by calling 800/270-7504. Hikers planning overnight stays beyond Boundary Camp in North Cascades National Park need campsite reservations and a free permit, which is available at the Glacier Public Service Center at 360/599-2714.

Maps: For a map of Mount Baker-Snoqualmie National Forest, contact the Outdoor Recreation Information Center, Seattle REI, 222 Yale Avenue North, Seattle, WA 98109; 206/470-4060. Green Trails, Inc.'s excellent topographic map of the region is available for $3.99 at outdoor retail outlets; ask for map number 14, Mount Shuksan. Ask the USGS for a topographic map of the Mount Sefrit area.

Directions: From Seattle drive 90 miles north on I-5 to Bellingham and Exit 255/Mount Baker Highway. Drive 31 miles east on Mount Baker Highway to the town of Glacier and another 13 miles to Forest Service Road 32. Turn left and drive 1.3 miles, keeping to the left on Forest Service Road 32 at the fork. Continue another four miles to Hannegan Campground and the trailhead, both at the road's end.

Contact: Mount Baker-Snoqualmie National Forest, Glacier Public Service Center, 1094 Mount Baker Highway, Glacier, WA 98244; 360/599-2714.

🔟2 Nooksack Cirque
9.0 mi/7.0 hrs

This is an unusual, spectacular hike. Normally, hiking to a remote alpine cirque surrounded by stone walls everywhere except the way you came requires a long struggle up a creek drainage. Make that a long, steep struggle. Nooksack Cirque, however, is a glacier-carved masterpiece awaiting you at the end of a mostly flat, albeit wild, hike up the North Fork Nooksack to the very foot of Mount Shuksan. Keep in mind that this is no Sunday afternoon stroll. The route is on a riverbed most of the way and is passable only when the river is low enough (in late summer or fall) to negotiate the gravel-bar path. Consult the ranger at the Glacier Public Service Center for advice on the route, which varies with the season. And make wise footwear choices: You'll be in and out of the water no matter how careful you are. Bring extra socks or abandon the pretense of dry feet altogether and wear rubber-soled sandals. Those who persevere are richly rewarded. Nooksack Cirque is truly amazing, with jutting waterfalls, hanging glaciers, and the near-vertical, 5,000-foot walls of Mount Shuksan. The negotiable segment of the trail ends at about 4.5 miles, where you can gaze into the cirque from the riverbed. Venturing farther upstream into the brush is for the truly insane or someone who really wants to be alone.

Location: Northeast of Mount Baker in the North Fork Nooksack River drainage; see Northern Cascades Map 1, grid a4.

User Groups: Hikers and dogs. No horses or mountain bikes are allowed. No wheelchair facilities.

Permits: Parking and access are free. Free overnight permits, required for anyone camping within North Cascades National Park boundaries, are available at the Glacier Public Service Center at 360/599-2714.

Maps: For a map of Mount Baker-Snoqualmie National Forest, contact the Outdoor Recreation Information Center, Seattle REI, 222 Yale Avenue North, Seattle, WA 98109; 206/470-4060. Green Trails, Inc.'s excellent topographic map of the region is available for $3.99 at outdoor retail outlets; ask for map number 14, Mount Shuksan. Ask the USGS for topographic maps of the Mount Larrabee, Shuksan Arm, and Mount Shuksan areas.

Directions: From Seattle drive 90 miles north on I-5 to Bellingham and Exit 255/Mount Baker Highway. Drive 31 miles east on Mount Baker Highway to the town of Glacier and another 13 miles to Forest Service Road 32. Turn left and drive 1.3 miles, veering right onto Forest Service Road 34. Proceed one mile to the trailhead at the road's end, at a Ruth Creek washout.

Contact: Mount Baker-Snoqualmie National Forest, Glacier Public Service Center, 1094 Mount Baker Highway, Glacier, WA 98244; 360/599-2714.

🔢 Copper Mountain via Hannegan Pass

18.9 mi one way/
2.0–3.0 days

There's no easy way onto Copper Ridge, so it stands to reason that the place should be special—and that reasoning is correct. The Copper Mountain Trail, an extension of the Hannegan Pass Trail (see hike in this chapter), takes you through some of the most spectacular scenery in the North Cascades. Once the ridgeline is gained by huffing and puffing 900 feet from Boundary Camp, the grade eases out, and the views are sublime.

Most of this trail is so high that it's passable only in the late summer and fall. You pass the Copper Mountain lookout, two ridgetop lakes and unsurpassed views off the north and south sides of the ridge. Those who continue straight down to the Chilliwack River Trail (see hike below), where this trail ends, better tighten their laces: the path plummets nearly 2,500 feet in five miles. Still, it's an excellent, 14-mile middle leg in a triangular loop combining the Hannegan, Copper Ridge, and Chilliwack River Trails (roughly 35 miles from car and back; allow five or six days).

Location: In the northwest corner of North Cascades National Park; see Northern Cascades Map 1, grid a4.

User Groups: Hikers only. No dogs, horses, or mountain bikes are allowed. No wheelchair facilities.

Permits: A federal Northwest Forest Pass, $5 per day or $30 annually, is required to park at the trailhead. Passes are available from ranger stations and many private vendors, online at website: www.wta.org, or by calling 800/270-7504. Backcountry campsite reservations (required) and free overnight permits are available at the Glacier Public Service Center at 360/599-2714.

Maps: For a map of North Cascades National Park, contact the Outdoor Recreation Information Center, Seattle REI, 222 Yale Avenue North, Seattle, WA 98109; 206/470-4060. Green Trails, Inc.'s excellent topographic map of the area is available at most outdoor retail outlets; ask for map number 15, Mount Challenger. Ask the USGS for topographic maps of the Mount Sefrit and Copper Mountain areas.

Directions: From Seattle drive 90 miles north on I-5 to Bellingham and Exit 255/Mount Baker Highway. Drive 31 miles east on Mount Baker Highway to the town of Glacier and another 13 miles to Forest Service Road 32. Turn left and drive 1.3 miles, keeping to the left on Forest Service Road 32 at the fork. Continue another four miles to Hannegan Campground and the trailhead, both at the road's end. Hike five miles on the Hannegan Pass Trail to Boundary Camp, where the Copper Ridge Trail forks to the left (north).

Contact: Mount Baker-Snoqualmie National Forest, Glacier Public Service Center, 1094 Mount Baker Highway, Glacier, WA 98244; 360/599-2714.

14 Chilliwack River
42.0 mi/6.0 days

Technically, the Chilliwack River Trail (also known as the Hannegan-Whatcom Trail) doesn't start until about seven miles beyond Boundary Camp (see hike Hannegan Pass, this chapter). But for all practical purposes, it begins when you hit the head of the Chilliwack Valley, right at the camp. Boundary Camp is a good first-night stop for the coming trip to Canada. First thing in the morning, head south, bound for Whatcom Pass. About 5.5 miles down the trail, one mile below U.S. Cabin Camps, you need to cross the Chilliwack River. In early summer, it might be necessary to use the handy cable car, instructions for which are found on the trail. Hang on tight and don't drop your glasses.

Safely across, proceed to the intersection with the Brush Creek Trail (see hike below), seven miles from Boundary Camp. This is one of the North Cascades' major intersections. Go right (south) on the Brush Creek Trail to Little Beaver Creek at Whatcom Pass for uninterrupted trail all the way to Ross Lake. But go left, staying on the Chilliwack River Trail, and you're headed due north along the Chilliwack to Canada. (Good camping can be found at Bear Creek Camp, 5.3 miles beyond the junction, and at Little Chilliwack Camp, 7.7 miles beyond the junction.) Either way, the Canadian border is the turnaround point (although many people head back from Brush Creek). This is a good early season hike (from June to July), when North Cascades high points remain buried in snow. Beware of high brush, nettles, and windfalls, all of which tend to proliferate on this wild trail.

Location: In the northwest corner of North Cascades National Park; see Northern Cascades Map 1, grid a4.

User Groups: Hikers and horses. No dogs or mountain bikes are allowed. No wheelchair facilities.

Permits: A federal Northwest Forest Pass, $5 per day or $30 annually, is required to park at the trailhead. Passes are available from ranger stations and many private vendors, online at website: www.wta.org, or by calling 800/270-7504. Mandatory overnight permits (free) and backcountry campsite reservations are available at the Glacier Public Service Center at 360/599-2714.

Maps: For a map of North Cascades National Park, contact the Outdoor Recreation Information Center, Seattle REI, 222 Yale Avenue North, Seattle, WA 98109; 206/470-4060. Green Trails, Inc.'s excellent topographic map of the region is available for $3.99 from outdoor retail outlets; ask for map number 15, Mount Challenger. Ask the USGS for topographic maps of the Mount Sefrit and Copper Mountain areas.

Directions: From Seattle drive 90 miles north on I-5 to Bellingham and Exit 255/Mount Baker Highway. Drive 31 miles east on Mount Baker Highway to the town of Glacier and another 13 miles to Forest Service Road 32. Turn left and drive 1.3 miles, keeping to the left on Forest Service Road 32 at the fork. Continue another four miles to Hannegan Campground and the trailhead, both at the road's end. Hike five miles to Boundary Camp, where the Chilliwack

River/Hannegan-Whatcom Trail forks to the right (south).

Contact: Mount Baker-Snoqualmie National Forest, Glacier Public Service Center, 1094 Mount Baker Highway, Glacier, WA 98244; 360/599-2714.

🔢 Brush Creek to Whatcom Pass

34.0 mi/4.0–5.0 days 👢 🥾

Backpackers, it doesn't get much better than this. The Whatcom Pass hike up the Brush Creek Trail (and, if you're up to it, all the way east on the Little Beaver Trail to Ross Lake) is a classic Northwest alpine traverse through some of the region's best scenery. From the Chilliwack River Trail (see hike in this chapter for cable car information), you climb about 2,500 feet in five miles, moving steadily upward through magnificent glacial valleys.

Good campsites are found along the way at Graybeat Camps (2.2 miles from the trail junction) and Tapto Camp (3.5 miles). Since there's no camping at the magnificent vista on Whatcom Pass, plan on spending a night at one of these camps and then striking out the next day to the pass and one of many side trails to the north, where you can explore and camp near Tapto Lakes, Middle Lakes, and other destinations on the south slopes of Red Face Mountain (elevation 7,174 feet). Whatcom Pass (elevation 5,206 feet) is the high point, and roughly the midpoint, on a 39-mile (one-way) cross-the-park hike from Hannegan Campground to Ross Lake. (See hike Big/Little Beaver Loop, this chapter, for the eastern leg of the loop.) If you turn around at Whatcom Pass, your total round-trip to and from Hannegan Campground will be 34 miles.

Location: In North Cascades National Park, north of Whatcom Peak and Mount Challenger; see Northern Cascades Map 1, grid a4.

User Groups: Hikers and horses. No dogs and mountain bikes are allowed. No wheelchair facilities. Note: Horse riders should check with rangers for trail conditions and closures.

Permits: A federal Northwest Forest Pass, $5 per day or $30 annually, is required to park at the trailhead. Passes are available from ranger stations and many private vendors, online at website: www.wta.org, or by calling 800/270-7504. Free overnight permits and backcountry campsite reservations (both mandatory) are available at the Glacier Public Service Center at 360/599-2714 and at all North Cascades National Park information centers.

Maps: For a map of North Cascades National Park, contact the Outdoor Recreation Information Center, Seattle REI, 222 Yale Avenue North, Seattle, WA 98109; 206/470-4060. Green Trails, Inc.'s excellent topographic maps of the region are available for $3.99 each from outdoor retail outlets; ask for map numbers 14 and 15, Mount Shuksan and Mount Challenger. Ask the USGS for topographic maps of the Mount Sefrit, Copper Mountain, Mount Redoubt, Mount Challenger, and Mount Blum areas.

Directions: From Seattle drive 90 miles north on I-5 to Bellingham and Exit 255/Mount Baker Highway. Drive 31 miles east on Mount Baker Highway to the town of Glacier and another 13 miles to Forest Service Road 32. Turn left and drive 1.3 miles, keeping to the left on Forest Service Road 32 at the fork. Continue another four miles to Hannegan Campground and the trailhead, both at the road's end. Hike five miles on the Hannegan Pass Trail to Boundary Camp. Head right on the Chilliwack River/Hannegan-Whatcom Trail for seven miles to the junction with the Brush Creek Trail. Follow the Brush Creek

Trail to the right (southeast) toward Whatcom Pass.

Contact: Mount Baker-Snoqualmie National Forest, Glacier Public Service Center, 1094 Mount Baker Highway, Glacier, WA 98244; 360/599-2714.

⏹ Big/Little Beaver Loop to Ross Lake

28.2 mi/4.0–5.0 days   🥾 🎒

The Big/Little Beaver Loop puts a chill in your spine and blisters on your feet. The trail, a 28.2-mile triangular loop, mixes plenty of up-and-down, rugged hiking with a water-taxi ride up one of America's most remote and beautiful lakes. The experience is unique, to say the least. From the south end of Ross Lake, a water taxi jets you 10 miles north up the Seattle City Light Reservoir, which flooded the upper Skagit Valley, to Little Beaver Camp. The trail climbs swiftly to Perry Creek Camp (4.4 miles) and ultimately to a junction with the Big Beaver Trail (11.4 miles). From here, it's 6.1 miles straight ahead to Whatcom Pass, an excellent destination for a 35-mile round-trip, or a 40.4-mile round-trip returning to Ross Lake via the Big Beaver Trail.

If you're just doing the Beaver Loop, turn left (south) at the Big/Little Beaver Trail junction and begin hiking the 16.8 miles back to the lake. You are puffing a bit over the first mile, which climbs to Beaver Pass (elevation 3,600 feet). The scenery all the way down is impressive, with massive, ancient trees (notice the incredible cedars, some 18 feet thick and 1,000 years old), deep creek gorges, views of the glaciated Luna Cirque and the Pickett Range, and much more than can be described here. The trail ends at Big Beaver Landing, where you can hike out to Ross Dam on the lakeside trail (about six miles) or be picked up by the water taxi, with prior arrangements.

In recent years upper portions of both Beaver Valley trails have been poorly maintained and can become quite brushy and difficult to follow. Also, bruins are commonly sighted here, so practice good bear-camping techniques.

Location: Between Ross Lake and Whatcom Pass in North Cascades National Park; see Northern Cascades Map 1, grid c8.

User Groups: Hikers and horses. No dogs or mountain bikes are allowed. No wheelchair facilities.

Permits: Free overnight permits are required and available at the Marblemount Ranger Station, 360/873-4500, and all park information centers. Parking at the Ross Dam Trailhead requires a federal Northwest Forest Pass, $5 per day or $30 annually. Passes are available from ranger stations and many private vendors, online at website: www.wta.org, or by calling 800/270-7504.

Maps: For a map of North Cascades National Park, contact the Outdoor Recreation Information Center, Seattle REI, 222 Yale Avenue North, Seattle, WA 98109; 206/470-4060. Green Trails, Inc.'s excellent topographic maps of the region are available for $3.99 each at outdoor retail outlets; ask for map numbers 15 and 16, Mount Challenger and Ross Lake. Ask the USGS for topographic maps of the Pumpkin Mountain and Mount Prophet areas.

Directions: From I-5 north of Mount Vernon, take Exit 230/Anacortes/Burlington. Follow Highway 20/North Cascades Highway east for 68 miles to the Diablo Ferry landing. Take the Diablo Ferry to Ross Dam for prearranged pickup by the Ross Lake Resort water taxi (call 206/386-4437 for reservations and price information). Ask for a drop-off at the Little Beaver Camp Trailhead, approximately 10 miles north of Ross Lake Resort. For an alternate route, follow Highway 20 east to the Ross Dam

Trail near milepost 134. Hike 0.8 mile to the gravel service road, go left, and then right on the road down an incline to the top of Ross Dam. Cross the dam and hike six miles north to Big Beaver Creek; hike the loop described below, but in the opposite direction. Note: Highway 20 is closed in winter at milepost 134. Call North Cascades National Park at 360/856-5700 for current road conditions.

Contact: North Cascades National Park/ Mount Baker Ranger District Information Center, 2105 Highway 20, Sedro-Woolley, WA 98284; 360/856-5700; Marblemount Ranger Station, 728 Ranger Station Road, Marblemount, WA 98267; 360/873-4500; Ross Lake Resort, Rockport, WA 98283; 206/386-4437.

🔳 Desolation Peak
13.6 mi/8.0 hrs

In the early summer this is a popular hike for visitors taking a rental boat to Ross Lake Resort, and also for beatnik-generation weekenders (more on that later) entering via the East Bank Trail. Whichever crowd you belong to, make sure to bring plenty of water from July on. From its origins at Lightning Creek's mysterious flooded-gorge entry to Ross Lake, the trail follows the lake north for about two miles. At this point, it's only buttering you up. From here, it gets steep and opens up into luscious wildflower meadows, often covered with snow until mid- to late summer.

At six miles, you have some serious altitude, and the views begin to tantalize. Below you—straight below—is Ross Lake. Snow-covered peaks stretch as far as the eye can see. Seemingly close enough to touch are spectacular Hozomeen Mountain (elevation 8,066 feet) and, to the south, 9,066-foot-high Jack Mountain and the rugged Nohokomeen Glacier. It's rather like sitting atop a cloud, and the scene might seem reminiscent of

something described by the late beat writer Jack Kerouac. Well, it is. Kerouac spent part of 1956 here in the lookout tower above and behind this knoll, left barren by a forest fire. The many mood-altering storms and changing vistas he witnessed served as inspiration for Desolation Angels. The total elevation gain is 4,400 feet. Desolation Peak is usually snow-free by mid- to late June.

Location: Above and east of Ross Lake in Ross Lake National Recreation Area; see Northern Cascades Map 1, grid a8.

User Groups: Hikers, dogs, and horses. No mountain bikes are allowed. No wheelchair facilities.

Permits: Free overnight permits are required and available at the Marblemount Ranger Station, 360/873-4500, and all park information centers. Parking and access are free.

Maps: For a map of North Cascades National Park and Ross Lake National Recreation Area, contact the Outdoor Recreation Information Center, Seattle REI, 222 Yale Avenue North, Seattle, WA 98109; 206/470-4060. Green Trails, Inc.'s excellent topographic map of the region is available for $3.99 at outdoor retail outlets; ask for map number 16, Ross Lake. Ask the USGS for a topographic map of the Hozomeen Mountain area.

Directions: For a water-taxi drop-off or pickup at the trailhead or at Desolation Landing on Ross Lake (cutting 4.2 miles off the round-trip hike, which many hikers choose to do), see hike Big/Little River Loop, this chapter.

To hike the trail from its trailhead: From I-5 north of Mount Vernon, take Exit 230/Anacortes/Burlington. Follow Highway 20/North Cascades Highway east to Colonial Creek Campground and continue another nine miles to the large trailhead parking lot near the Panther Creek Bridge. Hike the Ruby Creek Trail 2.8 miles west to its junction with the East Bank Ross Lake Trail. Hike the East Bank Trail approximately 13 miles north to the Lightning Creek Trailhead at Lightning Creek. Note: Highway 20 is closed at milepost 134 in winter. Call North Cascades National Park at 360/856-5700 for current road conditions.

Contact: North Cascades National Park/ Mount Baker Ranger District Information Center, 2105 Highway 20, Sedro-Woolley, WA 98284; 360/856-5700; Marblemount Ranger Station, 728 Ranger Station Road, Marblemount, WA 98267; 360/873-4500; Ross Lake Resort, Rockport, WA 98283; 206/386-4437.

18 Elbow Lake
7.0 mi/4.0 hrs

Hildebrand, Elbow, and Doreen Lakes, all set in a valley northeast of the beautiful Twin Sisters Mountains, are easily accessible both from the north and south. On this northern route, it's about 2.75 gradually ascending miles to the half-dry Lake Hildebrand. Just beyond is Elbow Lake (3.5 miles), the largest of the lakes and the most productive for trout fishing. Above Elbow is Lake Doreen, which is small and deep and lures anglers. Note that bugs are typically horrendous up here in midsummer. Hikers continuing through to the south access off Forest Service Road 12 discover that the trail has been rerouted and lengthened by three miles. It now exits at Pioneer Camp; Forest Service Road 12 is closed beyond this point.

Location: In the Middle Fork Nooksack River drainage, south of Mount Baker; see Northern Cascades Map 1, grid c2.

User Groups: Hikers and dogs. Horses are permitted August 1 through November 1 only. No mountain bikes are allowed. No wheelchair facilities.

Permits: A federal Northwest Forest Pass, $5 per day or $30 annually, is required to park at the trailhead. Passes are available from

ranger stations and many private vendors, online at website: www.wta.org, or by calling 800/270-7504.

Maps: For a map of Mount Baker-Snoqualmie National Forest, contact the Outdoor Recreation Information Center, Seattle REI, 222 Yale Avenue North, Seattle, WA 98109; 206/470-4060. Green Trails, Inc.'s excellent topographic map of the region is available for $3.99 at outdoor retail outlets. Ask for map number 45, Hamilton. Ask the USGS for topographic maps of the Twin Sisters Mountains and Baker Pass areas.

Directions: From Seattle drive approximately 90 miles north on I-5 to Bellingham and take Exit 255/Mount Baker. Drive 16.8 miles east on Highway 542/Mount Baker Highway to the Highway 9 junction. Proceed about two miles east on Mount Baker Highway and turn right (south) on Mosquito Lake Road. At 4.6 miles, miles turn east on Porter Creek Road (Forest Service Road 38). The trailhead is on the right, at the Middle Fork Nooksack River, 11.5 miles from Mosquito Lake Road and about 1.5 miles past the national forest boundary. Note: The road is gated at the forest boundary from December through mid-June to protect elk herds.

Contact: Mount Baker-Snoqualmie National Forest, Glacier Public Service Center, 1094 Mount Baker Highway, Glacier, WA 98244; 360/599-2714.

19 Park Butte/Railroad Grade/Scott Paul Trail
7.0 mi/6.0 hrs

"Caution: Earth still under construction." Somebody should post that sign near Park Butte, a high alpine lookout where you can survey the magnificent glaciation—past and present—of Mount Baker's south side. The Park Butte Trail climbs a total of 2,250 feet through the open boulder fields, wildflower-laced meadows, heather fields, and glacial vistas for which the Mount Baker area is famous. But it offers a bonus—a bird's-eye view that's sure to make you wish you hadn't left that camera in the car.

In the first mile, the trail crosses Schreibers Meadow (a good place to take a nap) and then climbs through forest. At mile two, the newly constructed Scott Paul Trail, which crosses the Sulphur Moraine and drops back to the road, exits to the right (you can combine the Scott Paul Trail and the lower leg of the Park Butte Trail for a nice loop of about eight miles.) Soon after, you reach broad, impressive Morovitz Meadow. Here the trail splits. The right fork climbs beneath (not over, as the old Baker Pass Trail did) Cathedral Crag to Mazama Park, while the left fork climbs about one mile directly to Park Butte Lookout, elevation 5,450 feet, for spectacular views. From Morovitz Meadow a side trail leads north, climbing the Railroad Grade (an old moraine) of the Easton Glacier, to the tip of the glacier itself, at about a 7,000-foot elevation. Be careful as you descend from the moraine to the glacier valley. Loose rocks can make the going dangerous. Overnighters usually camp at Morovitz Meadows (1,400 feet from the trailhead), an excellent base camp for exploration of the Deming and Easton Glaciers, Pocket Lake, Survey Point, and other nearby off-trail destinations. Note: This is a common access route for Baker summit climbers using the Easton Glacier route.

Location: In the South Fork Nooksack River drainage, south of Mount Baker; see Northern Cascades Map 1, grid c2.

User Groups: Hikers and dogs. No horses or mountain bikes are allowed. No wheelchair facilities.

Permits: A federal Northwest Forest Pass, $5 per day or $30 annually, is required to park at the trailhead. Passes are available from ranger stations and many private vendors, online at website: www.wta.org, or by calling 800/270-7504.

Maps: For a map of Mount Baker-Snoqualmie National Forest, contact the Outdoor Recreation Information Center, Seattle REI, 222 Yale Avenue North, Seattle, WA 98109; 206/470-4060. Green Trails, Inc.'s excellent topographic map of the region is available for $3.99 at outdoor retail outlets. Ask for map number 45, Hamilton. Ask the USGS for a topographic map of the Baker Pass area.

Directions: From Mount Vernon, take I-5 north to Exit 230/Anacortes/Burlington. Turn east on Highway 20 and drive seven miles to Sedro-Woolley and proceed to Baker Lake-Grandy Road, near milepost 82. Turn left and drive 12.5 miles to South Fork Nooksack Road/Forest Service Road 12. Turn left and drive 3.5 miles to Sulphur Creek Road/Forest Service Road 13. Follow Forest Service Road 13 about six miles to the trailhead near Sulphur Creek.

Contact: Mount Baker-Snoqualmie National Forest, Mount Baker Ranger District, 2105 Highway 20, Sedro-Woolley, WA 98284; 360/856-5700.

20 Bell Pass/Cathedral Pass/Mazama Park
10.0 mi/6.0 hrs

Backpackers who want to slowly expose themselves to the wonders of the Mount Baker backcountry—but away from crowds of day hikers—might consider this trail, a back-door entry to the Park Butte/Mazama Park area (see hike in this chapter). The trail climbs quickly to Bell Pass (the divide between the gurgling Nooksack's Middle and South Forks, at elevation 3,960 feet), and then skirts beneath the neck-craning cliffs ascending Park Butte. At four miles, the trail empties into Mazama Park, where it connects with the Ridley Creek Trail. From here, the old Baker Pass Trail used to climb the final half mile around the back side of Cathedral Crag to Baker Pass. The new trail takes a more direct route beneath the crag. This is an excellent hike for late summer or early fall, but expect plenty of company at Mazama Park. And before the fall's first big freeze, hikers who forget the bug dope will never forgive themselves.

Location: In the South Fork Nooksack River drainage, south of Mount Baker; see Northern Cascades Map 1, grid c2.

User Groups: Hikers and dogs. Horses are permitted, but not recommended as of this time, due to narrow trail sections. Mountain bikes are not allowed. No wheelchair facilities.

Permits: No permits are required. Parking and access are free.

Maps: For a map of Mount Baker-Snoqualmie National Forest, contact the Outdoor Recreation Information Center, Seattle REI, 222 Yale Avenue North, Seattle, WA 98109; 206/470-4060. Green Trails, Inc.'s excellent topographic map of the region is available for $3.99 at outdoor retail outlets. Ask for map number 45, Hamilton. Ask the USGS for a topographic map of the Baker Pass area.

Directions: From Mount Vernon, take I-5 north to Exit 230/Anacortes/Burlington. Turn east on Highway 20 and drive seven miles to Sedro-Woolley and proceed to Baker Lake-Grandy Road, near milepost 82. Turn left and drive 12.5 miles to South Fork Nooksack Road/Forest Service Road 12. Turn left and drive another 3.5 miles, staying left on Forest Service Road 12 at the fork. It's about 15 miles to the trailhead, marked as Baker Pass Trail 603.

Contact: Mount Baker-Snoqualmie National Forest, Mount Baker Ranger District, 2105 Highway 20, Sedro-Woolley, WA 98284; 360/856-5700.

21 Chain Lakes Loop
6.5 mi one way/4.0 hrs

You've seen the photos of pure-white Mount Baker reflected in a quaint alpine lake, perhaps with a chunk of ice floating off to the side. This is where you go to take your own. The Chain Lakes Trail, an up-and-down loop around flat-topped Table Mountain, begins either at Artist Point or farther down Mount Baker Highway, at Austin Pass south of the Mount Baker Ski Area.

Thanks to a major improvement project by Mount Baker-Snoqualmie National Forest, the entire area (collectively referred to as Heather Meadows) has been improved, with ample parking, easy access, and good facilities. It's much more scenic than tourist-grabbing sites such as Paradise at Mount Rainier, but you won't find a fraction of the crowds here, especially if you set off on this loop hike midweek. From Artist Point, the trail drops beneath the high cliffs of Table Mountain to Mazama, Iceberg, Hayes, and Arbuthnot Lakes. It then rises sharply to Herman Saddle, which has a Kodak (Fuji?) moment of Mount Shuksan on one side and Mount Baker on the other. It then drops again to Bagley Lakes, where you can watch snowboarders fly down Table Mountain all summer long. From here, a side trail leads back up (steeply) to Artist Point, or you can continue ahead to the exit at the Heather Park parking area.

This area receives an average annual snowfall of nearly 700 inches, among the heaviest in the United States. It's not unusual to find a 20-foot snowpack in mid-winter. The road may not be open above the Mount Baker Ski Area until early to mid-August.

Location: On the northeast slopes of Mount Baker; see Northern Cascades Map 1, grid b3.

User Groups: Hikers and dogs. No horses or mountain bikes are allowed. No wheelchair facilities.

Permits: A federal Northwest Forest Pass, $5 per day or $30 annually, is required to park at the trailhead. Passes are available from ranger stations and many private vendors, online at website: www.wta.org, or by calling 800/270-7504.

Maps: For a map of Mount Baker-Snoqualmie National Forest, contact the Outdoor Recreation Information Center, Seattle REI, 222 Yale Avenue North, Seattle, WA 98109; 206/470-4060. Green Trails, Inc.'s excellent topographic map of the region is available for $3.99 at outdoor retail outlets; ask for map number 14, Mount Shuksan. Ask the USGS for a topographic map of the Shuksan Arm area.

Directions: From Seattle drive 90 miles north on I-5 to Bellingham and Exit 255/Mount Baker Highway. Drive approximately 58 miles east on Mount Baker Highway, about 2.5 miles beyond the Mount Baker Ski Area, to the road's end and the large parking lot at Artist Point. The trailhead is at the south end of the parking lot, toward Mount Baker.

Contact: Mount Baker-Snoqualmie National Forest, Glacier Public Service Center, 1094 Mount Baker Highway, Glacier, WA 98244; 360/599-2714.

22 Table Mountain
3.6 mi/2.0 hrs

Not many tourist-attracting trailheads departing from large, paved parking lots provide a challenge for the seasoned hiker. Table Mountain is an exception. From the Artist Point parking lot, Table Mountain's flat top beckons high above, and the trail gets you to it perhaps quicker than you prefer. You switchback up the lava cliffs, peer over the side, get weak-kneed, and keep going. The scenery—fantastic views of Mount Shuksan, in particular—keep you juiced as you chug to the top. Once there, pause and soak in the views and the cleanest air in the Northwest. Take the summit as your turnaround point for a 3.6-mile round-trip or continue on the trail, straight over the other side. Unless you like to slide very fast in the snow in an awkward position, it might be best to leave that side to die-hard summertime snowboarders. The Mount Baker area, including Table Mountain, gave birth to snowboarding in the Northwest, and you're likely to see new generations of the Mount Baker Hard Core anywhere snow lingers on Table Mountain. Sit back and watch. They put on a better show than racing marmots.

This area receives an average annual snowfall of 700 inches, among the heaviest in the United States. It's not unusual to find a 20-foot snowpack in midwinter. The road may not be open above the Mount Baker Ski Area until early to mid-August.

Location: Northeast of Mount Baker at the end of Mount Baker Highway; see Northern Cascades Map 1, grid b3.

User Groups: Hikers and dogs. No horses or mountain bikes are allowed. No wheelchair facilities.

Permits: A federal Northwest Forest Pass, $5 per day or $30 annually, is required to park at the trailhead. Passes are available from ranger stations and many private vendors, online at website: www.wta.org, or by calling 800/270-7504.

Maps: For a map of Mount Baker-Snoqualmie National Forest, contact the Outdoor Recreation Information Center, Seattle REI, 222 Yale Avenue North, Seattle, WA 98109; 206/470-4060. Green Trails, Inc.'s excellent topographic map of the region is available for $3.99 at outdoor retail outlets; ask for map number 14, Mount Shuksan. Ask the USGS for a topographic map of the Shuksan Arm area.

Directions: From Seattle drive 90 miles north on I-5 to Bellingham and Exit 255/Mount Baker Highway. Drive about 58 miles east on Mount Baker Highway, about 2.5 miles beyond the Mount Baker Ski Area, to the road's end and the large parking lot at Artist Point. The trailhead is at the south end of the parking lot, toward Mount Baker.

Contact: Mount Baker-Snoqualmie National Forest, Glacier Public Service Center, 1094 Mount Baker Highway, Glacier, WA 98244; 360/599-2714.

23 Ptarmigan Ridge
9.0 mi/7.0 hrs

To many an auto-bound sightseer, this ridgetop walk from beautiful Artist Point south up the shoulders of Mount Baker looks easily negotiable. Looks can be deceiving. Snow lingers on the route for much of the year. Good boots and an ice ax are considered essential equipment, along with some knowledge of how to use both in the snow. But for the experienced, Ptarmigan Ridge is a magical walk, spring through fall, with uncountable mountain vistas, meadow views, and thousands of alpine country acres to explore. The route follows the ridge upward around Coleman Pinnacle to Camp Kiser, a snow flat for climbers on this secondary route to Mount Baker's summit. Watch for goats, sudden fog banks, and cairn trail markers in the snow. This is no place to lose track of where you are. The elevation gain to Coleman Pinnacle is about 1,000 feet.

This area receives an average annual snowfall of 700 inches, among the heaviest in the United States. It's not unusual to find a 20-foot snowpack in midwinter. The road may not be open above the Mount Baker Ski Area until early to mid-August.

Location: On the northeast slopes of Mount Baker; see Northern Cascades Map 1, grid b3

User Groups: Hikers and dogs. No horses or mountain bikes are allowed. No wheelchair facilities.

Permits: A federal Northwest Forest Pass, $5 per day or $30 annually, is required to park at the trailhead. Passes are available from ranger stations and many private vendors, online at website: www.wta.org, or by calling 800/270-7504.

Maps: For a map of Mount Baker-Snoqualmie National Forest, contact the Outdoor Recreation Information Center, Seattle REI, 222 Yale Avenue North, Seattle, WA 98109; 206/470-4060. Green Trails, Inc.'s excellent topographic map of the region is available for $3.99 at outdoor retail outlets; ask for map number 14, Mount Shuksan. Ask the USGS for topographic maps of the Shuksan Arm and Mount Baker areas.

Directions: From Seattle drive 90 miles north on I-5 to Bellingham and Exit 255/Mount Baker Highway. Drive about 58 miles east on Mount Baker Highway, about 2.5 miles beyond the Mount Baker Ski Area, to the road's end and the large parking lot at Artist Point. Hike the Chain Lakes Trail/Trail 682 1.2 miles to the Ptarmigan Ridge Trailhead.

Contact: Mount Baker-Snoqualmie National Forest, Glacier Public Service Center, 1094 Mount Baker Highway, Glacier, WA 98244; 360/599-2714.

24 Lake Ann
8.0 mi/5.0 hrs

The first time we saw the Lower Curtis Glacier from the Lake Ann Trail, it scared us to death. Appearing suddenly out of a misty fog that hung in the valley like a shroud all day, the heavily crevassed glacier lay right at our feet. Above it, magnificent Mount Shuksan gradually came into view, displaying its 8,268-foot summit before disappearing into the fog again for the day. That's a typical experience at Lake Ann, a beautiful alpine lake with up-close views of the rugged south Mount Shuksan face. The trail, which is also popular among climbers making their way to the peak, drops about two miles and 800 feet to a meadow at Swift Creek and then gains ground quickly as it switches back across open boulder fields and over a small saddle to Lake Ann, which lies nestled in the elbow of Shuksan Arm. From the lake, which has many good, if overused, campsites, it's a two-mile round-trip walk up the climber's trail to a prime gazing space above the Lower Curtis Glacier. The upper stretches of this extremely popular trail sometime stay covered with snow well into August. The elevation gain is about 900 feet.

This area receives an average annual snowfall of 700 inches, among the heaviest in the United States. It's not unusual to find a 20-foot snowpack in midwinter. The road may not be open above the Mount Baker Ski Area until early to mid-August.

Location: On the south slope of Mount Shuksan, north of Mount Baker; see Northern Cascades Map 1, grid b3.

User Groups: Hikers and dogs. No horses or mountain bikes are allowed. No wheelchair facilities.

Permits: A federal Northwest Forest Pass, $5 per day or $30 annually, is required to park at the trailhead. Passes are available from ranger stations and many private vendors, online at website: www.wta.org, or by calling 800/270-7504.

Maps: For a map of Mount Baker-Snoqualmie National Forest, contact the Outdoor Recreation Information Center, Seattle REI, 222 Yale Avenue North, Seattle, WA 98109; 206/470-4060. Green Trails, Inc.'s excellent topographic map of the region is available for $3.99 at outdoor retail outlets; ask for map number 14, Mount Shuksan. Ask the USGS for a topographic map of the Shuksan Arm area.

Directions: From Seattle drive 90 miles north on I-5 to Bellingham and Exit 255/Mount Baker Highway. Drive about 57 miles east on Mount Baker Highway, about one mile beyond the Mount Baker Ski Area, to the Austin Pass trailhead parking lot on the left, just before the last switchback to the Artist Point parking lot.

Contact: Mount Baker-Snoqualmie National Forest, Glacier Public Service Center, 1094 Mount Baker Highway, Glacier, WA 98244; 360/599-2714.

25 Baker Lake
8.0 mi–28.0 mi/
3.0 hrs–2.0 days

Viewed from a map, the Baker Lake Trail (formerly called East Bank Trail) looks like a long, gentle walk along the shores of Baker Lake. That's technically true, but this is primarily a forest walk, winding through lush, mossy (and often drippy!) trees, including a handful of magnificent old-growth Douglas firs. Most of the trail stays several hundred feet above the lake, with occasional grand views of the water and Mount Baker. The path proceeds at a pleasing pace for about four miles to Maple Grove Camp, popular with kayakers and canoeists who paddle over from campgrounds such as Panorama Point, Horseshoe Cove, and Baker Lake Resort.

Maple Grove Camp is the preferred turn-around point for most day hikers, although a shorter trip can be made by watching for an unnamed side trail down to the lakeshore at about two miles. But backpackers and long-haul day hikers now can continue much farther on this pleasant trail. Forest Service crews have added more mileage to the trail's north end year by year. The trail now crosses the Baker River on a footbridge at the head of the lake, where it connects with the Baker River Trail, as well as roads on the lake's west side. The completed trail allows a one-way shuttle hike of about 14 miles between the East Bank and Baker River Trailheads. Because it's below the normal winter snowfall, this is a pleasant, leg-stretching walk all year long.

Location: On the east shore of Baker Lake Reservoir; see Northern Cascades Map 1, grid c3.

User Groups: Hikers, dogs, and horses. No mountain bikes are allowed. No wheelchair facilities.

Permits: A federal Northwest Forest Pass, $5 per day or $30 annually, is required to park at the trailhead. Passes are available from ranger stations and many private vendors, online at website: www.wta.org, or by calling 800/270-7504.

Maps: For a map of Mount Baker-Snoqualmie National Forest, contact the Outdoor Recreation Information Center, Seattle REI, 222 Yale Avenue North, Seattle, WA 98109; 206/470-4060. Green Trails, Inc.'s excellent topographic map of the region is available for $3.99 at outdoor retail outlets; ask for map number 46, Lake Shannon. Ask the USGS for a topographic map of the Welker Peak area.

Directions: From I-5 north of Mount Vernon, take Exit 230/Anacortes/Burlington. Follow Highway 20/North Cascades Highway about 16 miles east of Sedro-Woolley to Baker Lake-Grandy Road/Forest Service Road 11, near milepost 82. Turn left (north), and at 14 miles turn right on Forest Service Road 1106, signed for Baker Lake/Koma Kulshan Campground. In about one mile, turn right over the Puget Sound Energy dam. On the far side of the dam, veer left on Forest Service Road 1107. The trailhead is on the left, about 0.75 mile down the road.

Contact: North Cascades National Park/Mount Baker Ranger District Information Center, 2105 Highway 20, Sedro-Woolley, WA 98284; 360/856-5700.

26 Thornton Lakes
10.6 mi/6.0 hrs

The views are great from Thornton Lakes, which lie nestled in the armpits of mighty rock ridges that appear to have been carved by glaciers as recently as yesterday. In a way, they have. On 7,270-foot Mount Triumph, looming to the north, glaciers are still at work, chewing away at slopes below the summit. On a clear day, you can watch them from the end of this half-day walk north from the upper Skagit River Valley. In the summer, the crowds can be heavy, too, but don't let that scare you away. The trail follows an old logging road through a clear-cut, then up to views of lower Thornton Lake. Just before the trail begins to drop toward it, a side trail lures you north (right) to the top of Trapper's Peak, where views of the jagged Southern Pickett Range are grand. The lakeshores themselves are camped out and have sustained major vegetation damage. Fishing is marginal here. The upper lakes are accessed via a side trail on the lower lake's west side. Expect snow in the upper lakes well into summer. The elevation gain is about 2,350 feet.

Location: In the Skagit River drainage of North Cascades National Park; see Northern Cascades Map 1, grid c6.

User Groups: Hikers only. No dogs, horses, or mountain bikes are allowed. No wheelchair facilities.

Permits: A federal Northwest Forest Pass, $5 per day or $30 annually, is required to park at the trailhead. Passes are available from ranger stations and many private vendors, online at website: www.wta.org, or by calling 800/270-7504. Free overnight permits and backcountry campsite reservations (both mandatory) are available at all North Cascades National Park information centers.

Maps: For a map of North Cascades National Park, contact the Outdoor Recreation Information Center, Seattle REI, 222 Yale Avenue North, Seattle, WA 98109; 206/470-4060. Green Trails, Inc.'s excellent topographic map of the region is available for $3.99 at outdoor retail outlets; ask for map number 47, Marblemount. Ask the USGS for a topographic map of the Mount Triumph area.

Directions: From I-5 north of Mount Vernon, take Exit 230/Anacortes/Burlington. Follow Highway 20/North Cascades Highway about 46 miles east to Marblemount. About 11 miles beyond Marblemount (three miles west of Newhalem), turn left (north) on Thornton Creek Road. Follow this road about five miles to the trailhead at the end of the steep road, at 2600 feet.

Contact: North Cascades National Park/Mount Baker Ranger District Information Center, 2105 Highway 20, Sedro-Woolley, WA 98284; 360/856-5700.

27 Trail of the Cedars Interpretive Loop
0.3 mi/0.25 hr

If you're in a rush and can only get out of the car in one or two places on your way through the North Cascades on Highway 20, make this one of them. The trail loops through some magnificent western red cedars, with interpretive signs describing the natural forest processes. It's a great leg stretcher for the dog or kids, and from here you can walk the suspension bridge to bustling downtown Newhalem.

Location: Near Newhalem on the upper Skagit River; see Northern Cascades Map 1, grid c7.

User Groups: Hikers and dogs. No horses or mountain bikes are allowed. No wheelchair facilities.

Permits: No permits are required. Parking and access are free.

Maps: For a map of North Cascades National Park, contact the Outdoor Recreation Information Center, Seattle REI, 222 Yale Avenue North, Seattle, WA 98109; 206/470-4060. Green Trails, Inc.'s excellent topographic map of the region is available for $3.99 at outdoor retail outlets; ask for map number 48, Diablo Dam. Ask the USGS for a topographic map of the Mount Triumph area.

Directions: From I-5 north of Mount Vernon, take Exit 230/Anacortes/Burlington. Follow Highway 20/North Cascades Highway approximately 62 miles east to Newhalem. Look for the trailhead near the Gorge Powerhouse, on the south side of Highway 20. Note: Call North Cascades National Park at 360/856-5700 to ascertain winter road conditions.

Contact: North Cascades National Park/Mount Baker Ranger District Information Center, 2105 Highway 20, Sedro-Woolley, WA 98284; 360/856-5700; Marblemount Ranger Station, 728 Ranger Station Road, Marblemount, WA 98267; 360/873-4500.

28 Ladder Creek Falls
0.4 mi/0.5 hr

Not really a walk through natural wildlands, this is more of a stroll through the hillside garden of a truly inspired landscaper, J. D. Ross, an early Seattle City Light superintendent. Ross, seeking to lure Seattle tourists to the wonders of the unfolding City Light project on the upper Skagit, built a wondrous botanical garden behind the Gorge Powerhouse in the early 1920s. Drawing water from the nearby river, he constructed a sprinkler system designed to water exotic plants and feed carefully crafted ponds and ornate fountains. He even installed a crude ground-heating system to keep warm-weather plants alive. The star of the show, however, was Ladder Creek Falls, a magnificent string of gracefully plunging falls that have carved a 40-foot gorge (in many places almost a tunnel) through the smooth mountain rock. The whole thing used to be lit at night, and the falls still are.

The garden's interior was filled with perfectly placed benches and natural stone stairs. Today, much of the garden has fallen into disrepair, a stretch of the original trail has closed, and exotic plants have been replaced by native species. But the trail that runs through it still offers a mysteriously wonderful walk, capped by the ever-present falls. In the fall, the planted maples here offer visitors a brilliant display of fire-engine red leaves. As you cross the suspension bridge back to the car, look carefully in the crystal-clear waters of the Skagit. Those hundreds of dark rocks along the river bottom might actually be spawning sockeye salmon, pooled up to die and wondering why they can't get farther up the river.

Location: Near Newhalem on the upper Skagit River; see Northern Cascades Map 1, grid c7.

User Groups: Hikers and dogs. No horses or mountain bikes are allowed. No wheelchair facilities.

Permits: No permits are required. Parking and access are free.

Maps: For a map of North Cascades National Park, contact the Outdoor Recreation Information Center at 206/470-4060. Green Trails, Inc.'s excellent topographic map of the region is available for $3.99 at outdoor retail outlets; ask for map number 48, Diablo Dam. Ask the USGS for a topographic map of the Mount Triumph area.

Directions: From I-5 north of Mount Vernon, take Exit 230/Anacortes/Burlington. Follow Highway 20/North Cascades Highway east about 62 miles to Newhalem. On the far side of town, park near the Gorge Powerhouse on the highway's south side. Cross the suspension footbridge to the powerhouse and look for the trailhead in the trees, straight ahead. Note: Call North Cascades National Park at 360/856-5700 for winter road conditions.

Contact: Outdoor Recreation Information Center, Seattle REI, 222 Yale Avenue North, Seattle, WA 98109; 206/470-4060.

29 Newhalem Campground Loop
0.5 mi/0.5 hr

Though short, this walk through a cool forest on the Newhalem Campground outskirts is still refreshing. Accessible all year (usually even when the North Cascades Highway is closed just up the road at milepost 134, from December to April), it's an easy walk, with many interpretive displays to greet hikers, whether on foot or in a wheelchair (the surface is compact gravel). Bring the kids.

Location: In the upper Skagit River drainage, North Cascades National Park; see Northern Cascades Map 1, grid c7.

User Groups: Hikers only. Wheelchair accessible. No dogs, horses, or mountain bikes are allowed.

Permits: No permits are required. Parking and access are free.

Maps: For a map of North Cascades National Park and Ross Lake National Recreation Area, contact the Outdoor Recreation Information Center, Seattle REI, 222 Yale Avenue North, Seattle, WA 98109; 206/470-4060. Green Trails, Inc.'s excellent topographic map of the region is available for $3.99 at outdoor retail outlets; ask for map number 47, Marblemount. Ask the USGS for a topographic map of the Mount Triumph area.

Directions: From I-5 north of Mount Vernon, take Exit 230/Anacortes/Burlington. Follow Highway 20/North Cascades Highway east about 62 miles to Newhalem. Follow the signs to the Newhalem Campground entrance station and amphitheater on the south (right) side of the highway. Note: Call North Cascades National Park at 360/856-5700 for winter road conditions.

Contact: North Cascades National Park/Mount Baker Ranger District Information Center, 2105 Highway 20, Sedro-Woolley, WA 98284; 360/856-5700.

◪ Sourdough Mountain
12.5 mi/1.0 day

Two legs of this trail—one from Diablo to the west of Sourdough, the other from Ross Lake to the east—lead to the lookout on Sourdough Mountain, and neither one is easy. Both routes, in fact, are so steep that many people who set out in search of this truly amazing, 360-degree North Cascades view never make it. The trail described here—the main route—departs from the western trailhead in Diablo and climbs 3,000 feet in just over two miles. If you're still alive after that, it gets even tougher, climbing another 2,100 or so feet in the remaining four miles. What could be worse? Try lack of motivation. The first three miles are completely forested. It's like climbing up the stairs to downtown Seattle's Washington Mutual Tower—in the dark, about four times. Even though the trail is usually well maintained, the grade is relentless. We can seriously say this is one of the most grueling day hikes in all the Northwest.

For the survivors, however, rich views await. At a fork at about three miles, you can turn left to a satellite dish or right to the summit lookout. Views from both are unbelievable. You can camp at Sourdough Creek (at four miles) or on the ridge near the summit (no

water) and rest up for the steep descent, either the way you came (for a 12.5-mile round-trip) or by continuing straight and dropping six miles to Ross Lake on the Sourdough Trail's eastern leg. From here, continue about 4.5 miles south on the Big Beaver Trail to a shuttle car or pickup at the Ross Dam Trailhead (see hike Big/Little Beaver Loop, this chapter for directions).

Whatever you do, don't do this hike early in the summer (before mid-July), when snow keeps you off the top, or on a cloudy day; the only reward for killing yourself getting here are the killer views at the very top. Miss 'em, and you'll be sorry you came.

Location: West of Ross Lake in North Cascades National Park; see Northern Cascades Map 1, grid c7.

User Groups: Hikers and horses. No dogs or mountain bikes are allowed. No wheelchair facilities.

Permits: No day-use permits are required. Free overnight permits (required) are available at the Marblemount Ranger Station at 360/873-4500. Parking and access are free.

Maps: For a map of North Cascades National Park, contact the Outdoor Recreation Information Center, Seattle REI, 222 Yale Avenue North, Seattle, WA 98109; 206/470-4060. Green Trails, Inc.'s excellent topographic maps of the area are available for $3.99 each at outdoor retail outlets; ask for map numbers 16 and 48, Ross Lake and Diablo. Ask the USGS for topographic maps of the Mount Prophet, Pumpkin Mountain, Ross Dam, and Diablo Dam areas.

Directions: From I-5 north of Mount Vernon, take Exit 230/Anacortes/Burlington. Follow Highway 20/North Cascades Highway about 70 miles east to the Seattle City Light town of Diablo (about five miles east of Newhalem). The trailhead is behind the dome-covered swimming pool in Diablo. Look for the sign along the hillside and park along the road's shoulder. Note: Highway 20 is closed in winter at milepost 134. Call North Cascades National Park at 360/856-5700 for current road conditions.

Contact: North Cascades National Park/Mount Baker Ranger District Information Center, 2105 Highway 20, Sedro-Woolley, WA 98284; 360/856-5700; Marblemount Ranger Station, 728 Ranger Station Road, Marblemount, WA 98267; 360/873-4500.

31 Stetattle Creek
8.0 mi/5.0 hrs

For all you day-trippers who venture north to Diablo to see the City Light power project, this is a great hike. The trail heads north along the creek, which often carries glacial dust from glaciers on McMillan Spires and Davis Peak. Farther up, you find small patches of trillium, bleeding heart, orchid, lily, dogwood, Indian pipe, and other flower species. The trail eventually leaves the creek for a leisurely stroll through forests of moss-bearded trees. It's quiet, peaceful, soothing, and particularly colorful in the fall. The trail just sort of dies away in the forest at about four miles. Don't let the lack of a whiz-bang main attraction at the end keep you from this walk, however. The creek itself is beautiful, and the shrubby vine maples along its banks make the greens of spring and yellows of autumn practically light the way.

Location: North of Diablo Lake in North Cascades National Park; see Northern Cascades Map 1, grid c7.

User Groups: Hikers and horses. No dogs or mountain bikes are allowed. No wheelchair facilities.

Permits: No day-use permits are required. Free overnight permits (required) are available at the Marblemount Ranger Station at 360/873-4500. Parking and access are free.

Maps: For a map of North Cascades National Park and Ross Lake National Recreation Area, contact the Outdoor Recreation Information Center, Seattle REI, 222 Yale Avenue North, Seattle, WA 98109; 206/470-4060. Green Trails, Inc.'s excellent topographic map of the region is available for $3.99 at outdoor retail outlets; ask for map number 48, Diablo Dam. Ask the USGS for a topographic map of the Diablo Dam area.

Directions: From I-5 north of Mount Vernon, take Exit 230/Anacortes/Burlington. Drive about 70 miles east on Highway 20/North Cascades Highway to the Seattle City Light town of Diablo. Watch for the green bridge over Stetattle Creek just before the town. The trailhead is just over the green bridge, on the left, with a small parking area on the right. Note: Highway 20 is closed in winter at milepost 134. Call North Cascades National Park at 360/856-5700 for current road conditions.

Contact: North Cascades National Park/Mount Baker Ranger District Information Center, 2105 Highway 20, Sedro-Woolley, WA 98284; 360/856-5700; Marblemount Ranger Station, 728 Ranger Station Road, Marblemount, WA 98267; 360/873-4500.

32 Diablo Lake
7.6 mi/4.0 hrs

Scenic views of aqua green Diablo Lake and the surrounding awesome peaks await on this easy, mostly flat hike. The trail begins at the lake near the metal dock where the Seattle City Light tugboat picks up passengers for its twice-daily jaunt to the base of Ross Dam. Near the trail's end, you get a close encounter with Ross Dam when you cross a suspension bridge spanning the narrow gap that was once the Skagit River Gorge, but now is merely the head of Diablo Lake. Many hikers prefer to make this a one-way trek by taking the tugboat-ferry up Diablo Lake and walking back to the car.

Location: Near Diablo Dam in Ross Lake National Recreation Area; see Northern Cascades Map 1, grid c8.

User Groups: Hikers, dogs, and horses. No mountain bikes are allowed. No wheelchair facilities.

Permits: No permits are required. Parking and access are free.

Maps: For a map of Ross Lake National Recreation Area and North Cascades National Park, contact the Outdoor Recreation Information Center, Seattle REI, 222 Yale Avenue North, Seattle, WA 98109; 206/470-4060. Green Trails, Inc.'s excellent topographic map of the region is available for $3.99 at outdoor retail outlets; ask for map number 48, Diablo Dam. Ask the USGS for a topographic map of the Ross Dam area.

Directions: From I-5 north of Mount Vernon, take Exit 230/Anacortes/Burlington. Follow Highway 20/North Cascades Highway east about 72 miles to the Diablo Dam turnoff on the left. Head north at the turnoff, cross the dam, and drive just over a mile to Old Diablo Lake Resort. The trailhead is on the left; park on the right along the lake. Note: Highway 20 is closed in winter at milepost 134. Call North Cascades National Park at 360/856-5700 for current road conditions.

Contact: For trail reports and the Diablo Lake tugboat schedule, contact the North Cascades National Park/Mount Baker Ranger District Information Center, 2105 Highway 20, Sedro-Woolley, WA 98284; 360/856-5700.

33 Thunder Creek
12.0 mi/6.0 hrs

The Thunder Creek Trail is a flat, easy path that makes a great day hike or a fine weekend backpack trip through lush forests. It's a favorite early season (May to early June) hike, when higher North Cascades remain snowbound. It's also a long, classic north-south traverse of the North Cascades and an access trail to greater glories at Easy Pass and Fourth of July Pass.

Many day hikers prefer to take the short route here, ambling up the first several broad, cool, relatively flat miles along the south side of Diablo Lake's Thunder Arm. You come to a junction with the Fourth of July/Panther Lake Trail (see hike in this chapter) at about two miles and pass numerous pleasant picnic spots and campsites in beautiful, deep forest with occasional mountain views on the way up to McAlester Creek Camp, about six miles in. Good campsites are plentiful here, and it's a fine turnaround spot for overnighters or day hikers.

For those looking for a multiday trip, the trail leads on to a junction, at just before 10 miles, with the Fisher Creek/Easy Pass Trail and the Park Creek Trail. The Fisher Creek Trail leads 10.5 miles east to Easy Pass (see hike in this chapter) and back down to the eastern portion of Highway 20. The Park Creek Trail leads another nine miles due south to 6,100-foot Park Creek Pass (see hike in this chapter) and another eight miles to the Stehekin River—a classic 36-mile round-trip, with splendid views, ample camping, and abundant wildlife all along the route. (If you decide to extend your trip to Park Creek Pass, note that it's snowbound much of the summer, so ice axes are recommended.)

If you are considering staying overnight, note that camping is restricted at Park Creek Pass. Heed camping closure signs and give the trampled meadows a chance to recover.

Location: South of Ross Lake in North Cascades National Park; see Northern Cascades Map 1, grid c8.

User Groups: Hikers, dogs, and horses. Pets are allowed only to the national park border, six miles in. No mountain bikes are allowed. No wheelchair facilities.

Permits: A federal Northwest Forest Pass, $5 per day or $30 annually, is required to park at the Panther Creek trailhead. Passes are available from ranger stations and many private vendors, online at website: www.wta.org, or by calling 800/270-7504. Free overnight permits (required) are available at the Marblemount Ranger Station at 360/873-4500.

Maps: For a map of North Cascades National Park and Ross Lake National Recreation Area, contact the Outdoor Recreation Information Center, Seattle REI, 222 Yale Avenue North, Seattle, WA 98109; 206/470-4060. Green Trails, Inc.'s excellent topographic maps of the region are available for $3.99 each at outdoor retail outlets; ask for map numbers 48 and 49, Diablo Dam and Mount Logan. Ask the USGS for topographic maps of the Ross Dam, Forbidden Peak, Mount Logan, and Goode Mountain areas.

Directions: From I-5 north of Mount Vernon, take Exit 230/Anacortes/Burlington. Drive about 74 miles east on Highway 20/North Cascades Highway to Colonial Creek Campground, four miles east of the Diablo Lake turnoff at milepost 130. Park in the lot above the boat ramp and find the trail just up the hill, near the amphitheater. To leave a car for a shuttle-hike exit via the Panther Creek Trail, proceed 8.2 miles east on Highway 20 and park in the East Bank Trailhead parking lot. Note: Highway 20 is closed in winter at milepost 134. Call North Cascades National Park at 360/856-5700 for current road conditions.

Contact: North Cascades National Park/ Mount Baker Ranger District Information Center, 2105 Highway 20, Sedro-Woolley, WA 98284; 360/856-5700; Marblemount Ranger Station, 728 Ranger Station Road, Marblemount, WA 98267; 360/873-4500.

34 Pyramid Lake
4.2 mi/2.0 hrs

Legs feeling a little cramped after that long drive up Highway 20 from Seattle? The Pyramid Lake Trail will take out a few of those kinks—and add a few new ones. The trail climbs swiftly up and away from the upper Skagit Valley, rising 1,500 feet in just over two miles. You pass through a pine and fir forest—burned at some point long ago—to a fantastically cool, damp spot on the creek at about one mile. Stop, catch your breath, drink something, and continue. At the top, you stumble on Pyramid Lake, actually more of a pond that's a bit of a biological oddity in its own right. You don't find fish here, but, according to biologists, you do find the rough-skinned newt, not to mention the famed sundew, an insect-eating plant that grows on old logs. The view around the lake is pleasant, and this is a fine lunch spot. You'll likely want to take a picture of 7,182-foot Pyramid Peak, one of the most distinctive (and aptly named) mountains in the region. Share your extra food with hungry climbers headed up to or back from ascents of Colonial and Pyramid Peaks.

Camping is not allowed at Pyramid Lake. It's a day hike only.

Location: South of Diablo in Ross Lake National Recreation Area; see Northern Cascades Map 1, grid c8.

User Groups: Hikers, dogs, and horses. No mountain bikes are allowed. No wheelchair facilities.

Permits: A federal Northwest Forest Pass, $5 per day or $30 annually, is required to park at the trailhead. Passes are available from ranger stations and many private vendors, online at website: www.wta.org, or by calling 800/270-7504. Free overnight permits are available at all North Cascades National Park visitor centers.

Maps: For a map of North Cascades National Park and Ross Lake National Recreation Area, contact the Outdoor Recreation Information Center, Seattle REI, 222 Yale Avenue North, Seattle, WA 98109; 206/470-4060. Green Trails, Inc.'s excellent topographic map of the region is available for $3.99 at outdoor retail outlets; ask for number 48, Diablo Dam. Ask the USGS for topographic maps of the Ross Dam and Diablo Dam areas.

Directions: From I-5 north of Mount Vernon, take Exit 230/Anacortes/Burlington. Follow Highway 20/North Cascades Highway east to a pullout on the north side of the road near milepost 127.5, just under a mile east of the spur road to the town of Diablo. The trailhead is on the south side of the highway near the creek. Note: Highway 20 is closed in winter. Call North Cascades National Park at 360/856-5700 for current road conditions.

Contact: North Cascades National Park/Mount Baker Ranger District Information Center, 2105 Highway 20, Sedro-Woolley, WA 98284; 360/856-5700.

35 East Bank Ross Lake
31.0 mi one way/
4.0–5.0 days

Every year around mid-September—when hiking crowds thin, the weather cools but remains dry, and summer-weary bones call out for an easy but isolated trip—the East Bank Ross Lake Trail comes to mind. For much of the more than 20 miles, the trail more or less follows the shores of Ross Lake, the grade is flat, and excellent campsites (complete with fire rings and tables) are almost embarrassingly accessible. Aside from one tough overland stretch along Lightning Creek about halfway in, this trail takes much of the work out of backpacking. An early autumn visit offers another advantage: Ross Lake Reservoir, which can be lowered 100 feet or more during drawdowns at Ross Dam, usually is full in the fall, creating beautiful reflections of fall foliage where only massive mudflats were visible in the spring, another time when the trail is a popular lowland alternative.

The most sensible way to backpack this route is to take the Ross Lake Resort water taxi to a northern point, such as the Lightning Creek area, and hike back. This avoids the repetition of the long, somewhat boring walk through the forest, with few views. Or do the whole stretch one way by starting all the way up by British Columbia. The 31-mile distance listed is a one-way trip from Highway 20 to Hozomeen Campground, near the Canadian border. This is where one of Washington's first recovering wolf packs is believed to haunt the woods. Hike the entire distance and arrange for a water-taxi pickup, or choose one of the dozen or more immaculate campgrounds along the lake and return when, and if, you feel like it. For an even more leisurely visit, rent a boat from Ross Lake Resort, head up the lake, pick a campsite, and day hike to your heart's content. For multiday backpackers, a side trip that shouldn't be missed is the 13.6-mile round-trip scramble up Desolation Peak. The trailhead is near the Lightning Creek crossing, where an impressive suspension bridge spans the creek gorge.

Black bears frequent this area, so don't forget to hang your food. Ross Lake offers hot fishing for large trout of various species, but most are caught by trolling from a boat. A state fishing license is required, and special restrictions are in effect.

Location: On the east bank of Ross Lake, in Ross Lake National Recreation Area; see Northern Cascades Map 1, grid c8.

User Groups: Hikers, dogs, and horses. No mountain bikes are allowed. No wheelchair facilities.

Permits: A federal Northwest Forest Pass, $5 per day or $30 annually, is required to park at the trailhead. Passes are available from ranger stations and many private vendors, online at website: www.wta.org, or by calling 800/270-7504. Free overnight permits (required) are available at the Marblemount Ranger Station, 360/873-4500, and all park information centers.

Maps: For a map of North Cascades National Park, contact the Outdoor Recreation Information Center, Seattle REI, 222 Yale Avenue North, Seattle, WA 98109; 206/470-4060. Green Trails, Inc.'s excellent topographic maps of the region are available for $3.99 each at outdoor retail outlets; ask for map numbers 16, 17, 48, and 49, Ross Lake, Jack Mountain, Diablo Dam, and Mount Logan. Ask the USGS for topographic maps of the Ross Dam, Pumpkin Mountain, Skagit Peak, and Hozomeen Mountain.

Directions: For a partial trip involving a water-taxi drop-off or pickup, see hike Desolation Peak, this chapter. To reach the trailhead: From I-north of Mount Vernon, take Exit 230/Anacortes/Burlington. Follow Highway 20/North Cascades Highway east about 74 miles to Colonial Creek Campground and another eight miles to the large trailhead parking lot near the Panther Creek Bridge, at mile 138. Hike the Ruby Creek Trail about three miles to its junction with the East Bank Trail. Note: Highway 20 is closed in winter at milepost 134. Call North Cascades National Park at 360/856-5700 for current road conditions.

Contact: North Cascades National Park/Mount Baker Ranger District Information Center, 2105 Highway 20, Sedro-Woolley, WA 98284; 360/856-5700; Marblemount Ranger Station, 728 Ranger Station Road, Marblemount, WA 98267; 360/873-4500.

36 Devil's Dome Loop
41.7 mi/8.0 days

If you're a hard-core mileage counter seeking a single, long-distance hike on which you can sample the varied fruits of the North Cascades, this might be the one for you. If you prefer short, tough treks to truly eye-popping scenery, however, you can probably find better alternatives in the same area. You have to work hard for what you get here. But you do get a lot: Much of this scenic trail is high in elevation, crossing ridgetops, dipping into and out of glacial valleys, alpine meadows and other wondrous spots, all below some of the more magnificently rugged peaks you'll see anywhere in the country. Highlights are numerous, including the Crater Mountain Lookout site, Devil's Park, and Devil's Pass, where you turn west toward Ross Lake. This traverse is spectacular, with larch trees shimmering golden in the fall, and 6,982-foot Devil's Dome offering excellent scrambling and mind-numbing views at approximately 20 miles. From here, the trail heads west to Dry Creek Pass, then literally plummets downward to the East Bank Trail near Ross Lake.

You can return by hiking the East Bank and Ruby Creek Trails 15 miles back to the trailhead, or taking the Ross Lake Resort water taxi (make prior arrangements; see hike Big/Little Beaver loop, this chapter) back for a pickup on Highway 20 near Ross Dam. Note: This trail is wild, and foul weather can turn the long trek from glorious to gloomy, particularly in light of the trail tread, which in many stretches has been pounded badly by horse hooves.

Location: West of Ross Lake in the Pasayten Wilderness and Ross Lake

National Recreation Area; see Northern Cascades Map 1, grid c8.

User Groups: Hikers, dogs, and horses. No mountain bikes are allowed. No wheelchair facilities.

Permits: Free overnight permits, required for camping in the Ross Lake National Recreation Area, are available at the Marblemount Ranger Station, 360/873-4500. Parking and access are free.

Maps: For a map of the Pasayten Wilderness and Okanogan National Forest or the Ross Lake National Recreation Area and North Cascades National Park, contact the Outdoor Recreation Information Center, Seattle REI, 222 Yale Avenue North, Seattle, WA 98109; 206/470-4060. Green Trails, Inc.'s excellent topographic maps of the region are available for $3.99 each at outdoor retail outlets; ask for map numbers 17 and 49, Jack Mountain and Mount Logan. Ask the USGS for topographic maps of the Crater Mountain, Azurite Peak, Shull Mountain, Jack Mountain, and Pumpkin Mountain areas.

Directions: From I-5 north of Mount Vernon, take Exit 230/Anacortes/Burlington. Follow Highway 20/North Cascades Highway about 85 miles east to the Canyon Creek Trailhead, on the left (north) side of the highway, approximately 11 miles east of Colonial Creek Campground. Begin the loop by crossing the footlog, turning right, and hiking the Jackita Ridge Trail 738 north toward McMillan Park. Note: Highway 20 is closed in winter at milepost 134. Call North Cascades National Park at 360/856-5700 for current road conditions.

Contact: North Cascades National Park/Mount Baker Ranger District Information Center, 2105 Highway 20, Sedro-Woolley, WA 98284; 360/856-5700; Marblemount Ranger Station, 728 Ranger Station Road, Marblemount, WA 98267; 360/873-4500.

37 Shadow of the Sentinels Nature Trail
0.5 mi/0.5 hr

Years ago, many, many giant Douglas firs stood watch in this valley, which has since been cleared and flooded by two Puget Sound Energy dams on the Baker River (which also all but destroyed a now-recovering sockeye salmon population). It's both inspiring and tragic to see this small remaining timber stand preserved in a short, easy, looped nature trail. One trip through and you find yourself muttering that at least this is better than nothing. The trees are truly magnificent, the grade flat and easy. Take your time and enjoy. This hike is accessible year-round and is a popular snowshoeing venue in the winter months. The path, which alternates between boardwalks and asphalt, is barrier-free.

Location: West of Baker Lake in Mount Baker-Snoqualmie National Forest; see Northern Cascades Map 1, grid d2.

User Groups: Hikers and dogs. Wheelchair accessible. No horses or mountain bikes are allowed.

Permits: A federal Northwest Forest Pass, $5 per day or $30 annually, is required to park at the trailhead. Passes are available from ranger stations and many private vendors, online at website: www.wta.org, or by calling 800/270-7504.

Maps: For a map of Mount Baker-Snoqualmie National Forest, contact the Outdoor Recreation Information Center, Seattle REI, 222 Yale Avenue North, Seattle, WA 98109; 206/470-4060. Green Trails, Inc.'s excellent topographic map of the region is available for $3.99 at outdoor retail outlets; ask for map number 46, Lake Shannon. Ask the USGS for a topographic map of the Welker Peak area.

Directions: From I-5 north of Mount Vernon, take Exit 230/Anacortes/Burlington. Follow

Highway 20/North Cascades Highway about 16 miles east of Sedro-Woolley to Baker Lake-Grandy Road/Forest Service Road 11, near milepost 82. Turn left (north) and follow this road about 15 miles to the marked trailhead on the right (less than a mile beyond the Koma Kulshan Guard Station).

Contact: North Cascades National Park/ Mount Baker Ranger District Information Center, 2105 Highway 20, Sedro-Woolley, WA 98284; 360/856-5700.

38 Sauk Mountain
4.2 mi/2.0 hrs

Parents, this one's for you. The relatively easy, gently graded Sauk Mountain Trail climbs 2.1 miles through a pleasant second-growth forest to a rounded hilltop with views in all directions. From the 5,537-foot summit, look northwest to Lake Shannon, west to the Skagit River Valley, south to Mount Rainier and north to Mount Baker. It's an excellent family hike in the early summer, when wildflowers bloom in full force in the meadows on the way up.

The trail gains only 1,200 feet on the way to the summit. If your legs want more, hop on the side trail that wanders 1.5 miles south and then east to Sauk Lake, elevation 4,100 feet. Notice Barr Creek exiting to the south and Bald Mountain looming to the north. Consider packing a lunch into Sauk Lake and then relaxing on the summit in late afternoon as the sun creeps toward the Pacific, before hurrying back down the trail to the fine campground at Rockport State Park. The latter, ironically, is in some ways more scenic than the trail up Sauk Mountain: the state park is home to one of the finest remaining patches of old-growth forest in this entire river drainage.

Location: In the Skagit River drainage of Mount Baker-Snoqualmie National Forest; see Northern Cascades Map 1, grid d4.

User Groups: Hikers and dogs. No horses or mountain bikes are allowed. No wheelchair facilities.

Permits: A federal Northwest Forest Pass, $5 per day or $30 annually, is required to park at the trailhead. Passes are available from ranger stations and many private vendors, online at website: www.wta.org, or by calling 800/270-7504.

Maps: For a map of Mount Baker-Snoqualmie National Forest, contact the Outdoor Recreation Information Center, Seattle REI, 222 Yale Avenue North, Seattle, WA 98109; 206/470-4060. Green Trails, Inc.'s excellent topographic map of the region is available for $3.99 at outdoor retail outlets; ask for map number 46, Lake Shannon. Ask the USGS for a topographic map of the Sauk Mountain area.

Directions: From I-5 north of Mount Vernon, take Exit 230/Anacortes/Burlington. Follow Highway 20/North Cascades Highway about 30 miles east, through Concrete. Go about 10 miles east of Concrete and turn left (north) onto Forest Service Road 1030, near Rockport State Park. Drive seven miles to Forest Service Spur Road 1036. Turn right and drive to the trailhead at road's end.

Contact: North Cascades National Park/ Mount Baker Ranger District Information Center, 2105 Highway 20, Sedro-Woolley, WA 98284; 360/856-5700.

39 Watson/Anderson Lakes
5.0 mi/2.5 hrs

On sunny summer days, Baker Lake's excellent campgrounds and fishing spots are tough to abandon. But after several days of basking on the shore, a hike usually is in order, and the Watson Lakes Trail is good for the whole family. You even have a choice of destinations. Just under a mile up the easy trail, a path leads a steep half mile up to

Anderson Butte, with prime views of Watson and Anderson Lakes and icy Mount Watson. The main trail leads another 0.6 mile to a spur to the right. This is the Watson Lakes Trail. Stroll down this path one easy mile to the smaller lake's northern shore, where you can pose for photos with hulking Bacon Peak in the background. Back at the main trail, continue straight to Anderson Lakes—less crowded, but less scenic. It's not difficult to do the entire circuit in an afternoon.

Location: East of Baker Lake in Mount Baker-Snoqualmie National Forest; see Northern Cascades Map 1, grid c4.

User Groups: Hikers and dogs. No horses or mountain bikes are allowed. No wheelchair facilities.

Permits: A federal Northwest Forest Pass, $5 per day or $30 annually, is required to park at the trailhead. Passes are available from ranger stations and many private vendors, online at website: www.wta.org, or by calling 800/270-7504.

Maps: For a map of Mount Baker-Snoqualmie National Forest, contact the Outdoor Recreation Information Center, Seattle REI, 222 Yale Avenue North, Seattle, WA 98109; 206/470-4060. Green Trails, Inc.'s excellent topographic map of the region is available for $3.99 at outdoor retail outlets; ask for map number 46, Lake Shannon. Ask the USGS for topographic maps of the Welker Peak and Bacon Peak areas.

Directions: From I-5 north of Mount Vernon, take Exit 230/Anacortes/Burlington. Follow Highway 20/North Cascades Highway about 16 miles east of Sedro-Woolley to Baker Lake-Grandy Road/Forest Service Road 11, near milepost 82. Turn left (north) and drive 14 miles to Forest Service Road 1106, signed for the Baker Lake/Koma Kulshan Campground. In about one mile, turn right over the Puget Sound Energy dam. On the far side of the dam, veer left on Forest Service Road 1107. Proceed about 10 miles to the trailhead parking lot.

Contact: North Cascades National Park/Mount Baker Ranger District Information Center, 2105 Highway 20, Sedro-Woolley, WA 98284; 360/856-5700.

40 Upper Newhalem Creek
9.0 mi/4.5 hrs

The Upper Newhalem Creek Trail is an easy, fairly well-traveled route running from the upper Skagit Valley into the well-preserved forest of North Cascades National Park. This path particularly shines during the fall, when the maple trees in the Newhalem area paint the valley blotchy red and yellow colors. We suggest trying this trail on a clear October morning; you'll be more than glad you made the drive out here. The grade is flat and wide, because this used to be a logging road. It's kept trampled in shape nowadays by day hikers out driving along Highway 20, as well as trout anglers who like to dip their lines in the creek every summer (a state fishing license is required). At the end of the trail is a hiker/horse camp, which offers plenty of sites and water.

Location: In the Skagit River drainage of Ross Lake National Recreation Area; see Northern Cascades Map 1, grid c7.

User Groups: Hikers and horses. No dogs or mountain bikes are allowed. No wheelchair facilities.

Permits: Free overnight permits are required inside the North Cascades National Park boundary (which is half a mile up the trail). They are available at the Marblemount Ranger Station, 360/873-4500. Parking and access are free.

Maps: For a map of North Cascades National Park and Ross Lake National Recreation Area, contact the Outdoor Recreation

Information Center, Seattle REI, 222 Yale Avenue North, Seattle, WA 98109; 206/470-4060. Green Trails, Inc.'s excellent topographic map of the region is available for $3.99 at outdoor retail outlets; ask for map number 48, Diablo Dam. Ask the USGS for topographic maps of the Diablo Dam and Eldorado Peak areas.

Directions: From I-5 north of Mount Vernon, take Exit 230/Anacortes/Burlington. Follow Highway 20/orth Cscades Highway east for approximately 62 miles to Newhalem. Turn south on the road at the Gorge Powerhouse and then drive 1.3 miles past Newhalem Campground to the trailhead, which is located close to the intake for the hydroelectric plant.

Contact: North Cascades National Park/Mount Baker Ranger District Information Center, 2105 Highway 20, Sedro-Woolley, WA 98284; 360/856-5700; Marblemount Ranger Station, 728 Ranger Station Road, Marblemount, WA 98267; 360/873-4500.

41 Monogram Lake
9.8 mi/7.5 hrs

After 2.8 miles of dizzying switchbacks up Lookout Creek, you're asked to make a choice: west to great views atop 5,719-foot Lookout Mountain or east to Monogram Lake, a gorgeous teardrop set in a glacial cirque. It isn't really fair to force a decision, as both are worth a visit. So leave early and plan to visit each. Whatever you choose to do, be ready for some deep breathing over the first two miles, which gain more than 2,200 feet. From the junction, you go 1.9 miles west—accompanied by wildflowers and fine views—to the lookout. In the other direction, you go 2.1 miles up and then down to Monogram Lake. It's an excellent lunch or camping spot, and a good jump-off point for exploring nearby Little Devil Peak. The total elevation gain to the lake is nearly 4,000 feet.

Location: In the Cascade River drainage of North Cascades National Park; see Northern Cascades Map 1, grid d6.

User Groups: Hikers and horses. No dogs or mountain bikes are allowed. No wheelchair facilities.

Permits: A federal Northwest Forest Pass, $5 per day or $30 annually, is required to park at trailheads along Cascade River Road. Passes are available from ranger stations and many private vendors, online at website: www.wta.org, or by calling 800/270-7504. Free overnight permits, required to camp inside North Cascades National Park, are available at the Mount Baker Ranger District Information Center, 360/856-5700.

Maps: For a map of North Cascades National Park, contact the Outdoor Recreation Information Center, Seattle REI, 222 Yale Avenue North, Seattle, WA 98109; 206/470-4060. Green Trails, Inc.'s excellent topographic map of the region is available for $3.99 at outdoor retail outlets; ask for map number 47, Marblemount. Ask the USGS for a topographic map of the Big Devil Peak area.

Directions: From I-5 north of Mount Vernon, take Exit 230/Anacortes/Burlington. Follow Highway 20/North Cascades Highway east for 46 miles to Marblemount. Turn right (east) on Cascade River Road. The trailhead is on the left at about seven miles, one mile west of Marble Creek Campground.

Contact: North Cascades National Park/Mount Baker Ranger District Information Center, 2105 Highway 20, Sedro-Woolley, WA 98284; 360/856-5700.

42 Hidden Lake Peaks
9.0 mi/5.0 rs

Like a magnet, this steep alpine walk to Hidden Lake and Hidden Lake Lookout attracts people in late summer, when snows finally recede and the North Cascades display stunning snowcapped peaks nestled between meadows bursting with wildflowers. Travel light; you gain 3,300 feet in 4.5 miles. After a steep climb through the forest, you arrive into the open high country and begin a long, exposed traverse to a saddle above Hidden Lake. On a clear day, gaze to the north at Mount Baker. From here, the lookout tower (elevation 6,890 feet) is a mere half mile and 300 feet up, but getting there might be trickier than you think. If snow still blocks the way and you don't have an ice ax (or know how to use one), admire the abandoned lookout from below. Good campsites are found below at the lake; stick to established sites. Use special care when crossing snowfields on the trail, both in and out. Snow remains on the ground very late into the summer.

Location: In the Cascade River drainage of North Cascades National Park; see Northern Cascades Map 1, grid d7.

User Groups: Hikers and horses. No dogs or mountain bikes are allowed. No wheelchair facilities.

Permits: A federal Northwest Forest Pass, $5 per day or $30 annually, is required to park at trailheads along Cascade River Road. Passes are available from ranger stations and many private vendors, online at website: www.wta.org, or by calling 800/270-7504. Free overnight permits are required and are available at the Mount Baker Ranger Station, 360/856-5700.

Maps: For a map of North Cascades National Park or the adjoining Mount Baker-Snoqualmie National Forest, contact the Outdoor Recreation Information Center, Seattle REI, 222 Yale Avenue North, Seattle, WA 98109; 206/470-4060. Green Trails, Inc.'s excellent topographic map of the region is available for $3.99 at outdoor retail outlets; ask for map number 80, Cascade Pass. Ask the USGS for topographic maps of the Eldorado Peak and Sonny Boy Lakes areas.

Directions: From I-5 north of Mount Vernon, take Exit 230/Anacortes/Burlington. Follow Highway 20/North Cascades Highway east for 46 miles to Marblemount. Turn east on Cascade River Road and follow it about 9.5 miles to Sibley Creek Road/Forest Service Road 1540. Turn left and drive 4.5 rough miles to the trailhead at the road's end.

Contact: North Cascades National Park/Mount Baker Ranger District Information Center, 2105 Highway 20, Sedro-Woolley, WA 98284; 360/856-5700.

43 Cascade River Trail
8.0 mi/5.5 hrs

Though it doesn't get much traffic, this out-of-the-way trail does provide a very nice walk through a lush North Cascades river valley. It's an excellent hike in the springtime, when upper trails are still covered with snow. The trail wanders for the first half mile, then splits, with the main trail following the river's south fork for a mile before turning into a little-used climber's access trail. The trail leading left (east) from the junction is also known as the Spaulding Mine Trail. It's not well maintained and can be quite brushy. The path ends about 3.5 miles up the valley between Cascade Peak and Mount Formidable.

Location: In the Mount Baker Ranger District of Mount Baker-Snoqualmie National Forest; see Northern Cascades Map 1, grid e8.

User Groups: Hikers, dogs, and horses. No mountain bikes are allowed. No wheelchair facilities.

Permits: A federal Northwest Forest Pass, $5 per day or $30 annually, is required to park at the trailhead. Passes are available from ranger stations and many private vendors, online at website: www.wta.org, or by calling 800/270-7504.

Maps: For a map of Mount Baker-Snoqualmie National Forest, contact the Outdoor Recreation Information Center, Seattle REI, 222 Yale Avenue North, Seattle, WA 98109; 206/470-4060. Green Trails, Inc.'s excellent topographic map of the region is available for $3.99 at outdoor retail outlets; ask for map number 80, Cascade Pass. Ask the USGS for topographic maps of the Sonny Boy Lakes and Cascade Pass.

Directions: From I-5 north of Mount Vernon, take Exit 230/Anacortes/Burlington. Follow Highway 20/North Cascades Highway east for 46 miles to Marblemount. Turn east on Cascade River Road and follow it approximately 16.5 miles to South Fork Cascade River Road/Forest Service Road 1590. Turn left and drive to the trailhead at the road's end. Note: The road is very rough. Many hikers choose to walk the final one to two miles to the trailhead.

Contact: North Cascades National Park/Mount Baker Ranger District Information Center, 2105 Highway 20, Sedro-Woolley, WA 98284; 360/856-5700.

44 Cascade Pass
7.4 mi/4.0 hrs

By the time you negotiate what seems like the 557th switchback on the way to Cascade Pass, you might feel like you've just spent five hours at the local auto showroom: dizzy. But the trail itself is not nearly as dizzying as the views you find up high at Cascade Pass. The first two miles lead through cool, clean forest. You breathe a bit harder as you switchback relentlessly through lovely meadows filled with glacier lilies. Before you know it, you're at Cascade Pass, elevation 5,400 feet, where there always seem to be about two dozen other folks, no matter when you go.

The fact that this is one of the most heavily (over)used trails in North Cascades National Park is made pungently clear by the compost toilet at the summit. Ignore it, plug your nose, and drink in the view. You're staring straight into the face of 8,065-foot Johannesburg Mountain, which spits out teeth frequently; chunks of the hanging glacier fall often, and if you're lucky, you'll see a piece of ice as big as your house explode on the rocks below. Camping in the area is limited (try the parking lot, where the view is better than from the summit of many other hikes), but this area calls out for exploring. Good side trips from Cascade Pass include Sahale Arm, Doubtful Lake, and the ridge to Mixup Peak. Also, the 1.5-mile jaunt north to Horseshoe Basin absolutely should not be missed. The total elevation gain to the pass is about 1,800 feet.

Location: In the North Fork Cascade River drainage of North Cascades National Park; see Northern Cascades Map 1, grid e8.

User Groups: Hikers only. No dogs, horses, or mountain bikes are allowed. No wheelchair facilities.

Permits: A federal Northwest Forest Pass, $5 per day or $30 annually, is required to park at the trailhead. Passes are available from ranger stations and many private vendors, online at website: www.wta.org, or by calling 800/270-7504. Free overnight permits (required) are available at the Marblemount Ranger Station, 360/873-4500.

Maps: For a map of North Cascades National Park or the adjoining Mount Baker-Snoqualmie National Forest, contact the Outdoor Recreation Information Center, Seattle REI, 222 Yale Avenue North, Seattle, WA 98109; 206/470-4060. Green Trails, Inc.'s excellent topographic map of the region is available for $3.99 at outdoor retail outlets; ask for map number 80, Cascade Pass. Ask the USGS for topographic maps of the Cascade Pass and Goode Mountain areas.

Directions: From I-5 north of Mount Vernon, take Exit

230/Anacortes/Burlington. Follow Highway 20/North Cascades Highway east for 46 miles to Marblemount. Turn east on Cascade River Road and follow it for approximately 22.3 very rough miles to the trailhead at the road's end. Note: This road might not be suitable for all vehicles. Call the Marblemount Ranger Station for road conditions.

Contact: North Cascades National Park/ Mount Baker Ranger District Information Center, 2105 Highway 20, Sedro-Woolley, WA 98284; 360/856-5700; Marblemount Ranger Station, 728 Ranger Station Road, Marblemount, WA 98267; 360/873-4500.

45 Park Creek Pass
15.8 mi/2.0–3.0 days

This eastern entrance to Park Creek Pass, described from the west in Thunder Creek (see hike in this chapter), is heavily used and fairly steep, but nonetheless spectacular. It's a great two- to three-day backpacking destination for vacationers staying in the Stehekin Valley. You quickly gain a lot of altitude, so be sure to carry plenty of water and pace yourself on those hot, arid August days. Good campsites are found at Five Mile and Buckner Camps. From Five Mile Camp on, it's mostly alpine meadows and glorious views. Look upward to Buckner, Booker, and Goode Mountains; the latter summit is one of the highest peaks in the Cascades at 9,160 feet. Time your visit right, and you see glaciers crackling and spitting ice into the valley.

No camping is allowed at the pass, so make Five Mile Camp your final resting spot on the way there. Stop and ponder at the pass. Ahead of you, all waters flow west toward Puget Sound. Behind you, everything runs east toward Lake Chelan. You, too, can go either way. From this 6,100-foot vantage point, it's eight miles back the way you came or 19.4

miles west to Colonial Creek Campground on Diablo Lake, via Thunder Creek.

Location: In the Stehekin River Valley of North Cascades National Park; see Northern Cascades Map 1, grid e8.

User Groups: Hikers only. No dogs, horses, or mountain bikes are allowed. No wheelchair facilities.

Permits: Free overnight permits (required) are available at the Golden West Visitor Center in Stehekin. Access to Stehekin requires a $25 round-trip boat ride from Chelan.

Maps: For a map of North Cascades National Park, contact the Outdoor Recreation Information Center, Seattle REI, 222 Yale Avenue North, Seattle, WA 98109; 206/470-4060. Green Trails, Inc.'s excellent topographic map of the region is available for $3.99 at outdoor retail outlets; ask for map number 81, McGregor Mountain. Ask the USGS for topographic maps of Goode Mountain and Mount Logan.

Directions: From Seattle take U.S. 2/Stevens Pass east to Wenatchee and U.S. 97 north to the city of Chelan. Catch the water taxi up Lake Chelan to Stehekin (contact the Outdoor Recreation Information Center at 206/470-4060, call 509/682-4584, or see website: www.ladyofthelake.com for boat schedules and shuttle bus information). Ride the shuttle bus from Stehekin 18.5 miles to the trailhead near Park Creek Camp.

Special access note: Flooding periodically damages Stehekin Valley Road, closing it to shuttle buses that normally operate there spring through fall. Check road conditions and shuttle schedules at 360/856-5700 before you depart for this or any other Stehekin Valley hike.

Contact: North Cascades National Park/Mount Baker Ranger District Information Center, 2105 Highway 20, Sedro-Woolley, WA 98284; 360/856-5700.

46 Boulder River/Boulder Falls
9.0 mi/4.0 hrs

This is an exceptionally good off-season hike. The trail can get quite muddy in the monsoon season; Boulder River gorge is beautiful and snow-free year-round.

The trail begins in a typical lowland Northwest forest (meaning clear cut) and follows an old railroad grade for a short distance before entering the Boulder River Wilderness, where it becomes a true trail amid the old-growth forest. After about 1.25 miles, a side trail leads to a misty waterfall, which seems to chug along all the time, even in the summer. Take a rest on one of the handy benches here. It's a gorgeous spot, particularly in the winter, when the falls gush superbly. If you're up for more, proceed. The trail then enters thick, dark forest as the river drops out of sight and sound, ultimately pouring back into the river gorge. At 4.5 miles, the trail ends abruptly at the river. On the other side of the river, there's a route heading to the Three Fingers Glacier Lookout; the Forest Service considers it dangerous, however, because of major trail degradation and a risky, often swift river crossing. One look at the river—and what passes for the trail—and you'll likely agree. If you see some hardy souls packing ice axes and other gear out of here, express your thanks. They're probably volunteers for the Washington Trails Association, which completed significant trail improvements here in 1997. Bravo! The total elevation gain is about 500 feet.

Location: East of Arlington in the Boulder River Wilderness; see Northern Cascades Map 1, grid f2.

User Groups: Hikers and dogs. No horses or mountain bikes are allowed. No wheelchair facilities.

Permits: A federal Northwest Forest Pass, $5 per day or $30 annually, is required to park at the trailhead. Passes are available from ranger stations and many private vendors, online at website: www.wta.org, or by calling 800/270-7504.

Maps: For a map of Mount Baker-Snoqualmie National Forest, contact the Outdoor Recreation Information Center, Seattle REI, 222 Yale Avenue North, Seattle, WA 98109; 206/470-4060. Green Trails, Inc.'s excellent topographic maps of the region are available for $3.99 each at outdoor retail outlets; ask for map numbers 77 and 109, Oso and Granite Falls. Ask the USGS for a topographic map of the Meadow Mountain area.

Directions: From Seattle drive 42 miles north on I-5 to Exit 208/Silvana/Arlington. Drive 19.5 miles east on Highway 530 to French Creek Road/Forest Service Road 2010. Turn right (south) and drive 3.8 miles to the trailhead at the end of the road.

Contact: Mount Baker-Snoqualmie National Forest, Darrington Ranger District, 1405 Emmens Street, Darrington, WA 98241; 360/436-1155.

47 Mount Higgins
9.0 mi/6.5 hrs

The Stillaguamish River Valley along Highway 530 is one of the most placid, unspoiled lowland valleys in the Puget Sound region, and this trail, which climbs to an old fire-lookout site, provides a bird's-eye view of it and a whole lot more. Getting there isn't exactly a joy, though. The trailhead is tricky to find, and the summit path is fairly nondescript.

The haphazardly maintained trail begins on Department of Natural Resources land and climbs 3.5 miles to a junction with another path, which drops a half mile and 100 feet west to Myrtle Lake. The main path (to the right) passes a swampy bog, numerous exposed rock-slide areas, and a pleasant, cool forest, before opening to Mount Higgins' 4,800-foot summit. The views of the valley below, nearby Whitehorse, Glacier Peak, Three Fingers, Puget Sound, and even Mount Rainier make you swiftly forget the 1,600 vertical feet you just climbed. A note on timing: The upper stretches of the trail typically are snowbound until midsummer. It's a good autumn hike.

Location: In the North Fork Stillaguamish River Valley east of Arlington; see Northern Cascades Map 1, grid f2.

User Groups: Hikers and dogs. No horses or mountain bikes. No wheelchair facilities.

Permits: A federal Northwest Forest Pass, $5 per day or $30 annually, is required to park at the trailhead. Passes are available from ranger stations and many private vendors, online at website: www.wta.org, or by calling 800/270-7504.

Maps: For a map of Mount Baker-Snoqualmie National Forest, contact the Outdoor Recreation Information Center, Seattle REI, 222 Yale Avenue North, Seattle, WA 98109; 206/470-4060. Green Trails, Inc.'s excellent topographic map of the region is available for $3.99 at outdoor retail outlets; ask for map number 77, Oso. Ask the USGS for a topographic map of the Oso area.

Directions: From Seattle drive 42 miles north on I-5 to Exit 208/Silvana/Arlington. Drive about 38 miles east on Highway 530 to the logging road marked SL-0-5500. (The No Trespassing sign is not intended to stop hikers driving to the trailhead.) Turn left (north) and drive a half mile to the North Fork Stillaguamish River. The trailhead is 2.9 miles from the bridge, on the right, just before the first switchback. Park alongside the road.

Contact: Mount Baker-Snoqualmie National Forest, Darrington Ranger District, 1405 Emmens Street, Darrington, WA 98241; 360/436-1155.

48 Meadow Mountain
11.6 mi/8.0 hrs

The Meadow Mountain Trail is an alternate route to Saddle Lake and Goat Flat (hike number 60). After a 2,200-foot vertical gain, the trail brings you to clear, ridgetop vistas overlooking jagged North Cascade peaks and an alpine lake. Along the way, it provides a world-class lunch spot on the crest of Meadow Mountain (4.5 miles, elevation 4,400 feet), where views are outstanding. From there you drop 500 feet in 1.3 miles, take in some lovely meadows, and merge with the Goat Flat Trail at Saddle Lake, where campsites are available. The trail to Goat Flat is an excellent day hike from the lake.

Location: Northeast of Granite Falls in the Boulder River Wilderness; see Northern Cascades Map 1, grid g2.

User Groups: Hikers, dogs, and horses. No mountain bikes are allowed. No wheelchair facilities.

Permits: A federal Northwest Forest Pass, $5 per day or $30 annually, is required to park at the trailhead. Passes are available from ranger stations and many private vendors, online at website: www.wta.org, or by calling 800/270-7504.

Maps: For a map of Mount Baker-Snoqualmie National Forest, contact the Outdoor Recreation Information Center, Seattle REI, 222 Yale Avenue North, Seattle, WA 98109; 206/470-4060. Green Trails, Inc.'s excellent topographic map of the region is available for $3.99 at outdoor retail outlets; ask for map number 109, Granite Falls. Ask the USGS for a topographic map of the Meadow Mountain areas.

Directions: From Seattle drive 28 miles north on I-5 to Exit 194/City Center/Stevens Pass.

Drive six miles east on Highway 2 to the Highway 9 exit near Snohomish. Follow Highway 9 north to Highway 92. Turn right and follow Highway 92 eight miles east to Granite Falls. At the end of town, turn left (north) on the Mountain Loop Highway. Drive three miles and turn left (north) on Tupso Pass Road/Forest Service Road 41. Continue for 11 miles to the trailhead on the right.

Contact: Mount Baker-Snoqualmie National Forest, Darrington Ranger District, 1405 Emmens Street, Darrington, WA 98241; 360/436-1155.

49 Squire Creek Pass
7.4 mi/3.5 hrs

If you're lucky, you might see mountain goats on the high reaches of this trail. If not, you are still treated to a fine, photogenic view of the rugged faces of Mount Bullen, as well as Whitehorse and Three Fingers Mountains, not to mention other wildlife, alpine heather, and various flowers. The trail starts on an abandoned road that eventually climbs beyond some pleasant waterfalls to the ridge top. Most likely the trail will leave you cursing because it's thick with irritating roots and rocks in places, and slippery when wet. It's also very dry in the summer, with few good water sources. But if you can get beyond those hurdles, this is a particularly pleasant walk in the fall, when ripe huckleberries draw pail-packing Seattleites and probably a few bears.

At about 3.5 miles, the trail comes to more good views among boulder fields at Squire Creek Pass, elevation 4,000 feet. From here, the trail continues an additional three miles to the ridge's east side and Forest Service Road 2065 in the Clear Creek drainage, an optional exit (not recommended). The total elevation gain is about 2,200 feet. Note: This trail melts out earlier than some of its neighbors, often by late May.

Location: South of Darrington in the Boulder River Wilderness; see Northern Cascades Map 1, grid g3.

User Groups: Hikers and dogs. No horses or mountain bikes are allowed. No wheelchair facilities.

Permits: A federal Northwest Forest Pass, $5 per day or $30 annually, is required to park at the trailhead. Passes are available from ranger stations and many private vendors, online at website: www.wta.org, or by calling 800/270-7504.

Maps: For a map of Mount Baker-Snoqualmie National Forest, contact the Outdoor Recreation Information Center, Seattle REI, 222 Yale Avenue North, Seattle, WA 98109; 206/470-4060. Green Trails, Inc.'s excellent topographic map of the region is available for $3.99 at outdoor retail outlets; ask for map number 110, Silverton. Ask the USGS for a map of the Silverton area.

Directions: From Seattle drive 40 miles north on I-5 to Exit 208/Silvana/Arlington. Drive about 32 miles east on Highway 530 to Darrington. Turn right (south) on Givens Street and continue several blocks to Darrington Street. Turn right (west) and continue on this road (it becomes Squire Creek Road 2040) about six miles to its end. Note: The last two miles of the road are very rough.

Contact: Mount Baker-Snoqualmie National Forest, Darrington Ranger District, 1405 Emmens Street, Darrington, WA 98241; 360/436-1155.

50 Old Sauk River
6.0 mi/3.0 hrs

One of our favorite rivers in the Northwest is the Sauk. It runs cold, clear, and most importantly, usually far away from people. That makes its treats—beautiful river vistas, occasional stretches of raucous white water and numerous species of fish—even more memorable. The Sauk is home to a thriving population of salmon and steelhead, many of which migrate all the way up here to spawn in the summer and fall. You can be there to watch, thanks to the Old Sauk Trail, which follows a long-since logged cedar forest up the river and back. It's a pleasant, mostly level (and often wet) walk along the banks of a river that time forgot. We can only hope it stays that way.

Location: On the Sauk River southeast of Darrington; see Northern Cascades Map 1, grid g4.

User Groups: Hikers and dogs. No horses or mountain bikes are allowed. No wheelchair faciliies.

Permits: A federal Northwest Forest Pass, $5 per day or $30 annually, is required to park at the trailhead. Passes are available from ranger stations and many private vendors, online at website: www.wta.org, or by calling 800/270-7504.

Maps: For a map of Mount Baker-Snoqualmie National Forest, contact the Outdoor Recreation Information Center, Seattle REI, 222 Yale Avenue North, Seattle, WA 98109; 206/470-4060. Green Trails, Inc.'s excellent topographic map of the region is available for $3.99 at outdoor retail outlets; ask for map number 110, Silverton. Ask the USGS for a topographic map of the Silverton area.

Directions: From Seattle drive 40 miles north on I-5 to Exit 208/Silvana/Arlington. Drive about 32 miles east on Highway 530 to Darrington. From the Darrington Ranger Station, take the Mountain Loop Highway along the west side of the Sauk River. Follow this road for four miles, past the Clear Creek Campground. The trailhead is on the left.

Contact: Mount Baker-Snoqualmie National Forest, Darrington Ranger District, 1405 Emmens Street, Darrington, WA 98241; 360/436-1155.

51 Mount Pugh (Stujack Pass)
7.0 mi/6.0 hrs

Mount Pugh is an oddity. Surrounded as it is by low, rolling green hills, its rocky top juts 7,201 feet straight skyward, thumbing its nose at the nearby west-side Cascade foothills. Not surprisingly, Stujack Pass, which sits in a saddle at nearly 6,000 feet, provides one of the grandest views around. Getting there can be a chore, however. In spite of the mountain's far-western position, snow lingers here until mid- to late July, and even when it melts, the summit trail is a rocky ankle-turner. But for most hikers who are merely hoofing it to Stujack and no farther, it's not a bad haul.

You break out of the trees and into rolling meadows at about three miles, lured upwards by progressively better views of surrounding peaks such as Whitehorse, Three Fingers, and from higher up, Glacier Peak. Don't venture farther than Stujack Pass without climbing gear and the ability to use it. The upper reaches of the trail are extremely rough going, which might explain why a lookout there was abandoned years ago. For the experienced, however, the views are worth the work.

Location: Off the Mountain Loop Highway southeast of Darrington; see Northern Cascades Map 1, grid g5.

User Groups: Hikers and dogs. No horses or mountain bikes are allowed. No wheelchair facilities.

Permits: A federal Northwest Forest Pass, $5 per day or $30 annually, is required to park at the trailhead. Passes are available from ranger stations and many private vendors, online at website: www.wta.org, or by calling 800/270-7504.

Maps: For a map of Mount Baker-Snoqualmie National Forest, contact the Outdoor Recreation Information Center, Seattle

REI, 222 Yale Avenue North, Seattle, WA 98109; 206/470-4060. Green Trails, Inc.'s excellent topographic map of the region is available for $3.99 at outdoor retail outlets; ask for map number 111, Sloan Peak. Ask the USGS for a topographic map of the Pugh Mountain area.

Directions: From Seattle drive 40 miles north I-5 to Exit 208/Silvana/Arlington. Drive about 32 miles east on Highway 530 to Darrington. From Darrington take Forest Service Road 20/Mountain Loop Highway 14 miles south to Mount Pugh Road/Forest Service Road 2095. Turn left (east) and travel one mile to the trailhead on the right.

Special access note: In the winter the Mount Pugh Road is closed at its junction with the Mountain Loop Highway. Call for road information. When the road is closed, park along the highway and add one mile to the round-trip hike mileage.

Contact: Mount Baker-Snoqualmie National Forest, Darrington Ranger District, 1405 Emmens Street, Darrington, WA 98241; 360/436-1155.

52 Huckleberry Mountain
14.0 mi/1.0 day

We hope you like the old-growth trees that guard the Huckleberry Mountain south slopes, because by the time you reach the former lookout site at the top of this trail, you'll be tired of them. Not that this trail is unpleasant. It just entails seven long, fairly steep miles in the forest before views begin up high. Still, the views are far better than average, and the forest walk itself is pleasant, thanks to a number of bubbling streams and some picturesque waterfalls. You might look for a campsite in this setting, as several are available. (Only very strong hikers will make it to the summit and back out in a single day.) At the top, the meadows and

views of White Chuck Mountain, Glacier Peak, Mount Baker, Whitehorse, and Mount Pugh are spectacular. At 5,900 feet, you're above most everything in the immediate vicinity. The total elevation gain is about 4,500 feet.

Location: In the Suiattle River drainage of Mount Baker-Snoqualmie National Forest; see Northern Cascades Map 1, grid f6.

User Groups: Hikers and dogs. No horses or mountain bikes are allowed. No wheelchair facilities.

Permits: A federal Northwest Forest Pass, $5 per day or $30 annually, is required to park at the trailhead. Passes are available from ranger stations and many private vendors, online at website: www.wta.org, or by calling 800/270-7504.

Maps: For a map of Mount Baker-Snoqualmie National Forest, contact the Outdoor Recreation Information Center, Seattle REI, 222 Yale Avenue North, Seattle, WA 98109; 206/470-4060. Green Trails, Inc.'s excellent topographic map of the region is available for $3.99 at outdoor retail outlets; ask for map number 79, Snowking Mountain. Ask the USGS for a topographic map of the Huckleberry Mountain area.

Directions: From Seattle drive 40 miles north on I-5 to Exit 208/Silvana/Arlington. Drive about 32 miles east on Highway 530 to Darrington. From Darrington drive seven miles north on Highway 530 to Suiattle River Road/Forest Service Road 26. Turn right (east) and drive 14.5 miles to the trailhead on the left (north) side of the road, approximately one mile west of Buck Creek Campground.

Contact: Mount Baker-Snoqualmie National Forest, Darrington Ranger District, 1405 Emmens Street, Darrington, WA 98241; 360/436-1155.

53 Green Mountain
8.0 mi/6.0 hrs

They call it green, but on sunny midsummer days, it's anything but. A hike up Green Mountain in July is a bonanza for wildflower fans, as the trail passes through many open meadows blazing with summer colors. At 2.5 miles, you drop down to a couple of small lakes, where good camping spots are found (camp in established sites only, please). From here, it's a fragrant walk up through even more meadows to the summit and lookout, elevation 6,500 feet. (Funny how they always put these lookouts in places with such great views.) This one, built in the 1920s, is closed to the public, but is used occasionally by the Forest Service.

The view from here is unobstructed in all directions, with North Cascade peaks too numerous to name lining up in your viewfinder. The view of Glacier Peak in particular is fantastic. If there's a better summertime lunch stop in Washington state, we've yet to find it. And if we do, we won't tell you, so enjoy this gem. The total elevation gain is 3,000 feet. The trail usually can be hiked by late June, although snow patches may linger longer.

Location: In the Suiattle River drainage of the Glacier Peak Wilderness; see Northern Cascades Map 1, grid f6.

User Groups: Hikers, dogs, and horses. No mountain bikes are allowed. No wheelchair facilities.

Permits: A federal Northwest Forest Pass, $5 per day or $30 annually, is required to park at the trailhead. Passes are available from ranger stations and many private vendors, online at website: www.wta.org, or by calling 800/270-7504.

Maps: For a map of the Glacier Peak Wilderness, contact the Outdoor Recreation Information Center, Seattle REI, 222 Yale Avenue North, Seattle, WA 98109; 206/470-4060. Green Trails, Inc.'s excellent topographic map of the region is available for $3.99 at outdoor retail outlets; ask for map number 80, Cascade Pass. Ask the USGS for a topographic map of the Glacier Peak area.

Directions: From Seattle drive 40 miles north on I-5 to Exit 208/Silvana/Arlington. Drive about 32 miles east on Highway 530 to Darrington. From Darrington drive seven miles north on Highway 530 to Suiattle River Road/Forest Service Road 26. Turn right (east) and drive about 20 miles to Forest Service Road 2680/Green Mountain Road. Turn left (north) and drive 5.9 miles to the trailhead and parking area near the road's end.

Contact: Mount Baker-Snoqualmie National Forest, Darrington Ranger District, 1405 Emmens Street, Darrington, WA 98241; 360/436-1155.

54 Meadow Mountain
17.5 mi one way/3.0 days

The five-mile jaunt up the gated logging road isn't exactly our idea of fun, and it probably won't be yours, either. But once you're in the high country of Meadow and Fire Mountains, you'll probably forget about it—especially if you've parked a second car at the White Chuck Trailhead and plan to do this trail as a 20-mile shuttle hike, in which case you only have to hike the road one way. Hit this hike in good weather, particularly in the early fall, and it'll be an experience you won't soon forget.

Once you're up and out of the forest, you're on ridge tops much of the time, and views of Glacier Peak, Washington's most underrated volcano, are spectacular. There's too much grand scenery to describe here, but highlights include four alpine lakes and a side trip up 6,591-foot Fire Mountain (12.5 miles). At 17.5 miles, the trail ends at its junction with the White Chuck River Trail (hike number 57). To the east, it's 5.2 miles to the Pacific Crest Trail and more wonders in Glacier Peak Wilderness. To the west, it's 1.5 miles back to the White Chuck Trailhead.

Location: In the western portion of the Glacier Peak Wilderness; see Northern Cascades Map 1, grid g6.

User Groups: Hikers, dogs, and horses. No mountain bikes are allowed. No wheelchair facilities.

Permits: A federal Northwest Forest Pass, $5 per day or $30 annually, is required to park at the trailhead. Passes are available from ranger stations and many private vendors, online at website: www.wta.org, or by calling 800/270-7504.

Maps: For a map of the Glacier Peak Wilderness, contact the Outdoor Recreation Information Center, Seattle REI, 222 Yale Avenue North, Seattle, WA 98109; 206/470-4060. Green Trails, Inc.'s excellent topographic map of the region is available for $3.99 at outdoor retail outlets; ask for map number 111, Sloan Peak. Ask the USGS for topographic maps of the Pugh Mountain and Glacier Peak areas.

Directions: From Seattle drive 40 miles north on I-5 to Exit 208/Silvana/Arlington. Drive about 32 miles east on Highway 530 to Darrington. From Darrington take the Forest Service Road 20/Mountain Loop Highway southeast about 10 miles to White Chuck Road/Forest Service Road 23. Turn left (east) and drive six miles to Rat Trap Pass Road/Forest Service Road 2700. Turn left (north) and drive about two miles to Forest Service Road 2710. Park at the gate and walk to the end of the road (about five miles) to the trailhead on the left.

Contact: Mount Baker-Snoqualmie National Forest, Darrington Ranger District, 1405 Emmens Street, Darrington, WA 98241; 360/436-1155.

55 Downey Creek/Bachelor Meadows
13.2 mi/7.0 hrs

The trees are the stars of this hike. The Downey Creek Trail climbs high into the Suiattle River drainage amid a grand display of old-growth fir, cedar, and hemlock. Of course, there's a reason the trees are so large, and before you know it, some of the life-giving rain might be seeping in through that long-neglected hole in the top of your boots. The trail can get quite swampy, especially in the early summer. Trail maintenance varies between poor and nonexistent, and deadfalls are a constant hassle. Nevertheless, when the weather is pleasant, this is a great trek. Good campsites are found at Sixmile Camp, where many backpackers stop for a first night (thus, our indicated turnaround point).

Those who are willing to sweat a bit more are in for a treat, however. From Sixmile Camp, you can set out the next day (with backpack or without) on Trail 796, which follows Bachelor Creek 3,000 vertical feet in about five miles to sublime views and campsites at Bachelor Meadows. Looming impressively above is Spire Point, elevation 8,264 feet. From the meadows, head back the way you came.

Location: In the Suiattle River drainage of the Glacier Peak Wilderness; see Northern Cascades Map 1, grid f7.

User Groups: Hikers and dogs. No mountain bikes or horses are allowed. No wheelchair facilities.

Permits: A federal Northwest Forest Pass, $5 per day or $30 annually, is required to park at the trailhead. Passes are available from ranger stations and many private vendors, online at website: www.wta.org, or by calling 800/270-7504.

Maps: For a map of the Glacier Peak Wilderness, contact the Outdoor Recreation Information Center, Seattle REI, 222 Yale Avenue North, Seattle, WA 98109; 206/470-4060. Green Trails, Inc.'s excellent topographic map of the region is available for $3.99 at outdoor retail outlets; ask for map number 80, Cascade Pass. Ask the USGS for a topographic map of the Downey Mountain area.

Directions: From Seattle drive 40 miles north on I-5 to Exit 208/Silvana/Arlington. Drive about 32 miles east on Highway 530 to Darrington. From Darrington drive seven miles north on Highway 530 to Suiattle River Road/Forest Service Road 26. Turn right (east) and drive 21 miles to the trailhead near Downey Creek Campground.

Contact: Mount Baker-Snoqualmie National Forest, Darrington Ranger District, 1405 Emmens Street, Darrington, WA 98241; 360/436-1155.

56 Sulphur Creek
3.6 mi/2.0 hrs

You can find your way up this trail using your nose. The route climbs steeply along the creek, passing several very pretty waterfalls, to the pungent hot springs, located across the creek. Alas, leave your beach towel at home. These are more like puddles than pools, and they're more warm (about 80 degrees) than hot. They are fascinating, however, with the unique colors and odors produced by their hydrogen-sulfide–laden waters. A friend once stuck his feet in here and six months later claimed to have lost 30 pounds. (The 60-day hike on the Pacific Crest Trail he completed later the same year probably had more to do with it, however.) The main trail ends here, while a side trail used mostly by anglers continues up the creek.

You might have to find your way up here using your nose. Our last visit revealed this trail no longer is maintained. It's brushy and rough but still navigable for the persistent. Consider yourself warned.

Location: In the Suiattle River drainage of the Glacier Peak Wilderness; see Northern Cascades Map 1, grid g7.

User Groups: Hikers, dogs, and horses. No mountain bikes are allowed. No wheelchair facilities.

Permits: A federal Northwest Forest Pass, $5 per day or $30 annually, is required to park at the trailhead. Passes are available from ranger stations and many private vendors, online at website: www.wta.org, or by calling 800/270-7504.

Maps: For a map of the Glacier Peak Wilderness, contact the Outdoor Recreation Information Center, Seattle REI, 222 Yale Avenue North, Seattle, WA 98109; 206/470-4060. Green Trails, Inc.'s excellent topographic map of the region is available for $3.99 at outdoor retail outlets; ask for map number 80, Cascade Pass. Ask the USGS for a topographic map of the Glacier Peak area.

Directions: From Seattle drive 40 miles north on I-5 to Exit 208/Silvana/Arlington. Drive about 32 miles east on Highway 530 to Darrington. From Darrington drive seven miles north on Highway 530 to Suiattle River Road/Forest Service Road 26. Turn right (east) and drive 21.5 miles to the trailhead on the left (north), located across from Sulphur Creek Campground.

Contact: Mount Baker-Snoqualmie National Forest, Darrington Ranger District, 1405 Emmens Street, Darrington, WA 98241; 360/436-1155.

57 Kennedy Ridge/Hot Springs via the White Chuck River
18.0 mi/1.0–2.0 days

The spectacular but heavily used White Chuck Trail draws mobs, and for good reason: It's a short, easy (at first) walk from here into the wonders of the Glacier Peak Wilderness, and ultimately to Glacier Peak itself. The trail runs high along the White Chuck River through magnificent forest with ample peek-through mountain views. At five miles, you come to a major junction. Go straight, across Kennedy Creek, and you soon arrive at tepid, scummy Kennedy Hot Springs (warning: fecal coliform conventions are booked solid here each summer) and a Forest Service guard station. Beyond the guard station, it's 1.8 miles to a junction with the Pacific Crest Trail at Sitkum Camp.

If you only have one day, skip the hot springs, turn left at the five-mile junction, and head up and east on the Kennedy Ridge Trail, following the Glacier Creek drainage to a higher (4,150-foot) junction with the PCT in 1.8 miles. From here, it's just under two miles to a delightful campsite at Glacier Creek (the first good water since the White Chuck Trail), at elevation 5,650 feet. From this camp, put on your cross-country gear and head east and up, toward moraines of the Kennedy and Scimitar Glaciers. The entire area is open and waiting to be explored. Views of 10,541-foot Glacier Peak and Scimitar Glacier are almost too good for mortals to comprehend. Farther north, the PCT passes through some of its most scenic sections. Take a week, hike north for three days, and see where you wind up. Elevation gain to the hot springs is about 1,000 feet; to the Glacier Creek campsite on the PCT, it's about 3,200 feet.

The Kennedy Hot Springs and Lake Byrne areas are a sorry site for lovers of true wilderness. They've become so overcrowded and misused over the years, we can't honestly recommend camping there overnight. Day hike or plan your camps at destinations farther into the Glacier Peak Wilderness. Also, hang your food in the Kennedy Hot Springs area, a noted bear hangout.

Location: On the east shoulder of Glacier Peak, in the Glacier Peak Wilderness; see Northern Cascades Map 1, grid g6.

User Groups: Hikers, dogs, and horses. No mountain bikes are allowed. No wheelchair facilities.

Permits: A federal Northwest Forest Pass, $5 per day or $30 annually, is required to park at the trailhead. Passes are available from ranger stations and many private vendors, online at website: www.wta.org, or by calling 800/270-7504.

Maps: For a map of the Glacier Peak Wilderness, contact the Outdoor Recreation Information Center at 206/470-4060. Green Trails, Inc.'s excellent topographic maps of the region are available for $3.99 each at outdoor retail outlets; ask for map numbers 111 and 112, Sloan Peak and Glacier Peak. Ask the USGS for topographic maps of the Pugh Mountain and Lime Mountain areas.

Directions: From Seattle drive 40 miles north on I-5 to Exit 208/Silvana/Arlington. Drive about 32 miles east on Highway 530 to Darrington. From Darrington take the Forest Service Road 20/Mountain Loop Highway about 10 miles to White Chuck Road/Forest Service Road 23. Turn left (east) and drive 11 miles to the trailhead at the road's end.

Contact: Outdoor Recreation Information Center, Seattle REI, 222 Yale Avenue North, Seattle, WA 98109; 206/470-4060.

58 Suiattle River to Image Lake/Suiattle Pass

42.0 mi/5.0–6.0 days

The freeway to the sublime, the Suiattle River Trail travels 10.8 miles through plain old, drop-dead gorgeous wild river valley scenery, gaining only about 1,000 feet in elevation. Then the fun begins. Pick a fork. Take the left one and you're on the Miner's Ridge Trail, a loop that leads to Image Lake and some of the most spectacular alpine camping anywhere. From here the trail drops back down to the Image Lake Trail and leads to Suiattle Pass, 21 miles from the car. Many Glacier Peak veterans say the latter stretch is one of the most beautiful in the entire wilderness area, if not the country. We can't argue. Or back at that first fork, take a right and connect with the Pacific Crest Trail, which you can hike north into North Cascades National Park. For an alpine highlight loop, take the PCT south from the Suiattle River Trail, across the north side of Glacier Peak, and then north on the Milk Creek Trail back to your car for a total loop of 32.8 miles.

If that's not enough, the Suiattle River Trail can be hiked straight through to the Railroad Creek Trail past Lyman Lake, 30 miles east to Holden, where it's 12 miles down a dirt road to Lake Chelan at Lucerne. It may well be the finest east-west Cascade traverse in Washington. Whichever of the above routes you choose, the scenery ranks up there with the best backpacking terrain in the United States. Please treat this land kindly; plenty of plodders will be following in your footsteps for generations to come.

Location: In the Glacier Peak Wilderness; see Northern Cascades Map 1, grid g7.

User Groups: Hikers, dogs, and horses. No mountain bikes are allowed. No wheelchair facilities.

Permits: A federal Northwest Forest Pass, $5 per day or $30 annually, is required to park at the trailhead. Passes are available from ranger stations and many private vendors, online at website: www.wta.org, or by calling 800/270-7504.

Maps: For a map of the Glacier Peak Wilderness, contact the Outdoor Recreation Information Center, Seattle REI, 222 Yale Avenue North, Seattle, WA 98109; 206/470-4060. Green Trails, Inc.'s excellent topographic maps of the region are available for $3.99 each at outdoor retail outlets; ask for map numbers 112 and 113, Glacier Peak and Holden. Ask the USGS for topographic maps of the Lime Mountain, Gamma Peak, and Suiattle Pass areas.

Directions: From Seattle drive 40 miles north on I-5 to Exit 208/Silvana/Arlington. Drive about 32 miles east on Highway 530 to Darrington. From Darrington drive seven miles north on Highway 530 to Suiattle River Road/Forest Service Road 26. Turn right (east) and drive 22.5 miles to the end of the road.

Contact: Mount Baker-Snoqualmie National Forest, Darrington Ranger District, 1405 Emmens Street, Darrington, WA 98241; 360/436-1155.

59 Upper Suiattle
37.4 mi/3.0–4.0 days

If you're seeking backpacking solitude in the Glacier Peak Wilderness, this trail offers a side trip into pristine backcountry or a jumping-off point for a more extensive five- to 10-day trip. The Upper Suiattle Trail begins deep in the wilderness on the northeast flank of Glacier Peak and skirts the peak to the east. Along the way are side trails to Gamma Ridge (six miles one way), Dusty Creek (3.5 miles one way), and Triad Creek (4.7 miles to Buck Creek Pass). All lead into the spectacular alpine glacier country of the Glacier Peak region. If you stick to the main trail, you wander a relatively level grade through massive old-growth trees all the way to Chocolate Creek, our destination, where the trail ends and true off-trail pathfinding begins. Mix and match for a backcountry adventure ranging from 42 to 60 miles, with enough memories to last you at least through the winter, if not forever. For the Lower Suiattle portion of this hike, see hike Suiattle River, this chapter.

Location: Northeast of Glacier Peak in the Glacier Peak Wilderness; see Northern Cascades Map 1, grid g8.

User Groups: Hikers, dogs, and horses. No mountain bikes are allowed. No wheelchair facilities.

Permits: A federal Northwest Forest Pass, $5 per day or $30 annually, is required to park at the trailhead. Passes are available from ranger stations and many private vendors, online at website: www.wta.org, or by calling 800/270-7504.

Maps: For a map of the Glacier Peak Wilderness, contact the Outdoor Recreation Information Center, Seattle REI, 222 Yale Avenue North, Seattle, WA 98109; 206/470-4060. Green Trails, Inc.'s excellent topographic map of the region is available for $3.99 at outdoor retail outlets; ask for map number 112, Glacier Peak. Ask the USGS for a topographic map of the Glacier Peak area.

Directions: From Seattle drive 40 miles north on I-5 to Exit 208/Silvana/Arlington. Drive about 32 miles east on Highway 530 to Darrington. From Darrington drive seven miles north on Highway 530 to Suiattle River Road/Forest Service Road 26. Turn right (east) and drive 22.5 miles to the end of the road. To reach the trailhead, hike the Suiattle River Trail 12.2 miles to the Pacific Crest Trail, and 1.2 miles to the Upper Suiattle Trail, or hike the Suiattle River Trail 0.8 mile to the Milk Creek Trail, and 14 miles to the Upper Suiattle Trail.

Contact: Mount Baker-Snoqualmie National Forest, Darrington Ranger District, 1405 Emmens Street, Darrington, WA 98241; 360/436-1155.

🗋 Goat Flat/Three Fingers
12.4 mi/8.0 hrs 🥾 🎒

The rugged, often frustrating path leads to some of the more scenic North Cascade high areas outside North Cascades National Park or the Mount Baker Wilderness. Heavy trail use and gully-washing weather in the spring and fall have left the path extremely rutted and filled with roots. If you can overcome those obstacles, you are rewarded richly.

The trail, very popular in the summer, begins at Tupso Pass and leads mostly through forest to Saddle Lake (2.5 miles), where campsites and a shelter await. From here you can climb the ridge to Meadow Mountain (see hike in this chapter) or continue 2.3 miles to Goat Flats. (A side trail a half mile from the Meadow Mountain Trail junction leads to campsites at the far side of Saddle Lake. Stay left to continue to Three Fingers and Goat Flats.) In midsummer, the wildflowers and alpine views at Goat Flats are excellent. Bring a big lunch and spend some time here. If you continue on to Tin Pan Gap (6.2 miles) high on the mountain, you have come as close to the Three Fingers Glacier as most people ever get. You can scan its 6,854-foot summit for the how-did-they-get-that-there lookout platform—it was built in the 1930s by blasting away the top of the mountain. The tricky, dangerous, and occasionally deadly route to the lookout from here is not for novices.

Location: Northeast of Granite Falls in the Boulder River Wilderness; see Northern Cascades Map 1, grid g3.

User Groups: Hikers and dogs. No horses or mountain bikes are allowed. No wheelchair facilities.

Permits: A federal Northwest Forest Pass, $5 per day or $30 annually, is required to park at the trailhead. Passes are available from ranger stations and many private vendors, online at website: www.wta.org, or by calling 800/270-7504.

Maps: For a map of Mount Baker-Snoqualmie National Forest, contact the Outdoor Recreation Information Center, Seattle REI,

222 Yale Avenue North, Seattle, WA 98109; 206/470-4060. Green Trails, Inc.'s excellent topographic map of the region is available for $3.99 at outdoor retail outlets; ask for map numbers 109 and 110, Granite Falls and Silverton. Ask the USGS for a topographic map of the Meadow Mountain area.

Directions: From Seattle drive 28 miles north on I-5 to Exit 194/City Center/Stevens Pass. Drive six miles east on Highway 2 to the Highway 9 exit near Snohomish. Follow Highway 9 north to Highway 92. Turn right and follow Highway 92 eight miles east to Granite Falls. At the end of town, turn left (north) on Mountain Loop Highway. Drive three miles and turn left (north) on Tupso Pass Road/Forest Service Road 41. Continue for 18 miles to the trailhead at the road's end.

Contact: Mount Baker-Snoqualmie National Forest, Darrington Ranger District, 1405 Emmens Street, Darrington, WA 98241; 360/436-1155.

61 Mount Pilchuck Lookout
6.0 mi/5.0 hrs

This is one of the most popular—and most underestimated—routes in the Puget Sound region. A year never goes by without headlines proclaiming "Hikers lost on Mount Pilchuck." Just why this trail, which is fairly well marked in most places, snares so many unsuspecting hikers is a mystery. But bad weather (fog) has something to do with it. So does the very nature of the hiker attracted to the high-mountain lookout. Many novices come without even one or two of the 10 essentials, get separated from their party and its trail veteran, detour down one of many shortcuts (such as a cleared grade for an abandoned ski area), and wind up spending one or more nights on the mountain, making themselves vulnerable to deadly hypothermia. Or worse, they tumble off a cliff, only to be found days later. We hate to sound preachy, but this happens so often it's almost beyond belief. Portions of the trail were significantly rebuilt during the summer of 1998, but the weather patterns won't change. Consider yourself forewarned. The hike itself is pleasant, climbing swiftly, first through forest and then open boulder fields, to the lookout at 5,300 feet—an elevation gain of about 2,200 feet. The views of the entire Puget Sound basin are outstanding, and so is the wind. Don't ever embark on this hike without carrying warm clothes in a daypack.

Location: Off Mountain Loop Highway east of Granite Falls, in the South Fork Stillaguamish River drainage; see Northern Cascades Map 1, grid h2.

User Groups: Hikers and dogs. No horses or mountain bikes are allowed. No wheelchair facilities.

Permits: A federal Northwest Forest Pass, $5 per day or $30 annually, is required to park at the trailhead. Passes are available from ranger stations and many private vendors, online at website: www.wta.org, or by calling 800/270-7504.

Maps: For a map of Mount Baker-Snoqualmie National Forest, contact the Outdoor Recreation Information Center, Seattle REI, 222 Yale Avenue North, Seattle, WA 98109; 206/470-4060. Green Trails, Inc.'s excellent topographic map of the region is available for $3.99 at outdoor retail outlets; ask for map number 109, Granite Falls. Ask the USGS for a topographic map of the Verlot area.

Directions: From Seattle drive 28 miles north on I-5 to Exit 194/City Center/Stevens Pass. Drive six miles east on Highway 2 to the Highway 9 exit near Snohomish. Follow Highway 9 north to Highway 92. Turn right and follow Highway 92 eight miles east to Granite Falls. At the end of town, turn left (north) on Mountain Loop Highway. Drive 13 miles (about one mile past the Verlot Public Service Center)

and turn right (south) on Mount Pilchuck Road/Forest Service Road 42. Drive seven miles to the parking lot at the end of the road.
Contact: Mount Baker-Snoqualmie National Forest, Darrington Ranger District, 1405 Emmens Street, Darrington, WA 98241; 360/436-1155.

62 Heather Lake
3.8 mi/2.0 hrs

Set in a cirque on Mount Pilchuck's north face, this pretty alpine lake is the source for Heather Creek, a tributary of the wild South Fork Stillaguamish, one of Washington's most scenic rivers. The heavily used Heather Lake Trail is accessible nearly all year, even drawing fans with ice skates—and, increasingly, snowshoes—in the winter. The trail, an old road at first, climbs steadily, gaining 1,100 feet in two miles. You pass through a lovely second-growth forest and then, about halfway up, enter a truly stunning old-growth stand of Douglas fir, hemlock, and massive western red cedar. The lake is heavily visited, and camping there isn't recommended. Make it a day hike, perhaps in combination with the climb to nearby (and slightly more impressive) Lake Twenty-Two (see below).
Location: Off Mountain Loop Highway east of Granite Falls, in the South Fork Stillaguamish River drainage; see Northern Cascades Map 1, grid h2.
User Groups: Hikers and dogs. No horses or mountain bikes are allowed. No wheelchair facilities.
Permits: A federal Northwest Forest Pass, $5 per day or $30 annually, is required to park at the trailhead. Passes are available from ranger stations and many private vendors, online at website: www.wta.org, or by calling 800/270-7504.
Maps: For a map of Mount Baker-Snoqualmie National Forest, contact the Outdoor Recreation Information Center, Seattle REI, 222 Yale Avenue North, Seattle, WA 98109; 206/470-4060. Green Trails, Inc.'s excellent topographic map of the region is available for $3.99 at outdoor retail outlets; ask for map number 109, Granite Falls. Ask the USGS for a topographic map of the Verlot area.
Directions: From Seattle drive 28 miles north on I-5 to Exit 194/City Center/Stevens Pass. Drive six miles east on Highway 2 to the Highway 9 exit near Snohomish. Follow Highway 9 north to Highway 92. Turn right and follow Highway 92 eight miles east to Granite Falls. At the end of town, turn left (north) on Mountain Loop Highway. Drive 13 miles (about one mile past the Verlot Public Service Center) and turn right (south) on Mount Pilchuck Road/Forest Service Road 42. Drive 1.2 miles to the parking lot and trailhead.
Contact: Mount Baker-Snoqualmie National Forest, Darrington Ranger District, 1405 Emmens Street, Darrington, WA 98241; 360/436-1155.

63 Lake Twenty-Two
4.0 mi/3.0 hrs

In the summer, this popular short hike seems like a freeway extension of the Mountain Loop Highway. But off-season, it can be a charming stroll along a frenetic creek, past a half dozen rushing waterfalls, to a peaceful alpine lake below the northeast ridge of Mount Pilchuck. Snow lingers on the far side of the lake almost all summer. The grade is fairly steep, but the atmosphere is truly cathedral-like. The old-growth forest here is magnificent, as it's under the protection of the surrounding Lake Twenty-Two Natural Research Area, set aside in 1947. Bring a lunch, a camera, and in the high summer, bug dope. This is an excellent late-autumn or late-spring walk, when the waterfalls reach their glorious full potential and everyone else is in school or at work. Every Puget Sound–area hiker does it every once in a while. Note: No overnight camping is allowed at the lake.

Location: East of Granite Falls in the South Fork Stillaguamish River drainage; see Northern Cascades Map 1, grid h2.

User Groups: Hikers and leashed dogs. No horses or mountain bikes are allowed. No wheelchair facilities.

Permits: A federal Northwest Forest Pass, $5 per day or $30 annually, is required to park at the trailhead. Passes are available from ranger stations and many private vendors, online at website: www.wta.org, or by calling 800/270-7504.

Maps: For a map of Mount Baker-Snoqualmie National Forest, contact the Outdoor Recreation Information Center, Seattle REI, 222 Yale Avenue North, Seattle, WA 98109; 206/470-4060. Green Trails, Inc.'s excellent topographic map of the region is available for $3.99 at outdoor retail outlets; ask for map number 109, Granite Falls. Ask the USGS for a topographic map of the Verlot area.

Directions: From Seattle drive north on I-5 to Exit 194/City Center/Stevens Pass. Drive six miles east on U.S. 2 to the Highway 9 exit near Snohomish. Follow Highway 9 north to U.S. 92. Turn right and follow U.S. 92 eight miles east to Granite Falls. At the end of town, turn left (north) on the Mountain Loop Highway. Drive 14 miles (about two miles beyond the Verlot Public Service Center), turn right, and continue to the parking area and trailhead.

Contact: Mount Baker-Snoqualmie National Forest, Darrington Ranger District, 1405 Emmens Street, Darrington, WA 98241; 360/436-1155.

64 Bald Mountain
21.4 mi/1.0–2.0 days

Managed by the Washington Department of Natural Resources, this seldom-used trail is a good, one-way, close-to-Seattle walk for solitude seekers. It skirts Ashland Lakes before climbing over Bald Ridge, where views of Three Fingers, Pilchuck, and Whitehorse Mountains begin at about three miles. Farther on, views of the entire Puget Sound lowland region unfold. From here the trail stays primarily high, crossing some meadows (many of which, in season, are filled with ripe huckleberries) before dropping into a pleasant, cool forest in the Sultan Basin. A side trail leads to Cutthroat Lakes and some campsites. It's best to stop here for lunch or for the night and return the way you came. But for a one-way trip, continue east and have a friend meet you at the east trailhead in the Sultan watershed off Williamson Creek Road.

Location: Between the South Fork Stillaguamish River drainage and Sultan Basin, Northern Cascades Map 1, grid h3.

User Groups: Hikers, dogs, and horses. No mountain bikes are allowed. No wheelchair facilities.

Permits: No permits are required. Parking and access are free.

Maps: For a map of Mount Baker-Snoqualmie National Forest, contact the Outdoor Recreation Information Center, Seattle REI, 222 Yale Avenue North, Seattle, WA 98109; 206/470-4060. Green Trails, Inc.'s excellent topographic map of the region is available for $3.99 at outdoor retail outlets; ask for map number 110, Silverton. Ask the USGS for a topographic map of the Silverton area.

Directions: From Seattle drive north on I-5 to Exit 194/City Center/Stevens Pass. Drive six miles east on U.S. 2 to the Highway 9 exit near Snohomish. Follow Highway 9 north to

U.S. 92. Turn right and follow U.S. 92 eight miles east to Granite Falls. At the end of ton, tun left (north) on the Mountain Loop Highway. Drive to the Verlot Public Service Center and another 4.5 miles to Schweitzer Creek Road/Forest Service Road 4020. Turn right and travel 2.3 miles to Bear Lake Road/Forest Service Road 4021. Turn right and drive 1.5 miles to a junction with Forest Service Road 4021-016. Turn left and follow the road for a short distance to the Department of Natural Resources parking lot at its end. Walk about one mile on the abandoned road to the Y; the trailhead is on your left.

Contact: Mount Baker-Snoqualmie National Forest, Darrington Ranger District, 1405 Emmens Street, Darrington, WA 98241; 360/436-1155.

65 Big Four Ice Caves
2.0 mi/1.0 hr

This is one of those hikes where halfway in you don't feel like you're going anywhere in particular. But soon after, you realize you're onto something quite special. The trail starts on a boardwalk through a marshy area, crosses the liquid-glass South Fork Stillaguamish, and then switches back gradually through the forest before opening onto a rocky plain below 6,153-foot Big Four Mountain.

At the base of the stony peak's north face, a permanent snowfield lies exposed in the summer months, with creeks carving massive ice caves from beneath its surface. It's an oddly magnificent site—as if the toe of a massive glacier had been picked up by a Chinook helicopter and deposited here, in seemingly lowland terrain, with no other visible snow or ice. Up closer, the walls of the ice caves are alluring, but venturing into the caves themselves can be—and often is—extremely dangerous. Early in the year, when snow still covers the cave openings,

avalanches are an all-too-common nemesis for hikers who venture too close to the base of Big Four. Ice can collapse from the cave ceilings any time of the year, and avalanches on this mountain face are common in winter. Note: Big Four was supposedly named for a large 4 visible on its face after heavy snows. Frankly, we've never seen it, but we know it must be there.

Location: In Mount Baker-Snoqualmie National Forest, off the Mountain Loop Highway; see Northern Cascades Map 1, grid h4.

User Groups: Hikers and dogs. No horses or mountain bikes are allowed. No wheelchair facilities.

Permits: A federal Northwest Forest Pass, $5 per day or $30 annually, is required to park at the trailhead. Passes are available from ranger stations and many private vendors, online at website: www.wta.org, or by calling 800/270-7504.

Maps: For a map of Mount Baker-Snoqualmie National Forest, contact the Outdoor Recreation Information Center, Seattle REI, 222 Yale Avenue North, Seattle, WA 98109; 206/470-4060. Green Trails, Inc.'s topographic map of the region is available for $3.99 at outdoor retail outlets; ask for map number 110, Silverton. Ask the USGS for a topographic map of the Silverton area.

Directions: From Seattle drive north on I-5 to Exit 194/City Center/Stevens Pass. Drive six miles east on U.S. 2 to the Highway 9 exit near Snohomish. Follow Highway 9 north to U.S. 92. Turn right and follow U.S. 92 eight miles east to Granite Falls. At the end of town, turn left (north) on the Mountain Loop Highway. Drive to the Verlot Public Service Center and another 14.5 miles to the Big Four Picnic Area on the right (south) side of the road.

Contact: Mount Baker-Snoqualmie National Forest, Darrington Ranger District,

1405 Emmens Street, Darrington, WA 98241; 360/436-1155.

66 Mount Forgotten/ Perry Creek
7.8 mi/6.5 hrs

Deep old-growth forest, misty waterfalls, open meadows, and alpine views—this far-western Cascade Mountains trail has it all. The pace is moderate and pleasing for the first two miles to Perry Creek Falls, which has a good lunch spot. In another 1.5 miles, the trail leaves the forest and enters the first of an expansive stretch of meadows. Most people stop here, relax, take a nap, and head back down. But more determined hikers and certainly climbers will want to continue, following the increasingly narrow trail, then just a lot of steep, crumbled rock, to the top of Mount Forgotten (elevation 6,005 feet). Views of surrounding peaks are outstanding here, from the main trail's end or the summit. We always intend to go back up Perry Creek and actually climb Mount Forgotten. But for reasons we can't really explain, it keeps slipping our minds. The total elevation gain is about 3,000 feet to the end of the trail, 1,100 feet to the falls overlook.

Location: Northeast of Granite Falls off the Mountain Loop Highway; see Northern Cascades Map 1, grid h5.

User Groups: Hikers and dogs. No horses or mountain bikes are allowed. No wheelchair facilities.

Permits: A federal Northwest Forest Pass, $5 per day or $30 annually, is required to park at the trailhead. Passes are available from ranger stations and many private vendors, online at website: www.wta.org, or by calling 800/270-7504.

Maps: For a map of Mount Baker-Snoqualmie National Forest, contact the Outdoor Recreation Information Center, Seattle REI, 222

Yale Avenue North, Seattle, WA 98109; 206/470-4060. Green Trails, Inc.'s excellent topographic map of the region is available for $3.99 at outdoor retail outlets; ask for map number 111, Sloan Peak. Ask the USGS for a topographic map of the Bedal area.

Directions: From Seattle drive north on I-5 to Exit 194/City Center/Stevens Pass. Drive six miles east on U.S. 2 to the Highway 9 exit near Snohomish. Follow Highway 9 north to U.S. 92. Turn right and follow U.S. 92 eight miles east to Granite Falls. At the end of town, turn left (north) on the Mountain Loop Highway. Drive 12 miles to the Verlot Public Service Center and another 15.2 miles to Perry Creek Road/Forest Service Road 4063. Turn left (north) and travel one mile to the road's end and the trailhead.

Contact: Mount Baker-Snoqualmie National Forest, Darrington Ranger District, 1405 Emmens Street, Darrington, WA 98241; 360/436-1155.

67 Mount Dickerman
8.6 mi/1.0 day

This very busy and very steep trail off the Mountain Loop Highway leads to a mountaintop escape from just about everything except open meadows, expansive views, and lingering snowfields. And huckleberries. Come fall (especially late September/early October) this is one of the Cascades' most noted producers of the tart little berries. They're thick. They're plump. They're everywhere. While they bloom, the bushes turn crimson in a wonderful autumn blush. Don't forget your camera. It's a tremendous sight. Getting here isn't easy, however; this is one steep trail, and if you're not in top condition, you'll find yourself pausing—often—to rest. Lucky for you, the ripe huckleberries provide the perfect natural excuse. A truly inspiring 360-degree view awaits at the

5,723-foot summit, with unobstructed views of two dozen major North Cascade peaks. Get those boots good and tight for the trip back down. You need all the leverage you can get. The total elevation gain is about 3,700 feet.

Location: In Mount Baker-Snoqualmie National Forest, north of the Mountain Loop Highway; see Northern Cascades Map 1, grid h5.

User Groups: Hikers, dogs, and horses. No mountain bikes are allowed. No wheelchair facilities.

Permits: A federal Northwest Forest Pass, $5 per day or $30 annually, is required to park at the trailhead. Passes are available from ranger stations and many private vendors, online at website: www.wta.org, or by calling 800/270-7504.

Maps: For a map of Mount Baker-Snoqualmie National Forest, contact the Outdoor Recreation Information Center, Seattle REI, 222 Yale Avenue North, Seattle, WA 98109; 206/470-4060. Green Trails, Inc.'s excellent topographic map of the region is available for $3.99 at outdoor retail outlets; ask for map number 111, Sloan Peak. Ask the USGS for a topographic map of the Bedal area.

Directions: From Seattle drive north on I-5 to Exit 194/City Center/Stevens Pass. Drive six miles east on U.S. 2 to the Highway 9 exit near Snohomish. Follow Highway 9 north to U.S. 92. Turn right and follow U.S. 92 eight miles east to Granite Falls. At the end of town, turn left (north) on the Mountain Loop Highway. Drive 12 miles to the Verlot Public Service Center and another 16.7 miles east to the trailhead on the left (north) side of the highway.

Contact: Mount Baker-Snoqualmie National Forest, Darrington Ranger District, 1405 Emmens Street, Darrington, WA 98241; 360/436-1155.

68 Monte Cristo Road

8.6 mi/5.0 hrs

As the name implies, this isn't a trail at all, but an old road to one of the Northwest's fascinating ghost towns. Hence, it draws all sorts of traffic on summer days, with everything from pedestrians to bicyclists to wiener dogs doing their thing on the mostly flat roadbed. This is likely the most popular one-day mountain bike ride in the Northwest—so popular, in fact, that it's become uncomfortable for some hikers. But for mountain bikers, particularly rookies, a day trip on this road can be immensely fun. With the recent addition of a bike-in campground near Monte Cristo, it's a good overnighter, as well.

At the abandoned townsite, trails lead in various directions past the ruins of what once was a thriving mining town. In recent years, proposals have been floated to build a full-fledged resort here. So far, so good—they haven't gotten far. If and when they do, this entry will be revised to suggest that Monte Cristo Road be hiked or biked in one direction only: out. Hikers, take note: at about two miles in on Monte Cristo Road, you see a trailhead for the Weden Creek Trail. It leads three miles into the Henry M. Jackson Wilderness and a truly spectacular destination at Gothic Basin (see hike in this chapter). No bikes are allowed.

Location: East of Granite Falls on the Mountain Loop Highway; see Northern Cascades Map 1, grid h5.

User Groups: Hikers, dogs, horses, and mountain bikes. No wheelchair facilities.

Permits: A federal Northwest Forest Pass, $5 per day or $30 annually, is required to park at the trailhead. Passes are available from ranger stations and many private vendors, online at website: www.wta.org, or by calling 800/270-7504.

Maps: For a map of Mount Baker-Snoqualmie National Forest, contact the Outdoor Recreation Information Center, Seattle REI, 222 Yale Avenue North, Seattle, WA 98109; 206/470-4060. Green Trails, Inc.'s excellent topographic map of the region is available for $3.99 at outdoor retail outlets; ask for map number 111, Sloan Peak. Ask the USGS for topographic maps of the Bedal and Monte Cristo areas.

Directions: From Seattle drive north on I-5 to Exit 194/City Center/Stevens Pass. Drive six miles east on U.S. 2 to the Highway 9 exit near Snohomish. Follow Highway 9 north to U.S. 92. Turn right and follow U.S. 92 eight miles east to Granite Falls. At the end of town, turn left (north) on the Mountain Loop Highway. Drive 12 miles to the Verlot Public Service Center and another 19.5 miles to Barlow Pass. Park on the left side of the highway.

Contact: Mount Baker-Snoqualmie National Forest, Darrington Ranger District, 1405 Emmens Street, Darrington, WA 98241; 360/436-1155.

69 Sunrise Mine
5.2 mi/4.5 hrs

Given the view from the parking lot, you know this hike promises to be spectacular—and rugged. The trail is most often used by climbers headed for encounters with the haggard faces of Del Campo, Morning Star, and Vesper Peaks, all visible from the parking lot. But experienced hikers can share the trail with them fairly comfortably. The trail is rough and ragged in places. You have to ford several streams early on, and as you gain altitude you usually are confronted by more than one snow slide, necessitating a snowfield crossing. Don't do this without an ice ax and the nerve and verve to use one. It might look safe from here; it might not when you're 10 feet out on it.

After you survive those obstacles, it seems the higher you go on this trail, the steeper it gets. The final climb—and we do mean climb—to Headlee Pass (elevation 4,700 feet) is a true calf-burner. The view from here, alas, is perhaps not quite what you expected. But don't complain. The only reason you can't see all the local mountains is that you're sitting on top of them. Pat yourself on the back and get back to the car before it starts getting dark. The total elevation gain to Headlee Pass is about 2,600 feet.

Location: South of the Mountain Loop Highway in Mount Baker-Snoqualmie National Forest; see Northern Cascades Map 1, grid h5.

User Groups: Hikers, dogs, and horses. No mountain bikes are allowed. No wheelchair facilities.

Permits: A federal Northwest Forest Pass, $5 per day or $30 annually, is required to park at the trailhead. Passes are available from ranger stations and many private vendors, online at website: www.wta.org, or by calling 800/270-7504.

Maps: For a map of Mount Baker-Snoqualmie National Forest, contact the Outdoor Recreation Information Center, Seattle REI, 222 Yale Avenue North, Seattle, WA 98109; 206/470-4060. Green Trails, Inc.'s excellent topographic map of the region is available for $3.99 at outdoor retail outlets; ask for map number 111, Sloan Peak. Ask the USGS for topographic maps of the Silverton and Bedal.

Directions: From Seattle drive north on I-5 to Exit 194/City Center/Stevens Pass. Drive six miles east on U.S. 2 to the Highway 9 exit near Snohomish. Follow Highway 9 north to U.S. 92. Turn right and follow U.S. 92 eight miles east to Granite Falls. At the end of town, turn left (north) on the Mountain Loop Highway. Drive 12 miles to the Verlot Public Service Center and another 17.5 miles to Sunrise Mine Road/Forest Service Road

4065. Turn right (south) and drive 2.2 miles to the trailhead in a clearing at the end of the road.

Contact: Mount Baker-Snoqualmie National Forest, Darrington Ranger District, 1405 Emmens Street, Darrington, WA 98241; 360/436-1155.

70 North Fork Sauk Falls
0.5 mi/0.5 hr

The road to the trailhead doesn't look like much. The trailhead doesn't look like much. In fact, we ignored it for years. The truth is, the trail doesn't look like much, either, dribbling down through the usually moist trees. But once there, the falls look like a lot. Too much, in fact, to experience in a few minutes. At the trail's end, 100 feet below the car, the North Fork Sauk River, as clean a stream as you're likely to find anywhere in western Washington, catches major air, splintering into a million droplets, each of which seems to earn unseemly air time on its way to the dark rocks below. It's an easy walk after an easy drive, an excellent place to sit and soak up the mist after a hard day.

Location: Southeast of Darrington, off the Mountain Loop Highway; see Northern Cascades Map 1, grid h6.

User Groups: Hikers, dogs, and horses. No mountain bikes are allowed. No wheelchair facilities.

Permits: A federal Northwest Forest Pass, $5 per day or $30 annually, is required to park at the trailhead. Passes are available from ranger stations and many private vendors, online at website: www.wta.org, or by calling 800/270-7504.

Maps: For a map of Mount Baker-Snoqualmie National Forest, contact the Outdoor Recreation Information Center, Seattle REI, 222 Yale Avenue North, Seattle,

WA 98109; 206/470-4060. Green Trails, Inc.'s excellent topographic map of the region is available for $3.99 at outdoor retail outlets; ask for map number 111, Sloan Peak. Ask the USGS for a topographic map of the Sloan Peak area.

Directions: From Seattle drive 40 miles north on I-5 to Exit 208/Silvana/Arlington. Drive about 32 miles east on Highway 530 to Darrington. From Darrington take the Forest Service Road 20/Mountain Loop Highway 19.7 miles south to Sloan Creek Road/Forest Service Road 49. Turn left (east) and travel one mile to the trailhead on the right.

Contact: Mount Baker-Snoqualmie National Forest, Darrington Ranger District, 1405 Emmens Street, Darrington, WA 98241; 360/436-1155.

71 Three Fools
27.0 mi one way/
5.0 days

Getting to this trail isn't easy. It's usually hiked one way, from the Pacific Crest National Scenic Trail's entrance in Manning Park, British Columbia, southwest to Ross Lake, where exit can be made via water taxi (see hike Big/Little Beaver Loop, this chapter) or by hiking the East Bank Trail south to a pickup point at the Panther Creek Trailhead on Highway 20. Another popular route is driving to Hart's Pass in Okanogan National Forest, hiking about 29 miles north on the Pacific Crest Trail to Castle Pass, and then 23 miles west to Ross Lake.

The good news is that the trail's remote nature thins out the crowds. The country is wild, and solitude is more easily obtainable than on perhaps any trail in this North Cascades portion. For most of the journey west, you stay high, with excellent views. Adequate, but by no means sprawling, campsites are located at approximate five-mile intervals along the route, but water is scarce in midsummer. Plan water stops carefully and be prepared for much up-and-down terrain. Somehow, the scenery keeps you going.

Location: Northeast of Ross Lake in the Pasayten Wilderness; see Northern Cascades Map 2, grid a1.

User Groups: Hikers, dogs, and horses. No mountain bikes are allowed. No wheelchair facilities.

Permits: A federal Northwest Forest Pass, $5 per day or $30 annually, is required to park at the trailhead. Passes are available from ranger stations and many private vendors, online at website: www.wta.org, or by calling 800/270-7504.

Maps: For a map of the Pasayten Wilderness and Okanogan National Forest, contact the Outdoor Recreation Information Center, Seattle REI, 222 Yale Avenue North, Seattle, WA 98109; 206/470-4060. Green Trails, Inc.'s excellent topographic map of the region is available for $3.99 at outdoor retail outlets; ask for map number 17, Jack Mountain. Ask the USGS for topographic maps of the Hozomeen Mountain, Skagit Peak, and Castle Peak areas.

Directions: From Manning Park, British Columbia, hike the Pacific Crest Trail four miles south to Castle Pass, where the Three Fools Trail starts to the right (west).

Contact: North Cascades National Park/Mount Baker Ranger District Information Center, 2105 Highway 20, Sedro-Woolley, WA 98284; 360/856-5700.

72 Coleman Ridge
35.4 mi/12.7 hrs

The first five miles of this hike are on the Andrews Creek Trail (see hike in this chapter), and although the river valley is pretty enough, the best of this trip doesn't begin until you start climbing the ridge route. Ascending the Ram Creek Valley, the trail leaves the noisy stream and traverses over to Meadow Lake, which, true to its name, is surrounded by lush heather and wildflower meadows. From the lake, the trail climbs to the turnaround point on a ridgetop with endless views of the Pasayten Wilderness, the Canadian Cascades, and east to Colville National Forest. Closer in, the views sweep across the Andrews and Chewuch Valleys, a pair of deep green grooves cut into the rugged landscape below. You can camp anywhere along the creek, but the best sites are at Meadow Lake.

Location: North of Winthrop in Okanogan National Forest; see Northern Cascades Map 2, grid b8.

User Groups: Hikers, dogs, and horses. No mountain bikes are allowed. No wheelchair facilities.

Permits: A federal Northwest Forest Pass, $5 per day or $30 annually, is required to park at the trailhead. Passes are available from ranger stations and many private vendors, online at website: www.wta.org, or by calling 800/270-7504.

Maps: For a trail information report, contact the Methow Valley Ranger District at 509/997-2131. For a map of Okanogan National Forest, contact the Outdoor Recreation Information Center, Seattle REI, 222 Yale Avenue North, Seattle, WA 98109; 206/470-4060. Ask the USGS for a topographic map of the Coleman Peak, Mount Barney, and Bauerman Ridge areas.

Directions: From Winthrop, drive 23 miles north on West Chewuch Road/Forest Service Road 51 to the trailhead at the end of the paved road. Hike five miles up the Andrews Creek Trail to the junction with the Coleman Ridge Trail.

Contact: Okanogan National Forest, Methow Valley Ranger District, 502 Glover Street, P.O. Box 188, Twisp, WA 98856; 509/997-2131.

Or contact Visitor Information Center, Building 49, Highway 20, Winthrop, WA 98862; 509/996-4000.

Contact: Okanogan National Forest, Tonasket Ranger District, 1 West Winesap Street, Tonasket, WA 98855; 509/486-2186.

73 Four Point
3.0 mi/1.5 hrs

You get no panoramic views on the Four Point Trail, but the diverse forest ecosystem and huge herds of mule deer offer plenty of visual stimulation to keep hikers happy. Autumn hikes here are particularly beautiful; the huge, evergreen Douglas firs and pines stand in lovely contrast with the golden aspens and larch. The trail ends on a small knoll overlooking the Pasayten Wilderness.

Location: North of Loomis in Okanogan National Forest; see Northern Cascades Map 2, grid a8.

User Groups: Hikers, dogs, and horses. No mountain bikes are allowed. No wheelchair facilities.

Permits: A federal Northwest Forest Pass, $5 per day or $30 annually, is required to park at the trailhead. Passes are available from ranger stations and many private vendors, online at website: www.wta.org, or by calling 800/270-7504.

Maps: For a trail information report, contact the Tonasket Ranger District at 509/486-2186. For a map of Okanogan National Forest, contact the Outdoor Recreation Information Center, Seattle REI, 222 Yale Avenue North, Seattle, WA 98109; 206/470-4060. Ask the USGS for topographic maps of the Corral Butte and Horseshoe Basin areas.

Directions: From Loomis drive two miles north on Sinlahekin Valley Road/County Road 9425 and turn left (west) onto Toats Coulee Road/Forest Service Road 39. Continue west on Toats Coulee Road for 16 miles to the marked trailhead on the right.

74 Clutch Creek
7.6 mi/3.8 hrs

Wildflower-filled meadows and a relatively new, clear path make the Clutch Creek Trail a beautiful summertime hike. But wildflowers of equal beauty bloom throughout the Pacific Northwest. The best time to appreciate this trail is in autumn, when the rare groves of aspen explode into color. Intermittent stands of larch—known locally as tamarack and common to many eastern Washington valleys—also blaze brightly here. In fact, this is as good as it gets when it comes to fall colors in the Pacific Northwest.

Location: North of Loomis in Okanogan National Forest; see Northern Cascades Map 2, grid a8.

User Groups: Hikers, dogs, and horses. No mountain bikes are allowed. No wheelchair facilities.

Permits: A federal Northwest Forest Pass, $5 per day or $30 annually, is required to park at the trailhead. Passes are available from ranger stations and many private vendors, online at website: www.wta.org, or by calling 800/270-7504.

Maps: For a trail information report, contact the Tonasket Ranger District at 509/486-2186. For a detailed map of Okanogan National Forest, contact the Outdoor Recreation Information Center, Seattle REI, 222 Yale Avenue North, Seattle, WA 98109; 206/470-4060. Ask the USGS for topographic maps of the Hurley Peak and Horseshoe Basin areas.

Directions: From Loomis drive approximately two miles north on Sinlahekin Valley Road/County Road 9425 and then turn left (west) onto Toats Coulee Road/Forest

Service Road 39. Continue west on Toats Coulee Road for 14 miles until you arrive at the Forest Service Road 39–500 junction. Turn right onto Forest Service Road 39–500 and drive to the road's end and the Iron Gate Trailhead. Hike about one mile up the Boundary Trail to reach the Clutch Creek Trail, which leads off to the left (west).

Contact: Okanogan National Forest, Tonasket Ranger District, 1 West Winesap Street, Tonasket, WA 98855; 509/486-2186.

75 Cathedral Driveway
4.0 mi/2.0 hrs

Leading to both the Windy Creek and Chewuch Valley Trails, this connector lets you customize a hike. The two-mile trail, which forms the stem of this Y-shaped trail network, also makes a pleasant, though rather tough, day hike. It starts out with gentle, rolling hills, but after crossing the Windy Creek Trail at one-half mile, it climbs steeply through a saddle in a ridge separating the two river valleys and then drops just as steeply into the Chewuch Valley. Views from the saddle are mediocre at best—for better views, scramble up the rocky sides of either unnamed high points flanking the saddle. Wildlife views are more readily attained, as this trail hits virtually all the likely wildlife hangouts. Look for deer grazing in the valley bottoms, on the saddle, and spots in between.

Location: North of Loomis in Okanogan National Forest, within the Pasayten Wilderness; see Northern Cascades Map 2, grid a8.

User Groups: Hikers, dogs, and horses. No mountain bikes are allowed. No wheelchair facilities.

Permits: A federal Northwest Forest Pass, $5 per day or $30 annually, is required to park at the trailhead. Passes are available from ranger stations and many private vendors,

online at website: www.wta.org, or by calling 800/270-7504.

Maps: For a trail information report, contact the Tonasket Ranger District at 509/486-2186. For a map of Okanogan National Forest, contact the Outdoor Recreation Information Center, Seattle REI, 222 Yale Avenue North, Seattle, WA 98109; 206/470-4060. Ask the USGS for topographic maps of the Corral Butte and Coleman Peak areas.

Directions: From Loomis drive approximately two miles north on Sinlahekin Valley Road/County Road 9425 and turn left (west) onto Toats Coulee Road/Forest Service Road 39. Continue west on Toats Coulee Road for 21 miles until you reach Long Swamp Campground. From the camp, continue driving on rough, gravel Forest Service Road 300 for three miles to the trailhead.

Contact: Okanogan National Forest, Tonasket Ranger District, 1 West Winesap Street, Tonasket, WA 98855; 509/486-2186.

76 Basin Creek
18.0 mi/1.0–2.0 days

Basin Creek empties into the Chewuch River, and the Basin Creek Trail branches off from the Chewuch River Trail. As a secondary trail, Basin Creek sees much less traffic and therefore offers more solitude. It also offers more scenery, both near and far, than many other area trails, and it is the only one that gives hikers a view of Horseshoe Basin from the Methow River side.

Climbing through second-growth lodgepole pine stands, you may think that the forest seems unremarkable, unless you visit in autumn, when the many tall, golden larch trees stand out from their evergreen brethren. The branches of those great trees also house several mated pairs of great horned owls, plus red-tailed hawks and at least one golden eagle. The trail tops out on a high ridge with great views of the surrounding peaks, particularly Topaz Mountain. Adventurers will find limitless possibilities for scrambling and bushwhacking excursions off trail.

Location: East of Winthrop in Okanogan National Forest, within the Pasayten Wilderness; see Northern Cascades Map 2, grid a8.

User Groups: Hikers, dogs, and horses. No mountain bikes are allowed. No wheelchair facilities.

Permits: A federal Northwest Forest Pass, $5 per day or $30 annually, is required to park at the trailhead. Passes are available from ranger stations and many private vendors, online at website: www.wta.org, or by calling 800/270-7504.

Maps: For a trail information report, contact the Methow Valley Ranger District at 509/997-2131. For a map of Okanogan National Forest, contact the Outdoor Recreation Information Center, Seattle REI, 222 Yale Avenue North, Seattle, WA 98109; 206/470-4060. Ask the USGS for topographic maps of the Coleman Peak, Mount Barney, and Remmel Mountain areas.

Directions: From Winthrop drive 29 miles north on West Chewuch Road/Forest Service Road 51 to the Chewuch trailhead. Hike the Chewuch Valley Trail 3.5 miles to the junction with Basin Creek.

Contact: Okanogan National Forest, Methow Valley Ranger District, 502 Glover Street, P.O. Box 188, Twisp, WA 98856; 509/997-2131. Or contact Visitor Information Center, Building 49, Highway 20, Winthrop, WA 98862; 509/996-4000.

77 West Fork Pasayten
31.0 mi/2.0–3.0 days

An unusual trail, this route begins in open wildflower meadows and leads into thick old-growth forest. The route drops under the west slope of Haystack Mountain and then into the West Fork Valley but doesn't reach the river for more than three miles. It then crosses the water via a footlog and hugs the west bank for the next dozen miles. Campsites are numerous, and so are the fishing opportunities. The best long-distance views are found along the first two miles, before you drop into the valley. Once in the valley, the scenery is limited to forest, river, and wildlife. Still, that's nothing to complain about, for the forest is thick and lush, the river spectacular, and the wildlife abundant. Your hike terminates at the river junction of the West Fork Pasayten and Soda Creek. Campsites are scattered every few miles along the riverbank.

Location: West of Winthrop in Okanogan National Forest, within the Pasayten Wilderness; see Northern Cascades Map 2, grid c3.

User Groups: Hikers, dogs, and horses. No mountain bikes are allowed. No wheelchair facilities.

Permits: A federal Northwest Forest Pass, $5 per day or $30 annually, is required to park at the trailhead. Passes are available from ranger stations and many private vendors, online at website: www.wta.org, or by calling 800/270-7504.

Maps: For a trail information report, contact the Methow Valley Ranger District at 509/997-2131. For a map of Okanogan National Forest, contact the Outdoor Recreation Information Center, Seattle REI, 222 Yale Avenue North, Seattle, WA 98109; 206/470-4060. Ask the USGS for topographic maps of the Slate Peak, Pasayten Peak, and Frosty Creek areas.

Directions: From Winthrop drive west on Highway 20 to Mazama and turn north on the Mazama Cutoff Road. Cross the river and turn left (west) onto Hart's Pass Road/County Road 1163. Continue 18.5 miles to Hart's Pass. Turn right onto Slate Peak Road/Forest Service Road

5400-600 and continue to the gate. Park here (but please not in front of the gate) and hike 100 yards up the gated road to the trailhead.

Contact: Okanogan National Forest, Methow Valley Ranger District, 502 Glover Street, P.O. Box 188, Twisp, WA 98856; 509/997-2131. Or contact Visitor Information Center, Building 49, Highway 20, Winthrop, WA 98862; 509/996-4000.

78 Azurite/Cady Pass Loop
24.7 mi/2.0–3.0 days

As you hike south for 10 miles on the Pacific Crest Trail, you have some great views of the surrounding craggy summits, including Slate Peak and Mount Ballard. At the junction with the Mill Creek Trail, you leave the PCT behind, but not the stunning vistas. Climbing to the west, this trail crosses the crest of the Cascades via Azurite Pass and drops into the lovely Mill Creek Valley. Follow the beautiful little raging stream west for several miles; then (just about when you start yearning for more high country) turn north onto the Cady Pass Trail and climb through a long series of relentlessly steep switchbacks to the high pass. More breathtaking panoramas await at the pass, just below the Cady Point summit. From here, drop down through more switchbacks and begin a long, descending traverse to the South Fork of Slate Creek, which the route parallels for the last two miles back to Slate Creek Road and the second trailhead.

Using a shuttle car makes hiking this loop easier, but if you can't shuttle a vehicle to the second trailhead, simply close the loop by walking the five miles up the road to the first trailhead (this walk is fast and easy, adding about two hours to the trip time).

Location: West of Winthrop in Okanogan National Forest, within the Pasayten Wilderness; see Northern Cascades Map 2, grid c3.

User Groups: Hikers, dogs, and horses. No mountain bikes are allowed. No wheelchair facilities.

Permits: A federal Northwest Forest Pass, $5 per day or $30 annually, is required to park at the trailhead. Passes are available from ranger stations and many private vendors, online at website: www.wta.org, or by calling 800/270-7504.

Maps: For a trail information report, contact the Winthrop Ranger District at 509/997-2131. For a map of Okanogan National Forest, contact the Outdoor Recreation Information Center, Seattle REI, 222 Yale Avenue North, Seattle, WA 98109; 206/470-4060. Ask the USGS for topographic maps of the Slate Peak, Pasayten Peak, and Frosty Creek areas.

Directions: From Winthrop drive west on Highway 20 to Mazama and turn north on the Mazama Cutoff Road. Cross the river and turn left (west) onto Hart's Pass Road/County Road 1163. Continue 18.5 miles to Hart's Pass and the trailhead. To reach the eastern trailhead at Cady Pass, continue past the first trailhead for 5.5 miles east; along the way, Hart's Pass Road becomes Slate Creek Road/Forest Service Road 374.

Contact: Okanogan National Forest, Methow Valley Ranger District, 502 Glover Street, P.O. Box 188, Twisp, WA 98856; 509/997-2131. Or contact Visitor Information Center, Building 49, Highway 20, Winthrop, WA 98862; 509/996-4000.

79 Jackita Ridge
30.4 mi/2.0–3.0 days

From the trailhead, cross Granite Creek via a footbridge; then turn left at the first fork and right at the second. Make sure you're ready for a workout before tackling the rest of this trail, though. A quick rundown of some of the geographic features you encounter will give you an idea of what's in store: The trail slices through Devil's Park, contours around the top of Hell Basin, and tops out on the Devil's Pass summit. But if you are in shape and willing to work, the beauty of the landscape makes this hike well worth the effort.

After ascending the steep ridge face, the trail evens out to a gradual climb along the ridge crest, largely above timberline. From the trail you enjoy breathtaking views of the surrounding peaks. The ridge is lined with beautiful wildflowers, but the broad, open meadows of Devil's and McMillan Parks are simply awash with startlingly vivid colors when wildflowers of every color explode in bloom. Backpackers find good campsites at the North Fork Dry Creek headwaters; cross this stream just two miles before the trail's end at Devil's Pass. Other campsites are located just below Devil's Peak, where the trail crosses Nichols Creek, and about eight miles into the trail where the route crosses several small spring creeks on the flank of Jackita Ridge.

Location: West of Winthrop in Okanogan National Forest; see Northern Cascades Map 2, grid c1.

User Groups: Hikers, dogs, and horses. No mountain bikes are allowed. No wheelchair facilities.

Permits: A federal Northwest Forest Pass, $5 per day or $30 annually, is required to park at the trailhead. Passes are available from ranger stations and many private vendors, online at website: www.wta.org, or by calling 800/270-7504.

Maps: For a trail information report, contact the Winthrop Ranger District at 509/997-2131. For a map of Okanogan National Forest, contact the Outdoor Recreation Information Center, Seattle REI, 222 Yale Avenue North,

Seattle, WA 98109; 206/470-4060. Ask the USGS for a topographic map of the Crater Mountain, Azurite Peak, and Shull Mountain areas.

Directions: From Winthrop drive 55 miles west on Highway 20, across Washington and Rainy Passes, to the Canyon Creek Trailhead in a well-marked parking area on the north side of the highway.

Contact: Okanogan National Forest, Methow Valley Ranger District, 502 Glover Street, P.O. Box 188, Twisp, WA 98856; 509/997-2131. Or contact Visitor Information Center, Building 49, Highway 20, Winthrop, WA 98862; 509/996-4000.

80 Chancellor
31.8 mi/2.0–3.0 days

This trail lies outside the Pasayten Wilderness, but just barely. It follows the south bank of Canyon Creek, while the wilderness boundary traces the north bank. That means you garner all the benefits of wilderness hiking without the drawback of big crowds. The hike begins in a heavily forested river bottom and leads past Rowley's Chasm. This 200-foot-deep hole gouged from solid rock lies 1.5 miles down a side trail, but it's worth considering making the detour, as the sight is truly awe-inspiring. Back on the main trail, the route crosses the creek, leaves the valley bottom at approximately six miles, climbs to ridge tops, and eventually leads to the Center Mountain flanks and great views of the Pasayten peaks. A bonus is the healthy fishery in Canyon Creek, where anglers can try for 12- to 14-inch rainbow, brown, and bull trout.

Location: West of Winthrop in Okanogan National Forest; see Northern Cascades Map 2, grid c1.

User Groups: Hikers, dogs, and horses. No mountain bikes are allowed. No wheelchair facilities.

Permits: A federal Northwest Forest Pass, $5 per day or $30 annually, is required to park at the trailhead. Passes are available from ranger stations and many private vendors, online at website: www.wta.org, or by calling 800/270-7504.

Maps: For a trail information report, contact the Methow Valley Ranger District at 509/997-2131. For a map of Okanogan National Forest, contact the Outdoor Recreation Information Center, Seattle REI, 222 Yale Avenue North, Seattle, WA 98109; 206/470-4060. Ask the USGS for topographic maps of the Crater Mountain, Azurite Peak, and Shull Mountain areas.

Directions: From Winthrop drive 55 miles west on Highway 20, across Washington and Rainy Passes, to the Canyon Creek Trailhead in a well-marked parking area on the north side of the highway.

Contact: Okanogan National Forest, Methow Valley Ranger District, 502 Glover Street, P.O. Box 188, Twisp, WA 98856; 509/997-2131. Or contact Visitor Information Center, Building 49, Highway 20, Winthrop, WA 98862; 509/996-4000.

81 Mill Creek to Azurite Pass
28.4 mi/3.0–4.0 days

Want to get out by yourself? This is your trail. Be careful, however, or you might get a little too much solitude for comfort. The Mill Creek Trail, which runs almost due south from the Canyon Creek Trail to the Pacific Crest Trail, is a rough, rugged, scarcely maintained path made worse by a 1987 forest fire. Make sure you're comfortable with navigating before you set out. For the experienced hiker, however, the trail is immensely scenic. It follows an old miners' route to Azurite Pass (elevation 6,200 feet) near Azurite Mine, which cranked out gold nuggets just before the turn of the century.

From the pass, it's 1.7 miles to the PCT, and 3.7 miles to a junction with the West Fork Methow Trail (see hike in this chapter), a possible exit route.

Location: In North Cascades National Park; see Northern Cascades Map 2, grid c1.

User Groups: Hikers, dogs, and horses. No mountain bikes are allowed. No wheelchair facilities.

Permits: No permits are required. Parking and access are free.

Maps: For a map of North Cascades National Park and Ross Lake National Recreation Area or the adjoining Okanogan National Forest, contact the Outdoor Recreation Information Center, Seattle REI, 222 Yale Avenue North, Seattle, WA 98109; 206/470-4060. Green Trails, Inc.'s excellent topographic maps of the region are available for $3.99 each at outdoor retail outlets; ask for map numbers 49 and 50, Mount Logan and Washington Pass. Ask the USGS for topographic maps of the Shull Mountain, Azurite Peak, and Slate Peak areas.

Directions: From I-5 north of Mount Vernon, take Exit 230/Anacortes/Burlington. Drive east on Highway 20/North Cascades Highway/North Cascades Highway about 72 miles to Colonial Creek Campground and another 11 miles to the Canyon Creek Trailhead/Trail 754 on the left. Walk over the Granite Creek Bridge and turn right, hiking the Canyon Creek Trail 5.9 miles to its junction with the Mill Creek Trail.

Contact: North Cascades National Park/Mount Baker Ranger District Information Center, 2105 Highway 20, Sedro-Woolley, WA 98284; 360/856-5700.

82 Robinson Pass
55.2 mi/5.0 days

Though long, this is essentially a valley hike. Make that a two-valley hike through old-growth pine and fir forests, with a short climb over a low pass in the middle. The first eight miles cut through the Robinson Creek Valley. Scattered along the valley bottom are the remains of a series of cabins and lean-tos erected up to a century ago by William "Billy" Robinson, the trapper for whom the valley was named. These cabins are largely in ruins, with just a few walls and collapsed roofs testifying to the existence of the trapper, but the river still bears the marks of his work. Beavers, which once thrived in the valley until trappers reduced their numbers, have started to make a strong recovery, and several of their dams can be found in the creek's side channels.

Some good campsites line the valley bottom. At the head of the valley, the trail climbs through low, narrow Robinson Pass and drops into Middle Fork Valley. Following the Middle Fork Creek downstream (north), the trail leads to Soda Creek. After descending to the Middle Fork Creek, you find no shortage of beautiful riverside campsites. The abundance of sites, in fact, makes choosing one difficult. The best bet is to hike as usual each day and then start looking for a good site about an hour before you stop for the night. Views throughout the trail's length are mostly limited to the beautiful old forests, with an occasional glimpse up the steep avalanche-prone chutes on the valley walls. In the autumn, these chutes are ablaze with brilliant hues as the leaves of slide alder and vine maple trees turn vibrant red and orange.

Location: West of Winthrop in Okanogan National Forest, within the Pasayten Wilderness; see Northern Cascades Map 2, grid c4.

User Groups: Hikers, dogs, and horses. No mountain bikes are allowed. No wheelchair facilities.

Permits: A federal Northwest Forest Pass, $5 per day or $30 annually, is required to park at the trailhead. Passes are available from ranger stations and many private vendors, online at website: www.wta.org, or by calling 800/270-7504.

Maps: For a trail information report, contact the Methow Valley Ranger District at 509/997-2131. For a map of Okanogan National Forest, contact the Outdoor Recreation Information Center, Seattle REI, 222 Yale Avenue North, Seattle, WA 98109; 206/470-4060. Ask the USGS for topographic maps of the Robinson Mountain, Slate Peak, Pasayten Peak, and Mount Lago areas.

Directions: From Winthrop drive west on Highway 20 to Mazama and turn north on the Mazama Cutoff Road. Cross the river and turn left (west) onto Hart's Pass Road/County Road 1163. Continue nine miles to the Robinson Trailhead on the right, at a hairpin turn.

Contact: Okanogan National Forest, Methow Valley Ranger District, 502 Glover Street, P.O. Box 188, Twisp, WA 98856; 509/997-2131. Or contact Visitor Information Center, Building 49, Highway 20, Winthrop, WA 98862; 509/996-4000.

83 Burch Mountain
9.4 mi/4.7 hrs

Old-growth pine forest, cold mountain streams, and lonely peaks with picturesque views sum up this trail's offerings. Hikers start out in the cool, shadowy world of old-growth trees. Spring creeks cross the trail in places before the route climbs into open meadows farther up the ridge. These sunny, hot meadows filled with wildflowers attract plentiful wildlife in the cool morning and evening hours, and more than enough bugs at midday. Climbing through the meadows, the trail switches around the flanks of Burch Mountain as it slowly climbs to the 7,700-foot summit. From the top enjoy views of Canada, the North Cascades, the Columbia River Basin, and beyond.

Location: North of Winthrop in Okanogan National Forest; see Northern Cascades Map 2, grid b6.

User Groups: Hikers and dogs. No horses or mountain bikes are allowed. No wheelchair facilities.

Permits: A federal Northwest Forest Pass, $5 per day or $30 annually, is required to park at the trailhead. Passes are available from ranger stations and many private vendors, online at website: www.wta.org, or by calling 800/270-7504.

Maps: For a trail information report, contact the Methow Valley Ranger District at 509/997-2131. For a map of Okanogan National Forest, contact the Outdoor Recreation Information Center, Seattle REI, 222 Yale Avenue North, Seattle, WA 98109; 206/470-4060. Ask the USGS for topographic maps of the Sweetgrass Butte and Billy Goat Mountain.

Directions: From Winthrop drive nine miles north on West Chewuch Road/Forest Service Road 51 to the Eightmile Ranch and a junction with Eightmile Creek Road/Forest Service Road 5130. Turn west (left) onto Eightmile Creek Road and drive 17 miles to the road's end and the trailhead.

Contact: Okanogan National Forest, Methow Valley Ranger District, 502 Glover Street, P.O. Box 188, Twisp, WA 98856; 509/997-2131. Or contact Visitor Information Center, Building 49, Highway 20, Winthrop, WA 98862; 509/996-4000.

84 Andrews Creek
31.0 mi/3.0 days

Climbing gradually through a valley, this route allows hikers time to relax and get into the spirit of the wilderness. The trail explores an old, sun-streaked forest that's periodically broken by open, flower-filled meadows. Along the way, the sounds of Andrews Creek fill the air, even when the water is out of view. You follow the creek for nearly the entire length of the valley before eventually angling up the valley head wall through subalpine forest and broad heather meadows. Look for deer and mountain goats in these meadows. The trail formally ends in Spanish Camp, a large, pleasant camp with picturesque views of the surrounding peaks and access to good fishing in the area's lakes and streams. Camping spots are plentiful—you find good ones about every half mile along the trail. When in season, huckleberries, too, are plentiful, and those who know what to look for can find a good crop of mushrooms in the forest along the trail.

Location: East of Winthrop in Okanogan National Forest, within the Pasayten Wilderness; see Northern Cascades Map 2, grid b8.

User Groups: Hikers, dogs, and horses. No mountain bikes are allowed. No wheelchair facilities.

Permits: A federal Northwest Forest Pass, $5 per day or $30 annually, is required to park at the trailhead. Passes are available from ranger stations and many private vendors, online at website: www.wta.org, or by calling 800/270-7504.

Maps: For a trail information report, contact the Methow Valley Ranger District at 509/997-2131. For a map of Okanogan National Forest, contact the Outdoor Recreation Information Center, Seattle REI, 222 Yale Avenue North, Seattle, WA 98109; 206/470-4060. Ask the USGS for topographic maps of the Coleman Peak, Mount Barney, and Remmel Mountain areas.

Directions: From Winthrop drive 23 miles north on West Chewuch Road/Forest Service Road 51 to the trailhead on the left.

Contact: Okanogan National Forest, Methow Valley Ranger District, 502 Glover Street, P.O. Box 188, Twisp, WA 98856; 509/997-2131. Or contact Visitor Information Center, Building 49, Highway 20, Winthrop, WA 98862; 509/996-4000.

85 Peepsight
28.1 mi/2.0–3.0 days

A long hike up Andrews Creek forms the leg of this backwards P-shaped route. After following the pretty creek and thick forest for eight miles, the trail turns due west and heads up the Peepsight Creek Valley, climbing gradually for a couple of miles. Suddenly it gives way to a steep ascent up the flank of Peepsight Mountain. A faint climbers' trail leads to a precipitous scramble to the 8,156-foot summit. The main trail angles on north past the mountain and gradually banks east past Rock Lake before rejoining Andrews Creek. Hiking back down the valley, you close the loop of the P and head back toward the trailhead. Backpackers find an assortment of campsites scattered throughout the Andrews Creek Valley, as well as one or two suitable tent sites located near the head of Peepsight Creek. From Peepsight north back to Andrews Creek, however, there is no suitable place for camping until you rejoin the river. As you walk south along the banks, the camping opportunities proliferate once again.

Location: East of Winthrop in Okanogan National Forest, within the Pasayten Wilderness; see Northern Cascades Map 2, grid b8.

User Groups: Hikers, dogs, and horses. No mountain bikes are allowed. No wheelchair facilities.

Permits: A federal Northwest Forest Pass, $5 per day or $30 annually, is required to park at the trailhead. Passes are available from ranger stations and many private vendors, online at website: www.wta.org, or by calling 800/270-7504.

Maps: For a trail information report, contact the Methow Valley Ranger District at 509/997-2131. For a map of Okanogan National Forest, contact the Outdoor Recreation Information Center, Seattle REI, 222 Yale Avenue North, Seattle, WA 98109; 206/470-4060. Ask the USGS for topographic maps of the Coleman Peak and Remmel Mountain areas.

Directions: From Winthrop drive 23 miles north on West Chewuch Road/Forest Service road 51 to the trailhead on the left.

Contact: Okanogan National Forest, Methow Valley Ranger District, 502 Glover Street, P.O. Box 188, Twisp, WA 98856; 509/997-2131. Or contact Visitor Information Center, Building 49, Highway 20, Winthrop, WA 98862; 509/996-4000.

86 Chewuch River
36.2 mi/3.0 days

A major wildfire impacted this area in the summer of 2001, and the damage to the trail at press time was not determined. Be sure to call before ahead to find out if the trail or access roads to the trailhead have been damaged or rerouted.

You won't find stunning panoramas here, but you also won't find a prettier river-valley hike anywhere else. The trail parallels the Chewuch River most of the way, while meandering through an ancient lodgepole and whitebark pine forest. Foot-long trout inhabit the river, but 18-inch rainbows hide out in the deep holes, too. The final few miles of the trail leave the river behind and climb to heather and wildflower meadows in the Cathedral area. You can camp anywhere along the river.

Location: North of Winthrop in Okanogan National Forest, within the Pasayten Wilderness; see Northern Cascades Map 2, grid b8.

User Groups: Hikers, dogs, and horses. No mountain bikes are allowed. No wheelchair facilities.

Permits: A federal Northwest Forest Pass, $5 per day or $30 annually, is required to park at the trailhead. Passes are available from ranger stations and many private vendors, online at website: www.wta.org, or by calling 800/270-7504.

Maps: For a trail information report, contact the Methow Valley Ranger District at 509/997-2131. For a map of Okanogan National Forest, contact the Outdoor Recreation Information Center, Seattle REI, 222 Yale Avenue North, Seattle, WA 98109; 206/470-4060. Ask the USGS for topographic maps of the Coleman Peak, Bauerman Ridge, and Remmel Mountain areas.

Directions: From Winthrop drive 29 miles north on West Chewuch Road/Forest Service Road 51 to the road's end and the trailhead.

Contact: Okanogan National Forest, Methow Valley Ranger District, 502 Glover Street, P.O. Box 188, Twisp, WA 98856; 509/997-2131. Or contact Visitor Information Center, Building 49, Highway 20, Winthrop, WA 98862; 509/996-4000.

87 Panther Creek to Fourth of July Pass
10.5 mi/6.0 hrs

One of the finest day hikes within easy distance of Highway 20 is right here. Bring the camera, lots of water, and repellent for bugs and people, both of which show in great numbers every summer. The first leg on the Thunder Creek Trail is an easy stroll through flat bottomlands. It's a setup. Once you turn east onto the Panther Creek Trail, elevation gains come in great gulps. Literally. You switchback and climb more than you'd like. But hang in there. At Fourth of July Pass, elevation 3,500 feet, you are rewarded by eastern views of Colonial Peak (elevation 7,771 feet), Snowfield Peak (elevation 8,347 feet) and Neve Glacier. This is also a great hike for one-way day-trippers. Continue past the pass and follow lovely Panther Creek Valley downstream

for five miles to the East Bank Ross Lake Trailhead (see hike in this chapter). Fast hikers can finish the trek in about the amount of time it takes for friends to drop them off, have lunch at Colonial Creek, play some blackjack, take a short nap, and meet them on the east side. Trust us.

Location: South of Ross Lake in North Cascades National Park; see Northern Cascades Map 2, grid c1.

User Groups: Hikers, dogs, and horses. No mountain bikes are allowed. No wheelchair facilities.

Permits: Free overnight permits (required) are available at the Marblemount Ranger Station at 360/873-4500. Parking and access are free.

Maps: For a map of North Cascades National Park and Ross Lake National Recreation Area, contact the Outdoor Recreation Information Center, Seattle REI, 222 Yale Avenue North, Seattle, WA 98109; 206/470-4060. Green Trails, Inc.'s excellent topographic map of the region is available for $3.99 at outdoor retail outlets; ask for map number 48, Diablo Dam. Ask the USGS for topographic maps of the Ross Dam and Crater Mountain areas.

Directions: From I-5 north of Mount Vernon, take Exit 230/Anacortes/Burlington. Follow Highway 20/North Cascades Highway east for about 74 miles to Colonial Creek Campground, four miles east of the Diablo Lake turnoff at milepost 130. Park in the lot above the boat ramp and find the trail just up the hill near the amphitheater. Hike the Thunder Creek Trail 1.8 miles south to the Panther Creek Trail, which splits off to the left (east).

Contact: North Cascades National Park/Mount Baker Ranger District Information Center, 2105 Highway 20, Sedro-Woolley, WA 98284; 360/856-5700; Marblemount Ranger Station, 728 Ranger Station Road, Marblemount, WA 98267; 360/873-4500.

88 East Creek to Mebee Pass
16.0 mi/8.0 hrs

Like its neighbor to the northeast, the Mill Creek Trail (see hike in this chapter), this one is likely to take you far from people, especially for a trail accessible from Highway 20. The East Creek Trail, also used as a link to the Pacific Crest Trail and Methow Valley to the east, follows the East Creek Valley through pleasant, cool forest and meadows to Mebee Pass (elevation 6,500 feet). The final two miles are up, up, and up. Breathe deeply, examine the former lookout site, and take in excellent views east to the Methow Valley. Keep your eyes peeled for bits of this area's rich mining past. True solitude seekers might consider making this trail the southern leg of a 27.5-mile loop connecting to the Pacific Crest and Mill Creek/Azurite Pass Trails. For a shuttle hike with an exit near Klipchuck Campground, see hike in this chapter.

Location: In Okanogan National Forest; see Northern Cascades Map 2, grid d2.

User Groups: Hikers, dogs, and horses. No mountain bikes are allowed. No wheelchair facilities.

Permits: A federal Northwest Forest Pass, $5 per day or $30 annually, is required to park at the trailhead. Passes are available from ranger stations and many private vendors, online at website: www.wta.org, or by calling 800/270-7504.

Maps: For a map of North Cascades National Park or the adjoining Okanogan National Forest, contact the Outdoor Recreation Information Center, Seattle REI, 222 Yale Avenue North, Seattle, WA 98109; 206/470-4060. Green Trails, Inc.'s excellent topographic maps of the region are available for $3.99 each at outdoor retail outlets; ask for map numbers 49 and 50, Mount Logan and Washington Pass. Ask the USGS for a topographic map of the Azurite Peak area.

Directions: From I-5 north of Mount Vernon, take Exit 230/Anacortes/Burlington. Drive east on Highway 20/North Cascades Highway/North Cascades Highway for 72 miles to Colonial Creek Campground and then approximately 15 miles more to the East Creek Trailhead on the left (northeast) side of the road. The trail begins on the far side of the bridge over the Creek. Note: Highway 20 is closed in winter. Call North Cascades National Park at 360/856-5700 for current road conditions.

Contact: Okanogan National Forest, Methow Valley Ranger District, 502 Glover Street, P.O. Box 188, Twisp, WA 98856; 509/997-2131. Or contact Visitor Information Center, Building 49, Highway 20, Winthrop, WA 98862; 509/996-4000.

89 Easy Pass
7.2 mi/7.0 hrs

Some friends insist this is the absolute, drop-dead, never-fail, bring-your-camera, best day hike in Washington state. To test their theory, we threw our gear in the car one August day and set off to throw cold water on their Easy Pass fire. We couldn't. It is gorgeous. Extremely gorgeous. But let's get one thing straight from the start: Easy Pass isn't easy. Whether you get there by hiking 21 miles from Colonial Creek Campground via the Thunder Creek Trail (see hike in this chapter), or a mere 3.6 miles from the eastern trailhead on Highway 20, you are sucking some wind. On the latter route, you start by crossing always-bustling Granite Creek (a bridge was here last time we checked, but sometimes it isn't) and then wind through a very fine forest. Breaking out of the trees at about two miles, you come upon great avalanche paths at the foot of Ragged Ridge. Look up to the east. Way up. There. See the tiny switchbacks? You'll be there soon. Assuming, that is, you brought boots sturdy enough to handle sharp rocks, and if you're here in early to midsummer, an ice ax to cross the snowfields.

At the pass, elevation 6,500 feet, you see what all the fuss was about. The views (Mount Logan, take a bow) are postcard spectacular, and the breeze is brisk and cleaner smelling than a freshly washed white cotton shirt. Deer and bears act as if they own the place. Time a trip right in early October and you get a rare visual feast: brilliant yellow larch trees against a backdrop of rocky peaks sporting their first coat of winter snow. Hikers continuing out to Colonial Creek or Stehekin via the Fischer Creek Trail should observe a moment of silence for the North Cascades' last (known) grizzly, which was shot here in 1968. All things considered, we're not sure we can say this is the best day hike in Washington, but it's in the ballpark. You'll be feeling it the next day and remembering it for life.

Although overnight camping is allowed at points beyond, there is no camping at Easy Pass. Make this a day hike.

Location: In the heart of North Cascades National Park; see Northern Cascades Map 2, grid d2.

User Groups: Hikers only. No dogs, horses, or mountain bikes are allowed. No wheelchair facilities.

Permits: Free overnight permits (required) are available at the Marblemount Ranger Station at 360/873-4500. Parking and access are free.

Maps: For a map of North Cascades National Park and Ross Lake National Recreation Area, contact the Outdoor Recreation Information Center, Seattle REI, 222 Yale Avenue North, Seattle, WA 98109; 206/470-4060. Green Trails, Inc.'s excellent topographic maps of the region are available for $3.99 each at outdoor retail outlets; ask for map numbers 48 and 49, Diablo Dam and Mount Logan. Ask the USGS for topographic maps of the Mount Arriva, Mount Logan, and Forbidden Peak areas.

Directions: From I-5 north of Mount Vernon, take Exit 230/Anacortes/Burlington. Drive about 96 miles east on Highway 20/North Cascades Highway, about 22 miles beyond Colonial Creek Campground (6.3 miles west of Rainy Pass). The trailhead is at the end of a short spur road on the south side of the highway.

Contact: North Cascades National Park/Mount Baker Ranger District Information Center, 2105 Highway 20, Sedro-Woolley, WA 98284; 360/856-5700; Marblemount Ranger Station, 728 Ranger Station Road, Marblemount, WA 98267; 360/873-4500.

90 Lake Ann/Maple Pass
6.2 mi/3.0 hrs

By the time you hit Rainy Pass, the kid in the back of the car has kicked his mother's seat back at least 1,000 times since you left Marblemount. Time to ditch the car, stretch the legs, and wear the little monster down by taking a refreshing afternoon walk to Maple Pass. The trail leaves the large parking lot in a forest, crossing through meadows and a slide area before reaching a junction at 1.5 miles. The left fork continues a half mile to Lake Ann (elevation 5,475 feet), and most people follow it, either to fish (cutthroat trout are stocked), sunbathe, or just gape. The other trail leads right (east) to Heather Pass (elevation 6,200 feet) and, at 3.1 miles, Maple Pass (elevation 6,800 feet). Enjoy the views of Corteo and Black Peaks, then strap what's left of Junior to your day pack and head on back down to the Subaru. He'll sleep all the way home.

There is no overnight camping within a quarter mile of Lake Ann or either of the passes described above.

Location: Near Rainy Pass on the eastern border of North Cascades National Park; see Northern Cascades Map 2, grid e3.

User Groups: Hikers and dogs. No horses or mountain bikes are allowed. No wheelchair facilities.

Permits: No permits are required. Parking and access are free.

Maps: For a map of North Cascades National Park or the adjoining Okanogan National Forest, contact the Outdoor Recreation Information Center, Seattle REI, 222 Yale Avenue North, Seattle, WA 98109; 206/470-4060. Green Trails, Inc.'s excellent topographic maps of the region are available for $3.99 each at outdoor retail outlets; ask for map numbers 49 and 50, Mount Logan and Washington Pass. Ask the USGS for topographic maps of the Washington Pass and McAlester Mountain areas.

Directions: From I-5 north of Mount Vernon, take Exit 230/Anacortes/Burlington. Drive about 46 miles east on Highway 20/North Cascades Highway to Marblemount and another 51 miles to the well-marked parking lot at Rainy Pass. Park in the south parking lot and walk several hundred yards east to the trailhead.

Contact: North Cascades National Park/Mount Baker Ranger District Information Center, 2105 Highway 20, Sedro-Woolley, WA 98284; 360/856-5700.

🖸 Rainy Lake Nature Trail
1.8 mi/1.0 hr

Anybody can walk this trail, and everybody should. Forest Service crews have eliminated any possible excuse someone could make for not venturing a short distance into the splendor of the North Cascades Highway wilderness. The broad, paved, and level path winds to the north end of Rainy Lake, where a large picnic spot awaits. Views across the lake are spectacular, much like views in North Cascades alpine cirques, which are much more difficult to reach. Lyall Glacier looms above, and waterfalls drop into the lake at the south end. It's even better in the fall. Low bushes turn spectacular shades of fiery red and burnt orange in October. This is a good break-up-the-trip walk any time of the year the North Cascades Highway is open, generally April through November.

Location: Near Rainy Pass on the eastern border of North Cascades National Park; see Northern Cascades Map 2, grid e3.

User Groups: Hikers and dogs. Wheelchair accessible. No mountain bikes are allowed.

Permits: No permits are required. Parking and access are free.

Maps: For a map of North Cascades National Park or the adjoining Okanogan National Forest, contact the Outdoor Recreation Information Center, Seattle REI, 222 Yale Avenue North, Seattle, WA 98109; 206/470-4060. Green Trails, Inc.'s excellent topographic map of the region is available for $3.99 at outdoor retail outlets; ask for map number 50, Washington Pass. Ask the USGS for a topographic map of the Washington Pass area.

Directions: From I-5 north of Mount Vernon, take Exit 230/Anacortes/Burlington. Drive 46 miles east on Highway 20/North Cascades Highway to Marblemount and another 51 miles to the well-marked parking lot at Rainy Pass. Park in the south parking lot.

Contact: North Cascades National Park/Mount Baker Ranger District Information Center, 2105 Highway 20, Sedro-Woolley, WA 98284; 360/856-5700.

92 Blue Lake
4.4 mi/2.0 hrs

Views of the surrounding peaks dominate the hike on the way in, but it's the picturesque lake at the trail's end that really grabs your attention. En route to the lake, enjoy the sweeping panoramas of Cutthroat Peak, the Early Winter Spires, and Liberty Bell Peak. At Blue Lake, those peaks are reflected in the deep, blue waters. If you want more than views and scenery to remember, cast a line into the lake and try to catch one of the many big cutthroat trout that reside in the cold waters.

Location: West of Winthrop in Okanogan National Forest; see Northern Cascades Map 2, grid d3.

User Groups: Hikers and dogs. No horses or mountain bikes are allowed. No wheelchair facilities.

Permits: A federal Northwest Forest Pass, $5 per day or $30 annually, is required to park at the trailhead. Passes are available from ranger stations and many private vendors, online at website: www.wta.org, or by calling 800/270-7504.

Maps: For a trail information report, contact the Methow Valley Ranger District at 509/997-2131. For a map of Okanogan National Forest, contact the Outdoor Recreation Information Center, Seattle REI, 222 Yale Avenue North, Seattle, WA 98109; 206/470-4060. Ask the USGS for a topographic map of the Washington Pass area.

Directions: From Winthrop drive west on Highway 20 across Washington Pass. Less than a mile west of the pass, turn into the trailhead parking area on the south side of the highway.

Contact: Okanogan National Forest, Methow Valley Ranger District, 502 Glover Street, P.O. Box 188, Twisp, WA 98856; 509/997-2131. Or contact Visitor Information Center, Building 49, Highway 20, Winthrop, WA 98862; 509/996-4000.

93 Washington Pass Overlook
0.5 mi/0.5 hr

A short walk on a paved trail brings you to a broad, bench-lined platform overlooking the actual Washington Pass (as opposed to the route that Highway 20 follows), as well as Silver Star Peak, the Wine Spires, the Early Winter Spires, and Liberty Bell Peak. The trail also offers a definitive overview of the two sides of the state. To the east, the mountains fall away into dry pine forests and even drier desert coulee country beyond. To the west, the mountains continue to rise into the sky and the lush forests are green swaths of Douglas fir and western red cedar. From the overlook at the top, it's a loooong way down to the dry side of the state. Watch your step and stay behind the rail.

Location: West of Winthrop in Okanogan National Forest; see Northern Cascades Map 2, grid d3.

User Groups: Hikers and dogs. Wheelchair accessible. No horses or mountain bikes are allowed.

Permits: No permits are required. Parking and access are free.

Maps: For a trail information report, contact the Methow Valley Ranger District at 509/997-2131. For a map of Okanogan National Forest, contact the Outdoor Recreation Information Center, Seattle REI, 222 Yale Avenue North, Seattle, WA 98109; 206/470-4060. Ask the USGS for a topographic map of the Washington Pass area.

Directions: From Winthrop drive west on Highway 20 to Washington Pass. The trailhead is north of the highway.

Contact: Okanogan National Forest, Methow Valley Ranger District, 502 Glover Street, P.O. Box 188, Twisp, WA 98856; 509/997-2131. Or contact Visitor Information Center, Building 49, Highway 20, Winthrop, WA 98862; 509/996-4000.

94 Cutthroat Pass
11.4 mi/8.0 hrs

You have your choice of access routes to the great views on Cutthroat Pass and the cool, clear waters of Cutthroat Lake. From Rainy Pass on Highway 20 (see hike in this chapter), it's a five-mile, 2,000-vertical-foot hike up the Pacific Crest Trail to the pass and then another 3.8 miles and 1,900 feet down to the lake. From the east side, at Cutthroat Campground, it's 1.7 miles and only 400 feet to the lake, and then 3.8 miles and 1,900 feet up to Cutthroat Pass. Choose your poison. Either way, this is an excellent, strenuous day hike in terrain described by long-distance trekkers as some of the most memorable on the entire length of the Pacific Crest Trail. If you can arrange transportation, try hiking the route one way, from Rainy Pass to Cutthroat Campground. It's 10.5 miles, and you'll save a bit of climbing if you hike west to east.

Location: In Okanogan National Forest; see Northern Cascades Map 2, grid d3.

User Groups: Hikers, dogs, and horses. No mountain bikes are allowed. No wheelchair facilities.

Permits: No permits are required. Parking and access are free.

Maps: For a map of North Cascades National Park or the adjoining Okanogan National Forest, contact the Outdoor Recreation Information Center, Seattle REI, 222 Yale Avenue North, Seattle, WA 98109; 206/470-4060. Green Trails, Inc.'s excellent topographic map of the region is available for $3.99 at outdoor retail outlets; ask for map number 50, Washington Pass. Ask the USGS for a topographic map of the Washington Pass area.

Directions: From I-5 north of Mount Vernon, take Exit 230/Anacortes/Burlington. Drive east on Highway 20/North Cascades Highway about five miles beyond Rainy and Washington Passes to Cutthroat Creek Road/Forest Service Road 400. Turn left (north) and drive one mile to the road's end and the trailhead at Cutthroat Campground.

Contact: Okanogan National Forest, Methow Valley Ranger District, 502 Glover Street, P.O. Box 188, Twisp, WA 98856; 509/997-2131. Or contact Visitor Information Center, Building 49, Highway 20, Winthrop, WA 98862; 509/996-4000.

95 Lone Fir
2.0 mi/1.0 hr

Old-fashioned standards went into the construction of this new barrier-free trail. Instead of placing long-lasting but ugly steel bridges over the creek, the trail builders erected classic log bridges that complement the natural setting. Four of these picturesque structures grace the trail; from the largest, hikers get great views down into Early Winters Creek. Interpretive signs line the route and offer insight into the workings of the surrounding ecosystem.

Location: West of Winthrop in Okanogan National Forest; see Northern Cascades Map 2, grid d4.

User Groups: Hikers and dogs. Wheelchair accessible. No horses or mountain bikes are allowed.

Permits: A federal Northwest Forest Pass, $5 per day or $30 annually, is required to park at the trailhead. Passes are available from ranger stations and many private vendors, online at website: www.wta.org, or by calling 800/270-7504.

Maps: For a trail information report, contact the Methow Valley Ranger District at 509/997-2131. For a map of Okanogan National Forest, contact the Outdoor Recreation Information Center, Seattle REI, 222 Yale Avenue North, Seattle, WA 98109; 206/470-4060. Ask the USGS for a topographic map of the Washington Pass area.

Directions: From Winthrop drive west on Highway 20 to Mazama. Continue another 11 miles to the Lone Fir Campground. Turn left (south) into the campground and find the trailhead near the camping fee station.

Contact: Okanogan National Forest, Methow Valley Ranger District, 502 Glover Street, P.O. Box 188, Twisp, WA 98856; 509/997-2131. Or contact Visitor Information Center, Building 49, Highway 20, Winthrop, WA 98862; 509/996-4000.

96 Indian Creek to Mebee Pass
23.4 mi one way/
3.0 days

Some of the most spectacular scenery and vistas outside of designated wilderness lands are accessible on this high, lonesome trail. Because the trail does not lie within a wilderness area, it doesn't attract much attention, so solitude is as good as guaranteed. You set out on an old logging road, but within half a mile it becomes a single-track path. Climbing gradually but continually, the trail eventually tops out on the Driveway Butte's summit, with views of Goat Wall, the Early Winter Spires, and the Methow Valley.

The route then drops down the north flank of the butte into the Methow drainage and, at the riverside, continues upstream to a junction with the Pacific Crest Trail. A short hike south on the PCT leads to another fork in the trail. This time bear right and climb west over Mebee Pass, the former site of a forest fire lookout tower. From here, drop through lush meadows and thick forest to a short boulder field and more forest before abruptly reaching the eastern trailhead. Campsites are scarce in the first four or five miles, but as the trail climbs into the Methow

River Valley and continues upstream along the riverbank, camping opportunities abound. All of them are good, and the river is beautiful from any vantage point. The sites thin out after the route links up with the Pacific Crest Trail. Once you're across the pass, though, and in the East Creek Basin, the number of sites increases; the East Creek isn't as spectacular as the Methow River, but the campsites are good.

To avoid retracing your steps, arrange to have a car waiting at one end of the trail. Highway 20 connects the two trailheads, making it easy to shuttle a vehicle.

Location: West of Winthrop in Okanogan National Forest; see Northern Cascades Map 2, grid d4.

User Groups: Hikers, dogs, and horses. No mountain bikes are allowed. No wheelchair facilities.

Permits: A federal Northwest Forest Pass, $5 per day or $30 annually, is required to park at the trailhead. Passes are available from ranger stations and many private vendors, online at website: www.wta.org, or by calling 800/270-7504.

Maps: For a trail information report, contact the Methow Valley Ranger District at 509/997-2131. For a map of Okanogan National Forest, contact the Outdoor Recreation Information Center, Seattle REI, 222 Yale Avenue North, Seattle, WA 98109; 206/470-4060. Ask the USGS for topographic maps of the Silver Star Mountain, Robinson Mountain, Crater Mountain, Azurite Peak, and Shull Mountain areas.

Directions: From Winthrop drive west on Highway 20 through Mazama and Early Winters to Forest Service Road 5310-300, signed for Klipchuck Campground. Drive to the end of Forest Service Road 5310-300 and find the trailhead near the campground fee station. To reach the eastern trailhead from Winthrop drive 50 miles west on Highway 20, across Washington and Rainy Passes, to the East Creek Trailhead in a well-marked parking area on the north side of the highway.

Contact: Okanogan National Forest, Methow Valley Ranger District, 502 Glover Street, P.O. Box 188, Twisp, WA 98856; 509/997-2131. Or contact Visitor Information Center, Building 49, Highway 20, Winthrop, WA 98862; 509/996-4000.

97 West Fork Methow
16.0 mi/1.0–2.0 days

The trail follows the Methow River upstream to Brush Creek. Campsites are found on the way, and the beautiful, sun-dappled river is easily accessible from the trail. Anglers love this route and the river—there's room and fish enough for everyone. Rainbow, brown, and cutthroat trout thrive in the waters, and trout-inhabited holes are found every few yards. The forest in the valley bottom opens up frequently, providing views of the surrounding peaks.

Location: West of Winthrop in Okanogan National Forest; see Northern Cascades Map 2, grid c4.

User Groups: Hikers, dogs, and horses. No mountain bikes are allowed. No wheelchair facilities.

Permits: A federal Northwest Forest Pass, $5 per day or $30 annually, is required to park at the trailhead. Passes are available from ranger stations and many private vendors, online at website: www.wta.org, or by calling 800/270-7504.

Maps: For a trail information report, contact the Methow Valley Ranger District at 509/997-2131. For a map of Okanogan National Forest, contact the Outdoor Recreation Information Center, Seattle REI, 222 Yale Avenue North, Seattle, WA 98109; 206/470-4060. Ask the USGS for topographic maps of the Robinson Mountain and Slate Peak areas.

Directions: From Winthrop drive west on Highway 20 to Mazama and turn north on the Mazama Cutoff Road. Cross the river and turn left (west) onto Hart's Pass Road/County Road 1163. Continue to the junction with the River Bend Access Road. Turn left onto the access road and drive a quarter mile to the River Bend Campground. The trailhead is a quarter mile beyond the campground.

Contact: Okanogan National Forest, Methow Valley Ranger District, 502 Glover Street, P.O. Box 188, Twisp, WA 98856; 509/997-2131. Or contact Visitor Information Center, Building 49, Highway 20, Winthrop, WA 98862; 509/996-4000.

98 Ferguson Lake
27.6 mi/2.0–3.0 days

For the first 11 miles, this trail leads through an old pine and fir forest in the Robinson Creek Valley (see hike in this chapter). Scattered along the valley bottom are the remains of dilapidated cabins and lean-tos erected some 100 years ago by the valley's namesake, fur trapper William "Billy" Robinson, as well as several good campsites. At mile 11, the Robinson Pass Trail continues north along the creek, and a side trail leads up a steep, open avalanche chute. Take this side trail, which travels 2.5 steep, rocky miles to Ferguson Lake. The climb is tough, but the views and lake environment are worth it. Anglers will have no trouble catching dinner in the cold waters, for both cutthroat and rainbow trout thrive in the rich lake. In season, wild strawberries are plentiful around the basin. The best campsites are on the west side of the lake. After setting up camp, hikers can relax and enjoy the views of the Wildcat Mountain's twin peaks behind the lake.

Location: West of Winthrop in Okanogan National Forest; see Northern Cascades Map 2, grid c5.

User Groups: Hikers, dogs, and horses. No mountain bikes are allowed. No wheelchair facilities.

Permits: A federal Northwest Forest Pass, $5 per day or $30 annually, is required to park at the trailhead. Passes are available from ranger stations and many private vendors, online at website: www.wta.org, or by calling 800/270-7504.

Maps: For a trail information report, contact the Methow Valley Ranger District at 509/997-2131. For a map of Okanogan National Forest, contact the Outdoor Recreation Information Center, Seattle REI, 222 Yale Avenue North, Seattle, WA 98109; 206/470-4060. Ask the USGS for topographic maps of the Silver Star Mountain and Robinson Mountain areas.

Directions: From Winthrop drive west on Highway 20 to Mazama and turn north on the Mazama Cutoff Road. Cross the river and turn left (west) onto Hart's Pass Road/County Road 1163. Continue nine miles to the Robinson Creek Trailhead.

Contact: Okanogan National Forest, Methow Valley Ranger District, 502 Glover Street, P.O. Box 188, Twisp, WA 98856; 509/997-2131. Or contact Visitor Information Center, Building 49, Highway 20, Winthrop, WA 98862; 509/996-4000.

99 Monument Creek
51.6 mi/5.0 days

Day hikers, do not be intimidated by the length of this trail. You don't have to hike the entire distance to have an enjoyable trip. The first few miles weave gently up the Lost Creek Valley, presenting beautiful views of the churning water and the cool, deep valley forests. After crossing Eureka Creek, a major tributary of Lost Creek, the trail turns up the steep ridge face and climbs through a series of switchbacks to the ridge top. From then on, it follows the ridge north, under the flanks of Pistol Peak, past Lake of the Woods, and back down into the Monument Creek Valley. The trail stays near the creek all the way up the valley to the headwaters before climbing yet again through steep switchbacks. The route ends at a junction with the Eureka Creek Trail at Shellrock Pass.

Campsites are common throughout the length of the trail. They are scarce at first, with a few possibilities in the first three miles, and another at eight miles (due south of Pistol Peak), where the trail passes a small spring. There is nothing more until you loop past Pistol Peak and drop into the Monument Creek Valley. Once the trail nears the creek, though, campsites become more plentiful, and you have no problem finding them on the rest of the trail. The ridgetop and pass both offer spectacular vistas stretching from the Canadian peaks to the north, the glacier-covered summits of the North Cascades to the west, and the Sawtooth Wilderness to the south. Both Eureka and Lost Creeks hold sizable rainbow and cutthroat trout. Hawks, falcons, and eagles grace the skies above, while mule deer, black bears, mountain goats, and even grizzly bears may prowl the ridges and valleys of this remote slice of the Pasayten Wilderness.

Location: West of Winthrop in Okanogan National Forest, within the Pasayten Wilderness; see Northern Cascades Map 2, grid c5.

User Groups: Hikers, dogs, and horses. No mountain bikes are allowed. No wheelchair facilities.

Permits: A federal Northwest Forest Pass, $5 per day or $30 annually, is required to park at the trailhead. Passes are available from ranger stations and many private vendors, online at website: www.wta.org, or by calling 800/270-7504.

Maps: For a trail information report, contact the Methow Valley Ranger District at 509/997-2131. For a map of Okanogan National Forest, contact the Outdoor Recreation Information Center, Seattle REI, 222 Yale Avenue North, Seattle, WA 98109; 206/470-4060. Ask the USGS for topographic maps of the Robinson Mountain, McLeod Mountain, Lost Peak, and Mount Lago areas.

Directions: From Winthrop drive west on Highway 20 to Mazama and turn north on the Mazama Cutoff Road. Cross the river and turn left (west) onto Hart's Pass Road/County Road 1163. Continue seven miles to the Lost River Trailhead, just beyond the Lost River airstrip.

Contact: Okanogan National Forest, Methow Valley Ranger District, 502 Glover Street, P.O. Box 188, Twisp, WA 98856; 509/997-2131. Or contact Visitor Information Center, Building 49, Highway 20, Winthrop, WA 98862; 509/996-4000.

100 Driveway Butte
8.0 mi/4.0 hrs

Steep, dry, and dusty, this trail is best attempted in the late spring or early fall. Midsummer excursions usually result in a sweat-drenched body that attracts blackflies and mosquitoes like a magnet. However, it's a different story in late September when the nighttime temperatures are cool enough to kill off the pesky insects, the sun isn't nearly as fierce and unyielding, and the local clumps of larch, alder, and heather have begun to don their brilliant autumn cloaks. By autumn, the resident deer are busy in their lust-driven rut (while they take no notice of late-season hikers, they do put on quite a show with their big antlers and shiny new winter coats). The trail leaves the campground on an old logging road but within half a mile becomes a primitive single-track path. Climbing gradually but contin-

ually, the trail eventually tops out on the butte's summit, where you find great views of the Early Winter Spires and Silver Star Mountain.

Autumn hikers should wear brightly colored clothing and stay on the trail, because deer hunters use this area heavily, particularly in October, and to a lesser degree during early hunts in late September. Contact the ranger district for details on hunting seasons.

Location: West of Winthrop in Okanogan National Forest; see Northern Cascades Map 2, grid d4.

User Groups: Hikers, dogs, and horses. No mountain bikes are allowed. No wheelchair facilities.

Permits: A federal Northwest Forest Pass, $5 per day or $30 annually, is required to park at the trailhead. Passes are available from ranger stations and many private vendors, online at website: www.wta.org, or by calling 800/270-7504.

Maps: For a trail information report, contact the Methow Valley Ranger District at 509/997-2131. For a map of Okanogan National Forest, contact the Outdoor Recreation Information Center, Seattle REI, 222 Yale Avenue North, Seattle, WA 98109; 206/470-4060. Ask the USGS for topographic maps of the Silver Star Mountain and Robinson Mountain areas.

Directions: From Winthrop drive west on Highway 20 through Mazama and Early Winters to Forest Service Road 5310-300, signed for Klipchuck Campground. Drive to the end of the road and find the trailhead near the campground fee station.

Contact: Okanogan National Forest, Methow Valley Ranger District, 502 Glover Street, P.O. Box 188, Twisp, WA 98856; 509/997-2131. Or contact Visitor Information Center, Building 49, Highway 20, Winthrop, WA 98862; 509/996-4000.

101 Goode Ridge Lookout
10.0 mi/8.0 hrs

Not many trails in the Northwest take you up 5,000 vertical feet in five miles or less. This one doesn't either, but it comes awfully close. The first three miles or so are mostly in forest, for which you should be thankful: the trail is often dry, and hikers who do not carry plenty of water shall surely perish less than two miles up the trail. At 3.5 miles, the sun comes out and so do views of the Stehekin drainage. The trail ends and your body drops to a lump of exhausted flesh at the summit, elevation 6,600 feet. A fire lookout used to stand here, but they closed it in the 1940s—maybe because they ran out of fools capable of hoofing it all the way up here.

Location: In the Stehekin River Valley of North Cascades National Park; see Northern Cascades Map 2, grid e1.

User Groups: Hikers only. No dogs, horses, or mountain bikes are allowed. No wheelchair facilities.

Permits: Free overnight permits (required) are available at the Golden West Visitor Center in Stehekin. Access to Stehekin requires a $25 round-trip boat ride from Chelan.

Maps: For a map of North Cascades National Park, contact the Outdoor Recreation Information Center, Seattle REI, 222 Yale Avenue North, Seattle, WA 98109; 206/470-4060. Green Trails, Inc.'s excellent topographic map of the region is available for $3.99 at outdoor retail outlets; ask for map number 81, McGregor Mountain. Ask the USGS for a topographic map of the Goode Mountain area.

Directions: From Seattle take U.S. 2/Stevens Pass east to Wenatchee and U.S. 97 north to the city of Chelan. Catch the water taxi up Lake Chelan to Stehekin (contact the Outdoor Recreation Information Center at 206/470-4060 or see website: www.ladyofthe lake.com for boat schedules and shuttle bus information). Ride the shuttle bus from Stehekin to the trailhead near the Bridge Creek Bridge. See the special access note in the Park Creek Pass hike in this chapter.

Contact: North Cascades National Park/ Mount Baker Ranger District Information Center, 2105 Highway 20, Sedro-Woolley, WA 98284; 360/856-5700.

102 North Fork Bridge Creek
19.0 mi/2.0–3.0 days

If you're in the Stehekin Valley, hoping to don a backpack and sample the area's magnificent scenery without dying in the process, the Bridge Creek trails are a good option. Start out by walking three miles up the Pacific Crest Trail. (Offer some chocolate to those poor-soul PCT hikers who come straggling down from the more remote North Cascades.) At three miles, rest at North Fork Camp and then hang a left on the North Fork/Walker Park Trail. Walker Camp at 5.5 miles is an unforgettable first-night destination. Stare across the valley to Stor King and Goode Mountain and marvel at the wall of glacial ice hanging below both on Memaloose Ridge. The trail ends among similarly superb views about 6.5 miles from North Fork Camp. Because the trail stays low throughout, it's a good bet early in the season.

Location: In the Stehekin River Valley of North Cascades National Park; see Northern Cascades Map 2, grid e2.

User Groups: Hikers only. No dogs, horses, or mountain bikes are allowed. No wheelchair facilities.

Permits: Free overnight permits are required and are available at the Golden West Visitor Center in Stehekin. Access to Stehekin requires a $25 round-trip boat ride from Chelan.

Maps: For a map of North Cascades National Park, contact the Outdoor Recreation Information Center, Seattle REI, 222 Yale Avenue North, Seattle, WA 98109; 206/470-4060. Green Trails, Inc.'s excellent topographic maps of the region are available for $3.99 each at outdoor retail outlets; ask for map numbers 81 and 49, McGregor Mountain and Mount Logan. Ask the USGS for topographic maps of the Goode Mountain, McGregor Mountain, and Mount Logan areas.

Directions: From Seattle take U.S. 2/Stevens Pass east to Wenatchee and U.S. 97 north to the city of Chelan. Catch the water taxi up Lake Chelan to Stehekin (contact the Outdoor Recreation Information Center at 206/470-4060 or see website: www.ladyofthelake.com for boat schedules and shuttle bus information). Ride the shuttle bus from Stehekin to the trailhead near the Bridge Creek Bridge. Hike the Bridge Creek Trail three miles to the North Fork Trail on the left (east). See the special access note in the Park Creek Pass hike.

Contact: North Cascades National Park/Mount Baker Ranger District Information Center, 2105 Highway 20, Sedro-Woolley, WA 98284; 360/856-5700.

103 McGregor Mountain
7.6 mi/1.0 day

Pull out a topographic map of McGregor Mountain and look at the trail to the peak. What appears to be a wild zigzag pattern left by a wayward sewing machine really is the trail, all 144 switchbacks, which runs between High Bridge and Heaton Camp at 6.6 miles. It will suck the life out of you as it climbs an incredible 6,400 feet in 7.6 miles, a rate that really should be illegal. Many hikers who survive the trek to Heaton Camp spend the night there or head back. The views are grand, and that last mile is often covered with snow. Those who left their ice axes at home (or stashed them three miles up the trail in a desperate attempt to lighten their loads) should consider this the end of the road. But if it's late summer or if all this altitude has gone straight to your head, follow the red-paint trail markers to the top. Be careful; it's easy to get lost, and no rescue team in its right mind is coming up here after you. At the 8,000-foot former lookout site, the view is predictably unbelievable. You are sitting in a place not many people see. Relish that for a second, then lace up your boots tighter than they have ever been as you prepare for the long plunge back down.

Location: In the Stehekin River Valley of North Cascades National Park; see Northern Cascades Map 2, grid e2.

User Groups: Hikers only. No dogs, horses, or mountain bikes are allowed. No wheelchair facilities.

Permits: Free overnight permits (required) are available at the Golden West Visitor Center in Stehekin. Access to Stehekin requires a $25 round-trip boat ride from Chelan.

Maps: For a map of North Cascades National Park, contact the Outdoor Recreation Information Center, Seattle REI, 222 Yale Avenue North, Seattle, WA 98109; 206/470-4060. Green Trails, Inc.'s excellent topographic map of the region is available for $3.99 at outdoor retail outlets; ask for map number 81, McGregor Mountain. Ask the USGS for a topographic map of the Goode Mountain area.

Directions: From Seattle take U.S. 2/Stevens Pass east to Wenatchee and U.S. 97 north to the city of Chelan. Catch the water taxi up Lake Chelan to Stehekin (contact the Outdoor Recreation Information Center at 206/470-4060 or see website: www.ladyofthelake.com for boat schedules and shuttle bus information). Ride the shuttle bus from Stehekin to the trailhead in the backyard of the High Bridge Ranger Station. See the special access note in the Park Creek Pass hike.

Contact: North Cascades National Park/Mount Baker Ranger District Information Center, 2105 Highway 20, Sedro-Woolley, WA 98284; 360/856-5700.

104 Agnes Gorge
5.0 mi/2.0 hrs

For starters, don't confuse this trail with the nearby Agnes Creek Trail. That's actually a stretch of the Pacific Crest Trail, described later in this chapter. The Agnes Gorge Trail, one of the better and more accessible day hikes from the Stehekin Valley, skirts the creek's west bank. Along the entire hike are great views of the skinny gorge below, as well as of 8,115-foot Agnes Mountain, which keeps a constant eye on you. At the end of the trail you find a good campsite/picnic spot. Treat it with care. The hike is mostly level and shouldn't be too difficult for children or seniors.

Location: In the Stehekin River Valley of North Cascades National Park; see Northern Cascades Map 2, grid e2.

User Groups: Hikers only. No dogs, horses, or mountain bikes are allowed. No wheelchair facilities.

Permits: Free overnight permits (required) are available at the Golden West Visitor Center in Stehekin. Access to Stehekin requires a $25 round-trip boat ride from Chelan.

Maps: For a map of North Cascades National Park, contact the Outdoor Recreation Information Center, Seattle REI, 222 Yale Avenue North, Seattle, WA 98109; 206/470-4060. Green Trails, Inc.'s excellent topographic map of the region is available for $3.99 at outdoor retail outlets; ask for map number 81, McGregor Mountain. Ask the USGS for topographic maps of the McGregor Mountain and Mount Lyall areas.

Directions: From Seattle take U.S. 2/Stevens Pass east to Wenatchee and U.S. 97 north to the city of Chelan. Catch the water taxi up Lake Chelan to Stehekin (contact the Outdoor Recreation Information Center at 206/470-4060 or see website: www.ladyofthelake.com for boat schedules and shuttle bus information). Ride the shuttle bus from Stehekin to the trailhead on the southwest side of the road near High Bridge Campground. See the special access note in the Park Creek Pass hike.

Contact: North Cascades National Park/Mount Baker Ranger District Information Center, 2105 Highway 20, Sedro-Woolley, WA 98284; 360/856-5700.

105 Rainbow Lake
20.0 mi/2.0 days

The Rainbow Lake Trail, which begins 5.4 miles up the Rainbow Loop (see hike in this chapter), can be hiked as a one-way access route to the Pacific Crest Trail at South Fork Camp on Bridge Creek, or as part of a long loop that includes the PCT, McAlester Pass, and Rainbow Creek Trails. But many backpackers settle for a satisfying, 20-mile round-trip jaunt to Rainbow Lake. From its genesis at Bench Creek Camp, the trail drops across Rainbow Creek and then climbs swiftly into pleasant meadows, where wildflowers are in full display in early summer. Following the creek's north fork, the trail leads to Rainbow Lake, which on a sunny day shimmers like a jewel amid a frame of green meadows. Fishing is fair in the lake, and no license is required. You find good established campsites here and excellent options for day hikes to other nearby lakes and Bowan Pass (elevation 6,200 feet). Farther north, the trail drops steadily to the Pacific Crest Trail junction.

Location: In the upper Stehekin River Valley of North Cascades National Park; see Northern Cascades Map 2, grid f3.

User Groups: Hikers only. No dogs, horses, or mountain bikes are allowed. No wheelchair facilities.

Permits: Free overnight permits (required) are available at the Golden West Visitor Center in Stehekin. Access to Stehekin requires a $25 round-trip boat ride from Chelan.

Maps: For a map of North Cascades National Park and Lake Chelan National Recreation Area, contact the Outdoor Recreation Information Center, Seattle REI, 222 Yale Avenue North, Seattle, WA 98109; 206/470-4060. Green Trails, Inc.'s excellent topographic map of the region is available for $3.99 at outdoor retail outlets; ask for map number 82, Stehekin. Ask the USGS for topographic maps of the Stehekin and McGregor Mountain areas.

Directions: From Seattle take U.S. 2/Stevens Pass east to Wenatchee and U.S. 97 north to the city of Chelan. Catch the water taxi up Lake Chelan to Stehekin (contact the Outdoor Recreation Information Center at 206/470-4060 or see website: www.ladyofthelake.com for boat schedules and shuttle bus information). Ride the shuttle bus for 2.5 miles up Stehekin Road to the Rainbow Creek Trailhead. See the special access note in the Park Creek Pass hike.

Contact: North Cascades National Park/Mount Baker Ranger District Information Center, 2105 Highway 20, Sedro-Woolley, WA 98284; 360/856-5700.

106 Company/Devore Creeks Loop
28.0 mi/3.0–4.0 days

Don't be fooled by guidebooks proclaiming "elevation gain: none" for this trail. It's a major haul, with 5,000 feet gained and lost again throughout the 28-mile loop. You just happen to wind up at the same elevation at which you began: about 1,200 feet. It can be particularly challenging early in the summer, when many snowfields linger (ice axes are a must) and stream fordings can be treacherous (carry a rope). When the conditions are right, however, it's a great getaway from the summer tourist crowds in the magnificent Stehekin Valley. It's at its best in the fall.

At five miles, you need to ford Company Creek. Check water levels with a ranger before departing. From here, climb steadily to Hilgard Pass and then Tenmile Pass. The farther you go down the Devore Creek drainage on the way out, the more impressive it becomes. The creek empties into Lake Chelan at your destination, Weaver Point. From here, it's a 3.5-mile walk down the Stehekin River Trail to Stehekin Road. Good campsites along the loop include camps at 3.5 and 10 miles on Company Creek and Tenmile Basin, and Tenmile Pass and Bird Creek in the Devore Creek drainage. You get great views of Tupshin and Devore Peaks from various spots along the route.

Portions of this trail haven't been cleared of brush since the days when steam engines ran.

Location: In the lower Stehekin River Valley of Lake Chelan National Recreation Area; see Northern Cascades Map 2, grid f3.

User Groups: Hikers, leashed dogs, and horses. No mountain bikes are allowed. No wheelchair facilities.

Permits: Free overnight permits are required and available at the Golden West Visitor Center in Stehekin. Access to Stehekin requires a $25 round-trip boat ride from Chelan.

Maps: For a map of North Cascades National Park, contact the Outdoor Recreation Information Center, Seattle REI, 222 Yale Avenue North, Seattle, WA 98109; 206/470-

4060. Green Trails, Inc.'s excellent topographic maps of the region are available for $3.99 each at outdoor retail outlets; ask for map numbers 81, 82, and 114, McGregor Mountain, Stehekin, and Lucerne. Ask the USGS for topographic maps of the Stehekin, Mount Lyall, Holden, and Pinnacle Mountain areas.

Directions: From Seattle take U.S. 2/Stevens Pass east to Wenatchee and U.S. 97 north to the city of Chelan. Catch the water taxi up Lake Chelan to Stehekin (contact the Outdoor Recreation Information Center at 206/470-4060 or see website: www.ladyofthelake.com for boat schedules and shuttle bus information). Ride the shuttle bus 5.5 miles from Stehekin to the trailhead on Company Creek Road.

Contact: North Cascades National Park/ Mount Baker Ranger District Information Center, 2105 Highway 20, Sedro-Woolley, WA 98284; 360/856-5700.

107 Copper Pass
13.0 mi/4.0 hrs

The first 2.5 miles follow the route to Twisp Pass. At the fork, stay right and slowly climb the valley of the North Fork Twisp River. This trout-filled stream is an angler's paradise as well as a scenic wonder: the pretty, churning water provides a perfect backdrop to the dry pine forest. Before long, the trail begins to get steeper, and as it climbs the head wall of the valley, it leaves the forest and enters subalpine meadows. The last mile to the pass is very steep, rocky, and, in midsummer, blisteringly hot. The trail leads up the south face of the hill, and the surrounding rocks bounce the sun's heat right back into your face. Carry plenty of water and apply sunscreen liberally. At the pass, you will want to sit down for a rest and enjoy the great views. To the south, the skyline is dominated by Gilbert Mountain; the north side of the pass looks toward the Early Winter Spires.

Location: West of Twisp in Okanogan National Forest, within the Lake Chelan/Sawtooth Wilderness; see Northern Cascades Map 2, grid e4.

User Groups: Hikers, dogs, and horses. No mountain bikes are allowed. No wheelchair facilities.

Permits: A federal Northwest Forest Pass, $5 per day or $30 annually, is required to park at the trailhead. Passes are available from ranger stations and many private vendors, online at website: www.wta.org, or by calling 800/270-7504.

Maps: For a trail information report, contact the Methow Valley Ranger District at 509/997-2131. For a map of Okanogan National Forest, contact the Outdoor Recreation Information Center, Seattle REI, 222 Yale Avenue North, Seattle, WA 98109; 206/470-4060. Ask the USGS for topographic maps of the Gilbert and McAlester Mountain areas.

Directions: From Twisp drive 25 miles west on Twisp River Road/Forest Service Road 44 to the road's end and the trailhead.

Contact: Okanogan National Forest, Methow Valley Ranger District, 502 Glover Street, P.O. Box 188, Twisp, WA 98856; 509/997-2131. Or contact Visitor Information Center, Building 49, Highway 20, Winthrop, WA 98862; 509/996-4000.

108 Twisp Pass
19.0 mi/1.0–2.0 days

The pass is actually the midpoint of this trail, not the destination. The first couple miles of trail head up the Twisp River. Then the route angles steeply up the valley wall and heads through a series of switchbacks to the pass, which offers moderate views. Crossing over to the west side of the ridge, the trail drops past Dagger Lake and on down the East Fork of McAlester Creek before ending at a junction with the Pacific Crest Trail. If views are what you're after, Dagger Lake is a good place to have lunch and then turn around; beyond that, the forest closes in, allowing hikers to see nothing but old pine trees and a small stream. From the shores of the lake, though, views of Stiletto Peak and Twisp Mountain are pretty, and the fishing is good, too. Beware, however, of the midsummer swarms of blackflies and mosquitoes. Camp at Dagger Lake or along McAlester Creek.

Location: West of Twisp in Okanogan National Forest, within the Lake Chelan/Sawtooth Wilderness; see Northern Cascades Map 2, grid e4.

User Groups: Hikers, dogs, and horses. No mountain bikes are allowed. No wheelchair facilities.

Permits: A federal Northwest Forest Pass, $5 per day or $30 annually, is required to park at the trailhead. Passes are available from ranger stations and many private vendors, online at website: www.wta.org, or by calling 800/270-7504.

Maps: For a trail information report, contact the Methow Valley Ranger District at 509/997-2131. For a map of Okanogan National Forest, contact the Outdoor Recreation Information Center, Seattle REI, 222 Yale Avenue North, Seattle, WA 98109; 206/470-4060. Ask the USGS for topographic maps of the Gilbert and McAlester Mountain areas.

Directions: From Twisp drive 25 miles west on Twisp River Road/Forest Service Road 44 to the road's end and the trailhead.

Contact: Okanogan National Forest, Methow Valley Ranger District, 502 Glover Street, P.O. Box 188, Twisp, WA 98856; 509/997-2131. Or contact Visitor Information Center, Building 49, Highway 20, Winthrop, WA 98862; 509/996-4000.

109 North Creek
9.6 mi/4.8 hrs

Start hiking north along the North Creek and follow the river valley as it loops through its fishhook-shaped path. As you near the trail end, you find yourself hiking due south into the North Lake Basin. That means you enjoy nearly five miles of scenic valley hiking en route to a lake that is only 2.2 miles as the crow flies from the trailhead. That's OK, though, because the shorter route would require a direct assault on 8,000-foot Gilbert Peak. Stay on the trail and you get to see that same peak from three sides and, from the lake, you enjoy stunning views across the water to Gilbert's rugged north face. The lake is surrounded by pretty but fragile alpine meadows, so restrict your wandering around the lake as much as possible to help minimize damage to the vegetation.

Location: West of Twisp in Okanogan National Forest, within the Lake Chelan/Sawtooth Wilderness; see Northern Cascades Map 2, grid e4.

User Groups: Hikers, dogs, and horses. No mountain bikes are allowed. No wheelchair facilities.

Permits: A federal Northwest Forest Pass, $5 per day or $30 annually, is required to park at the trailhead. Passes are available from ranger stations and many private vendors, online at website: www.wta.org, or by calling 800/270-7504.

Maps: For a trail information report, contact the Methow Valley Ranger District at 509/997-2131. For a map of Okanogan National Forest, contact the Outdoor Recreation Information Center, Seattle REI, 222 Yale Avenue North, Seattle, WA 98109; 206/470-4060. Ask the USGS for a topographic map of the Gilbert area.

Directions: From Twisp drive 25 miles west on Twisp River Road/Forest Service Road 44 to the trailhead on the right.

Contact: Okanogan National Forest, Methow Valley Ranger District, 502 Glover Street, P.O. Box 188, Twisp, WA 98856; 509/997-2131. Or contact Visitor Information Center, Building 49, Highway 20, Winthrop, WA 98862; 509/996-4000.

110 Louis Lake
11.4 mi/5.7 hrs

Hike 2.5 miles along South Creek before turning left (south) at the first trail fork and heading up toward the lake. The valley forest is thick with lodgepole pine, fir, and spruce, and these trees line the draw that you follow on a sometimes-steep climb to the lake. The forest is broken by large flower-filled fields, though, and the lake is surrounded by fragile heather meadows. Campers have trampled these lakeside fields, and a revegetation program is under way. For the new plants to survive and the meadows to return to top health, hikers and campers must respect the area closure signs and stay on designated trails.

Location: West of Twisp in Okanogan National Forest, within the Lake Chelan/Sawtooth Wilderness; see Northern Cascades Map 2, grid e4.

User Groups: Hikers, dogs, and horses. No mountain bikes are allowed. No wheelchair facilities.

Permits: A federal Northwest Forest Pass, $5 per day or $30 annually, is required to park at the trailhead. Passes are available from ranger stations and many private vendors, online at website: www.wta.org, or by calling 800/270-7504.

Maps: For a trail information report, contact the Methow Valley Ranger District at 509/997-2131. For a map of Okanogan National Forest, contact the Outdoor Recreation Information Center, Seattle REI, 222 Yale Avenue North, Seattle, WA 98109; 206/470-4060. Ask the USGS for a topographic map of the Gilbert area.

Directions: From Twisp drive 22 miles west on Twisp River Road/Forest Service Road 44 to the South Creek Campground and the trailhead.

Contact: Okanogan National Forest, Methow Valley Ranger District, 502 Glover Street, P.O. Box 188, Twisp, WA 98856; 509/997-2131. Or contact Visitor Information Center, Building 49, Highway 20, Winthrop, WA 98862; 509/996-4000.

111 Scatter Creek
8.4 mi/4.2 hrs

A 20-percent grade makes for a steep climb at any time, but when that pitch is maintained over the length of a four-mile trail, expect a tough hike. Make that trail rough and brushy, and the hike becomes almost nightmarishly tough. But put a crystal-clear, ice-cold alpine lake at the end of the trail and throw in spectacular views of an 8,320-foot peak, and your weariness is sure to miraculously melt away. That's the Scatter Creek Trail. A long, hot climb is the price you pay for the scenic splendor of Scatter Lake, a blue pool under the shadows of towering Gilbert Peak. The trail is seldom used, so solitude is probable. That lack of use also allows the vegetation to grow over the trail, adding yet another obstacle for hikers to overcome.

Location: West of Twisp in Okanogan National Frest, within the Lake Chelan/Sawtooth Wilderness; see Northern Cascades Map 2, grid e4.

User Groups: Hikers, dogs, and horses. No mountain bikes are allowed. No wheelchair facilities.

Permits: A federal Northwest Forest Pass, $5 per day or $30 annually, is required to park at the trailhead. Passes are available from ranger stations and many private vendors, online at website: www.wta.org, or by calling 800/270-7504.

Maps: For a trail information report, contact the Methow Valley Ranger District at 509/997-2131. For a map of Okanogan National Forest, contact the Outdoor Recreation Information Center, Seattle REI, 222 Yale Avenue North, Seattle, WA 98109; 206/470-4060. Ask the USGS for a topographic map of the Gilbert and Midnight Mountain areas.

Directions: From Twisp drive 22 miles west on Twisp River Road/Forest Service Road 44 to the trailhead opposite the South Creek Campground.

Contact: Okanogan National Forest, Methow Valley Ranger District, 502 Glover Street, P.O. Box 188, Twisp, WA 98856; 509/997-2131. Or contact Visitor Information Center, Building 49, Highway 20, Winthrop, WA 98862; 509/996-4000.

112 Slate Creek
10.2 mi/6.0 hrs

Survive the first half of this trail and you have it made. Nearly all of the 3,700 feet in elevation gain is accomplished in the first three miles. Making that section even tougher is the fact that the trail is faint and the tread disappears in places, so hikers must navigate with the assistance of rock cairns. Get through that section, though, and the final two miles consist of a scenic ridge hike to Slate Lake. Great views out over the splendid Lake Chelan/Sawtooth Wilderness are accented with closer views of open wildflower meadows.

Location: West of Twisp in Okanogan National Forest, within the Lake Chelan/Sawtooth Wilderness; see Northern Cascades Map 2, grid e5.

User Groups: Hikers, dogs, and horses. No mountain bikes are allowed. No wheelchair facilities.

Permits: A federal Northwest Forest Pass, $5 per day or $30 annually, is required to park at the trailhead. Passes are available from ranger stations and many private vendors, online at website: www.wta.org, or by calling 800/270-7504.

Maps: For a trail information report, contact the Methow Valley Ranger District at 509/997-2131. For a map of Okanogan National Forest, contact the Outdoor Recreation Information Center, Seattle REI, 222 Yale Avenue North, Seattle, WA 98109; 206/470-4060. Ask the USGS for a topographic map of the Midnight Mountain area.

Directions: From Twisp drive 17.4 miles west on Twisp River Road/Forest Service Road 44 to the trailhead on the right.

Contact: Okanogan National Forest, Methow Valley Ranger District, 502 Glover Street, P.O. Box 188, Twisp, WA 98856; 509/997-2131. Or contact Visitor Information Center, Building 49, Highway 20, Winthrop, WA 98862; 509/996-4000.

113 Williams Creek
15.0 mi/1.0 day

Before topping out at a high alpine lake with plenty of distant craggy peak views, this moderately steep trail parallels a pretty river, climbs through pine forests, and explores an area that was burned but is recovering. The most unusual part of the route is the old burn. After a couple of decades, the forest has recovered to a large degree and now provides an interesting exercise in forest study. Compare the characteristics of the old pine forests at the lower end of the trail to the new, young growth in the burned area. Note how different birds and animals browse through the two forest types and how different flowers and berries grow in each area. From William's Lake at the trail's end, look up on William's Butte to the west and War Creek Ridge to the south.

Location: West of Twisp in Okanogan National Forest, within the Lake Chelan/Sawtooth Wilderness; see Northern Cascades Map 2, grid e5.

User Groups: Hikers, dogs, and horses. No mountain bikes are allowed. No wheelchair facilities.

Permits: A federal Northwest Forest Pass, $5 per day or $30 annually, is required to park at the trailhead. Passes are available from ranger stations and many private vendors, online at website: www.wta.org, or by calling 800/270-7504.

Maps: For a trail information report, contact the Methow Valley Ranger District at 509/997-2131. For a map of Okanogan National Forest, contact the Outdoor Recreation Information Center, Seattle REI, 222 Yale Avenue North, Seattle, WA 98109; 206/470-4060. Ask the USGS for topographic maps of the Midnight Mountain, Gilbert, and Sun Mountain areas.

Directions: From Twisp drive 18 miles west on Twisp River Road/Forest Service Road 44 to the Mystery Campground; turn left at the campground and cross the river. Turn left immediately across the river onto Forest Service Road 4430 and drive one-half mile to the trailhead on the right.

Contact: Okanogan National Forest, Methow Valley Ranger District, 502 Glover Street, P.O. Box 188, Twisp, WA 98856; 509/997-2131. Or contact Visitor Information Center, Building 49, Highway 20, Winthrop, WA 98862; 509/996-4000.

114 North War Creek
19.0 mi/1.0–2.0 days

Old-growth pine and fir forest gives way to subalpine forests of spruce and scrub pine that eventually give way to alpine meadows at War Creek Pass. The first eight miles of the route run alongside the north bank of War Creek, a noisy, bouncing little stream. At the pass, the trail ends at a junction with the Purple Creek Trail. A short side trail leads down to Juanita Lake, a pretty alpine tarn. This is a good place to set up camp, but beware: it is also a breeding ground for mosquitoes.

Location: West of Twisp in Okanogan National Forest, within the Lake Chelan/Sawtooth Wilderness; see Northern Cascades Map 2, grid f5.

User Groups: Hikers, dogs, and horses. No mountain bikes are allowed. No wheelchair facilities.

Permits: A federal Northwest Forest Pass, $5 per day or $30 annually, is required to park at the trailhead. Passes are available from ranger stations and many private vendors, online at website: www.wta.org, or by calling 800/270-7504.

Maps: For a trail information report, contact the Methow Valley Ranger District at 509/997-2131. For a map of Okanogan National Forest, contact the Outdoor Recreation Information Center, Seattle REI, 222 Yale Avenue North, Seattle, WA 98109; 206/470-4060. Ask the USGS for topographic maps of the Oval Peak and Sun Mountain areas.

Directions: From Twisp drive 14.7 miles west on Twisp River Road/Forest Service Road 44 to the junction with Forest Service Road 4430-100. Turn left (south) onto Forest Service Road 4430-100 and drive 2.1 miles to the road's end and the trailhead.

Contact: Okanogan National Forest, Methow Valley Ranger District, 502 Glover Street, P.O. Box 188, Twisp, WA 98856; 509/997-2131.

Or contact Visitor Information Center, Building 49, Highway 20, Winthrop, WA 98862; 509/996-4000.

115 War Creek South
12.0 mi/6.0 hrs

The trail follows the War Creek main branch for two miles through old pine, fir, and spruce forest. Mule deer are abundant in this forest, especially up the creek's south fork. At the first fork in the trail, stay left and head up the faint, primitive trail that parallels the South Fork of War Creek. The path peters out in four miles near the creek's headwaters in the shadow of Sun Mountain. This little-used trail is a forest-lover's dream, and few views are available through the dense forest canopy. That dense forest provides a lot of protection for wildlife. Look for mule deer, black bears, rabbits, raccoons, and a host of birds and small mammals.

Location: West of Twisp in Okanogan National Forest, within the Lake Chelan/Sawtooth Wilderness; see Northern Cascades Map 2, grid f5.

User Groups: Hikers, dogs, and horses. No mountain bikes are allowed. No wheelchair facilities.

Permits: A federal Northwest Forest Pass, $5 per day or $30 annually, is required to park at the trailhead. Passes are available from ranger stations and many private vendors, online at website: www.wta.org, or by calling 800/270-7504.

Maps: For a trail information report, contact the Methow Valley Ranger District at 509/997-2131. For a map of Okanogan National Forest, contact the Outdoor Recreation Information Center, Seattle REI, 222 Yale Avenue North, Seattle, WA 98109; 206/470-4060. Ask the USGS for topographic maps of the Oval Peak and Sun Mountain areas.

Directions: From Twisp drive 14.7 miles west on Twisp River Road/Forest Service Road 44 to the junction with Forest Srvice Road 4430-100. Turn left (south) onto Forest Service Road 4430-100 and drive 2.1 miles to the road's end and the trailhead.

Contact: Okanogan National Forest, Methow Valley Ranger District, 502 Glover Street, P.O. Box 188, Twisp, WA 98856; 509/997-2131. Or contact Visitor Information Center, Building 49, Highway 20, Winthrop, WA 98862; 509/996-4000.

116 Eagle Creek
14.6 mi/1.0 day

Solitude is almost guaranteed on this primitive little path. The narrow, quiet trail winds through forest as it follows the north bank of Eagle Creek, which is small and tame but nevertheless beautiful. The forest is thick and dark, home to a multitude of wildlife, and the trail is faint and brushy. The route takes you under the north flank of Duckbill Mountain before climbing, steeply at times, across the side of Battle Mountain and eventually into the open meadows around Eagle Pass. In high, remote areas such as this, there are typically at least a few red-tailed or rough-legged hawks circling overhead, but these creatures are notably absent here. That's because, in recent years anyway, the creek and pass have lived up to their names: golden eagles have been spotted from the pass, and those large birds usually scare off the much smaller hawks.

Location: West of Twisp in Okanogan National Forest, within the Lake Chelan/Sawtooth Wilderness; see Northern Cascades Map 2, grid f6.

User Groups: Hikers, dogs, and horses. No mountain bikes are allowed. No wheelchair facilities.

Permits: A federal Northwest Forest Pass, $5 per day or $30 annually, is required to park at the trailhead. Passes are available from ranger stations and many private vendors, online at website: www.wta.org, or by calling 800/270-7504.

Maps: For a trail information report, contact the Methow Valley Ranger District at 509/997-2131. For a map of Okanogan National Forest, contact the Outdoor Recreation Information Center, Seattle REI, 222 Yale Avenue North, Seattle, WA 98109; 206/470-4060. Ask the USGS for a topographic map of the Oval Peak area.

Directions: From Twisp drive 11 miles west on Twisp River Road/Forest Service Road 44. Turn left (south) onto Buttermilk Creek Road/Forest Service 43 and cross the Twisp River. Just beyond the bridge, turn right (west) onto Forest Service Road 4420 and continue 3.4 miles to a junction with Forest Service Road 4420-80. Turn left (south) and drive two miles to the road's end and the trailhead.

Contact: Okanogan National Forest, Methow Valley Ranger District, 502 Glover Street, P.O. Box 188, Twisp, WA 98856; 509/997-2131. Or contact Visitor Information Center, Building 49, Highway 20, Winthrop, WA 98862; 509/996-4000.

⑪⑦ Wolf Creek
20.6 mi/2.0 days

Though unlikely, visitors to this deep wilderness valley might be treated to the howling of wolves. The remote wilderness areas of the North Cascades contain one of the last remaining populations of timber wolves in the Lower 48. Knowing that fact is enough to make this hike special, but there is more to this trail than just a name and a remote possibility of wolf visits. The wide, cold creek is alive with some big native cutthroat and

rainbow trout; the forests are home to mule deer, black bears, and a host of small mammals; and the skies are teeming with red-tailed and rough-legged hawks. Following the forest stream, the trail periodically breaks out into green meadows full of wild strawberries and fragrant wildflowers. Along the edges of the meadows, just inside the tree line, you'll find the biggest, juiciest huckleberries you'll ever hope to taste. If you can beat the bears to them, the forest is full of morel mushrooms.

If picking mushrooms, make absolutely sure you can tell the harmless ones from the deadly. Also, before heading out, ask rangers for the latest information on the mushroom crop and whether there are any seasonal restrictions or permits required for picking.

Location: West of Winthrop in Okanogan National Forest, within the Lake Chelan/Sawtooth Wilderness; see Northern Cascades Map 2, grid e7.

User Groups: Hikers, dogs, and horses. No mountain bikes are allowed. No wheelchair facilities.

Permits: A federal Northwest Forest Pass, $5 per day or $30 annually, is required to park at the trailhead. Passes are available from ranger stations and many private vendors, online at website: www.wta.org, or by calling 800/270-7504.

Maps: For a trail information report, contact the Methow Valley Ranger District at 509/997-2131. For a map of Okanogan National Forest, contact the Outdoor Recreation Information Center, Seattle REI, 222 Yale Avenue North, Seattle, WA 98109; 206/470-4060. Ask the USGS for topographic maps of the Thompson Ridge, Midnight Mountain, and Gilbert areas.

Directions: From Winthrop drive south on Highway 20 across the Methow River and turn right (west) onto Twin Lakes Road/County Road 9120. Continue 1.5 miles before turning right onto Wolf Creek Road/County Road 1131. Follow Wolf Creek Road for 4.5 miles to the trailhead.

Contact: Okanogan National Forest, Methow Valley Ranger District, 502 Glover Street, P.O. Box 188, Twisp, WA 98856; 509/997-2131. Or contact Visitor Information Center, Building 49, Highway 20, Winthrop, WA 98862; 509/996-4000.

118 Railroad Creek to Lyman Lakes
19.4 mi/2.0 days

Half the fun of the Railroad Creek Trail, the major east-side access to the Glacier Peak area, is getting there. From Lucerne, you catch the church bus to Holden, a former wild, backcountry mining town turned Lutheran retreat center. From a campground beyond the odd little village (which is packed with both black bears and backpackers in the summer months), you walk away from mining history and into natural history, passing Hart Lake and Crown Point Falls on the way to lower Lyman Lake (seven miles).

From here, turn south and follow a path through stunning meadows to the upper lakes, and finally, to the toe of the receding Lyman Glacier. It's a magnificent sight, as well as a magnificent campsite. Practicing low-impact camping techniques is essential here. The trail then becomes a side trail and skirts the east side of the glacier up to Spider Gap (elevation 7,100 feet). Skilled cross-country trekkers can drop down Spider Glacier to Phelps Creek Pass. From here, it's 6.5 miles down through Spider Meadow to Chiwawa River Road, an optional exit (see hike in this chapter). Don't try this traverse without some ice ax and route-finding know-how. The route isn't always easy to follow. Back on the main

trail stem before the lake, you can continue west to more spectacular scenery at Cloudy Pass in 1.5 miles and at Suiattle Pass, an additional 0.7 mile.

Location: In the northeastern portion of the Glacier Peak Wilderness, west of Lake Chelan; see Northern Cascades Map 2, grid g2.

User Groups: Hikers, dogs, and horses. No mountain bikes are allowed. No wheelchair facilities.

Permits: No permits are required. Access requires a $25 round-trip boat ride on Lake Chelan, a bus fee, and possibly a parking fee.

Maps: For a map of the Glacier Peak Wilderness, contact the Outdoor Recreation Information Center, Seattle REI, 222 Yale Avenue North, Seattle, WA 98109; 206/470-4060. Green Trails, Inc.'s excellent topographic map of the region is available for $3.99 at outdoor retail outlets; ask for map number 113, Holden. Ask the USGS for a topographic map of the Holden area.

Directions: From Seattle take U.S. 2/Stevens Pass east to Wenatchee and U.S. 97 north to the city of Chelan. Catch the water taxi up Lake Chelan to Lucerne (contact the Outdoor Recreation Information Center at 206/470-4060 or see website: www.ladyofthe lake.com for boat schedules and shuttle bus information). Walk or ride the bus 12 miles upstream (west) to Holden Campground.

Contact: North Cascades National Park/Chelan Ranger District, 428 Woodin Avenue, Chelan, WA 98816; 509/682-2576.

119 Rainbow Loop
7.5 mi/2.0 hrs

A classic Stehekin Valley day hike, this trail is very popular with valley campers and even single-day visitors. You can ride the shuttle bus to either trailhead, but starting at the upper one (the north end of the trail) seems to be the favorite choice. The trail climbs quickly to a ridge above the lower valley, with excellent views. At 2.4 miles, it comes to a junction. If time allows, hang a left and walk a bit north up the Rainbow Creek Trail. It goes another eight miles to High Camp and McAlester Pass, and another 5.3 miles from there to the Pacific Crest Trail just south of Rainy Lake (see hike this chapter) on North Cascades Highway. You only need to go about a mile to find side trails leading to spectacular views of the meadows, lakes, peaks, and open sky that make Stehekin famous among mountain lovers around the world.

On the way down, you pass through Rainbow Bridge Camp and a junction with the Boulder Creek Trail before landing back on the valley road. Wait for the shuttle bus here or strike out along the road; it's about 2.5 miles north to Harlequin Campground and three miles south to Stehekin Landing.

Location: In the lower Stehekin Valley of Lake Chelan National Recreation Area; see Northern Cascades Map 2, grid f3.

User Groups: Hikers, leashed dogs, and horses. No mountain bikes are allowed. No wheelchair facilities.

Permits: Free overnight permits are required and are available at the Golden West Visitor Center in Stehekin. Access to Stehekin requires a $25 round-trip boat ride from Chelan.

Maps: For a map of North Cascades National Park, contact the Outdoor Recreation Information Center, Seattle REI, 222 Yale Avenue North, Seattle, WA 98109; 206/470-4060. Green Trails, Inc.'s excellent topographic map of the region is available for $3.99 at outdoor retail outlets; ask for map number 82, Stehekin. Ask the USGS for a topographic map of the Stehekin area.

Directions: From Seattle take U.S. 2/Stevens Pass east to Wenatchee and U.S. 97 north to the city of Chelan. Catch the water taxi up Lake Chelan to Stehekin (contact the Outdoor Recreation Information Center at 206/470-4060 or see website: www.ladyofthelake.com for boat schedules and shuttle bus information). Ride the shuttle bus to the upper trailhead on the right, a half mile beyond Harlequin Bridge.

Contact: North Cascades National Park/Mount Baker Ranger District Information Center, 2105 Highway 20, Sedro-Woolley, WA 98284; 360/856-5700.

120 Domke Mountain/ Domke Lake
7.2 mi/3.5 hrs

This excellent family hike provides a good chance to get out and work up a sweat after a morning boat trip up Lake Chelan on the water taxi. Domke Lake, which can be reached in about 1.5 easy miles from Lucerne, offers visitors good fishing (a state fishing license is required; ask at the Domke Lake Resort), and the trail continues through the forest to Domke Lake Camp at about three miles. If you're up for a bit more vertical hiking, take the Domke Mountain Trail, which splits off from the main trail just under a mile from the trailhead. It climbs 2.8 miles and about 3,000 feet to a former lookout site with—surprise!—great views of Lake Chelan.

Location: West of Lake Chelan in Wenatchee National Forest; see Northern Cascades Map 2, grid g4.

User Groups: Hikers and dogs. Horses are allowed to Domke Lake, but not on the Domke Mountain Trail. No mountain bikes are allowed. No wheelchair facilities.

Permits: No permits are required. Access requires a $25 round-trip boat ride from Chelan.

Maps: For a map of Wenatchee National Forest, contact the Outdoor Recreation Information Center, Seattle REI, 222 Yale Avenue North, Seattle, WA 98109; 206/470-4060. Green Trails, Inc.'s excellent topographic map of the region is available for $3.99 at outdoor retail outlets; ask for map number 114, Lucerne. Ask the USGS for a topographic map of the Lucerne area.

Directions: From Seattle take U.S. 2/Stevens Pass east to Wenatchee and then proceed on U.S. 97 north to the city of Chelan. Take the water taxi from Chelan to Lucerne (contact the Outdoor Recreation Information Center at 206/470-4060 or see website: www.ladyofthelake.com to obtain the necessary boat schedules and shuttle bus information). Walk a quarter mile on Railroad Creek Road to the Domke Lake Trailhead.

Contact: North Cascades National Park/Chelan Ranger District, 428 Woodin Avenue, Chelan, WA 98816; 509/682-2576.

121 Emerald Park
16.0 mi/2.0 days

For hikers who love the high, dry, scenic eastern Glacier Peak Wilderness setting but can't stand the crowds, this route makes an excellent two- to three-day backpack trip. Thanks to the somewhat cumbersome access (either by boat or from other trails), Emerald Park—a long, green valley surrounded by the imposing Chelan Mountains to the south and high ridges to the east and west—isn't as heavily used as other Lake Chelan–area backpacking venues.

The trail begins in cool forest and climbs steadily, with good campsites and views of the Sawtooth Range beginning about four miles in. At about eight miles, stroll into the backcountry wonderland of Emerald Park. Camp here and make a day hike on to Millham Pass, elevation 6,663 feet, or take the worthwhile 2.5-mile day hike to Mirror Lake. From Millham Pass, the trail

continues five miles down Snowbrushy Creek to a junction with the Entiat River Trail. Combining the Emerald Park and Entiat River Trails makes a good one-way trip of just under 20 miles, with an exit at Cottonwood Campground (see hike in this chapter). The total elevation gain to Emerald Park is 3,000 feet.

Location: West of Lake Chelan in the Glacier Peak Wilderness; see Northern Cascades Map 2, grid g4.

User Groups: Hikers, leashed dogs, and horses. No mountain bikes are allowed. No wheelchair facilities.

Permits: No permits are required. Access to the trail requires a $25 round-trip boat ride from Chelan. Parking is free.

Maps: For a map of the Glacier Peak Wilderness, contact the Outdoor Recreation Information Center, Seattle REI, 222 Yale Avenue North, Seattle, WA 98109; 206/470-4060. Green Trails, Inc.'s excellent topographic map of the region is available for $3.99 at outdoor retail outlets; ask for map number 114, Lucerne. Ask the USGS for topographic maps of the Lucerne, Pinnacle Mountain, and Holden areas.

Directions: From Seattle take U.S. 2/Stevens Pass east to Wenatchee and U.S. 97 north to the city of Chelan. Take the water taxi from Chelan to Lucerne (contact the Outdoor Recreation Information Center at 206/470-4060 or see website: www.ladyofthelake.com for boat schedules and shuttle bus information). Walk along Railroad Creek Road to the Domke Lake Trail. Hike that trail 1.6 miles to the Emerald Park Trailhead.

Contact: North Cascades National Park/Chelan Ranger District, 428 Woodin Avenue, Chelan, WA 98816; 509/682-2576.

122 Chelan Summit Loops

19.3–48.0 mi/
5.0–10.0 days

High-country hikers, this one's for you. No matter which access trail you puff up to reach its arid heights, the Chelan Summit Trail starts out high and stays that way, rarely dropping below 5,500 feet on its ridgetop journey above the north shore of Lake Chelan. Views of surrounding peaks, open meadows, and, larch landscapes make this hike one you'll remember.

The beauty of this route is that it's adjustable. From the trailhead at War Creek Pass (elevation 6,800 feet), the Chelan Summit Trail runs nearly 30 miles southeast to South Navarre Campground, where friends can pick you up after a harrowing auto venture from Manson and Chelan. That long shuttle hike is only one option. For shorter, scenic loop hikes that make it easier on everyone, including yourself, consider returning to Stehekin by dropping southwest down the Fish Creek or Prince Creek Trails and then catching the water taxi or hoofing it back northwest up the Chelan Lakeshore Trail (see hike this chapter). The Fish Creek route is a 19.3-mile walk from Stehekin up and over the summit and back down to the Lakeshore Trail (just over 25 miles if you walk back to Stehekin). The Prince Creek route makes a 31-mile walk from Stehekin up and over the Chelan Summit Trail to a water pickup at Prince Creek Campground (just under 48 miles if you do the whole shebang and walk back on the Chelan Lakeshore Trail). Whichever way you choose, the alpine portion is a seemingly endless series of meadows and spectacular peaks, particularly in the Sawtooth Range to the east.

Location: High above the north shore of Lake Chelan; see Northern Cascades Map 2, grid f6.

User Groups: Hikers, dogs, and horses. No mountain bikes are allowed. No wheelchair facilities.

Permits: Free overnight permits are required and available at the Golden West Visitor Center in Stehekin. Access to Stehekin requires a $25 round-trip boat ride from Chelan.

Maps: For a map of North Cascades National Park and Lake Chelan National Recreation Area, contact the Outdoor Recreation Information Center, Seattle REI, 222 Yale Avenue North, Seattle, WA 98109; 206/470-4060. Green Trails, Inc.'s excellent topographic maps of the region are available for $3.99 each at outdoor retail outlets; ask for map numbers 82, 83, and 114, Stehekin, Buttermilk Butte, and Lucerne. Ask the USGS for topographic maps of the Stehekin and Sun Mountain areas.

Directions: The Chelan Summit Trail's southern reaches can be accessed by car at South Navarre Campground, but the route is difficult, and we recommend entry and exit via the water taxi on Lake Chelan. From Seattle take U.S. 2/Stevens Pass east to Wenatchee and U.S. 97 north to the city of Chelan. Catch the water taxi up Lake Chelan to Stehekin (contact the Outdoor Recreation Information Center at 206/470-4060 or see website: www.ladyofthelake.com for boat schedules and shuttle bus information). If you're starting the hike from Stehekin, take the boat to Stehekin Landing and find the Purple Creek Trailhead on the visitor center's southeast side. Hike the Purple Creek Trail eight miles to War Creek Pass and the beginning of the Summit Trail. Good southern access routes involve boat drop-offs at Fish Creek or Prince Creek, then a hike north to the Summit Trail, high above the lake.

Contact: North Cascades National Park/Mount Baker Ranger District Information Center, 2105 Highway 20, Sedro-Woolley, WA 98284; 360/856-5700; North Cascades National Park/Chelan Ranger District, 428 Woodin Avenue, Chelan, WA 98816; 509/682-2576.

123 West Fork Buttermilk
19.0 mi/2.0 days

A mosquito swamp sprawls across the trail at the six-mile point. Survive that, and you are sure to enjoy your hike. This valley has just enough pitch to keep the creek flowing and, since the trail stays close to the creek over its entire length, only a very gradual climb is required. Solitude is virtually assured, as the trail doesn't lead to a high alpine lake or a mountain pass with views. Instead, this route takes you to yet another forested valley. Still, solitude in a quiet, cool forest has its merits when compared to a crowded lake with views of craggy peaks. Especially when the forest features a trout-filled creek. Again, make sure to slather on plenty of bug dope and don't forget your fishing pole. The trail ends at Fish Creek Pass, but a small side trail leads a few hundred yards south to a small blue pool, Star Lake. You find the best camping here, though smaller sites dot the route as it climbs along the creek.

Location: West of Twisp in Okanogan National Forest, within the Lake Chelan/Sawtooth Wilderness; see Northern Cascades Map 2, grid f6.

User Groups: Hikers, dogs, and horses. No mountain bikes are allowed. No wheelchair facilities.

Permits: A federal Northwest Forest Pass, $5 per day or $30 annually, is required to park at the trailhead. Passes are available from ranger stations and many private vendors, online at website: www.wta.org, or by calling 800/270-7504.

Maps: For a trail information report, contact the Methow Valley Ranger District at 509/997-

2131. For a map of Okanogan National Forest, contact the Outdoor Recreation Information Center, Seattle REI, 222 Yale Avenue North, Seattle, WA 98109; 206/470-4060. Ask the USGS for topographic maps of the Hoodoo Peak and Oval Peak areas.

Directions: From Twisp drive 11 miles west on Twisp River Road/Forest Service Road 44 to the junction with Buttermilk Creek Road. Turn left (south) onto Buttermilk Creek Road and continue 4.5 miles to Forest Service Road 4300-500. Turn right (west) and drive three miles to the road's end and the trailhead.

Contact: Okanogan National Forest, Methow Valley Ranger District, 502 Glover Street, P.O. Box 188, Twisp, WA 98856; 509/997-2131. Or contact Visitor Information Center, Building 49, Highway 20, Winthrop, WA 98862; 509/996-4000.

124 East Fork Buttermilk
13.0 mi/6.5 hrs

Buttermilk Creek is a pretty little stream, and this route offers plenty of views of its noisy east fork. The trail parallels the creek for nearly five miles, climbing gradually through the dense forest on the valley bottom. Periodic breaks in the forest canopy provide views of Spirit Mountain, a long, steep ridge to the north that tapers up toward Spirit Peak. On the south side of the trail, due south of Spirit Peak, is the 8,400-foot Hoodoo Peak summit. Climbers' access trails lead up these peaks, but the way is steep, rocky, and difficult to find; only experienced map and compass users should attempt these bushwhacking excursions. Fortunately, the main trail leads to views equal to those found from the remote summits. The trail eventually leaves the creek (actually it just continues on past the creek's headwaters) and leads up a steep, rocky pitch to Hoodoo Pass. From the pass, the views north to Hoodoo and Spirit Peaks and beyond are unbeatable. Then look south to a panoramic sweep across Old Maid Mountain, Skookum Pass Mountain, and the Lake Chelan Valley.

Location: West of Twisp in Okanogan National Forest, within the Lake Chelan/Sawtooth Wilderness; see Northern Cascades Map 2, grid f7.

User Groups: Hikers, dogs, and horses. No mountain bikes are allowed. No wheelchair facilities.

Permits: A federal Northwest Forest Pass, $5 per day or $30 annually, is required to park at the trailhead. Passes are available from ranger stations and many private vendors, online at website: www.wta.org, or by calling 800/270-7504.

Maps: For a trail information report, contact the Methow Valley Ranger District at 509/997-2131. For a map of Okanogan National Forest, contact the Outdoor Recreation Information Center, Seattle REI, 222 Yale Avenue North, Seattle, WA 98109; 206/470-4060. Ask the USGS for topographic maps of the Hoodoo Pass and Martin Peak.

Directions: From Twisp drive 11 miles west on Twisp River Road/Forest Service Road 44. Turn left (south) onto Buttermilk Creek Road/Forest Service 43 and drive seven miles to the junction with Forest Service Road 400. Turn right (west) and drive three miles to the trailhead, at a sharp switchback turn. Parking is limited at the trailhead, but additional parking can be found at any of the wide turnouts just up the road.

Contact: Okanogan National Forest, Methow Valley Ranger District, 502 Glover Street, P.O. Box 188, Twisp, WA 98856; 509/997-2131. Or contact Visitor Information Center, Building 49, Highway 20, Winthrop, WA 98862; 509/996-4000.

125 Libby Creek
10.6 mi/5.3 hrs

Rolling over several small ridges and crossing a number of intermittent streams, this trail is not for the timid. The roller-coaster route at the trail's start is just a precursor to a steep, thigh-busting, lung-bursting climb under the south flank of Hoodoo Peak and ultimately up through a half-mile-long boulder field to Libby Lake. The tiny lake is very picturesque, if somewhat rugged; its shores are rocky and bare, and the views are impressive. Camping sites are available at the lake, but they are limited. And, when the sun goes down, the wind almost invariably picks up here. With few natural windbreaks, a strong, stable tent is a must for a comfortable night.

Location: South of Twisp in Okanogan National Forest; see Northern Cascades Map 2, grid f6.

User Groups: Hikers, dogs, and horses. No mountain bikes are allowed. No wheelchair facilities.

Permits: A federal Northwest Forest Pass, $5 per day or $30 annually, is required to park at the trailhead. Passes are available from ranger stations and many private vendors, online at website: www.wta.org, or by calling 800/270-7504.

Maps: For a trail information report, contact the Methow Valley Ranger District at 509/997-2131. For a map of Okanogan National Forest, contact the Outdoor Recreation Information Center, Seattle REI, 222 Yale Avenue North, Seattle, WA 98109; 206/470-4060. Ask the USGS for topographic maps of the Hoodoo Peak and Martin Peak.

Directions: From Twisp drive south on Highway 153 to the junction with Libby Creek Road/Forest Service Road 43. Turn right (west) onto Libby Creek Road and continue 7.5 miles before turning left (southwest) onto

Gold Creek Road/Forest Service Road 4340. In 0.75 mile, turn right onto Forest Service Road 700 and drive two miles to the trailhead on the left.

Contact: Okanogan National Forest, Methow Valley Ranger District, 502 Glover Street, P.O. Box 188, Twisp, WA 98856; 509/997-2131. Or contact Visitor Information Center, Building 49, Highway 20, Winthrop, WA 98862; 509/996-4000.

126 Martin Creek
22.8 mi/2.0 days

Sharing the first 2.5 miles with the Eagle Lake Trail (see hike this chapter), this route is popular and often crowded, but the crowds thin considerably after the trail forks. The Eagle Lake Trail angles steeply to the north, while this route continues southwest along the Martin Creek Valley. Access to the creek isn't provided simply because the trail stays high on the valley wall well above the creekbed, but periodic openings in the forest allow good views of the small, quiet creek. After reaching the Martin Creek headwaters, the trail climbs steeply across the valley's head wall and through the basin of Cooney Lake. This lake lies alongside the trail, but the more picturesque Martin Lakes are reached via a short, steep side trail that branches off the main path at about five miles from the trailhead. Moving on past Cooney Lake (take care when traveling through the revegetation areas), the trail eventually ends at a junction with the Foggy Dew Trail (see hike this chapter), just below the Merchants Basin.

If you have two cars and can arrange a shuttle, this trail combined with the Foggy Dew Trail makes a good one-way trip. The shuttle distance is only about seven miles.

Location: South of Twisp in Okanogan National Forest; see Northern Cascades Map 2, grid f6.

User Groups: Hikers, dogs, and horses. No mountain bikes are allowed. No wheelchair facilities.

Permits: A federal Northwest Forest Pass, $5 per day or $30 annually, is required to park at the trailhead. Passes are available from ranger stations and many private vendors, online at website: www.wta.org, or by calling 800/270-7504.

Maps: For a trail information report, contact the Methow Valley Ranger District at 509/997-2131. For a map of Okanogan National Forest, contact the Outdoor Recreation Information Center, Seattle REI, 222 Yale Avenue North, Seattle, WA 98109; 206/470-4060. Ask the USGS for a topographic map of the Martin Peak area.

Directions: From Twisp, proceed south on Highway 153 to the junction with North Fork Gold Creek Road/County Road 1029 and turn right (west). Stay right at the junction near the forest boundary, bearing onto Forest Service Road 4340. Continue 5.6 miles to Forest Service Road 300, a narrow dirt road leading off to the left (northwest). Drive five miles to the end of Forest Service Road 300 and the trailhead.

Contact: Okanogan National Forest, Methow Valley Ranger District, 502 Glover Street, P.O. Box 188, Twisp, WA 98856; 509/997-2131. Or contact Visitor Information Center, Building 49, Highway 20, Winthrop, WA 98862; 509/996-4000.

127 Crater Creek
7.8 mi/3.6 hrs

Hike half a mile on the wooded trail; then leave the main trail at the fork and angle off to the right, walking along small, babbling Crater

Creek. The route climbs steeply at times until the trail and the creek end at Crater Lake. Though not as spectacular as its famous Oregon namesake, this lake is a picturesque blue jewel just outside the Lake Chelan/Sawtooth Wilderness. Great horned owls frequent these woods and can often be seen in the early morning and late afternoon hours, particularly in the spring. Stellar's jays and whiskey jacks prowl the lakeshores; the jacks, a.k.a. camp robber jays, are particularly bold little fellows that have been known to try to swipe gorp out of my pack pockets while I was wearing the pack.

Location: South of Twisp in Okanogan National Forest; see Northern Cascades Map 2, grid f6.

User Groups: Hikers, dogs, and horses. No mountain bikes are allowed. No wheelchair facilities.

Permits: A federal Northwest Forest Pass, $5 per day or $30 annually, is required to park at the trailhead. Passes are available from ranger stations and many private vendors, online at website: www.wta.org, or by calling 800/270-7504.

Maps: For a trail information report, contact the Methow Valley Ranger District at 509/997-2131. For a map of Okanogan National Forest, contact the Outdoor Recreation Information Center, Seattle REI, 222 Yale Avenue North, Seattle, WA 98109; 206/470-4060. Ask the USGS for a topographic map of the Martin Peak area.

Directions: From Twisp drive south on Highway 153 to the junction with North Fork Gold Creek Road/County Road 1029 and turn right (west). Stay right at the junction near the forest boundary, bearing onto Forest Service Road 4340. Continue for 5.6 miles to Forest Service Road 300, a narrow dirt road leading off to the left (northwest). Drive five miles to the end of Forest Service Road 300 and the trailhead.

Contact: Okanogan National Forest, Methow Valley Ranger District, 502 Glover Street, P.O. Box 188, Twisp, WA 98856; 509/997-2131. Or contact Visitor Information Center, Building 49, Highway 20, Winthrop, WA 98862; 509/996-4000.

128 Eagle Lake
14.0 mi/1.0 day

Traversing a steep hillside, this route climbs gradually but steadily toward Horsehead Pass. The thick forest offers few views and little variety for the first few miles, but as it nears Sawtooth Ridge, there are several side trip options. The main trail splits a ridge almost dead center between Upper and Lower Eagle Lakes, and faint side trails lead to each of the lake basins. Head north to Upper Eagle Lake and find views of Mount Bigelow reflected in the cold blue waters. Or head south to Lower Eagle Lake to enjoy trout fishing while looking out on Martin Peak. The benefit of visiting the lower lake is that another trail loops back to the main trail and on to the pass, eliminating the need to backtrack. From the pass, a short side trail takes you to yet another lake, Boiling Lake.

Location: South of Twisp in Okanogan National Forest; see Northern Cascades Map 2, grid g6.

User Groups: Hikers, dogs, and horses. No mountain bikes are allowed. No wheelchair facilities.

Permits: A federal Northwest Forest Pass, $5 per day or $30 annually, is required to park at the trailhead. Passes are available from ranger stations and many private vendors, online at website: www.wta.org, or by calling 800/270-7504.

Maps: For a trail information report, contact the Methow Valley Ranger District at 509/997-2131. For a map of Okanogan National Forest, contact the Outdoor Recreation Information

Center, Seattle REI, 222 Yale Avenue North, Seattle, WA 98109; 206/470-4060. Ask the USGS for a topographic map of the Martin Peak area.

Directions: From Twisp drive south on Highway 153 to the junction with North Fork Gold Creek Road/County Road 1029 and turn right (west). Stay right at the junction near the forest boundary, bearing onto Forest Service Road 4340. Continue 5.6 miles to Forest Service Road 300, a narrow dirt road leading off to the left (northwest). Drive five miles to the end of the road and the trailhead.

Contact: Okanogan National Forest, Methow Valley Ranger District, 502 Glover Street, P.O. Box 188, Twisp, WA 98856; 509/997-2131. Or contact Visitor Information Center, Building 49, Highway 20, Winthrop, WA 98862; 509/996-4000.

129 Blackpine Lake Loop
0.6 mi/0.5 hr

The trail arcs around the blue waters of Blackpine Lake and crosses a couple of small feeder and outlet streams. These little creeks are used extensively by the beaver colony that calls this lake home. Few visitors to this trail leave without at least hearing the hard kersplash of a beaver tail slapping against the water. Wheelchairs are prevented from rolling off the slightly sloping path by a log curb that runs the length of the trail. A pair of fishing piers attest to the quality fishery in the lake, but neither of the piers is wheelchair-accessible, so wheelchair users have to cast from the shore. That could be a blessing, though, as the best fishing holes are far from the piers.

Location: West of Twisp in Okanogan National Forest; see Northern Cascades Map 2, grid f7.

User Groups: Hikers and dogs. Wheelchair accessible. No horses or mountain bikes are allowed.

Permits: A federal Northwest Forest Pass, $5 per day or $30 annually, is required to park at the trailhead. Passes are available from ranger stations and many private vendors, online at website: www.wta.org, or by calling 800/270-7504.

Maps: For a trail information report, contact the Methow Valley Ranger District at 509/997-2131. For a map of Okanogan National Forest, contact the Outdoor Recreation Information Center, Seattle REI, 222 Yale Avenue North, Seattle, WA 98109; 206/470-4060. Ask the USGS for a topographic map of the Mission Peak area.

Directions: From Twisp drive 10.6 miles west on Twisp River Road/Forest Service Road 44, then turn left (south) onto Buttermilk Creek Road/Forest Service Road 43. Drive 8.2 miles to the Blackpine Lake Campground. The trailhead and parking area are near the boat ramp and day-use area.

Contact: Okanogan National Forest, Methow Valley Ranger District, 502 Glover Street, P.O. Box 188, Twisp, WA 98856; 509/997-2131. Or contact Visitor Information Center, Building 49, Highway 20, Winthrop, WA 98862; 509/996-4000.

130 Lookout Mountain
2.6 mi/1.3 hrs

This short, rugged trail climbs 1,200 vertical feet in less than a mile and a half. But after that strenuous ascent, the trail tops out on the Lookout Mountain summit, where visitors can sit back and enjoy the great views of the web of river valleys at the foot of the mountain and beyond to the high peaks of the Sawtooth Ridge, North Cascades National Park, and Glacier Peak Wilderness. The peak's namesake is an old, working fire lookout tower perched on the rocky summit.

During late summer months, hikers may be greeted at the

mountaintop by a Forest Service volunteer living in the small boxlike house.

Location: West of Twisp in Okanogan National Forest; see Northern Cascades Map 2, grid g7.

User Groups: Hikers, dogs, and horses. No mountain bikes are allowed. No wheelchair facilities.

Permits: A federal Northwest Forest Pass, $5 per day or $30 annually, is required to park at the trailhead. Passes are available from ranger stations and many private vendors, online at website: www.wta.org, or by calling 800/270-7504.

Maps: For a trail information report, contact the Methow Valley Ranger District at 509/997-2131. For a map of Okanogan National Forest, contact the Outdoor Recreation Information Center, Seattle REI, 222 Yale Avenue North, Seattle, WA 98109; 206/470-4060. Ask the USGS for a topographic map of the Twisp West area.

Directions: From Twisp drive one-quarter mile west on Twisp River Road/Forest Service Road 44. Turn left (south) onto Alder Creek Road/Forest Service Road 4345-200 and continue eight miles to the road's end and the trailhead.

Contact: Okanogan National Forest, Methow Valley Ranger District, 502 Glover Street, P.O. Box 188, Twisp, WA 98856; 509/997-2131. Or contact Visitor Information Center, Building 49, Highway 20, Winthrop, WA 98862; 509/996-4000.

131 Buck Creek Pass
19.2 mi/2.0 days

This trail might be as good as it gets anywhere in the Glacier Peak Wilderness, which can be awfully good at times. The Buck Creek Trail is heavily used by summertime backpackers drawn by million-dollar views of Glacier Peak, and billion-dollar whiffs and snapshots of some of the most spectacular wildflower meadows this side of heaven. The path, at first an old mining road, skirts then crosses the Chiwawa River, which gets smaller and smaller as you enter high alpine meadows. The grade steepens, eventually topping out at about 6,000 feet near Buck Creek Pass. Camping is possible here, but there are better sites down the trail a ways.

Buck Creek Pass is an excellent base camp for a number of spectacular scrambles in this area. Consult a map and find the side trails to Liberty Cap, the aptly named Flower Dome, and if you're up to a bit of snow travel, find your way to High Pass, where the views melt your Thor-Lo socks. The main trail continues five miles north to the Pacific Crest Trail, just short of Suiattle Pass. It's also possible to travel due east to Glacier Peak itself on the Triad Creek Trail. The trip to Buck Creek Pass can be made in a single, long day (a total elevation gain of about 3,000 feet). But one crimson sunset from this alpine vantage point will make you wish you'd brought your pack and planned to spend several days. Guaranteed.

Location: East of Glacier Peak in the Glacier Peak Wilderness; see Northern Cascades Map 2, grid h2.

User Groups: Hikers, dogs, and horses. No mountain bikes are allowed. No wheelchair facilities.

Permits: A federal Northwest Forest Pass, $5 per day or $30 annually, is required to park at the trailhead. Passes are available from ranger stations and many private vendors, online at website: www.wta.org, or by calling 800/270-7504.

Maps: For a map of the Glacier Peak Wilderness, contact the Outdoor Recreation Information Center, Seattle REI, 222 Yale Avenue North, Seattle, WA 98109; 206/470-4060. Green Trails, Inc.'s excellent topographic map of the region is available for $3.99 at outdoor retail outlets; ask for map number 113, Holden. Ask the USGS for topographic maps of the Trinity, Clark Mountain, and Suiattle Pass areas.

Directions: From I-5 at Everett, take U.S. 2/Stevens Pass east to Cole's Corner, about 20 miles east of Stevens Pass summit. Turn left (north) toward Lake Wenatchee on Highway 207. Bear right toward Fish Lake and turn left on Forest Service Road 62, which becomes Chiwawa River Road/Forest Service Road 6200. Stay left at the fork with Phelps Creek Road and continue to the trailhead just beyond Phelps Creek Campground, about 29 miles from U.S. 2, near the old mining town of Trinity.

Contact: Wenatchee National Forest, Lake Wenatchee Ranger District, 22976 Highway 207, Leavenworth, WA 98826; 509/763-3103.

132 Spider Meadow (Phelps Creek)
16.0 mi/2.0 days

This is an excellent overnighter for Seattle-area residents looking to get out in it without getting in over their heads. It's less than a three-hour drive from Seattle to this excellent alpine getaway, which follows Phelps Creek up an old road with a gentle grade for 5.5 miles to Spider Meadow, where evidence of glaciation lies all around. At about 6.5 miles, cross the creek and examine the old cabin ruins.

Beyond this excellent campsite, the trail splits, with the right fork continuing through more of the same terrain to 5,500 feet, with good views of Dumbell Mountain. The other fork meanders west up, up, and up—1,000 feet or so—to the foot of the spectacular, wormlike snowfield of Spider Glacier. From here it's a mile straight up snow or a narrow rock side trail to Spider Gap, with great views

of the Lyman Lakes Valley (see hike in this chapter). Inexperienced mountaineers should not attempt the snow traverse. Even for the practiced, snow conditions can make crossing difficult.

Location: In the Chiwawa River drainage on the eastern border of the Glacier Peak Wilderness; see Northern Cascades Map 2, grid h2.

User Groups: Hikers, dogs, and horses (stock prohibited on spur trail to Upper Phelps Basin). No mountain bikes are allowed. No wheelchair facilities.

Permits: A federal Northwest Forest Pass, $5 per day or $30 annually, is required to park at the trailhead. Passes are available from ranger stations and many private vendors, online at website: www.wta.org, or by calling 800/270-7504.

Maps: For a map of the Glacier Peak Wilderness, contact the Outdoor Recreation Information Center, Seattle REI, 222 Yale Avenue North, Seattle, WA 98109; 206/470-4060. Green Trails, Inc.'s excellent topographic map of the region is available for $3.99 at outdoor retail outlets; ask for map number 113, Holden. Ask the USGS for topographic maps of the Trinity, Holden, and Suiattle Pass areas.

Directions: From I-5 at Everett, take U.S. 2/Stevens Pass east to Cole's Corner, about 20 miles east of Stevens Pass summit. Bear right toward Fish Lake and turn left onto Forest Service Road 62, which becomes Chiwawa River Road/Forest Service Road 6200. Follow that road to Phelps Creek Road/Forest Service Road 6211 and turn right. Drive about two miles to the trailhead at the gate, about 30 miles from U.S. 2.

Contact: Wenatchee National Forest, Lake Wenatchee Ranger District, 22976 Highway 207, Leavenworth, WA 98826; 509/763-3103.

133 Pyramid Mountain
18.4 mi/1.0–2.0 days

For a view this good, and this high, above Lake Chelan, you have two options: rent a Cessna or hike the Pyramid Mountain Trail. You have to be determined, however, to make the long, often rough car trip to the trailhead. If you make it that far, you find yourself on a path that climbs, drops, then climbs some more through open, brushy terrain with good views. At 6.3 miles, the Pyramid Lookout Trail departs to the right. Suck it up and attack. About 2.5 miles later, you stagger to the summit, which is littered with remnants of an old lookout. If you're sucking wind, consider the altitude: You're standing at 8,245 feet. It's 7,000 feet straight down to Lake Chelan. Most people who make this a two-day venture camp at the lookout.

Location: West of Lake Chelan in the Glacier Peak Wilderness; see Northern Cascades Map 2, grid h4.

User Groups: Hikers, dogs, and horses. Mountain bikes are allowed only outside wilderness boundaries. No wheelchair facilities.

Permits: A federal Northwest Forest Pass, $5 per day or $30 annually, is required to park at the trailhead. Passes are available from ranger stations and many private vendors, online at website: www.wta.org, or by calling 800/270-7504.

Maps: For a map of Wenatchee National Forest, contact the Outdoor Recreation Information Center, Seattle REI, 222 Yale Avenue North, Seattle, WA 98109; 206/470-4060. Green Trails, Inc.'s excellent topographic map of the region is available for $3.99 at outdoor retail outlets; ask for map number 114, Lucerne. Ask the USGS for topographic maps of the Pyramid Mountain and Saksa Peak areas.

Directions: From I-5 at Everett, take U.S. 2/Stevens Pass about 110 miles east to U.S. 97. Drive north on U.S. 97A to Entiat. Drive about 29 miles northwest on Entiat River Road/Forest Service Road 51, just past Lake Creek Campground, to Big Hill Road/Forest Service Road 5900. Turn right and proceed 8.5 miles, keeping left at Shady Pass. At 10.5 miles, stay straight, getting onto Forest Service Road 113. The trailhead is at the road's end, just less than 11 miles from Entiat River Road.

Contact: Wenatchee National Forest, Entiat Ranger District, 2108 Entiat Way, P.O. Box 476, Entiat, WA 98822; 509/784-1511.

134 Chelan Lakeshore
18.0 mi one way/ 3.0–4.0 days

Some people simply can't get enough of Lake Chelan. This trail gives you all you can get—on foot, anyway. Whether hiked from the north or south, the Lakeshore Trail is a pleasant stroll above the cold, clear waters of Chelan. It's slightly hilly, though never too steep, allowing you to carry some of those extra goodies you'd normally shed for weight. (The backpack espresso maker is a fine appliance to have on a crisp autumn morning at Meadow Creek.) Good campsites are found at numerous points along the route. Be sure to explore Moore's Point, the site of an old resort near Fish Creek.

We highly recommend this hike for spring, when other Stehekin-area destinations remain snowbound. The trail is at its best in May and June, when fires are still allowed (they're banned by midsummer because it's so dry) and wildflowers light up the meadows. Later in the year, the trail gets hot, dry and less interesting.

Location: On the north bank of Lake Chelan; see Northern Cascades Map 2, grid h5.

User Groups: Hikers, dogs, and horses. No mountain bikes are allowed. No wheelchair facilities.

Permits: Free overnight permits, required for camping inside the Lake Chelan National Recreation Area, are available at the Golden West Visitor Center in Stehekin. The trip to Stehekin requires a $25 round-trip boat ride from Chelan.

Maps: For a map of North Cascades National Park and Lake Chelan National Recreation Area, contact the Outdoor Recreation Information Center, Seattle REI, 222 Yale Avenue North, Seattle, WA 98109; 206/470-4060. Green Trails, Inc.'s excellent topographic maps of the region are available for $3.99 each at outdoor retail outlets; ask for map numbers 82 and 114, Stehekin and Lucerne. Ask the USGS for topographic maps of the Stehekin, Sun Mountain, Lucerne, and Prince Creek areas.

Directions: From Seattle take U.S. 2/Stevens Pass east to Wenatchee and U.S. 97 north to the city of Chelan. Catch the water taxi up Lake Chelan to Stehekin (contact the Outdoor Recreation Information Center at 206/470-4060 or see lady-ofthelake.com for boat schedules and shuttle bus information). The trip can be hiked from the north or the south. For a southern starting point, arrange to be dropped off at Prince Creek. For a northern departure, ride the boat to Stehekin, where the trail begins at the south end of the settlement, and arrange for a boat pickup at Prince Creek.

Contact: North Cascades National Park/Mount Baker Ranger District Information Center, 2105 Highway 20, Sedro-Woolley, WA 98284; 360/856-5700.

135 Foggy Dew
15.4 mi/7.6 hrs

The forest here is old, and the canopy is broken and varied, allowing sunlight to reach the forest floor and feed the light-hungry undergrowth. That means huckleberries are sweet and juicy. A couple miles up the trail the noisy, raucous Foggy Dew Creek turns into a raging torrent as it crashes over the granite slabs of Foggy Dew Falls, then mellows out again above the falls into a babbling stream. Wildflowers thrive along the valley trail, but as the route climbs into Merchants Basin and on to the Chelan Divide, the forest gives way to open meadows where flowers explode in colorful blooms: Indian paintbrush, an assortment of lilies (from avalanche to bear grass), and countless other varieties. Campsites can be found virtually anywhere along the trail.

Location: South of Twisp in Okanogan National Forest; see Northern Cascades Map 2, grid h5.

User Groups: Hikers, dogs, and horses. No mountain bikes are allowed. No wheelchair facilities.

Permits: A federal Northwest Forest Pass, $5 per day or $30 annually, is required to park at the trailhead. Passes are available from ranger stations and many private vendors, online at website: www.wta.org, or by calling 800/270-7504.

Maps: For a trail information report, contact the Methow Valley Ranger District at 509/997-2131. For a map of Okanogan National Forest, contact the Outdoor Recreation Information Center, Seattle REI, 222 Yale Avenue North, Seattle, WA 98109; 206/470-4060. Ask the USGS for topographic maps of the Hungry Mountain and Martin Peak areas.

Directions: From Twisp drive south on Highway 153 to the junction with North Fork Gold Creek Road/County Road 1029 and turn right (west). Stay right at the junction near the forest boundary, bearing onto Forest Service Road 4340. Continue 4.1 miles and veer left onto Forest Service Road 200, a narrow dirt road. Drive four miles to the road's end and the trailhead.

Contact: Okanogan National Forest, Methow Valley Ranger District, 502 Glover Street, P.O. Box 188, Twisp, WA 98856; 509/997-2131. Or contact Visitor Information Center, Building 49, Highway 20, Winthrop, WA 98862; 509/996-4000.

136 Windy Creek
10.0 mi/5.0 hrs

Winding upward through the narrow valley of Windy Creek, this trail intercepts the Windy Peak Trail about five miles in, on the ridge top. While the entire Windy Peak Trail entails only high ridge walking, this creekside route offers more climbing, as well as more variety for the senses. The booming calls of blue grouse complement the noise of the rushing creek, while the dusky, gray trunks of the lodgepole pine and blue spruce trees provide a stark backdrop to the landscape. You probably see some of the buckskin-colored white-tailed deer and mule deer that populate (almost overpopulate, in fact) this area.

Location: Northwest of Loomis in Okanogan National Forest, within the Pasayten Wilderness; see Northern Cascades Map 3, grid a1.

User Groups: Hikers, dogs, and horses. No mountain bikes are allowed. No wheelchair facilities.

Permits: A federal Northwest Forest Pass, $5 per day or $30 annually, is required to park at the trailhead. Passes are available from ranger stations and many private vendors, online at website: www.wta.org, or by calling 800/270-7504.

Maps: For a trail information report, contact the Tonasket Ranger District at 509/486-2186. For a map of Okanogan National Forest, con-

tact the Outdoor Recreation Information Center, Seattle REI, 222 Yale Avenue North, Seattle, WA 98109; 206/470-4060. Ask the USGS for topographic maps of the Corral Butte and Horseshoe Basin areas.

Directions: From Loomis drive approximately two miles north on Sinlahekin Valley Road/County Road 9425 until you reach the junction with Toats Coulee Road/Forest Service Road 39. Turn left (west) onto Toats Coulee Road and continue 20.5 miles to the trailhead found in the Long Swamp Campground. From here, turn right (north) onto Forest Service Road 39–300 and drive about three miles to the trailhead on the right. The first half mile of the hike follows the Cathedral Driveway trail.

Contact: Okanogan National Forest, Tonasket Ranger District, 1 West Winesap Street, Tonasket, WA 98855; 509/486-2186.

137 Windy Peak
24.0 mi/2.5 days

Rolling up and down along the high ridge, this trail is no mild stroll in the park. But the workout won't prevent you from appreciating all there is to see on the route. The variety of forest types, which range from old-growth Douglas fir and lodgepole pine to subalpine fir and hemlock, offers an introductory lesson in forestry. With wide, open meadows filled with wild strawberries, paintbrush, alpine daisies, lupine, and other blooms, this landscape is a wildflower lover's paradise, and the combination of meadow and forest makes this a favorite haunt of mule deer and black bears. The trail climbs along a ridge just under the Windy Peak summit, then rolls on north, offering panoramic views of Topaz Mountain and the craggy peaks of the Canadian Cascades. Good campsites are available at Windy Lake, roughly eight miles from the trailhead. The trail ends at the mouth of Horseshoe Basin.

Location: Northwest of Loomis in Okanogan National Forest, within the Pasayten Wilderness; see Northern Cascades Map 3, grid b1.

User Groups: Hikers, dogs, and horses. No mountain bikes are allowed. No wheelchair facilities.

Permits: A federal Northwest Forest Pass, $5 per day or $30 annually, is required to park at the trailhead. Passes are available from ranger stations and many private vendors, online at website: www.wta.org, or by calling 800/270-7504.

Maps: For a trail information report, contact the Tonasket Ranger District at 509/486-2186. For a map of Okanogan National Forest, contact the Outdoor Recreation Information Center, Seattle REI, 222 Yale Avenue North, Seattle, WA 98109; 206/470-4060. Ask the USGS for topographic maps of the Corral Butte and Horseshoe Basin areas.

Directions: From Loomis drive two miles north on Sinlahekin Valley Road/County Road 9425 to the junction with Toats Coulee Road/Forest Service Road 39. Turn left (west) onto Toats Coulee Road and continue about 20.5 miles to the trailhead, located in the Long Swamp Campground.

Contact: Okanogan National Forest, Tonasket Ranger District, 1 West Winesap Street, Tonasket, WA 98855; 509/486-2186.

138 Boundary
73.0 mi one way/7.0 days 5

Heavily used by horse packers, this great wilderness trail leads through Horseshoe Basin, past the Teapot Dome, and around, over, or through a dozen other wonderful settings. The trail bisects the Pasayten Wilderness, running roughly parallel to the Canadian border. Numerous high points along the trail offer views north into Canada, west to the glacier-covered Cascades, and east to the Salmo-Priest Wilderness. Between these high points, several side trails link up to the Boundary Trail, which makes loops, side trips, and alternative destinations easy to plan. Wildlife thrives throughout the area, and the countless lakes, streams, and rivers here swarm with rainbow, cutthroat, and brook trout. The trail climbs from one creek valley to the adjoining ridge and then down into the next creek valley, and ends at the Pacific Crest Trail, just south of the Canadian border. You can camp in any of the valley bottoms.

Location: Northwest of Loomis in Okanogan National Forest, within the Pasayten Wilderness; see Northern Cascades Map 3, grid a2.

User Groups: Hikers, dogs, and horses. No mountain bikes. No wheelchair facilities.

Permits: A federal Northwest Forest Pass, $5 per day or $30 annually, is required to park at the trailhead. Passes are available from ranger stations and many private vendors, online at website: www.wta.org, or by calling 800/270-7504.

Maps: For a trail information report, contact the Tonasket Ranger District at 509/486-2186. For a map of Okanogan National Forest, contact the Outdoor Recreation Information Center, Seattle REI, 222 Yale Avenue North, Seattle, WA 98109; 206/470-4060. Ask the USGS for topographic maps of the Horseshoe Basin, Bauerman Ridge, Remmel Mountain, and Ashnola Pass areas.

Directions: From Loomis drive two miles north on Sinlahekin Valley Road/County Road 9425 to the junction with Toats Coulee Road/Forest Service Road 39. Turn left (west) onto Toats Coulee Road and continue 14 miles to the Iron Gate Road. Turn right onto Iron Gate Road and drive 5.2 miles to the trailhead.

Contact: Okanogan National Forest, Tonasket Ranger

District, 1 West Winesap Street, Tonasket, WA 98855; 509/486-2186.

139 Fire Creek
20.2 mi/2.0 days

A major wildfire impacted this area in the summer of 2001, and the damage to the trail at press time was not determined. Be sure to call before ahead to find out if the trail or access roads to the trailhead have been damaged or rerouted.

For the first five miles this is an easy and relaxing hike through an ancient lodgepole pine forest along the Chewuch River. Anglers might want to cast a line on a few of the productive fishing holes along the creek. The trail forks where Fire Creek empties into the Chewuch. Turn left (west) onto the Fire Creek Trail and hike up the valley between a pair of sheer cliffs. The lodgepole forest continues up this valley nearly all the way to the valley head. Climbing up away from the creek, the trail finally breaks out of the forest and bisects broad, flower-filled meadows at the top of the wide Coleman Ridge, your turnaround point. From the ridge, enjoy views of Cal Peak, Peepsight Mountain, and Vic Meadows. The trail ends at Coleman Ridge. Camping sites are common along both the Chewuch River and Fire Creek, with the best site on the upper reaches of Fire Creek, just upstream from the cliffs.

Location: North of Winthrop in Okanogan National Forest, within the Pasayten Wilderness; see Northern Cascades Map 3, grid b1.

User Groups: Hikers, dogs, and horses. No mountain bikes are allowed. No wheelchair facilities.

Permits: A federal Northwest Forest Pass, $5 per day or $30 annually, is required to park at the trailhead. Passes are available from ranger stations and many private vendors,

online at website: www.wta.org, or by calling 800/270-7504.

Maps: For a trail information report, contact the Methow Valley Ranger District at 509/997-2131. For a map of Okanogan National Forest, contact the Outdoor Recreation Information Center, Seattle REI, 222 Yale Avenue North, Seattle, WA 98109; 206/470-4060. Ask the USGS for topographic maps of the Coleman Peak, Bauerman Ridge, and Remmel Mountain areas.

Directions: From Winthrop drive 29 miles north on West Chewuch Road/Forest Service Road 51 to the road's end and the trailhead.

Contact: Okanogan National Forest, Methow Valley Ranger District, 502 Glover Street, P.O. Box 188, Twisp, WA 98856; 509/997-2131. Or contact Visitor Information Center, Building 49, Highway 20, Winthrop, WA 98862; 509/996-4000.

140 Smarty Creek
23.4 mi/3.0 days

Just outside the designated wilderness area, this trail has all the benefits of formal wilderness without the drawbacks. Benefits include pristine forest, fragrant wildflower meadows, and abundant wildlife. What you avoid is a crowd. Without the official designation to guide them, most people miss this trail, so you can revel in solitude. Hike through the beautiful North and South Twentymile Meadows and then along the bank of the noisy Smarty Creek.

Location: Northwest of Conconully in Okanogan National Forest; see Northern Cascades Map 3, grid c1.

User Groups: Hikers, dogs, and horses. No mountain bikes are allowed. No wheelchair facilities.

Permits: A federal Northwest Forest Pass, $5 per day or $30 annually, is required to park

at the trailhead. Passes are available from ranger stations and many private vendors, online at website: www.wta.org, or by calling 800/270-7504.

Maps: For a trail information report, contact the Tonasket Ranger District at 509/486-2186. For a map of Okanogan National Forest, contact the Outdoor Recreation Information Center, Seattle REI, 222 Yale Avenue North, Seattle, WA 98109; 206/470-4060. Ask the USGS for topographic maps of the Tiffany Mountain, Spur Peak, Coleman Peak, and Corral Butte areas.

Directions: From Conconully drive 3.5 miles west on the West Fork Road/County Road 2017 to the junction with Forest Service Road 37. Turn right (northwest) onto Forest Service Road 37 and proceed 16.5 miles to Forest Service Road 39. Turn right (north) onto this road and drive 10 miles to the trailhead on the left (just past Tiffany Springs Campground).

Contact: Okanogan National Forest, Tonasket Ranger District, 1 West Winesap Street, Tonasket, WA 98855; 509/486-2186.

141 Tiffany Lake
8.5 mi one way/4.5 hrs

Rolling across the north shore of Tiffany Lake and around the north flank of Tiffany Mountain, this trail provides an assortment of picturesque views. From the western trailhead the trail climbs gradually along Boulder Creek, passing through dense pine and fir forest before reaching the blue waters of the lake. This is a cool place to rest before you finish the climb to the low saddle—Honeymoon Pass—between Tiffany Mountain and Middle Tiffany Mountain. Views from the pass are lovely; you can also scramble to the summit of either peak for more, although it's easier to reach Tiffany by way of Freezeout Ridge to the south. As you descend the east side of

Honeymoon Pass, you enjoy pretty views over Clark Peak and Clark Basin, a deep green valley to the north of the peak. At the valley floor, the trail enters a deep, shadowy forest, which continues to the end of the route at the eastern trailhead.

The best way to experience this trail is traveling west to east and having a vehicle waiting at the far end to avoid backtracking. Or split your group into two parties. Have one party start from each end and swap car keys when you meet in the middle.

Location: Northwest of Conconully in Okanogan National Forest; see Northern Cascades Map 3, grid c1.

User Groups: Hikers, dogs, and horses. No mountain bikes are allowed. No wheelchair facilities.

Permits: A federal Northwest Forest Pass, $5 per day or $30 annually, is required to park at the trailhead. Passes are available from ranger stations and many private vendors, online at website: www.wta.org, or by calling 800/270-7504.

Maps: For a trail information report, contact the Tonasket Ranger District at 509/486-2186. For a map of Okanogan National Forest, contact the Outdoor Recreation Information Center, Seattle REI, 222 Yale Avenue North, Seattle, WA 98109; 206/470-4060. Ask the USGS for topographic maps of the Tiffany Mountain and Coxit Mountain areas.

Directions: For the western trailhead, from Conconully drive 3.5 miles west on the West Fork Road/County Road 2017 to the junction with Forest Service Road 37. Turn right (northwest) onto Forest Service Road 37 and proceed 16.5 miles to Forest Service Road 39. Turn right (north) onto this road and drive seven miles to the Tiffany Springs Campground on the right. A second car can be dropped at the eastern end of the trail. To get there from Conconully, drive nine miles

north on Salmon Creek Road/Forest Service Road 38 to the trailhead, which is on the left.
Contact: Okanogan National Forest, Tonasket Ranger District, 1 West Winesap Street, Tonasket, WA 98855; 509/486-2186.

142 Angel Pass
3.0 mi/1.5 hrs

Angel Pass is actually not a pass, but a saddle set between Coxit Mountain and Cougar Mountain. Faint side trails lead from the end of the official trail up to the summit of each of these peaks, where you can rest and enjoy stunning vistas. Even the lower pass, however, offers fantastic views.

Location: Northwest of Conconully in Okanogan National Forest; see Northern Cascades Map 3, grid c1.

User Groups: Hikers, dogs, and horses. No mountain bikes are allowed. No wheelchair facilities.

Permits: A federal Northwest Forest Pass, $5 per day or $30 annually, is required to park at the trailhead. Passes are available from ranger stations and many private vendors, online at website: www.wta.org, or by calling 800/270-7504.

Maps: For a trail information report, contact the Tonasket Ranger District at 509/486-2186. For a map of Okanogan National Forest, contact the Outdoor Recreation Information Center, Seattle REI, 222 Yale Avenue North, Seattle, WA 98109; 206/470-4060. Ask the USGS for a topographic map of the Coxit Mountain area.

Directions: From Conconully drive north 8.5 miles on Salmon Creek Road to the Salmon Meadows Campground. The trailhead is just inside the campground.

Contact: Okanogan National Forest, Tonasket Ranger District, 1 West Winesap Street, Tonasket, WA 98855; 509/486-2186.

143 Mutton Creek
2.0 mi/1.0 hr

We're not sure how this modest trail and the creek it follows were named, but we're guessing that whoever cut the trail started dreaming about a pot of lamb stew back at camp. Although the trail offers few vistas, it does provide views of the picturesque little creek as it meanders in and out of the trees. The gentle slope of the route makes travel easy for children and the elderly, too.

Location: North of Conconully in Okanogan National Forest; see Northern Cascades Map 3, grid c1.

User Groups: Hikers, dogs, and horses. No mountain bikes are allowed. No wheelchair facilities.

Permits: A federal Northwest Forest Pass, $5 per day or $30 annually, is required to park at the trailhead. Passes are available from ranger stations and many private vendors, online at website: www.wta.org, or by calling 800/270-7504.

Maps: For a trail information report, contact the Tonasket Ranger District at 509/486-2186. For a map of Okanogan National Forest, contact the Outdoor Recreation Information Center, Seattle REI, 222 Yale Avenue North, Seattle, WA 98109; 206/470-4060. Ask the USGS for a topographic map of the Coxit Mountain area.

Directions: From Conconully drive 8.5 miles northwest on Salmon Creek Road/Forest Service Road 38 to Salmon Meadows Campground. The trailhead is just inside the campground. Parking is near the day-use area.

Contact: Okanogan National Forest, Tonasket Ranger District, 1 West Winesap Street, Tonasket, WA 98855; 509/486-2186.

144 Freezeout Ridge

7.4 mi/3.7 hrs

This ridgetop trail is hot, dusty, and dry, but it's beautiful nonetheless, climbing to an elevation of more than 7,000 feet. The forests here are sparse and low, but between them lie wide, sun-streaked meadows that are chock-full of red paintbrush, lavender lupine, yellow and white mountain daisies, and many other colorful wildflowers. Look for marmots, mule deer, and high-flying hawks across the length of the ridge. If the long-distance views from the ridge aren't enough for you, scramble up the rocky flanks of Tiffany Mountain near the end of the trail for more.

Location: Northwest of Conconully in Okanogan National Forest; see Northern Cascades Map 3, grid c1.

User Groups: Hikers, dogs, and horses. No mountain bikes are allowed. No wheelchair facilities.

Permits: A federal Northwest Forest Pass, $5 per day or $30 annually, is required to park at the trailhead. Passes are available from ranger stations and many private vendors, online at website: www.wta.org, or by calling 800/270-7504.

Maps: For a trail information report, contact the Tonasket Ranger District at 509/486-2186. For a map of Okanogan National Forest, contact the Outdoor Recreation Information Center, Seattle REI, 222 Yale Avenue North, Seattle, WA 98109; 206/470-4060. Ask the USGS for topographic maps of the Corral Butte and Horseshoe Basin areas.

Directions: From Conconully drive 3.5 miles west on West Fork Road/County Road 2017 to Forest Service Road 37. Turn right (northwest) onto Forest Service Road 37 and proceed 16.5 miles to Forest Service Road 39. Turn right (north) onto this road and drive three miles to the trailhead on the right.

Contact: Okanogan National Forest, Tonasket Ranger District, 1 West Winesap Street, Tonasket, WA 98855; 509/486-2186.

145 Bernhardt Mine

6.0 mi/3.0 hrs

An old cabin and a deep mine shaft still mark the site where a prospector staked his claim. The trail leads through a dry pine and fir forest, and you find no water past the first few hundred yards, so bring plenty. The mining site is fun to explore, but both the cabin and mine are virtual death traps. For your own safety and for the safety of potential rescuers, stay outside of both structures. Plenty of other evidence of mining activity lies scattered around the area, so even the most curious should be satisfied.

Location: Southwest of Tonasket in Okanogan National Forest; see Northern Cascades Map 3, grid c1.

User Groups: Hikers, dogs, and horses. No mountain bikes are allowed. No wheelchair facilities.

Permits: A federal Northwest Forest Pass, $5 per day or $30 annually, is required to park at the trailhead. Passes are available from ranger stations and many private vendors, online at website: www.wta.org, or by calling 800/270-7504.

Maps: For a trail information report, contact the Tonasket Ranger District at 509/486-2186. For a map of Okanogan National Forest, contact the Outdoor Recreation Information Center, Seattle REI, 222 Yale Avenue North, Seattle, WA 98109; 206/470-4060. Ask the USGS for a topographic map of the Tiffany Mountain area.

Directions: From Conconully drive 3.5 miles southwest on West Fork Road/County Road 2017 before turning right (north) onto Forest Service Road 37. Continue 16.5 miles west on Forest Service Road 37 to the junction with Forest Service Road 39. Turn right (north) onto this road and continue 1.5 miles to the trailhead at a wide switchbacking corner. The parking area and trailhead are on the right.

Contact: Okanogan National Forest, Tonasket Ranger District, 1 West Winesap Street, Tonasket, WA 98855; 509/486-2186.

146 Muckamuck
8.0 mi/4.0 hrs

The trail name doesn't sound like much, but there's more to Muckamuck than its name. Climbing over the ridge between Pelican and Muckamuck Creeks, the trail accesses plenty of great, long-distance views, as well as close-ups of wildflowers and wildlife. From the top of the saddle, look back to the west at Starvation Mountain, Old Baldy, and Granite Mountain and north to Clark Peak. The repeated ups and downs of the trail entail frequent dips into small creek basins and draws, where wildlife often hole up during the midday heat. If you enter these forest sanctuaries quietly, you may see mule deer, white-tailed deer, or wild sheep up close.

Location: Northwest of Conconully in Okanogan National Forest; see Northern Cascades Map 3, grid d1.

User Groups: Hikers, dogs, and horses. No mountain bikes are allowed. No wheelchair facilities.

Permits: A federal Northwest Forest Pass, $5 per day or $30 annually, is required to park at the trailhead. Passes are available from ranger stations and many private vendors, online at website: www.wta.org, or by calling 800/270-7504.

Maps: For a trail information report, contact the Tonasket Ranger District at 509/486-2186. For a map of Okanogan National Forest, contact the Outdoor Recreation Information Center, Seattle REI, 222 Yale Avenue North, Seattle, WA 98109; 206/470-4060. Ask the USGS for topographic maps of the Old Baldy, Conconully West, and Coxit Mountain areas.

Directions: From Conconully drive 3.5 miles west on West Fork Road/County Road 2017 to the junction with Forest Service Road 37. Turn right (northwest) onto Forest Service Road 37 and proceed approximately eight miles to the trailhead on the right.

Contact: Okanogan National Forest, Tonasket Ranger District, 1 West Winesap Street, Tonasket, WA 98855; 509/486-2186.

147 Golden Stairway
12.4 mi/8.0 hrs

The "golden" refers not to the stairway, but to the panoramic views. Climbing up steep switchbacks to a high ridge along the flank of Mount Baldy (elevation 6,750 feet), this trail presents first-rate views of the North Cascade peaks. From Glacier Peak to Jack Mountain, the craggy, glaciated summits of the Washington Cascades rise up on the western horizon. The early morning hours are by far the most spectacular, as the rising sun blazes off the stark peaks. The flower-filled Beaver Meadow highlights the views during the long, steep climb to the trail's end.

Location: Northwest of Conconully in Okanogan National Forest; see Northern Cascades Map 3, grid d1.

User Groups: Hikers, dogs, and horses. No mountain bikes are allowed. No wheelchair facilities.

Permits: A federal Northwest Forest Pass, $5 per day or $30 annually, is required to park at the trailhead. Passes are available from ranger stations and many private vendors, online at website: www.wta.org, or by calling 800/270-7504.

Maps: For a trail information report, contact the Tonasket Ranger District at 509/486-2186.

For a map of Okanogan National Forest, contact the Outdoor Recreation Information Center, Seattle REI, 222 Yale Avenue North, Seattle, WA 98109; 206/470-4060. Ask the USGS for a topographic map of the Old Baldy area.

Directions: From Conconully drive 3.5 miles west on the West Fork Road/County Road 2017 to the junction with Forest Service Road 37. Turn right (northwest) and proceed 2.5 miles to Forest Service Road 37-400. Turn left onto this road and then bear left onto Forest Service Road 37-420. Continue to the road's end and the trailhead.

Contact: Okanogan National Forest, Tonasket Ranger District, 1 West Winesap Street, Tonasket, WA 98855; 509/486-2186.

148 North Summit
32.0 mi/3.0 days

The most difficult part of the hike is the two-mile climb up the Golden Stairway Trail, where it joins with the ridge trail. Once you reach that point, though, the trail stays along the ridge and provides nonstop vistas of the far-off Washington and Canadian Cascades. To the east, the rocky pinnacles of the Selkirk Mountains in northern Idaho appear as shadowy spikes on the horizon. If views from the ridge aren't spectacular enough (in which case I'd say something's wrong with your capacity for wonder), small side trails lead intrepid travelers to the Clark Peak and Tiffany Mountain summits. Expect to see bald and golden eagles, as well as an assortment of hawks and falcons, along the ridge. Backpackers find good campsites anywhere along the ridge; the best are usually a few yards under the crest to escape the wind.

The campsites along this trail are dry sites, so you need to carry extra water. Early summer hikers may find some lingering snow-

banks that can be used as a second source of water, but remember to boil it thoroughly.

Location: Northwest of Conconully in Okanogan National Forest; see Northern Cascades Map 3, grid d2.

User Groups: Hikers, dogs, and horses. No mountain bikes are allowed. No wheelchair facilities.

Permits: A federal Northwest Forest Pass, $5 per day or $30 annually, is required to park at the trailhead. Passes are available from ranger stations and many private vendors, online at website: www.wta.org, or by calling 800/270-7504.

Maps: For a trail information report, contact the Tonasket Ranger District at 509/486-2186. For a map of Okanogan National Forest, contact the Outdoor Recreation Information Center, Seattle REI, 222 Yale Avenue North, Seattle, WA 98109; 206/470-4060. Ask the USGS for topographic maps of the Old Baldy and Tiffany Mountain areas.

Directions: From Conconully drive 3.5 miles west on West Fork Road/County Road 2017 to the junction with Forest Service Road 37. Turn right (northwest) onto Forest Service Road 37 and proceed another 2.5 miles to Forest Service Road 37-400. Turn left onto that road and drive to the trailhead on the right. Hike the Golden Stairway Trail two miles to the junction with the North Summit Trail.

Contact: Okanogan National Forest, Tonasket Ranger District, 1 West Winesap Street, Tonasket, WA 98855; 509/486-2186.

149 Granite Mountain
11.0 mi/5.5 hrs

The great fun on this hike is the plethora of opportunities to scramble off trail. The official trail leads past both Little Granite Mountain and Granite Mountain proper;

boot-beaten side trails lead to their summits. The trail is steep and these side routes are even steeper, but the views are worth the sweat. Starvation Mountain, Old Baldy, and the great, craggy peaks of the North Cascades dominate the incredible views from the trail and the summits. Plan to carry plenty of water; the route is hot and dry in the summer months. Even in the cooler fall days, you find no potable water along the route.

Location: Northwest of Conconully in Okanogan National Forest; see Northern Cascades Map 3, grid d2.

User Groups: Hikers, dogs, and horses. No mountain bikes are allowed. No wheelchair facilities.

Permits: A federal Northwest Forest Pass, $5 per day or $30 annually, is required to park at the trailhead. Passes are available from ranger stations and many private vendors, online at website: www.wta.org, or by calling 800/270-7504.

Maps: For a trail information report, contact the Tonasket Ranger District at 509/486-2186. For a map of Okanogan National Forest, contact the Outdoor Recreation Information Center, Seattle REI, 222 Yale Avenue North, Seattle, WA 98109; 206/470-4060.

Directions: From Conconully drive 3.5 miles west on the West Fork Road/County Road 2017 to the junction with Forest Service Road 37–100. Bear left (west) onto this road and proceed one-quarter mile to the trailhead on the right.

Contact: Okanogan National Forest, Tonasket Ranger District, 1 West Winesap Street, Tonasket, WA 98855; 509/486-2186.

150 Wallace Falls State Park

7.0 mi/4.0 hrs

A close friend measures her level of conditioning (not to mention age) by degrees of soreness after making tracks on the 1,700 vertical feet up the Wallace Falls Trail once

every year. Plenty of other people do the same, and little wonder: this high-traffic state park trail is one that gets very familiar, but in a good way. The route up either of the two trails to Wallace Falls is rather ordinary, but the falls themselves are just spellbinding enough to keep their fans returning year after year.

A short distance up the main trailhead near the tiny camping area, the trail splits. The left fork is the old railroad grade—easier on the calves but a mile longer than the one-mile straight-shot route, also called the Woody Trail. Your best bet is to take the railroad grade on the way up and the Woody Trail down. The two paths meet at a spectacular bridge over the North Fork Wallace River; then a single path leads another 1.3 miles to a lower viewpoint and about 1.5 miles up a steep final pitch to a viewpoint above the falls. The falls, a magnificent 250-foot leap of faith of the South Fork Wallace, are probably the tallest you'll ever see in the Cascades. If you're standing above them at the upper viewpoint, a view of the Skykomish Valley is an added treat.

Keep a tight rein on kids and dogs in the area above the falls. When this book went to press, Washington State Parks were considering implementing a day-use parking fee; call the contact number for current information.

Location: North of Gold Bar near U.S. 2; see Northern Cascades Map 4, grid b3.

User Groups: Hikers and dogs. No horses or mountain bikes are allowed. No wheelchair facilities.

Permits: No permits are required. Parking and access are free.

Maps: Green Trails, Inc.'s excellent topographic map of the region is available for $3.99 at outdoor retail outlets; ask for map number 142, Mount Index. Ask the USGS for a topographic map of the Wallace Lake area.

Directions: From Seattle drive 28 miles north on I-5 to Exit 194/City Center/Stevens Pass. Drive 23 miles east on U.S. 2 to Gold Bar. Turn left at the sign for Wallace Falls State Park and proceed about two miles north to the park entrance.

Contact: Wallace Falls State Park, P.O. Box 230, Gold Bar, WA 98251; 360/793-0420; Washington State Parks and Recreation Commission, Public Affairs Office, P.O. Box 42650, Olympia, WA 98504-2650; 800/233-0321.

151 Gothic Basin
9.4 mi/1.0–2.0 days

Gothic Basin is one of the more spectacular alpine destinations within a short drive of the Puget Sound basin. It can also be one of the most difficult of these getaways to reach. From its start on the deceptively tame Monte Cristo Road, the trail generally follows the route of an aerial tram that ran to mines in the basin early in the 20th century. Not far up the trail, you understand why the miners didn't want to haul rock in and out of here on foot. This trail is very steep in places, and from early to midsummer you have to make as many as three potentially tricky snow-gully crossings. Bring the ice ax and dress warmly; it's not uncommon for snow to linger in the basin until mid-September.

For those who persevere, Gothic Basin, nestled between the craggy peaks of Del Campo (elevation 6,610 feet) and Gothic (elevation 6,213 feet), is a spectacular mix of carved stone and crystal-clear lakes. In season, the basin around Foggy Lake is filled with a rainbow of wildflowers, which sprout amid the healthy display of mining artifacts. Don't plan on making this a day hike, because you'll really regret it. And don't even think about making the climb before late summer. The total elevation gain to Foggy Pass is 2,600 feet.

Location: South of Monte Cristo; see Northern Cascades Map 4, grid a5.

User Groups: Hikers and dogs. Mountain bikes are allowed on the first four miles, to Monte Cristo. No wheelchair facilities.

Permits: A federal Northwest Forest Pass, $5 per day or $30 annually, is required to park at the trailhead. Passes are available from ranger stations and many private vendors, online at website: www.wta.org, or by calling 800/270-7504.

Maps: For a map of the Henry M. Jackson Wilderness, contact the Outdoor Recreation Information Center, Seattle REI, 222 Yale Avenue North, Seattle, WA 98109; 206/470-4060. Green Trails, Inc.'s excellent topographic maps of the region are available for $3.99 each at various outdoor retail outlets; ask for map numbers 111 and 143, Sloan Peak and Monte Cristo. Ask the USGS for a topographic map of the Monte Cristo area.

Directions: From Seattle drive 28 miles north on I-5 to Exit 194/City Center/Stevens Pass. Drive six miles east on U.S. 2 to the Highway 9 exit near Snohomish. Follow Highway 9 north to U.S. 92. Turn right and follow U.S. 92 eight miles east to Granite Falls. At the end of town, turn left (north) on the Mountain Loop Highway. Drive 12 miles to the Verlot Public Service Center and another 19.5 miles to Barlow Pass. Parking is on the left side of the highway. Walk 1.2 miles up to Monte Cristo Road to the Gothic Basin trailhead on the right (south) side of the road, just before the bridge over the Sauk River.

Contact: Mount Baker-Snoqualmie National Forest, Darrington Ranger District, 1405 Emmens Street, Darrington, WA 98241; 360/436-1155.

152 Poodle Dog Pass to Twin Lakes

16.8 mi/1.0 day

This is a great day hike for people camping in the Monte Cristo area, and an equally great—though painfully long—day hike for those who walk it all the way from the parking lot at Barlow Pass. The round-trip mileage above includes the eight-mile round-trip walk on Monte Cristo Road.

The trail, which starts on private property, is steep, rutted, and aggravating all the way to Poodle Dog Pass (1.7 miles, 4,400 feet). From this point, it's one-third of a mile and 150 feet down to Silver Lake (no fish, poor campsites). If you're heading back to Barlow Pass on the same day, this is a good stopping place. But the young of heart and legs can take the left fork at Poodle Dog Pass, continue another 2.7 miles up, then sharply down a rutted old miners' trail leading to Twin Lakes, which offer good camping, fishing, and respite from the masses who drive their four-wheel-drive rigs to Barlow Pass and flock to Monte Cristo. The total elevation gain to Twin Lakes is about 2,600 feet.

Location: Southeast of Monte Cristo in the Henry M. Jackson Wilderness; see Northern Cascades Map 4, grid a6.

User Groups: Hikers, dogs, and horses. Mountain bikes are allowed on the first four miles, to Monte Cristo. No wheelchair facilities.

Permits: A federal Northwest Forest Pass, $5 per day or $30 annually, is required to park at the trailhead. Passes are available from ranger stations and many private vendors, online at website: www.wta.org, or by calling 800/270-7504.

Maps: For a map of the Henry M. Jackson Wilderness, contact the Outdoor Recreation Information Center, Seattle REI, 222 Yale Avenue North, Seattle, WA 98109; 206/470-4060.

Green Trails, Inc.'s excellent topographic map of the region is available for $3.99 at outdoor retail outlets; ask for map number 143, Monte Cristo. Ask the USGS for topographic maps of the Monte Cristo and Sloan Peak areas.

Directions: From Seattle drive 28 miles north on I-5 to Exit 194/City Center/Stevens Pass. Drive six miles east on U.S. 2 to the Highway 9 exit near Snohomish. Follow Highway 9 north to U.S. 92. Turn right and follow U.S. 92 eight miles east to Granite Falls. At the end of town, turn left (north) on the Mountain Loop Highway. Drive 12 miles to the Verlot Public Service Center and another 19.5 miles to Barlow Pass. Parking is on the left side of the highway. Walk four miles on Monte Cristo Road to the junction with the Monte Cristo Campground road. Go right across the bridge to the trailhead signed for Silver Lake.

Contact: Mount Baker-Snoqualmie National Forest, Darrington Ranger District, 1405 Emmens Street, Darrington, WA 98241; 360/436-1155.

153 Glacier Basin

12.2 mi/1.0–2.0 days

For people whose first loves include Vibram soles and rusty old mining relics, the Glacier Basin Trail is a treasure trove. It can be completed in one long day (the round-trip mileage listed includes the eight-mile round-trip walk on Monte Cristo Road; riding to Monte Cristo on a mountain bike is a good option). The road, incidentally, was open to traffic until 1980, when a winter storm washed it out once and for all. Since then, once-popular day hiking venues such as Glacier Basin have benefited mightily from the added eight miles, which tend to weed out the aerobically challenged.

Given the long distance and interesting terrain, you might want to plan several days to explore this historically unique mining area. The trail is usually somewhat of a mess, worn by many boots and gully-washing spring melts. But for those who endure the two miles from Monte Cristo, Glacier Basin spreads out before you like a seven-course meal. It's truly beautiful, with wildflower meadows, lingering snowfields, and many climbers buzzing about and preparing to attack the Wilmon Spires, Monte Cristo Peak, or Cadet Peak, all jagged-edge monsters topping 7,000 feet. Stay on footpaths and please camp in existing sites at Ray's Knoll and Mystery Ridge.

Location: East of Monte Cristo in the Henry M. Jackson Wilderness; see Northern Cascades Map 4, grid a6.

User Groups: Hikers and dogs. Mountain bikes are allowed on the first four miles, to Monte Cristo. No wheelchair facilities.

Permits: A federal Northwest Forest Pass, $5 per day or $30 annually, is required to park at the trailhead. Passes are available from ranger stations and many private vendors, online at website: www.wta.org, or by calling 800/270-7504.

Maps: For a map of the Henry M. Jackson Wilderness, contact the Outdoor Recreation Information Center, Seattle REI, 222 Yale Avenue North, Seattle, WA 98109; 206/470-4060. Green Trails, Inc.'s excellent topographic map of the region is available for $3.99 at outdoor retail outlets; ask for map number 143, Monte Cristo. Ask the USGS for a topographic map of the Monte Cristo area.

Directions: From Seattle drive 28 miles north on I-5 to Exit 194/City Center/Stevens Pass. Drive six miles east on U.S. 2 to the Highway 9 exit near Snohomish. Follow Highway 9 north to U.S. 92. Turn right and follow U.S. 92 eight miles east to Granite Falls. At the end of town, turn left (north) on the Mountain Loop Highway. Drive 12 miles to the Verlot Public Service Center and another 19.5 miles to Barlow Pass. Parking is on the left side of the highway. Walk four miles on Monte Cristo Road to the trailhead in Monte Cristo.

Contact: Mount Baker-Snoqualmie National Forest, Darrington Ranger District, 1405 Emmens Street, Darrington, WA 98241; 360/436-1155.

154 West Cady Ridge
17.0 mi/2.0 days

The not-too-crowded trail begins in the deep forest of the Skykomish Valley and climbs to pleasant alpine meadows. From here it becomes a ridgetop walk for more than five miles, with excellent views throughout. Bring plenty of water, because you won't find any on the trail's high stretches. You pass within 200 feet of the Benchmark Mountain summit (elevation 5,816 feet) and shortly thereafter drop to Saddle Gap, where the trail joins the Pacific Crest Trail.

From here, you can hike 1.3 miles north on the PCT and then cut back east on Pass Creek and the North Fork Skykomish Trails to form a two-day, 15-mile loop. Or hike farther north on the PCT, through some of the most scenic stretches of the entire route, to Dishpan Gap, and then hike the full length of the North Fork Skykomish Trail back to the road about 1.5 miles from where you started. The latter loop, sometimes called the North Fork/Benchmark Loop, is 23.4 miles and takes two to four days, depending on your load. Longer-distance hikers can use the West Cady Ridge Trail as an entry or exit to a big (30-mile) loop involving the PCT, Bald Mountain, and Quartz Creek Trails. Take care in the fall, however; this is a popular footpath for bear hunters.

Location: In the North Fork Skykomish River drainage of the Henry M.

Jackson Wilderness; see Northern Cascades Map 4, grid a6.

User Groups: Hikers, dogs, and horses. No mountain bikes are allowed. No wheelchair facilities.

Permits: A federal Northwest Forest Pass, $5 per day or $30 annually, is required to park at the trailhead. Passes are available from ranger stations and many private vendors, online at website: www.wta.org, or by calling 800/270-7504.

Maps: For a map of the Henry M. Jackson Wilderness, contact the Outdoor Recreation Information Center, Seattle REI, 222 Yale Avenue North, Seattle, WA 98109; 206/470-4060. Green Trails, Inc.'s excellent topographic map of the region is available for $3.99 at outdoor retail outlets; ask for map number 143, Monte Cristo. Ask the USGS for topographic maps of the Benchmark Mountain and Blanca Lake areas.

Directions: From Seattle drive 28 miles north on I-5 to Exit 194/City Center/Stevens Pass. Drive about 30 miles east on U.S. 2 to the Index turnoff. Turn left (north) on North Fork Skykomish River Road/Forest Service Road 63. At 15 miles, stay left on Forest Service Road 63 at the fork. Proceed another 4.5 miles to the trailhead on the south side of the road.

Contact: Mount Baker-Snoqualmie National Forest, Skykomish Ranger District, 74920 Northeast Stevens Pass Highway, Skykomish, WA 98288; 360/677-2414.

155 Fortune Ponds

17.0 mi/2.0 days

Fortune Ponds, a set of four to six pleasant alpine lakes (depending on which bodies of water you include), are a popular Stevens Pass–area destination accessible via two trailheads on U.S. 2. The above description takes you to the Meadow Creek Trail, which climbs through a 1960s burn, rises gently, and then drops into the first of the ponds, where the Pacific Crest Trail intersects. The total distance one way is 6.5 miles. Nearby are Pear, Peach, Top, and Grass Lakes, where camping is available but meadows are heavily, heavily damaged. Use existing sites only. One-way backpackers can camp in the Fortune Ponds basin and exit via an 11.8-mile walk south on the PCT to Forest Service Road 6700, which exits U.S. 2 near the Stevens Pass Ski Area, or take a longer walk farther south to U.S. 2 via Lake Valhalla and Stevens Creek.

Location: In the Henry M. Jackson Wilderness, northwest of Stevens Pass; see Northern Cascades Map 4, grid b8.

User Groups: Hikers, dogs, and horses. No mountain bikes are allowed. No wheelchair facilities.

Permits: A federal Northwest Forest Pass, $5 per day or $30 annually, is required to park at the trailhead. Passes are available from ranger stations and many private vendors, online at website: www.wta.org, or by calling 800/270-7504.

Maps: For a map of the Henry M. Jackson Wilderness, contact the Outdoor Recreation Information Center, Seattle REI, 222 Yale Avenue North, Seattle, WA 98109; 206/470-4060. Green Trails, Inc.'s excellent topographic map of the region is available for $3.99 at outdoor retail outlets; ask for map number 144, Benchmark Mountain. Ask the USGS for topographic maps of the Captain Point and Benchmark Mountain areas.

Directions: From Seattle drive 28 miles north on I-5 to Exit 194/City Center/Stevens Pass. Drive east on U.S. 2 one-half mile west of the Skykomish Ranger Station to Beckler River Road/Forest Service Road 65. Turn left (north) and drive about seven miles to Rapid River Road/Forest Service Road 6530. Turn right and travel about four miles to the trailhead on the left.

Contact: Mount Baker-Snoqualmie National Forest, Skykomish Ranger District, 74920 Northeast Stevens Pass Highway, Skykomish, WA 98288; 360/677-2414.

156 Iron Goat
8.0 mi/3.5 hrs

This successful rails-to-trails project is a more scenic, more interesting version of the Iron Horse Trail system on the I-90 corridor. Many, many volunteer hours from Volunteers for Outdoor Washington have been poured into turning a four-mile stretch of the abandoned Great Northern Railway into a broad, smooth hiking path.

It wasn't easy. This stretch of railroad was abandoned by Burlington Northern in 1929 when the railway's second Cascade Tunnel, a 7.8-mile passage under Stevens Pass, made it obsolete. The present Iron Goat Trail follows the path of a switchback the railway made to reduce the grade on the climb to Stevens Pass. The lower section of the switchback, 1.2 miles long from the Martin Creek trailhead to an abandoned tunnel, is barrier-free. The surface is crushed rock, with a 2.2 percent downhill grade. The upper section, 2.4 miles, is linked to the lower near the west end by paths at the Martin Creek and Corea crossovers. By combining all sections, you can make a loop of more than six miles. It's a historically fascinating walk, with trail markers indicating the distance by rail from St. Paul. Old railroad debris—ranging from collapsed snowsheds to rusty spikes and crumbling tunnels—is ever present. When skies are clear, you get a bonus: great views, including Deception Falls and Cathedral Rock in the Alpine Lakes Wilderness.

The Wellington Trailhead, a more recent addition, offers a three-mile, barrier-free walk to Windy Point Tunnel. Note that the Martin Creek Trailhead melts out earlier in the summer.

Location: On an abandoned railroad grade near Stevens Pass; see Northern Cascades Map 4, grid c6.

User Groups: Hikers and dogs. More than one mile of the lower path is wheelchair accessible. No horses or mountain bikes are allowed.

Permits: A federal Northwest Forest Pass, $5 per day or $30 annually, is required to park at the trailhead. Passes are available from ranger stations and many private vendors, online at website: www.wta.org, or by calling 800/270-7504.

Maps: Ask the USGS for topographic maps of the Skykomish and Scenic areas.

Directions: To reach the Martin Creek (western) trailhead: From U.S. 2 at Skykomish, drive six miles east to the Old Cascade Highway/Forest Service Road 67 near milepost 55. Turn left (north) and drive 2.3 miles to a junction with Forest Service Road 6710. Turn left and drive 1.4 miles to the trailhead parking lot. To reach the Wellington (eastern) trailhead: From U.S. 2 near milepost 64, just west of Stevens Pass, turn north on Old Stevens Pass Highway. Proceed 2.8 miles to Forest Service Road 50. Turn right into the parking lot.

Contact: Mount Baker-Snoqualmie National Forest, Skykomish Ranger District, 74920 Northeast Stevens Pass Highway, Skykomish, WA 98288; 360/677-2414.

157 Tonga Ridge
9.2 mi/4.5 hrs

Tonga Ridge starts high and stays high, starts great and stays great. It's an easy hike for the whole family, with outstanding views and, in the fall, one of the better huckleberry crops in the western Cascades. The trail

Alpine Lakes Wilderness Restrictions and Reservations

After decades of overuse and, all too often, abuse, the Forest Service has lowered the boom on unfettered use of the Alpine Lakes Wilderness, one of the most spectacular—and heavily traveled—wilderness areas in the United States. Recent regulations place new group-size limits; camping, stock, and pet restrictions; and permit requirements on much of the wilderness.

Day use: Free day-use permits, available at all trailheads and ranger stations, are required for all Alpine Lakes Wilderness hikes. These self-issuing permits are found at trailhead dispensers. In addition, because the wilderness is administered by two national forests (Mount Baker-Snoqualmie and Wenatchee), parking at most of the 47 Alpine Lakes trailheads also requires a federal Northwest Forest Pass, $5 per day or $30 annually. Passes are available from ranger stations and many private vendors, online at www.wta.org, or by calling 800/270-7504.

Overnight use: Free overnight permits, available at trailheads and ranger stations, are required for all overnight Alpine Lakes hikes. In the mid-1990s, Forest Service managers announced plans to issue limited numbers of overnight permits in many popular Alpine Lakes destinations, such as an expanded Enchantments region in the Leavenworth Ranger District, the West Fork Foss Lakes area in the Skykomish Ranger District, and a large area north of I-90 and Snoqualmie Pass that includes Snow Lake and Rampart Ridge. To date, however, those restrictions have been enacted only for the expanded Enchantments permit area, which now includes Eightmile and Caroline Lakes, the upper Ingalls drainage, and Mount Stuart. It's unclear whether limited overnight-permit requirements will expand, or when. Be sure to call the ranger district listed with the hike of your choice to inquire about permit availability before you go.

Enchantments permit reservations: At this writing Alpine Lakes advance overnight permits are required only for the expanded Enchantments permit area. To reserve a permit, required for trips between June 15 and October 15, call the Leavenworth Ranger Station at 509/548-6977.

Other restrictions: Group size is limited to 12 souls (human and/or stock) throughout the wilderness, eight in the Enchantments area. No fires are allowed within one-half mile of most lakes and anywhere above 5,000 feet. Horses are banished from many sensitive areas; dogs are banished or allowed on leashes only in most Alpine Lakes Wilderness areas. Mountain bikes are prohibited from all wilderness trails. Forest officials say they will strictly enforce rules requiring camping in established sites only. Specific restrictions are listed with individual trails, but it's important to call ahead to ensure rules haven't changed.

Contact: Contact the Mount Baker-Snoqualmie or Wenatchee National Forest ranger district office nearest your destination for complete rules and updated permit-reservation instructions before departing. This is important!

starts in second-growth forest but passes meadows after about a mile and continues to do so for much of the route. Good campsites are found at Sawyer Pass, about 3.5 miles, in the midst of the mother of all huckleberry patches. The trail continues on over another ridge to a side trail leading two miles south to Fisher Lake, where you find—surprise—fishers (a state license is required to fish). The path ends back on gravel near the end of Tonga Ridge Road. Like other Alpine Lakes trails within easy driving distance of U.S. 2 or I-90, this one is likely to be painfully overcrowded on weekends and increasingly even on summer weekdays.

Location: Southeast of Skykomish in the Alpine Lakes Wilderness; see Northern Cascades Map 4, grid c6.

User Groups: Hikers, leashed dogs, and horses. No mountain bikes are allowed. No wheelchair facilities.

Permits: Free day-use and overnight permits, required for all Alpine Lakes Wilderness trails, are available at all local ranger stations and trailheads. For more on Alpine Lakes restrictions and reservations, see sidebar. A federal Northwest Forest Pass, $5 per day or $30 annually, also is required to park at this trailhead. Passes are available from ranger stations and many private vendors, online at website: www.wta.org, or by calling 800/270-7504.

Maps: For a map of the Alpine Lakes Wilderness, contact the Outdoor Recreation Information Center, Seattle REI, 222 Yale Avenue North, Seattle, WA 98109; 206/470-4060. Green Trails, Inc.'s excellent topographic map of the region is available for $3.99 at outdoor retail outlets; ask for map number 175, Skykomish. Ask the USGS for topographic maps of the Scenic and Skykomish areas.

Directions: From the Skykomish Ranger Station on U.S. 2, drive one-half mile east and turn right (south) on Foss River Road/Forest Service Road 68. Follow Foss River Road 3.5 miles to Tonga Ridge Road/Forest Service Road 6830. Turn left and drive about six miles to Spur Road 310. Bear right on Spur Road 310 and drive about 1.5 miles to the trailhead at the road's end.

Contact: Mount Baker-Snoqualmie National Forest, Skykomish Ranger District, 74920 Northeast Stevens Pass Highway, Skykomish, WA 98288; 360/677-2414.

158 Deception Creek
20.6 mi/2.0 days

Don't be fooled by the listed mileage. This is another one of those excellent Cascade convertible hikes that can be walked a mile with a child or for days with a full pack to Salmon La Sac. For short-distance hikers looking to break in those new boots just off U.S. 2, it's primarily a forested valley walk. The grade is moderate, making this a good place to haul a lunch, wander until a good sweat breaks, and then find a cool, private log along Deception Creek to park your body, nibble cheese, sip wine, or suck down a Gatorade—however the spirit moves you.

The old-growth forest is awe-inspiring, rife with spongy green moss that looks almost fluorescent when highlighted by a laser ray of sunshine. For longer-distance hikes, continue 7.3 miles to the Deception Lakes Trail and walk about a mile east and 600 feet up to the Pacific Crest Trail and the lakes. Continuing straight, it's three miles to Deception Pass, which divides Deception Creek from the Cle Elum River drainage (see hike in this chapter).

Location: West of Stevens Pass in the Alpine Lakes Wilderness; see Northern Cascades Map 4, grid c7.

User Groups: Hikers and dogs. No horses or mountain bikes are allowed. No wheelchair facilities.

Permits: Free day-use and overnight permits, required for all Alpine Lakes Wilderness trails, are available at all local ranger stations and trailheads. For more on Alpine Lakes restrictions and reservations, see sidebar. In addition, a federal Northwest Forest Pass, $5 per day or $30 annually, is required to park at the trailhead. Passes are available from ranger stations and many private vendors, online at website: www.wta.org, or by calling 800/270-7504.

Maps: For a map of the Alpine Lakes Wilderness, contact the Outdoor Recreation Information Center, Seattle REI, 222 Yale Avenue North, Seattle, WA 98109; 206/470-4060. Green Trails, Inc.'s excellent topographic map of the region is available for $3.99 at outdoor retail outlets; ask for map number 175, Stevens Pass. Ask the USGS for topographic maps of the Scenic and Mount Daniel areas.

Directions: From Skykomish drive eight miles east on U.S. 2. Just before the Deception Falls parking area, turn right (south) on Deception Creek Road/Forest Service Road 6088. Drive one mile to the trailhead.

Contact: Mount Baker-Snoqualmie National Forest, Skykomish Ranger District, 74920 Northeast Stevens Pass Highway, Skykomish, WA 98288; 360/677-2414.

159 Surprise Creek to Surprise Lake
8.0 mi/4.0 hrs

Pick a hot day, pack a frozen water bottle and your swim trunks, and head south on the Surprise Creek Trail. As soon as you get off the old road and onto the trail, you are in a delightful forest with many places to stop and gape at lively waterfalls and stream cross-ings. The trail gets steeper closer to Surprise Lake, which is what you want. When you get there all hot and irritated, take a plunge. Aim for one of those big rocks sticking out of the water. Climb up on it, stare at the view, and pat yourself on the back.

You might want to lounge indefinitely, but the trail does go on. You're on the Pacific Crest Trail now, and it's just over a mile to Glacier Lake, at the base of Surprise Mountain (elevation 6,330 feet). If you're still itching to move, continue straight for a short but very steep haul up to Pieper Pass (elevation 6,000 feet); it's worth the walk. The views make you feel like a relative molecule. A couple more miles ahead are Deception Lakes (see hike in this chapter), both of which have good camping in designated sites only. It's about 10 miles back to the car from here.

Location: South of Stevens Pass in the Alpine Lakes Wilderness; see Northern Cascades Map 4, grid c7.

User Groups: Hikers and dogs. No horses or mountain bikes are allowed. No wheelchair facilities.

Permits: Free day-use and overnight permits, required for all Alpine Lakes Wilderness trails, are available at all local ranger stations and trailheads. For more on Alpine Lakes restrictions and reservations, see sidebar. In addition, a federal Northwest Forest Pass, $5 per day or $30 annually, is required to park at the trailhead. Passes are available from ranger stations and many private vendors, online at website: www.wta.org, or by calling 800/270-7504.

Maps: For a map of the Alpine Lakes Wilderness, contact the Outdoor Recreation Information Center, Seattle REI, 222 Yale Avenue North, Seattle, WA 98109; 206/470-4060. Green Trails, Inc.'s excellent topographic map of the region is available for $3.99 at outdoor retail outlets; ask for map number 176,

Stevens Pass. Ask the USGS for topographic maps of the Scenic area.

Directions: From Skykomish, take U.S. 2 east 10 miles to the town of Scenic. Turn right (south) on a dirt road just before the railroad underpass. Turn right again on the spur road marked with the hiker symbol, which denotes the trailhead.

Contact: Mount Baker-Snoqualmie National Forest, Skykomish Ranger District, 74920 Northeast Stevens Pass Highway, Skykomish, WA 98288; 360/677-2414.

160 Chain Lakes
24.2 mi/3.0–4.0 days

First, consider your options. The Chain Lakes Valley, one of the Alpine Lakes area's truly spectacular backpacking destinations, is accessible both from Stevens Pass and Icicle Creek Road from Leavenworth. But considering that the Hatchery Creek fire near Leavenworth destroyed 6,000 acres of forest, closed The Enchantments for half a season, and made a general mess of Icicle Valley, this is probably the best entrance, at least for now.

From Stevens Pass hike past Lake Josephine to the Icicle Creek Trail and then walk south two miles to the Chain Lakes Trail. From here, it's 4.5 miles up, up, up, and east to the Chain Lakes Valley. Chain and Doelle Lakes lie in a cirque below 6,807-foot Bull's Tooth, one of the most awesome granite peaks you'll ever encounter. The high lake basin stays snowbound until late summer. Come equipped; bring a stove (no fires) and camp in designated sites.

If you prefer a one-way hike through this spectacular region, the route between Stevens Pass and Icicle Creek Road can be hiked 31.5 miles straight through via Frosty Pass, Frosty Creek, and Icicle Creek Trails. The lakes also make an excellent centerpiece

to long loop hikes combining the Chain Lakes Trail with the Whitepine Creek Trail to the north or the Icicle Creek Trail to the south. Both can be hiked with either Stevens Pass or Icicle Creek Road as the starting point. Pick and win.

Location: South of Stevens Pass in the Alpine Lakes Wilderness; see Northern Cascades Map 4, grid b8.

User Groups: Hikers, dogs, and horses. No mountain bikes are allowed. No wheelchair facilities.

Permits: Free day-use and overnight permits, required for all Alpine Lakes Wilderness trails, are available at all local ranger stations and trailheads. For more on Alpine Lakes restrictions and reservations, see sidebar. In addition, a federal Northwest Forest Pass, $5 per day or $30 annually, is required to park at the trailhead. Passes are available from ranger stations and many private vendors, online at website: www.wta.org, or by calling 800/270-7504.

Maps: For a map of the Alpine Lakes Wilderness, contact the Outdoor Recreation Information Center, Seattle REI, 222 Yale Avenue North, Seattle, WA 98109; 206/470-4060. Green Trails, Inc.'s excellent topographic maps of the region are available for $3.99 each at outdoor retail outlets; ask for map numbers 176 and 177, Stevens Pass and Chiwaukum Mountains. Ask the USGS for topographic maps of the Stevens Pass and Chiwaukum Mountains areas.

Directions: From I-5 at Everett, take U.S. 2 east to Stevens Pass. Park in the large lot on the right (south) side of the highway, just east of the ski area. Find the trailhead signed for Pacific Crest Trail 2000.

Contact: Mount Baker-Snoqualmie National Forest, Skykomish Ranger District, 74920 Northeast Stevens Pass Highway, Skykomish, WA 98288; 360/677-2414.

161 Rock Mountain to Rock Lake

10.0 mi/10.0 hrs

You'd have to be nuts to choose this as your route to the top of otherwise pleasant Nason Ridge, which stretches from near Stevens Pass all the way east to Lake Wenatchee. If you're not nuts yet, you may well be by the time you get there. The Rock Mountain Trail rises so steeply you get a kink in your neck just looking up to your hiking partners. The first time they shout down at you, "On belay!" it'll be funny. By the third time, you're ready to kill.

This enjoyable little stroll gains 3,500 feet in just over four miles, and in spite of an almost unbelievable number of switchbacks, it sucks most of the life out of you. If it doesn't, the indefatigable blackfly air force will. Oh, there's no water, either.

For easier access to Rock Mountain, hike the 4.5-mile Snowy Creek Trail, accessible via Smith Brook Road/Forest Service Road 6700, which turns north 4.5 miles east of Stevens Pass. But if you're stuck on this one, go ahead and get it out of your system. Some people have to do everything once. At the top, the view is, well, almost worth the effort. To the left just over a mile is the Rock Mountain summit, elevation 6,852 feet. To the right about a half mile and several hundred feet down is Rock Lake. If you're going out the way you came in, something in your brain won't quite let you relax up here, in spite of the splendor.

Location: North of U.S. 2 in Wenatchee National Forest; see Northern Cascades Map 4, grid b8.

User Groups: Hikers, dogs, and mountain bikes. Horses are allowed, but not recommended. No wheelchair facilities.

Permits: A federal Northwest Forest Pass, $5 per day or $30 annually, is required to park at the trailhead. Passes are available from ranger stations and many private vendors, online at website: www.wta.org, or by calling 800/270-7504.

Maps: For a map of Wenatchee National Forest, contact the Outdoor Recreation Information Center, Seattle REI, 222 Yale Avenue North, Seattle, WA 98109; 206/470-4060. Green Trails, Inc.'s excellent topographic map of the region is available for $3.99 at outdoor retail outlets; ask for map number 145, Wenatchee Lake. Ask the USGS for a topographic map of the Mount Howard area.

Directions: From I-5 at Everett, take U.S. 2 east to Stevens Pass and about nine miles beyond to the marked trailhead on the right (north) side of the highway near milepost 73.

Contact: Wenatchee National Forest, Lake Wenatchee Ranger District, 22976 Highway 207, Leavenworth, WA 98826; 509/763-3103.

162 Merritt Lake

6.0 mi/3.0 hrs

A tarn that marks the entrance of the Nason Ridge high country is the destination of this day hike from Stevens Pass, suitable for families and the mildly aerobically challenged. Head up the first switchbacks and inhale a good lungful of the sweet, ponderosa pine–scented air. You won't breathe air like this in Tukwila, or anywhere near it. The grade is moderate for two miles, where you meet the Nason Ridge Trail. Stay right and hike another mile and about 1,000 feet of vertical to Merritt Lake, where foot-soaking and perhaps fishing (a state license is required; the lake is probably overfished) are in order. A short distance east on the Nason Ridge Trail, a side trail leads a mile north to Lost Lake. It's a very steep downward grade, not easily negotiable. Consider whether it's worth the hike and then either take the plunge or cut your losses and head home.

Location: North of U.S. 2 in Wenatchee National Forest; see Northern Cascades Map 4, grid b8.

User Groups: Hikers, dogs, and horses. No mountain bikes are allowed. No wheelchair facilities.

Permits: A federal Northwest Forest Pass, $5 per day or $30 annually, is required to park at the trailhead. Passes are available from ranger stations and many private vendors, online at website: www.wta.org, or by calling 800/270-7504.

Maps: For a map of Wenatchee National Forest, contact the Outdoor Recreation Information Center, Seattle REI, 222 Yale Avenue North, Seattle, WA 98109; 206/470-4060. Green Trails, Inc.'s excellent topographic map of the region is available for $3.99 at outdoor retail outlets; ask for map number 145, Wenatchee Lake. Ask the USGS for topographic maps of the Lake Wenatchee and Mount Howard areas.

Directions: From I-5 at Everett, drive east on U.S. 2 over Stevens Pass and about 12 miles beyond the summit to a spur road signed for Merritt Lake, near milepost 76. Turn left (north) and follow the road 1.5 miles to the trailhead.

Contact: Wenatchee National Forest, Lake Wenatchee Ranger District, 22976 Highway 207, Leavenworth, WA 98826; 509/763-3103.

⊞ Tiger Mountain State Forest

1.0–12.0 mi/0.5–6.0 hrs 🥾 ⚞

Tiger Mountain may well be the most heavily trod-upon 3,000-foot hill in the United States. Since 1980, when the popular wooded peak in Issaquah's backyard was designated a state forest—thus set aside for non-ammunition-related recreation—trails on this mountain have thrived, and hikers have flocked here in record numbers. There are no views of snowy peaks, stunning alpine basins, or exotic wildlife. But hey, it's a hill and it's close. The mountain is literally webbed with trails—about 60 miles worth, and counting.

The best way to check it out is to just go there and set out on foot. You can make loop trips ranging from a mile to a dozen miles, and the upper trails do provide some excellent views of Mount Rainier and the Puget Sound lowlands. An easy, representative example of the park's trails is the popular Tradition Lake Loop, a heavily traveled trail/road loop of about 2.5 miles from the High Point Trailhead. You see a shallow lake, plenty of trees, various local wildlife—and lots of friendly company. Nary a day goes by anymore when you don't see 50 to 250 cars at the High Point Trailhead. And that just represents a portion of the visitors to this mountain, which also has trailheads near downtown Issaquah, Issaquah High School, and Highway 18, among other places. This trail network is accessible year-round and keeps getting better, thanks to a quadrillion volunteer hours from members of the Issaquah Alps and other hiking clubs.

Location: Near Issaquah south of I-90; see Northern Cascades Map 4, grid c8.

User Groups: Hikers, dogs, and horses. Mountain bikes are allowed on some trails. No wheelchair facilities.

Permits: No permits are required. Parking and access are free.

Maps: For a Tiger Mountain State Forest trail map, contact the Washington Department of Natural Resources at 360/825-1631. Ask the USGS for topographic maps of the Hobart and Fall City areas.

Directions: From Seattle drive 20 miles east on I-90 to Exit 20/High Point. Drive south under the freeway and immediately turn right on the frontage road. Park along the road or in a small turn-around at the road's end.

Contact: Washington Department of Natural Resources, P.O. Box 68, Enumclaw, WA 98022; 360/825-1631.

164 Little Si
5.0 mi/3.0 hrs

The haven of rock climbers and hikers seeking to escape the masses who frequent the Mount Si Trail (see hike this chapter), Little Si is another hugely popular route offering views of the Upper Snoqualmie Valley. The trail weaves through a marshy area, below several massive rock cliffs (one of which stretches directly and disconcertingly over your head) to impressive views at the 1,575-foot summit. The grade is a killer at the start and again at the finish, where the hike occasionally turns into a scramble over steep rock. In between, the walk is a pleasant, easy stroll through mossy forest marked by intriguing rock formations. In recent years, user groups have planned more trails from this area to the Middle Fork Snoqualmie and some other destinations high on Mount Si. A new state management plan buys into that concept—at least partially—and calls for the Little Si Trail to remain open as a key link.

Location: On the southwest slopes of Mount Si east of Seattle near North Bend; see Northern Cascades Map 4, grid d1.

User Groups: Hikers and dogs. No horses or mountain bikes are allowed. No wheelchair facilities.

Permits: No permits are required. Parking and access are free.

Maps: For a map of the Mount Si Natural Resources Conservation Area, contact the Washington Department of Natural Resources at 360/825-1631. Green Trails, Inc.'s excellent topographic maps of the region are available for $3.99 each at various outdoor retail outlets; ask for map numbers 174 and 206, Mount Si and Bandera. To obtain some USGS topographic area maps, ask for Mount Si and Chester Morse Lake areas.

Directions: From Seattle drive 32 miles east on I-90 to Exit 32/436th Avenue Southeast. Turn left (north) over the freeway and drive one-half mile to North Bend Way. Turn left (west) and in a quarter mile, turn right (north) on Mount Si Road. After a third of a mile, cross the river and turn left on 434th Street. The small parking lot and trailhead are on the left. Overflow parking is available on the shoulder of North Bend Way. The trailhead is a quarter mile down the street to the west. It's in a residential neighborhood. Be quiet, keep pets leashed, and do not park along the road.

Contact: Washington Department of Natural Resources, P.O. Box 68, Enumclaw, WA 98027; 360/825-1631.

165 Mount Si
8.0 mi/4.0 hrs

When native Washington hikers assemble at salmon barbecues to lament the overcrowding of their once wide-open state, example number one usually is Mount Si. The immensely popular 4,167-foot peak, which looms above North Bend like a hulking guardian rock, offers views of the Upper Snoqualmie Valley and far beyond. And the trail switching back up its glacier-carved south face draws people in numbers you really might not believe. Managers estimate the trail draws between 30,000 and 50,000 visitors a year, making it the most heavily used trail in the state, and likely one of the more popular in the nation.

Two things draw the crowds: the vertical climb and the location. The steep ascent (3,200 feet) makes it an optimal workout course for those seeking to buff the quads for hiking season, ski season, or even a day on the beach at Lake Sammamish. The only thing separating Mount Si (which was named for homesteader Josiah "Uncle Si" Merritt) from people-scrunched Seattle is 30 miles of four-lane freeway. That sounds like a recipe for overuse, and it is. The parking lot often looks more like a shopping mall lot than a trailhead, and we've counted more than 400 hikers (and 65 dogs!) coming up the four-mile trail while we scoot down. We can't recommend it for a natural experience. Still, if you're like everyone else, you'll probably go anyway. If so, pace yourself. The grade is a killer. The trail tops out at 3,900 feet, with expansive views in Haystack Basin. Above you is the nearly vertical Haystack rock face, which leads up to the summit. Do not attempt it unless you're an experienced rock climber. The rock is crumblier than freezer-burnt cookies.

Recent improvements to the parking area and lower trail have resulted in a short, barrier-free path and picnic area on lower Mount Si.

Location: East of Seattle near North Bend in the Cascade foothills; see Northern Cascades Map 4, grid d2.

User Groups: Hikers and dogs. No horses or mountain bikes are allowed. No wheelchair facilities.

Permits: No permits are required. Parking and access are free.

Maps: For a map of the Mount Si Natural Resources Conservation Area, contact the Washington Department of Natural Resources at 360/825-1631. Green Trails, Inc.'s excellent topographic maps of the region are available for $3.99 each at outdoor retail outlets; ask for map numbers 174 and 206, Mount Si and Bandera. Ask the USGS for topographic maps of the Mount Si and Chester Morse Lake areas.

Directions: From Seattle drive 30 miles east on I-90 to Exit 32/436th Avenue Southeast. Turn left (north) over the freeway and drive one-half mile to North Bend Way. Turn left (west), and in a quarter mile, turn right (north) on Mount Si Road. The unsettlingly large trailhead parking lot is on the left, 2.5 miles down the road.

Contact: Washington Department of Natural Resources, P.O. Box 68, Enumclaw, WA 98022; 360/825-1631.

166 Rattlesnake Ledge
2.6 mi/3.0 hrs

Portions of this trail were rebuilt recently by the city of Seattle (which manages the surrounding Cedar River Watershed) and volunteers from the Issaquah Alps Trails Club to replace an older, treacherous path to the bird's-eye perch atop Rattlesnake Ledge. In the winter of 1998-99, the entire Rattlesnake Lake Park got its own major facelift, including lots of new parking for this fine trail. From the parking lot, round the gate and walk the old road a quarter mile to one of several side trails leading to the real thing. (The main path is signed; stay on the road and you'll see it.) The trail doesn't mess around. You huff and puff up 1,300 vertical feet in 1.3 miles, nearly all of it under the canopy of second-growth forest.

At the top (elevation 2,080 feet), the trail shoots out onto the nose of the ledge rather abruptly. On a sunny day, it's like walking outside into the sunlight after a long day in the office. The views are superb, particularly to the southeast, into the rarely seen Cedar River Watershed. Chester Morse Lake, which supplies Seattle with a good share of its drinking water, is visible, as is the rich forest (closed to hikers) that hides perhaps the greatest population of wild animals in the Puget Sound region. (The watershed's elk herd is the stuff of legend.) To the north is the Upper Snoqualmie Valley, the bursting little city of North Bend (drop to your knees and pay homage to the Super Safeway), and directly across, Mount Si. Be extremely careful at this overlook; it's 400 to 500 feet straight down on three sides, and the rock is crumbly and dangerous. From this point, it's possible to follow the side trail west another 1,500 feet up to Rattlesnake Mountain's (logged) east summit. Since you asked: fret not over rattlesnakes. The mountain is named after wind-rattled seedpods, which someone once thought sounded something like rattlesnakes.

Location: On the border of the Cedar River Watershed, above Rattlesnake Lake south of North Bend; see Northern Cascades Map 4, grid d3.

User Groups: Hikers and dogs. No horses or mountain bikes are allowed. No wheelchair facilities.

Permits: No permits are required. Parking and access are free.

Maps: Ask the USGS for a topographic map of the North Bend area.

Directions: From Seattle drive 32 miles east on I-90 to Exit 32. Turn right (south) on 436th Avenue Southeast/Cedar Falls Road and drive about four miles to the Rattlesnake Lake parking area. A sign points to the trailhead; there is ample parking on the right side of the road, near a metal gate.

Contact: Issaquah Alps Trails Club, P.O. Box 351, Issaquah, WA 98027; 206/328-0480; website: www.issaquahalps.org.

167 Iron Horse
4.0–114.0 mi one way/
2.0 hrs–10.0 days

Imagine a state where you could step off a ship from the Far East, hop a bus 35 miles east, and start walking on a railroad-grade trail that gives you direct foot access to more

than 2,000 hiking trails in one of the nation's most spectacular alpine regions. Washington now qualifies, thanks to the developing Iron Horse Trail (also known as John Wayne Pioneer Trail), which intersects the Pacific Crest Trail—and the edge of the Alpine Lakes Wilderness—at Snoqualmie Pass.

The converted railroad grade, home to the Milwaukee Road railway that ran from Cedar Falls near North Bend to Chicago early in the 20th century, now belongs to the state and surely qualifies as the longest, skinniest state park in the United States. The route already is secured (with several interruptions) as far as Vantage, although some land-swapping with railroads in 1996 made it necessary to take some detours in central Washington. But most of the action on this trail in the future is likely to be found on the west side. Two major trail developments of late have given the western Snoqualmie Pass portions of this trail a much higher profile. First, a major new Cedar Falls Trailhead—at the extreme western end of the cross-state trail—was built in 2000, next to a remodeled City of Seattle park at Rattlesnake Lake, southeast of North Bend (see trailhead directions, above). And already in place about five miles up the trail is a new, decked-and-railed span across the long-washed-out Hall Creek Trestle, near I-90 Exit 38. The Hall Creek washout required a long, torturous detour down one side of the 165-foot-deep gorge and then back up the other to the railroad grade. No more. The trail now is complete and uninterrupted all the way from Cedar Falls to Thorp. Bridging the gap at Hall Creek allows hikers and cyclists a unique, one-way opportunity: catch a ride east on I-90 to Lake Easton or Keechelus Lake and ride the flat, wide trail west, through the Snoqualmie Tunnel (see hike this chapter), and—at a gentle, downhill pace—all the way to the new trailhead at Cedar Falls. The distance is about 25 miles. Several other mini-trips are possible by linking the multiple trailheads along the route.

Portions of this trail near Snoqualmie Pass have become quite popular with cross-country skiers. The stretch from Hyak east around Keechelus Lake to Lake Easton is especially spectacular.

Location: Between east King County and the Columbia River at Vantage; see Northern Cascades Map 4, grid e2.

User Groups: Hikers, dogs, horses, and mountain bikes. Note: Equestrians should not ride trail portions with undecked train trestles. Limited wheelchair access.

Permits: No permits are required. Parking and access are free.

Maps: For a free trail map and brochure, contact Washington State Parks at 800/233-0321. Green Trails, Inc.'s excellent topographic maps show some western portions of the trail and are available for $3.99 each at outdoor retail outlets; ask for map numbers 206, 207, 208, 240, 241, and 242, Bandera, Snoqualmie Pass, Kachess Lake, Easton, Cle Elum, and Thorp. Ask the USGS for topographic maps of the series bordering I-90 that begins with North Bend and ends with Vantage.

Directions: From Seattle drive east on I-90 to Exit 34. Turn south on 436th Avenue Southeast and proceed about four miles to the Cedar Falls Trailhead parking area near Rattlesnake Lake. Trailheads at I-90 Exit 38/Olallie Natural Area, McClellan Butte, Annette Lake, and Snoqualmie Tunnel (see hikes this chapter) also provide access to the Iron Horse Trail.

Contact: Washington State Parks and Recreation Commission, Public Affairs Office, P.O. Box 42650, Olympia, WA 98504-2650; 800/233-0321; Lake Easton State Park, P.O. Box 26, Easton, WA 98925; 509/656-2230.

168 Dingford Creek to Myrtle/Hester Lakes
11.2 mi/6.0 hrs

Children, especially those who like to fish, will enjoy this good family day hike. The trail climbs at a lung-testing pace through second-growth forest to a Y at about three miles. The left fork leads for 2.5 miles to scenic Myrtle Lake, with a side trail climbing for another mile to Little Myrtle Lake and views of Big Snow Mountain to the south and Lake Dorothy and the East Fork Miller River drainage to the north. The right fork heads for 2.5 brushy, muddy miles to Hester Lake, which is set in a cirque beneath Mount Price. You can fish in both lakes (a state fishing license is required), but you shouldn't expect to fish alone.

Location: In the Middle Fork Snoqualmie River drainage of Mount Baker-Snoqualmie National Forest; see Northern Cascades Map 4, grid e2.

User Groups: Hikers, dogs, and horses. No mountain bikes are allowed. No wheelchair facilities.

Permits: A federal Northwest Forest Pass, $5 per day or $30 annually, is required to park at the trailhead. Passes are available from ranger stations and many private vendors, online at website: www.wta.org, or by calling 800/270-7504.

Maps: For a map of Mount Baker-Snoqualmie National Forest, contact the Outdoor Recreation Information Center, Seattle REI, 222 Yale Avenue North, Seattle, WA 98109; 206/470-4060. Green Trails, Inc.'s excellent topographic map of the region is available for $3.99 at outdoor retail outlets; ask for map number 175, Skykomish. Ask the USGS for a topographic map of the Snoqualmie Lake area.

Directions: From Seattle drive 34 miles east on I-90 to Exit 34/Edgewick Road.

Follow Edgewick Road north to the junction with Forest Service Road 5620, then bear right on Middle Fork Snoqualmie Road/Forest Service Road 56. After one mile, the road turns left. Continue another five very rough miles to the Dingford Creek Trailhead.

Contact: Mount Baker-Snoqualmie National Forest, Snoqualmie Ranger District, North Bend office, 42404 Southeast North Bend Way, North Bend, WA 98045; 425/888-1421.

169 Middle Fork Snoqualmie River
21.6 mi/1.0 day

A pleasant, mostly flat walk up the Middle Fork Snoqualmie River, the trail follows an abandoned logging railroad grade 3.5 miles downstream and about 6.5 miles upstream from the Dingford Creek Trailhead. It's an easy trail, made slightly complicated by the necessity of crossing several unbridged streams (a very wet undertaking in the winter or spring). Also, remember that the only bridge over this section of the Middle Fork is at Dingford Creek. Upstream, pass a junction with the Rock Creek Trail that leads 4.3 miles to Snow Lake (see hike this chapter) at 1.5 miles and winds up near a private campground at Goldmeyer Hot Springs. The Middle Fork Trail is frequently being extended in both directions, but the current trail makes a welcome retreat year-round.

Location: Northwest of Snoqualmie Pass in Mount Baker-Snoqualmie National Forest; see Northern Cascades Map 4, grid e3.

User Groups: Hikers, dogs, and horses. No mountain bikes are allowed. No wheelchair facilities.

Permits: A federal Northwest Forest Pass, $5 per day or $30 annually, is required to park at the trailhead. Passes are available from ranger stations and many private vendors, online at website: www.wta.org, or by calling 800/270-7504.

Maps: For a map of Mount Baker-Snoqualmie National Forest, contact the Outdoor Recreation Information Center, Seattle REI, 222 Yale Avenue North, Seattle, WA 98109; 206/470-4060. Green Trails, Inc.'s excellent topographic map of the region is available for $3.99 at outdoor retail outlets; ask for map number 175, Skykomish. Ask the USGS for a topographic map of the Snoqualmie Lake area.

Directions: From Seattle drive 34 miles east on Intestate 90 to Exit 34/Edgewick Road. Follow Edgewick Road north to the junction with Forest Service Road 5620 and then bear right on Middle Fork Snoqualmie Road/Forest Service Road 56. After one mile, the road turns left. Continue another five very rough miles to the Dingford Creek Trailhead.

Contact: Mount Baker-Snoqualmie National Forest, Snoqualmie Ranger District, North Bend office, 42404 Southeast North Bend Way, North Bend, WA 98045; 425/888-1421.

170 Lake Dorothy/ Snoqualmie Lake
4.0–18.0 mi/2.0–8.0 hrs

On this designer route, you choose your distance and even the final exit point, so it's a fun bet for families. It can be a great shady day hike of only four miles round-trip to Lake Dorothy's northern shore or an 18-mile round-trip marathon that includes stops at Dorothy, Bear, Deer, and Snoqualmie Lakes. For even more adventure, hike straight through—for about two miles beyond Snoqualmie Lake—to the abandoned Taylor River Road, where you can walk another six miles to a waiting car on the Middle Fork Snoqualmie Road, not far from I-90's Edgewick Junction. You find good views of Big Snow Mountain, elevation 6,680 feet, along the route. Campers should use designated sites only. Since this lake system is accessible from both U.S. 2 and I-90, expect large crowds. Fishing in the lakes is decent; a state fishing license is required.

Location: In the Alpine Lakes Wilderness, south of Skykomish; see Northern Cascades Map 4, grid e3.

User Groups: Hikers and leashed dogs. No horses or mountain bikes are allowed. No wheelchair facilities.

Permits: Free day-use and overnight permits, required for all Alpine Lakes Wilderness trails, are available at all local ranger stations and trailheads. For more on Alpine Lakes restrictions and reservations, see sidebar. In addition, a federal Northwest Forest Pass, $5 per day or $30 annually, is required to park at the trailhead. Passes are available from ranger stations and many private vendors, online at website: www.wta.org, or by calling 800/270-7504.

Maps: To receive a map of the Alpine Lakes Wilderness, contact the Outdoor Recreation Information Center, Seattle REI, 222 Yale Avenue North, Seattle, WA 98109; 206/470-4060. Green Trails, Inc.'s excellent topographic map of the region is available for $3.99 at outdoor retail outlets; ask for map number 175, Skykomish. Ask the USGS for topographic maps of the Skykomish, Grotto, and Snoqualmie Lake areas.

Directions: From U.S. 2 at Gold Bar, drive 17.5 miles east on U.S. 2/Stevens Pass to Old Cascade Highway, just before the tunnel. Turn right (south) and drive one mile to Miller River Road/Forest Service Road 6410. Turn right (south) and travel four miles until the road becomes Forest Service Road 6412. Continue straight to the trailhead at the road's end.

Contact: Mount Baker-Snoqualmie National Forest, Skykomish Ranger District, 74920 Northeast Stevens Pass Highway, Skykomish, WA 98288; 360/677-2414.

171 West Fork Foss Lakes
13.6 mi/8.0 hrs

Guidebook authors cringe as they type descriptions of trails such as this into the computer, knowing it's already so trampled that adding even a few Vibram soles could lead to permanent disaster, not to mention a major guilty conscience. Nevertheless, the West Fork Foss Lakes Trail is included in this book for the same reason millions of feet have made their way here throughout the century: it's a special spot, one likely to hook everyone who gravitates toward seemingly endless alpine lakes surrounded by rugged glacier-carved peaks, clear streams, and waterfalls.

The first in this chain of easily accessed lakes is Trout Lake, a scant 1.5 miles from the car. The rest of the lineup includes Malachite at 3.5 miles, Copper at 4.0, Little Heart at 6.0, Delta at 7.5, and many more found off-trail to the south and east. The good news is that the trail steepens significantly after Trout Lake. It gains 1,800 feet in the two miles to Malachite Lake and, in the process, weeds out the aerobically challenged and many small children. Still, if you're looking for even small bits of solitude, we can't honestly recommend this hike for a weekend day or nearly any day in midsummer. If you do go, make it a day hike. There aren't enough campsites to go around, and you're likely to have about as much privacy in the mall parking lot the day after Thanksgiving—and fewer bugs, to boot.

Location: South of Skykomish in the Alpine Lakes Wilderness; see Northern Cascades Map 4, grid d5.

User Groups: Hikers and leashed dogs. No horses or mountain bikes are allowed. No wheelchair facilities.

Permits: Free day-use permits, required for all Alpine

Lakes Wilderness trails, are available at all local ranger stations and trailheads. Limited numbers of overnight permits have been under consideration for West Fork Foss Lakes. Contact the Skykomish Ranger District at 360/677-2414. For more on Alpine Lakes restrictions and reservations, see sidebar. In addition, a federal Northwest Forest Pass, $5 per day or $30 annually, is required to park at the trailhead. Passes are available from ranger stations and many private vendors, online at website: www.wta.org, or by calling 800/270-7504.

Maps: For a map of the Alpine Lakes Wilderness, contact the Outdoor Recreation Information Center, Seattle REI, 222 Yale Avenue North, Seattle, WA 98109; 206/470-4060. Green Trails, Inc.'s excellent topographic map of the region is available for $3.99 at outdoor retail outlets; ask for map number 175, Skykomish. Ask the USGS for topographic maps of the Big Snow Mountain and Skykomish areas.

Directions: From the Skykomish Ranger Station on U.S. 2, drive one-half mile east and turn right (south) on Foss River Road/Forest Service Road 68. Follow Foss River Road to Forest Service Road 6835. Turn left and drive to the trailhead at the road's end.

Contact: Mount Baker-Snoqualmie National Forest, Skykomish Ranger District, 74920 Northeast Stevens Pass Highway, Skykomish, WA 98288; 360/677-2414.

172 Necklace Valley
15.0 mi/2.0 days

True to its name, this one's a jewel. A steep trail leads upward to Jade, Locket, Jewel, Emerald, Opal, and a handful of other stunning alpine lakes, each with its own charm and most set in dramatic alpine cirques that look like they belong on nature calendar photos. No doubt some are. The first five miles of

trail are easy and almost flat, following a former narrow-gauge railroad grade used by miners early in the century. Then you cross the river and start straight up, about 2,500 feet in 2.2 long miles. You emerge into a monument to the handiwork of glaciers: deep cirques with sparkling, clear lakes. You'll find clean streams, rocks polished Formica-smooth by tons of ice, and good campsites all around. Visit midweek or off-season, pick a lake off the beaten path, and you might actually find some privacy.

Location: In the western interior of the Alpine Lakes Wilderness; see Northern Cascades Map 4, grid d6.

User Groups: Hikers and leashed dogs. No horses or mountain bikes are allowed. No wheelchair facilities.

Permits: Free day-use and overnight permits, required for all Alpine Lakes Wilderness trails, are available at all local ranger stations and trailheads. For more on Alpine Lakes restrictions and reservations, see sidebar. In addition, a federal Northwest Forest Pass, $5 per day or $30 annually, is required to park at the trailhead. Passes are available from ranger stations and many private vendors, online at website: www.wta.org, or by calling 800/270-7504.

Maps: For a map of the Alpine Lakes Wilderness, contact the Outdoor Recreation Information Center, Seattle REI, 222 Yale Avenue North, Seattle, WA 98109; 206/470-4060. Green Trails, Inc.'s excellent topographic maps of the region are available for $3.99 each at outdoor retail outlets; ask for map numbers 175 and 176, Skykomish and Stevens Pass. Ask the USGS for topographic maps of the Scenic, Skykomish, Mount Daniel, and Big Snow Mountain areas.

Directions: From the Skykomish Ranger Station on U.S. 2, drive one-half mile east and turn right (south) on Foss River Road/Forest Service Road 68. Follow this road 4.1

miles to the trailhead and parking area on the left.

Contact: Mount Baker-Snoqualmie National Forest, Skykomish Ranger District, 74920 Northeast Stevens Pass Highway, Skykomish, WA 98288; 360/677-2414.

173 Dutch Miller Gap
15.2 mi/2.0 days

Ever sit in the Salish Lodge, watch the water whoosh over Snoqualmie Falls, and let your mind wander to the alpine source of the flow? Let your feet do the wandering instead. This trail follows the Middle Fork Snoqualmie for four miles and then heads into thick brush (somebody get a machete up here!) as it climbs steeply to a wide marshy plain, good campsites, and the remains of an old miner's cabin. At seven miles there's a Y. Go left one mile to Williams Lake and farther beyond it on side trails to excellent campsites near Chain Lakes, La Bohn Lakes, and La Bohn Gap. The main trail continues to Dutch Miller Gap near Lake Ivanhoe, with good campsites and spectacular alpine-peak scenery in every direction. This spot also can be reached from the Salmon La Sac area to the east by hiking the Waptus River Trail to Waptus Lake (see hike in this chapter). All in all, recent improvements to the trail and road system here, coupled with its close proximity to Seattle, make this a good first-timer's backpack trip.

Location: Northwest of Waptus Lake in the Alpine Lakes Wilderness; see Northern Cascades Map 4, grid d6.

User Groups: Hikers, dogs, and horses. No mountain bikes are allowed. No wheelchair facilities.

Permits: Free day-use and overnight permits, required for all Alpine Lakes Wilderness trails, are available at all local ranger stations and trailheads. For more on Alpine Lakes restrictions and reservations, see

sidebar. In addition, a federal Northwest Forest Pass, $5 per day or $30 annually, is required to park at the trailhead. Passes are available from ranger stations and many private vendors, online at website: www.wta.org, or by calling 800/270-7504.

Maps: For a map of the Alpine Lakes Wilderness, contact the Outdoor Recreation Information Center, Seattle REI, 222 Yale Avenue North, Seattle, WA 98109; 206/470-4060. Green Trails, Inc.'s excellent topographic maps of the region are available for $3.99 each at outdoor retail outlets; ask for map numbers 175 and 176, Skykomish and Stevens Pass. Ask the USGS for topographic maps of the Big Snow Mountain and Mount Daniel areas.

Directions: From Seattle drive east on I-90 to Exit 34/Edgewick Road. Turn right on Middle Fork Road/Forest Service Road 56 and continue approximately 30 miles to the trailhead at the road's end.

Contact: Mount Baker-Snoqualmie National Forest, Snoqualmie Ranger District, North Bend office, 42404 Southeast North Bend Way, North Bend, WA 98045; 425/888-1421.

174 Deception Pass Loop
15.0 mi/2.0 days

Alpine Lakes scenery doesn't get much better than this. On some summer days you might think backcountry crowds don't get much bigger, either. But hike this excellent loop early or late in the season, explore some of its many off-trail possibilities, and you just might secure for yourself a bit of solitary alpine heaven. The loop goes both ways, of course, but to hit the best stuff first, head clockwise. Hike 4.7 miles west on the Cathedral Rock Trail to Cathedral Pass, elevation 5,600 feet. A good side trip is to Deep Lake, three miles south on the Pacific Crest Trail. Continue north on one of the most memorable stretches of the PCT to Deception Pass, elevation 4,500 feet. Along the way, you pass awesome, 6,722-foot Cathedral Rock.

At Deception Pass, take an extra day to run 3.5 miles north to spectacular, vertical-walled Marmot Lake. To complete the loop, head south on the Deception Pass Trail, which follows the Cle Elum River downstream past Little Hyas and Hyas Lakes. Less than a mile down the trail, notice a side trail to the left that appears to have accommodated the First Infantry Division on recent maneuvers. The heavily traveled trail leads two miles up and east to Tuck and Robin Lakes below Granite Mountain. These two lakes offer such fine camping and awesome views of Mount David and other peaks that they've been literally trampled to death over the years. Lack of trail maintenance and other measures have done nothing to curb the crowds. To see these lakes, do the world a favor and make it a day hike. Beyond this sideshow, it's an easy, flat exit down the Cle Elum back to the car.

Day hikers can get a taste of this area without making a multiday investment by hiking the loop in the opposite direction. The walk to Hyas Lake makes a fine day hike of about four miles round-trip. It's relatively flat, and a half-dozen good campsites near the lake make this a good first-time overnight route for kids.

Location: In the Cle Elum River drainage of the Alpine Lakes Wilderness; see Northern Cascades Map 4, grid d6.

User Groups: Hikers, horses, and dogs. No mountain bikes are allowed. No wheelchair facilities.

Permits: Free day-use and overnight permits, required for all Alpine Lakes Wilderness trails, are available at all local ranger stations and trailheads. For more on Alpine Lakes restrictions and reservations, see sidebar. In addition, a federal Northwest Forest

Pass, $5 per day or $30 annually, is required to park at the trailhead. Passes are available from ranger stations and many private vendors, online at website: www.wta.org, or by calling 800/270-7504.

Maps: For a map of the Alpine Lakes Wilderness, contact the Outdoor Recreation Information Center, Seattle REI, 222 Yale Avenue North, Seattle, WA 98109; 206/470-4060. Green Trails, Inc.'s excellent topographic map of the region is available for $3.99 at outdoor retail outlets; ask for map number 176, Stevens Pass. Ask the USGS for topographic maps of the The Cradle and Mount Daniel areas.

Directions: From Seattle drive east on I-90 to Exit 80. Travel north on Highway 903 to Roslyn. Continue north on the highway, which becomes Forest Service Road 4330, to the end of the pavement at Salmon La Sac Campground. Veer right on the steep gravel road and continue to its end at Tucquala Meadows Campground. The trailhead is at the north end of the campground.

Contact: Wenatchee National Forest, Cle Elum Ranger District, 803 West Second Street, Cle Elum, WA 98922; 509/674-4411.

175 Paddy Go Easy Pass
6.0 mi/4.0 hrs

Take your pick: this is either a good day hike, or merely the front-door entry to longer, cross-Cascades treks to the Icicle Creek drainage via the French Creek and Meadow Creek Trails (see hike this chapter). The ascent is steep, passing through forest for the first two miles, with good views from here on. Watch for signs of past mining activity along the route. At Easy Pass, elevation 6,100 feet, prop up your feet, pat yourself on the fanny pack for climbing 2,700 feet, and gaze east to the Cradle, elevation 7,467 feet.

Location: In the Cle Elum River drainage of the Alpine Lakes Wilderness; see Northern Cascades Map 4, grid d8.

User Groups: Hikers, dogs, and horses. No mountain bikes are allowed. No wheelchair facilities.

Permits: Free day-use and overnight permits, required for all Alpine Lakes Wilderness trails, are available at all local ranger stations and trailheads. For more on Alpine Lakes restrictions and reservations, see sidebar. In addition, a federal Northwest Forest Pass, $5 per day or $30 annually, is required to park at the trailhead. Passes are available from ranger stations and many private vendors, online at website: www.wta.org, or by calling 800/270-7504.

Maps: For a map of the Alpine Lakes Wilderness, contact the Outdoor Recreation Information Center, Seattle REI, 222 Yale Avenue North, Seattle, WA 98109; 206/470-4060. Green Trails, Inc.'s excellent topographic map of the region is available for $3.99 at outdoor retail outlets; ask for map number 176, Stevens Pass. Ask the USGS for a topographic map of the Cradle area.

Directions: From Seattle drive east on I-90 to Exit 80. Travel north on Highway 903 to Roslyn. Continue north on the highway, which becomes Forest Service Road 4330, to the trailhead on the right about two miles north of Scatter Creek Campground.

Contact: Wenatchee National Forest, Cle Elum Ranger District, 803 West Second Street, Cle Elum, WA 98922; 509/674-4411.

176 Waptus/Spade Lakes
28.0 mi/3.0–4.0 days

This excellent river-valley trail leads to some of the more spectacular Alpine Lakes scenery that you can walk to in a single day. The first section stays low, following the beautiful valley along the Waptus River to a junction near Waptus Lake at about eight miles. Veer left along the lakeshore to campsites and the Waptus Pass Trail. A walk from here to Waptus Pass, then south on the Polallie Ridge Trail, makes an excellent two- to three-day, 22-mile loop back to your car. Back at the junction near the lake, the right fork leads about a mile to a junction with the Spinola Creek access to the Pacific Crest Trail. Beyond the junction, the trail follows the shore of Waptus Lake and turns up the valley to the eastern access to Dutch Miller Gap (see hike this chapter). Excellent camps are located along the lake, one of the largest in the Alpine Lakes area. Views of Bears Breast Mountain, Summit Chief, and other local peaks are magnificent.

Halfway up the northern lakeshore, the Spade Lake Trail, an old sheep path, leads a startling 2,200 feet up in 3.5 miles to Spade Lake, frozen until midsummer near the base of Mount Daniel. Water is scarce and horses are forbidden on this part of the trail. Eat your Wheaties.

Location: North of Salmon La Sac in the Alpine Lakes Wilderness; see Northern Cascades Map 4, grid d8.

User Groups: Hikers, dogs, and horses. No mountain bikes are allowed. No wheelchair facilities.

Permits: Free day-use and overnight permits, required for all Alpine Lakes Wilderness trails, are available at all local ranger stations and trailheads. For more on Alpine Lakes restrictions and reservations, see sidebar. In addition, a federal Northwest Forest Pass, $5 per day or $30 annually, is required to park at the trailhead. Passes are available from ranger stations and many private vendors, online at website: www.wta.org, or by calling 800/270-7504.

Maps: For a map of the Alpine Lakes Wilderness, contact the Outdoor Recreation Information Center, Seattle REI, 222 Yale

Avenue North, Seattle, WA 98109; 206/470-4060. Green Trails, Inc.'s excellent topographic map of the region is available for $3.99 at outdoor retail outlets; ask for map number 208, Kachess Lake. Ask the USGS for topographic maps of the Davis Peak, Polallie Ridge, and Mount Daniel areas.

Directions: From Seattle drive east on I-90 to Exit 80. Travel north on Highway 903 through Roslyn, where it becomes Salmon La Sac Road. Follow the signs to Salmon La Sac Campground. The trailhead for Waptus River Trail 1310 is on the right side of the road after you cross the river.

Contact: Wenatchee National Forest, Cle Elum Ranger District, 803 West Second Street, Cle Elum, WA 98922; 509/674-4411.

177 Jolly Mountain
12.4 mi/8.0 hrs

What a view, no matter which direction you look. Getting to the top isn't quite a jolly experience, however. You need to cross Salmon La Sac Creek, which can be rippin' in the early summer, and avoid wrong turns in the intricate Salmon La Sac–area trail network. At 3.2 miles, turn right. At 4.2 miles, turn left (up). At 4.6 miles, stay straight. At 5.2 miles, turn right and head for the summit. In all, it's about 4,043 vertical feet. But you are able to see just about everything within 100 miles of here, including Cle Elum Lake to the west and the Stuart Range to the northeast. Listen to the sounds of dirt bikes close by, gaze at the Enchantments, and wish again that you'd remembered to send in that reservations request for the Enchantment Basin.

Location: East of Salmon La Sac in the Alpine Lakes Wilderness; see Northern Cascades Map 4, grid d8.

User Groups: Hikers, dogs, and horses. No mountain bikes are allowed. No wheelchair facilities.

Permits: Free day-use and overnight permits, required for all Alpine Lakes Wilderness trails, are available at all local ranger stations and trailheads. Parking and access are free. For more on Alpine Lakes restrictions and reservations, see sidebar.

Maps: For a map of Wenatchee National Forest, contact the Outdoor Recreation Informaion Center, Seattle REI, 222 Yale Avenue North, Seattle, WA 98109; 206/470-4060. Green Trails, Inc.'s excellent topographic map of the region is available for $3.99 at outdoor retail outlets; ask for map number 208, Kachess Lake. Ask the USGS for topographic maps of the Davis Peak and Cle Elum Lake areas.

Directions: From Seattle drive east on I-90 to Exit 80. Travel north on Highway 903 to Roslyn. Continue north on the highway, which becomes Forest Service Road 4330, to Salmon La Sac. Look for the trailhead on the right, between Cayuse Horse Camp and the picnic area.

Contact: Wenatchee National Forest, Cle Elum Ranger District, 803 West Second Street, Cle Elum, WA 98922; 509/674-4411.

178 County Line/ Forgotten Trail
23.0 mi one way/ 3.0–4.0 days

Here's a hidden treasure. This occasionally obscure, universally scenic trail follows the Wenatchee Mountains ridgetop marking the boundary between Chelan and Kittitas Counties. The old Forgotten Trail, once a grand mountain route, long ago fell into disrepair, but the Forest Service has rebuilt portions as the County Line Trail. However, some of the route on private land has not been maintained and can be occasionally difficult to follow. In short, get a good map, such as one of those listed here.

Think of the County Line Trail as the top rung in a ladder lying on its side. The bottom rung is the trail's parallel companion, Ingalls Creek to the north. The rungs in between are five steep creek drainages (Turnpike, Fourth, Hardscrabble, Cascade, and Falls Creeks), all about 1.5 miles apart, that link the two and provide loop-hike options too numerous to mention. Figure out the intricacies of the County Line Trail, and the entire high, dry alpine area between Blewett Pass and the North Fork Teanaway River is open to you.

It's possible to spend weeks making short or long trips, all under the watchful eye of the majestic Stuart Range to the north. Most hikers make loops from the west access, including trails such as Beverly-Turnpike and Fourth Creek. The eastern end is bisected at times by logging roads and requires several off-trail ridge walks, most notably the Miller Peak to Navajo Peak section. But the entire route is scenic and awaits exploring. A truly determined soul can follow the path more than 30 miles—all the way from Blewett Pass to the Cle Elum River.

Those on two wheels will be pleased to learn that large non-wilderness portions of this trail and many others in this area of Wenatchee National Forest are accessible to mountain bikes and motorcycles.

Location: On the southeast border of the Alpine Lakes Wilderness; see Northern Cascades Map 4, grid d8.

User Groups: Hikers, dogs, horses, and mountain bikes. No wheelchair facilities.

Permits: Free day-use and overnight permits, required for all Alpine Lakes Wilderness trails, are available at all local ranger stations and trailheads. For more on Alpine Lakes restrictions and reservations, see sidebar. In addition, a federal Northwest Forest Pass, $5 per day or $30 annually, is required to park at the trailhead. Passes are available from ranger stations and many private vendors, online at website: www.wta.org, or by calling 800/270-7504.

Maps: For a map of the Alpine Lakes Wilderness and Wenatchee National Forest, contact the Outdoor Recreation Information Center, Seattle REI, 222 Yale Avenue North, Seattle, WA 98109; 206/470-4060. Green Trails, Inc.'s excellent topographic maps of the region are available for $3.99 each at outdoor retail outlets; ask for map numbers 209 and 210, Mount Stuart and Liberty. Ask the USGS for topographic maps of the Liberty, Blewett, Enchantment Lakes, and Mount Stuart areas.

Directions: To reach the western trailhead, drive Teanaway River Road north from Highway 970 east of Cle Elum. The road becomes Forest Service Road 9737 at 29 Pines Campground. Continue about 16 miles to Spur Road 112, just before Beverly Creek. Turn right and drive to the Beverly-Turnpike Trailhead on the south side of the decrepit bridge. Hike 2.7 miles north to the County Line/Forgotten Trail. To reach the eastern trailhead, drive U.S. 97 north from Ellensburg. Turn north on Old Blewett Pass Road/Forest Service Road 7320. Drive just under four miles to Blewett Pass and turn left on Spur Road 200. The trailhead is on the west side of the road.

Contact: Wenatchee National Forest, Cle Elum Ranger District, 803 West Second Street, Cle Elum, WA 98922; 509/674-4411.

179 Beverly-Turnpike
13.0 mi/8.0 hrs

We have observed that this trail clinks a lot. It's not the trail itself, but squadrons of climbers zooming up behind you, carabiners clinking together like backcountry wind chimes, as they head toward Mount Stuart, one of Washington's more challenging alpine ascents. In addition to being a climber's route, this trail is the closest west-side access to the Ingalls Creek Trail and Stuart Pass. It's also a wildflower-lover's dream, with persistent fields of blooms all along the route for much of the summer. And from the Ingalls Creek Trail, it's possible to make any number of excellent two- or three-day loops. A return via the Fourth Creek Trail to the east makes a 15-mile loop that should sate your appetite for high, dry alpine scenery for at least another week.

Location: Between the North Fork Teanaway drainage and the Ingalls Creek Valley in the Alpine Lakes Wilderness; see Northern Cascades Map 4, grid d8.

User Groups: Hikers, dogs, and horses. No mountain bikes are allowed. No wheelchair facilities.

Permits: Free day-use and overnight permits, required for all Alpine Lakes Wilderness trails, are available at all local ranger stations and trailheads. For more on Alpine Lakes restrictions and reservations, see sidebar. In addition, a federal Northwest Forest Pass, $5 per day or $30 annually, is required to park at the trailhead. Passes are available from ranger stations and many private vendors, online at website: www.wta.org, or by calling 800/270-7504.

Maps: For a map of the Alpine Lakes Wilderness, contact the Outdoor Recreation Information Center, Seattle REI, 222 Yale Avenue North, Seattle, WA 98109; 206/470-4060. Green Trails, Inc.'s topographic map of the region is available for $3.99 at outdoor retail outlets; ask for map number 209, Mount Stuart. Ask the USGS for topographic maps of the Red Top Mountain, Enchantment Lakes, and Mount Stuart areas.

Directions: From Highway 970 east of Cle Elum, drive north on Teanaway River Road. The road becomes Forest Service Road 9737 at 29 Pines Campground. Continue about 16 miles to Spur Road 112, just before Beverly Creek. Turn right and drive to the Beverly-Turnpike Trailhead on the south side of the decrepit bridge.

Contact: Wenatchee National Forest, Cle Elum Ranger District, 803 West Second Street, Cle Elum, WA 98922; 509/674-4411.

180 Twin Falls
2.6 mi/1.0 hr

A relatively easy walk through a cool forest leads to a 150-foot waterfall. Just about anyone can make it, and being this close to the city, many people do. Still, this is a keen place to visit in the fall or winter, when snows choke off all the "real" trails in the high country and the Twin Falls get down to some serious water pumping.

Trodding up the 1.6-mile trail to Twin Falls gives you the same feeling as a serious hike, and it somehow seems more precious in the winter months. The first mile is almost flat, great for kids. The route follows the clear, cold South Fork Snoqualmie, with plenty of sandy spots for little Jamie to plunk her feet in the water on hot summer days. The surrounding forest is enchanting, with a unique rainforest feel. It's easy to explain the moss: About 90 inches of rain fall in this gorge during an average year—two to three times the amount that falls on Seattle, only 32 miles away. All that water gets put to good use, and the falls are glorious. Here, the South Fork shoots through a thin gorge, building up steam for a series of upper falls and then the showstopper—a 150-foot cascade over the lower falls.

The trail, after a level walk along the river and then a series of long switchbacks up several hundred feet, leads to an excellent viewpoint of both falls, although from a distance. Up the trail another half mile is a bridge that takes you over the canyon, directly between the two falls. If you feel the need to walk on, continue straight to a nearby link with the Iron Horse Trail (see hike this chapter). Walk east to the washed-out trestle and stare 125 feet down into the creek gorge below.

Location: East of North Bend in Twin Falls Natural Area, near Olallie State Park; see Northern Cascades Map 4, grid d8.

User Groups: Hikers and leashed dogs. No horses or mountain bikes are allowed. No wheelchair facilities.

Permits: No permits are required. Parking and access are free.

Maps: Green Trails, Inc.'s excellent topographic map of the region is available for $3.99 at outdoor retail outlets; ask for map number 207, Snoqualmie Pass. Ask the USGS for a topographic map of the Chester Morse Lake area.

Directions: From Seattle drive east on I-90 to Exit 34/Edgewick Road. Turn south on 468th Avenue Southeast and proceed about one half mile. Immediately before the South Fork Snoqualmie River Bridge, turn left (east) on Southeast 159th Street and drive one-half mile to the trailhead parking lot at the road's end.

Contact: Washington State Parks and Recreation Commission, Public Affairs Office, P.O. Box 42650, Olympia, WA 98504-2650; 800/233-0321.

181 McClellan Butte
8.8 mi/6.0 hrs

It's steep. It can be crowded. Views at the top are so-so. But it's a 3,700-vertical-foot outdoor workout within 40 minutes of downtown Seattle, so you're likely to wind up here eventually. Actually, this isn't a bad weekend alternative to the nearby Mount Si Trail. But don't expect to find much solitude here, either. The trail climbs through second-growth timber for about a mile before getting steeper and better, thanks to an indescribably old patch of trees. Beware of slippery snow spots, even in July. The first good view spot is at about three miles, which might be a turnaround spot for some. From

here, the trail opens to a mix of rocky slopes and forest before coming to a clearing about 100 feet below the summit. The rock scramble to the true summit is usually slippery and always dangerous. The view? Good, but probably not worth that final leap of faith.

Location: West of Snoqualmie Pass on the south side of I-90; see Northern Cascades Map 4, grid e3.

User Groups: Hikers and dogs. No horses or mountain bikes are allowed. No wheelchair facilities.

Permits: A federal Northwest Forest Pass, $5 per day or $30 annually, is required to park at the trailhead. Passes are available from ranger stations and many private vendors, online at website: www.wta.org, or by calling 800/270-7504.

Maps: For a map of Mount Baker-Snoqualmie National Forest, contact the Outdoor Recreation Information Center, Seattle REI, 222 Yale Avenue North, Seattle, WA 98109; 206/470-4060. Green Trails, Inc.'s excellent topographic map of the region is available for $3.99 at outdoor retail outlets; ask for map number 206, Bandera. Ask the USGS for a topographic map of the Bandera area.

Directions: From Seattle drive east on I-90 to Exit 42/West Tinkham Road. Turn right from the off-ramp and continue past the Department of Transportation office. The parking lot and trailhead are just past the office driveway on the right (west) side of the road.

Contact: Mount Baker-Snoqualmie National Forest, Snoqualmie Ranger District, North Bend office, 42404 Southeast North Bend Way, North Bend, WA 98045; 425/888-1421.

182 Talapus/Olallie Lakes
4.0 mi/2.5 hrs

By all means, bring the kids. As Alpine Lakes Wilderness hikes go, this one is a relative snoozer. But the competition is tough in these parts. And besides, a nice hike to two even nicer alpine lakes is a great way to wear down the kids, whether on a day trip or an overnighter. You tolerate the crowds, and the little ones will have a trip they'll talk about until, well, until they turn 13 and pretend you no longer exist.

Talapus Lake is virtually surrounded by campsites, and yes, they'll all be full on weekends. Take a day off and do this midweek, and your enjoyment factor will increase tenfold. From Talapus Lake, it's only another mile up the trail to Olallie Lake, also outfitted with many campsites. You can come out the way you came in or catch the nearby Pratt Lake Trail (see hike this chapter). No fires are allowed at either lake. The trail is only moderately steep and should pose no major problems for the mildly aerobically challenged. The total elevation gain is 1,200 feet.

Location: In the Alpine Lakes Wilderness, north of I-90 near Bandera Mountain; see Northern Cascades Map 4, grid e4.

User Groups: Hikers and leashed dogs. No horses or mountain bikes are allowed. No wheelchair facilities.

Permits: Free day-use and overnight permits, required for all Alpine Lakes Wilderness trails, are available at all local ranger stations and trailheads. For more on Alpine Lakes restrictions and reservations, see sidebar. In addition, a federal Northwest Forest Pass, $5 per day or $30 annually, is required to park at the trailhead. Passes are available from ranger stations and many private vendors, online at website: www.wta.org, or by calling 800/270-7504.

Maps: For a map of the Alpine Lakes Wilderness, contact the Outdoor Recreation Information Center, Seattle REI, 222 Yale Avenue North, Seattle, WA 98109; 206/470-4060. Green Trails, Inc.'s excellent topographic map of the region is available for $3.99 at outdoor retail

outlets; ask for map number 206, Bandera. Ask the USGS for topographic maps of the Bandera area.

Directions: From Seattle take I-90 east to Exit 45/Lookout Point Road. Turn left under the freeway on Forest Service Road 9030. In one mile, bear right at the junction with Forest Service Road 9031. Continue straight to the trailhead at the road's end.

Contact: Mount Baker-Snoqualmie National Forest, Snoqualmie Ranger District, North Bend office, 42404 Southeast North Bend Way, North Bend, WA 98045; 425/888-1421.

183 Pratt Lake
11.0 mi/6.5 hrs

Who says you can't drive less than an hour from Seattle and be able to hike alone? In general, we do. But we must admit it's still feasible on the Pratt Lake trail system, which offers literally hundreds of opportunities to search for solitude on side trails, next to small hidden lakes, or on tough-to-reach ridgetops. The trail climbs quickly beyond the Granite Mountain turnoff and side trails to Olallie Lake to a vista near Pratt Mountain, with good views of Pratt Lake, at about four miles. From here the trail goes on past a half dozen other explorable (and fishable—a state license is required) lakes to Mount Defiance and Thompson Lake, both of which receive relatively little use.

Back on the main trail at about 4.3 miles, a spur trail runs 1.5 miles north to Pratt Lake. You won't want to camp here. Continue on to a junction with Trail 1011, which leads a half mile east to Tuscohatchie Lakes and another 2.5 miles east to Melakwa Lakes, Hemlock Pass, and a junction with the Denny Creek Trail (loop-trippers, take note). Other, more remote lakes lie a fairly short walk north of Tuscohatchie Lakes or a quick hike west of Pratt Mountain. The total elevation gain to the Pratt Lake vista is 2,400 feet.

Location: North of I-90 in the Alpine Lakes Wilderness; see Northern Cascades Map 4, grid e4.

User Groups: Hikers and leashed dogs. No horses or mountain bikes are allowed. No wheelchair facilities.

Permits: Free day-use and overnight permits, required for all Alpine Lakes Wilderness trails, are available at all local ranger stations and trailheads. For more on Alpine Lakes restrictions and reservations, see sidebar. In addition, a federal Northwest Forest Pass, $5 per day or $30 annually, is required to park at the trailhead. Passes are available from ranger stations and many private vendors, online at website: www.wta.org, or by calling 800/270-7504.

Maps: For a map of the Alpine Lakes Wilderness, contact the Outdoor Recreation Information Centr, Seattle REI, 222 Yale Avenue North, Seattle, WA 98109; 206/470-4060. Green Trails, Inc.'s excellent topographic map of the region is available for $3.99 at outdoor retail outlets; ask for map number 207, Snoqualmie Pass. Ask the USGS for topographic maps of the Bandera area and Snoqualmie Pass areas.

Directions: From Seattle drive east on I-90 to Exit 47/Asahel Curtis/Denny Creek. Turn north over the freeway, turn left at the T, and drive to the nearby Pratt Lake parking area.

Contact: Mount Baker-Snoqualmie National Forest, Snoqualmie Ranger District, North Bend office, 42404 Southeast North Bend Way, North Bend, WA 98045; 425/888-1421.

184 Granite Mountain
8.6 mi/7.5 hrs

A leading cause of Thighus Fryus among Snoqualmie Pass hikers, the Granite Mountain Trail—the most heavily traveled summit path

along I-90—starts steep and stays that way, climbing 3,800 feet in 4.3 miles to an old fire lookout at the 5,600-foot summit. Near the top, you find late-lingering snow, open slopes, a fire lookout, and good views in all directions. Take a picture of Mount Rainier. Like other trails in this area, this one draws enormous crowds on weekends.

Use caution in snow-covered areas, especially the upper trail portions, which are dangerous when snow-covered. Much of the route is exposed, and no water is available. Carry plenty.

Location: North of I-90 in the Alpine Lakes Wilderness; see Northern Cascades Map 4, grid e5.

User Groups: Hikers and leashed dogs. No horses or mountain bikes are allowed. No wheelchair facilities.

Permits: Free day-use and overnight permits, required for all Alpine Lakes Wilderness trails, are available at all local ranger stations and trailheads. For more on Alpine Lakes restrictions and reservations, see sidebar. In addition, a federal Northwest Forest Pass, $5 per day or $30 annually, is required to park at the trailhead. Passes are available from ranger stations and many private vendors, online at website: www.wta.org, or by calling 800/270-7504.

Maps: For a map of the Alpine Lakes Wilderness, contact the Outdoor Recreation Information Center, Seattle REI, 222 Yale Avenue North, Seattle, WA 98109; 206/470-4060. Green Trails, Inc.'s excellent topographic map of the region is available for $3.99 at outdoor retail outlets; ask for map number 207, Snoqualmie Pass. Ask the USGS for a topographic map of the Snoqualmie Pass area.

Directions: From Seattle drive east on I-90 to Exit 47/Asahel Curtis/Denny Creek. Turn north over the freeway, turn left t the T, and drive to the nearby Pratt Lake parking area. Hike the Pratt Lake Trail 1.2 miles to the Granite Mountain Trail.

Contact: Mount Baker-Snoqualmie National Forest, Snoqualmie Ranger District, North Bend office, 42404 Southeast North Bend Way, North Bend, WA 98045; 425/888-1421.

185 Annette Lake
7.0 mi/6.0 hrs

Be patient with this one. Walking the first section of the Annette Lake Trail—below the intersection with the old railroad grade-turned-Iron Horse Trail (see hike in this chapter)—is like ducking into a tunnel, so thick is the second-growth shrubbery that sprang up in the wake of a mondo clear-cut. After that, however, things get a bit more scenic. The section above the Iron Horse right-of-way enters more pleasant forest, open and older, where some actual daylight filters through. Views are rare, but pleasant little Humpback Creek treats you to a couple of minor waterfalls.

The path continues at a steady uphill pace to a ridge top at about three miles and then flattens out for the final half mile to small but pretty Annette Lake, set beneath Silver Peak. You'll find some good campsites on the north side of the lake; on weekends, they'll probably be taken (this is a popular hike for Scouts and parents of fledgling backpackers). Make it a day hike, and you'll enjoy it more. This is one Snoqualmie Pass trail that's actually not all that unpleasant to walk in the rain, as the footing is generally quite good all the way up. The total elevation gain is 1,700 feet.

Location: South of I-90 near Asahel Curtis Picnic Area; see Northern Cascades Map 4, grid e5.

User Groups: Hikers and dogs. No horses or mountain bikes are allowed. No wheelchair facilities.

Permits: A federal Northwest Forest Pass, $5 per day or $30 annually, is required to park at the trailhead. Passes are available from ranger stations and many private vendors, online at website: www.wta.org, or by calling 800/270-7504.

Maps: To receive a map of the Mount Baker-Snoqualmie National Forest, contact the Outdoor Recreation Information Center, Seattle REI, 222 Yale Avenue North, Seattle, WA 98109; 206/470-4060. Green Trails, Inc.'s excellent topographic map of the region is available for $3.99 at outdoor retail outlets; ask for map number 207, Snoqualmie Pass. Ask the USGS for a topographic map of the Snoqualmie Pass area.

Directions: From Seattle drive east on I-90 to Exit 47/Asahel Curtis/Denny Creek. Turn right (south) at the stop sign, then left (north) at the next stop sign. The parking area is in one-half mile. The trailhead is at the east end of the parking lot.

Contact: Mount Baker-Snoqualmie National Forest, Snoqualmie Ranger District, North Bend office, 42404 Southeast North Bend Way, North Bend, WA 98045; 425/888-1421.

186 Denny Creek to Hemlock Pass
8.0 mi/4.0 hrs

Denny Way. Denny Park. Denny Creek Trail. Which one would David Denny, a prominent Seattle settler, be glad to see memorialized by his name? If you're stuck in traffic on Denny Way and can see Denny Park, you correctly answer "C," Denny Creek Trail. The route bearing his name is one of the most spectacular in the Snoqualmie Pass area, with several waterfalls on Denny Creek—most notably Keekwulee Falls—providing the highlights. The trail turns up under I-90 and climbs gently, reaching lovely Keekwulee and Snowshoe Falls at 1.5 and two miles. At about four miles, rest at Hemlock Pass, elevation 4,800 feet—for many, the turnaround point. But consider that, from here, it's only about a half mile to Melakwa Lake and a three-mile walk to the west to the Pratt Lake Trail. Expect big crowds down below, fewer at the pass, and fewer still on the connecting leg to Pratt Lake. The elevation gain to Melakwa Lake is 2,200 feet.

Location: North of I-90, just west of Snoqualmie Pass; see Northern Cascades Map 4, grid e5.

User Groups: Hikers and leashed dogs. No horses or mountain bikes are allowed. No wheelchair facilities.

Permits: Free day-use and overnight permits, required for all Alpine Lakes Wilderness trails, are available at all local ranger stations and trailheads. For more on Alpine Lakes restrictions and reservations, see sidebar. In addition, a federal Northwest Forest Pass, $5 per day or $30 annually, is required to park at the trailhead. Passes are available from ranger stations and many private vendors, online at website: www.wta.org, or by calling 800/270-7504.

Maps: For a map of the Alpine Lakes Wilderness, contact the Outdoor Recreation Information Center, Seattle REI, 222 Yale Avenue North, Seattle, WA 98109; 206/470-4060. Green Trails, Inc.'s excellent topographic map of the region is available for $3.99 at outdoor retail outlets; ask for map number 207, Snoqualmie Pass. Ask the USGS for a topographic map of the Snoqualmie Pass area.

Directions: From Seattle drive east on I-90 to Exit 47/Asahel Curtis/Denny Creek. Turn left over the overpass and proceed to a T. Turn right and travel one-quarter mile to Denny Creek Road/Forest Service Road 58. Turn left and drive 2.5 miles, turning left on the paved road just after the Denny Creek Campground. The trailhead is at the road's end. Don't block driveways when you park here.

Contact: Mount Baker-Snoqualmie National Forest, Snoqualmie Ranger District, North Bend office, 42404 Southeast North Bend Way, North Bend, WA 98045; 425/888-1421.

187 Snow Lake
7.0 mi/3.0 hrs

Start with a lovely alpine lake. Add easy access and a good parking area. Mix in a dash of pleasant trail grade blended with a moderate ascent rate. What do you get? Company, in the case of Snow Lake. This might be the second-most popular trail in Washington, behind only Mount Si for consistent overcrowding.

The trail climbs gradually at first, across Source Creek Valley from the Alpental Ski Area, before launching you into some steep switchbacks to the ridge top. From here, it's downhill to Snow Lake, which on a sunny summer day draws a bigger lunchtime crowd than the downtown Seattle McDonald's. At three miles, the High Lakes Trail leads two miles north to Gem Lake, then another two miles to Wildcat Lakes, which should provide a break from the throngs. Also, at three miles, the Rock Creek Trail leads 4.3 miles north to the Middle Fork Snoqualmie River Trail (see hike this chapter). It's a pretty area, particularly at Gem Lake, but the traffic level really does detract from the experience. Crowds of 500 to 800 people a day are common on summer weekends. If not for volunteer trail maintenance (give a nod of thanks to the Cascade Designs, Inc. step-building crew, among others), this trail would be in trouble in a hurry. The elevation gain to Snow Lake is 1,300 feet.

Location: Due north of Alpental Ski Area at Snoqualmie Pass, in the Alpine Lakes Wilderness; see Northern Cascades Map 4, grid e5.

User Groups: Hikers and leashed dogs. No horses or

mountain bikes are allowed. No wheelchair facilities.

Permits: Free day-use and overnight permits, required for all Alpine Lakes Wilderness trails, are available at all local ranger stations and trailheads. For more on Alpine Lakes restrictions and reservations, see sidebar. In addition, a federal Northwest Forest Pass, $5 per day or $30 annually, is required to park at the trailhead. Passes are available from ranger stations and many private vendors, online at website: www.wta.org, or by calling 800/270-7504.

Maps: For a map of the Alpine Lakes Wilderness, contact the Outdoor Recreation Information Center, Seattle REI, 222 Yale Avenue North, Seattle, WA 98109; 206/470-4060. Green Trails, Inc.'s excellent topographic map of the region is available for $3.99 at outdoor retail outlets; ask for map number 207, Snoqualmie Pass. Ask the USGS for a topographic map of the Snoqualmie Pass area.

Directions: From Seattle take I-90 east to Exit 52/Snoqualmie Pass. Turn left, and in one-quarter mile, turn right and drive two miles to the Alpental Ski Area. The trailhead is to the right of the Road Closed sign in the parking lot at the road's end.

Contact: Mount Baker-Snoqualmie National Forest, Snoqualmie Ranger District, North Bend office, 42404 Southeast North Bend Way, North Bend, WA 98045; 425/888-1421.

188 Commonwealth Basin/ Red Pass
10.0 mi/6.0 hrs

This trail is used less heavily than many in the Snoqualmie Pass vicinity and is at its best in the fall, when autumn colors and solitude abound. We like to hike it in mid-October, just before the season's first snows raise many (false) hopes at nearby Alpental Ski Area. The trail begins in deep, dark forest on the Pacific Crest Trail, switching back gently and then opening onto rocky slopes, where the climbing begins. The Commonwealth Trail is reached in 2.5 miles and, just beyond that, good campsites can be found for quick-trip overnighters. The trail continues up Commonwealth Basin to good campsites and excellent views of Red Mountain from a cirque below its rocky slopes. The basin shows off a rainbow of color in October. The trail ends at five miles, at Red Pass, elevation 5,300 feet. Views are great, as far as Rainier to the south and as close as the Middle Fork Snoqualmie at your feet. It might be the best lunch spot within 20 miles of Snoqualmie Pass. The elevation gain to Red Pass is 2,300 feet.

Location: North of Snoqualmie Pass in the Alpine Lakes Wilderness; see Northern Cascades Map 4, grid e5.

User Groups: Hikers and dogs. No horses or mountain bikes are allowed. No wheelchair facilities.

Permits: Free day-use and overnight permits, required for all Alpine Lakes Wilderness trails, are available at all local ranger stations and trailheads. For more on Alpine Lakes restrictions, see sidebar. In addition, a federal Northwest Forest Pass, $5 per day or $30 annually, is required to park at the trailhead. Passes are available from ranger stations and many private vendors, online at website: www.wta.org, or by calling 800/270-7504.

Maps: For a map of the Alpine Lakes Wilderness, contact the Outdoor Recreation Information Center, Seattle REI, 222 Yale Avenue North, Seattle, WA 98109; 206/470-4060. Green Trails, Inc.'s excellent topographic map of the region is available for $3.99 at outdoor retail outlets; ask for map number 207, Snoqualmie Pass. Ask the USGS for a topographic map of the Snoqualmie Pass area.

Directions: From Seattle drive east on I-90 to Exit 52/West Summit. Turn north beneath the freeway and immediately head right on a spur road to the Pacific Crest Trail parking lot. Hike the PCT 2.5 miles to Commonwealth Basin Trailhead.

Contact: Mount Baker-Snoqualmie National Forest, Snoqualmie Ranger District, North Bend office, 42404 Southeast North Bend Way, North Bend, WA 98045; 425/888-1421.

189 Snoqualmie Pass to Spectacle Lake
36.0 mi/4.0 days

You've done the short overnighters to get your backpacking feet wet. You progressed to a weeklong loop trip in the Olympics. Now you're ready to take a bite out of the fabled Pacific Crest Trail. Well, open wide for the Spectacle Lake route from Snoqualmie Pass, which offers relatively easy access to one of the PCT's more memorable stretches. The trail climbs to Kendall Ridge (at about five miles) and on to the aptly named Kendall Katwalk, a trail section chipped and blasted from solid rock, with vertical cliffs below and vertical cliffs above.

If you even think about crossing this before all the snow's gone, you're nuttier than you look. After the melt, it's a hoot; smile and be glad you're not riding a mule. Just beyond is a good first night's camp at either Gravel or Ridge Lake (7.3 miles). Next day, continue beneath Alaska and Huckleberry Mountains, past Alaska and Joe Lakes, and across the top of Chikamin Ridge to a fine viewpoint above Park Lakes, near the junction with the Mineral Creek Trail. The scenery is already spectacular. But hang on: just beyond is Spectacle Point, a rock that juts out into oblivion above Spectacle Lake, about three miles ahead. The Park and Spectacle Lakes area also can be hiked as a shorter trip from the Mineral Creek or Pete Lake Trails north of Kachess Lake, with access from the Salmon La Sac Road.

Location: In the Alpine Lakes Wilderness, northeast of Snoqualmie Pass on the Pacific Crest Trail; see Northern Cascades Map 4, grid e5.

User Groups: Hikers and leashed dogs. No horses or mountain bikes are allowed. No wheelchair facilities.

Permits: Free day-use and overnight permits, required for all Alpine Lakes Wilderness trails, are available at all local ranger stations and trailheads. For more on Alpine Lakes restrictions and reservations, see sidebar. In addition, a federal Northwest Forest Pass, $5 per day or $30 annually, is required to park at the trailhead. Passes are available from ranger stations and many private vendors, online at website: www.wta.org, or by calling 800/270-7504.

Maps: For a map of the Alpine Lakes Wilderness, cotact the Outdoor Recreation Information Center, Seattle REI, 222 Yale Avenue North, Seattle, WA 98109; 206/470-4060. Green Trails, Inc.'s excellent topographic map of the region is available for $3.99 at outdoor retail outlets; ask for map number 207, Snoqualmie Pass. Ask the USGS for topographic maps of the Snoqualmie Pass and Chikamin Peak areas.

Directions: From Seattle drive east on I-90 to Exit 52/West Summit. Turn north beneath the freeway and immediately head right on a spur road to the Pacific Crest Trail parking lot.

Contact: Wenatchee National Forest, Cle Elum Ranger District, 803 West Second Street, Cle Elum, WA 98922; 509/674-4411.

190 Snoqualmie Tunnel
5.6 mi/2.5 hrs

Three words of advice: Check flashlight batteries. It's not much for scenery, but the Snoqualmie Tunnel may well be one of the more unusual day hikes in the country.

From its entrance behind giant wooden doors near the Summit East (formerly Hyak) ski area, the concrete-lined tunnel, built in 1912 and finally abandoned by the Milwaukee Road Railway in 1979, leads 2.3 miles under millions of solid rock tons at the crest of Snoqualmie Pass. The tunnel, which opened to the public as part of the Iron Horse Trail in the fall of 1994, is almost pitch dark. It's also cold. Even on the hottest summer days, the temperature rarely breaks 55 degrees. Bring a sweater. Also bring good boots. The floor often is covered by puddles of groundwater that leaches through the old but strong concrete liner.

At the west end, turn around and walk back past the trailhead and around Keechelus Lake. For a one-way trip, keep going west to one of many Iron Horse Trail accesses along I-90, including the McClellan Butte and Annette Lake Trailheads. Either way, the tunnel, built for one of the nation's few all-electric railways, is a fascinating walk through railroad history. In days of yore, attendants stood at the east gates, opening the wooden doors to let trains through. The doors were kept closed to prevent strong winds from sweeping through the tunnel, creating massive icicles inside. At various points in history, the tunnel was heated, first with smudge pots, then with electricity, to stave off ice buildup. Walk up to the tunnel today, and you find that it's still very much alive. An icy blast roars out of its Hyak mouth, daring you to enter. When the weather is right, steam billows out of the opening, like the musty breath of a snoozing mountain dragon. It's creepy. It's historical. It's mildly aerobic. And in every sense of the word, it's very, very cool.

In winter months, the tunnel is too cool. Due to ice buildup that can result in six-foot icicles, the Snoqualmie Tunnel is gated and closed from November 1 to May 1. Should unseasonably cold weather cause icicles to form earlier, don't put your tongue on one—it might stick.

Location: On the Iron Horse Trail, beneath Snoqualmie Pass; see Northern Cascades Map 4, grid e5.

User Groups: Hikers, dogs, horses, and mountain bikes. Wheelchair accessible.

Permits: No permits are required. Parking and access are free.

Maps: Green Trails, Inc.'s excellent topographic map of the area is available for $3.99 at outdoor retail outlets; ask for map number 207, Snoqualmie Pass. Ask the USGS for a topographic map of the Snoqualmie Pass area.

Directions: From Seattle drive east on I-90 to Exit 54/Hyak/Gold Creek. At the stop sign, go straight on the road toward the Department of Transportation facility. After about a half mile, turn right on Forest Service Road 22191, signed for Keechelus Lake Boat Launch and Iron Horse Trail Access. Take an immediate right into the new parking area and trailhead. Hike west (right, as you face the trailhead sign in the parking lot) back toward Hyak about one-quarter mile to the tunnel.

Contact: Washington State Parks and Recreation Commission, Public Affairs Office, P.O. Box 42650, Olympia, WA 98504-2650; 800/233-0321; Lake Easton State Park, P.O. Box 26, Easton, WA 98925; 509/656-2230.

191 Gold Creek Valley
10.0 mi/8.0 hrs

Early in the season, head here. This trail is haphazardly maintained, and route-finding on its upper stretches can (and does) prove difficult. But for good route-finders and those who don't mind an occasional deadfall, it's a good early-season alternative route to the high country of Alaska Lake/Alaska Mountain, which otherwise is reached only via the

Pacific Crest Trail and Kendall Katwalk (see hike in this chapter). Nobody wants to cross Kendall Katwalk when snow lingers. Nobody. This path turns to a side trail in spots, circling around a beaver pond and crossing several creeks before splitting at four miles. The right fork is a dead end. The left fork goes one rough mile to Alaska Lake. Don't expect lots of company up here in the late summer or fall.

Location: Northeast of Snoqualmie Pass in the Alpine Lakes Wilderness; see Northern Cascades Map 4, grid e5.

User Groups: Hikers and leashed dogs. No horses or mountain bikes are allowed. No wheelchair facilities.

Permits: Free day-use and overnight permits, required for all Alpine Lakes Wilderness trails, are available at all local ranger stations and trailheads. For more on Alpine Lakes restrictions and reservations, see sidebar. In addition, a federal Northwest Forest Pass, $5 per day or $30 annually, is required to park at the trailhead. Passes are available from ranger stations and many private vendors, online at website: www.wta.org, or by calling 800/270-7504.

Maps: For a map of the Alpine Lakes Wilderness, contact the Outdoor Recreation Information Center, Seattle REI, 222 Yale Avenue North, Seattle, WA 98109; 206/470-4060. Green Trails, Inc.'s excellent topographic map of the region is available for $3.99 at outdoor retail outlets; ask for map number 207, Snoqualmie Pass. Ask the USGS for a topographic map of the Chikamin Peak area.

Directions: From Seattle drive east on I-90 to Exit 54/Hyak/Gold Creek. Turn left (north) under the freeway and right on the frontage road marked Gold Creek. After about one-half mile, turn left (north) on Gold Creek Road (often unsigned). After a third of a mile, bear right on Forest Service Road 9080 and drive north to the locked gate. Walk to the trailhead at the road's end.

Contact: Wenatchee National Forest, Cle Elum Ranger District, 803 West Second Street, Cle Elum, WA 98922; 509/674-4411.

192 Rampart Ridge/Mount Margaret/Lake Lillian
7.4 mi/4.0 hrs

The hike starts on a private road, and many more roads will try to lure you off course on lower portions of the trail. When the trail actually becomes a trail, it switches back furiously up to a junction at about 2.7 miles. The right fork leads a mile down to a pretty and sometimes private cirque containing Lakes Margaret, Stonesthrow, Swan, and Rock Rabbit. You can camp here and day hike to the summit of Mount Margaret. The left fork continues north 1.8 miles to Twin Lakes and, ultimately, Lake Lillian, where the trail ends at the foot of Rampart Ridge. Expect Lake Lillian to be heavily visited.

Location: East of Snoqualmie Pass near Keechelus Lake, in the Alpine Lakes Wilderness; see Northern Cascades Map 4, grid e6.

User Groups: Hikers and leashed dogs. No horses or mountain bikes are allowed. No wheelchair facilities.

Permits: Free day-use and overnight permits, required for all Alpine Lakes Wilderness trails, are available at all local ranger stations and trailheads. For more on Alpine Lakes restrictions and reservations, see sidebar. In addition, a federal Northwest Forest Pass, $5 per day or $30 annually, is required to park at the trailhead. Passes are available from ranger stations and many private vendors, online at website: www.wta.org, or by calling 800/270-7504.

Maps: For a map of the Alpine Lakes Wilderness, contact the Outdoor Recreaton Information Center, Seattle REI, 222 Yale Avenue North, Seattle, WA 98109; 206/470-4060. Green Trails, Inc.'s excellent topographic map of the region is available for $3.99 at outdoor retail outlets; ask for map number 207, Snoqualmie Pass. Ask the USGS for a topographic map of the Chikamin Peak area.

Directions: From Seattle drive east on I-90 to Exit 54/Hyak/Gold Creek. Turn left (north) under the freeway and right on the frontage road signed Gold Creek. At about four miles, turn left on Forest Service Road 4934. Park less than one-half mile down the road and then walk to the gated road and the trailhead on the left.

Contact: Wenatchee National Forest, Cle Elum Ranger District, 803 West Second Street, Cle Elum, WA 98922; 509/674-4411.

193 Rachel Lake
9.6 mi/7.0 hrs

Let's be honest. This trail to a series of scenic ponds and lakes on the shoulders of Rampart Ridge is so overused, beaten, stripped, and denuded that we honestly can't recommend it as a day hike, let alone an overnight wilderness trek. The setting is spectacular, but the damage is disheartening. If you must come (other nearby hikes are as scenic and far less crowded), try to do it off-season and as a day hike. At Rachel Lake, take a good look around and imprint upon your brain a permanent mental image of what years of happy feet can do to fragile alpine environments. This is the kind of trail the Forest Service has in mind as it continues to mull limited overnight permits to many Alpine Lakes destinations. Now, how about making Rachel and Rampart Lakes the area's first local day-hiking-only zone? It's food for thought. The main trail leads four miles to Rachel Lake. The elevation

gain is about 1,600 feet. From here, follow the right trail fork for a path that continues north up Rampart Ridge, later splitting into separate paths to Mount Alta (6,250 feet), Lila Lake, and the Rampart Lakes. The round-trip distance to Rampart Lakes, where lesser-used campsites are found, is about 11 miles, with an elevation gain of 2,300 feet.

Location: North of Kachess Lake in the Alpine Lakes Wilderness; see Northern Cascades Map 4, grid e6.

User Groups: Hikers and leashed dogs. No horses or mountain bikes are allowed. No wheelchair facilities.

Permits: Free day-use and overnight permits, required for all Alpine Lakes Wilderness trails, are available at all local ranger stations and trailheads. For more on Alpine Lakes restrictions and reservations, see sidebar. In addition, a federal Northwest Forest Pass, $5 per day or $30 annually, is required to park at the trailhead. Passes are available from ranger stations and many private vendors, online at website: www.wta.org, or by calling 800/270-7504.

Maps: For a map of the Alpine Lakes Wilderness, contact the Outdoor Recreation Information Center, Seattle REI, 222 Yale Avenue North, Seattle, WA 98109; 206/470-4060. Green Trails, Inc.'s excellent topographic maps of the region are available for $3.99 each at outdoor retail outlets; ask for map numbers 207 and 208, Snoqualmie Pass and Kachess Lake. Ask the USGS for a topographic map of the Chikamin Peak area.

Directions: From Seattle take I-90 east to Exit 62/Crystal Springs and travel northeast on Forest Service Road 49 toward Lake Kachess. Follow the signs to Lake Kachess Campground. Turn left on Forest Service Road 4930, which leads about four miles to the large parking lot and the trailhead at the road's end.

Contact: Wenatchee National Forest, Cle Elum Ranger District, 803 West Second Street, Cle Elum, WA 98922; 509/674-4411.

194 Kachess Ridge
14.5 mi one way/
2.0–3.0 days

Forest, a few clear-cuts, and miles of blue water to the west. Same to the east! This long, usually dry north-south traverse between Kachess and Cle Elum Lakes (OK, reservoirs) is a unique hike that's best walked one way. To do so, leave one car at the trailhead above and in the other, continue east on I-90 to Exit 80. Travel north on Highway 903 to Roslyn. Continue north on the highway, which becomes Forest Service Road 4330, to Cooper Lake Road/Forest Service Road 46, one mile south of Salmon La Sac. Turn left and drive east over Cooper Pass to Forest Service Road 125. Turn left (south) and drive to the trailhead about three miles on the left.

Hike south through the clear-cut and up onto No Name Ridge. It's 5.5 steep miles to Thorp Mountain (elevation 5,854 feet), where the Thorp Creek Trail brings day hikers three miles up from Forest Service Road 4308 and the Salmon La Sac Road. The side trip up toward Thorp Mountain lookout is well worth the time. Just down the main trail are junctions with the Knox Creek, French Cabin, and Silver Creek Trails. The latter connects with the Domerie Peak Trail. It's smooth sailing from here, 4.5 miles and 2,200 feet to the lower trailhead.

Location: East of Kachess Lake in Wenatchee National Forest; see Northern Cascades Map 4, grid e6.

User Groups: Hikers, dogs, and horses. No mountain bikes are allowed. No wheelchair facilities.

Permits: A federal Northwest Forest Pass, $5 per day or $30 annually, is required to park at the trailhead. Passes are available from ranger stations and many private vendors, online at website: www.wta.org, or by calling 800/270-7504.

Maps: For a map of Wenatchee National Forest, contact the Outdoor Recreation Information Center, Seattle REI, 222 Yale Avenue North, Seattle, WA 98109; 206/470-4060. Green Trails, Inc.'s excellent topographic map of the region is available for $3.99 at outdoor retail outlets; ask for map number 208, Kachess Lake. Ask the USGS for topographic maps of the Kachess Lake and Polallie Ridge areas.

Directions: From Seattle drive east on I-90 over Snoqualmie Pass. Take Exit 70/Easton/Sparks, drive north, turn left on Sparks Road, and drive parallel to the freeway for about five miles to Forest Service Road 4818. Turn right (north) and drive about four miles to the first road after the Kachess Dam turnoff. Turn right and follow the power line to the next trailhead sign. Turn left. Keep left at the fork and drive to the trailhead at the road's end.

Contact: Wenatchee National Forest, Cle Elum Ranger District, 803 West Second Street, Cle Elum, WA 98922; 509/674-4411.

195 West Fork Teanaway River
9.6 mi one way/5.0 hrs

This long, scenic, and little-used trail makes an excellent day hike (if you turn back at a reasonable distance), a medium-length hike, or one leg of a large Teanaway Valley loop trail in conjunction with the Yellow Hill or Middle Fork Teanaway Trails to the east. The trail gains 3,000 feet, although gradually, and crosses the scenic West Fork Teanaway River enough times to cool your broiling feet. It's a great midsummer hike, although you should check snowmelt conditions with rangers to make sure river crossings are safe and practical. The trail climbs 9.6 miles to a junction with the Jolly Creek Trail (see hike this chapter). Loopers can continue east to Jolly Mountain and then south over Elbow Peak and Yellow Hill (see hike this chapter). Along the way you find the wide-open views that make the Teanaway drainage a favorite destination for many fans of high, arid pinecone country. Don't forget your sunscreen—and earplugs if you're in this area when stream crossings are easy and motorcycles proliferate.

Location: In the Teanaway River drainage north of I-90 and east of Cle Elum Lake; see Northern Cascades Map 4, grid f7.

User Groups: Hikers, leashed dogs, horses, and mountain bikes. No wheelchair facilities.

Permits: No permits are required. Parking and access are free.

Maps: For a Wenatchee National Forest map, contact the Outdoor Recreation Information Center, Seattle REI, 222 Yale Avenue North, Seattle, WA 98109; 206/470-4060. Green Trails, Inc.'s excellent topographic maps of the region are available for $3.99 each at outdoor retail outlets. Ask for map numbers 208 and 209, Kachess Lake and Mount Stuart. Ask the USGS for topographic maps of the Cle Elum Lake, Teanaway Butte, and Davis Peak areas.

Directions: From Seattle drive 80 miles east on I-90 over Snoqualmie Pass to Exit 80 and proceed several miles north to Roslyn. Follow Highway 903 Salmon La Sac Road several miles north to Forest Service Road 4305, just south of Wish Poosh Campground. Turn right (east) and drive past two junctions with Spur Road 113. The trailhead is on the left about 1.5 miles beyond the second junction.

Contact: Wenatchee National Forest, Cle Elum Ranger District, 803 West Second Street, Cle Elum, WA 98922; 509/674-4411.

196 Yellow Hill/Elbow Peak
10.0 mi/5.0 hrs

If the Forest Service would boot motorcycles off this trail, it would be first class. As it is, it's a strong second, with spectacular open views from Yellow Hill and Elbow Peak almost compensating for the dirt bikes. The gas vehicles are worst at the start, especially on the trail's (road's?) first few miles. After that it's almost all backcountry pedestrians, as they'll undoubtedly be known someday in Forest Service parlance. Views of the Teanaway Valley start to get good several miles in. You pass directly below, zoom straight up to great views at Yellow Hill (elevation 5,527 feet), and then continue to even more stupendous views of Rainier, Stuart, and many other mountains from the Elbow Peak summit (five miles, 5,673 feet). Most day hikers turn around here. But long-haul day hikers can continue north 5.5 miles to Jolly Mountain, where the Jolly Creek Trail leads to the Salmon La Sac area or east to the Middle Fork Teanaway Trail. A big, dry, and lonesome loop utilizing either trail system is possible, perhaps even probable, once you get a taste of the Teanaway high country.

Location: In the Teanaway River drainage of Wenatchee National Forest; see Northern Cascades Map 4, grid f8.

User Groups: Hikers, leashed dogs, and horses. No mountain bikes. No wheelchair facilities.

Permits: No permits are required. Parking and access are free.

Maps: For a map of the Wenatchee National Forest, contact the Outdoor Recreation Information Center, Seattle REI, 222 Yale Avenue North, Seattle, WA 98109; 206/470-4060. Green Trails, Inc.'s excellent topographic maps of the region are available for $3.99 each at outdoor retail outlets. Ask for map numbers 208 and 209, Kachess Lake and

Mount Stuart. Ask the USGS for topographic maps of the Cle Elum Lake, Teanaway Butte, and Davis Peak areas.

Directions: From Seattle drive east on I-90 over Snoqualmie Pass to Exit 80 and proceed north to Roslyn. Follow Highway 903, Salmon La Sac Road, several miles north to Forest Service Road 4305, just south of Wish Poosh Campground. Turn right (east) and drive to Spur Road 113. Follow the spur road to the trailhead on the left, up a rough second spur to the north (walking it isn't a bad idea since the road is rough).

Contact: Wenatchee National Forest, Cle Elum Ranger District, 803 West Second Street, Cle Elum, WA 98922; 509/674-4411.

197 Summit Lake/ Bearhead Mountain

5.0–22.0 mi/
2.0 hrs–3.0 days

Mount Rainier would be a great place to go if it weren't for all the people. That's what you think while slurping from a water bottle as you recline on the shores of Summit Lake, with Mount Rainier's north face in full view, and nary a soul in sight to disturb you if you come here on a weekday. Summit Lake, a picturesque little alpine lake, is the reward for a short, easy hike suitable for children, or a long hike up Carbon Trail 1179, which leads through the Clearwater Wilderness forest.

For overnighters, the long route is a great opportunity to get away from it (and them) all. At one mile, you pass a junction with the Clearwater Trail, which leads 8.1 miles to the northern part of the wilderness. Go straight and you cross the Clearwater River and, about eight miles in, find excellent views of Mount Rainier. For even better views, hike north for less than a mile on the Bearhead Mountain Trail, which climbs to a lookout site at 6,069 feet. As you hike west on the main

trail, go straight to a junction with Upper Summit Lake Trail (9.4 miles), then the lake itself (11.1 miles).

From the western trailhead, a moderate grade leads under a mile to a junction with the Carbon Trail. Turn left (north) and go 1.7 miles to the lake, where a side trail leads to the northwest side. Views of Rainier are splendid here, offering rarely seen vistas of the north face and Willis Wall. Although the short route begins in a clear-cut, much of both trails is in old-growth forest. If you can arrange transportation to both ends, you can enjoy a nice, 11-mile one-way shuttle walk.

Location: In the Clearwater Wilderness north of Mount Rainier National Park; see Northern Cascades Map 4, grid f8.

User Groups: Hikers and leashed dogs. No horses or mountain bikes are allowed. No wheelchair facilities.

Permits: A federal Northwest Forest Pass, $5 per day or $30 annually, is required to park at the trailhead. Passes are available from ranger stations and many private vendors, online at website: www.wta.org, or by calling 800/270-7504.

Maps: For a map of the Mount Baker-Snoqualmie National Forest and the Clearwater Wilderness, contact the Outdoor Recreation Information Center, Seattle REI, 222 Yale Avenue North, Seattle, WA 98109; 206/470-4060. Green Trails, Inc.'s excellent topographic maps of the region are available for $3.99 each at outdoor retail outlets. Ask for map number 237, Enumclaw. Ask the USGS for a topographic map of the Bearhead Mountain area.

Directions: To reach the western trailhead of this five-mile round-trip hike, from Enumclaw drive west on Highway 410 to Highway 165. Proceed on Highway 165 to the Carbon River Road/Mowich Lake Highway junction. Turn left onto Carbon River Road and follow it to Cayada Creed Road/Forest Service Road 7810, just before the national park entrance. Turn left (north) and drive about 6.8 miles to the trailhead at the end of the road. To make the longer hike (including Bearhead Mountain) from Enumclaw, drive east on Highway 410 to West Fork Road 74. Turn right (south) and proceed 11 miles to Forest Service Road 7450. Turn left (north) and follow the road to the Carbon/Clearwater trailhead at the road's end.

Contact: Mount Baker-Snoqualmie National Forest, Snoqualmie Ranger District, Enumclaw office, 450 Roosevelt Avenue East, Enumclaw, WA 98022; 360/825-6585.

198 Noble Knob
7.0 mi/4.5 hrs

Here's a grand alternative to overcrowded hiking trails in Mount Rainier National Park. It offers some comparable sights (Rainier view, magnificent wildflowers), a reasonable distance, and easier access. And you just might have a few moments to yourself if your timing is good.

From the trailhead near Corral Pass, start north along Dalles Ridge on the mostly level trail, which alternates between footpath and abandoned road. At about 1.5 miles the trail is joined by the Deep Creek Trail, which leads sharply downhill to the west to a trailhead near Highway 410. After another two miles of meadows, forest, and occasional excellent views, you reach a junction with the Dalles Ridge Trail, which also leads down to Highway 410. A short distance farther (downhill) is a three-way junction. The left fork drops past George Lake to a trailhead on Forest Service Road 72. The right fork drops to Lost Lake and, ultimately, the Greenwater River Trail (see hike in this chapter). Take the middle trail and circle the mountaintop to Noble Knob,

site of an old forest lookout. The views of Rainier are grand, and in season the entire mountaintop is ablaze with the color of bursting wildflowers and wild strawberries. Bring binoculars and watch for mountain goats.

Location: Northeast of Mount Rainier National Park in Norse Peak Wilderness; see Northern Cascades Map 4, grid h3.

User Groups: Hikers, leashed dogs, horses, and mountain bikes. No wheelchair facilities.

Permits: A federal Northwest Forest Pass, $5 per day or $30 annually, is required to park at the trailhead. Passes are available from ranger stations and many private vendors, online at website: www.wta.org, or by calling 800/270-7504. Free day-hiking and overnight wilderness permits are available at the trailhead.

Maps: For a map of the William O. Douglas and Norse Peak Wilderness, contact the Outdoor Recreation Information Center, Seattle REI, 222 Yale Avenue North, Seattle, WA 98109; 206/470-4060. Green Trails, Inc.'s excellent topographic maps of the region are available for $3.99 each at outdoor retail outlets. Ask for map number 239, Lester. Ask the USGS for a topographic map of the Noble Knob area.

Directions: From Enumclaw drive approximately 30 miles east on Highway 410 to Corral Pass Road/Forest Service Road 7174, just north of the Mount Rainier National Park boundary. Turn left (east) on Corral Pass Road and drive about six miles to the parking lot and trailhead, just before the large parking area at Corral Pass.

Contact: Mount Baker-Snoqualmie National Forest, Snoqualmie Ranger District, Enumclaw office, 450 Roosevelt Avenue East, Enumclaw, WA 98022; 360/825-6585.

199 Greenwater River
15.2 mi/1.0–2.0 days

This old-growth forest makes you feel young again, particularly after passing through the various clear-cuts on Highway 410 on the way down here, and once again on the first stretches of this trail. The Greenwater River Trail, a beautiful, valley-bottom hike, is always worth the effort for the trees alone. Tall, proud, majestic, and silent, they're an elixir for any number of ills. But the trail offers a bonus: Echo Lake, a large alpine jewel just over seven miles up the trail.

The path begins with a gradual ascent, passing Lower and Upper Greenwater Lakes, both of which offer fair fishing (state license required). The trail then enters Norse Peak Wilderness and passes a junction with the Lost Lake Trail, which leads about three miles to the lake and about 5.3 miles to the top of Noble Knob (see hike this chapter). From here things get steeper, topping out at about 6.5 miles after passing a junction with the Maggie Creek Trail, which departs to the left (east). The final mile is all downhill. You'll find good campsites near the lake (set up camp at least 100 feet away) and near the horse camp at the south end. The trail continues on around the lake, ending in another five miles at Corral Pass.

Location: Northeast of Mount Rainier in Norse Peak Wilderness; see Northern Cascades Map 4, grid h4.

User Groups: Hikers, leashed dogs, and horses. No mountain bikes. No wheelchair facilities.

Permits: A federal Northwest Forest Pass, $5 per day or $30 annually, is required to park at the trailhead. Passes are available from ranger stations and many private vendors, online at website: www.wta.org, or by calling 800/270-7504. Free day-hiking and overnight wilderness permits are available at the trailhead.

Maps: For a map of the William O. Douglas and Norse Peak Wilderness, contact the Outdoor Recreation Information Center, Seattle REI, 222 Yale Avenue North, Seattle, WA 98109; 206/470-4060. Green Trails, Inc.'s excellent topographic maps of the region are available for $3.99 each at outdoor retail outlets. Ask for map number 239, Lester. Ask the USGS for a topographic map of the Noble Knob area.

Directions: From Enumclaw drive 20 miles east on Highway 410 to Greenwater Road/Forest Service Road 70. Turn left and drive 8.5 miles to Forest Service Road 7033, just beyond the Greenwater River crossing. Turn right and find the trailhead after about a quarter mile on the right.

Contact: Mount Baker-Snoqualmie National Forest, Snoqualmie Ranger District, Enumclaw office, 450 Roosevelt Avenue East, Enumclaw, WA 98022; 360/825-6585.

200 Cady Creek/Little Wenatchee Loop
18.8 mi/3.0–4.0 days

Fairly close to home for most Seattleites, this excellent loop trip puts hikers into the high country fast and gives them a taste of the Pacific Crest Trail at its very best. Begin at the Little Wenatchee Ford Campground (elevation 3,000 feet) on the Cady Creek Trail, which climbs gently through the woods for about 4.8 miles to Cady Pass (elevation 4,300 feet). Hang a right here and walk north on the PCT, which becomes a ridgetop walk that skirts Skykomish Peak (elevation 6,368 feet) and then drops to an excellent but overused camp at Lake Sally Ann, about four miles north of Cady Pass. From here, it's only 1.5 miles north to Dishpan Gap (elevation 5,600 feet), and another mile over Sauk Pass to a right-hand turn on the Little Wenatchee

Trail near Meander Meadows, a grand second-night destination.

The meadows are rife with good campsites and, of course, wildflowers in season. Don't forget repellent for bears (common sense usually suffices) and bugs (heavy doses of DEET kill bugs and eat your clothing). It's seven mostly pleasant miles and 2,500 vertical feet out the Little Wenatchee Trail to your car, and two hours' worth of highway between your stomach and a Zeke's Burger at the bottom of U.S. 2. Add a peanut butter milkshake if you carried the whole tent out by yourself.

Location: In the Henry M. Jackson Wilderness, north of Stevens Pass; see Northern Cascades Map 4, grid h4.

User Groups: Hikers, dogs, and horses. No mountain bikes are allowed. No wheelchair facilities.

Permits: A federal Northwest Forest Pass, $5 per day or $30 annually, is required to park at the trailhead. Passes are available from ranger stations and many private vendors, online at website: www.wta.org, or by calling 800/270-7504.

Maps: For a map of the Henry M. Jackson Wilderness, contact the Outdoor Recreation Information Center, Seattle REI, 222 Yale Avenue North, Seattle, WA 98109; 206/470-4060. Green Trails, Inc.'s excellent topographic map of the region is available for $3.99 at outdoor retail outlets; ask for map number 144, Benchmark Mountain. Ask the USGS for topographic maps of the Poe Mountain and Benchmark Mountain areas.

Directions: From Seattle drive 28 miles north on I-5 to Exit 194/City Center/Stevens Pass. Follow U.S. 2 east for 19 miles beyond Stevens Pass to Highway 207. Turn left (north) toward Lake Wenatchee. Drive around the north shore of the lake, 1.5 miles beyond the ranger station, to Forest Service

Road 6500. Turn left and travel to the trailhead at the end of the road.

Contact: Wenatchee National Forest, Lake Wenatchee Ranger District, 22976 Highway 207, Leavenworth, WA 98826; 509/763-3103.

201 Little Giant Pass
10.0 mi/1.0–2.0 days

Better do plenty of squat thrusts to get in shape for this one. We've always speculated that the Little Giant Trail, bounding up and plunging down as it does, was named for the thighs of some mythical hiker who traveled this route at least once a week for much of his or her life. But if you believe pristine alpine valleys are worth a drop—OK, a bucket—of sweat, you won't be disappointed. From Chiwawa River Road, you have to immediately ford the Chiwawa River (easy if footlogs are to be found, harrowing otherwise) and then walk up a torturously steep, haphazardly maintained path with wet feet. And don't forget about the flies, which make you begin searching for Dr. Kevorkian's phone number in the depths of your pack. Nevertheless, the trail is very pretty as it ascends, with good campsites found once you meet Little Giant Creek at about 2.5 miles. The remaining 2.5 miles are steep and tiring but scenic, with good campsites all along the way. Count on good views from Little Giant Pass, and better views from the ridge top in either direction. This is the turnaround point, but if you go on from here, the trail drops steeply into the wild Napeequa Valley, where in 3.3 miles it meets the Boulder Creek Trail, which continues to the head of the valley and the High Pass area.

Location: In the Glacier Peak Wilderness, south of Buck Creek Pass; see Northern Cascades Map 5, grid a1.

User Groups: Hikers and dogs. Horses are permitted, but as of early 1999, the trail was considered hazardous for equestrian use. No mountain bikes are allowed. No wheelchair facilities.

Permits: A federal Northwest Forest Pass, $5 per day or $30 annually, is required to park at the trailhead. Passes are available from ranger stations and many private vendors, online at website: www.wta.org, or by calling 800/270-7504.

Maps: For a map of the Glacier Peak Wilderness, contact the Outdoor Recreation Information Center, Seattle REI, 222 Yale Avenue North, Seattle, WA 98109; 206/470-4060. Green Trails, Inc.'s excellent topographic map of the region is available for $3.99 at outdoor retail outlets; ask for map number 113, Holden. Ask the USGS for topographic maps of the Trinity and Clark Mountain areas.

Directions: From Seattle take I-5 north to U.S. 2 and then take U.S. 2 east to Highway 207, which turns left (north) toward Lake Wenatchee. Bear right toward Fish Lake and turn left on Forest Service Road 62, which becomes Chiwawa River Road/Forest Service Road 6200. Follow the road for about one mile beyond Nineteen Mile Camp to the trailhead on the left.

Contact: Wenatchee National Forest, Lake Wenatchee Ranger District, 22976 Highway 207, Leavenworth, WA 98826; 509/763-3103.

202 Mount David
14.0 mi/7.0 hrs

Scoot to the top of this snowy peak (elevation 7,400 feet), and you might catch a glimpse of the highest-altitude stone outhouse in the state of Washington (a remnant from an old lookout tower). If that doesn't entice you, the exhilarating climb and thrilling view should. This is a tough hike, gaining more than 5,000 feet. At times, the trail gets a bit lost in the scree and is difficult to follow, especially at the top, where snow can remain into August. The final steps are a bit hairy, and you are thankful for the work done by the old lookout crew, which probably saved you the trouble of a full rope-up ascent. Nevertheless, be careful. It's a long way down.

Location: North of Stevens Pass Highway in Wenatchee National Forest; see Northern Cascades Map 5, grid a2.

User Groups: Hikers and dogs. Trail is open to horses, but not recommended. No mountain bikes are allowed. No wheelchair facilities.

Permits: A federal Northwest Forest Pass, $5 per day or $30 annually, is required to park at the trailhead. Passes are available from ranger stations and many private vendors, online at website: www.wta.org, or by calling 800/270-7504.

Maps: For a map of Wenatchee National Forest, contact the Outdoor Recreation Information Center, Seattle REI, 222 Yale Avenue North, Seattle, WA 98109; 206/470-4060. Green Trails, Inc.'s excellent topographic map of the region is available for $3.99 at various outdoor retail outlets; ask for map number 145, Wenatchee Lake. Ask the USGS for a topographic map of the Mount David area.

Directions: From Seattle take I-5 north to U.S. 2 and then take U.S. 2 east to Highway 207, which turns left (north) toward Lake Wenatchee. Drive around the north shore of Lake Wenatchee to Forest Service Road 6400. Follow the road to its end and the Indian Creek Trailhead. Hike the Indian Creek Trail a short distance to the Panther Creek Trail. Hike one mile on the Panther Creek Trail to the Mount David Trail.

Contact: Wenatchee National Forest, Lake Wenatchee Ranger District, 22976 Highway 207, Leavenworth, WA 98826; 509/763-3103.

203 Dirty Face
9.0 mi/8.0 hrs

Another steep (4,000 vertical feet), dry haul into arid Wenatchee National Forest, Dirty Face pays off with a terrific view of the sparkling lake and surrounding valley. About halfway up a series of switchbacks that drag on far longer than the slide show at Uncle Fred's house, the views begin and spirits lift. You follow an old logging road for a short distance and then break out on a ridge, with the summit in view. At the top (elevation 6,000 feet) is an old lookout site. Rest your aching toes and gaze across Nason Ridge and straight down to tiny Lake Wenatchee. Warning: Carry plenty of water. It's scarce and you'll need it.

Location: Above the north shore of Lake Wenatchee; see Northern Cascades Map 5, grid a1.

User Groups: Hikers, dogs, and horses. No mountain bikes are allowed. No wheelchair facilities.

Permits: A federal Northwest Forest Pass, $5 per day or $30 annually, is required to park at the trailhead. Passes are available from ranger stations and many private vendors, online at website: www.wta.org, or by calling 800/270-7504.

Maps: For a map of Wenatchee National Forest, contact the Outdoor Recreation Information Center, Seattle REI, 222 Yale Avenue North, Seattle, WA 98109; 206/470-4060. Green Trails, Inc.'s excellent topographic map of the region is available for $3.99 at outdoor retail outlets; ask for map number 145, Wenatchee Lake. Ask the USGS for topographic maps of the Lake Wenatchee and Schaefer Lake areas.

Directions: From Seattle take I-5 north to U.S. 2 and then take U.S. 2 east to Highway 207, which turns left (north) toward Lake Wenatchee. Drive around the north shore of Lake Wenatchee to the Wenatchee Ranger District office. The trailhead is on the right side of the ranger station access road, near Dirty Face Campground.

Contact: Wenatchee National Forest, Lake Wenatchee Ranger District, 22976 Highway 207, Leavenworth, WA 98826; 509/763-3103.

204 Ice Lakes/Entiat Meadows
29.4 mi/3.0–5.0 days

The long, well-used trail travels into the heart of the Glacier Peak Wilderness, offering up-close encounters with the hanging glaciers, fertile valleys, and magnificent peaks that make this area a national treasure. From the trailhead at 3,140 feet, the path follows the Entiat River north and slightly west, with mountain bikes and a few motorcycles buzzing by for the first 4.3 miles, until you reach the wilderness boundary and leave them all behind.

The trail passes junctions with the Larch Lakes and Snowbrushy Creek Trails and then climbs to a major junction with the Icicle Creek Trail at about eight miles. Turn left (west) on the Icicle Creek Trail and hike 3.7 miles to a truly awesome campsite near a waterfall from Upper Ice Lake. From here a side trail leads up to the Ice Lakes, which hang in a cirque below Mount Maude, elevation 9,082 feet. They're the very type of isolated alpine lakes you might have flown over at some point, leading to daydreams of being dropped in to strike a private camp. By continuing straight back on the Entiat River Trail, it's five miles to the opening of the seemingly endless Entiat Meadows, which entice hikers toward the awesome peaks of Seven Fingered Jack (elevation 9,077 feet), Mount Fernow (elevation 9,249 feet), and once again, Mount Maude, this time accompanied by the awesome Entiat Glacier. Plan a long-enough trip to partake of both trail destinations, and keep in mind that the mileage listed above is round-trip to the end of the Entiat River Trail. The Ice Lakes side trip adds about seven miles to the total.

Location: East of Glacier Peak in the Glacier Peak Wilderness; see Northern Cascades Map 5, grid a2.

User Groups: Hikers, dogs, horses, and mountain bikes (mountain bikes are allowed for the first 4.3 miles, up to the wilderness boundary). No wheelchair facilities.

Permits: A federal Northwest Forest Pass, $5 per day or $30 annually, is required to park at the trailhead. Passes are available from ranger stations and many private vendors, online at website: www.wta.org, or by calling 800/270-7504.

Maps: For a map of the Glacier Peak Wilderness, contact the Outdoor Recreation Information Center, Seattle REI, 222 Yale Avenue North, Seattle, WA 98109; 206/470-4060. Green Trails, Inc.'s excellent topographic maps of the region are available for $3.99 each at outdoor retail outlets; ask for map numbers 113 and 114, Holden and Lucerne. Ask the USGS for topographic maps of the Saska Peak, Pinnacle Mountain, and Holden areas.

Directions: From I-5 at Everett, take U.S. 2 east to U.S. 97A at Wenatchee. Drive north on U.S. 97 to Entiat. Drive 38 miles northwest on Entiat River Road/Forest Service Road 51 to the Entiat River trailhead at Cottonwood Campground, at the road's end.

Contact: Wenatchee National Forest, Entiat Ranger District, 2108 Entiat Way, P.O. Box 476, Entiat, WA 98822; 509/784-1511.

205 Devil's Backbone
6.2 mi/3.0 hrs

The name of this popular hiking and off-road vehicle trail took on a frightful new meaning in the summer of 1994. From the first viewpoint on the Devil's Backbone at Angle Peak as far south as the eye can see, the ravenous Tyee Creek wildfire consumed more than 100,000 acres of tinder-dry recreation lands. The Devil's Backbone Trail itself was closed, much of its southern sections destroyed. It reopened the following year, with a goodly portion of the former trail grade now converted to bulldozed fire road.

Still, this route is worth walking if only for the expansive views and up-close introduction to the aftereffects of this horrific fire. Forest Service wilderness experts said the damage was some of the worst they had ever seen. In many places, even organic matter ground deep into trail grades was consumed, leaving scorched trenches up to a foot deep where a trail once existed. Many trails in the area thus appear to have been stricken by literal rivers of fire. Today, the upper Devil's Backbone trail to Angle Peak, elevation 6,700 feet, provides a prime vantage point. It's a humbling sight; forest rehabilitation in the vast area spread before you is likely to continue long after all of us are gone.

Location: South of Lake Chelan in the Entiat River drainage of Wenatchee National Forest; see Northern Cascades Map 5, grid a5.

User Groups: Hikers, dogs, horses, and mountain bikes. No wheelchair facilities.

Permits: No permits are required. Parking and access are free.

Maps: For a map of Wenatchee National Forest, contact the Outdoor Recreation Information Center, Seattle REI, 222 Yale Avenue North, Seattle, WA 98109; 206/470-4060. Green Trails, Inc.'s topographic map of the region is available for $3.99 at outdoor retail outlets; ask for map number 147, Brief. Ask the USGS for topographic maps of the Brief and Stormy Mountain areas.

Directions: From Seattle take U.S. 2 east to Wenatchee

and U.S. 97A north to South Shore Road near Chelan. Follow South Shore Road past Twenty-Five Mile Creek Campground to Shady Pass Road. Turn left (south) and then follow Shady Pass Road for 15 miles to the trailhead near Handy Springs Campground.

Contact: Wenatchee National Forest, Entiat Ranger District, 2108 Entiat Way, P.O. Box 476, Entiat, WA 98822; 509/784-1511.

206 French Creek to Paddy Go Easy Pass

22.8 mi/2.0–3.0 days

This moderately easy trail, which begins in the Icicle Creek drainage and travels east all the way to the Cle Elum River, is a favorite backpacking destination for families and hikers seeking a quiet alternative to the crowds found on other local Alpine Lakes trails. It can be hiked as part of a pleasant, two- to four-day loop trip in conjunction with the French Ridge, Snowall Creek, or Meadow Creek Trails to the south; as a day hike to Klonaqua Lake (8.8 miles one way); or as a one-way, 14.4-mile traverse from Icicle Creek to the Cle Elum River north of Salmon La Sac. But it is also an excellent destination for those who would rather hike both in and out on the French Creek Trail. After 11.4 green miles of creek valleys, good campsites, and pleasant forest, the trail climbs to Paddy Go Easy Pass, elevation 6,100 feet. Here, you find lovely Sprite Lake, fantastic views, meadows, and campsites—and plenty of other hikers who have come in the short, three-mile route from the Salmon La Sac area.

Location: In the interior of the Alpine Lakes Wilderness; see Northern Cascades Map 5, grid a6.

User Groups: Hikers, dogs, and horses. No mountain bikes are allowed. No wheelchair facilities.

Permits: Free day-use and overnight permits, required for all Alpine Lakes Wilderness trails, are available at all local ranger stations and trailheads. For more on Alpine Lakes restrictions and reservations, see sidebar. In addition, a federal Northwest Forest Pass, $5 per day or $30 annually, is required to park at the trailhead. Passes are available from ranger stations and many private vendors, online at website: www.wta.org, or by calling 800/270-7504.

Maps: For a map of the Alpine Lakes Wilderness, contact the Outdoor Recreation Information Center, Seattle REI, 222 Yale Avenue North, Seattle, WA 98109; 206/470-4060. Green Trails, Inc.'s excellent topographic map of the region is available for $3.99 at outdoor retail outlets; ask for map number 177, Chiwaukum Mountains. Ask the USGS for topographic maps of the Chiwaukum Mountains, Stevens Pass, and Cradle areas.

Directions: From U.S. 2 at Leavenworth, turn south on Icicle Creek Road/Forest Service Road 7600. Drive all the way to the end of the road at Blackpine Campground. Hike the Icicle Creek Trail/Trail 1551 1.5 miles and turn left (west) on the French Creek Trail.

Contact: Wenatchee National Forest, Leavenworth Ranger Station, 600 Sherbourne Street, Leavenworth, WA 98826; 509/548-6977.

207 Trout Creek to Eightmile Lake

12.6 mi one way/2.0 days

Want a lesson in recovery? This enchanting trail, found between three tempting alpine lakes in true nature-calendar settings, was hit by the westernmost edge of the ferocious Hatchery Creek fire in the summer of 1994. Flames swept through the forest on the lower trail, burned to near the shores of Eightmile Lake, and stopped just short of Lake Caroline, forever changing the face of this area. Nevertheless, now that access has been reestablished, this alpine region is likely to remain a rare treat, blackened trees or not. In the past, most hikers entered the area from the east, via the now-damaged Eightmile Lake Trail off Forest Service Road 7601. But by hiking into the lakes from the western (Trout Creek) access described above, you should avoid much of the fire-devastated area.

You follow Trout Creek for 3.8 miles to a junction with the Eightmile Trout Creek Trail. Hike east to spectacular, larch-dotted Windy Pass (elevation 7,200 feet) and then on to Lake Caroline, whose awe-inspiring, nearly vertical rock wall backdrop is an Alpine Lakes classic. From here, it's only about two miles to the Eightmile Lake Trail and another three miles to Forest Service Road 7601, assuming you can get there. If you can, arrange for transportation and hike the entire trail one way.

Location: West of Leavenworth in the Icicle Creek drainage of the Alpine Lakes Wilderness; see Northern Cascades Map 5, grid d1.

User Groups: Hikers and dogs. Dogs not permitted south of Windy Pass. No horses or mountain bikes are allowed. No wheelchair facilities.

Permits: Free day-use permits, required for all Alpine Lakes Wilderness trails, are available at all local ranger stations and trailheads. Limited numbers of overnight permits are issued for the expanded Enchantments permit area, which includes Eightmile Lake and Caroline Lake. For permit information, contact the Leavenworth Ranger Station at 509/548-6977. For more information on Alpine Lakes restrictions and reservations, see sidebar. Day hikers need a federal Northwest Forest Pass, $5 per day or $30 annually. Passes are available from ranger stations and many private vendors,

online at website: www.wta.org, or by calling 800/270-7504.

Maps: For a map of the Alpine Lakes Wilderness, contact the Outdoor Recreation Information Center, Seattle REI, 222 Yale Avenue North, Seattle, WA 98109; 206/470-4060. Green Trails, Inc.'s excellent topographic map of the region is available for $3.99 at outdoor retail outlets; ask for map number 177, Chiwaukum Mountains. Ask the USGS for topographic maps of the Cashmere Mountain and Jack Ridge areas.

Directions: From U.S. 2 just west of Leavenworth, turn south on Icicle Creek Road/Forest Service Road 7600. Drive past Ida Creek Campground. Just before Chatter Creek Campground, find the trailhead for the Trout Creek Trail/Trail 1555 on the left (south) side of the road.

Contact: Wenatchee National Forest, Leavenworth Ranger Station, 600 Sherbourne Street, Leavenworth, WA 98826; 509/548-6977.

208 Chatter Creek to Lake Edna
11.5 mi/7.5 hrs

Ready for a tough, thigh-burning day hike capped by a relaxing foot soak in a sparkling little alpine lake? Head this way. The Chatter Creek Trail climbs a steep 3,400 vertical feet in five miles to the Icicle Valley and the Icicle Ridge Trail (see hike this chapter). Once there, hang a left and walk one-half mile east to Lake Edna, a charming pond set in its own glacial bathtub enclosure looking out upon miles and miles of wilderness. Edna, we're glad we met ya. If you still feel like moving, continue a half mile east to Ladies Pass, elevation 6,800 feet, with more great views and a junction with the South Fork Chiwaukum Creek Trail. Looper special: Chatter Creek to Icicle Ridge; west to Lake Edna, Ladies Pass, and Frosty Pass; south along Frosty Creek to Icicle Creek;

east to Blackpine Campground and the end of Icicle Creek Road. The total trip is about 16 miles and two rolls of moleskin.

Location: East of Leavenworth in the Icicle Creek drainage of the Alpine Lakes Wilderness; see Northern Cascades Map 5, grid d2.

User Groups: Hikers, dogs, and horses. No mountain bikes are allowed. No wheelchair facilities.

Permits: Free day-use and overnight permits, required for all Alpine Lakes Wilderness trails, are available at all local ranger stations and trailheads. For more on Alpine Lakes restrictions and reservations, see sidebar. In addition, a federal Northwest Forest Pass, $5 per day or $30 annually, is required to park at the trailhead. Passes are available from ranger stations and many private vendors, online at website: www.wta.org, or by calling 800/270-7504.

Maps: For a map of the Alpine Lakes Wilderness, contact the Outdoor Recreation Information Center, Seattle REI, 222 Yale Avenue North, Seattle, WA 98109; 206/470-4060. Green Trails, Inc.'s excellent topographic map of the region is available for $3.99 at outdoor retail outlets; ask for map number 177, Chiwaukum Mountains. Ask the USGS for topographic maps of the Jack Ridge and Chiwaukum Mountains areas.

Directions: From U.S. 2 just west of Leavenworth, turn south on Icicle Creek Road/Forest Service Road 7600. Travel about 16 miles to the trailhead on the right near the Chatter Creek Campground.

Contact: Wenatchee National Forest, Leavenworth Ranger Station, 600 Sherbourne Street, Leavenworth, WA 98826; 509/548-6977.

209 Jack Creek to Stuart Pass
24.0 mi/3.0–4.0 days

Like French Creek to the west, Jack Creek is another long, valley-bottom trail in the Icicle Creek drainage, providing excellent backpacking camps and access to dozens of other side and loop trips, including a loop all the way around—but not into—the Enchantment Basin via the Ingalls Creek Trail. Many hikers turn the trail into a 10.5-mile one- or two-day loop by hiking three miles south on the Jack Creek Trail, turning east and climbing 3.5 steep miles on the Jack Ridge Trail to Trout Lake, then returning to Icicle Creek Road via the Trout Creek Trail. Hikers who stay on the Jack Creek Trail will experience an excellent, moderate-grade walk through ancient forest. At 9.3 miles, pass the junction with the Van Epps Creek Trail. Just beyond the 12-mile point is Stuart Pass and the junction with the Ingalls Creek Trail. Take this as the turnaround point or continue 14.5 miles east along the southern edge of the Stuart Range.

Location: Northeast of the Enchantments in the Alpine Lakes Wilderness; see Northern Cascades Map 5, grid d2.

User Groups: Hikers, dogs, and horses. No mountain bikes are allowed. No wheelchair facilities.

Permits: Free day-use and overnight permits, required for all Alpine Lakes Wilderness trails, are available at all local ranger stations and trailheads. For more on Alpine Lakes restrictions and reservations, see sidebar. In addition, a federal Northwest Forest Pass, $5 per day or $30 annually, is required to park at the trailhead. Passes are available from ranger stations and many private vendors, online at website: www.wta.org, or by calling 800/270-7504.

Maps: For a map of the Alpine Lakes Wilderness, contact the Outdoor Recreation Information Center, Seattle REI, 222 Yale Avenue North, Seattle, WA 98109; 206/470-4060. Green Trails, Inc.'s excellent topographic maps of the region are available for $3.99 each at outdoor retail outlets; ask for map numbers 177 and 209, Chiwaukum Mountains and Mount Stuart. Ask the USGS for topographic maps of the Jack Ridge and Mount Stuart areas.

Directions: From U.S. 2 just west of Leavenworth, turn south on Icicle Creek Road. Drive past the Ida Creek Campground. Just before the Chatter Creek Campground, find the Trout Creek Trailhead/Trail 1555 on the left (south) side of the road. Hike the Trout Creek Trail 0.8 mile to the Jack Creek Trail.

Contact: Wenatchee National Forest, Leavenworth Ranger Station, 600 Sherbourne Street, Leavenworth, WA 98826; 509/548-6977.

210 Stuart/Colchuck Lakes
8.2–9.0 mi/1.0–2.0 days

Wildfire may well have done what the U.S. Forest Service could not: keep people out of Stuart and Colchuck Lakes. Well, temporarily, anyway. The lakes—extremely popular backpacking destinations since our grandfathers were hiking (and a rugged, backdoor entry to the area)—have been extremely overpopulated for years, thanks to their irresistible alpine scenery. The Hatchery Creek fire, which swept across the lower flanks of the Stuart Lake Trail in the summer of 1994, gave the lakes a two-year reprieve. But the area has reopened, and these alpine jewels are luring crowds equal to or greater than before.

The trail follows Mountaineer Creek 2.5 miles to a split, with Stuart Lake lying two miles to the right and Colchuck 1.6 miles to the left. When you get to either, be good. Use designated campsites and absolutely no fires. From Colchuck Lake, a steep, difficult side trail leads 3.7 miles south over Aasgard Pass to Isolation Lake, the easternmost lake in the Enchantments chain. It's extremely difficult going. Unless fire damage prevents

timely reopening of the other major entry point, the Snow Lake Trail (see hike in this chapter), leave Aasgard Pass to serious mountaineers.

Location: North of the Enchantments in the Alpine Lakes Wilderness; see Northern Cascades Map 5, grid d2.

User Groups: Hikers only. No dogs, horses, or mountain bikes are allowed. No wheelchair facilities.

Permits: Free day-use permits, required for all Alpine Lakes Wilderness trails, are available at all local ranger stations and trailheads. Limited numbers of overnight permits are issued for the Enchantments permit area, which includes Stuart and Colchuck Lakes. Contact the Leavenworth Ranger Station at 509/548-6977 for more information. For more on Alpine Lakes restrictions and reservations, see sidebar. Day hikers also must have a federal Northwest Forest Pass, $5 per day or $30 annually. Passes are available from ranger stations and many private vendors, online at website: www.wta.org, or by calling 800/270-7504.

Maps: To receive a map of the Alpine Lakes Wilderness, contact the Outdoor Recreation Information Center, Seattle REI, 222 Yale Avenue North, Seattle, WA 98109; 206/470-4060. Green Trails, Inc.'s excellent topographic map of the region is available for $3.99 at outdoor retail outlets; ask for map number 177, Chiwaukum Mountains. Ask the USGS for topographic maps of the Cashmere Mountain, Enchantment Lakes, and Mount Stuart areas.

Directions: From U.S. 2 just west of Leavenworth, turn right (south) on Icicle Creek Road/Forest Service Road 7600. Drive about 8.5 miles and turn left over the bridge to Forest Service Road 7601. The trailhead is at the end of the road.

Contact: Wenatchee National Forest, Leavenworth

Ranger Station, 600 Sherbourne Street, Leavenworth, WA 98826; 509/548-6977.

211 The Enchantments via Snow Lake
28.0 mi/2.0–4.0 days 🥾

Many a lifetime memory has been made here. In spite of the great gnashing of teeth over overcrowding, permit systems, and regulations in recent years, the Enchantments remain one of the most spectacular spots on planet Earth to just sit outside a tent, stare in awe at the surroundings, and give in to nature.

A series of jewel-like alpine lakes set amid the most ruggedly beautiful, glacier-carved valley the mind can imagine, the Enchantments almost seem otherworldly. Sitting up here, it's easy to imagine you are witnessing the first or last geological breaths of some faraway world, with mythological forces of rock, water, and sky wildly competing, yet somehow melding into a perfect natural harmony. And yes, too, there are many people. Permits to this area are sharply limited and fully booked.

The Snow Lake Trail, whose lower sections were scorched by the white-hot Hatchery Creek fire of 1994 (and since repaired), is steep and occasionally very difficult, covering 4,100 feet in the first 6.5 miles. Plan to spend one very long day or two average hiking days getting to the Upper Enchantment Lakes. Most hikers make Snow Lake a first night's camping goal. Bring lots of film. The Enchantments are a photographer's dream—and nightmare: too much to shoot, from too many angles. The lakes are crystal clear, their rocky shores polished countertop smooth by glaciers. All around you are jagged, snow-covered, 8,000-foot-plus peaks. In the fall, brilliantly golden larch trees add to the splendor. The upper basin, filled with snow until mid- to late summer, is truly breathtaking.

The total party-size limit in the Enchantments Basin is eight. Fires are prohibited above 5,000 feet and near lakeshores.

Location: Southwest of Leavenworth in the Alpine Lakes Wilderness; see Northern Cascades Map 5, grid d2.

User Groups: Hikers only. No dogs, horses, or mountain bikes are allowed. No wheelchair facilities.

Permits: Free day-use permits, required for all Alpine Lakes Wilderness trails, are available at all local ranger stations and most trailheads. A limited number of overnight permits are issued for the Enchantment Lakes between June 15 and October 15, and demand far exceeds supply. Reservations are suggested. For more on Alpine Lakes restrictions and reservations, contact the Leavenworth Ranger Station at 509/548-6977 and see sidebar. Day hikers must have a federal Northwest Forest Pass, $5 per day or $30 annually. Passes are available from ranger stations and many private vendors, online at website: www.wta.org, or by calling 800/270-7504.

Maps: For a map of the Alpine Lakes Wilderness, contact the Outdoor Recreation Information Center, Seattle REI, 222 Yale Avenue North, Seattle, WA 98109; 206/470-4060. Green Trails, Inc.'s excellent topographic map of the region is available for $3.99 at outdoor retail outlets; ask for map number 209S, the Enchantments. Ask the USGS for topographic maps of the Leavenworth, Blewett, and Enchantment Lakes areas.

Directions: From U.S. 2 just west of Leavenworth, turn south on Icicle Creek Road/Forest Service Road 7600. Follow the road for four miles to the marked trailhead on the left.

Contact: Wenatchee National Forest, Leavenworth Ranger Station, 600 Sherbourne Street, Leavenworth, WA 98826; 509/548-6977.

212 Icicle Ridge
26.0 mi one way/
2.0–3.0 days

This up-and-down ridgetop trail, which stretches from Leavenworth 26 miles east to the upper reaches of the Icicle Creek drainage, not far from Stevens Pass, has a bird's-eye view of the Hatchery Creek fire burn zone. Its eastern portion was at the heart of the fire and today serves as a showcase for the power of a rampaging wildfire.

The trail overlooks much of the burn, and in its western stages, provides access to a number of trails leading north toward the popular Mormon Lakes area south of Highway 2. Good loop trips that run in that direction (near—but not in—the burn zone) can be made by hiking the Hatchery Creek, Painter Creek, Index Creek, Chiwaukum Creek, or Frosty Creek Trails north from Icicle Ridge, and then back south on another of those trails. For day hikers, Icicle Ridge also can be accessed from Icicle Valley via the Chatter Creek to Lake Edna and Fourth of July Creek Trails, both excellent day hikes west of the burn zone that should provide tremendous views of the Alpine Lakes Wilderness and the burn area itself.

Location: East of Leavenworth in the Alpine Lakes Wilderness; see Northern Cascades Map 5, grid d3.

User Groups: Hikers, dogs, and horses. No mountain bikes are allowed. No wheelchair facilities.

Permits: Free day-use and overnight permits, required for all Alpine Lakes Wilderness trails, are available at all local ranger stations and trailheads. For more on Alpine Lakes restrictions and reservations, see sidebar. In addition, a federal Northwest Forest Pass, $5 per day or $30 annually, is required to park at the trailhead. Passes are available from ranger stations and many private vendors, online at website: www.wta.org, or by calling 800/270-7504.

Maps: For a map of the Alpine Lakes Wilderness, contact the Outdoor Recreation Information Center, Seattle REI, 222 Yale Avenue North, Seattle, WA 98109; 206/470-4060. Green Trails, Inc.'s excellent topographic maps of the region are available for $3.99 each at outdoor retail outlets; ask for map numbers 177 and 178, Chiwaukum Mountains and Leavenworth. Ask the USGS for topographic maps of the Leavenworth, Cashmere Mountain, Big Jim Mountain, and Chiwaukum Mountains areas.

Directions: From U.S. 2 just west of Leavenworth, turn south on Icicle Creek Road/Forest Service Road 7600. Travel about 1.5 miles to the trailhead parking lot on the right.

Contact: Wenatchee National Forest, Leavenworth Ranger Station, 600 Sherbourne Street, Leavenworth, WA 98826; 509/548-6977.

213 Longs Pass/Ingalls Lake/Esmeralda Basin
6.0 mi/3.0 hrs

Pack the kids. Pack a lunch. Pack a zoom lens. This trail packs a lot of punch per mile. From a single trailhead sprouts three rare, relatively easy opportunities to introduce the entire family to your old friend Mount Stuart, one of Washington's highest—and inarguably most rugged—alpine peaks. From the trailhead at the end of the road that seemed to those in the backseat to go on forever and a little farther, work out the kinks by heading up the old miners' road marked Esmeralda Basin. (If old miners should arrive in a truck, make them walk behind you at your pace.) A short distance from the trailhead, the road becomes a trail where one path departs to the left into the lovely wildflower meadows of Esmeralda Basin and Fortune Creek Pass. Go that way for a short, pleasant overnighter with the kids. Day hikers, stay straight, and in another two miles, the trail splits again.

The left spur goes 1.5 miles up to Ingalls Pass, where you could reach out and kiss Mount Stuart—if your lips protruded only another eight or 10 miles. Straight ahead and down from here is Ingalls Lake, a lovely little spot where Mount Stuart does the seemingly impossible by getting closer yet. Nobody camps here anymore; it's too crowded. Back at the first Y, a right turn takes you a long half mile to Longs Pass, elevation 6,250 magnificent feet, where you definitely should take off your boots, lean back against your pack, and speculate about just what ungodly forces conspired to give Mount Stuart that pitted facial.

Location: South of Mount Stuart in the Alpine Lakes Wilderness; see Northern Cascades Map 5, grid d3.

User Groups: Hikers and dogs. No horses or mountain bikes are allowed. No wheelchair facilities.

Permits: Free day-use and overnight permits, required for all Alpine Lakes Wilderness trails, are available at all local ranger stations and trailheads. For more on Alpine Lakes restrictions and reservations, see sidebar. In addition, a federal Northwest Forest Pass, $5 per day or $30 annually, is required to park at the trailhead. Passes are available from ranger stations and many private vendors, online at website: www.wta.org, or by calling 800/270-7504.

Maps: For a map of the Alpine Lakes Wilderness, contact the Outdoor Recreation Information Center, Seattle REI, 222 Yale Avenue North, Seattle, WA 98109; 206/470-4060. Green Trails, Inc.'s excellent topographic map of the region is available for $3.99 at outdoor retail outlets; ask for map number 209, Mount Stuart. Ask the USGS for a topographic map of the Mount Stuart area.

Directions: From Highway 970 east of Cle Elum, drive north on Teanaway River Road, which be-

comes Forest Service Road 9737 at 29 Pines Campground. Continue to the road's end.

Contact: Wenatchee National Forest, Cle Elum Ranger District, 803 West Second Street, Cle Elum, WA 98922; 509/674-4411.

214 Ingalls Creek to Stuart Pass
29.0 mi/3.0–5.0 days

The Ingalls Creek Valley is an expressway to many Alpine Lakes interior hikes. Few expressways treat hikers so well. The first half of the trail is a gentle, relaxing grade, one of those rare routes on which you can have long discussions with hiking buddies without ever gulping for air. Falls Creek, just less than six miles in, is a great place to camp, or if you're a day tripper, to consume lunch and relax. Good views, open meadows, and excellent campsites increase in number as you climb higher and cross the Falls, Cascade, Hardscrabble, Fourth, and Turnpike Creeks drainages. Views of the Stuart Range are scrumptious. After the trail skirts 9,415-foot Stuart, the going gets tougher. You climb about 1,600 feet in the last two miles to Stuart Pass, elevation 6,400 feet. From here it's not too difficult to find an off-trail route down to Lake Ingalls and the North Fork Teanaway drainage via the Esmeralda Basin Trail. Or continue ahead for a gigantic one-way walk to Icicle Creek via the Jack Creek Trail.

Location: South of the Stuart Range in the Alpine Lakes Wilderness; see Northern Cascades Map 5, grid e1.

User Groups: Hikers, dogs, and horses. No mountain bikes are allowed. No wheelchair facilities.

Permits: Free day-use and overnight permits, required for all Alpine Lakes Wilderness trails, are available at all local ranger stations and most trailheads. For more on Alpine Lakes restrictions and reservations, see sidebar. In addition, a federal Northwest Forest Pass, $5 per day or $30 annually, is required to park at the trailhead. Passes are available from ranger stations and many private vendors, online at website: www.wta.org, or by calling 800/270-7504.

Maps: For a map of the Alpine Lakes Wilderness, contact the Outdoor Recreation Information Center, Seattle REI, 222 Yale Avenue North, Seattle, WA 98109; 206/470-4060. Green Trails, Inc.'s excellent topographic map of the region is available for $3.99 at outdoor retail outlets; ask for map numbers 209 and 210, Mount Stuart and Liberty. Ask the USGS for topographic maps of the Blewett, Enchantment Lakes, and Mount Stuart areas.

Directions: From Ellensburg drive U.S. 97 north to Swauk/Blewett Pass and continue about 12.5 miles to Ingalls Creek Road. Turn left (west) and drive about a mile to the trailhead at the end of the spur road.

Contact: Wenatchee National Forest, Leavenworth Ranger Station, 600 Sherbourne Street, Leavenworth, WA 98826; 509/548-6977.

PCT-14 Snoqualmie Pass to Stevens Pass

68.0 mi/6.0–7.0 days

What a difference crossing I-90 makes. Scenery on the Pacific Crest Trail improves markedly as the trail enters the Alpine Lakes Wilderness and makes its way through scenic, unspoiled wilderness to Stevens Pass. This has not failed to attract the attention of the quadrillion hikers in the Puget Sound region, who note the Snoqualmie Pass Trailhead's proximity to their homes and flock here in hordes. For those seeking solitude, this is not the best PCT section, but it is spectacular at times and very pleasant at others.

From Snoqualmie Pass, the trail gets serious immediately, climbing to the precarious Kendall Katwalk (see hike in this chapter)

and continuing to Alaska and Joe Lakes, Park Lakes, Spectacle Point, and Summit Chief Mountain. Other highlights include Waptus Lake, Cathedral Rock, Mount Daniel, and Deception Pass (see hike in this chapter). From here, head north and then northeast via Surprise Lake (see hike in this chapter), Mig Lake, and Josephine Lake to an exit at U.S. 2 near the Stevens Pass Ski Area.

Location: From Snoqualmie Pass north through the Alpine Lakes Wilderness to Stevens Pass on U.S. 2; see Northern Cascades Map 4, grid e5.

User Groups: Hikers, dogs, and horses. No mountain bikes are allowed. No wheelchair facilities.

Permits: Free Alpine Lakes Wilderness permits are required for both day hikes and overnight stays. Some popular areas have limits on overnight permits. Pacific Crest Trail through-hikers should consult with Forest Service officials for permit information. In addition, a federal Northwest Forest Pass, $5 per day or $30 annually, is required to park at most PCT trailheads. Passes are available from ranger stations and many private vendors, online at website: www.wta.org, or by calling 800/270-7504.

Maps: For a map of the Pacific Crest Trail, Washington North, contact the Outdoor Recreation Information Center at 206/470-4060. Ask the USGS for topographic maps of the Snoqualmie Pass, Chikamin Peak, Big Snow Mountain, Mount Daniel, the Cradle, and Stevens Pass areas.

Directions: To reach the Snoqualmie Pass Trailhead, drive east on I-90 from Seattle to Exit 52/West Summit. Cross under the freeway to the north and look for the PCT trailhead parking area on the right side of the road. To reach the Stevens Pass Trailhead, drive east on U.S. 2 from Everett to Stevens Pass; park in the easternmost parking area south of the highway.

Contact: Outdoor Recreation Information Center, Seattle REI, 222 Yale Avenue North, Seattle, WA 98109; 206/470-4060.

PCT-15 Stevens Pass to Stehekin Valley
97.0 mi/10.0–12.0 days

If you hike only one Northwest section of the magnificent, Canada-to-Mexico Pacific Crest Trail, this should be it. Not that the endeavor will be a breeze. This section, which travels through the best of the spectacular Glacier Peak and Henry M. Jackson Wilderness, isn't easy. At times, it can be downright difficult. Whether your experience here is good or bad, it certainly will be memorable.

From Stevens Pass the trail is fairly gentle at first, meandering east and west of the Pacific Crest, with only minor ups and downs. You pass Lake Valhalla, Janice Cabin, Grizzly Peak, Wenatchee Pass, Lake Sally Ann, Dishpan Gap, and Cady Pass in the first 30 miles. Then comes White Pass, directly south of Glacier Peak, and the going gets tough. You skirt Glacier Peak to the west, near the headwaters of the White Chuck River (see hike in this chapter), on a steep, up-and-down grade to Fire Creek Pass and Mica Lake. Here the trail turns east to Dolly Vista Camp, Lyman Camp on the Suiattle River, Glacier Creek Mines, and Suiattle Pass before turning north again, following South Fork Agnes Creek to the High Bridge Trailhead.

Some hikers prefer to skirt the east slopes of Glacier Peak by turning northeast at White Pass and taking a route that includes Little Giant Pass, the town of Trinity, and Buck Creek Pass. The route is somewhat gentler but involves a five-mile road walk between the Little Giant Trail and Trinity.

Location: From U.S. 2 at Stevens Pass to High Bridge east of Stehekin; see Northern Cascades Map 4, grid c8.

User Groups: Hikers, dogs, and horses. No mountain bikes are allowed. No wheelchair facilities.

Permits: A federal Northwest Forest Pass, $5 per day or $30 annually, is required to park at the trailhead. Passes are available from ranger stations and many private vendors, online at website: www.wta.org, or by calling 800/270-7504.

Maps: For a map of the Pacific Crest Trail, Washington North, contact the Outdoor Recreation Information Center at 206/470-4060. Ask the USGS for topographic maps of the Labyrinth Mountain, Captain Point, Benchmark Mountain, Poe Mountain, Glacier Peak West, Glacier Peak East, Clark Mountain, Suiattle Pass, Dome Peak, and Agnes Mountain areas.

Directions: To reach the Stevens Pass Trailhead, drive east on U.S. 2 from Everett to Stevens Pass and park in the easternmost parking area south of the highway. To reach the Stehekin Valley Trailhead, take U.S. 2 or Highway 20 from Seattle to U.S. 97 and the city of Chelan. Catch the water taxi up Lake Chelan to Stehekin. Ride the shuttle bus from Stehekin to the trailhead on the southwest side of the road near High Bridge Campground.

Contact: Outdoor Recreation Information Center, Seattle REI, 222 Yale Avenue North, Seattle, WA 98109; 206/470-4060.

PCT-16 Stehekin Valley to Monument 78
81.0 mi/9.0–10.0 days

At long last, the finish line. This northernmost portion of the Pacific Crest Trail offers a combination of agony and bliss for through-hikers who've made it all the way from Mexico. It's beautiful, rugged, trying, and rewarding, and leads through some of the wildest country in the Northwest, if not the Lower 48. From High Bridge, the trail heads northwest along the Stehekin River to Bridge Creek Campground and Ranger Station and then swings northeast, following Bridge Creek to Highway 20 at Rainy Pass (14 miles from Bridge Creek). Across the road, the trail climbs to Cutthroat Pass, skirts south of Azurite and Mebee Passes (see hikes this chapter), and then climbs north to road access at Hart's Pass, 30 miles north of Highway 20. From here, it's a straight, 30-mile northward march through the Pasayten Wilderness via Holman, Woody, Hopkins, and Castle Passes to Monument 78 at the Canadian border.

Location: From High Bridge on the Stehekin River north through North Cascades National Park and the Pasayten Wilderness to Monument 78, at the Canadian border; see Northern Cascades Map 2, grid f2.

User Groups: Hikers, dogs, and horses. No mountain bikes. No wheelchair facilities.

Permits: A federal Northwest Forest Pass, $5 per day or $30 annually, is required to park at the trailhead. Passes are available from ranger stations and many private vendors, online at website: www.wta.org, or by calling 800/270-7504.

Maps: For a map of the Pacific Crest Trail, Washington North, contact the Outdoor Recreation Information Center, 915 Second Avenue, Suite 442, Seattle, WA 98174; 206/220-7450. Ask the USGS for topographic maps of the Dome Peak, Cascade Pass, Goode Mountain, Mount Logan, Mount Arriva, Washington Pass, Azurite Peak, Slate Peak, Pasayten Peak, Frosty Creek, Skagit Peak, and Castle Peak areas.

Directions: To reach the Stehekin Valley Trailhead, take U.S. 2 or Highway 20 from Seattle to U.S. 97 and the city of Chelan. Catch the water taxi up Lake Chelan to Stehekin. Ride the shuttle bus from Stehekin to the trailhead on the southwest side of the road, near High Bridge Campground. To reach the northern trailhead, take Canada 3 east to Manning Provincial Park and the Allison Pass Trailhead. Hike south along Castle Creek to Monument 78 at the U.S. border.

Contact: Outdoor Recreation Information Center, 915 Second Avenue, Suite 442, Seattle, WA 98174; 206/220-7450.

NORTHEAST WASHINGTON

Northeast Washington

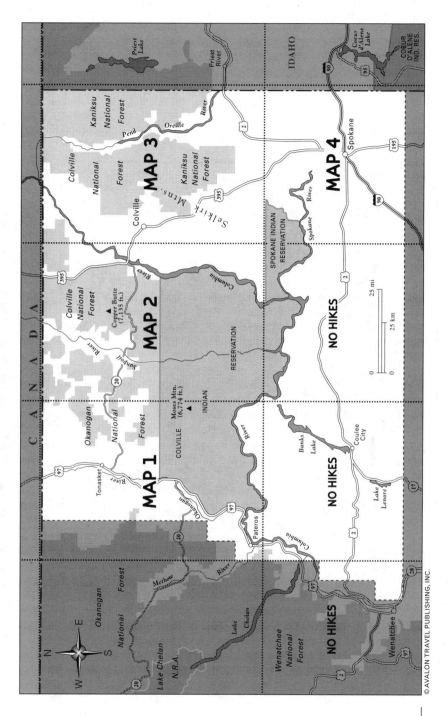

© AVALON TRAVEL PUBLISHING, INC.

Map 1

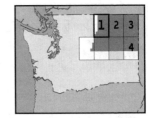

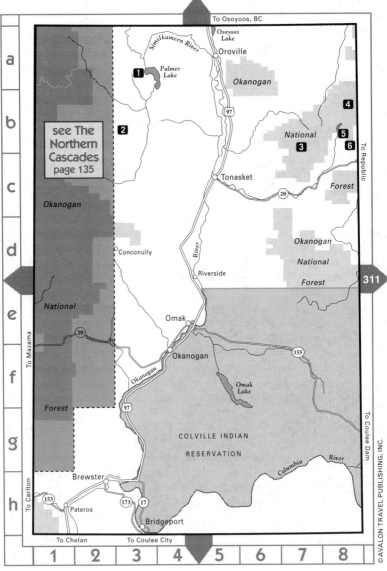

To Osoyoos, BC

a

1

Palmer Lake

Similkameen River

Osoyoos Lake

Oroville

Okanogan

b

see The Northern Cascades page 135

2

97

National

4

5

3

6

To Republic

c

Tonasket

20

Forest

Okanogan

d

Conconully

River

Riverside

Okanogan

National

Forest

311

To Mazama

e

20

National

Omak

f

Okanogan

Okanogan

155

Omak Lake

97

Forest

g

COLVILLE INDIAN RESERVATION

Columbia River

To Coulee Dam

To Carlton

h

Brewster

153

Pateros

173

17

Bridgeport

To Chelan

To Coulee City

© AVALON TRAVEL PUBLISHING, INC.

1   2   3   4   5   6   7   8

Map 2

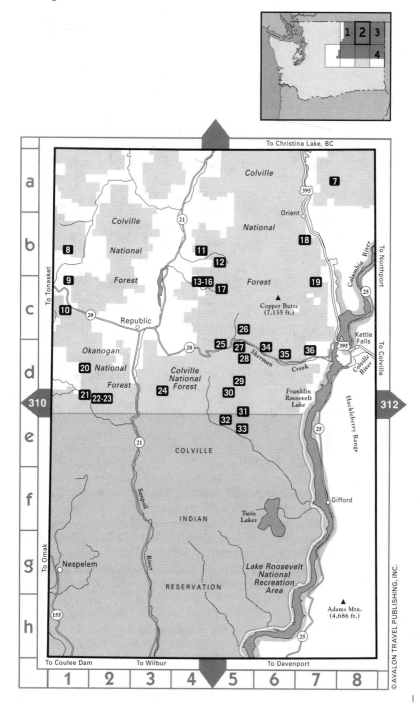

To Christina Lake, BC

Colville

a

Colville

National

b

Colville

National

Forest

c

Copper Butte
(7,135 ft.)

Republic

Okanogan

d

Colville
National
Forest

Sherman

Creek

Franklin
Roosevelt
Lake

National

Forest

Orient

Kettle
Falls

Huckleberry Range

e

COLVILLE

f

INDIAN

Gifford

Twin
Lakes

g

Nespelem

River

Lake Roosevelt
National
Recreation
Area

RESERVATION

h

Adams Mtn.
(4,686 ft.)

To Tonasket

To Coulee Dam

To Wilbur

To Davenport

To Omak

Columbia River

To Northport

To Colville

Colville River

© AVALON TRAVEL PUBLISHING, INC.

Map 3

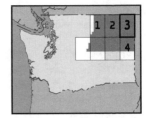

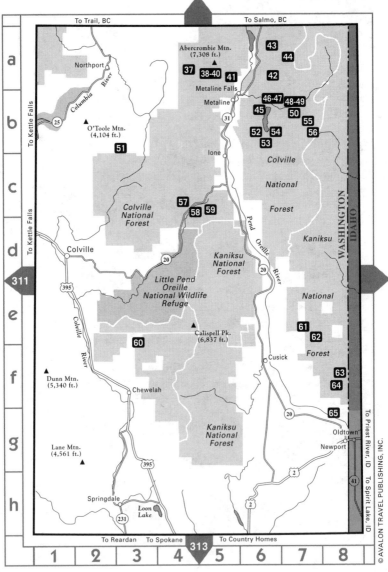

Map 4

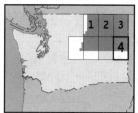

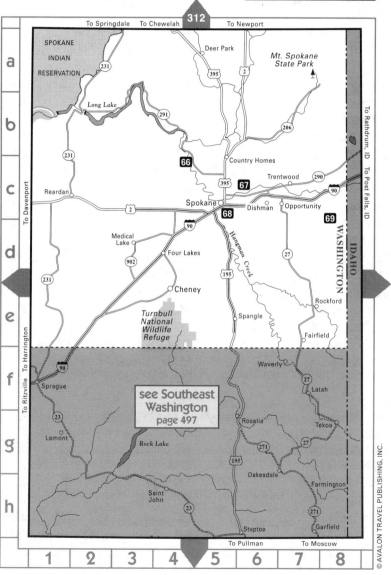

To Springdale   **To Chewelah**   **312**   **To Newport**

SPOKANE
INDIAN
RESERVATION

Deer Park

Mt. Spokane
State Park

231

395   2

Long Lake

291

206

To Rathdrum, ID   To Post Falls, ID

231

66

Country Homes

395   67   Trentwood   290

Reardan

2   Spokane   68   Dishman   Opportunity   69

90

Medical
Lake

Four Lakes

902

Hangman Creek

27

WASHINGTON   IDAHO

231

Cheney   195

Rockford

Turnbull
National
Wildlife
Refuge

Spangle

Fairfield

To Davenport

90

Waverly

Sprague

23

27   Latah

To Harrington   To Ritzville

see Southeast
Washington
page 497

Rosalia

Tekoa

Lamont

Rock Lake

271   27

195

Oakesdale

Farmington

Saint
John

23

271   Garfield

Steptoe

To Pullman   **To Moscow**

1   2   3   4   5   6   7   8

a   b   c   d   e   f   g   h

© AVALON TRAVEL PUBLISHING, INC.

Northeast Washington

◻ Albert Camp

17.0 mi/1.0–2.0 days

The trail starts on land owned by the state Department of Natural Resources, climbs into Okanogan/Wenatchee National Forest, and ends in the Pasayten Wilderness. Along the way it passes through thick, second-growth forests of lodgepole pine and white pine, as well as old-growth forests of Douglas fir and pine. Wide, sunny meadows offer wildflowers and wild strawberries. As the trail climbs through Horseshoe Basin and nears the 7,400-foot summit of Horseshoe Mountain, the views expand from local wonders to distant panoramas. The jagged peaks of the Canadian Cascades seem just a stone's throw away to the north; the high, rocky peaks of Washington's Cascades are just to the west; and the distant peaks of the Salmo-Priest Wilderness jut up against the eastern sky.

Location: North of Tonasket in Okanogan/Wenatchee National Forest, partially within the Pasayten Wilderness; see Northeast Washington Map 1, grid a3.

User Groups: Hikers, dogs, and horses. No mountain bikes are allowed. No wheelchair facilities.

Permits: A federal Northwest Forest Pass, $5 per day or $30 annually, is required to park at the trailhead. Passes are available from ranger stations and many private vendors, online at website: www.wta.org, or by calling 800/270-7504.

Maps: For a trail information report, contact the Tonasket Ranger District at 509/486-2186. For a map of Okanogan/Wenatchee National Forest, send $3 to Outdoor Recreation Information Center, 915 Second Avenue, Suite 442, Seattle, WA 98174; 206/220-7450. Ask the USGS for topographic maps of the Hurley Peak and Horseshoe Basin areas.

Directions: From Loomis drive two miles north on Sinlahekin Valley Road/County Road 9425 to the junction with Toats Coulee Road/Forest Service Road 39. Turn left (west) onto Toats Coulee Road and continue 8.5 miles to State Road T-1000. Turn right (north) onto State Road T-1000 and drive five miles to the road's end and the trailhead in the Fourteen Mile Campground.

Contact: Okanogan/Wenatchee National Forest, Tonasket Ranger District, 1 West Winesap Street, Tonasket, WA 98855; 509/486-2186.

◻ Ninemile

5.0 mi/3.5 hrs

This trail doesn't lead to a beautiful mountain lake, and it doesn't end at a high promontory with stunning views. Instead, it's a short, casual forest trail on which hikers can walk along a small stream, relax, and enjoy the forest for its own sake. And believe me, this forest is very enjoyable, especially in autumn. Evergreen conifers dominate the forest, but come fall, the dark green forest canopy is broken and highlighted with brilliant gold spears of larch trees and yellow bundles of aspen tree leaves. Mule deer crunch around the fallen leaves on the forest floor; the lucky hiker may also see a hawk or falcon perched up in a larch, his shiny brown plumage offset by the tree's shimmering gold needles.

Location: North of Tonasket in Loomis State Forest; see Northeast Washington Map 1, grid b3.

User Groups: Hikers, dogs, and horses. No mountain bikes are allowed. No wheelchair facilities.

Permits: A federal Northwest Forest Pass, $5 per day or $30 annually, is required to park at the trailhead. Passes are available from ranger stations and many private vendors, online at website: www.wta.org, or by calling 800/270-7504. Campfires are restricted on a seasonal basis as the threat of wildfire develops; check with the Colville office of the Department of Natural Resources at 509/684-7474 for current restrictions and pass information.

Maps: For a map of Okanogan/Wenatchee National Forest, which includes Loomis State Forest, send $3 to Outdoor Recreation Information Center, 915 Second Avenue, Suite 442, Seattle, WA 98174; 206/220-7450. Ask the USGS for topographic maps of the Hurley Peak and Horseshoe Basin Canadian areas.

Directions: From Loomis drive two miles north on Sinlahekin Valley Road/County Road 9425 to the junction with Toats Coulee Road/Forest Service Road 39. Turn left (west) onto Toats Coulee Road and continue eight miles to the North Fork Campground. The trailhead is at the west end of the campground.

Contact: Department of Natural Resources, Special Lands Unit-Recreation, P.O. Box 190, Colville WA 99114; 509/684-7474.

❸ Fourth of July Ridge
14.6 mi/1.0–2.0 days

What better place to explore a bit of American history than on the Fourth of July Ridge Trail? Prospectors, ranchers, and farmers settled along this ridge more than a century ago, and several of the long-abandoned cabins still stand near the trail. Just remember: if you take souvenirs no one else will be able to enjoy them. Leave all artifacts, no matter how small and seemingly insignificant, right where you found them. (Photos make better mementos.) Once you pass all the cabins, the trail leads to stunning views of Mount Bonaparte and other peaks to the south. The turnaround point is right at the ridge above the cabins.

Location: Northeast of Tonasket in Okanogan/Wenatchee National Forest; see Northeast Washington Map 1, grid b7.

User Groups: Hikers, dogs, and horses. No mountain bikes are allowed. No wheelchair facilities.

Permits: A federal Northwest Forest Pass, $5 per day or $30 annually, is required to park at the trailhead. Passes are available from ranger stations and many private vendors, online at website: www.wta.org, or by calling 800/270-7504.

Maps: For a trail information report, contact the Tonasket Ranger District at 509/486-2186. For a map of Okanogan/Wenatchee National Forest, send $3 to Outdoor Recreation Information Center, 915 Second Avenue, Suite 442, Seattle, WA 98174; 206/220-7450. Ask the USGS for topographic maps of the Havillah and Mount Bonaparte areas.

Directions: From Tonasket drive 15 miles east on Tonasket-Havillah Road/County Road 9467 and turn right (south) onto Mill Creek Road/County Road 3230. Continue four miles on Mill Creek Road to the trailhead.

Contact: Okanogan/Wenatchee National Forest, Tonasket Ranger District, 1 West Winesap Street, Tonasket, WA 98855; 509/486-2186.

❹ Strawberry Mountain
3.2 mi/1.7 hrs

You'll find no better early summer stroll than this one. The aptly named Strawberry Mountain (wild strawberries truly grow on its hillsides) offers pretty views down onto Lost and Bonaparte Lakes, as well as across to Mount Bonaparte. The trail climbs gently, rising just 600 feet in a little more than a 1.5 miles, but the summit is high enough to look north into Canada; on a clear day, you can recognize individual peaks in the Canadian Cascades.

Location: Northeast of Tonasket in Okanogan/Wenatchee National Forest; see Northeast Washington Map 1, grid b8.

User Groups: Hikers, dogs, and horses. No mountain bikes are allowed. No wheelchair facilities.

Permits: A federal Northwest Forest Pass, $5 per day or $30 annually, is required to park at the trailhead. Passes are available from ranger stations and many private vendors, online at website: www.wta.org, or by calling 800/270-7504.

Maps: For a trail information report, contact the Tonasket Ranger District at 509/486-2186. For a map of Okanogan/Wenatchee National Forest, send $3 to Outdoor Recreation Information Center, 915 Second Avenue, Suite 442, Seattle, WA 98174; 206/220-7450. Ask the USGS for topographic maps of Mount Bonaparte area.

Directions: From Tonasket drive 20 miles east on Highway 20, then turn left (north) onto Bonaparte Creek Road/County Road 4953. Continue north to Bonaparte Lake where the road becomes Forest Service Road 32. Drive five miles beyond Bonaparte Lake to the junction with Forest Service Road 33. Turn left (northwest) onto Forest Service Road 33 and continue to the Lost Lake Campground. The trailhead is about 50 yards beyond the entrance to the campground, but parking is limited at the actual trailhead. Take advantage of the extra parking spaces at the campground instead and walk the short distance up the road to the trailhead.

Contact: Okanogan/Wenatchee National Forest, Tonasket Ranger District, 1 West Winesap Street, Tonasket, WA 98855; 509/486-2186.

5 South Side Bonaparte
11.2 mi/5.6 hrs

Rising well above the other peaks in the vicinity, Mount Bonaparte offers the best views of the eastern reaches of Okanogan/Wenatchee National Forest. A short side trail

near the trail's end leads to the summit and 360-degree views, which include the peaks of the Pasayten Wilderness to the northwest, the peaks of British Columbia to the north, and the far-off peaks of the Salmo-Priest Wilderness to the east. Hikers find wild strawberries or huckleberries (depending on the season) to nibble upon while gazing at the panoramas before them.

Location: Northeast of Tonasket in Okanogan/Wenatchee National Forest; see Northeast Washington Map 1, grid b8.

User Groups: Hikers, dogs, and horses. No mountain bikes are allowed. No wheelchair facilities.

Permits: A federal Northwest Forest Pass, $5 per day or $30 annually, is required to park at the trailhead. Passes are available from ranger stations and many private vendors, online at website: www.wta.org, or by calling 800/270-7504.

Maps: For a trail information report, contact the Tonasket Ranger District at 509/486-2186. For a map of Okanogan/Wenatchee National Forest, send $3 to Outdoor Recreation Information Center, 915 Second Avenue, Suite 442, Seattle, WA 98174; 206/220-7450. Ask the USGS for a topographic map of the Mount Bonaparte area.

Directions: From Tonasket drive 20 miles east on Highway 20, then turn left (north) onto Bonaparte Creek Road/County Road 4953. Continue north to Bonaparte Lake, where the road becomes Forest Service Road 32. Drive five miles beyond Bonaparte Lake to the junction with Forest Service Road 33. Turn left (northwest) onto Forest Service Road 33 and continue past the Lost Lake Campground to Forest Service Road 100. Turn left (south) onto that road and drive four miles to the trailhead.

Contact: Okanogan/Wenatchee National Forest, Tonasket Ranger District, 1 West Winesap Street, Tonasket, WA 98855; 509/486-2186.

6 Pipsissewa

2.0 mi/1.0 hr

The hike may be short, but the rewards are great indeed. This gentle but steady climb winds through a series of rocky clearings and then tops out on a broad overlook perched 400 feet above Bonaparte Lake. The sparkling blue waters of the lake dominate the views here, making it a great place to stop and enjoy a picnic lunch and a long, relaxing rest. Don't be surprised if the sun and a gentle breeze lull you to sleep for a peaceful midday nap—it has happened to us more than once.

Location: Northeast of Tonasket in Okanogan/Wenatchee National Forest; see Northeast Washington Map 1, grid b8.

User Groups: Hikers, dogs, and horses. No mountain bikes are allowed. No wheelchair facilities.

Permits: A federal Northwest Forest Pass, $5 per day or $30 annually, is required to park at the trailhead. Passes are available from ranger stations and many private vendors, online at website: www.wta.org, or by calling 800/270-7504.

Maps: For a trail information report, contact the Tonasket Ranger District at 509/486-2186. For a map of Okanogan/Wenatchee National Forest, send $3 to Outdoor Recreation Information Center, 915 Second Avenue, Suite 442, Seattle, WA 98174; 206/220-7450. Ask the USGS for a topographic map of the Mount Bonaparte area.

Directions: From Tonasket drive 20 miles east on Highway 20, and turn left (north) onto Bonaparte Creek Road/County Road 4953. Continue north to Bonaparte Lake, where the road becomes Forest Service Road 32. Drive five miles beyond Bonaparte Lake to the junction with Forest Service Road 33. Turn left (northwest) onto Forest Service Road 33 and continue past the Lost Lake Campground to Forest Service Road 100. Turn left (south) onto that road and drive four miles to the trailhead.

Contact: Okanogan/Wenatchee National Forest, Tonasket Ranger District, 1 West Winesap Street, Tonasket, WA 98855; 509/486-2186.

7 Pierre Lake

1.6 mi/0.8 hr

With cozy car-camping facilities and a beautiful lake, this trail makes a great evening hike for campers who want a leisurely stroll through a pleasant lakeside forest. The trail follows the west shore of the trout-filled lake and generally is flat and wide enough for wheelchairs. Seasonal soft spots or ruts, however, could necessitate an assistant.

Location: Northwest of Kettle Falls in Colville National Forest; see Northeast Washington Map 2, grid a7.

User Groups: Hikers and dogs. Limited wheelchair access. No horses or mountain bikes are allowed.

Permits: A federal Northwest Forest Pass, $5 per day or $30 annually, is required to park at the trailhead. Passes are available from ranger stations and many private vendors, online at website: www.wta.org, or by calling 800/270-7504.

Maps: For a map of Colville National Forest, contact the Outdoor Recreation Information Center, 915 Second Avenue, Suite 442, Seattle, WA 98174; 206/220-7450. Ask the USGS for a topographic map of the Laurier area.

Directions: From Kettle Falls drive north on U.S. 395 to Barstow. At Barstow turn northeast onto Barstow-Pierre Lake Road/County Road 4013 and continue nine miles to the Pierre Lake Campground. The trailhead is inside the campground.

Contact: Colville National Forest, Kettle Falls Ranger

District, 255 West 11th Street, Kettle Falls, WA 99141; 509/738-7700.

8 Beth Lake
3.8 mi/1.9 hrs

Linking a pair of quiet, lakefront campgrounds, this trail is gentle but scenic. It skirts both Beaver Lake and Beth Lake, providing plenty of opportunities to enjoy their pretty waters and wildflower-lined banks. The first mile of trail parallels the west shore of Beaver Lake. Then it enters Beth Lake Campground (at just about the midway point), where hikers walk along the camp's dirt road before rejoining the single-track trail at a small dam at the mouth of the lake. The final mile angles north along the lakeshore.

Location: Northeast of Tonasket in Okanogan/Wenatchee National Forest; see Northeast Washington Map 2, grid b1.

User Groups: Hikers, dogs, and horses. No mountain bikes are allowed. No wheelchair facilities.

Permits: A federal Northwest Forest Pass, $5 per day or $30 annually, is required to park at the trailhead. Passes are available from ranger stations and many private vendors, online at website: www.wta.org, or by calling 800/270-7504.

Maps: For a trail information report, contact the Tonasket Ranger District at 509/486-2186. For a map of Okanogan/Wenatchee National Forest, send $3 to Outdoor Recreation Information Center, 915 Second Avenue, Suite 442, Seattle, WA 98174; 206/220-7450. Ask the USGS for a topographic map of the Bodie area.

Directions: From Tonasket drive approximately 20 miles east on Highway 20, and turn left (north) onto Bonaparte Creek Road/County Road 4953. Continue north to Bonaparte Lake, where the road becomes Forest Service Road 32. Continue driving north on Forest Service Road 32 until you reach Beaver Lake Campground. The trailhead is located within the campground, near the first set of campsites. Parking is available opposite Campsite 4.

Contact: Okanogan/Wenatchee National Forest, Tonasket Ranger District, 1 West Winesap Street, Tonasket, WA 98855; 509/486-2186.

9 Big Tree Botanical Loop
1.6 mi/1.0 hr

Ponderosa, lodgepole, and whitebark pines mingle with giant and very old (that's 500-plus years old) larch trees along this route, giving a rare look at a truly ancient old-growth forest, eastern Washington style. Eastern forests are dry and brown, but no less beautiful than their wetter, greener old-growth cousins across the Cascade Crest. Wheelchair users will appreciate the broad, packed gravel and dirt trail, but a few short, steep sections may necessitate an assistant.

Location: Northeast of Tonasket in Okanogan/Wenatchee National Forest; see Northeast Washington Map 2, grid c1.

User Groups: Hikers and dogs. Fully wheelchair accessible. No horses or mountain bikes are allowed.

Permits: A federal Northwest Forest Pass, $5 per day or $30 annually, is required to park at the trailhead. Passes are available from ranger stations and many private vendors, online at website: www.wta.org, or by calling 800/270-7504.

Maps: For a trail information report, contact the Tonasket Ranger District at 509/486-2186. For a map of Okanogan/Wenatchee National Forest, send $3 to Outdoor Recreation Information Center, 915 Second Avenue, Suite 442, Seattle, WA 98174; 206/220-7450. Ask the

USGS for a topographic map of the Mount Bonaparte area.

Directions: From Tonasket drive east on Highway 20 to the junction with Bonaparte Lake Road/Forest Service Road 4935. Turn left (north) onto the Bonaparte Lake Road, continue north five miles, and then turn right onto Forest Service Road 32. Follow the road for 3.9 miles to the junction with Forest Service Road 33. Bear left onto Forest Service Road 33 and continue 4.7 miles to the trailhead and well-marked parking area.

Contact: Okanogan/Wenatchee National Forest, Tonasket Ranger District, 1 West Winesap Street, Tonasket, WA 98855; 509/486-2186.

10 Fir Mountain
4.0 mi/3.5 hrs

Built more by boot than by shovel, this short trail minimizes switchbacks by keeping the grade steep (in excess of 25 percent at times). In addition, the tread is dusty and often littered with loose rocks and debris. You forget the workout when you see the views from this 5,600-foot summit, however. It rises above the surrounding countryside and stands alone, away from the other peaks, creating stunning panoramic views of northeastern Washington and southern British Columbia.

Location: South of Republic in Colville National Forest; see Northeast Washington Map 2, grid c1.

User Groups: Hikers and dogs. No horses or mountain bikes are allowed. No wheelchair facilities.

Permits: A federal Northwest Forest Pass, $5 per day or $30 annually, is required to park at the trailhead. Passes are available from ranger stations and many private vendors, online at website: www.wta.org, or by calling 800/270-7504.

Maps: For a trail information report, contact the Tonasket Ranger District at 509/486-2186. For a map of Okanogan/Wenatchee National Forest, send $3 to Outdoor Recreation Information Center, 915 Second Avenue, Suite 442, Seattle, WA 98174. 206/220-7450. Ask the USGS for a topographic map of the Wauconda Summit area.

Directions: From Republic drive 8.5 miles west on Highway 20 to the Sweat Creek Campground. Turn left (south) onto Forest Service Road 31 opposite the campground. Continue 1.5 miles to the trailhead and small parking area on the right. Additional parking is available on wide turnouts farther down the road.

Contact: Okanogan/Wenatchee National Forest, Tonasket Ranger District, 1 West Winesap Street, Tonasket, WA 98855; 509/486-2186.

11 Marcus
8.8 mi/4.4 hrs

A "whoomp, whoomp, whoomp" sound emanates from the forest for the entire length of this trail. That booming echo is the call of the blue grouse that thrive in the area. Look closely in the tree branches and under the brush and you might spot one of these big tame birds. About the size of a chicken, the blues and their cousins, spruce grouse, are generally unafraid of humans. Often you can approach within eight or 10 feet of them. The Native Americans and early white settlers took advantage of this characteristic to get an easy meal. Keep an eye out, too, for the resident white-tailed deer herd. They love to graze along the trail where wild strawberries grow in abundance. The trail itself climbs to and then along the Kettle Crest, breaking out of the forest often and presenting clear views down into the valleys and out over the distant scenery.

Location: Northeast of Republic in Colville National Forest; see Northeast Washington Map 2, grid b4.

User Groups: Hikers, dogs, and horses. No mountain bikes are allowed. No wheelchair facilities.

Permits: A federal Northwest Forest Pass, $5 per day or $30 annually, is required to park at the trailhead. Passes are available from ranger stations and many private vendors, online at website: www.wta.org, or by calling 800/270-7504.

Maps: For a map of Colville National Forest, send $3 to Outdoor Recreation Information Center, 915 Second Avenue, Suite 442, Seattle, WA 98174; 206/220-7450. Ask the USGS for topographic maps of the Cooke Mountain and Copper Mountain areas.

Directions: From Republic drive east for 14 miles on Highway 20 and turn left (north) onto Forest Service Road 2040/Karamip Road. Continue north for 12 miles to Forest Service Road 250 (marked with a large sign proclaiming Marcus Trail #8). Turn right onto Forest Service Road 250 and continue two miles to the road's end and the trailhead.

Contact: Colville National Forest, Republic Ranger District, 180 North Jefferson Street, Republic, WA 99166; 509/775-7400.

🖫 Old Stage Road
3.4 mi/1.7 hrs

Hiking this trail gives you an idea of the rugged lifestyles of the past. In the late 1880s, stagecoaches really did use this rough, rolling trail. Riding in those stiff carriages must have been a bone-jarring experience, but hikers find the route much more enjoyable, with its clear, smooth tread and gentle grade (less than 600 feet of elevation gain in 1.5 miles). As visitors muse on earlier times,

they can also enjoy the open, sun-dappled forest—with its requisite huckleberries. Near the end of the trail, the forest gives way to clearings and magnificent views from Kettle Crest.

Location: Northwest of Kettle Falls in Colville National Forest; see Northeast Washington Map 2, grid b5.

User Groups: Hikers, dogs, and horses. No mountain bikes are allowed. No wheelchair facilities.

Permits: A federal Northwest Forest Pass, $5 per day or $30 annually, is required to park at the trailhead. Passes are available from ranger stations and many private vendors, online at website: www.wta.org, or by calling 800/270-7504.

Maps: For a map of Colville National Forest, send $3 to Outdoor Recreation Information Center, 915 Second Avenue, Suite 442, Seattle, WA 98174; 206/220-7450. Ask the USGS for a topographic map of the Copper Butte area.

Directions: From Kettle Falls drive 22 miles west on Highway 20 to the Albian Hill Road junction. Turn north onto Albian Hill Road/Forest Service Road 2030 and continue 7.1 miles to the trailhead parking area on the left side of the road.

Contact: Colville National Forest, Kettle Falls Ranger District, 255 West 11th Street, Kettle Falls, WA 99141; 509/738-7700.

🖫 Leona
2.0 mi/1.0 hr

A primitive campsite at the trailhead offers an unbeatable opportunity: spend the night and then hit the trail at first light in the morning. This puts you at the junction with the Kettle Crest Trail right around sunrise, and you start the day enjoying the brilliant orange glow over the Columbia River Valley. A bit of casual wandering along the Kettle

Crest Trail (in either direction) is sure to provide some close encounters with the native wildlife. Overhead, hawks and falcons are searching for their morning meals; around the meadows, deer—both white-tailed and mule—are browsing through their breakfasts; and you find hungry rabbits, raccoons, and a host of other small mammals scurrying through the brush.

Location: Northeast of Republic in Colville National Forest; see Northeast Washington Map 2, grid c4.

User Groups: Hikers, dogs, and horses. No mountain bikes are allowed. No wheelchair facilities.

Permits: A federal Northwest Forest Pass, $5 per day or $30 annually, is required to park at the trailhead. Passes are available from ranger stations and many private vendors, online at website: www.wta.org, or by calling 800/270-7504.

Maps: For a map of Colville National Forest, send $3 to Outdoor Recreation Information Center, 915 Second Avenue, Suite 442, Seattle, WA 98174; 206/220-7450. Ask the USGS for a topographic map of the Mount Leona area.

Directions: From Republic drive north on Highway 21 past Curlew Lake to the small town of Malo and a junction with St. Peters Creek Road/County Road 584. Turn right (east) onto St. Peters Creek Road and continue 2.5 miles to the forest boundary where the road becomes Forest Service Road 400. Continue another 2.7 miles beyond the forest boundary to a fork. Stay left and continue on Forest Service Road 2040. The trailhead is at the road's end. A word of caution: Forest Service Road 2040 may be unsuitable for passenger cars. If it becomes too rough for your vehicle, use the wide turnout to park. Hike the short distance up the road to the trailhead.

Contact: Colville National Forest, Republic Ranger District, 180 North Jefferson Street, Republic, WA 99166; 509/775-7400.

14 Ryan Cabin
5.0 mi/2.5 hrs

Sections of this route border 12-year-old logging sites, but rather than detracting from the setting, the new growth in these areas illustrates the power of natural restoration. Tree clearing occurred in the early 1980s as part of a program to fight an infestation of mountain pine beetle, a voracious species that feeds on the tender sprouts and needles of the conifers and can devastate entire forests. The trail leads up a small tributary of the South Fork Boulder River, ending at an old log cabin, called Ryan Cabin, at a junction with the Kettle Crest Trail. For views of the surrounding country, hike about one-half mile south on the Kettle Crest Trail and then scramble a few hundred yards off-trail to the Ryan Hill summit.

Location: Northwest of Kettle Falls in Colville National Forest; see Northeast Washington Map 2, grid c4.

User Groups: Hikers, dogs, and horses. No mountain bikes are allowed. No wheelchair facilities.

Permits: A federal Northwest Forest Pass, $5 per day or $30 annually, is required to park at the trailhead. Passes are available from ranger stations and many private vendors, online at website: www.wta.org, or by calling 800/270-7504.

Maps: For a map of Colville National Forest, send $3 to Outdoor Recreation Information Center, 915 Second Avenue, Suite 442, Seattle, WA 98174; 206/220-7450. Ask the USGS for a topographic map of the Mount Leona area.

Directions: From Kettle Falls drive 22 miles west on Highway 20. Then turn right (north) onto Albian Hill Road/Forest Service Road 2030 and drive north 22.1 miles to the trailhead parking area on the west side of the road. The Stick Pin Trail (see hike this chapter) takes off to the left; for this trail, stay right.

Contact: Colville National Forest, Kettle Falls Ranger District, 255 West 11th Street, Kettle Falls, WA 99141; 509/738-7700.

ⓟ Profanity
2.4 mi/1.2 hrs

This scenic little trail is a secondary access route to the Kettle Crest Trail, but it's worth a visit in its own right. Rising a little more than 700 feet in the first mile, the moderately steep trail climbs through a sunny forest. The trees frequently give way to clearings that provide startling vistas to the west, looking down into the Curlew Creek and Curlew Lake Valley, and beyond to the peaks of the Cascades. One of the most enjoyable elements of the trail, though, is the human one. About one mile in, a faint side trail (it looks like a game path) weaves for one-quarter mile through the forest to a small, old log cabin. This is the Lindsey Cabin, which provides a glimpse into the lives of the area's early settlers.

Location: Northeast of Republic in Colville National Forest; see Northeast Washington Map 2, grid c4.

User Groups: Hikers, dogs, and horses. No mountain bikes are allowed. No wheelchair facilities.

Permits: A federal Northwest Forest Pass, $5 per day or $30 annually, is required to park at the trailhead. Passes are available from ranger stations and many private vendors, online at website: www.wta.org, or by calling 800/270-7504.

Maps: For a map of Colville National Forest, send $3 to Outdoor Recreation Information Center, 915 Second Avenue, Suite 442, Seattle, WA 98174; 206/220-7450. Ask the USGS for a topographic map of the Mount Leona area.

Directions: From Republic drive north on Highway 21 past Curlew Lake to the junction with Aeneas Creek Road/County Road 566. Turn right (east) onto Aeneas Creek Road and continue another 3.5 miles to Forest Service Road 2160. Turn right (south) onto Forest Service Road 2160 and drive six miles to the trailhead, located at the road's end.

Contact: Colville National Forest, Republic Ranger District, 180 North Jefferson Street, Republic, WA 99166; 509/775-7400.

ⓠ Stick Pin
5.2 mi/2.6 hrs

This trail is plagued by mosquitoes and deerflies, climbs more than 2,000 feet through thick timber, and offers views only of the nearby babbling creek and the aquatic life in the marshes at the lower end of the route. Despite these drawbacks, it's not all bad. The forest provides good concealing cover for lots of wildlife, especially deer; water keeps the critters close by. And just when the forest begins to seem a bit too closed in, the trail tops out at the Kettle Crest and the forest gives way to a broad meadow and pretty vistas.

Location: West of Kettle Falls in Colville National Forest; see Northeast Washington Map 2, grid c4.

User Groups: Hikers, dogs, and horses. No mountain bikes are allowed. No wheelchair facilities.

Permits: A federal Northwest Forest Pass, $5 per day or $30 annually, is required to park at the trailhead. Passes are available from ranger stations and many private vendors, online at website: www.wta.org, or by calling 800/270-7504.

Maps: For a map of Colville National Forest, send $3 to Outdoor Recreation Information Center, 915 Second Avenue, Suite 442, Seattle, WA 98174; 206/220-7450. Ask the USGS for topographic maps of the Mount Leona and Copper Butte areas.

Directions: From Kettle Falls drive 22 miles west on Highway 20. Then turn right (north) onto Albian Hill Road/Forest Service Road 2030 and drive north 22.1 miles to the trailhead parking area on the west side of the road. The Ryan Cabin Trail (see hike this chapter) takes off to the right; for this trail, stay left.

Contact: Colville National Forest, Kettle Falls Ranger District, 255 West 11th Street, Kettle Falls, WA 99141; 509/738-7700.

🔟 U.S. Mountain
10.8 mi/5.4 hrs

The trail begins almost due west of U.S. Mountain, but loops around to approach the summit from the northeast. Steep, rocky pitches periodically interrupt this moderate climb, but they seldom last more than a few hundred yards. Some ranchers still graze cattle in the thin forests and open clearings around the mountain, so wildlife may be scarce and not-so-wild life may be more plentiful than you'd like (especially in late summer). The good news is that few people use this trail, so solitude is almost guaranteed. So is the view from the summit: it's one of the best around.

Location: Northwest of Kettle Falls in Colville National Forest; see Northeast Washington Map 2, grid c5.

User Groups: Hikers, dogs, and mountain bikes. No horses are allowed. No wheelchair facilities.

Permits: A federal Northwest Forest Pass, $5 per day or $30 annually, is required to park at the trailhead. Passes are available from ranger stations and many private vendors, online at website: www.wta.org, or by calling 800/270-7504.

Maps: For a map of Colville National Forest, send $3 to Outdoor Recreation Information Center, 915 Second Avenue, Suite 442, Seattle, WA 98174; 206/220-7450. Ask the USGS for a topographic map of the Copper Butte area.

Directions: From Kettle Falls drive 22 miles west on Highway 20 to the junction with Albian Hill Road/Forest Service Road 2030. Turn north onto Albian Hill Road and continue 7.5 miles, then turn right (east) onto a short, rough dirt road. The trailhead is at the end of this road.

Contact: Colville National Forest, Kettle Falls Ranger District, 255 West 11th Street, Kettle Falls, WA 99141; 509/738-7700.

🔟 Hoodoo Canyon
5.0 mi/2.5 hrs

The view from the top of this trail is unbeatable. Looking out from the summit of a broad bluff above Hoodoo Canyon, you see the whole glacier-carved Hoodoo Basin open up before you, and the south end of the Kettle Range appears as a tall, pine-lined wall. Still, you have to bear with some ugliness on the way up. Soon after the trailhead, the trail crosses the sparkling waters of the South Fork of Deadman Creek. Then, as it begins to climb, it meanders in and out of thick stands of larch, cedar, and spruce—and stark, ugly clear-cuts. Though small and quickly left behind, these scars are long-term blemishes on an otherwise beautiful trail.

Location: Southwest of Barstow in Colville National Forest; see Northeast Washington Map 2, grid b7.

User Groups: Hikers, dogs, and horses. No mountain bikes are allowed. No wheelchair facilities.

Permits: A federal Northwest Forest Pass, $5 per day or $30 annually, is required to park at the trailhead. Passes are available from ranger stations and many private vendors, online at website: www.wta.org, or by calling 800/270-7504.

Maps: For a map of Colville National Forest, contact the Outdoor Recreation Information Center, 915 Second Avenue, Suite 442, Seattle, WA 98174; 206/220-7450. Ask the USGS for a topographic map of the Jackknife Mountain area.

Directions: From Kettle Falls drive 10 miles north on U.S. 395. Turn left (west) onto Deadman Creek Road/Forest Service Road 9565 and continue another 10 miles to the trailhead, on the left (south) side of the road at a broad meadow. There is a large parking area at the trailhead.

Contact: Colville National Forest, Kettle Falls Ranger District, 255 West 11th Street, Kettle Falls, WA 99141; 509/738-7700.

19 Gillette Ridge
12.0 mi/6.0 hrs

This relatively easy trail is chock-full of views and opportunities to see all kinds of wildlife, from big blue grouse to big black bears. Best of all, though, is the chance to enjoy spectacular views while munching on plump huckleberries. There are, in fact, more open views than shaded segments, but the views come with a price: blazing sunshine. Be sure to bring plenty of water and sunscreen. One word of warning: the worst sunburn can be on the back of the neck, which is often exposed and is easily forgotten when applying a coat of sunscreen. If you're like me, you spend a lot of time bent over picking berries, so lather up your neck and ears or wear a hat with a neck cape to block the sun.

Location: West of Aladdin in Colville National Forest; see Northeast Washington Map 2, grid c7.

User Groups: Hikers, dogs, and horses. No mountain bikes are allowed. No wheelchair facilities.

Permits: A federal Northwest Forest Pass, $5 per day or $30 annually, is required to park at the trailhead. Passes are available from ranger stations and many private vendors, online at website: www.wta.org, or by calling 800/270-7504.

Maps: For a map of Colville National Forest, contact the Outdoor Recreation Information Center, 915 Second Avenue, Suite 442, Seattle, WA 98174; 206/220-7450. Ask the USGS for topographic maps of the Gillette Mountain, Aladdin, and Spirit areas.

Directions: From Colville drive north on Colville-Aladdin-Northport Road to the junction with Rogers Mountain Road/Forest Service Road 500. Continue to the point where the road is blocked. The trail begins here. Parking is available along the roadside on the wide turnouts.

Contact: Colville National Forest, Colville Ranger District, 755 South Main Street, Colville, WA 99114; 509/684-7000.

20 Fish Lake
0.8 mi/0.5 hr

Like the Long Lake Loop (see hike this chapter), this is a short, flat trail that offers relaxation and pretty views across the cool, blue waters of a mountain lake. The trail stays close to the west shore of Fish Lake and provides plenty of access to good fishing spots. If you're angling, expect to catch some moderate-sized rainbow trout and occasionally a brown trout.

Location: South of Republic in Colville National Forest; see Northeast Washington Map 2, grid d2.

User Groups: Hikers and dogs. No horses or mountain bikes are allowed. No wheelchair facilities.

Permits: A federal Northwest Forest Pass, $5 per day or $30 annually, is required to park at the trailhead. Passes are available from ranger stations and many private vendors, online at website: www.wta.org, or by calling 800/270-7504.

Maps: For a map of Colville National Forest, send $3 to Outdoor Recreation Information Center, 915 Second Avenue, Suite 442, Seattle, WA 98174; 206/220-7450. Ask the USGS for topographic maps of the Bear Mountain and Swan Lake areas.

Directions: From Republic drive 7.5 miles south on Highway 21/Sanpoil River Road to the junction with Scatter Creek Road/Forest Service Road 53. Turn right (west) onto Scatter Creek Road and drive 6.5 miles before turning south (left) onto Long Lake Road/Forest Service Road 400. Continue one-half mile to the well-marked trailhead. The trailhead and parking area are near the campground's day-use area.

Contact: Colville National Forest, Republic Ranger District, 180 North Jefferson Street, Republic, WA 99166; 509/775-7400.

21 Long Lake Loop
1.2 mi/1.0 hr

Looping around pretty Long Lake, this trail is flat and easy. One short section crosses a broad slope of loose talus; you need to exercise some caution, as the footing can be loose and tricky in places. Once you get across, the rest of the route is smooth and well graded, so you can amble along comfortably while enjoying the view of the lake and the surrounding hills.

Location: South of Republic in Colville National Forest; see Northeast Washington Map 2, grid d1.

User Groups: Hikers and dogs. No horses or mountain bikes are allowed. No wheelchair facilities.

Permits: A federal Northwest Forest Pass, $5 per day or $30 annually, is required to park at the trailhead. Passes are available from ranger stations and many private vendors, online at website: www.wta.org, or by calling 800/270-7504.

Maps: For a map of Colville National Forest, send $3 to Outdoor Recreation Information Center, 915 Second Avenue, Suite 442, Seattle, WA 98174; 206/220-7450. Ask the USGS for topographic maps of the Bear Mountain and Swan Lake areas.

Directions: From Republic drive 7.5 miles south on Highway 21/Sanpoil River Road to the junction with Scatter Creek Road/Forest Service Road 53. Turn right (west) onto Scatter Creek Road and drive 6.5 miles before turning south (left) onto Long Lake Road/Forest Service Road 400. Continue one mile to Long Lake Campground. The trailhead and parking area are near the campground's day-use area.

Contact: Colville National Forest, Republic Ranger District, 180 North Jefferson Street, Republic, WA 99166; 509/775-7400.

22 Swan Lake Loop
1.5 mi/1.0 hr

Huckleberries, swimming holes, and campsites abound on this short loop trail. The trail circles the lake, staying close to the water, and meanders in and out of the cool forest. In the clearings between trees you find fields full of huckleberries. We recommend picking enough both for an evening dessert and for garnishing pancakes in the morning. This is a popular trail for families since it is generally flat and smooth, and the numerous campsites along the trail route offer a good alternative to car camping. Kids can hike in a half mile or so and feel like they're really backpacking instead of sleeping next to their car.

Location: South of Republic in Colville National Forest; see Northeast Washington Map 2, grid d2.

User Groups: Hikers, dogs, and horses. No mountain bikes are allowed. No wheelchair facilities.

Permits: A federal Northwest Forest Pass, $5 per day or $30 annually, is required to park at the trailhead. Passes are available from ranger stations and many private vendors, online at website: www.wta.org, or by calling 800/270-7504.

Maps: For a map of Colville National Forest, send $3 to Outdoor Recreation Information Center, 915 Second Avenue, Suite 442, Seattle, WA 98174; 206/220-7450. Ask the USGS for topographic maps of the Bear Mountain and Swan Lake areas.

Directions: From Republic drive 7.5 miles south on Highway 21/Sanpoil River Road to the junction with Scatter Creek Road/Forest Service Road 53. Turn right (west) onto Scatter Creek Road and drive eight miles to the Swan Lake Campground. The trailhead and parking area are at the north end of the campground, near the day-use area.

Contact: Colville National Forest, Republic Ranger District, 180 North Jefferson Street, Republic, WA 99166; 509/775-7400.

23 Tenmile
5.0 mi/2.5 hrs

This long, steady climb up Tenmile Creek Valley rewards hikers with a forest experience unlike most others. The dry, pine-based forest consists largely of untouched old growth,

but it is entirely unlike the old growth of western Washington. The forest here is dominated by huge old ponderosa, lodgepole pine, whitebark pine, blue spruce, and fir; the dominant animals of the area are black bears and rattlesnakes instead of spotted owls and marmots; and the weather is hot and dry rather than cool and moist. To truly enjoy the trail, you need to carry lots of water and sunscreen.

Location: South of Republic in Colville National Forest; see Northeast Washington Map 2, grid d2.

User Groups: Hikers, dogs, and horses. No mountain bikes are allowed. No wheelchair facilities.

Permits: A federal Northwest Forest Pass, $5 per day or $30 annually, is required to park at the trailhead. Passes are available from ranger stations and many private vendors, online at website: www.wta.org, or by calling 800/270-7504.

Maps: For a map of Colville National Forest, send $3 to Outdoor Recreation Information Center, 915 Second Avenue, Suite 442, Seattle, WA 98174; 206/220-7450. Ask the USGS for topographic maps of the Bear Mountain and Swan Lake areas.

Directions: From Republic drive 10 miles south on Highway 21/Sanpoil River Road to the Tenmile Campground on the left (east) side of the highway. The trailhead is near the day-use parking lot.

Contact: Colville National Forest, Republic Ranger District, 180 North Jefferson Street, Republic, WA 99166; 509/775-7400.

24 Edds Mountain
8.4 mi/6.0 hrs

This faint, rocky trail accesses the Kettle Crest South Trail and provides endless views. It also provides endless thirst and wicked sunburn if attempted during the height of summer. Although the elevation gain is minimal—just 900 feet—the trail is difficult because it can be hard to find in places. It starts off traversing a broad, smooth slab of granite, which requires you to keep a sharp eye out for the trail as you near the far side of the rock. From here, the trail repeatedly crosses talus and scree. If the trail does disappear, look around for small piles of rocks or cairns that mark the route. Despite the arduous going, you can expect good views of the Southern Kettle Range peaks and beyond.

Location: East of Republic in Colville National Forest; see Northeast Washington Map 2, grid d3.

User Groups: Hikers, dogs, and horses. No mountain bikes are allowed. No wheelchair facilities.

Permits: A federal Northwest Forest Pass, $5 per day or $30 annually, is required to park at the trailhead. Passes are available from ranger stations and many private vendors, online at website: www.wta.org, or by calling 800/270-7504.

Maps: For a map of Colville National Forest, send $3 to Outdoor Recreation Information Center, 915 Second Avenue, Suite 442, Seattle, WA 98174; 206/220-7450. Ask the USGS for topographic maps of the Edds Mountain and Sherman Pass areas.

Directions: From Republic drive east 6.5 miles on Highway 20 and turn right (south) onto Hall Creek Road/County Road 99. Continue south for 2.5 miles to Forest Service Road 300. Turn left (east) onto Forest Service Road 300 and drive 2.5 miles to the road's end and the trailhead. Note: the final one-half mile of Forest Service Road 300 is impassable to passenger cars. Only high-clearance vehicles should attempt it. There is a large parking area at the end of the passable section for passenger cars.

Contact: Colville National Forest, Republic Ranger District, 180 North Jefferson Street, Republic, WA 99166; 509/775-7400.

25 Sherman

2.4 mi/1.2 hrs

Dense forest and a steep, rocky trail are the trademarks here. The route climbs more than 1,500 feet of elevation in just over one trail mile. That means this hike is short, but not always sweet. After you finish the steep climb to the trail's end at the Kettle Crest, however, you get great views back along the Crest Trail to Sherman Pass and north to the assorted peaks and valleys of Colville National Forest. Before heading back down the trail, explore the crest to the north and enjoy a broad, sunny meadow full of wildflowers.

Location: West of Kettle Falls in Colville National Forest; see Northeast Washington Map 2, grid d5.

User Groups: Hikers, dogs, and horses. No mountain bikes are allowed. No wheelchair facilities.

Permits: A federal Northwest Forest Pass, $5 per day or $30 annually, is required to park at the trailhead. Passes are available from ranger stations and many private vendors, online at website: www.wta.org, or by calling 800/270-7504.

Maps: For a map of Colville National Forest, send $3 to Outdoor Recreation Information Center, 915 Second Avenue, Suite 442, Seattle, WA 98174; 206/220-7450. Ask the USGS for a topographic map of the Cooke Mountain area.

Directions: From Republic drive east 14 miles on Highway 20 and turn left (north) onto Forest Service Road 2040. Continue north for 2.5 miles, cross the Sanpoil River, then turn right (east) onto Forest Service Road 65, and drive two miles to the trailhead at the road's end. Note: Forest Service Road 65 is maintained for high-clearance vehicles only. It is not suitable for passenger cars and other low-clearance vehicles.

Contact: Colville National Forest, Republic Ranger District, 180 North Jefferson Street, Republic, WA 99166; 509/775-7400.

26 Kettle Crest North
28.9 mi one way/3.0 days 🥾 👟

Kettle Crest North is one of the most popular trails in Colville National Forest, but hikers find plenty of wilderness solitude. Leading north from Sherman Pass, the trail stays high and lonesome along the crest of the Kettle Range, passing over or near the summits of Columbia Mountain, Jungle Hill, Wapaloosie Mountain, Scar Mountain, Copper Butte, Mount Leona, and Profanity Peak, among others. Between the peaks are wide, sun-dappled meadows filled with wildflowers, huckleberries, and wildlife. You find good camping sites around the small springs and creeks in the area, and you can expect to see red-tailed and rough-legged hawks, white-tailed deer, mule deer, rabbits, coyotes, and many other small birds and mammals. From the high peaks, you can enjoy views of the Columbia River Valley to the east and the craggy peaks of the North Cascades to the west.

To best enjoy this long, one-way trail, hike from south to north and arrange a car-drop at the northern end to avoid backtracking the entire length of the trail. Or if you can find a willing group, divide into two hiking teams. Have one team start at one end, the other team on the other end, and trade car keys when you meet in the middle.

Location: West of Kettle Falls in Colville National Forest; see Northeast Washington Map 2, grid c5.

User Groups: Hikers, dogs, and horses. No mountain bikes are allowed. No wheelchair facilities.

Permits: A federal Northwest Forest Pass, $5 per day or $30 annually, is required to park at the trailhead. Passes are available from ranger stations and many private vendors, online at website: www.wta.org, or by calling 800/270-7504.

Maps: For a map of Colville National Forest, send $3 to Outdoor Recreation Information Center, 915 Second Avenue, Suite 442, Seattle, WA 98174; 206/220-7450. Ask the USGS for topographic maps of the Mount Leona and Copper Butte areas.

Directions: From Kettle Falls drive west 25 miles on Highway 20 to the summit of Sherman Pass. Turn north onto a short, well-marked spur road that leads into the trailhead parking area. To reach the northern trailhead from Kettle Falls, drive north on U.S. 395 to the junction with Boulder Creek Road. Turn left (west) onto Boulder Creek Road and continue 12 miles to the pass and the well-marked northern terminus of the trail.

Contact: Colville National Forest, Republic Ranger District, 180 North Jefferson Street, Republic, WA 99166; 509/775-7400.

27 Columbia Mountain
4.0 mi/2.5 hrs 🥾 👟

The first stretch of this trail is shared with the Kettle Crest North Trail (see hike above). About 1.5 miles from the trailhead, watch for an unmarked trail leading off to the right. (You'll know you're close when the peak of Columbia Mountain looms in the east.) At the junction, leave the Kettle Crest Trail and head around the northeast flank of Columbia Mountain. The trail climbs gently to the 6,500-foot summit, where you can lunch and relax. Lean back against the timbers of the old Forest Service lookout building and enjoy the far-reaching views in all directions.

Location: West of Kettle Falls in Colville National Forest; see Northeast Washington Map 2, grid d5.

User Groups: Hikers, dogs, and horses. No mountain bikes are allowed. No wheelchair facilities.

Permits: A federal Northwest Forest Pass, $5 per day or $30 annually, is required to park at the trailhead. Passes are available from ranger stations and many private vendors, online at website: www.wta.org, or by calling 800/270-7504.

Maps: To receive a map of Colville National Forest, send $3 to Outdoor Recreation Information Center, 915 Second Avenue, Suite 442, Seattle, WA 98174; 206/220-7450. Ask the USGS for a topographic map of the Sherman Peak area.

Directions: From Kettle Falls drive west for approximately 25 miles on Highway 20 to the Sherman Pass summit. Turn north onto a short, well-marked spur road that leads into the trailhead parking area.

Contact: Colville National Forest, Republic Ranger District, 180 North Jefferson Street, Republic, WA 99166; 509/775-7400.

28 Jungle Hill
5.0 mi/2.5 hrs

Although the Jungle Hill Trail doesn't really take you through a jungle, it is heavily wooded, and it's so steep your sweat will raise the humidity in the area to jungle levels. Leaving the trailhead, the route crosses a cool, babbling creek before getting down to the serious business of climbing to the top of Kettle Crest. The heavy forest cover occasionally gives way to sun-filled clearings, but it isn't until you top out on the crest that the views become clear. From your vantage point on the crest, look south to see Colum-

bia Mountain, east to the Columbia River, and west to the Cascade Peaks.

Location: Northwest of Kettle Falls in Colville National Forest; see Northeast Washington Map 2, grid d5.

User Groups: Hikers, dogs, and horses. No mountain bikes are allowed. No wheelchair facilities.

Permits: A federal Northwest Forest Pass, $5 per day or $30 annually, is required to park at the trailhead. Passes are available from ranger stations and many private vendors, online at website: www.wta.org, or by calling 800/270-7504.

Maps: For a trail information report, contact the Kettle Falls Ranger District at 509/738-7700. For a map of Colville National Forest, send $3 to Outdoor Recreation Information Center, 915 Second Avenue, Suite 442, Seattle, WA 98174; 206/220-7450. Ask the USGS for topographic maps of the Copper Butte and Cooke Mountain areas.

Directions: From Kettle Falls drive approximately 22 miles west on Highway 20 until you reach the Albian Hill Road junction. Turn north onto Albian Hill Road/Forest Service Road 2030 and continue about three-quarters of a mile to a gravel pit and short side road. Follow the small gravel road around the gravel pit for one-quarter mile to the trailhead.

Contact: Colville National Forest, Kettle Falls Ranger District, 255 West 11th Street, Kettle Falls, WA 99141; 509/738-7700.

29 Kettle Crest South
29.0 mi/2.0–3.0 days

Just like the northern section of the Kettle Crest Trail (see hike in this chapter), this route stays high and thus provides hikers with picturesque long-distance vistas and stunning meadow views. The granite cliffs and craggy peaks found on this southern route, however, mean that you encounter different wildlife species, too. Golden eagles soar in the skies above, instead of the usual hawks and falcons, and a few bighorn sheep range through the area. (Keep your camera handy.) You get the best views by climbing a small spur trail that leads to the 7,103-foot summit of Snow Peak. From here, enjoy a 360-degree view that sweeps in the Columbia River Valley, the scars from the massive 1988 forest fires to the south (not too far to the south, as you discover as you continue down the trail), and the Cascades and Glacier Peak to the west.

Unlike the northern section of the Kettle Crest, it isn't practical to make a one-way hike out of this route. Although the trail terminates at an old road on the southern end, it isn't passable to passenger cars.

Location: West of Kettle Falls in Colville National Forest; see Northeast Washington Map 2, grid d5.

User Groups: Hikers, dogs, and horses. No mountain bikes are allowed. No wheelchair facilities.

Permits: A federal Northwest Forest Pass, $5 per day or $30 annually, is required to park at the trailhead. Passes are available from ranger stations and many private vendors, online at website: www.wta.org, or by calling 800/270-7504.

Maps: To receive a map of Colville National Forest, send $3 to the Outdoor Recreation Information Center, 915 Second Avenue, Suite 442, Seattle, WA 98174; 206/220-7450. Ask the USGS for topographic maps of the Sherman Peak and Sitdown Mountain areas.

Directions: From Kettle Falls drive approximately 25 miles west on Highway 20 to the Sherman Pass summit. Turn south into the trailhead parking area.

Contact: Colville National Forest, Republic Ranger District, 180 North Jefferson Street, Republic, WA 99166; 509/775-7400.

30 Sherman Pass Tie
1.0 mi/1.0 hr

Park your car and camp at Kettle Range Campground before setting out on the trail. This short, casual hike through a pretty forest provides direct access to the main, scenic Kettle Creek Trail. From the three gurgling stream crossings and the raised puncheon (boardwalk) sections, you get a good look at the regenerative powers of the forest. Two fires have left their mark on the area. The eastern slope burned in 1929 and has largely recovered, while a more recent fire blackened more than 20,000 acres of forest. This makes for great wildlife habitat and offers an excellent opportunity to see and hear pileated woodpeckers at work on the tall snags that tower over the ravaged landscape.

Location: West of Kettle Falls in Colville National Forest; see Northeast Washington Map 2, grid d5.

User Groups: Hikers and dogs. Fully wheelchair accessible. No horses or mountain bikes are allowed.

Permits: A federal Northwest Forest Pass, $5 per day or $30 annually, is required to park at the trailhead. Passes are available from ranger stations and many private vendors, online at website: www.wta.org, or by calling 800/270-7504.

Maps: For a map of Colville National Forest, send $3 to Outdoor Recreation Information Center, 915 Second Avenue, Suite 442, Seattle, WA 98174; 206/220-7450. Ask the USGS for topographic maps of the Sherman Peak and Sitdown Mountain areas.

Directions: From Kettle Falls drive west 24 miles on Highway 20 to the Kettle Range

Campground, just one mile short of the Sherman Pass summit. Turn north into the trailhead parking area.

Contact: Colville National Forest, Kettle Falls Ranger District, 255 West 11th Street, Kettle Falls, WA 99141; 509/738-7700.

31 ThirteenMile
26.0 mi/3.0 days

This trail is a real treat, as the surrounding forest is filled with massive, old-growth ponderosa pine. Between the enormous orange trunks, brightly colored lupine stalks and blooms color the forest floor. (Late in the summer and early fall, you find lush huckleberry patches, too.) The trail rolls up and down but has no dramatic ascents or descents. Strenuous climbs occur only if you take the optional side excursions to the summits of the nearby peaks. Explore Fire Mountain and ThirteenMile Mountain. From their tops, enjoy views of the rest of the state's northeastern corner and beyond into the craggy peaks of the Canadian Cascades and the Rocky Mountains of Idaho.

Location: East of Republic in Colville National Forest; see Northeast Washington Map 2, grid e5.

User Groups: Hikers, dogs, and horses. No mountain bikes are allowed. No wheelchair facilities.

Permits: A federal Northwest Forest Pass, $5 per day or $30 annually, is required to park at the trailhead. Passes are available from ranger stations and many private vendors, online at website: www.wta.org, or by calling 800/270-7504.

Maps: For a map of Colville National Forest, send $3 to Outdoor Recreation Information Center, 915 Second Avenue, Suite 442, Seattle, WA 98174; 206/220-7450. Ask the USGS for topographic maps of the Edds Mountain and Sherman Pass areas.

Directions: From Republic drive east 6.5 miles on Highway 20 and turn right (south) onto Hall Creek Road/County Road 99. Continue south for 2.5 miles to Forest Service Road 300. Turn left (east) onto Forest Service Road 300 and drive 2.5 miles to the road's end and the trailhead. Note: the final half mile of Forest Service Road 300 is impassable to passenger cars, and only high-clearance vehicles should attempt it. There is a large parking area at the end of the passable section.

Contact: Colville National Forest, Republic Ranger District, 180 North Jefferson Street, Republic, WA 99166; 509/775-7400.

32 Barnaby Butte
3.4 mi/2.0 hrs

This trail is actually an old road, but it provides a wonderful hiking experience. Wild strawberries and huckleberries thrive along the route, and during their respective seasons, they offer sweet delights to both two-legged and four-legged berry fans. Keep a watchful eye out when hiking here. If you're fortunate, you'll spot a white-tailed deer or even a small black bear snacking. The views from the Barnaby Butte summit, high above the Kettle Crest South Trail, are unbeatable.

Location: East of Republic in Colville National Forest; see Northeast Washington Map 2, grid e5.

User Groups: Hikers, dogs, and horses. No mountain bikes are allowed. No wheelchair facilities.

Permits: A federal Northwest Forest Pass, $5 per day or $30 annually, is required to park at the trailhead. Passes are available from ranger stations and many private vendors, online at website: www.wta.org, or by calling 800/270-7504.

Maps: For a map of Colville National Forest, send $3 to

Outdoor Recreation Information Center, 915 Second Avenue, Suite 442, Seattle, WA 98174; 206/220-7450. Ask the USGS for a topographic map of the Sherman Peak area.

Directions: From Republic drive east 6.5 miles on Highway 20 and turn right (south) onto Hall Creek Road/County Road 99. Continue south until the road turns left and becomes Forest Service Road 600. Continue on Forest Service Road 600 to Forest Service Road 680, turn left, and drive to the road's end and the trailhead.

Contact: Colville National Forest, Republic Ranger District, 180 North Jefferson Street, Republic, WA 99166; 509/775-7400.

33 Barnaby Butte East
9.6 mi/3.0 hrs

The first couple miles of the trail are a primitive, rough jeep road, but this is a fine trail for those seeking wildlife, wild scenery, and wild adventure. The trail climbs to the crest of the Kettle Range's southern half and provides stunning panoramic views to the east throughout the trail length. The broad, open clearings also provide great wildlife habitat and juicy wild berries of all kinds. Water is plentiful and cold along the way—please remember to treat all your drinking water—and a large selection of campsites makes this a good choice for backpackers. Most campers will see deer, perhaps during their regular evening and early morning feedings in the forest meadows.

Location: West of Kettle Falls in Colville National Forest; see Northeast Washington Map 2, grid e5.

User Groups: Hikers, dogs, and horses. No mountain bikes are allowed. No wheelchair facilities.

Permits: A federal Northwest Forest Pass, $5 per day or $30 annually, is required to park at the trailhead. Passes are available from

ranger stations and many private vendors, online at website: www.wta.org, or by calling 800/270-7504.

Maps: For a map of Colville National Forest, send $3 to Outdoor Recreation Information Center, 915 Second Avenue, Suite 442, Seattle, WA 98174; 206/220-7450. Ask the USGS for a topographic map of the Sherman Peak area.

Directions: From Kettle Falls drive west 18 miles on Highway 20 and then turn left (south) onto South Sherman Road/Forest Service Road 2020. Continue south 6.2 miles to the junction with Forest Service Road 2014. Turn right (west) and continue one-half mile to the junction with a primitive dirt road leading to the west. Park in the wide turnout here and hike two miles farther down this primitive, impassable road to the actual marked trailhead.

Contact: Colville National Forest, Republic Ranger District, 180 North Jefferson Street, Republic, WA 99166; 509/775-7400.

34 Log Flume
0.5 mi/1.0 hr

The logging industry in Washington is slowing down, but this flat trail offers an important reminder of the crucial role timber production played in Northwest history. Before chain saws and diesel tractors, loggers used muscle-powered saws and fast-flowing water to get the logs out of the mountains. In some cases, river channels provided the water. In other cases, including here, loggers channeled nearby stream water with a wood trough elevated on stilts above the forest floor, thereby creating a several-mile-long water flume. Logs were loaded into this flume and sent racing down the mountain to the valley floor and a collection pond. When machines replaced the flume system, the nature (and magnitude) of logging changed.

Parts of the elevated flume still stand, however, and this trail explores those remnants of a bygone era. Along the way, you discover that nature has started to recover, with young trees beginning to refoliate the area.

Location: West of Kettle Falls in Colville National Forest; see Northeast Washington Map 2, grid d6.

User Groups: Hikers and dogs. Fully wheelchair accessible. No horses or mountain bikes are allowed.

Permits: A federal Northwest Forest Pass, $5 per day or $30 annually, is required to park at the trailhead. Passes are available from ranger stations and many private vendors, online at website: www.wta.org, or by calling 800/270-7504.

Maps: For a map of Colville National Forest, contact the Outdoor Recreation Information Center, 915 Second Avenue, Suite 442, Seattle, WA 98174; 206/220-7450. Ask the USGS for a topographic map of the Canyon Creek area.

Directions: From Kettle Falls drive approximately 10 miles west on Highway 20 to a well-marked trailhead parking area on the south side of the highway. The trail begins behind the information kiosk.

Contact: Colville National Forest, Kettle Falls Ranger District, 255 West 11th Street, Kettle Falls, WA 99141; 509/738-7700.

35 Canyon Creek
2.0 mi/1.5 hrs

Ambling along the loud, rushing waters of Sherman Creek, this barrier-free, level, and hard-packed trail offers both a lush forest walk and a water-lover's stroll. The forest consists of second-growth lodgepole pine and Douglas fir. The original old growth disappeared in the 1929 Dollar Mountain fire, which swept through the area and blackened thousands of forest acres. But the new forest is healthy and beautiful—evidence that fire damage doesn't permanently blemish the landscape.

Providing even greater evidence of the forest's health are the many animals found here, even this close to a highway. Many of the large pines, for instance, have gouges and scratches several feet up from the ground, left by black bears marking their territory. Though seldom seen, the shy bruins still haunt the surrounding forests. White-tailed deer, raccoons, coyotes, and a multitude of birds also fill the woods. Rainbow, brown, and bull trout lurk in the creek's cold pools. Wheelchair-accessible fishing platforms are provided along the trail, so everyone can fully enjoy the area.

Location: West of Kettle Falls in Colville National Forest; see Northeast Washington Map 2, grid d6.

User Groups: Hikers and dogs. Fully wheelchair accessible. No horses or mountain bikes are allowed.

Permits: A federal Northwest Forest Pass, $5 per day or $30 annually, is required to park at the trailhead. Passes are available from ranger stations and many private vendors, online at website: www.wta.org, or by calling 800/270-7504.

Maps: For a map of Colville National Forest, contact the Outdoor Recreation Information Center, 915 Second Avenue, Suite 442, Seattle, WA 98174; 206/220-7450. Ask the USGS for a topographic map of the Canyon Creek area.

Directions: From Kettle Falls drive approximately nine miles west on Highway 20 to Canyon Creek Campground on the south side of the highway. The trail begins from the day-use parking area inside the campground.

Contact: Colville National Forest, Kettle Falls Ranger District, 255 West 11th Street, Kettle Falls, WA 99141; 509/738-7700.

36 Sherry Loop
3.8 mi/2.0 hrs

Paralleling the banks of the Little Pend Oreille River, this big loop trail (which connects with smaller side trails) offers a flat, smooth trail surface and plenty of opportunities to view wildlife. Cross-country skiers love this trail network, but the real joy is visiting in early summer, when the wildflowers bloom along the banks of the river. Fly fishers will also enjoy the access to some largely unfished sections of a top-notch trout stream.

Location: East of Colville in Colville National Forest; see Northeast Washington Map 2, grid d7.

User Groups: Hikers and dogs only. No horses or mountain bikes are allowed. No wheelchair facilities.

Permits: Winter visitors must have a state Sno-Park Permit. No other permits are required.

Maps: For a trail information report, contact the Colville Ranger District at the address below. For a map of Colville National Forest, contact the Outdoor Recreation Information Center, 915 Second Avenue, Suite 442, Seattle, WA 98174; 206/220-7450. To obtain a USGS topographic map of the area, ask for Lake Gillette.

Directions: From Colville, drive 23 miles east on U.S. 20 to the entrance sign for Colville National Forest (just before Sherry Lake). The trailhead is on the south side of the highway.

Contact: Colville National Forest, Colville Ranger District, 755 South Main Street, Colville, WA 99114; 509/684-7000.

37 Springboard Interpretive Loop
2.4 mi/1.0 hr

European settlers claimed and worked this fertile lakeside area into a homestead more than a hundred years ago. Later, the settlers abandoned the homestead, leaving nature to reclaim the site. Artifacts still line the loop trail route, and interpretive signs explain the historic background of the region, so history buffs will love this trail. Pick up a detailed brochure and trail guide at a trailhead kiosk and remember to leave relics where they lie so others may enjoy them as well.

Location: East of Colville in Colville National Forest; see Northeast Washington Map 3, grid a4.

User Groups: Hikers and dogs. Limited wheelchair accessibility. No horses or mountain bikes are allowed.

Permits: A federal Northwest Forest Pass, $5 per day or $30 annually, is required to park at the trailhead. Passes are available from ranger stations and many private vendors, online at website: www.wta.org, or by calling 800/270-7504.

Maps: For a map of Colville National Forest, contact the Outdoor Recreation Information Center, 915 Second Avenue, Suite 442, Seattle, WA 98174; 206/220-7450. Ask the USGS for a topographic map of the Lake Gillette area.

Directions: From Colville drive 26 miles east on U.S. 20 to the East Gillette Lake Campground on the south side of the highway. The trail begins in the campground at the southeast end of Lake Gillette.

Contact: Colville National Forest, Colville Ranger District, 755 South Main Street, Colville, WA 99114; 509/684-7000.

38 Abercrombie Mountain
6.4 mi/3.2 hrs

The open ridgetop and easy water availability make this a great place to view both large and small wildlife. From the trailhead, the route climbs through an old pine forest to an open ridge. The first mile of trail winds across several small spring creeks before topping out on the ridge. The lower end of the ridge was clear-cut long ago, but new forest growth is slowly obscuring those scars. Still, the local herds of deer and elk take advantage of the break in the forest canopy to browse among tender plants in the sunny meadow. Moving up the ridge, the trail leaves the clear-cut and briefly passes through a young stand of forest before entering yet another cleared area three miles in. A forest fire leveled this forest several decades ago, leaving a meadow full of silvery snags and stumps. Sit here and enjoy the wildlife attracted to this new environment. Woodpeckers drill into the snags in search of beetles and bugs; red-tailed and rough-legged hawks soar overhead; and rabbits, ground squirrels, and badgers scurry about the brush and decaying logs. Carry plenty of water, as the open ridge creates not only great views, but hot, dry hiking in the summer.

Location: North of Metaline in Colville National Forest; see Northeast Washington Map 3, grid a5.

User Groups: Hikers, dogs, and horses. No mountain bikes are allowed. No wheelchair facilities.

Permits: A federal Northwest Forest Pass, $5 per day or $30 annually, is required to park at the trailhead. Passes are available from ranger stations and many private vendors, online at website: www.wta.org, or by calling 800/270-7504.

Maps: For a map of Colville National Forest, contact the Outdoor Recreation Information Center, 915 Second Avenue, Suite 442, Seattle, WA 98174; 206/220-7450. Ask the USGS for a topographic map of the Abercrombie Mountain area.

Directions: From Colville drive north on the Colville-Aladdin-Northport Road to its junction with Deep Creek Road at Spirit. Follow Deep Creek Road north for seven miles to Leadpoint. Turn east on Silver Creek Road/Forest Service Road 4720 and continue 1.5 miles to a junction with Forest Service Road 7078. Drive north on Forest Service Road 7078 for 2.3 miles to the junction with Forest Service Road 300. Take Forest Service Road 300 for about 1.5 miles to the trailhead at the end of the road.

Contact: Colville National Forest, Colville Ranger District, 755 South Main Street, Colville, WA 99114; 509/684-7000.

39 North Fork Silver Creek
7.0 mi/3.5 hrs

Paralleling the North Fork of Silver Creek for three-quarters of a mile, this trail follows an old horse road before leaving the river and climbing the ridge via a long series of switchbacks. In early summer, a variety of wildflowers brighten the route. In late summer, you find thick huckleberry patches around the second mile of the trail. These juicy purple berries are irresistible to hikers and wildlife alike—including black bears. The trail ends at the junction with the Abercrombie Mountain Trail (see hike this chapter).

Location: Northwest of Metaline in Colville National Forest; see Northeast Washington Map 3, grid a5.

User Groups: Hikers, dogs, and horses. No mountain bikes are allowed. No wheelchair facilities.

Permits: A federal Northwest Forest Pass, $5 per day or $30 annually, is required to park at the trailhead. Passes are available from ranger stations and many private vendors, online at website: www.wta.org, or by calling 800/270-7504.

Maps: For a map of Colville National Forest, contact the Outdoor Recreation Information Center, 915 Second Avenue, Suite 442, Seattle, WA 98174; 206/220-7450. Ask the USGS for topographic maps of the Leadpoint and Abercrombie Mountain areas.

Directions: From Colville drive north on the Colville-Aladdin-Northport Road to its junction with Deep Creek Road at Spirit. Follow Deep Creek Road north for seven miles to Leadpoint. Turn east on Silver Creek Road/Forest Service Road 4720 and continue 1.5 miles to a junction with Forest Service Road 070. Take Forest Service Road 070 for about 1.5 miles to the trailhead at the end of the road.

Contact: Colville National Forest, Colville Ranger District, 755 South Main Street, Colville, WA 99114; 509/684-7000.

40 South Fork Silver Creek
7.2 mi/3.6 hrs

Where it starts on an old logging road, this trail seems to offer little visual stimulation. But soon the clear-water creek becomes an attractive and constant companion as the trail repeatedly crosses it via bridges and footlogs. After three miles, the trail climbs steeply to the grassy ridge between Sherlock and Abercrombie Mountains. Here, at the end of the trail, you find stunning panoramic views of the Columbia and Pend Oreille River Valleys and the high peaks of the Salmo-Priest Wilderness. Several campsites line this trail.

Location: Northwest of Metaline in Colville National Forest; see Northeast Washington Map 3, grid a5.

User Groups: Hikers, dogs, and horses. No mountain bikes are allowed. No wheelchair facilities.

Permits: A federal Northwest Forest Pass, $5 per day or $30 annually, is required to park at the trailhead. Passes are available from ranger stations and many private vendors, online at website: www.wta.org, or by calling 800/270-7504.

Maps: For a map of Colville National Forest, contact the Outdoor Recreation Information Center, 915 Second Avenue, Suite 442, Seattle, WA 98174; 206/220-7450. Ask the USGS for topographic maps of the Leadpoint and Abercrombie Mountain areas.

Directions: From Colville drive north on the Colville-Aladdin-Northport Road to its junction with Deep Creek Road at Spirit. Follow Deep Creek Road north for seven miles to Leadpoint. Turn east on Silver Creek Road/Forest Service Road 4720 and continue 1.5 miles to a junction with Forest Service Road 070. Take Forest Service Road 070 for about 1.5 miles to the trailhead at the end of the road.

Contact: Colville National Forest, Colville Ranger District, 755 South Main Street, Colville, WA 99114; 509/684-7000.

41 Sherlock Peak
2.4 mi/1.2 hrs

Though short, this trail offers plenty to hold the interest of visitors. After crossing a small stream at the start of the route, you quickly climb into a steep, rocky section that requires both skill and patience to cross, as the trail fades and disappears in places. Once past this half-mile stretch, though, you are rewarded with stunning panoramic vistas sweeping from the Columbia River Basin to the Deep Lake and Deep Creek Valleys. To the north, you'll see Abercrombie Mountain and to the west the jagged peaks of the Salmo-Priest Wilderness.

Location: Northwest of Metaline in Colville National Forest; see Northeast Washington Map 3, grid a5.

User groups: Hikers, dogs, and horses only. No mountain bikes are allowed. No wheelchair facilities.

Permits: No permits are required.

Maps: For a trail information report, contact the Colville Ranger District at the address below. For a map of Colville National Forest, contact the Outdoor Recreation Information Center, 915 Second Avenue, Suite 442, Seattle, WA 98174; 206/220-7450. To obtain USGS topographic maps of the area, ask for Leadpoint and Deep Lake.

Directions: From Colville, drive north on the Colville-Aladdin-Northport Road to its junction with Deep Creek Road at Spirit. Follow Deep Creek Road north for seven miles to Leadpoint. Turn east on Silver Creek Road (Forest Service Road 4720) and continue 1.5 miles to a junction with Forest Service Road 070. Take Forest Service Road 070 approximately one-half mile to Windy Ridge Road (Forest Service Road 075). Continue on Windy Ridge Road to the trailhead at the road's end.

Contact: Colville National Forest, Colville Ranger District, 755 South Main Street, Colville, WA 99114; 509/684-7000.

42 Flume Creek
8.0 mi/4.0 hrs

Solitude and scenery are the order of the day here. The ruggedness of this trail, which climbs more than 2,000 feet in just four miles, explains why so few people visit. But those who come find some of the best country in the Colville National Forest. From the 7,000-foot high point, hikers get broad views that sweep from the Kokanee Mountains in eastern British Columbia to the Salmo-Priest Wilderness ranges to the east, the Pend Oreille River to the south and the Columbia River Valley to the west. The fortunate few who strike the trail in the early morning or late afternoon may also see the resident mountain goats grazing on the ridge and Abercrombie Mountain to the west.

Location: North of Metaline in Colville National Forest; see Northeast Washington Map 3, grid a6.

User Groups: Hikers and dogs. No horses or mountain bikes are allowed. No wheelchair facilities.

Permits: A federal Northwest Forest Pass, $5 per day or $30 annually, is required to park at the trailhead. Passes are available from ranger stations and many private vendors, online at website: www.wta.org, or by calling 800/270-7504.

Maps: For a map of Colville National Forest, contact the Outdoor Recreation Information Center, 915 Second Avenue, Suite 442, Seattle, WA 98174; 206/220-7450. Ask the USGS for topographic maps of the Abercrombie Mountain and Boundary Dam areas.

Directions: From Metaline drive north one-quarter mile on Highway 31, then turn west onto Boundary Road/County Road 2975. Drive four miles to the junction with Flume Creek Road/Forest Service Road 350. Turn left onto Flume Creek Road and continue seven miles to the trailhead on the right side of the road. Note: Flume Creek Road is rough and may be inaccessible to low-clearance vehicles.

Contact: Colville National Forest, Sullivan Lake Ranger District, 12641 Sullivan Lake Road, Metaline Falls, WA 99153; 509/446-7500.

43 Halliday
15.6 mi/7.8 hrs

Winding through deep, old pine forests, this trail is a good connector to other trails of the Salmo-Priest Wilderness, notably the North Fork Sullivan Trail and the Red Bluff Trail (see hikes this chapter). It's also a good forest hike in its own right. White-tailed and mule deer are often seen grazing here, while elk browse along the valley bottom in spring and autumn. Rarely, you may also spot a moose wading in the beaver ponds just a mile up the trail. The trail ends alongside the pretty North Fork Sullivan River. Campsites are found near its shore.

Location: Northeast of Metaline in Colville National Forest; see Northeast Washington Map 3, grid a6.

User Groups: Hikers, dogs, and horses. No mountain bikes are allowed. No wheelchair facilities.

Permits: A federal Northwest Forest Pass, $5 per day or $30 annually, is required to park at the trailhead. Passes are available from ranger stations and many private vendors, online at website: www.wta.org, or by calling 800/270-7504.

Maps: For a map of Colville National Forest, contact the Outdoor Recreation Information Center, 915 Second Avenue, Suite 442, Seattle, WA 98174; 206/220-7450. Ask the USGS for topographic maps of the Boundary Dam and Gypsy Peak areas.

Directions: From Metaline Falls drive north for eight miles on Highway 31 to the junction with Forest Service Road 180. The trailhead is at the junction (on the east side of Highway 31).

Contact: Colville National Forest, Sullivan Lake Ranger District, 12641 Sullivan Lake Road, Metaline Falls, WA 99153; 509/446-7500.

44 Slate Creek
8.4 mi/4.0 hrs

The net elevation gain over the trail's length is just 770 feet, but thanks to all the up-and-down action, the gross gain is closer to 3,000 feet. Climbing over several ridges, the trail repeatedly breaks out into ridgetop meadows with gorgeous views, and then drops back down into valley forests that echo with the calls of grouse and the chatter of rabbits. The constantly changing scenery gives

you a good chance of spotting deer, elk, or other wildlife. Hikers should be aware that the opportunity to see animals makes this a popular trail for hunters in the autumn, so all visitors should wear bright colors, preferably blaze orange or neon pink.

Location: Northeast of Metaline in Colville National Forest, partially within the Salmo-Priest Wilderness; see Northeast Washington Map 3, grid a7.

User Groups: Hikers, dogs, and horses. No mountain bikes are allowed. No wheelchair facilities.

Permits: A federal Northwest Forest Pass, $5 per day or $30 annually, is required to park at the trailhead. Passes are available from ranger stations and many private vendors, online at website: www.wta.org, or by calling 800/270-7504.

Maps: For a map of Colville National Forest, contact the Outdoor Recreation Information Center, 915 Second Avenue, Suite 442, Seattle, WA 98174; 206/220-7450. Ask the USGS for a topographic map of the Abercrombie Mountain area.

Directions: From Metaline drive north for nine miles on Highway 31 and then turn east onto Slate Creek Road/Forest Service Road 3155. Drive seven miles to the trailhead, which is clearly marked on the right side of the road.

Contact: Colville National Forest, Sullivan Lake Ranger District, 12641 Sullivan Lake Road, Metaline Falls, WA 99153; 509/446-7500.

45 North Fork Sullivan
19.2 mi/2.0 days

The first mile of the North Fork Sullivan Trail traverses a wooded hillside before entering the North Fork Sullivan Valley. From here the route parallels the river for nearly the remainder of its length but seldom gets near the water.

Passing under the southern flank of Crowell Mountain, the trail enters the Salmo-Priest Wilderness and begins to climb steeply to the top of Crowell Ridge. Keep an eye out for mountain goats on both Crowell Mountain and the ridge. The trail ends at a junction with the Crowell Ridge Trail (see hike in this chapter). Campsites are scattered along the first seven miles of this route, most notably where it dips closer to the river.

Location: Northeast of Metaline in Colville National Forest, partially within the Salmo-Priest Wilderness; see Northeast Washington Map 3, grid b6.

User Groups: Hikers, dogs, and horses. No mountain bikes are allowed. No wheelchair facilities.

Permits: A federal Northwest Forest Pass, $5 per day or $30 annually, is required to park at the trailhead. Passes are available from ranger stations and many private vendors, online at website: www.wta.org, or by calling 800/270-7504.

Maps: For a map of Colville National Forest, contact the Outdoor Recreation Information Center, 915 Second Avenue, Suite 442, Seattle, WA 98174; 206/220-7450. Ask the USGS for topographic maps of the Boundary Dam and Gypsy Peak areas.

Directions: From Metaline drive east for 1.1 miles on Sullivan Lake Road/County Road 9345. Turn north on County Road 3911 and continue for one mile to Lime Lake. The marked trailhead is at the north end of the lake, on the right side of the road.

Contact: Colville National Forest, Sullivan Lake Ranger District, 12641 Sullivan Lake Road, Metaline Falls, WA 99153; 509/446-7500.

46 Red Bluff
10.4 mi/5.2 hrs

This lowland trail is best visited in late spring and early autumn but is enjoyable all sum-mer long. The trail goes up and down repeatedly as it crosses several small- to medium-sized ridges, making this a strenuous hike, even though the net elevation gain is just 1,000 feet in five miles. Spring hikers find plenty of fresh morel mushrooms growing in the shady forest; early autumn hikers enjoy abundant plump huckleberries in the clearings. Other forest travelers often appear, too, including deer, elk, grouse, rabbit, black bear, and cougar, among others.

Unless you are skilled in identifying mushrooms, don't eat any you may find here. While some are delicious and harmless, others are deadly.

Location: Northeast of Metaline in Colville National Forest; see Northeast Washington Map 3, grid b6.

User Groups: Hikers, dogs, and horses. No mountain bikes are allowed. No wheelchair facilities.

Permits: A federal Northwest Forest Pass, $5 per day or $30 annually, is required to park at the trailhead. Passes are available from ranger stations and many private vendors, online at website: www.wta.org, or by calling 800/270-7504.

Maps: For a map of Colville National Forest, contact the Outdoor Recreation Information Center, 915 Second Avenue, Suite 442, Seattle, WA 98174; 206/220-7450. Ask the USGS for topographic maps of the Metaline Falls and Boundary Dam areas.

Directions: From Metaline Falls drive east on Sullivan Lake Road/County Road 9345 for approximately four miles to the marked trailhead on the north side of the road (opposite Mill Pond).

Contact: Colville National Forest, Sullivan Lake Ranger District, 12641 Sullivan Lake Road, Metaline Falls, WA 99153; 509/446-7500.

47 Crowell Ridge
15.6 mi/1.0–2.0 days

Beginning high and staying high, this trail is a treat for those who love beautiful views but hate steep climbs. The trail runs the length of Crowell Ridge, entering the Salmo-Priest Wilderness early on. Water is scarce along the ridgetop, while the panoramic views are abundant. From the wildflower-filled meadows, hikers can look north to the craggy summits of Gypsy Peak, Salmo Mountain, and the Kokanees of British Columbia. To the south is the Pend Oreille Valley and Sullivan Lake. To make the views even more enjoyable, visit in late summer and snack on the plentiful, plump huckleberries. This is primarily a dry trail, so carry enough water for your entire trip. Backpackers can pitch a tent just about anywhere, but if you don't use an established site (and these are common here), move at least 150 feet away from the trail before setting up camp. This will give the vegetation in your spot a chance to recover.

Location: Northeast of Metaline in Colville National Forest, mostly within the Salmo-Priest Wilderness; see Northeast Washington Map 3, grid b6.

User Groups: Hikers, dogs, and horses. No mountain bikes. No wheelchair facilities.

Permits: A federal Northwest Forest Pass, $5 per day or $30 annually, is required to park at the trailhead. Passes are available from ranger stations and many private vendors, online at website: www.wta.org, or by calling 800/270-7504.

Maps: For a map of Colville National Forest, contact the Outdoor Recreation Information Center, 915 Second Avenue, Suite 442, Seattle, WA 98174; 206/220-7450. Ask the USGS for a topographic map of the Gypsy Peak area.

Directions: From Metaline Falls drive east on Sullivan Lake Road/County Road 9345 to the junction with Forest Service Road 2212, just beyond Mill Pond Campground. Drive east for three miles on Forest Service Road 2212 and then turn left onto Forest Service Road 245. Passenger cars should park here. High-clearance vehicles may continue on for five miles to the trailhead, at a switchback three-quarters of a mile below the Sullivan Mountain summit.

Contact: Colville National Forest, Sullivan Lake Ranger District, 12641 Sullivan Lake Road, Metaline Falls, WA 99153; 509/446-7500.

48 Sullivan Lake
4.1 mi one way/2.0 hrs

Following the east shore of Sullivan Lake, this flat trail links two camps for car campers: Sullivan Lake Campground on the north end of the lake and Noisy Creek Campground on the south end. The lake is pretty, and the trail offers brilliant colors in the autumn, especially in October. The surrounding forest is largely hardwood—bigleaf maple, some oak and walnut—and a surprisingly large number of aspen. This blend of deciduous trees, annual conifers, and evergreens creates a visual cornucopia that's hard to beat. Also be on the lookout for white-tailed and mule deer along the lakeshore and surrounding forest, and for bighorn sheep on the flanks of Hall Mountain above the trail.

Location: East of Metaline at Sullivan Lake in Colville National Forest; see Northeast Washington Map 3, grid b7.

User Groups: Hikers, dogs, and horses. No mountain bikes are allowed. No wheelchair facilities.

Permits: A federal Northwest Forest Pass, $5 per day or $30 annually, is required to park at the trailhead. Passes are available from ranger stations and many private vendors,

online at website: www.wta.org, or by calling 800/270-7504.

Maps: For a map of Colville National Forest, contact the Outdoor Recreation Information Center, 915 Second Avenue, Suite 442, Seattle, WA 98174; 206/220-7450. Ask the USGS for a topographic map of the Metaline Falls area.

Directions: From Metaline Falls drive east on Sullivan Lake Road/County Road 9345 to Sullivan Lake and the junction with Forest Service Road 22. Take Forest Service Road 22 east for one-half mile and then turn right on Forest Service Road 241. Continue one-quarter mile south to the trailhead parking area on the left side of the road. To reach the pickup point, continue south on County Road 9345, past the junction with Forest Service Road 22, to the southern end of Sullivan Lake and the Noisy Creek Campground. The trailhead is at the camp.

Contact: Colville National Forest, Sullivan Lake Ranger District, 12641 Sullivan Lake Road, Metaline Falls, WA 99153; 509/446-7500.

49 Salmo Loop
18.0 mi/2.0 days

The best way to experience this beautiful wilderness trail is by taking your time. A three-day backpacking trip is ideal, as it allows plenty of time for casual exploration and worthwhile ventures. For the better views, travel this route clockwise, which means you start with a steep descent three miles down Trail 506 into the South Salmo River Valley. This river is teeming with succulent, pan-sized rainbow trout. Once at the river, the trail turns west and parallels the water upstream to a junction with the Shedroof Divide Trail (see hike in this chapter). Turn right and follow this south for nearly seven miles to another junction, this time with Trail 535, just before reaching Shedroof

Mountain. Adventurers may choose to climb either or both Shedroof Mountain and Old Snowy Top (near the first junction of Trail 506 and the Shedroof Divide Trail). Both mountains offer fantastic views of the surrounding wilderness, but the climbs are steep and strenuous. The main trail heads north from the flank of Shedroof Mountain, along a long ridge back to the trailhead, completing the loop. Campsites exist throughout the Salmo River Valley—pitch a tent wherever there's a wide spot and good access to fishing. Other camping spots can be found along the ridge between Shedroof and Little Snowy Top. A few small creeks and springs provide adequate water for overnight stops.

Location: North of Metaline in Colville National Forest, within the Salmo-Priest Wilderness; see Northeast Washington Map 3, grid b7.

User Groups: Hikers, dogs, and horses. No mountain bikes are allowed. No wheelchair facilities.

Permits: A federal Northwest Forest Pass, $5 per day or $30 annually, is required to park at the trailhead. Passes are available from ranger stations and many private vendors, online at website: www.wta.org, or by calling 800/270-7504.

Maps: For a map of Colville National Forest, contact the Outdoor Recreation Information Center, 915 Second Avenue, Suite 442, Seattle, WA 98174; 206/220-7450. Ask the USGS for a topographic map of the Salmo Mountain area.

Directions: From Metaline Falls drive east on Sullivan Lake Road/County Road 9345 to Sullivan Lake and the junction with Forest Service Road 22. Take Forest Service Road 22 east. After six miles, the road changes to Forest Service Road 2220. Continue for one-half mile past the junction with Forest Service Road 270 to the trailhead at the end of Forest Service Road 2220.

Contact: Colville National Forest, Sullivan Lake Ranger District, 12641 Sullivan Lake Road, Metaline Falls, WA 99153; 509/446-7500.

50 Thunder Creek
5.8 mi/2.9 hrs

Traversing a hillside in a steep valley, the trail begins in a lush, virgin forest. As the route drops into the creek-lined valley floor, this forest takes on an emerald glow. The deep, rich soil; the steep, shaded valley; and the old-growth forest all combine to create an environment filled with hanging mosses, luscious ferns, and thick underbrush. This is as close as an eastern Washington pine forest gets to resembling the temperate rainforests of the Olympic Peninsula. But it goes one step better because while this area might look like rainforest, it tastes like dry eastern pine and fir forests: the plentiful huckleberries found in this valley are as plump and sweet as any in Washington State.

Location: Northeast of Metaline in Colville National Forest, within the Salmo-Priest Wilderness; see Northeast Washington Map 3, grid b7.

User Groups: Hikers, dogs, and horses. No mountain bikes are allowed. No wheelchair facilities.

Permits: A federal Northwest Forest Pass, $5 per day or $30 annually, is required to park at the trailhead. Passes are available from ranger stations and many private vendors, online at website: www.wta.org, or by calling 800/270-7504.

Maps: For a map of Colville National Forest, contact the Outdoor Recreation Information Center, 915 Second Avenue, Suite 442, Seattle, WA 98174; 206/220-7450. Ask the USGS for topographic maps of the Salmo Mountain and Helmer Mountain areas.

Directions: From Metaline Falls drive east on Sullivan Lake Road/County Road 9345 to Sullivan Lake and the junction with Forest Service Road 22. Take Forest Service Road 22 east. After six miles, the road changes to Forest Service Road 2220. Continue to the junction with Thunder Creek Road/Forest Service Road 345. Turn right at the junction and park near the gate across the road (but make sure not to block the gated road, as Forest Service people may need to get through). The trailhead begins at the junction.

Contact: Colville National Forest, Sullivan Lake Ranger District, 12641 Sullivan Lake Road, Metaline Falls, WA 99153; 509/446-7500.

51 Shedroof Cutoff
3.4 mi/1.7 hrs

For the first mile, this trail rolls easily along a long-abandoned logging road. The route parallels Sullivan Creek, so here and there the sparkling waters appear through the young forest. As the old roadbed peters out and the trail reverts to a narrow single track, the route steepens and leaves the creek behind. The second mile of the trail is a steep climb to a junction with the Shedroof Divide Trail. The junction is a good place for day hikers and wildlife lovers to stop and turn around—deer often graze in the lower river valley. If you wish to continue, see the description of Shedroof Divide (see hike in this chapter).

Location: Northeast of Metaline in Colville National Forest, within the Salmo-Priest Wilderness; see Northeast Washington Map 3, grid b3.

User Groups: Hikers, dogs, and horses. No mountain bikes are allowed. No wheelchair facilities.

Permits: A federal Northwest Forest Pass, $5 per day or $30 annually, is required to park at the trailhead. Passes are available from

ranger stations and many private vendors, online at website: www.wta.org, or by calling 800/270-7504.

Maps: For a map of Colville National Forest, contact the Outdoor Recreation Information Center, 915 Second Avenue, Suite 442, Seattle, WA 98174; 206/220-7450. Ask the USGS for a topographic map of the Salmo Mountain area.

Directions: From Metaline Falls drive east on Sullivan Lake Road/County Road 9345 to Sullivan Lake and the junction with Forest Service Road 22. Take Forest Service Road 22 east. After six miles, the road changes to Forest Service Road 2220. Continue for another seven miles on Forest Service Road 2220 to the trailhead on the right side of the road.

Contact: Colville National Forest, Sullivan Lake Ranger District, 12641 Sullivan Lake Road, Metaline Falls, WA 99153; 509/446-7500.

52 Taylor Ridge
19.0 mi/2.0 days

Like most ridge walks, Taylor Ridge offers stunning vistas, wildflower meadows, and plenty of opportunities to see wildlife. But this one is different: there's water. You cross several streams and pass by several cold-water springs scattered across the hillsides. Some of these are mere seeps. Others fill natural rock bowls, out of which water can be siphoned with a microfilter pump. Backpackers enjoy watching the sun set over the Okanogan/Wenatchee National Forest and the North Cascade Peaks. On a clear evening, you may even see the top of Glacier Peak on the horizon. Come morning, watch the sun rise over the Columbia River Valley. And during the afternoon, enjoy views of Copper, Lambert, Midnight, Stick Pin, and Twin Sisters Mountains.

Location: Northwest of Kettle Falls in Colville National Forest; see Northeast Washington Map 3, grid b6.

User Groups: Hikers, dogs, and horses. No mountain bikes are allowed.

Permits: A federal Northwest Forest Pass, $5 per day or $30 annually, is required to park at the trailhead. Passes are available from ranger stations and many private vendors, online at website: www.wta.org, or by calling 800/270-7504.

Maps: For a map of Colville National Forest, contact the Outdoor Recreation Information Center, 915 Second Avenue, Suite 442, Seattle, WA 98174; 206/220-7450. Ask the USGS for topographic maps of the Orient, Bulldog Mountain, and Mount Leona areas.

Directions: From Kettle Falls drive north on U.S. 395 for 22 miles to Boulder Creek Road/Forest Service Road 61. Turn left (west) onto Boulder Creek Road and continue two miles to South Boulder Creek Road/Forest Service Road 6110. Follow South Boulder Creek Road two miles to the trailhead.

Contact: Colville National Forest, Kettle Falls Ranger District, 255 West 11th Street, Kettle Falls, WA 99141; 509/738-7700.

53 Noisy Creek
10.6 mi/5.3 hrs

Day hikers, especially those based in one of the waterfront campgrounds at Sullivan Lake, will enjoy this trail despite its constant—and at times steep—climb. The trail leads through a cool, old forest and parallels a rather loud creek (hence the name). The trees periodically open up and allow great views into the Sullivan Lake Valley and beyond. The first of these viewpoints is at the 1.25-mile mark, but a much better view is from the top of the trail, at the junction with the Hall Mountain Trail, your turn-around point. For the best scenic vistas, take the right fork at the junction and continue two miles up the Hall Mountain Trail to the summit of Hall Mountain. Here you find views of distant peaks, wide river valleys, and, if you're lucky, herds of deer and bighorn sheep.

Location: East of Metaline at Sullivan Lake in Colville National Forest; see Northeast Washington Map 3, grid b6.

User Groups: Hikers, dogs, and horses. No mountain bikes are allowed. No wheelchair facilities.

Permits: A federal Northwest Forest Pass, $5 per day or $30 annually, is required to park at the trailhead. Passes are available from ranger stations and many private vendors, online at website: www.wta.org, or by calling 800/270-7504.

Maps: For a map of Colville National Forest, contact the Outdoor Recreation Information Center, 915 Second Avenue, Suite 442, Seattle, WA 98174; 206/220-7450. Ask the USGS for topographic maps of the Metaline Falls and Pass Creek areas.

Directions: From Metaline Falls drive east on Sullivan Lake Road/County Road 9345 to Sullivan Lake and continue along the western shore to the south end of the lake and Noisy Creek Campground. Turn left at the entrance to the campground and then turn right at the first junction, a small dirt road. The trailhead is about 50 feet down this path.

Contact: Colville National Forest, Sullivan Lake Ranger District, 12641 Sullivan Lake Road, Metaline Falls, WA 99153; 509/446-7500.

54 Hall Mountain

5.0 mi/2.5 hrs

This trail passes through one of the few places in the Northwest where bighorn sheep live in sizable numbers, so you have ample opportunities to see the agile mountain climbers. For most of the way, you traverse

pine forests until you reach the upper flanks of Hall Mountain, a steep peak whose summit offers wide views on every horizon, plus a good chance of seeing the sheep. State wildlife managers reintroduced these majestic animals to the area a few years ago and have been trying to help the animals develop a stable, healthy population. The rangers place salt blocks near the summit, which keeps the herd close to the area and accessible for viewing. Despite their proximity, remember that these animals are wild and unpredictable. Don't approach or feed them.

Location: East of Metaline in Colville National Forest; see Northeast Washington Map 3, grid b6.

User Groups: Hikers, dogs, and horses. No mountain bikes are allowed. No wheelchair facilities.

Permits: A federal Northwest Forest Pass, $5 per day or $30 annually, is required to park at the trailhead. Passes are available from ranger stations and many private vendors, online at website: www.wta.org, or by calling 800/270-7504.

Maps: For a map of Colville National Forest, contact the Outdoor Recreation Information Center, 915 Second Avenue, Suite 442, Seattle, WA 98174; 206/220-7450. Ask the USGS for topographic maps of the Pass Creek and Metaline Falls areas.

Directions: From Metaline Falls drive east on Sullivan Lake Road/County Road 9345 to Sullivan Lake and the junction with Forest Service Road 22. Take Forest Service Road 22 east for four miles and then turn right on Forest Service Road 500. Continue eight miles to the end of the road and the trailhead. Note: Forest Service Road 500 is closed from August 15 through June 30 each year to protect wildlife, especially bighorn sheep, during the autumn mating season and the spring birthing season.

Contact: Colville National Forest, Sullivan Lake Ranger District, 12641 Sullivan Lake Road, Metaline Falls, WA 99153; 509/446-7500.

55 Hall Mountain-Grassy Top
10.2 mi/5.1 hrs 🥾 🔍6

The first three-quarters of a mile of this trail covers the same ground as the Hall Mountain Trail (see hike this chapter). At the first junction, stay left and follow the trail southeast along a rocky ridgeline. The ridge is a rough, up-and-down route, but because the trail stays under the ridge crest on the wooded slope, it doesn't present many open views of the surrounding countryside. As the trail climbs through the fifth mile and nears the junction with the Pass Creek/Grassy Top Trail (see hike in this chapter), the forest opens up into flower-filled meadows and limited views of the distant peaks. (For the real panoramic views, you need to go farther.) This trail terminates at the junction with the Pass Creek Trail. At that point, turn right and continue one mile to a small side trail that offers a 15-minute climb to the Grassy Top Mountain summit. This old lookout site provides a 360-degree view of the surrounding Salmo-Priest Wilderness.

Location: East of Metaline in Colville National Forest; see Northeast Washington Map 3, grid b7.

User Groups: Hikers, dogs, and horses. No mountain bikes are allowed. No wheelchair facilities.

Permits: A federal Northwest Forest Pass, $5 per day or $30 annually, is required to park at the trailhead. Passes are available from ranger stations and many private vendors, online at website: www.wta.org, or by calling 800/270-7504.

Maps: For a map of Colville National Forest, contact the Outdoor Recreation Information Center, 915 Second Avenue, Suite 442, Seattle, WA 98174; 206/220-7450. Ask the USGS for a topographic map of the Pass Creek area.

Directions: From Metaline Falls drive east on Sullivan Lake Road/County Road 9345 to Sullivan Lake and the junction with Forest Service Road 22. Take Forest Service Road 22 east for four miles and then turn right on Forest Service Road 500. Continue eight miles to the end of the road and the trailhead. Note: Forest Service Road 500 is closed from August 15 through June 30 each year to protect wildlife, especially bighorn sheep, during the autumn mating season and the spring birthing season.

Contact: Colville National Forest, Sullivan Lake Ranger District, 12641 Sullivan Lake Road, Metaline Falls, WA 99153; 509/446-7500.

56 Shedroof Divide
31.4 mi/4.0 days 🥾 🔍9

Lying completely within the Salmo-Priest Wilderness, this trail is part of a 23-mile national scenic trail. The trail hugs a rocky ridge between a series of high peaks, with an initial elevation gain of less than 200 feet. In other words, the trail starts high and stays high, so you get the kind of breathtaking views for which you usually have to work. At various points, the Divide Trail intersects the Thunder Creek, Shedroof Cutoff, and Salmo Loop Trails. It also offers the chance to view and scramble up Helmer, Old Snowy, Round Top, Shedroof, and Thunder Mountains. Old lookout trails once led to most of these peaks, and while the trails are partially obscured now, a bit of searching and close examination will usually reveal fragments here and there. The trail ends deep in the wilderness, tapering into other Idaho trails.

Location: Northeast of Metaline in Colville National Forest, within the

Salmo-Priest Wilderness; see Northeast Washington Map 3, grid b7.

User Groups: Hikers, dogs, and horses. No mountain bikes are allowed. No wheelchair facilities.

Permits: A federal Northwest Forest Pass, $5 per day or $30 annually, is required to park at the trailhead. Passes are available from ranger stations and many private vendors, online at website: www.wta.org, or by calling 800/270-7504.

Maps: For a map of Colville National Forest, contact the Outdoor Recreation Information Center, 915 Second Avenue, Suite 442, Seattle, WA 98174; 206/220-7450. Ask the USGS for topographic maps of the Pass Creek, Helmer Mountain, and Salmo Mountain areas.

Directions: From Metaline Falls drive east on Sullivan Lake Road/County Road 9345 to Sullivan Lake and the junction with Forest Service Road 22. Take Forest Service Road 22 east. After six miles Forest Service Road 22 turns sharply right while Forest Service Road 2220 continues straight. Turn to stay on Forest Service Road 22 and continue for six miles to the trailhead, one-quarter mile past Pass Creek Pass on the north side of the road (opposite the Pass Creek/Grassy Top Trailhead).

Contact: Colville National Forest, Sullivan Lake Ranger District, 12641 Sullivan Lake Road, Metaline Falls, WA 99153; 509/446-7500.

57 Pass Creek/Grassy Top
15.4 mi/7.7 hrs

The best time to hike this trail is late spring, when the bulbous beargrass blossoms are in full splendor. Meandering through second-growth forest, the trail gently climbs to meadows at the ridgetop, where the beargrass fields begin. At the height of the blooming season, it's possible to stand amid the four-foot-tall stalks and their great, white flowers and admire the panorama sprawled out beyond. The trail follows the ridge for several miles, passing under Grassy Top Mountain. To reach its summit, look for an old side trail 3.5 miles from the trailhead. After a short scramble up this access trail, you reach the old lookout site with its commanding view of the surrounding countryside.

Location: East of Metaline in Colville National Forest; see Northeast Washington Map 3, grid c4.

User Groups: Hikers, dogs, and horses. No mountain bikes are allowed. No wheelchair facilities.

Permits: A federal Northwest Forest Pass, $5 per day or $30 annually, is required to park at the trailhead. Passes are available from ranger stations and many private vendors, online at website: www.wta.org, or by calling 800/270-7504.

Maps: For a map of Colville National Forest, contact the Outdoor Recreation Information Center, 915 Second Avenue, Suite 442, Seattle, WA 98174; 206/220-7450. Ask the USGS for a topographic map of the Pass Creek area.

Directions: From Metaline Falls drive east on Sullivan Lake Road/County Road 9345 to Sullivan Lake and the junction with Forest Service Road 22. Take Forest Service Road 22 east. After six miles Forest Service Road 22 turns sharply right while Forest Service Road 2220 continues straight. Turn to stay on Forest Service Road 22 and continue for six miles to the trailhead, one-quarter mile past Pass Creek Pass on the south side of the road (opposite the Shedroof Divide Trailhead).

Contact: Colville National Forest, Sullivan Lake Ranger District, 12641 Sullivan Lake Road, Metaline Falls, WA 99153; 509/446-7500.

58 Wapaloosie
5.0 mi/2.5 hrs

A midsummer hike on the Wapaloosie stimu-lates all your senses. The warm sunshine brings out sweet, fresh odors of the tall lodgepole and ponderosa pines, a fragrance so pungent, in fact, you can almost taste it. You can eat your fill of plump, sweet huck-leberries and feast your eyes on the stun-ning display of peaks and valleys that open up before you as you ascend the trail. Graves and Mack Mountains rise up majestically in the east, and Paradise and Sherman Peaks are seen to the south. Between them all lie deep valleys that seem to have been colored with a blue-tinted brush, the result of bright sunshine reflecting off the bluish-green nee-dles of the pine and spruce trees there. The trail ends at the ridgetop where it meets the Kettle Crest Trail, the main artery through the area.

Location: West of Kettle Falls in Colville Na-tional Forest; Northeast Washington Map 3, .

User Groups: Hikers, dogs, and horses. No mountain bikes are allowed. No wheelchair facilities.

Permits: A federal Northwest Forest Pass, $5 per day or $30 annually, is required to park at the trailhead. Passes are available from ranger stations and many private vendors, online at website: www.wta.org, or by call-ing 800/270-7504.

Maps: For a map of Colville National Forest, contact the Outdoor Recreation Information Center, 915 Second Avenue, Suite 442, Seat-tle, WA 98174; 206/220-7450. Ask the USGS for a topographic map of the Copper Butte area.

Directions: From Kettle Falls drive 20 miles west on U.S. 20. Turn right onto Albian Hill Road/Forest Service Road 2030 and continue 3.2 miles to the trailhead on the left side of the road. Limited parking is available at the trailhead. Additional parking is possible at wide turnouts alongside the road, both above and below the trailhead.

Contact: Colville National Forest, Kettle Falls Ranger District, 255 West 11th Street, Kettle Falls, WA 99141; 509/738-7700.

59 Tiger/Coyote Rock Loops
10.0 mi/5.0 hrs

This pair of five-mile loop trails explores the shore of Frater Lake, nearby meadows, and several small knolls. The Tiger Loop passes through the flower-filled Tiger Meadow along the southeast shore of the lake. The Coyote Rock Loop, on the other hand, leaves the meadows behind and explores an open forest of lodgepole pine and Douglas fir before climbing to picturesque views at the top of Coyote Rock. Though enjoyable year-round, these loops provide especially fine winter recreation for cross-country skiers and snowshoers.

Location: East of Colville on Frater Lake in Colville National Forest; see Northeast Washington Map 3, grid c5.

User Groups: Hikers and dogs. No horses or mountain bikes are allowed. No wheel-chair facilities.

Permits: A federal Northwest Forest Pass, $5 per day or $30 annually, is required to park at the trailhead. Passes are available from ranger stations and many private vendors, online at website: www.wta.org, or by call-ing 800/270-7504.

Maps: For a map of Colville National Forest, contact the Outdoor Recreation Information Center, 915 Second Avenue, Suite 442, Seat-tle, WA 98174; 206/220-7450. Ask the USGS for a topographic map of the Ione area.

Directions: From Colville drive 29 miles east on U.S. 20 to Frater Lake. The trailhead and parking area are on the north side of the highway at the east end of the lake.

Contact: Colville National Forest, Colville Ranger District, 755 South Main Street, Colville, WA 99114; 509/684-7000.

60 Indian Creek
6.0 mi/3.0 hrs

The chances of encountering a mountain bike or even a motorcycle are greater on this trail than any other in the area. But it's still likely that you'll have the trail to yourself. The route climbs up a steep, rocky valley wall to the Iron Mountain Ridge and a junction with the Iron Mountain Road. Tall timber here blocks the vistas, but red-tailed hawks, goshawks, and a large herd of white-tailed deer all live here.

Location: East of Colville in Colville National Forest; see Northeast Washington Map 3, grid e2.

User Groups: Hikers, dogs, horses, and mountain bikes. No wheelchair facilities.

Permits: A federal Northwest Forest Pass, $5 per day or $30 annually, is required to park at the trailhead. Passes are available from ranger stations and many private vendors, online at website: www.wta.org, or by calling 800/270-7504.

Maps: For a map of Colville National Forest, contact the Outdoor Recreation Information Center, 915 Second Avenue, Suite 442, Seattle, WA 98174; 206/220-7450. Ask the USGS for topographic maps of the Addy and Addy Mountain areas.

Directions: From Colville drive approximately 13 miles south on U.S. 395 to Indian Creek Road, a narrow, single-lane dirt road. Turn east onto Indian Creek Road and continue three-quarters of a mile to the boundary of Colville National Forest. Park in one of the wide turnouts; the trailhead is near the National Forest sign.

Contact: Colville National Forest, Colville Ranger District, 755 South Main Street, Colville, WA 99114; 509/684-7000.

61 Brown's Lake
0.5 mi/1.0 hr

This trail is at its best in autumn, when red-cheeked cutthroat trout move up out of the lake and into the river to spawn. The barrier-free trail has a raised boardwalk route that provides the perfect view of one of the best spawning beds here. A dense forest of pine, fir, and larch surrounds the lake and the stream, providing a stunning backdrop both to the crimson-sided fish thrashing passionately in their spawning beds and the autumnal gold of the larch. Fishing is allowed (barring special closure, which rarely occurs), but this trail has something for everyone. It's settled in a deep, narrow valley, which makes it seem like an untouched wilderness, but the trail is just developed enough to accommodate everyone, regardless of physical abilities. We always recommend this trail for friends (especially those with kids), the elderly, physically challenged, or just anyone who wants a leisurely stroll.

Location: North of Newport in Colville National Forest; see Northeast Washington Map 3, grid e7.

User Groups: Hikers and dogs. Fully wheelchair accessible. No horses or mountain bikes are allowed.

Permits: A federal Northwest Forest Pass, $5 per day or $30 annually, is required to park at the trailhead. Passes are available from ranger stations and many private vendors, online at website: www.wta.org, or by calling 800/270-7504.

Maps: For a map of Colville National Forest, contact the Outdoor Recreation Information Center, 915 Second Avenue, Suite 442, Seattle, WA 98174; 206/220-7450. Ask the USGS for a topographic map of the Brown's Lake area.

Directions: From Newport drive about 16 miles north on Highway 20 to Usk. Turn east onto Kings Lake Road and cross the Pend Oreille River. Continue northeast on Kings Lake Road to a junction with Forest Service Road 5030. Turn left (north) onto this road and drive one-quarter mile past Brown's Lake Campground to the trailhead and parking area.

Contact: Colville National Forest, Newport Ranger District, 315 North Warren Avenue, Newport, WA 99156; 509/447-7300.

62 South Skookum Loop
1.3 mi/1.0 hr

This trail's low level of difficulty belies the rewards it offers. The trail loops along the south and west shores of South Skookum Lake, offering postcard views of the surrounding peaks, fronted by beautiful hardwood and conifer forests. Lucky visitors may see something that so far has eluded me—one of the many resident moose wading through shallow waters along the lake's edge or grazing through the adjoining meadows. To improve your odds of seeing one, visit in late summer and spend the day picnicking along the trail.

Location: North of Newport in Colville National Forest; see Northeast Washington Map 3, grid e7.

User groups: Hikers and dogs only. No horses or mountain bikes are allowed. No wheelchair facilities.

Permits: No permits are required.

Maps: For a trail information report, contact the Newport Ranger District at the address below. For a map of Colville National Forest, contact the Outdoor Recreation Information Center, 915 Second Avenue, Suite 442, Seattle, WA 98174; 206/220-7450. To obtain a USGS

topographic map of the area, ask for Brown's Lake.

Directions: From Newport, drive about 16 miles north on U.S. 20 to Usk. Turn east onto Kings Lake Road and cross the Pend Oreille River. Continue along Kings Lake Road for 10 miles to a junction with Skookum Lake Road (Forest Service Road 50). Turn right (east) onto Skookum Lake Road and drive to the South Skookum Lake Campground. The trailhead is near the boat-launch area. Parking is provided in the day-use parking lot.

Contact: Colville National Forest, Newport Ranger District, 315 North Warren Street, Newport, WA 99156; 509/447-7300.

63 Bead Lake
11.8 mi/5.9 hrs

Big trees, a beautiful blue lake, and shoreline meadows filled with wildflowers await hikers on this trail. The first four miles of the route amble along the east shore of Bead Lake. Deer and occasionally moose wander along the trail, sipping out of the clean, clear lake and browsing in the fragrant lupine and wood violets that fill the forest clearings. At the north end of the lake, the trail turns and briefly follows Lodge Creek, the lake's main water source, as it angles up the ridge toward Mosquito Point. The scenery is striking, and the skeeters are, too. Carry plenty of bug repellent and hope for a stiff breeze.

Location: North of Newport in Colville National Forest; see Northeast Washington Map 3, grid f8.

User Groups: Hikers and dogs. No horses or mountain bikes are allowed. No wheelchair facilities.

Permits: A federal Northwest Forest Pass, $5 per day or $30 annually, is required to park at the trailhead. Passes are available from ranger stations and many private

vendors, online at website: www.wta.org, or by calling 800/270-7504.

Maps: For a map of Colville National Forest, contact the Outdoor Recreation Information Center, 915 Second Avenue, Suite 442, Seattle, WA 98174; 206/220-7450. Ask the USGS for a topographic map of the Bead Lake area.

Directions: From Newport drive east on U.S. 2 across the Pend Oreille River into Idaho. Just across the river, turn north onto LeClerc Creek Road and continue 3.8 miles to a junction with Bead Lake Road. Bear right (north) onto Bead Lake Road. As you near Bead Lake, turn right onto County Road 3215, a gravel road leading around the south shore of the lake. The trailhead is at the end of County Road 3215, near the Mineral Bay Campground.

Contact: Colville National Forest, Newport Ranger District, 315 North Warren Avenue, Newport, WA 99156; 509/447-7300.

64 Pioneer Park Interpretive Trail

0.5 mi/1.0 hr

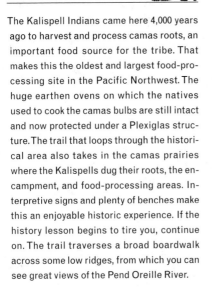

The Kalispell Indians came here 4,000 years ago to harvest and process camas roots, an important food source for the tribe. That makes this the oldest and largest food-processing site in the Pacific Northwest. The huge earthen ovens on which the natives used to cook the camas bulbs are still intact and now protected under a Plexiglas structure. The trail that loops through the historical area also takes in the camas prairies where the Kalispells dug their roots, the encampment, and food-processing areas. Interpretive signs and plenty of benches make this an enjoyable historic experience. If the history lesson begins to tire you, continue on. The trail traverses a broad boardwalk across some low ridges, from which you can see great views of the Pend Oreille River.

Location: North of Newport in Colville National Forest; see Northeast Washington Map 3, grid f8.

User Groups: Hikers and dogs. Fully wheelchair accessible. No horses or mountain bikes allowed.

Permits: A federal Northwest Forest Pass, $5 per day or $30 annually, is required to park at the trailhead. Passes are available from ranger stations and many private vendors, online at website: www.wta.org, or by calling 800/270-7504.

Maps: For a map of Colville National Forest, contact the Outdoor Recreation Information Center, 915 Second Avenue, Suite 442, Seattle, WA 98174; 206/220-7450. Ask the USGS for a topographic map of the Newport area.

Directions: From Newport drive east on U.S. 2 across the Pend Oreille River into Idaho. Turn left (north) immediately after crossing the river onto Forest Service Road 9305. Continue 2.3 miles to the Pioneer Park Campground. The trailhead is at the day-use parking area.

Contact: Colville National Forest, Newport Ranger District, 315 North Warren Avenue, Newport, WA 99156; 509/447-7300.

65 Wolf Donation Trail System

2.0 mi/1.0 hr

An old logging road is the foundation of this trail. The area was logged fairly recently, but the surrounding forest shows little evidence of the activity. That's because the loggers used draft horses, instead of huge diesel skidders and bulldozers, to thin the dense lodgepole forest. Using horses in place of machines allows loggers to manage the operation more precisely, so while you may notice the loss of a few trees, you probably won't feel offended. The net result is a series of trails for hikers and cross-country skiers to explore and enjoy. A short side trail leads off the main route to an overlook of the sparkling Pend Oreille River.

Location: Just north of Newport in Colville National Forest; see Northeast Washington Map 3, grid g8.

User groups: Hikers, dogs, and mountain bikes only. No horses. No wheelchair facilities.

Permits: No permits are required.

Maps: For a trail information report, contact the Newport Ranger District at the address below. For a map of Colville National Forest, contact the Outdoor Recreation Information Center, 915 Second Avenue, Suite 442, Seattle, WA 98174; 206/220-7450. To obtain a USGS topographic map of the area, ask for Newport.

Directions: From downtown Newport, drive north on Route 20 to the north edge of town. Turn left onto Larch Street and, after two blocks, turn right onto Laurelhurst Drive and continue one-half mile. There is no designated parking area, so trail users have to park along the street.

Contact: Colville National Forest, Newport Ranger District, 315 North Warren Street, Newport, WA 99156; 509/447-7300.

66 Little Spokane River Natural Area
12.0 mi/6.0 hrs

Though close to the metropolitan area of Spokane, this is truly a natural wonderland. A wild menagerie of creatures prowls the clear, cold waters of the Little Spokane River. Rainbow, cutthroat, and brown trout swim in the deep holes; beavers work tirelessly to create their pools; and muskrats swim and splash among them all. As you wander along the flat, broad trail, don't be surprised to see white-tailed deer, coyotes, porcupines, white-tailed rabbits, hoary marmots, and a variety of birds, ranging from hummingbirds to bald eagles. A great blue heron rookery occupies

the tall cottonwoods on the river's south shore. Other wildlife to be seen and enjoyed are the wild river runners—the humans that inhabit long, sleek canoes and ride them down the white-crested river.

Sections of the trail may be closed or detoured from February to August, the nesting season of the great blue heron.

Location: Northwest of Spokane; see Northeast Washington Map 4, grid c4.

User Groups: Hikers only. No dogs, horses, or mountain bikes are allowed. No wheelchair facilities.

Permits: No permits are required.

Maps: For a map of the area, contact Riverside State Park at 509/456-3964. Ask the USGS for topographic maps of the Nine Mile Falls and Dartford areas.

Directions: From Spokane drive six miles north on Highway 291. Turn right (east) onto Rutter Parkway and continue a short distance to the trailhead on the banks of the river.

Contact: Little Spokane River Natural Area, c/o Riverside State Park, Spokane, WA 99205; 509/456-3964.

67 Spokane River Centennial Trail
40.0 mi/2.0–3.0 days

The history of this trail extends back hundreds of thousands of years to a time when a massive ice dam burst, releasing pent-up waters from the melting Ice Age glaciers. The ensuing flood carved out the Spokane River Valley and prepared the way for this trail. In relatively more recent times, native tribes etched images into the cliffs around Long Lake. These petroglyphs are thousands of years old, but you can still see them from the trail. Even more recently, during the 1880s, Colonel Wright brutally raided the native tribes at Horse Slaughter Island Camp, just off the pathway. The trail here is broad, hard-surfaced, and parallels the banks of the beautiful Spokane River. Eventually the existing 20-mile trail will be extended to 39 miles in Washington and will link to another 21 miles in Idaho. There are many access points along the trail route, including several in the city of Spokane.

Location: North of Spokane in Riverside State Park; see Northeast Washington Map 4, grid c6.

User Groups: Hikers, dogs, horses, and mountain bikes. Fully wheelchair accessible.

Permits: No permits are required.

Maps: For a trail information report, contact Riverside State Park at 509/456-3964. Ask the USGS for topographic maps of the Nine Mile Falls and Airway Heights areas.

Directions: From downtown Spokane drive six miles north on Highway 291 to the entrance of Riverside State Park at the junction of Highway 291 and Gun Club Road. The trail begins in the park.

Contact: Riverside State Park, Spokane, WA 99205; 509/456-3964.

68 Dishman Hills Nature Trails
4.0 mi/2.5 hrs

Looping through 450 acres of nearly pristine wildlands on the outskirts of the large Spokane urban center, these trails are a testament to the power of the people. Once destined for a life under asphalt and condominiums, the Dishman Hills Natural Area was preserved through the joint efforts of a retired high school teacher and his grassroots supporters, as well as the county parks planners and the Nature Conservancy. The best way to experience the Dishman Hills is on the gentle trail that weaves through old stands of dry ponderosa pine, past a quartet of frog-filled ponds, and through wildflower meadows, mushroom patches, and berry brambles. The trail rolls up and down the hills, dropping from the trailhead at Camp Caro—a county park—into the Enchanted Ravine, where birds serenade visitors. Leaving the ravine, the trail angles off to the right, climbing for a mile to East and West Ponds. Let the kids study the tadpoles and toads that lurk here before moving on to the high point of the trail. About 2.5 miles from your car, the trail crosses the 2,400-foot unnamed peak that tops the Dishman Hills. From here, it's a gentle drop along a narrow path to the two Lost Ponds (possibly named because by the end of a long, dry summer, they have lost all their water) and then back to the trailhead through groves of cottonwood and pine. Deer, coyotes, and raccoons are abundant, and the trees house more than a hundred species of birds, according to a member of the local Audubon Society.

Location: East of Spokane in Dishman Hills Natural Area; see Northeast Washington Map 4, grid c5.

User Groups: Hikers and dogs. No horses or mountain bikes are allowed. No wheelchair facilities.

Permits: No permits are required.

Maps: Ask the USGS for a topographic map of the Spokane Southeast area.

Directions: From downtown Spokane drive east on I-90 to the East Sprague exit/Exit 95 and drive east on Sprague Avenue for nearly two miles to Sargent Road. Turn south (right) onto Sargent Road and continue a half mile to the buildings of Camp Caro. The trailhead is found on the southeast side of the parking area.

Contact: A nonprofit group and a county agency jointly manage this area. Dishman Hills Natural Area Association, E10820 Maxwell, Spokane, WA 99206; Spokane County Parks and Recreation Department, W1115 Broadway, Spokane, WA 99260; 509/456-4730.

69 Liberty Creek

6.0 mi/3.2 hrs

You have to fight your way past picnickers, Frisbee throwers, and volleyball players in the popular lakeside park at the beginning of this trail. But we promise that you'll soon leave behind the madding crowds. The trail is easy at first, as it follows and sometimes crosses the tumbling waters of Liberty Creek. A little more than a mile up the creek valley, the trail cuts through a large group campsite. Then the workout begins. The trail climbs up the hillside behind the campsite, switchbacking repeatedly until, at the last hairpin turn about two miles in from the trailhead, a stunning view of the valley and lake lies at your feet. Enjoy the view, but don't stop. Follow the trail another mile to the even better views found on the end of a long ridge. From here, you can admire the lake, Liberty Creek Valley, and the mountains of Idaho. Return the way you came or continue along the trail as it climbs up over a short rock ledge and then drops into shady pine forest. The trail quickly loops back down the hill to the trailhead, passing a pretty little waterfall and a scenic old log bridge along the way.

Location: East of Spokane in Liberty Lake County Park; see Northeast Washington Map 4, grid c8.

User Groups: Hikers and dogs. No horses or mountain bikes are allowed. No wheelchair facilities.

Permits: No permits are required.

Maps: Ask the USGS for topographic maps of the Liberty Lake and Mica Peak areas.

Directions: From downtown Spokane drive east on I-90 to the Liberty Lake exit. Turn right (south) onto Liberty Lake Road and, in just a block, turn left (east) onto Mission Avenue. Drive three-quarters of a mile to Molter Street and turn right (south). Continue nearly a mile to Valley Way and turn left (east). Drive two miles to the entrance of Liberty Lake County Park. Valley Way becomes Lakeside Road when it loops around the east end of the golf course. After entering the park, continue past the tollbooth and drive straight ahead to the trailhead parking area at the southeast end of the campground. The trailhead is near campsite 21.

Contact: Spokane County Parks and Recreation Department, W1115 Broadway, Spokane, WA 99260; 509/456-4730.

MOUNT RAINIER AND THE COLUMBIA RIVER GORGE

Mount Rainier and the Columbia River Gorge

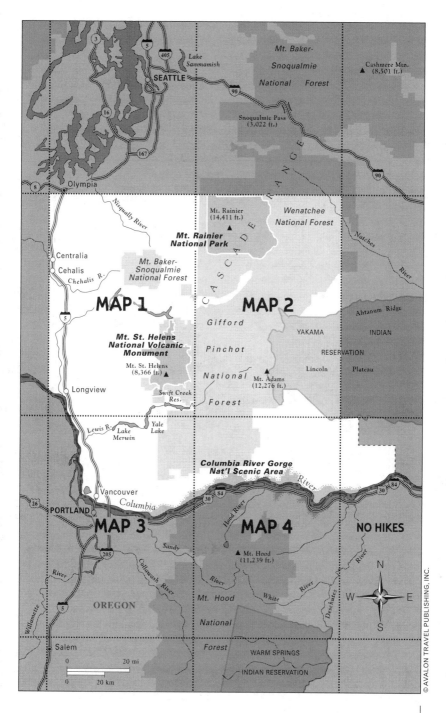

Map 1

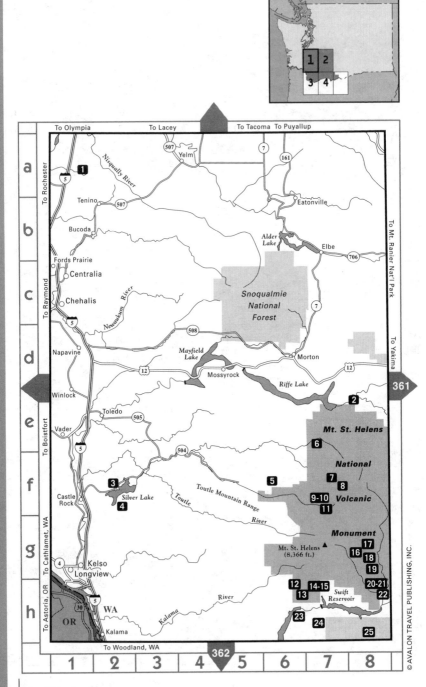

To Olympia To Lacey To Tacoma To Puyallup

a
To Rochester
507
Yelm
7
161
1
5

b
Tenino
507
Bucoda
Eatonville
Alder Lake
Elbe
706
To Mt. Ranier Nat'l Park

c
Fords Prairie
Centralia
Chehalis
Newaukum River
Snoqualmie National Forest
7
To Raymond

d
Napavine
508
Mayfield Lake
Morton
12
12
To Yakima
Winlock
Mossyrock
Riffe Lake
2
361
To Boistfort

e
Toledo
505
Vader
Mt. St. Helens
6

f
Castle Rock
3
Silver Lake
504
Toutle
Toutle Mountain Range
5
National
7
8
9-10
Volcanic
11
To Cathlamet, WA

g
Kelso
Longview
River
Mt. St. Helens (8,366 ft.)
Monument
17
16
18
19
12
14-15
20-21
13
Swift Reservoir
22
To Astoria, OR

h
30
WA
OR
5
Kalama
Kalama
River
23
24
25

To Woodland, WA

362

© AVALON TRAVEL PUBLISHING, INC.

1 2 3 4 5 6 7 8

Map 2

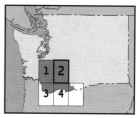

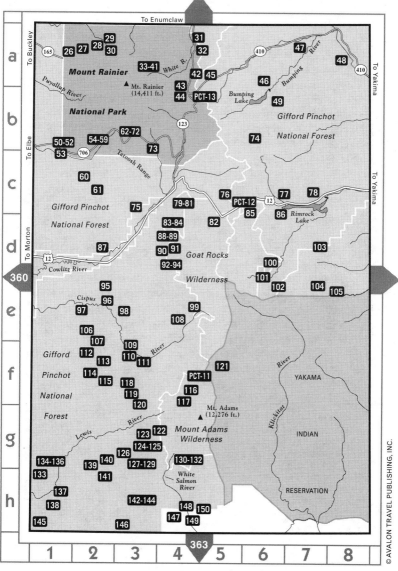

© AVALON TRAVEL PUBLISHING, INC.

Map 3

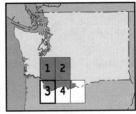

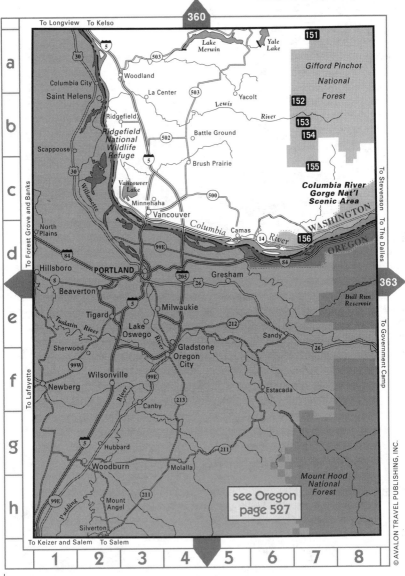

To Longview   To Kelso

151

Lake
Merwin

Yale
Lake

a

30

5

503

Woodland

Gifford Pinchot

Columbia City

La Center

503

Yacolt

National

Saint Helens

152

Forest

Lewis

b

Ridgefield

153

River

Ridgefield
National
Wildlife
Refuge

502

Battle Ground

154

Scappoose

5

Brush Prairie

155

30

Vancouver
Lake

Columbia River
Gorge Nat'l
Scenic Area

c

To Forest Grove and Banks

Minnehaha

500

Vancouver

WASHINGTON

To Stevenson

To The Dalles

North
Plains

99E

Columbia

Camas

River

14

156

OREGON

d

84

PORTLAND

205

Gresham

84

363

Hillsboro

8

26

Bull Run
Reservoir

Beaverton

To Lafayette

Tigard

5

Milwaukie

To Government Camp

e

Tualatin

River

Lake
Oswego

212

Sandy

Sherwood

Gladstone

26

99W

Oregon
City

f

Newberg

Wilsonville

99E

River

Estacada

Canby

213

g

5

Hubbard

211

To Keizer and Salem

99E

Woodburn

Molalla

Mount Hood
National
Forest

h

Pudding

Mount
Angel

211

see Oregon
page 527

Silverton

To Keizer and Salem   To Salem

© AVALON TRAVEL PUBLISHING, INC.

Map 4

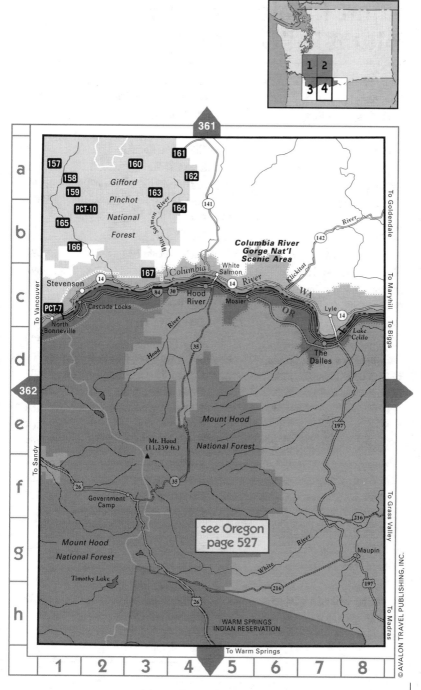

a

157 **160** **161**

158 *Gifford* **162**

159 *Pinchot* **163** **164** (141)

PCT-10 *National* River

b

165 *Forest* **142** To Goldendale

166

Columbia River
Gorge Nat'l
Scenic Area

167 Columbia White Klickitat **WA**
Salmon River

c

Stevenson (14) 84 30 (14)

PCT-7 Hood Mosier **OR** Lyle (14)

Cascade Locks River

North Lake
Bonneville Celilo

d

Hood The
Dalles

River (35)

e

Mount Hood (197)

Mt. Hood
(11,239 ft.) *National Forest*

f

(26) (35)

Government
Camp (216)

g

Mount Hood White (197)

National Forest River Maupin

Timothy Lake (216)

h

(26) (197)

WARM SPRINGS
INDIAN RESERVATION

To Warm Springs

see Oregon
page 527

To Vancouver

To Sandy

To Grass Valley

To Madras

To Maryhill

To Biggs

© AVALON TRAVEL PUBLISHING, INC.

1 2 3 4 5 6 7 8

Mount Rainier and the Columbia River Gorge

(CONTINUED ON NEXT PAGE)

❶ Millersylvania Memorial State Park

0.5–6.0 mi/0.5–3.0 hrs

Millersylvania has something for everyone: a 1.5-mile fitness trail, 6.6 miles of hiking trails, fine campground among stately Douglas fir and waterfront on Deep Lake, which is stocked with rainbow trout (a state license is required to fish here). The trail system is well developed and relaxing, with paths leading to all of the 842-acre park's destinations. It's a great place to bring the kids, and the fitness trail is an excellent blood flow–restoration tool for Seattle-to-Portland drivers. The entire park was donated to the state in 1921 by the Miller family, survivors of Johann Mueller, an Austrian general exiled to the United States in the early 1880s.

Location: Near I-5 south of Olympia; see Mount Rainier and the Columbia River Gorge Map 1, grid a1.

User Groups: Hikers, leashed dogs, and mountain bikes (check with rangers for open trails). No horses are allowed. No wheelchair facilities.

Permits: Day-use parking permits may be required. Contact the Washington State Parks and Recreation Commission at 800/233-0321.

Maps: For a Washington State Parks brochure, contact Washington State Parks at 800/233-0321. Ask the USGS for a topographic map of the Maytown area.

Directions: From Olympia drive 11 miles south on I-5 to Exit 99. Drive east on 113th Street Southwest, turn south onto Southwest Tilley Road, and drive to the park. Note: Carbon River Road was washed out in 1996 and had not been repaired at press time. See the special highway access note in the Mount Rainier Sidebar.

Contact: Washington State Parks and Recreation Commission, Public Affairs Office, P.O. Box 42650, Olympia, WA 98504-2650; 800/233-0321.

❷ Strawberry Mountain

21.4 mi/1.0–2.0 days

A steep, dark climb through thick second-growth Douglas fir leads to a forested ridgetop here. This route levels off along the ridgetop, where views are limited to occasional breaks in the trees. The Strawberry Mountain summit does afford some pleasant views, but the best scenery is located at the far end of the trail. The route dips, crosses Forest Service Road 2516, and climbs once more to an unnamed peak. At the top of this mountain are the remnants of an old fire lookout tower. The tower is gone, but the views are still here. The southern vistas include Mount St. Helens and all the devastation wrought by its May 18, 1980, eruption. The trail ends just at the other side of this summit, which is actually the best place to turn and retrace your steps.

Location: South of Randle in Gifford Pinchot National Forest; see Mount Rainier and the Columbia River Gorge Map 1, grid e8.

User Groups: Hikers, leashed dogs, horses, and mountain bikes. No wheelchair facilities.

Permits: A federal Northwest Forest Pass, $5 per day or $30 annually, is required to park at the trailhead. Passes are available from ranger stations and many private vendors, online at website: www.wta.org, or by calling 800/270-7504.

Maps: For a trail information report, contact the Cowlitz Valley Ranger District at 360/497-1100. For a map of Gifford Pinchot National Forest, send $3 to Outdoor Recreation Information Center, 915 Second Avenue, Suite 442, Seattle, WA 98174; 206/220-7450. Green Trails, Inc.'s excellent topographic maps of the region are available for $3.99 each at outdoor retail outlets. Ask for map number 332, Spirit Lake. Ask the USGS for topographic maps of the Spirit Lake East and Cowlitz Falls areas.

Directions: From Randle drive about eight miles south on Forest Service Road 25 and cross the Cispus River. Just beyond the river turn right (west) onto Forest Service Road 26. Continue two miles on this road to a junction with Forest Service Road 26-045 and turn left. Follow this primitive dirt road 1.8 miles to the road's end and the trailhead.

Contact: Gifford Pinchot National Forest, Cowlitz Valley Ranger District, 10024 U.S. Highway 12, Randle, WA 98377; 360/497-1100.

⓫ Seaquest Trails
7.0 mi/3.5 hrs

Deep, old Douglas fir and hemlock forest lines this heavily used trail. Despite the number of visitors that hike the trail, expect to see deer, owls, assorted squirrels, a couple jay varieties, and maybe even cougar or black bear tracks. The trail is level and weaves through the trees with no particular destination. Hike as long as you like before turning back and returning to the day-use part of the park.

Location: North of Vancouver in Seaquest State Park; see Mount Rainier and the Columbia River Gorge Map 1, grid f2.

User Groups: Hikers and leashed dogs. No mountain bikes are allowed. No wheelchair facilities.

Permits: Day-use parking permits may be required. Contact the Washington State Parks and Recreation Commission at 800/233-0321.

Maps: Ask the USGS for a topographic map of the Silver Lake area.

Directions: From Vancouver, Washington, drive north on I-5 to the Castle Rock exit/Exit

49 and turn east on Highway 504. Drive 5.5 miles east to Silver Lake and Seaquest State Park.

Contact: Washington State Parks and Recreation Commission, Public Affairs Office, P.O. Box 42650, Olympia, WA 98504-2650; 800/233-0321.

⓬ Silver Lake
0.5 mi/0.5 hr

Big, beautiful Silver Lake is entering old age. Like all living things, the lake is changing, and it will die someday. Death, for a lake, is disappearance. The shoreline of Silver Lake is extending out into the water, the water is getting shallower, and lush meadows flourish where fish once swam. The wide, paved trail loops through meadows and shoreline wetlands, exploring the changing ecosystem and variety of wildlife in each area.

Location: West of Castle Rock in Gifford Pinchot National Forest within the Mount St. Helens National Volcanic Monument; see Mount Rainier and the Columbia River Gorge Map 1, grid f2.

User Groups: Hikers, leashed dogs, and wheelchairs. No horses or mountain bikes are allowed.

Permits: A federal Northwest Forest Pass, $5 per day or $30 annually, is required to park at the trailhead. Passes are available from ranger stations and many private vendors, online at website: www.wta.org, or by calling 800/270-7504. Visitors to any developed site in the Mount St. Helens Monument—including visitor centers, paved overlooks, and interpretive areas—are required to pay an $8 fee per person for a Monument Pass. The pass is valid for three days. Anyone attempting to climb the peak or just scramble on the upper slopes must register in the town of Cougar and pay a $15 climbing fee per person. Contact the Mount St. Helens National Volcanic Monument at 360/247-3900.

Maps: For a trail information report, contact the Mount St. Helens National Volcanic Monument at 360/247-3900. For a map of Gifford Pinchot National Forest, send $3 to Outdoor Recreation Information Center, 915 Second Avenue, Suite 442, Seattle, WA 98174; 206/220-7450. Green Trails, Inc.'s excellent topographic maps of the region are available for $3.99 each at outdoor retail outlets. Ask for map number 364S, Mount St. Helens Northwest. Ask the USGS for a topographic map of the Mount St. Helens area.

Directions: From Castle Rock drive five miles east on Highway 504 to the Mount St. Helens Silver Lake Visitor Center on the right. The trailhead is on the left side of the parking area.

Contact: Gifford Pinchot National Forest, Mount St. Helens National Volcanic Monument, 42218 Northeast Yale Bridge Road, Amboy, WA 98601-9715; 360/247-3900.

5 Coldwater Lake View Trail
5.0 mi/4.0 hrs

Before May 18, 1980, this was a forest, not a lake. The volcanic eruption that day, however, swept away the forest, and the massive mudflows in the Toutle River Basin created a huge earthen dam that trapped the waters of Coldwater Creek and formed the new lake. This trail leaves the new visitor center and drops several hundred feet on a moderately steep trail to the north shore of the lake. At the shoreline you meet the main Coldwater Lake Trail. A left turn on this route leads, in a half mile, to a permanent trail closure—the devastating floods of 1996 destroyed a huge section of the trail and turned the surrounding fragile hillside into a sheer cliff. Monument officials want to find a way to bypass

the washout, but it will require a lot of special funding and engineering magic.

For the time being, hikers should enjoy this short dead-end trail segment and then head back down the right-hand fork, which leads down the lake to the boat launch area. This trail section stays high above the waterline, affording great views of the young lake and the devastated hillside just to the south. It's not unusual to see the resident elk herd grazing somewhere on that far bank—a good pair of binoculars can help pick them out of the gray stumps and dead logs that litter the slope. The trail ends at the fishing pier near the boat launch. You can end the hike here if you arranged to have a car shuttled down to the lakeside; otherwise, you need to retrace your steps to the visitor center.

Location: West of Castle Rock in Gifford Pinchot National Forest within the Mount St. Helens National Volcanic Monument; see Mount Rainier and the Columbia River Gorge Map 1, grid f6.

User Groups: Hikers only. No dogs, horses, or mountain bikes. No wheelchair facilities.

Permits: A federal Northwest Forest Pass, $5 per day or $30 annually, is required to park at the trailhead. Passes are available from ranger stations and many private vendors, online at website: www.wta.org, or by calling 800/270-7504. Visitors to any developed site in the Mount St. Helens Monument—including visitor centers, paved overlooks, and interpretive areas—are required to pay an $8 fee per person for a Monument Pass. The pass is valid for three days. Anyone attempting to climb the peak or just scramble on the upper slopes must register in the town of Cougar and pay a $15 climbing fee per person. Contact the Mount St. Helens National Volcanic Monument at 360/247-3900.

Maps: For a trail information report, contact the Mount St. Helens National Volcanic

Monument at 360/247-3900. For a map of Gifford Pinchot National Forest, send $3 to Outdoor Recreation Information Center, 915 Second Avenue, Suite 442, Seattle, WA 98174; 206/220-7450. Green Trails, Inc.'s excellent topographic maps of the region are available for $3.99 each at outdoor retail outlets. Ask for map number 364S, Mount St. Helens Northwest. Ask the USGS for a topographic map of the Mount St. Helens area.

Directions: From Castle Rock drive about 25 miles east on Highway 504 to the Coldwater Visitor Center. The trailhead is on the north side of the road, at the visitor center.

Contact: Gifford Pinchot National Forest, Mount St. Helens National Volcanic Monument, 42218 Northeast Yale Bridge Road, Amboy, WA 98601-9715; 360/247-3900.

6 Quartz Creek Big Trees
1.5 mi/1.0 hr

As the name implies, this trail passes under some big trees. Big, in fact, is too small a word for these trees. Massive, gigantic, or enormous is more appropriate. Douglas firs tower more than 200 feet over the trail, hemlocks as wide as your car are scattered throughout the forest, and western red cedars (comparable in size to the hemlocks and firs) provide a pleasant fragrance to the trek. Trail-guide pamphlets are available at the trailhead kiosk; they offer helpful interpretive comments on the forest ecosystem, inhabitants and structure.

Location: South of Randle in Gifford Pinchot National Forest; see Mount Rainier and the Columbia River Gorge Map 1, grid e7.

User Groups: Hikers, leashed dogs, and wheelchairs. No horses or mountain bikes are allowed.

Permits: A federal Northwest Forest Pass, $5 per day or $30 annually, is required to park at the trailhead. Passes are available from ranger stations and many private vendors, online at website: www.wta.org, or by calling 800/270-7504.

Maps: For a map of the Gifford Pinchot National Forest, send $3.60 to Outdoor Recreation Information Center, 915 Second Avenue, Suite 442, Seattle, WA 98174; 206/220-7450. Green Trails, Inc.'s excellent topographic maps of the region are available for $3.99 each at outdoor retail outlets. Ask for map number 332, Spirit Lake. Ask the USGS for a topographic map of the Cowlitz Falls area.

Directions: From Randle drive about eight miles south on Forest Service Road 25 and cross the Cispus River. Just beyond the river turn right (west) onto Forest Service Road 26. Continue about seven miles to a junction with Forest Service Road 2608 and turn right. Follow Forest Service Road 2608 about one mile to the trailhead on the right.

Contact: Gifford Pinchot National Forest, Cowlitz Valley Ranger District, 10024 U.S. Highway 12, Randle, WA 98377; 360/497-1100.

7 Goat Mountain
12.0 mi/6.0 hrs

Traversing a high ridge due north of Mount St. Helens, this trail offers some of the best views of the volcano's massive crater and huge blast area. It climbs steeply from the trailhead near Ryan Lake for about two miles (a 1,500-foot elevation gain) to the long ridge of Goat Mountain and then heads west along its southern flank. Goat Mountain hikers can see the yawning crater and the piled rubble of the new lava dome, as well as the incredible changes to the land in front of the blast. You can look out over vast hillsides that used to be covered in thick, green forest; in a matter of minutes in 1980, they were reduced to stark gray wastelands. Vegetation has only begun to come back in the last few years, and the new greenery is especially vivid against the sterile ash backdrop. Even the ridge along which the trail runs was scarred by the blast, and streaks of ash are evident everywhere.

The remnants of Mount St. Helens are put in proper context when you turn north from the summit of Goat Mountain and view noble, towering Mount Rainier. The low, gray hulk of St. Helens used to be white-capped and, some say, even more majestic in appearance than Rainier, the King of the Cascades. Even kings can be laid low—Mount Rainier is considered active and expected to erupt in the next 100 years.

Location: South of Randle in Gifford Pinchot National Forest partially within the Mount St. Helens National Volcanic Monument; see Mount Rainier and the Columbia River Gorge Map 1, grid f7.

User Groups: Hikers, leashed dogs, and horses. No mountain bikes are allowed. No wheelchair facilities.

Permits: A federal Northwest Forest Pass, $5 per day or $30 annually, is required to park at the trailhead. Passes are available from ranger stations and many private vendors, online at website: www.wta.org, or by calling 800/270-7504.

Maps: For a map of Gifford Pinchot National Forest, send $3 to Outdoor Recreation Information Center, 915 Second Avenue, Suite 442, Seattle, WA 98174; 206/220-7450. Green Trails, Inc.'s excellent topographic maps of the region are available for $3.99 each at outdoor retail outlets. Ask for map number 332, Spirit Lake. Ask the USGS for topographic maps of the Spirit Lake East, Spirit Lake West, and Cowlitz Falls areas.

Directions: From Randle drive about eight miles south on Forest Service Road 25 and cross the Cispus River. Just beyond the river turn right (west) onto Forest Service Road 26. Continue to a junction with Forest Service Road 2612 and turn right. Follow Forest Service Road 2612 one-half mile to the trailhead on the right.

Contact: Gifford Pinchot National Forest, Cowlitz Valley Ranger District, 10024 U.S. Highway 12, Randle, WA 98377; 360/497-1100.

8 Ryan Lake Interpretive Loop
0.6 mi/1.0 hr

This interpretive trail loops around a broad clearing just south of Ryan Lake. It includes several steep sections, but none is longer than a few dozen yards. Generally speaking, this is an easy, relaxing trail on which to explore a small segment of the Mount St. Helens blast area—the trailhead is just 12 miles from the volcano's crater. The interpretive signs along the route are well designed and very informative; they help explain the way the incredible blast behaved, how it affected the landscape, and the land's subsequent recovery from the fiery destruction.

Location: South of Randle in Gifford Pinchot National Forest partially within the Mount St. Helens National Volcanic Monument; see Mount Rainier and the Columbia River Gorge Map 1, grid f7.

User Groups: Hikers, leashed dogs, and horses. No mountain bikes are allowed. No wheelchair facilities.

Permits: A federal Northwest Forest Pass, $5 per day or $30 annually, is required to park at the trailhead. Passes are available from ranger stations and many private vendors, online at website: www.wta.org, or by calling 800/270-7504.

Maps: For a map of Gifford Pinchot National Forest, send $3 to Outdoor Recreation Information Center, 915 Second Avenue, Suite 442, Seattle, WA 98174; 206/220-7450. Green Trails, Inc.'s excellent topographic maps of the region are available for $3.99 each at various outdoor retail outlets. Ask for map number 332, Spirit Lake. Ask the USGS for topographic maps of the Spirit Lake East, Spirit Lake West, and Cowlitz Falls areas.

Directions: From Randle drive about eight miles south on Forest Service Road 25 and cross the Cispus River. Just beyond the river turn right (west) onto Forest Service Road 26. Continue for about 10 miles on Forest Service Road 26 to the Ryan Lake Interpretive Center on the right. The trailhead is near the center's parking area.

Contact: Gifford Pinchot National Forest, Cowlitz Valley Ranger District, 10024 U.S. Highway 12, Randle, WA 98377; 360/497-1100.

9 Boundary, West End
12.0 mi/8.0 hrs

Even people who don't want to hike the full Boundary Trail will love this section: it's a pleasant 12-mile round-trip day hike. The Boundary Trail is a 36-mile ridgetop route that bisects Gifford Pinchot National Forest from east to west. Prior to the May 18, 1980, eruption of Mount St. Helens, it was possible to hike the full length of the trail without backtracking. After the eruption, however, road access to the trail's western end was destroyed, and the trailhead had to be relocated six miles east of there. As a result, a lot of hikers who plan to hike the full length of the trail skip the six western miles—and they are missing out on the route's best part. From Norway Pass the trail climbs west along a ridge to Bear Pass and continues to Mount Margaret. The views are stunning throughout the length of the hike, but from Mount Margaret on, they surpass belief. Mount Margaret's 5,858-foot summit is due north of the Mount St. Helens crater. It looks directly south at the lava dome inside the crater and across once-fertile, green Spirit Lake Basin. From Mount Margaret the trail stays high and leapfrogs

from one beautiful wildflower meadow to another until it ends at Coldwater Peak. You can enjoy more spectacular views from Coldwater before retracing your steps to Norway Pass.

Location: South of Randle in Gifford Pinchot National Forest partially within the Mount St. Helens National Volcanic Monument; see Mount Rainier and the Columbia River Gorge Map 1, grid f7.

User Groups: Hikers, leashed dogs, horses, and mountain bikes. No wheelchair facilities.

Permits: A federal Northwest Forest Pass, $5 per day or $30 annually, is required to park at the trailhead. Passes are available from ranger stations and many private vendors, online at website: www.wta.org, or by calling 800/270-7504. Visitors to any developed site in the Mount St. Helens Monument—including visitor centers, paved overlooks, and interpretive areas—are required to pay an $8 fee per person for a Monument Pass. The pass is valid for three days. Anyone attempting to climb the peak or just scramble on the upper slopes must register in the town of Cougar and pay a $15 climbing fee per person.

Maps: For a map of the Gifford Pinchot National Forest, send $3 to Outdoor Recreation Information Center, 915 Second Avenue, Suite 442, Seattle, WA 98174; 206/220-7450. Green Trails, Inc.'s excellent topographic maps of the region are available for $3.99 each at outdoor retail outlets. Ask for map number 332, Spirit Lake. Ask the USGS for topographic maps of the Spirit Lake East and Spirit Lake West areas.

Directions: From Randle drive about eight miles south on Forest Service Road 25 and cross the Cispus River. Just beyond the river turn right (west) onto Forest Service Road 26. Continue to Norway Pass and the trailhead on the left.

Contact: Gifford Pinchot National Forest, Cowlitz Valley Ranger District, 10024 U.S. Highway 12, Randle, WA 98377; 360/497-1100.

🔟 Boundary, East End
30.0 mi one way/
3.0–4.0 days

Heading east from Norway Pass, this trail slices across the heart of the Gifford Pinchot National Forest; it rides the crest of a long series of east/west ridges. The route starts in the Mount St. Helens blast zone, and the incredible destruction wrought by the eruption more than 19 years ago is still very evident. Gray ash streaks the hillsides, and bleached-white skeletons of massive Douglas firs litter the area. At about 2.5 miles the route passes Ghost Lake and its forest of young, fortunate trees—fortunate because there was a heavy snow load on the area in the 1980 winter, and when the mountain erupted, these youngsters were buried in a cold, protective layer. All the older, larger trees that poked above the deep snow cover were destroyed.

From the lake the trail continues east and climbs high enough to give occasional views of hulking Mount Rainier to the north and Mount Adams to the east. Several small, suitable camps are scattered along the route, but the best overnight stops are found at Badger Lake on the flank of Badger Mountain, roughly nine miles east of the trailhead, or at Dark Meadows in the shadow of Dark Mountain, at about 20 miles in. Side trails lead to the tops of several peaks within a mile of the main trail. Many of these summits are former fire-lookout locations, and they offer fantastic panoramas of the surrounding forest. The trail ends at Council Lake Campground, on the western edge of the Mount Adams Wilderness.

Location: South of Randle in Gifford Pinchot National Forest partially within the Mount St. Helens National Volcanic Monument; see Mount Rainier and the Columbia River Gorge Map 1, grid f7.

User Groups: Hikers, leashed dogs, horses, and mountain bikes. No wheelchair facilities.

Permits: A federal Northwest Forest Pass, $5 per day or $30 annually, is required to park at the trailhead. Passes are available from ranger stations and many private vendors, online at website: www.wta.org, or by calling 800/270-7504. Visitors to any developed site in the Mount St. Helens Monument—including visitor centers, paved overlooks, and interpretive areas—are required to pay an $8 fee per person for a Monument Pass. The pass is valid for three days. Anyone attempting to climb the peak or just scramble on the upper slopes must register in the town of Cougar and pay a $15 climbing fee per person.

Maps: For a map of Gifford Pinchot National Forest, send $3 to Outdoor Recreation Information Center, 915 Second Avenue, Suite 442, Seattle, WA 98174; 206/220-7450. Green Trails, Inc.'s excellent topographic maps of the region are available for $3.99 each at outdoor retail outlets. Ask for map numbers 332 and 333, Spirit Lake and McCoy Peak. Ask the USGS for topographic maps of the Spirit Lake East, Spirit Lake West, French Butte, and McCoy Peak areas.

Directions: From Randle drive about eight miles south on Forest Service Road 25 and cross the Cispus River. Just beyond the river turn right (west) onto Forest Service Road 26. Continue to Norway Pass and the trailhead on the left. To reach the eastern trailhead from Randle, drive about one mile south on Forest Service Road 25 and then turn right onto Forest Service Road 23. Continue east for about 35 miles to the junction with Forest Service

Road 2329 at Takhlakh Meadow. Turn left (north) onto Forest Service Road 2329 and continue a short distance to the Council Lake Campground. The trailhead is near the day-use parking area.

Contact: Gifford Pinchot National Forest, Cowlitz Valley Ranger District, 10024 U.S. Highway 12, Randle, WA 98377; 360/497-1100.

⓫ Meta Lake
0.5 mi/0.5 hr

The Meta Lake Trail celebrates life that miraculously escaped devastation during the 1980 eruption of Mount St. Helens. This broad, paved trail weaves through a lush forest of alpine and noble firs; these trees survived the fiery blast because of their youth and diminutive size. The early-spring eruption leveled tall, mature trees in the area, but, because there was still more than 10 feet of snow on the ground at the time of the blast, the younger, smaller trees along this trail were shielded by a deep snow blanket. The trail rolls past the rusty hulk of a mangled car caught by the blast. This route also visits the lakeshore and cuts through the thick new grass growing in the meadows. Other plants and animals are moving back into the region, including a family of beavers at Meta Lake. Listen and you might hear the solid kersplash of a big dam-builder slapping his tail on the water, alerting his friends to your presence.

Location: South of Randle in Gifford Pinchot National Forest within the Mount St. Helens National Volcanic Monument; see Mount Rainier and the Columbia River Gorge Map 1, grid f7.

User Groups: Hikers only. Fully wheelchair accessible. No dogs, horses, or mountain bikes are allowed.

Permits: A federal Northwest Forest Pass, $5 per day or $30 annually, is required to park at the trailhead. Passes are available from ranger stations and many private vendors, online at website: www.wta.org, or by calling 800/270-7504. Visitors to any developed site in the Mount St. Helens Monument—including visitor centers, paved overlooks, and interpretive areas—are required to pay an $8 fee per person for a Monument Pass. The pass is valid for three days. Anyone attempting to climb the peak or just scramble on the upper slopes must register in the town of Cougar and pay a $15 climbing fee per person. Contact the Mount St. Helens National Volcanic Monument at 360/247-3900.

Maps: For a trail information report, contact the Mount St. Helens National Volcanic Monument at 360/247-3900. For a map of the Gifford Pinchot National Forest, send $3 to Outdoor Recreation Information Center, 915 Second Avenue, Suite 442, Seattle, WA 98174; 206/220-7450. Green Trails, Inc.'s excellent topographic maps of the region are available for $3.99 each at various outdoor retail outlets. Ask for map number 364S, Mount St. Helens Northwest. Ask the USGS for a topographic map of the Spirit Lake East area.

Directions: From Randle drive about eight miles south on Forest Service Road 25 and cross the Cispus River. Just beyond the river turn right (west) onto Forest Service Road 26. Continue to Forest Service Road 99. Turn right (west) onto Forest Service Road 99 and continue one-half mile to the trailhead.

Contact: Gifford Pinchot National Forest, Mount St. Helens National Volcanic Monument, 42218 Northeast Yale Bridge Road, Amboy, WA 98601-9715; 360/247-3900.

⓬ Sheep Canyon
4.4 mi/2.2 hrs

Offering great views down the mud-filled Toutle River Valley, this trail explores areas of destruction as well as healthy old forests that miraculously escaped the ravages of the

1980 eruption. From a viewing platform near the start of the trail, you can see the upper Toutle River Basin with its deep mudflows and new contours. The trail then winds into the deep shadows of an old fir and hemlock forest, where it stays during a sometimes steep climb to the west flank of Mount St. Helens and its junction with the Loowit Trail (see hike in this chapter). At the junction, turn back, retrace your steps, and take advantage of the periodic breaks in the forest to look down on Sheep Canyon and the Toutle. Before you start back, however, we suggest wandering around the Loowit Trail a bit. A short walk in either direction on this trail leads to great views of the mountain. Remember that a permit is needed from May 15 to November 1 to go above 4,800 feet (the trail junction is at 4,600 feet), so don't go too far off trail to find views.

Location: North of Cougar in Gifford Pinchot National Forest within the Mount St. Helens National Volcanic Monument; see Mount Rainier and the Columbia River Gorge Map 1, grid h6.

User Groups: Hikers and leashed dogs. No horses or mountain bikes are allowed. No wheelchair facilities.

Permits: A federal Northwest Forest Pass, $5 per day or $30 annually, is required to park at the trailhead. Passes are available from ranger stations and many private vendors, online at website: www.wta.org, or by calling 800/270-7504. Visitors to any developed site in the Mount St. Helens Monument—including visitor centers, paved overlooks, and interpretive areas—are required to pay an $8 fee per person for a Monument Pass. The pass is valid for three days. Anyone attempting to climb the peak or just scramble on the upper slopes must register in the town of Cougar and pay a $15 climbing fee per person. Contact the Mount St. Helens National Volcanic Monument at 360/247-3900.

Maps: For a trail information report, contact the Mount St. Helens National Volcanic Monument at 360/247-3900. For a map of Gifford Pinchot National Forest, send $3 to Outdoor Recreation Information Center, 915 Second Avenue, Suite 442, Seattle, WA 98174; 206/220-7450. Green Trails, Inc.'s excellent topographic maps of the region are available for $3.99 each at outdoor retail outlets. Ask for map number 364S, Mount St. Helens Northwest. Ask the USGS for topographic maps of the Goat Mountain and Mount St. Helens areas.

Directions: From Cougar drive east on Forest Service Road 90 just one mile beyond the Swift Dam and turn left (north) onto Forest Service Road 83. Continue three miles on this road and then turn left onto Forest Service Road 81. Continue to the road's junction with Forest Service Road 8123. Take a right (north) turn onto Forest Service Road 8123 and drive to the road's end and the trailhead.

Contact: Gifford Pinchot National Forest, Mount St. Helens National Volcanic Monument, 42218 Northeast Yale Bridge Road, Amboy, WA 98601-9715; 360/247-3900.

🔢 Toutle

6.0 mi/3.0 hrs

As you climb from the Blue Lake Basin along Coldspring Creek, you find a forest of old noble firs; these deep-green, soft-needled conifers seem to live up to their regal name. The trail leaves the creek and runs up and over a low ridge before dropping into the Toutle River Valley. From the ridgetop you find great views of the mountain, and as you near the Toutle, you see evidence of the vast destruction that took place on May 18, 1980. On that day the normally placid, clear Toutle River turned into a massive raging torrent of mud—more than 100 feet deep—that scoured the valley clean and left new land formations throughout the basin. Explore the area near the Toutle before retracing your steps to Blue Lake.

Location: North of Cougar in Gifford Pinchot National Forest within the Mount St. Helens National Volcanic Monument; see Mount Rainier and the Columbia River Gorge Map 1, grid h6.

User Groups: Hikers and leashed dogs. No horses or mountain bikes are allowed. No wheelchair facilities.

Permits: A federal Northwest Forest Pass, $5 per day or $30 annually, is required to park at the trailhead. Passes are available from ranger stations and many private vendors, online at website: www.wta.org, or by calling 800/270-7504. Visitors to any developed site in the Mount St. Helens Monument—including visitor centers, paved overlooks, and interpretive areas—are required to pay an $8 fee per person for a Monument Pass. The pass is valid for three days. Anyone attempting to climb the peak or just scramble on the upper slopes must register in the town of Cougar and pay a $15 climbing fee per person. Mount St. Helens National Volcanic Monument at 360/247-3900.

Maps: For a trail information report, contact the Mount St. Helens National Volcanic Monument at 360/247-3900. For a map of Gifford Pinchot National Forest, send $3 to Outdoor Recreation Information Center, 915 Second Avenue, Suite 442, Seattle, WA 98174; 206/220-7450. Green Trails, Inc.'s excellent topographic maps of the region are available for $3.99 each at outdoor retail outlets. Ask for map number 364S, Mount St. Helens Northwest. Ask the USGS for a topographic map of the Mount St. Helens area.

Directions: From Cougar drive east on Forest Service Road 90 just one mile beyond the Swift Dam and turn left (north) onto Forest Service Road 83. Continue three miles on this road and then turn left onto Forest Service Road 81. Continue to its junction with Forest Service Road 8123. Turn right (north) and drive to the trailhead near the junction with Forest Service Road 8123-170.

Contact: Gifford Pinchot National Forest, Mount St. Helens National Volcanic Monument, 42218 Northeast Yale Bridge Road, Amboy, WA 98601-9715; 360/247-3900.

14 Butte Camp
6.8 mi/3.4 hrs

You start hiking through a stark, rough lava bed, climb through second-growth forest to a stand of ancient Douglas fir, and cross a small spring-fed creek before you even reach Butte Camp. Backpackers are well advised to drop their gear, set up camp, and then push on up the trail (with a light day sack) for another 1.3 miles to the route's junction with the Loowit Trail. You can enjoy alpine meadows and fields of wildflowers—made all the more colorful by the dull-gray ash background—on this trail stretch. The jagged edge of the mammoth crater at the top of Mount St. Helens rises above all this glory.

Location: North of Cougar in Gifford Pinchot National Forest within the Mount St. Helens National Volcanic Monument; see Mount Rainier and the Columbia River Gorge Map 1, grid h7.

User Groups: Hikers and leashed dogs. No horses or mountain bikes are allowed. No wheelchair facilities.

Permits: A federal Northwest Forest Pass, $5 per day or $30 annually, is required to park at the trailhead. Passes are available from ranger stations and many private vendors, online at website: www.wta.org, or by calling 800/270-7504. Visitors to any developed site in the Mount St. Helens Monument—including visitor centers, paved overlooks, and interpretive areas—are required to pay an $8 fee per person for a Monument Pass. The pass is valid for three days. Anyone attempting to climb the peak or just scramble on the upper slopes must register in the town of Cougar and pay a $15 climbing fee per person. Contact the Mount St. Helens National Volcanic Monument at 360/247-3900.

Maps: For a trail information report, contact the Mount St. Helens National Volcanic Monument at 360/247-3900. For a map of Gifford Pinchot National Forest, send $3 to Outdoor Recreation Information Center, 915 Second Avenue, Suite 442, Seattle, WA 98174; 206/220-7450. Green Trails, Inc.'s excellent topographic maps of the region are available for $3.99 each at outdoor retail outlets. Ask for map number 364S, Mount St. Helens Northwest. Ask the USGS for a topographic map of the Mount St. Helens area.

Directions: From Cougar drive east on Forest Service Road 90 just one mile beyond the Swift Dam and then turn left (north) onto Forest Service Road 83. Drive three more miles on Forest Service Road 83 and turn left onto Forest Service Road 81. Continue for three miles to the trailhead on the right.

Contact: Gifford Pinchot National Forest, Mount St. Helens National Volcanic Monument, 42218 Northeast Yale Bridge Road, Amboy, WA 98601-9715; 360/247-3900.

15 Ape Cave
1.0 mi one way/2.0 hrs

The primates who gave their name to lava tubes found along this trail weren't monkeys—they were members of a 1950s outdoor club who found and explored the tubes. They called themselves the Mount St. Helens Apes, and the lava tubes became known as their caves. The tubes are long tunnels in the thick lava beds; they run roughly parallel to the surface of the land. Interpretive signs

line both the trail through the forest and the tubes' mouth. Descending into the tubes requires a jacket—it's a constant, cool 42 degrees under the earth, regardless of what happens on the surface—and a powerful flashlight or lantern. The tube bed is rough and uneven. There are two routes you can take: The lower route is the easiest (but still requires a certain amount of care) and the upper tube is larger. A pleasant, flat trail through the old forest links the two tubes and leads from the trailhead to these underworld entrances.

Powerful flashlights with well-charged batteries or a strong lantern are required for walking in the caves. Do not try to explore these spots without a good light.

Location: North of Cougar in Gifford Pinchot National Forest within the Mount St. Helens National Volcanic Monument; see Mount Rainier and the Columbia River Gorge Map 1, grid h7.

User Groups: Hikers and leashed dogs. No horses or mountain bikes are allowed. No wheelchair facilities.

Permits: A federal Northwest Forest Pass, $5 per day or $30 annually, is required to park at the trailhead. Passes are available from ranger stations and many private vendors, online at website: www.wta.org, or by calling 800/270-7504. Visitors to any developed site in the Mount St. Helens Monument—including visitor centers, paved overlooks, and interpretive areas—are required to pay an $8 fee per person for a Monument Pass. The pass is valid for three days. Anyone attempting to climb the peak or just scramble on the upper slopes must register in the town of Cougar and pay a $15 climbing fee per person. Contact the Mount St. Helens National Volcanic Monument at 360/247-3900.

Maps: For a trail information report, contact the Mount St. Helens National Volcanic

Monument at 360/247-3900. For a map of the Gifford Pinchot National Forest, send $3 to Outdoor Recreation Information Center, 915 Second Avenue, Suite 442, Seattle, WA 98174; 206/220-7450. Green Trails, Inc.'s excellent topographic maps of the region are available for $3.99 each at outdoor retail outlets. Ask for map number 364S, Mount St. Helens Northwest. Ask the USGS for a topographic map of the Mount St. Helens area.

Directions: From Cougar drive east on Forest Service Road 90 just one mile beyond the Swift Dam and turn left (north) onto Forest Service Road 83. Drive two miles on Forest Service Road 83 and turn left onto Forest Service Road 8303. Continue for one mile on Forest Service Road 8303 to the trailhead on the right.

Contact: Gifford Pinchot National Forest, Mount St. Helens National Volcanic Monument, 42218 Northeast Yale Bridge Road, Amboy, WA 98601-9715; 360/247-3900.

16 Independence Pass
7.0 mi/4.5 hrs

What more could you want from a trail in this area? Here you enjoy stunning views of Mount St. Helens and its gaping crater, the new mountain growing inside the crater (the lava dome), and reshaped Spirit Lake. You find these vistas within the first 15 minutes of hiking. Keep going and you weave through ash-covered boulder fields, rocky spires, and carpets of wildflowers. The trail ends at its junction with the Boundary Trail (see hikes this chapter). Explore the area around the junction—it's directly in front of the crater breach—before retracing your steps.

Location: South of Randle in Gifford Pinchot National Forest within the Mount St. Helens National Volcanic Monument; see Mount Rainier and the Columbia River Gorge Map 1, grid g8.

User Groups: Hikers only. No dogs, horses, or mountain bikes are allowed. No wheelchair facilities.

Permits: A federal Northwest Forest Pass, $5 per day or $30 annually, is required to park at the trailhead. Passes are available from ranger stations and many private vendors, online at website: www.wta.org, or by calling 800/270-7504. Visitors to any developed site in the Mount St. Helens Monument—including visitor centers, paved overlooks, and interpretive areas—are required to pay an $8 fee per person for a Monument Pass. The pass is valid for three days. Anyone attempting to climb the peak or just scramble on the upper slopes must register in the town of Cougar and pay a $15 climbing fee per person. Contact the Mount St. Helens National Volcanic Monument at 360/247-3900.

Maps: For a trail information report, contact the Mount St. Helens National Volcanic Monument at 360/247-3900. For a map of Gifford Pinchot National Forest, send $3 to Outdoor Recreation Information Center, 915 Second Avenue, Suite 442, Seattle, WA 98174; 206/220-7450. Green Trails, Inc.'s excellent topographic maps of the region are available for $3.99 each at outdoor retail outlets. Ask for number 364S, Mount St. Helens Northwest. Ask the USGS for topographic maps of the Spirit Lake East and Spirit Lake West areas.

Directions: From Randle drive about eight miles south on Forest Service Road 25 and cross the Cispus River. Just beyond the river turn right (west) onto Forest Service Road 26. Continue about 15 miles to Forest Service Road 99. Turn right (west) on Forest Service Road 99 and continue 1.6 miles to the trailhead.

Contact: Gifford Pinchot National Forest, Mount St. Helens National Volcanic Monument, 42218 Northeast Yale Bridge Road, Amboy, WA 98601-9715; 360/247-3900.

17 Harmony
2.0 mi/1.0 hr

Overlooking the east bay of Spirit Lake, this trail drops from the Harmony Falls Viewpoint on gentle switchbacks. Harmony Trail's name seems appropriate so long after the eruption, but as you hike down this route you recognize the lack of harmony—in fact, the ultimate chaos—that reigned here years ago. You'll be awed by the precise pattern of the fallen trees laid low by the huge blast. The trees lie parallel to each other like matches in a matchbook, pointing away from the volcano's crater. At the bottom of the trail are volcano-redesigned Spirit Lake and Harmony Falls. Once a beautiful high cascade, Harmony Falls was reduced in height by half. The massive mudflows that accompanied the eruption dammed the outlet of Spirit Lake, raising its water level by 200 feet. The shoreline is rough and treacherous, lined with gritty ash and loose rock.

Location: South of Randle in Gifford Pinchot National Forest within the Mount St. Helens National Volcanic Monument; see Mount Rainier and the Columbia River Gorge Map 1, grid g8.

User Groups: Hikers only. No dogs, horses, or mountain bikes are allowed. No wheelchair facilities.

Permits: A federal Northwest Forest Pass, $5 per day or $30 annually, is required to park at the trailhead. Passes are available from ranger stations and many private vendors, online at website: www.wta.org, or by calling 800/270-7504. Visitors to any developed site in the Mount St. Helens Monument—including visitor centers, paved overlooks, and interpretive areas—are required to pay an $8 fee per person for a Monument Pass. The pass is valid for three days. Anyone attempting to climb the peak or just scramble on the upper slopes must register in the town of Cougar and pay a $15 climbing fee per person. Contact the Mount St. Helens National Volcanic Monument at 360/247-3900.

Maps: For a trail information report, contact the Mount St. Helens National Volcanic Monument at 360/247-3900. For a map of Gifford Pinchot National Forest, send $3 to Outdoor Recreation Information Center, 915 Second Avenue, Suite 442, Seattle, WA 98174; 206/220-7450. Green Trails, Inc.'s excellent topographic maps of the region are available for $3.99 each at outdoor retail outlets. Ask for map number 364S, Mount St. Helens Northwest. Ask the USGS for a topographic map of the Spirit Lake East area.

Directions: From Randle drive about eight miles south on Forest Service Road 25 and cross the Cispus River. Just beyond the river turn right (west) onto Forest Service Road 26. Continue about 15 miles to Forest Service Road 99. Turn right (west) and continue three miles to the trailhead.

Contact: Gifford Pinchot National Forest, Mount St. Helens National Volcanic Monument, 42218 Northeast Yale Bridge Road, Amboy, WA 98601-9715; 360/247-3900.

18 Loowit
28.0 mi one way/
3.0–4.0 days

There are at least seven ways to access the Loowit Trail, but the Windy Ridge Trailhead is (in our opinion) the best starting point—from here the hike runs clockwise around the mountain. The advantage of this trailhead is that you start with a clear, stunning, close-up view of the crater, the origin of the May 18, 1980, eruption. As you travel farther around the trail, you see less destruction (though it is always present) and more of the old, long-established ecosystem that has flourished here for years.

At times the trail dips into lush old-growth forest before rising back above timberline and into the gray, ashy world of the volcano. As you work your way north along the west side of the mountain, the incredible magnitude of the destruction becomes evident. After crossing over the mudflows in Sheep Canyon and the main Toutle River Valley, you enter the main blast zone. Devastation is the only thing to be found here. After the long hike around the still-beautiful forests on the south side of Mount St. Helens, you enter the wastelands in front of the crater, see the destruction that occurred, and (because of your experience on the other side of the mountain) know the beauty that was lost.

Through the ash and pumice, however, the beauty of nature is still evident. The forests were leveled, the rivers filled with mud, and the lakes buried in rafts of dead trees, but the area has a raw sort of beauty. After more than two decades, plants have recolonized the ashes, and animals are returning to feed on the new grasses and flowers. During the early summer, masses of wildflowers seem particularly vibrant against the shimmering gray landscape.

This is a relatively new trail and can be difficult in places. Loose rocks, deep gravel, sand, ash, and steep climbs and traverses make hiking dangerous in places. Use extreme caution in areas where footing is questionable. Also the dry, gritty ash here is very abrasive and can cause damage to cameras, stoves, and water filters. Carry your camera in a tightly sealed case, be prepared to field-clean your cook stove, and carry iodine tablets to treat your water in case your microfilter is put out of service by the fine ash. Campground information must be obtained from the monument headquarters.

Location: South of Randle in Gifford Pinchot National Forest within the Mount St. Helens National Volcanic Monument; see Mount Rainier and the Columbia River Gorge Map 1, grid g8.

User Groups: Hikers, leashed dogs, and horses. No mountain bikes. No wheelchair facilities.

Permits: A federal Northwest Forest Pass, $5 per day or $30 annually, is required to park at the trailhead. Passes are available from ranger stations and many private vendors, online at website: www.wta.org, or by calling 800/270-7504. Visitors to any developed site in the Mount St. Helens Monument—including visitor centers, paved overlooks, and interpretive areas—are required to pay an $8 fee per person for a Monument Pass. The pass is valid for three days. Anyone attempting to climb the peak or just scramble on the upper slopes must register in the town of Cougar and pay a $15 climbing fee per person. Contact the Mount St. Helens National Volcanic Monument at 360/247-3900.

Maps: For a trail information report, contact the Mount St. Helens National Volcanic Monument at 360/247-3900. For a map of Gifford Pinchot National Forest, send $3 to Outdoor Recreation Information Center, 915 Second Avenue, Suite 442, Seattle, WA 98174; 206/220-7450. Green Trails, Inc.'s excellent topographic maps of the region are available for $3.99 each at outdoor retail outlets. Ask for number 364S, Mount St. Helens Northwest. Ask the USGS for topographic maps of the Mount St. Helens, Spirit Lake West, and Goat Mountain areas.

Directions: From Randle drive about eight miles south on Forest Service Road 25 and cross the Cispus River. Just beyond the river turn right (west) onto Forest Service Road 26. Continue about 15 miles to Forest Service Road 99. Turn right (west) onto this road and continue to the road's end and the trailhead at the Windy Ridge Interpretive Center.

Contact: Gifford Pinchot National Forest, Mount St. Helens National Volcanic Monument, 42218 Northeast Yale Bridge Road, Amboy, WA 98601-9715; 360/247-3900.

19 Plains of Abraham
8.2 mi/4.1 hrs

The Plains of Abraham—broad, barren, ash-strewn meadows that are just beginning to recover from the devastation wrought by the eruption—allow you to experience the power of an active volcano. The trail begins with spectacular views from the trailhead; Windy Ridge is the best road-accessible vantage point in the monument. The trail traverses a stark hillside on the edge of the major blast area before entering the plains from the north end, skirts the Plains of Abraham on its east side, and loops around the west flank of Pumice Butte before reaching a junction with the Ape Cave Trail (see hike in this chapter). Retrace your steps from here.

Just before leaving the north end of the plains, you find an alternate route. For a more strenuous return trip, stay on the Loowit Trail (see above) as it slants away to the left. This trail adds one-half mile to the length of the return hike and climbs an extra 600 feet, but it is worth it. The trail leads up and through Windy Pass before dropping back down to a short spur trail that leads up to Windy Ridge.

Location: South of Randle in Gifford Pinchot National Forest within the Mount St. Helens National Volcanic Monument; see Mount Rainier and the Columbia River Gorge Map 1, grid g8.

User Groups: Hikers, leashed dogs, horses, and mountain bikes. No wheelchair facilities.

Permits: A federal Northwest Forest Pass, $5 per day or $30 annually, is required to park at the trailhead. Passes are available from ranger stations and many private vendors, online at website: www.wta.org, or by calling 800/270-7504. Visitors to any developed site in the Mount St. Helens Monument—including visitor centers, paved overlooks, and interpretive areas—are required to pay an $8 fee per person for a Monument Pass. The pass is valid for three days. Anyone attempting to climb the peak or just scramble on the upper slopes must register in the town of Cougar and pay a $15 climbing fee per person. Contact the Mount St. Helens National Volcanic Monument at 360/247-3900.

Maps: For a trail information report, contact the Mount St. Helens National Volcanic Monument at 360/247-3900. For a map of Gifford Pinchot National Forest, send $3 to Outdoor Recreation Information Center, 915 Second Avenue, Suite 442, Seattle, WA 98174; 206/220-7450. Green Trails, Inc.'s excellent topographic maps of the region are available for $3.99 each at outdoor retail outlets. Ask for map number 364S, Mount St. Helens Northwest. Ask the USGS for topographic maps of the Mount St. Helens and Spirit Lake West areas.

Directions: From Randle drive about eight miles south on Forest Service Road 25 and cross the Cispus River. Just beyond the river, turn right (west) onto Forest Service Road 26. Continue about 15 miles to Forest Service Road 99. Turn right (west) onto this road and continue to the road's end and the trailhead at the Windy Ridge Interpretive Center.

Contact: Gifford Pinchot National Forest, Mount St. Helens National Volcanic Monument, 42218 Northeast Yale Bridge Road, Amboy, WA 98601-9715; 360/247-3900.

20 Lava Canyon Interpretive Trail
0.5 mi/0.5 hr

The wide, paved Lava Canyon Interpretive Trail leads to a viewing platform overlooking a stunning canyon—a deep jagged cut through a thick layer of ancient lava.

From the viewing area the trail loops down to the canyon rim in a long series of steep (for wheelchair users) switchback turns offering excellent views. The Muddy River cuts through the heart of this basalt canyon, which was scoured clean by the rushing mudflows during the 1980 eruption. This interpretive trail offers an excellent lesson in the awesome power of nature. Numerous benches line the route, offering welcome rest stops on the climb up the eight-percent grade back to the trailhead.

Location: North of Cougar in Gifford Pinchot National Forest within the Mount St. Helens National Volcanic Monument; see Mount Rainier and the Columbia River Gorge Map 1, grid h8.

User Groups: Hikers, leashed dogs, and wheelchairs. No horses or mountain bikes are allowed.

Permits: A federal Northwest Forest Pass, $5 per day or $30 annually, is required to park at the trailhead. Passes are available from ranger stations and many private vendors, online at website: www.wta.org, or by calling 800/270-7504. Visitors to any developed site in the Mount St. Helens Monument—including visitor centers, paved overlooks, and interpretive areas—are required to pay an $8 fee per person for a Monument Pass. The pass is valid for three days. Anyone attempting to climb the peak or just scramble on the upper slopes must register in the town of Cougar and pay a $15 climbing fee per person. Contact the Mount St. Helens National Volcanic Monument at 360/247-3900.

Maps: For a trail information report, contact Mount St. Helens National Volcanic Monument at 360/247-3900. For a map of Gifford Pinchot National Forest, send $3 to Outdoor Recreation Information Center, 915 Second Avenue, Suite 442, Seattle, WA 98174; 206/220-7450. Green Trails, Inc.'s excellent topographic maps of the region are available for $3.99 each at outdoor retail outlets. Ask for map number 364S, Mount St. Helens Northwest. Ask the USGS for a topographic map of the Mount St. Helens area.

Directions: From Cougar drive east on Forest Service Road 90 just one mile beyond the Swift Dam and turn left (north) onto Forest Service Road 83. Drive about 12 miles to the trailhead on the left.

Contact: Gifford Pinchot National Forest, Mount St. Helens National Volcanic Monument, 42218 Northeast Yale Bridge Road, Amboy, WA 98601-9715; 360/247-3900.

21 Jackpine Shelter Interpretive Trail
0.8 mi/0.5 hr

The Jackpine Shelter Interpretive Trail explores an old forest and its interaction with the surrounding volcanic environment. Despite the catastrophe of May 18, 1980, this beautiful, ancient forest grove remains wonderfully intact. The trees, primarily Douglas and noble firs, were sheltered—the blast's heat was most severely felt to the north of this area. The trees and forest ecosystem here survived the eruption, but some damage did occur. This trail explores the Pine Creek Basin, which was gouged deeply by massive mudflows that followed the blast. Farther on, the south flank of Mount St. Helens is visible with all its scars and mantle of gray ash. The route also passes historic Jackpine Shelter, a shack that was built in 1932 to keep backcountry visitors (primarily rangers and hunters) warm and dry.

Location: North of Cougar in Gifford Pinchot National Forest within the Mount St. Helens National Volcanic Monument; see Mount Rainier and the Columbia River Gorge Map 1, grid h8.

User Groups: Hikers and leashed dogs. No horses or mountain bikes are allowed. No wheelchair facilities.

Permits: A federal Northwest Forest Pass, $5 per day or $30 annually, is required to park at the trailhead. Passes are available from ranger stations and many private vendors, online at website: www.wta.org, or by calling 800/270-7504. Visitors to any developed site in the Mount St. Helens Monument—including visitor centers, paved overlooks, and interpretive areas—are required to pay an $8 fee per person for a Monument Pass. The pass is valid for three days. Anyone attempting to climb the peak or just scramble on the upper slopes must register in the town of Cougar and pay a $15 climbing fee per person. Contact the Mount St. Helens National Volcanic Monument at 360/247-3900.

Maps: For a trail information report, contact the Mount St. Helens National Volcanic Monument at 360/247-3900. For a map of Gifford Pinchot National Forest, send $3 to Outdoor Recreation Information Center, 915 Second Avenue, Suite 442, Seattle, WA 98174; 206/220-7450. Green Trails, Inc.'s excellent topographic maps of the region are available for $3.99 each at outdoor retail outlets. Ask for map number 364S, Mount St. Helens Northwest. Ask the USGS for topographic maps of the Smith Creek Butte and Mount St. Helens areas.

Directions: From Cougar, drive east on Forest Service Road 90 for one mile beyond Swift Dam. Turn left onto Forest Service Road 83and drive 11 miles to the trailhead on the left.

Contact: Gifford Pinchot National Forest, Mount St. Helens National Volcanic Monument, 42218 Northeast Yale Bridge Road, Amboy, WA 98601-9715; 360/247-3900.

22 June Lake
2.8 mi/1.5 hr

This scenic trail climbs gently to the shore of June Lake, a small blue pool near the timberline on Mount St. Helens' southern flank. The surrounding wildflowers are examples of the resiliency of nature, the meadows are once again lush and green, and the lake seems to host a healthy population of frogs and salamanders. The south bank of the lake is a gorgeous tapered beach of gray sand. While the cinder cone summit is hidden behind a ridge, there are good views of the south end of the Worm Flows, an interesting network of mud and lava flows.

Location: North of Cougar in Gifford Pinchot National Forest within the Mount St. Helens National Volcanic Monument; see Mount Rainier and the Columbia River Gorge Map 1, grid h8.

User Groups: Hikers and leashed dogs. No horses or mountain bikes are allowed. No wheelchair facilities.

Permits: A federal Northwest Forest Pass, $5 per day or $30 annually, is required to park at the trailhead. Passes are available from ranger stations and many private vendors, online at website: www.wta.org, or by calling 800/270-7504. Visitors to any developed site in the Mount St. Helens Monument—including visitor centers, paved overlooks, and interpretive areas—are required to pay an $8 fee per person for a Monument Pass. The pass is valid for three days. Anyone attempting to climb the peak or just scramble on the upper slopes must register in the town of Cougar and pay a $15 climbing fee per person. Contact the Mount St. Helens National Volcanic Monument at 360/247-3900.

Maps: For a trail information report, contact the Mount St. Helens National Volcanic Monument at 360/247-3900. For a map of

Gifford Pinchot National Forest, send $3 to Outdoor Recreation Information Center, 915 Second Avenue, Suite 442, Seattle, WA 98174; 206/220-7450. Green Trails, Inc.'s excellent topographic maps of the region are available for $3.99 each at outdoor retail outlets. Ask for map number 364S, Mount St. Helens Northwest. Ask the USGS for a topographic map of the Mount St. Helens area.

Directions: From Cougar drive east on Forest Service Road 90 just one mile beyond the Swift Dam and turn left (north) onto Forest Service Road 83. Drive 10 miles on Forest Service Road 83 to the trailhead on the left.

Contact: Gifford Pinchot National Forest, Mount St. Helens National Volcanic Monument, 42218 Northeast Yale Bridge Road, Amboy, WA 98601-9715; 360/247-3900.

23 Trail of Two Forests Loop
0.6 mi/0.5 hr

The two forests in question are separated in age by 2,000 years, but they stand side by side. One forest is a lush, old-growth Douglas fir and western red cedar ecosystem that surrounds this boardwalk trail. The other is a young forest that was originally engulfed and consumed by the lava flows from an eruption of Mount St. Helens more than two millennia ago. The trees from that ancient forest are gone, and all that remains are the imprints left by their burning hulks in the cooling lava. The lava solidified faster than the trees burned, and as a result there are hollow impressions of trees engulfed by the river of rock. These three-dimensional imprints of trees are called lava tubes, and this scenic loop trip offers plenty of opportunity to study them.

Location: North of Cougar in Gifford Pinchot National Forest within the Mount St. Helens National Volcanic Monument; see Mount Rainier and the Columbia River Gorge Map 1, grid h6.

User Groups: Hikers, leashed dogs, and wheelchairs. No horses or mountain bikes are allowed.

Permits: A federal Northwest Forest Pass, $5 per day or $30 annually, is required to park at the trailhead. Passes are available from ranger stations and many private vendors, online at website: www.wta.org, or by calling 800/270-7504. Visitors to any developed site in the Mount St. Helens Monument—including visitor centers, paved overlooks, and interpretive areas—are required to pay an $8 fee per person for a Monument Pass. The pass is valid for three days. Anyone attempting to climb the peak or just scramble on the upper slopes must register in the town of Cougar and pay a $15 climbing fee per person. Contact the Mount St. Helens National Volcanic Monument at 360/247-3900.

Maps: For a trail information report, contact the Mount St. Helens National Volcanic Monument at 360/247-3900. For a map of Gifford Pinchot National Forest, send $3 to Outdoor Recreation Information Center, 915 Second Avenue, Suite 442, Seattle, WA 98174; 206/220-7450. Green Trails, Inc.'s excellent topographic maps of the region are available for $3.99 each at outdoor retail outlets. Ask for map number 364S, Mount St. Helens Northwest. Ask the USGS for a topographic map of the Mount St. Helens area.

Directions: From Cougar drive east on Forest Service Road 90 just one mile beyond the Swift Dam and turn left (north) onto Forest Service Road 83. Drive two miles and turn left onto Forest Service Road 8303. Continue for one-half mile to the trailhead on the right.

Contact: Gifford Pinchot National Forest, Mount St. Helens National Volcanic Monument, 42218 Northeast Yale Bridge Road, Amboy, WA 98601-9715; 360/247-3900.

24 Lower Siouxon
6.4 mi/3.2 hrs

Lower Siouxon is first section of the Siouxon River Trail; it makes a great day hike and is often ignored by those planning to hike the length of the main trail. This short route parallels the access road and links the upper and lower trailheads. The route features a gradual descent, but doesn't drop all the way down to river level. You may be able to see and hear the river occasionally, but Lower Siouxon isn't really a river trail. It is, instead, a beautiful forest hike that offers a history lesson.

The history of the area is exemplified by mossy little Hickmans Cabin. It was built in the early 1930s by the firefighters who moved into the area to suppress and battle the fires that frequently plagued the area. The cabin was used as an advance supply hut, and firefighters stored and sharpened their tools and cooked their meals here. The scars of the fires they fought are still visible. Much of the fallen timber rotting along the route was killed by the fires and later toppled over. At the end of the trail is the second Siouxon Trailhead. Either arrange for a shuttle vehicle to pick you up here, or simply turn around and retrace your steps to the lower trailhead.

Location: East of Woodland in Gifford Pinchot National Forest; see Mount Rainier and the Columbia River Gorge Map 1, grid h7.

User Groups: Hikers, leashed dogs, horses, and mountain bikes. No wheelchair facilities.

Permits: A federal Northwest Forest Pass, $5 per day or $30 annually, is required to park at the trailhead. Passes are available from ranger stations and many private vendors, online at website: www.wta.org, or by calling 800/270-7504.

Maps: For a trail information report, contact the Wind River Information/Work Center at 509/427-3200. For a map of Gifford Pinchot National Forest, send $3 to Outdoor Recreation Information Center, 915 Second Avenue, Suite 442, Seattle, WA 98174; 206/220-7450. Green Trails, Inc.'s excellent topographic maps of the region are available for $3.99 each at outdoor retail outlets. Ask for map number 396, Lookout Mountain. Ask the USGS for a topographic map of the Gifford Peak area.

Directions: From Woodland drive about 22 miles east on Highway 503 past Lake Merwin and south across the Lewis River. Just south of the Lewis River Bridge, turn left (east) onto Forest Service Road 54 and continue about 10 miles to its junction with Forest Service Road 57. Turn left and within one-quarter mile turn left again onto Forest Service Road 5701. Continue to the road's end and the trailhead.

Contact: Gifford Pinchot National Forest, Wind River Information/Work Center, 1262 Hemlock Road, Carson, WA 98610; 509/427-3200.

25 Curly Creek Waterfalls
0.3 mi/0.3 hr

A pair of waterfalls are visible from this broad, compact-gravel trail. Climbing through a thick stand of Douglas and noble fir, the route breaks into the open at a viewpoint overlooking Curly Falls, a pretty cascade on the Lewis River. Enjoy the crashing water before moving up the trail to a second viewing platform. At this point the scenery consists of Miller Creek Falls, a smaller cascade that is as picturesque as Curly Falls. The trail doesn't provide river access, but it is a good place to watch the falls and the autumn anglers trying to catch spawning steelhead trout.

Although this trail is outside the official boundary of Mount St. Helens National

Volcanic Monument, the monument office administers the whole area.

Location: East of Cougar in Gifford Pinchot National Forest; see Mount Rainier and the Columbia River Gorge Map 1, grid h8.

User Groups: Hikers, leashed dogs, and wheelchairs. No horses or mountain bikes are allowed.

Permits: A federal Northwest Forest Pass, $5 per day or $30 annually, is required to park at the trailhead. Passes are available from ranger stations and many private vendors, online at website: www.wta.org, or by calling 800/270-7504. Visitors to any developed site in the Mount St. Helens Monument—including visitor centers, paved overlooks, and interpretive areas—are required to pay an $8 fee per person for a Monument Pass. The pass is valid for three days. Anyone attempting to climb the peak or just scramble on the upper slopes must register in the town of Cougar and pay a $15 climbing fee per person. Contact the Mount St. Helens National Volcanic Monument at 360/247-3900.

Maps: For a trail information report, contact the Mount St. Helens National Volcanic Monument at 360/247-3900. For a map of Gifford Pinchot National Forest, send $3 to Outdoor Recreation Information Center, 915 Second Avenue, Suite 442, Seattle, WA 98174; 206/220-7450. Green Trails, Inc.'s excellent topographic maps of the region are available for $3.99 each at outdoor retail outlets. Ask for map number 364, Mount St. Helens. Ask the USGS for a topographic map of the Mount St. Helens area.

Directions: From Cougar drive about 20 miles east on Forest Service Road 90 to its junction with Forest Service Road 9039. Turn left (north) onto this road and continue three-quarters of a mile. Cross the Lewis River and then turn into the parking area on the left, just beyond the bridge.

Contact: Gifford Pinchot National Forest, Mount St. Helens National Volcanic Monument, 42218 Northeast Yale Bridge Road, Amboy, WA 98601-9715; 360/247-3900.

26 Green Lake
3.6 mi/1.5 hrs

It might not seem right that one of the loveliest spots in Mount Rainier National Park lies a mere 1.8 miles off a semi-major highway. It will seem right once you get there. Everything seems right, in fact, on the shores of Green Lake and along the trail leading to it. It's an easy, mile-long walk through spectacular old-growth forest to spellbinding Ranger Creek Falls, just off the main trail. A mile later you're at the lake, which always seems peaceful no matter how rowdy the weather. Rest here for a short time and offer a brief thanks to the Park Service, which unlike its cousin the Forest Service, long ago saw the need to make some fragile areas off-limits to overnight camping. This is one such place. Enjoy it with the kids and then bring them back here with their kids someday and see how the lake has fared. You might be pleasantly surprised. The trail is usually snow-free from June through October.

Location: In the Carbon River drainage of Mount Rainier National Park; see Mount Rainier and the Columbia River Gorge Map 2, grid a1.

User Groups: Hikers only. No dogs, horses, or mountain bikes are allowed. No wheelchair facilities.

Permits: A $10-per-car access fee is collected at all park entrances. Day-hiking permits are not required. Wilderness permits are required for all backcountry camping. Some permits can be reserved in advance for a fee. Others are issued free no more than 24 hours before departure. Contact the Outdoor Recreation Information Center at 206/470-4060.

Maps: For a free map of Mount Rainier National Park, contact the Outdoor Recreation Information Center at 206/470-4060. Green Trails, Inc.'s excellent topographic maps of the region are available for $3.99 each at outdoor retail outlets. Ask for map number 269, Mount Rainier West. Ask the USGS for a topographic map of the Mowich Lake area.

Directions: From Puyallup drive 13 miles east on Highway 410 to Buckley. Turn right (south) onto Highway 165. Proceed to the bridge over the Carbon River Gorge and then bear left to Mount Rainier National Park's Carbon River entrance. Just over three miles beyond the entrance station, look for the trailhead on the right, where Ranger Creek runs beneath the road.

Contact: Outdoor Recreation Information Center, Seattle REI, 222 Yale Avenue North, Seattle, WA 98109; 206/470-4060.

27 Windy Gap
13.0 mi/9.0 hrs

The Windy Gap Trail is a good overnighter for hikers who want to escape the mass-transit crowds on many Rainier day-hiking trails. From Ipsut Creek Campground, stay left at the junctions to Ipsut Creek and Spray Park (see hike in this chapter) and cross the Carbon River on a footlog, at about 2.1 miles. On the other side, you turn sharply left, leaving the Wonderland Trail and climbing up over many switchbacks to Yellowstone Cliff Meadows, where a campsite awaits amid bear grass run amok. It's about a mile farther (up) beyond several small lakes to 5,800-foot Windy Gap, where it seems as if the mountain gods got carried away one day and began flipping large boulders around like Vegas dice.

It's well worth the time to venture another long mile past Lake James and then about a mile northeast to a viewpoint of the Natural Bridge, a massive rock arch across a ravine. Continue east from here to hike Rainier's Northern Loop, which leads to the Fire Creek and Berkeley Camps near Sunrise; it then swings back west on the Wonderland Trail over Skyscraper Pass to Granite Creek Park, the Winthrop Glacier, Mystic Lake, and (ultimately) the start at Ipsut Creek Campground. The total loop is about 35 miles and leads through some of the most unspoiled and untrammeled alpine areas of the park. Allow four or five days, but if you've got a week, you'll be glad you took it. Upper portions of this trail are snow-covered until midsummer.

Location: Near the Carbon Glacier on the northern slopes of Mount Rainier; see Mount Rainier and the Columbia River Gorge Map 2, grid a2.

User Groups: Hikers only. No dogs, horses, or mountain bikes are allowed. No wheelchair facilities.

Permits: A $10-per-car access fee is collected at all park entrances. Day-hiking permits are not required. Wilderness permits are required for all backcountry camping. Some permits can be reserved in advance for a fee. Others are issued free no more than 24 hours before departure. Contact the Outdoor Recreation Information Center at 206/470-4060.

Maps: For a free map of Mount Rainier National Park, contact the Outdoor Recreation Information Center at 206/470-4060. Green Trails, Inc.'s excellent topographic maps of the region are available for $3.99 each at outdoor retail outlets. Ask for map number 269, Mount Rainier West. Ask the USGS for topographic maps of the Mowich Lake and Sunrise areas.

Directions: From Puyallup drive 13 miles east on Highway 410 to Buckley. Turn right (south) onto Highway 165. Proceed to the

Highway Access: Roads in and around Mount Rainier National Park close frequently because of flooding or winter weather. One, Carbon River Road, has washed out several times in the past five years, and as this book went to press, was open to traffic. The washed-out section, about five miles below the road's end at Ipsut Creek Campground, has been patched back together somewhat temporarily. It's rough, but most cars can maneuver across it. But don't assume this road—or, for that matter, the Mowich Lake Road—will be open or in good shape when you go. If the Carbon River Road is closed at the perennial washout, or if you don't want to risk your passenger car on its rocky grade, add appropriate mileage (6 to 10 miles round-trip) to all Carbon River–area hikes listed in this section (many hikers prefer to mountain bike the closed road section.) Call the park before embarking on any Carbon River–area hike.

West Side Road: Also worth noting is the state of the West Side Road, home to many of the park's most popular day hikes before frequent washouts caused its closure three miles north of the Paradise-Longmire Road near the Park's Nisqually Entrance Station. At this writing, much of the worst washout damage on this road has been repaired. However, the park service, citing safety concerns about potentially violent Tahoma Creek, has no plans to open it to auto traffic. The park does plan to implement a shuttle service on the road, from the parking area at the washout to trailheads farther up the road. At this writing, no funding for the shuttle exists, and it might be several years away or more. Call the park for current West Side Road information.

Winter access: Most of Highway 123 (Cayuse Pass) and Highway 410 (Chinook Pass) and all roads within Mount Rainier National Park are closed in winter—roughly from November through May—except the road between the Nisqually entrance and Paradise, which is kept open year-round, conditions permitting. Always call Mount Rainier National Park's recorded information line at 360/569-2211 for current road conditions before setting out.

Backcountry Permits: After several years of experimenting with a wilderness

bridge over the Carbon River Gorge and bear left to Mount Rainier National Park's Carbon River entrance. Proceed five miles to the trailhead at the road's end at Ipsut Creek Campground. Hike the Wonderland Trail 2.1 miles to the Northern Loop Trailhead near the Carbon River. Note: Carbon River Road was washed out in 1996 and at press time had not been repaired.

Contact: Outdoor Recreation Information Center, Seattle REI, 222 Yale Avenue North, Seattle, WA 98109; 206/470-4060.

28 Carbon Glacier/Mystic Lake
15.2 mi/1.0–2.0 days

Many a Northwesterner got his or her first close rub with a glacier here, on a trail that can be an easy day hike to the Carbon Glacier or an overnight trip/exhausting day hike to Mystic Lake. The Carbon Glacier Trail, actually part of Rainier's Wonderland Trail (see hike in this chapter), leads gradually upward two miles from Ipsut Creek Campground to a junction with the Northern Loop Trail and permit/fee system, Mount Rainier National Park has settled on one that seems to please most hikers—or at least not anger as many as previous attempts. It works thusly: No day-use permits are required. Wilderness permits, required for all overnight backcountry camping, are free—unless you're making a reservation, which you'll likely need at popular backcountry camps in the summer. The vast majority of the park's backcountry areas are under an overnight-quota system between May 1 and September 30. Overnight hikers bound for popular backcountry destinations in the summertime thus face a choice: Pay for a reserved permit or try your luck at getting one on the day of departure. For a flat, nonrefundable fee of $20, hiking parties can reserve a backcountry campsite up to 60 days in advance by calling 360/569-HIKE. Roughly 60 percent of the site permits for each quota area will be made available for these reservations. Remaining sites will be dispensed free at ranger stations, no more than 24 hours in advance, on a first-come, first-served basis.

Note: Reservations are not available for backcountry trips outside the May 1 to September 30 quota period. Reservations aren't always necessary for midweek, early, or late-season hikes. But if you're planning to backpack in the park on Friday through Sunday in the summer, a reservation is a good idea. Also, park officials say the volume of calls seeking reservations has been extremely heavy, prompting complaints about long waits. If you want to avoid the long phone call, you can download a Wilderness Permit Reservation form from the Mount Rainier website, www.nps.gov/mora/recreation/rsvpform.htm. Fill it out and fax it to 360/569-3131 or mail it to: Wilderness Information Center, Mount Rainier National Park, Tahoma Woods, Star Route, Ashford, WA 98304-9751. Include contact information with your fax. The Wilderness Information Center at Longmire, which processes wilderness permit reservations, typically opens to the public in late May. If you don't have a backcountry reservation but are flexible regarding destinations, it's usually worth stopping in. They often have space available somewhere in the park.

Reservations also are accepted for space at Camp Muir and Camp Schurman, Mount Rainier's two alpine climbing bivouac camps. Be warned that the park continues to tinker with its fee system. These rules could change! Call the park at 360/569-2211, or visit the website www.nps.gov/mora, for current permit information.

then turns upward along the Carbon River to a junction with the Spray Park/Seattle Park Trail at about three miles. Just beyond here you come to a rather lanky suspension bridge over the river. The bridge is not for the faint-hearted, who can bypass it by backtracking, hiking east 0.3 mile on the Northern Loop Trail, then turning right and proceeding up the other side of the river on the Mystic Lake Trail. Once safely across, turn right and follow the moraine steeply upward to an excellent viewpoint of the glacier, the lowest-elevation glacier in the Lower 48 states and one of the more melt-resistant ice fingers on Rainier. Most people stop here at about 3.5 miles; the trail beyond shows why, as it gets steep, rocky, and downright ornery for approximately the next mile up to Dick Creek Camp.

Beyond, you enter the delightful Moraine Park area, where wildflowers and views collide to leave you spellbound. Continue onward and upward on the Wonderland Trail toward Curtis Ridge and you find yourself at Mystic Lake, so named because early explorers noticed an unexplained whirlpool in the water. Look for it yourself by plunging your head into the icy water, removing it, then screaming quite loudly. Shake your head and close your eyes. See the spinning water? We thought you would. When you recover, gaze south at to-die-for views of Rainier's extremely handsome north face, marked by the unmistakable, 3,500-foot rock face known as the Willis Wall. You also find a summer ranger camp here and, rest assured, the ranger will remind you to camp in designated sites one-half mile farther down the trail, not at the lake. Heed the advice.

Location: On the north side of the Carbon Glacier, in the Carbon River drainage of Mount Rainier National Park; see Mount Rainier and the Columbia River Gorge Map 2, grid a2.

User Groups: Hikers only. No dogs, horses, or mountain bikes are allowed. No wheelchair facilities.

Permits: A $10-per-car access fee is collected at all park entrances. Day-hiking permits are not required. Wilderness permits are required for all backcountry camping. Some permits can be reserved in advance for a fee. Others are issued free no more than 24 hours before departure. Contact the Outdoor Recreation Information Center at 206/470-4060.

Maps: For a map of Mount Rainier National Park, contact the Outdoor Recreation Information Center at 206/470-4060. Green Trails, Inc.'s excellent topographic maps of the region are available for $3.99 each at outdoor retail outlets. Ask for map number 269, Mount Rainier West. Ask the USGS for a topographic map of the Mowich Lake area.

Directions: From Puyallup drive 13 miles east on Highway 410 to Buckley. Turn right (south) onto Highway 165. Proceed to the bridge over the Carbon River Gorge and then bear left to Mount Rainier National Park's Carbon River entrance. Proceed five miles to the trailhead at the road's end at Ipsut Creek Campground. Note: Carbon River Road was washed out in early 1999 and at press time had not been repaired.

Contact: Outdoor Recreation Information Center, Seattle REI, 222 Yale Avenue North, Seattle, WA 98109; 206/470-4060.

29 Tolmie Peak Lookout
6.4 mi/3.5 hrs

Bring the kids for this one so they can join everyone else's kids in trooping up to see grand views at a lovely alpine lake, with none of those raspy-looking backpacker types fouling the air along the trail. Tolmie Peak is a day-hiker's special. It's about the right distance, offers the right touch of outdoor magic at its destination, and has been ruled off-limits to overnighters, except for a few who receive special permits to camp in the bush, away from fragile Eunice Lake. The trail meanders about 1.25 miles to Ipsut Pass (elevation 5,100 feet), where more ambitious hikers can continue north along Ipsut Creek to the Carbon River and the Wonderland Trail. Stay left and walk another 1.75 miles to Eunice Lake, which offers grand views of Tolmie Peak and its lookout tower, not to mention a little molehill to the east known as Tahoma. Cinch down your knapsack and head on up the trail, climbing steeply another mile to Tolmie Peak, where the panorama is worth every one of the painful steps it took to get here. Mount Rainier National Park ranks this hike as one of its better family day hikes. Whether the kids make it beyond Eunice Lake or not, we have to agree. Expect crowds on weekends—big ones.

Location: Northwest of Mount Rainier in the Carbon River drainage of Mount Rainier

National Park; see Mount Rainier and the Columbia River Gorge Map 2, grid a2.

User Groups: Hikers only. No dogs, horses, or mountain bikes are allowed. No wheelchair facilities.

Permits: A $10-per-car access fee is collected at all park entrances. Day-hiking permits are not required. Wilderness permits are required for all backcountry camping. Some permits can be reserved in advance for a fee. Others are issued free no more than 24 hours before departure. Contact the Outdoor Recreation Information Center at 206/470-4060.

Maps: For a free map of Mount Rainier National Park, contact the Outdoor Recreation Information Center at 206/470-4060. Green Trails, Inc.'s excellent topographic maps of the region are available for $3.99 each at outdoor retail outlets. Ask for map number 269, Mount Rainier West. Ask the USGS for topographic maps of the Mowich Lake and Golden Lakes areas.

Directions: From Puyallup drive 13 miles east on Highway 410 to Buckley. Turn right (south) onto Highway 165 and proceed through Carbonado. Just beyond the Carbon River Gorge bridge, bear right onto Mowich Lake Road. Follow the road about 17 miles to its end and find the trailhead on the left (north) side of the road, near Mowich Lake. Note: Carbon River Road was washed out in early 1999 and at press time had not been repaired. See the highway access note in the Mount Rainier sidebar in this chapter.

Contact: Outdoor Recreation Information Center, Seattle REI, 222 Yale Avenue North, Seattle, WA 98109; 206/470-4060.

30 Spray Park
6.0 mi/3.0 hrs

In many ways, you never recover from your first walk into Spray Park. The trail isn't difficult to follow. It's just difficult to forget. The three-mile walk leads to seemingly endless open meadows of heather and alpine blossoms that tease the nose, ease the mind, and tickle the imagination. The place is a virtual lily factory. The so-called park itself—actually a vast corridor of open meadows interspersed among rocky moraines, lingering snow patches, whistling marmots, and sunbasking hikers—is a wonder to behold in the summer and truly qualifies as one of Rainier's most magnificent day-hike destinations. Even though the Mowich entrance to Rainier is a lesser-used, backdoor way into the park, this trail also can be (understandably) quite crowded. But Spray Park is a broad enough area, rife with so many hidden pockets of meadow between rock formations, that it's still possible to grab some solitude among the blossoms.

From Mowich Lake the trail drops quickly to a junction with the Wonderland Trail and then climbs gradually to a side trail leading down to Spray Falls, a short, worthwhile side trip. You climb steeply to a vista of Mount Rainier at Eagle's Cliff overlook before winding into the open alpine area of Spray Park. Rainier is in full glory from here, offering great views of the Russell and North Mowich Glaciers. Lower down, the remnants of the Flett Glacier are reached via an easy off-trail jaunt to the east. And there's a bonus: Spray Park isn't really a destination, per se, it's just a section of a magnificent trail that continues north between Mount Pleasant and Mount Rainier, through alpine country to similarly beautiful Seattle Park, Cataract Camp, and (ultimately) Carbon River Camp at the toe of the Carbon Glacier, the lowest-altitude glacier in the Lower 48. From here a backpacker or sturdy day hiker can turn northwest on the Wonderland Trail for 2.5 miles and then southwest on the Ipsut Creek Trail for a five-mile walk back to the Mowich Lake parking lot. The total mileage for this tough-to-beat loop is about 15.5 miles. Your feet might not be glad you did it, but your soul will.

Location: On the northwest slope of Mount Rainier in the Carbon River area; see Mount Rainier and the Columbia River Gorge Map 2, grid a2.

User Groups: Hikers only. No dogs, horses, or mountain bikes are allowed. No wheelchair facilities.

Permits: A $10-per-car access fee is collected at all park entrances. Day-hiking permits are not required. Wilderness permits are required for all backcountry camping. Some permits can be reserved in advance for a fee. Others are issued free no more than 24 hours before departure. Contact the Outdoor Recreation Information Center at 206/470-4060.

Maps: For a free map of Mount Rainier National Park, contact the Outdoor Recreation Information Center at 206/470-4060. Green Trails, Inc.'s excellent topographic maps of the region are available for $3.99 each at outdoor retail outlets. Ask for map number 269, Mount Rainier West. Ask the USGS for a topographic map of the Mowich Lake area.

Directions: From Puyallup drive 13 miles east on Highway 410 to Buckley. Turn right (south) onto Highway 165 and proceed through Carbonado. Just beyond the Carbon River Gorge bridge, bear right onto Mowich Lake Road. Follow the road about 17 miles to its end; the trailhead is at the far end of the Mowich Lake Campground. See the highway access note in the Mount Rainier Sidebar.

Contact: Outdoor Recreation Information Center, Seattle REI, 222 Yale Avenue North, Seattle, WA 98109; 206/470-4060.

31 Crystal Mountain
9.0 mi one way/5.0 hrs

Wild, this trail is not. Right in the middle of it is a high-tech, high-powered, high-visibility six-holer ski lift and a ridgetop restaurant. And part of the trail below is a road. But the surrounding countryside viewed from here is quite wild, making the Crystal Mountain loop a good summer day hike. It can be done a multitude of ways by connecting with Crystal Mountain Road and other local trails at various points. But most people prefer to do the hike as a one-way trip, beginning at Sand Flats. The trail climbs steadily three miles to its first excellent Rainier views. Continue another three miles along the ridgetop, through several alpine basins to the chairlift/restaurant on top, at an elevation of 6,500 feet. From here you drop to Hen Skin Lakes and hang a left on the Silver Creek Trail 1192, which drops quickly 1.5 miles back to the Crystal Mountain parking area. Then hop in your strategically placed second car or hoof it some two miles back down Road 7190-410, cross the highway, and wind up back where you started. Another option is to pay Crystal Mountain to jet you to the top on the chairlift and hike the loop downhill in either direction to a waiting vehicle. Whichever way you go, Crystal's high country is beautiful, easily accessible terrain. And if you get up early, you might even see an elk or two.

Location: Near Crystal Mountain Ski Area northeast of Mount Rainier; see Mount Rainier and the Columbia River Gorge Map 2, grid a4.

User Groups: Hikers, leashed dogs, horses, and mountain bikes. No wheelchair facilities.

Permits: A federal Northwest Forest Pass, $5 per day or $30 annually, is required to park at the trailhead. Passes are available from ranger stations and many private vendors,

online at website: www.wta.org, or by calling 800/270-7504.

Maps: For a map of the Mount Baker-Snoqualmie National Forest, contact the Outdoor Recreation Information Center, Seattle REI, 222 Yale Avenue North, Seattle, WA 98109; 206/470-4060. Green Trails, Inc.'s excellent topographic maps of the region are available for $3.99 each at outdoor retail outlets. Ask for map number 271, Bumping Lake. Ask the USGS for topographic maps of the Bumping Lake and White River Park areas.

Directions: From Enumclaw drive 33 miles east on Highway 410 to Crystal Mountain Road/Forest Service Road 7190. Turn left and drive 4.4 miles to Forest Service Road 7190-510. Turn right and drive half a mile to the trailhead, horse ramp, and camping area at Sand Flats.

Contact: Mount Baker-Snoqualmie National Forest, Snoqualmie Ranger District, 42404 SE North Bend Way, North Bend, WA 98045; 425/888-1421.

32 Norse Peak
9.4 mi/5.5 hrs

You've got your abandoned lookout site with sweeping views of Mount Rainier; you've got your splendid alpine meadows, rich with wildflowers and complemented by a small lake. And you'd better have your boots laced up tight: this baby climbs. The trail begins on the road to Crystal Mountain Ski Area and gains ground rapidly, quickly opening to views of Mount Rainier beyond the ridge to the southwest. At four miles, when you've exhausted most of this trail's 3,000 vertical feet, you arrive at a junction. The trail to the left (north) drops quickly to the Pacific Crest Trail and then enters Crow Creek Basin, which has good campsites surrounded by much summer greenery. The right fork climbs another three-fourths of a mile to Norse

Peak (elevation 6,856 feet). Day hikers with gumption can visit the green meadows and stony summit on one long trip. Long-distance hikers note: You can continue down the PCT from Big Crow Basin and hit a short connecting trail to the right to the Crow Creek Trail, which leads about six miles east to Crow Creek Lake and then seven miles south to Highway 410 east of Pleasant Valley Campground.

Location: Northeast of Crystal Mountain Ski Area in the Norse Peak Wilderness; see Mount Rainier and the Columbia River Gorge Map 2, grid a4.

User Groups: Hikers, leashed dogs, and horses. No mountain bikes. No wheelchair facilities.

Permits: A federal Northwest Forest Pass, $5 per day or $30 annually, is required to park at the trailhead. Passes are available from ranger stations and many private vendors, online at website: www.wta.org, or by calling 800/270-7504.

Maps: For a map of the William O. Douglas and Norse Peak Wilderness, contact the Outdoor Recreation Information Center, Seattle REI, 222 Yale Avenue North, Seattle, WA 98109; 206/470-4060. Green Trails, Inc.'s excellent topographic maps of the area are available for $3.99 each at outdoor retail outlets. Ask for map number 271, Bumping Lake. Ask the USGS for a topographic map of the Norse Peak area.

Directions: From Enumclaw drive 33 miles east on Highway 410 to Crystal Mountain Road/Forest Service Road 7190. Turn left and drive 4.2 miles to a parking area on the shoulder. Walk a short distance up Forest Service Road 7190-410 to the trailhead on the left.

Contact: Mount Baker-Snoqualmie National Forest, Snoqualmie Ranger District, 42404 SE North Bend Way, North Bend, WA 98045; 425/888-1421.

33 Grand Park/Berkeley Park
13.0 mi/7.0 hrs

This is wildflower central. In July when the deep, oppressive snows of Rainier finally recede far enough for the park to dig out the Sunrise Lodge and patch up Sunrise Road, open meadows burst into brilliant fireworks displays all around Sunrise. Berkeley and Grand Parks are as good a place as you'll find to plop down in their midst, stare up at the summit, and attempt to etch the magic of the moment forever onto your brain. Berkeley Park, tucked up against the north indent of Burroughs Mountain, comes first, just less than a mile after Frozen Lake. You come to a junction here with the Wonderland Trail, which continues west to Skyscraper Pass and Granite Creek Camp, part of the Northern Loop Hike. Keep right at the junction and follow the Northern Loop Trail through a fascinating series of split-level meadows, each filled with its own splash of low-level summer color. Beyond Berkeley Camp, the trail drops a bit, passing a waterfall on Lodi Creek, and then climbs again to Grand Park, a massive, flat meadow that almost looks bizarre among the steep, rocky gullies of this region. Stroll the length of this spectacular parkland, and if time allows, continue three miles east to a campsite at Lake Eleanor, below 6,100-foot Scarface. The Grand Park area, about 6.5 miles from the car, is alive with wildlife—and people. Arriving midweek helps to avoid the crush, but not much. If you're after solitude, try hitting this one (and other Sunrise-area trails, for that matter) very early in the day. Whatever time of the day it is, don't tromp on the meadows, or we will hunt you down and insist you recite the 10 essentials immediately.

Location: Near Sunrise on the northeast slopes of Mount Rainier; see Mount Rainier and the Columbia River Gorge Map 2, grid a3.

User Groups: Hikers only. No dogs, horses, or mountain bikes. No wheelchair facilities.

Permits: A $10-per-car access fee is collected at all park entrances. Day-hiking permits are not required. Wilderness permits are required for all backcountry camping. Some permits can be reserved in advance for a fee. Others are issued free no more than 24 hours before departure. Contact the Outdoor Recreation Information Center at 206/470-4060.

Maps: For a free map of Mount Rainier National Park, contact the Outdoor Recreation Information Center at 206/470-4060. Green Trails, Inc.'s excellent topographic maps of the region are available for $3.99 each at outdoor retail outlets. Ask for map number 270, Mount Rainier East. Ask the USGS for a topographic map of the Sunrise area.

Directions: From Enumclaw drive 43 miles east on Highway 410 to the Mount Rainier National Park White River Entrance Station. Proceed to Sunrise Road and follow it 17 miles west to the large parking lot and visitor center at the road's end. The trailhead is at the north end of the parking lot, near the picnic area. Hike to Frozen Lake and continue straight on the main stem. Note: Sunrise Road usually doesn't open until early July. Call the park at 360/569-2211 for road information.

Contact: Outdoor Recreation Information Center, Seattle REI, 222 Yale Avenue North, Seattle, WA 98109; 206/470-4060.

34 Mount Fremont Lookout
5.6 mi/3.0 hrs

The Mount Fremont Trail, an easy half-day hike from the popular (and spectacular) Sunrise area, is an extremely popular hike that can be combined with other Sunrise-area destinations for a full day of wandering among some of the most spectacular mountain and alpine parkland scenery in the United States. From its common trailhead at Sunrise, the trail climbs a third of a mile to the top of Sourdough Ridge, and then turns left (west) along the ridgetop for 1.2 miles, passing small Frozen Lake. Watch for winking blond marmots in the rocks. At lake's end is a three-way intersection. The left trail goes to Burroughs Mountain and the center trail to Berkeley Park and Grand Park. For Mount Fremont turn due north (right). It's an easy 1.3 miles through magnificent meadow and rugged rock-ridge terrain to the lookout, situated to keep watch on hundreds of miles of rolling green (or clear-cut) forest all the way to the Central Cascades and Olympics. If conditions are right, your binoculars might even find downtown Seattle. Look for the brown haze. Up closer if your timing is right, you might see mountain goats. Excellent Rainier views, of course, tantalize you all along the route. Expect heavy traffic (many, many gapers) on this trail, which gains 1,200 feet one way, all summer long. It's a good family hike—even if you're here without a family. Long-distance hikers can continue straight on the Huckleberry Creek Trail, which leads about 10 miles downhill to the northern National Park Boundary.

Location: Near Sunrise on the northeast slopes of Mount Rainier; see Mount Rainier and the Columbia River Gorge Map 2, grid a3.

User Groups: Hikers only. No dogs, horses, or mountain bikes. No wheelchair facilities.

Permits: A $10-per-car access fee is collected at all park entrances. Day-hiking permits are not required. Wilderness permits are required for all backcountry camping. Some permits can be reserved in advance for a fee. Others are issued free no more than 24 hours before departure. Contact the Outdoor Recreation Information Center at 206/470-4060.

Maps: For a free map of Mount Rainier National Park, contact the Outdoor Recreation Information Center at 206/470-4060. Green Trails, Inc.'s excellent topographic maps of the region are available for $3.99 each at outdoor retail outlets. Ask for map number 270, Mount Rainier East. Ask the USGS for a topographic map of the Sunrise area.

Directions: From Enumclaw drive 43 miles east on Highway 410 to the Mount Rainier National Park White River Entrance Station. Proceed to Sunrise Road and follow it 17 miles west to the large parking lot and visitor center at the road's end. The trailhead is at the north end of the parking lot, near the picnic area. Note: Sunrise Road usually doesn't open until early July. Call the park at 360/569-2211 for road information.

Contact: Outdoor Recreation Information Center, Seattle REI, 222 Yale Avenue North, Seattle, WA 98109; 206/470-4060.

35 Sourdough Ridge/Dege Peak
4.0 mi/2.0 hrs

If you're looking for a quick way to get away from the car and into Mount Rainier's alpine splendor, this is your express lane to ecstasy. The Sourdough Ridge Trail, which begins in the thick of the tourist-choked Sunrise Visitor Center, leaves it all fairly quickly, climbing to a ridgetop and turning east beneath Antler Peak. The trail follows the ridgetop east, with absolutely stunning views of brilliant white and ice-blue Rainier to the south, occasional views of national forest lands to the north, and the almost unnaturally brilliant green parklands of Yakima Park constantly at your feet. At Dege Peak (elevation 7,006 feet) scan the distant view of Mount Adams and the close-up view of the Cowlitz Chimneys and Sarvent Glacier to the south.

Bring water. Bring a camera. Bring a friend. Years later,

you'll look at the cheesy poses against the stunning Rainier backdrop and remember when times were really good. Whenever you're up here in the summer, times truly are.

If you can arrange transportation, this trail makes a good three-mile, one-way shuttle hike between the Sunrise Visitor Center and Sunrise Point Trailhead on Sunrise Road (see hike in this chapter).

Location: North of Sunrise in Mount Rainier National Park; see Mount Rainier and the Columbia River Gorge Map 2, grid a3.

User Groups: Hikers only. No dogs, horses, or mountain bikes. No wheelchair facilities.

Permits: A $10-per-car access fee is collected at all park entrances. Day-hiking permits are not required. Wilderness permits are required for all backcountry camping. Some permits can be reserved in advance for a fee. Others are issued free no more than 24 hours before departure. Contact the Outdoor Recreation Information Center at 206/470-4060.

Maps: For a free map of Mount Rainier National Park, contact the Outdoor Recreation Information Center at 206/470-4060. Green Trails, Inc.'s excellent topographic maps of the region are available for $3.99 each at outdoor retail outlets. Ask for map number 270, Mount Rainier East. Ask the USGS for a topographic map of the Sunrise area.

Directions: From Enumclaw drive 43 miles east on Highway 410 to the Mount Rainier National Park White River Entrance Station. Proceed to Sunrise Road and follow it 17 miles west to the large parking lot and visitor center at the road's end. The trailhead is at the north end of the parking lot, near the picnic area. Note: Sunrise Road usually doesn't open until early July. Call the park at 360/569-2211 for road information.

Contact: Outdoor Recreation Information Center, Seattle REI, 222 Yale Avenue North, Seattle, WA 98109; 206/470-4060.

36 Palisades Lakes
7.0 mi/4.0 hrs

This extremely popular Mount Rainier trail might be a disappointment if you're coming just to look at the mountain. Unless you hike the trail from Sunrise along Sourdough Ridge (doubling the distance), you won't see Rainier. But you will see a fine chain of alpine lakes and a big rock outcrop, the Palisades. Good campsites are found at Dick's Lake (2.5 miles) and Upper Palisades Lake (3.5 miles), although they're liable to be crowded. You gain and lose plenty of altitude, but only short stretches leave you gasping.

Location: Southeast of Sunrise in Mount Rainier National Park; see Mount Rainier and the Columbia River Gorge Map 2, grid a3.

User Groups: Hikers only. No dogs, horses, or mountain bikes. No wheelchair facilities.

Permits: A $10-per-car access fee is collected at all park entrances. Day-hiking permits are not required. Wilderness permits are required for all backcountry camping. Some permits can be reserved in advance for a fee. Others are issued free no more than 24 hours before departure. Contact the Outdoor Recreation Information Center at 206/470-4060.

Maps: For a free map of Mount Rainier National Park, contact the Outdoor Recreation Information Center at 206/470-4060. Green Trails, Inc.'s excellent topographic maps of the region are available for $3.99 each at outdoor retail outlets. Ask for map number 270, Mount Rainier East. Ask the USGS for a topographic map of the White River Park area.

Directions: From Enumclaw drive 43 miles east on Highway 410 to the Mount Rainier National Park White River Entrance Station. Proceed 10.5 miles on Sunrise Road to the large parking lot at Sunrise Point, on the hairpin corner on the road. Note: Sunrise Road usually doesn't open until early July. Contact Mount Rainier National Park at 360/569-2211 for road information.

Contact: Outdoor Recreation Information Center, Seattle REI, 222 Yale Avenue North, Seattle, WA 98109; 206/470-4060.

³⁷ Burroughs Mountain
7.0 mi/5.0 hrs

Double Jeopardy. Burroughs Mountain is one of Rainier's most spectacular alpine walks. It's also the trail most often underestimated by day hikers. The route crosses a large snowfield that usually doesn't melt until early August, if at all. You might consider an alternative if you're uncomfortable with crossing snow with an ice ax. The snow notwithstanding, Burroughs Mountain is a great experience. The trail begins by skirting Shadow Lake to Sunrise Camp and then shoots up sharply to a viewpoint with an awesome vantage point of the Emmons Glacier and moraine. Continuing up the ridgeline, cross the snowfield and climb to First Burroughs Mountain (7,300 feet), where the trail joins with a path to Frozen Lake at about 2.8 miles. Continuing upward, you find a magnificent, fragile tundra environment, considered the best of its kind in the Northwest. Do not for any reason venture off the trail. The plants you stomp on will take as long to grow back as you'll be alive, which might not be long, if you're spotted lurching through the meadows by a backcountry ranger. Second Burroughs Mountain (elevation 7,400 feet) is about half a mile beyond the first. The views are stupendous. For the return trip you have three choices: the way you came, the Frozen Lake route via Sourdough Ridge, or dropping sharply south to the Glacier Basin Trail and then walking a section of the Wonderland Trail back to your vehicle.

Location: Near Sunrise in northeast Mount Rainier National Park; see Mount Rainier and the Columbia River Gorge Map 2, grid a3.

User Groups: Hikers only. No dogs, horses, or mountain bikes. No wheelchair facilities.

Permits: A $10-per-car access fee is collected at all park entrances. Day-hiking permits are not required. Wilderness permits are required for all backcountry camping. Some permits can be reserved in advance for a fee. Others are issued free no more than 24 hours before departure. Contact the Outdoor Recreation Information Center at 206/470-4060.

Maps: For a free map of Mount Rainier National Park, contact the Outdoor Recreation Information Center at 206/470-4060. Green Trails, Inc.'s excellent topographic maps of the region are available for $3.99 each at outdoor retail outlets. Ask for map number 270, Mount Rainier East. Ask the USGS for a topographic map of the Sunrise area.

Directions: From Enumclaw drive 43 miles east on Highway 410 to the Mount Rainier National Park White River Entrance Station. Proceed to Sunrise Road and follow it 17 miles west to the large parking lot and visitor center at the road's end. The trailhead is on the south side of the parking lot. Note: Sunrise Road usually doesn't open until early July. Contact Mount Rainier National Park at 360/569-2211 for road information.

Contact: Outdoor Recreation Information Center, Seattle REI, 222 Yale Avenue North, Seattle, WA 98109; 206/470-4060.

³⁸ Glacier Basin
7.0 mi/4.0 hrs

Metal detectors are optional. Glacier Basin offers many reminders that this land wasn't always protected as a park. Quite the contrary, in fact. Remnants of an old mining operation that began in the late nineteenth century still are found at various points in this glacial valley. The hike is relatively uneventful, following an old road up through the headwaters of the White River. About one mile in, veer left to get an up-close view of the snout of the Emmons Glacier, the granddaddy of all Rainier ice sheets. Continuing straight, you'll climb beyond a junction with the Burroughs Mountain Trail to Glacier Basin Camp, a nice meadow area that serves as a springboard to Camp Schurman at the crux of the Emmons and Winthrop Glaciers. You're likely to see mountain climbers headed there, taking advantage of a secondary route to Rainier's summit. This is another good place to watch for mountain goats.

Location: South of Sunrise and north of the Emmons Glacier in Mount Rainier National Park; see Mount Rainier and the Columbia River Gorge Map 2, grid a3.

User Groups: Hikers only. No dogs, horses, or mountain bikes. No wheelchair facilities.

Permits: A $10-per-car access fee is collected at all park entrances. Day-hiking permits are not required. Wilderness permits are required for all backcountry camping. Some permits can be reserved in advance for a fee. Others are issued free no more than 24 hours before departure. Contact the Outdoor Recreation Information Center at 206/470-4060.

Maps: For a free map of Mount Rainier National Park, contact the Outdoor Recreation Information Center at 206/470-4060. Green Trails, Inc.'s excellent topographic maps of the region are available for $3.99 each at outdoor retail outlets. Ask for map number 270, Mount Rainier East. Ask the USGS for a topographic map of the Sunrise area.

Directions: From Enumclaw drive 43 miles east on Highway 410 to the Mount Rainier National Park White River Entrance Station. Proceed five miles to White River Campground and park in the day-use parking lot. The trailhead is in the upper campground area.

Contact: Outdoor Recreation Information Center, Seattle REI, 222 Yale Avenue North, Seattle, WA 98109; 206/470-4060.

39 Summerland/ Panhandle Gap
8.6 mi/4.5 hrs

This is the best—and therefore typically most crowded—high-country backpack trip in the park. The trail follows Fryingpan Creek up at a good clip for about four miles before opening into an upper valley. Views begin here and don't end for the rest of the day, sudden fogouts notwithstanding. You cross the creek in an avalanche area and then embark on some serious steepness for the final mile or so. Then, boom: Summerland. Meadows sprawl. Breezes tickle. Views entice. Shoulders ache. Drop the pack and look to your left, into the trees, for an unoccupied campsite (in the dead of summer, good luck). Campsite or no, the scenery is splendid, with great views of Rainier, Little Tahoma Peak (11,138 feet), Goat Island Mountain, and the Fryingpan Glacier. Ahead about 1.5 miles is Panhandle Gap, which has unique views all its own, plus a bonus—it's not unusual to look up and see mountain goats. An all-time Rainier classic hike awaits those who continue ahead to Indian Bar and make the two- to three-day trip south on the Wonderland Trail to Indian Bar and an exit on Stevens Canyon Road. Total trip: about 16 miles, through some of the park's more unoccupied trail stretches. For average backpackers the latter trip isn't a good idea early in the season, when much of the trail remains covered in snow.

Location: In the upper White River drainage of Mount Rainier National Park; see Mount

Rainier and the Columbia River Gorge Map 2, grid a3.

User Groups: Hikers only. No dogs, horses, or mountain bikes. No wheelchair facilities.

Permits: A $10-per-car access fee is collected at all park entrances. Day-hiking permits are not required. Wilderness permits are required for all backcountry camping. Some permits can be reserved in advance for a fee. Others are issued free no more than 24 hours before departure. Contact the Outdoor Recreation Information Center at 206/470-4060.

Maps: For a free map of Mount Rainier National Park, contact the Outdoor Recreation Information Center at 206/470-4060. Green Trails, Inc.'s excellent topographic maps of the region are available for $3.99 each at outdoor retail outlets. Ask for map number 270, Mount Rainier East. Ask the USGS for topographic maps of the Sunrise and White River Park areas.

Directions: From Enumclaw drive 43 miles east on Highway 410 to the Mount Rainier National Park White River Entrance Station. Proceed three miles to the limited parking area near the Fryingpan Creek Bridge. The trailhead is across the road.

Contact: Outdoor Recreation Information Center, Seattle REI, 222 Yale Avenue North, Seattle, WA 98109; 206/470-4060.

40 Sunrise-Area Nature Trails
3.0 mi/1.5 hrs

Aside from the considerable crowds, Sunrise might well be one of the more lovely spots on the planet to bring a picnic lunch, snare a table, and alternate between snacking, sunbathing, and walking in a lush alpine environment, with the snow- and ice-encrusted dome of Mount Rainier keeping close watch nearby. The cold cuts and olives are up to you, but the National Park Service has already set the short-hiking table. From the main Sunrise parking lot, the Emmons Vista Trail leads a short half mile to a viewpoint of the Emmons Glacier. It's as good a place to photograph Rainier as you'll ever find (best early in the morning or late afternoon). Interpretive signs along the way tell you what you're looking at and urge you not to tromp on it. An offshoot of the Emmons Vista Trail is the Sunrise Rim Trail, which leads 1.5 miles to the walk-in campground at Shadow Lake. Nearby is the Silver Forest/Yakima Park Trail, which leads 1.2 miles east through bleached snags and delicious Rainier views. Starting from the other (north) side of the parking lot near the picnic area, the Sourdough Ridge Nature Trail makes a nice, hour-long loop on the hillside. Watch for mountain goats, deer, marmots, and Rocky Mountain elk.

Location: Near the Sunrise parking area in northeastern Mount Rainier National Park; see Mount Rainier and the Columbia River Gorge Map 2, grid a3.

User Groups: Hikers only. No dogs, horses, or mountain bikes. No wheelchair facilities.

Permits: A $10-per-car access fee is collected at all park entrances. Day-hiking permits are not required.

Maps: For a free map of Mount Rainier National Park, contact the Outdoor Recreation Information Center at 206/470-4060. Green Trails, Inc.'s excellent topographic maps of the region are available for $3.99 each at outdoor retail outlets. Ask for map number 270, Mount Rainier East. Ask the USGS for a topographic map of the Sunrise area.

Directions: From Enumclaw drive 43 miles east on Highway 410 to the Mount Rainier National Park White River Entrance Station. Proceed to Sunrise Road and follow it 17 miles west to the large parking lot and visitor center at the road's end. Note: Sunrise Road usually doesn't open until early July. Call the park at 360/569-2211 for road information.

Contact: Outdoor Recreation Information Center, Seattle REI, 222 Yale Avenue North, Seattle, WA 98109; 206/470-4060.

41 Owyhigh Lakes
7.0 mi/4.0 hrs

Once you've seen enough awesome mountain views of Rainier to last a lifetime, you might want to head out for a relaxing overnighter away from the hustle and bustle of glacier photographers. Owyhigh Lakes is a good place to do that. The trail can be walked as a seven-mile round-trip from the White River side or as a nine-mile, one-way trip to Deer Creek Camp near Highway 123. Overnighters should note that the only established campsite on the route is three miles in from the Owyhigh Lakes Trailhead. Owyhigh Lakes lie half a mile ahead, nestled in green meadows with jagged Governors Ridge as a backdrop. It's a quiet lunch spot.

Location: In the White River drainage of Mount Rainier National Park; see Mount Rainier and the Columbia River Gorge Map 2, grid a3.

User Groups: Hikers only. No dogs, horses, or mountain bikes. No wheelchair facilities.

Permits: A $10-per-car access fee is collected at all park entrances. Day-hiking permits are not required. Wilderness permits are required for all backcountry camping. Some permits can be reserved in advance for a fee. Others are issued free no more than 24 hours before departure. Contact the Outdoor Recreation Information Center at 206/470-4060.

Maps: For a free map of Mount Rainier National Park, contact the Outdoor Recreation Information Center at 206/470-4060. Green Trails, Inc.'s excellent topographic maps of the region are available for $3.99 each at outdoor retail outlets. Ask for map number 270, Mount Rainier East. Ask the USGS for topographic maps of the White River Park and Chinook Pass areas.

Directions: From Enumclaw drive 43 miles east on Highway 410 to the Mount Rainier National Park White River entrance station. Proceed two miles to the parking lot on the right. The Owyhigh Lakes Trailhead is on the opposite side of the road from the parking lot.

Contact: Outdoor Recreation Information Center, Seattle REI, 222 Yale Avenue North, Seattle, WA 98109; 206/470-4060.

42 Crystal Lakes
6.0 mi/3.0 hrs

On a clear winter day atop Crystal Mountain Ski Area, you look across what appears to be a frozen wonderland of lakes, trees, and ridges. Crystal Lake is one of those objects of wonder, and you might be surprised how inviting it is in the summer. The trail climbs through the forest and then breaks into the open for occasional views of Mount Rainier. At 1.5 miles a rarely maintained trail departs to the right to the top of rocky, 6,615-foot Crystal Peak, which offers superior views of Rainier and other Cascade volcanoes. On the main trail you reach the lower lake at about 2.5 miles, while the much-larger upper lake is in a basin half a mile above. At both lakes you find good campsites, plentiful wildflowers, and if your timing is right, perhaps even elk or goats. Pack the binoculars.

Location: East of Mount Rainier in Mount Rainier National Park; see Mount Rainier and the Columbia River Gorge Map 2, grid a4.

User Groups: Hikers only. No dogs, horses, or mountain bikes. No wheelchair facilities.

Permits: A $10-per-car access fee is collected at all park entrances. Day-hiking permits are not required. Wilderness permits are required for all backcountry camping. Some permits can be reserved in advance for a fee. Others are issued free no more than 24 hours before departure. Contact the Outdoor Recreation Information Center at 206/470-4060.

Maps: For a free map of Mount Rainier National Park, contact the Outdoor Recreation Information Center at 206/470-4060. Green Trails, Inc.'s excellent topographic maps of the region are available for $3.99 each at outdoor retail outlets. Ask for map number 270, Mount Rainier East. Ask the USGS for a topographic map of the White River Park area.

Directions: From Enumclaw drive 33 miles east on Highway 410 to the Mount Rainier National Park boundary. Proceed to the trailhead on the east side of the road near Crystal Creek, just before Department of Transportation maintenance sheds on the right.

Contact: Outdoor Recreation Information Center, Seattle REI, 222 Yale Avenue North, Seattle, WA 98109; 206/470-4060.

43 Tipsoo Lakes/ Naches Peak Loop

4.5 mi/3.0 hrs

On a clear day a drive over Chinook Pass near Mount Rainier is one of the more stunning mountain drives in the United States. Trails in the Tipsoo Lakes area are even better. From the parking lot a paved loop trail, fully wheelchair accessible, leads around Upper Tipsoo Lake. It's an easy walk for anyone. For a better taste of the area, hike the Naches Loop, one of the more heavily walked trails in the Northwest. The easily negotiated loop can be hiked in either direction, but most people favor a clockwise approach to take best advantage of the Rainier views. To do so, head north around Tipsoo Lake, over the Highway 410 overpass to the Pacific Crest Trail, which leads

south below Naches Peak. In 2.2 miles you reach a junction. You can go left 1.2 miles to Dewey Lakes, where good campsites await and long-distance hikers can catch the south end of the American River Trail, which leads nine miles downriver to a trailhead just west of Lodgepole Campground on Highway 410. But to continue the Tipsoo Lakes/Naches Peak loop, go straight on the Naches Trail, which leads back to Tipsoo Lakes from the south. Wildflowers and alpine views all along the route are sublime, with flowers peaking in July and August. Snow is likely to linger on some trail portions in the summer.

Location: At Chinook Pass on the east side of Mount Rainier; see Mount Rainier and the Columbia River Gorge Map 2, grid b4.

User Groups: Hikers and wheelchairs. No dogs, horses, or mountain bikes.

Permits: No day-use permits are required. Parking and access are free.

Maps: For a free map of Mount Rainier National Park contact the Outdoor Recreation Information Center at 206/470-4060. Green Trails, Inc.'s excellent topographic maps of the region are available for $3.99 each at outdoor retail outlets. Ask for map numbers 270 and 271, Mount Rainier East and Bumping Lake. Ask the USGS for topographic maps of the Chinook Pass and Cougar Lake areas.

Directions: From Enumclaw drive 47 miles east on Highway 410 to the Tipsoo Lake parking lot, half a mile west of Chinook Pass. Note: Chinook Pass/Highway 410 is closed in the winter. Call the Washington Department of Transportation's toll-free hotline at 888/766-4636 for current road conditions.

Contact: Outdoor Recreation Information Center, Seattle REI, 222 Yale Avenue North, Seattle, WA 98109; 206/470-4060.

44 Sourdough/Pickhandle Gaps
17.4 mi/1.0 day 🥾 ⚡9

For those millions of us who've always fancied a top-to-bottom trip on the Pacific Crest Trail but just never seem to be able to carve time out from raking leaves, small bites of the main course must serve as pacifiers. This is one of the tastiest nibbles of all—easily accessible, easily walkable, and downright gorgeous. From the parking lot at Chinook Pass, the PCT climbs slightly (400 feet in 2.5 miles) northeast to Sheep Lake. The wildflowers on this stretch are sublime in July and August. Beyond, the trail climbs gradually to Sourdough Gap (3.3 miles), where views aren't worth writing to your sister in Ohio about, and your feet might tell you to turn around for the day. Long-distance lunatics can continue straight, down a little bit to Bear Gap and then up to Pickhandle Point, Pickhandle Gap, and Blue Bell Pass, where great views await. It's a long round-trip day hike, so consider making it a one-way venture by dropping straight down from Pickhandle or Bear Gap to a pickup point at Crystal Mountain Ski Area (see hike this chapter). Total one-way distance: about nine miles. A more scenic day hike in this region would be tough to come by. For an even longer one-way special, continue beyond Blue Bell Pass about 8.5 miles on the PCT over Norse Peak to Big Crow Basin and a trailhead on Crystal Mountain Road. Or turn east from the Pickhandle Gap area to the Union Creek Trail, which loops seven dry, dusty miles back to a trailhead, west of Pleasant Valley Campground on Highway 410.

Location: From Chinook Pass to the Crystal Mountain area east of Mount Rainier; see Mount Rainier and the Columbia River Gorge Map 2, grid b4.

User Groups: Hikers, leashed dogs, and horses. No mountain bikes. No wheelchair facilities.

Permits: A federal Northwest Forest Pass, $5 per day or $30 annually, is required to park at the trailhead. Passes are available from ranger stations and many private vendors, online at website: www.wta.org, or by calling 800/270-7504.

Maps: For a map of Mount Baker-Snoqualmie National Forest, contact the Outdoor Recreation Information Center, Seattle REI, 222 Yale Avenue North, Seattle, WA 98109; 206/470-4060. Green Trails, Inc.'s excellent topographic maps of the area are available for $3.99 each at outdoor retail outlets. Ask for map number 271, Bumping Lake. Ask the USGS for topographic maps of the White River Park and Norse Peak areas.

Directions: From Enumclaw drive 47 miles east on Highway 410 to the Pacific Crest Trail parking lot at Chinook Pass. Note: Chinook Pass/Highway 410 is closed in the winter. Call the Washington Department of Transportation's toll-free hotline at 888/766-4636 for current road conditions.

Contact: Okanogan/Wenatchee National Forest, Naches Ranger District, 10061 Highway 12, Naches, WA 98937; 509/653-2205.

45 Mesatchee Creek
10.6 mi/6.5 hrs 🥾 ⚡8

This is a beautiful creek-valley walk, interrupted by the occasional proud gush of a waterfall, a delightful ridgetop plateau filled with straight, loyal white pine trees, and a side trip to a scenic backcountry lake. The Mesatchee Creek Trail, whether hiked as a day hike or as an appetizer to a greater thrill farther on, is a great sampler tray of the William O. Douglas Wilderness' wonders. The trail climbs moderately for 1.5 miles on an old road, crosses the American River on a footlog, and then comes to a junction with the American River Trail to Dewey Lakes (see hike in this chapter). Stay left and begin climbing the first of many switchbacks on the east side of Mesatchee Creek. You reach the American Ridge Trail (see hike in this chapter) at about 5.3 miles. Enjoy the views slightly east of here and turn around or follow the ridge an additional 5.5 miles southwest to Cougar Lakes (stay left at the intersection with the American Lake Trail). Note: If Cougar Lakes are your primary goal, consider a shorter, 12-mile round-trip route on the Swamp Lake Trail, which departs from the Upper Bumping Road west of Bumping Lake.

Location: South of Highway 410 in the William O. Douglas Wilderness; see Mount Rainier and the Columbia River Gorge Map 2, grid a5.

User Groups: Hikers, leashed dogs, and horses. No mountain bikes. No wheelchair facilities.

Permits: A federal Northwest Forest Pass, $5 per day or $30 annually, is required to park at the trailhead. Passes are available from ranger stations and many private vendors, online at website: www.wta.org, or by calling 800/270-7504.

Maps: For a map of the William O. Douglas Wilderness, contact the Outdoor Recreation Information Center, Seattle REI, 222 Yale Avenue North, Seattle, WA 98109; 206/470-4060. Green Trails, Inc.'s excellent topographic maps of the region are available for $3.99 each at outdoor retail outlets. Ask for map number 271, Bumping Lake. Ask the USGS for topographic maps of the Norse Peak and Cougar Lake areas.

Directions: From Enumclaw drive 47 miles east on Highway 410 to Chinook Pass and proceed another 6.75 miles to Forest Service Road 1700-460. Turn right (south) and drive half a mile to the trailhead. Note: Chinook Pass/Highway 410 is closed in the winter. Call the Washington Department of Transportation's toll-free hotline at 888/766-4636 for current road conditions.

Contact: Okanogan/Wenatchee National Forest, Naches Ranger District, 10061 Highway 12, Naches, WA 98937; 509/653-2205.

46 Bumping Lake
20.2 mi/2 days

Listen closely and you hear the prancing of hooves. OK, so they are horses. Wait for them to pass, and listen closely again: elk, most likely. A herd has taken up permanent residence in the Bumping River Valley. Little wonder. They're probably attracted by the same things that appeal to you: a cool, flat valley trail along a river that you can look into and see yourself peering back. It's a great early-summer day hike and midsummer backpack trip with an adjustable length. Starting the trail at the upper access lops off the lakeside walk but also shaves about eight miles off the round-trip. Be advised, though, that the access for the shorter route requires fording the Bumping River, which can be a harrowing experience until mid- to late summer. The trail follows an easy grade along the river drainage, gradually gaining elevation to its upper reaches south of Crag Mountain. Good campsites are found at several sites along the way. At 10.1 miles the trail intersects the Pacific Crest Trail. Either make this your turnaround point or continue 0.3 mile straight from the junction to campsites at Fish Lake. From here you can hike north for a scenic side trip to One Lake and Two Lakes, or seven miles north to Dewey Lakes and Chinook Pass.

Location: East of Mount Rainier National Park in the William O. Douglas Wilderness; see Mount Rainier and the Columbia River Gorge Map 2, grid a6.

User Groups: Hikers, leashed dogs, and horses. No mountain bikes. No wheelchair facilities.

Permits: A federal Northwest Forest Pass, $5 per day or $30 annually, is required to park at the trailhead. Passes are available from ranger stations and many private vendors, online at website: www.wta.org, or by calling 800/270-7504.

Maps: For a map of the William O. Douglas Wilderness, contact the Outdoor Recreation Information Center, Seattle REI, 222 Yale Avenue North, Seattle, WA 98109; 206/470-4060. Green Trails, Inc.'s excellent topographic maps of the region are available for $3.99 each at outdoor retail outlets. Ask for map number 271, Bumping Lake. Ask the USGS for topographic maps of the Bumping Lake and Cougar Lake areas.

Directions: From Enumclaw drive 47 miles east on Highway 410 to Chinook Pass and proceed another 19 miles to Bumping Road/Forest Service Road 18. Turn right (south) and follow the road to Forest Service Road 394 at Bumping Lake. Turn right and continue about two miles to the trailhead along the lake at the road's end. Alternate access: Drive Forest Service Road 18 until it becomes Forest Service Road 1800 at the end of the pavement and follow it to the trailhead for Trail 790 at the road's end. Note: Chinook Pass/Highway 410 is closed in the winter. Call the Washington Department of Transportation's toll-free hotline at 888/766-4636 for current road conditions.

Contact: Okanogan/Wenatchee National Forest, Naches Ranger District, 10061 Highway 12, Naches, WA 98937; 509/653-2205.

47 American Ridge
26.7 mi one way/
4.0–5.0 days

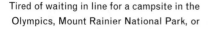

Tired of waiting in line for a campsite in the Olympics, Mount Rainier National Park, or the North Cascades? It might be time to introduce yourself to William O. Douglas and his best friend, the American Ridge Trail. The trail itself is not drop-to-the-ground-and-writhe spectacular, but some of the places it leads to come close. And it's likely to be far less crowded than similar long treks elsewhere in the Cascades. Not that it's without fault: by late summer finding water anywhere on American Ridge can be next to impossible. Backpackers should consult rangers and time their trip after the most harrowing snowfields have gone, but before the trail dries up altogether.

One-way trekkers often begin at the eastern trailhead and hike over Goat Peak to Kettle Lake, Mesatchee Creek, then Swamp, Cougar, and American Lakes to the Pacific Crest Trail and an exit either northwest to Chinook Pass via Dewey Lakes or to Bumping Lake via the Swamp Lake Trail (the mileage above reflects the latter route). But enterprising hikers can design a loop trip to suit their own taste (and leg strength) by combining the American Ridge Trail with the Mesatchee Creek, Kettle Creek, Pleasant Valley Lake, or Goat Peak Trails, all of which have trailheads on Highway 410. Or combine the ridge trail with the Swamp Lake, Goose Prairie, or Goat Creek Trails, all of which exit to Bumping Road or Upper Bumping Road to the south. The trail stays high, but the ups and downs are trying, and we can assure you the cumulative impact makes your legs feel like canned hams after a few days with a backpack. But the scenery makes up for it. Highlights include the grand view from the lookout site on Goat Peak, 6,473 feet and about eight miles from the eastern trailhead; and beautiful Big Basin, which offers the best campsites and wildlife viewing along the ridge. (Big Basin is about 20 miles in from the eastern trailhead or eight miles one way from the Goose Prairie Trailhead.)

Day hikers often prefer the short, steep climb to Goat Peak (5.3 miles one way from the Goat Creek Trailhead on Forest Service Road 18) or the Goose Prairie hike, which climbs 2,600 feet in 5.1 miles to the ridgetop. After a short walk west along the ridge, you find excellent views of Mount Rainier, where people are jostling for position for views not much better than this. Pity them and pat yourself on the back.

Location: South of Highway 410 in the William O. Douglas Wilderness; see Mount Rainier and the Columbia River Gorge Map 2, grid a7.

User Groups: Hikers, leashed dogs, and horses. No mountain bikes. No wheelchair facilities.

Permits: A federal Northwest Forest Pass, $5 per day or $30 annually, is required to park at the trailhead. Passes are available from ranger stations and many private vendors, online at website: www.wta.org, or by calling 800/270-7504.

Maps: For a map of the William O. Douglas Wilderness, contact the Outdoor Recreation Information Center, Seattle REI, 222 Yale Avenue North, Seattle, WA 98109; 206/470-4060. Green Trails, Inc.'s excellent topographic maps of the region are available for $3.99 each at outdoor retail outlets. Ask for map number 271, Bumping Lake. Ask the USGS for topographic maps of the Norse Peak, Cougar Lake, Bumping Lake, Goose Prairie and Old Scab Mountain areas.

Directions: From Enumclaw drive 47 miles east on Highway 410 to Chinook Pass and proceed another 19 miles to Bumping Road/Forest Service Road 18. Turn south and find the eastern trailhead in about half a mile off a spur road to the right (west). For the shortest route to Goat Peak, proceed about three miles to the Goat Peak Trailhead, on the right (west) side of the road. For more direct day-hiking access to

the central ridge, proceed on Bumping Road about nine miles beyond the eastern trailhead to the Goose Prairie Trailhead, on the right (west) side of the road. To leave a shuttle at the far western (Swamp Lake) trailhead, proceed approximately eight additional miles to the end of the road. Note: Chinook Pass/Highway 410 is closed in the winter. Call the Washington Department of Transportation's toll-free hotline at 888/766-4636 for current road conditions.

Contact: Okanogan/Wenatchee National Forest, Naches Ranger District, 10061 Highway 12, Naches, WA 98937; 509/653-2205.

48 Boulder Cave Nature Trail
1.6 mi/1.0 hr

This is a kids' special. Bring a lunch, a flashlight, and the patience to answer a lot of questions as you lead the youngsters into Boulder Cave, a natural stone tunnel nearly 200 feet long. Actually, interpretive signs answer many of the questions for you if you take time to read them. A short distance up the path, the trail splits. Choose a direction, because the trail is a loop that winds through both ends of the cave. Plug your ears inside— if your own kids aren't screaming to test the echo, someone else's will be. And keep your eyes open for bats. Back near the parking area, the barrier-free nature trail is a good alternative for members of your party who don't care for dark, clammy places.

Location: In the Naches River drainage near Highway 410; see Mount Rainier and the Columbia River Gorge Map 2, grid a8.

User Groups: Hikers and leashed dogs. No horses or mountain bikes. A 1.4-mile paved, barrier-free nature loop circles the Boulder Cave parking lot along the Naches River.

Permits: No permits are required. Parking and access are free.

Maps: For a map of the Okanogan/Wenatchee National Forest, contact the Outdoor Recreation Information Center, Seattle REI, 222 Yale Avenue North, Seattle, WA 98109; 206/470-4060. Green Trails, Inc.'s excellent topographic maps of the region are available for $3.99 each at outdoor retail outlets. Ask for map number 272, Old Scab Mountain. Ask the USGS for a topographic map of the Cliffdell area.

Directions: From Enumclaw drive 47 miles east on Highway 410 to Cliffdell. Cross the Naches River and turn north on Forest Service Road 1706. In a short distance turn right, following signs to Boulder Cave Campground. The trailhead is on the left in just over a mile, near Boulder Cave Campground. Note: Chinook Pass/Highway 410 is closed in the winter. Call the Washington Department of Transportation's toll-free hotline at 888/766-4636 for current road conditions.

Contact: Okanogan/Wenatchee National Forest, Naches Ranger District, 10061 Highway 12, Naches, WA 98937; 509/653-2205.

49 Mount Aix
11.5 mi/9.0 hrs

The aerobically challenged need not apply. This one is for all you muscle lungs who can't sleep at night unless you've sauntered up some 4,000 feet of vertical before bedtime. You sleep well after a visit to Mount Aix. The trail gains 4,200 vertical feet in about five miles, but you are rewarded by splendid views, clean air, and probably not as much company as you might expect from an easily accessible wilderness trail. You climb steeply through a pine forest with Mount Rainier keeping watch behind you. At 3.7 miles you conquer a ridgetop, and the Nelson Ridge Trail departs to the north. You get great views all along this nice ridgetop walk for about 2.5 miles before the trail drops into the North

Fork Rattlesnake Creek drainage and then exits back to Forest Service Road 18 north of Bumping Lake via the Thunder Creek or Nile Ridge Trails. Nice loops both, for those of you with transportation options. But dead ahead, the Mount Aix Trail climbs a short distance farther to a fine lookout over the entire wilderness, not to mention the Goat Rocks, Mount Rainier, and Mount Adams. The summit lies beyond, up a lengthy scramble on rock and scree to the site of a former lookout tower on the 7,766-foot summit. The trail continues east to the Hindoo Creek drainage, exiting on Forest Service Road 1502 near McDaniel Lake. This trail absolutely is not for the out-of-shape, timid, or tired. Carry plenty of water; it's scarce in the summer. Expect some slippery stream crossings, steep switchbacks, and nasty talus slopes.

Location: High above the south side of Bumping Lake in the William O. Douglas Wilderness; see Mount Rainier and the Columbia River Gorge Map 2, grid b6.

User Groups: Hikers, leashed dogs, and horses. No mountain bikes. No wheelchair facilities.

Permits: A federal Northwest Forest Pass, $5 per day or $30 annually, is required to park at the trailhead. Passes are available from ranger stations and many private vendors, online at website: www.wta.org, or by calling 800/270-7504.

Maps: For a map of the William O. Douglas Wilderness, contact the Outdoor Recreation Information Center, Seattle REI, 222 Yale Avenue North, Seattle, WA 98109; 206/470-4060. Green Trails, Inc.'s excellent topographic maps of the region are available for $3.99 each at outdoor retail outlets. Ask for map number 271, Bumping Lake. Ask the USGS for topographic maps of the Timberwolf Mountain and Bumping Lake areas.

Directions: From Enumclaw drive 47 miles east on Highway 410 to Chinook Pass and proceed 19 miles east to Bumping Road/Forest Service Road 18. Turn right (south) and follow the road to the end of the pavement, where it becomes Forest Service Road 1800. Proceed to a junction and stay straight on what now is Deep Creek Road/Forest Service Road 395. Drive about 1.5 miles to the Mount Aix Trailhead on the left (east) side of the road just before the Copper Creek bridge. Note: Chinook Pass/Highway 410 is closed in the winter. Call the Washington Department of Transportation's toll-free hotline at 888/766-4636 for current road conditions.

Contact: Okanogan/Wenatchee National Forest, Naches Ranger District, 10061 Highway 12, Naches, WA 98937; 509/653-2205.

50 Klapatche Park
21.0 mi/2.0 days

Klapatche Park and the surrounding area, all on the west shoulders of Mount Rainier, make a classic Northwest overnight hike. Campsites near Aurora Lake offer truly spectacular views of the mountain and have been heavily used over the years. The lake is only 2.5 miles from the road. The good thing about the additional eight-mile walk due to the West Side Road closure is that it weeds out the excessive number of hikers who come here. The bad news is that when they get here, they're tired enough to stay. But however long you stay, cherish this spot. The view of the mountain is unsurpassed, sunsets are brilliant, and there's a fair chance you'll encounter a mountain goat on the rocks above.

From the lake, which sometimes dries up in late summer, you can follow the trail around Aurora Peak to Aurora Park and the North Puyallup Creek Trail, which leads back west to the end of West Side Road. But the real show is to the south of the lake, where a short trail leads three-quarters of a mile up to Saint Andrews Lake and Saint Andrews

Park, one of Rainier's most spectacular vistas. It's a view to be savored. The wildflowers carry you to another place. So might the bugs, if you forget your DEET. For an added treat on the way out on the Klapatche Park Trail, cross West Side Road at the trailhead and walk a short distance down the hill to where Saint Andrews Creek plunges over Denman Falls. It's a lovely spot.

Location: In the Puyallup River drainage of Mount Rainier National Park; see Mount Rainier and the Columbia River Gorge Map 2, grid b1.

User Groups: Hikers and mountain bikes. Mountain bikes are allowed on West Side Road between the washout and the trailhead. No dogs or horses are allowed. No wheelchair facilities.

Permits: A $10-per-car access fee is collected at all park entrances. Day-hiking permits are not required. Wilderness permits are required for all backcountry camping. Some permits can be reserved in advance for a fee. Others are issued free no more than 24 hours before departure. Contact the Outdoor Recreation Information Center at 206/470-4060.

Maps: For a free map of Mount Rainier National Park, contact the Outdoor Recreation Information Center at 206/470-4060. Green Trails, Inc.'s excellent topographic maps of the region are available for $3.99 each at outdoor retail outlets. Ask for map number 269, Mount Rainier West. Ask the USGS for topographic maps of the Mount Wow and Mount Rainier West areas.

Directions: From Tacoma drive south on Highway 7 to Elbe and continue east on Highway 706 to the Mount Rainier National Park Nisqually Entrance Station. Proceed one mile; then turn left (north) onto West Side Road and drive to the parking area at the washout. Walk or bicycle approximately eight miles up the closed road to the trailhead on the right (east) side of the road. See the highway access note in the Mount Rainier National Park Sidebar.

Contact: Outdoor Recreation Information Center, Seattle REI, 222 Yale Avenue North, Seattle, WA 98109; 206/470-4060.

51 Emerald Ridge
16.0 mi/10.0 hrs

If you're up for the long haul, day hikes in Mount Rainier—or on the planet, for that matter—don't get too much better than this. After a 4.5-mile trek up West Side Road, the trail climbs steadily toward Emerald Ridge, first through old forest then up through a truly tundralike fragile alpine environment. Just over a mile up the initially forested trail, notice the large columns of andesite rock that formed in almost unbelievable geometric shapes when lava cooled here a short hop back in geologic history.

You encounter a junction with the Wonderland Trail, and a big decision, at 1.5 miles. The left fork leads north about two miles and 2,500 vertical feet up to Saint Andrews Park and Saint Andrews Lake. The right fork continues up and east to the foot of the Tahoma Glacier and then cuts south around Glacier Island, a spectacular rock formation that was fully surrounded by ice about the time your dad was a little kid, but now is surrounded only by choppy moraines. You really can't go wrong. Pick a path and continue up for several hours to truly memorable alpine views and some of the sweetest, cleanest alpine air you can imagine. Pack a big lunch. And on the way out you'll be a much happier camper if you rode a bike, rather than walked, up West Side Road. Trust us. Besides, how many other places in the Northwest combine a spectacular mountain bike ride with a breathtaking alpine hike? Not too many.

Overnight camping is not allowed on Emerald Ridge. Remember that the left-fork route to Saint Andrews Park can be hiked as a loop that exits on the Klapatche Park Trail, which leads to the far northern end of West Side Road.

Location: In the Puyallup River drainage of Mount Rainier National Park; see Mount Rainier and the Columbia River Gorge Map 2, grid b1.

User Groups: Hikers and mountain bikes. Mountain bikes are allowed on West Side Road between the washout and the trailhead. No dogs or horses are allowed. No wheelchair facilities.

Permits: A $10-per-car access fee is collected at all park entrances. Day-hiking permits are not required. Wilderness permits are required for all backcountry camping. Some permits can be reserved in advance for a fee. Others are issued free no more than 24 hours before departure. Contact the Outdoor Recreation Information Center at 206/470-4060.

Maps: For a free map of Mount Rainier National Park, contact the Outdoor Recreation Information Center at 206/470-4060. Green Trails, Inc.'s excellent topographic maps of the region are available for $3.99 each at outdoor retail outlets. Ask for map number 269, Mount Rainier West. Ask the USGS for topographic maps of the Mount Wow and Mount Rainier West areas.

Directions: From Tacoma drive south on Highway 7 to Elbe and continue east on Highway 706 to the Mount Rainier National Park Nisqually Entrance Station. Proceed one mile, turn left (north) onto West Side Road, and drive to the parking area at the washout. Walk or bicycle approximately 4.5 miles up the closed road to the trailhead on the right (east) side of the road, just before the road crosses the South Fork Puyallup River. See the highway access note in the Mount Rainier Sidebar.

Contact: Outdoor Recreation Information Center, Seattle REI, 222 Yale Avenue North, Seattle, WA 98109; 206/470-4060.

52 Glacier View/Lake Christine
9.4 mi/5.0 hrs

Glacier View Wilderness trails offer the advantage of seeing Mount Rainier up close and personal. Under the aegis of the Forest Service, which allows dogs on most trails, this one is for hikers whose love of Rainier is surpassed only by their love of their favorite quadruped hiking companion. So put dog packs on the mutt, fill them with enough Diet Pepsi to weigh the beast down to crawling speed, and proceed. Lake Christine (reached a short distance from Forest Service Road 5920) is quite heavily used, and better views lie beyond. Continue north for two miles around Mount Beljica to a junction with the Puyallup Trail, which exits to the right (east) and leads to Goat Lake, Gobbler's Knob, and West Side Road in Mount Rainier National Park (see hike this chapter). Stay left and cross Beljica Meadows to an upper trailhead about 10 miles up Forest Service Road 59 (the lower trail portion can be bypassed by starting here). The trail then climbs 900 feet in two miles to a viewpoint atop Glacier View, a 5,450-foot former fire lookout, where you can see Mount Rainier in full glory to the east. If you think the mountain view is better here than inside the park, you're right. For those who began at the lower trailhead, this is a grand turnaround spot. But the main stem trail leads another 2.3 miles to West and Helen Lakes, both far less visited than Christine. The entire circuit is about 15.5 miles—enough to keep the pooch snoozing all the way back to town.

Location: In the Glacier View Wilderness immediately west of Mount Rainier National Park; see Mount Rainier and the Columbia River Gorge Map 2, grid b1.

User Groups: Hikers, leashed dogs, and horses. No mountain bikes are allowed. No wheelchair facilities.

Permits: A federal Northwest Forest Pass, $5 per day or $30 annually, is required to park at the trailhead. Passes are available from ranger stations and many private vendors, online at website: www.wta.org, or by calling 800/270-7504.

Maps: For a map of the Glacier View Wilderness and Mount Baker-Snoqualmie National Forest, contact the Outdoor Recreation Information Center, Seattle REI, 222 Yale Avenue North, Seattle, WA 98109; 206/470-4060. Green Trails, Inc.'s excellent topographic maps of the region are available for $3.99 each at outdoor retail outlets. Ask for map number 269, Mount Rainier West. Ask the USGS for a topographic map of the Mount Wow area.

Directions: From Tacoma drive south on Highway 7 to Elbe and continue east on Highway 706 to Ashford. Proceed approximately 3.5 miles east to Copper Creek Road/Forest Service Road 59. Turn left (north) and drive to Forest Service Road 5920. Turn right (east) and follow the road to the trailhead at the road's end.

Contact: Gifford Pinchot National Forest, Cowlitz Valley Ranger District, 10024 U.S. Highway 12, Randle, WA 98377; 360/497-1100.

53 Gobbler's Knob/ Lake George
12.0 mi/6.0 hrs

When Aunt Millie and Uncle Jed from Omaha come to town in August, and they want to trek just far enough into the wilderness to gaze at Rainier from an unpaved viewpoint, consider bringing them here. Not that you won't enjoy it yourself. Hundreds of thousands of people have over the years. It's a moderate hike to a spectacular Rainier vista. After your three-mile get-acquainted session with the upper portion of West Side Road (you'll wish you'd brought your mountain bike), start up the easy, mile-long path to Lake George. The moderate grade used to make this trail a favorite for parents, but the four-mile road walk at the start has thinned them out somewhat. Nevertheless, Lake George is a pleasant place to have lunch or camp, if crowds aren't too huge. Deer and wildflowers are in great abundance. When the last dill pickle is consumed, hop back on the trail and hike the slightly steeper 1.2 miles west to a side trail that leads another half mile right (north) to Gobbler's Knob, site of a fire lookout. The straight-on view of Rainier from here is one of the best in the park. You're just far enough away to get the full effect, but close enough to make out spectacular details, such as the Tahoma Glacier (from top to bottom) and Puyallup Cleaver. Back on the main trail, those with plenty of untapped leg muscle can continue another mile into the Glacier View Wilderness to Goat Lake and then another 1.5 miles on the Puyallup Trail to the Glacier View/Lake Christine Trail (see hike this chapter).

Location: In the Puyallup River drainage of Mount Rainier National Park; see Mount Rainier and the Columbia River Gorge Map 2, grid c1.

User Groups: Hikers and mountain bikes. Mountain bikes are allowed on West Side Road between the washout and the trailhead. No dogs or horses are allowed. No wheelchair facilities.

Permits: A $10-per-car access fee is collected at all park entrances. Day-hiking permits are not required. Wilderness permits are required for all backcountry camping. Some permits can be reserved in advance

for a fee. Others are issued free no more than 24 hours before departure. Contact the Outdoor Recreation Information Center at 206/470-4060.

Maps: For a free map of Mount Rainier National Park, contact the Outdoor Recreation Information Center at 206/470-4060. Green Trails, Inc.'s excellent topographic maps of the region are available for $3.99 each at outdoor retail outlets. Ask for map number 269, Mount Rainier West. Ask the USGS for a topographic map of the Mount Wow area.

Directions: From Tacoma drive south on Highway 7 to Elbe and continue east on Highway 706 to the Mount Rainier National Park Nisqually Entrance Station. Proceed one mile, turn left (north) onto West Side Road, and drive to the parking area at the washout. Walk or bicycle three miles up the closed road to the trailhead on the left (west) side of the road at Round Pass. See the highway access note in the Mount Rainier Sidebar.

Contact: Outdoor Recreation Information Center, Seattle REI, 222 Yale Avenue North, Seattle, WA 98109; 206/470-4060.

54 Comet Falls/ Van Trump Park
5.5 mi/4.0 hrs

The combination of a spectacular waterfall less than two miles from the road, beautiful alpine parklands, and plentiful wildlife—including some mountain goats—draws lots of hikers to this trail. The problem is that the trail often doesn't melt out until midsummer, just when the tourists arrive, so it's difficult to hike this trail off-season. Try early October.

The trail begins steeply, with a blister-raising first half mile giving way to a more moderate grade. Soon, you're crossing just-melted snowfields. (Use good judgment if they're still-frozen snowfields; the run-out at the bottom of an impromptu glissade from here is harrowing.) At about 1.5 miles the falls come into view. It's an amazing sight, with water gushing 320 feet down. Van Trump is located about a mile up more switchbacks and steep rock. You'll want to spend some time among the wildflowers, checking out the great views. In late June and early July, keep your eyes open for mountain goats. For even more views, cross the creek and turn north, climbing a mile up to Mildred Point (elevation 5,800 feet) and a stunning view of the recalcitrant Kautz Glacier. If the creek proves uncrossable, take the spur trail to the right, following the east side of the creek to another viewpoint. From Van Trump Park, you can hike south 4.2 miles on Rampart Ridge to Longmire (see hike this chapter).

Note: A melting finger of the Kautz Glacier sent a torrent of muddy debris down Van Trump Creek—temporarily closing the path—in the unusually warm summer of 2001. The trail has been reopened, but always be on the lookout for geologic events here.

Check the level of Van Trump Creek with rangers before departing. High flows might prevent the upper crossing, which provides access to the Mildred Point viewpoint.

Location: North of Longmire in Mount Rainier National Park; see Mount Rainier and the Columbia River Gorge Map 2, grid b2.

User Groups: Hikers only. No dogs, horses, or mountain bikes are allowed. No wheelchair facilities.

Permits: A $10-per-car access fee is collected at all park entrances. Day-hiking permits are not required. Wilderness permits are required for all backcountry camping. Some permits can be reserved in advance for a fee. Others are issued free no more than 24 hours before departure. Contact the Outdoor Recreation Information Center at 206/470-4060.

Maps: For a free map of Mount Rainier National Park, contact the Outdoor Recreation

Information Center at 206/470-4060. Green Trails, Inc.'s excellent topographic maps of the region are available for $3.99 each at outdoor retail outlets. Ask for map number 269, Mount Rainier West. Ask the USGS for a topographic map of the Mount Rainier West area.

Directions: From Tacoma drive south on Highway 7 to Elbe and continue east on Highway 706 to the Mount Rainier National Park Nisqually Entrance Station. Proceed six miles to Longmire and four miles to the trailhead parking lot on the left side, just before the Christine Falls Bridge. It's often full. See the highway access note in the Mount Rainier Sidebar.

Contact: Outdoor Recreation Information Center, Seattle REI, 222 Yale Avenue North, Seattle, WA 98109; 206/470-4060.

55 Kautz Creek/Indian Henry's Hunting Ground
11.4 mi/6.0 hrs

The Kautz Creek Trail—named for Lieutenant August V. Kautz, one of Rainier's early climbers—is one of two remaining routes into Indian Henry's Hunting Ground, one of Mount Rainier National Park's most alluring day-hike destinations. (The meadow was named for a Klickitat guide who aided Rainier climbers in the late 19th century.) Along the way, you get a chance to view the awesome force of glaciation at work. The first mile of this trail is carved atop a giant mudflat, the result of an ice dam (located at the toe of Kautz Glacier) that burst in 1947, carving a giant, muddy swath out of this hillside. Similar, though smaller-scale, floods from the same glacier still result in frequent flash floods, wreaking havoc with roads such as the washout-plagued West Side Road.

The mudflat makes good walking, and you stay with it until crossing the creek and heading up a series of steep, forested switchbacks out of the valley. Near the top, you skirt Mount Ararat (named by an optimistic explorer who believed he found traces of Noah's Ark here) and drop a bit into Indian Henry's Hunting Ground, a vast meadow that lights your eyes with wildflowers in early summer. To camp, head back down the Wonderland Trail toward Longmire about a mile to Devil's Dream Camp. To take photos, continue straight up the trail beyond a junction with the Emerald Ridge Trail (see hike this chapter) to Mirror Lakes, where you can attempt to duplicate Asahel Curtis' famous postage-stamp photo of Mount Rainier reflected in the water.

Indian Henry's Hunting Ground also can be reached from Longmire via the Rampart Ridge Trail. That round-trip route is about a mile longer. The shortest route, along Tahoma Creek, is washed out and impassable.

Location: Northwest of Longmire in Mount Rainier National Park; see Mount Rainier and the Columbia River Gorge Map 2, grid b2.

User Groups: Hikers only. No dogs, horses, or mountain bikes are allowed. No wheelchair facilities.

Permits: A $10-per-car access fee is collected at all park entrances. Day-hiking permits are not required. Wilderness permits are required for all backcountry camping. Some permits can be reserved in advance for a fee. Others are issued free no more than 24 hours before departure. Contact the Outdoor Recreation Information Center at 206/470-4060.

Maps: For a free map of Mount Rainier National Park, contact the Outdoor Recreation Information Center at 206/470-4060. Green Trails, Inc.'s excellent topographic maps of the region are available for $3.99 each at outdoor retail outlets. Ask for map number 269,

Mount Rainier West. Ask the USGS for a topographic map of the Mount Rainier West area.

Directions: From Tacoma drive south on Highway 7 to Elbe and continue east on Highway 706 to the Mount Rainier National Park Nisqually Entrance Station. Proceed for three miles; the Kautz Creek Trailhead is near the Kautz Creek Bridge. See the highway access note in the Mount Rainier Sidebar.

Contact: Outdoor Recreation Information Center, Seattle REI, 222 Yale Avenue North, Seattle, WA 98109; 206/470-4060.

56 Rampart Ridge Loop
4.6 mi/2.5 hrs

It's 9 A.M., telemark skis are on the roof, gaiters are on your calves, and Paradise Road is closed for another two hours while snowplows do their thing up above. What to do? Park the rig at the National Park Inn and stretch those legs on the Rampart Ridge Trail. This is a pleasant loop that can be hiked with equal ease in either direction. It's a bit steep at first, but only until you gain the ridge atop the Ramparts, created by an ancient lava flow from Rainier. The views are good in all directions—assuming you can see more than 50 feet—as you walk about 1.25 miles along the ridge and then drop back into the forest. If you're hiking clockwise, you arrive at a junction with the Wonderland Trail at three miles (1.5 miles counterclockwise). Turn right to go back to Longmire and left to reach Pyramid Creek Camp, Squaw Lake, and Indian Henry's Hunting Grounds. The path straight ahead is the Van Trump Park Trail, which leads three miles to Mildred Point (offering an awesome view of the Kautz Glacier), over the rushing stream in Van Trump Park, past spectacular Comet Falls and Christine Falls, and back 5.7 miles to a higher point on the Nisqually-Paradise Road. If transportation can be arranged, the latter route makes a pleasant 8.2-mile day-hike loop. The elevation gain for the short loop is about 1,340 feet.

Location: Near Longmire in Mount Rainier National Park; see Mount Rainier and the Columbia River Gorge Map 2, grid b2.

User Groups: Hikers only. No dogs, horses, or mountain bikes are allowed. No wheelchair facilities.

Permits: A $10-per-car access fee is collected at all park entrances. Day-hiking permits are not required. Wilderness permits are required for all backcountry camping. Some permits can be reserved in advance for a fee. Others are issued free no more than 24 hours before departure. Contact the Outdoor Recreation Information Center at 206/470-4060.

Maps: For a free map of Mount Rainier National Park, contact the Outdoor Recreation Information Center at 206/470-4060. Green Trails, Inc.'s excellent topographic maps of the region are available for $3.99 each at outdoor retail outlets. Ask for map number 269, Mount Rainier West. Ask the USGS for a topographic map of the Mowich Lake area.

Directions: From Tacoma drive south on Highway 7 to Elbe and continue east on Highway 706 to the Mount Rainier National Park Nisqually Entrance Station. Proceed six miles to Longmire and look for the Trail of the Shadows Nature Trail directly across the highway from the National Park Inn. See the highway access note in the Mount Rainier Sidebar.

Contact: Outdoor Recreation Information Center, Seattle REI, 222 Yale Avenue North, Seattle, WA 98109; 206/470-4060.

57 Trail of the Shadows Nature Trail
0.75 mi/0.5 hr

Accessible to the whole family, this leg-stretcher offers a historic link as well. You pass the former site of the Longmire Springs Hotel, a cabin restored from the original 1888 Longmire family mining settlement, several steaming mineral springs, and other interesting artifacts. One is a restored cabin that was part of the original Longmire settlement and now rates as the oldest structure in the park. The trail is self-guided, so pick up an interpretive pamphlet at the trailhead and proceed counterclockwise. Unlike most Mount Rainier trails, this one is snow-free for much of the year and makes a good, brisk early-winter walk for patrons of the National Park Inn at Longmire. (The Nisqually-Paradise Road is the only Mount Rainier National Park road that is kept open all winter.) The entire gravel-and-boardwalk route is wheelchair accessible, with a grade ranging 3–12 percent.

Some important last words: Don't drink the water from the springs. It's nasty.

Location: Near Longmire in Mount Rainier National Park; see Mount Rainier and the Columbia River Gorge Map 2, grid b2.

User Groups: Hikers and wheelchairs. No dogs, horses, or mountain bikes are allowed.

Permits: A $10-per-car access fee is collected at all park entrances. Day-hiking permits are not required.

Maps: For a free map of Mount Rainier National Park, contact the Outdoor Recreation Information Center at 206/470-4060. Green Trails, Inc.'s excellent topographic maps of the region are available for $3.99 each at outdoor retail outlets. Ask for number 269, Mount Rainier West. Ask the USGS for a topographic map of the Mowich Lake area.

Directions: From Tacoma drive south on Highway 7 to Elbe and continue east on Highway 706 to the Mount Rainier National Park Nisqually Entrance Station. Proceed six miles to Longmire and look for the Trail of the Shadows Nature Trail directly across the highway from the National Park Inn. See the highway access note in the Mount Rainier Sidebar.

Contact: Outdoor Recreation Information Center, Seattle REI, 222 Yale Avenue North, Seattle, WA 98109; 206/470-4060.

58 Carter Falls/Paradise River
2.0 mi/1.0 hr

You might feel a surge of power on this trail. Relax, it's not coming from the Power Bar you inhaled in the car on the way up. It's emanating from the ground. Or at least it used to be. The Carter Falls Trail takes you across the Nisqually River and along remnants of an old hydroelectric power project that once lit Longmire. You pass the site of an old power plant and are accompanied for some distance by an old wooden pipeline that once carried water to spin turbines. But this hike is mostly natural, winding through spectacular old-growth forest on the banks of the Paradise River. Carter Falls makes a good photo-shoot destination. If you're left with extra frames, venture a short distance beyond to Madcap Falls.

Location: North of Longmire in Mount Rainier National Park; see Mount Rainier and the Columbia River Gorge Map 2, grid b2.

User Groups: Hikers only. No dogs, horses, or mountain bikes are allowed. No wheelchair facilities.

Permits: A $10-per-car access fee is collected at all park entrances. Day-hiking permits are not required.

Maps: For a free map of Mount Rainier National Park, contact the Outdoor Recreation Information Center at 206/470-4060. Green Trails, Inc.'s excellent topographic maps of the region are available for $3.99 each at outdoor retail outlets. Ask for map number 269, Mount Rainier West. Ask the USGS for a topographic map of the Mowich Lake area.

Directions: From Tacoma drive south on Highway 7 to Elbe and continue east on Highway 706 to the Mount Rainier National Park Nisqually Entrance Station. Proceed six miles to Longmire and find the trailhead on the right shoulder, just before the entrance to Cougar Rock Campground. See the highway access note in the Mount Rainier Sidebar.

Contact: Outdoor Recreation Information Center, Seattle REI, 222 Yale Avenue North, Seattle, WA 98109; 206/470-4060.

59 Eagle Peak
7.2 mi/5.0 hrs

The Eagle Peak Trail is the number one cause of sweaty, bedraggled hikers pulling their bodies into Longmire's National Park Inn and ordering hot fudge sundaes to resuscitate themselves. In an area littered with short, relatively easy hikes, Eagle Peak stands out as a thigh-burner. It's serious business, climbing nearly 3,000 feet in 3.6 miles. But the magnificent virgin forest on the way up and the stupendous Rainier views once you reach the 5,700-foot saddle below the summit are more than worth the effort. The final stretches of the trail are steep, and the last several hundred feet to the summit should be attempted by trained climbers only. The view of the Nisqually River below is lovely; don't fall into it and mess it up. Besides, there's a sundae down at the inn with your name on it. The elevation gain to the saddle is 2,955 feet.

You won't find a designated backcountry campsite up here, but overnight camping is allowed to those who can practice low-impact techniques in available space.

Location: Near Longmire in Mount Rainier National Park; see Mount Rainier and the Columbia River Gorge Map 2, grid b2.

User Groups: Hikers only. No dogs, horses, or mountain bikes are allowed. No wheelchair facilities.

Permits: A $10-per-car access fee is collected at all park entrances. Day-hiking permits are not required. Wilderness permits are required for all backcountry camping. Some permits can be reserved in advance for a fee. Others are issued free no more than 24 hours before departure. Contact the Outdoor Recreation Information Center at 206/470-4060.

Maps: For a free map of Mount Rainier National Park, contact the Outdoor Recreation Information Center at 206/470-4060. Green Trails, Inc.'s excellent topographic maps of the region are available for $3.99 each at outdoor retail outlets. Ask for map number 269, Mount Rainier West. Ask the USGS for topographic maps of the Mount Rainier West and Wahpenayo Peak areas.

Directions: From Tacoma drive south on Highway 7 to Elbe and continue east on Highway 706 to the Mount Rainier National Park Nisqually Entrance Station. Proceed six miles to Longmire, cross the suspension bridge over the Nisqually River, and park in front of the community building. Walk a short distance back toward the bridge; you find the trailhead on the right, 50 yards from the bridge. See the highway access note in the Mount Rainier Sidebar.

Contact: Outdoor Recreation Information Center, Seattle REI, 222 Yale Avenue North, Seattle, WA 98109; 206/470-4060.

60 Osborne Mountain
11.0 mi/6.0 hrs

A short hop away from the crowded trails of Mount Rainier National Park, Osborne Mountain combines a solid aerobic workout with good views of Rainier and three alpine lakes. From Big Creek Campground, the trail begins a gentle climb through forest and then switches back steeply up the north slopes of Osborne Mountain, passing through a clear-cut before dropping onto the mountain's south side. Here you turn southeast and proceed about two miles to a junction with the Teeley Lake Trail. Turn left to visit Pothole Lake or right to continue a short distance to Bertha May Lake. From both, gaze to the south at the impressive Sawtooth Ridge, which ranges from 5,100 to 5,700 feet.

If you prefer to navigate this trail on a motorcycle, note that this trail is open to motorized use in the summer after June 30.

Location: In the Nisqually River drainage of Gifford Pinchot National Forest; see Mount Rainier and the Columbia River Gorge Map 2, grid c2.

User Groups: Hikers, leashed dogs, and horses. Mountain bikes are permitted, but not recommended. No wheelchair facilities.

Permits: A federal Northwest Forest Pass, $5 per day or $30 annually, is required to park at the trailhead. Passes are available from ranger stations and many private vendors, online at website: www.wta.org, or by calling 800/270-7504.

Maps: For a map of the Gifford Pinchot National Forest, contact the Outdoor Recreation Information Center, Seattle REI, 222 Yale Avenue North, Seattle, WA 98109; 206/470-4060. Green Trails, Inc.'s excellent topographic maps of the region are available for $3.99 each at various outdoor retail outlets. Ask for map number 301, Randle. Ask the USGS for a topographic map of the Randle area.

Directions: From Tacoma drive south on Highway 7 to Elbe and continue east on Highway 706 for about seven miles to Forest Service Road 52. Turn south, proceed about five miles, and turn right (south) into Big Creek Campground. The trailhead is in the campground.

Contact: Gifford Pinchot National Forest, Cowlitz Valley

Ranger District, 10024 U.S. Highway 12, Randle, WA 98377; 360/497-1100.

61 High Rock
3.2 mi/2.0 hrs

High Rock is one of the more impressive stone formations on which you're ever likely to sit, not so much for its sheer height (5,700 feet) but for its sheer north face (about 600 feet straight down). The trail begins near a clear-cut and rises 1,400 feet through increasingly thin forest before opening to the grand spectacle at the top: a 1929-vintage fire lookout on the tip-top of what appears to be a massive, stone-walled ship's bow. Look straight ahead for one of the most magnificent views of Rainier anywhere in Washington. Look straight down, about 1,400 feet, for an overhead view of Cora Lake. You'll want to spend some time here watching Rainier make its own weather, which in turn performs magical shadow-and-light shows across the mountain's full south face; you'll see these displays in better detail here than from anywhere inside Mount Rainier National Park. High Rock is a favorite early-morning and late-afternoon hangout for nature photographers. The fire lookout, the only one left in the Cowlitz Valley Ranger District (and one of only three in the Gifford Pinchot National Forest) is staffed in the summer.

Location: In the Gifford Pinchot National Forest south of Mount Rainier National Park; see Mount Rainier and the Columbia River Gorge Map 2, grid c2.

User Groups: Hikers, leashed dogs, horses, and mountain bikes. Horses and mountain bikes are not recommended because of steep cliffs and exposures. No wheelchair facilities.

Permits: A federal Northwest Forest Pass, $5 per day or $30 annually, is required to park at the trailhead. Passes are available from ranger stations and many private vendors, online at website: www.wta.org, or by calling 800/270-7504.

Maps: For a map of the Gifford Pinchot National Forest, contact the Outdoor Recreation Information Center, Seattle REI, 222 Yale Avenue North, Seattle, WA 98109; 206/470-4060. Green Trails, Inc.'s excellent topographic maps of the region are available for $3.99 each at various outdoor retail outlets. Ask for map number 301, Randle. Ask the USGS for a topographic map of the Randle area.

Directions: From Tacoma drive Highway 7 east to Elbe and continue on Highway 706 to Ashford. Continue east and turn right onto Kernahan Road. At about 1.5 miles turn right onto Forest Service Road 85. Proceed 5.8 miles to Forest Service Road 8440. Turn left and continue 4.5 miles to the trailhead on the left.

Contact: Gifford Pinchot National Forest, Cowlitz Valley Ranger District, 10024 U.S. Highway 12, Randle, WA 98377; 360/497-1100.

62 Camp Muir
9.0 mi/9.0 hrs

Think twice before embarking on this one. If you don't have a good reason to get to Camp Muir, the main staging area for Mount Rainier summit attempts, easier trails with comparable views can be found elsewhere in the Paradise area. But for accomplished hikers who want to hit the high spot (10,000 feet), or for mental mountaineers seeking a taste of what a Rainier summit attempt might be like, Camp Muir calls. Faintly. It's 4,600 feet up from the Paradise parking lot. The first half of the route isn't difficult: it's the Skyline Trail (see hike in this chapter). Hike to Panorama Point (elevation 6,800 feet) on the lower Skyline Trail or to the Pebble Creek crossing of the upper trail and turn due north, straight up the mountain. It's only 2.7 more miles to

Camp Muir, but it seems like the equivalent of 27 miles on a flat, easy trail. From here your hike becomes a snow slog, difficult any time of the year, downright hazardous with poor snow or weather conditions. Crevasses can open on the route, and weather can turn from bright and sunny to dark, foggy, and lethal in minutes. This trip shouldn't be attempted by anyone without proper climbing gear and prior knowledge of snow traverses.

That said, however, a night at Camp Muir can be an exhilarating experience—sort of a mini-summit all of its own. By keeping your sights on Gibraltar Rock and climbing up established steps, you might make it to Muir, where the stone and concrete shelters are likely to be occupied by climbers preparing for an early morning summit attempt. Tent sites are available, and a toilet is provided. Use it. The view below is stupendous. Sunsets from the camp will be emblazoned on your memory for the rest of your life. The site is named for writer and outdoor luminary John Muir, a member of the sixth successful Rainier summit group in 1888.

Location: High above the Paradise area on the south side of Mount Rainier; see Mount Rainier and the Columbia River Gorge Map 2, grid b3.

User Groups: Hikers only. No dogs, horses, or mountain bikes. No wheelchair facilities.

Permits: A $10-per-car access fee is collected at all park entrances. Day-hiking permits are not required. Wilderness permits are required for all backcountry camping. Some permits can be reserved in advance for a fee. Others are issued free no more than 24 hours before departure. Contact the Outdoor Recreation Information Center at 206/470-4060.

Maps: For a free map of Mount Rainier National Park, contact the Outdoor Recreation Information Center at 206/470-4060. Green Trails, Inc.'s excellent topographic maps of the region are available for $3.99 each at outdoor retail outlets. Ask for map number 270, Mount Rainier East, or number 270S, Paradise. Ask the USGS for a topographic map of the Mount Rainier East area.

Directions: From Tacoma drive 40 miles south on Highway 7 to Elbe and then continue 10 miles east on Highway 706 to the Mount Rainier National Park Nisqually Entrance Station. Proceed 20 miles to the upper Paradise parking lot at Paradise Ranger Station. The trailhead is near the restrooms to the left of the ranger station.

Contact: Outdoor Recreation Information Center, Seattle REI, 222 Yale Avenue North, Seattle, WA 98109; 206/470-4060.

63 Skyline Loop
5.8 mi/4.0 hrs

Get in the mood for altitude. The Skyline Trail above Paradise takes you quickly to nearly 7,000 feet—about as high as you can get in a short hike from the car anywhere in Washington state. The loop trip is spectacular on clear days, with views to the Rainier summit above, wildflowers all around and a view south as far as Mount Hood below.

Most people hike the loop clockwise, following the Skyline Trail north past the Alta Vista Nature Trail, then turning directly up the mountain, and passing the short Glacier Vista Loop, which offers prime views of the massive Nisqually Glacier. At about two miles you come to a split. Your direction might be dictated by the season and the weather. If it's late in the year or a very warm day, the snowfield blocking the lower route should be well-stomped and fairly easy to traverse. If it's early in the season or in the day, when snow is likely to remain hard, take the upper route and detour. That adds about three-fourths of a mile to the loop, but you'll be glad later. The lower route leads directly to aptly named Panorama Point, where views in all directions are magnificent. When the upper and lower paths meet, the trail turns south below McClure Rock, leading in about half a mile to a junction with the Golden Gate Trail. For the quickest exit back to Paradise, turn right here for the 1.5-mile walk back to the parking lot. Or continue straight toward Mazama Ridge and a 2.5-mile return via the first portion of the Lakes Trail (see hike in this chapter). This trail is crowded on nice summer days. You might be more pleased with a hike very early in the day or in late afternoon. Carry water and note that no camping is allowed.

Location: Above Paradise on the south slopes of Mount Rainier; see Mount Rainier and the Columbia River Gorge Map 2, grid b3.

User Groups: Hikers only. No dogs, horses, or mountain bikes. No wheelchair facilities.

Permits: No day-use permits are required. A $10-per-vehicle access fee is collected at the Nisqually Entrance Station.

Maps: For a free map of Mount Rainier National Park, contact the Outdoor Recreation Information Center at 206/470-4060. Green Trails, Inc.'s excellent topographic maps of the region are available for $3.99 each at outdoor retail outlets. Ask for map number 270, Mount Rainier East, or number 270S, Paradise. Ask the USGS for a topographic map of the Mount Rainier East area.

Directions: From Tacoma drive 40 miles south on Highway 7 to Elbe and go east 10 miles on Highway 706 to the Mount Rainier National Park Nisqually Entrance Station. Proceed 20 miles to the upper Paradise parking lot near Paradise Ranger Station. The trailhead is near the restrooms to the left of the ranger station.

Contact: Outdoor Recreation Information Center, Seattle REI, 222 Yale Avenue North, Seattle, WA 98109; 206/470-4060.

64 Paradise Glacier
6.0 mi/4.0 hrs

The Paradise Glacier hike provides a high-altitude refuge from the teeming summertime throngs at Paradise. From the parking lot trek up the Skyline Trail described in this chapter. Beyond Myrtle Falls take a right (east) turn onto the Skyline Trail and then hike 1.3 miles uphill, over the Paradise River, up Mazama Ridge, and beyond the Stevens-Van Trump monument to famous 1870 Rainier climbers. Go right at the fork and climb 1.3 miles and 400 vertical feet to the toe of Paradise Glacier, 6,400 feet.

The upper portion of the trail is an otherworldly experience. You rise and fall over an ancient moraine in desolate, tundra-like conditions. Depending on weather and snowpack, this upper stretch can be quite difficult, particularly if deep, sloppy snow lingers. (In spring and early summer, this is a popular backcountry ski destination.) It's tempting to wander off in this wide-open country, but stick to the trail or to marker posts, whichever is more visible. Hazardous pitfalls await on either side of the trail.

This trail became one of the most famous in the United States years ago as a route to the world-renowned Paradise Glacier ice caves—massive, wind-carved caverns of deep blue ice that were widely photographed. But in recent years glacial movement has effectively destroyed or closed off the caves. Trekking on the glacier, parts of which are quite thin, can be extremely hazardous. This glacier keeps many secrets, however. From time to time an adventurous climber or telemark skier will return with tales of new ice-cave exploration. Leave it to the risk-takers and enjoy the view of the glacier, which is hard to beat.

Location: On the south slopes of Mount Rainier; see Mount Rainier and the Columbia River Gorge Map 2, grid b3.

User Groups: Hikers only. No dogs, horses, or mountain bikes. No wheelchair facilities.

Permits: A $10-per-car access fee is collected at all park entrances. Day-hiking permits are not required. Wilderness permits are required for all backcountry camping. Some permits can be reserved in advance for a fee. Others are issued free no more than 24 hours before departure. Contact the Outdoor Recreation Information Center at 206/470-4060.

Maps: For a free map of Mount Rainier National Park, contact the Outdoor Recreation Information Center at 206/470-4060. Green Trails, Inc.'s excellent topographic maps of the region are available for $3.99 each at outdoor retail outlets. Ask for map number 270, Mount Rainier East, or number 270S, Paradise. Ask the USGS for a topographic map of the Mount Rainier East area.

Directions: From Tacoma drive 40 miles south on Highway 7 to Elbe and go east 10 miles on Highway 706 to the Mount Rainier National Park Nisqually Entrance Station. Proceed 20 miles to the upper Paradise parking lot at Paradise Ranger Station. The trailhead is near the restrooms to the left of the ranger station.

Contact: Outdoor Recreation Information Center, Seattle REI, 222 Yale Avenue North, Seattle, WA 98109; 206/470-4060.

65 Mazama Ridge/Lakes Loop
5.0 mi/4.0 hrs

You climb up, you drop down, but most of the time, you just gape. The Lakes Loop, which begins above Paradise, turns south along Mazama Ridge to the Reflection Lakes area, and then ascends north back to Paradise, is the best daylong sampler of Rainier's unique and spectacular alpine country. Start on the Skyline Trail, paved for the first half mile, and then turn east just beyond Myrtle Falls, saving the upward (left) branch toward Golden Gate and the Skyline Trail for another day. After an up-and-down mile beyond Myrtle Falls, turn right (south) at the junction with the Mazama Ridge Trail. In the next 1.5 miles, you drop downhill, leaving spectacular wildflower meadows for dry, scrubby forest and occasional lakes. At the next junction you're left with a choice: Turn right (west) on the High Lakes Trail and pass high above Reflection Lakes, with outstanding views to the south Cascades, and return two miles to Paradise parking lot. Or continue straight (south) along the ridge to the memorable views of Rainier from Faraway Rock and, 0.75 mile farther south, Reflection Lakes. If you choose the latter route, you exit onto Stevens Canyon Road about a quarter mile east of the Reflection Lakes parking lot, where you can hook up with the Lakes Trail and return 1.5 miles uphill to Paradise. The lower Reflection Lakes route adds about one mile to the trip mileage noted above.

Location: Near the Henry M. Jackson Visitor Center at Paradise, on the south slopes of Mount Rainier; see Mount Rainier and the Columbia River Gorge Map 2, grid b3.

User Groups: Hikers only. No dogs, horses, or mountain bikes. No wheelchair facilities.

Permits: A $10-per-car access fee is collected at all park entrances. Day-hiking permits are not required. Wilderness permits are required for all backcountry camping. Some permits can be reserved in advance for a fee. Others are issued free no more than 24 hours before departure. Contact the Outdoor Recreation Information Center at 206/470-4060.

Maps: For a free map of Mount Rainier National Park, contact the Outdoor Recreation Information Center at 206/470-4060. Green Trails, Inc.'s excellent topographic maps of the region are available for $3.99 each at outdoor retail outlets. Ask for map number 270, Mount Rainier East or number 270S, Paradise. Ask the USGS for a topographic map of the Mount Rainier East area.

Directions: From Tacoma drive 40 miles south on Highway 7 to Elbe and continue east 10 miles on Highway 706 to the Mount Rainier National Park Nisqually Entrance Station. Proceed 20 miles to the upper parking lot near Paradise Ranger Station. Find the trailhead near the restrooms.

Contact: Outdoor Recreation Information Center, Seattle REI, 222 Yale Avenue North, Seattle, WA 98109; 206/470-4060.

66 Pinnacle Saddle
2.6 mi/2.0 hrs

If you're at Paradise for one day and want to head straight for the best camera angle in the area, here's your trail. Unlike other Paradise vistas, which actually traverse the lower slopes of the mountain, Pinnacle Saddle is a bit more detached, keeping a constant watch on Rainier from the Tatoosh Range to the south. The trail starts out gradually and then turns upward sharply enough to crimp the style of even the most aerobically fit. The trail ends at an elevation of 6,000 feet in the saddle between Pinnacle Peak (6,562 feet) and Plummer Peak (6,370 feet). The view of Rainier is framable, and the view backward, to the south, is almost as magnificent. Try to pick out Mount Adams in the haze.

Sections of this trail remain snowbound until midsummer and should not be attempted by hikers without experience crossing snow. Sturdy, waterproof, and deep-lugged boots are recommended, if not essential. Several scrambles from the saddle to the top are inviting but should be avoided by most.

Location: South of the Henry M. Jackson Visitor Center at Paradise, on the south slopes of Mount Rainier; see Mount Rainier and the Columbia River Gorge Map 2, grid b3.

User Groups: Hikers only. No dogs, horses, or mountain bikes. No wheelchair facilities.

Permits: A $10-per-car access fee is collected at all park entrances. Day-hiking permits are not required. Wilderness permits are required for all backcountry camping. Some permits can be reserved in advance for a fee. Others are issued free no more than 24 hours before departure. Contact the Outdoor Recreation Information Center at 206/470-4060.

Maps: For a free map of Mount Rainier National Park, contact the Outdoor Recreation Information Center at 206/470-4060. Green Trails, Inc.'s excellent topographic maps of the region are available for $3.99 each at outdoor retail outlets. Ask for map number 270, Mount Rainier East, or 270S, Paradise. Ask the USGS for a topographic map of the Mount Rainier East area.

Directions: From Tacoma drive 40 miles south on Highway 7 to Elbe and go east 10 miles on Highway 706 to the Mount Rainier National Park Nisqually Entrance Station. Proceed 15 miles to Stevens Canyon Road. Turn right (south) and drive 1.5 miles south to the Reflection Lakes parking area. The trailhead is on the south side of the road.

Contact: Outdoor Recreation Information Center, Seattle REI, 222 Yale Avenue North, Seattle, WA 98109; 206/470-4060.

67 Bench and Snow Lakes
2.6 mi/1.5 hrs

Bring the camera. Bring the mudboots. Bring the kids. Bench and Snow Lakes, two easily accessible Kodak moments near Paradise (the park's most popular destination) rank high on the tennis-shoe-stuck-in-the-mud list. Situated about 700 feet below the Paradise parking lot, the lakes seem to be at a relatively low elevation. But they're actually set at 4,700 feet and happen to lie in a basin that receives as much snow in a single season as any spot on the planet. That means lovely, snow-spotted views throughout the summer. It also means slow-thawing lakes (July) and lingering mud on the trail (late July). Be prepared. The muddy areas, once dry, actually become quite dusty due to heavy use. Other than that it's a delightful walk, with several major blood-pumping ups and downs (total round-trip elevation gain is 700 feet). The first lake, Bench, is reached in three-quarters of a mile. Half a mile beyond is Snow Lake, a gorgeous droplet beneath barren 6,940-foot Unicorn Peak. Examine the top of the peak and guess the source of its name. In early summer wildflowers are abundant along the route. Keep your eyes peeled for black bears. Extremely limited—and extremely stunning—campsites are available by permit only at Snow Lake and elsewhere off-trail along the surrounding Tatoosh Ridge.

Location: South of Henry M. Jackson Visitor Center at Paradise, on the south slopes of Mount Rainier; see Mount Rainier and the Columbia River Gorge Map 2, grid b3.

User Groups: Hikers only. No dogs, horses, or mountain bikes. No wheelchair facilities.

Permits: A $10-per-car access fee is collected at all park entrances. Day-hiking permits are not required. Wilderness permits are required for all backcountry camping. Some permits can be reserved in advance for a fee. Others are issued free no more than 24 hours before departure. Contact the Outdoor Recreation Information Center at 206/470-4060.

Maps: For a free map of Mount Rainier National Park, contact the Outdoor Recreation Information Center at 206/470-4060. Green Trails, Inc.'s excellent topographic maps of

the region are available for $3.99 each at outdoor retail outlets. Ask for map numbers 270 or 270S, Mount Rainier East or Paradise. Ask the USGS for a topographic map of the Mount Rainier East area.

Directions: From Tacoma drive 40 miles south on Highway 7 to Elbe and go east 10 miles on Highway 706 to the Mount Rainier National Park Nisqually Entrance Station. Proceed beyond Longmire and Narada Falls to Stevens Canyon Road. Turn right and drive just under three miles to the trailhead, about 1.2 miles east of the Reflection Lakes parking area. The trailhead is on the south side of the road. Note: The trailhead also can be reached from the east by driving Stevens Canyon Road about 16 miles west from its junction with Highway 123.

Contact: Outdoor Recreation Information Center, Seattle REI, 222 Yale Avenue North, Seattle, WA 98109; 206/470-4060.

68 Wonderland Trail
93.0 mi/14.0 days

This is the mother of all Northwest backpacking experiences: no less than 93 miles, all the way around Rainier, through some of the more magical—and frustrating—terrain you could ever wish or fear to encounter. Along the way, you participate in all of Rainier's microclimates and environments, ranging from lowland forest to high, exposed snowfield crossings. Eighteen campsites, some with shelters, are found along the route, spaced between three and seven miles apart. Don't plan on skipping by three or four of them in one day. The Wonderland Trail rarely lollygags. It's steep: you gain 20,000 feet over the whole route, and gains and losses of 3,500 feet a day are common. Wonderland veterans advise that you plan to travel only seven to 10 miles a day. Even if you proceed more quickly, there's a good chance that weather will slow you down or stop you cold somewhere along the route. The trail is at its best from mid-July to September, when snow has receded far enough for you to follow most of the trail without resorting to compass skills. Even late in the summer, you should know how to navigate with a compass, and carrying an ice ax is a good idea any time of the year. Go prepared and you'll bring home memories that last a lifetime.

The Wonderland Trail is filled with amazingly beautiful vistas, surprise revelations, and completely unpredictable climatic conditions. Be flexible. Be resilient. A word about supplies: trust us, you won't want to carry two weeks' worth of food over the entire route. Plan at least one ranger-station food cache, two if possible. Paradise, Longmire, and Sunrise are the most dependable, and some self-serve (unsecured) cache barrels are available elsewhere. Food must be in weather- and rodent-proof containers, and you can't cache fuel. Contact the park for detailed cache-planning information. Our advice: arrange for friends to meet you with a cache. They'll enjoy it, and so will your stomach.

Now, wondering where to start and in which direction? It doesn't really matter. Pick an easy entrance point and make sure it's one that allows timely pickup of your cached goods at a convenient place. Parting advice: rainproof everything you carry. Everything.

Location: All the way around Mount Rainier with trailheads at various spots throughout Mount Rainier National Park; see Mount Rainier and the Columbia River Gorge Map 2, grid b3.

User Groups: Hikers only. Horses are allowed on several stretches of the trail; consult park rangers for details. No dogs or mountain bikes. No wheelchair facilities.

Permits: A $10-per-car access fee is collected at all park entrances. Day-hiking permits are not required. Wilderness permits are required for all backcountry camping. Some permits can be reserved in advance for a fee. Others are issued free no more than 24 hours before departure. Contact the Outdoor Recreation Information Center at 206/470-4060.

Maps: For a free map of Mount Rainier National Park, contact the Outdoor Recreation Information Center at 206/470-4060. Green Trails, Inc.'s excellent topographic maps of the region are available for $3.99 each at outdoor retail outlets. Ask for map numbers 269, 270, and 270S, Mount Rainier West, Mount Rainier East, and Paradise. To obtain USGS topographic maps, ask for Mount Rainier West, Mount Rainier East, Mowich Lake, Sunrise, Golden Lakes, Mount Wow, White River Park, and Chinook Pass areas.

Directions: The Wonderland Trail can be accessed from dozens of trailheads, but the most popular are the Paradise/Reflection Lakes area and Longmire. To reach either from Tacoma, drive 40 miles south on Highway 7 to Elbe and continue east 10 miles on Highway 706 to the Mount Rainier National Park Nisqually Entrance Station. Proceed six miles to the trailhead at Longmire or continue nine miles to Stevens Canyon Road. Turn right (south) and drive 1.5 miles to the Reflection Lakes parking area on the right. Or park at the main Paradise parking lot and hike the Lakes Trail 1.2 miles south to the Wonderland Trail. Consult with rangers about campsites before departing.

Contact: Outdoor Recreation Information Center, Seattle REI, 222 Yale Avenue North, Seattle, WA 98109; 206/470-4060.

69 Paradise Nature Trails
1.0–2.5 mi/0.5–1.5 hrs

Few places in the Northwest offer as much alpine splendor such a short distance from the car as Paradise. For some of the splendor, you don't even have to venture off pavement. Favorite short day hikes from the Paradise parking lot include Alta Vista, a loop that departs from the lower Paradise parking lot and also from the Skyline Trail. It winds through wildflower meadows to the top of a knoll overlooking Paradise, with views south as far as Mount St. Helens and Mount Adams. Alta Vista is 1.5 miles long and can be hiked in an hour or less. For a longer walk hike the Deadhorse Creek Trail three-quarters of a mile from the lower Paradise parking lot to the Moraine Trail, which leads just over a half mile to a viewpoint above the Nisqually Glacier. Another good choice from the lower parking area is the Nisqually Vista Trail, which leads west to a loop overlooking the Upper Nisqually River and Nisqually Glacier. It's a 1.2-mile loop that can be hiked in an hour or less. For a higher-altitude walk, hike the Skyline Trail about a mile and 600 vertical feet to the short Glacier Vista Loop, a round-trip of just under two miles. When the weather cooperates, you can't go wrong on any of these trails—assuming, that is, you stay on the path and off the fragile plants, some of which bloom only every several years and can take years to recover from a stomping.

Location: In the Paradise area on the south side of Mount Rainier; see Mount Rainier and the Columbia River Gorge Map 2, grid b3.

User Groups: Hikers only. No dogs, horses, or mountain bikes. No wheelchair facilities.

Permits: A $10-per-car access fee is collected at all park entrances. Day-hiking permits are not required.

Maps: For a free map of Mount Rainier National Park, contact the Outdoor Recreation Information Center at 206/470-4060. Green Trails, Inc.'s excellent topographic maps of the region are available for $3.99 each at outdoor retail outlets. Ask for map number 270, Mount Rainier East, or number 270S, Paradise. Ask the USGS for a topographic map of the Mount Rainier East area.

Directions: From Tacoma drive 40 miles south on Highway 7 to Elbe and then go east 10 miles on Highway 706 to the Mount Rainier National Park Nisqually Entrance Station. Proceed 20 miles to the Paradise area and park in the lower lot, near the Henry M. Jackson Visitor Center.

Contact: Outdoor Recreation Information Center, Seattle REI, 222 Yale Avenue North, Seattle, WA 98109; 206/470-4060.

70 Grove of the Patriarchs
1.3 mi/1.0 hr

Cross a bridge and go back in time. You can do both on the Grove of the Patriarchs Trail, which crosses the Ohanapecosh River on a suspension bridge and loops on a boardwalk through a grove of ancient Douglas fir, western red cedar, and hemlock, estimated to be 1,000 years old. The trees, protected from fire and other intrusions by a lot of water and a little luck, are spectacular. Some of the trunks are more than 35 feet in circumference and they're plentiful here. This is an easy hike, suitable for families with small children. The value of the experience is much higher than the energy you expend. If you're still up for more miles on the spectacularly clear Ohanapecosh River, cross the highway at the trailhead and head about a mile down the Eastside Trail (see hike this chapter) to spectacular Silver Falls and beyond to Ohanapecosh Campground. It's a slam-dunk winner of a day hike.

Location: Near the Stevens Canyon Entrance to Mount

Rainier National Park; see Mount Rainier and the Columbia River Gorge Map 2, grid b3.

User Groups: Hikers only. No dogs, horses, or mountain bikes. No wheelchair facilities.

Permits: No day-use permits are required. A $10-per-vehicle entrance fee is collected at the Stevens Canyon Entrance Station. Parking is free.

Maps: For a free map of Mount Rainier National Park, contact the Outdoor Recreation Information Center at 206/470-4060. Green Trails, Inc.'s excellent topographic maps of the region are available for $3.99 each at outdoor retail outlets. Ask for map number 270, Mount Rainier East. Ask the USGS for a topographic map of the Ohanapecosh Hot Springs area.

Directions: From Enumclaw drive 41 miles east on Highway 410 to Highway 123. Follow Highway 123 south for 11 miles to the Stevens Canyon Entrance to Mount Rainier National Park. The trailhead is just west of the entrance station on Stevens Canyon Road.

Contact: Outdoor Recreation Information Center, Seattle REI, 222 Yale Avenue North, Seattle, WA 98109; 206/470-4060.

🔟 Eastside Trail
9.0 mi one way/4.5 hrs 🥾

You can't see Mount Rainier from here, which is actually more of a blessing than a curse for the Eastside Trail. Thanks to its lack of a summit view, the trail receives far less traffic than its counterparts high on the mountain. On a hot summer day when tourists are huffing and puffing their way toward Glacier Vista, you could be lying back and soaking your feet in the crystal-clear waters of the Ohanapecosh River and strolling at great length beneath magnificent timber.

If you can arrange transportation, this is one of the best one-way hikes in Mount Rainier National Park. Start at Deer Creek and hike south, crossing gushing Chinook Creek on a bridge above a picturesque waterfall. Continue on this cool, quiet trail all the way to Ohanapecosh Campground, adding a nice side trip on the Grove of the Patriarchs loop trail or Silver Falls (see hikes this chapter) near the finish line.

Location: Along the upper Ohanapecosh River in southeastern Mount Rainier National Park; see Mount Rainier and the Columbia River Gorge Map 2, grid b3.

User Groups: Hikers only. No dogs, horses, or mountain bikes. No wheelchair facilities.

Permits: A $10-per-car access fee is collected at all park entrances. Day-hiking permits are not required. Wilderness permits are required for all backcountry camping. Some permits can be reserved in advance for a fee. Others are issued free no more than 24 hours before departure. Contact the Outdoor Recreation Information Center at 206/470-4060.

Maps: For a free map of Mount Rainier National Park, contact the Outdoor Recreation Information Center at 206/470-4060. Green Trails, Inc.'s excellent topographic maps of the region are available for $3.99 each at outdoor retail outlets. Ask for map number 270, Mount Rainier East. Ask the USGS for a topographic map of the Ohanapecosh Hot Springs area.

Directions: From Enumclaw drive 41 miles east on Highway 410 to Highway 123. Follow Highway 123 south over Cayuse Pass and five miles to the trailhead parking area, half a mile south of Deer Creek on the right (west) side of the road. From the Longmire-Paradise area, drive on Stevens Canyon Road east to Highway 123 and then about six miles north to the trailhead. Note: Highway 123/Cayuse Pass and upper portions of Highway 4/Chinook Pass are closed in winter. Call the Washington Department of Transportation's toll-free hotline at 888/766-4636 for current road conditions.

Contact: Outdoor Recreation Information Center, Seattle REI, 222 Yale Avenue North, Seattle, WA 98109; 206/470-4060.

72 Laughingwater Creek (Three Lakes)
12.0 mi/7.0 hrs

Three Lakes is another excellent, low-altitude river hike that should be less crowded than upper trails near visitor centers at Paradise and Sunrise. The trail treats you kindly for the first several miles, then gets serious about gaining the 2,700 feet necessary to reach Three Lakes. At about 5.5 miles the trail tops out as you pass a junction with the East Boundary Trail. You drop about half a mile along the ridgetop to Three Lakes, where good campsites and a backcountry ranger cabin are found (this is the standard turnaround point). You can get a good view of Rainier by walking a short distance beyond the third lake. A mile farther on the same route is an intersection with the Pacific Crest Trail.

Location: Near the Stevens Canyon Entrance to Mount Rainier National Park; see Mount Rainier and the Columbia River Gorge Map 2, grid b3.

User Groups: Hikers and horses. No dogs or mountain bikes. No wheelchair facilities.

Permits: A $10-per-car access fee is collected at all park entrances. Day-hiking permits are not required. Wilderness permits are required for all backcountry camping. Some permits can be reserved in advance for a fee. Others are issued free no more than 24 hours before departure. Contact the Outdoor Recreation Information Center at 206/470-4060.

Maps: For a free map of Mount Rainier National Park, contact the Outdoor Recreation Information Center at 206/470-4060. Green Trails, Inc.'s excellent topographic maps of the region are available for $3.99 each at outdoor retail outlets. Ask for map number 270, Mount Rainier East. Ask the USGS for a topographic map of the Chinook Pass area.

Directions: From Enumclaw drive 41 miles east on Highway 410 to Highway 123. Follow Highway 123 south over Cayuse Pass to the Stevens Canyon Entrance. Proceed one mile south to the Laughingwater Creek parking area, on the right (west) side of the highway. The trailhead is across the highway. Note: Highway 123/Cayuse Pass and upper portions of Highway 4/Chinook Pass are closed in winter. Call the Washington Department of Transportation's toll-free hotline at 888/766-4636 for current road conditions.

Contact: Outdoor Recreation Information Center, Seattle REI, 222 Yale Avenue North, Seattle, WA 98109; 206/470-4060.

73 Silver Falls Loop
3.0 mi/1.5 hrs

Look up pure in the dictionary and there's a picture of the Ohanapecosh River. There should be, anyway. After a walk up and down its banks on the Silver Falls Trail, you might be tempted to go home and amend the dictionary yourself. The trail starts near the Ohanapecosh Visitor Center, passes the site of a former health resort at Ohanapecosh Hot Springs, and leads over mostly flat, forested terrain 1.5 miles to the thundering falls, which produce a fine mist thanks to a 75-foot drop. Cross the bridge over the breathtaking gorge below the falls and return on the west side of the river, staying left at the trail junctions. The trail exits in Loop B of Ohanapecosh Campground. (At this same trail junction, turning right takes you just over a mile uphill to the Grove of the Patriarchs Trail near the Stevens Canyon Entrance Station.) The falls also can be reached via a shorter hike on a lower extension of the Laughingwater Creek Trail, near the Laughingwater Bridge off Highway 123. Park rangers recommend this as a good family day trip, and they're right. It's snow free from May to November or December, when some higher park trails remain snowed in.

Location: Near the Stevens Canyon Entrance to Mount Rainier National Park; see Mount Rainier and the Columbia River Gorge Map 2, grid b3.

User Groups: Hikers only. No dogs, horses, or mountain bikes. No wheelchair facilities.

Permits: No day-use permits are required. Parking and access are free.

Maps: For a free map of Mount Rainier National Park, contact the Outdoor Recreation Information Center at 206/470-4060. Green Trails, Inc.'s excellent topographic maps of the region are available for $3.99 each at outdoor retail outlets. Ask for map number 270, Mount Rainier East. Ask the USGS for topographic maps of the Ohanapecosh Hot Springs and Chinook Pass areas.

Directions: From Enumclaw drive 41 miles east on Highway 410 to Highway 123. Follow Highway 123 south for 14 miles to Ohanapecosh Campground and Visitor Center. The trailhead is behind the visitor center. Note: Highway 123/Cayuse Pass and upper portions of Highway 4/Chinook Pass are closed in winter. Call the Washington Department of Transportation's toll-free hotline at 888/766-4636 for current road conditions.

Contact: Outdoor Recreation Information Center, Seattle REI, 222 Yale Avenue North, Seattle, WA 98109; 206/470-4060.

7.4 Twin Sisters
5.0 mi/3.5 hrs

Elbow room can be hard to come by here. Two scenic lakes that are set a short distance from the road make this one of the more popular William O. Douglas Wilderness day hikes, especially for parents with children. The first of the twins is only about two miles down a moderate climbing trail, so plenty of people make their way here. The second lake is half a mile ahead. Campsites at both lakes are superb, as are the lakes themselves, which have clean, sandy beaches. Designated sites are likely to be filled early on weekends and even summer weekdays. You must camp 200 feet from the lakes. If you do snare a site, plenty of opportunities await to leave the crowds behind and venture out on your own. By utilizing the nearby Pacific Crest Trail and other paths, you can day hike from here to Snow Lake, Fryingpan Mountain, and Fryingpan Lake, or hike to any of hundreds of other small lakes waiting at the end of local side trails. The premiere day hike side trip, however, is to Tumac Mountain, 2.2 miles beyond the smaller of the Twin Sisters on the Cowlitz Trail. The cratered, 6,340-foot peak, topped by an old lookout site, is a prime example of a volcanic mountain in its younger years. The trail receives heavy horse use, so watch your step.

Location: South of Bumping Lake in the William O. Douglas Wilderness; see Mount Rainier and the Columbia River Gorge Map 2, grid b6.

User Groups: Hikers, leashed dogs, and horses. No mountain bikes. No wheelchair facilities.

Permits: A federal Northwest Forest Pass, $5 per day or $30 annually, is required to park at the trailhead. Passes are available from ranger stations and many private vendors, online at website: www.wta.org, or by calling 800/270-7504. Contact the Outdoor Recreation Information Center at 206/470-4060.

Maps: For a map of the William O. Douglas Wilderness, contact the Outdoor Recreation Information Center, Seattle REI, 222 Yale

Avenue North, Seattle, WA 98109; 206/470-4060. Green Trails, Inc.'s excellent topographic maps of the region are available for $3.99 each at outdoor retail outlets. Ask for map numbers 271 and 303, Bumping Lake and White Pass. Ask the USGS for topographic maps of the Bumping Lake, Spiral Butte, and White Pass areas.

Directions: From Enumclaw drive 47 miles east on Highway 410 to Chinook Pass and proceed 19 miles east to Bumping Road/Forest Service Road 18. Turn right (south) and follow the road to the end of the pavement, where it becomes Forest Service Road 1800. Proceed to a junction and stay straight on what is now Deep Creek Road/Forest Service Road 395. Drive to the end of the road and walk to the Twin Sisters Trailhead in Deep Creek Campground. Note: Highway 123/Cayuse Pass and upper portions of Highway 4/Chinook Pass are closed in winter. Call the Washington Department of Transportation's toll-free hotline at 888/766-4636 for current road conditions.

Contact: Okanogan/Wenatchee National Forest, Naches Ranger District, 10061 Highway 12, Naches, WA 98937; 509/653-2205.

⁊⁊ Tatoosh Ridge

9.0 mi/5.0 hrs

It was a cruel injustice that Tatoosh Ridge, a verifiable bit of alpine heaven, got left outside the squared-off boundaries of Mount Rainier National Park. That made it all the more fitting that the ridge should later be protected within the boundaries of the Tatoosh Wilderness. Much of the thanks for that must go to forest-fire spotter Martha Hardy, who made this ridge famous in her 1940s bestseller, *Tatoosh*. The Tatoosh Ridge Trail takes you to the lookout building where she once kept watch, as well as a half dozen other spectacular viewpoints. The trail climbs

steeply at first through forest and then breaks into the open at about two miles. The first good views come quickly and continue as you turn south along the ridge. At about 4.5 miles turn north on a side trail and plummet three-quarters of a mile down to Tatoosh Lakes (no camping). Or continue another mile to another side trail, this one leading north to the Tatoosh Lookout site. If you have two cars available, the entire ridge can be hiked as a long day hike, with a southern pickup (after a steep last couple of miles downhill) at the south trailhead off Forest Service Road 5292.

Location: In the Tatoosh Wilderness south of Mount Rainier National Park; see Mount Rainier and the Columbia River Gorge Map 2, grid c3.

User Groups: Hikers, dogs, and horses. No mountain bikes. No wheelchair facilities.

Permits: A federal Northwest Forest Pass, $5 per day or $30 annually, is required to park at the trailhead. Passes are available from ranger stations and many private vendors, online at website: www.wta.org, or by calling 800/270-7504.

Maps: For a map of the Glacier View and Tatoosh Wildernesses, contact the Outdoor Recreation Information Center, Seattle REI, 222 Yale Avenue North, Seattle, WA 98109; 206/470-4060. Green Trails, Inc.'s excellent topographic maps of the region are available for $3.99 each at outdoor retail outlets. Ask for map number 302, Packwood. Ask the USGS for a topographic map of the Packwood area.

Directions: From I-5 south of Chehalis, drive 64 miles east on Highway 12 to Packwood. Turn left (north) on Forest Service Road 52. In approximately four miles, turn right on Forest Service Road 5270. Proceed to a junction with Forest Service Road 5272. Stay right (north) and continue 1.5 miles on Forest

Service Road 5272 to the trailhead on the right side of the road.

Contact: Gifford Pinchot National Forest, Cowlitz Valley Ranger District, 10024 U.S. Highway 12, Randle, WA 98377; 360/497-1100.

76 Dumbbell Lake Loop
15.7 mi/2.0 days

Lots of lakes—more than you can count. Lots of people—at times more than you can tolerate. Lots of mosquitoes—more than you ever thought you'd slap in your entire lifetime. The combination can be grim, but this White Pass hike can still be a gem if you hit it off-season, such as in late September, after the first frost has removed the bugs and crowds from the picture. Start north on the Pacific Crest Trail and stay left at the trail junction in 1.3 miles, continuing another 1.5 miles to Sand Lake. This is a fine day-hiking destination, but backpackers will want to keep moving upward and north on the PCT for 3.8 miles to Buesch Lake and another half a mile to Dumbbell Lake, both of which have campsites. Local day hikes abound, ranging from short walks to Pipe and Jess Lakes north on the PCT, or to Cramer Lake and Otter Lake on Trail 1106 to the east. Cowlitz Pass and Tumac Mountain also are within easy reach, as is Shellrock Lake. For the return trip it's 8.6 miles south to the car on the Cramer Lake and Dark Meadows Trails, or 5.8 miles to a pickup near Dog Lake, farther east on Highway 12. The loop is typical of the William O. Douglas Wilderness north of White Pass: lots of wide-open, arid snow-shadow peaks and valleys dotted by sprawling lakes lined with sandy volcanic discharge. It's beautiful in the summer, but more palatable in the fall when the marauding mosquito armies have gone to sleep for good.

Location: Near White Pass in the William O. Douglas Wilderness; see Mount Rainier and the Columbia River Gorge Map 2, grid c5.

User Groups: Hikers, leashed dogs, and horses. No mountain bikes. No wheelchair facilities.

Permits: A federal Northwest Forest Pass, $5 per day or $30 annually, is required to park at the trailhead. Passes are available from ranger stations and many private vendors, online at website: www.wta.org, or by calling 800/270-7504.

Maps: For a map of the William O. Douglas Wilderness, contact the Outdoor Recreation Information Center, Seattle REI, 222 Yale Avenue North, Seattle, WA 98109; 206/470-4060. Green Trails, Inc.'s excellent topographic maps of the region are available for $3.99 each at outdoor retail outlets. Ask for map number 303, White Pass. Ask the USGS for a topographic map of the White Pass area.

Directions: From I-5 south of Chehalis, drive about 85 miles east on Highway 12 to White Pass and just under another mile to White Pass Campground on the north side of the highway. Turn left (north) and find the trailhead for Pacific Crest Trail near Leech Lake.

Contact: Okanogan/Wenatchee National Forest, Naches Ranger District, 10061 Highway 12, Naches, WA 98937; 509/653-2205.

77 Spiral Butte
12.0 mi/6.0 hrs

White Pass commuters can find some peace and quiet—not to mention a fair amount of vertical—on the Spiral Butte Trail, which climbs 2,500 vertical feet to reach some of the best mountain views in this region. Begin on the Sandy Trail and walk northwest, staying left at two major trail junctions, until you meet Spiral Butte (Trail 1108), which exits left. Follow it another 2.2 miles to the summit (elevation 5,900 feet) and grand views of the entire White Pass area.

Location: North of White Pass in the William O. Douglas Wilderness; see Mount Rainier and the Columbia River Gorge Map 2, grid c6.

User Groups: Hikers, leashed dogs, and horses. No mountain bikes. No wheelchair facilities.

Permits: A federal Northwest Forest Pass, $5 per day or $30 annually, is required to park at the trailhead. Passes are available from ranger stations and many private vendors, online at website: www.wta.org, or by calling 800/270-7504.

Maps: For a map of the William O. Douglas Wilderness, contact the Outdoor Recreation Information Center, Seattle REI, 222 Yale Avenue North, Seattle, WA 98109; 206/470-4060. Green Trails, Inc.'s excellent topographic maps of the region are available for $3.99 each at outdoor retail outlets. Ask for map number 303, White Pass. Ask the USGS for a topographic map of the Spiral Butte area.

Directions: From I-5 south of Chehalis, drive about 85 miles east on Highway 12 to White Pass and another six miles east to the marked trailhead on the left (north) side of the highway.

Contact: Okanogan/Wenatchee National Forest, Naches Ranger District, 10061 Highway 12, Naches, WA 98937; 509/653-2205.

78 Ironstone Mountain
10.4 mi one way/
1.0–2.0 days

Start high on a ridgetop and stay there through some of the most scenic stretches of the William O. Douglas Wilderness. Take a short day hike to memorable views or drop into privacy and good campsites in the dry, quiet environment of the Rattlesnake Creek drainage. All of these options are possible from the Cash Prairie Trailhead. But you are forced to make decisions quickly. In one mile is a junction, with the right branch leading 3.5 miles sharply down the Burnt Mountain Trail to the lovely Rattlesnake/Strawberry Meadows area of Rattlesnake Creek drainage. Go straight to reach excellent day-hike summit views. The first series of views is at the crest of Burnt Mountain (6,536 feet) a short distance ahead. The second is about two miles farther east atop Shellrock Peak (6,835 feet). Backpackers can and must continue on to the first good water stop at Fox Meadow, which you hit at 6.5 miles. Camp between the stone countenances of Ironstone Mountain to the north and Bootjack Rock to the south. The trail follows Russell Ridge northwest two miles to McNeil Peak and exits into the Indian Creek Meadows area, making possible a long one-way trip to the Bumping Lake area on Chinook Pass/Highway 410. A combination Ironstone Mountain/Rattlesnake Creek loop is also a challenging alternative for creative route planners. Our advice: plan your water stops carefully, or bring plenty of your own. The upper ridges are extremely dry in midsummer.

Location: Between Highway 410 and Highway 12 in the William O. Douglas Wilderness; see Mount Rainier and the Columbia River Gorge Map 2, grid c7.

User Groups: Hikers, leashed dogs, and horses. No mountain bikes. No wheelchair facilities.

Permits: A federal Northwest Forest Pass, $5 per day or $30 annually, is required to park at the trailhead. Passes are available from ranger stations and many private vendors, online at website: www.wta.org, or by calling 800/270-7504.

Maps: For a map of the William O. Douglas Wilderness, contact the Outdoor Recreation Information Center, Seattle REI,

222 Yale Avenue North, Seattle, WA 98109; 206/470-4060. Green Trails, Inc.'s excellent topographic maps of the region are available for $3.99 each at outdoor retail outlets. Ask for map numbers 303 and 304, White Pass and Rimrock. Ask the USGS for topographic maps of the Rimrock Lake and Spiral Butte areas.

Directions: From I-5 south of Chehalis, drive about 85 miles east on Highway 12 over White Pass and proceed to Forest Service Road 1500, between Hause Creek and Riverbend Campgrounds east of Rimrock Lake. Turn left (north) and proceed to Forest Service Road 199. Turn left and find the Cash Prairie Trailhead at the road's end after about 1.5 miles.

Contact: Okanogan/Wenatchee National Forest, Naches Ranger District, 10061 Highway 12, Naches, WA 98937; 509/653-2205.

79 Bluff Lake
13.2 mi/6.6 hrs

The best thing about this trail to Bluff Lake and beyond is that the hardest climbing is taken care of in the first few miles. Not only does that mean the work is out of the way quickly, but it also means the weak of heart (and leg) will leave the back half of the route to the select few who are willing to break a sweat for the pleasures that lie ahead. And what pleasures there are along this trail. Climbing past the picturesque, pristine Bluff Lake, the trail levels off to a gentle ascent along the long, scenic ridge that links the multiple peaks of Coal Creek Mountain. The alpine and subalpine ecosystems along the ridge offer a nice combination of cooling shade, sun-streaked meadows, and awesome views of the Goat Rocks Range northern end. As if the stunning vistas and lack of crowds weren't enticing enough, this trail is also widely used by the local populations of mountain goats and mule deer, making a

chance observation of a majestic animal a strong possibility. To top it all off, late-summer visitors are swept away by the heavenly abundance of huge, juicy huckleberries.

Location: Northeast of Packwood in Gifford Pinchot National Forest partially within the Goat Rocks Wilderness; see Mount Rainier and the Columbia River Gorge Map 2, grid c4.

User Groups: Hikers, leashed dogs, and horses. No mountain bikes. No wheelchair facilities.

Permits: A federal Northwest Forest Pass, $5 per day or $30 annually, is required to park at the trailhead. Passes are available from ranger stations and many private vendors, online at website: www.wta.org, or by calling 800/270-7504.

Maps: For a map of Gifford Pinchot National Forest, contact the Outdoor Recreation Information Center, Seattle REI, 222 Yale Avenue North, Seattle, WA 98109; 206/470-4060. Green Trails, Inc.'s excellent topographic maps are available for $3.99 each at outdoor retail outlets. Ask for map number 302, Packwood. Ask the USGS for a topographic map of the Packwood area.

Directions: From Packwood drive 4.6 miles east on U.S. 12 and turn right (south) onto Forest Service Road 4610. Continue two miles before turning left onto Forest Service Road 4612. Drive 2.6 miles to the trailhead on the right.

Contact: Gifford Pinchot National Forest, Cowlitz Valley Ranger District, 10024 U.S. Highway 12, Randle, WA 98377; 360/497-1100.

80 Three Peaks
10.8 mi/5.4 hrs

The first section of this trail is far from spectacular, but those who persevere to the end get to experience the unbeatable views from the trail's ridgetop. As much as those first couple of miles through second-growth forest and old clear-cuts are uninspiring, the last miles of the trail are sublime. Actually it may just be a coincidence, but the trail really improves shortly after it enters the wilderness area. The forest gets lighter—old growth with a varied canopy to let in more light—and the views start to open up more. You find a great vista down into the Packwood Lake Basin and south to Johnson Peak. Be sure to carry plenty of water since there is no water at the trailhead and the only water along the route is at the turnaround point near Mosquito Lake.

Location: Northeast of Packwood in Gifford Pinchot National Forest partially within the Goat Rocks Wilderness; see Mount Rainier and the Columbia River Gorge Map 2, grid c4.

User Groups: Hikers, leashed dogs, and horses. No mountain bikes. No wheelchair facilities.

Permits: A federal Northwest Forest Pass, $5 per day or $30 annually, is required to park at the trailhead. Passes are available from ranger stations and many private vendors, online at website: www.wta.org, or by calling 800/270-7504.

Maps: For a map of Gifford Pinchot National Forest, contact the Outdoor Recreation Information Center, Seattle REI, 222 Yale Avenue North, Seattle, WA 98109; 206/470-4060. Green Trails, Inc.'s excellent topographic maps are available for $3.99 each at outdoor retail outlets. Ask for map number 302, Packwood. Ask the USGS for a topographic map of the Packwood area.

Directions: From Packwood drive two miles east on U.S. 12 and turn right (south) onto Forest Service Road 1266. Continue to the end of the road where there is a large barrier. The trail begins less than 50 yards beyond the roadblock.

Contact: Gifford Pinchot National Forest, Cowlitz Valley Ranger District, 10024 U.S. Highway 12, Randle, WA 98377; 360/497-1100.

81 Clear Fork
19.2 mi/9.6 hrs

Paralleling the beautiful Cowlitz River, this trail is flat and smooth, making it a wonderful hiking adventure for families with small children or for those who simply want to enjoy the wilderness without a lot of exertion. Over the entire trail length, the elevation gain is less than 1,200 feet. Walking ease doesn't correspond to a lack of interesting sites, though. The best and most dominant feature of this hike is the ever-beautiful Clear Fork of the Cowlitz River. We enjoy simply listening to the river; watching the cold, clear water roll over the rocks; admiring the thirsty wildlife that gathers on its shores; or casting a fly into the river and feeling the raw energy of the strong, toothy trout that prowl the icy pools and eddies. In addition to the river, the trail passes by Lily Lake, a small meadow tarn that is the favorite haunt of muskrats and mule deer.

Location: Northeast of Packwood in Gifford Pinchot National Forest partially within the Goat Rocks Wilderness; see Mount Rainier and the Columbia River Gorge Map 2, grid c4.

User Groups: Hikers, leashed dogs, and horses. No mountain bikes. No wheelchair facilities.

Permits: A federal Northwest Forest Pass, $5 per day or $30 annually, is required to park at the trailhead. Passes are available from ranger stations and many private vendors, online at website: www.wta.org, or by calling 800/270-7504.

Maps: For a map of Gifford Pinchot National Forest, contact the Outdoor Recreation Information Center, Seattle REI, 222 Yale Avenue North, Seattle, WA 98109; 206/470-4060. Green Trails, Inc.'s excellent topographic maps are available for $3.99 each at outdoor retail outlets. Ask for map number 303, White Pass. Ask the USGS for topographic maps of the White Pass and Packwood areas.

Directions: From Packwood drive 4.6 miles east on U.S. 12 and turn right (south) onto Forest Service Road 46. Continue 9.2 miles to the road's end and the trailhead.

Contact: Gifford Pinchot National Forest, Cowlitz Valley Ranger District, 10024 U.S. Highway 12, Randle, WA 98377; 360/497-1100.

82 Clear Lost
13.2 mi/6.6 hrs

A steep descent and a cold-water ford in the first two miles of the hike discourage a lot of hikers from pursuing the rewards offered by this trail. After crossing the Clear Fork of the Cowlitz River, though, the trail begins to gradually climb up the opposite wall of the Clear Fork Valley. As you gain elevation, you gain views, and by the time you reach the subalpine meadows of Coyote Ridge, you enjoy sweeping vistas that encompass Mount Rainier and all the long, green valleys between you and the mountain. The trail winds past Lost Hat Lake before ending near Lost Lake. Camp at either lake (going on to Lost Lake adds nearly another mile to the total distance) and return the way you came.

Location: Northeast of Packwood in Gifford Pinchot National Forest partially within the Goat Rocks Wilderness; see Mount Rainier and the Columbia River Gorge Map 2, grid d5.

User Groups: Hikers, leashed dogs, and horses. No mountain bikes. No wheelchair facilities.

Permits: A federal Northwest Forest Pass, $5 per day or $30 annually, is required to park at the trailhead. Passes are available from ranger stations and many private vendors, online at website: www.wta.org, or by calling 800/270-7504.

Maps: For a map of Gifford Pinchot National Forest, contact the Outdoor Recreation Information Center, Seattle REI, 222 Yale Avenue North, Seattle, WA 98109; 206/470-4060. Green Trails, Inc.'s excellent topographic maps are available for $3.99 each at outdoor retail outlets. Ask for map number 303, White Pass. Ask the USGS for topographic maps of the White Pass and Packwood areas.

Directions: From Packwood drive 17 miles east on U.S. 12 to the well-marked trailhead on the right.

Contact: Gifford Pinchot National Forest, Cowlitz Valley Ranger District, 10024 U.S. Highway 12, Randle, WA 98377; 360/497-1100.

83 Packwood Lake
19.2 mi/1.0–2.0 days

Surrounded on three sides by wilderness, Packwood Lake is a big, trout-filled lake that is just remote enough to thin out the crowds of campers. Until a few years ago, a road accessed the north end of the lake, and even after that was closed to the public, a private boat rental agency and outfitter operated a business on the lakeshore. Fortunately for wilderness lovers, the operating permit wasn't renewed, and for the past few years, the lake has been enjoyed in its pristine state. This trail leads through a pair of small clear-cuts in the first mile. The logged areas certainly can't be called pretty, but they do offer beautiful views of Mount Rainier to the north. Shortly after leaving the last clear-cut, the trail enters thick second-growth forest before dipping just inside the wilderness boundary at two miles and rolling through a beautiful stand of old-growth forest. As the route nears the lake, it leaves the wilderness area and crosses the north shore of the lake at 3.5 miles. Just past the Forest Service Guard Station, the trail reenters the wilderness on the east side of Packwood Lake and climbs a steep ridge to Mosquito Lake (be warned, the name is appropriate). From here the trail continues east to Lost Lake at 9.6 miles. The ridge walk offers nice views, and Lost Lake is a good place to camp.

Location: Southwest of Packwood in Gifford Pinchot National Forest; see Mount Rainier and the Columbia River Gorge Map 2, grid d4.

User Groups: Hikers, leashed dogs, and horses. No mountain bikes. No wheelchair facilities.

Permits: A federal Northwest Forest Pass, $5 per day or $30 annually, is required to park at the trailhead. Passes are available from ranger stations and many private vendors, online at website: www.wta.org, or by calling 800/270-7504.

Maps: For a map of Gifford Pinchot National Forest, contact the Outdoor Recreation Information Center, 915 Second Avenue, Suite 442, Seattle, WA 98174; 206/220-7450. Green Trails, Inc.'s excellent topographic maps are available for $3.99 each at outdoor retail outlets. Ask for map number 302, Packwood. Ask the USGS for a topographic map of the Packwood area.

Directions: From Packwood drive six miles south on Snyder Road/Forest Service Road 1260. The trailhead is at the end of the road on the large parking area's south end.

Contact: Gifford Pinchot National Forest, Cowlitz Valley Ranger District, 10024 U.S. Highway 12, Randle, WA 98377; 360/497-1100.

84 Coyote
25.6 mi/2.0–3.0 days
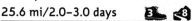

This trail leads past Packwood Lake and climbs steeply to Mosquito Lake until it reaches a fork at about six miles. The trail angles to the right and continues to climb through broken forest and subalpine meadow before topping out in Packwood Saddle,

roughly 11 miles in from the trailhead. A small pond is found at the head of Saddle Creek, just under the lip of the saddle, providing a water source for campers who want to sleep high and wake up to great views. From here the sweeping views from the saddle continue as the trail drops down the other side of the ridge and leads to a junction with the Pacific Crest Trail near Elk Pass. This is a great out-and-back trail because the scenery is so stunning, but it's easy to miss some of the gorgeous views the first time. The only way to see it all is to enjoy the scenery to the east as you hike in, then turn around, and as you return to the trailhead, enjoy the views to the west. This way you can take in the Goat Rocks, Mount Adams, Mount Rainier, and everything in between, including an array of wildlife, from mountain goats and marmots to elk and eagles.

Location: Southwest of Packwood in Gifford Pinchot National Forest partially within the Goat Rocks Wilderness; see Mount Rainier and the Columbia River Gorge Map 2, grid d4.

User Groups: Hikers, leashed dogs, and horses. No mountain bikes. No wheelchair facilities.

Permits: A federal Northwest Forest Pass, $5 per day or $30 annually, is required to park at the trailhead. Passes are available from ranger stations and many private vendors, online at website: www.wta.org, or by calling 800/270-7504.

Maps: For a map of Gifford Pinchot National Forest, contact the Outdoor Recreation Information Center, 915 Second Avenue, Suite 442, Seattle, WA 98174; 206/220-7450. Green Trails, Inc.'s excellent topographic maps are available for $3.99 each at outdoor retail outlets. Ask for map number 302, Packwood. Ask the USGS for a topographic map of the Packwood area.

Directions: From Packwood drive six miles south on Snyder Road/Forest Service Road 1260. The trailhead is at the end of the road on the large parking area's south end.

Contact: Gifford Pinchot National Forest, Cowlitz Valley Ranger District, 10024 U.S. Highway 12, Randle, WA 98377; 360/497-1100.

85 Shoe Lake

12.0 mi/7 hrs

A long series of switchbacks through a thin stand of young forest leads to a number of rolling alpine meadows, then a subalpine mountain cirque, and finally a blue lake bounded by brilliant fields of wildflowers.

The trail climbs more than 1,500 feet in the first two miles as it skirts the eastern flank of the White Pass Ski Area. There isn't a lot of scenery to hold your attention here, but there are lots of deer browsing in the open forest—keep an eye out for them and keep pressing on.

As the trail levels out past the two-mile mark, you see a small side trail on the right leading to the head of the ski lifts. Stay on the main track and you climb gradually now as the trail rolls through a series of open meadows. Marmots can be seen in the rockier sections of these, and gray jays swoop from tree to tree, watching every hiker in hopes of getting a bite of gorp or granola bar.

There are occasional views from these meadows, with the surrounding peaks providing most of the scenery, but now and then Mount Rainier can be seen on the northwestern horizon.

The trail eventually leaves the forest glades and starts a long traverse of the barren, rocky slope on the upper flank of Hogback Mountain. For more than a mile, you can see the trail laid out before you as it follows the curving mountain flank. At about 6.5 miles the trail rolls through one steep switchback and

crosses a 6,500-foot saddle on the ridge. Directly ahead is Shoe Lake, though it requires a descent of nearly 800 feet and about a mile of trail to reach its shores. This would be a great place to camp if not for the unfortunate fact that camping in the lake basin is prohibited.

Location: West of Yakima in Okanogan/Wenatchee National Forest; see Mount Rainier and the Columbia River Gorge Map 2, grid c6.

User Groups: Hikers, horses, and dogs. No mountain bikes. No wheelchair facilities.

Permits: A federal Northwest Forest Pass, $5 per day or $30 annually, is required to park at the trailhead. Passes are available from ranger stations and many private vendors, online at website: www.wta.org, or by calling 800/270-7504.

Maps: Green Trails, Inc.'s excellent topographic maps of the region are available for $3.99 each at outdoor retail outlets. Ask for map number 303, White Pass. Ask the USGS for topographic maps of the White Pass area.

Directions: From Yakima drive west on U.S. 12 for 45 miles and turn left onto a small, dirt road, signed for the Pacific Crest Trail trailhead, near the summit of White Pass. The trailhead is found about a half mile east of the ski area at the crest of the pass.

Contact: Okanogan/Wenatchee National Forest, Naches Ranger District, 10061 Highway 12, Naches, WA 98937; 509/653-2205.

86 Round Mountain

4.0 mi/2.5 hrs

This is a steep but short trail with incredible views and great wildlife viewing opportunities. The trail climbs relentlessly from the first step, first through cool forest and then finally, near the top, in open meadow. There are no views until the trail nears the summit, but deer and elk browse in the forest around the trail, and black bears frequent the area as well. An impressive array of birds is also found in this area; from cedar waxwings to golden eagles, the forests—and the skies above them—are filled with feathered beasts.

The trail leads from the lake, switching up through forest to a trail junction in about a mile and a half. The right fork leads to the Pacific Crest Trail by way of Twin Peaks, while the Round Mountain route rolls straight ahead. The last half mile of climb to the top of Round Mountain is steep and strenuous, but it leads to a prominent knob with outstanding views of the eastern flank of the South Cascades. From the summit look north to the cindercone of Spiral Butte. Look down onto the blue waters of Rimrock and Clear Lakes (actually reservoirs) and look west to Goat Rocks Wilderness with its tall rocky spires and glaciated peaks.

Location: West of Yakima in Okanogan/Wenatchee National Forest; see Mount Rainier and the Columbia River Gorge Map 2, grid c6.

User Groups: Hikers, horses, and dogs. No mountain bikes. No wheelchair facilities.

Permits: A federal Northwest Forest Pass, $5 per day or $30 annually, is required to park at the trailhead. Passes are available from ranger stations and many private vendors, online at website: www.wta.org, or by calling 800/270-7504.

Maps: Green Trails, Inc.'s excellent topographic maps of the region are available for $3.99 each at outdoor retail outlets. Ask for map number 303, White Pass. Ask the USGS for topographic maps of the White Pass area.

Directions: From Yakima drive west on U.S. 12 for about 40 miles and turn onto the Upper Tieton Road. Drive 2.8 miles and turn right onto Forest Service Road 830. Follow this to its end, about five miles, to find the trailhead.

Contact: Okanogan/Wenatchee National Forest, Naches Ranger District, 10061 Highway 12, Naches, WA 98937; 509/653-2205.

87 Purcell Lookout
7.2 mi/5.0 hrs

To get to the site of the old Purcell Lookout, you have a choice: hike all the way from U.S. 12, or let your car do part of the work. The Purcell Mountain Trail, which begins just west of the left-hand turn to Forest Service Road 63 described above, leads 7.6 pleasant miles up the mountain to grand views at the lookout. The Purcell Lookout Trail, which begins higher on the mountain, cuts straight to the chase. If you're a backpacker looking for a more leisurely stroll with fewer people around, take the long trail. If you're more into peak-bagging and great views, choose the upper frontal assault. After about an hour on the Purcell Lookout Trail, you might wonder if you're assaulting the trail or vice versa. The grade is steep, gaining 2,100 feet (about half in an open, hot clear-cut) in about three miles. Here you join the main trail from the bottom and climb a more moderate half-mile pitch to the lookout site. You get great views in all directions. Funny how they keep putting lookouts in places like this.

Location: In the Cowlitz River drainage of Gifford Pinchot National Forest; see Mount Rainier and the Columbia River Gorge Map 2, grid d2.

User Groups: Hikers, leashed dogs, horses, and mountain bikes. Note: Because of frequent trail-collapse damage caused by mountain beavers, horses and mountain bikes are not recommended. No wheelchair facilities.

Permits: A federal Northwest Forest Pass, $5 per day or $30 annually, is required to park at the trailhead. Passes are available from ranger stations and many private vendors, online at website: www.wta.org, or by calling 800/270-7504.

Maps: For a map of the Gifford Pinchot National Forest,

contact the Outdoor Recreation Information Center, Seattle REI, 222 Yale Avenue North, Seattle, WA 98109; 206/470-4060. Green Trails, Inc.'s excellent topographic maps of the region are available for $3.99 each at various outdoor retail outlets. Ask for map number 301, Randle. Ask the USGS for a topographic map of the Randle area.

Directions: From Seattle or Portland drive south or north (respectively) on I-5 to U.S. 12. Turn east onto U.S. 12 and drive approximately 47 miles to Randle. Continue six miles east to the old highway (unmarked) on the left. Turn left (north) and drive about one mile to Forest Service Road 63. Turn left and drive north to Forest Service Road 6310. Bear left on Forest Service Road 6310 and you find the trailhead on the right in less than a mile.

Contact: Gifford Pinchot National Forest, Cowlitz Valley Ranger District, 10024 U.S. Highway 12, Randle, WA 98377; 360/497-1100.

88 Upper Lake Creek
20.0 mi/1.0–2.0 days

This trail leads through a pair of small clearcuts in the first mile, but shortly after leaving the last one, it enters thick second-growth forest. Then it dips just inside the wilderness boundary and rolls through a beautiful stand of old-growth forest. As the route nears Packwood Lake, it leaves the wilderness area and heads across the north shore of the lake. Here, when the trail forks at 3.5 miles, turn right and continue south along the east shore of the lake and on up the Upper Lake Creek Valley. The trail stays fairly level and easy as it rolls upstream from the lake; camping is good along this stretch. But after about four miles of that gentle ride, the land suddenly tilts at a drastic angle and the trail climbs steeply up the valley headwall to the ridge crest and a junction with the Coyote Trail. Enjoy the views from the ridge and return the way you came, or combine this

hike with Coyote (see hike this chapter) to make a loop trip back to Packwood Lake.

Location: Southwest of Packwood in Gifford Pinchot National Forest partially within the Goat Rocks Wilderness; see Mount Rainier and the Columbia River Gorge Map 2, grid d3.

User Groups: Hikers, leashed dogs, and horses. No mountain bikes. No wheelchair facilities.

Permits: A federal Northwest Forest Pass, $5 per day or $30 annually, is required to park at the trailhead. Passes are available from ranger stations and many private vendors, online at website: www.wta.org, or by calling 800/270-7504.

Maps: For a map of Gifford Pinchot National Forest, contact the Outdoor Recreation Information Center, 915 Second Avenue, Suite 442, Seattle, WA 98174; 206/220-7450. Green Trails, Inc.'s excellent topographic maps are available for $3.99 each at outdoor retail outlets. Ask for map number 302, Packwood. Ask the USGS for a topographic map of the Packwood area.

Directions: From Packwood drive six miles south on Snyder Road/Forest Service Road 1260. The trailhead is at the end of the road on the large parking area's south end. For the first 3.5 miles, the trail follows the Packwood Lake Trail and then branches off onto the Upper Lake Creek Trail.

Contact: Gifford Pinchot National Forest, Cowlitz Valley Ranger District, 10024 U.S. Highway 12, Randle, WA 98377; 360/497-1100.

89 Dry Creek
7.0 mi/3.5 hrs

This steep forest trail offers few views and not much of interest other than thick second-growth fir forest, until near the route's end. But spectacular views await the patient and persistent. The 4,400-foot elevation gain brings hikers to a vantage point that is unrivaled in the area. Once a Forest Service lookout tower stood here, but now all that is left are great views of the Cowlitz River Valley to the north and west; the high, craggy Smith Ridge to the east; and Goat Divide, a precipitous cliff, directly below on the north side of the ridge. On clear days the top of Mount Rainier can also be seen peeking up over the ridges to the north.

Location: West of Packwood in Gifford Pinchot National Forest; see Mount Rainier and the Columbia River Gorge Map 2, grid d4.

User Groups: Hikers, leashed dogs, horses, and mountain bikes. No wheelchair facilities.

Permits: A federal Northwest Forest Pass, $5 per day or $30 annually, is required to park at the trailhead. Passes are available from ranger stations and many private vendors, online at website: www.wta.org, or by calling 800/270-7504.

Maps: For a map of Gifford Pinchot National Forest, contact the Outdoor Recreation Information Center, 915 Second Avenue, Suite 442, Seattle, WA 98174; 206/220-7450. Green Trails, Inc.'s excellent topographic maps are available for $3.99 each at outdoor retail outlets. Ask for map number 302, Packwood. Ask the USGS for a topographic map of the Packwood area.

Directions: From Packwood drive four miles west on U.S. 12 to a junction with Forest Service Road 20. Turn left (south) onto this road and continue half a mile to the trailhead on the right.

Contact: Gifford Pinchot National Forest, Cowlitz Valley Ranger District, 10024 U.S. Highway 12, Randle, WA 98377; 360/497-1100.

90 Lily Basin
24.0 mi/2.0–3.0 days

The worst part of this moderate climb is knocked off in the first few miles. After that the trail rambles along a beautiful, rugged ridge to the west flank of 7,487-foot Johnson Peak before turning sharply south to intercept the Angry Mountain Trail. From that junction the trail veers back to the southeast to Jordan Basin. Just before dropping into the basin, though, the trail crosses the most scenic part of the trip and possibly the best views in this part of the forest. Just two miles beyond the Angry Mountain junction, the trail climbs to 7,431-foot Hawkeye Point, a high, lonesome peak that offers stunning views in all directions. Past the point, the trail traverses Jordan Basin and angles across the ridge to Goat Lake, a deep, cold lake of sapphire-blue water that is filled with broken ice long into the summer. The first trail section can make a pleasant loop trip, utilizing the Angry Mountain Trail, provided a car shuttle can be arranged. That loop is roughly 16 miles.

Location: Southwest of Packwood in Gifford Pinchot National Forest partially within Goat Rocks Wilderness; see Mount Rainier and the Columbia River Gorge Map 2, grid d3.

User Groups: Hikers, leashed dogs, and horses. No mountain bikes. No wheelchair facilities.

Permits: A federal Northwest Forest Pass, $5 per day or $30 annually, is required to park at the trailhead. Passes are available from ranger stations and many private vendors, online at website: www.wta.org, or by calling 800/270-7504.

Maps: For a map of Gifford Pinchot National Forest, contact the Outdoor Recreation Information Center, 915 Second Avenue, Suite 442, Seattle, WA 98174; 206/220-7450. Green Trails, Inc.'s excellent topographic maps are available for $3.99 each at outdoor retail outlets. Ask for map number 302, Packwood. Ask the USGS for a topographic map of the Packwood area.

Directions: From Packwood drive two miles west on U.S.

12 to a junction with Forest Service Road 48. Turn left (south) onto this road and continue 10 miles to the trailhead on the right.

Contact: Gifford Pinchot National Forest, Cowlitz Valley Ranger District, 10024 U.S. Highway 12, Randle, WA 98377; 360/497-1100.

91 South Point Lookout
7.0 mi/3.5 hrs

This is largely an open, sunlit trail thanks to an old forest fire that leveled much of the forest canopy and created a series of new wildflower meadows and deer-filled clearings. After passing the old burn sites and meandering through thick second-growth forest, the moderately steep trail tops out at the 5,900-foot South Point summit. Look for remains of the old lookout tower that stood here during the middle of this century. The adventurous hiker can scramble along an old trail (no longer maintained) that rides the crest of the South Point Ridge south for a few miles. There is no source of drinking water along the entire trail, so be sure to carry all you need.

Location: West of Packwood in Gifford Pinchot National Forest; see Mount Rainier and the Columbia River Gorge Map 2, grid d4.

User Groups: Hikers, leashed dogs, and horses. No mountain bikes. No wheelchair facilities.

Permits: A federal Northwest Forest Pass, $5 per day or $30 annually, is required to park at the trailhead. Passes are available from ranger stations and many private vendors, online at website: www.wta.org, or by calling 800/270-7504.

Maps: For a map of Gifford Pinchot National Forest, contact the Outdoor Recreation Information Center, 915 Second Avenue, Suite 442, Seattle, WA 98174; 206/220-7450. Green Trails, Inc.'s excellent topographic maps are available for $3.99 each at outdoor retail out-

lets. Ask for map number 302, Packwood. Ask the USGS for topographic maps of the Packwood and Steamboat Mountain areas.

Directions: From Packwood drive four miles west on U.S. 12 to a junction with Forest Service Road 20. Turn left (south) onto this road and continue four miles to the trailhead on the left.

Contact: Gifford Pinchot National Forest, Cowlitz Valley Ranger District, 10024 U.S. Highway 12, Randle, WA 98377; 360/497-1100.

92 Glacier Lake
4.0 mi/2.0 hrs

Climbing just 800 feet in two miles, this is one of the best trails for families and kids. Not only is the going easy, but it's also a pretty hike that ends at a beautiful alpine wilderness lake. The trail follows Glacier Creek through old Douglas fir and hemlock forest the entire way. Late-summer hikers find bushels of huckleberries growing along the route, and anglers can try for the big rainbow trout that lurk in the depths of Glacier Lake at the trail's end. A rough path circles the lake, accessing the top casting locations and also offering the best views of the lake and lake basin.

Location: West of Packwood in Gifford Pinchot National Forest partially within the Goat Rocks Wilderness; see Mount Rainier and the Columbia River Gorge Map 2, grid d4.

User Groups: Hikers, leashed dogs, and horses. No mountain bikes. No wheelchair facilities.

Permits: A federal Northwest Forest Pass, $5 per day or $30 annually, is required to park at the trailhead. Passes are available from ranger stations and many private vendors, online at website: www.wta.org, or by calling 800/270-7504.

Maps: For a map of Gifford Pinchot National Forest, contact the Outdoor Recreation

Information Center, 915 Second Avenue, Suite 442, Seattle, WA 98174; 206/220-7450. Green Trails, Inc.'s excellent topographic maps are available for $3.99 each at outdoor retail outlets. Ask for map number 302, Packwood. Ask the USGS for a topographic map of the Packwood area.

Directions: From Packwood drive 2.1 miles west on U.S. 12 to a junction with Forest Service Road 21. Turn left (south) onto this road and continue five miles. Turn right onto Forest Service Road 2110 and drive half a mile to the trailhead on the right.

Contact: Gifford Pinchot National Forest, Cowlitz Valley Ranger District, 10024 U.S. Highway 12, Randle, WA 98377; 360/497-1100.

93 Angry Mountain
16.8 mi/1.0–2.0 days

Though this trail starts off climbing gently through second-growth forest, it doesn't take long before the forest shifts to old-growth and the trail's pitch turns steep and rugged. A long series of steep switchbacks tops out on an open ridge on the north flank of Angry Mountain, elevation 5,245 feet. Obscure climber's routes lead up Angry Mountain, but unless you're a skilled bushwhacker and route-finder, leave the off-trail travel to someone else. Stay on the trail and ride the ridge about six miles east to a fork. This is the turnaround point unless you're planning a loop trip on the Lily Basin Trail, which is the left fork at the junction. The ridge walk provides countless views of the surrounding peaks and river valleys, as well as peeks at Mount Rainier to the north on clear days.

Location: Southwest of Packwood in Gifford Pinchot National Forest partially within the Goat Rocks Wilderness; see Mount Rainier and the Columbia River Gorge Map 2, grid d4.

User Groups: Hikers, leashed dogs, and horses. No mountain bikes. No wheelchair facilities.

Permits: A federal Northwest Forest Pass, $5 per day or $30 annually, is required to park at the trailhead. Passes are available from ranger stations and many private vendors, online at website: www.wta.org, or by calling 800/270-7504.

Maps: For a map of Gifford Pinchot National Forest, contact the Outdoor Recreation Information Center, 915 Second Avenue, Suite 442, Seattle, WA 98174; 206/220-7450. Green Trails, Inc.'s excellent topographic maps are available for $3.99 each at outdoor retail outlets. Ask for map number 302, Packwood. Ask the USGS for a topographic map of the Packwood area.

Directions: From Packwood drive 2.1 miles west on U.S. 12 to a junction with Forest Service Road 21. Turn left (south) onto this road and continue 7.9 miles. Turn right onto Forest Service Road 2120 and drive half a mile to the trailhead on the right.

Contact: Gifford Pinchot National Forest, Cowlitz Valley Ranger District, 10024 U.S. Highway 12, Randle, WA 98377; 360/497-1100.

94 Jordan Creek
10.2 mi/5.0 hrs

This trail starts with a quick, one-mile hop over a low ridge before it settles into a comfortably gentle climb upstream along Jordan Creek. Pretty, old Douglas fir, hemlock, and western red cedar forest surrounds the trail, but the beauty of the trees is secondary to the beauty (and flavor) of the thick huckleberry patches. Late summer brings the heavy berries to sweet ripeness, and in early autumn, you find many of the ripe berries still on the bushes, the deep-blue and purple fruit highlighted by bright red and orange leaves. This makes a beautiful setting for picnics, from both a visual as well as a gastronomic perspective.

Location: Southwest of Packwood in Gifford Pinchot National Forest within the Goat Rocks Wilderness; see Mount Rainier and the Columbia River Gorge Map 2, grid d4.

User Groups: Hikers, leashed dogs, and horses. No mountain bikes. No wheelchair facilities.

Permits: A federal Northwest Forest Pass, $5 per day or $30 annually, is required to park at the trailhead. Passes are available from ranger stations and many private vendors, online at website: www.wta.org, or by calling 800/270-7504.

Maps: For a map of Gifford Pinchot National Forest, contact the Outdoor Recreation Information Center, 915 Second Avenue, Suite 442, Seattle, WA 98174; 206/220-7450. Green Trails, Inc.'s excellent topographic maps are available for $3.99 each at outdoor retail outlets. Ask for map number 302, Packwood. Ask the USGS for topographic maps of the Packwood and Hamilton Butte areas.

Directions: From Packwood proceed 2.1 miles west on U.S. 12 to a junction with Forest Service Road 21. Take a left (south) turn onto this road and continue for 10 miles to Forest Service Road 2140. Turn right onto Forest Service Road 2140 and drive 1.5 miles to Forest Service Road 2142. Turn right and drive to the road's end and the trailhead.

Contact: Gifford Pinchot National Forest, Cowlitz Valley Ranger District, 10024 U.S. Highway 12, Randle, WA 98377; 360/497-1100.

95 Pompey Peak
10.0 mi/5.0 hrs

Clear, cool Kilborn Springs provides a fine place to rest and refresh yourself just a couple miles into this hike. From the springs continue climbing to the Pompey Peak summit and enjoy breathtaking views of surrounding forests and deep river valleys. From the peak the trail continues east along the ridge between the Twin Sisters Peaks and past Castle Butte before dropping into a steep valley. The trail ends abruptly at the edge of the forest, both literally and figuratively—it dead-ends at the property line between the national forest and privately owned land. The landowner of the private parcel has clear-cut this spot.

Even though the springwater seems crystal clear and pure, filter or treat it before you drink it.

Location: Southwest of Packwood in Gifford Pinchot National Forest; see Mount Rainier and the Columbia River Gorge Map 2, grid e2.

User Groups: Hikers, leashed dogs, horses, and mountain bikes. No wheelchair facilities.

Permits: A federal Northwest Forest Pass, $5 per day or $30 annually, is required to park at the trailhead. Passes are available from ranger stations and many private vendors, online at website: www.wta.org, or by calling 800/270-7504.

Maps: For a map of Gifford Pinchot National Forest, send $3 to Outdoor Recreation Information Center, 915 Second Avenue, Suite 442, Seattle, WA 98174; 206/220-7450. Green Trails, Inc.'s excellent topographic maps of the region are available for $3.99 each at outdoor retail outlets. Ask for map numbers 301, 302, and 334, Randle, Packwood, and Blue Lake. Ask the USGS for topographic maps of the Randle, Packwood, Blue Lake, and Tower Rock areas.

Directions: From Randle drive one mile south on Forest Service Road 25 and turn left (east) onto Forest Service Road 23. Continue east for 3.5 miles on Forest Service Road 23 and turn left (north) onto Forest Service Road 2304. Drive to the end of the road; you find the trailhead on the left.

Contact: Gifford Pinchot National Forest, Cowlitz Valley Ranger District, 13068 U.S. 12, Packwood, WA 98361; 360/494-0600.

96 Northfork
1.6 mi one way/1.0 hr

The gentle Northfork loop trail is ideal for families with kids, especially when they stay at the serene trailhead campground. The route begins near an old Civilian Conservation Corps structure (which was used as a ranger station) and loops through a varied forest with great views of the sparklingly clear Cispus River. Ancient Douglas fir and western hemlocks are scattered throughout the area, and huckleberries—though widely dispersed—are around and worth searching out. Anglers find big trout lurking in the cold river, just waiting for something that looks good to eat.

Location: Southeast of Randle in Gifford Pinchot National Forest; see Mount Rainier and the Columbia River Gorge Map 2, grid e2.

User Groups: Hikers and leashed dogs. No horses or mountain bikes are allowed. No wheelchair facilities.

Permits: A federal Northwest Forest Pass, $5 per day or $30 annually, is required to park at the trailhead. Passes are available from ranger stations and many private vendors, online at website: www.wta.org, or by calling 800/270-7504.

Maps: For a map of Gifford Pinchot National Forest, send $3 to Outdoor Recreation Information Center, 915 Second Avenue, Suite 442, Seattle, WA 98174; 206/220-7450. Green Trails, Inc.'s excellent topographic maps of the region are available for $3.99 each at outdoor retail outlets. Ask for map number 333, McCoy Peak. Ask the USGS for a topographic map of the Tower Rock area.

Directions: From Randle drive south for one mile on Forest Service Road 25 and then turn left (east) onto Forest Service Road 23. Continue on Forest Service Road 23 to the North Fork Campground. The trailhead begins near the overflow parking area.

Contact: Gifford Pinchot National Forest, Cowlitz Valley Ranger District, 10024 U.S. Highway 12, Randle, WA 98377; 360/497-1100.

97 Cispus Braille
1.0 mi one way/1.0 hr

It's hard to believe this area was leveled twice by forest fire, but it's true. But those fires are in the past, and the forest has recovered beautifully. This barrier-free interpretive trail explores the new forest and explains the changes wrought by the fires, as well as the processes of recovery. Trail guide pamphlets are available at the Cispus Learning Center, and the interpretive signs along the route are printed in bold, easy-to-read lettering and in Braille. A guide-rope is strung along the right side of the trail; it helps the visually impaired move from station to station. The compact-dirt trail is smooth and free of those toe-grabbing roots so often found on forest trails.

Location: South of Randle in Gifford Pinchot National Forest; see Mount Rainier and the Columbia River Gorge Map 2, grid e2.

User Groups: Hikers and leashed dogs. Fully wheelchair accessible. No horses or mountain bikes are allowed.

Permits: A federal Northwest Forest Pass, $5 per day or $30 annually, is required to park at the trailhead. Passes are available from ranger stations and many private vendors, online at website: www.wta.org, or by calling 800/270-7504.

Maps: For a map of the Gifford Pinchot National Forest, send $3 to Outdoor Recreation Information Center, 915 Second Avenue, Room 442, Seattle, WA 98174; 206/220-7450. Green Trails, Inc.'s excellent topographic maps of the region are available for $3.99 each at outdoor retail outlets. Ask for number 333, McCoy Peak. Ask the USGS for a topographic map of the Tower Rock area.

Directions: From Randle drive one mile south on Forest Service Road 25 and then turn left (east) onto Forest Service Road 23. Continue on Forest Service Road 23 to its junction with Forest Service Road 21. Bear right on Forest Service Road 21, cross the Cispus River, turn left onto Forest Service Road 76, and continue to the Cispus Learning Center. Parking is on the left near the Elderberry Lodge.

Contact: Gifford Pinchot National Forest, Cowlitz Valley Ranger District, 10024 U.S. Highway 12, Randle, WA 98377; 360/497-1100.

98 Klickitat
20.0 mi one way/
1.0–2.0 days   4 6

This east-to-west trail travels along ridgetops for most of its route and explores deep old-growth forest, thick second-growth forest, sparkling alpine lakes, and wildflower-filled alpine meadows. The trail is best enjoyed if a shuttle car can be positioned at one end, but if you have to hike it out and back, don't worry. The scenery changes frequently enough that doing it twice is something of a benefit; there's so much to see and explore that you probably won't take it all in on one trip. Hiking east to west, the first 6.5 miles climb gradually from the 4,400-foot trailhead to the 5,700-foot summit of Mission Mountain. Enjoy the great views from the peak before continuing another two miles west to the first—and best—campsite on the shores of Saint John Lake. After a night near the cool lake, hike a long, looping five miles with very little elevation gain as the trail contours around the flanks of Cold Spring Butte (elevation 5,724 feet). About

16 miles from the trailhead, the route passes Jackpot Lake at 4,600 feet, the second worthwhile camping spot. From here it's a quick, 2.5-mile climb to Castle Butte, at 5,767 feet, before the trail tapers in a long descent to the route's western end near Forest Service Road 55-024.

Location: Southeast of Randle in Gifford Pinchot National Forest; see Mount Rainier and the Columbia River Gorge Map 2, grid e3.

User Groups: Hikers, leashed dogs, horses, and mountain bikes. No wheelchair facilities.

Permits: A federal Northwest Forest Pass, $5 per day or $30 annually, is required to park at the trailhead. Passes are available from ranger stations and many private vendors, online at website: www.wta.org, or by calling 800/270-7504.

Maps: For a map of Gifford Pinchot National Forest, contact the Outdoor Recreation Information Center, 915 Second Avenue, Suite 442, Seattle, WA 98174; 206/220-7450. Green Trails, Inc.'s excellent topographic maps are available for $3.99 each at outdoor retail outlets. Ask for map numbers 333 and 334, McCoy Peak and Blue Lake. Ask the USGS for topographic maps of the Tower Rock, Hamilton Butte, and Blue Lake areas.

Directions: To reach the western trailhead from Randle, drive one mile south on Forest Service Road 25 and then turn left (east) onto Forest Service Road 23. Continue to the junction with Forest Service Road 55, turn left (east) onto this road, and follow it to Forest Service Road 55-024. Turn left onto Forest Service Road 55-024 and drive two miles to the road's end and trailhead. To reach the eastern trailhead from Packwood, drive two miles west on U.S. 12 and turn left (south) on Forest Service Road 21. Follow Forest Service Road 21 for 15 miles and then turn right onto Forest Service Road 22. Drive to the end of the road, where you find the trailhead.

Contact: Gifford Pinchot National Forest, Cowlitz Valley Ranger District, 10024 U.S. Highway 12, Randle, WA 98377; 360/497-1100.

99 Goat Ridge
9.2 mi/4.6 hrs

As the name implies, this is a great place to see mountain goats. The trail follows a high ridge into the Jordan Basin, and, along the way, provides stunning views of the Goat Rocks Peaks. These jagged summits are the remnants of a massive volcano after a cataclysmic eruption and centuries of erosion. The rocky, glacier-covered spires make for scenic vistas and excellent goat habitat. As the trail continues along the ridge, it crosses from the eastern slope to the west side. Though the panoramas of the Goat Rocks disappear along the way, they are replaced with views down into the emerald world of the Jordan Basin and farther down the Johnson Creek Valley. In addition to mountain goats, keep an eye out for black-tailed deer and black bears, which like to roam this area in late summer, munching happily on the plentiful huckleberries.

It's possible to take a side loop to the high point on the ridge, the site of an old lookout tower. The side trail takes off from the main trail at the 1.4-mile point, loops up 400 feet to the ridgetop and lookout site, and then drops back down to rejoin the main trail. The loop trail length is 1.7 miles, and it bypasses half a mile of the main trail.

Location: Southwest of Packwood in Gifford Pinchot National Forest partially within Goat Rocks Wilderness; see Mount Rainier and the Columbia River Gorge Map 2, grid e4.

User Groups: Hikers, leashed dogs, and horses. No mountain bikes. No wheelchair facilities.

Permits: A federal Northwest Forest Pass, $5 per day or $30 annually, is required to park at the trailhead. Passes are available from ranger stations and many private vendors, online at website: www.wta.org, or by calling 800/270-7504.

Maps: For a map of Gifford Pinchot National Forest, contact the Outdoor Recreation Information Center, 915 Second Avenue, Suite 442, Seattle, WA 98174; 206/220-7450. Green Trails, Inc.'s excellent topographic maps are available for $3.99 each at outdoor retail outlets. Ask for map number 334, Blue Lake. Ask the USGS for topographic maps of the Hamilton Butte and Packwood areas.

Directions: From Packwood drive 2.1 miles west on U.S. 12 to a junction with Forest Service Road 21. Turn left (south) onto this road, continue 15 miles, and then turn left onto Forest Service Road 2150. Drive to the road's end and the trailhead (signed for the Berrypatch Trailhead).

Contact: Gifford Pinchot National Forest, Cowlitz Valley Ranger District, 10024 U.S. Highway 12, Randle, WA 98377; 360/497-1100.

100 Tieton Meadows
9.4 mi/4.7 hrs

The name may say meadow, but the trail says hill. After a brief visit to the broad, wildflower-filled meadows, the trail angles up the south wall of the Tieton River Valley. A moderately steep 4.7-mile climb leads to the top of Pinegrass Ridge (elevation about 7,000 feet), just west of Bear Creek Mountain, and offers nice views into the Tieton Valley as well as the Bear Creek Valley. There is no water along the route after starting up the ridge, and no campsites either. The meadows offer camping and plentiful water, but in midsummer you find the meadows abuzz with bugs.

Location: East of Packwood in Gifford Pinchot National Forest partially within the Goat Rocks Wilderness; see Mount

Rainier and the Columbia River Gorge Map 2, grid d6.

User Groups: Hikers, leashed dogs, and horses. No mountain bikes. No wheelchair facilities.

Permits: A federal Northwest Forest Pass, $5 per day or $30 annually, is required to park at the trailhead. Passes are available from ranger stations and many private vendors, online at website: www.wta.org, or by calling 800/270-7504.

Maps: For a map of Okanogan/Wenatchee National Forest, contact the Outdoor Recreation Information Center, 915 Second Avenue, Suite 442, Seattle, WA 98174; 206/220-7450. Green Trails, Inc.'s excellent topographic maps are available for $3.99 each at outdoor retail outlets. Ask for map number 303, White Pass. Ask the USGS for a topographic map of the Pinegrass Ridge area.

Directions: From Packwood drive about 29 miles east on U.S. 12 across White Pass to Clear Lake. Just east of the lake, turn right (south) onto Forest Service Road 12 and drive about 2.5 miles south and east around the lake to a junction with Forest Service Road 1207. Turn right (south) onto this road and continue to the road's end and the trailhead.

Contact: Okanogan/Wenatchee National Forest, Naches Ranger District, 10061 U.S. 12, Naches, WA 98937; 509/653-2205.

101 Bear Creek Mountain
7.0 mi/4 hrs

For a grand view of the craggy peaks of the Goat Rocks Wilderness, there is no better hike than this one. The trail climbs gradually, but continually, as it passes through dense pine forests and open wildlife meadows. From Section Lake the trail rolls uphill through the timber for nearly a mile, with occasional breaks in the trees before opening up into a series of large meadows. Through these meadows, Bear Creek Mountain is seen directly ahead.

The trail continues to weave through forest and meadow, past small babbling streams, for another mile and a half. Then flowers and trees give way to rocks, and the trail gets steep. The path is rough and often the footing is poor, so use care on the climb. The effort you expend to scramble up the steep trail is certainly worthwhile as the views grow better and better the higher you go. Finally, the 7,300-foot summit is reached at 3.5 miles, and the stunningly beautiful Goat Rocks peaks dominate the horizon.

Location: West of Yakima in Okanogan/Wenatchee National Forest; see Mount Rainier and the Columbia River Gorge Map 2, grid e6.

User Groups: Hikers, horses, and dogs. No mountain bikes. No wheelchair facilities.

Permits: A federal Northwest Forest Pass, $5 per day or $30 annually, is required to park at the trailhead. Passes are available from ranger stations and many private vendors, online at website www.wta.org, or by calling 800/270-7504.

Maps: Green Trails, Inc.'s excellent topographic maps of the region are available for $3.99 each at outdoor retail outlets. Ask for map number 303, White Pass. Ask the USGS for a topographic map of the White Pass area.

Directions: From Yakima drive west on U.S. 12 for 33.2 miles and turn left onto Tieton River Road. Drive 10 miles, passing Rimrock Lake, and turn left onto Forest Service Road 1205. Continue about seven miles and turn right on a narrow dirt access road to Section Lake. Drive two miles to the lake and find the trailhead on the right side of the small lake.

Contact: Okanogan/Wenatchee National Forest, Naches Ranger District, 10061 Highway 12, Naches, WA 98937; 509/653-2205.

102 Surprise Lake
10.0 mi/5 hrs

Most hikers enter the Goat Rocks Wilderness from the western side, but those who come in from the east find the wilderness just as beautiful and wild, and much less crowded. The Surprise Lake Trail is one of the few that enter from the east, and it is also one of the most gentle and scenic.

The trail climbs gradually from Conrad Meadow—a broad grassy meadow in the valley bottom—to the high alpine lake at trail's end. Along the way it passes through a seemingly endless series of forest meadows. These elk pastures are broken up by beautiful stands of ponderosa pine and spruce forests and are home to not only elk but white-tailed and mule deer and a host of small critters.

Indeed, so great is the number of meadows that many hikers find it more enjoyable to leave the trail all together and journey up to the lake by going cross-country through the forest glades. This is a great place to practice your off-trail rambling, but before leaving the trail, be sure you have map and compass and the skill to use them effectively.

The first 3.5 miles of trail pierces these patchwork wildflower meadows, but the upper end of the route is enclosed in denser forests until, near the lake, the route breaks out into alpine clearings. Above the pretty little lake loom some of the great craggy peaks that give this Wilderness its first name. With a pair of binoculars and a little patience, it's possible to spot the creatures that contribute the second half of the area's name. Mountain goats scramble among the rocky slopes high above the lake, jumping lightly about the cliffs that lie between the forest and the glaciers. Look for them on the bare rocks above green fields of moss and grass.

There are good campsites at the lake and along the numerous meadows further down the trail. If you choose to camp in a meadow, though, wander as far off trail as reasonable and look for a campsite that is sheltered from the trail by a stand of trees. This will shield your camp from other hikers so they can continue to enjoy their sense of solitude in this wild, beautiful area.

Location: West of Yakima in Okanogan/Wenatchee National Forest; see Mount Rainier and the Columbia River Gorge Map 2, grid e6.

User Groups: Hikers, horses, and dogs. No mountain bikes. No wheelchair facilities.

Permits: A federal Northwest Forest Pass, $5 per day or $30 annually, is required to park at the trailhead. Passes are available from ranger stations and many private vendors, online at website www.wta.org, or by calling 800/270-7504.

Maps: Green Trails, Inc.'s excellent topographic maps of the region are available for $3.99 each at outdoor retail outlets. Ask for map number 304, Rimrock. Ask the USGS for a topographic map of the Rimrock Lake area.

Directions: From Yakima drive west on U.S. 12 for 33.2 miles and turn left onto Tieton River Road. Drive 3.5 miles, passing Rimrock Lake, and turn left onto Forest Service Road 100. Continue 14 miles to the trailhead parking area at Conrad Meadows.

Contact: Okanogan/Wenatchee National Forest, Naches Ranger District, 10061 Highway 12, Naches, WA 98937; 509/653-2205.

103 Jump Off
6.0 mi/3.5 hrs

An old fire lookout station is perched at the top of the oddly named Jump Off Peak, and that old, squat building is one of the main reasons for doing this hike. The Jump

Off Lookout is the last fire lookout building in the southern Okanogan/Wenatchee National Forest, and it is worth the hike to see this remnant of a bygone era. The fact that the views are fantastic from the peak (as you would expect from a lookout station) is merely icing on the cake.

The trail begins at Long Lake, on an old abandoned logging road found just across the main road from the Pickle Prairie Trailhead. The road leads around Long Lake to the trail's start near the outlet end of the lake. The trail climbs steeply almost from the beginning and doesn't let up until you near the top. The early section climbs through young pine and spruce forests, but the upper end of the trail is in open, semi-desert environment. Sagebrush, tiny cactus, and cheat grass dominate this area. Down low, hikers might see—or hear—spruce grouse, quail, owls, and gray jays. But as you climb, look for soaring eagles and hawks, chukar, rattlesnakes, and scorpions. Deer browse throughout the area, though the chances of seeing them are greater on the upper end simply because the field of view is greater.

The trail tops out on a ridge and joins an old two-track (i.e., jeep trail) along the ridge crest. Follow this a few hundred yards to the high point of the ridge where the lookout cabin sits. And this is just a cabin. While some lookout stations where built on high towers to increase their field of view, this location is high enough that the station was built flat on the ground at the edge of the ridge. The square structure has the traditional broad deck completely encircling it, and glass windows on every wall.

Location: West of Yakima in Okanogan/Wenatchee National Forest; see Mount Rainier and the Columbia River Gorge Map 2, grid d7.

User Groups: Hikers, horses, and dogs. No mountain bikes. No wheelchair facilities.

Permits: A federal Northwest Forest Pass, $5 per day or $30 annually, is required to park at the trailhead. Passes are available from ranger stations and many private vendors, online at website: www.wta.org, or by calling 800/270-7504.

Maps: Green Trails, Inc.'s excellent topographic maps of the region are available for $3.99 each at outdoor retail outlets. Ask for map number 304, Rimrock. Ask the USGS for a topographic map of the Rimrock Lake area.

Directions: From Yakima drive west on U.S. 12 for 33.2 miles and turn left onto Tieton River Road. Make a quick left onto Forest Service Road 1201—look for signs for Lost Lake—and continue nearly eight miles to the Pickle Prairie Trailhead.

Contact: Okanogan/Wenatchee National Forest, Naches Ranger District, 10061 Highway 12, Naches, WA 98937; 509/653-2205.

▊104▊ North Fork Tieton
9.8 mi/4.9 hrs

The total elevation gain isn't much—under 2,000 feet—but most of that comes in the second half of this hike. The first couple of miles offer a gentle climb through lush old-growth forest. By mile three the trail tilts considerably and the steep climb brings you into alpine heather meadows and rock-lined wildflower patches. The hiking is more difficult here, but the scenery is worth every labored breath. The contrast between the rough, gray rocks and the vibrant flowers is spectacular, and farther afield, the broad blue sky is a backdrop for the jagged peaks of the glacier-covered Goat Rocks, including Old Snow Mountain, Ives Peak, and Gilbert Peak. The trail merges with the Pacific Crest Trail at Tieton Pass. This is the place to turn around and retrace your steps, unless you plan to spend the night, in which case we recommend a 1.5-mile hike south on the PCT to McCall Basin, a beautiful high-alpine meadow basin complete with a babbling creek and small waterfall.

Location: East of Packwood in Gifford Pinchot National Forest partially within the Goat Rocks Wilderness; see Mount Rainier and the Columbia River Gorge Map 2, grid e7.

User Groups: Hikers, leashed dogs, and horses. No mountain bikes. No wheelchair facilities.

Permits: A federal Northwest Forest Pass, $5 per day or $30 annually, is required to park at the trailhead. Passes are available from ranger stations and many private vendors, online at website: www.wta.org, or by calling 800/270-7504.

Maps: For a map of Wenatchee Pinchot National Forest, contact the Outdoor Recreation Information Center, 915 Second Avenue, Suite 442, Seattle, WA 98174; 206/220-7450. Green Trails, Inc.'s excellent topographic maps are available for $3.99 each at outdoor retail outlets. Ask for map number 303, White Pass. Ask the USGS for a topographic map of the Pinegrass Ridge area.

Directions: From Packwood drive about 29 miles east on U.S. 12 across White Pass to Clear Lake. Just east of the lake, turn right (south) onto Forest Service Road 12 and drive about 2.5 miles south and east around the lake to a junction with Forest Service Road 1207. Turn right (south) onto this road and continue to the road's end and the trailhead.

Contact: Okanogan/Wenatchee National Forest, Naches Ranger District, 10061 U.S. 12, Naches, WA 98937; 509/653-2205.

105 Hidden Springs
9.4 mi/4.7 hrs

A gentle climb up the North Fork Tieton River Valley through a beautiful fir and cedar forest begins this hike. At the first fork in the trail (about 1.5 miles in), turn left and climb somewhat steeply up the north side of the valley to a beautiful meadow around Hidden Springs at mile 3.4. This is a great place to set up camp: there's plenty of cold, clear water available; the surroundings are as beautiful as any you find in the region; and the views of the distant peaks are incredible. If you want more stimuli, push on past the springs to the trail's end at a junction with the Pacific Crest Trail. Turn north on the PCT and walk a short mile to Shoe Lake. A two-mile loop trail circles the clear, blue lake, allowing you to visit all the best vantage points before heading back down the trail to the springs and the trailhead.

Location: East of Packwood in Gifford Pinchot National Forest partially within the Goat Rocks Wilderness; see Mount Rainier and the Columbia River Gorge Map 2, grid e8.

User Groups: Hikers, leashed dogs, and horses. No mountain bikes. No wheelchair facilities.

Permits: A federal Northwest Forest Pass, $5 per day or $30 annually, is required to park at the trailhead. Passes are available from ranger stations and many private vendors, online at website: www.wta.org, or by calling 800/270-7504.

Maps: For a map of the Okanogan/Wenatchee National Forest, contact the Outdoor Recreation Information Center, 915 Second Avenue, Suite 442, Seattle, WA 98174; 206/220-7450. Green Trails, Inc.'s excellent topographic maps are available for $3.99 each at outdoor retail outlets. Ask for map number 303, White Pass. Ask the USGS for a topographic map of the Pinegrass Ridge area.

Directions: From Packwood drive about 29 miles east on U.S. 12 across White Pass to Clear Lake. Just east of the lake, turn right (south) onto Forest Service Road

12 and drive about 2.5 miles south and east around the lake to a junction with Forest Service Road 1207. Turn right (south) onto this road and continue to the road's end and the trailhead.

Contact: Okanogan/Wenatchee National Forest, Naches Ranger District, 10061 U.S. 12, Naches, WA 98937; 509/653-2205.

106 Burley Mountain
6.0 mi/3.0 hr

A pleasant forest hike, with pretty views of a crystal-clear mountain river and a crashing waterfall, is all that awaits you here. There are no grandiose vistas, no high, craggy peaks—just a beautiful old-growth forest, a short side trail to a broad overlook of the Cispus River down among the ancient trees, and a modest waterfall near the trail. The trail ends at a rough, nearly impassable old access road, so you're pretty much required to retrace your steps, but don't spend much time worrying about it. This hike is so enjoyable that you won't mind experiencing the forest twice.

Location: South of Randle in Gifford Pinchot National Forest; see Mount Rainier and the Columbia River Gorge Map 2, grid e2.

User Groups: Hikers, leashed dogs, and horses. No mountain bikes are allowed. No wheelchair facilities.

Permits: A federal Northwest Forest Pass, $5 per day or $30 annually, is required to park at the trailhead. Passes are available from ranger stations and many private vendors, online at website: www.wta.org, or by calling 800/270-7504.

Maps: For a map of Gifford Pinchot National Forest, send $3 to Outdoor Recreation Information Center, 915 Second Avenue, Suite 442, Seattle, WA 98174; 206/220-7450. Green Trails, Inc.'s excellent topographic maps of the region are available for $3.99 each at outdoor retail outlets. Ask for number 333, McCoy Peak. Ask the USGS for a topographic map of the Tower Butte area.

Directions: From Randle drive one mile south on Forest Service Road 25 and then turn left (east) onto Forest Service Road 23. Continue on Forest Service Road 23 to its junction with Forest Service Road 21. Bear right on Forest Service Road 21, cross the Cispus River, turn left onto Forest Service Road 76, and continue to the Cispus Learning Center. Parking is on the left near the Elderberry Lodge.

Contact: Gifford Pinchot National Forest, Cowlitz Valley Ranger District, 10024 U.S. Highway 12, Randle, WA 98377; 360/497-1100.

107 Langille Ridge
20.4 mi/2.0 days

A forest of thick Douglas fir (punctuated by fat, juicy huckleberries) runs for nearly two miles here before it begins to thin and open up into broad, windswept meadows on the ridgetop. This trail—one of the long octopus arms that make up the wild, remote Dark Divide region of the forest—stays high and open during most of the route's remainder. Early-summer hikers find the snow melted and wildflowers in full bloom. In addition to the bonanza of color underfoot, the Langille Ridge Trail is renowned for its beautiful vistas of distant peaks and valleys. Mount St. Helens, Mount Adams, and Mount Rainier can all be seen on clear days, and the deep, dark valleys on either side of the ridge give this area a true feeling of wilderness, even without an official wilderness designation.

Location: South of Randle in Gifford Pinchot National Forest; see Mount Rainier and the Columbia River Gorge Map 2, grid e2.

User Groups: Hikers, leashed dogs, horses, and mountain bikes. No wheelchair facilities.

Permits: A federal Northwest Forest Pass, $5 per day or $30 annually, is required to park at the trailhead. Passes are available from ranger stations and many private vendors, online at website: www.wta.org, or by calling 800/270-7504.

Maps: For a map of the Gifford Pinchot National Forest, send $3 to Outdoor Recreation Information Center, 915 Second Avenue, Suite 442, Seattle, WA 98174; 206/220-7450. Green Trails, Inc.'s excellent topographic maps of the region are available for $3.99 each at outdoor retail outlets. Ask for map number 333, McCoy Peak. Ask the USGS for topographic maps of the Tower Rock and McCoy Peak areas.

Directions: From Randle drive one mile south on Forest Service Road 25 and then turn left (east) onto Forest Service Road 23. Continue to a junction with Forest Service Road 28. Turn right (south) on Forest Service Road 28, drive 6.8 miles, and turn left onto Forest Service Road 2809. Continue to the road's end and the trailhead.

Contact: Gifford Pinchot National Forest, Cowlitz Valley Ranger District, 10024 U.S. Highway 12, Randle, WA 98377; 360/497-1100.

108 Hamilton Peak
2.0 mi/1.0 hr

Mount Adams, Mount Rainier, the Goat Rocks, and the Tatoosh Range are all visible from this 5,800-foot peak. The views are stunning and well worth the hike up, which is important to remember while hurrying over the first half mile of the trail. In this early section the route follows an old access road and the views are restricted by dense second-growth forest and alder thickets. After leaving that old road and starting up the single-track path, your enjoyment level increases exponentially until you reach the summit, a former lookout site. This is a great

trail for late-afternoon hiking—it's short enough that you can enjoy the sunset from the summit, hurry down, and be back at your vehicle before the evening twilight completely fades into darkness.

Location: Southeast of Randle in Gifford Pinchot National Forest; see Mount Rainier and the Columbia River Gorge Map 2, grid e4.

User Groups: Hikers, leashed dogs, horses, and mountain bikes. No wheelchair facilities.

Permits: A federal Northwest Forest Pass, $5 per day or $30 annually, is required to park at the trailhead. Passes are available from ranger stations and many private vendors, online at website: www.wta.org, or by calling 800/270-7504.

Maps: For a map of Gifford Pinchot National Forest, contact the Outdoor Recreation Information Center, 915 Second Avenue, Suite 442, Seattle, WA 98174; 206/220-7450. Green Trails, Inc.'s excellent topographic maps are available for $3.99 each at outdoor retail outlets. Ask for map number 334, Blue Lake. Ask the USGS for a topographic map of the Hamilton Butte area.

Directions: From Randle drive one mile south on Forest Service Road 25 and turn left (east) onto Forest Service Road 23. Continue to a junction with Forest Service Road 22. Turn left onto Forest Service Road 22, drive 4.1 miles, and turn right onto Forest Service Road 2208. Continue 2.6 miles and turn right onto Forest Service Road 78. Follow Forest Service Road 78 to Forest Service Road 7807. Bear left and continue on Forest Service Road 7807 to Forest Service Road 7807-29. Drive to the trailhead at the end of the road.

Contact: Gifford Pinchot National Forest, Cowlitz Valley Ranger District, 10024 U.S. Highway 12, Randle, WA 98377; 360/497-1100.

109 Bishop Ridge
17.4 mi/1.0–2.0 days

Hikers might feel like there's no end in sight on the long, steep climb that characterizes the first few miles of the Bishop Ridge Trail. But most of the elevation gain is achieved by the time you reach the three-mile marker. The trail levels out somewhat on the ridge and then leapfrogs from one ridgetop meadow to another, passing through intermittent sections of dense fir forest. Once on the ridge, you loop around the headwaters of Smoothrock Creek and traverse the mountainside to the east of Blue Lake before the trail ends at a junction with the Blue Lake Ridge Trail. A long mile hike north on this side trail leads to the shores of Blue Lake. But this route is popular with motorcyclists, and hikers who don't want to encounter them may choose to skip the excursion to the lake and retrace their steps from the junction.

Location: Southeast of Randle in Gifford Pinchot National Forest; see Mount Rainier and the Columbia River Gorge Map 2, grid f3.

User Groups: Hikers, leashed dogs, and horses. No mountain bikes. No wheelchair facilities.

Permits: A federal Northwest Forest Pass, $5 per day or $30 annually, is required to park at the trailhead. Passes are available from ranger stations and many private vendors, online at website: www.wta.org, or by calling 800/270-7504.

Maps: For a map of the Gifford Pinchot National Forest, contact the Outdoor Recreation Information Center, 915 Second Avenue, Suite 442, Seattle, WA 98174; 206/220-7450. Green Trails, Inc.'s excellent topographic maps are available for $3.99 each at outdoor retail outlets. Ask for map number 333, McCoy Peak. Ask the USGS for topographic maps of the Tower Rock and Blue Lake areas.

Directions: From Randle drive one mile south on Forest Service Road 25 and then turn left (east) onto Forest Service Road 23. Continue to the trailhead, which is 2.8 miles beyond North Fork Campground.

Contact: Gifford Pinchot National Forest, Cowlitz Valley Ranger District, 10024 U.S. Highway 12, Randle, WA 98377; 360/497-1100.

110 Tongue Mountain
10.8 mi/5.4 hrs

The main trail on this hike traverses the mountain, but the real treat is the scramble-path that leads to the summit. Just 1.2 miles in from the trailhead, look for the faint path leading off to the right. This is the summit trail, and it's well worth the extra 1.5 miles round-trip to climb to the top and back. From the summit you'll love the views out over the Cispus River Valley to the north and the many long arms of the Dark Divide, a network of high, wild ridges in the heart of the forest between Mount Adams and Mount St. Helens. Back on the main trail, continue north to the long ridge high above the Cispus River before turning and retracing your steps back to the trailhead.

Location: Southeast of Randle in Gifford Pinchot National Forest; see Mount Rainier and the Columbia River Gorge Map 2, grid f3.

User Groups: Hikers, leashed dogs, horses, and mountain bikes. No wheelchair facilities.

Permits: A federal Northwest Forest Pass, $5 per day or $30 annually, is required to park at the trailhead. Passes are available from ranger stations and many private vendors, online at website: www.wta.org, or by calling 800/270-7504.

Maps: For a map of Gifford Pinchot National Forest, contact the Outdoor Recreation Information Center, 915 Second Avenue, Suite 442, Seattle, WA 98174; 206/220-7450. Green Trails, Inc.'s excellent topographic maps are available for $3.99 each at outdoor retail outlets. Ask for map number 333, McCoy Peak. Ask the USGS for a topographic map of the Tower Rock area.

Directions: From Randle drive one mile south on Forest Service Road 25 and then turn left (east) onto Forest Service Road 23. Continue on Forest Service Road 23 to the junction with Forest Service Road 28. Turn right (south) onto Forest Service Road 28 and then left on Forest Service Road 29. Follow the road about 4.5 miles before turning left on Forest Service Road 2904. Drive two miles to the trailhead on the left.

Contact: Gifford Pinchot National Forest, Cowlitz Valley Ranger District, 10024 U.S. Highway 12, Randle, WA 98377; 360/497-1100.

111 Juniper Ridge
23.2 mi/1.0–2.0 days

A wonderful wilderness experience is in store for hikers at Juniper Ridge, despite the lack of official recognition as a wilderness area. Juniper Ridge is the heart of the Dark Divide Roadless Area, and it offers some of the largest and most stunning wildflower meadows in the Pacific Northwest. In early summer the hundreds of acres of blooming wildflowers are rendered even more spectacular because of their setting against a backdrop of the snow-capped peaks of Mount Adams, Mount Rainier, or Mount St. Helens, depending on which direction you look. The trail climbs moderately in the first two miles and then just rolls along the ridgetop past Juniper, Sunrise, and Jumbo Peaks.

This makes a great backpacking trip, except for the lack of water. The primary water sources for campers are a few large snowdrifts that linger well into the summer in shady coves off the trail. It's a good idea not to bank on finding these and to carry all the water you need for your trip.

Location: Southeast of Randle in Gifford Pinchot National Forest; see Mount Rainier and the Columbia River Gorge Map 2, grid f3.

User Groups: Hikers, leashed dogs, horses, and mountain bikes. No wheelchair facilities.

Permits: A federal Northwest Forest Pass, $5 per day or $30 annually, is required to park at the trailhead. Passes are available from ranger stations and many private vendors, online at website: www.wta.org, or by calling 800/270-7504.

Maps: For a map of Gifford Pinchot National Forest, contact the Outdoor Recreation Information Center, 915 Second Avenue, Suite 442, Seattle, WA 98174; 206/220-7450. Green Trails, Inc.'s excellent topographic maps are available for $3.99 each at outdoor retail outlets. Ask for map number 333, McCoy Peak. Ask the USGS for topographic maps of the Tower Rock and McCoy Peak areas.

Directions: From Randle drive one mile south on Forest Service Road 25 and turn left (east) onto Forest Service Road 23. Continue to a junction with Forest Service Road 28. Turn right (south) on Forest Service Road 28, and after 1.2 miles, turn left (east) on Forest Service Road 29. Drive to the junction with Forest Service Road 2904 and turn left. Continue two miles to the trailhead on the right.

Contact: Gifford Pinchot National Forest, Cowlitz Valley Ranger District, 10024 U.S. Highway 12, Randle, WA 98377; 360/497-1100.

112 Badger Ridge
2.0 mi/1.0 hr

A rough road and short trail may deter you from making this hike, but remember the great views and solitude that await at the top. Badger Ridge Trail, steep in places and a bit primitive, traverses the ridge on the north flank of Badger Mountain. There are pleasant views from the trail, but the best panoramas of the surrounding forests and mountains are found at the top of Badger Mountain. Three-quarters of the way in, a faint side trail leads to the south. This little path climbs almost straight to the summit, a short (approximately one-half mile) but strenuous scramble. The summit is a great place to recuperate, however. Once home to a fire lookout station, the 5,560-foot peak offers views ranging from Mount Rainier to Mount St. Helens. The most impressive sight is Pinto Rock, the craggy remains of a long-gone volcano.

Location: South of Randle in Gifford Pinchot National Forest; see Mount Rainier and the Columbia River Gorge Map 2, grid f2.

User Groups: Hikers, leashed dogs, horses, and mountain bikes. No wheelchair facilities.

Permits: A federal Northwest Forest Pass, $5 per day or $30 annually, is required to park at the trailhead. Passes are available from ranger stations and many private vendors, online at website: www.wta.org, or by calling 800/270-7504.

Maps: For a map of Gifford Pinchot National Forest, send $3 to Outdoor Recreation Information Center, 915 Second Avenue, Suite 442, Seattle, WA 98174; 206/220-7450. Green Trails, Inc.'s excellent topographic maps of the region are available for $3.99 each at outdoor retail outlets. Ask for map number 333, McCoy Peak. Ask the USGS for a topographic map of the French Butte area.

Directions: From Randle drive one mile south on Forest Service Road 25 and then turn left (east) onto Forest Service Road 23. Continue to the road's junction with Forest Service Road 28. Take a right (south) turn onto Forest Service Road 28 and drive 13 miles to Forest Service Road 2816. Turn left (east) and follow Forest Service Road 2816 for three miles to the trailhead.

Contact: Gifford Pinchot National Forest, Cowlitz Valley Ranger District, 10024 U.S. Highway 12, Randle, WA 98377; 360/497-1100.

113 French Creek
8.2 mi/4.1 hrs

Few people visit this trail, so you should have the deep-forest path to yourself. From the trailhead, hike west about three-quarters of a mile on the Boundary Trail to the first fork. Turn left and start up the French Creek Valley. Enjoy the closed, dark forest and babbling creek. If you are quiet and listen closely, you may hear and even see great horned owls, barred owls, and white-tailed deer. The forest, though thick and lush now, was once ravaged by fire; silvery gray snags stand like bright beacons among the dark living trees. The trail ends at a junction with the Quartz Creek Trail, so turn around when you arrive at that point.

Location: South of Randle in Gifford Pinchot National Forest; see Mount Rainier and the Columbia River Gorge Map 2, grid f2.

User Groups: Hikers and leashed dogs. No horses or mountain bikes are allowed. No wheelchair facilities.

Permits: A federal Northwest Forest Pass, $5 per day or $30 annually, is required to park at the trailhead. Passes are available from ranger stations and many private vendors, online at website: www.wta.org, or by calling 800/270-7504. Visitors to any developed site in the Mount St. Helens Monument—including visitor centers, paved overlooks, and interpretive areas—are required to pay an $8 fee per person for a Monument Pass. The pass is valid for three days. Anyone attempting to climb the peak or just scramble on the upper slopes must register in the town of Cougar and pay a $15 climbing fee per person. Contact the

Mount St. Helens National Volcanic Monument at 360/247-3900.

Maps: For a trail information report, contact the Mount St. Helens National Volcanic Monument at 360/247-3900. For a map of the Gifford Pinchot National Forest, send $3 to Outdoor Recreation Information Center, 915 Second Avenue, Suite 442, Seattle, WA 98174; 206/220-7450. Green Trails, Inc.'s excellent topographic maps of the region are available for $3.99 each at outdoor retail outlets. Ask for map number 333, McCoy Peak. Ask the USGS for topographic maps of the Quartz Creek Butte and McCoy Peak areas.

Directions: From Randle drive one mile south on Forest Service Road 25 and then turn left (east) onto Forest Service Road 23. Continue to its junction with Forest Service Road 28. Turn right (south) on Forest Service Road 28 and, in 1.2 miles, turn left (southeast) onto Forest Service Road 29. Drive south to the road's end and the trailhead.

Contact: Gifford Pinchot National Forest, Mount St. Helens National Volcanic Monument, 42218 Northeast Yale Bridge Road, Amboy, WA 98601-9715; 360/247-3900.

114 Yellow Jacket/Hat Rock
5.0 mi/2.5 hrs

The Yellow Jacket/Hat Rock Trail allows you to enjoy the beauty of the Langille Ridge Meadows and the views from Hat Rock without making the long hike from the ridge's north end. This trail climbs steeply for less than a mile to the top of Langille Ridge. At the path's junction with the ridge trail, turn south and hike to the flank of Hat Rock, savoring the views of Mount St. Helens and Mount Adams as you go. Turn around at the flank of Hat Rock, or if you have a lot of climbing experience, scramble to the summit's rocky peak.

Location: South of Randle in Gifford Pinchot National Forest; see Mount Rainier and the Columbia River Gorge Map 2, grid f2.

User Groups: Hikers, leashed dogs, horses, and mountain bikes. No wheelchair facilities.

Permits: A federal Northwest Forest Pass, $5 per day or $30 annually, is required to park at the trailhead. Passes are available from ranger stations and many private vendors, online at website: www.wta.org, or by calling 800/270-7504.

Maps: For a map of Gifford Pinchot National Forest, send $3 to Outdoor Recreation Information Center, 915 Second Avenue, Suite 442, Seattle, WA 98174; 206/220-7450. Green Trails, Inc.'s excellent topographic maps of the region are available for $3.99 each at outdoor retail outlets. Ask for map number 333, McCoy Peak. Ask the USGS for a topographic map of the McCoy Peak area.

Directions: From Randle drive one mile south on Forest Service Road 25 and then turn left (east) onto Forest Service Road 23. Continue to its junction with Forest Service Road 28. Turn right (south), drive 7.8 miles, and turn left onto Forest Service Road 2810. Continue to the trailhead just before the road's end.

Contact: Gifford Pinchot National Forest, Cowlitz Valley Ranger District, 10024 U.S. Highway 12, Randle, WA 98377; 360/497-1100.

115 Snagtooth
4.0 mi/2.0 hrs

A pleasant walk with some better than average views, this trail is a good choice when time is limited or weather is less than perfect. Many of the best vistas along the route are found close in to the trailhead, and they are not dependent on crystal-clear skies. The trail rolls under the Snagtooth

Mountain summit—a rocky, jagged peak—before climbing higher on the rough ridge to its junction with the Boundary Trail (see hikes this chapter). It is possible to scramble to the summit of Snagtooth, but extreme care should be taken when navigating loose rocks and scree.

A section of the Snagtooth Trail leads from the trailhead down into the Quartz Creek drainage, but logging has obliterated the trail in places and generally reduced the enjoyability of that section.

Location: South of Randle in Gifford Pinchot National Forest; see Mount Rainier and the Columbia River Gorge Map 2, grid f2.

User Groups: Hikers, leashed dogs, and horses. No mountain bikes are allowed. No wheelchair facilities.

Permits: A federal Northwest Forest Pass, $5 per day or $30 annually, is required to park at the trailhead. Passes are available from ranger stations and many private vendors, online at website: www.wta.org, or by calling 800/270-7504. Visitors to any developed site in the Mount St. Helens Monument—including visitor centers, paved overlooks, and interpretive areas—are required to pay an $8 fee per person for a Monument Pass. The pass is valid for three days. Anyone attempting to climb the peak or just scramble on the upper slopes must register in the town of Cougar and pay a $15 climbing fee per person. Contact the Mount St. Helens National Volcanic Monument at 360/247-3900.

Maps: For a trail information report, contact the Mount St. Helens National Volcanic Monument at 360/247-3900. For a map of Gifford Pinchot National Forest, send $3 to Outdoor Recreation Information Center, 915 Second Avenue, Suite 442, Seattle, WA 98174; 206/220-7450. Green Trails, Inc.'s excellent topographic maps of the region are available for $3.99 each at outdoor retail outlets. Ask for map numbers 333 and 365, McCoy Peak and Lone Butte. Ask the USGS for topographic maps of the Quartz Creek and McCoy Peak areas.

Directions: From Cougar drive east on Forest Service Road 90 to the Lewis River Campground and the junction with Forest Service Road 93. Turn left (north) onto Forest Service Road 93 and drive to its junction with Forest Service Road 9341. Turn right (east) and drive to the road's end and the trailhead on the left.

Contact: Gifford Pinchot National Forest, Mount St. Helens National Volcanic Monument, 42218 Northeast Yale Bridge Road, Amboy, WA 98601-9715; 360/247-3900.

116 Spring Creek
4.6 mi/2.3 hrs

This trail leads through small meadows, old fir forest, and huckleberry patches to the shore of blue-green Horseshoe Lake. Along the way you can enjoy the views of Mount Adams rising in the south and Green Mountain to the north. After relaxing on the lakeshore for a time, start back on the trail, and midway back to the trailhead, look for the small side trail that leads off to the left (northwest) to the 5,007-foot Green Mountain summit. If you decide to make this climb, keep in mind that the trail is rough, brushy, and unmaintained. The going is tough, but the rewards from the top make it worth the extra sweat—you'll have wonderful views of the Cispus River Valley, the Goat Rocks, and Mount Adams. This side trail adds nearly four miles to the round-trip distance.

Location: Southeast of Randle in Gifford Pinchot National Forest; see Mount Rainier and the Columbia River Gorge Map 2, grid f4.

User Groups: Hikers, leashed dogs, horses, and mountain bikes. No wheelchair facilities.

Permits: A federal Northwest Forest Pass, $5 per day or $30 annually, is required to park at the trailhead. Passes are available from ranger stations and many private vendors, online at website: www.wta.org, or by calling 800/270-7504.

Maps: For a map of Gifford Pinchot National Forest, contact the Outdoor Recreation Information Center, 915 Second Avenue, Suite 442, Seattle, WA 98174; 206/220-7450. Green Trails, Inc.'s excellent topographic maps are available for $3.99 each at outdoor retail outlets. Ask for map number 334, Blue Lake. Ask the USGS for a topographic map of the Green Mountain area.

Directions: From Randle drive approximately one mile south on Forest Service Road 25 and turn left (east) onto Forest Service Road 23. Continue to the junction with Forest Service Road 21. Turn left onto Forest Service Road 21, drive to the Adams Fork Campground, and then turn left (south) onto Forest Service Road 56. Cross the Cispus River and continue left to Forest Service Road 5603. Turn right and drive to the spur road (Forest Service Road 042). Turn right onto Forest Service Road 042 and follow it to the road's end and the trailhead. The Spring Creek Trail begins in the Spring Creek Campground, near the boat ramp.

Contact: Gifford Pinchot National Forest, Cowlitz Valley Ranger District, 10024 U.S. Highway 12, Randle, WA 98377; 360/497-1100.

117 High Lakes
6.7 mi/3.3 hrs

Set in the middle of a broad meadow and thin forest, the Chain Lakes lie strung out like a strand of jewels in Gifford Pinchot National Forest. Sparkling blue-green waters reflect the glacier-covered north face of Mount Adams. Huckleberries, wild strawberries, and an assortment of mushrooms thrive in the area around the lakes, and wildlife—from white-tailed deer and black bear to deer mice and blackbirds—linger close by to feed on the bountiful harvest. The trail climbs gently from the campground and between the six or seven lakes and ponds before continuing west across Adams Creek to Horseshoe Lake.

Unless you are skilled in identifying mushrooms, don't eat any of them. While some are delicious, others are deadly.

Location: Southeast of Randle in Gifford Pinchot National Forest; see Mount Rainier and the Columbia River Gorge Map 2, grid f4.

User Groups: Hikers, leashed dogs, horses, and mountain bikes. No wheelchair facilities.

Permits: A federal Northwest Forest Pass, $5 per day or $30 annually, is required to park at the trailhead. Passes are available from ranger stations and many private vendors, online at website: www.wta.org, or by calling 800/270-7504.

Maps: For a map of Gifford Pinchot National Forest, contact the Outdoor Recreation Information Center, 915 Second Avenue, Suite 442, Seattle, WA 98174; 206/220-7450. Green Trails, Inc.'s excellent topographic maps are available for $3.99 each at outdoor retail outlets. Ask for map number 334, Blue Lake. Ask the USGS for a topographic map of the Green Mountain area.

Directions: From Randle drive one mile south on Forest Service Road 25 and turn left (east) onto Forest Service Road 23. Continue to a junction with Forest Service Road 2329. Turn left and drive south to Forest Service Spur Road 022. Turn left and drive to the end of the road at Chain Lakes Campground. The trailhead is on the east end of the campground.

Contact: Gifford Pinchot National Forest, Cowlitz Valley Ranger District, 10024 U.S. Highway 12, Randle, WA 98377; 360/497-1100.

118 Snowgrass
10.6 mi/5.0 hrs

This trail traverses a long hillside, drops through the Goat Creek Basin, and climbs moderately to Snowgrass Flats and a junction with the Pacific Crest Trail. Yes, the views for most of the route are limited, the forest consists of middle-aged second growth, and the trail is somewhat dusty, but don't be discouraged. We heartily recommend this hike for a number of reasons. The destination, Snowgrass Flats, is a beautiful wildflower meadow, not to mention one of the best places in the state for viewing mountain goats. Also, even if the views in the first few miles were the best in the world, most late-summer hikers would find themselves so tempted by the thick huckleberry patches along the trail that they would never look up. Fat, juicy berries literally turn the trail purple at times as the fruit falls or is knocked loose onto the ground and trampled into the dirt path. In addition to mountain goats, keep an eye out for mule deer, black bears, and great horned owls. Occasionally golden eagles visit the area. Spend some time exploring and enjoying the flats before retracing your steps through this berry heaven.

This trail can be combined with the Goat Ridge Trail (see hike this chapter) and a short section of the Pacific Crest Trail to create a wonderful loop backpacking trip.

Location: Southwest of Packwood in Gifford Pinchot National Forest partially within the Goat Rocks Wilderness; see Mount Rainier and the Columbia River Gorge Map 2, grid f3.

User Groups: Hikers, leashed dogs, and horses. No mountain bikes. No wheelchair facilities.

Permits: A federal Northwest Forest Pass, $5 per day or $30 annually, is required to park at the trailhead. Passes are available from ranger stations and many private vendors, online at website: www.wta.org, or by calling 800/270-7504.

Maps: For a map of Gifford Pinchot National Forest, contact the Outdoor Recreation Information Center, 915 Second Avenue, Suite 442, Seattle, WA 98174; 206/220-7450. Green Trails, Inc.'s excellent topographic maps are available for $3.99 each at outdoor retail outlets. Ask for map numbers 334 and 335, Blue Lake and Walupt Lake. Ask the USGS for a topographic map of the Walupt Lake area.

Directions: From Packwood drive 2.1 miles west on U.S. 12 to a junction with Forest Service Road 21. Turn left (south) onto Forest Service Road 21, continue 15 miles, and then turn left onto Forest Service Road 2150. Drive to the road's end and the trailhead (signed for the Berrypatch Trailhead).

Contact: Gifford Pinchot National Forest, Cowlitz Valley Ranger District, 10024 U.S. Highway 12, Randle, WA 98377; 360/497-1100.

119 Nannie Ridge
9.0 mi/4.0 hrs

A moderately steep climb through a long series of open switchbacks takes hikers to the crest of Nannie Ridge, and a junction with a small side trail leading to the Nannie Peak summit at 2.5 miles. The half-mile side trip to an old lookout site is worth the effort; it provides the first great views of Mount Adams to the south and Gilbert Peak to the east. The main trail continues along the south side of the ridge, rolling east under a long, tall cliff face, past countless huckleberry bushes and wildflower patches, and around the shores of small, clean Sheep Lake. This little tarn is ideal for a rejuvenating swim—it's deep enough to be clean and swimmable but shallow and warm enough to permit a quick plunge or two. There are some wonderful campsites around the lake, the best being on the south shore with down-valley views of Mount Adams. From Sheep Lake at 4.5 miles, the trail continues a few hundred yards to a junction with the Pacific Crest Trail. Unless you plan to hike part of that trail, you might as well turn around at the lake and retrace your steps from there. The PCT is a dusty, rutted trail, and horses are commonly seen here, as are black bears. The horses are easy to deal with—step off the trail and let them pass—and the bears can be dealt with, too. Practice safe bear-country camping techniques and you'll be fine.

This trail can be combined with the Walupt Creek Trail (see below) and a five-mile section of the Pacific Crest Trail to create a wonderful 15-mile loop trip.

Location: Southwest of Packwood in Gifford Pinchot National Forest within the Goat Rocks Wilderness; see Mount Rainier and the Columbia River Gorge Map 2, grid f3.

User Groups: Hikers, leashed dogs, and horses. No mountain bikes. No wheelchair facilities.

Permits: A federal Northwest Forest Pass, $5 per day or $30 annually, is required to park at the trailhead. Passes are available from ranger stations and many private vendors, online at website: www.wta.org, or by calling 800/270-7504.

Maps: For a map of Gifford Pinchot National Forest, contact the Outdoor Recreation Information Center, 915 Second Avenue, Suite 442, Seattle, WA 98174; 206/220-7450. Green Trails, Inc.'s excellent topographic maps are available for $3.99 each at outdoor retail outlets. Ask for map number 335, Walupt Lake. Ask the USGS for a topographic map of the Walupt Lake area.

Directions: From Packwood drive 2.1 miles west on U.S. 12 to a junction with Forest Service Road 21. Turn left (south), go 16 miles, and then turn left onto Forest Service Road 2160. Drive three miles to the road's end at Walupt Lake Campground. The trailhead is at the far east end of the campground, near the walk-in campsites.

Contact: Gifford Pinchot National Forest, Cowlitz Valley Ranger District, 10024 U.S. Highway 12, Randle, WA 98377; 360/497-1100.

120 Walupt Creek
8.6 mi/4.3 hrs

Leading along the north shore of cold, blue Walupt Lake, this trail accesses several lakefront campsites in the first couple miles before leaving the lake and climbing up Walupt Creek Valley. Crossing the creek far upstream, the trail continues east while the creek angles north. The trail pushes upward into a high-alpine basin with some modest views and small flower meadows before intersecting with the Pacific Crest Trail. Backpackers can stop just short of the PCT and stay at Short Trail Camp in the alpine meadow area before retracing their steps to Walupt Lake.

This trail can be combined with the Nannie Ridge Trail (see above) and a five-mile section of the Pacific Crest Trail to create a wonderful 15-mile loop trip.

Location: Southwest of Packwood in Gifford Pinchot National Forest within the Goat Rocks Wilderness; see Mount Rainier and the Columbia River Gorge Map 2, grid f3.

User Groups: Hikers, leashed dogs, and horses. No mountain bikes. No wheelchair facilities.

Permits: A federal Northwest Forest Pass, $5 per day or $30 annually, is required to park at the trailhead. Passes are available from ranger stations and many private vendors, online at website: www.wta.org, or by calling 800/270-7504.

Maps: For a map of Gifford Pinchot National Forest, contact the Outdoor Recreation

Information Center, 915 Second Avenue, Suite 442, Seattle, WA 98174; 206/220-7450. Green Trails, Inc.'s excellent topographic maps are available for $3.99 each at outdoor retail outlets. Ask for map number 335, Walupt Lake. Ask the USGS for a topographic map of the Walupt Lake area.

Directions: From Packwood drive 2.1 miles west on U.S. 12 to a junction with Forest Service Road 21. Turn left (south), continue 16 miles, and then turn left onto Forest Service Road 2160. Drive three miles to the road's end at the Walupt Lake Campground. The trailhead is at the far east end of the campground, near the walk-in campsites.

Contact: Gifford Pinchot National Forest, Cowlitz Valley Ranger District, 10024 U.S. Highway 12, Randle, WA 98377; 360/497-1100.

121 Coleman Weedpatch
6.0 mi/3.0 hrs

Popular with equestrians, this trail is deeply rutted and dusty, but don't let appearances stop you. The plentiful berries, fragrant wildflowers, and picturesque views of Elk Peak and Nannie Ridge are incentive enough to venture out on this trail. But we love to hike it because of the herds of mule deer that are almost always seen along the route, not to mention the red-tailed hawks that soar endlessly overhead.

Location: Southwest of Packwood in Gifford Pinchot National Forest within the Goat Rocks Wilderness; see Mount Rainier and the Columbia River Gorge Map 2, grid f5.

User Groups: Hikers, leashed dogs, and horses. No mountain bikes. No wheelchair facilities.

Permits: A federal Northwest Forest Pass, $5 per day or $30 annually, is required to park at the trailhead. Passes are available from ranger stations and many private vendors,

online at website: www.wta.org, or by calling 800/270-7504.

Maps: For a map of Gifford Pinchot National Forest, contact the Outdoor Recreation Information Center, 915 Second Avenue, Suite 442, Seattle, WA 98174; 206/220-7450. Green Trails, Inc.'s excellent topographic maps are available for $3.99 each at outdoor retail outlets. Ask for map numbers 334 and 335, Blue Lake and Walupt Lake. Ask the USGS for topographic maps of the Walupt Lake and Hamilton Butte areas.

Directions: From Packwood drive 2.1 miles west on U.S. 12 to a junction with Forest Service Road 21. Turn left (south) onto this road, continue 16 miles, and then turn left onto Forest Service Road 2160. Drive three miles to the trailhead on the right.

Contact: Gifford Pinchot National Forest, Cowlitz Valley Ranger District, 10024 U.S. Highway 12, Randle, WA 98377; 360/497-1100.

122 Dark Meadow
6.4 mi/3.2 hrs

This is a wonderful and diverse hike. Beginning in a pretty creek valley, the trail parallels the water for nearly 1.4 miles before climbing to the top of Juniper Ridge. As the trail ascends, the views begin to develop, and the thick fir forest thins and fades away entirely when the trail enters Dark Meadow near the ridgetop. The stunning meadow is filled with wildflowers, panoramic vistas, and a wide variety of wildlife. The views encompass Mount Adams, Mount St. Helens, and Jumbo Peak just to the north.

Location: South of Randle in Gifford Pinchot National Forest; see Mount Rainier and the Columbia River Gorge Map 2, grid g4.

User Groups: Hikers, leashed dogs, horses, and mountain bikes. No wheelchair facilities.

Permits: A federal Northwest Forest Pass, $5 per day or $30 annually, is required to park

at the trailhead. Passes are available from ranger stations and many private vendors, online at website: www.wta.org, or by calling 800/270-7504.

Maps: For a map of Gifford Pinchot National Forest, contact the Outdoor Recreation Information Center, 915 Second Avenue, Suite 442, Seattle, WA 98174; 206/220-7450. Green Trails, Inc.'s excellent topographic maps are available for $3.99 each at outdoor retail outlets. Ask for map numbers 333 and 334, McCoy Peak and Blue Lake. Ask the USGS for topographic maps of the East Canyon Ridge and McCoy Peak areas.

Directions: From Randle drive one mile south on Forest Service Road 25 and then turn left (east) onto Forest Service Road 23. Continue to the trailhead on the left.

Contact: Gifford Pinchot National Forest, Cowlitz Valley Ranger District, 10024 U.S. Highway 12, Randle, WA 98377; 360/497-1100.

123 Takhlakh Loop
1.1 mi one way/1.0 hr 🥾 ⭐

A flat lakeside trail with absolutely astounding views of Mount Adams—what more could you want? If your answer is a nearby campground and maybe some decent trout fishing, well, this is your kind of place. It's all here, as well as wildflowers and moderately large patches of huckleberries in the fall.

Location: Southeast of Randle in Gifford Pinchot National Forest; see Mount Rainier and the Columbia River Gorge Map 2, grid g3.

User Groups: Hikers and leashed dogs. No horses or mountain bikes. No wheelchair facilities.

Permits: A federal Northwest Forest Pass, $5 per day or $30 annually, is required to park at the trailhead. Passes are available from ranger stations and many private vendors, online at website: www.wta.org, or by calling 800/270-7504.

Maps: For a map of Gifford Pinchot National Forest, contact the Outdoor Recreation Information Center, 915 Second Avenue, Suite 442, Seattle, WA 98174; 206/220-7450. Green Trails, Inc.'s excellent topographic maps are available for $3.99 each at outdoor retail outlets. Ask for map number 334, Blue Lake. Ask the USGS for a topographic map of the Green Mountain area.

Directions: From Randle drive one mile south on Forest Service Road 25 and then turn left (east) onto Forest Service Road 23. Continue 29 miles to a junction with Forest Service Road 2329. Turn left and drive south to Takhlakh Lake Campground. The trail begins in the campground, near the boat ramp.

Contact: Gifford Pinchot National Forest, Cowlitz Valley Ranger District, 10024 U.S. Highway 12, Randle, WA 98377; 360/497-1100.

124 Divide Camp
5.6 mi/2.8 hrs 🥾 ⭐

Adams Glacier hangs directly above the end of this trail, making the gentle climb through beautiful old forest seem almost too easy for such wonderful rewards. But the views of Mount Adams and its heavy glacier system, and the serenity of nearby Divide Camp, are as enjoyable as they would have been after a grueling hike. To find the best views of the mountain, climb to the trail's end at a junction with the Pacific Crest Trail. After you have your fill of the scenery (or darkness forces you to head for camp), retrace your steps about half a mile down the trail and follow a short side trail to Divide Camp. After spending a peaceful night in the wilderness camp, head back up to the PCT junction for a look at the mountain in the soft morning light and then retrace your way back to the trailhead.

Location: North of Trout Lake in Gifford Pinchot National Forest within the Mount Adams Wilderness; see Mount Rainier and the Columbia River Gorge Map 2, grid g3.

User Groups: Hikers, leashed dogs, and horses. No mountain bikes. No wheelchair facilities.

Permits: A federal Northwest Forest Pass, $5 per day or $30 annually, is required to park at the trailhead. Passes are available from ranger stations and many private vendors, online at website: www.wta.org, or by calling 800/270-7504.

Maps: For a map of Gifford Pinchot National Forest, contact the Outdoor Recreation Information Center, 915 Second Avenue, Suite 442, Seattle, WA 98174; 206/220-7450. Green Trails, Inc.'s excellent topographic maps are available for $3.99 each at outdoor retail outlets. Ask for map numbers 334 and 366, Blue Lake and Mount Adams West. Ask the USGS for topographic maps of the Green Mountain and Mount Adams West areas.

Directions: From Trout Lake drive 26 miles north on Forest Service Road 23 to the Takhlakh Lake Campground and the junction with Forest Service Road 2329. Turn right (south) onto this road and drive three miles to the trailhead on the left.

Contact: Gifford Pinchot National Forest, Mount Adams Ranger District, 2455 Highway 141, Trout Lake, WA 98650; 509/395-3400.

125 Quartz Butte Trail
3.0 mi/1.5 hrs

A quick, straight drop into the Quartz Creek Valley brings you to a beautiful, sparkling river flanked by thick, dry forest. Look for deer and elk hiding along the hillside above the river. The creekside environment is a great place for a lunchtime nap before the tough climb back to the trailhead.

Location: South of Randle in Gifford Pinchot National Forest; see Mount Rainier and the Columbia River Gorge Map 2, grid g3.

User Groups: Hikers, leashed dogs, horses, and mountain bikes. No wheelchair facilities.

Permits: A federal Northwest Forest Pass, $5 per day or $30 annually, is required to park at the trailhead. Passes are available from ranger stations and many private vendors, online at website: www.wta.org, or by calling 800/270-7504. Visitors to any developed site in the Mount St. Helens Monument—including visitor centers, paved overlooks, and interpretive areas—are required to pay an $8 fee per person for a Monument Pass. The pass is valid for three days. Anyone attempting to climb the peak or just scramble on the upper slopes must register in the town of Cougar and pay a $15 climbing fee per person.

Maps: For a map of Gifford Pinchot National Forest, contact the Outdoor Recreation Information Center, 915 Second Avenue, Suite 442, Seattle, WA 98174; 206/220-7450. Green Trails, Inc.'s excellent topographic maps are available for $3.99 each at outdoor retail outlets. Ask for map number 365, Lone Butte. Ask the USGS for topographic maps of the Steamboat Mountain and Blue Lake areas.

Directions: From Cougar drive about 30 miles east on Forest Service Road 90 to Island Shelter and the trailhead on the left.

Contact: Gifford Pinchot National Forest, Mount St. Helens National Volcanic Monument, 42218 Northeast Yale Bridge Road, Amboy, WA 98601-9715; 360/750-3900.

126 Summit Prairie
18.0 mi/1.0–2.0 days

The Summit Prairie Trail is a gentle hike for 6.5 miles along the crest of Quartz Creek Ridge—gentle, that is, after you make the steep and dusty climb about 2.5 miles from the Lewis River to the ridgetop. At least the surrounding forest on the way up is thick and shady, which keeps hikers from baking in the hot summer sun. There are even a few huckleberries along the route to provide nourishment. At the ridgetop the walking is easy, and the views are spectacular. The network of broad, meadow-topped ridges of the Dark Divide sprawls across the scenery to the west, the white summits of Mount Adams and Mount Rainier punctuate the vistas to the east and north, and the beautiful valley of the Lewis River stretches away to the south. Dry campsites can be found anywhere along the ridgetop. Bring plenty of water.

Location: South of Randle in Gifford Pinchot National Forest; see Mount Rainier and the Columbia River Gorge Map 2, grid g3.

User Groups: Hikers, leashed dogs, horses, and mountain bikes. No wheelchair facilities.

Permits: A federal Northwest Forest Pass, $5 per day or $30 annually, is required to park at the trailhead. Passes are available from ranger stations and many private vendors, online at website: www.wta.org, or by calling 800/270-7504. Visitors to any developed site in the Mount St. Helens Monument—including visitor centers, paved overlooks, and interpretive areas—are required to pay an $8 fee per person for a Monument Pass. The pass is valid for three days. Anyone attempting to climb the peak or just scramble on the upper slopes must register in the town of Cougar and pay a $15 climbing fee per person.

Maps: For a map of Gifford Pinchot National Forest, contact the Outdoor Recreation Information Center, 915 Second Avenue, Suite 442, Seattle, WA 98174; 206/220-7450. Green Trails, Inc.'s excellent topographic maps are available for $3.99 each at outdoor retail outlets. Ask for map number 365, Lone Butte. Ask the USGS for topographic maps of the Steamboat Mountain and Blue Lake areas.

Directions: From Cougar drive about 30 miles east on Forest Service Road 90 to Island Shelter and the trailhead on the left.

Contact: Gifford Pinchot National Forest, Mount St. Helens National Volcanic Monument, 42218 Northeast Yale Bridge Road, Amboy, WA 98601-9715; 360/750-3900.

127 Steamboat Viewpoint
1.4 mi/1.0 hr

This short trail climbs a moderately steep slope to the former lookout site on the Steamboat Mountain summit. From here enjoy the stunning views of Mount Adams and the surrounding valleys. The rocky mountaintop is frequently visited by mountain goats, and if they aren't around, just enjoy the thick carpet of wildflowers before heading back the way you came.

Location: West of Trout Lake in Gifford Pinchot National Forest; see Mount Rainier and the Columbia River Gorge Map 2, grid g3.

User Groups: Hikers, leashed dogs, horses, and mountain bikes. No wheelchair facilities.

Permits: A federal Northwest Forest Pass, $5 per day or $30 annually, is required to park at the trailhead. Passes are available from ranger stations and many private vendors, online at website: www.wta.org, or by calling 800/270-7504.

Maps: For a map of Gifford Pinchot National Forest, contact the Outdoor Recreation Information Center, 915 Second Avenue, Suite 442, Seattle, WA 98174; 206/220-7450. Green Trails, Inc.'s excellent topographic maps are available for $3.99 each at outdoor retail outlets. Ask for map number 366, Mount Adams West. Ask the USGS for a topographic map of the Steamboat Mountain area.

Directions: From Trout Lake drive west on Highway 141 and turn right (north) on

Forest Service Road 88 just outside of town. Continue on Forest Service Road 88 for roughly 12 miles, turn left on Forest Service Road 8851, and then bear right on Forest Service Road 8854. Follow Forest Service Road 8854 to Access Road 021 on the left and continue on the spur a quarter mile to the trailhead.

Contact: Gifford Pinchot National Forest, Mount Adams Ranger District, 2455 Highway 141, Trout Lake, WA 98650; 509/395-3400.

128 Langfield Falls Interpretive Trail
0.5 mi/1.0 hr

This trail follows Mosquito Creek to a viewing platform and a monument dedicating the trail to K. C. Langfield, a former Mount Adams district ranger. From the platform enjoy the close-up views of the tall cascade in front of you. Interpretive signs explain the flora and fauna of the area, and well-placed benches invite leisurely rest stops and contemplative breaks.

Location: West of Trout Lake in Gifford Pinchot National Forest; see Mount Rainier and the Columbia River Gorge Map 2, grid g3.

User Groups: Hikers and leashed dogs. No horses or mountain bikes. No wheelchair facilities.

Permits: A federal Northwest Forest Pass, $5 per day or $30 annually, is required to park at the trailhead. Passes are available from ranger stations and many private vendors, online at website: www.wta.org, or by calling 800/270-7504.

Maps: For a map of Gifford Pinchot National Forest, contact the Outdoor Recreation Information Center, 915 Second Avenue, Suite 442, Seattle, WA 98174; 206/220-7450. Green Trails, Inc.'s excellent topographic maps are available for $3.99 each at outdoor retail outlets. Ask for map number 366, Mount Adams

West. Ask the USGS for a topographic map of the Sleeping Beauty area.

Directions: From Trout Lake drive west on Highway 141 and turn right (north) on Forest Service Road 88. Continue about 12 miles to the trailhead, just a quarter mile past the junction with Forest Service Road 8851. The trailhead is on the right.

Contact: Gifford Pinchot National Forest, Mount Adams Ranger District, 2455 Highway 141, Trout Lake, WA 98650; 509/395-3400.

129 High Line
16.6 mi/2.0 days

Though this hike starts with a steep climb up the Killen Creek Trail—actually a ridge trail, not a creek trail—the worst of the elevation gain is taken care of in the first three miles. At that point the trail intercepts the Pacific Crest Trail and offers the first great views of the northern face of Mount Adams. Heading east for a mile on the PCT leads to the second junction of the route. Leave the PCT here and continue east around the flank of the 12,000-foot volcano. At times the trail tilts steeply, forcing hikers above 7,500 feet in a couple places, but the workout is always compensated with priceless scenery: high alpine meadows, massive hanging glaciers, and the ever-present monolith of Mount Adams, the cinder cone to the south. If that isn't enough, turn west and study the craggy peaks of the Goat Rocks or look northwest to the high, glacier-capped cone of Mount Rainier.

Location: North of Trout Lake in Gifford Pinchot National Forest within the Mount Adams Wilderness; see Mount Rainier and the Columbia River Gorge Map 2, grid g3.

User Groups: Hikers, leashed dogs, and horses. No mountain bikes. No wheelchair facilities.

Permits: A federal Northwest Forest Pass, $5 per day or $30 annually, is required to park at the trailhead. Passes are available from ranger stations and many private vendors, online at website: www.wta.org, or by calling 800/270-7504.

Maps: For a map of Gifford Pinchot National Forest, contact the Outdoor Recreation Information Center, 915 Second Avenue, Suite 442, Seattle, WA 98174; 206/220-7450. Green Trails, Inc.'s excellent topographic maps are available for $3.99 each at outdoor retail outlets. Ask for map numbers 334 and 366, Blue Lake and Mount Adams West. Ask the USGS for topographic maps of the Green Mountain, Mount Adams West, and Mount Adams East areas.

Directions: From Trout Lake drive north on Forest Service Road 23 to the Takhlakh Lake Campground and the junction with Forest Service Road 2329. Turn right (south) onto this Forest Service road and drive 4.2 miles to the trailhead on the left.

Contact: Gifford Pinchot National Forest, Mount Adams Ranger District, 2455 Highway 141, Trout Lake, WA 98650; 509/395-3400.

130 Around the Mountain
26.4 mi/2.0–3.0 days   5 10

This route follows the Pacific Crest Trail for the first five miles and then angles northwest as it enters the Mount Adams Wilderness. Just a few miles past the wilderness boundary, the trail forks. The left fork continues up around the west and north sides of the mountain on the Pacific Crest Trail. But the right fork is the one you should take. Just past the fork, good camping can be found at Horseshoe Meadows (at mile eight), and there's plenty of waterside camping available beyond the meadows, too.

Though the trail is called Around the Mountain, it actually only goes around the southern third of Mount Adams. It's a beautiful route, offering unbelievable views of the nearly perfect volcanic cone and exploring a multitude of ecosystems. You hike through old-growth forest, subalpine and even true alpine meadows. Despite the beauty, there's at least one difficulty with this trail. While Mount Adams is a relatively inactive volcano, the trail is dusted with a fine gritty ash that seems to penetrate all your gear. That ash isn't the product of a long-ago Adams eruption, but rather the not-so-long ago eruption of Mount Adams' hot-headed sister, Mount St. Helens. It seems the Around the Mountain Trail is just high enough to have caught a load of the ash as it spewed out across eastern Washington. The trail ends at the boundary of the Yakima Indian Reservation, and since there's no access on the reservation side, returning the way you came is the only option.

Location: North of Trout Lake in Gifford Pinchot National Forest within the Mount Adams Wilderness; see Mount Rainier and the Columbia River Gorge Map 2, grid g4.

User Groups: Hikers, leashed dogs, and horses. No mountain bikes. No wheelchair facilities.

Permits: A federal Northwest Forest Pass, $5 per day or $30 annually, is required to park at the trailhead. Passes are available from ranger stations and many private vendors, online at website: www.wta.org, or by calling 800/270-7504.

Maps: For a map of Gifford Pinchot National Forest, contact the Outdoor Recreation Information Center, 915 Second Avenue, Suite 442, Seattle, WA 98174; 206/220-7450. Green Trails, Inc.'s excellent topographic maps are available for $3.99 each at outdoor retail outlets. Ask for map number 366, Mount Adams West. Ask the USGS for topographic maps of the Mount Adams East and Mount Adams West areas.

Directions: From Trout Lake drive about 12 miles north on Forest Service Road 23 to the junction with Forest Service Road 8810. The trailhead is on the right, opposite Forest Service Road 8810, and is signed Pacific Crest Trail.

Contact: Gifford Pinchot National Forest, Mount Adams Ranger District, 2455 Highway 141, Trout Lake, WA 98650; 509/395-3400.

131 Stagman Ridge
8.6 mi/4.3 hrs

Always remember: when you start a hike in a clear-cut, things can only get better. This trail proves that point. Beginning in a relatively new clear-cut, the trail quickly dips into thick second-growth forest before reaching the subalpine environments on the southern flank of Mount Adams. Enjoy great views of the snowy peak while carefully negotiating the rocky slope. Don't stare too much at the distant vistas, though. The scenery underfoot is startlingly beautiful. Wildflowers peek up around the gray boulders, and scraggy low firs punctuate the area's rugged beauty. At the junction with the Pacific Crest Trail, enjoy a hearty lunch before retracing your steps.

Location: North of Trout Lake in Gifford Pinchot National Forest within the Mount Adams Wilderness; see Mount Rainier and the Columbia River Gorge Map 2, grid g4.

User Groups: Hikers, leashed dogs, and horses. No mountain bikes. No wheelchair facilities.

Permits: A federal Northwest Forest Pass, $5 per day or $30 annually, is required to park at the trailhead. Passes are available from ranger stations and many private vendors, online at website: www.wta.org, or by calling 800/270-7504.

Maps: For a map of Gifford Pinchot National Forest, contact the Outdoor Recreation Information Center, 915 Second Avenue, Suite 442, Seattle, WA 98174; 206/220-7450. Green Trails, Inc.'s excellent topographic maps are available for $3.99 each at outdoor retail outlets. Ask for map number 366, Mount Adams West. Ask the USGS for a topographic map of the Mount Adams West area.

Directions: From Trout Lake drive about 8.5 miles north on Forest Service Road 23 and turn right (east) onto Forest Service Road 8031. Drive a quarter mile to Forest Service Road 8031-70. Turn left and drive about three miles to Forest Service Spur Road 120. Drive three-quarters of a mile west on the spur road. The trailhead is on the left side of the road.

Contact: Gifford Pinchot National Forest, Mount Adams Ranger District, 2455 Highway 141, Trout Lake, WA 98650; 509/395-3400.

132 Shorthorn
5.6 mi/2.8 hrs

You catch wonderful views of the glaciated summit of Mount Adams from this short, gentle trail. The route climbs moderate slopes through scraggly pine and fir to the alpine meadows on the southern flank of the mountain before ending at the timberline, where you can enjoy unobstructed views of the peak. Scramble around for the best vistas and photo opportunities before returning the way you came.

Location: North of Trout Lake in Gifford Pinchot National Forest within the Mount Adams Wilderness; see Mount Rainier and the Columbia River Gorge Map 2, grid g5.

User Groups: Hikers, leashed dogs, and horses. No mountain bikes. No wheelchair facilities.

Permits: A federal Northwest Forest Pass, $5 per day or $30 annually, is required to park at the trailhead. Passes are available from

ranger stations and many private vendors, online at website: www.wta.org, or by calling 800/270-7504.

Maps: For a map of Gifford Pinchot National Forest, contact the Outdoor Recreation Information Center, 915 Second Avenue, Suite 442, Seattle, WA 98174; 206/220-7450. Green Trails, Inc.'s excellent topographic maps are available for $3.99 each at outdoor retail outlets. Ask for map number 366, Mount Adams West. Ask the USGS for a topographic map of the Mount Adams West area.

Directions: From Trout Lake drive north on Forest Service Road 23 and then turn right (east) onto Forest Service Road 80 just outside of town. Continue about one mile on Forest Service Road 80 (which becomes Forest Service Road 8040) to the Morrison Creek Campground. The trailhead is on the north side of the camp.

Contact: Gifford Pinchot National Forest, Mount Adams Ranger District, 2455 Highway 141, Trout Lake, WA 98650; 509/395-3400.

⬛133 Cedar Flats Nature Trail
1.0 mi/1.0 hr

Looping through a cathedral forest of massive western red cedars and Douglas fir, this trail offers a lesson in forest ecology. There are countless examples of life springing from death. Huge logs lie across the valley floor—the remains of ancient trees that finally died of age. Vibrant, young trees now grow from these great logs, nourished by the decaying wood of the old giants. Lush mosses, lichens, and ferns carpet the forest and give the trail an emerald glow. From the second half of the trail, you can enjoy views of the Muddy River.

Although this trail is outside the official boundary of Mount St. Helens National Volcanic Monument, the monument office administers the whole area.

Location: North of Cougar in Gifford Pinchot National Forest; see Mount Rainier and the Columbia River Gorge Map 2, grid h1.

User Groups: Hikers, leashed dogs, and wheelchairs. No horses or mountain bikes are allowed.

Permits: A federal Northwest Forest Pass, $5 per day or $30 annually, is required to park at the trailhead. Passes are available from ranger stations and many private vendors, online at website: www.wta.org, or by calling 800/270-7504. Visitors to any developed site in the Mount St. Helens Monument—including visitor centers, paved overlooks, and interpretive areas—are required to pay an $8 fee per person for a Monument Pass. The pass is valid for three days. Anyone attempting to climb the peak or just scramble on the upper slopes must register in the town of Cougar and pay a $15 climbing fee per person. Contact the Mount St. Helens National Volcanic Monument at 360/247-3900.

Maps: For a trail information report, contact the Mount St. Helens National Volcanic Monument at 360/247-3900. For a map of Gifford Pinchot National Forest, send $3 to Outdoor Recreation Information Center, 915 Second Avenue, Suite 442, Seattle, WA 98174; 206/220-7450. Green Trails, Inc.'s excellent topographic maps of the region are available for $3.99 each at outdoor retail outlets. Ask for map number 364, Mount St. Helens. Ask the USGS for a topographic map of the Mount St. Helens area.

Directions: From Cougar drive east on Forest Service Road 90 to its junction with Forest Service Road 9039. Turn left (north) and continue three-quarters of a mile. Cross the Lewis River and park in the lot on the left just beyond the bridge.

Contact: Gifford Pinchot National Forest, Mount St. Helens National Volcanic Monument, 42218

Northeast Yale Bridge Road, Amboy, WA 98601-9715; 360/247-3900.

134 Spencer Butte
6.0 mi/3.0 hrs

A broad, flower-filled meadow lies just to the west of this trailhead. Spend a few minutes exploring fragrant Spencer Meadow before turning south and hiking down the trail. If you arrive early in the morning, you will probably find deer, elk, or both grazing in the lush forest clearing. If you don't see any of these big animals in the meadow, keep your eyes open as you hike up the butte trail.

The elevation gain to the butte top is only 800 feet, but that distance is enough to provide some startlingly clear views of distant peaks: from Mount Rainier to Mount Hood and from Mount Adams to Mount St. Helens. If you missed spotting deer, elk, or black bear earlier, scan the forest and valleys closer to you—this might be your opportunity. The rocky butte top is carpeted with wildflowers in early summer, and huckleberries line the lower trail later in the year.

Although this trail is outside the official boundary of Mount St. Helens National Volcanic Monument, the monument office administers the whole area.

Location: North of Cougar in Gifford Pinchot National Forest; see Mount Rainier and the Columbia River Gorge Map 2, grid g1.

User Groups: Hikers, leashed dogs, horses, and mountain bikes. No wheelchair facilities.

Permits: A federal Northwest Forest Pass, $5 per day or $30 annually, is required to park at the trailhead. Passes are available from ranger stations and many private vendors, online at website: www.wta.org, or by calling 800/270-7504. Visitors to any developed site in the Mount St. Helens Monument—including visitor centers, paved overlooks, and interpretive areas—are required to pay an $8 fee

per person for a Monument Pass. The pass is valid for three days. Anyone attempting to climb the peak or just scramble on the upper slopes must register in the town of Cougar and pay a $15 climbing fee per person. Contact the Mount St. Helens National Volcanic Monument at 360/247-3900.

Maps: For a trail information report, contact the Mount St. Helens National Volcanic Monument at 360/247-3900. For a map of Gifford Pinchot National Forest, send $3 to Outdoor Recreation Information Center, 915 Second Avenue, Suite 442, Seattle, WA 98174; 206/220-7450. Green Trails, Inc.'s excellent topographic maps of the region are available for $3.99 each at outdoor retail outlets. Ask for map number 365, Lone Butte. Ask the USGS for a topographic map of the Spencer Butte area.

Directions: From Cougar drive about 30 miles east on Forest Service Road 90 to the Lewis River Campground and the junction with Forest Service Road 93. Turn left (north) and continue 16 miles to the trailhead on the right. If you so desire, you can take a shuttle car to the lower trailhead, just three miles farther down Forest Service Road 93.

Contact: Gifford Pinchot National Forest, Mount St. Helens National Volcanic Monument, 42218 Northeast Yale Bridge Road, Amboy, WA 98601-9715; 360/247-3900.

135 Wright Meadow
7.8 mi/3.9 hrs

The Wright Meadow Trail follows Copper Creek upstream for more than two miles before crossing the stream, angling steeply up the ridge wall and climbing to the broad wildflower meadow near the end of the trail. Elk are frequently seen in the Copper Creek Valley and the meadow above, so stay alert and you may see the big beasts. If you visit in September, you might get lucky and hear the haunting bugling of rutting bulls. The route ends at a trailhead just off Forest Service Road 93. Either retrace your steps from this point or arrange for a shuttle or pickup vehicle prior to your hike.

This trail is frequently used as part of a loop trip with either the Cussed Hollow Trail or the Bluff Trail (see hikes this chapter). Although this trail is outside the official boundary of Mount St. Helens National Volcanic Monument, the monument office administers the whole area.

Location: North of Cougar in Gifford Pinchot National Forest; see Mount Rainier and the Columbia River Gorge Map 2, grid g1.

User Groups: Hikers, leashed dogs, horses, and mountain bikes. No wheelchair facilities.

Permits: A federal Northwest Forest Pass, $5 per day or $30 annually, is required to park at the trailhead. Passes are available from ranger stations and many private vendors, online at website: www.wta.org, or by calling 800/270-7504. Visitors to any developed site in the Mount St. Helens Monument—including visitor centers, paved overlooks, and interpretive areas—are required to pay an $8 fee per person for a Monument Pass. The pass is valid for three days. Anyone attempting to climb the peak or just scramble on the upper slopes must register in the town of Cougar and pay a $15 climbing fee per person. Contact the Mount St. Helens National Volcanic Monument at 360/247-3900.

Maps: For a trail information report, contact Mount St. Helens National Volcanic Monument at 360/247-3900. For a map of the Gifford Pinchot National Forest, send $3 to Outdoor Recreation Information Center, 915 Second Avenue, Suite 442, Seattle, WA 98174; 206/220-7450. Green Trails, Inc.'s excellent topographic maps of the region are available for $3.99 each at outdoor retail outlets. Ask for map number 365, Lone

Butte. Ask the USGS for topographic maps of the Spencer Butte, Quartz Creek, and McCoy Peak areas.

Directions: From Cougar drive east on Forest Service Road 90 to the Lewis River Campground and the trailhead on the left side of the road.

Contact: Gifford Pinchot National Forest, Mount St. Helens National Volcanic Monument, 42218 Northeast Yale Bridge Road, Amboy, WA 98601-9715; 360/247-3900.

136 Bluff

5.4 mi/2.7 hrs

The Bluff Trail is relatively short but steep. This route parallels the Lewis River downstream for a quarter mile, crosses the mouth of Cussed Hollow Creek, turns steeply uphill, and then ends at Forest Service Road 93. During the climb up the ridge face, pause often to enjoy the startlingly beautiful southern and eastern views of Mount Adams, the Lewis River drainage, and Hungry Peak. If shuttle cars are available, you only need to hike one way, since Forest Service Road 93 is very accessible. Otherwise, turn around at the top of the route and retrace your steps back to the valley floor, which will allow you to really enjoy the views.

Although this trail is outside the official boundary of Mount St. Helens National Volcanic Monument, the monument office administers the whole area.

Location: North of Cougar in Gifford Pinchot National Forest; see Mount Rainier and the Columbia River Gorge Map 2, grid g1.

User Groups: Hikers, leashed dogs, and wheelchairs. No horses or mountain bikes are allowed.

Permits: A federal Northwest Forest Pass, $5 per day or $30 annually, is required to park at the trailhead. Passes are available from ranger stations and many private vendors, online at website: www.wta.org, or by calling 800/270-7504. Visitors to any developed site in the Mount St. Helens Monument—including visitor centers, paved overlooks, and interpretive areas—are required to pay an $8 fee per person for a Monument Pass. The pass is valid for three days. Anyone attempting to climb the peak or just scramble on the upper slopes must register in the town of Cougar and pay a $15 climbing fee per person. Contact the Mount St. Helens National Volcanic Monument at 360/247-3900.

Maps: For a trail information report, contact the Mount St. Helens National Volcanic Monument at 360/247-3900. For a map of Gifford Pinchot National Forest, send $3 to Outdoor Recreation Information Center, 915 Second Avenue, Suite 442, Seattle, WA 98174; 206/220-7450. Green Trails, Inc.'s excellent topographic maps of the region are available for $3.99 each at outdoor retail outlets. Ask for map number 365, Lone Butte. Ask the USGS for a topographic map of the Spencer Butte area.

Directions: From Cougar drive east on Forest Service Road 90 past the Lewis River Campground to the trailhead. The trailhead is located just after the bridge on the north side of the Lewis River on the left.

Contact: Gifford Pinchot National Forest, Mount St. Helens National Volcanic Monument, 42218 Northeast Yale Bridge Road, Amboy, WA 98601-9715; 360/247-3900.

137 Speed

2.0 mi/1.0 hr

If you want to reach the beautiful Lewis River quickly, this is your trail. It drops steeply from the road into the Lewis River Basin, slicing through thick old-growth pine and fir forest. Anglers love this trail because it takes them right to water that's chock-full of big rainbow, brown, and brook trout. In the spring and fall, ocean-running steelhead return en masse. Even if you don't plan on fishing, we recommend bringing a pair of polarized sunglasses to help you peer into the swirling cold water and spot the big fish. Look for ripples as the fish lunge up from under big rocks to snatch insects off the surface of the river. The climb back up to the car is a workout, so go slow and enjoy the deep-forest environment.

Although this trail is outside the official boundary of Mount St. Helens National Volcanic Monument, the monument office administers the whole area.

Location: North of Cougar in Gifford Pinchot National Forest; see Mount Rainier and the Columbia River Gorge Map 2, grid h1.

User Groups: Hikers, leashed dogs, horses, and mountain bikes. No wheelchair facilities.

Permits: A federal Northwest Forest Pass, $5 per day or $30 annually, is required to park at the trailhead. Passes are available from ranger stations and many private vendors, online at website: www.wta.org, or by calling 800/270-7504. Visitors to any developed site in the Mount St. Helens Monument—including visitor centers, paved overlooks, and interpretive areas—are required to pay an $8 fee per person for a Monument Pass. The pass is valid for three days. Anyone attempting to climb the peak or just scramble on the upper slopes must register in the town of Cougar and pay a $15 climbing fee per person. Contact the Mount St. Helens National Volcanic Monument at 360/247-3900.

Maps: For a trail information report, contact the Mount St. Helens National Volcanic Monument at 360/247-3900. For a map of Gifford Pinchot National Forest, send $3 to Outdoor Recreation Information Center, 915 Second Avenue, Suite 442, Seattle, WA 98174;

206/220-7450. Green Trails, Inc.'s excellent topographic maps of the region are available for $3.99 each at outdoor retail outlets. Ask for map number 365, Lone Butte. Ask the USGS for a topographic map of the Burnt Peak area.

Directions: From Cougar drive about 25 miles east on Forest Service Road 90 up the Lewis River Valley to the well-marked trailhead on the left.

Contact: Gifford Pinchot National Forest, Mount St. Helens National Volcanic Monument, 42218 Northeast Yale Bridge Road, Amboy, WA 98601-9715; 360/247-3900.

138 Big Creek Falls
0.2 mi/0.2 hr

Along this trail, interpretive signs offer information on the flora, fauna, and geography of the area, but you won't need signs to figure out that this land is beautiful and wild. The wide, compacted trail meanders through ancient Douglas fir forest before reaching the viewing platform overlooking the falls. As you near the viewing area, you hear crashing water echoing through the tall trees. Once you see it, the falling white water is awe-inspiring. The waterfall leaps into view as you round the last bend of the trail and immediately grabs your attention. The sight of the falls, the sound of the crashing water, and the mute vibrations caused by the pounding water dominate your senses. It is a wonderful experience.

Although this trail is outside the official boundary of Mount St. Helens National Volcanic Monument, the monument office administers the whole area.

Location: North of Cougar in Gifford Pinchot National Forest; see Mount Rainier and the Columbia River Gorge Map 2, grid h1.

User Groups: Hikers, leashed dogs, and wheelchairs. No horses or mountain bikes are allowed.

Permits: A federal Northwest Forest Pass, $5 per day or $30 annually, is required to park at the trailhead. Passes are available from ranger stations and many private vendors, online at website: www.wta.org, or by calling 800/270-7504. Visitors to any developed site in the Mount St. Helens Monument—including visitor centers, paved overlooks, and interpretive areas—are required to pay an $8 fee per person for a Monument Pass. The pass is valid for three days. Anyone attempting to climb the peak or just scramble on the upper slopes must register in the town of Cougar and pay a $15 climbing fee per person. Contact the Mount St. Helens National Volcanic Monument at 360/247-3900.

Maps: For a trail information report, contact the Mount St. Helens National Volcanic Monument at 360/247-3900. For a map of the Gifford Pinchot National Forest, send $3 to Outdoor Recreation Information Center, 915 Second Avenue, Suite 442, Seattle, WA 98174; 206/220-7450. Green Trails, Inc.'s excellent topographic maps of the region are available for $3.99 each at outdoor retail outlets. Ask for map number 365, Lone Butte. Ask the USGS for a topographic map of the Burnt Peak area.

Directions: From Cougar drive about 25 miles east on Forest Service Road 90 up the Lewis River Valley to the well-marked trailhead on the left.

Contact: Gifford Pinchot National Forest, Mount St. Helens National Volcanic Monument, 42218 Northeast Yale Bridge Road, Amboy, WA 98601-9715; 360/247-3900.

139 Cussed Hollow
6.6 mi/3.3 hrs

The steep Cussed Hollow Trail runs for almost a mile nearly straight up a ridge face before turning west, traversing the ridge, and crossing the Cussed Hollow Creek Basin. From the basin it heads directly uphill once more to the trail's end. The thick Douglas fir, noble fir, and pine forest limits the views, but after reaching the trail's end (at an upper trailhead on Forest Service Road 93) and turning back to retrace your steps down the hill, you find that the forest breaks enough to give periodic southern views. The Lewis River Valley stretches out below you, and Cussed Hollow—a deep, steep basin to the west—can be seen from the upper section of the trail.

It's possible to drop a shuttle car at the upper trailhead. This trail can be combined with either the Bluff Trail (see hike in this chapter) or the Wright Meadow Trail (see hike in this chapter) to create a loop trip. Both options require short walks on Forest Service Road 93 to complete the loop. Also, although this trail is outside the official boundary of Mount St. Helens National Volcanic Monument, the monument office administers the whole area.

Location: North of Cougar in Gifford Pinchot National Forest; see Mount Rainier and the Columbia River Gorge Map 2, grid g2.

User Groups: Hikers, leashed dogs, horses, and mountain bikes. No wheelchair facilities.

Permits: A federal Northwest Forest Pass, $5 per day or $30 annually, is required to park at the trailhead. Passes are available from ranger stations and many private vendors, online at website: www.wta.org, or by calling 800/270-7504. Visitors to any developed site in the Mount St. Helens Monument—including visitor centers, paved overlooks, and interpretive areas—are required to pay an $8 fee per person for a Monument Pass. The pass is valid for three days. Anyone attempting to climb the peak or just scramble on the upper slopes must register in the town of Cougar and pay a $15 climbing fee per person. Contact the Mount St. Helens National Volcanic Monument at 360/247-3900.

Maps: For a trail information report, contact the Mount St. Helens National Volcanic Monument at 360/247-3900. For a map of Gifford Pinchot National Forest, send $3 to Outdoor Recreation Information Center, 915 Second Avenue, Suite 442, Seattle, WA 98174; 206/220-7450. Green Trails, Inc.'s excellent topographic maps of the region are available for $3.99 each at outdoor retail outlets. Ask for map number 365, Lone Butte. Ask the USGS for topographic maps of the Spencer Butte and Quartz Creek Butte areas.

Directions: From Cougar drive about 30 miles east on Forest Service Road 90 to the Lewis River Campground and the trailhead on the left.

Contact: Gifford Pinchot National Forest, Mount St. Helens National Volcanic Monument, 42218 Northeast Yale Bridge Road, Amboy, WA 98601-9715; 360/247-3900.

140 Craggy Peak
8.0 mi/4.0 hrs

The thick forest canopy here effectively shuts out most of the potential views from the trail, but that's OK. This is a beautiful forest to hike in. The old-growth fir, hemlock, and cedar forest is home to countless species of wildlife. Although the forest canopy is thick, it is like all old-growth canopies—staggered in height so that light filters down to the forest floor, which creates ideal growing conditions for the large patches of bear grass that thrive here. If you want more to look at than forest, you will enjoy the small flower-filled meadows dotting the route. These lush green fields also offer the best long-distance views; the top of Mount Rainier occasionally peeks up in the north.

Although this trail is outside the official boundary of Mount St. Helens National Volcanic Monument, the monument office administers this whole area.

Location: South of Randle in Gifford Pinchot National Forest; see Mount Rainier and the Columbia River Gorge Map 2, grid g2.

User Groups: Hikers, leashed dogs, horses, and mountain bikes. No wheelchair facilities.

Permits: A federal Northwest Forest Pass, $5 per day or $30 annually, is required to park at the trailhead. Passes are available from ranger stations and many private vendors, online at website: www.wta.org, or by calling 800/270-7504. Visitors to any developed site in the Mount St. Helens Monument—including visitor centers, paved overlooks, and interpretive areas—are required to pay an $8 fee per person for a Monument Pass. The pass is valid for three days. Anyone attempting to climb the peak or just scramble on the upper slopes must register in the town of Cougar and pay a $15 climbing fee per person. Contact the Mount St. Helens National Volcanic Monument at 360/247-3900.

Maps: For a trail information report, contact Mount St. Helens National Volcanic Monument at 360/247-3900. For a map of Gifford Pinchot National Forest, send $3 to Outdoor Recreation Information Center, 915 Second Avenue, Suite 442, Seattle, WA 98174; 206/220-7450. Green Trails, Inc.'s excellent topographic maps of the region are available for $3.99 each at outdoor retail outlets. Ask for map number 332, Spirit Lake. Ask the USGS for topographic maps of the Spencer Butte, Quartz Creek, and McCoy Peak areas.

Directions: From Cougar drive about 16 miles east on Forest Service Road 90 to the east end of Swift Reservoir and turn left (north) onto Forest Service Road 25. Continue north to its junction with Forest Service Road 93, one-half mile past the Muddy River Bridge. Turn right (east) onto Forest Service Road 93 and continue 12 more miles to Forest Service Road 9327. Turn left (north) onto this road and drive one-half mile to the trailhead on the left.

Contact: Gifford Pinchot National Forest, Mount St. Helens National Volcanic Monument, 42218 Northeast Yale Bridge Road, Amboy, WA 98601-9715; 360/247-3900.

141 Quartz Creek
21.2 mi/10.6 hrs

The Quartz Creek route is a river trail, but not a river valley trail. Sure, it follows the creek upstream, but it doesn't exactly parallel it. This path weaves in and out of side canyons and up and down small rises and ridges, always working upstream, but seldom coming very close to the waters of Quartz Creek. When it does dip down and access the creek, however, the views are stunning. The creek is a rugged, swift mountain river teeming with trout. Several good campsites are easily accessible, many of them near the shores of the creek, and the scenery near and away from the river is spectacular. The side canyons and ravines are often cut down the middle by rushing tributary creeks that thunder through narrow slots and bound over steep drops. The forest that shades the entire route is dominated by deep, old groves of Douglas fir and western red cedar, and the high, shimmering cliff walls of Quartz Canyon are beautiful.

Although this trail is outside the official boundary of Mount St. Helens National Volcanic Monument, the monument office administers the whole area.

Location: North of Cougar in Gifford Pinchot National Forest; see Mount Rainier and the Columbia River Gorge Map 2, grid h2.

User Groups: Hikers, leashed dogs, horses, and mountain bikes. No wheelchair facilities.

Permits: A federal Northwest Forest Pass, $5 per day or $30 annually, is required to park at the trailhead. Passes are available from ranger stations and many private

vendors, online at website: www.wta.org, or by calling 800/270-7504. Visitors to any developed site in the Mount St. Helens Monument—including visitor centers, paved overlooks, and interpretive areas—are required to pay an $8 fee per person for a Monument Pass. The pass is valid for three days. Anyone attempting to climb the peak or just scramble on the upper slopes must register in the town of Cougar and pay a $15 climbing fee per person. Contact the Mount St. Helens National Volcanic Monument at 360/247-3900.

Maps: For a trail information report, contact the Mount St. Helens National Volcanic Monument at 360/247-3900. For a map of Gifford Pinchot National Forest, send $3 to Outdoor Recreation Information Center, 915 Second Avenue, Suite 442, Seattle, WA 98174; 206/220-7450. Green Trails, Inc.'s excellent topographic maps of the region are available for $3.99 each at outdoor retail outlets. Ask for map number 365, Lone Butte. Ask the USGS for topographic maps of the Quartz Creek Butte and Steamboat Mountain areas.

Directions: From Cougar drive about 30 miles east on Forest Service Road 90 to the Lewis River Campground. The trailhead is on the left (north) side of the road, just past Forest Service Road 90's junction with Forest Service Road 93.

Contact: Gifford Pinchot National Forest, Mount St. Helens National Volcanic Monument, 42218 Northeast Yale Bridge Road, Amboy, WA 98601-9715; 360/247-3900.

142 Indian Heaven
6.6 mi/3.3 hrs

What more could you want? This is a moderate climb up a beautiful creek valley past several sparkling blue alpine lakes and stunning panoramic views. Throw in a collage of brilliant wildflower blooms mixed with an assortment of juicy wild berries, and you have hikers' heaven—or Indian Heaven, since the Native Americans found it first. The trail climbs under the shadow of Bird Mountain to the shores of beautiful Cultus Lake. Camp here, catch a few trout for dinner, and enjoy the sunset views of Mount Hood. Or continue on as the trail drops down the other side of the ridge above Clear Lake to the shores of Pacific Lake (more of a pond, really). At Pacific Lake, rest up and retrace your steps back through heaven to the earthly world at the trailhead.

Location: West of Trout Lake in Gifford Pinchot National Forest within the Indian Heaven Wilderness; see Mount Rainier and the Columbia River Gorge Map 2, grid h3.

User Groups: Hikers, leashed dogs, and horses. No mountain bikes. No wheelchair facilities.

Permits: A federal Northwest Forest Pass, $5 per day or $30 annually, is required to park at the trailhead. Passes are available from ranger stations and many private vendors, online at website: www.wta.org, or by calling 800/270-7504.

Maps: For a map of Gifford Pinchot National Forest, contact the Outdoor Recreation Information Center, 915 Second Avenue, Suite 442, Seattle, WA 98174; 206/220-7450. Green Trails, Inc.'s excellent topographic maps are available for $3.99 each at outdoor retail outlets. Ask for map number 365, Lone Butte. Ask the USGS for topographic maps of the Sleeping Beauty and Lone Butte areas.

Directions: From Trout Lake drive about 16 miles west on Highway 141 (which becomes Forest Service Road 24 at the forest boundary) to the Cultus Creek Campground. The trailhead is near the day-use parking area.

Contact: Gifford Pinchot National Forest, Mount Adams Ranger District, 2455 Highway 141, Trout Lake, WA 98650; 509/395-3400.

143 Hidden Lakes
1.0 mi/0.5 hr

Three beautiful small lakes nestle into a grassy meadow just outside the Indian Heaven Wilderness, and this gentle hike takes you to their shores. The beauty factor, combined with the easy accessibility to good roads and campgrounds, makes this a very attractive trail for families with small children, hikers with mobility limitations, and those who simply want a pleasant hike. Late summer is the prime time to go, when the flowers are still in bloom and the resident huckleberries are beginning to ripen.

Location: West of Trout Lake in Gifford Pinchot National Forest; see Mount Rainier and the Columbia River Gorge Map 2, grid h3.

User Groups: Hikers, leashed dogs, horses, and mountain bikes. No wheelchair facilities.

Permits: A federal Northwest Forest Pass, $5 per day or $30 annually, is required to park at the trailhead. Passes are available from ranger stations and many private vendors, online at website: www.wta.org, or by calling 800/270-7504.

Maps: For a map of Gifford Pinchot National Forest, contact the Outdoor Recreation Information Center, 915 Second Avenue, Suite 442, Seattle, WA 98174; 206/220-7450. Green Trails, Inc.'s excellent topographic maps are available for $3.99 each at outdoor retail outlets. Ask for map number 366, Mount Adams West. Ask the USGS for a topographic map of the Sleeping Beauty area.

Directions: From Trout Lake drive about 14 miles west on Highway 141 (which becomes Forest Service Road 24 at the forest boundary) to Little Goose Horse Camp. Continue 2.2 miles beyond the camp to the trailhead on the right.

Contact: Gifford Pinchot National Forest, Mount Adams Ranger District, 2455 Highway 141, Trout Lake, WA 98650; 509/395-3400.

144 Sleeping Beauty Peak
2.8 mi/1.4 hrs

Climbing steeply through a long series of switchbacks, this trail tops out on the summit of Sleeping Beauty Peak, with views worthy of inclusion in any fairy tale. The former lookout site provides great vistas of Mount Adams and the emerald ridges and valleys of the Indian Heaven Wilderness to the southwest. This trail may have a storybook name, but it offers real-life views and scenic wonders.

Location: West of Trout Lake in Gifford Pinchot National Forest; see Mount Rainier and the Columbia River Gorge Map 2, grid h3.

User Groups: Hikers, leashed dogs, and horses. No mountain bikes. No wheelchair facilities.

Permits: A federal Northwest Forest Pass, $5 per day or $30 annually, is required to park at the trailhead. Passes are available from ranger stations and many private vendors, online at website: www.wta.org, or by calling 800/270-7504.

Maps: For a map of Gifford Pinchot National Forest, contact the Outdoor Recreation Information Center, 915 Second Avenue, Suite 442, Seattle, WA 98174; 206/220-7450. Green Trails, Inc.'s excellent topographic maps are available for $3.99 each at outdoor retail outlets. Ask for map number 366, Mount Adams West. Ask the USGS for a topographic map of the Sleeping Beauty area.

Directions: From Trout Lake drive west on Highway 141 and turn right (north) on Forest Service Road 88 just outside of town. Continue about 11 miles to a junction with Forest Service Road 8810-40. Drive a quarter mile north to the trailhead on the left.

Contact: Gifford Pinchot National Forest, Mount Adams Ranger District, 2455 Highway 141, Trout Lake, WA 98650; 509/395-3400.

145 Lemei
10.6 mi/5.3 hrs

Prior to entering the wilderness boundary, this trail is wide and rough—the result of following an old logging trail through second-growth forest. But within a mile it dips into the Indian Heaven Wilderness and the forest reverts to old-growth. The trail climbs into lush green meadows painted bright by a multitude of wildflowers. Sweeping views of the surrounding peaks await, as do crystal-clear lakes farther up the trail. Look down on the blue waters of Lake Comcomly and Lake Wapiki before sliding around the northern flank of Lemei Rock. Side trails lead to the small lakes, but we recommend sticking to the main trail. If you like lakes, it's just a matter of time before you reach the trail's end at Cultus Lake, where you can stop and relax, even camp, for as long as you like before retracing your steps along this pretty trail.

Location: West of Trout Lake in Gifford Pinchot National Forest within the Indian Heaven Wilderness; see Mount Rainier and the Columbia River Gorge Map 2, grid h1.

User Groups: Hikers, leashed dogs, and horses. No mountain bikes. No wheelchair facilities.

Permits: A federal Northwest Forest Pass, $5 per day or $30 annually, is required to park at the trailhead. Passes are available from ranger stations and many private vendors, online at website: www.wta.org, or by calling 800/270-7504.

Maps: For a map of Gifford Pinchot National Forest, contact the Outdoor Recreation Information Center, 915 Second Avenue, Suite 442, Seattle, WA 98174; 206/220-7450. Green Trails, Inc.'s excellent topographic maps are available for $3.99 each at outdoor retail outlets. Ask for map numbers 365 and 366, Lone Butte and Mount Adams West. Ask the USGS for topographic maps of the Sleeping Beauty and Lone Butte areas.

Directions: From Trout Lake drive about 14 miles west on Highway 141 (which becomes Forest Service Road 24 at the forest boundary) to Little Goose Horse Camp. The trailhead is near the south end of the parking area.

Contact: Gifford Pinchot National Forest, Mount Adams Ranger District, 2455 Highway 141, Trout Lake, WA 98650; 509/395-3400.

146 Crofton Butte
5.4 mi/2.7 hrs

Rolling along the lower slope of Mount Adams, this trail offers mountain views and during the early season, a forest floor carpeted with lush clumps of bear grass with bulbous white flowers. Though much of the trail is under the old fir and pine forest canopy, there are enough breaks and clearings to keep Mount Adams frequently in view. The best panoramas of the peak are found at the top of 5,272-foot Crofton Butte. There you also find fields of wildflowers. After the trail ends at the Crofton Butte summit, turn around and retrace your steps.

Location: North of Trout Lake in Gifford Pinchot National Forest within the Mount Adams Wilderness; see Mount Rainier and the Columbia River Gorge Map 2, grid h3.

User Groups: Hikers, leashed dogs, and horses. No mountain bikes. No wheelchair facilities.

Permits: A federal Northwest Forest Pass, $5 per day or $30 annually, is required to park at the trailhead. Passes are available from ranger stations and many private vendors, online at website: www.wta.org, or by calling 800/270-7504.

Maps: For a map of Gifford Pinchot National Forest, contact the Outdoor Recreation Information Center, 915 Second Avenue, Suite 442, Seattle, WA 98174; 206/220-7450. Green

Trails, Inc.'s excellent topographic maps are available for $3.99 each at outdoor retail outlets. Ask for map number 366, Mount Adams West. Ask the USGS for a topographic map of the Mount Adams West area.

Directions: From Trout Lake drive about 8.5 miles north on Forest Service Road 23 and turn right (east) onto Forest Service Road 8031. Continue 1.4 miles to Forest Service Road 8031-50. Turn left and drive a quarter mile to the trailhead.

Contact: Gifford Pinchot National Forest, Mount Adams Ranger District, 2455 Highway 141, Trout Lake, WA 98650; 509/395-3400.

147 Snipes Mountain
11.4 mi/5.7 hrs

Weaving through hot, dry pine forest and even hotter, drier lava beds, this trail sucks the moisture out of you, so bring plenty of water. But bring lots of film, too. The scenery is great along the trail—stark moonscapes of the lava beds; pine forests carpeted with tall, lush bear grass; an assortment of wildflowers; and distant views that are even better still. The trail itself is moderately steep, with a constant grade climbing 2,500 vertical feet in 5.5 miles. At several points it runs along Gotchen Creek. The white-capped peak of Mount Adams stands nobly above it all, while the deep green valleys and ridges of the south Cascades provide a scenic mosaic to the south.

Location: North of Trout Lake in Gifford Pinchot National Forest within the Mount Adams Wilderness; see Mount Rainier and the Columbia River Gorge Map 2, grid h4.

User Groups: Hikers, leashed dogs, and horses. No mountain bikes. No wheelchair facilities.

Permits: A federal Northwest Forest Pass, $5 per day or $30 annually, is required to park at the trailhead. Passes are available from ranger stations and many private vendors, online at website: www.wta.org, or by calling 800/270-7504.

Maps: For a map of Gifford Pinchot National Forest, contact the Outdoor Recreation Information Center, 915 Second Avenue, Suite 442, Seattle, WA 98174; 206/220-7450. Green Trails, Inc.'s excellent topographic maps are available for $3.99 each at outdoor retail outlets. Ask for map number 366, Mount Adams West. Ask the USGS for a topographic map of the Mount Adams East area.

Directions: From Trout Lake drive north on Forest Service Road 23, turn right (east) onto Forest Service Road 80 just outside of town, and then bear right on Forest Service Road 82 almost immediately. Continue three miles to Forest Service Road 8225. Turn left and drive about three miles to Forest Service Road 150. Turn left and continue half a mile to the trailhead on the left.

Contact: Gifford Pinchot National Forest, Mount Adams Ranger District, 2455 Highway 141, Trout Lake, WA 98650; 509/395-3400.

148 Gotchen Creek
6.0 mi/3.0 hrs

Climbing along an old sheep trail, this route begins at a livestock corral and climbs gently through a forest that has seen selective timber harvest. The logging scars are faint but noticeable, though they are left behind once you cross Hole in the Wall Creek and begin the climb along McDonald Ridge. Views are moderate to good from the ridge, and the chances of seeing wildlife are great. Keep an eye out for deer, elk, and a variety of songbirds and raptors.

Location: North of Trout Lake in Gifford Pinchot National Forest; see Mount Rainier and the Columbia River Gorge Map 2, grid h4.

User Groups: Hikers, leashed dogs, horses, and mountain bikes. No wheelchair facilities.

Permits: A federal Northwest Forest Pass, $5 per day or $30 annually, is required to park at the trailhead. Passes are available from ranger stations and many private vendors, online at website: www.wta.org, or by calling 800/270-7504.

Maps: For a map of Gifford Pinchot National Forest, contact the Outdoor Recreation Information Center, 915 Second Avenue, Suite 442, Seattle, WA 98174; 206/220-7450. Green Trails, Inc.'s excellent topographic maps are available for $3.99 each at outdoor retail outlets. Ask for map number 366, Mount Adams West. Ask the USGS for topographic maps of the Mount Adams East and Mount Adams West areas.

Directions: From Trout Lake drive north on Forest Service Road 23 and turn right (east) onto Forest Service Road 80 just outside of town. Continue three miles to Forest Service Road 8020. Turn right and drive 3.5 miles to the trailhead on the left.

Contact: Gifford Pinchot National Forest, Mount Adams Ranger District, 2455 Highway 141, Trout Lake, WA 98650; 509/395-3400.

149 Cold Springs
8.4 mi/4.2 hrs

Half a mile up the trail, bear right at the fork and climb through thick, young, second-growth forest to Cold Springs Camp, due south of Mount Adams' snow-capped summit. On the way, you cross broad lava flows laid down hundreds of years ago during Mount Adams' last eruption. The views of Mount Adams are great and the local wildflower bloom is spectacular, especially the huge carpets of bear grass. Cold Springs Camp is commonly used by horse packers and four-wheel-drive enthusiasts willing to brave the deeply rutted (up to two-foot-deep

ruts) road leading to the camp. Hikers who want to camp on the northern end of this trail are advised to pitch their tents just a quarter mile south of Cold Springs Camp at an old Forest Service trail crew shelter (Cold Springs Shelter), which is much closer than the camp to its namesake springs.

Location: North of Trout Lake in Gifford Pinchot National Forest; see Mount Rainier and the Columbia River Gorge Map 2, grid h4.

User Groups: Hikers, leashed dogs, horses, and mountain bikes. No wheelchair facilities.

Permits: A federal Northwest Forest Pass, $5 per day or $30 annually, is required to park at the trailhead. Passes are available from ranger stations and many private vendors, online at website: www.wta.org, or by calling 800/270-7504.

Maps: For a map of Gifford Pinchot National Forest, contact the Outdoor Recreation Information Center, 915 Second Avenue, Suite 442, Seattle, WA 98174; 206/220-7450. Green Trails, Inc.'s excellent topographic maps are available for $3.99 each at outdoor retail outlets. Ask for map number 366, Mount Adams West. Ask the USGS for topographic maps of the Mount Adams East and Mount Adams West areas.

Directions: From Trout Lake drive north on Forest Service Road 23 and turn right (east) onto Forest Service Road 80 just outside of town. Continue three miles to Forest Service Road 8020. Turn right and drive 3.5 miles to the trailhead on the left.

Contact: Gifford Pinchot National Forest, Mount Adams Ranger District, 2455 Highway 141, Trout Lake, WA 98650; 509/395-3400.

150 Upper Siouxon
17.0 mi/1.0–2.0 days

Upper Siouxon Trail drops quickly to the river level, crosses West Creek, and proceeds up the beautiful Siouxon Creek Valley. Some of the most picturesque waterfalls in a woodland environment grace this trail, and every cascade is accompanied by a deep pool of clear, cold water. These pools are shaded by the thick second-growth forest and usually flanked by moss-laden rocks and logs—just the kind of place where big lunker trout like to hide and feed. Anglers will think they've gone to heaven when they see this river trail.

The route continues along the river until its last couple of miles, when it turns and climbs a long series of switchbacks up the steep valley wall and ends at a junction with Forest Service Road 58. There is no designated parking area or trailhead off Forest Service Road 58, so don't plan on dropping a shuttle vehicle. Instead, enjoy retracing your steps or, better yet, skip the last mile or so and turn around when the going gets too steep. The views from the top of the trail aren't particularly impressive, and the real highlights are found in the valley bottom. Camping is good all along the river.

Location: East of Woodland in Gifford Pinchot National Forest; see Mount Rainier and the Columbia River Gorge Map 2, grid h5.

User Groups: Hikers, leashed dogs, horses, and mountain bikes. No wheelchair facilities.

Permits: A federal Northwest Forest Pass, $5 per day or $30 annually, is required to park at the trailhead. Passes are available from ranger stations and many private vendors, online at website: www.wta.org, or by calling 800/270-7504.

Maps: For a trail information report, contact the Wind River Information/Work Center at 509/427-3200. For a map of Gifford Pinchot National Forest, send $3 to Outdoor Recreation Information Center, 915 Second Avenue, Suite 442, Seattle, WA 98174; 206/220-7450. Green Trails, Inc.'s excellent topographic maps of the region are available for $3.99 each at outdoor retail outlets. Ask for number 396, Lookout Mountain. Ask the

USGS for topographic maps of the Siouxon Peak and Bare Mountain areas.

Directions: From Woodland drive about 22 miles east on Highway 503 past Lake Merwin and south across the Lewis River. Just south of the Lewis River Bridge, turn left (east) onto Forest Service Road 54 and continue about 10 miles to its junction with Forest Service Road 57. Turn left and within one-quarter mile turn left again onto Forest Service Road 5701. Continue to the road's end and the trailhead.

Contact: Gifford Pinchot National Forest, Wind River Information/Work Center, 1262 Hemlock Road, Carson, WA 98610; 509/427-3200.

151 Battle Ground Lake Loop
7.0 mi/3.0 hrs

This trail loops around the shoreline of interesting Battle Ground Lake. Like better-known Crater Lake in Oregon, Battle Ground was formed when a volcano erupted and collapsed in on itself, leaving a deep cauldron eventually filled by rain, streams, and springs. The heavy vegetation on the shore often breaks and allows hikers to reach the waterline, soak their feet, cast a fishing line, or even jump in for a cold swim.

Location: North of Vancouver in Battle Ground State Park; see Mount Rainier and the Columbia River Gorge Map 3, grid a7.

User Groups: Hikers, leashed dogs, and horses. No mountain bikes are allowed. No wheelchair facilities.

Permits: Day-use parking permits may be required. Contact the Washington State Parks and Recreation Commission at 800/233-0321.

Maps: Ask the USGS for topographic maps of the Battle Ground and Yacolt areas.

Directions: From Vancouver drive about eight miles north on Highway 503 to the town of Battle Ground. Turn north onto Heissen Road and continue to the park entrance. The trail begins near the day-use parking area.

Contact: Washington State Parks and Recreation Commission, Public Affairs Office, P.O. Box 42650, Olympia, WA 98504-2650; 800/233-0321.

152 Observation
16.4 mi/1.0-2.0 days

Wild is the key word here. Wildflowers, wild berries, and wildlife thrive throughout this area. The trail climbs for more than a mile alongside Canyon Creek through a pleasant young forest before angling sharply up Howe Ridge. After more than five miles, this route climbs past Observation Peak and Sisters Rocks. A short (three-quarter-mile) trail leads to the Observation Peak summit. Enjoy great views from the ridge trail and the summit, including a panorama of Mount Adams, Mount Rainier, Mount St. Helens, and Mount Hood.

The main trail continues around the eastern flank of Observation Peak and rolls north out of the Wilderness before ending at an unmarked junction with an old dirt logging road. Don't plan on driving to the end of this trail—this is an out-and-back hike. Remember, too, that once you leave the river, this trail is dry. The campsites are also dry, so be sure to carry plenty of water.

Location: North of Carson in Gifford Pinchot National Forest within the Trapper Creek Wilderness; see Mount Rainier and the Columbia River Gorge Map 3, grid b7.

User Groups: Hikers, leashed dogs, horses, and mountain bikes. No wheelchair facilities.

Permits: A federal Northwest Forest Pass, $5 per day or $30 annually, is required to park at the trailhead. Passes are available from ranger stations and many private vendors, online at website: www.wta.org, or by calling 800/270-7504.

Maps: For a trail information report, contact the Wind River Information/Work Center at 509/427-3200. For a map of Gifford Pinchot National Forest, send $3 to Outdoor Recreation Information Center, 915 Second Avenue, Suite 442, Seattle, WA 98174; 206/220-7450. Green Trails, Inc.'s excellent topographic maps of the region are available for $3.99 each at outdoor retail outlets. Ask for map numbers 396 and 397, Lookout Mountain and Wind River. Ask the USGS for a topographic map of the Termination Point area.

Directions: From Carson proceed approximately eight miles north on Wind River Road/County Road 30 to the fork at Mineral Springs. Veer to the left on Mineral Springs Road and in one-half mile take a right turn onto Forest Service Road 5401. Continue one-half mile to the trailhead.

Contact: Gifford Pinchot National Forest, Wind River Information/Work Center, 1262 Hemlock Road, Carson, WA 98610; 509/427-3200.

153 West Crater
1.6 mi/0.8 hr

Considering the skyscraping volcanoes that surround the south Cascades, it should be no surprise that the entire area was formed by repeated eruptions and volcanic activity, and not always from the big cinder cones that decorate the horizons. This trail loops around the east side of a large volcanic crater, on the edge of one of its last massive lava flows. The route tops out on the crater's south rim, offering good southern views over the lava beds created by this crater's eruptions. The views of the big volcanoes aren't nearly as good—you can barely make out the top of Mount Adams and Mount St. Helens if you find the right spot on the crater rim. If you are really adventurous and a skilled scrambler, you can work your way down into the brushy crater. Be warned: the rocks are rough and very abrasive—they have a tendency to wear holes in boots, pants, and hands.

Location: North of Carson in Gifford Pinchot National Forest within the Trapper Creek Wilderness; see Mount Rainier and the Columbia River Gorge Map 3, grid b7.

User Groups: Hikers and leashed dogs. No horses or mountain bikes are allowed. No wheelchair facilities.

Permits: A federal Northwest Forest Pass, $5 per day or $30 annually, is required to park at the trailhead. Passes are available from ranger stations and many private vendors, online at website: www.wta.org, or by calling 800/270-7504.

Maps: For a trail information report, contact the Wind River Information/Work Center at 509/427-3200. For a map of Gifford Pinchot National Forest, send $3 to Outdoor Recreation Information Center, 915 Second Avenue, Suite 442, Seattle, WA 98174; 206/220-7450. Green Trails, Inc.'s excellent topographic maps of the region are available for $3.99 each at outdoor retail outlets. Ask for map number 396, Lookout Mountain. Ask the USGS for a topographic map of the Lookout Mountain area.

Directions: From Carson drive 8.4 miles north on Wind River Road/County Road 30 to the town of Stabler and the junction with Hemlock Road. Turn left (west) onto Hemlock Road, cross the river, and bear right (north) onto Forest Service Road 54. Continue 12 miles and then turn left onto Forest Service Road 34. Drive one mile to the trailhead.

Contact: Gifford Pinchot National Forest, Wind River Information/Work Center, 1262 Hemlock Road, Carson, WA 98610; 509/427-3200.

154 Zig Zag Lake Loop
1.0 mi/1.0 hr

Old-growth forest, a deep, green lake stocked with big, toothy brook trout and a lush aquatic environment are the highlights of this trail. The short but steep path penetrates a cool, lush, ancient forest before bursting out of the trees on the lakeshore. If you aren't interested in angling for brookies, study the water anyway—you may see six-inch geckos darting around the shallows or lounging on the submerged logs.

Location: North of Carson in Gifford Pinchot National Forest; see Mount Rainier and the Columbia River Gorge Map 3, grid b7.

User Groups: Hikers, leashed dogs, horses, and mountain bikes. No wheelchair facilities.

Permits: A federal Northwest Forest Pass, $5 per day or $30 annually, is required to park at the trailhead. Passes are available from ranger stations and many private vendors, online at website: www.wta.org, or by calling 800/270-7504.

Maps: For a map of Gifford Pinchot National Forest, send $3 to Outdoor Recreation Information Center, 915 Second Avenue, Suite 442, Seattle, WA 98174; 206/220-7450. Green Trails, Inc.'s excellent topographic maps of the region are available for $3.99 each at outdoor retail outlets. Ask for map number 396, Lookout Mountain. Ask the USGS for a topographic map of the Lookout Mountain area.

Directions: From Carson drive 8.4 miles north on Wind River Road/County Road 30 to the town of Stabler and the junction with Hemlock Road. Turn left (west) onto Hemlock Road, cross the river, and bear right (north) onto Forest Service Road 54. Continue for six miles and then turn left onto Forest Service Road 42. Drive seven miles west to the trailhead on the right.

Contact: Gifford Pinchot National Forest, Mount Adams

Ranger District, 2455 Highway 141, Trout Lake, WA 98650; 509/395-3400.

155 East Fork Lewis River
6.0 mi/3.0 hrs

Although this trail is unmaintained, it generally receives enough traffic to keep it fairly clear and very enjoyable. The first mile is usually the brushiest, but the path opens up and improves dramatically. The trail climbs alongside the East Fork Lewis River before looping up around the valley head wall and gently climbing the flank of Lookout Mountain. It ends at Forest Service Road 41, but there is no trailhead or parking off the road, which makes it difficult to use a shuttle car. Simply retrace your steps and enjoy the views down the East Fork Valley as you drop back down to the valley floor.

Location: North of Carson in Gifford Pinchot National Forest; see Mount Rainier and the Columbia River Gorge Map 3, grid c7.

User Groups: Hikers and leashed dogs. No horses or mountain bikes are allowed. No wheelchair facilities.

Permits: A federal Northwest Forest Pass, $5 per day or $30 annually, is required to park at the trailhead. Passes are available from ranger stations and many private vendors, online at website: www.wta.org, or by calling 800/270-7504.

Maps: For a map of Gifford Pinchot National Forest, send $3 to Outdoor Recreation Information Center, 915 Second Avenue, Suite 442, Seattle, WA 98174; 206/220-7450. Green Trails, Inc.'s excellent topographic maps of the region are available for $3.99 each at outdoor retail outlets. Ask for map number 397, Wind River. Ask the USGS for a topographic map of the Gifford Peak area.

Directions: From Carson drive 8.4 miles north on Wind River Road/County Road 30 to the town of Stabler and the junction with Hemlock Road. Turn left (west) onto Hemlock Road, cross the river, and then bear right (north) onto Forest Service Road 54. Continue six more miles on this road and then turn left onto Forest Service Road 42. Drive 15.2 miles to Forest Service Road 42–514. Turn left and drive to the road's end and the trailhead.

Contact: Gifford Pinchot National Forest, Mount Adams Ranger District, 2455 Highway 141, Trout Lake, WA 98650; 509/395-3400.

156 Beacon Rock
2.0 mi/2.0 hrs

Beacon Rock earned its name when Captains Lewis and Clark camped in its shadow on their way to the Pacific Ocean in 1805. The rock is an 848-foot basalt column that formed the core of an ancient volcano. It towers over the Columbia River, and its sheer walls were unscaled until 1901—the date of the first recorded ascent of the rock. Notably, that first climb followed the route now covered by the intricate system of paths, bridges, and stairs that make up the trail today. The hike begins as a gentle walk through the forest as the trail leads hikers around to the southern face of the rock. Then the climbing begins. Traversing and climbing sheer rock walls, the trail is daunting to consider but easy to hike. The iron works that make up the bridges and stairs are solid and braced well on the indestructible rock face. The trail was built between 1915 and 1918 by Henry Biddle, who owned the rock and all the land about it at the time. The structures have been repaired, replaced, and reinforced in places over the years, but the trail built by Biddle is the one now used by thousands of recreationists every year. The route covers nearly a mile as it switches back and forth up the rock, but there are plenty of places folks can pause and catch their breath while enjoying the magnificent views of the Columbia River Gorge. At the top the views are even better, and there is never any question that the climb is worth the effort, for even when the gorge is filled with rain or fog, the view is splendid, wrapped in mists and shrouded in mantles of gray.

The trail itself is safe for travel, but anyone who leaves the trail is putting himself in danger. The route is steep and occasionally lined with loose rocks. Do not leave the designated trail at any time.

Location: East of Vancouver near Bonneville Dam; see Mount Rainier and the Columbia River Gorge Map 3, grid d8.

User Groups: Hikers and leashed dogs. No horses or mountain bikes. No wheelchair facilities.

Permits: Day-use parking permits may be required. Contact the Washington State Parks and Recreation Commission at 800/233-0321.

Maps: For a U.S. Forest Service Trails of the Columbia Gorge map, contact the Nature of the Northwest Information Center, 800 Northeast Oregon Street, Suite 177, Portland, OR 97232; 503/872-2750. Green Trails, Inc.'s excellent topographic maps of the region are available for $3.99 each at outdoor retail outlets. Ask for map number 429, Bonneville Dam. Ask the USGS for topographic maps of the Bonneville Dam and Tanner Butte areas.

Directions: From I-205 in Vancouver, drive east on State Highway 14 for 30 miles to the Beacon Rock Parking area on the north side of the highway. The trail is found on the south side of the highway.

Contact: Washington State Parks and Recreation Commission, Public Affairs Office, P.O. Box 42650, Olympia, WA 98504-2650; 800/233-0321.

Lava Butte
1.2 mi/0.6 hr

The Lava Butte Trail is convenient for people staying at the trailhead campground. The hike begins at a short valley meadow, fords a stream, and climbs steeply through a dense second-growth forest. The forest ends abruptly near the summit in a broad clear-cut. Cross the clear-cut to the top of the butte to obtain fine views of the surrounding countryside. The trail ends at an old logging road. Forget about driving a shuttle car up here, though—it's quicker and easier to return on the trail.

Location: North of Carson in Gifford Pinchot National Forest; see Mount Rainier and the Columbia River Gorge Map 4, grid a1.

User Groups: Hikers, leashed dogs, and mountain bikes. No horses are allowed. No wheelchair facilities.

Permits: A federal Northwest Forest Pass, $5 per day or $30 annually, is required to park at the trailhead. Passes are available from ranger stations and many private vendors, online at website: www.wta.org, or by calling 800/270-7504.

Maps: For a trail information report, contact the Wind River Information/Work Center at 509/427-3200. For a map of Gifford Pinchot National Forest, send $3 to Outdoor Recreation Information Center, 915 Second Avenue, Suite 442, Seattle, WA 98174; 206/220-7450. Green Trails, Inc.'s excellent topographic maps of the region are available for $3.99 each at outdoor retail outlets. Ask for map number 397, Wind River. Ask the USGS for a topographic map of the Termination Point area.

Directions: From Carson drive 21 miles north on Wind River Road/County Road 30 to the Paradise Creek Campground. The trailhead is in the campground at site 30D.

Contact: Gifford Pinchot National Forest, Wind River Information/Work Center, 1262 Hemlock Road, Carson, WA 98610; 509/427-3200.

158 Paradise
5.0 mi/2.5 hrs

A moderate 1.5-mile climb to the top of Paradise Ridge (1,000-foot elevation gain) starts off this scenic route. Once at the top of the ridge, your walking is easy; the trail follows the ridge crest north to the northern trailhead. Wildflowers brighten the way and huckleberries sweeten it. The ridge is pretty and the views are great. At the end of the trail, turn around and retrace your steps—you'll be amazed at how much scenery you missed the first time.

Location: North of Carson in Gifford Pinchot National Forest; see Mount Rainier and the Columbia River Gorge Map 4, grid a1.

User Groups: Hikers, leashed dogs, horses, and mountain bikes. No wheelchair facilities.

Permits: A federal Northwest Forest Pass, $5 per day or $30 annually, is required to park at the trailhead. Passes are available from ranger stations and many private vendors, online at website: www.wta.org, or by calling 800/270-7504.

Maps: For a trail information report, contact the Wind River Information/Work Center at 509/427-3200. For a map of Gifford Pinchot National Forest, send $3 to Outdoor Recreation Information Center, 915 Second Avenue, Suite 442, Seattle, WA 98174; 206/220-7450. Green Trails, Inc.'s excellent topographic maps of the region are available for $3.99 each at outdoor retail outlets. Ask for map number 397, Wind River. Ask the USGS for a topographic map of the Termination Point area.

Directions: From Carson drive 16 miles north on Wind River Road/County Road 30 and turn left (west) on Forest Service Road 64. Continue to its junction with Forest Service Road 201. Turn right (east) onto Forest Service Road 201 and continue 1.4 miles to the trailhead on the left. To reach the northern trailhead from here, return to Forest Service Road 64 and continue north on it to Forest Service Road 6401. Turn right and drive to the road's end and the trailhead.

Contact: Gifford Pinchot National Forest, Wind River Information/Work Center, 1262 Hemlock Road, Carson, WA 98610; 509/427-3200.

159 Upper Falls Creek
8.0 mi/4.0 hrs

One-hundred-foot Upper Falls may be this hike's key attraction, but it's by no means the only one. The thick forest along the lower half of the trail shelters plump huckleberries in the autumn and clumps of bear grass in the early summer.

The waterfall comes into view about 2.5 miles into the hike, and you find a wide, deep pool of crystal-clear water just above the falls. Local populations of white-tailed deer and elk frequent this 50-foot-wide pool, and there is a beaver den along the shore—don't be surprised if the big wood eaters make themselves scarce, but you might hear them slipping into the water and signaling their family with a loud kersplashing slap of the tail. Lounge around the pool, admire the thundering falls, and explore the surrounding area before returning the way you came.

Location: North of Carson in Gifford Pinchot National Forest; see Mount Rainier and the Columbia River Gorge Map 4, grid a1.

User Groups: Hikers, leashed dogs, and horses. No mountain bikes are allowed. No wheelchair facilities.

Permits: A federal Northwest Forest Pass, $5 per day or $30 annually, is required to park at the trailhead. Passes are available from ranger stations and many private vendors, online at website: www.wta.org, or by calling 800/270-7504.

Maps: To receive a trail information report, contact the Wind River Information/Work Center at 509/427-3200. To receive a map of Gifford Pinchot National Forest, send $3 to Outdoor Recreation Information Center, 915 Second Avenue, Suite 442, Seattle, WA 98174; 206/220-7450. Green Trails, Inc.'s excellent topographic maps of the region are available for $3.99 each at various outdoor retail outlets. Ask for map number 397, Wind River. Ask the USGS for topographic maps of the Termination Point and Gifford Peak areas.

Directions: From Carson drive 15 miles north on Wind River Road/County Road 30 to its junction with Forest Service Road 3062. Turn right (east) and drive to the road's end and the trailhead.

Contact: Gifford Pinchot National Forest, Wind River Information/Work Center, 1262 Hemlock Road, Carson, WA 98610; 509/427-3200.

160 Race Track
6.2 mi/3.1 hrs

Native tribes used to gather in the broad meadows of this area to collect abundant berries. In addition to work, the gatherings generated a lot of play, and one such activity lent its name to the meadow at the end of the trail—a rough, no-holds-barred horse race. If you climb the gentle trail through the old second-growth fir and pine forest in late summer, you first find the big, juicy berries that drew the natives' attention. As you climb out of the forest, you enter an enormous meadow full of lush, thick grass; it's painted a mosaic of colors by a multitude of flower blooms. A small lake lies at the southern end of the meadows, and it is easy to imagine an encampment of hundreds of Native Americans living here, collecting baskets full of berries and celebrating their good fortune. Sitting quietly beside the lake, one can almost hear the thunder of hooves throughout the long, flat meadow. Red Mountain rises above the lake, and a short side trail leads to its summit. We recommend the 1.5-mile round-trip hike to the top. You'll appreciate the views, especially looking north over the large, impressive Indian Race Track area.

Location: West of Trout Lake in Gifford Pinchot National Forest within the Indian Heaven Wilderness; see Mount Rainier and the Columbia River Gorge Map 4, grid a3.

User Groups: Hikers, leashed dogs, and horses. No mountain bikes are allowed. No wheelchair facilities.

Permits: A federal Northwest Forest Pass, $5 per day or $30 annually, is required to park at the trailhead. Passes are available from ranger stations and many private vendors, online at website: www.wta.org, or by calling 800/270-7504.

Maps: For a trail information report, contact the Wind River Information/Work Center at 509/427-3200. For a map of the Gifford Pinchot National Forest, send $3 to Outdoor Recreation Information Center, 915 Second Avenue, Suite 442, Seattle, WA 98174; 206/220-7450. Green Trails, Inc.'s excellent topographic maps of the region are available for $3.99 each at outdoor retail outlets. Ask for map number 397, Wind River. Ask the USGS for a topographic map of the Gifford Peak area.

Directions: From Trout Lake drive about six miles west on Highway 141 (which becomes Forest Service Road 24 at the forest boundary) and turn left on Forest Service Road 60. Continue about 12 miles west on Forest Service Road 60 to its junction with Forest Service Road 65. Turn right and drive to Falls Creek Horse Camp. The trailhead is located across the road from the camp.

Contact: Gifford Pinchot National Forest, Wind River Information/Work Center, 1262 Hemlock Road, Carson, WA 98610; 509/427-3200.

161 Buck Creek

4.8 mi/2.4 hrs

The White Salmon River rushes through a deep gorge. This trail follows along the river and offers good views down the rugged banks of the swift-flowing stream. The trail crosses several small streams but never accesses the main river, largely because of the precipitous nature of the gorge walls. If you like watching wild water, this is the trail for you. If you like trails with steep drops on one side, this, again, is the trail for you.

Location: North of Trout Lake in Gifford Pinchot National Forest, within the Indian Heaven Wilderness; see Mount Rainier and the Columbia River Gorge Map 4, grid a4.

User Groups: Hikers, leashed dogs, horses, and mountain bikes. No wheelchair facilities.

Permits: A federal Northwest Forest Pass, $5 per day or $30 annually, is required to park at the trailhead. Passes are available from ranger stations and many private vendors, online at website: www.wta.org, or by calling 800/270-7504.

Maps: For a map of Gifford Pinchot National Forest, contact the Outdoor Recreation Information Center, 915 Second Avenue, Suite 442, Seattle, WA 98174; 206/220-7450. Green Trails, Inc.'s excellent topographic maps are available for $3.99 each at outdoor retail outlets. Ask for map number 366, Mount Adams West. Ask the USGS for a topographic map of the Trout Lake area.

Directions: From Trout Lake drive north on Forest Service Road 23 and turn right (east) onto Forest Service Road 80 just outside of town. Continue 2.4 miles to Forest Service Road 80–031. Turn left and drive to the road's end and the trailhead.

Contact: Gifford Pinchot National Forest, Mount Adams Ranger District, 2455 Highway 141, Trout Lake, WA 98650; 509/395-3400.

162 Monte Cristo

8.2 mi/4.1 hrs

This is an easy hike—a gentle climb with less than a 1,000-foot elevation gain in four miles—to an old fire lookout site where you find great views of the surrounding region. Unlike most summit trails, this one leads to two peaks. After gaining the summit of Monte Cristo, you can continue along a ridge to a second summit, Monte Carlo. From there you can look south to the Columbia River and into the dry lands of eastern Washington. You won't find any water near this trail, so pack plenty.

Location: South of Trout Lake in Gifford Pinchot National Forest; see Mount Rainier and the Columbia River Gorge Map 4, grid a4.

User Groups: Hikers, leashed dogs, horses, and mountain bikes. No wheelchair facilities.

Permits: A federal Northwest Forest Pass, $5 per day or $30 annually, is required to park at the trailhead. Passes are available from ranger stations and many private vendors, online at website: www.wta.org, or by calling 800/270-7504.

Maps: For a map of Gifford Pinchot National Forest, contact the Outdoor Recreation Information Center, 915 Second Avenue, Suite 442, Seattle, WA 98174; 206/220-7450. Green Trails, Inc.'s excellent topographic maps are available for $3.99 each at outdoor retail outlets. Ask for map number 398, Willard. Ask the USGS for a topographic map of the Guler Mountain area.

Directions: From Trout Lake drive about three miles west on Highway 141 and turn south on Forest Service Road 86. Continue about four miles to the junction with Forest Service Road 86-080. Turn left (west) onto this road and drive to the road's end and the trailhead.

Contact: Gifford Pinchot National Forest, Mount Adams Ranger District, 2455 Highway 141, Trout Lake, WA 98650; 509/395-3400.

163 Little Huckleberry
5.0 mi/2.5 hrs 🥾 ⚡9

Steep, hot, and dusty is an accurate description of this hike, but the views from the summit of Little Huckleberry Mountain are astoundingly beautiful. And don't be fooled by the name—there is nothing little about the big, juicy huckleberries you gobble down while plodding along the ridge trail. The route leads up through a thick stand of timber along a ridge on the north face of the mountain. Near the top the trees fall away to reveal a broad, open meadow on the summit. Enjoy the views west over the scarred landscape of the Big Lava Beds and beyond to Goose Lake.

Location: West of Trout Lake in Gifford Pinchot National Forest; see Mount Rainier and the Columbia River Gorge Map 4, grid a3.

User Groups: Hikers, leashed dogs, horses, and mountain bikes. No wheelchair facilities.

Permits: A federal Northwest Forest Pass, $5 per day or $30 annually, is required to park at the trailhead. Passes are available from ranger stations and many private vendors, online at website: www.wta.org, or by calling 800/270-7504.

Maps: For a map of Gifford Pinchot National Forest, contact the Outdoor Recreation Information Center, 915 Second Avenue, Suite 442, Seattle, WA 98174; 206/220-7450. Green Trails, Inc.'s excellent topographic maps are available for $3.99 each at outdoor retail outlets. Ask for map number 366, Mount Adams West. Ask the USGS for a topographic map of the Sleeping Beauty area.

Directions: From Trout Lake drive about 14 miles west on Highway 141 (which becomes Forest Service Road 24 at the forest boundary) to Little Goose Horse Camp. Continue 2.2 miles beyond Little Goose Horse Camp to the trailhead on the right.

Contact: Gifford Pinchot National Forest, Mount Adams Ranger District, 2455 Highway 141, Trout Lake, WA 98650; 509/395-3400.

164 Monte Carlo
12.4 mi/6.2 hrs 🥾 ⚡5

Thick second-growth forest lines this route, with occasional old-growth trees poking through the low, thick canopy. Those infrequent big trees are the survivors of several old logging operations as well as some more recent cuts. A few small clear-cuts and selective-cut harvest areas cross the trail before the route turns steeply up the south flank of Monte Carlo at 2.5 miles. Enjoy the views from the summit, which include peeks at the Columbia River and Big Lava Beds.

Location: South of Trout Lake in Gifford Pinchot National Forest; see Mount Rainier and the Columbia River Gorge Map 4, grid b4.

User Groups: Hikers, leashed dogs, horses, and mountain bikes. No wheelchair facilities.

Permits: A federal Northwest Forest Pass, $5 per day or $30 annually, is required to park at the trailhead. Passes are available from ranger stations and many private vendors, online at website: www.wta.org, or by calling 800/270-7504.

Maps: For a map of Gifford Pinchot National Forest, contact the Outdoor Recreation Information Center, 915 Second Avenue, Suite 442, Seattle, WA 98174; 206/220-7450. Green Trails, Inc.'s excellent topographic maps are available for $3.99 each at outdoor retail outlets. Ask for map number 398, Willard. Ask the USGS for a topographic map of the Guler Mountain area.

Directions: From Trout Lake drive about three miles west on Highway 141 and turn south on Forest Service Road 86. Continue about 14 miles to the White Salmon River and a junction with Forest Service Road 18. Turn left onto Forest Service Road 18 and continue 1.1 miles to the trailhead on the right.

Contact: Gifford Pinchot National Forest, Mount Adams Ranger District, 2455 Highway 141, Trout Lake, WA 98650; 509/395-3400.

165 Lower Falls Creek
3.4 mi/1.7 hrs

After climbing gradually through young second-growth fir and pine to a rough-hewn log bridge over Falls Creek, this trail continues along the north side of the pretty little river to the base of a 100-foot cascade. On hot days this is a wonderful place to stretch out on the mossy carpet that lines the riverbank. You enjoy the cool mist that wafts out from the waterfall and settles over the area.

Location: North of Carson in Gifford Pinchot National Forest; see Mount Rainier and the Columbia River Gorge Map 4, grid b1.

User Groups: Hikers, leashed dogs, and mountain bikes. No horses are allowed. No wheelchair facilities.

Permits: A federal Northwest Forest Pass, $5 per day or $30 annually, is required to park at the trailhead. Passes are available from ranger stations and many private vendors, online at website: www.wta.org, or by calling 800/270-7504.

Maps: For a trail information report, contact the Wind River Information/Work Center at 509/427-3200. For a map of Gifford Pinchot National Forest, send $3 to Outdoor Recreation Information Center, 915 Second Avenue, Suite 442, Seattle, WA 98174; 206/220-7450. Green Trails, Inc.'s excellent topographic maps of the region are available for $3.99 each at outdoor retail outlets. Ask for map number 397, Wind River. Ask the USGS for topographic maps of the Termination Point and Gifford Peak areas.

Directions: From Carson drive 15 miles north on Wind River Road/County Road 30 to its junction with Forest Service Road 3062. Turn right (east), drive 1.5 miles, and turn right onto Forest Service Road 057. Continue one-quarter mile to the trailhead.

Contact: Gifford Pinchot National Forest, Wind River Information/Work Center, 1262 Hemlock Road, Carson, WA 98610; 509/427-3200.

166 Bunker Hill
4.0 mi/2.0 hrs

After following the Pacific Crest Trail east for a mile, this trail turns north and climbs steeply for another mile to the top of lonesome Bunker Hill. This peak stands apart from other mountains in the area and therefore offers great unobstructed views in all directions. The Forest Service used to maintain a fire lookout station at the summit, and it's easy to see why. The views of the Wind River Basin and the southern Washington Cascades are fantastic. The summit is a maze of rocky outcroppings, which (while fun to scramble over) are potentially dangerous; they end abruptly at tall cliffs that drop hundreds of feet to jagged rocky slopes. Enjoy the views, but stay away from the edges.

Location: North of Carson in Gifford Pinchot National Forest; see Mount Rainier and the Columbia River Gorge Map 4, grid b1.

User Groups: Hikers and leashed dogs. No horses or mountain bikes are allowed. No wheelchair facilities.

Permits: A federal Northwest Forest Pass, $5 per day or $30 annually, is required to park at the trailhead. Passes are available from ranger stations and many private vendors, online at website: www.wta.org, or by calling 800/270-7504.

Maps: For a trail information report, contact the Wind River Information/Work Center at 509/427-3200. For a map of Gifford Pinchot National Forest, send $3 to Outdoor Recreation Information Center, 915 Second Avenue, Suite 442, Seattle, WA 98174; 206/220-7450. Green Trails, Inc.'s excellent topographic maps of the region are available for $3.99 each at outdoor retail outlets. Ask for map number 397, Wind River. Ask the USGS for a topographic map of the Stabler area.

Directions: From Carson drive 8.4 miles north on Wind River Road/County Road 30 to the town of Stabler and the junction with Hemlock Road. Turn left (west) onto Hemlock Road, cross the river, and continue 1.2 miles to Forest Service Road 43. Turn right and drive 0.6 mile to the junction with Forest Service Road 43-417. Drive one-quarter mile to the trailhead on the right, which is marked as the Pacific Crest Trail.

Contact: Gifford Pinchot National Forest, Wind River Information/Work Center, 1262 Hemlock Road, Carson, WA 98610; 509/427-3200.

167 Dog Mountain
6.0 mi/3.0 hrs

With a trailhead on the Columbia River banks and the end of the trail on a mountaintop, you can bet that you'll enjoy great views of the Columbia River Gorge and beyond to Mount Hood. This is a popular trail that offers great views and a pleasant trail experience; wildflowers grace the forest meadows and clearings, and wildlife roams the area. The route begins with a steep, half-mile climb before the trail forks. Flip a coin and take either route—they rejoin at the top. Keep in mind, though, that the left fork climbs steeply up the northern flank of the mountain, putting you on top quickly so you have more time to enjoy the views from there. The right fork loops around to the east and climbs more gradually through broken forest that offers periodic views across the gorge. Our choice: get to the top fast via the northern route and enjoy a leisurely exploration of the summit, a former lookout site. Then descend on the eastern trail, enjoying the vistas as they stretch out before you.

Location: East of Carson in Gifford Pinchot National Forest; see Mount Rainier and the Columbia River Gorge Map 4, grid c3.

User Groups: Hikers, leashed dogs, and mountain bikes. No horses. No wheelchair facilities.

Permits: A federal Northwest Forest Pass, $5 per day or $30 annually, is required to park at the trailhead. Passes are available from ranger stations and many private vendors, online at website: www.wta.org, or by calling 800/270-7504.

Maps: For a trail information report, contact the Wind River Information/Work Center at 509/427-3200. For a map of Gifford Pinchot National Forest, contact the Outdoor Recreation Information Center, 915 Second Avenue, Suite 442, Seattle, WA 98174; 206/220-7450. Ask the USGS for a topographic map of the Mount Defiance area.

Directions: From Carson drive approximately nine miles east on Highway 14 to the trailhead, just beyond milepost 53. The parking area and trailhead are on the left (north) side of the highway.

Contact: Gifford Pinchot National Forest, Wind River Information/Work Center, 1262 Hemlock Road, Carson, WA 98610; 509/427-3200.

PCT-9 Columbia River to Big Lava Bed
52.3 mi one way/
4.0–5.0 days

The Columbia River to Big Lava Bed section of the Pacific Crest Trail (PCT) begins by traversing nearly 10 miles of broken forest (including some clear-cuts) along state and privately owned land. These young forests are within the protective boundaries of the Columbia River Gorge National Scenic Area. This is far from pristine forest, but you find the best camping in the first 20 miles of this section of the PCT along the small creeks you encounter here.

After leaving the gorge area, the trail enters another 10-mile stretch; this time it cuts across a patchwork area of unprotected state-owned forest and private timber lands. Once this route enters Gifford Pinchot National Forest, the forest gets thicker and the scenery improves dramatically. The path rolls over the low summit of Sedum Point, just a few miles inside the national forest, and drops to a good camp at the Trout River. From here the trail continues northeast through the Wind River Valley before climbing again, this time to the top of Big Huckleberry Mountain. Enjoy the stunning views of the Columbia River Gorge to the south; then turn due north and roll along the western flank of the stark Big Lava Bed landscape to the northern trailhead.

Location: East of Vancouver, Washington, in the Columbia River Gorge National Scenic Area; see Mount Rainier and the Columbia River Gorge Map 4, grid c1.

User Groups: Hikers, leashed dogs, and horses. No mountain bikes are allowed. No wheelchair facilities.

Permits: A federal Northwest Forest Pass, $5 per day or $30 annually, is required to park at the trailhead. Passes are available from ranger stations and many private vendors, online at website: www.wta.org, or by calling 800/270-7504.

Maps: For a trail information report, contact the Wind River Information/Work Center at 509/427-3200. For a map of Gifford Pinchot National Forest, send $3 to Outdoor Recreation Information Center, 915 Second Avenue, Suite 442, Seattle, WA 98174; 206/220-7450. Green Trails, Inc.'s excellent topographic maps of the region are available for $3.99 each at outdoor retail outlets. Ask for map numbers 396 and 397, Lookout Mountain and Wind River. Ask the USGS

for topographic maps of the Bonneville Dam, Beacon Rock, Lookout Mountain, Stabler, and Big Huckleberry Mountain areas.

Directions: From Vancouver drive about 32 miles east on Highway 14 to the trailhead near the Cascade Salmon Hatchery. Park at the small lot near the Bridge of the Gods; the trailhead is clearly marked.

Contact: Gifford Pinchot National Forest, Wind River Information/Work Center, 1262 Hemlock Road, Carson, WA 98610; 509/427-3200.

PCT-10 Big Lava Bed to Potato Hill

52.3 mi one way/ 4.0–5.0 days

After climbing three miles through uniformly sized second-growth forest, this section of the PCT dips into the Indian Heaven Wilderness. As it moves through the old-growth forest and broad meadows of the wilderness, the route gains elevation and scenic appeal. Shortly after entering the wilderness (within the first two miles), the trail erupts into an enormous field of wildflowers spreading north to a beautiful little alpine lake. This is the Indian Race Track, a historic gathering place for native tribes. They came together to harvest an incredible bounty of huckleberries and to enjoy a communal celebration. Reputedly, the highlights of the gatherings were rough-and-tumble horse races through the vast meadows. Spend at least one night here to fully appreciate the area.

Beyond the race track, the trail continues through the wilderness, past a number of cool alpine lakes and ponds—most full of trout—and grassy meadows. The north end of the wilderness, roughly eight to 10 miles from the race track, is a good area in which to pitch a tent for the night. After leaving the north end of the wilderness, the trail swings northeast and runs directly to the Mount Adams Wilderness. It winds north through this Wilderness (around the west flank of the volcano) and enjoys spectacular vistas; these views are dominated by Mount Adams on the one side and Mount St. Helens, Mount Rainier, and various other peaks on the other side. The Mount Adams Wilderness trail section stays high and traverses numerous alpine meadows, full of tiny spring-fed creeks and carpeted with fragrant wildflowers. Camping opportunities abound. The beautiful tent sites are so numerous, in fact, that it can be hard to choose sometimes.

Location: North of Trout Lake in Gifford Pinchot National Forest partially within the Mount Adams Wilderness; see Mount Rainier and the Columbia River Gorge Map 4, grid b2.

User Groups: Hikers, leashed dogs, and horses. No mountain bikes are allowed. No wheelchair facilities.

Permits: A federal Northwest Forest Pass, $5 per day or $30 annually, is required to park at the trailhead. Passes are available from ranger stations and many private vendors, online at website: www.wta.org, or by calling 800/270-7504.

Maps: For a map of Gifford Pinchot National Forest, send $3 to Outdoor Recreation Information Center, 915 Second Avenue, Suite 442, Seattle, WA 98174; 206/220-7450. Green Trails, Inc.'s excellent topographic maps of the region are available for $3.99 each at outdoor retail outlets. Ask for map numbers 334, 366, and 365, Blue Lake, Mount Adams West, and Lone Butte. Ask the USGS for topographic maps of the Big Huckleberry Mountain, Gifford Peak, Lone Butte, Sleeping Butte, Steamboat Mountain, Mount Adams West, and Green Mountain areas.

Directions: From Trout Lake drive west on Highway 141 (which becomes Forest Service

Road 24 at the forest boundary) and turn left (south) onto Forest Service Road 60. Continue to Crest Horse Camp and the southern trailhead. To reach the northern trailhead from Randle, drive one mile south on Forest Service Road 25 and then turn left (east) onto Forest Service Road 23. Continue to its junction with Forest Service Road 21. Bear right onto Forest Service Road 21 and drive to the Adams Fork Campground and a junction with Forest Service Road 56. Turn right onto Forest Service Road 56, cross the Cispus River, drive 3.5 miles, and turn right onto Forest Service Road 5603. Continue to the trailhead, just one-half mile before the road ends at the Yakima Indian Reservation boundary.

Contact: Gifford Pinchot National Forest, Mount Adams Ranger District, 2455 Highway 141, Trout Lake, WA 98650; 509/395-3400.

PCT-11 Potato Hill to White Pass

36.6 mi one way/ 3.0–4.0 days

By all accounts this section of the 2,600-mile Pacific Crest Trail is in the top three for sheer scenic value. The dozen or so hikers that we've talked to who have hiked the trail's entire length feel that Goat Rocks offers the same wonderful experiences as the rugged North Cascades and the noble Yosemite/Tahoe area of California.

The first few miles of the trail are in poor condition. Four-wheel enthusiasts routinely wrench out the barricades and drive down the PCT itself. The route has been chewed into a broad, muddy mess by the illegal drivers, but fortunately this section is short (less than three miles) and the walking is fast and easy. Beyond this the trail climbs through second-growth forest to the Mount Adams Wilderness, found about 10 miles from the trailhead. About one mile inside the wilderness, you reach a 5,700-foot scenic overlook with views of Walupt Lake and, just below, the Coleman Weedpatch. Look for herds of mountain goats browsing the precipitous slopes around you. The weed patch is actually a wildflower meadow dotted with sparking blue ponds—it's a great camping area. Farther north, about 23 miles from the trailhead, you can also see goats around Cispus Pass. Also keep an eye out for berry-hungry black bears. North of Cispus, you enter open talus slopes that are still powdered with the fine white ash of the 1980 eruption of Mount St. Helens. That white powder provides a dramatic background to the bright green and red heather that grows between the talus slopes and boulder fields. Rolling along the crest of a high, jagged ridge, the trail takes in the ancient hanging glaciers that cling to the rocky slopes, and the distant volcanic peaks of Mount Rainier, Mount Adams, and, on clear days, Mount St. Helens. From Cispus Pass the trail rolls north through Elk Pass (30 miles in), past Lutz Lake (great campsites), Tieton Pass, and Shoe Lake. Camp at Shoe, enjoy a pleasant 6.5-mile hike the last day along the high ridge of Hogback Mountain, and drop down into White Pass past the alpine ski lifts.

Location: Southeast of Packwood in Gifford Pinchot National Forest partially within the Goat Rocks Wilderness; see Mount Rainier and the Columbia River Gorge Map 2, grid f4.

User Groups: Hikers, dogs, and horses. No mountain bikes. No wheelchair facilities.

Permits: A federal Northwest Forest Pass, $5 per day or $30 annually, is required to park at the trailhead. Passes are available from ranger stations and many private vendors, online at website: www.wta.org, or by calling 800/270-7504.

Maps: For a map of Gifford Pinchot National Forest, contact the Outdoor Recreation Information Center, 915 Second Avenue, Suite 442, Seattle, WA 98174; 206/220-7450. Green Trails, Inc.'s excellent topographic maps are available for $3.99 each at outdoor retail outlets. Ask for map numbers 303, 334, and 335, White Pass, Blue Lake, and Walupt Lake. Ask the USGS for topographic maps of the White Pass, Walupt Lake, Hamilton Butte, and Green Mountain areas.

Directions: From Randle drive one mile south on Forest Service Road 25 and turn left (east) onto Forest Service Road 23. Continue to a junction with Forest Service Road 21. Bear right and drive to Adams Fork Campground and a junction with Forest Service Road 56. Turn right, cross the Cispus River, drive 3.5 miles, and turn right onto Forest Service Road 5603. Continue on to the trailhead, just half a mile before the road ends at the Yakima Indian Reservation boundary. To reach the northern trailhead from Packwood, drive 20 miles east on U.S. 12 to the White Pass Ski Area. The trailhead is just east of the ski area, across the highway from Leech Lake.

Contact: Gifford Pinchot National Forest, Cowlitz Valley Ranger District, 10024 U.S. Highway 12, Randle, WA 98377; 360/497-1100.

PCT-12 White Pass to Chinook Pass
29.5 mi/3.0 days

Much of this Pacific Crest Trail section traverses recently designated federal wilderness that draws thousands of day hikers every summer. From White Pass you immediately enter the William O. Douglas Wilderness, named for the late Supreme Court justice who grew up hiking on trails in this area. Pass beyond Deer Lake and Sand Lake, with Spiral Butte (see hike in this chapter) looking on to the east. It's downhill into the basin containing Buesch Lake, the first of many on this trail stretch. You hike by Cowlitz Pass and Snow Lake, with great views of Mounts Rainier, Adams, and St. Helens along the way, before eventually reaching Dewey Lakes, a popular overnight spot for Mount Rainier National Park visitors. Just ahead is an intersection with the Tipsoo Lake Trail, where you're bound to stumble upon hundreds of wildflower-sniffing day hikers from the popular Naches Loop Trail (see hike in this chapter) departing from the trailhead at Chinook Pass. Walk over the log bridge to the other side and make a beeline for Crystal Mountain to escape the mobs. The total elevation gain for this short Pacific Crest Trail stretch is about 2,500 feet.

Several miles of this section pass within Mount Rainier National Park. Overnight permits are required there, but good campsites are scarce anyway. Better campsites can be scouted on Forest Service lands east of the park.

Location: From White Pass near the White Pass Ski Area north through the William O. Douglas Wilderness to Chinook Pass, east of Mount Rainier; see Mount Rainier and the Columbia River Gorge Map 2, grid c5.

User Groups: Hikers, horses, and dogs. No mountain bikes. No wheelchair facilities.

Permits: A federal Northwest Forest Pass, $5 per day or $30 annually, is required to park at the trailhead. Passes are available from ranger stations and many private vendors, online at website: www.wta.org, or by calling 800/270-7504.

Maps: For a map of the Pacific Crest Trail, Washington South, contact the Outdoor Recreation Information Center at 206/220-7450. Ask the USGS for topographic maps of the White Pass, Chinook Pass, and Cougar Lake areas.

Directions: To reach the White Pass Trailhead, follow Highway 12 east to White Pass and the Pacific Crest Trailhead on the left

near Leech Lake. To reach the Chinook Pass Trailhead, follow Highway 410 east from Enumclaw to Chinook Pass and the well-marked Pacific Crest Trailhead. Note: Portions of Highway 123/Cayuse Pass and Highway 4/Chinook Pass and all roads within Mount Rainier National Park are closed in winter, except the road between the Nisqually entrance and Paradise, which is kept open as conditions permit. Contact the park at 360/569-2211 for current road conditions.

Contact: Outdoor Recreation Information Center, 915 Second Avenue, Suite 442, Seattle, WA 98174; 206/220-7450; Mount Baker-Snoqualmie National Forest, White River Ranger District, 857 Roosevelt Avenue East, Enumclaw, WA 98022; 360/825-6585.

PCT-13 Chinook Pass to Snoqualmie Pass
69.0 mi/7.0 days

This section of the Pacific Crest Trail is a mixture of good and bad—the good being the Norse Peak Wilderness on the northeast side of Mount Rainier, the bad being what comes after it. The trail starts off on a route that is highly popular with day hikers, passing Sheep Lake and making its way to Sourdough Gap and Bear Gap. More good scenery and great views continue from here to the Crystal Mountain Ski Area and the Pickhandle Point/Hen Skin Lakes area. Scenery remains excellent as you skirt around Norse Peak to prime campsites in Big Crow Basin. Continue north to Little Crow Basin, Arch Rock Camp, Rod's Gap, Government Meadows, and Windy Gap. Note the rustic cabin at the edge of the broad fields of Government Meadows—campers are free to spend the night in this shelter, provided they pick up after themselves and leave the place as clean as (or cleaner than) they found it. From here to Blowout Mountain, much of the trail's normal grandeur is lost in a maze of bulldozer roads and clear-cuts. A lot of the trail in this section traverses the forest, much of which is logged. Views are rare. From Blowout Mountain the route leads north to Tacoma Pass, Lizard Lake, and the well-peopled Stampede Pass, where Forest Service Road 54 brings auto traffic. Continuing north, the trail follows the ridgetop above Keechelus Lake, past Mirror Lake, Tinkham and Silver Peaks, and Lodge Lake to the Snoqualmie Pass Ski Area. Follow the chair lifts down and cross under I-90 at the underpass.

Location: From State Route 410 to I-90 through the Norse Peak Wilderness area in the central Cascades; see Mount Rainier and the Columbia River Gorge Map 2, grid b5.

User Groups: Hikers, dogs, and horses. No mountain bikes. No wheelchair facilities.

Permits: A federal Northwest Forest Pass, $5 per day or $30 annually, is required to park at the trailhead. Passes are available from ranger stations and many private vendors, online at website: www.wta.org, or by calling 800/270-7504.

Maps: For maps of the Pacific Crest Trail, Washington North and South, contact the Outdoor Recreation Information Center, 915 Second Avenue, Suite 442, Seattle, WA 98174; 206/220-7450. Ask the USGS for topographic maps of the White River Park, Norse Peak, Noble Knob, Lester, Blowout Mountain, Stampede Pass, Lost Lake, and Snoqualmie Pass areas.

Directions: To reach the Chinook Pass Trailhead, follow Highway 410 east from Enumclaw to Chinook Pass and the well-marked Pacific Crest Trailhead. To reach the Snoqualmie Pass Trailhead, drive east on I-90 from Seattle to Exit 52/West Summit. Cross under the freeway to the north and find the Pacific Crest Trailhead parking area on the right side of the road. Note: Portions of Highway 123/Cayuse Pass and Highway 4/Chinook Pass and all roads within Mount Rainier National Park are closed in winter, except the road between the Nisqually entrance and Paradise, which is kept open as conditions permit. Contact the park at 360/569-2211 for current road conditions.

Contact: Outdoor Recreation Information Center, 915 Second Avenue, Suite 442, Seattle, WA 98174; 206/220-7450.

SOUTHEAST WASHINGTON

Southeast Washington

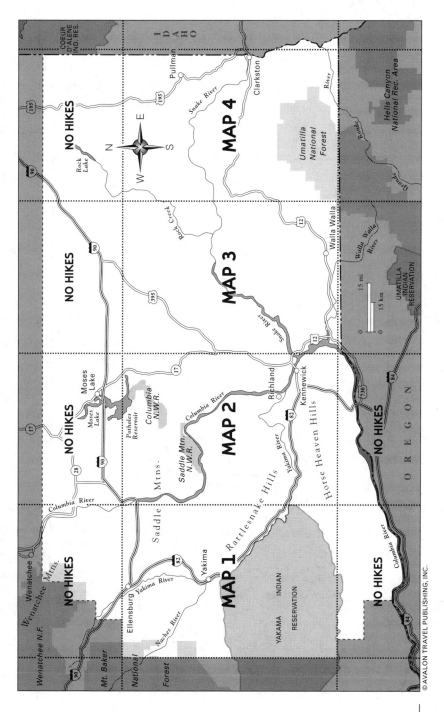

© AVALON TRAVEL PUBLISHING, INC.

Map 1

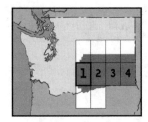

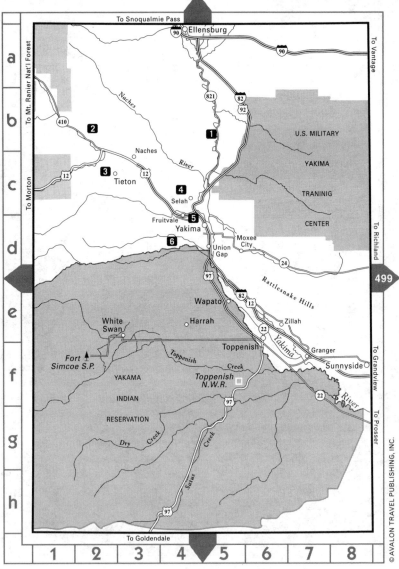

Map 2

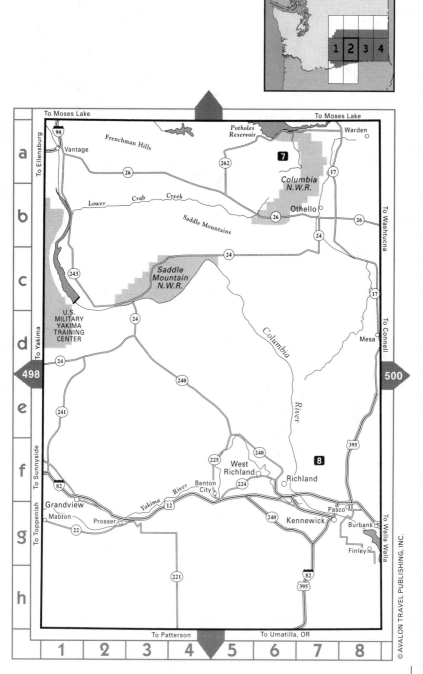

To Moses Lake · To Moses Lake

To Ellensburg · To Yakima · To Toppenish · To Sunnyside

90 · Vantage · Frenchman Hills · Potholes Reservoir · Warden

262 · **7**

Columbia N.W.R. · 17

26 · Lower · Crab · Creek · Othello · 26

Saddle Mountains · 26 · 24

24

Saddle Mountain N.W.R. · 243

U.S. MILITARY YAKIMA TRAINING CENTER · 24 · Mesa · To Connell

498 · 24 · 240 · **500**

241 · Columbia · River

395 · To Washtucna

225 · West Richland · 240 · **8**

224 · Richland

82 · Yakima · River · Benton City

Grandview · 12

Mabton · Prosser · 240 · Kennewick · Pasco

22 · Burbank · To Walla Walla

Finley

221 · 82 · 395

To Patterson · To Umatilla, OR

© AVALON TRAVEL PUBLISHING, INC.

1 · 2 · 3 · 4

Map 3

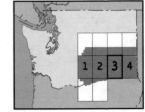

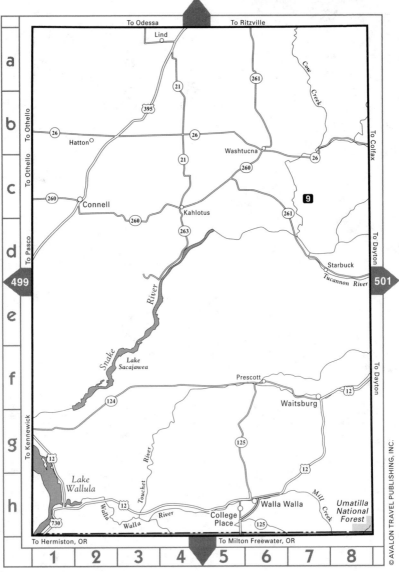

Map 4

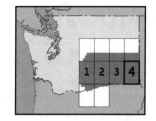

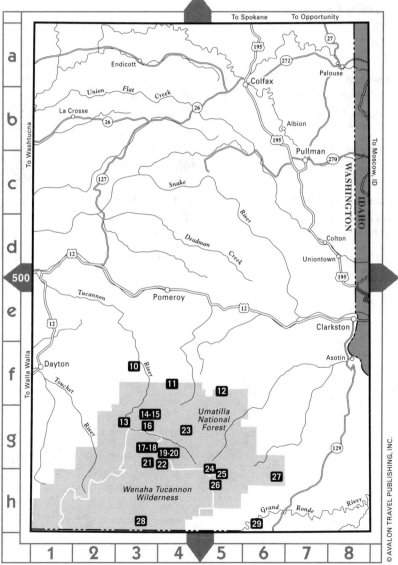

Southeast Washington

◳ Umtanum Creek
2.5 mi/2.0 hrs

Once over the bouncy suspension bridge, cross the railroad tracks on the far side of the river and find the official start of the Umtanum Creek Trail. The small but beautiful creek drains a dry valley that harbors lots of sagebrush, cheat grass, and a few old locust and alder trees. The route follows the creek upstream, crossing it once, and a sometimes-tricky traverse of a steep cliff face near the upper end of the trail. The traverse is generally safe, but heavy rains can soften the outer edge of the trail, making the path narrow and slippery. Also, during late fall and early spring, when the overnight temperatures still dip below freezing, the upper trail may be icy as spray from the Umtanum Falls drifts over the rocks. The narrow canyon prevents the ice from thawing as fast as you might expect, so use caution. That said, spring and fall are the ideal times to visit this creek-side trail. Not only are the chances of encountering spectacular wildflower displays great in the spring, but these seasons are when the wildlife is most active—with the notable exception of snakes. Come high summer, rattlesnakes are out in force in this region, so to avoid the vipers, visit in the cool months when they aren't active.

Location: Northwest of Yakima in the L.T. Murray Wildlife Recreation Area; see Southeast Washington Map 1, grid b5.

User Groups: Hikers and dogs. No horses or mountain bikes. No wheelchair facilities.

Permits: A Stewardship Access Decal is required on any vehicle parking at the trailhead. These annual permits are required on all lands managed by the Washington Department of Fish and Wildlife. The permits are free with the purchase of a state fishing or hunting license. They can also be purchased separately for $10 from any retailer

selling fishing licenses, online at website: www.wa.gov/wdfw/ or by calling 206/976-3200.

Maps: Ask the USGS for topographic maps of the Wymer and Ellensburg areas.

Directions: From Selah drive north on Highway 821 toward Ellensburg. Park in the large lot found just past Milepost 17. The trail begins on the pedestrian-only suspension bridge over the Yakima River.

Contact: Washington Department of Fish and Wildlife, 600 Capitol Way North, Olympia, WA 98501-7091; 360/902-2200 or 509/457-9312 (Yakima regional office).

◲ Mount Cleman
5.5 mi/3.0 hrs

There is some dispute over the best way to get to the top of Mount Cleman. There is an old, beat-up road that weaves its way most of the way to the top, but it is rough and dusty, and you still have to hike to make the summit. The better bet is to park at the base of the hill. From here hikers can enjoy the views as they unfold during the moderate ascent. The hike begins from the shoulder of SR 410. Walk through the ditch at roadside and slip through a gap in the elk drift fence. The trail is really nothing more than a series of game trails leading upward through the rich meadows and sagebrush fields. The lower section follows Waterworks Creek along game trails widened by frequent human usage. In a few miles the creek basin forks. Good scenery and wildlife viewing can be found in either drainage, but to get to the top of Cleman, stay right. In just a few hundred yards, the path, growing fainter here, veers to the right and begins to climb the valley wall. It quickly reaches a low saddle in the ridgeline above the creek. Turn south and follow this well-defined ridge crest to its high point and you find yourself on top of Mount Cleman in no time. The route climbs steeply at times, especially in the later sections near the top. But if the way is too steep, simply weave back and forth as if you are climbing a series of switchbacks. Or just stop and enjoy the views more often. Looking down the valley, you see a series of ridges just like the one you're on leading down to the river valley below. As you gain elevation, the views grow, including the snow-capped summits of Mount Adams and Mount Rainier. Deer (muleys and white-tailed), elk, coyotes, hares, raptors-eagles, hawks, and falcons, as well as an array of small animals, can be seen along the route. Bring a pair of binoculars and a camera to take advantage of all wonderful scenery.

Location: Northwest of Yakima; see Southeast Washington Map 1, grid b2.

User Groups: Hikers and dogs. No horses or mountain bikes. No wheelchair facilities.

Permits: A Stewardship Access Decal is required on any vehicle parking at the trailhead. These annual permits are required on all lands managed by the Washington Department of Fish and Wildlife. The permits are free with the purchase of a state fishing or hunting license. They can also be purchased separately for $10 from any retailer selling fishing licenses, online at website: www.wa.gov/wdfw/ or by calling 206/976-3200.

Maps: Ask the USGS for topographic map of the Milk Creek area.

Directions: From Yakima drive west on U.S. 12 for 16 miles to a Y in the road. Bear right onto Highway 410 and continue a half-mile to the parking area on the right at either end of a small bridge.

Contact: Washington Department of Fish and Wildlife, 600 Capitol Way North, Olympia, WA 98501-7091; 360/902-2200 or 509/457-9312 (Yakima regional office).

❸ Tieton River Interpretive Trail

8.0 mi/3.5 hrs

Come here in winter and the trail will be snow covered within the first mile or so, but in that first mile, you are likely to see hundreds of elk. The State Department of Fish and Wildlife maintains a winter feeding station for the great beasts just across the river from the trail's start. The herds congregate here as snows fill their grazing areas in the high country, and the feeding station keeps them out of towns and fields where they could cause problems. But as fine as it is to visit in winter, the best seasons to be here are spring and fall. Come spring, the elk are still moving around, though singly or in small groups. But by April or May, the trail is mostly snow-free so hikers can get a good walk in while watching the wildlife. In autumn the elk return as snow falls in the high country, and bald eagles swoop in to feed on the plentiful fish in the river.

You follow the river upstream, but the trail stays well back from its banks for the first couple miles. But that's okay; the forest the trail pierces is picturesque enough to capture your full attention. In addition to elk, the woods are home to white-tailed and mule deer, coyotes, weasels, badgers, beavers (near the river), and other small critters. Hikers here at dawn and dusk might witness great horned owls winging silently through the trees, or hear grouse barking out their deep "whomp, whomp, whomp" in the underbrush.

At two miles the trail rejoins the river bank, and a small foot bridge offers access back to the main road (this bridge can serve as an alternative trailhead if the lower, main trailhead is made inaccessible by a temporary wildlife protection closure—these closures are sometimes put in effect in late winter if the elk and/or bald eagles are enduring a particularly brutal winter).

Beyond this bridge, the trail continues upstream, now generally staying near the water, until it reaches an old, rough dirt road at four miles. Hikers should turn around here.

Location: West of Yakima in Okanogan/Wenatchee National Forest; see Southeast Washington Map 1, grid c2.

User Groups: Hikers and dogs. No horses or mountain bikes. No wheelchair facilities.

Permits: A federal Northwest Forest Pass, $5 per day or $30 annually, is required to park at the trailhead. Passes are available from ranger stations and many private vendors, online at website: www.wta.org, or by calling 800/270-7504.

Maps: Green Trails, Inc.'s excellent topographic maps of the region are available for $3.99 each at outdoor retail outlets. Ask for map number 305, Tieton. Ask the USGS for topographic map of the Tieton Basin area.

Directions: From Yakima drive west on U.S. 12 to the Y junction with Highway 410. Bear left to continue on U.S. 12 for another two miles to the parking area at entrance to the Tieton Elk Feeding Station. Walk across the bridge to find the beginning of the trail on the other side of the river.

Contact: Okanogan/Wenatchee National Forest, Naches Ranger District, 10061 Highway 12, Naches, WA 98937; 509/653-2205.

4 Yakima Rim
12.0 mi/7.0 hrs

The route along the Yakima Rim Trail begins with neither trail nor rim. Rather, hikers leave their vehicles and squeeze through a small gap in a seemingly endless drift fence designed to keep elk in the Wildlife Recreation Area. The route then follows the fence up through open country; there is no formal trail here, but many game and hiker paths are cut into the sagebrush desert. In just over two miles of shadowing the drift fence, you find the old, true trail on the true Yakima Rim. This path was created more than two decades ago, but because of some bureaucratic snafus the Department of Fish and Wildlife didn't secure a road easement to the original trailhead. But all in all, this isn't bad. The meandering route through the sagebrush provides ample opportunity for hikers to see some desert wildflowers and quite possibly, some desert wildlife. Red-tailed hawks soar overhead, ever in search of deer mice, bull snakes, rattlesnakes, sage grouse, pheasants, quail, hares, and other dry-country critters. There are also plenty of mule deer, fewer white-tailed deer, coyotes, and occasionally a cougar or two prowling the region. And come winter, herds of elk browse the area while the high country is full of snow. The main Yakima Rim Trail follows the crest of the ridge north and offers stunning views of the surrounding country for miles on end. This is truly a wonderful place to hike in early spring—the first part of March until early May—and in late autumn. Springtime brings vibrant colors and an array of wildflowers. Autumn brings out the strong essence of the ever-present sagebrush. Autumn is also the best time to see wildlife, as the animals are active for longer periods of time each day as they fight for as much nourishment as they can consume before the cold winter months set in. Hike the length of the trail or just as much of it as your legs and time allow. Whether it's 2 or all 12 miles, the hike gives you a taste of the high desert environment of the Columbia River drainage.

Location: Northwest of Yakima in the L.T. Murray Wildlife Recreation Area; see Southeast Washington Map 1, grid c4.

User Groups: Hikers and leashed dogs. No horses or mountain bikes. No wheelchair facilities.

Permits: A Stewardship Access Decal is required on any vehicle parking at the trailhead. These annual permits are required on all lands managed by the Washington Department of Fish and Wildlife. The permits are free with the purchase of a state fishing or hunting license. They can also be purchased separately for $10 from any retailer selling fishing licenses, online at website: www.wa.gov/wdfw/ or by calling 206/976-3200.

Maps: Ask the USGS for topographic maps of the Badger Pocket and Ellensburg areas.

Directions: From Selah drive north on Naches Avenue as it leaves town. Turn left onto North Wenas Road. Continue 2.8 miles to a fork in the road. Continue straight ahead onto Gibson Road. After just a quarter mile, turn right onto Buffalo Road and continue three-quarters of a mile to the trailhead (found at very wide area along a sharp bend in the road).

Contact: Washington Department of Fish and Wildlife, 600 Capitol Way North, Olympia, WA 98501-7091; 360/902-2200 or 509/457-9312 (Yakima regional office).

5 Cowiche Canyon
6.4 mi/4.0 hrs

The Cowiche Canyon Trail borders a major urban center, but it is wild and scenic throughout its length. The path follows the route of the old Burlington Northern Railroad line through the deep gorge of the Cowiche River. The railroad abandoned the route in 1984, and the Conservancy was formed to transform the old freight line into a hikers' paradise. The trail follows the bottom of the canyon, crosses some old redecked railroad trestles, and skirts some beautiful old stands of deciduous trees. There are wild-

flowers aplenty in the spring, which comes early to this near-desert environment. Hike here in March and April for springtime scenery, or in early October for an autumn color panorama. Since the trail follows an old railroad grade, the path is gentle in pitch and broad enough to make this an ideal route for families to explore with the little ones.

Location: West of Yakima; see Southeast Washington Map 1, grid d4.

User Groups: Hikers and leashed dogs. No horses or mountain bikes. No wheelchair facilities.

Permits: No permits are required.

Maps: Ask the USGS for topographic maps of the Naches, Wiley City, and Yakima West areas.

Directions: Drive west through Yakima on Summitview Drive. Continue out of town for six miles and turn right on to Weikel Road. Find the trailhead on the right in about a quarter mile.

Contact: Cowiche Canyon Conservancy, P.O. Box 877, Yakima, WA 98907; Okanogan/Wenatchee National Forest, Naches Ranger District, 10061 U.S. 12, Naches, WA 98937; 509/653-2205.

6 Yakima River Greenway
14.0 mi/7.0 hrs

Expect a little of everything here. Explore the wild banks of the Yakima River with its large migratory populations of heron, osprey, Canadian geese, a variety of ducks, and an ever-growing number of American bald eagles. The route dips through several small hardwood and conifer forests that are swarming with cottontail rabbits and therefore watched closely by falcons and hawks. When not in the trees, the trail is near the water, and in addition to the native wildlife, you can see other people enjoying a leisurely float trip down the river, anglers prowling the banks in search of big trout, and during the spawn, salmon and steelhead. The broad, paved trail is wonderfully flat and accessible, making it enjoyable for people of all ages and abilities.

Location: In north Yakima along the riverfront; see Southeast Washington Map 1, grid d4.

User Groups: Hikers, leashed dogs, horses, mountain bikes, and wheelchairs.

Permits: No permits are required.

Maps: Ask the USGS for a topographic map of the Yakima area.

Directions: From Yakima there are numerous access points. To reach the best one, from Yakima drive north on I-82 to the Resthaven Road exit. At the bottom of the exit ramp, turn west and drive about 1.5 miles on Resthaven Road to the trailhead.

Contact: Yakima Greenway Foundation, 111 South 18th Street, Yakima, WA 98901; 509/453-8280.

◼ Potholes Sand Dunes
0.5–10.0 mi/0.5–5.0 hrs 🥾 ⬅️6

Don't look for trails here. This is a sand dune landscape punctuated by a series of small ponds and lakes, or potholes, which are interesting to explore. Shifting sands would quickly obscure any trails here, so no one built them. That makes visiting this area all the more enjoyable.

Climb over dunes, leap off their crests into the soft sandy flanks, and watch the ever-present breeze push fresh layers of sand into your tracks. Prowl the edges of the fish-rich ponds and lakes. Admire the incredible diversity of animal life that thrives here, including mule deer, large and small migratory birds, rattlesnakes, scorpions, mice, rabbits, hawks, owls, and coyotes. Those animals you don't spot will likely have left tracks in the soft sand, giving you a chance to practice your tracking skills.

Location: South of Moses Lake in Potholes Wildlife Area; see Southeast Washington Map 2, grid a6.

User Groups: Hikers and dogs. No horses or mountain bikes are allowed. No wheelchair facilities.

Permits: A Stewardship Access Decal is required on any vehicle parking at the trailhead. These annual permits are required on all lands managed by the Washington Department of Fish and Wildlife. The permits are free with the purchase of a state fishing or hunting license. They can also be purchased separately for $10 from any retailer selling fishing licenses, online at website: www.wa.gov/wdfw/ or by calling 206/976-3200.

Maps: For more information contact the Washington Department of Fish and Wildlife at 360/902-2200. Ask the USGS for a topographic map of the Moses Lake area.

Directions: From Moses Lake drive three miles east on I-90 to the junction with Highway 17. Exit onto Highway 17 and drive three-quarters of a mile south to Base Line Road. Turn right (west) and continue on Base Line Road to Potato Hill Road. Turn left (south) and drive to the junction with Sand Dunes Road. Turn right (west) and follow this road to its end and the parking area.

Contact: Washington State Department of Fish and Wildlife, 600 Capitol Way North, Olympia, WA 98501; 360/902-2200.

◼ Juniper Dunes
1.0–8.0 mi/1.0–6.0 hrs 🥾 ⬅️9

The only trail in this small, desert preserve is an old jeep track that slices across its southern end. Hike along this track for as long as you care to; then turn north and disappear into the sand dunes and desert juniper groves. You find six large groves of the desert juniper trees, the largest concentration of this species this far north. But between the well-spaced groves are individual trees, some of which are hundreds of years old. The mild hills here are sand dunes, by the way, but not in the Sahara Desert sense of the word. A few barren mounds of shifting sand do exist, but sagebrush, wild rye grass, desert flowers—such as phlox, larkspur, and blue-eyed Marys—and a web of animal tracks cover the rest. As you explore the tiny Wilderness, watch for huge mule deer, wily coyotes, fear-inducing rattlesnakes, deer mice, kangaroo rats, porcupines, badgers, rabbits, and skunks, among others. Red-tailed hawks circle overhead, and great horned owls stare from the thick branches of the junipers. Bring plenty of water (none is available in the area) and a compass to help you navigate through the maze of dunes. If you get lost, a hike of not more than 4.5 miles in any direction takes you to the boundary of the Wilderness, marked with a strong, steel barbed-wire fence. This keeps out the motorcycle and four-wheel-drive enthusiasts who recreate on the surrounding BLM property; it can also lead weary hikers back to where they started.

Location: North of Pasco in the Juniper Dunes Wilderness; see Southeast Washington Map 2, grid f7.

User Groups: Hikers, dogs, and horses. No mountain bikes are allowed. No wheelchair facilities.

Permits: No permits are required.

Maps: For more information contact the Bureau of Land Management at 509/353-2570. Ask the USGS for topographic maps of the Rye Grass Coulee, Levy Southwest, Levy Southeast, and Levy Northeast areas.

Directions: From Pasco drive east on U.S. 12 to the junction with the Pasco-Kahlotus Highway. Turn left (north) onto the Pasco-Kahlotus Highway and drive 5.6 miles to Peterson Road. The junction is at a small crop duster airstrip and grain silo. Turn left onto an unnamed wide gravel road and continue four miles northeast. The road quickly turns to rough dirt as it leaves the farmlands and enters Bureau of Land Management property. At the four-mile point, follow the signs to the right. A large parking area is 100 yards down this road. If you're driving a low-clearance passenger vehicle or the conditions are very wet, park here and walk 3.5 miles on the rough road to the wilderness boundary. If you're in a high-clearance vehicle, drive along the rough, rutted sand road to the wilderness boundary marked by a barbed-wire fence and gate. Park near the gate.

Contact: Bureau of Land Management, Spokane District, 1103 North Fancher, Spokane, WA 99212; 509/536-1200.

9 Palouse Falls
0.5 mi/1.0 hr

The 185-foot Palouse waterfall thunders into a deep circular bowl in the black basalt rock of this desert region, and this primitive trail loops around the west side of the pool. One of the best views of the falls is found just a few yards down the trail, where a deep cut in the bowl's rim perfectly frames the crashing waters (it makes a good photo opportunity). Continue around the rim, being careful to always keep a safe distance from the edge, and you find a great vantage point overlooking the river above the falls and the unique rock formation that stands nearby. From a distance the basalt core looks like a tall castle or multi-masted sailing ship just waiting to launch itself into the churning waters. When you've had your fill of the view (if you ever do), return to the parking area, taking note of the beautiful, aromatic sagebrush and pretty blue bachelor buttons along the way.

This is rattlesnake country. Be cautious and alert when walking here, even in the gravel parking area. Given a chance, the snakes would rather slither away than attack something as big as a human. It is important that you be alert enough to know when they need to get away and give them enough room.

Location: North of Dayton in Palouse Falls State Park; see Northeast Washington Map 3, grid c7.

User Groups: Hikers and dogs. No mountain bikes are allowed. No wheelchair facilities.

Permits: Day-use parking permits may be required. Contact the Washington State Parks and Recreation Commission at 800/233-0321.

Maps: Ask the USGS for a topographic map of the Palouse Falls area.

Directions: From Dayton drive 15 miles north on U.S. 12 to Delaney Junction. Turn west on Highway 261 and continue west past Starbuck and across the Snake River. Continue five miles up the hill to the junction with Palouse Falls Road. Turn right and drive 2.8 miles to the state park. The trail begins to the left of the parking area.

Contact: Washington State Parks and Recreation Commission, Public Affairs Office, P.O. Box 42650, Olympia, WA 98504-2650; 800/233-0321.

🔟 Rattlesnake
10.0 mi/5.0 hrs

Steep, dry, hot, and appropriately named, this trail scares off most visitors before they even start up the hill. A sparse forest lines the first three-quarters of a mile, but as the trail climbs, the forest falls behind and shade comes only from the few trees that have ventured out onto the rocky slope. The reddish soil is baked dry by long, hot summer days, and the dearth of ground cover creates a loose, dusty layer of topsoil. That combination results in two things: a strenuous, dirty hike and ideal rattlesnake habitat. At the ridgetop there are great views back down over the Tucannon Valley. There is water at the top and the bottom but nothing on the long climb up.

This is truly rattlesnake country. Keep eyes and ears open for the serpents sunning themselves on the rocks. Given a chance, they will either escape or warn you to escape. Their warning is less of a rattle than a high-pitched buzz. If you hear that buzz, freeze, locate the snake, and move away slowly.

Location: Southeast of Dayton in Umatilla National Forest within the Wenaha-Tucannon Wilderness; see Northeast Washington Map 4, grid f3.

User Groups: Hikers, dogs, and horses. No mountain bikes are allowed. No wheelchair facilities.

Permits: A federal Northwest Forest Pass, $5 per day or $30 annually, is required to park at the trailhead. Passes are available from ranger stations and many private vendors, online at website: www.wta.org, or by calling 800/270-7504.

Maps: For a trail information report, contact the Pomeroy Ranger District at 509/843-1891. For a map of Umatilla National Forest, contact Nature of the Northwest Information Center, 800 Northeast Oregon Street, Suite 177, Portland, OR 97232; 503/872-2750. Ask the USGS for a topographic map of the Panjab Creek area.

Directions: From Dayton drive 14 miles northeast on U.S. 12 to Tucannon Road. Turn right (south) onto Tucannon Road and continue 35 miles to a junction. Take the right fork up Panjab Road/Forest Service Road 4713 and continue a few hundred yards to a campground. The trailhead is near the campground entrance.

Contact: Umatilla National Forest, Pomeroy Ranger District, 71 West Main Street, Pomeroy, WA 99347; 509/843-1891.

11 Bear Creek
6.0 mi/3.0 hrs

Enjoy yourself on the hike in, as you drop down from the ridgetop road, because the workout begins when you head back out. The trail descends gradually through open hillside meadows lined with basaltic rimrock. These dry, hot clearings provide pleasant views into the Tucannon River basin, your ultimate destination. Between the rimrock and cheat grass meadows lie stands of whitebark pine, blue spruce, and tamarack forest, all home to big mule deer, spruce, blue grouse, and the occasional black bear and cougar. (Early Westerners called the grouse "stupid chickens" because they let hunters get within a few feet. In fact, many trappers and other wilderness explorers reportedly saved precious bullets and gunpowder by killing the birds by clubbing them or throwing rocks.) Three miles from the trailhead, the route ends at a junction with the Tucannon River Trail (see hike in this chapter) near the water's edge. Take a dip in the cool, clean, clear river.

Campers need to hang all food and packs, not just to guard against hungry bears, but also against the potentially more damaging attacks by hordes of mice. Remember, too, that mice are eaten by snakes, and around here snakes usually come with rattles on their tails. Keep an alert eye and ear out for these slithering mousetraps.

Location: South of Pomeroy in Umatilla National Forest; see Northeast Washington Map 4, grid f4.

User Groups: Hikers, dogs, and horses. No mountain bikes are allowed. No wheelchair facilities.

Permits: A federal Northwest Forest Pass, $5 per day or $30 annually, is required to park at the trailhead. Passes are available from ranger stations and many private vendors, online at website: www.wta.org, or by calling 800/270-7504.

Maps: For a trail information report, contact the Pomeroy Ranger District at 509/843-1891. For a map of Umatilla National Forest, contact Nature of the Northwest Information Center, 800 Northeast Oregon Street, Suite 177, Portland, OR 97232; 503/872-2750. Ask the USGS for a topographic map of the Stentz Spring area.

Directions: From Pomeroy drive 10 miles south on Benjamin Gulch Road/County Road 128 to a fork. Bear left onto Mountain Road/Forest Service Road 40. Follow Mountain Road nearly 18 miles to Hunter Springs and the Bear Creek Trailhead.

Contact: Umatilla National Forest, Pomeroy Ranger District, 71 West Main Street, Pomeroy, WA 99347; 509/843-1891.

12 North Fork Asotin
11.0 mi one way/5.0 hrs

The trail follows Asotin Creek for about eight miles before turning steeply up the valley wall. It then climbs high on the flank of Pinkham Butte, turns 90 degrees, and angles under the north face of Jumpoff Joe Peak and then on west to Elk Point and the west trailhead. For much of the route, you see mostly heavy pine forest and the cold, clear river. The western end of the trail provides some views. If really picturesque vistas are your goal, leave the trail and scramble up Pinkham Butte and/or Jumpoff Joe Point. Just don't jump off.

Location: West of Asotin in Umatilla National Forest; see Northeast Washington Map 4, grid f5.

User Groups: Hikers, dogs, horses, and mountain bikes. No wheelchair facilities.

Permits: A federal Northwest Forest Pass, $5 per day or $30 annually, is required to park at the trailhead. Passes are available from ranger stations and many private vendors, online at website: www.wta.org, or by calling 800/270-7504.

Maps: For a trail information report, contact the Pomeroy Ranger District at 509/843-1891. For a map of Umatilla National Forest, contact Nature of the Northwest Information Center, 800 Northeast Oregon Street, Suite 177, Portland, OR 97232; 503/872-2750. Ask the USGS for topographic maps of the Pinkham Butte and Harlow Ridge areas.

Directions: From Asotin drive 2.8 miles west on Asotin Creek Road. Turn right onto Asotin Road and continue to a fork at the Asotin Wildlife Area. Stay right on Lickfork Road/Forest Service Road 41 and drive 0.7 mile. Turn left onto a secondary dirt road and continue five miles to the east trailhead. To reach the west trailhead, stay on Lickfork Road for 10 miles. The trailhead and parking area are on the left.

Contact: Umatilla National Forest, Pomeroy Ranger District, 71 West Main Street, Pomeroy, WA 99347; 509/843-1891.

🔳 Sawtooth
24.0 mi/2.0–3.0 days

This is a dry trail with no water source until you reach the Wenaha River at the far end. For a great day trip, hike just the first one to four miles of the trail, which stretches along the scenic Sawtooth Ridge. Here the trail wanders in and out of old pine forests and wildflower meadows on the ridgetop, from which you get lovely views out over the upper Wenaha River Drainage, as well as views of peaks to the west, including Table Rock and Squaw Peak. The trail ultimately runs out of ridge at four miles and drops steeply for about eight miles into the Wenaha River Valley. There it joins the Wenaha River Trail. The only water available is in the river, so camp near its banks or make a dry camp along the ridge before returning up the trail.

Location: South of Dayton in Umatilla National Forest within the Wenaha-Tucannon Wilderness; see Northeast Washington Map 4, grid g3.

User Groups: Hikers, dogs, and horses. No mountain bikes are allowed. No wheelchair facilities.

Permits: A federal Northwest Forest Pass, $5 per day or $30 annually, is required to park at the trailhead. Passes are available from ranger stations and many private vendors, online at website: www.wta.org, or by calling 800/270-7504.

Maps: For a trail information report, contact the Pomeroy Ranger District at 509/843-1891. For a map of Umatilla National Forest, contact Nature of the Northwest Information Center, 800 Northeast Oregon Street, Suite 177, Portland, OR 97232; 503/872-2750. Ask the USGS for topographic maps of the Godman Springs and Wenaha Forks areas.

Directions: From Dayton drive south on Fourth Avenue. This road becomes North Touchet Road at the city limits and then Forest Service Road 64 at the forest boundary. Continue on up the valley past Ski Bluewood Ski Area. At the fork at the top of the long climb, turn left (east) onto Forest Service Road 46 (about 26 miles from Dayton). Drive 3.5 miles to the broad meadow marked Burnt Flat. Drive about a hundred yards south on a faint dirt road to the top of a knoll. Hike one-quarter mile along this faint road to the wilderness boundary where the trail actually starts.

Contact: Umatilla National Forest, Pomeroy Ranger District, 71 West Main Street, Pomeroy, WA 99347; 509/843-1891.

14 Panjab

11.2 mi/5.6 hrs

A pretty valley hike ending at a large, popular camping area complete with great views is the reward for hikers who hit this trail. Old-growth pine—lodgepole, whitebark, some ponderosa—fir, and spruce trees create a cool, shadowy corridor along the banks of Panjab Creek. Three miles from the trailhead, the route turns uphill and climbs steeply through a few switchbacks to the ridgetop and along the ridge to Indian Corral, a popular horse-camping area and the intersection of several wilderness trails.

Location: Southeast of Dayton in Umatilla National Forest within the Wenaha-Tucannon Wilderness; see Northeast Washington Map 4, grid g3.

User Groups: Hikers, dogs, and horses. No mountain bikes are allowed. No wheelchair facilities.

Permits: A federal Northwest Forest Pass, $5 per day or $30 annually, is required to park at the trailhead. Passes are available from ranger stations and many private vendors, online at website: www.wta.org, or by calling 800/270-7504.

Maps: For a trail information report, contact the Pomeroy Ranger District at 509/843-1891. For a map of Umatilla National Forest, contact Nature of the Northwest Information Center, 800 Northeast Oregon Street, Suite 177, Portland, OR 97232; 503/872-2750. Ask the USGS for topographic maps of the Panjab Creek, Oregon Butte, Diamond Peak, and Eden areas.

Directions: From Dayton drive 14 miles northeast on U.S. 12 to Tucannon Road. Turn right (south) onto Tucannon Road and continue 35 miles to a junction. Take the right fork up Panjab Road/Forest Service Road 4713 and continue 2.8 miles to the Panjab Trailhead on the right.

Contact: Umatilla National Forest, Pomeroy Ranger District, 71 West Main Street, Pomeroy, WA 99347; 509/843-1891.

15 Crooked Creek

**22.1 mi one way/
1.0–2.0 days**

If possible, arrange for transportation at this trail's far end to avoid a long backtrack through the forest. This is one of several trails that slice across the Wenaha-Tucannon Wilderness, and one of the few that actually cross through the drainages of the two rivers that give their names to the area. From the Panjab Trailhead the trail climbs gradually alongside Panjab Creek and then up the headwall of the creek valley to Dunlop Springs and Indian Corral at roughly 5.3 miles. This large horse-camping area is one of the busiest places in this uncrowded wilderness because it serves as a central hub for several trails that radiate out into the pristine valleys around it.

The Crooked Creek Trail leaves Indian Corral and drops slowly into the Trout Creek Valley. On the way down the valley wall, you get occasional views out over the U-shaped valley and can often see all the way down to your ultimate destination, the Wenaha River. Fortunate hikers see bighorn sheep, elk, and black bears. The unlucky have to settle for the graceful, yet somewhat fearless, blue grouse, as well as white-tailed and mule deer and maybe a rattlesnake.

Once in the valley bottom, the trail follows cold, trout-filled Trout Creek for about three miles until it spills into Third Creek. The trail then continues downstream for another three miles to the mouth of Third Creek at Crooked Creek and joins that river as it weaves its way south for three more miles. Just before crossing over into Oregon, leave the Crooked Creek Trail at Slide

Creek and climb Three Forks Trail to the southern trailhead.

If you plan to retrace your steps rather than exit at the southern end of the trail, skip the hike up the Three Forks Trail. Instead, continue south on the Crooked Creek Trail for a few miles to its junction with the Wenaha River Trail. The Wenaha, a beautiful, clear wilderness river, really is worth seeing. Plan to spend at least a lunch break along its banks before heading back north.

Location: Southeast of Dayton in Umatilla National Forest within the Wenaha-Tucannon Wilderness; see Northeast Washington Map 4, grid g3.

User Groups: Hikers, dogs, and horses. No mountain bikes are allowed. No wheelchair facilities.

Permits: A federal Northwest Forest Pass, $5 per day or $30 annually, is required to park at the trailhead. Passes are available from ranger stations and many private vendors, online at website: www.wta.org, or by calling 800/270-7504.

Maps: For a trail information report, contact the Pomeroy Ranger District at 509/843-1891. For a map of Umatilla National Forest, contact Nature of the Northwest Information Center, 800 Northeast Oregon Street, Suite 177, Portland, OR 97232; 503/872-2750. Ask the USGS for topographic maps of the Panjab Creek, Oregon Butte, Diamond Peak, and Eden areas.

Directions: From Dayton drive 14 miles northeast on U.S. 12 to Tucannon Road. Turn right (south) onto Tucannon Road and continue 35 miles to a junction. Take the right fork up Panjab Road/Forest Service Road 4713 and continue 2.8 miles to the Panjab Trailhead on the right. To reach the southern trailhead, from Pomeroy drive 35 miles south on Mountain Road/Forest Service Road 40, around the eastern boundary of the Wenaha-Tucannon Wilderness, to a junction with Forest Service Road 4039. Turn right onto Forest Service Road 4039 and continue to the Three Forks Trailhead.

Contact: Umatilla National Forest, Pomeroy Ranger District, 71 West Main Street, Pomeroy, WA 99347; 509/843-1891.

16 Meadow Creek
8.0 mi/4.0 hrs

Both ends of the trail are accessible by car, and the two trailheads are only four trail miles apart. But shuttling cars between the trailheads can require nearly 90 miles of driving, making this hike a better round-trip than one-way trip. Until recently, the trail weaved back and forth across Meadow Creek several times, but a reconstruction project eliminated those repeat fords and keeps hikers from crossing the creek until near the end of the trail—and then there is a bridge. Even with the new trail, the creek is always close enough to see and enjoy, and it provides for lush greenery. Some campsites are set up along the way, and because this is a short trail, few campers compete for them. Families with small children will enjoy the trail, thanks to the short hike into the campsites and the plentiful water supply (both for drinking and playing in).

Location: South of Dayton in Umatilla National Forest; see Northeast Washington Map 4, grid g3.

User Groups: Hikers, dogs, horses, and mountain bikes. No wheelchair facilities.

Permits: A federal Northwest Forest Pass, $5 per day or $30 annually, is required to park at the trailhead. Passes are available from ranger stations and many private vendors, online at website: www.wta.org, or by calling 800/270-7504.

Maps: For a trail information report, contact the Pomeroy Ranger District at 509/843-1891. For a map of Umatilla National Forest, contact Nature of the Northwest Information Center, 800 Northeast Oregon Street, Suite 177, Portland, OR 97232; 503/872-2750. Ask the USGS for topographic maps of the Eckler Mountain and Panjab Spring areas.

Directions: From Dayton drive 14 miles northeast on U.S. 12 to Tucannon Road. Turn right (south) onto Tucannon Road and continue 35 miles to a junction. Take the right fork up Panjab Creek Road/Forest Service Road 4713 and continue 4.1 miles to the road's end and the trailhead. To reach the upper trailhead, from Dayton drive south on Fourth Avenue and turn left onto Eckler Mountain Road/County Road 9124. Follow this road about 28 miles south (it becomes Forest Service Road 46 at the forest boundary) to Godman Camp, an old ranger guard station and camping area. The Meadow Creek Trail begins here.

Contact: Umatilla National Forest, Pomeroy Ranger District, 71 West Main Street, Pomeroy, WA 99347; 509/843-1891.

🔲 East Butte
12.0 mi/6.0 hrs

The trailhead sits on a broad bench overlooking the Wenaha Valley. At the left end of the bench, one trail leads up to the old fire lookout on the top of Oregon Butte. The East Butte Trail drops straight off the edge of the bench and winds down through a series of switchbacks into the valley. Before starting, take a minute to look down onto the ponderosa pine and rimrock meadows that you will be venturing through. A close look almost always reveals deer or elk somewhere in the thousands of acres of viewable wilderness before you. If you don't see anything, don't worry. Start down the steep trail and keep a keen eye out as you hike. You may see mule deer, elk, or—if you are really lucky—a big, silent cougar. The steep descent tapers

off at the headwaters of East Butte Creek and then almost levels off as it follows the water downstream to its junction with King Creek. The official maintained trail ends here, but horse packers frequently push onward to a faint trail that leads all the way down to the main branch of Butte Creek. That bushwhacking adventure adds just over seven miles to the total round-trip distance of the hike.

Location: South of Dayton in Umatilla National Forest within the Wenaha-Tucannon Wilderness; see Northeast Washington Map 4, grid g3.

User Groups: Hikers, dogs, and horses. No mountain bikes are allowed. No wheelchair facilities.

Permits: A federal Northwest Forest Pass, $5 per day or $30 annually, is required to park at the trailhead. Passes are available from ranger stations and many private vendors, online at website: www.wta.org, or by calling 800/270-7504.

Maps: For a trail information report, contact the Pomeroy Ranger District at 509/843-1891. For a map of Umatilla National Forest, contact Nature of the Northwest Information Center, 800 Northeast Oregon Street, Suite 177, Portland, OR 97232; 503/872-2750. Ask the USGS for a topographic map of the Oregon Butte area.

Directions: From Dayton drive south on Fourth Avenue and turn left onto Eckler Mountain Road/County Road 9124. Follow this road about 28 miles south (it becomes Forest Service Road 46 at the forest boundary) to Godman Camp, an old ranger guard station and camping area. Turn left (east) onto Forest Service Road 4608 and drive seven miles to the Teepee Trailhead at the road's end.

Contact: Umatilla National Forest, Pomeroy Ranger District, 71 West Main Street, Pomeroy, WA 99347; 509/843-1891.

18 Turkey Creek
8.0 mi/4.0 hrs

Enjoy the views at the trailhead, which is one of the best overlook points of the upper Wenaha River drainage. Once you start down the trail, the views are pretty much limited to the surrounding forest. Of course, if you like forest hikes, this is a fantastic trail. It drops from Teepee down into the Turkey Creek Basin and then follows the creek from its headwaters down to its mouth, emptying into Panjab Creek. Huckleberries grow along the trail, and deer often graze here. Cougars and bobcats live here, but they're elusive and seldom seen. You find campsites scattered along the route, with the best sites at the bottom of the trail, where Panjab and Turkey Creeks join. The hike back to Teepee isn't too difficult, and the views at the trailhead provide a welcome change from the dark forest.

Location: South of Dayton in Umatilla National Forest within the Wenaha-Tucannon Wilderness; see Northeast Washington Map 4, grid g3.

User Groups: Hikers, dogs, and horses. No mountain bikes are allowed. No wheelchair facilities.

Permits: A federal Northwest Forest Pass, $5 per day or $30 annually, is required to park at the trailhead. Passes are available from ranger stations and many private vendors, online at website: www.wta.org, or by calling 800/270-7504.

Maps: For a trail information report, contact the Pomeroy Ranger District at 509/843-1891. For a map of Umatilla National Forest, contact Nature of the Northwest Information Center, 800 Northeast Oregon Street, Suite 177, Portland, OR 97232; 503/872-2750. Ask the USGS for topographic maps of the Oregon Butte, Eden, and Diamond Peak areas.

Directions: From Dayton drive south on Fourth Avenue and turn left onto Eckler Mountain Road/County Road 9124. Follow this road about 28 miles south (it becomes Forest Service Road 46 at the forest boundary) to Godman Camp, an old ranger guard station and camping area. Turn left (east) onto Forest Service Road 4608 and drive seven miles to the Teepee Trailhead at the road's end.

Contact: Umatilla National Forest, Pomeroy Ranger District, 71 West Main Street, Pomeroy, WA 99347; 509/843-1891.

19 Smooth Ridge
40.0 mi/2.0–3.0 days

Start with a 3.5-mile hike to 6,401-foot Oregon Butte. After enjoying the panoramic views from the lookout tower, continue out along a long, narrow ridge to Danger Point. From Danger Point the route continues to descend gradually while passing an assortment of cold springs—McBain, Ruth, Taylor, Huckleberry, Rettkowski, and Lodgepole. The trail climbs slightly from Lodgepole Spring to Weller Butte, then after another long ridge run, drops steeply into the Wenaha River Valley. The high, lonesome nature of this trail, with the abundance of fresh, cool water, makes this a great trip for backpackers. The views are endless and fantastic, the wildlife is plentiful and visible, and the hiking is easy and enjoyable.

Location: South of Dayton in Umatilla National Forest within the Wenaha-Tucannon Wilderness; see Northeast Washington Map 4, grid g3.

User Groups: Hikers, dogs, and horses. No mountain bikes are allowed. No wheelchair facilities.

Permits: A federal Northwest Forest Pass, $5 per day or $30 annually, is required to park at the trailhead. Passes are available from ranger stations and many private

vendors, online at website: www.wta.org, or by calling 800/270-7504.

Maps: For a trail information report, contact the Pomeroy Ranger District at 509/843-1891. For a map of Umatilla National Forest, contact Nature of the Northwest Information Center, 800 Northeast Oregon Street, Suite 177, Portland, OR 97232; 503/872-2750. Ask the USGS for topographic maps of the Oregon Butte, Eden, and Diamond Peak areas.

Directions: From Dayton drive south on Fourth Avenue and turn left onto Eckler Mountain Road/County Road 9124. Follow this road about 28 miles south (it becomes Forest Service Road 46 at the forest boundary) to Godman Camp, an old ranger guard station and camping area. Turn left (east) onto Forest Service Road 4608 and drive seven miles to the Teepee Trailhead at the road's end.

Contact: Umatilla National Forest, Pomeroy Ranger District, 71 West Main Street, Pomeroy, WA 99347; 509/843-1891.

20 Oregon Butte
6.0 mi/3.0 hrs

Oregon Butte isn't the tallest of the Blue Mountain peaks, but it does claim the greatest local prominence. That is, it rises significantly higher than the surrounding peaks, so the views from the summit are particularly stunning. That prominence inspired the Forest Service to build a fire lookout tower here, one of the few wilderness fire lookouts still staffed in the summer months. The trail leaves the north end of the parking area at Teepee and climbs slowly but steadily through a series of open meadow switchbacks and patches of thick pine and larch forest. A pair of springs provide cold water along the way. At the 6,401-foot summit, enjoy views south to the Wallowa and Seven Devil ranges flanking Hells Canyon on the Snake River.

Location: South of Dayton in Umatilla National Forest within the Wenaha-Tucannon Wilderness; see Northeast Washington Map 4, grid g4.

User Groups: Hikers, dogs, and horses. No mountain bikes. No wheelchair facilities.

Permits: A federal Northwest Forest Pass, $5 per day or $30 annually, is required to park at the trailhead. Passes are available from ranger stations and many private vendors, online at website: www.wta.org, or by calling 800/270-7504.

Maps: For a trail information report, contact the Pomeroy Ranger District at 509/843-1891. For a map of Umatilla National Forest, contact Nature of the Northwest Information Center, 800 Northeast Oregon Street, Suite 177, Portland, OR 97232; 503/872-2750. Ask the USGS for a topographic map of the Oregon Butte area.

Directions: From Dayton drive south on Fourth Avenue and turn left onto Eckler Mountain Road/County Road 9124. Follow this road about 28 miles south (it becomes Forest Service Road 46 at the forest boundary) to Godman Camp, an old ranger guard station and camping area. Turn left (east) onto Forest Service Road 4608 and drive seven miles to the Teepee Trailhead at the road's end.

Contact: Umatilla National Forest, Pomeroy Ranger District, 71 West Main Street, Pomeroy, WA 99347; 509/843-1891.

21 West Butte
16.0 mi/1.0–2.0 days

Godman Camp is in a scenic little basin of meadows and forest, with a deep, cold spring just across the road from the ranger buildings. The trailhead is on the upper end of the largest meadow and drops off the south side of the road. It begins with a traverse across a hillside meadow, then gradually drops into a network of small creek valleys that feed into Butte Creek Valley, which in turn drops into the Wenaha River Valley. The biggest and prettiest creek you cross en route to Butte Creek is Rainbow, a small, gurgling stream with good campsites along its banks. The trail continues past Rainbow Creek to Butte Creek and a junction with the East Butte Trail (see hike this chapter). Backtrack to the Godman Trailhead, or if you have arranged a car shuttle, follow the East Butte Trail north to Teepee.

Location: South of Dayton in Umatilla National Forest within the Wenaha-Tucannon Wilderness; see Northeast Washington Map 4, grid g3.

User Groups: Hikers, dogs, and horses. No mountain bikes are allowed. No wheelchair facilities.

Permits: A federal Northwest Forest Pass, $5 per day or $30 annually, is required to park at the trailhead. Passes are available from ranger stations and many private vendors, online at website: www.wta.org, or by calling 800/270-7504.

Maps: For a trail information report, contact the Pomeroy Ranger District at 509/843-1891. For a map of Umatilla National Forest, contact Nature of the Northwest Information Center, 800 Northeast Oregon Street, Suite 177, Portland, OR 97232; 503/872-2750. Ask the USGS for topographic maps of the Oregon Butte, Eden, and Diamond Peak areas.

Directions: From Dayton drive south on Fourth Avenue and turn left onto Eckler Mountain Road/County Road 9124. Follow this road about 28 miles south (it becomes Forest Service Road 46 at the forest boundary) to Godman Camp, an old ranger guard station and camping area. The trailhead is near the ranger station's horse barn. For a one-way hike, shuttle a car to Teepee Camp. To get there from Godman, turn left (east) onto Forest Service Road 4608 and drive

seven miles to the Teepee Trailhead at the road's end.

Contact: Umatilla National Forest, Pomeroy Ranger District, 71 West Main Street, Pomeroy, WA 99347; 509/843-1891.

22 Grizzley Bear
15.0 mi/7.5 hrs

The first few miles of trail are on an old, reclaimed road that was once abandoned and then converted into a single track after the wilderness area was created in the late 1970s. Still, the route is scenic and barely resembles a road. (Of course even when it was open as a road, it barely resembled a road!) One short, steep climb is all that interrupts the tranquil pleasure of hiking the first few ridgetop miles. As the route breaks out of the ponderosa pine forest for good at the end of the ridge, the trail drops through a long series of steep, dusty switchbacks to the Wenaha River, nearly 2,000 feet below. Summer hikers will do well to follow an example set by longtime wilderness travelers here (especially horse packers): stash some cold beverages in the deep, shaded recess under the rotted-out roots of "the beer tree" at the crest of the hill. The deep, dark hole keeps them from getting hot, although they won't stay ice cold. But after making the long, dusty, hot climb out of the valley in the full glare of the sun, any liquid that's even mildly cold tastes great. At the lower end of the trail, a series of pleasant and cool campsites lie in the open ponderosa pine forest along the north bank of the Wenaha River.

The grizzly bears that gave their name to this trail (even if it is misspelled) left long ago, but plenty of black bears are near. If you are planning to catch some of the big trout in the Wenaha, make sure you kill the fish at least a hundred yards from camp. Hang all food and cooking utensils well outside camp.

Location: South of Pomeroy in Umatilla National Forest within the Wenaha-Tucannon Wilderness; see Northeast Washington Map 4, grid g3.

User Groups: Hikers, dogs, and horses. No mountain bikes are allowed. No wheelchair facilities.

Permits: A federal Northwest Forest Pass, $5 per day or $30 annually, is required to park at the trailhead. Passes are available from ranger stations and many private vendors, online at website: www.wta.org, or by calling 800/270-7504.

Maps: For a trail information report, contact the Pomeroy Ranger District at 509/843-1891. For a map of Umatilla National Forest, contact Nature of the Northwest Information Center, 800 Northeast Oregon Street, Suite 177, Portland, OR 97232; 503/872-2750. Ask the USGS for a topographic map of the Stentz Spring area.

Directions: From Dayton drive south on Fourth Avenue, which becomes North Touchet Road at the city limits and then Forest Service Road 64 at the forest boundary. Continue on up the valley past Ski Bluewood Ski Area. At the fork at the top of the long hill, turn left (east) onto Forest Service Road 46 (about 26 miles from Dayton). Drive nearly five miles to the junction with Forest Service Road 300 (marked Twin Buttes). Turn right and drive about five miles to Twin Buttes Spring. Stay left at the fork and continue another half mile to the road's end and the trailhead.

Contact: Umatilla National Forest, Pomeroy Ranger District, 71 West Main Street, Pomeroy, WA 99347; 509/843-1891.

23 Tucannon River

8.2 mi/4.1 hrs

This pleasant river hike provides plenty of opportunities to step off the trail and relax alongside a rushing trout stream. You often see deer and elk in the valley, and sometimes you see bighorn sheep on the valley walls. Several good campsites line the route, the largest being Ruchert Camp less than a mile up the trail. The fishing is fine here, and the trail's gentle slope, easy water availability, and assortment of campsites make this a wonderful trail for backpacking with kids. Youngsters will enjoy playing near the water and catching trout in the river's deep pools and eddies. With less than 200 feet of elevation gain per mile, the route makes for easy hiking, both for short-legged kids and parents carrying heavy packs.

Location: Southeast of Dayton in Umatilla National Forest; see Northeast Washington Map 4, grid g4.

User Groups: Hikers, dogs, and horses. No mountain bikes are allowed. No wheelchair facilities.

Permits: A federal Northwest Forest Pass, $5 per day or $30 annually, is required to park at the trailhead. Passes are available from ranger stations and many private vendors, online at website: www.wta.org, or by calling 800/270-7504.

Maps: For a trail information report, contact the Pomeroy Ranger District at 509/843-1891. For a map of Umatilla National Forest, contact Nature of the Northwest Information Center, 800 Northeast Oregon Street, Suite 177, Portland, OR 97232; 503/872-2750. Ask the USGS for a topographic map of the Stentz Spring area.

Directions: From Dayton drive 14 miles northeast on U.S. 12 to Tucannon Road. Turn right (south) onto Tucannon Road and continue 35 miles to a junction. Take the left fork up Forest Service Road 4712 and continue five miles to the road's end and the trailhead.

Contact: Umatilla National Forest, Pomeroy Ranger District, 71 West Main Street, Pomeroy, WA 99347; 509/843-1891.

24 Mount Misery
32.0 mi/2.0–3.0 days

Don't be daunted by the length of this trail. It is long, but it's also very pleasant, gaining just 400 feet in elevation over the 16-mile length. The trail weaves through open pine and fir forests, as well as broad, sun-filled meadows. The first point of interest is Diamond Springs at mile two, a large campsite at the intersection of three wonderful wilderness trails. The Mount Misery Trail is the middle one and heads due west on the long, flat top of Horse Ridge. The views from the meadows along the route take in the surrounding Wenaha-Tucannon Wilderness peaks and the more distant summits of the Wallowa and Seven Devil ranges in Oregon. About three miles into the hike, you reach Sheephead Springs, a popular horse camp and a good source of water. You see a corral made from native lodgepole pines against the trees at the edge of a large camp. Farther down the trail, other springs (some routed through troughs hewn of single logs) provide cold water for hikers and for wildlife—these are good places to find deer and elk in the summer. Campsites are numerous along the route all the way to its end; the best are in the immediate vicinity of the springs. We can't decide which spring offers the prettiest setting, but you really can't go wrong at any of them.

Location: South of Pomeroy in Umatilla National Forest within the Wenaha-Tucannon Wilderness; see Northeast Washington Map 4, grid g5.

User Groups: Hikers, dogs, and horses. No mountain bikes are allowed. No wheelchair facilities.

Permits: A federal Northwest Forest Pass, $5 per day or $30 annually, is required to park at the trailhead. Passes are available from ranger stations and many private vendors,

online at website: www.wta.org, or by calling 800/270-7504.

Maps: For a trail information report, contact the Pomeroy Ranger District at 509/843-1891. For a map of Umatilla National Forest, contact Nature of the Northwest Information Center, 800 Northeast Oregon Street, Suite 177, Portland, OR 97232; 503/872-2750. Ask the USGS for a topographic map of the Diamond Peak area.

Directions: From Pomeroy drive about 10 miles south on Benjamin Gulch Road/County Road 128 to a fork. Continue along the left fork onto Mountain Road/Forest Service Road 40 and then proceed some 24 miles to Misery Springs and a junction with Forest Service Road 4030. Turn right (west) onto the Forest Service road and drive five miles to the Diamond Trailhead at the road's end.

Contact: Umatilla National Forest, Pomeroy Ranger District, 71 West Main Street, Pomeroy, WA 99347; 509/843-1891.

25 Melton Creek
22.4 mi/1.0–2.0 days

Hike 1.5 miles up the Mount Misery Trail (see hike above) to the first fork, Diamond Springs, and turn left. That first stretch is popular, but only because Diamond Springs is the hub of activity in this neck of the woods. Fortunately, most of the traffic at Diamond Springs continues up the other two trails that leave from there. This route, by contrast, is seldom used, although why people ignore it is a mystery.

The trail stays up on a ridgetop for roughly 2.5 miles, offering great views of Diamond Peak, Chaparral Basin, and Halsey Butte. The route then drops several miles into the Melton Creek Valley, a deep, steep-walled canyon. Sparse ponderosa pine forest lines the valley floor, and steep cheat-grass meadows lined with black basalt rimrock cliffs make up the walls. Campsites are scarce, but people are even scarcer, so there should be no problem finding a good site. The best camping is found at the end of the trail, where Melton Creek empties into Crooked Creek. From there turn around and head back up the hot, dry Melton Creek Canyon to the trailhead.

Location: South of Pomeroy in Umatilla National Forest within the Wenaha-Tucannon Wilderness; see Northeast Washington Map 4, grid h5.

User Groups: Hikers, dogs, and horses. No mountain bikes are allowed. No wheelchair facilities.

Permits: A federal Northwest Forest Pass, $5 per day or $30 annually, is required to park at the trailhead. Passes are available from ranger stations and many private vendors, online at website: www.wta.org, or by calling 800/270-7504.

Maps: For a trail information report, contact the Pomeroy Ranger District at 509/843-1891. For a map of Umatilla National Forest, contact Nature of the Northwest Information Center, 800 Northeast Oregon Street, Suite 177, Portland, OR 97232; 503/872-2750. Ask the USGS for a topographic map of the Diamond Peak area.

Directions: From Pomeroy drive about 10 miles south on Benjamin Gulch Road/County Road 128 to a fork. Continue along the left fork onto Mountain Road/Forest Service Road 40 and then proceed some 24 miles to Misery Springs and a junction with Forest Service Road 4030. Turn right (west) onto the Forest Service road and drive five miles to the Diamond Trailhead and the road's end.

Contact: Umatilla National Forest, Pomeroy Ranger District, 71 West Main Street, Pomeroy, WA 99347; 509/843-1891.

26 Jelly Springs
9.0 mi/4.5 hrs

On the flank of Diamond Peak, the Jelly Springs Trail begins high, offering fine views of the 6,300-foot summit, and then gradually drops into the Tucannon River Valley. For the first 1.5 miles, Jelly Springs follows the same route as the Mount Misery Trail (see hike in this chapter).

At the first fork in the trail, turn right and continue down the valley wall through thick lodgepole and whitebark pine into the upper Tucannon Valley. The river is clear and cold, fed by numerous deep springs, including Jelly Springs, which you pass well up the trail. Anglers will appreciate the healthy population of rainbow trout in the river and the paucity of biting insects.

Location: South of Pomeroy in the Umatilla National Forest within the Wenaha-Tucannon Wilderness; see Northeast Washington Map 4, grid h5.

User Groups: Hikers, dogs, and horses. No mountain bikes are allowed. No wheelchair facilities.

Permits: A federal Northwest Forest Pass, $5 per day or $30 annually, is required to park at the trailhead. Passes are available from ranger stations and many private vendors, online at website: www.wta.org, or by calling 800/270-7504.

Maps: For a trail information report, contact the Pomeroy Ranger District at 509/843-1891. For a map of Umatilla National Forest, contact Nature of the Northwest Information Center, 800 Northeast Oregon Street, Suite 177, Portland, OR 97232; 503/872-2750. Ask the USGS for topographic maps of the Stentz Spring and Diamond Peak areas.

Directions: From Pomeroy, drive about 10 miles south on Benjamin Gulch Road/County Road 128 until you reach a fork in the road. Continue along the left fork on Mountain

Road/Forest Service Road 40 and then proceed some 24 miles to Misery Springs and a junction with Forest Service Road 4030. Turn right (west) onto the Forest Service road and drive five more miles to the Diamond Trailhead at the road's end.

Contact: Umatilla National Forest, Pomeroy Ranger District, 71 West Main Street, Pomeroy, WA 99347; 509/843-1891.

☐☐ Ranger Creek
6.0 mi/3.0 hrs

This trail quickly turns steep, dropping into the Ranger Creek Basin and following that creek down to the Menatchee River. The trailhead offers the only views, but the scenic vistas are enough to satisfy. Before dropping into the valley, look southeast to the rising forms of the Wallowa and Seven Devil ranges bordering Hells Canyon on the Snake River. When you have your fill, continue down to the Menatchee River, which is small and soothing and has plenty of places to camp along its pretty banks. The trail follows the river downstream, and while the official maintained trail peters out, an old, faint packer's trail continues downstream into the scrub-brush and rimrock country near the Grande Ronde River before disappearing and forcing hikers to retrace their steps. Look for bighorn sheep at this far end of the trail.

Location: South of Pomeroy in Umatilla National Forest; see Northeast Washington Map 4, grid h6.

User Groups: Hikers, dogs, and horses. No mountain bikes are allowed. No wheelchair facilities.

Permits: A federal Northwest Forest Pass, $5 per day or $30 annually, is required to park at the trailhead. Passes are available from ranger stations and many private vendors, online at website: www.wta.org, or by calling 800/270-7504.

Maps: For a trail information report, contact the Pomeroy Ranger District at 509/843-1891. For a map of Umatilla National Forest, contact Nature of the Northwest Information Center, 800 Northeast Oregon Street, Suite 177, Portland, OR 97232; 503/872-2750. Ask the USGS for a topographic map of the Diamond Peak area.

Directions: From Pomeroy drive 10 miles south on Benjamin Gulch Road/County Road 128 to a fork. Continue along the left fork onto Mountain Road/Forest Service Road 40 and then proceed some 24 miles to a three-way fork, marked Troy Junction. Turn left onto Forest Service Road 44 and drive four miles to another junction. Bear left onto Forest Service Road 43 and drive 2.5 miles to the trailhead on the right.

Contact: Umatilla National Forest, Pomeroy Ranger District, 71 West Main Street, Pomeroy, WA 99347; 509/843-1891.

☐☐ Slick Ear
10.4 mi/5.0 hrs

The upper trail weaves through old-growth pine forest, accented by the "whomp, whomp, whomp" calls of the local grouse population. Shortly after passing a sign marking the Washington/Oregon state line about 1.5 miles in, the trail drops into a clearing with awesome views down into the Wenaha River Valley. From here the trail drops steeply through a long series of rocky switchbacks for roughly 2.5 miles before returning to the forest. The last mile is brushy and muddy in places; the hillside spring along the trail contributed to both conditions. At the bottom of the route, the trail intercepts the Wenaha River Trail at a broad, open campsite. For better camping areas, head downstream along the river trail for a few hundred yards. The Wenaha River supports a healthy population of wild rainbow trout, and the

surrounding valley supports healthy populations of deer, elk, and black bear.

Location: South of Dayton in Umatilla National Forest within the Wenaha-Tucannon
Wilderness; see Northeast Washington Map
4, grid h3.

User Groups: Hikers, dogs, and horses. No
mountain bikes are allowed. No wheelchair
facilities.

Permits: A federal Northwest Forest Pass,
$5 per day or $30 annually, is required to park
at the trailhead. Passes are available from
ranger stations and many private vendors,
online at website: www.wta.org, or by calling 800/270-7504.

Maps: For a trail information report, contact
the Pomeroy Ranger District at 509/843-1891.
For a map of Umatilla National Forest, contact Nature of the Northwest Information
Center, 800 Northeast Oregon Street, Suite
177, Portland, OR 97232; 503/872-2750. Ask
the USGS for topographic maps of the Godman Springs and Wenaha Forks areas.

Directions: From Dayton drive south on Fourth
Avenue, which becomes North Touchet Road at
the city limits and Forest Service Road 64 at
the forest boundary. Continue on up the valley
past Ski Bluewood Ski Area. At the fork at the
top of the long hill, turn left (east) onto Forest
Service Road 46 (about 26 miles from Dayton).
Drive nearly five miles to the junction with Forest Service Road 300 (marked Twin Buttes).
Turn right and drive to Twin Buttes Spring. Stay
right at the fork and continue another 1.5 miles
to the road's end and the trailhead.

Contact: Umatilla National Forest, Pomeroy
Ranger District, 71 West Main Street,
Pomeroy, WA 99347; 509/843-1891.

29 Packers Trail
18.0 mi/1.0–2.0 days

The route drops three miles down to the
Crooked Creek Valley and then goes upstream

for a half mile, where the actual Packers Trail
starts. It then turns right off the Crooked
Creek Trail and climbs gradually to the top of
Moore Flat and Smooth Ridge. From the trail's
end at the ridgetop, enjoy views into the
sparsely wooded valleys of Crooked Creek
and Three Fork Drainage. One note: the
scarcity of trees makes the hike hot on long
summer days and wet on rainy days.

Location: South of Pomeroy in Umatilla National Forest within the Wenaha-Tucannon
Wilderness; see Northeast Washington Map
4, grid h6.

User Groups: Hikers, dogs, and horses. No
mountain bikes are allowed. No wheelchair
facilities.

Permits: A federal Northwest Forest Pass,
$5 per day or $30 annually, is required to park
at the trailhead. Passes are available from
ranger stations and many private vendors,
online at website: www.wta.org, or by calling 800/270-7504.

Maps: For a trail information report, contact
the Pomeroy Ranger District at 509/843-1891.
For a map of Umatilla National Forest, contact Nature of the Northwest Information
Center, 800 Northeast Oregon Street, Suite
177, Portland, OR 97232; 503/872-2750. Ask
the USGS for a topographic map of the Diamond Peak area.

Directions: From Pomeroy drive 35 miles
south on Mountain Road/Forest Service
Road 40 around the eastern boundary of the
Wenaha-Tucannon Wilderness to a junction
with Forest Service Road 4039. Turn right and
continue to the Three Forks Trailhead.

Contact: Umatilla National Forest, Pomeroy
Ranger District, 71 West Main Street,
Pomeroy, WA 99347; 509/843-1891.

OREGON
THE OREGON COAST

Oregon Regions

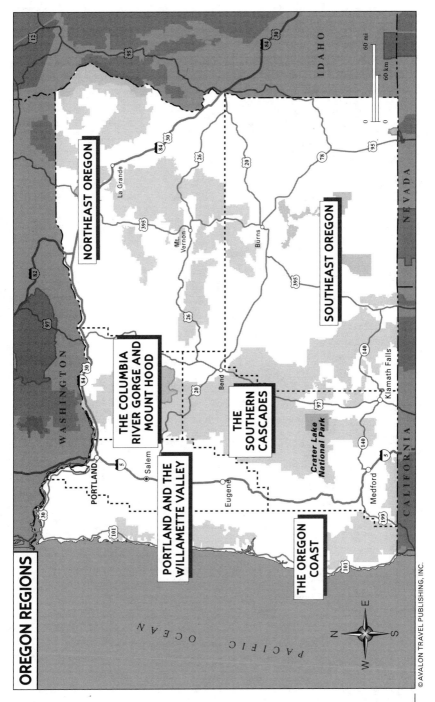

OREGON REGIONS

NORTHEAST OREGON

SOUTHEAST OREGON

THE COLUMBIA RIVER GORGE AND MOUNT HOOD

THE SOUTHERN CASCADES

PORTLAND AND THE WILLAMETTE VALLEY

THE OREGON COAST

WASHINGTON

IDAHO

NEVADA

CALIFORNIA

PACIFIC OCEAN

La Grande

Mt. Vernon

Burns

Bend

Klamath Falls

Crater Lake National Park

Salem

PORTLAND

Eugene

Medford

© AVALON TRAVEL PUBLISHING, INC.

60 mi

60 km

The Oregon Coast

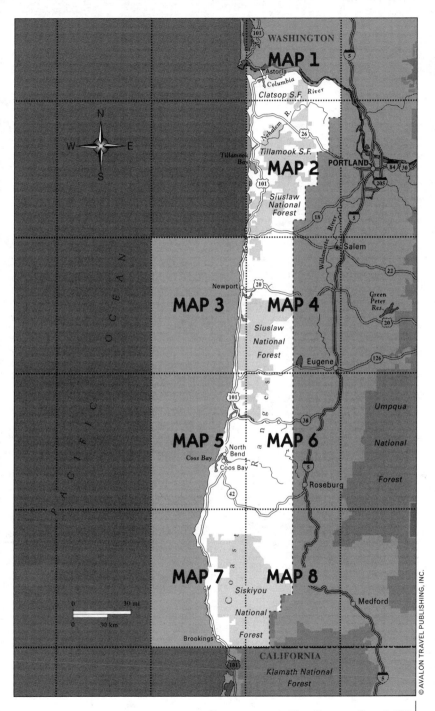

Map 1

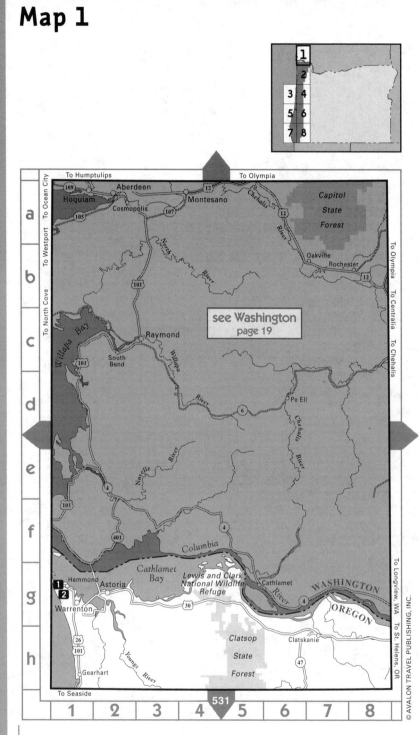

Map 2

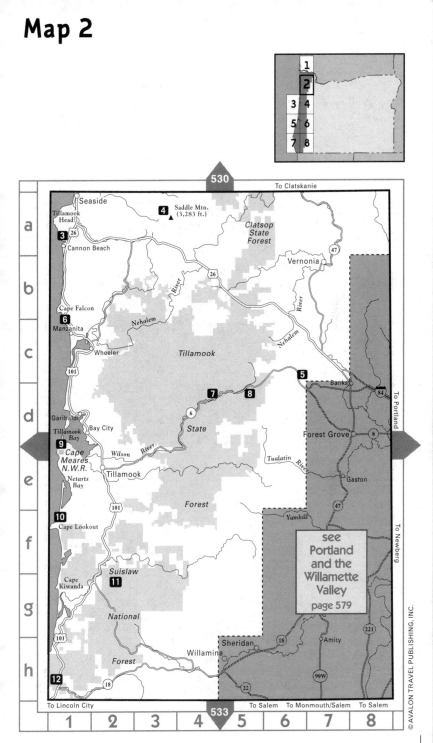

530

To Clatskanie

a

Seaside
Tillamook
Head
3 26
Cannon Beach
Saddle Mtn.
(3,283 ft.)
4

Clatsop
State
Forest

47
Vernonia

b

26

River

Cape Falcon
6
Manzanita

Nehalem

River

Nehalem

c

Wheeler

101

Tillamook

5
Banks

84

To Portland

7   **8**

d

6

State

Garibaldi
Tillamook
Bay
Bay City
9
Cape
Meares
N.W.R.

Wilson   River

Forest Grove

8

Tualatin   River

e

Netarts
Bay

Tillamook

Gaston

47

10

Forest

Yamhill

To Newberg

f

Cape Lookout

101

see
Portland
and the
Willamette
Valley
page 579

g

Cape
Kiwanda

Suislaw
11

National

221

h

Cape
Kiwanda
12

18

Sheridan
18
Amity

Willamina

Forest

99W

22

To Lincoln City

To Salem   To Monmouth/Salem   To Salem

© AVALON TRAVEL PUBLISHING, INC.

533

1   2   3   4   5   6   7   8

1 2 3 4 5 6 7 8

Map 3

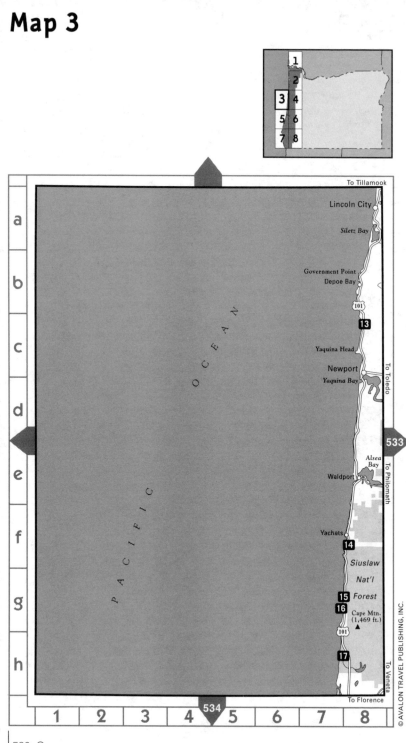

Lincoln City

Siletz Bay

Government Point
Depoe Bay

101

13

Yaquina Head

Newport
Yaquina Bay

To Toledo

533

To Philomath

Alsea Bay

Waldport

Yachats

14

Siuslaw

Nat'l

15 *Forest*

16

Cape Mtn.
(1,469 ft.)
▲

101

17

To Veneta

To Florence

534

© AVALON TRAVEL PUBLISHING, INC.

1 2 3 4 5 6 7 8

Map 4

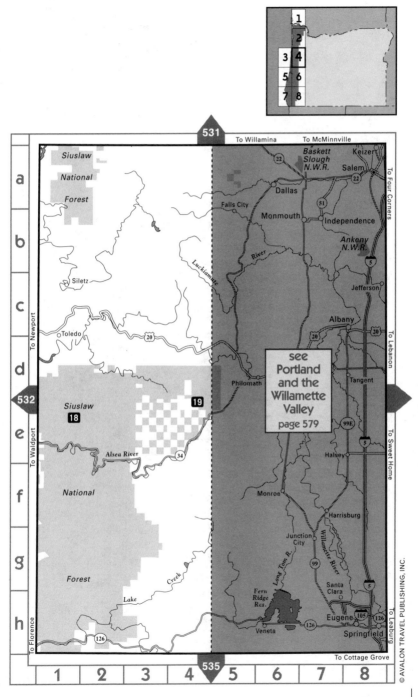

531
To Willamina   To McMinnville

a

Siuslaw

National

Forest

Baskett
Slough
N.W.R.
Keizer
22
Salem
22

To Four Corners

Falls City
Dallas
51
Monmouth   Independence

b

Siletz
Luckiamute River
Ankeny
N.W.R.
5

c

To Newport
Toledo
20
Jefferson

Albany
20
20

To Lebanon

d

532

Siuslaw
18   19

Philomath
Tangent

see
**Portland
and the
Willamette
Valley**
page 579

e

To Waldport

Alsea River
34
99E
5

Halsey

To Sweet Home

f

National

Monroe

Harrisburg

g

Forest
Creek

Lake
Junction
City
99
Willamette River
5

To Leaburg

h

To Florence
126
Fern
Ridge
Res.
Veneta
126
Long Tom R.
Santa
Clara
Eugene
105   126
Springfield

To Cottage Grove

535

1   2   3   4   5   6   7   8

© AVALON TRAVEL PUBLISHING, INC.

Map 5

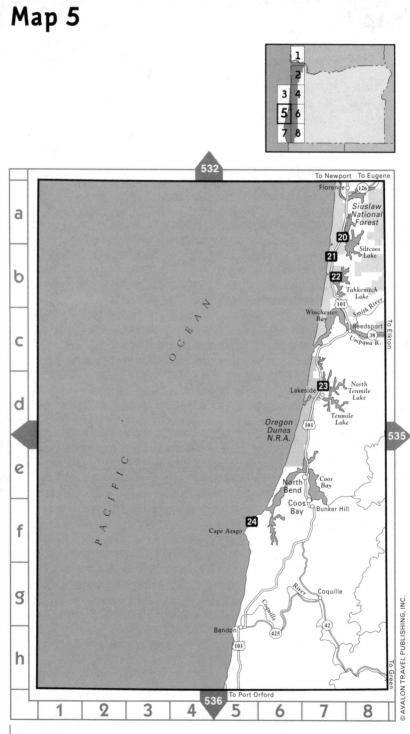

To Newport   To Eugene
Florence 126

Siuslaw
National
Forest

20

21 Siltcoos
Lake

22

Tahkenitch
Lake

101

Winchester Smith River
Bay

Reedsport
38 To Elkton

Umpqua R.

North
Tenmile
Lake

23

Lakeside

Tenmile
Lake

Oregon
Dunes
N.R.A.

101 535

Coos
Bay

North
Bend

Coos
Bay Bunker Hill

24

Cape Arago

Coquille

River

Coquille

42

Bandon

425

101

To Port Orford

536

© AVALON TRAVEL PUBLISHING, INC.

To Green

a b c d e f g h
1 2 3 4 5 6 7 8

P A C I F I C   O C E A N

Map 6

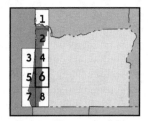

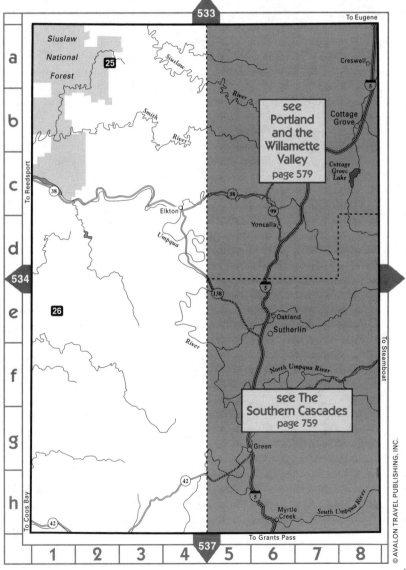

© AVALON TRAVEL PUBLISHING, INC.

Map 7

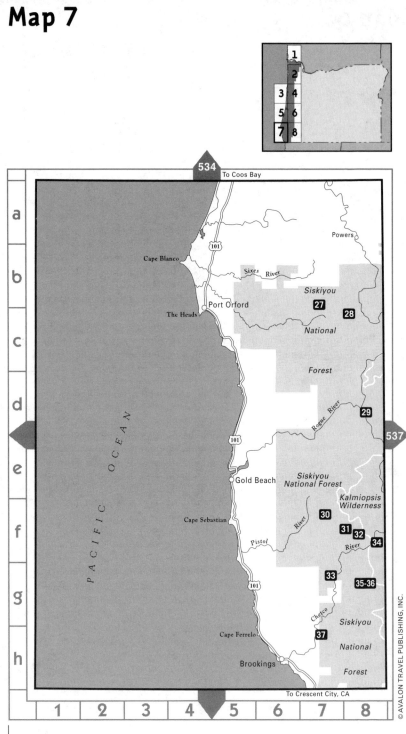

Powers

Cape Blanco

Sixes   River

Siskiyou

27   28

Port Orford

The Heads

National

Forest

Rogue River

29

PACIFIC   OCEAN

Gold Beach

Siskiyou
National Forest

Kalmiopsis
Wilderness

Cape Sebastian

River

30

31 32

34

Pistol

33

35-36

Chetco

Siskiyou

37

Cape Ferrelo

National

Brookings

Forest

537

Map 8

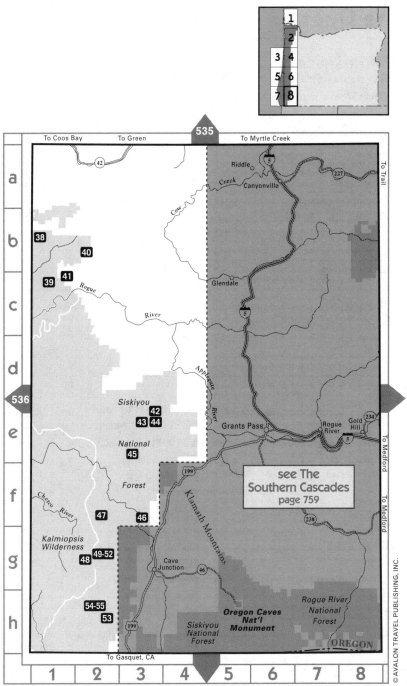

To Coos Bay   To Green   To Myrtle Creek
535

a

42
Riddle
Canyonville
227
To Trail

Cow
Creek

b

38
40
39 41
Rogue
Glendale

c

River
5

d

Applegate

536

e

Siskiyou
42
43 44
National
45
Grants Pass
Rogue River
Gold Hill
234
To Medford

f

Forest
46
199
see The
Southern Cascades
page 759
238
To Medford

Chetco River

g

47
46
Klamath Mountains
Cave Junction
46

Kalmiopsis
Wilderness
48 49-52

h

54-55
53
199
Siskiyou
National
Forest
Oregon Caves
Nat'l
Monument
Rogue River
National
Forest
OREGON

To Gasquet, CA

1   2   3   4   5   6   7   8

© AVALON TRAVEL PUBLISHING, INC.

The Oregon Coast

① Oregon Coast Trail
360 mi one way/
1.0 hr–1.0 lifetime

Call this a work in progress—and quite a fantastic one, at that. Eventually the distinctive gray cedar-post markers for the Oregon Coast Trail will be visible along the entire length of the rugged, spectacular coastline. Today about 80 percent of it is well developed, marked, and fairly heavily traveled. Much of the trail is on sandy beaches, some on footpaths over headlands, and some on roads and even city streets. The northern 60 miles between Fort Stevens and Tillamook Bay offer the best hiking. Many of those stretches are described in detail in other hike descriptions in this guide.

Whichever portion of this highly scenic trail you hike, make sure you come prepared. Weather changes rapidly, and you might be surprised at just how remote the Pacific beach can be even when you are fewer than a half dozen miles from the nearest seaside hotel. Unlike Washington coastal beach hikes, beach camping on this trail is either impractical or impossible. Be sure to obtain a copy of the Oregon Coast Trail brochure described below for route planning. It's an essential starting point for planning trips of any length on the Coastal Trail.

Location: Spanning the entire Oregon coast from the Columbia River west of Astoria to the California border south of Brookings; see The Oregon Coast Map 1, grid g1.

User Groups: Hikers, dogs, and horses. No mountain bikes are allowed. No wheelchair facilities.

Permits: No permits are required. A $3-per-vehicle access fee is collected at the Fort Stevens State Park entrance. Annual Oregon Parks and Recreation Passes, which replace the daily parking fee, are available for $25; contact Oregon Parks and Recreation Department, 1115 Commercial Street Northeast, Salem, OR 97301; 800/551-6949.

Maps: For an Oregon Coast Trail brochure, contact the Oregon Parks and Recreation Department at 800/551-6949. Ask the USGS for maps of popular northern portions of the trail, including the Clatsop Spit, Warrenton, Gearhart, Tillamook Head, Arch Cape, Nehalem, Garibaldi, Kilchis River, Tillamook, Netarts, and Sand Lake areas.

Directions: From Astoria drive four miles south on U.S. 101 (or about nine miles north of Seaside) to a signed turnoff to Fort Stevens State Park on the left. Turn left (west) and follow signs about four miles to the park. Inside the park follow signs to the South Jetty, four miles to the north.

Contact: Oregon Parks and Recreation Department, 1115 Commercial Street Northeast, Salem, OR 97301; 800/551-6949.

② Fort Stevens State Park
1.0–9.0 mi/0.5–4.5 hrs

Buried deep in the hearts of native Northwesterners worldwide are warm memories of childhood days spent exploring wonderful Fort Stevens State Park. The 3,700-acre park, weighing in as Oregon's third largest, combines sprawling sand dunes, pockets of forest, and miles of Oregon's vaunted pristine coastline into a package as convenient and accessible as any in the Pacific Northwest. It's also a historically fascinating region, with its own shipwreck and a handful of war relics.

But the true beauty of the park for hikers and cyclists is a magnificent trail system—the ribbon holding the Fort Stevens package together. The park's designers were far ahead of their time in establishing paved trails for cyclists and hikers, and years of heavy use haven't diminished the appeal of the trail network, which includes some nine miles of walking trails and 8.5 miles of cycle paths.

Hiking trails crisscross the park, but one of our lasting favorites is the mile-long path from the campground to the beach and what's left of the rusting hulk of the wreck of the Peter Iredale, a four-masted British ship that came ashore in 1906. Other trails lead three miles to an ocean observation platform, where there's good whale watching in season; about a mile to the explorable bunkers and gun emplacements of Battery Russell; and 2.4 miles in a loop around Coffenbury Lake, with a dozen other interesting points in between. The park also provides the northernmost access to the Oregon Coast Trail (see hike above). As a bonus, backpackers and cyclists have a section of the campground all to themselves, where no drive-in camping is permitted. By all means bring the kids to this one. It's an ideal place to break them in slowly—and instill some priceless outdoor memories they'll always treasure.

Location: Ten miles west of Astoria on the extreme northwest tip of Oregon; see The Oregon Coast Map 1, grid g1.

User Groups: Hikers, leashed dogs, and mountain bikes. No horses are allowed. Some of Fort Stevens' trails are paved and wheelchair accessible.

Permits: No permits are required. A $3 parking fee is collected at the park entrance. Annual Oregon Parks and Recreation Passes, which replace the daily parking fee, are available for $25; contact Oregon Parks and Recreation Department, 800/551-6949. The Oregon Pacific Coast Passport, a joint federal-state parking pass valid at 16 sites along the Oregon Coast, can be used in lieu of the parking fee. Coast Passports, $35 a year or $10 for five days, are available at local visitor centers.

Maps: For a free park brochure and map, contact Oregon Parks and Recreation Department at 800/551-6949. Ask the USGS for topographic maps of the Warrenton and Clatsop Spit areas.

Directions: From Astoria drive four miles south on U.S. 101 (or about nine miles north of Seaside) to a signed turnoff to Fort Stevens State Park on the left. Turn left (west) and follow signs about four miles to the park.

Contact: Oregon Parks and Recreation Department, 1115 Commercial Street Northeast, Salem, OR 97301; 800/551-6949.

🔳 Tillamook Head
5.0 mi/3.0 hrs

First-time visitors to Tillamook Head might have the feeling they've been here before. It could be the ghost of explorer William Clark fooling with your memory banks. But most likely you've seen the view on at least 100 nature calendars and other scenic photos. The Tillamook Head National Recreation Trail, which runs 6.9 miles from Ecola State Park north to Sunset Boulevard at the south end of Seaside, is quintessential Oregon Coast: views of the roiling Pacific foaming over jagged, rocky headlands, with a pinch of salty breeze and a hint of history accompanying every step. The trail, now part of the Oregon Coast Trail, follows the route Clark and other cohorts from the Lewis and Clark Expedition took over Tillamook Head in 1806. Clark "discovered" a path that likely had been used for time and eternity by both animals and local natives. Nevertheless, put on something wool and try to imagine you're Clark making the journey for the very first time. Come here off-season (dress warm), and it doesn't require an extensive leap of imagination.

Most people do a round-trip hike from the trailhead at Indian Creek, an ancient Native American village site. From here the trail climbs a short distance to Indian Point, which offers prime views of the offshore Tillamook Lighthouse. Stand here and watch the bashing the light takes during a storm, and you understand why it's now abandoned. Continue another mile to an old hikers' camp, and just to the west, an abandoned bunker and viewpoint atop Tillamook Head, where views are sublime. More good photo opportunities await at the turnaround point, Clark's Point of View, an ocean overlook about a mile farther up the trail. Farther north on the trail, gaze at outstanding views of oceanscapes as near as Seaside and as far as Cape Disappointment on the Washington side of the mighty Columbia.

For an easier, 3.5-mile hike that's gentle enough for kids and seniors, turn left at the entrance booth into the Ecola Point picnic area lot and follow the trail toward Indian Creek parking area. A good viewpoint is reached about 1.75 miles up the trail.

Location: Two miles north of Cannon Beach on the Oregon coast; see The Oregon Coast Map 2, grid a1.

User Groups: Hikers and leashed dogs. Check with park rangers for local mountain-bike restrictions. No horses are allowed. No wheelchair facilities.

Permits: No permits are required. A $3-per-vehicle access fee is collected at the Ecola State Park entrance. Annual Oregon State Parks passes are available for $25; contact the Oregon State Parks and Recreation Department at 800/551-6949. The Oregon Pacific Coast Passport, a joint federal-state parking pass valid at 16 sites along the Oregon Coast, can be used in lieu of the parking fee. Coast Passports, $35 a year or $10 for five days, are available at local visitor centers.

Maps: For a free park brochure and map, contact Oregon State Parks at 800/551-6949. Ask the USGS for a topographic map of the Tillamook Head area.

Directions: From Portland drive about 73 miles west on U.S. 26 and four miles south on U.S. 101 to Cannon Beach. At the north end of town (or the north Cannon Beach exit off U.S. 101), follow signs to the park road and drive two miles west to the park entrance. Trailheads are found at Ecola Point and Indian Creek (closed in winter) picnic areas. To access the trail's northern entrance (and avoid the Ecola parking fee), follow Sunset Boulevard south from Seaside.

Contact: Oregon Parks and Recreation Department, 1115 Commercial Street Northeast, Salem, OR 97301; 800/551-6949.

❹ Saddle Mountain
5.0 mi/4.0 hrs

Saddle Mountain, the grandest viewpoint in Oregon's North Coast Range, used to be topped by a fire lookout. Now its pillow-basalt bald head is vacant, just waiting to be adorned by your Vibram soles. From the trailhead in primitive Saddle Mountain State Natural Area, the trail climbs through a mixed forest to a side trail leading to a good viewpoint at about one-quarter mile. The route steepens above, crossing more than one rock ledge before opening onto the ridgetop at about two miles. The final mile or so to the summit can be a bit treacherous, especially for the ill-equipped fool in tennis shoes. But the view from the 3,283-foot summit makes up for all that. Gaze west to the ocean and north to the Columbia River and the Cascades of southern Washington. Keep your eyes open for deer, elk, and unique plants, all of which thrive on Saddle Mountain. Unfortunately, so do summertime crowds. Try to hit this one on a weekday or an off-season weekend. Total elevation gain: about 1,600 feet.

Location: In Saddle Mountain State Natural Area northeast of Cannon Beach; see The Oregon Coast Map 2, grid a3.

User Groups: Hikers and leashed dogs. Check with park rangers for local mountain-bike restrictions. No horses are allowed. No wheelchair facilities.

Permits: No permits are required. Parking and access are free.

Maps: For a free park brochure and map, contact Oregon State Parks at 800/551-6949. Ask the USGS for a topographic map of the Saddle Mountain area.

Directions: From Portland drive about 65 miles west (or 10 miles east from Seaside) on U.S. 26 and turn north at the Saddle Mountain State Park road sign. Proceed seven miles northeast on Saddle Mountain Road to the trailhead in Saddle Mountain State Park.

Contact: Oregon Parks and Recreation Department, 1115 Commercial Street Northeast, Salem, OR 97301; 800/551-6949.

5 Banks-Vernonia Railroad Trail
21 mi one way/2.0 days

The Banks-Vernonia Trail, a 21-mile-long, former Burlington Northern right-of-way, is a great getaway for hikers, cyclists, and equestrians. The most-traveled section to date is the northern portion, which leads from Vernonia eight miles south to the Tophill Trailhead. That portion is in the best condition, with a 12-foot-wide path split into a paved trail for hikers and cyclists and a gravel portion for horses.

But the full 21-mile route is passable now, either on an improved, wide (cycle- and horse-friendly) tread or more traditional footpaths that skirt trail highlights such as the impressive Buxton and Horseshoe trestles.

The path certainly isn't the most scenic in Northwest Oregon, but it's a peaceful walk that passes peaceful streams and meadows, and it's only half an hour from downtown Portland. Better yet, at this writing, anyway, the trail is free. No trail park pass is required to recreate here.

Location: A railroad grade between the towns of Banks and Vernonia off Highway 47, northwest of the Portland area; see The Oregon Coast Map 2, grid c6.

User Groups: Hikers, dogs, horses, and mountain bikes are allowed. There are no wheelchair facilities.

Permits: No permits are required. Parking and access are free.

Maps: For a trail map and brochure, contact Oregon Parks and Recreation at 800/551-6949. Ask the USGS for topographic maps of Vernonia and Forest Grove.

Directions: From the Portland area drive approximately 28 miles west on U.S. 26 to Buxton and turn right (north) on Highway 47. Watch for signs for several trailheads on the route to Vernonia, including Manning, Buxton, Tophill, and Beaver Creek. The far north trailhead is located at Anderson Park in Vernonia.

Contact: Oregon Parks and Recreation Department, 1115 Commercial Street Northeast, Salem, OR 97301; 800/551-6949; oregonstateparks.org.

6 Neahkahnie Mountain
5.0 mi/3.0 hrs

Somewhere on Neahkahnie Mountain, hidden treasure awaits. So goes the local legend, which holds that early Spanish explorers were shipwrecked on the nearby spit in the early 18th century and buried riches somewhere on the 1,631-foot mountain. Whether the treasure is gold and jewels or just a magnificent taste of Oregon coastal scenery, Neahkahnie Mountain always seems to pay off.

The trail climbs steeply through a meadow for the first mile, passes through a forest and a high meadow, and then climbs from a saddle to the summit at about 2.5 miles. Gaze below to Cape Falcon, Nehalem Spit, Tillamook Head, and mountain peaks inland. Return via the same route or continue straight on the Oregon Coast Trail another two miles back to U.S. 101 and a short walk along the (narrow) highway to your car.

Back at the trailhead, don't overlook Oswald West Park's (named for the former Oregon governor who first protected these beaches) excellent oceanside hikes. A four-mile round-trip walk on the Oregon Coast Trail from the picnic area to forested, 750-foot-high Cape Falcon is a memorable experience when weather cooperates.

Location: In Oswald West State Park on the northern Oregon coast; see The Oregon Coast Map 2, grid c1.

User Groups: Hikers and leashed dogs. Check with park rangers for local mountain-bike restrictions. No horses are allowed. No wheelchair facilities.

Permits: No permits are required. Parking and access are free.

Maps: For a park brochure contact Oregon State Parks at 800/551-6949. Ask the USGS for topographic maps of the Nehalem and Arch Cape areas.

Directions: From Cannon Beach drive about 10 miles south on U.S. 101 to Oswald West State Park. About a mile beyond the campground, turn east at the trail sign between mileposts 41 and 42. Proceed about half a mile to the parking area on the right. Look for the gray Oregon Coast Trail marker on the opposite side of the road.

Contact: Oregon Parks and Recreation Department, 1115 Commercial Street Northeast, Salem, OR 97301; 800/551-6949.

7 Elk Mountain/Kings Mountain Loop

9.0 mi/6.0 hrs

Lingering scars from the massive wildfires that decimated 350,000 acres of this Tillamook Burn region in the 1930s and 1940s are awesome reminders of the destructive power of nature. But today, with second-growth forest taking firm hold and a sense of peace prevailing, some of those same scars provide truly awesome mountaintop portals to a largely under-appreciated Oregon natural area.

The parallel twin trails to the summits of Elk and Kings Mountains both climb through fire-scarred second-growth forest to magnificent views of the Cascade volcano chain. The icy heads of Mounts Adams, Hood, and Jefferson are all visible from the top, as are much of the Coast Range and Cascades. If you're camping in the area, the trails can be hiked individually for round trips of about five miles each. But it's possible to make a loop trip across both summits by using an unnamed old road connecting the two summits and dropping to a waiting second car at the Kings Mountain Trailhead, about three miles east on Highway 6. Or for a loop on Elk Mountain alone, turn right rather than left at the old road after the summit and make a logging-road loop back to Elk Creek Forest Park.

Whichever route you choose, be prepared for a steady upward pace that's sure to make your lungs really pump. You gain about 2,000 feet of vertical on the way up Elk Mountain, and about 2,700 feet on Kings Mountain. Hikers doing the shuttle hike between the two trailheads gain about 3,500 feet. The upper stretches of both trails are the highlights, with straight, silvery snags standing as silent reminders of the fires. In season, wildflowers on the upper stretches dance on the breeze and entice you to stay.

Location: North of Highway 6 in Tillamook State Forest; see The Oregon Coast Map 2, grid d4.

User Groups: Hikers, dogs, horses, and mountain bikes. No wheelchair facilities.

Permits: No permits are required. Parking and access are free.

Maps: For a Tillamook Forest Trails brochure, contact the Nature of the Northwest Information Center at 503/872-2750. Ask the USGS for a topographic map of the Timber area.

Directions: To reach the Elk Mountain Trailhead from Portland, drive about 45 miles west via U.S. 26 and Highway 6, the Wilson River Highway, to Elk Creek Forest Park Campground on the right (north) side of the highway near milepost 28. The Elk Mountain Trailhead is at the far end of the campground across the bridge. To reach the Kings Mountain Trailhead, proceed 3.2 miles east on Wilson River Highway to the hiker sign on the north side of the road near milepost 25.

Contact: Nature of the Northwest Information Center, 800 Northeast Oregon Street, Suite 177, Portland, OR 97232; 503/872-2750.

8 University Falls Loop
8.5 mi/6.0 hrs

If you can stand the sound of roaring off-road vehicles on nearby trails—and even on some shared-road portions of the loop—this loop trip to University Falls is a great spring or summer day hike. Focus on the lowland forest greenery and crystal stream trickles of Elliott Creek instead of the blue smoke of Yamahas, and it's a trip well worth making.

The loop trail marches through young Douglas fir forest and crosses several roads, one of which is a historic wagon trail leading to a former camp above the falls. The falls themselves, about 5.5 miles in, are magnificent, dropping some 65 feet in a wide, almost gentle drop over stair-step rock. Bring your cam-

era if you're here early in the summer, when the falls are gushing. By fall they're usually reduced to a trickle.

Location: South of Highway 6 in Tillamook State Forest; see The Oregon Coast Map 2, grid d5.

User Groups: Hikers, dogs, horses, and mountain bikes. No wheelchair facilities.

Permits: No permits are required. Parking and access are free.

Maps: For a Tillamook Forest Trails brochure, contact the Nature of the Northwest Information Center at 503/872-2750. Ask the USGS for a topographic map of the Timber area.

Directions: From Portland drive about 40 miles west via U.S. 26 and Highway 6/Wilson River Highway to the Summit Trailhead on the north side of the road near milepost 33. The trail begins on the other side of the road.

Contact: Nature of the Northwest Information Center, 800 Northeast Oregon Street, Suite 177, Portland, OR 97232; 503/872-2750.

9 Cape Meares
2.0 mi one way/1.0 hr

Here's a good, short leg-stretcher for those short legs in the backseat. The Cape Meares trail allows parents to take kids on an easy one-way hike that leaves them feeling like they've actually been somewhere. And they actually have been. The trail leads a short distance to the Cape Meares Lighthouse, installed in 1890 and replaced by an automatic light in 1963. Bring the binoculars and watch for common murres and other seabirds (this is one of the nation's most populous nesting seabird sites), sea lions, and whales in the offshore Cape Meares National Wildlife Refuge. Follow the loop trail back along the south side of the headland, with views of the seabird-rich Three Arch Rocks National

Wildlife Refuge, south past the restrooms to the Octopus Tree, a large spruce whose six branches form a massive cradle. Turn around here or continue another half a mile to an exit and pick up the Three Capes Scenic Loop just south of the turnoff to Cape Meares.

Location: In Cape Meares State Park northwest of Tillamook; see The Oregon Coast Map 2, grid e1.

User Groups: Hikers and leashed dogs. Check with park rangers for local mountain-bike restrictions. No horses are allowed. No wheelchair facilities.

Permits: No permits are required. Parking and access are free.

Maps: For a park brochure contact the Oregon Parks and Recreation Department at 800/551-6949. Ask the USGS for a topographic map of the Netarts area.

Directions: From U.S. 101 at Tillamook, follow signs to Three Capes Scenic Loop. Proceed about 10 miles west to Cape Meares State Park. The trailhead parking area is at the end of the road.

Contact: Oregon Parks and Recreation Department, 1115 Commercial Street Northeast, Salem, OR 97301; 800/551-6949.

10 Cape Lookout
5.0 mi/3.0 hrs

An easy path through old-growth spruce and hemlock leads along a magnificent rock finger jutting into the Pacific, while migrating gray whales, sea lions, and other creatures frolic in the surf offshore. What more could you want? Probably more time to explore once you get out on the Cape Lookout Trail.

First, pick the correct trail. At the trailhead the path to the right leads to the campground. Take the left (south) trail and stay straight where the Oregon Coast Trail departs to the left a short way down the path. Your trail starts on the south side of the

ridge, dropping into forest before meandering to northern views of Cape Meares at a point just beyond a mile down the path. The trail then skirts the edge of magnificent, 400-foot cliffs on the southern cape and ends at a surprisingly small viewpoint. Views are limited to the south, toward impressive Cape Kiwanda, rich with sea birds. During whale migration seasons in the spring and winter, volunteer whale watchers are likely to be here, recording movement of the magnificent beasts. After you spot one, haul your own magnificent beast, whoever he or she might be, 2.5 easy miles back to the car.

If you make it back without getting soaked, consider yourself lucky. Cape Lookout gets drenched by about 100 inches of rain a year. A visit here in early autumn, sometime after Labor Day, gives you a fair shot at avoiding both crowds and rain squalls. The total elevation gain to the cape is about 400 feet.

Location: On U.S. 101, 12 miles southwest of Tillamook; see The Oregon Coast Map 2, grid f1.

User Groups: Hikers and leashed dogs. Check with park rangers for local mountain-bike restrictions. No horses are allowed. No wheelchair facilities.

Permits: No permits are required. A $3-per-vehicle access fee is collected at the park entrance. Annual Oregon State Parks passes are available for $25; contact the Oregon State Parks and Recreation Department at 800/551-6949. The Oregon Pacific Coast Passport, a joint federal-state parking pass valid at 16 sites along the Oregon Coast, can be used in lieu of the parking fee. Coast Passports, $35 a year or $10 for five days, are available at local visitor centers.

Maps: For a park brochure contact the Oregon Parks and Recreation Department at 800/551-6949. Ask the USGS for a topographic map of the Sand Lake area.

Directions: From Tillamook turn west on Third Street and follow the signs for about 13 miles west to Cape Lookout State Park. Proceed about 2.5 miles beyond the campground to the Cape Lookout Trailhead on the right side of the road.

Contact: Oregon Parks and Recreation Department, 1115 Commercial Street Northeast, Salem, OR 97301; 800/551-6949.

11 Pioneer Trail
8.0 mi one way/7.0 hrs

This old, interesting trail climbs over 3,144-foot Mount Hebo and travels east to Mount Hebo and South Lake Campgrounds, making it a challenging one-way day hike or more leisurely overnight backpacking trip. The path, part of the old Grande Ronde Indian Trail linking the Willamette and Tillamook Valleys, was later used by white settlers in the Tillamook area. Today it's just used by hikers, who enjoy its tour through the second-growth (fire got the old stuff) forest. The trail meanders through meadows, climbs steeply through forest, and offers a variety of excellent viewpoints along the way.

Overnighters can camp at Mount Hebo Campground and then proceed southeast the next day for a pickup at North or South Lakes, reached via bumpy Forest Service Road 1428, which turns south from Forest Service Road 14 about seven miles east of South Lake Campground. Day hikers without a shuttle car can hike to the West Summit for a round-trip of about 6.5 miles. Total elevation gain is about 1,500 feet. Watch for elk along the trail.

Location: Between Hebo Lake and South Lake in the Oregon Coast Range in Siuslaw National Forest; see The Oregon Coast Map 2, grid g2.

User Groups: Hikers, dogs, and horses. Mountain bikes are not allowed. No wheelchair facilities.

Permits: A federal Northwest Forest Pass, $5 per day or $30 annually, is required to park at the trailhead. Passes are available from ranger stations and many private vendors, online at website: www.wta.org, or by calling 800/270-7504. The Oregon Pacific Coast Passport, a joint federal-state pass valid at 16 sites along the Oregon Coast, can be used in lieu of the parking fee at this site. Coast Passports, $35 a year or $10 for five days, are available at local visitor centers.

Maps: For a map of the Siuslaw National Forest, contact the Nature of the Northwest Information Center, 800 Northeast Oregon Street, Suite 177, Portland, OR 97232; 503/872-2750. Ask the USGS for topographic maps of the Hebo and Niagara Creek areas.

Directions: From U.S. 101 19 miles south of Tillamook, turn east on Highway 22 at Hebo. In less than half a mile, turn left on Forest Service Road 14 (following signs to Hebo Lake) about four miles east to the trailhead near Hebo Lake Campground.

Contact: Siuslaw National Forest, Hebo Ranger District, 31525 Highway 22, Hebo, OR 97122; 503/392-3161.

12 Cascade Head Scenic Research Area
2.0–5.5 mi/1.0–3.0 hrs

Three trails of very different stripes await your feet on this wild Pacific Ocean bluff protected as the Cascade Head Scenic Research Area. The preserve, a 9,600-acre living outdoor laboratory, is a spectacular piece of real estate, with rocks jutting as high as 1,800 feet above the Pacific and several streams cascading (hence the name) into the ocean from spectacular, smooth gorges.

In the heart of the research area, an interpretive trail leads between trailheads on Three Rocks Road and Road 1861. The path, which runs through the Nature Conservancy Preserve, makes an excellent two-mile, one-way day hike through magnificent stands of spruce. Or opt for a longer, more dramatic day hike by following Road 1861 to the Hart's Cove Trail. That path leads down through truly awesome old-growth Sitka spruce to a viewpoint above the cliff-lined cove, where Chilwood Creek drops into the sea. Look north to spot Cape Lookout and Cape Kiwanda in the mist. It's a great whale-watching vantage point. Back near Highway 101 the Cascade Head Trail begins on Three Rocks Road and parallels the highway six miles to the north, passing through more magnificent stands of spruce and offering good ocean views from the north end.

Location: North of Lincoln City in Cascade Head Scenic Research Area; see The Oregon Coast Map 2, grid h1.

User Groups: Hikers, dogs, and horses. Note: Dogs are not allowed on the Nature Conservancy Trail. No mountain bikes are allowed. No wheelchair facilities.

Permits: No permits are required. Parking and access are free.

Maps: For a map of Siuslaw National Forest, contact the Nature of the Northwest Information Center, 800 Northeast Oregon Street, Suite 177, Portland, OR 97232; 503/872-2750. Ask the USGS for topographic maps of the Cascade Head and Neskowin areas.

Directions: To reach the Nature Conservancy Interpretive Trail or Cascade Head Trail, drive on U.S. 101 north a short distance from Lincoln City, about one-half mile north of the Highway 18 junction, to Three Rocks Road. Turn left (west) and drive a short distance to the marked Cascade Head Trailhead or 2.2 miles to the arched Nature Conservancy Trailhead, both on the right (north) side of the road. To reach the Hart's Cove Trail, follow U.S. 101 about 3.5 miles north of Highway 18 to Cascade Head Road 1861. Turn left (west) and drive about four miles to the trailhead parking lot on the left. Note: The latter trailhead is closed January 1 to July 15.

Contact: Siuslaw National Forest, Hebo Ranger District, P.O. Box 324, Hebo, OR 97122; 503/392-3161.

13 Beverly Beach State Park
0.75–10.0 mi/0.5–5.0 hrs 2 🥾 🔟9

Streamside protected forests or open, breezy, and stunning ocean beaches: Beverly Beach State Park has something to please the palate of just about any day hiker. For a short jaunt through the woods, cross the highway to the campground and embark on the Spencer Creek Nature Trail, a three-quarter-mile loop that wanders through skunk cabbage, alder, spruce, and the dead-soldier reminders of old-growth that once was.

To hike the ocean beach north, go to the west section of the campground and through the U.S. 101 underpass. Cross Spencer Creek and hike the rocky shoreline toward Otter Rock. At just over a mile, stairs lead up to the Marine Gardens tidepools and a view of the fascinating Devil's Punchbowl, a large, bowl-shaped collapsed sea cave that fills with rolling seawater from tunnels beneath it, creating quite a spectacle when tides are right.

The beach hike south leads about three miles beneath rocky cliffs toward Yaquina Head, Colony Rock, and Yaquina Head Lighthouse. The latter is worth an auto side trip for great photo opportunities and a perfect vantage point of the Yaquina Head Rocks National Wildlife Refuge, one of the Oregon coast's most productive seabird habitats. It's also another fantastic seasonal whale-watching post.

Location: North of Newport, east of U.S. 101; see The Oregon Coast Map 3, grid c8.

User Groups: Hikers, dogs, and horses. Check with park rangers for local mountain bike restrictions. No wheelchair facilities.

Permits: No permits are required. Parking and access are free.

Maps: For a park brochure contact Oregon State Parks at 800/551-6949. For a nature-trail interpretive brochure, stop at the campground toll booth. Ask the USGS for a topographic map of the Newport North area.

Directions: From Newport drive about seven miles north on U.S. 101 to the day-use parking lot on the east side of the highway.

Contact: Oregon Parks and Recreation Department, 1115 Commercial Street Northeast, Salem, OR 97301; 800/551-6949.

14 Cape Perpetua
5.0 mi/3.0 hrs

Three trails near Cape Perpetua Campground and Visitors Center will get you of your car and into one of the more intriguing regions of Oregon's fabled U.S. 101 coastal tour. From the visitor center, follow the Giant Spruce Trail a mile to—you guessed it—a rather large tree of definite spruce origin. The Sitka spruce is 190 feet high (the top got knocked out in the infamous Columbus Day storm of 1962) and estimated to be 500 years old, so don't give it any grief. In the spring, you're likely to share this trail with elk, wildflowers, and skunk cabbages with brilliant green leaves bigger than your head. Return the same way and hang a right at the Saint Perpetua Trail leading north to the campground and cape viewpoint. It connects to the Whispering Spruce Trail. Here you'll find a short loop trail leading to two Civilian Conservation Corps–era stone structures, the Parapet and West Shelter, high atop Cape Perpetua. The views in al-

most all directions are magnificent. Gaze as far along the coast as the Heceta Head Lighthouse, Cape Blanco, and Cape Foulweather. Return to the visitor center via the same route or have one pick you up in the car at the upper loop, which connects to the Cape Perpetua Viewpoint parking lot. If you're up for a longer hike, take the Cook's Ridge/Gwynn Creek Loop Trail from a trailhead just south of the visitor center. It follows an old wagon road for 5.5 miles through forest on a moderate grade.

Location: Near Cape Perpetua Campground, south of Yachats off U.S. 101; see The Oregon Coast Map 3, grid f8.

User Groups: Hikers and dogs. No mountain bikes or horses are allowed. A portion of the Whispering Spruce Trail is barrier-free and wheelchair accessible.

Permits: No permits are required. Parking requires an Oregon Pacific Coast Passport, a joint federal-state parking pass valid at 16 sites along the Oregon Coast. The passport, $10 for five days or $35 a year, is available at local visitor centers.

Maps: For a map of Siuslaw National Forest, contact the Nature of the Northwest Information Center, 800 Northeast Oregon Street, Suite 177, Portland, OR 97232; 503/872-2750. To obtain a USGS topographic map, ask for Yachats.

Directions: From Newport go 23 miles south on U.S. 101 to the town of Yachats. Continue south three miles on U.S. 101 to the trailhead at the Cape Perpetua Visitors Center on the left (east) side of the highway.

Contact: Siuslaw National Forest, Waldport Ranger District, 1094 Southwest Pacific Highway, Waldport, OR 97394; 541/563-3211.

15 Carl G. Washburne State Park Loop
4.5 mi/2.0 hrs

Washburne has plenty of good day-strolling potential. From the campground area, hike south on the Valley Trail, which parallels the highway, intersects the five-mile dead-end China Creek Trail, and then opens to a viewing platform at large Twin Beaver Ponds. The Valley Loop, a short walk through a meadow area, leads north off the trail. Continue south on the Valley Trail back toward the highway, cross the road, and enter the Hobbit Trail, a fascinating little path that drops quickly to the beach on the north side of Heceta Head. From here it's a pleasant, 1.5-mile walk north on the beach back to the day-use area and your car. Or continue south on a newly constructed path leading about a half mile up Heceta Head to the lighthouse.

Location: Between Florence and Yachats on U.S. 101; see The Oregon Coast Map 3, grid g7.

User Groups: Hikers, dogs, and horses. Check with park rangers for local mountain bike restrictions. No wheelchair facilities.

Permits: No permits are required. Parking and access are free.

Maps: For a park brochure contact Oregon State Parks at 800/551-6949. Ask the USGS for a topographic map of Heceta Head.

Directions: From Florence drive 14 miles north on U.S. 101 to the day-use area of Washburne State Park, on the west side of the highway. Park here and cross the highway to find the trailhead on the right, near China Creek.

Contact: Oregon Parks and Recreation Department, 1115 Commercial Street Northeast, Salem, OR 97301; 800/551-6949.

16 Heceta Head Lighthouse
1.0 mi/0.5 hrs

Anyone can walk the short, half-mile stretch of trail between the Devil's Elbow day-use area and Heceta Head. And everyone will want to stay. This is one of the most-visited and oft-photographed scenes on the entire Oregon coast. The lighthouse, built in 1894 and named after Portuguese explorer Bruno Heceta (thankfully, "Bruno Head" was dismissed as a title), is a spectacular sight, with the two-ton Fresnel lens still operating. Nearby is Sea Lion Caves, of bumper-sticker and marine-mammal fame.

Location: 13 miles north of Florence, near Devil's Elbow State Park off U.S. 101; see The Oregon Coast Map 3, grid g7.

User Groups: Hikers, dogs, and horses. No mountain bikes are allowed. No wheelchair facilities.

Permits: A $3 day-use parking fee is charged. Annual Oregon Parks and Recreation parking permits are available for $25; call Oregon Parks and Recreation at 800/551-6949. The Oregon Pacific Coast Passport, a joint federal-state parking pass valid at 16 sites along the Oregon Coast, can be used in lieu of the parking pass. Coast Passports, $35 a year or $10 for five days, are available at local visitor centers.

Maps: For a map of Siuslaw National Forest, contact the Nature of the Northwest Information Center, 800 Northeast Oregon Street, Suite 177, Portland, OR 97232; 503/872-2750. Ask the USGS for a topographic map of Heceta Head.

Directions: From Florence drive 12 miles north on U.S. 101 to Devil's Elbow State Park on the left (west) side of the road. The trail begins in the parking lot.

Contact: Siuslaw National Forest, Waldport Ranger District, 1094 Southwest Pacific Highway, Waldport, OR 97394; 541/563-3211.

17 Sutton Creek Sand Dunes
6.0 mi/3.0 hrs

Forest, dunes, and ocean combine for great day hikes of any length on the Sutton trail system, which also offers access to fishing, boating, and swimming in Sutton Lake. From the western trailhead, a short barrier-free trail leads to Holman Vista, a great place to watch for blue herons and other wild birds in the estuary below. From the other side of the parking area, three loops—one 1.25 miles, one 2.4 miles, and the final one three-quarters of a mile—travel through the Sutton sand dunes area. The loop system also is accessible by entering the upper loop from Sutton Campground. Hike them all, plus a trail east to Alder Lake, and you'll put in about six miles. Heceta Head (see hike in this chapter) and Sea Lion Caves are a short drive away.

Location: North of Florence along U.S. 101; see The Oregon Coast Map 3, grid h8.

User Groups: Hikers, dogs, and horses. No mountain bikes are allowed. There is one barrier-free trail.

Permits: A federal Northwest Forest Pass, $5 per day or $30 annually, is required to park at the trailhead. Passes are available from ranger stations and many private vendors, online at website: www.wta.org, or by calling 800/270-7504. The Oregon Pacific Coast Passport, a joint federal-state parking pass valid at 16 sites along the Oregon Coast, can be used in lieu of the Forest Service parking pass. Coast Passports, $35 a year or $10 for five days, are available at local visitor centers.

Maps: For a map of Siuslaw National Forest, contact the Nature of the Northwest Information Center, 800 Northeast Oregon Street, Suite 177, Portland, OR 97232; 503/872-2750. Ask the USGS for a topographic map of the Mercer Lake area.

Directions: From Florence proceed 2.5 miles north on U.S. 101 to Sutton Road. Turn west and follow the road to Sutton Campground. Trailheads are found throughout the campground and 2.5 miles west at Holman Vista on Sutton Beach Road.

Contact: Siuslaw National Forest, Mapleton Ranger District, 4480 Highway 101, Building G, Florence, OR 97439; 541/902-8526.

18 Horse Creek
4.5 mi/3.0 hrs

Old growth keeps you young at heart. If that's true, then frequent trips to Horse Creek in the Drift Creek Wilderness should keep you heading down the trail for years. The fragile beauty of this forested area earned it federal wilderness protection in 1984, making the Horse Creek Trail something of an anomaly—a trail called horse where no horses are allowed. Be thankful you're not a horse. The path drops through superb Douglas fir stands to Drift Creek, where peaceful meadows, clean water, and, if you're lucky, solitude await. It's a good mind-soothing hike any time of the year. If the creek is passable, as it usually is in late summer only, you can continue across the stream to the northern portion of the Horse Creek Trail. Crossing the creek also allows access to the Harris Ranch Trail, permitting a shuttle hike from the Horse Creek area to the Harris Ranch Trailhead off Forest Service Spur Road 346.

Location: East of Waldport in the Drift Creek Wilderness; see The Oregon Coast Map 4, grid e1.

User Groups: Hikers and dogs. No mountain bikes or horses are allowed. No wheelchair facilities.

Permits: No permits are required. Parking and access are free.

Maps: For a map of Siuslaw National Forest and Drift

Creek Wilderness, contact the Nature of the Northwest Information Center, 800 Northeast Oregon Street, Suite 177, Portland, OR 97232; 503/872-2750. Ask the USGS for topographic maps of the Hellion Rapids and Tidewater areas.

Directions: From Corvallis drive six miles west on U.S. 20 to Highway 34. Turn southwest and drive 50 miles to Risley Creek Road, about seven miles east of Waldport. Turn right (north) on Risley Creek Road/Forest Service Road 3446. Drive just over seven miles to Forest Service Road 3464. Turn left and drive 1.5 miles to the trailhead at the end of the road.

Contact: Siuslaw National Forest, Waldport Ranger District, 1094 Southwest Pacific Highway, Waldport, OR 97394; 541/563-3211.

19 Mary's Peak
7.2 mi/4.0 hrs

The Mary's Peak summit, to which you can walk from the north or south or drive from the southwest, is one of the most magnificent viewpoints in western Oregon on a clear day. Stand at the 4,097-foot peak and take it all in: Mount Jefferson, Mount Hood, Mount Bachelor, the Sisters, Mount Adams, Mount St. Helens, Mount Rainier. They're all here, lined up in a semicircle for your viewing and photographing pleasure. The St. Mary's Trail, part of which follows an old sheepherder's route, is the longest access to the St. Mary's summit but probably the nicest. The southern route, the East Ridge Trail, is 4.6 miles round-trip. Whichever route you choose, plan to spend some time on the summit, where the two-mile Meadow Edge Loop is a marvelous stroll, particularly during the wildflower explosions of the spring. Total elevation gain via the St. Mary's Trail is about 2,000 feet.

Location: West of Philomath in the Oregon Coast Range; see The Oregon Coast Map 4, grid e4.

User Groups: Hikers, dogs, mountain bikes, and horses. No wheelchair facilities.

Permits: A federal Northwest Forest Pass, $5 per day or $30 annually, is required to park at the trailhead. Passes are available from ranger stations and many private vendors, online at website: www.wta.org, or by calling 800/270-7504. The Oregon Pacific Coast Passport, a joint federal-state parking pass valid at 16 sites along the Oregon Coast, can be used in lieu of the Forest Service parking pass. Coast Passports, $35 a year or $10 for five days, are available at local visitor centers.

Maps: For a map of Siuslaw National Forest, contact the Northwest Information Center, 800 Northeast Oregon Street, Suite 177, Portland, OR 97232; 503/872-2750. Ask the USGS for a topographic map of the Mary's Peak area.

Directions: From Corvallis drive west on U.S. 20 through Philomath to the U.S. 34 junction. Proceed 1.8 miles west on U.S. 20 to Woods Creek Road near milepost 48. Turn left (west) and drive six miles to the locked gate. Walk to the trailhead at the end of the road.

Contact: Siuslaw National Forest, Waldport Ranger District, 1094 Southwest Pacific Highway, Waldport, OR 97394; 541/563-3211.

20 Siltcoos Lake
5.0 mi/2.5 hrs

Spectacular this trail is not. It's mostly dark, bare, second-growth fir forest, with not a lot to see until you break out of the darkness at Siltcoos Lake. Fortunately, there is a lot to see once you get there, including a thriving bird congregation and a healthy herd of deer, among other critters. At about three-quarters of a mile, the trail divides. Pick either route, because the trails form a loop along the lakeshore, with several campsites at the north and south ends of the shoreline portion of the loop. It's not a prime backpacking destination, but it does provide a nice change-of-pace day hike for vacationers who have seen enough coastal landscapes to last a lifetime, or at least for the rest of the week.

Location: South of Florence in the Oregon Dunes National Recreation Area; see The Oregon Coast Map 5, grid a8.

User Groups: Hikers, dogs, horses, and mountain bikes. No wheelchair facilities.

Permits: A federal Northwest Forest Pass, $5 per day or $30 annually, is required to park at the trailhead. Passes are available from ranger stations and many private vendors, online at website: www.wta.org, or by calling 800/270-7504. The Oregon Pacific Coast Passport, a joint federal-state parking pass valid at 16 sites along the Oregon Coast, can be used in lieu of the Northwest Forest Pass. The passport, $10 for five days or $35 a year, is available at local visitor centers.

Maps: For a map of the Oregon Dunes National Recreation Area, contact the Nature of the Northwest Information Center, 800 Northeast Oregon Street, Suite 177, Portland, OR 97232; 503/872-2750. Ask the USGS for topographic maps of the Goose Prairie, Tahkenitch Creek, Florence, and Fivemile Creek areas.

Directions: From the U.S. 101/Highway 126 junction in Florence, travel 7.7 miles south on U.S. 101 to the trailhead turnoff on the east side of the road, opposite the Siltcoos Road turnoff.

Contact: Oregon Dunes National Recreation Area, 855 Highway 101, Reedsport, OR 97467; 541/271-3611.

21 River of No Return Loop
1.0 mi/0.5 hrs

This is a bird-watcher's delight. The short, level, easy loop off Siltcoos Road travels through tall cattails, marsh grass, sand, and willows—all the ingredients for productive birding. Aiding and abetting is the marsh itself, actually an old meander scar closed off at both ends. Wildlife is plentiful, people are not, and the air is sweet. Take your time and bring binoculars.

Location: Near Waxmyrtle and Lagoon Campgrounds in the Oregon Dunes National Recreation Area; see The Oregon Coast Map 5, grid b7.

User Groups: Hikers, dogs, and horses. No mountain bikes are allowed. No wheelchair facilities.

Permits: A federal Northwest Forest Pass, $5 per day or $30 annually, is required to park at the trailhead. Passes are available from ranger stations and many private vendors, online at website: www.wta.org, or by calling 800/270-7504. The Oregon Pacific Coast Passport, a joint federal-state parking pass valid at 16 sites along the Oregon Coast, can be used in lieu of the Northwest Forest Pass. The passport, $10 for five days or $35 a year, is available at local visitor centers.

Maps: For a map of the Oregon Dunes National Recreation Area, contact the Nature of the Northwest Information Center, 800 Northeast Oregon Street, Suite 177, Portland, OR 97232; 503/872-2750. Ask the USGS for a topographic map of Goose Prairie.

Directions: From Florence drive eight miles south on U.S. 101 to Siltcoos Road. Turn right and drive to the trailhead on the right (north) side of the road across from Waxmyrtle Campground.

Contact: Oregon Dunes National Recreation Area, 855 Highway 101, Reedsport, OR 97467; 541/271-3611.

22 Tahkenitch Dunes/ Threemile Lake Loop

6.5 mi/3.0 hrs

Be prepared to participate in the sand dune. At Tahkenitch Dunes, they tend to sneak up on you. This is a fascinating walk through a massive, ever-shifting sand dune that's taking over a forest. You'll also walk for about a mile on an ocean beach, where off-road vehicles can be a nuisance in warm months. But that section is swift, and ORVs aren't allowed on the dunes portion of the trail. Begin clockwise and alternate between forest and open dunes to the lake, which you'll reach after about 3.5 miles. It's a fascinating spot, with windblown sand constantly changing the shape and nature of the shoreline. Camping is permitted at the lake. From here hike just over a mile north to the beach and return to complete the loop. A blue-topped post marks the path back up through the dunes to the campground and the car.

Location: South of Florence in the Oregon Dunes National Recreation Area; see The Oregon Coast Map 5, grid b8.

User Groups: Hikers, dogs, and horses. Mountain bikes are not recommended due to soft sand. No wheelchair facilities.

Permits: A federal Northwest Forest Pass, $5 per day or $30 annually, is required to park at the trailhead. Passes are available from ranger stations and many private vendors, online at website: www.wta.org, or by calling 800/270-7504. The Oregon Pacific Coast Passport, a joint federal-state parking pass valid at 16 sites along the Oregon Coast, can be used in lieu of the Northwest Forest pass. The passport, $10 for five days or $35 a year, is available at local visitor centers.

Maps: For a map of the Oregon Dunes National Recreation Area, contact the Nature of the Northwest Information Center, 800 Northeast Oregon Street, Suite 177, Portland, OR 97232; 503/872-2750. Ask the USGS for a topographic map of Tahkenitch Creek.

Directions: From the U.S. 101/Highway 38 junction at Reedsport, drive 7.5 miles north on U.S. 101 to the trailhead in the southwest portion of Tahkenitch Lake Campground. From Florence drive 12.5 miles south to the campground.

Contact: Oregon Dunes National Recreation Area, 855 Highway 101, Reedsport, OR 97467; 541/271-3611.

23 Umpqua Dunes

5.0 mi/3.0 hrs

If sand is your bag, this is your trail. Actually, it's not much of a trail at all, but rather an established route between Eel Creek Campground and the beach. Along the way, you'll encounter a magnificent set of desert-like dunes, some measuring 400 feet tall. Kids will have a blast jettisoning themselves off the top and landing in soft, warm sand. Better yet, this area is closed to off-road vehicles, so hikers and sand fans won't have to watch their backs constantly. Leave the sturdy hiking boots at home for this one. Sandals or tennis shoes are more appropriate. One word of caution: Make sure you pick a landmark on the horizon to establish your route. The path isn't well marked, and it's easy to lose your way. From the trailhead, aim for the tallest dune and the visible "island" of trees. From the trees, the trail turns north to the beach. Watch for the blue markers. And be prepared to have sand all over yourself by the time you return.

Location: South of Reedsport in the Umpqua Dunes Scenic Area, west of U.S. 101; see The Oregon Coast Map 5, grid d7.

User Groups: Hikers, dogs, and horses. Mountain bikes are not recommended due to soft sand. No wheelchair facilities.

Permits: A federal Northwest Forest Pass, $5 per day or $30 annually, is required to park at the trailhead. Passes are available from ranger stations and many private vendors, online at website: www.wta.org, or by calling 800/270-7504. The Oregon Pacific Coast Passport, a joint federal-state parking pass valid at 16 sites along the Oregon Coast, can be used in lieu of the Northwest Forest Pass. The passport, $10 for five days or $35 a year, is available at local visitor centers.

Maps: For a map of the Oregon Dunes National Recreation Area, contact the Nature of the Northwest Information Center, 800 Northeast Oregon Street, Suite 177, Portland, OR 97232; 503/872-2750. Ask the USGS for a topographic map of the Lakeside area.

Directions: From Reedsport drive 10 miles south on U.S. 101 to Eel Creek Campground. Turn west and find the trailhead in the campground's south loop.

Contact: Oregon Dunes National Recreation Area, 855 Highway 101, Reedsport, OR 97467; 541/271-3611.

24 Sunset Cove to Cape Arago
6.0 mi/3.0 hrs

This stretch of the Oregon Coast Trail is one of the more special spots on a coastline that is littered with them. From the amazingly calm, sheltered waters of Sunset Cove, a three-mile stretch of the Oregon Coast Trail leads south past Shore Acres State Park to the North Cove area of Cape Arago State Park. In between is a photographer's dream: plenty of outstanding, high-bank vistas bring uncountable offshore rock formations—one of them supporting the Cape Arago Lighthouse—into your viewfinder. At the outset, a short side trail leads east to the mansion of the Simpson family, who once owned this entire plot. Continue past the helter-skelter rock formations and breathtaking seascape views. Views to the north include sea lion–littered Simpson Reef. You can hike the trail one way by arranging a pickup at the Simpson Reef Viewpoint or North Cove at Cape Arago State Park, both a short drive. But you'll want to include a south-to-north walk to take in good views of the lighthouse, connected to the mainland by a tiny footbridge.

Location: South of Coos Bay between Cape Arago State Park and Cape Arago Lighthouse; see The Oregon Coast Map 5, grid f5.

User Groups: Hikers, horses, and dogs. No mountain bikes are allowed. No wheelchair facilities.

Permits: No permits are required. Parking and access are free.

Maps: For a free park brochure, contact Oregon Parks and Recreation at the address below. Ask the USGS for a topographic map of Cape Arago.

Directions: From Coos Bay drive south on Cape Arago Highway, following signs to Sunset Bay State Park, about 13 miles southwest. Park in the day-use area on the east side of the highway and cross under the highway near Big Creek to reach the trailhead in the picnic area.

Contact: Oregon Parks and Recreation Department, 1115 Commercial Street Northeast, Salem, OR 97301; 800/551-6949.

25 Kentucky Falls
4.2 mi/2.0 hrs

Tired of the gaper parade and jam-packed trails along the Oregon coast? Head inland a short distance and leave it all behind on the Kentucky Falls Trail, which climbs through some luscious old-growth forest to a spectacular waterfall. Make that three waterfalls, each upwards of 80 feet high. If you're here in the winter, when streams flow full and trees with fallen leaves afford better views, the noise and

mist might be enough to distract you from seeing the elk that may be standing in the woods right behind you. You'll reach the upper falls first, then drop down to viewpoints of the Lower Kentucky Falls and the Smith River Falls.

Location: On Kentucky Creek in the North Fork Smith River drainage of Siuslaw National Forest; see The Oregon Coast Map 6, grid a2.

User Groups: Hikers, dogs, and horses. No mountain bikes are allowed. No wheelchair facilities.

Permits: No permits are required. Parking and access are free.

Maps: For a map of Siuslaw National Forest, contact the Nature of the Northwest Information Center, 800 Northeast Oregon Street, Suite 177, Portland, OR 97232; 503/872-2750. Ask the USGS for a topographic map of the Mercer Lake area.

Directions: From Eugene drive 33 miles east on Highway 126 to a signed turnoff for Whittaker Creek Recreation Area, between mileposts 26 and 27 (about 12.5 miles east of Mapleton.) Proceed 1.5 miles south and turn right across a bridge on a sometimes-unsigned road. Proceed 1.5 miles to Dunn Ridge Road. Veer left and drive 6.9 miles, then turn left on Knowles Creek Road (at signs for Reedsport). Proceed 2.7 miles to Forest Service Road 23. Turn right and head 1.6 miles to Forest Service Road 2300-919. Turn right and proceed 2.7 miles to the trailhead on the left side of the road. Parking is on the right shoulder. (This route is usually well marked at the main intersections.)

Contact: Siuslaw National Forest, Mapleton Ranger District, 4480 Highway 101, Building G, Florence, OR 97439; 541/902-8526.

26 Golden and Silver Falls
3.3 mi/2.0 hrs

Golden and Silver Falls are not exactly easy to reach. The upper stretches of the access road are rough enough to put a major hitch in your getalong, if not a rock through your transmission pan. That fact tends to weed out visitors, making these two falls, set in old-growth forest, all the more impressive for the resilient few who push on. After you cross Silver Creek, the trail to 160-foot Silver Falls starts on the left, and the trail to 200-foot Golden Falls starts on the right. The Silver Falls Trail climbs about one-third of a mile to a falls overlook, then another half a mile east to a high (and very exposed—stay away from the edge) viewpoint at the top of Golden Falls. The Golden Falls Trail is a straight shot of about a quarter mile to a vantage point below the falls. A short, separate trail leads one-third of a mile from the road before the picnic area north to a viewpoint of Silver Falls on the west side of Silver Creek. All three trails can be hiked pleasantly in a couple of hours.

Location: Northeast of Coos Bay; see The Oregon Coast Map 6, grid e1.

User Groups: Hikers and dogs. No horses are allowed. Check with park rangers for local mountain bike restrictions. No wheelchair facilities.

Permits: No permits are required. Parking and access are free.

Maps: For a free park brochure, contact Oregon State Parks at 800/551-6949. Ask the USGS for a topographic map of the Golden Falls area.

Directions: From U.S. 101 at the south end of Coos Bay, turn east on Coos River Highway, following signs about 13.5 miles to Allegany. From Allegany, follow signs about 9.5 miles to Golden and Silver Falls State Park. The trailhead is in the picnic area. Note: The final five miles of the access road are extremely rough.

Contact: Oregon Parks and Recreation Department, 1115 Commercial Street Northeast, Salem, OR 97301; 800/551-6949.

27 Barklow Mountain
2.2 mi/1.0 hr

The short trail gains just 400 feet over its length, making it a fine route for families hoping to give the kids a taste of nature or those just looking for a quiet afternoon in a cool forest. The trail leads to the mountain summit, where there are wonderful views of the surrounding peaks and valleys. That is to be expected, of course, considering this was, for many years, the site of a U.S. Forest Service fire lookout station. But those mountaintop vistas aren't the only reason to explore this trail. The narrow path pierces deep old forests and passes some classic old USFS relics at Barklow Camp, including an old log hut once used by fire lookouts and other ranger-types in the area.

The trail climbs from the end of the road in a gentle swing north, rolling upward through rhododendron-filled fir forests. At a half mile the trail forks. The left path leads to the 3,579-foot summit, with its astounding views and welcome sunshine. It's less than a quarter mile to the top, and with a long, restful stay at the summit, you should have plenty of energy and daylight to return to the trail junction and take the other fork. This leads to the old log cabin at Barklow Camp in less than a half mile. Poke around the old camp at your leisure. Admire the old, hand-beaten square nails, the tin cups, and rusted out cookware and stove, and then leave it all where it lies and head for home. Please do not remove any of the artifacts—if you need a remembrance of your visit, take plenty of pictures, but leave the relics for the next group to admire.

Location: Northeast of Gold Beach in Siskiyou National Forest; see The Oregon Coast Map 7, grid b7.

User Groups: Hikers and dogs. No horses or mountain bikes are allowed. No wheelchair facilities.

Permits: A federal Northwest Forest Pass, $5 per day or $30 annually, is required to park at the trailhead. Passes are available from ranger stations and many private vendors, online at website: www.wta.org, or by calling 800/270-7504.

Maps: Ask the USGS for topographic maps of the Powers and Agness areas.

Directions: From Gold Beach drive north on U.S. 101, passing through the small town of Port Orford, and turn right (east) onto Elk River Road. Continue about 18 miles and turn right onto Forest Service Road 5325. Drive nine miles and turn left onto Forest Service Road 3353. In 9.5 miles turn right on Forest Service Road 220—a small, dirt two-laner—and drive about a mile to the trailhead at the end of the road.

Contact: Siskiyou National Forest, Powers Ranger District, Highway 242, Powers, OR 97446; 541/439-3011.

28 Sucker Creek's Fern Forest
4.9 mi/3.0 hr

From open, sun-drenched slopes to shadowy creek beds, to steep, fern-covered canyon walls, this trail has it all despite its relatively short length. From the trailhead the route descends to the Sucker Creek valley bottom by way of an open, rocky slope. The trail traverses the hillside, which can be difficult at times, depending on the number of slides that have occurred since the last trail crews came through and cleaned off the slide debris. The trail passes through open areas with stands of madrona, sometimes called "peely trees" because of the way the bark peels off the trunks in long curls. There are also some old oaks, and a few nasty clumps of poison oak (remember: "Leaves of three, leave it be.").

In less than mile the trail passes Yontz Camp—a fine place for an overnight stay, especially in early spring when the abundant rhododendrons around camp are in full, glorious bloom. Just past the camp the trail reaches Sucker Creek. Though the path stays well above the creek at this point, the influence of the water is evident on the surrounding vegetation. The forests around the trail are lush and rich in mosses, lichens, and ferns. In fact, the ferns fill the slopes between the trunks of the massive cedars and hemlocks, giving the forest a green tint and cool texture that is wonderful to experience year-round, but especially in the hot summer months.

From camp the trail angles northeast, gradually dropping closer and closer to the creek, until at 2.3 miles the trail finally edges alongside the water. At 2.4 miles the trail crosses the creek and, 0.1 mile later, ends at Forest Service Road 5591. Rather than cross the creek just to see a road, stay on the western bank and take a relaxing break along the babbling waters. Dip your feet, take a nap, or enjoy a quiet lunch among the ferns at creekside before retracing your steps to the starting point.

Location: Northeast of Gold Beach in Siskiyou National Forest; see The Oregon Coast Map 7, grid c8.

User Groups: Hikers and dogs. No horses or mountain bikes are allowed. No wheelchair facilities.

Permits: A federal Northwest Forest Pass, $5 per day or $30 annually, is required to park at the trailhead. Passes are available from ranger stations and many private vendors, online at website: www.wta.org, or by calling 800/270-7504.

Maps: Ask the USGS for topographic maps of the Powers and Agness areas.

Directions: From Gold Beach drive north on U.S. 101, passing through the small town of Port Orford, and turn right (east) onto Elk River Road. Continue about 18 miles and turn right onto Forest Service Road 5325. Drive nine miles and turn left onto Forest Service Road 3353. In about 15 miles turn left (east) onto Forest Service Road 260. Continue east 1.5 miles to the trailhead on the right.

Contact: Siskiyou National Forest, Powers Ranger District, Highway 242, Powers, OR 97446; 541/439-3011.

29 Illinois River
16 mi/8.0 hrs or 2.0 days 🥾 🥾

The Illinois is a designated National Wild and Scenic River, and the trail along its banks—and valley walls—is also wild and scenic. The trail covers more than 27 miles total, but difficult access makes some sections virtually unusable, while too much access, i.e., road crossings, mar other parts of it. But this eight-mile stretch is easy to reach and just wild and scenic enough to meet anyone's taste.

The trail starts out with a steep climb to a high promontory overlooking the river. In the first mile the trail includes great views of the river and a walk through one of the rarest forests of the world. Here grow the renowned myrtle trees, a magnificent hardwood found only on the southern Oregon coast and in parts of the Middle East. It is much prized by wood workers, for it has beautiful grain patterns and can be polished to a high shine.

Still within that first mile, the trail crosses picturesque Nancy Creek. Deer are frequently seen browsing this area, and flocks of song birds can often be seen or heard in the blackberry brambles along the creek banks. Farther along the route, the trail crosses Buzzard's Roost for more panoramic views, descends to the river just past an old but still active (and occupied) ranch homestead, and finally enters the Kalmiopsis Wilderness at 7.5 miles. Just inside the wilderness there are great campsites near the mouth of Silver Creek. Pitch camp at Silver Creek, try for some of the big, beautiful trout in either Silver Creek or Illinois River, and enjoy the quiet beauty of the area.

The trail continues through the wilderness area, exiting near Flat Top just west of Grants Pass if you desire a longer journey and can arrange for a car shuttle between trailheads.

Location: Northeast of Gold Beach in Siskiyou National Forest; see The Oregon Coast Map 7, grid d8.

User Groups: Hikers and dogs. No horses or mountain bikes are allowed. No wheelchair facilities.

Permits: A federal Northwest Forest Pass, $5 per day or $30 annually, is required to park at the trailhead. Passes are available from ranger stations and many private vendors, online at website: www.wta.org, or by calling 800/270-7504.

Maps: For a map of Siskiyou National Forest, contact Nature of the Northwest Information Center, 800 Northeast Oregon Street, Suite 177, Portland, OR 97232; 503/872-2750. Ask the USGS for topographic maps of the Agness, Collier, and Pearsoll Peak areas.

Directions: From Gold Beach drive north on U.S. 101 and turn right (east) onto South Bank Road/Forest Service Road 33 just north of town. Drive 27 miles and turn right onto Forest Service Road 450. Follow signs 3.2 miles to the trailhead on the left.

Contact: Siskiyou National Forest, Powers Ranger District, Powers, OR 97446; 541/439-3011.

30 Snow Camp Lookout
10.4 mi/7.0 hrs

A long, moderate drop leads down the east ridge of the thickly forested Windy Creek Valley. After crossing the cold, clear creek, the trail continues straight up the opposite valley wall and doesn't stop until the summit of Snow Camp Mountain. The views from this summit—the site of an old fire lookout—are great, especially facing east into the Kalmiopsis Wilderness. (The views to the west are marred by clear-cuts.) Campsites are available in the Windy Creek basin if you want to spend the night.

Location: Northeast of Brookings in Siskiyou National Forest; see The Oregon Coast Map 7, grid f7.

User Groups: Hikers, dogs, and horses. No mountain bikes are allowed. No wheelchair facilities.

Permits: A federal Northwest Forest Pass, $5 per day or $30 annually, is required to park at the trailhead. Passes are available from ranger stations and many private vendors, online at website: www.wta.org, or by calling 800/270-7504.

Maps: For a trail information report, contact the Chetco Ranger District at 541/469-2196. For a map of Siskiyou National Forest, contact Nature of the Northwest Information Center, 800 Northeast Oregon Street, Suite 177, Portland, OR 97232; 503/872-2750. Ask the USGS for a topographic map of the Collier Butte area.

Directions: From Brookings drive northeast on County Road 784 (which becomes Forest Service Road 1376 at the forest boundary) to Cedar Camp. The trailhead is on the left at the camp.

Contact: Siskiyou National Forest, Chetco Ranger District, 555 Fifth Street, Brookings, OR 97415; 541/469-2196.

31 Mislatnah
7.2 mi/3.6 hrs

There's something for everyone on this hike. Beginning as a riverside trail, the route leaves the Chetco River after less than a mile and begins a long, steep climb to fantastic views from the summit of the high, isolated Mislatnah Peak. From where a fire lookout tower once stood, you can look down into the wild valley of the Big Craggies Botanical Area. The lush green forest below is rich in plants, both large and small, rare and common. For a closer look at the trees, continue across the summit of Mislatnah and drop down the peak's northern flank a short distance into the botanical area. The trail dead-ends in less than a mile, so enjoy the diversity of flora while you can. On the way back out, pay close attention to your surroundings and you should see at least some of the abundant wildlife that lives among the rich forage, including black-tailed deer and coyotes.

Location: Northeast of Brookings in Siskiyou National Forest partially within the Kalmiopsis Wilderness; see The Oregon Coast Map 7, grid f8.

User Groups: Hikers, dogs, and horses. No mountain bikes are allowed. No wheelchair facilities.

Permits: A federal Northwest Forest Pass, $5 per day or $30 annually, is required to park at the trailhead. Passes are available from ranger stations and many private vendors, online at website: www.wta.org, or by calling 800/270-7504. Party size is limited to 12 people.

Maps: For a trail information report, contact the Chetco Ranger District at 541/469-2196. For a map of Siskiyou National Forest, contact Nature of the Northwest Information Center, 800 Northeast Oregon Street, Suite 177, Portland, OR 97232; 503/872-2750. Ask the USGS for a topographic map of the Big Craggies area.

Directions: From Brookings drive about 24 miles northeast on County Road 784 (which becomes Forest Service Road 1376 at the forest boundary) to Forest Service Road 360.

Turn right (north) onto the junction with this road and drive about two miles to Forest Service Road 365. Turn right and continue to the road's end and the trailhead.

Contact: Siskiyou National Forest, Chetco Ranger District, 555 Fifth Street, Brookings, OR 97415; 541/469-2196.

32 Tincup
19.4 mi/1.0–2.0 days

Isolation-seekers take note! This is the sole trail into a deep, unmarred section of the Kalmiopsis Wilderness. It dead-ends in the center of the trailless section of forest, so if you don't see anyone on this trail, you know you're alone in the wilderness. From the trailhead amble on up the gently sloping trail as it follows the north bank of the Chetco River. Initially the trail sticks to a route well above the river, but as you dip deeper into the old-growth wilderness, the trail creeps nearer to the sparkling water. At the sharp bend in the river, the trail leaves the Chetco and switches over to paralleling Tincup Creek for the final few miles. The route ends abruptly at Darling Creek, where you can pitch a tent for the night if you want to make this a two-day hike.

Location: Northeast of Brookings in Siskiyou National Forest partially within the Kalmiopsis Wilderness; see The Oregon Coast Map 7, grid f8.

User Groups: Hikers, dogs, and horses. No mountain bikes are allowed. No wheelchair facilities.

Permits: A federal Northwest Forest Pass, $5 per day or $30 annually, is required to park at the trailhead. Passes are available from ranger stations and many private vendors, online at website: www.wta.org, or by calling 800/270-7504. Party size is limited to 12 people.

Maps: For a trail information report, contact the Chetco Ranger District at 541/469-2196. For a map of Siskiyou National Forest, contact Nature of the Northwest Information Center, 800 Northeast Oregon Street, Suite 177, Portland, OR 97232; 503/872-2750. Ask the USGS for a topographic map of the Big Craggies area.

Directions: From Brookings drive about 24 miles northeast on County Road 784 (which becomes Forest Service Road 1376 at the forest boundary) to the junction with Forest Service Road 360. Turn right (north) onto this road and drive about two miles to Forest Service Road 365. Turn right and continue to the road's end and the trailhead.

Contact: Siskiyou National Forest, Chetco Ranger District, 555 Fifth Street, Brookings, OR 97415; 541/469-2196.

33 Chetco Gorge
3.4 mi/1.7 hrs

The trail briefly follows the east bank of the river before reaching a wide ford with slow water. Carefully wade across (a hiking staff helps) and continue climbing upstream along the west bank of the wild river. The gorge is pretty, the river is picturesque, and on a hot summer day, the water is very inviting. Enjoy the wide, grassy banks farther upstream by stopping for a picnic lunch. The trail ends at the junction of Eagle Creek and the Chetco River. Generations of hikers have enjoyed a refreshing dip in the deep pool near the mouth of the creek.

Location: Northeast of Brookings in Siskiyou National Forest; see The Oregon Coast Map 7, grid g7.

User Groups: Hikers, dogs, and horses. No mountain bikes are allowed. No wheelchair facilities.

Permits: A federal Northwest Forest Pass, $5 per day or $30 annually, is required to park

at the trailhead. Passes are available from ranger stations and many private vendors, online at website: www.wta.org, or by calling 800/270-7504.

Maps: For a trail information report, contact the Chetco Ranger District at 541/469-2196. For a map of Siskiyou National Forest, contact Nature of the Northwest Information Center, 800 Northeast Oregon Street, Suite 177, Portland, OR 97232; 503/872-2750. Ask the USGS for a topographic map of the Big Craggies area.

Directions: From Brookings drive about 13 miles northeast on County Road 784 (which becomes Forest Service Road 1376 at the forest boundary) to Forest Service Road 150. Turn left onto Forest Service Road 150 and drive a short distance to the old bridge over the Chetco River. Park just before you reach the bridge. The trailhead is on the east end of the bridge, on the right.

Contact: Siskiyou National Forest, Chetco Ranger District, 555 Fifth Street, Brookings, OR 97415; 541/469-2196.

34 Johnson Butte
12.6 mi/6.3 hrs

This long trail is relatively gentle. It flows north, tracing a long ridge to Dry Butte, on past Salamander Lake, around the shore of Valen Lakes, to its terminus on the east flank of Johnson Butte. There are good views the entire way and great views from the two buttes, and the local scenery is stunning. The forest and meadows on the ridges are pretty, and the lakes are shiny pools full of life. Look for tadpoles, frogs, salamanders, water snakes, and muskrats in the ponds, as well as a variety of aquatic plants. The trail ends at a junction with the Chetco trail network. Return the way you came once you reach the end.

Location: Northeast of Brookings in Siskiyou National Forest within the Kalmiopsis Wilderness; see The Oregon Coast Map 7, grid f8.

User Groups: Hikers, dogs, and horses. No mountain bikes are allowed. No wheelchair facilities.

Permits: A federal Northwest Forest Pass, $5 per day or $30 annually, is required to park at the trailhead. Passes are available from ranger stations and many private vendors, online at website: www.wta.org, or by calling 800/270-7504. Party size is limited to 12 people.

Maps: For a trail information report, contact the Chetco Ranger District at 541/469-2196. For a map of Siskiyou National Forest, contact Nature of the Northwest Information Center, 800 Northeast Oregon Street, Suite 177, Portland, OR 97232; 503/872-2750. Ask the USGS for topographic maps of the Chetco Peak and Tincup Peak areas.

Directions: From Brookings drive about 12.5 miles northeast on County Road 784 (which becomes Forest Service Road 1376 at the forest boundary) to the junction with Forest Service Road 1909. Turn right (north) onto this road and drive about seven miles to Forest Service Road 260. Turn right and continue to the road's end and the trailhead.

Contact: Siskiyou National Forest, Chetco Ranger District, 555 Fifth Street, Brookings, OR 97415; 541/469-2196.

35 Vulcan Peak
2.4 mi/1.2 hrs

You gain nearly 1,000 feet in just over a mile on this steep, rough trail, but the workout is forgotten once you hit the 4,655-foot summit of Vulcan Peak. The former site of a fire lookout tower, this mountaintop presents some of the best views in southwest Oregon. Scan the panorama of Siskiyou National Forest and notice how the dark green valleys, filled with ancient, huge Douglas fir trees, are highlighted

by the raggedy ridges and knobby peaks scattered throughout the region. The trail ends at the summit of Vulcan Peak. Sit and enjoy the views before returning down the steep trail.

Location: Northeast of Brookings in Siskiyou National Forest within the Kalmiopsis Wilderness; see The Oregon Coast Map 7, grid g8.

User Groups: Hikers, dogs, and horses. No mountain bikes are allowed. No wheelchair facilities.

Permits: A federal Northwest Forest Pass, $5 per day or $30 annually, is required to park at the trailhead. Passes are available from ranger stations and many private vendors, online at website: www.wta.org, or by calling 800/270-7504. Party size is limited to 12 people.

Maps: For a trail information report, contact the Chetco Ranger District at 541/469-2196. For a map of Siskiyou National Forest, contact Nature of the Northwest Information Center, 800 Northeast Oregon Street, Suite 177, Portland, OR 97232; 503/872-2750. Ask the USGS for a topographic map of the Chetco Peak area.

Directions: From Brookings drive about 12.5 miles northeast on County Road 784 (which becomes Forest Service Road 1376 at the forest boundary) to Forest Service Road 1909. Turn right (north) and drive about seven miles to Forest Service Road 260. Turn right and continue about two miles east to a junction with Forest Service Road 261. Turn right and drive less than a mile to the road's end and the trailhead.

Contact: Siskiyou National Forest, Chetco Ranger District, 555 Fifth Street, Brookings, OR 97415; 541/469-2196.

36 Vulcan Lake
3.4 mi/1.7 hrs

Few lakes are as pretty as Vulcan Lake. Its azure waters are best viewed during calm winds, when the glassy surface perfectly mirrors Vulcan Peak. If the wind is blowing, try your hand at angling; some big trout prowl the deep pool, but the clarity of the water makes them spook easily when the surface is glassy. The trail to the lake is a gentle, mostly flat (less than 500 feet elevation gain) route that leads through old stands of Douglas fir and hemlock.

Location: Northeast of Brookings in Siskiyou National Forest within the Kalmiopsis Wilderness; see The Oregon Coast Map 7, grid g8.

User Groups: Hikers, dogs, and horses. No mountain bikes are allowed. No wheelchair facilities.

Permits: A federal Northwest Forest Pass, $5 per day or $30 annually, is required to park at the trailhead. Passes are available from ranger stations and many private vendors, online at website: www.wta.org, or by calling 800/270-7504. Party size is limited to 12 people.

Maps: For a trail information report, contact the Chetco Ranger District at 541/469-2196. For a map of Siskiyou National Forest, contact Nature of the Northwest Information Center, 800 Northeast Oregon Street, Suite 177, Portland, OR 97232; 503/872-2750. Ask the USGS for a topographic map of the Chetco Peak area.

Directions: From Brookings drive about 12.5 miles northeast on County Road 784 (which becomes Forest Service Road 1376 at the forest boundary) to Forest Service Road 1909. Turn right (north) onto this road and drive about seven miles to Forest Service Road 260. Turn right and continue to the road's end, where you find the trailhead.

Contact: Siskiyou National Forest, Chetco Ranger District, 555 Fifth Street, Brookings, OR 97415; 541/469-2196.

37 Redwood Nature Loop
1.0 mi/0.5 hr

If you think you have to go to California to see massive redwood trees, think again. This flat, wide loop trail explores a pristine grove of 300- to 800-year-old redwoods that

tower up to 350 feet above the forest floor. The diameter of the widest tree is approximately 20 feet, meaning the circumference of that trunk is at least 60 feet. If you want to link hands around this beast, bring 10 or 12 friends. The trail is marked with interpretive signs, and a guide brochure is available at the trailhead.

Location: Northeast of Brookings in Siskiyou National Forest; see The Oregon Coast Map 7, grid h7.

User Groups: Hikers and dogs. No horses or mountain bikes are allowed. No wheelchair facilities.

Permits: A federal Northwest Forest Pass, $5 per day or $30 annually, is required to park at the trailhead. Passes are available from ranger stations and many private vendors, online at website: www.wta.org, or by calling 800/270-7504.

Maps: For a trail information report, contact the Chetco Ranger District at 541/469-2196. For a map of Siskiyou National Forest, contact Nature of the Northwest Information Center, 800 Northeast Oregon Street, Suite 177, Portland, OR 97232; 503/872-2750. Ask the USGS for a topographic map of the Brookings area.

Directions: From Brookings drive about seven miles northeast on County Road 784 to Alfred A. Loeb State Park. The trailhead is one-half mile beyond the state park on the left.

Contact: Siskiyou National Forest, Chetco Ranger District, 555 Fifth Street, Brookings, OR 97415; 541/469-2196.

38 Elk Falls and Big Tree
3 mi/1.5 hrs

This hike offers two trails for the price of one. The first is short with an incredibly beautiful view at its end, and the other offers a good stretch of the legs with a remarkable natural feature to ponder at its end.

The trails begin at the same point at the trailhead. The left (northern) path leads to the falls on Elk Creek. This trail is relatively flat and just a quarter mile in length (round trip), so begin here to warm up for the longer trail. The trail climbs through lush old-growth rainforests. Cedar, bigleaf maples, and hemlocks tower over the path, and long beards of lichens trail from the branches overhead. The falls of Elk Creek are pretty horsetail-type falls on a stark, black rock face. There is great viewing of the falls from the end of the maintained trails, and a small path leads even closer—right up to the base of the cascade. Don't get too close, though, as waterfalls frequently bring down lots of rock, too. And while a shower of water on a hot day can be a great way to cool off, a conk on the head with a large rock can end an enjoyable day in a hurry.

After getting your fill of the cascade, return to the trailhead and head up the other trail. This one climbs over 500 feet in nearly 1.4 miles as it rolls east through equally lush forests. At the trail's end is the Big Tree—the world's largest Port Orford Cedar. If you want to measure just how big the tree is by putting your arms around it, plan on bringing six or eight friends—the cedar measures more than 38 feet in circumference and stands 220 feet tall.

Location: Northeast of Gold Beach in Siskiyou National Forest; see The Oregon Coast Map 8, grid b1.

User Groups: Hikers and dogs. No horses or mountain bikes are allowed. No wheelchair facilities.

Permits: A federal Northwest Forest Pass, $5 per day or $30 annually, is required to park at the trailhead. Passes are available from ranger stations and many private vendors, online at website: www.wta.org, or by calling 800/270-7504.

Maps: For a map of Siskiyou National Forest, contact Nature of the Northwest Information Center, 800 Northeast Oregon Street, Suite 177, Portland, OR 97232; 503/872-2750. Ask the USGS for topographic maps of the Powers area.

Directions: From Powers drive south on Forest Service Road 33 for six miles to the trailhead. Park in the wide turnout on the left (east) side of the road.

Contact: Siskiyou National Forest, Powers Ranger District, Powers, OR 97446; 541/439-3011.

🕉 Panther Ridge
12 mi/7.0 hrs

Find your way to this trail in early spring—April or May—and you'll think you're hiking a Hawaiian trail. The ridge's old, dense rainforests are filled with huge rhododendrons, and when they bloom in spring, the trail becomes a path with a fragrant pink tunnel. The huge rhody bushes are literally covered in giant pink blooms, and when the sunlight filters down through the forest canopy and hits these flowers, it's like a tropical paradise.

The trail rolls gently up and down along the ridge, passing Buck Point in less than a half mile before ending at the Bald Knob Lookout, the site of an old Forest Service fire watch tower. In addition to the glorious vegetation along the way, there are also awe-inspiring views and plenty of opportunities to see wildlife.

The first great views come just over a mile and a half out, when the trail passes Hanging Rock. This promontory is a flat shelf set atop high vertical walls, and it overlooks the center of the Rogue River Valley and a host of Siskiyou peaks. You can make this the end point of your hike if you are short of time or energy. But those looking for a longer stretch of the legs can continue southwest along Panther Ridge to Bald Knob. The trail passes a great campsite at five miles out, nestled alongside a broad meadow and another rhody jungle.

Location: Northeast of Gold Beach in Siskiyou National Forest; see The Oregon Coast Map 8, grid c1.

User Groups: Hikers and dogs. No horses or mountain bikes are allowed. No wheelchair facilities.

Permits: A federal Northwest Forest Pass, $5 per day or $30 annually, is required to park at the trailhead. Passes are available from ranger stations and many private vendors, online at website: www.wta.org, or by calling 800/270-7504.

Maps: For a map of Siskiyou National Forest, contact Nature of the Northwest Information Center, 800 Northeast Oregon Street, Suite 177, Portland, OR 97232; 503/872-2750. Ask the USGS for topographic maps of the Agness, Marial, and Bone Mountain areas.

Directions: From Powers drive south on Forest Service Road 33 for about 17 miles and turn left (east) onto Forest Service Road 3348. Continue nine miles and then turn right onto Forest Service Road 5520 at Buck Creek. Drive a little over a mile and turn left onto Forest Service Road 230. The trailhead is found just a half mile down this small, dirt spur road, on the right.

Contact: Siskiyou National Forest, Powers Ranger District, Powers, OR 97446; 541/439-3011.

🕐 Mount Bolivar

3.2 mi/2.0 hrs

This short trail leads in a serpentine route to the 4,319-foot Mount Bolivar summit. Though not a particularly tall peak, in relation to the surrounding mountains, this is a high pinnacle. The views from the top are panoramic splendor. The blue and green braid of the Rogue River Valley, the long backbone of Panther Ridge, and the paradise of Eden Valley are all spread out at your feet as your stand (or recline) at the trail's end.

From the trailhead the path climbs gradually but continually through a long series of switchbacks. The forest around the mountain's flanks are filled with old cedars and firs, and between the widely spaced trunks are groves of rhododendrons and meadows of beargrass, making spring the prime time for a visit. Come when the rhodies are blooming or, if you miss those, when the tall stalks of beargrass are topped with their white bulbous blooms. Spring is also when the vistas are most splendid, as the deep valleys around the mountain are filled with an array of greens.

Location: South of Powers in Siskiyou National Forest; see The Oregon Coast Map 8, grid b2.

User Groups: Hikers and dogs. No horses or mountain bikes are allowed. No wheelchair facilities.

Permits: A federal Northwest Forest Pass, $5 per day or $30 annually, is required to park at the trailhead. Passes are available from ranger stations and many private vendors, online at website: www.wta.org, or by calling 800/270-7504.

Maps: For a map of Siskiyou National Forest, contact Nature of the Northwest Information Center, 800 Northeast Oregon Street, Suite 177, Portland, OR 97232; 503/872-2750. Ask the USGS for topographic maps of the Bone Mountain area.

Directions: From Powers drive south on Forest Service Road 33 for about 17 miles and turn left (east) onto Forest Service Road 3348. Continue about 20 miles to a small access road signed for Mount Bolivar on the right. Turn here and drive a couple hundred yards to the road's end and trailhead parking area.

Contact: Siskiyou National Forest, Powers Ranger District, Powers, OR 97446; 541/439-3011.

41 Hanging Rock
21.6 mi/2.0 days

Skirting a high, open ridge above the wild and scenic Rogue River, this trail rolls gently past fantastic scenery and stunning views. The trail leaves Buck Point at the trailhead and moves south along Panther Ridge, past Hanging Rock, a high, heavy rock overhang that defies the laws of gravity. A short side trail leads to the summit of the rock; exploring there is well worth the time and effort. From here the main trail continues south along Panther Ridge, skirting the headwater basins of several pretty little creeks that feed into the Rogue River, visible as a thin blue ribbon in the deep valley on the east side of the ridge.

Midway through the hike, the trail passes the Devil's Backbone, a long, jagged rocky ridge that juts out perpendicular to Panther Ridge. The trail continues south of the Devil's Backbone, but the quality of the scenery quickly diminishes, and the thick forest increasingly obscures the views. The trail ends near the headwaters of Tate Creek. Retrace your steps to the trailhead, taking in the great views once again.

Location: West of Grants Pass in Siskiyou National Forest within the Wild Rogue Wilderness Area; see The Oregon Coast Map 8, grid c1.

User Groups: Hikers and dogs. No horses or mountain bikes are allowed. No wheelchair facilities.

Permits: A federal Northwest Forest Pass, $5 per day or $30 annually, is required to park at the trailhead. Passes are available from ranger stations and many private vendors, online at website: www.wta.org, or by calling 800/270-7504. Party size is limited to 12 people.

Maps: For a trail information report, contact the Powers Ranger District at 541/439-3011. For a map of Siskiyou National Forest, contact Nature of the Northwest Information Center, 800 Northeast Oregon Street, Suite 177, Portland, OR 97232; 503/872-2750. Ask the USGS for topographic maps of the Eden Ridge Valley, Marial, and Illahe areas.

Directions: From Grants Pass drive north on I-5. Take Exit 76 and turn left (west) onto Glendale Valley Road. Follow the road west to Glendale and turn right (north). Cross the river and then turn left (west) onto Cow Creek Road/BLM Road 32-9-3. Continue west up the Cow Creek Valley until you reach Dutch Henry Road/Forest Service Road 3348. Turn left and follow Dutch Henry Road southwest to Buck Creek Campground and the junction with Forest Service Road 5520. Turn left (east) and continue to Forest Service Road 230. Turn left and drive to the trailhead on the right side of the road.

Contact: Siskiyou National Forest, Powers Ranger District, Powers, OR 97446; 541/439-3011.

42 Big Pine
1.2 mi/0.7 hr

With their long, green needles and orange-brown scaly bark, ponderosa pines are quite beautiful. Few people, however, think of these trees as huge, an honor usually reserved for Douglas firs, redwoods, or even western red cedars. But this short trail offers proof that the ponderosa can scrape the skies with the best of them.

As you hike along this route, you weave among countless massive specimens of the ponderosa family, but it's not until you reach the trail's end that you find the really big one. Towering hundreds of feet above the valley floor is the world's tallest ponderosa pine. Its massive girth and incredible height are truly awesome, and the short hike to this great natural beauty is well worth the effort.

Location: West of Grants Pass in Siskiyou National Forest; see The Oregon Coast Map 8, grid e3.

User Groups: Hikers and dogs. No horses or mountain bikes are allowed. No wheelchair facilities.

Permits: A federal Northwest Forest Pass, $5 per day or $30 annually, is required to park at the trailhead. Passes are available from ranger stations and many private vendors, online at website: www.wta.org, or by calling 800/270-7504.

Maps: For a trail information report, contact the Galice Ranger District at 541/471-6500. For a map of Siskiyou National Forest, contact Nature of the Northwest Information Center, 800 Northeast Oregon Street, Suite 177, Portland, OR 97232; 503/872-2750. Ask the USGS for a topographic map of the Chrome Ridge area.

Directions: From Grants Pass drive about four miles north on I-5 to the Merlin exit. Turn left onto Merlin-Galice Road and drive about 12 miles west to Taylor Creek Road/Forest Service Road 25. Turn right onto Taylor Creek Road and continue to the Big Pine Campground and the trailhead.

Contact: Siskiyou National Forest, Galice Ranger District, 200 Northeast Greenfield Road, P.O. Box 440, Grants Pass, OR 97528-0242; 541/471-6500.

43 Dutchy Creek
15.8 mi/1.0–2.0 days

You'll find plenty of mining relics along this forest trail, including rusted equipment and old, narrow-gauge rails. The route follows the hillside up the Dutchy Creek Valley, sticking to the heavily forested slope and providing only moderate views of the creek and valley. The trail ends in the headwater basin of Silver Creek after crossing the high ridge at the junction of several creek basins. The best views over the valley are from this high point; unfortunately an old, rough logging road cuts across the ridge, somewhat diminishing the quality of the experience.

Location: West of Grants Pass in Siskiyou National Forest; see The Oregon Coast Map 8, grid e3.

User Groups: Hikers and dogs. No horses or mountain bikes are allowed. No wheelchair facilities.

Permits: A federal Northwest Forest Pass, $5 per day or $30 annually, is required to park at the trailhead. Passes are available from ranger stations and many private vendors, online at website: www.wta.org, or by calling 800/270-7504.

Maps: For a trail information report, contact the Galice Ranger District at 541/471-6500. For a map of Siskiyou National Forest, contact Nature of the Northwest Information Center, 800 Northeast Oregon Street, Suite 177, Portland, OR 97232; 503/872-2750. Ask the USGS for topographic maps of the Chrome Ridge and York Butte areas.

Directions: From Grants Pass drive about four miles north on I-5 to the Merlin exit. Turn left onto Merlin-Galice Road and drive approximately 12 miles west to Taylor Creek Road/Forest Service Road 25. Turn right onto Taylor Creek Road and continue 12 more miles before turning right onto Forest Service Road 2512. Follow this road for one-half mile and then turn right onto Forest Service Road 2512-015. Drive just one-half mile to the trailhead on the left side of the road.

Contact: Siskiyou National Forest, Galice Ranger District, 200 Northeast Greenfield Road, P.O. Box 440, Grants Pass, OR 97528-0242; 541/471-6500.

⓸⓸ Briggs Creek
17.0 mi/2.0 days

Briggs Creek and the surrounding valley were named in honor of George Briggs, a robust old mule driver who ran pack trains into this century-old mining region to supply gold-hungry miners. Moving upstream along the creek, this trail provides a gently rolling hike past several former mining sites—you can still see the tailing heaps and chunks of wood from the placer mine operations. Farther up the Briggs, you discover more evidence of the mineral-rich nature of this land, as mining operations are still in business along the creek.

The scenery offered by this hike is limited to the creek and surrounding valley forests (with the occasional clear-cutting scars). The route ends at the confluence of Briggs and Soldier Creeks near Forest Service Road 4105. (There's no trail access to the road, but a short bushwhacking adventure gets you there if you must see it.)

Location: West of Grants Pass in Siskiyou National Forest; see The Oregon Coast Map 8, grid e3.

User Groups: Hikers and dogs. No horses or mountain bikes are allowed. No wheelchair facilities.

Permits: A federal Northwest Forest Pass, $5 per day or $30 annually, is required to park at the trailhead. Passes are available from ranger stations and many private vendors, online at website: www.wta.org, or by calling 800/270-7504.

Maps: For a trail information report, contact the Galice Ranger District at 541/471-6500. For a map of Siskiyou National Forest, contact Nature of the Northwest Information Center, 800 Northeast Oregon Street, Suite 177, Portland, OR 97232; 503/872-2750. Ask the USGS for topographic maps of the Chrome Ridge, York Butte, Pearsoll Peak, and Eight Dollar Mountain areas.

Directions: From Grants Pass drive about four miles north on I-5 to the Merlin exit. Turn left onto Merlin-Galice Road and drive about 12 miles west to Taylor Creek Road/Forest Service Road 25. Turn right onto Taylor Creek Road and continue 12 miles before turning right onto Forest Service Road 2512. Follow this road to Sam Brown Campground and the trailhead.

Contact: Siskiyou National Forest, Galice Ranger District, 200 Northeast Greenfield Road, P.O. Box 440, Grants Pass, OR 97528-0242; 541/471-6500.

⓸⓹ York Butte
2.4 mi/1.2 hrs

After crossing the headwaters of Panther Creek, this trail climbs gently to the York Peak summit on the northeastern edge of the Kalmiopsis Wilderness. Enjoy the explosions of wildflower blooms you see throughout the sweeping meadows on the peak's flanks in early summer. The York Peak summit yields great views of the Illinois River Basin.

Location: West of Grants Pass in Siskiyou National Forest partially within the Kalmiopsis Wilderness Area; see The Oregon Coast Map 8, grid e3.

User Groups: Hikers and dogs. No horses or mountain bikes are allowed. No wheelchair facilities.

Permits: A federal Northwest Forest Pass, $5 per day or $30 annually, is required to park at the trailhead. Passes are available from ranger stations and many private vendors, online at website: www.wta.org, or by calling 800/270-7504. Party size is limited to 12 people.

Maps: For a trail information report, contact the Galice Ranger District at 541/471-6500. For a map of Siskiyou National Forest, contact Nature of the Northwest Information Center, 800 Northeast Oregon Street, Suite 177, Portland, OR 97232; 503/872-2750. Ask the USGS for a topographic map of the York Butte area.

Directions: From Grants Pass drive about four miles north on I-5 to the Merlin exit. Turn left onto Merlin-Galice Road and drive about 12 miles west to Taylor Creek Road/Forest Service Road 25. Turn right onto Taylor Creek Road and continue 12 miles before turning right onto Forest Service Road 2512. Follow this road for eight miles and turn left onto Forest Service Road 2512-675. Drive just over 1.5 miles and turn right onto Forest Service Road 678. Drive one-quarter mile to the trailhead on the left.

Contact: Siskiyou National Forest, Galice Ranger District, 200 Northeast Greenfield Road, P.O. Box 440, Grants Pass, OR 97528-0242; 541/471-6500.

46 Fall Creek
13.2 mi/6.6 hrs

Classic old-growth forests of Douglas fir, hemlock, and cedar shelter the rusting remains of 19th-century dreams. Gold-rush miners, who found the valleys of northern California already staked and claimed, moved into this area in search of the elusive big gold strike. Evidence of their quest lies scattered along the beautiful river valley, from the tools used by placer miners to excavations dug by hard-rock miners. Nature is slowly healing from the damage wrought by gold fever.

From the trailhead the trail climbs gently alongside Fall Creek for nearly its entire length. As you near the head of the valley, the route slants up the valley wall, works across a small feeder stream, and traverses to the ridgetop at the head of the river basin. The trail ends just east of Eagle Gap. Head back down the valley the way you came.

Location: Northwest of Cave Junction in Siskiyou National Forest; see The Oregon Coast Map 8, grid f3.

User Groups: Hikers and dogs. No horses or mountain bikes are allowed. No wheelchair facilities.

Permits: A federal Northwest Forest Pass, $5 per day or $30 annually, is required to park at the trailhead. Passes are available from ranger stations and many private vendors, online at website: www.wta.org, or by calling 800/270-7504. Party size is limited to 12 people.

Maps: For a trail information report, contact the Illinois Valley Ranger District at 541/592-4000. For a map of Siskiyou National Forest, contact Nature of the Northwest Information Center, 800 Northeast Oregon Street, Suite 177, Portland, OR 97232; 503/872-2750. Ask the USGS for topographic maps of the Josephine Mountain and Pearsoll Peak areas.

Directions: From Grants Pass drive about 20 miles west on U.S. 199 to Selma. Turn left (west) onto County Road 5070, which becomes Forest Service Road 4103 at the forest boundary. Continue about nine miles west on Forest Service Road 4103 to the Illinois River Falls day-use recreation area. The trailhead is near the parking lot.

Contact: Siskiyou National Forest, Illinois Valley Ranger District, 26568 Redwood Highway 199, Cave Junction, OR 97523; 541/592-4000.

47 Upper Chetco
57.2 mi/5.0 days

Slashing east to west across the heart of the Kalmiopsis Wilderness, this trail drops along the southern edge of Sourdough Flats and down the Slide Creek Valley. The trail is actually a long-abandoned wagon road into an old mining district, and the first stretch is marred by mining claims. You hike parallel to the creek about 6.5 miles upstream to Taggarts Bar (a good overnight camping destination) and then veer to the left and climb over a low ridge. After crossing through Canyon Creek Valley, the trail begins a long, sometimes steep, climb at mile 8.5 over Johnson Butte.

From the top of the peak (elevation 3,779 feet), enjoy sweeping views of the beautiful, pristine wilderness peaks and valleys around you and then head north on a long, rolling ridge crest for about six miles to Lately Prairie (another good camping spot). This wildflower field is home to dozens of rare plant species, as well as not-so-rare plants such as phlox, paintbrush, tiger lily, and trillium. From the prairie it's a quick drop to Boulder Creek and a long (about eight miles), gentle climb to the western trailhead on the flanks of Quail Mountain. Retrace your steps from there.

You can do this trail as a one-way hike if you shuttle a vehicle to one end or arrange for a pickup at the trail's end.

Location: Northwest of Cave Junction in Siskiyou National Forest within the Kalmiopsis Wilderness; see The Oregon Coast Map 8, grid f2.

User Groups: Hikers, dogs, and horses. No mountain bikes are allowed. No wheelchair facilities.

Permits: A federal Northwest Forest Pass, $5 per day or $30 annually, is required to park at the trailhead. Passes are available from ranger stations and many private vendors, online at website: www.wta.org, or by calling 800/270-7504. Party size is limited to 12 people.

Maps: For a trail information report, contact the Illinois Valley Ranger District at 541/592-4000. For a map of Siskiyou National Forest, contact Nature of the Northwest Information Center, 800 Northeast Oregon Street, Suite 177, Portland, OR 97232; 503/872-2750. Ask the USGS for topographic maps of the Pearsoll Peak, Tincup Peak, Big Craggies, and Quail Prairie Mountain areas.

Directions: From Grants Pass drive about 20 miles west on U.S. 199 to Selma. Turn left (west) onto County Road 5070, which becomes Forest Service Road 4103 at the forest boundary. Continue about nine miles west on Forest Service Road 4103 to the Illinois

River Falls day-use recreation area. Turn left (south) onto Forest Service Road 087 and drive to McCaleb Ranch. High-clearance vehicles may cross the low-water bridge and continue four miles to the road's end and the trailhead. The road is unfit for low-clearance vehicles, so those hikers should park near the ranch and hike to the road's end.

The western end of the trail is accessed from Brookings. Drive northeast on County Road 784, which becomes Forest Service Road 1376 at the forest boundary. Turn right (north) on Forest Service Road 1917 and drive to the road's end and the trailhead.

Contact: Siskiyou National Forest, Illinois Valley Ranger District, 26568 Redwood Highway 199, Cave Junction, OR 97523; 541/592-4000.

48 Bailey Mountain
25.8 mi/2.5 days

Moving down the Slide Creek Valley past several old mining claims, the Bailey Mountain Trail sticks to a long-abandoned wagon road before forking to the south, away from the Chetco Trail. At the shores of the Chetco River, stay left and continue south, hiking upstream alongside the noisy, trout-packed river. Over the course of several miles, you get to simply enjoy the cool beauty of the river valley, but just after crossing Carter Creek, the trail turns and climbs a moderately steep slope to Bailey Mountain. Be on the lookout for animals—big and small—in the forest clearings on this climb, as everything from deer to kangaroo mice thrive in the forage-rich wilderness.

From the top of Mount Bailey, the views are pleasing but not spectacular until you look skyward. If you don't see a rough-legged or red-tailed hawk winging overhead, it's probably because there's a bald eagle soaring nearby on the thermals. These beautiful raptors hunt, fish, and fly throughout this wonderful wilderness, but Bailey seems to have more than its fair share of the big birds.

The trail drops off the southern flank of Mount Bailey and ends at the north shore of the Little Chetco River. There are great campsites scattered around this area. Camp and enjoy the serenity of the Little Chetco before retracing your steps home.

Location: Northeast of Cave Junction in Siskiyou National Forest within the Kalmiopsis Wilderness Area; see The Oregon Coast Map 8, grid g2.

User Groups: Hikers, dogs, and horses. No mountain bikes are allowed. No wheelchair facilities.

Permits: A federal Northwest Forest Pass, $5 per day or $30 annually, is required to park at the trailhead. Passes are available from ranger stations and many private vendors, online at website: www.wta.org, or by calling 800/270-7504. Party size is limited to 12 people.

Maps: For a trail information report, contact the Illinois Valley Ranger District at 541/592-4000. For a map of Siskiyou National Forest, contact Nature of the Northwest Information Center, 800 Northeast Oregon Street, Suite 177, Portland, OR 97232; 503/872-2750. To obtain some USGS topographic maps of the area, ask for Pearsoll Peak, Josephine Mountain, and Chetco Peak.

Directions: From Grants Pass drive about 20 miles west on U.S. 199 to Selma. Turn left (west) onto County Road 5070, which becomes Forest Service Road 4103 at the forest boundary. Continue about nine miles west on Forest Service Road 4103 to the Illinois River Falls day-use recreation area. Turn left (south) onto Forest Service Road 087 and drive to McCaleb Ranch. High-clearance vehicles may cross the low-water bridge and continue four miles to the road's end and the trailhead. The road is unfit for low-clearance vehicles, so those hikers should park near the ranch and hike to the road's end.

Contact: Siskiyou National Forest, Illinois Valley Ranger District, 26568 Redwood Highway 199, Cave Junction, OR 97523; 541/592-4000.

49 Kalmiopsis Rim South
24.8 mi/3.0 days

Rather than slicing deep into the wilderness, this trail skirts the wilderness boundary, weaving south over, around, and along a series of high ridges and peaks. You'll be awed by the great vistas presented from the high points and impressed by the thick, diverse old-growth forest along the valley bottoms. The trail primarily sticks to a ridge as it moves south past Cold Springs Camp (where you find good camping), Canyon Peak (elevation 4,903 feet), and Doe Gap, where the trail terminates. Retrace your steps from there.

Location: West of Cave Junction in Siskiyou National Forest within the Kalmiopsis Wilderness; see The Oregon Coast Map 8, grid g2.

User Groups: Hikers, dogs, and horses. No mountain bikes are allowed. No wheelchair facilities.

Permits: A federal Northwest Forest Pass, $5 per day or $30 annually, is required to park at the trailhead. Passes are available from ranger stations and many private vendors, online at website: www.wta.org, or by calling 800/270-7504. Party size is limited to 12 people.

Maps: For a trail information report, contact the Illinois Valley Ranger District at 541/592-4000. For a map of Siskiyou National Forest, contact Nature of the Northwest Information Center, 800 Northeast Oregon Street, Suite 177, Portland, OR 97232; 503/872-2750. Ask the USGS for topographic maps of the Josephine Mountain and Buckskin Peak areas.

Directions: From Cave Junction drive four miles north on U.S. 199. Turn left (west) onto County Road 5240, which becomes Forest

Service Road 4201 at the forest boundary. Continue about 11 miles west on Forest Service Road 4201 to the junction with Forest Service Road 141. Turn left and drive to the road's end and the trailhead.

Contact: Siskiyou National Forest, Illinois Valley Ranger District, 26568 Redwood Highway 199, Cave Junction, OR 97523; 541/592-4000.

50 Kalmiopsis Rim North
9.0 mi/4.5 hrs

The northern section of this trail lies outside the wilderness area, but it is as beautiful as the longer, more rugged southern portion. The route follows a high, mostly open ridge covered with wildflower meadows. Panoramic views of the surrounding Siskiyou National Forest valleys and peaks await at every turn. North from the trailhead, the trail leads over Whetstone Butte, which offers some of the best views, and back down into a thick old-growth forest on the ridge. Continue north past Eagle Gap to Eagle Mountain for more great vistas. From Eagle Mountain the trail drops to Chetco Pass; retrace your steps from here.

This trail can be hiked as a one-way trip if you get picked up or drop a shuttle car off at the Upper Chetco Trailhead.

Location: West of Cave Junction in Siskiyou National Forest; see The Oregon Coast Map 8, grid g2.

User Groups: Hikers, dogs, horses, and mountain bikes. No wheelchair facilities.

Permits: A federal Northwest Forest Pass, $5 per day or $30 annually, is required to park at the trailhead. Passes are available from ranger stations and many private vendors, online at website: www.wta.org, or by calling 800/270-7504. Party size is limited to 12 people.

Maps: For a trail information report, contact the Illinois Valley Ranger District at 541/592-4000. For a map of Siskiyou National Forest,

contact Nature of the Northwest Information Center, 800 Northeast Oregon Street, Suite 177, Portland, OR 97232; 503/872-2750. Ask the USGS for topographic maps of the Josephine Mountain and Pearsoll Peak areas.

Directions: From Cave Junction drive four miles north on U.S. 199. Turn left (west) onto County Road 5240, which becomes Forest Service Road 4201 at the forest boundary. Continue about 11 miles west to the junction with Forest Service Road 141. Turn left and drive to the road's end and the trailhead.

The northern end of the trail is at the Chetco Pass Trailhead. To get there from Grants Pass, drive about 20 miles west on U.S. 199 to Selma. Turn left (west) onto County Road 5070, which becomes Forest Service Road 4103 at the forest boundary. Continue about nine miles west to the Illinois River Falls area. Turn left (south) onto Forest Service Road 087 and drive to McCaleb Ranch. High-clearance vehicles may cross the low-water bridge and continue four miles to the trailhead. The road is unfit for low-clearance vehicles, so those hikers should park near the ranch and hike to the road's end.

Contact: Siskiyou National Forest, Illinois Valley Ranger District, 26568 Redwood Highway 199, Cave Junction, OR 97523; 541/592-4000.

51 Emily Cabin
16.6 mi/1.0–2.0 days

A short walk south on the ridgetop Kalmiopsis Rim Trail leads to the route to Emily Cabin. Turn right at the first fork in the trail and head down a long ridge to the Little Chetco River. Along the way you find old-growth Douglas fir and hemlock forests, sunny meadows, and great views. As you near the river, the rustic Emily Cabin appears off to one side. Though it lies within the wilderness, the cabin and all the associated equipment are on private property, and the owner asks that hikers in the area avoid the cabin. The trail ends at the Little Chetco River at a junction with the Upper Chetco Trail (see hike this chapter). Some good campsites are available near the picturesque creek. Spend time in the area and then return the way you came.

Location: West of Cave Junction in Siskiyou National Forest within the Kalmiopsis Wilderness; The Oregon Coast Map 87, grid g2.

User Groups: Hikers, dogs, and horses. No mountain bikes are allowed. No wheelchair facilities.

Permits: A federal Northwest Forest Pass, $5 per day or $30 annually, is required to park at the trailhead. Passes are available from ranger stations and many private vendors, online at website: www.wta.org, or by calling 800/270-7504. Party size is limited to 12 people.

Maps: For a trail information report, contact the Illinois Valley Ranger District at 541/592-4000. For a map of Siskiyou National Forest, contact Nature of the Northwest Information Center, 800 Northeast Oregon Street, Suite 177, Portland, OR 97232; 503/872-2750. Ask the USGS for topographic maps of the Josephine Mountain and Chetco Peak areas.

Directions: From Cave Junction drive four miles north on U.S. 199. Turn left (west) onto County Road 5240, which becomes Forest Service Road 4201 at the forest boundary. Continue about 11 miles west to the junction with Forest Service Road 141. Turn left and drive to the road's end and the trailhead.

Contact: Siskiyou National Forest, Illinois Valley Ranger District, 26568 Redwood Highway 199, Cave Junction, OR 97523; 541/592-4000.

52 Babyfoot Lake
5.2 mi/2.6 hrs

The rich diversity of life in this area is evident from the fact that the land has been set aside for national research and protected as the Babyfoot Lake Botanical Area. Bring your field guidebook to wild plants, as there's a vast assortment of plant species from rare mushrooms and grasses to common wildflowers and massive trees. The trail is short and easy, so take the time to stop and try to identify some of the interesting, unusual specimens.

Midway up the gently sloping trail, you pass the cool, blue waters of Babyfoot Lake. This pretty alpine pool is a good place to stop and rest, pulling out the field guide for a little botanical study time. When you've enough of that pursuit, continue on up to the trail's end at a junction with the Chetco Trail before turning around and returning the way you came.

Location: West of Cave Junction in Siskiyou National Forest partially within the Kalmiopsis Wilderness; see The Oregon Coast Map 8, grid g2.

User Groups: Hikers, dogs, and horses. No mountain bikes are allowed. No wheelchair facilities.

Permits: A federal Northwest Forest Pass, $5 per day or $30 annually, is required to park at the trailhead. Passes are available from ranger stations and many private vendors, online at website: www.wta.org, or by calling 800/270-7504. Party size is limited to 12 people.

Maps: For a trail information report, contact the Illinois Valley Ranger District at 541/592-4000. For a map of Siskiyou National Forest, contact Nature of the Northwest Information Center, 800 Northeast Oregon Street, Suite 177, Portland, OR 97232; 503/872-2750. Ask the USGS for a topographic map of the Josephine Mountain area.

Directions: From Cave Junction drive four miles north on U.S. 199. Turn left (west) onto County Road 5240, which becomes Forest Service Road 4201 at the forest boundary. Continue about 11 miles west on Forest Service Road 4201 to the junction with Forest

Service Road 140. Turn left and drive to the trailhead on the right side of the road.

Contact: Siskiyou National Forest, Illinois Valley Ranger District, 26568 Redwood Highway 199, Cave Junction, OR 97523; 541/592-4000.

53 Baldface
13.6 mi/1.0–2.0 days

Beginning at the head of the Biscuit Creek Valley, this trail stays high on a ridge as it traverses to the west, offering good views into the pretty valley below. Midway along the route, you curve around the southern flank of Biscuit Hill; there you find a short side trail that leads up to the summit. The views are worth the extra effort needed to make this easy climb. From the top of Biscuit Hill, you look out over the southern end of the Siskiyous, as well as the whole Kalmiopsis Wilderness stretching out to the north—a wonderful dark green world of old-growth forest valleys and knobby peaks.

The trail then continues west from Biscuit Hill and drops into the Baldface Creek Basin. Rainbow, golden, and brown trout thrive in the cold creek waters, so bring a rod and reel if you're a trout hunter. If not, bring a camera and plan on spending some time just enjoying the noisy, splashing creek.

Location: Southwest of Cave Junction in Siskiyou National Forest; see The Oregon Coast Map 8, grid h2.

User Groups: Hikers, dogs, horses, and mountain bikes. No wheelchair facilities.

Permits: A federal Northwest Forest Pass, $5 per day or $30 annually, is required to park at the trailhead. Passes are available from ranger stations and many private vendors, online at website: www.wta.org, or by calling 800/270-7504. Party size is limited to 12 people.

Maps: For a trail information report, contact the Illinois Valley Ranger District at 541/592-4000. For a map of Siskiyou National Forest,

contact Nature of the Northwest Information Center, 800 Northeast Oregon Street, Suite 177, Portland, OR 97232; 503/872-2750. Ask the USGS for topographic maps of the Buckskin Peak and Biscuit Hill areas.

Directions: From Cave Junction drive about eight miles south on U.S. 199 to O'Brien. Turn right (west) onto County Road 5550, which becomes Forest Service Road 4402 at the forest boundary. Continue about nine miles west to the junction with Forest Service Road 112 and turn right (north). Drive three miles to the trailhead on the left.

Contact: Siskiyou National Forest, Illinois Valley Ranger District, 26568 Redwood Highway 199, Cave Junction, OR 97523; 541/592-4000.

54 Frantz Meadow
5.4 mi/2.7 hrs

You have to work for your views here, but this area is so beautiful you won't mind the effort. The trail is steep, rocky, and in several sections, deeply rutted, as motorcycles occasionally churn things up. The route drops from the trailhead along the side of a wide, shallow valley to the meadow wetlands. There you find an assortment of wildflowers, scores of bird species, and wildlife ranging from big mule deer to tiny kangaroo mice. If you are a wildlife enthusiast, this is the hike for you. Bring binoculars and a camera.

Location: Southwest of Cave Junction in Siskiyou National Forest; see The Oregon Coast Map 8, grid h2.

User Groups: Hikers, dogs, horses, and mountain bikes. No wheelchair facilities.

Permits: A federal Northwest Forest Pass, $5 per day or $30 annually, is required to park at the trailhead. Passes are available from ranger stations and many private vendors, online at website: www.wta.org, or by calling 800/270-7504. Party size is limited to 12 people.

Maps: For a trail information report, contact the Illinois Valley Ranger District at 541/592-4000. For a map of Siskiyou National Forest, contact Nature of the Northwest Information Center, 800 Northeast Oregon Street, Suite 177, Portland, OR 97232; 503/872-2750. Ask the USGS for topographic maps of the Josephine Mountain and Pearsoll Peak areas.

Directions: From Cave Junction drive about eight miles south on U.S. 199 to O'Brien. Turn right (west) onto County Road 5550, which becomes Forest Service Road 4402 at the forest boundary. Continue about nine miles to the junction with Forest Service Road 112 and turn right (north). Drive to the road's end and the trailhead.

Contact: Siskiyou National Forest, Illinois Valley Ranger District, 26568 Redwood Highway 199, Cave Junction, OR 97523; 541/592-4000.

55 Chetco Divide
33.0 mi/3.0 days

A pure wilderness trail, this route cuts east to west across the southern end of the protected area and explores some of its wildest sections. Climbing an old rutted wagon road, the first few trail miles traverse the west side of Buckskin Peak, elevation 3,253 feet, and roll north to Doe Gap, a 3,712-foot saddle on an open ridge. The view from the gap is indescribable—awesome, incredible, stunning—there simply aren't enough adjectives to do it justice. Even more incredible, though, is the fact that as you hike west, the views are as good and sometimes even better.

A long ridge walk from Doe Gap leads past 4,540-foot Chetlo Peak (take a side trail to the summit and Chetlo Lookout) and on to Chetco Peak, elevation 4,660 feet. Drop from the Chetco summit to Chetco Lake, with its fine campsites. Then continue on over Red Mountain before reaching the trail's end at 4,655-foot Vulcan Peak. Retrace your steps from here and thrill to the scenery all over again.

Location: Southwest of Cave Junction in Siskiyou National Forest; see The Oregon Coast Map 8, grid h2.

User Groups: Hikers, dogs, horses, and mountain bikes. No wheelchair facilities.

Permits: A federal Northwest Forest Pass, $5 per day or $30 annually, is required to park at the trailhead. Passes are available from ranger stations and many private vendors, online at website: www.wta.org, or by calling 800/270-7504. Party size is limited to 12 people.

Maps: For a trail information report, contact the Illinois Valley Ranger District at 541/592-4000. For a map of Siskiyou National Forest, contact Nature of the Northwest Information Center, 800 Northeast Oregon Street, Suite 177, Portland, OR 97232; 503/872-2750. Ask the USGS for topographic maps of the Josephine Mountain and Pearsoll Peak areas.

Directions: From Cave Junction drive about eight miles south on U.S. 199 to O'Brien. Turn right (west) onto County Road 5550, which becomes Forest Service Road 4402 at the forest boundary. Continue about nine miles to the junction with Forest Service Road 112 and turn right (north). Drive to the road's end and the trailhead.

Contact: Siskiyou National Forest, Illinois Valley Ranger District, 26568 Redwood Highway 199, Cave Junction, OR 97523; 541/592-4000.

PORTLAND AND THE WILLAMETTE VALLEY

Portland and the Willamette Valley

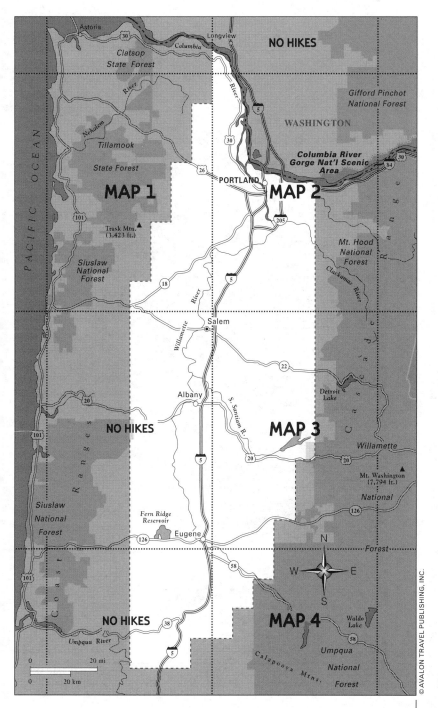

Map 1

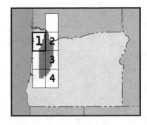

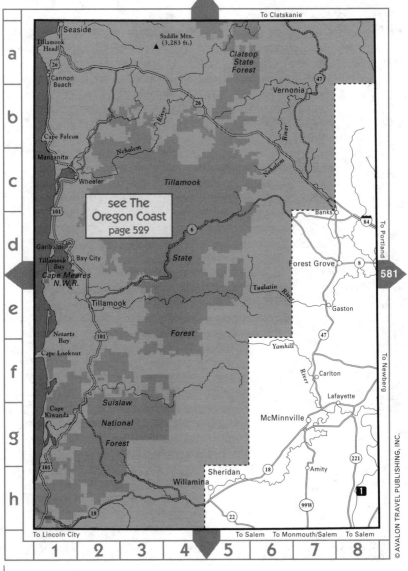

see The
Oregon Coast
page 529

To Clatskanie

Seaside

Saddle Mtn.
(3,283 ft.)

Tillamook
Head

Clatsop
State
Forest

Cannon
Beach

Vernonia

River

Cape Falcon

Nehalem

Manzanita

Tillamook

Nehalem

Wheeler

Banks

To Portland

Garibaldi

State

Bay City

Forest Grove

Tillamook
Bay

Cape Meares
N.W.R.

Tillamook

Tualatin River

Gaston

Netarts
Bay

Forest

Yamhill

Cape Lookout

Carlton

To Newberg

Lafayette

Cape
Kiwanda

Suislaw

McMinnville

National

Forest

Sheridan

Amity

Willamina

To Lincoln City

To Salem   To Monmouth/Salem   To Salem

Map 2

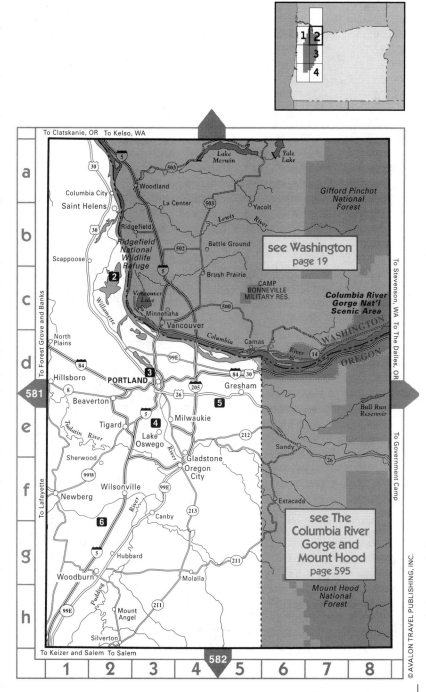

To Clatskanie, OR   To Kelso, WA

Lake Merwin

Yale Lake

To Forest Grove and Banks

Columbia City

Saint Helens

Woodland

La Center

Yacolt

Gifford Pinchot National Forest

Ridgefield

Ridgefield National Wildlife Refuge

Scappoose

Lewis River

Battle Ground

see Washington page 19

Brush Prairie

CAMP BONNEVILLE MILITARY RES.

Columbia River Gorge Nat'l Scenic Area

Vancouver Lake

Minnehaha

Vancouver

Camas

Columbia River

WASHINGTON

OREGON

North Plains

Hillsboro

PORTLAND

Gresham

Bull Run Reservoir

To Stevenson, WA   To The Dalles, OR

581

Beaverton

Tigard

Lake Oswego

Milwaukie

Sandy

To Government Camp

Sherwood

Gladstone

Oregon City

Newberg

Wilsonville

Canby

Estacada

see The Columbia River Gorge and Mount Hood page 595

To Lafayette

Hubbard

Woodburn

Molalla

Mount Hood National Forest

Mount Angel

Silverton

To Keizer and Salem   To Salem

582

1   2   3   4   5   6   7   8

© AVALON TRAVEL PUBLISHING, INC.

Map 3

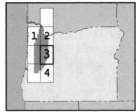

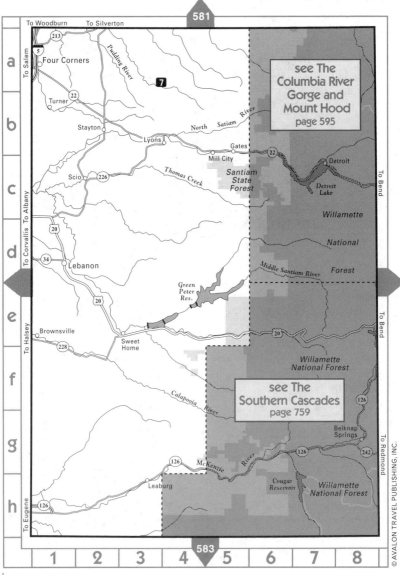

see The Columbia River Gorge and Mount Hood
page 595

see The Southern Cascades
page 759

To Woodburn   To Silverton

To Salem

213

5

Four Corners

Pudding River

7

Turner   22

Stayton

Lyons

North Santiam River

Gates

Mill City

Detroit

To Corvallis   To Albany

Scio   226

Thomas Creek

Santiam State Forest

Detroit Lake

Willamette

20

34

Lebanon

National

Middle Santiam River

Forest

To Bend

Green Peter Res.

20

To Halsey

Brownsville

228

Sweet Home

20

Willamette National Forest

To Bend

Calapooia River

126

Belknap Springs

126

126

McKenzie River

242

To Redmond

Cougar Reservoir

Willamette National Forest

To Eugene

126

Leaburg

© AVALON TRAVEL PUBLISHING, INC.

581

583

1   2   3   4   5   6   7   8

a b c d e f g h

Map 4

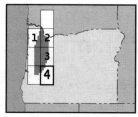

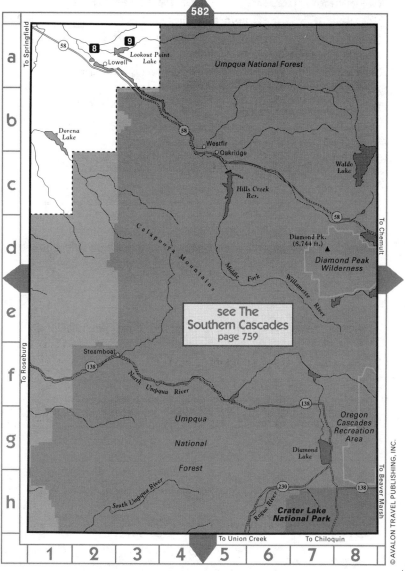

To Springfield

a

58

8   **9**

Lowell   Lookout Point Lake

Umpqua National Forest

b

Dorena Lake

58

Westfir
Oakridge

Waldo Lake

c

Hills Creek Res.

58

Calapooya Mountains

d

To Roseburg

To Chemult

Diamond Pk. (8,744 ft.)

Diamond Peak Wilderness

Middle Fork

Willamette River

e

see The
Southern Cascades
page 759

f

Steamboat

138

North Umpqua River

138

Oregon Cascades Recreation Area

g

Umpqua

National

Forest

Diamond Lake

To Beaver Marsh

h

South Umpqua River

230

Rogue River

138

Crater Lake National Park

© AVALON TRAVEL PUBLISHING, INC.

To Union Creek   To Chiloquin

1   2   3   4   5   6   7   8

Portland and the Willamette Valley

1 Willamette Mission State Park Loop
2.7 mi/1.5 hrs

The biggest cottonwood tree in the world is here. We've seen it. Unless you're really bored, that might not be enough to get you to drive south to Willamette Mission State Park. But a loop trail along the Willamette River might be, especially when you spice it up a bit with a ride across the river on the Wheatland Ferry.

Park in the Filbert Grove day-use area and follow the trail along the river to the ferry landing and a bit beyond. Whether or not you ride the ferry, backtrack a bit when you're through and turn left on a bicycle/wheelchair trail that leads along the north shore of Mission Lake, an old meander scar (the massive flood of 1861 that wiped out Champoeg also eliminated this river bend) outfitted with a boat launch and a pair of barrier-free fishing piers. Walnuts and great blue herons are commonly sighted here. That big cottonwood is on the west end of the lake. It's 155 feet tall, more than 26 feet around, and estimated to be more than 260 years old. Take a picture of it and imagine how tall it was when the Reverend Jason Lee built a homestead and Methodist mission on this fertile soil in 1834. Continue straight to the parking lot where you started.

Location: North of Salem on the Willamette River; see Portland and the Willamette Valley Map 1, grid h8.

User Groups: Hikers, dogs, horses, and mountain bikes. A short barrier-free trail leads to twin wheelchair-accessible fishing piers on Mission Lake.

Permits: No permits are required. A $3 parking fee is collected at the park. Annual Oregon Parks and Recreation permits are available for $25; contact Oregon State Parks at 800/551-6949.

Maps: For a free park brochure, contact the Oregon Parks and Recreation Department at 800/551-6949. Ask the USGS for a topographic map of the Mission Bottom area.

Directions: From Portland drive 39 miles south on I-5 to Exit 263. Drive about 1.8 miles west on Brooklake Road to Wheatland Road. Turn right and proceed about 2.5 miles to the Willamette Mission State Park entrance.

Contact: Oregon Parks and Recreation Department, 1115 Commercial Street Northeast, Salem, OR 97301; 800/551-6949.

2 Warrior Rock
7.0 mi/3.5 hrs

Bald eagles and bulging freighters keep you company on this island trail that just might be at its best in the winter, when higher-elevation Northwest trails are snowbound and migratory birds stop here to rest. Some portions of the Sauvie Island Wildlife Area, in fact, close between October and April to allow solitude to migratory birds. But the Warrior Rock Trail is open all year. Wildlife experts say September through March is the best time for viewing waterfowl and sandhill cranes, January through March for spotting bald eagles. The path, on the north end of 16-mile-long Sauvie Island, is actually a road, which you have to share with a cow or two. It leads three miles north along the island edge to the tiny Warrior Rock Lighthouse at the tip of the island. The lighthouse is off-limits, but a beach is nearby. Follow the trail about half a mile farther to its end on the tip of the island, across from the town of St. Helens.

If you have time stop on the drive back for a short loop hike around Oak Island, an island within an island that sits in the middle of Sauvie Island's Sturgeon Lake. The trailhead is on Oak Island Road, which departs north from the beginning stretches of Reeder

Road. Swans, sandhill cranes, and other migratory birds can all be seen here in the winter.

Location: On Sauvie Island between the Columbia River and Multnomah Channel; see Portland and the Willamette Valley Map 2, grid c2.

User Groups: Hikers only. No horses, mountain bikes, or dogs are allowed. No wheelchair facilities.

Permits: No day-use permits are required. A $3 Sauvie Island Wildlife Area parking permit ($10.50 annually) is required and available at outdoors stores, merchants in the Sauvie Island Area, or Sauvie Island Wildlife Area at the address below.

Maps: Ask the USGS for a topographic map of the St. Helens area.

Directions: From Portland drive 10 miles west on U.S. 30 to Sauvie Island Bridge. Turn right and drive north on Northwest Sauvie Island Road to Reeder Road. Turn right and follow Reeder Road 12.5 miles to the parking area. To reach the trail, climb over the stile in the parking area.

Contact: Sauvie Island Wildlife Area, 18330 NW Sauvie Island Road, Portland, OR 97231; 503/621-3488.

3 Wildwood National Recreation Trail

**26.3 mi. total/
0.5 hr–1.0 day**

Quiet it isn't, but convenient it is. You find plenty of company on the Wildwood Trail, which begins in Portland and runs farther north than most hikers can walk in a day or two. Most of the trail is broad and easy to walk, with multiple entry points and well-marked side trails combining to make route-finding easy to the trail newcomer. The southern portion is more urban and, naturally, more crowded. Here the trail winds through the Hoyt Arboretum, where kids—and parents—are challenged to identify as many of the 650 tree species as possible. Continuing north, you cross bustling Burnside Street, providing one of the more challenging moments of your hike. Farther north, the trail passes the grounds of the Pittock Mansion and comes to a dividing line at the Cornell Street Trailhead. Farther north from here the trail gets more wild as you make your way into the city's Forest Park. Combining the Wildwood Trail with the popular Maple Trail or one of a series of closed roads that bisect the area can produce pleasant day hikes of three to five miles through mixed forest. For a trail that spends as much time as this one does within the city limits of a major metropolis, the Wildwood Trail is a true gem.

If you were hoping to ride a bike or horse, note that mountain bikes and horses are allowed on abandoned roads adjacent to the Wildwood Trail. Call the Portland Parks and Recreation Department at the number below for more information.

Location: Between Portland's Washington Park and Germantown Road in North Forest Park; see Portland and the Willamette Valley Map 2, grid d3.

User Groups: Hikers only. No horses, dogs, or mountain bikes are allowed. No wheelchair facilities.

Permits: No permits are required. Parking and access are free.

Maps: For a free trail map, contact the Portland Parks and Recreation Department at 503/823-7529. Ask the USGS for topographic maps of the Portland, Linnton, Hillsboro, and Dixie Mountain areas.

Directions: To reach the southern trailhead from downtown Portland, drive on U.S. 26 west to the Washington Park Zoo exit and follow signs to parking at the MAX station and World Forestry Center. The trailhead is near the Vietnam Veterans Memorial. To reach the northern trailhead, drive on U.S. 30 to the Northwest Germantown Road exit and follow signs to the trailhead.

Contact: Portland Parks and Recreation Department, 1120 Southwest Fifth Avenue, Suite 1302, Portland, OR 97204; 503/823-PLAY (7529).

4 Tryon Creek State Park
2.0–4.0 mi/1.0–2.0 hrs

This relatively new 631-acre state park was created of the hiker, by the hiker, and for the hiker, not to mention bikers as well as those who ride horses or use wheelchairs. Everyone has a place at Tryon Creek, which has eight miles of hiking trails, 3.5 miles of horse trails, three miles of bike paths, and a one-third mile barrier-free nature path, the Trillium Trail.

At the main park entrance, stop at the Nature Center for a trail map, which you need to navigate the myriad trail junctions in the park. You can spend days here exploring the second-growth mixed forest of the Tryon Creek drainage. One of the more popular routes is the three-mile hiker loop, which drops to the lush banks of Tryon Creek, climbs to the opposite ridge, and returns after several bridge crossings. The route is steep in places and can be very muddy when it's wet. But the terrain is beautiful, particularly in the early spring, when trillium is in bloom and the forest floor is a study in vivid greens.

For mountain bikers a 2.6-mile path starts at Lewis and Clark Law School outside the park and follows the park's eastern boundary to Highway 43. Equestrians have their own parking lot and two loop trails from which to choose. If you're looking for a short day hike in the relative quiet of the forest, several half-mile loops begin and end at the Nature Center.

Friends of Tryon Creek State Park operates a nature store, summer day camps, and guided nature walks here. For schedules and information, call 503/636-4398.

Tryon Creek is one of many Portland-area parks expected to be connected by the "40-mile Trail" network in the future. The 40-Mile Trail was originally conceived in 1904 by the Olmsted Brothers, famed park designers, who envisioned a nature trail circling the city. The concept now has been expanded to a 140-mile trail forming a wide circle around the metro area, connecting with parks along the Columbia, Sandy, and Willamette rivers.

Location: Between downtown Portland and Lake Oswego in suburban Portland; see Portland and the Willamette Valley Map 2, grid e3.

User Groups: Hikers, leashed dogs (six-foot leash maximum), horses, and mountain bikes are allowed. The park includes a barrier-free nature trail for wheelchair users.

Permits: No permits are required. Parking and access are free.

Maps: For a free brochure and map, stop at the park's Nature Center or contact the Oregon Parks and Recreation Department at 800/551-6949. Ask the USGS for a topographic map of the Lake Oswego area.

Directions: From downtown Portland drive on I-5 a short distance south to Exit 297/Terwilliger Boulevard and follow signs for 2.5 miles to the park's main entrance on the right. Note: Don't leave valuables in your car.

Contact: Oregon Parks and Recreation Department, 1115 Commercial Street Northeast, Salem, OR 97301; 800/551-6949.

5 Powell Butte Loop
3.1 mi/1.5 hrs

In the depths of winter, when your friends are all watching the Rose Bowl on a perfectly fine day, Powell Butte is a prime getaway.

The park's 3.1-mile loop is a good leg-stretcher, close to the city but just far enough away to provide some pleasant scenery and remind you of what entices you out onto trails in the warm summer months. From the top (about 630 feet) views of Mount Hood, Mount Adams, and what's left of Mount St. Helens await.

Location: South of U.S. 26 between Portland and Gresham; see Portland and the Willamette Valley Map 2, grid e4.

User Groups: Hikers, horses, and dogs. The first half mile of the trail is paved and accessible to wheelchairs. No mountain bikes are allowed.

Permits: No permits are required. Parking and access are free.

Maps: For a free park brochure and map, contact the Portland Department of Parks and Recreation at 503/823-2223. Trail brochures are provided at the trailhead. Ask the USGS for a topographic map of the Gladstone area.

Directions: From I-205 east of Portland, take Exit 19/Powell Boulevard. Follow Southeast Powell Boulevard about 3.5 miles east to 162nd Avenue. Turn right (south) and follow the road to the parking lot and the trailhead.

Contact: Portland Parks and Recreation Department, 1120 Southwest Fifth Avenue, Suite 1302, Portland, OR 97204; 503/823-PLAY (503/823-7529).

6 Champoeg State Park Loop
3.0 mi/1.5 hrs

Champoeg, site of an ancient Indian village on the banks of the Willamette, reeks of history. The Hudson's Bay Company brought the earliest white settlement in the region here in 1811, and the West Coast's first provisional government was organized at a meeting here in 1843. Later the town of Champoeg developed here,

only to be wiped out by an 1861 flood. Plenty of history remains, and a popular, well-developed trail system leads you to most of it.

The 615-acre park contains about 10 miles of hiking and cycle trails, but most people pick a three-mile loop that serves as sort of a sampler. The loop trail starts near the Champoeg Creek Bridge and winds along the banks of the river to pageant grounds that are used for historical re-creations. Farther west, you pass an old Daughters of the American Revolution cabin and then loop back east on the park's cycle trail, crossing Mission Creek and returning to the campground. Another cycle trail starts at the campground and makes an eight-mile round-trip ride to the rustic old town of Butteville. A short distance down the trail, a half-mile nature trail is worth your time, as is the park's fascinating visitor center and the Newell House Museum.

Location: Southeast of Newburg on the south banks of the Willamette River; see Portland and the Willamette Valley Map 2, grid g2.

User Groups: Hikers, dogs, and mountain bikes. No horses are allowed. No wheelchair facilities.

Permits: No permits are required. A $3 parking fee is collected at the park entrance. Annual Oregon Parks and Recreation passes are available for $25; contact the Oregon Parks and Recreation Department at 800/551-6949.

Maps: For a free park brochure, contact the Oregon Parks and Recreation Department at 800/551-6949. Ask the USGS for a topographic map of the Newberg area

Directions: From Portland drive south on I-5 to Exit 278 and follow the signs to the park, which is about 5.5 miles west on Champoeg Road.

Contact: Oregon Parks and Recreation Department, 1115 Commercial Street Northeast, Salem, OR 97301; 800/551-6949.

7 Silver Falls State Park Loop
7.0 mi/4.0 hrs

This is Oregon's largest state park, with a geological and historical fascination to match its physical size. The 8,706-acre park encompasses equestrian and bicycle trails, jogging paths, youth camp and conference center, horse camp, public campground, and a fascinating loop trail (the Canyon Trail) that leads past 10 waterfalls on the North and South Forks of Silver Creek.

This seven-mile loop takes hikers past sights such as dramatic South Falls, where the former owner of this property, D.E. Geiser, once charged onlookers to watch humans and old automobiles plunge over the abyss. Later the land was purchased for public use and at one point was even considered for national park status. That wasn't to be, but the park remains a fascinating place to spend a free day. Whether you're into hiking, running, horseback riding, or cycling, Silver Falls has ample space to roam. It's pleasant all year long, but arriving here in the spring usually ensures the best display from the 10 waterfalls, ranging in height from 27 to 178 feet. The loop trail actually passes behind three of the falls. Cyclists are funneled onto two separate loop trails in the park, and horseback riders can explore miles of paths around Buck Mountain, including a 14-mile loop (also open to hikers). Wildlife and wildflowers are plentiful. The place is big, so get an early start if you want to see even a portion of this fascinating park.

Location: Twenty-six miles east of Salem off Highway 214; see Portland and the Willamette Valley Map 3, grid b3.

User Groups: Hikers, leashed dogs, and horses. Pets are not allowed on the Canyon Trail. Some trails are open to mountain bikes (check with park rangers). Some trail portions are wheelchair accessible.

Permits: A $3-per-vehicle day-use fee is charged at the park entrance. Annual Oregon Parks and Recreation permits are available for $25 at 800/551-6949.

Maps: For a free park brochure, contact Oregon Parks and Recreation at 800/551-6949. Ask the USGS for topographic maps of the Lyons and Elk Prairie areas.

Directions: From Salem drive about five miles east on Highway 22, then turn east on Highway 214, and follow signs for about 15 miles to the well-marked park.

Contact: Oregon Parks and Recreation Department, 1115 Commercial Street Northeast, Salem, OR 97301; 800/551-6949.

8 Elijah Bristow State Park Loop
3.2 mi/1.5 hrs

Plenty of easy, flat day-hiking trails are found in Bristow State Park, an 847-acre park that adjoins the Willamette River Greenway Recreation and Recovery Area. The trails crisscross the park through mixed forest, and it's easy to get lost while you're out wandering. So much the better, perhaps. But most people stop by Bristow Park to stroll the 3.2-mile riverfront loop that begins on the park's access road at its first crossing of Lost Creek. The terrain varies from mixed forest to open fields to riverfront, the latter being a pleasant diversion in summer, when cool breezes greet hikers. Many of the park's trails are designated horse trails, but horses and walkers share the uncrowded paths with no noticeable problems. Another interesting hiking option is a side trail that leads from the eastern edge of park development up the river to the base of Dexter Dam, water conditions permitting.

Location: On the Middle Fork Willamette River southeast

of Eugene; see Portland and the Willamette Valley Map 4, grid a2.

User Groups: Hikers, horses, and dogs. Check with park rangers for local mountain bike restrictions. No wheelchair facilities.

Permits: No permits are required. Parking and access are free.

Maps: For a free park brochure, contact the Oregon Parks and Recreation Department, 800/551-6949. Ask the USGS for a topographic map of the Lowell area.

Directions: From I-5 south of Eugene drive east on Willamette Pass Highway/Highway 58 about seven miles and follow signs to Bristow Park on the left (north) side of the highway.

Contact: Oregon Parks and Recreation Department, 1115 Commercial Street Northeast, Salem, OR 97301; 800/551-6949.

9 Fall Creek National Recreation Trail
13.7 mi one way/6.0 hrs

This is a good day hike any time of the year, with the length of your own choosing. The Fall Creek Trail winds 13.7 miles along Fall Creek but crosses Forest Service Road 18 several times, allowing shuttle hikes of various lengths from one trailhead to another. The route, except for a stretch near Bedrock Creek where the trail climbs steeply to join the Jones Trail, is mostly smooth, flat, and creekside. You'll venture through both old-growth and mature second-growth forest, passing numerous excellent fishing and swimming holes. The upper portion of the trail, which extends east to Forest Service Road 1833, is more lightly used. This is a

good hike for children, who will find enough nature to keep them fascinated virtually any time of the year.

Location: Southeast of Eugene near the Middle Fork Willamette River; see Portland and the Willamette Valley Map 4, grid a3.

User Groups: Hikers, horses, and dogs. No mountain bikes are allowed. No wheelchair facilities.

Permits: A federal Northwest Forest Pass, $5 per day or $30 annually, is required to park at the trailhead. Passes are available from ranger stations and many private vendors, online at website: www.wta.org, or by calling 800/270-7504.

Maps: For a map of the Willamette National Forest, contact the Nature of the Northwest Information Center, 800 Northeast Oregon Street, Suite 177, Portland, OR 97232; 503/872-2750. Ask the USGS for topographic maps of the Fall Creek Lake, Saddleblanket Mountain, and Sinker Mountain areas.

Directions: From I-5 south of Eugene, drive about 14 miles east on Willamette Pass Highway/Highway 58. Head north across Dexter Reservoir on the covered bridge and proceed to Lowell. Continue about one mile north on County Road 6220 and then turn right on County Road 6240. Proceed a short distance to Fall Creek Road/Forest Service Road 18 and continue about 10 miles up the north shore of Fall Creek Reservoir to the trailhead sign on the right, just before the bridge near Dolly Varden Campground.

Contact: Willamette National Forest, Middle Fork Ranger District, Lowell Office, 60 South Pioneer Street, Lowell, OR 97452; 541/937-2129.

THE COLUMBIA RIVER GORGE AND MOUNT HOOD

The Columbia River Gorge and Mount Hood

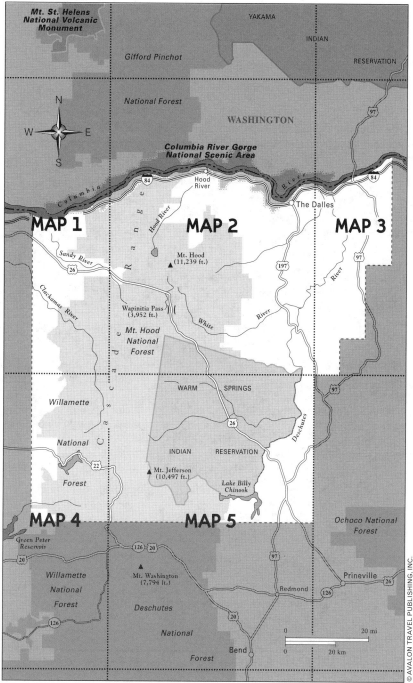

Map 1

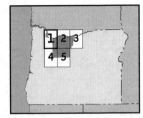

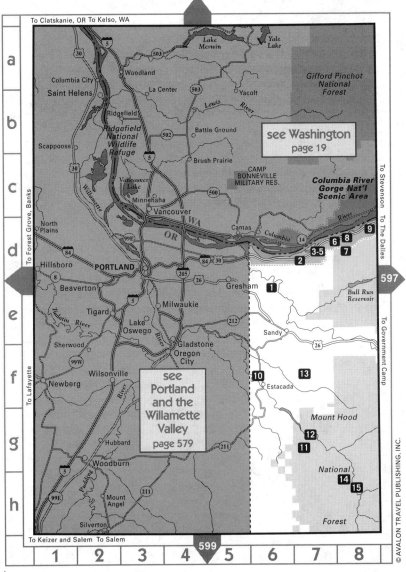

To Clatskanie, OR To Kelso, WA

a

Lake Merwin
Yule Lake
Woodland
Columbia City
Saint Helens
La Center
Yacolt
Gifford Pinchot National Forest

b

Ridgefield
Ridgefield National Wildlife Refuge
Lewis River
Battle Ground
see Washington
page 19
Scappoose
Brush Prairie

c

Vancouver Lake
CAMP BONNEVILLE MILITARY RES.
Columbia River Gorge Nat'l Scenic Area
To Stevenson
Minnehaha
Vancouver
WA
To The Dalles

d

North Plains
OR
Camas
Columbia
River
3-5 **6** **8** **9**
7
To Forest Grove, Banks
Hillsboro
PORTLAND
99E
84 30
2
597

e

Beaverton
Tualatin River
Tigard
Lake Oswego
Gresham
1
Bull Run Reservoir
Sandy
To Government Camp

f

Sherwood
Wilsonville
Gladstone
Oregon City
see Portland and the Willamette Valley page 579
10
Estacada
13
To Lafayette
Newberg

g

Hubbard
Mount Hood
Woodburn
12
11

h

Mount Angel
National
14
15
Silverton
Forest

To Keizer and Salem To Salem
599

1 2 3 4 5 6 7 8

© AVALON TRAVEL PUBLISHING, INC.

Map 2

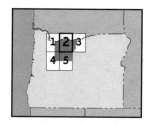

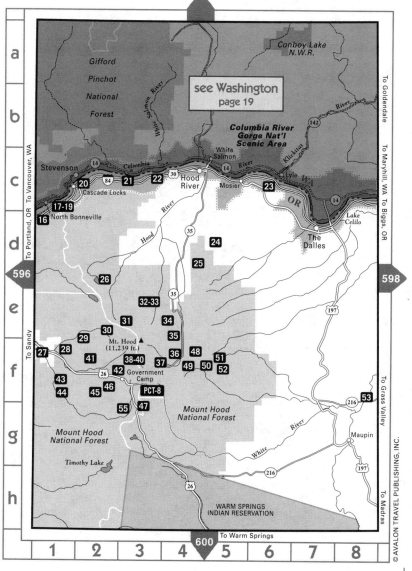

Map 3

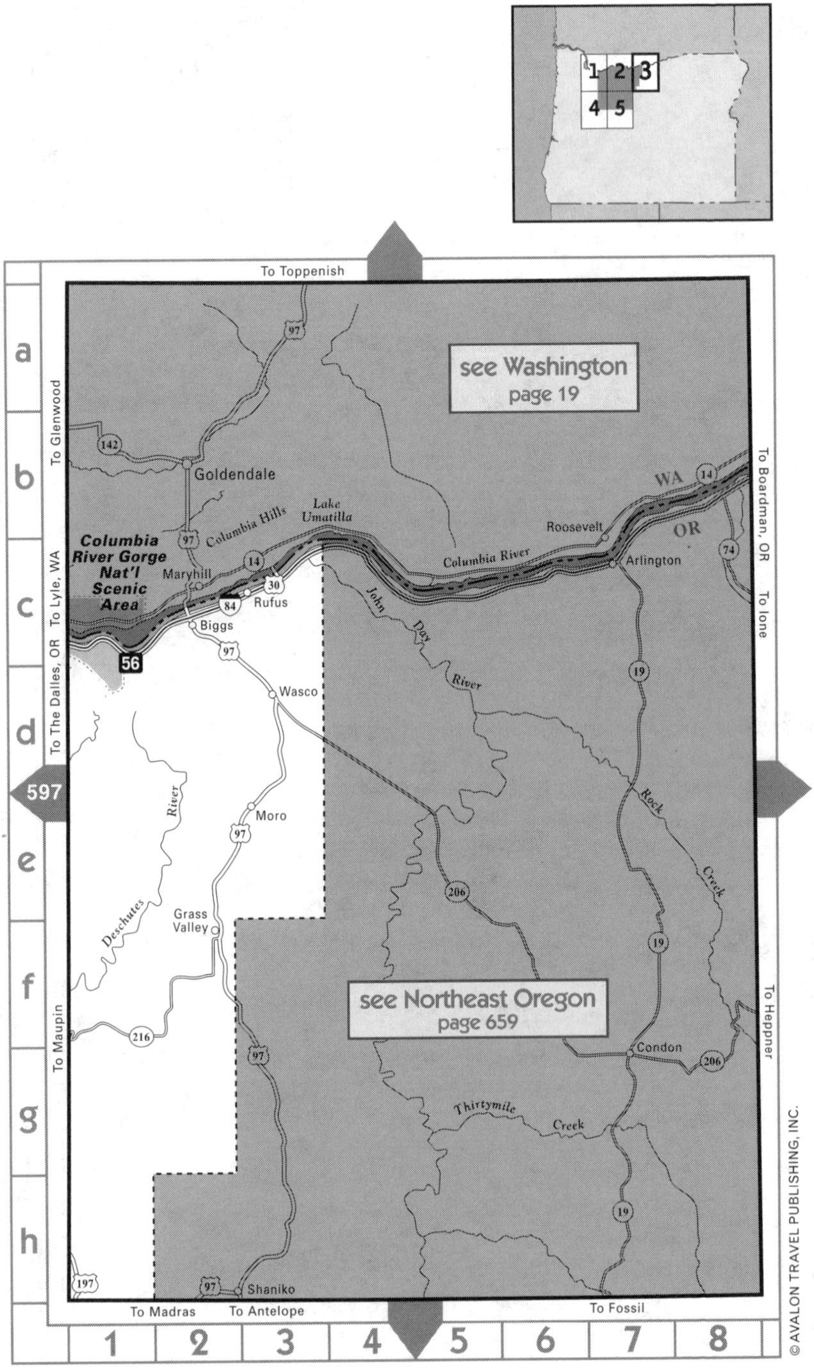

see Washington
page 19

see Northeast Oregon
page 659

To Toppenish

To Glenwood

Goldendale

Columbia Hills

Lake Umatilla

Columbia River Gorge Nat'l Scenic Area

Maryhill

Rufus

Biggs

Wasco

Moro

Grass Valley

Deschutes River

John Day River

Rock Creek

Roosevelt

Arlington

WA
OR

To Boardman, OR

To Ione

To Lyle, WA

To The Dalles, OR

To Maupin

Condon

To Heppner

Thirtymile Creek

Shaniko

To Madras   To Antelope

To Fossil

© AVALON TRAVEL PUBLISHING, INC.

Map 4

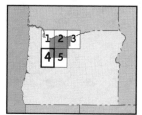

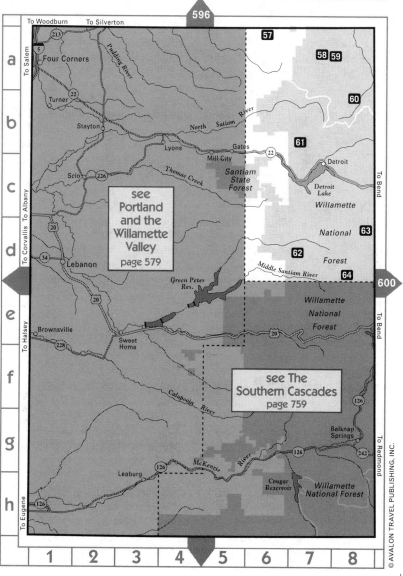

To Woodburn   To Silverton

To Salem

213

Four Corners

Turner 22

Stayton

Lyons

Scio 226

To Corvallis To Albany

28

34 Lebanon

Green Peter
Res.

Brownsville

228

Sweet
Home

To Halsey

Calapooia River

Leaburg 126

To Eugene

126

Padding River

North Santiam River

Gates
Mill City

Thomas Creek

Santiam
State
Forest

22

Detroit

Detroit
Lake

Willamette

National 63

Forest

Middle Santiam River 64

62

20

Willamette

National

Forest

To Bend

20

McKenzie River

Cougar
Reservoir

Willamette
National Forest

126

Belknap
Springs

242

To Redmond

126

To Bend

57

58 59

60

61

see
Portland
and the
Willamette
Valley
page 579

see The
Southern Cascades
page 759

1 2 3
4 5

© AVALON TRAVEL PUBLISHING, INC.

1 2 3 4 5 6 7 8

a b c d e f g h

Map 5

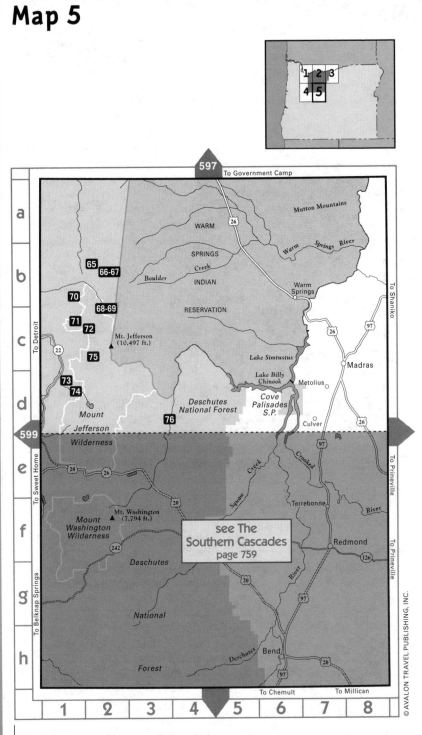

597
To Government Camp

a

Mutton Mountains

WARM

SPRINGS

Creek

Boulder

INDIAN

Warm Springs River

65
66-67

70

68-69

71
72

75

Mt. Jefferson
(10,497 ft.)

73
74

Mount
Jefferson

76

599

Wilderness

RESERVATION

Warm
Springs

Lake Simtustus

Lake Billy
Chinook

Metolius

Deschutes
National Forest

Cove
Palisades
S.P.

Culver

26

97

Madras

To Detroit

22

To Shaniko

97

26

To Prineville

b

c

d

e

f

g

h

To Sweet Home

20

26

20

Mt. Washington
(7,794 ft.)

Mount
Washington
Wilderness

242

Deschutes

see The
Southern Cascades
page 759

Squaw Creek

Crooked

Terrebonne

River

Redmond

126

To Prineville

To Belknap Springs

National

Forest

Deschutes

River

Bend

97

20

97

To Chemult

To Millican

1   2   3   4   5   6   7   8

© AVALON TRAVEL PUBLISHING, INC.

600 Oregon

The Columbia River
Gorge and Mount Hood

(CONTINUED ON NEXT PAGE)

▮ Oxbow Regional Park
2.0–3.5 mi/1.0–2.0 hrs

Oxbow, one of the Portland area's most popular parks, is 1,000 acres of sprawling forest, green grass, and a curving, luscious bend of the soothing Sandy River. Tying it all together are three loop trails of 3.5, 2.25, and 2.0 miles. The shortest of the group, the Upper Bend Loop, passes through two group camps and a forested area on the east side of the park. The 2.25-mile Alder Ridge Loop travels through an old-growth forest area frequented by elk.

The most scenic trail, the 3.5-mile Downstream Loop Trail, follows the south bank of the Sandy River through occasional old-growth forest and passes easy access points to the river, which offers good swimming and fishing (state license required). In the summer watch the many rafters starting off down the river. In the winter watch the many chinook salmon returning. It's a year-round adventure, close to home, safe and convenient, and quite crowded in the summer months. For longer hikes be sure to consult the park brochure. Some trail junctions are not well marked and can be fairly confusing.

Location: East of Gresham on the Sandy River; see The Columbia River Gorge and Mount Hood Map 1, grid e6.

User Groups: Hikers and horses. No dogs are allowed. Check with park rangers for local restrictions on mountain bikes. No wheelchair facilities.

Permits: A $3-per-vehicle access fee is charged at the park entrance.

Maps: For a free park brochure, contact Oxbow Park at 503/663-4708. Brochures are also available at the park entrance station. Ask the USGS for topographic maps of the Washougal and Sandy areas.

Directions: From Portland follow U.S. 26 east to Gresham. Take Division Street southeast; within several miles it becomes Oxbow Parkway. Continue on Oxbow Parkway four miles to the park entrance.

Contact: Oxbow Regional Park, 3010 Southeast Oxbow Parkway, Gresham, OR 97080; 503/663-4708.

▮ Latourell Falls
2.0 mi/1.5 hrs

This easy, moderately paced trail is a delight all year long. Close to ever-eastward-creeping Portland, it's likely to be crowded in the summer. But in the winter and early spring it's especially enticing.

From the parking lot a paved trail leads a very short way up a very steep grade to a viewpoint overlooking Latourell Falls, a tall (250 feet), thin ribbon of whitewater. It's without a doubt the most graceful and serene waterfall in the gorge. And that's saying something. Many people venture no further, but the trail beyond is a great walk, especially for children. You climb gradually up the east side of Latourell Creek to the less-impressive Upper Falls, cross the creek, and then wander down the west bank back to the parking lot. A side trail leads to the top of the falls, where the view down the sheer rock face makes you dizzy. Use extreme caution and go nowhere near the edge—there's no railing. From here the trail drops like a rock to the creek below and then rejoins the trail above the parking lot, forming a loop. Another option is to continue north on the loop trail, dropping to Guy Talbot State Park and then returning to the parking lot. In the spring when trillium plants proliferate, the combination of vivid greens in the upper valley here is particularly memorable.

Location: On the Columbia River Scenic Highway in the Columbia River Gorge; see The Columbia River Gorge and Mount Hood Map 1, grid d7.

User Groups: Hikers and dogs. No horses or mountain bikes are allowed. No wheelchair facilities.

Permits: No permits are required. Parking and access are free.

Maps: For a U.S. Forest Service Trails of the Columbia Gorge map, contact the Nature of the Northwest Information Center, 800 Northeast Oregon Street, Suite 177, Portland, OR 97232; 503/872-2750. Green Trails, Inc.'s excellent topographic maps of the region are available for $3.99 each at outdoor retail outlets. Ask for map number 428, Bridal Veil. Ask the USGS for a topographic map of the Bridal Veil area.

Directions: From Portland drive 28 miles east on I-84 to Exit 28/Bridal Veil. Travel about three miles west on Columbia River Highway to the trailhead parking lot on the left (south) side of the road.

Contact: Columbia River Gorge National Scenic Area, 902 Wasco Avenue, Suite 200, Hood River, OR 97031; 541/386-2333 or 503/668-1440 (Portland number).

❸ Columbia Gorge Trail
35.5 mi one way/7.0 days 🥾 🎒

For the enterprising hiker with the patience and energy to put up with a bit of route finding, crowd avoidance, and often unpleasant weather, the Gorge Trail in its entirety is one of the more spectacular long-distance trails in the United States. A compilation of existing gorge hiking trails and new connector links, the Gorge Trail begins at Bridal Veil and connects with side trails at Angel's Rest, Multnomah Falls, Triple Falls, Ponytail Falls, Ainsworth State Park, Yeon State Park, Elowah Falls, Tanner Creek, Wahclella Falls, Eagle Creek, and Cascade Locks. The trail varies from a narrow footpath to a broad, dilapidated roadbed—actually portions of the abandoned Columbia River Highway.

While the present eastern trailhead is at Wyeth, future construction will turn this trail into a hiking corridor from Portland all the way to Hood River. Already the trail includes a grand collection of sites, from some of the nation's most beautiful waterfalls to old-growth forest, sheer basalt cliffs, and spectacular narrow creek gorges—and of course, sublime views of the Columbia River itself. If you don't mind the intrusion of Highway 84 traffic noise, it's a grand hiking experience, especially in the winter and early spring, when higher trails remain snowbound and gorge forests explode in green underbrush.

In case you're considering staying overnight, note that camping opportunities are limited. Most overnight hikers seek shelter in Ainsworth or Yeon State Parks. Portions of the trail have washed out from time to time. Check with rangers for updates before attempting a through hike.

Location: Between Bridal Veil and Wyeth along I-84; see The Columbia River Gorge and Mount Hood Map 1, grid d7.

User Groups: Hikers, dogs, and horses. Some sections are open to mountain bikes; check with rangers. No wheelchair facilities.

Permits: A federal Northwest Forest Pass, $5 per day or $30 annually, is required to park at the trailhead. Passes are available from ranger stations and many private vendors, online at website: www.wta.org, or by calling 800/270-7504.

Maps: For a U.S. Forest Service Trails of the Columbia Gorge map, contact the Nature of the Northwest Information Center, 800 Northeast Oregon Street, Suite 177, Portland, OR 97232; 503/872-2750. Green Trails, Inc.'s excellent topographic maps of the region are available for $3.99 each at outdoor retail outlets. Ask for map number 428, Bridal Veil. Ask the USGS for topographic maps of the Bridal Veil, Multnomah Falls, Tanner Butte, Bonneville Dam, and Carson areas.

Directions: From Portland drive about 30 miles east on I-84 to Exit 28/Bridal Veil. Travel a short distance off the exit and find a gravel parking lot on the right, at the junction with the Columbia River Highway. The trailhead is across the Columbia River Highway and slightly east.

Contact: Columbia River Gorge National Scenic Area, 902 Wasco Avenue, Suite 200, Hood River, OR 97031; 541/386-2333 or 503/668-1440 (Portland number).

▲ Bridal Veil Falls
1.0 mi/0.5 hr

First off, the falls don't really look like a bridal veil—unless the bride had a head like a sideways watermelon. Some guidebooks prefer to describe the falls as "uniquely shaped." We can't say they're that, either. But they are big, voluminous, sparkling, wet, and awesome, not to mention easily accessible to the whole family. What more do you want? The trail drops a short distance through nondescript forest to the creek and then climbs a long set of stairs to a falls viewing platform. Take in the roar and whoosh of wind and decide for yourself what the falls most closely resemble.

This is a good, short day hike that can be done on the same visit as nearby Latourell Falls, and, if you're up for it, Multnomah Falls farther east (see hike in this chapter). Another short, interesting trail at the same trailhead is the Overlook Loop Trail, a paved path that winds its way through a field of camas to a viewpoint high above the Columbia River. Across the way on the Washington side, spot the train tunnel where miles-long trains disappear into one end and emerge out the other, with ends visible on either side of the tunnel.

Location: On the Columbia River Scenic Highway in the Columbia River Gorge; see

The Columbia River Gorge and Mount Hood Map 1, grid d7.

User Groups: Hikers and dogs. No horses or mountain bikes are allowed. No wheelchair facilities.

Permits: No permits are required. Parking and access are free.

Maps: For a U.S. Forest Service Trails of the Columbia Gorge map, contact the Nature of the Northwest Information Center, 800 Northeast Oregon Street, Suite 177, Portland, OR 97232; 503/872-2750. Green Trails, Inc.'s excellent topographic maps of the region are available for $3.99 each at outdoor retail outlets. Ask for map number 428, Bridal Veil. Ask the USGS for a topographic map of the Bridal Veil area.

Directions: From Portland drive 28 miles east on I-84 to Exit 28/Bridal Veil. Travel a mile west on the Columbia River Highway to Bridal Veil State Park. The trailhead is at the far end of the parking lot.

Contact: Columbia River Gorge National Scenic Area, 902 Wasco Avenue, Suite 200, Hood River, OR 97031; 541/386-2333 or 503/668-1440 (Portland number).

▲ Angel's Rest
4.4 mi/3.0 hrs

Angels rest, but you certainly won't. At least not until you're perched atop the prime viewpoint at the top of this 1,400-foot climb. This is a good workout, and probably not the best place to drag the kids. The trail climbs quickly and skirts to within sweating distance of some fairly substantial cliffs. Great views await at the top, far east and west in the Columbia River Gorge. The trail continues on another 2.6 miles to Wahkeena Springs and ultimately the far reaches of the Gorge Trail (see hike in this chapter).

Location: On the Columbia River Scenic Highway in the

Columbia River Gorge; see The Columbia River Gorge and Mount Hood Map 1, grid d7.

User Groups: Hikers and dogs. No horses or mountain bikes are allowed. No wheelchair facilities.

Permits: No permits are required. Parking and access are free.

Maps: For a U.S. Forest Service Trails of the Columbia Gorge map, contact the Nature of the Northwest Information Center, 800 Northeast Oregon Street, Suite 177, Portland, OR 97232; 503/872-2750. Green Trails, Inc.'s excellent topographic maps of the region are available for $3.99 each at outdoor retail outlets. Ask for map number 428, Bridal Veil. Ask the USGS for topographic maps of the Bridal Veil and Multnomah Falls areas.

Directions: From Portland drive 28 miles east on I-84 to Exit 28/Bridal Veil. Travel a short distance off the exit and find a gravel parking lot on the right, at the junction with the Columbia River Highway. The trailhead is across the Columbia River Highway and slightly east.

Contact: Columbia River Gorge National Scenic Area, 902 Wasco Avenue, Suite 200, Hood River, OR 97031; 541/386-2333 or 503/668-1440 (Portland number).

6 Wahkeena Falls Loop
5.0 mi/4.0 hrs

The trip to Wahkeena Falls is short (about one mile round-trip), pleasant, and impressive, but it's just a sampler of what awaits on the Wahkeena trail system. Above Wahkeena Falls the trail continues more than a mile uphill to Wahkeena Springs and then cuts east to the Larch Mountain Trail, which drops past Upper Multnomah Falls. From here continue downhill to lower Multnomah Falls and return west to the trailhead on the Perdition Trail, forming a spectacular five-mile loop. The trail avoids some of the mob

scene at Multnomah Falls and leads you into wilderness you would never see by sticking to the primary, lower falls trails. Also connecting to the upper Wahkeena system are day-hike trails to Devil's Rest and Angel's Rest (see above).

Location: On the Columbia River Scenic Highway in the Columbia River Gorge; see The Columbia River Gorge and Mount Hood Map 1, grid d7.

User Groups: Hikers and dogs. No horses or mountain bikes are allowed. No wheelchair facilities.

Permits: No permits are required. Parking and access are free.

Maps: For a U.S. Forest Service Trails of the Columbia Gorge map, contact the Nature of the Northwest Information Center, 800 Northeast Oregon Street, Suite 177, Portland, OR 97232; 503/872-2750. Green Trails, Inc.'s excellent topographic maps of the region are available for $3.99 each at outdoor retail outlets. Ask for map number 428, Bridal Veil. Ask the USGS for topographic maps of the Bridal Veil and Multnomah Falls areas.

Directions: From Portland drive 28 miles east on I-84 to Exit 28/Bridal Veil. Drive just under three miles east on the Columbia River Scenic Highway to the trailhead on the right (south) side of the road.

Contact: Columbia River Gorge National Scenic Area, 902 Wasco Avenue, Suite 200, Hood River, OR 97031; 541/386-2333 or 503/668-1440 (Portland number).

7 Larch Mountain
5.5 mi/3.5 hrs

The view from the top of this retired volcanic peak knocks your socks off. And the hike down below may well melt your soles. From the parking lot take a short walk to Sherrard Point and drink in the view. Then head down into the gorge on the Larch Mountain

Trail, which leads into the remnants of the mountain's volcanic crater. At about two miles a side trail leads east across Multnomah Creek to Trail 444, which climbs back out of the crater to the summit. Take the side trail for the 5.5-mile loop or continue straight down, a total of 6.8 miles to the Multnomah Falls Lodge. If a car shuttle can be arranged, it's a fun downhill, one-way hike. For longer loops or one-way shuttle hikes, the Larch Mountain trail system also connects with Oneonta trails (see hike in this chapter) to the east.

Location: High above the Columbia River Gorge and Multnomah Falls; see The Columbia River Gorge and Mount Hood Map 1, grid d8.

User Groups: Hikers, dogs, and mountain bikes. No wheelchair facilities.

Permits: A federal Northwest Forest Pass, $5 per day or $30 annually, is required to park at the trailhead. Passes are available from ranger stations and many private vendors, online at website: www.wta.org, or by calling 800/270-7504.

Maps: For a U.S. Forest Service Trails of the Columbia Gorge map, contact the Nature of the Northwest Information Center, 800 Northeast Oregon Street, Suite 177, Portland, OR 97232; 503/872-2750. Green Trails, Inc.'s excellent topographic maps of the region are available for $3.99 each at outdoor retail outlets. Ask for map number 428, Bridal Veil. Ask the USGS for a topographic map of the Multnomah Falls area.

Directions: From Portland drive 22 miles east on I-84 to Exit 22/Corbett. Proceed up Corbett Hill to the Columbia River Scenic Highway. Turn left (east) and travel to Larch Mountain Road. Turn right and follow Larch Mountain Road about 14 miles to the trailhead in the Larch Mountain Picnic Area.

Contact: Columbia River Gorge National Scenic Area, 902 Wasco Avenue, Suite 200, Hood River, OR 97031; 541/386-2333 or 503/668-1440 (Portland number).

🖪 Multnomah Falls
2.5 mi/1.5 hrs

This is the Mother of all Columbia Gorge waterfalls, and it usually comes equipped with the Mother of all Mobs, even in the winter. The falls is Oregon's number one natural attraction, so be prepared for company whenever you visit. The trail, paved all the way to the top of the falls, switches back up the creek face, crossing a graceful bridge right in front of the falls and climbing to a viewpoint at the top.

No matter how many times you return to see it, the 540-foot waterfall is truly an awesome sight. Most people only venture about a half mile up the trail to the bridge crossing, or hike to the top of the trail and back for a round-trip walk of about 2.5 miles. But venturing beyond is well worth the effort. From the top, hikers can start up the Larch Mountain Trail, which leads five spectacular miles uphill to the Sherrard Point viewpoint on Larch Mountain (see hike above). Remember: It's also possible to combine Wahkeena and Multnomah Falls in a five-mile loop (see hike in this chapter).

Location: On the Columbia River Scenic Highway in the Columbia River Gorge; see The Columbia River Gorge and Mount Hood Map 1, grid d8.

User Groups: Hikers and dogs. No horses or mountain bikes are allowed. No wheelchair facilities.

Permits: No permits are required. Parking and access are free.

Maps: For a U.S. Forest Service Trails of the Columbia Gorge map, contact the Nature of the Northwest Information Center, 800 Northeast Oregon Street, Suite 177, Portland,

OR 97232; 503/872-2750. Green Trails, Inc.'s excellent topographic maps of the region are available for $3.99 each at outdoor retail outlets. Ask for map number 428, Bridal Veil. Ask the USGS for a topographic map of the Multnomah Falls areas.

Directions: From Portland drive 31 miles east on I-84 to Exit 31/Multnomah Falls. The trailhead is visible just east of the Multnomah Falls Lodge, a short distance from the exit.

Contact: Columbia River Gorge National Scenic Area, 902 Wasco Avenue, Suite 200, Hood River, OR 97031; 541/386-2333 or 503/668-1440 (Portland number).

9 Oneonta/Horsetail Falls
2.8 mi/1.5 hrs

The trail system in the Horsetail Falls area provides the most waterfall bang for your buck of any single stop in the Columbia River Gorge. From the parking lot follow the trail a short distance up beside Horsetail Falls and turn right on the Ponytail Falls Trail. Soon you have the unusual pleasure of walking behind a waterfall, as the path leads directly behind Ponytail Falls. Continue ahead just under a mile to a high footbridge above Oneonta Falls in the dramatic Oneonta Gorge. From here a trail leads south up the hill to spectacular Triple Falls, three dramatic waterfalls dropping into a single splash pool on Oneonta Creek. If you include the Triple Falls leg up and back, the loop trip described here grows to about 5.5 miles. But if time is short, turn right at the junction and continue downhill to the Gorge Trail and the highway, about half a mile west of the parking lot on the other side of Oneonta Gorge. If the weather is good, a wade into the gorge is a spectacular experience, leading to a rarely visited waterfall and magnificent displays of flora on the canyon walls.

Location: On the Columbia River Scenic Highway in the Columbia River Gorge; see The Columbia River Gorge and Mount Hood Map 1, grid d8.

User Groups: Hikers and dogs. No horses or mountain bikes are allowed. No wheelchair facilities.

Permits: No permits are required. Parking and access are free.

Maps: For a U.S. Forest Service Trails of the Columbia Gorge map, contact the Nature of the Northwest Information Center, 800 Northeast Oregon Street, Suite 177, Portland, OR 97232; 503/872-2750. Green Trails, Inc.'s excellent topographic maps of the region are available for $3.99 each at outdoor retail outlets. Ask for map number 428, Bridal Veil. Ask the USGS for a topographic map of the Multnomah Falls area.

Directions: From Portland drive 35 miles east on I-84 to Exit 3/Ainsworth State Park. Drive 1.5 miles west on the Columbia River Scenic Highway to the Horsetail Falls Trailhead parking area on the left (south) side of the highway.

Contact: Columbia River Gorge National Scenic Area, 902 Wasco Avenue, Suite 200, Hood River, OR 97031; 541/386-2333 or 503/668-1440 (Portland number).

10 Milo McIver State Park Loop
4.5 mi/2.0 hrs

River rafters, anglers, and equestrians flock to McIver State Park for its fine equestrian trail and access to the Clackamas River. But it's an equally pleasant stop for day hikers. The horse trail, a 4.5-mile loop also open to hikers, begins near the campground entrance and has several other access points throughout the 952-acre park. (Horse rentals are available in the park during summer months.) The trail passes forest, a state chinook salmon hatchery, River Mill Dam, and open riverfront, all in the southern portion of the park. Trail junctions can be confusing, so watch your turns. The park isn't really large enough to get very lost in, so even zigging when you should have zagged is easily rectifiable with a short detour back to the route.

In the north end of the park, a short nature trail loops for a mile through a second-growth forest. A separate path leads along the riverfront. For wheelchair users a paved path leads to a memorable viewpoint of the park and the nearby Clackamas River bend. It's found in the central park area.

Location: Four miles northwest of Estacada off Highway 211 in McIver State Park; see The Columbia River Gorge and Mount Hood Map 1, grid f6.

User Groups: Hikers, horses, and leashed dogs. Check with rangers for trails open to mountain bikes. One short hiking trail is open to wheelchair use.

Permits: No permits are required. A $3 parking fee is collected during summer months. Annual Oregon Parks and Recreation passes are available for $25; contact the Oregon Parks and Recreation and Recreation Department at 800/551-6949.

Maps: For a free park brochure, contact Oregon Parks and Recreation at 800/551-6949. Ask the USGS for a topographic map of the Estacada area.

Directions: From Portland drive about 25 miles east on U.S. 26 to Highway 211. Turn south on Highway 211 and proceed about seven miles, following signs to the park.

Contact: Oregon Parks and Recreation Department, 1115 Commercial Street Northeast, Salem, OR 97301; 800/551-6949.

🔢 Memaloose Lake/ South Fork Mountain
4.6 mi/3.0 hrs   🥾 ⛰️

This can be an easy family hike to pretty Memaloose Lake (2.6 miles round-trip) or a longer, pleasant 4.6-mile round-trip hike that includes the lake and fine views above the glacial cirque on South Fork Mountain. The trail to the lake is a delightful walk through old-growth forest on a good, steeply graded path along Memaloose Creek. The lake has several campsites on the south side and good trout fishing in the summer (state license required). The mountain above, also reachable by road, has tremendous views of the entire Cascade volcano chain. You gain about 500 feet of elevation on the walk to the lake, and an additional 700 to the summit of South Fork Mountain (elevation 4,853 feet).

Location: Southeast of Estacada in the Clackamas River drainage of Mount Hood National Forest; see The Columbia River Gorge and Mount Hood Map 1, grid g7.

User Groups: Hikers, dogs, and mountain bikes. No horses are allowed. No wheelchair facilities.

Permits: No permits are required. Parking and access are free.

Maps: For a map of the Mount Hood National Forest, contact the Nature of the Northwest Information Center, 800 Northeast Oregon Street, Suite 177, Portland, OR 97232; 503/872-2750. Green Trails, Inc.'s excellent topographic maps of the region are available for $3.99 each at outdoor retail outlets. Ask for map number 492, Fish Creek Mountain. Ask the USGS for a topographic map of the Wanderers Peak area.

Directions: From Estacada drive about 9.5 miles south on Highway 224 to Memaloose Road/Forest Service Road 45. Turn right and drive 12 miles—staying right at the end of the pavement—to the trailhead on the left (west) side of the road.

Contact: Mount Hood National Forest, Clackamas River Ranger District, Estacada Ranger Station, 595 Northwest Industrial Way, Estacada, OR 97023; 503/630-6861.

12 Clackamas River
7.8 mi one way/5.0 hrs

This winding, low-elevation trail along the federally protected Clackamas River is a treasure of Oregon's central Cascades. The path's rich supply of surprising beaches, waterfalls, wildlife, and whitewater creates a pleasing diversion from city life any time of the year. Arrange for car transportation at one of the two trailheads, pack a lunch, and head out to enjoy the lowland forest, clean water, and clean air. The trail, rebuilt in 1999, leaves the riverbank briefly, but you spend most of your time along the water. For an out-and-back trip involving only the northern trailhead, hike to beautiful, 100-foot-high Pup Creek Falls for a round-trip of about seven miles. The upper part of the trail skirts the edge of a bluff high above the churning river. Winter or summer, it's a day-hiker's delight. The elevation gain is only about 400 feet.

Location: Between Fish Creek and Indian Henry campgrounds in Mount Hood National Forest; see The Columbia River Gorge and Mount Hood Map 1, grid g7.

User Groups: Hikers and dogs only. The trail as of 1999 is no longer open to mountain bikes. No horses are allowed. No wheelchair facilities.

Permits: A federal Northwest Forest Pass, $5 per day or $30 annually, is required to park at the trailhead. Passes are available from ranger stations and many private vendors, online at website: www.wta.org, or by calling 800/270-7504.

Maps: For a map of the Mount Hood National Forest, contact the Nature of the Northwest Information Center, 800 Northeast Oregon Street, Suite 177, Portland, OR 97232; 503/872-2750. Green Trails, Inc.'s excellent topographic maps of the region are available for $3.99 each at outdoor retail outlets. Ask for map number 492, Fish Creek Mountain. Ask the USGS for topographic maps of the Bedford Point, Three Lynx, and Fish Creek Mountain areas.

Directions: From Portland drive 12 miles south on I-5 to Exit 288/West Linn. Drive 12 miles east on I-205 to the town of Gladstone. Turn east on Highway 224 and drive 15 miles to Estacada. Continue about 16 miles southeast on Highway 224 to Fish Creek Road/Forest Service Road 54, just beyond Fish Creek Campground. Turn right across the bridge and park in the trailhead parking lot. The trail is now located at the far end of the parking lot, across Road 54.

Contact: Mount Hood National Forest, Clackamas River Ranger District, Estacada Ranger Station, 595 Northwest Industrial Way, Estacada, OR 97023; 503/630-6861.

13 Old Baldy
7.5 mi/4.0 hrs

Here's a great daylong getaway for Portland-area residents seeking a solid, lung-testing trail, with great views of the Salmon-Huckleberry Wilderness and Mount Hood as a reward. The Old Baldy Trail, accessible by a number of good and decaying trails, is most easily accessed from the trailhead described above. Walk on a moderate grade around Githens Mountain and stay right at the junction with the old Old Baldy Trail. Soon you're on a ridgetop at a 4,000-foot viewpoint, standing on the far western edge of the Salmon-Huckleberry Wilderness, with Mount Adams and Mount Hood as snowy backdrops. It's about a mile from here to the old lookout site on top of Old Baldy (elevation 4,200 feet).

Location: On the western edge of the Salmon-Huckleberry Wilderness, southeast of Estacada; see The Columbia River Gorge and Mount Hood Map 1, grid f7.

User Groups: Hikers, dogs, and horses. Not suitable for mountain bikes. No wheelchair facilities.

Permits: No permits are required. Parking and access are free.

Maps: For a map of the Salmon-Huckleberry Wilderness, contact the Nature of the Northwest Information Center, 800 Northeast Oregon Street, Suite 177, Portland, OR 97232; 503/872-2750. Green Trails, Inc.'s excellent topographic maps of the region are available for $3.99 each at outdoor retail outlets. Ask for map numbers 460 and 492, Cherryville and Fish Creek Mountain. Ask the USGS for a topographic map of the Three Lynx area.

Directions: From Estacada follow Highway 224 south for one mile to Fall Creek Road. Turn left (north) and drive 2.5 miles to the road's end. Jog left on Divers Road for 0.2 mile and then turn right on Squaw Mountain Road. Proceed nine miles to a junction with Forest Service Road 4615. Ignore the Baldy Trail sign pointing left and stay straight on the road, now Forest Service Road 4614. Continue until the road tops out and starts downhill; look for the Old Baldy Trailhead at the end of a very short spur road on the right.

Contact: Mount Hood National Forest, Clackamas River Ranger District, Estacada Ranger Station, 595 Northwest Industrial Way, Estacada, OR 97023; 503/630-6861.

🏴 Fish Creek Mountain
4.2 mi/3.0 hrs

The long access route to this trailhead makes it a rarely visited day-hike destination. That means it's a good choice on those sunny summer weekends when you know the trailheads at your favorite Mount Hood–area trail will look more like the mall on the day after Thanksgiving. And there's another good reason to come here: old-growth forest accompanies you for much of the trail length, at

least until you break out of the forest near the top. The upper trail follows the ridgeline to a junction with a side trail that leads three-quarters of a mile to High Lake, a good lunching, swimming, and trout-fishing spot (state license required). Continue on the main trail half a mile to the site of the old lookout atop Fish Creek Mountain, elevation 5,100 feet. Grand views beckon in all directions.

Location: South of Highway 224 in the Clackamas River drainage of Mount Hood National Forest; see The Columbia River Gorge and Mount Hood Map 1, grid h8.

User Groups: Hikers, dogs, horses, and mountain bikes. No wheelchair facilities.

Permits: A federal Northwest Forest Pass, $5 per day or $30 annually, is required to park at the trailhead. Passes are available from ranger stations and many private vendors, online at website: www.wta.org, or by calling 800/270-7504.

Maps: For a map of the Mount Hood National Forest, contact the Nature of the Northwest Information Center, 800 Northeast Oregon Street, Suite 177, Portland, OR 97232; 503/872-2750. Green Trails, Inc.'s excellent topographic maps of the region are available for $3.99 each at outdoor retail outlets. Ask for map number 492, Fish Creek Mountain. Ask the USGS for topographic maps of the Wanderers Peak and Fish Creek Mountain areas.

Directions: From Estacada drive about 15 miles south on Highway 224 to Fish Creek Road/Forest Service Road 54. Turn right (south) and proceed 1.6 miles to a junction with Forest Service Road 5410. Veer left on Forest Service Road 5410 and then immediately right on Forest Service Road 5420. Follow the road about 12 miles to the end of pavement and turn left on Forest Service Road 5420-290. The trailhead is 1.3 miles down the road on the right (east) side.

Contact: Mount Hood National Forest, Clackamas River Ranger District, Estacada Ranger Station, 595 Northwest Industrial Way, Estacada, OR 97023; 503/630-6861.

15 Riverside National Recreation Trail
4.0 mi one way/2.0 hrs

This is another excellent, year-round lowland river hike through old-growth trees on the wild Clackamas River. In the winter, when Rainbow Campground is closed, the hike is equally pleasant. Just start at the gate on the road instead of the trailhead in the campground. If you arrange for a pickup at Riverside Campground at the other end, the trail makes a pleasant, four-mile one-way hike for the whole family. A popular alternative to the auto drop-off is a mountain-bike loop or shuttle. Drop off a bike at one end, park at the other, hike to the bike, ride to the car. Or ride the entire circuit on your mountain bike, combining the trail and Forest Service Road 46. Of course, it's possible to do this as an eight-mile round-trip as well.

Location: On the Clackamas River between Rainbow and Riverside Campgrounds in Mount Hood National Forest; see The Columbia River Gorge and Mount Hood Map 1, grid h8.

User Groups: Hikers, dogs, and mountain bikes. No horses are allowed. No wheelchair facilities.

Permits: A federal Northwest Forest Pass, $5 per day or $30 annually, is required to park at the trailhead. Passes are available from ranger stations and many private vendors, online at website: www.wta.org, or by calling 800/270-7504.

Maps: For a map of the Mount Hood National Forest, contact the Nature of the Northwest Information Center, 800 Northeast Oregon Street, Suite 177, Portland, OR 97232; 503/872-

2750. Green Trails, Inc.'s excellent topographic maps of the region are available for $3.99 each at outdoor retail outlets. Ask for map number 492, Fish Creek Mountain. Ask the USGS for a topographic map of the Fish Creek Mountain area.

Directions: From Estacada follow Highway 224 about 27 miles southeast to Forest Service Road 46. Continue about 100 yards beyond Ripplebrook Campground and then turn right (south) into Rainbow Campground. The trailhead is at the far end of the campground.

Contact: Mount Hood National Forest, Clackamas River Ranger District, Estacada Ranger Station, 595 Northwest Industrial Way, Estacada, OR 97023; 503/630-6861.

16 Nesmith Point/Elowah Falls
10.0 mi/8.0 hrs

The Nesmith Trail is no place for the aerobically challenged. Trust us. Climbing 3,800 feet in just over 4.5 miles is no easy feat. The trail, in fact, is commonly used as a training route by climbers and other athletes looking to get in shape for summer alpine climbs. But strong hikers will enjoy the hike for its own aesthetics. The trail climbs to the highest spot on the gorge's south wall, and the view from Nesmith Point is tremendous. For an even better workout, turn west just before the top and walk five miles to the Oneonta trail system (see hike in this chapter), exiting on top or bottom of the gorge, depending on your route. More placid hikers will enjoy the two-mile hike from the same trailhead to Elowah and Upper McCord Creek Falls. Good viewpoints are found both above and below these falls, each of which would be worth a hike three times as long.

Location: High above the Columbia River Gorge in John Yeon State Park near Dodson; see The Columbia River Gorge and Mount Hood Map 2, grid d1.

User Groups: Hikers and dogs. No horses or mountain bikes are allowed. No wheelchair facilities.

Permits: No permits are required. Parking and access are free.

Maps: For a U.S. Forest Service Trails of the Columbia Gorge map, contact the Nature of the Northwest Information Center, 800 Northeast Oregon Street, Suite 177, Portland, OR 97232; 503/872-2750. Green Trails, Inc.'s excellent topographic maps of the region are available for $3.99 each at outdoor retail outlets. Ask for map number 428, Bridal Veil. Ask the USGS for topographic maps of the Multnomah Falls and Tanner Butte areas.

Directions: From Portland drive 35 miles east on I-84 to Exit 35/Ainsworth State Park. Travel 2.5 miles east on the Columbia River Highway and Frontage Road to the trailhead parking lot on the right (south) side of the road.

Contact: Columbia River Gorge National Scenic Area, 902 Wasco Avenue, Suite 200, Hood River, OR 97031; 541/386-2333 or 503/668-1440 (Portland number).

🆗 Wahclella Falls
2.0 mi/1.0 hr

This is a good family hike up Tanner Creek. The trail starts as a gravel road and then narrows as it heads up beyond an intake dam for the Bonneville Fish Hatchery and up into the canyon. At about seven-tenths of a mile, the trail splits. Choose either route: it's a loop. (Note: If you're hiking with small children, stay on the lower trail to avoid the sheer-sided return loop.) Near the top is a great viewpoint below the falls, which is a true gusher, particularly during periods of heavy rainfall or snowmelt. The falls, one of the mightiest in the gorge, is a 350-foot, two-tiered plunge with a final 60-foot section creating a horsetail fall into a wide splash pool.

Check out the massive 1973 slide area on the upper trail, evidenced by the slide impression above and much rubble below. Return the way you came.

Location: Near Bonneville Dam in the Columbia River Gorge; see The Columbia River Gorge and Mount Hood Map 2, grid d1.

User Groups: Hikers and dogs. No horses or mountain bikes are allowed. No wheelchair facilities.

Permits: A federal Northwest Forest Pass, $5 per day or $30 annually, is required to park at the trailhead. Passes are available from ranger stations and many private vendors, online at website: www.wta.org, or by calling 800/270-7504.

Maps: For a U.S. Forest Service Trails of the Columbia Gorge map, contact the Nature of the Northwest Information Center, 800 Northeast Oregon Street, Suite 177, Portland, OR 97232; 503/872-2750. Green Trails, Inc.'s excellent topographic maps of the region are available for $3.99 each at outdoor retail outlets. Ask for map number 429, Bonneville Dam. Ask the USGS for topographic maps of the Bonneville Dam and Tanner Butte areas.

Directions: From Portland drive 40 miles east on I-84 to Exit 40. The trailhead is visible on the south side of the exit.

Contact: Columbia River Gorge National Scenic Area, 902 Wasco Avenue, Suite 200, Hood River, OR 97031; 541/386-2333 or 503/668-1440 (Portland number).

🔢 Wauna Point/Dublin Lake
10.0 mi/7.0 hrs

This is a good place to get away from gorge crowds for some time—and deep breaths—to yourself. After the rough access road, head south uphill on the trail for about two miles, where a side trail leads 0.4 mile up to Wauna Point, which offers excellent views of Bonneville Dam and the gorge both east and west. Turn around here, or if you're up to it, return to the main trail and hike south for two miles to another eastward-leading spur, this one dropping to Dublin Lake, a quiet, seldom-visited spot at 3,500 feet. You can return the way you came or, if you don't mind road walking, hike three miles east on the Tanner Creek Cutoff Trail to Forest Service Road 777, which leads 2.5 miles north back to the car. If you're really feeling your oats, continue south from Dublin Lake another 4.5 miles to the Tanner Butte area, where you can connect with the Eagle Creek Trail (see below).

Location: South of Bonneville Dam in the Columbia River Gorge; see The Columbia River Gorge and Mount Hood Map 2, grid c1.

User Groups: Hikers and dogs. No horses or mountain bikes are allowed. No wheelchair facilities.

Permits: A federal Northwest Forest Pass, $5 per day or $30 annually, is required to park at the trailhead. Passes are available from ranger stations and many private vendors, online at website: www.wta.org, or by calling 800/270-7504.

Maps: For a U.S. Forest Service Trails of the Columbia Gorge map, contact the Nature of the Northwest Information Center, 800 Northeast Oregon Street, Suite 177, Portland, OR 97232; 503/872-2750. Green Trails, Inc.'s excellent topographic maps of the region are available for $3.99 each at outdoor retail outlets. Ask for map number 429, Bonneville Dam. Ask the USGS for topographic maps of the Bonneville Dam and Tanner Butte areas.

Directions: From Portland drive 40 miles east on I-84 to Exit 40/Bonneville Dam. Drive 2.5 mile south on Forest Service Road 777 to the trailhead on the left (east) side of the road.

Contact: Columbia River Gorge National Scenic Area, 902 Wasco Avenue, Suite 200,

Hood River, OR 97031; 541/386-2333 or 503/668-1440 (Portland number).

19 Eagle Creek
12.0 mi/8.0 hrs

If you could pick only one Columbia Gorge Trail to hike, this would likely be it. And plenty of people do pick this one. Gorge visitors for a day or a lifetime flock to Eagle Creek, largely because it samples the best scenery the gorge has to offer while managing to maintain a fairly friendly pace. On the long, winding path to Wahtum Lake in the Columbia Wilderness, you pass half a dozen waterfalls, any one of which would be worth a substantial hike on its own. It's almost an embarrassment of riches.

For a short hike of just over four miles round-trip, trek to aptly named Punchbowl Falls. Hikers can continue to the spectacular High Bridge, which spans a frighteningly deep gorge on the creek, for a 6.5-mile round-trip. If you're up to it, go all the way to Tunnel Falls for a 12-mile round-trip you won't soon forget. Go as far as you can. You won't regret it. Even the longer trip has a net elevation gain of only about 1,200 feet. For a bonus, watch salmon spawning in the creek in the fall.

Location: In the Columbia River Gorge east of Bonneville Dam; see The Columbia River Gorge and Mount Hood Map 2, grid c1.

User Groups: Hikers and dogs. No horses or mountain bikes are allowed. No wheelchair facilities.

Permits: A federal Northwest Forest Pass, $5 per day or $30 annually, is required to park at the trailhead. Passes are available from ranger stations and many private vendors, online at website: www.wta.org, or by calling 800/270-7504.

Maps: For a U.S. Forest Service Trails of the Columbia Gorge map, contact the Nature of the Northwest Information Center, 800 North-east Oregon Street, Suite 177, Portland, OR 97232; 503/872-2750. Green Trails, Inc.'s excellent topographic maps of the region are available for $3.99 each at outdoor retail outlets. Ask for map number 429, Bonneville Dam. Ask the USGS for topographic maps of the Bonneville Dam, Tanner Butte, and Wahtum Lake areas.

Directions: From Portland drive 41 miles east on I-84 to Exit 41/Eagle Creek. Drive south on Eagle Creek Road to the trailhead. Note: There is no westbound exit to Eagle Creek Road. Take the Bonneville Dam exit and backtrack on the freeway. The trailhead parking lot has been plagued by car break-ins.

Contact: Columbia River Gorge National Scenic Area, 902 Wasco Avenue, Suite 200, Hood River, OR 97031; 541/386-2333 or 503/668-1440 (Portland number).

20 Herman Creek to Indian Point

8.0 mi/6.0 hrs

Herman Creek Canyon and its neighbor to the east, Nick Eaton Ridge, are alive with trails that venture far north, creating a spectacular 26-mile backpacking loop through ancient cedar forests to Wahtum Lake and back. But day hikers find plenty of scenery, too, such as Indian Point, a grand vista above the Columbia Gorge.

Go left at the first junction and walk 1.3 miles on trail and old road to Herman Camp. Turn left and head up Gorton Creek Trail, which leads 2.6 miles to the turnaround, Indian Point, where you can see north to Mount St. Helens and beyond. For a varied return route, follow the Ridge Cutoff Trail half a mile downhill to the Nick Eaton Trail, which follows rocky, scenic Eaton Ridge about two miles back to Herman Camp and a well-earned exit. Loop hik-ers generally continue straight on the Herman Creek Trail from Herman Camp to Wahtum Lake and return to the west via the Pacific Crest Trail. It's one of the better multi-day trips in the gorge.

Location: In the Columbia Wilderness of the Columbia River Gorge between Cascade Locks and Wyeth; see The Columbia River Gorge and Mount Hood Map 2, grid c2.

User Groups: Hikers, dogs, and horses. No mountain bikes are allowed. No wheelchair facilities.

Permits: A federal Northwest Forest Pass, $5 per day or $30 annually, is required to park at the trailhead. Passes are available from ranger stations and many private vendors, online at website: www.wta.org, or by calling 800/270-7504.

Maps: For a U.S. Forest Service Trails of the Columbia Gorge map, contact the Nature of the Northwest Information Center, 800 Northeast Oregon Street, Suite 177, Portland, OR 97232; 503/872-2750. Green Trails, Inc.'s excellent topographic maps of the region are available for $3.99 each at outdoor retail outlets. Ask for map number 429, Bonneville Dam. Ask the USGS for topographic maps of the Carson and Wahtum Lake areas.

Directions: From Portland drive 44 miles east on I-84 to Exit 44/Cascade Locks. Continue east through the town of Cascade Locks. Just before the freeway on-ramp, turn sharply right on Forest Lane, following signs for the Oxbow Hatchery and Herman Creek Work Center. About 1.6 miles from town, turn right into Herman Creek Campground. Follow the road a short distance beyond the camping area to the trailhead.

Contact: Columbia River Gorge National Scenic Area, 902 Wasco Avenue, Suite 200, Hood River, OR 97031; 541/386-2333 or 503/668-1440 (Portland number).

21 Mount Defiance
11.9 mi/1.0 day

This is where you go when all the other Columbia Gorge trails start to seem easy. It gains nearly 5,000 feet in just over five miles, and it's as tough a climb as it sounds. Still up to it? After a glance at the bizarre Hole-in-the-Wall Falls, stay right at the junction with the Starvation Creek Trail at about half a mile. (Short day hikers, go left to make a short loop back to the car near Starvation Creek Falls.) You'll pass below Lancaster Falls, and a short distance later start up the elevator shaft. About three miles later stay right at the trail junction and walk the final quarter mile through rock slides to the antenna farm at the summit, 4,960 feet. Views of the gorge are predictably gorgeous. Return via the same route, or preferably, turn east from the summit to Warren Lake, gain the top of the exposed Starvation Ridge, and follow it down some four miles to the parking lot where you started about seven blisters ago.

Before you make the climb, consider that the summit of Mount Defiance also can be reached from the south side by walking about three miles round-trip from a trailhead on Forest Service Road 2820, or by walking an even shorter distance up a gated road off Forest Service Road 2821. But that wouldn't be nearly as much fun. Right? Right.

Location: In the Columbia River Gorge at Starvation Creek State Park east of Wyeth; see The Columbia River Gorge and Mount Hood Map 2, grid c3.

User Groups: Hikers and dogs. No horses or mountain bikes are allowed. No wheelchair facilities.

Permits: No permits are required. Parking and access are free.

Maps: For a U.S. Forest Service Trails of the Columbia Gorge map, contact the Nature of the Northwest Information Center, 800 Northeast Oregon Street, Suite 177, Portland, OR 97232; 503/872-2750. Green Trails, Inc.'s excellent topographic maps of the region are available for $3.99 each at outdoor retail outlets. Ask for map number 430, Hood River. Ask the USGS for topographic maps of the Carson and Mount Defiance areas.

Directions: From Portland drive east on I-84 to Starvation Creek State Park near milepost 54. The trailhead is to the west of the parking area.

Contact: Columbia River Gorge National Scenic Area, 902 Wasco Avenue, Suite 200, Hood River, OR 97031; 541/386-2333 or 503/668-1440 (Portland number).

22 Wygant
8.0 mi/5.0 hrs

When it pours in the Columbia Gorge, which is often, even a short walk up a southside trail can be an exercise in endurance. With cold rain trickling down your back, even the grandest waterfall looks like just so much more water. When water is the enemy, that's bad. On those days, savvy gorge hikers stray farther east, past that magic line in the central gorge where rain squalls peter out. Thankfully trails like Wygant Peak are on the dry side of that line.

This is a lonesome, pleasant walk with a 2,200-foot elevation gain to an old lookout site. It starts on a stretch of the historic, abandoned Columbia River Scenic Highway and climbs moderately up forested slopes to a view of the eastern portion of the gorge and southern Washington landmarks such as Dog Mountain and Drano Lake. You can return via the new Chetwoot Trail, which drops down the east side of Perham Creek back to the trailhead.

Location: Between Viento State Park and Hood River in the Columbia River Gorge; see

The Columbia River Gorge and Mount Hood Map 2, grid c3.

User Groups: Hikers and dogs. No horses or mountain bikes are allowed. No wheelchair facilities.

Permits: No permits are required. Parking and access are free.

Maps: For a U.S. Forest Service Trails of the Columbia Gorge map, contact the Nature of the Northwest Information Center, 800 Northeast Oregon Street, Suite 177, Portland, OR 97232; 503/872-2750. Green Trails, Inc.'s excellent topographic maps of the region are available for $3.99 each at outdoor retail outlets. Ask for map number 430, Hood River. Ask the USGS for topographic maps of the Mount Defiance and Hood River areas.

Directions: From Portland drive east on I-84 to Exit 58. Park at the east end of Vinzenz Lausmann Rest Area and find the trailhead a short distance up a gated road to the west.

Contact: Columbia River Gorge National Scenic Area, 902 Wasco Avenue, Suite 200, Hood River, OR 97031; 541/386-2333 or 503/668-1440 (Portland number).

23 Tom McCall Preserve
5.6 mi/3.5 hrs

There's something for both the stroller and the climber in all of us at the 231-acre Tom McCall Preserve, a Nature Conservancy project just off I-84, east of Mosier. Two trails depart from the Rowena Crest Viewpoint. The first, an easy, 2.2-mile round-trip, heads west toward two plateau ponds before ending at a viewpoint overlooking the Gorge. It's a good hike for children, although the Nature Conservancy advises—correctly—that it's best to bring them here in spring or early summer, as days later in the summer make this a hot, dry, exposed walk. The second trail climbs more than 1,000 feet in 1.7 miles on a rather relentless switchback ladder to Tom McCall Point (elevation 1,720

feet). The view is awesome. Wildflowers dot both trails in the spring, before the dry season sucks the life out of the eastern Columbia Gorge. More than 300 plant species have been documented here in grasslands and rocky basalt outcrops. Four species—Thompson's waterleaf, Hood River milkvetch, Columbia desert parsley, and Thompson's broadleaf lupine—are unique to the Columbia River Gorge. Visits from March to May usually are best for wildflower viewing. The area is named after a former governor of Oregon.

Long pants are advised here to avoid close encounters with poison oak. Also keep an eye out for rattlesnakes.

Location: East of Hood River near Mosier in the Columbia River Gorge; see The Columbia River Gorge and Mount Hood Map 2, grid c6.

User Groups: Hikers only. No dogs, horses, or mountain bikes are allowed. No wheelchair facilities.

Permits: No permits are required. Parking and access are free.

Maps: Trail brochures are usually available at the trailhead. Ask the USGS for a topographic map of the White Salmon area.

Directions: From Portland drive 65 miles east on I-84 to Hood River and proceed to Mosier, Exit 69. Follow signs to the Rowena Crest Viewpoint. Park on the west side of the road, next to the Nature Conservancy sign or at the Rowena Viewpoint.

Contact: The Nature Conservancy, 821 Southeast 14th Avenue, Portland, OR 97214; 503/230-1221.

24 Surveyors Ridge
11.7 mi one way/
1.0–2.0 days

If the high, drier country east of Mount Hood is more to your liking than the soggy west side, chances are that something along the sprawling ridgetop Surveyors Ridge route will catch your fancy. From its northern terminus, the trail leads south to several sites: 3,780-foot Bald Butte (see below), a junction with the Oak Ridge Trail, Rimrock Viewpoint, Forest Service Road 17 and Gibson Prairie Horse Camp. You can also follow the Zigzag Trail about three-quarters of a mile west to an exit (or entry) at the Polallie Trailhead on Highway 35.

Views of Mount Hood and the Hood River valley are splendid throughout, and well-used campsites are frequent. The terrain varies widely, from clear-cut to deep forest to open meadows to exposed peaks. The path itself varies from broad, beaten horse path to gravel road to more normal, single-track footpath. Lately the trail has been a particular hit with mountain bikers. In the fall it's a haven for hunters, who flock to the horse camp.

Location: East of Highway 35 near Mount Hood; see The Columbia River Gorge and Mount Hood Map 2, grid d5.

User Groups: Hikers, horses, dogs, and mountain bikes. No wheelchair facilities.

Permits: A federal Northwest Forest Pass, $5 per day or $30 annually, is required to park at the trailhead. Passes are available from ranger stations and many private vendors, online at website: www.wta.org, or by calling 800/270-7504.

Maps: For a map of the Mount Hood National Forest and Badger Creek Wilderness, contact the Nature of the Northwest Information Center, 800 Northeast Oregon Street, Suite 177, Portland, OR 97232; 503/872-2750. Green Trails, Inc.'s excellent topographic maps of the region are available for $3.99 each at outdoor retail outlets. Ask for map numbers 430 and 462, Hood River and Mount Hood. Ask the USGS for topographic maps of the Parkdale and Dog River areas.

Directions: North trailhead: From Hood River drive 14 miles south on Highway 35 to Pinemont Drive/Forest Service Road 17. Turn left (east) and drive about five miles to Road 630, a spur road immediately south of the power lines. Turn right and follow Road 630 a short distance to the parking area.

South trailhead: From Hood River, drive 26 miles south on Highway 35 to Forest Service Road 44. Turn left and proceed for 3.6 miles to Road 620. The trail crosses Road 620 near its junction with Road 44. Parking is limited. Other access points along the trail are at Gibson Prairie Horse Camp and on Forest Service Roads 640, 670, and 680.

Contact: Mount Hood National Forest, Hood River Ranger District, 6780 Highway 35, Mount Hood-Parkdale, OR 97041; 541/352-6002.

25 Oak Ridge to Bald Butte/Rimrock
8.2 mi/5.0 hrs

Want to sample the best views of the Surveyors Ridge Trail without committing to the whole thing? Taste a slice of the northern portion by walking to a good viewpoint atop 3,780-foot Bald Butte or 4,300-foot Rimrock. From the parking area follow the Oak Ridge Trail through a delightful forest of white oak on the lower portions before climbing to pine forests at about 1.5 miles. Good views of Mount Hood begin in this area. At 2.3 miles is a junction with the Surveyors Ridge Trail. The trail leads south 2.3 miles to Rimrock Viewpoint, perched atop a sheer cliff. For Bald Butte turn left (north) and follow the ridgetop for about a mile to a dirt road beneath a set of large power lines. Follow the road straight about 0.8 mile to the old lookout site, where views extend far into southern Washington.

Location: East of the Hood River Ranger Station in Mount Hood National Forest; see The

Columbia River Gorge and Mount Hood Map 2, grid d4.

User Groups: Hikers, horses, dogs, and mountain bikes. No wheelchair facilities.

Permits: No permits are required. Parking and access are free.

Maps: For a map of the Mount Hood National Forest, contact the Nature of the Northwest Information Center, 800 Northeast Oregon Street, Suite 177, Portland, OR 97232; 503/872-2750. Green Trails, Inc.'s excellent topographic maps of the region are available for $3.99 each at outdoor retail outlets. Ask for map number 430, Hood River. Ask the USGS for a topographic map of the Parkdale area.

Directions: From Hood River drive approximately 16 miles south on Highway 35 to Smullin Road (one mile beyond Hood River Ranger Station). Turn left (east) and proceed about one-third mile to a sharp turn to the south. Turn left onto an unmarked gravel road and proceed about a quarter mile to the parking area on the right side of the road.

Contact: Mount Hood National Forest, Hood River Ranger District, 6780 Highway 35, Mount Hood-Parkdale, OR 97041; 541/352-6002.

⁨26⁩ Lost Lake Loop
3.2 mi/2.0 hrs

Bring your camera. Lost Lake is famous for its expansive views of Mount Hood, and the Lost Lake Trail is a pleasant loop all the way around the lake, easy and inviting enough for the whole family. Pick up an interpretive pamphlet at the trailhead. The occasionally planked trail loops through an awesome grove of old-growth cedars and follows the lakeshore closely for the entire 3.2-mile route. An optional side trip is the four-mile round-trip to Lost Lake Butte (4,468 feet), which offers great views from a dilapidated hilltop lookout. The trail begins in the large Forest Service campground on the northeast side of the lake. Another pleasant family hike from the same parking area is the Old-Growth Trail, a two-mile, barrier-free loop that splits off the Lost Lake Trail. Watch for signs along the main path. Because the lake is at 3,100 feet, it's usually only accessible from May through October.

Location: Northwest of Mount Hood in the Mount Hood Wilderness; see The Columbia River Gorge and Mount Hood Map 2, grid e2.

User Groups: Hikers, horses, and dogs. No mountain bikes are allowed. One mile of the path is barrier-free and wheelchair accessible.

Permits: No permits are required. Parking costs $3.

Maps: For a map of the Mount Hood Wilderness, contact the Nature of the Northwest Information Center, 800 Northeast Oregon Street, Suite 177, Portland, OR 97232; 503/872-2750. Green Trails, Inc.'s excellent topographic maps of the region are available for $3.99 each at outdoor retail outlets. Ask for map number 461, Government Camp. Ask the USGS for a topographic map of the Bull Run Lake area.

Directions: From Portland drive about 40 miles east on U.S. 26 to Zigzag. Turn left (north) on Lolo Pass Road/Forest Service Road 18 and drive 10.5 miles to Lolo Pass and McGee Creek Road/Forest Service Road 1810. Turn right and proceed four miles until the road rejoins Forest Service Road 18. Proceed to the junction with Forest Service Road 13. Turn left and drive to the trailhead on the Lost Lake shores at the far end of the picnic area parking lot.

Contact: Mount Hood National Forest Information Center, 65000 East Highway 26, Welches, OR 97067; 503/622-7674.

27 Huckleberry Mountain/ Boulder Ridge
11.1 mi/6.5 hrs

Boulder Ridge and Huckleberry Mountain, both popular day-hike destinations for Portland-area hikers, can be reached from the Wildwood Trailhead described below or from the Huckleberry Mountain Trailhead, about four miles east on Welches Road. Since parking is difficult at the latter trailhead, many hikers arrange a pickup and hike both trails as a shuttle walk. Or try stashing a bicycle at the eastern trailhead.

On the Boulder Ridge Trail, cross the Salmon River and start up, with good views of Mount Hood beginning at about two miles. Continue up Boulder Ridge and, at just beyond four miles, turn right on the Plaza Trail and walk the final mile to Huckleberry Mountain (elevation 4,300 feet). Return the way you came or continue along the ridge a half mile to a sharp, downhill left turn on the Bonanza Trail, which includes a stop at Bonanza Mine on the trail's five-mile journey to the eastern trailhead.

Location: South of U.S. 26 in the Salmon-Huckleberry Wilderness; see The Columbia River Gorge and Mount Hood Map 2, grid f1.

User Groups: Hikers, horses, and dogs. No mountain bikes are allowed. No wheelchair facilities.

Permits: No permits are required. A parking fee is charged at the Wildwood trailhead only.

Maps: For a map of the Salmon-Huckleberry Wilderness, contact the Nature of the Northwest Information Center, 800 Northeast Oregon Street, Suite 177, Portland, OR 97232; 503/872-2750. Green Trails, Inc.'s excellent topographic maps of the region are available for $3.99 each at outdoor retail outlets. Ask for map numbers 460 and 461, Cherryville and Government Camp. Ask the USGS for topographic maps of the Salmon and Rhododendron areas.

Directions: From Portland drive east on U.S. 26 to signs for Wildwood Recreation Site on the right (south) side of the highway. Turn right and proceed to the trailhead near the picnic area.

Contact: Mount Hood National Forest Information Center, 65000 East Highway 26, Welches, OR 97067; 503/622-7674.

28 West Zigzag Mountain
11.4 mi/8.0 hrs

A strong, leg-testing climb and grand views at an old lookout site on top make the West Zigzag Trail a popular spring and summer getaway for Portland-area hikers. The trail starts out fairly steep and never really allows you to catch your breath. Carry plenty of water in mid- to late summer. The first 3.5 miles are relentless switchbacks; then the mountain ridge is gained and the trail eases up a bit. Soon you're alternately gaining and losing altitude on the up-and-down final 1.5 miles to the West Zigzag lookout. Good views begin when you first break onto the ridge and culminate at the old lookout site, where the top of Mount Jefferson is in sight to the south and rugged, desolate Castle Canyon is directly below to the west. You gain more than 3,000 feet on the way up to the lookout site, elevation 4,468 feet. For one-way hikers, take the trails that continue east to Cast Lake, Horseshoe Ridge, and the East Zigzag Mountain area, or southeast to the trailhead near Henry Creek on Forest Service Road 207 (see hike East Zigzag Mountain Loop, this chapter).

Location: On the west slopes of Zigzag Mountain in the Mount Hood Wilderness, north of U.S. 26; see The Columbia River Gorge and Mount Hood Map 2, grid f1.

User Groups: Hikers, dogs, and horses. No mountain bikes are allowed. No wheelchair facilities.

Permits: A federal Northwest Forest Pass, $5 per day or $30 annually, is required to park at the trailhead. Passes are available from ranger stations and many private vendors, online at website: www.wta.org, or by calling 800/270-7504.

Maps: For a map of the Mount Hood Wilderness, contact the Nature of the Northwest Information Center, 800 Northeast Oregon Street, Suite 177, Portland, OR 97232; 503/872-2750. Green Trails, Inc.'s excellent topographic maps of the region are available for $3.99 each at outdoor retail outlets. Ask for map number 461, Government Camp. Ask the USGS for topographic maps of the Rhododendron, Government Camp, and Bull Run Lake areas.

Directions: From Portland drive about 40 miles east on U.S. 26 to Zigzag. Turn left (north) on East Lolo Pass Road/Forest Service Road 18. Travel about half a mile and turn right (east) on East Mountain Drive. The trailhead is about three-quarters of a mile ahead on the left (north) side of the road.

Contact: Mount Hood National Forest Information Center, 65000 East Highway 26, Welches, OR 97067; 503/622-7674.

29 Ramona Falls/ Bald Mountain Loop
10.5 mi/7.0 hrs

This highly popular loop hike can be a short, 4.5-mile trek to cool, beautiful Ramona Falls or a longer, 10.5-mile looping march to a great viewpoint at Bald Mountain on the Pacific Crest Trail. Hike the loop in either direction to Ramona Falls and then proceed on the Pacific Crest Trail 5.5 miles to Bald Mountain. In the midst of that stretch, you face fording the often raging Muddy Fork River. Keep in mind that crossings are easier early in the day. Views of Mount Hood from Bald Mountain (4,400

feet) are superb. Return to the car by hiking the Bald Mountain Trail 2.8 miles out, again crossing the Muddy Fork River, but this time with the help of a bridge, for which you will be most thankful. The elevation gain from the upper trailhead to Bald Mountain is about 1,600 feet.

Location: In the Sandy River drainage of the Mount Hood Wilderness; see The Columbia River Gorge and Mount Hood Map 2, grid f2.

User Groups: Hikers and dogs. No horses or mountain bikes are allowed. No wheelchair facilities.

Permits: A federal Northwest Forest Pass, $5 per day or $30 annually, is required to park at the trailhead. Passes are available from ranger stations and many private vendors, online at website: www.wta.org, or by calling 800/270-7504.

Maps: For a map of the Mount Hood Wilderness, contact the Nature of the Northwest Information Center, 800 Northeast Oregon Street, Suite 177, Portland, OR 97232; 503/872-2750. Green Trails, Inc.'s excellent topographic maps of the region are available for $3.99 each at outdoor retail outlets. Ask for map numbers 461 and 462, Government Camp and Mount Hood. Ask the USGS for a topographic map of the Bull Run Lake.

Directions: From Portland drive about 40 miles east on U.S. 26 to Zigzag. Turn left (north) on Lolo Pass Road/Forest Service Road 18. Drive five miles, veer right on Forest Service Road 1825, and then turn left on Spur Road 100. The lower trailhead (which adds 2.5 miles to the round-trip hike) is on the left. Or continue 1.25 miles up (rough) Spur Road 100 to the upper trailhead at the road's end.

Contact: Mount Hood National Forest Information Center, 65000 East Highway 26, Welches, OR 97067; 503/622-7674.

30 McNeil Point
7.0 mi/4.5 hrs

McNeil Point, site of an old stone CCC-era backcountry shelter, is a wildly magnificent place, high on Mount Hood's rugged north-western shoulder. Two trails (take your pick) skirt around either side of Bald Mountain and join the Timberline Trail (see hikes in this chapter). You climb up a ridge through bear-grass to stunning wildflower meadows with Mount Hood as a close-up backdrop. From the uppermost part of the meadow near a small lake, a side trail leads up to the stone McNeil Point Shelter. It rejoins the Timberline Trail after about a mile, but the route is quite rough and its use is discouraged by trail managers. Return the way you came. More so than ever, tread lightly in this delicate and beautiful alpine area.

Camping is not allowed in the open mead-ows or close to the lakeshore. No fires are allowed within 500 feet of the CCC shelter. Bring a stove.

Location: On the west slopes of Mount Hood; see The Columbia River Gorge and Mount Hood Map 2, grid e2.

User Groups: Hikers and dogs. No horses or mountain bikes are allowed. No wheel-chair facilities.

Permits: A federal Northwest Forest Pass, $5 per day or $30 annually, is required to park at the trailhead. Passes are available from ranger stations and many private vendors, online at website: www.wta.org, or by call-ing 800/270-7504.

Maps: For a map of the Mount Hood Wilder-ness, contact the Nature of the Northwest Information Center, 800 Northeast Oregon Street, Suite 177, Portland, OR 97232; 503/872-2750. Green Trails, Inc.'s excellent topo-graphic maps of the region are available for $3.99 each at outdoor retail outlets. Ask for map numbers 461 and 462, Government Camp and Mount Hood. Ask the USGS for topo-graphic maps of the Mount Hood North and Bull Run Lake areas.

Directions: From Portland drive about 40 miles east on U.S. 26 to Zigzag. Turn left (north) on Lolo Pass Road/Forest Service Road 18 and drive to Forest Service Road 1825. Veer right and in about a half mile stay straight on Forest Service Road 1828. Drive about seven miles to the Top Spur Trail park-ing area along the road.

Contact: Mount Hood National Forest Infor-mation Center, 65000 East Highway 26, Welch-es, OR 97067; 503/622-7674.

31 Vista Ridge to Eden Park, Cairn, and Wy'East Basins
8.0 mi/6.0 hrs

This is the most direct route into the spec-tacular northern alpine country of Mount Hood. The Vista Ridge Trail begins on an old road and climbs in the forest beyond an old trail junction at about a half mile (stay right). Mount Hood pops increasingly into view as you gain the ridge and eventually join Tim-berline Trail 600 at about 2.5 miles. From here choose your spellbinding alpine destination. Turn right (west) and begin a three-mile loop that visits Eden Park, Cairn Basin, and Wy'East Basin. Go east and Elk Cove awaits in two miles. Or go off-trail to the south-east from Wy'East Basin to the top of rugged Barrett Spur (elevation 7,853 feet), where the views of the Ladd and Coe Glaciers are truly awesome.

Views and August wildflowers at Eden Park and Cairn and Wy'East Basins make you kick yourself (not recommended if you're wear-ing mountaineering boots) for not discover-ing this trail years before. It's the kind of terrain you normally have to hike much, much farther to see. Be careful not to con-tribute to the meadow-stomping and other degradation that overuse already has brought to this area. Return the way you came, or for a shuttle hike, exit via the Mc-Neil Point Trail (see above), reached by walking about two miles west on the Timberline Trail (see hike in this chapter).

Location: On the northwestern slopes of Mount Hood in the Hood River Ranger District; see The Columbia River Gorge and Mount Hood Map 2, grid e3.

User Groups: Hikers and dogs. No horses or mountain bikes are allowed. No wheelchair facilities.

Permits: A federal Northwest Forest Pass, $5 per day or $30 annually, is required to park at the trailhead. Passes are available from ranger stations and many private vendors, online at website: www.wta.org, or by calling 800/270-7504.

Maps: For a map of the Mount Hood Wilderness, contact the Nature of the Northwest Information Center, 800 Northeast Oregon Street, Suite 177, Portland, OR 97232; 503/872-2750. Green Trails, Inc.'s excellent topographic maps of the region are available for $3.99 each at outdoor retail outlets. Ask for map numbers 461 and 462, Government Camp and Mount Hood. Ask the USGS for a topographic map of the Mount Hood North area.

Directions: From Portland drive about 40 miles east on U.S. 26 to Zigzag. Turn left (north) on Lolo Pass Road/Forest Service Road 18 and drive 10.5 miles to Lolo Pass and McGee Creek Road/Forest Service Road 1810. Turn right and proceed until the road rejoins Forest Service Road 18. Proceed east for just under 3.5 miles and turn right on Forest Service Road 16. Follow signs on Forest Service Roads 16 and 1650 to Vista Ridge Trailhead at the end of Forest Service Road 1650.

Contact: Mount Hood National Forest, Hood River Ranger District, 6780 Highway 35, Mount Hood-Parkdale, OR 97041; 541/352-6002.

🖸 Elk Cove
9.6 mi/6.0 hrs

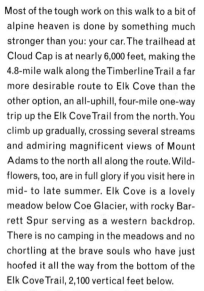

Most of the tough work on this walk to a bit of alpine heaven is done by something much stronger than you: your car. The trailhead at Cloud Cap is at nearly 6,000 feet, making the 4.8-mile walk along the Timberline Trail a far more desirable route to Elk Cove than the other option, an all-uphill, four-mile one-way trip up the Elk Cove Trail from the north. You climb up gradually, crossing several streams and admiring magnificent views of Mount Adams to the north all along the route. Wildflowers, too, are in full glory if you visit here in mid- to late summer. Elk Cove is a lovely meadow below Coe Glacier, with rocky Barrett Spur serving as a western backdrop. There is no camping in the meadows and no chortling at the brave souls who have just hoofed it all the way from the bottom of the Elk Cove Trail, 2,100 vertical feet below.

Location: On the north slopes of Mount Hood, west of Cloud Cap Campground; see The Columbia River Gorge and Mount Hood Map 2, grid e3.

User Groups: Hikers and dogs. No horses or mountain bikes are allowed. No wheelchair facilities.

Permits: A federal Northwest Forest Pass, $5 per day or $30 annually, is required to park at the trailhead. Passes are available from ranger stations and many private vendors, online at website: www.wta.org, or by calling 800/270-7504.

Maps: For a map of the Mount Hood Wilderness, contact the Nature of the Northwest Information Center, 800 Northeast Oregon Street, Suite 177, Portland, OR 97232; 503/872-2750. Green Trails, Inc.'s excellent topographic maps of the region are available for $3.99 each at outdoor retail outlets. Ask for map number 462, Mount Hood. Ask the

USGS for a topographic map of the Mount Hood North areas.

Directions: From Portland drive about 55 miles east on U.S. 26 or to Highway 35. Drive north on Highway 35 to signs for the Cooper Spur Ski Area, between mileposts 73 and 74. Drive west on Cooper Spur Road/Forest Service Road 3510 for about three miles to a junction with Forest Service Road 3512. Turn left and follow signs about 10 rough miles to Cloud Cap Campground. Watch for the sign for the Timberline Trail near the campground.

Contact: Mount Hood National Forest, Hood River Ranger District, 6780 Highway 35, Mount Hood-Parkdale, OR 97041; 541/352-6002.

33 Cooper Spur
7.0 mi/4.0 hrs

Breathe deeply. Step. Breathe deeply again. It's a technique taught to all alpine climbers, especially those who aren't accustomed to vigorous exercise in the thin-air environment at high altitudes. And it might come in handy on the Cooper Spur Trail, which literally looks down upon all other trails in the state of Oregon. You start at almost 6,000 feet and wind up at 8,500, a little worn, a lot winded, and very much exhilarated.

From the trailhead choose the middle trail and walk straight south for one mile to the remains of the stone Cooper Spur Shelter. Turn uphill on the Cooper Spur Trail. Pace yourself and enjoy the magnificent, though exposed, view. Be sure to carry warm clothes; nasty winter weather can catch you off guard here, even in August. Go until you've had enough altitude and great views. Or continue all the way up to the large boulder in the distance, Tie-In-Rock. For something different on the way out, instead of retracing your steps on the Timberline Trail, follow the Tilly Jane Trail a mile downhill from the Cooper Spur Shelter area to an excellent viewpoint

above Polallie Canyon and then walk back uphill about half a mile to the car.

Location: On the north slopes of Mount Hood, west of Cloud Cap Campground; see The Columbia River Gorge and Mount Hood Map 2, grid e3.

User Groups: Hikers and dogs. No horses or mountain bikes are allowed. No wheelchair facilities.

Permits: A federal Northwest Forest Pass, $5 per day or $30 annually, is required to park at the trailhead. Passes are available from ranger stations and many private vendors, online at website: www.wta.org, or by calling 800/270-7504.

Maps: For a map of the Mount Hood Wilderness, contact the Nature of the Northwest Information Center, 800 Northeast Oregon Street, Suite 177, Portland, OR 97232; 503/872-2750. Green Trails, Inc.'s excellent topographic maps of the region are available for $3.99 each at outdoor retail outlets. Ask for map number 462, Mount Hood. Ask the USGS for a topographic map of the Mount Hood North area.

Directions: From Portland drive about 55 miles east on U.S. 26 to Highway 35. Drive north on Highway 35 to signs for the Cooper Spur Ski Area, between mileposts 73 and 74. Drive west on Cooper Spur Road/Forest Service Road 3510 for about three miles to a junction with Forest Service Road 3512. Turn left and follow signs about 10 rough miles to Cloud Cap Campground. Watch for the sign for the Timberline Trail near the campground.

Contact: Mount Hood National Forest, Hood River Ranger District, 6780 Highway 35, Mount Hood-Parkdale, OR 97041; 541/352-6002.

34 Tilly Jane/ Polallie Ridge Loop
5.0 mi/4.0 hrs

This trail is a major workout and it leads to a destination that you can also drive to. But getting here on foot is half the fun on this loop trail, which begins in Cooper Spur Ski Area, climbs up the Polallie Ridge or Tilly Jane Ski Trail (choose one), and exits on the opposite, parallel leg. Views are grand from the entire route, which gains 1,400 feet from bottom to top.

Location: Between Cooper Spur Ski Area and Tilly Jane Campground on the northeastern slopes of Mount Hood; see The Columbia River Gorge and Mount Hood Map 2, grid e4.

User Groups: Hikers, dogs, and horses. No mountain bikes are allowed. No wheelchair facilities.

Permits: A federal Northwest Forest Pass, $5 per day or $30 annually, is required to park at the trailhead. Passes are available from ranger stations and many private vendors, online at website: www.wta.org, or by calling 800/270-7504.

Maps: For a map of the Mount Hood Wilderness and National Recreation Area, contact the Nature of the Northwest Information Center, 800 Northeast Oregon Street, Suite 177, Portland, OR 97232; 503/872-2750. Green Trails, Inc.'s excellent topographic maps of the region are available for $3.99 each at outdoor retail outlets. Ask for map number 462, Mount Hood. Ask the USGS for topographic maps of the Dog River and Mount Hood North areas.

Directions: From Portland drive about 55 miles east on U.S. 26 to Highway 35. Drive north on Highway 35 to signs for the Cooper Spur Ski Area, between mileposts 73 and 74. Turn west on Cooper Spur Road/Forest Service Road 3510 and follow signs for the Tilly Jane Ski Trailhead on the left, just beyond the ski area.

Contact: Mount Hood National Forest, Hood River Ranger District, 6780 Highway 35, Mount Hood-Parkdale, OR 97041; 541/352-6002.

35 Tamanawas Falls Loop
4.0 mi/2.0 hrs

This is an often crowded but always pleasant stroll to an impressive waterfall. Most of the route is a cool, shaded walk along Cold Spring Creek. A straight-shot round-trip to the falls is about four miles, with a vertical rise of only 450 feet, making this a good family hike. But the route can be lengthened to a 5.5-mile loop.

From the trailhead cross the bridge and hike north on the East Fork Trail for about half a mile to a junction with Tamanawas Falls Trail. Stay left for the broad, impressive falls (elevation 3,450 feet), 1.4 miles ahead. Linger here for a while and return the same way. For the loop trip, turn left about half a mile below the falls on the return trip and walk 1.5 miles to the Polallie overlook, where you can survey the damage of a massive 1980 flood. Return on the East Fork Trail. The trail is usually snow-free April through November.

Location: On the east side of Mount Hood near Highway 35; see The Columbia River Gorge and Mount Hood Map 2, grid f4.

User Groups: Hikers and dogs. No horses or mountain bikes are allowed. No wheelchair facilities.

Permits: A federal Northwest Forest Pass, $5 per day or $30 annually, is required to park at the trailhead. Passes are available from ranger stations and many private vendors, online at website: www.wta.org, or by calling 800/270-7504.

Maps: For a map of the Mount Hood Wilderness and National Recreation Area, contact the Nature of the Northwest Information Center, 800 Northeast Oregon Street, Suite 177, Portland, OR 97232; 503/872-2750. Green Trails, Inc.'s excellent topographic maps of the region are available for $3.99 each at various outdoor retail outlets. Ask for map number 462, Mount Hood. Ask the USGS for a topographic map of the Dog River area.

Directions: From Portland drive about 55 miles east on U.S. 26 to Highway 35. Proceed north to the East Fork Trailhead, a quarter of a mile north of Sherwood Campground near milepost 72.

Contact: Mount Hood National Forest, Hood River Ranger District, 6780 Highway 35, Mount Hood-Parkdale, OR 97041; 541/352-6002.

36 East Fork Trail
6.0 mi one way/3.0 hrs

This is a mountain-bikers' special. The long, straight, fairly level East Fork Trail is a great one-way ride between Robin Hood Campground and Polallie Trailhead along the East Fork Hood River. Arrange for a drop-off at one trailhead and a pickup at the other. The trail can easily be done on bike (or foot) in either direction. The elevation change is only about 250 feet, one way. Some day hikers combine portions of this trail with the Tamanawas Falls Trail to lengthen day-hiking loops. The trail is usually snow-free April through November. It's particularly beautiful in the fall, when crowds are light and vine maples put on a fine color show.

Location: Parallel to Highway 35 on the East Fork of the Hood River; see The Columbia River Gorge and Mount Hood Map 2, grid f4.

User Groups: Hikers, dogs, and mountain bikes. Horses are not allowed. No wheelchair facilities.

Permits: A federal Northwest Forest Pass, $5 per day or $30 annually, is required to park at the trailhead. Passes are available from ranger stations and many private vendors, online at website: www.wta.org, or by calling 800/270-7504.

Maps: For a map of the Mount Hood Wilderness and National Recreation Area, contact the Nature of the Northwest Information Center, 800 Northeast Oregon Street, Suite 177, Portland, OR 97232; 503/872-2750. Green Trails, Inc.'s excellent topographic maps of the region are available for $3.99 each at outdoor retail outlets. Ask for map number 462, Mount Hood. To obtain USGS topographic maps, ask for the Dog River and Badger Lake areas.

Directions: From Portland drive about 55 miles east on U.S. 26 to Highway 35. Drive north on Highway 35 to Robin Hood Campground on the left side of the highway, near milepost 68. Find the trailhead at the north end of the campground.

Contact: Mount Hood National Forest, Hood River Ranger District, 6780 Highway 35, Mount Hood-Parkdale, OR 97041; 541/352-6002.

37 Elk Meadows/Gnarl Ridge
7.0 mi/4.0 hrs

Some of the most fantastic, sprawling wildflower meadows anywhere on Mount Hood are found at the top of this excellent, long day hike from the Hood River Meadows area. The trail follows Clark Creek upward at a moderate pace and then switches back sharply to a four-way junction (at about 2.5 miles) on a plateau atop Gnarl Ridge, where Elk Meadows unfolds before you like a feast for the eyes. From here the left trail leads up about 2.5 miles to Gnarl Ridge, a fantastic viewpoint at 6,500 feet on the edge of a massive chasm containing Newton Creek. Lamberson Butte, a rock outcrop at 6,663 feet, is above and to the north. This route to Gnarl Ridge is 10 miles round-trip. For Elk Meadows go straight and travel in either direction on a loop trail through the fields of lupine, huckleberries, and lilies. The Elk Meadows Shelter is found off a side trail at the top of this 1.2-mile loop. Also near the upper portion of the loop, a side trail leads west, joining the trail to Gnarl Ridge about two miles below the high point. Loop hikers can continue on the Gnarl Ridge Trail to its junction with the Newton Creek Trail and follow the other side of the canyon back to the trailhead.

For yet another variation, hike the same route from the Sno-Park Trailhead and at the junction at 2.5 miles, turn right on the Bluegrass Ridge Trail and walk about a mile to a stunning summit viewpoint atop Elk Mountain, at 5,600 feet. Loops of various distances can be made by continuing half a mile north on the Bluegrass Ridge Trail and taking a short side trail west to the Elk Meadow Loop Trail.

In case you consider camping, note that it is not allowed in Elk Meadows.

Location: On the southeast side of Mount Hood above Hood River Meadows; see The Columbia River Gorge and Mount Hood Map 2, grid f4.

User Groups: Hikers, dogs, and horses. No mountain bikes are allowed. No wheelchair facilities.

Permits: A federal Northwest Forest Pass, $5 per day or $30 annually, is required to park at the trailhead. Passes are available from ranger stations and many private vendors, online at website: www.wta.org, or by calling 800/270-7504.

Maps: For a map of the Mount Hood Wilderness and National Recreation Area, contact the Nature of the Northwest Information Center, 800 Northeast Oregon Street, Suite 177, Portland, OR 97232; 503/872-2750. Green Trails, Inc.'s excellent topographic maps of the region are available for $3.99 each at various outdoor retail outlets. Ask for map number 462, Mount Hood. Ask the USGS for a topographic map of the Dog River area.

Directions: From Portland drive about 55 miles east on U.S. 26 to Highway 35. Proceed north about eight miles and follow signs to Clark Creek Sno-Park. The trailhead is in the parking area on the left.

Contact: Mount Hood National Forest, Hood River Ranger District, 6780 Highway 35, Mount Hood-Parkdale, OR 97041; 541/352-6002.

⏣ Mountaineer Trail to Silcox Hut

2.0 mi/1.5 hrs

Revenge. Any skier who's ever endured the freezing chairlift ride to the top of the Magic Mile should return and enjoy the summer climes. Actually, you can cheat on this route and (for a fee) ride the Magic Mile Chair to the top of this arching trail and then walk back down. The Magic Mile Chair runs through Labor Day, providing access to the Palmer Glacier, one of the only lift-accessed, all-summer ski slopes in the United States. But that would be cheating, so start at the lodge, climb the side trail on the right side of the building, and turn up the Mountaineer Trail, setting your sights on Silcox Hut, tucked neatly into the mountainside a mile above. Much of the route to the hut is on a gravel road/cat track. Stop at the historic 1939 Civilian Conservation Corps hut, recently renovated and reopened with bunk-style accommodations, and then continue down the path for a downhill mile on the west side of the Magic Mile lift. Or trek a bit farther west at the top and follow the side trail down to the Pacific Crest Trail about three-fourths of a mile west of the lodge.

Even though this is a short walk from a major tourist area, always be prepared for surprising weather changes this high on Mount Hood. Unlucky travelers have perished in whiteout conditions even in early summer within a stone's throw of the

Palmer Glacier chairlift at the top of this hike (7,000 feet).

Location: High on Mount Hood above Timberline Lodge; see The Columbia River Gorge and Mount Hood Map 2, grid f3.

User Groups: Hikers and dogs. No horses or mountain bikes are allowed. No wheelchair facilities.

Permits: No permits are required. Parking and access are free.

Maps: For a map of the Mount Hood Wilderness, contact the Nature of the Northwest Information Center, 800 Northeast Oregon Street, Suite 177, Portland, OR 97232; 503/872-2750. Green Trails, Inc.'s excellent topographic maps of the region are available for $3.99 each at outdoor retail outlets. Ask for map number 462, Mount Hood. Ask the USGS for a topographic map of the Mount Hood South area.

Directions: From Portland drive about 52 miles east on U.S. 26 to Government Camp. Follow signs to the Timberline Lodge and ski area parking lot, six miles north of U.S. 26 on Timberline Road/Forest Service Road 50. The trail departs from the east side of Timberline Lodge.

Contact: Mount Hood National Forest Information Center, 65000 East Highway 26, Welches, OR 97067; 503/622-7674.

39 Timberline Lodge to Zigzag Canyon/Paradise Park

12.2 mi/8.0 hrs 4 10

This is the perfect daylong taste of wilderness for summertime visitors to magnificent Timberline Lodge. From the lodge follow the Pacific Crest Trail west, beyond the base area for the Magic Mile chairlift. Traverse through open meadows with spectacular views of 11,235-foot Mount Hood, as well as Mount Jefferson and the Three Sisters to the south. About a mile down the path, you drop to the Little Zigzag River and then climb up the other side. It's a bit steep, but it's just prepping you for the grand show ahead. About a mile farther you arrive at an overlook on the lip of Zigzag Canyon. The aerobically challenged should call it a day here. Just beyond, the bottom drops out. You plunge almost 800 feet straight down, directly to the bottom of the awesome canyon, a steep, barren reminder of the combined impact that weather and erosion have on this volcanic peak.

A pleasant spot at the bottom, next to the icy Zigzag River, allows you to catch your breath for the climb back up the other side. (Watch for falling rocks.) About 1.5 miles later at the top, stop, wheeze, gasp, and then turn right on the Paradise Park Trail, which loops up (way up) to absolutely spectacular wildflower meadows in Paradise Park. A grander lunch spot in the entire universe just might not exist. Turn around here or continue on the loop trail to the Pacific Crest Trail for the full 12-mile loop.

Remember: Save some juice for that climb back out of Zigzag Canyon on the way home. And don't forget to bring a coat. Weather can turn bad in an instant any time of the year on Mount Hood.

Location: West of Timberline Lodge on Mount Hood; see The Columbia River Gorge and Mount Hood Map 2, grid f3.

User Groups: Hikers and dogs. No horses or mountain bikes are allowed. No wheelchair facilities.

Permits: No permits are required. Parking and access are free.

Maps: For a map of the Mount Hood Wilderness, contact the Nature of the Northwest Information Center, 800 Northeast Oregon Street, Suite 177, Portland, OR 97232; 503/872-2750. Green Trails, Inc.'s excellent topographic maps of the region are available for $3.99 each at outdoor retail outlets. Ask for map number 462, Mount Hood. Ask the USGS for a topographic map of the Mount Hood South area.

Directions: From Portland drive about 52 miles east on U.S. 26 to Government Camp. Follow signs to the Timberline Lodge and ski area parking lot, six miles north of U.S. 26 on Timberline Road/Forest Service Road 50. The trail departs from the west side of Timberline Lodge.

Contact: Mount Hood National Forest Information Center, 65000 East Highway 26, Welches, OR 97067; 503/622-7674.

🔟 Timberline Trail
40.7 mi/4.0–5.0 days 🔢 👟

This is one of the grandest—and certainly most challenging—backpacking experiences in all of Oregon, if not the whole Northwest. The Timberline Trail, a shorter, more compact version of the Wonderland Trail around Mount Rainier, is a rewarding experience for the well-prepared backpacker. It can be a nightmare experience for novices, however. Even in the dead of summer, weather can be life-threateningly nasty on Mount Hood, often with little or no warning. Go prepared for extreme cold and a fair amount of snow travel, no matter what time of year you visit. Ice axes and the ability to use them are essential. Even when the path is snow free, it often is less of a path than a route—in places the trail is not visible. Know how to use a compass and map for route-finding. And you will be tested by plenty of ups and downs; you gain and lose some 9,000 feet of elevation along the route. You are climbing into and out of glacial canyons, and that means you face a bevy of stream crossings.

That said, it's a magnificent walk. Any time after mid-July, much of the route is snow free, and wildflower displays are sublime. Views are grand from start to finish. Much of the route was built in the 1930s by the Civilian

Conservation Corps, and like many similar Depression-era Northwest mountain projects, this one is a true national treasure.

Be prepared to get very wet crossing streams. When route-planning, keep in mind that most streams are best crossed in the morning, when flow is at its lowest.

Location: All the way around Mount Hood; see The Columbia River Gorge and Mount Hood Map 2, grid f3.

User Groups: Hikers and dogs. No mountain bikes are allowed. Horses are allowed only on the south and west portions where the route joins the Pacific Crest Trail. No wheelchair facilities.

Permits: A federal Northwest Forest Pass, $5 per day or $30 annually, is required to park at the Cloud Cap, Ramona Falls, and Top Spur trailheads. Passes are available from ranger stations and many private vendors, online at website: www.wta.org, or by calling 800/270-7504.

Maps: For a map of the Mount Hood Wilderness and a Timberline Trail brochure, contact the Nature of the Northwest Information Center, 800 Northeast Oregon Street, Suite 177, Portland, OR 97232; 503/872-2750. Green Trails, Inc.'s excellent topographic maps of the region are available for $3.99 each at outdoor retail outlets. Ask for map numbers 461 and 462, Government Camp and Mount Hood. Ask the USGS for topographic maps of the Mount Hood South, Mount Hood North, and Bull Run Lake areas.

Directions: From Portland drive about 52 miles east on U.S. 26 to Government Camp. Follow signs to the Timberline Lodge and ski area parking lot, six miles north of U.S. 26 on Timberline Road/Forest Service Road 50. Hike two miles east on the Pacific Crest Trail to Timberline Trail number 600. Other popular access points include a northern trailhead at Cloud Cap, reached via Highway 35 and Forest Service Road 3512; and a western trailhead in the Lolo Pass area, at the Ramona Falls (see hike in this chapter) or Top Spur Trailheads.

Contact: Mount Hood National Forest Information Center, 65000 East Highway 26, Welches, OR 97067; 503/622-7674.

41 East Zigzag Mountain Loop
11.1 mi/8.0 hrs

Thanks to its always-stunning scenery, lung-busting bravado, and infinite flexibility, the East Zigzag Mountain Loop is one of our favorite Mount Hood hikes. The views are spectacular, fields of wildflowers are sublime, and when you get back to the car, your calves will be mooing so loudly that you won't soon forget you've been somewhere.

The trail starts on an old road grade and heads up and east to Devil's Meadow, where we guarantee you'll want to linger in wildflower season (don't forget bug juice). About a mile ahead the Kodak-moment views of Mount Hood begin. Turn left (west) at the junction of the Burnt Lake and Paradise Park Trails (see hike in this chapter, Hidden Lake/Southern Paradise Park Access) and climb to East Zigzag Peak, 4,971 feet. The views of Hood are absolutely first-rate. Continue about a mile and take the side trail to Cast Lake, a pleasant midway rest stop. Tighten the boots, pack up, and head a short distance south to a side trail leading down to the Devil's Meadow area. Take this trail for a loop of just under eight miles, or turn west and follow the Zigzag Mountain Trail two miles up and along the ridgetop, beyond the Horseshoe Ridge Junction to West Zigzag Mountain (see hike in this chapter). Walk to your second grand lookout of the day and then backtrack a short distance to the junction with the West Zigzag Trail. From here it's 2.3 miles back

down to the car and, if you're smart, several gallons of cold liquid.

Location: On the east side of Zigzag Mountain just west of Mount Hood in the Mount Hood Wilderness; see The Columbia River Gorge and Mount Hood Map 2, grid f2.

User Groups: Hikers, dogs, and horses. No mountain bikes are allowed. No wheelchair facilities.

Permits: No permits are required. Parking and access are free.

Maps: For a detailed map of the Mount Hood Wilderness, contact the Nature of the Northwest Information Center, 800 Northeast Oregon Street, Suite 177, Portland, OR 97232; 503/872-2750. Green Trails, Inc.'s excellent topographic maps of the region are available for $3.99 each at various outdoor retail outlets. Ask for map number 461, Government Camp. Ask the USGS for a topographic map of the Government Camp area.

Directions: From Portland drive east on U.S. 26 to Forest Service Road 27, approximately 1.5 miles east of the town of Rhododendron. Turn left (north) and follow Forest Service Road 27 about a half-mile to Forest Service Road 207. Turn left on Forest Service Road 207 and drive about 4.5 miles to the trailhead at the road's end. Note: Forest Service Road 207 is very rough and might not be suitable for low-clearance vehicles.

Contact: Mount Hood National Forest Information Center, 65000 East Highway 26, Welches, OR 97067; 503/622-7674.

42 Hidden Lake/ Southern Paradise Park
4.0 mi/2.5 hrs

This is a popular, easy hike up the east side of Zigzag Canyon to an alpine lake. Wait until June, when the many wild rhododendrons that line this trail are in full, brilliant pink bloom. The grade is moderate for most of the way to the lake, which is a wonderful lunch spot. Let the kids soak their feet before the trek back down. For true aerobic junkies the trail leads on (and up) another three miles to a junction with the Pacific Crest Trail near Timberline. This route can be hiked one way, up or down, for a shuttle hike of just under seven miles to Timberline Lodge. Or for a full loop from this trailhead, hike five miles to the Pacific Crest Trail, turn left (west), and climb into and out of Zigzag Canyon (whew!); then turn south on the Paradise Park Trail and proceed five miles back to the Paradise Park Trailhead farther west on Forest Service Road 2639. It's a 13-mile loop, and we guarantee that it feels more like 26. Consider that Paradise Park and upper Zigzag Canyon are reached by a relatively easy walk from Timberline Lodge (see hike in this chapter). The loop trip from the bottom does provide a degree of solitude that is tough to obtain in this people-packed region: if you're up to it, go for it. The trail is usually snow-free from June through October.

Location: In the Mount Hood Wilderness north of Government Camp; see The Columbia River Gorge and Mount Hood Map 2, grid f2.

User Groups: Hikers, dogs, and horses. No mountain bikes are allowed. No wheelchair facilities.

Permits: A federal Northwest Forest Pass, $5 per day or $30 annually, is required to park at the trailhead. Passes are available from ranger stations and many private vendors, online at website: www.wta.org, or by calling 800/270-7504.

Maps: For a map of the Mount Hood Wilderness, contact the Nature of the Northwest Information Center, 800 Northeast Oregon Street, Suite 177, Portland, OR 97232; 503/872-2750. Green Trails, Inc.'s excellent topographic maps of the region are available for $3.99 each at outdoor retail outlets. Ask for map numbers 461 and 462, Government Camp and Mount Hood. Ask the USGS for topographic maps of the Government Camp and Mount Hood South areas.

Directions: From Portland drive east on U.S. 26 to Rhododendron, continuing six miles beyond the Zigzag Ranger Station to Kiwanis Camp Road/Forest Service Road 2639. Turn left (north) and proceed about two miles to the trailhead on the left, just beyond the Kiwanis Camp entrance.

Contact: Mount Hood National Forest Information Center, 65000 East Highway 26, Welches, OR 97067; 503/622-7674.

43 Salmon River
16.6 mi one way/
1.0–2.0 days

Whether a pleasant, 2.6-mile riverside stroll or a more challenging, 16-mile trek is on your itinerary, Salmon River fits the bill. The river trail, which can be hiked in its entirety or in portions accessed by several roads, skirts one of Oregon's most spectacular wilderness streams. On the route are many good picnic and camping spots, deep pools, plunging falls, and an awesome river canyon. If you're in the mood for altitude, detour onto the Kinzel Lake Trail and climb 3.5 steep miles to Devil's Peak lookout. But it's tough to leave the Salmon River Trail once you get started. Much of the path wanders below massive old-growth cedar and Douglas fir. At about 4.5 miles the trail leaves the river and climbs to good views above the upper river canyon. Several good designated campsites are found along the way. To complete the full-length, one-way hike, arrange for a pickup or second car at the eastern Mud Creek Trailhead, reached via Forest Service Road 309 near Trillium Lake. Forest Service Road 309 exits via Forest Service Road 2656 onto U.S. 26, three miles east of Government Camp. The trail is snow-free most of the year. Elevation gain on the main route is minimal.

Location: South of Highway 26 in the Salmon-Huckleberry Wilderness; see The Columbia River Gorge and Mount Hood Map 2, grid f1.

User Groups: Hikers and dogs only. Horses are not allowed. Mountain bikes are allowed on the lower trail only; call for details. No wheelchair facilities.

Permits: A federal Northwest Forest Pass, $5 per day or $30 annually, is required to park at the trailhead. Passes are available from ranger stations and many private vendors, online at website: www.wta.org, or by calling 800/270-7504.

Maps: For a map of the Salmon-Huckleberry Wilderness, contact the Nature of the Northwest Information Center, 800 Northeast Oregon Street, Suite 177, Portland, OR 97232; 503/872-2750. Green Trails, Inc.'s excellent topographic maps of the region are available for $3.99 each at outdoor retail outlets. Ask for map numbers 461 and 493, Government Camp and High Rock. Ask the USGS for topographic maps of the High Rock, Rhododendron, and Wolf Peak areas.

Directions: From Portland drive about 40 miles east on U.S. 26 to Zigzag. Turn right (south) on Salmon River Road. Drive east about 2.7 miles to the trailhead on the right, just beyond the Mount Hood National Forest boundary marker. For alternative access you can skip the heavily used first 2.6 miles of trail that parallel the road by driving about five miles past the first trailhead to the Upper Salmon River Trailhead, just before the bridge over the river, and proceeding upstream.

Contact: Mount Hood National Forest Information Center, 65000 East Highway 26, Welches, OR 97067; 503/622-7674.

44 Salmon Butte
8.4 mi/6.0 hrs

This trail is best in June, when the shoulders of Salmon Butte are covered with vivid pink wild rhododendron blossoms. But any time of the year, it's a pleasant walk to an old lookout site with great views of Mount Hood. The trail passes through a clear-cut, old-growth forest, and open slopes before connecting with an old road at about four miles for the final push to the summit (elevation 4,877 feet). Mounts Hood, Jefferson, and St. Helens are visible from the peak. The total elevation gain is about 2,850 feet. The trail is usually snow-free from June through October.

Location: In the Salmon River drainage of the Salmon-Huckleberry Wilderness, south of Welches; see The Columbia River Gorge and Mount Hood Map 2, grid f1.

User Groups: Hikers, dogs, and horses. No mountain bikes are allowed. No wheelchair facilities.

Permits: A federal Northwest Forest Pass, $5 per day or $30 annually, is required to park at the trailhead. Passes are available from ranger stations and many private vendors, online at website: www.wta.org, or by calling 800/270-7504.

Maps: For a map of the Salmon-Huckleberry Wilderness, contact the Nature of the Northwest Information Center, 800 Northeast Oregon Street, Suite 177, Portland, OR 97232; 503/872-2750. Green Trails, Inc.'s excellent topographic maps of the region are available for $3.99 each at outdoor retail outlets. Ask for map numbers 461 and 493, Government Camp and High Rock. Ask the USGS for a topographic map of the High Rock area.

Directions: From Portland drive about 40 miles east on U.S. 26 to Zigzag. Turn right (south) on Salmon River Road and proceed about 6.5 miles to the signed parking area.

Walk a quarter-mile up the gated spur road to the right to find the trailhead.

Contact: Mount Hood National Forest Information Center, 65000 East Highway 26, Welches, OR 97067; 503/622-7674.

⁴⁵ Devil's Peak Lookout/ Hunchback Mountain

8.0 mi/6.0 hrs

It's a thigh-burner, but the ready-made platform for taking Mount Hood portraits at the Devil's Peak Lookout makes the climb worth the pain. This trail goes up in a hurry, gaining 3,200 feet in about four miles on its way to the lookout at 5,045 feet. Actually, this is only one of three routes to the popular lookout. The shortest, a 1.2-mile walk from Forest Service Road 2613, is accessed by a brutal gravel-road maze from the Trillium Lake area. The longest, an eight-mile trek along Hunchback Mountain, starts just behind the Zigzag Ranger Station off Highway 26.

Our recommended route, the Cool Creek Trail, is probably best if you're pressed for time (also, at this writing you don't have to pay a parking fee at this trailhead). Some hikers who truly enjoy pain make this a one-way shuttle hike by climbing the Cool Creek Trail (definitely not cool in summer), then turning north on the Hunchback Trail, and returning to a pickup or second car at the Zigzag Ranger Station. Whichever route you choose, carry plenty of water. You'll need it to wash the sticky gunk off your hands after applying roll after roll of moleskin to your blistered heels.

Location: On Hunchback Mountain, south of U.S. 26 in the Salmon-Huckleberry Wilderness; see The Columbia River Gorge and Mount Hood Map 2, grid f2.

User Groups: Hikers and dogs. No horses or mountain bikes are allowed. No wheelchair facilities.

Permits: No permits are required. Parking and access are free.

Maps: For a map of the Salmon-Huckleberry Wilderness, contact the Nature of the Northwest Information Center, 800 Northeast Oregon Street, Suite 177, Portland, OR 97232; 503/872-2750. Green Trails, Inc.'s excellent topographic maps of the region are available for $3.99 each at outdoor retail outlets. Ask for map number 461, Government Camp. Ask the USGS for topographic maps of the Wolf Peak and Government Camp areas.

Directions: From Portland drive about 40 miles east on U.S. 26 to Zigzag and another 1.5 miles east to Still Creek Road. Turn right (south) and drive three miles to the Cool Creek Trail on the right side of the road near the Cool Creek crossing.

Contact: Mount Hood National Forest Information Center, 65000 East Highway 26, Welches, OR 97067; 503/622-7674.

⁴⁶ Mirror Lake

3.2 mi/2.5 hrs

Here's a perfect leg-stretcher for that long, arduous drive back to Portland from Bend. From U.S. 26 the trail crosses Camp Creek near Yocum Falls and climbs gently and steadily about 1.5 miles to Mirror Lake, which offers prime snapshot views of Mount Hood. A trail circles the lake and passes by some designated campsites and picnic spots. If you're up for more, catch the trail on the west shore of the lake, which leads 1.8 miles and 900 vertical feet to a lake and mountain overview on Tom, Dick, and Harry Mountain. To the east are the two far summits of this three-headed peak, and just beyond, Mount Hood Ski Bowl. This is one of the Mount Hood–area's busiest trails during the summer season.

Tom, Dick, and Harry Mountain is closed annually between approximately

July 30 and September 10 for peregrine falcon releases.

Location: In the Mount Hood Wilderness east of Mount Hood Ski Bowl; see The Columbia River Gorge and Mount Hood Map 2, grid f2.

User Groups: Hikers and dogs. No horses or mountain bikes are allowed. No wheelchair facilities.

Permits: A federal Northwest Forest Pass, $5 per day or $30 annually, is required to park at the trailhead. Passes are available from ranger stations and many private vendors, online at website: www.wta.org, or by calling 800/270-7504.

Maps: For a map of the Mount Hood Wilderness, contact the Nature of the Northwest Information Center, 800 Northeast Oregon Street, Suite 177, Portland, OR 97232; 503/872-2750. Green Trails, Inc.'s excellent topographic maps of the region are available for $3.99 each at outdoor retail outlets. Ask for map number 461, Government Camp. Ask the USGS for a topographic map of the Government Camp area.

Directions: From Portland drive east on U.S. 26 to the Yocum Falls Sno-Park near the footbridge over Camp Creek, between mileposts 51 and 52 (just under two miles west of Government Camp). Park on the south shoulder. The trail begins at the footbridge.

Contact: Mount Hood National Forest Information Center, 65000 East Highway 26, Welches, OR 97067; 503/622-7674.

47 Twin Lakes/Palmateer Point
9.0 mi/5.0 hrs

This is a pleasant (and busy) daylong stroll from Highway 26 to a pair of backcountry lakes and an impressive vista at Palmateer Point. From the Sno-Park set out on the Pacific Crest Trail and proceed about 1.25 miles to a junction. Veer right for Twin Lakes. The first lake comes up quickly. Stay left around the top to continue to the smaller upper lake. To continue to Palmateer Point, stay right around the lake and walk by good Mount Hood views for about 1.25 miles to a side trail that leads a third of a mile up to the viewpoint on the right. Gaze off the steep bank east to the valley holding Devil's Half Acre, an old high camp on the Barlow Road, an early pioneer wagon-train route. Return by the same route or continue just under a mile west on the main trail back to the Pacific Crest Trail, where a right (south) turn takes you back to the Frog Lake Trailhead.

Location: Southeast of Mount Hood in the Barlow Creek drainage of Mount Hood National Forest; see The Columbia River Gorge and Mount Hood Map 2, grid g3.

User Groups: Hikers, dogs, and horses. No mountain bikes are allowed. No wheelchair facilities.

Permits: No permits are required. Parking and access are free.

Maps: For a map of Mount Hood National Forest, contact the Nature of the Northwest Information Center, 800 Northeast Oregon Street, Suite 177, Portland, OR 97232; 503/872-2750. Green Trails, Inc.'s excellent topographic maps of the region are available for $3.99 at outdoor retail outlets. Ask for map numbers 462 and 494, Mount Hood and Mount Wilson. Ask the USGS for a topographic map of the Mount Hood South area.

Directions: From Portland drive east on U.S. 26 to Frog Lake Sno-Park, about eight miles east of Government Camp and 4.5 miles south of the Highway 35 junction. Start hiking from the Pacific Crest Trail marker on the left side of the parking lot.

Contact: Mount Hood National Forest, Barlow Ranger District, Bear Springs Work Center, 73558 Highway 216, Maupin, OR 97037; 541/467-2291.

48 Lookout Mountain/ Palisade Point

6.4 mi/4.5 hrs

This is one of the most scenic trails in the Badger Creek Wilderness. It starts by following an old road for 1.2 miles and gaining about 600 vertical feet to reach the top of 6,525-foot Lookout Mountain, which offers a spellbinding view of Mount Hood's glacier-draped eastern countenance. This is the shorter "cheater" route to Lookout Mountain, the other option being the trail from Highway 35 up 2.4 steep miles to Gumjuwac Saddle, then across Forest Service Road 3550 and another 2.25 miles on the Divide Trail to Lookout Mountain. The beauty of this shorter route is that it allows you time to venture about 1.75 miles further on the Divide Trail down the jagged-peak ridgeline to the Fret Creek Trail, which leads a quarter mile to beautiful Oval Lake (and ultimately two miles beyond to Fifteen Mile Campground). You might get some solitude there on a weekday or off-season weekend. From Oval Lake return to the Divide Trail, walk another quarter mile east, and find yourself at the turnaround, Palisade Point, a spectacular high-cliff viewpoint. For one-way shuttle hikers, the Divide Trail continues another 1.2 miles to a trailhead on Forest Service Road 200, for a one-way hike of about 4.5 miles from the original trailhead.

Location: East of Mount Hood on the border of Badger Creek Wilderness; see The Columbia River Gorge and Mount Hood Map 2, grid f4.

User Groups: Hikers, dogs, and horses. No mountain bikes are allowed. No wheelchair facilities.

Permits: No permits are required. Parking and access are free.

Maps: For a map of the Mount Hood National Forest and Badger Creek Wilderness, contact the Nature of the Northwest Information Center, 800 Northeast Oregon Street, Suite 177, Portland, OR 97232; 503/872-2750. Green Trails, Inc.'s excellent topographic maps of the region are available for $3.99 each at outdoor retail outlets. Ask for map numbers 462 and 463, Mount Hood and Flag Point. Ask the USGS for topographic maps of the Flag Point and Badger Lake areas.

Directions: From Highway 35 east of Mount Hood, turn right (east) on Dufur Mill Road/Forest Service Road 44, 2.5 miles north of Robin Hood Campground. Proceed about four miles east to High Prairie Road 4410. Turn right and travel 4.75 miles south to a T junction and the end of the pavement. Turn left and find the trailhead on the right.

Contact: Mount Hood National Forest, Barlow Ranger District, Dufur Ranger Station, 780 Northeast Court Street, Dufur, OR 97021; 541/467-2291.

49 Divide to Badger Lake

5.2 mi/3.0 hrs

Take your pick here. Many trails lead from the Gumjuwac Saddle/Gunsight Butte area into Badger Lake. It's possible to walk the western edge of the ridge and enjoy good views of Mount Hood and then drop into the lake basin on the Camp Windy Trail, returning on the Divide Trail for an 8.5-mile loop. But the easiest and probably most popular way into and out of the lake is the Divide Trail, which drops 2.6 miles and 600 vertical feet to the lake, a popular place to link up with the Badger Creek Trail (see hike in this chapter). At the lake you find an old CCC-constructed dam, roads, and other developments that are now locked in a wilderness area. You'll also find a handful of established campsites and perhaps some trout in the lake (state fishing license required).

Another hiking option is to take the plunging trail from Gumjuwac Saddle 1,300 vertical feet and 2.2 miles down Gumjuwac Creek, then 2.2 miles up through a delightful old-growth forest on the Badger Creek Trail to the lake. Returning on the Divide Trail makes an excellent seven-mile loop. Take your pick. Everyone's a winner in this game.

Location: Southeast of Mount Hood in the western portion of Badger Creek Wilderness; see The Columbia River Gorge and Mount Hood Map 2, grid f4.

User Groups: Hikers, dogs, and horses. No mountain bikes. No wheelchair facilities.

Permits: A federal Northwest Forest Pass, $5 per day or $30 annually, is required to park at the trailhead. Passes are available from ranger stations and many private vendors, online at website: www.wta.org, or by calling 800/270-7504.

Maps: For a map of the Mount Hood National Forest and Badger Creek Wilderness, contact the Nature of the Northwest Information Center, 800 Northeast Oregon Street, Suite 177, Portland, OR 97232; 503/872-2750. Green Trails, Inc.'s excellent topographic maps of the region are available for $3.99 each at outdoor retail outlets. Ask for map number 462, Mount Hood. Ask the USGS for topographic maps of the Flag Point and Badger Lake areas.

Directions: From Highway 35 east of Mount Hood, turn right (east) on Dufur Mill Road/Forest Service Road 44, 2.5 miles north of Robin Hood Campground. Turn right (east) and proceed about four miles to High Prairie Road 4410. Turn right and proceed about 4.8 miles to Bennett Pass Road 3550. Turn right and travel about 3.3 miles south to the well-marked trailhead at Gumjuwac Saddle.

Contact: Mount Hood National Forest, Barlow Ranger District, Dufur Ranger Station, 780 Northeast Court Street, Dufur, OR 97021; 541/467-2291.

50 Gordon Butte/Flag Point
7.0 mi/4.0 hrs

At Flag Point you get good views without even getting out of the car. You should get out, though, to enjoy the wildflowers and vistas on the 3.5-mile ridgetop trail to 4,820-foot Gordon Butte, high above the Badger Creek drainage. From the Flag Point lookout, the trail drops south, passes Sunrise Springs, and loses about 800 feet in elevation on the way to Gordon Butte, which is a perfect place to have lunch, enjoy grand views, and bolster yourself for the uphill walk back to the car. This trail also can be hiked as a loop of about nine miles by continuing half a mile beyond Gordon Butte to a Forest Service road, hiking half a mile north on the road to Gordon Butte Trail 470A, and climbing back to Forest Service Road 200 via the Little Badger Trail.

Location: In the Badger Creek drainage of Badger Creek Wilderness; see The Columbia River Gorge and Mount Hood Map 2, grid f4.

User Groups: Hikers, dogs, and horses. No mountain bikes are allowed. No wheelchair facilities.

Permits: No permits are required. Parking and access are free.

Maps: For a map of the Mount Hood National Forest and Badger Creek Wilderness, contact Nature of the Northwest Information Center, 800 Northeast Oregon Street, Suite 177, Portland, OR 97232; 503/872-2750. Green Trails, Inc.'s excellent topographic maps of the region are available for $3.99 each at outdoor retail outlets. Ask for map number 463, Flag Point. Ask the USGS for a topographic map of the Flag Point area.

Directions: From Highway 35 east of Mount Hood, turn right (east) on Dufur Mill Road/Forest Service Road 44, 2.5 miles north of Robin Hood Campground. Turn right (east) and proceed about 10 miles to Forest Service Road 4420. Turn right (south) and drive about five miles. Veer left at the fork onto Forest Service Road 2730 and continue beyond Fifteen Mile Campground to Forest Service Road 200. Turn right and proceed about 4.5 miles to the Flag Point Trailhead at the road's end.

Contact: Mount Hood National Forest, Barlow Ranger District, Dufur Ranger Station, 780 Northeast Court Street, Dufur, OR 97021; 541/467-2291.

51 School Canyon/Ball Point
6.4 mi/3.5 hrs

In the spring when most of the Mount Hood area remains snow-slogged, the Badger Creek Wilderness trades its own winter coat for a light jacket of wildflowers and, usually, dry skies. That makes lightly used trails such as School Canyon particularly inviting for hikers who have been cooped up far too long. The School Canyon Trail, an old road through grassy ridgetop meadows, is one of the best. It leads up at a moderate grade about 800 feet to a panoramic viewing point below 3,959-foot Ball Point, then skirts the north side of the peak and continues along the ridge to a cliff-top with excellent views, just beyond a junction with the Little Badger Creek Trail. Continuing straight, the trail leads another 3.3 miles to an exit on Forest Service Road 200 just west of Flag Point. Return the way you came on the School Canyon Trail, or turn south, heading downhill for four miles on the Little Badger Trail to a shuttle pickup on Forest Service Road 2710.

Location: In the Little Badger Creek drainage of Badger Creek Wilderness; see The Columbia River Gorge and Mount Hood Map 2, grid f5.

User Groups: Hikers, dogs, and horses. No mountain bikes are allowed. No wheelchair facilities.

Permits: A federal Northwest Forest Pass, $5 per day or $30 annually, is required to park at the trailhead. Passes are available from ranger stations and many private vendors, online at website: www.wta.org, or by calling 800/270-7504.

Maps: For a map of the Mount Hood National Forest and Badger Creek Wilderness, contact Nature of the Northwest Information Center, 800 Northeast Oregon Street, Suite 177, Portland, OR 97232; 503/872-2750. Green Trails, Inc.'s excellent topographic maps of the region are available for $3.99 each at outdoor retail outlets. Ask for map number 463, Flag Point. Ask the USGS for topographic maps of the Friend and Flag Point areas.

Directions: From Highway 35 north of Barlow Pass, turn east on Forest Service Road 48. Proceed toward Rock Creek Reservoir and Forest Service Road 4810. Turn left (north), keep right just before the reservoir, and proceed about two miles to Forest Service Road 4811. Turn right and proceed just over one mile to Forest Service Road 2710. Turn right and drive about 6.5 miles to Forest Service Road 27. Turn left and you find the School Canyon Trailhead in about two miles on the left.

Contact: Mount Hood National Forest, Barlow Ranger District, Dufur Ranger Station, 780 Northeast Court Street, Dufur, OR 97021; 541/467-2291.

52 Badger Creek National Recreation Trail
12.2 mi one way/2.0 days

This is a fine walk through the heart of the Badger Creek Wilderness, a fascinating transition zone between the dry, high plains of central Oregon and the alpine country around Mount Hood. It's a good late-spring hike, when dancing wildflowers keep time with the robust creek. A good campsite is found at Pine Creek, about halfway up the trail. On the upper half of the trail, the path leaves the creek and climbs out of its sight for much of the way. It's a good, strenuous daylong shuttle hike, or a more pleasant overnighter, hiking to a pickup above Badger Lake (see hike in this chapter) or back to the car at Bonney Crossing. Another good option is to hike the lower, more scenic half to Pine Creek, and then return to Bonney Crossing for a round-trip hike of about 11.5 miles.

Location: Between Badger Lake and Bonney Crossing Campground in the Badger Creek Wilderness; see The Columbia River Gorge and Mount Hood Map 2, grid f5.

User Groups: Hikers, dogs, and horses. No mountain bikes are allowed. No wheelchair facilities.

Permits: A federal Northwest Forest Pass, $5 per day or $30 annually, is required to park at the trailhead. Passes are available from ranger stations and many private vendors, online at website: www.wta.org, or by calling 800/270-7504.

Maps: For a map of the Mount Hood National Forest and Badger Creek Wilderness, contact Nature of the Northwest Information Center, 800 Northeast Oregon Street, Suite 177, Portland, OR 97232; 503/872-2750. Green Trails, Inc.'s excellent topographic maps of the region are available for $3.99 each at outdoor retail outlets. Ask for map numbers 462 and 463, Mount Hood and Flag Point. Ask the USGS for topographic maps of the Friend, Flag Point, and Badger Lake areas.

Directions: From Highway 35 north of Barlow Pass, turn east on Forest Service Road 48. Proceed toward Rock Creek Reservoir and turn left (north) onto Forest Service Road 4810. Keep right just before the reservoir and proceed about two miles to Forest Service Road 4811. Turn right and proceed about 1.3 miles to Forest Service Road 2710.

Turn right and drive about two miles to the trailhead, across a bridge over Badger Creek on the left side of the road, just beyond Bonney Crossing Campground. Park at the campground.

Contact: Mount Hood National Forest, Barlow Ranger District, Dufur Ranger Station, 780 Northeast Court Street, Dufur, OR 97021; 541/467-2291.

53 Tygh Valley Falls
1.5 mi/1.0 hr

The short, paved trail doesn't amount to much, but the scenery does. The whole family will enjoy the short walk to a platform overlooking Tygh Valley Falls, which drops 100 feet in a magnificent, multitiered cascade. Beyond the overlook, walk down to the abandoned powerhouse, filled with massive turbines and swooping swallows. A side trail continues down the river for some distance, but beware of ticks and poison oak. Watch for lizards, too. When you've finished here, drive east on Highway 216 a short distance to Sherars Bridge on the Deschutes River, site of annual salmon dipping by members of the Confederated Tribes of Warm Springs Reservation.

Location: Near the confluence of the White and Deschutes Rivers, east of the Highway 216/U.S. 197 junction; see The Columbia River Gorge and Mount Hood Map 2, grid f8.

User Groups: Hikers and dogs. No mountain bikes or horses are allowed. Wheelchair access to the falls overlook only.

Permits: No permits are required. Parking and access are free.

Maps: For a park brochure contact Oregon Parks and Recreation at 800/551-6949. Ask the USGS for a topographic map of the Maupin area.

Directions: From U.S. 197 at Tygh Valley north of Maupin, drive approximately four miles east on Highway 216 toward Sherars Bridge to White River Falls State Park on the right. Park in the picnic area.

Contact: Oregon Parks and Recreation Department, 1115 Commercial Street Northeast, Salem, OR 97301; 800/551-6949.

54 Rock Lakes Loop
8.0 mi/5.0 hrs

This loop trail that encompasses a chain of high-plateau Cascade lakes can be hiked as a short day hike, a great overnight backpack, or an ample, full-day walk with stops at as many as five different alpine lakes. For the full loop start hiking west on the Serene Lake Trail to side trails leading north and south to Upper, Middle, and Lower Rock Lakes. For day hikers with children, exploring these three scenic lakes and then walking back to the car is a good day's work. On the main trail, Serene Lake, by far the largest of the group, is reached in another two miles. Campsites are found on the western shore. Continue south about a mile up to a junction with the Grouse Point Trail. Turn left (southeast) here and hike just under a mile to a high viewpoint with great views of Mount Hood, Mount Adams, Mount Rainier, and Mount St. Helens, as well as Serene Lake to the north. Continue south another mile downhill to Cache Meadow, site of an old shelter and good campsites. After that it's two relatively uneventful miles north on an old road grade back to the car.

Location: North of Highway 224 in the Clackamas River drainage of Mount Hood National Forest; see The Columbia River Gorge and Mount Hood Map 2, grid g1.

User Groups: Hikers, dogs, mountain bikes, and horses. No wheelchair facilities.

Permits: No permits are required. Parking and access are free.

Maps: For a map of the Mount Hood National Forest, contact the Nature of the Northwest Information Center, 800 Northeast Oregon Street, Suite 177, Portland, OR 97232; 503/872-2750. Green Trails, Inc.'s excellent topographic maps of the region are available for $3.99 each at outdoor retail outlets. Ask for map numbers 492 and 493, Fish Creek Mountain and High Rock. Ask the USGS for a topographic map of the High Rock area.

Directions: From Estacada drive about 25 miles southeast on Highway 224 to Clackamas Ranger Station at Ripplebrook and turn left on Forest Service Road 57. Proceed about 7.5 miles to Forest Service Road 58. Turn left and drive seven miles to Forest Service Road 4610. Turn left and drive 1.2 miles to Forest Service Road 4610-240. Follow the road 4.4 very rough miles to the trailhead at Frazier Turnaround. Begin hiking on the Serene Lake Trail. Note: For a longer hike avoiding the upper, gravel-road access to Frazier Turnaround, you can begin this loop below at Hideaway Lake Campground. Hike north on the Shellrock Trail to its intersection with the loop trail. This adds nearly five miles and 500 vertical feet to the loop.

Contact: Mount Hood National Forest, Clackamas River Ranger District, 595 Northwest Industrial Way, Estacada, OR 97023; 503/630-6861.

55 Timothy Lake Loop
12.0 mi/7.0 hrs

For hikers, cyclists, and equestrians whose idea of a grand day hike is a long, flat, scenic path with stunning views and plenty of local curiosities, the Timothy Lake Loop ranks at the very top of the Northwest pecking order. Curiosity number one is Little Crater Lake, a miniature version of the one in Crater Lake National Park. This one owes its existence to an artesian spring, which created the al- most surreal emerald-blue color. But that's just for starters. Proceed to the Timothy Lake Trail, which skirts the lakeshore all the way around to the dam on the other side. Just before the dam is curiosity number two: a log boom protecting the dam. Notice that the boom has a plank walkway along the top. You can hike it if you dare. You can bike it if you're more than a half-bubble off plumb. Cooler heads can continue on the trail and cross at the dam. The trail grade is excellent, smooth, and flat, all the way around. You pass four campgrounds, several of which (Pine Point, Hood View, and Gone Creek on the southeast shore) provide lakeside trail access for wheelchairs. Hikers should remember to yield to horses, and mountain bikers should remember to yield to everyone or face a forced crossing of the log boom.

Location: Around Timothy Lake, south of Mount Hood and west of U.S. 26 in Mount Hood National Forest; see The Columbia River Gorge and Mount Hood Map 2, grid g3.

User Groups: Hikers, dogs, horses, and mountain bikes. Some wheelchair access.

Permits: No permits are required. Parking and access are free.

Maps: For a map of Mount Hood National Forest, contact the Nature of the Northwest Information Center, 800 Northeast Oregon Street, Suite 177, Portland, OR 97232; 503/872-2750. Green Trails, Inc.'s excellent topographic maps of the region are available for $3.99 at outdoor retail outlets. Ask for map numbers 493 and 494, High Rock and Mount Wilson. Ask the USGS for topographic maps of the Timothy Lake and Wolf Peak areas.

Directions: From Portland drive east on U.S. 26 to Skyline Road/Forest Service Road 42, just beyond milepost 65 and about 3.5 miles southeast of Wapinitia Pass. Turn right (west) and proceed about four miles to Abbott Road/Forest Service Road 58. Turn right on Abbott Road and drive approximately 1.5 miles to the trailhead at the far end of Little Crater Campground.

Contact: Mount Hood National Forest, Barlow Ranger District, Bear Springs Work Center, 73558 Highway 216, Maupin, OR 97037; 541/467-2291.

56 Lower Deschutes River
4.0 mi/2.5 hrs

The dry, dusty desert of the eastern Columbia Gorge is interrupted here by a hiking and mountain-biking oasis—dual trails along the rushing lower Deschutes River. Two hiking trails, one beside the river, the other slightly higher, lead about four miles up the valley, passing some scenic rapids and links with trails that skirt the upper canyon. Unfortunately, winter flooding often damages sections of the lower-river trail, as well as a separate, 16.5-mile mountain bike path that follows an old service road up the valley. Call for trail-construction updates before you assume you can take a long hike here.

This is rattlesnake country. Keep your eyes peeled.

Location: At the confluence of the Deschutes and Columbia Rivers in the eastern Columbia River Gorge; see The Columbia River Gorge and Mount Hood Map 3, grid c1.

User Groups: Hikers, mountain bikes, leashed dogs, and horses. No wheelchair facilities.

Permits: No permits are required. Parking and access are free.

Maps: For a free park brochure, contact the Nature of the Northwest Information Center, 800 Northeast Oregon Street, Suite 177, Portland, OR 97232; 503/872-2750. Ask the USGS for topographic maps of the Wishram and Emerson areas.

Directions: From Portland drive about 85 miles east on I-84 to The Dalles and another

12 miles to Exit 97/Deschutes Park. Follow signs to Deschutes State Park and Recreation Area.

Contact: Oregon Parks and Recreation Department, 1115 Commercial Street Northeast, Salem, OR 97301; 800/551-6949.

57 Table Rock
7.4 mi/5.5 hrs

This is the place to get away from it all, and, more importantly, get away from "them" all. By that we mean the hordes of day hikers who inundate Northwest Oregon's trails. Not many of them make it all the way out to Table Rock Wilderness during midweek, when you're liable to find some cherished privacy. The trail climbs moderately and brushes up against the near-vertical north face of Table Rock, where you can count the multiple layers of volcanic basalt flows. On the ridgetop at about two miles, turn left on the half-mile side trail to the top of Table Rock (elevation 4,881 feet). On a clear day views of the Cascade peaks north into Washington are as magnificent as any we've seen. The entire chain is laid out before you like a topographic map. Turn around at the top or backtrack to the main trail and continue another 1.5 miles to Rooster Rock, an even more fascinating geologic remnant. The trail continues down to a lower trailhead on the Molalla River, making possible an 11.5-mile one-way hike.

Location: In the Table Rock Wilderness, east of Salem and north of Highway 22; see The Columbia River Gorge and Mount Hood Map 4, grid a6.

User Groups: Hikers, dogs, and horses. No mountain bikes are allowed. No wheelchair facilities.

Permits: No permits are required. Parking and access are free.

Maps: For a map of the Table Rock Wilderness and vicinity, contact the Nature of the Northwest Information Center, 800 Northeast Oregon Street, Suite 177, Portland, OR 97232; 503/872-2750. Ask the USGS for a topographic map of the Rooster Rock area.

Directions: From Molalla drive half a mile east on Highway 211 to South Mathias Road. Turn right and proceed to South Feyrer Park Road. Continue 1.6 miles to South Dickey Prairie Road. Turn right and drive 5.3 miles, turning right on a bridge across the Molalla River. Drive 12.8 miles to a fork and veer left onto Middle Fork Road. Drive about 2.7 miles and turn right on Table Rock Road. The trailhead is on the right at 5.6 miles.

Contact: Bureau of Land Management, Salem District, 1717 Fabry Road Southeast, Salem, OR 97306; 503/375-5646.

58 Bagby Hot Springs/ Silver King Lake
15.0 mi/8.0 hrs

For day hikers headed for a short walk to Bagby Hot Springs or backpackers seeking to sample the whole of the Bull of the Woods Wilderness, the Bagby Hot Springs Trail is the front door. From the trailhead on Forest Service Road 70, it's a short 1.5-mile walk along the Hot Springs Fork of the Collawash to the well-developed hot springs, which have soaking tubs made from cedar logs. The route is entirely within cool, old-growth forest, making this a favorite midsummer getaway. Expect a long line at the free hot tubs, which are filled by a common hot water trough running through the bath house. Baths lasting longer than an hour are a no-no, and you're not likely to see many swimsuits up here. A guard station and campsites lie beyond.

For backpackers or long-haul day hikers, the trail continues up the Hot Springs Fork for 7.3 miles to a side trail leading to campsites at Silver King Lake, about 2,000 feet above your starting point. Another three-fourths of a mile ahead is a junction. Go right for the Whetstone Trail, which leads 3.5 miles west along a ridgetop to Whetstone Mountain and beyond to the Whetstone Trailhead on Forest Service Road 7020 (an overnight shuttle-hike possibility). Back at the main Bagby Hot Springs Trail junction, turning left below Silver King Mountain leads to a trail fork in just under a mile. The right fork is the continuation of the Bagby Trail, leading south to Battle Ax and Elk Lake. The left path travels two miles east to Twin Lakes and ultimately upward on the Mother Lode Trail, which provides access to the Bull of the Woods, Big Slide Mountain, Pansy Basin, and Dickey Creek trail systems (see Pansy Basin hike, this chapter). All of these make fine shuttle-hike backpack trips in this prime, uncrowded wilderness terrain.

Location: On the Hot Springs Fork of the Collawash River in Bull of the Woods Wilderness; see The Columbia River Gorge and Mount Hood Map 4, grid a7.

User Groups: Hikers and dogs only to the hot springs. Horses are allowed above but not recommended. No mountain bikes are allowed. No wheelchair facilities.

Permits: A federal Northwest Forest Pass, $5 per day or $30 annually, is required to park at the trailhead. Passes are available from ranger stations and many private vendors, online at website: www.wta.org, or by calling 800/270-7504.

Maps: For a map of Bull of the Woods Wilderness, contact the Nature of the Northwest Information Center, 800 Northeast Oregon Street, Suite 177, Portland, OR 97232; 503/872-2750. Green Trails, Inc.'s excellent topographic maps of the region are available for $3.99 each at outdoor retail outlets. Ask for map number 524, Battle Ax. Ask the USGS for topographic maps of the Bagby Hot Springs, Battle Ax, and Mother Lode Mountain areas.

Directions: From Estacada drive about 28 miles southeast on Highway 224 to Forest Service Road 46. Proceed 3.5 miles south on Forest Service Road 46 to Forest Service Road 63 at Riverford Campground. Bear right and travel 3.5 miles to Forest Service Road 70. Turn right and drive six miles to the trailhead parking area on the left.

Contact: Mount Hood National Forest, Clackamas River Ranger District, Estacada Ranger Station, 595 Northwest Industrial Way, Estacada, OR 97023; 503/630-6861.

59 Pansy Basin/Bull of the Woods Loop

7.0 mi/4.0 hrs

The geology is fascinating, the lake crystal clear, and the high-mountain lookout well worth the climb. It all adds up to a hiking wonderland in one concentrated area of the Bull of the Woods Wilderness. The recently reconstructed trail into Pansy Lake and Pansy Basin is a pleasant walk that begins in magnificent ancient forest. It's easy at first, and then more challenging as the path switchbacks toward Pansy Basin. Still, you gain only about 500 feet on the 1.2 miles to the lake. Go left at the first trail junction with an abandoned Pansy Basin trail and find Pansy Lake about one-third mile ahead on the right. Short day hikers or parents with children can stop here and enjoy the view. To continue the loop walk south from the lake to a junction with the Mother Lode Trail. Turn left and climb two miles to the Bull of the Woods lookout tower, elevation 5,523 feet. The view is truly panoramic, with wild country as far as the eye can see. Continue north on Bull of the Woods Trail toward South Dickey Peak. Just over a mile from the lookout, turn left (west) on the Dickey Lake Trail, which drops 1.6 miles back to the Pansy Lake area, and exit the way you came.

Location: In the heart of Bull of the Woods Wilderness; see The Columbia River Gorge and Mount Hood Map 4, grid a7.

User Groups: Hikers, dogs, and horses. No mountain bikes are allowed. No wheelchair facilities.

Permits: A federal Northwest Forest Pass, $5 per day or $30 annually, is required to park at the trailhead. Passes are available from ranger stations and many private vendors, online at website: www.wta.org, or by calling 800/270-7504.

Maps: For a map of the Bull of the Woods Wilderness, contact the Nature of the Northwest Information Center, 800 Northeast Oregon Street, Suite 177, Portland, OR 97232; 503/872-2750. Green Trails, Inc.'s excellent topographic maps of the region are available for $3.99 each at outdoor retail outlets. Ask for map number 524, Battle Ax. Ask the USGS for a topographic map of the Bull of the Woods area.

Directions: From Estacada drive 27 miles southeast on Highway 224 to Forest Service Road 46. Proceed 3.5 miles south on Forest Service Road 46 to Forest Service Road 63 at Riverford Campground. Turn right and travel to Forest Service Road 6340. Turn right and proceed just under eight miles to a fork. Veer right on Forest Service Road 6341. The trailhead is at about four miles on the left (east) side of the road, just before a sweeping right turn.

Contact: Mount Hood National Forest, Clackamas River Ranger District, Estacada Ranger Station, 595 Northwest Industrial Way, Estacada, OR 97023; 503/630-6861.

60 Hawk Mountain
8.5 mi/5.0 hrs

You have to envy the guys who used to live in the lookout cabin atop Hawk Mountain. Not for the ease of access to their house, but certainly for the view of Mount Jefferson. To get to the lookout, follow the Rho Ridge Trail, which runs straight north and south through a semi-maze of clearcuts, logging roads, and undisturbed forest. At about 3.5 miles the Hawk Mountain Trail exits to the left (east) in a meadow, with the Rho Ridge Trail continuing south. Go left and walk 0.6 mile to the meadow mountaintop with the lookout cabin, remains of a lookout tower, and a grand view of not only Mount Jefferson, but also of Mount Washington, the Three Sisters, Olallie Butte, and Park Ridge.

Location: On Rhododendron Ridge north of Breitenbush Campground in Mount Hood National Forest; see The Columbia River Gorge and Mount Hood Map 4, grid b8.

User Groups: Hikers, dogs, horses, and mountain bikes. No wheelchair facilities.

Permits: No permits are required. Parking and access are free.

Maps: For a map of Mount Hood National Forest, contact the Nature of the Northwest Information Center, 800 Northeast Oregon Street, Suite 177, Portland, OR 97232; 503/872-2750. Green Trails, Inc.'s excellent topographic maps of the region are available for $3.99 each at outdoor retail outlets. Ask for map number 525, Breitenbush. Ask the USGS for a topographic map of the Breitenbush Hot Springs area.

Directions: From Estacada drive 27 miles southeast on Highway 224 to Forest Service Road 46. Proceed 3.5 miles south on Forest Service Road 46 to Forest Service Road 63 at Riverford Campground. Turn right and proceed just under nine miles to Forest Service Road 6350. Turn left and proceed to a fork at 1.2 miles. Veer right for about 4.5 miles and then veer left back onto Forest Service Road 6350. The trailhead is on the right, 1.5 miles beyond Graham Pass.

Contact: Mount Hood National Forest, Clackamas

River Ranger District, Estacada Ranger Station, 595 Northwest Industrial Way, Estacada, OR 97023; 503/630-6861.

61 Phantom Bridge
5.4 mi/3.0 hrs

No hiking season would be complete without a walk to the local geological curiosity—sort of the circus freak of the mountain range. This fine ridge walk to a peculiar natural wonder certainly qualifies. From the road the trail cuts through a clear-cut and skirts the north side of Dog Rock—you'll know it when you see it. You then wind along the scenic ridgetop, looking down on Opal Lake. From here you drop like a rock to tiny Cedar Lake and a junction with a side trail to an exit higher on Forest Service Road 2207. Stay straight and keep plodding 1.25 (steep!) miles to the Phantom Bridge, accompanied by excellent views of Three Fingered Jack, Coffin Mountain, Three Sisters, Mount Hood, Mount Jefferson, and Mount Washington. The Phantom Bridge, the turnaround point, is a large rock bridge, about 40 feet across, probably formed by the collapse of a cave. Through its center is a peek-a-boo view of Opal Lake. Pose for your picture on top of it if you dare.

Location: North of Detroit in the Little North Santiam River drainage of Willamette National Forest; see The Columbia River Gorge and Mount Hood Map 4, grid b7.

User Groups: Hikers, dogs, horses, and mountain bikes. No wheelchair facilities.

Permits: No permits are required. Parking and access are free.

Maps: For a map of Willamette National Forest, contact the Nature of the Northwest Information Center, 800 Northeast Oregon Street, Suite 177, Portland, OR 97232; 503/872-2750. Green Trails, Inc.'s excellent topographic maps of the region are available for $3.99 each at outdoor retail outlets. Ask for map number 524, Battle Ax. Ask the USGS for a topographic map of the Battle Ax area.

Directions: From Highway 22 at the west end of the town of Detroit, turn north on French Creek Road/Forest Service Road 2233 at the west end of the bridge. Proceed about four miles to Forest Service Road 2207. Turn right and drive about 3.75 miles to the trailhead on the left.

Contact: Willamette National Forest, Detroit Ranger District, HC 73, Box 320, Mill City, OR 97360; 503/854-3366.

62 Chimney Peak
12.2 mi/8.0 hrs

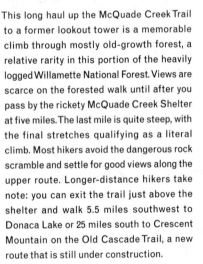

This long haul up the McQuade Creek Trail to a former lookout tower is a memorable climb through mostly old-growth forest, a relative rarity in this portion of the heavily logged Willamette National Forest. Views are scarce on the forested walk until after you pass by the rickety McQuade Creek Shelter at five miles. The last mile is quite steep, with the final stretches qualifying as a literal climb. Most hikers avoid the dangerous rock scramble and settle for good views along the upper route. Longer-distance hikers take note: you can exit the trail just above the shelter and walk 5.5 miles southwest to Donaca Lake or 25 miles south to Crescent Mountain on the Old Cascade Trail, a new route that is still under construction.

Location: Between Sweet Home and Detroit in the Middle Santiam Wilderness; see The Columbia River Gorge and Mount Hood Map 4, grid d7.

User Groups: Hikers, dogs, and horses. No mountain bikes are allowed. No wheelchair facilities.

Permits: Free day-hiking and overnight wilderness permits, required for all hikers, can be obtained at trailheads or ranger stations. A federal Northwest Forest Pass, $5 per day or $30 annually, is required to park at the trailhead. Passes are available from ranger stations and many private vendors, online at website: www.wta.org, or by calling 800/270-7504.

Maps: For a map of Willamette National Forest and Middle Santiam Wilderness, contact the Nature of the Northwest Information Center, 800 Northeast Oregon Street, Suite 177, Portland, OR 97232; 503/872-2750. Ask the USGS for topographic maps of the Quartzville and Chimney Peak areas.

Directions: From Sweet Home drive four miles east on U.S. 20 to Quartzville Drive. Turn left (north) and drive nearly 25 miles northeast to Forest Service Road 11. Turn right and proceed about three miles to Forest Service Road 1142. Turn right and drive about four miles to the McQuade Creek Trailhead.

Contact: Willamette National Forest, Sweet Home Ranger District, 3225 Highway 20, Sweet Home, OR 97386; 541/367-5168.

63 Coffin Mountain
3.0 mi/2.0 hrs

For the minor investment of 1,000 feet of vertical and a couple hours of your time, you can climb through pleasant wildflower meadows to a grand overlook of the Cascade Mountains at the unsettlingly titled Coffin Mountain Lookout. Viewed from far below at Detroit Lake, it's easy to see how Coffin Mountain's straight, box-like walls gave it its name. People who have only seen the mountain from a distance will be impressed if you tell them you've walked to the top, but it's really not that daunting. Trails run up both the north and south sides of the peak, and each trail is only moderately difficult. The southern route switches back through some pleasant wildflower and beargrass meadows to the lookout tower (elevation 5,771 feet). The views

are fabulous, including the entire Oregon Cascade volcano chain. Mount Jefferson to the east is close by and particularly stunning. It's easy to pick out the nearby wilderness areas: just let your eye follow the clear-cuts up to the borders. Nearby to the east is a trail that leads to another viewpoint atop 5,953-foot Mount Bachelor. That trailhead is reached via Forest Service Road 1168 and Forest Service Spur Road 430.

Bring your own water. None is available at the trailhead, on the summit, or anywhere along the route.

Location: South of Highway 22 in the North Santiam River drainage of Willamette National Forest; see The Columbia River Gorge and Mount Hood Map 4, grid d8.

User Groups: Hikers, dogs, horses, and mountain bikes. No wheelchair facilities.

Permits: A federal Northwest Forest Pass, $5 per day or $30 annually, is required to park at the trailhead. Passes are available from ranger stations and many private vendors, online at website: www.wta.org, or by calling 800/270-7504.

Maps: For a map of the Willamette National Forest, contact the Nature of the Northwest Information Center, 800 Northeast Oregon Street, Suite 177, Portland, OR 97232; 503/872-2750. Green Trails, Inc.'s excellent topographic maps of the region are available for $3.99 each at outdoor retail outlets. Ask for map number 556, Detroit. Ask the USGS for a topographic map of the Coffin Mountain area.

Directions: From Salem drive about 52 miles east on Highway 22 to Detroit and then continue southeast on Highway 22 to Marion Forks and another three miles to Straight Creek Road/Forest Service Road 11. Turn right (west) and drive 4.2 miles to Forest Service Road 1168. Turn right and drive 3.8 miles to Forest Service Spur Road 450. Drive a short distance on this road to the trailhead parking area on the left.

Contact: Willamette National Forest, Detroit Ranger District, HC 73, P.O. Box 320, Mill City, OR 97360; 503/854-3366.

64 Three Pyramids
4.2 mi/3.0 hrs

Call them Curly, Moe, and Larry. Call them rough, wild, and rocky. Call them anything you want, but don't call them young. The Three Pyramids are ancient, played-out volcanic peaks, ranging in height from 5,486 to 5,690 feet. This trail leads up the left shoulder to the top of the center peak, opening up to grand views of the other two and of additional peaks beyond. The trail begins in old-growth forest and climbs steadily up the east side, around the north face, and up to the summit's west side. The views to the west are sufficiently awesome to quell the pain in your aching calves. Try to pick out nearby Iron Mountain and Chimney Peak to the southwest. Return the way you came, with views of the Three Sisters and Mount Jefferson accompanying you down and back.

Location: Northwest of Santiam Pass in Willamette National Forest; see The Columbia River Gorge and Mount Hood Map 4, grid d8.

User Groups: Hikers and dogs. The trail is unsuitable for horses and mountain bikes. No wheelchair facilities.

Permits: A federal Northwest Forest Pass, $5 per day or $30 annually, is required to park at the trailhead. Passes are available from ranger stations and many private vendors, online at website: www.wta.org, or by calling 800/270-7504.

Maps: For a map of Willamette National Forest, contact the Nature of the Northwest Information Center, 800 Northeast Oregon Street, Suite 177, Portland, OR 97232;

503/872-2750. Ask the USGS for topographic maps of the Echo Mountain and Coffin Mountain areas.

Directions: From the U.S. 20/Highway 22 junction, drive northwest on Highway 22 about five miles to Forest Service Road 2067. Turn left (west) and drive about two miles to Forest Service Road 560, just beyond Park Creek. Turn right and drive 3.5 miles to the trailhead on the left.

Contact: Willamette National Forest, Sweet Home Ranger District, 3225 Highway 20, Sweet Home, OR 97386; 541/367-5168.

65 Potato Butte via Red Lake
7.4 mi/4.0 hrs

They should have called this pockmarked plateau north of Mount Jefferson "Land of 10,000 Lakes." But apparently some folks in Minnesota had already laid claim to the name, so "Olallie Lake Scenic Area" had to suffice. The scenery takes a backseat to no place, however, as you'll see on this nice day hike that takes you to several of the lakes and one of the cinder cone mountains that helped create the local topography. The trail quickly takes you beneath a big power line and into the scenic area, reaching Red Lake in less than two easy miles. Just ahead in the next mile are Averill, Wall, and Sheep Lakes, all of which lie just south of the trail and all of which are worth exploring. To top off the hike, turn left at the north end of Sheep Lake and take the side trail 510 vertical feet for about three-quarters of a mile to the summit of Potato Butte (elevation 5,300 feet). The best view is actually a bit below the summit, but you'll want to take the summit just to say you did. For longer-distance hikers, continue east on the Red Lake Trail to the Pacific Crest Trail, Olallie Lake, and Double Peaks (see hike in this chapter).

Location: North of Mount Jefferson in Olallie Lake Scenic Area; see The Columbia River Gorge and Mount Hood Map 5, grid b2.

User Groups: Hikers, dogs, horses, and mountain bikes. No wheelchair facilities.

Permits: No permits are required. Parking and access are free.

Maps: For a map of Mount Hood National Forest and Olallie Lake Scenic Area, contact the Nature of the Northwest Information Center, 800 Northeast Oregon Street, Suite 177, Portland, OR 97232; 503/872-2750. Green Trails, Inc.'s excellent topographic maps of the region are available for $3.99 each at outdoor retail outlets. Ask for map number 525, Breitenbush. Ask the USGS for a topographic map of the Olallie Butte area.

Directions: From Estacada follow Highway 224 southeast 27 miles to Forest Service Road 46 just beyond Ripplebrook Campground. Continue straight on Forest Service Road 46, proceeding about 27 miles to Forest Service Road 380 and turn left, following the sign to Red Lake Trail. The trailhead is on the left side of the road, just under a mile from the turnoff.

Contact: Mount Hood National Forest, Clackamas River Ranger District, 595 Northwest Industrial Way, Estacada, OR 97023; 503/630-6861.

66 Double Peaks Loop
5.5 mi/3.5 hrs

This can be an easy loop hike that's a favorite with children, or it can be extended to a tougher day hike by adding a short, steep climb to Double Peaks in the middle of the hike. Start on the Red Lake Trail and hike an easy, pleasant (OK, maybe a few too many bugs) mile past a couple of small lakes to Top Lake, a good place to linger for a while. To loop back to the car, turn north here on the Pacific Crest Trail and walk back to Head

Lake and the road near the Olallie Lake Guard Station. From this point it's a quarter-mile walk back down the road to the car. To add Double Peaks to the hike, turn left at the Top Lake junction, hike about half a mile to the PCT and Cigar Lake, and in a short distance turn right up the Double Peaks Trail. It's steep but mercifully short. You can get to both summits, with good views of the entire Olallie Lakes area from each. Long-distance hikers can continue south on the PCT from the Double Peaks turnoff to reach the Ruddy Hill/Breitenbush Lake trail system (see hike in this chapter).

Location: North of Mount Jefferson in Olallie Lake Scenic Area; see The Columbia River Gorge and Mount Hood Map 5, grid b2.

User Groups: Hikers and dogs. Horses and mountain bikes are allowed only on the lower Red Lake Trail. No wheelchair facilities.

Permits: A federal Northwest Forest Pass, $5 per day or $30 annually, is required to park at the trailhead. Passes are available from ranger stations and many private vendors, online at website: www.wta.org, or by calling 800/270-7504.

Maps: For a map of the Mount Hood National Forest and Olallie Lake Scenic Area, contact the Nature of the Northwest Information Center, 800 Northeast Oregon Street, Suite 177, Portland, OR 97232; 503/872-2750. Green Trails, Inc.'s excellent topographic maps of the region are available for $3.99 each at outdoor retail outlets. Ask for map number 525, Breitenbush. Ask the USGS for a topographic map of the Olallie Butte area.

Directions: From Estacada follow Highway 224 southeast 27 miles to Forest Service Road 46 just beyond Ripplebrook Campground. Continue straight on Forest Service Road 46, proceeding about 22 miles to Forest Service Road 4690. Turn left and drive eight miles to Forest Service Road 4220.

Turn right and follow signs to Olallie Lake Resort. Keep right at the junction and proceed about one-quarter mile to the trailhead on the right (west) side of the road.

Contact: Mount Hood National Forest, Clackamas River Ranger District, 595 Northwest Industrial Way, Estacada, OR 97023; 503/630-6861.

🔢 Olallie/Monon Lake Loop
6.1 mi/3.0 hrs

This is an easy day's walk for single-day visitors to Olallie Lake or overnight campers at Paul Dennis or Peninsula Campgrounds, which are both on the lake. Start walking on the crystal-clear lake's northeast shore, with postcard-perfect reflections of Mount Jefferson awaiting. At about one mile turn right on the Monon Lake Loop Trail, which leads past more small lakes to Monon Lake's east shore. Hike the three-mile loop (a short distance on the southwest side is on Forest Service Road 4220) in either direction and return the way you came. It's a pleasant trip. Bring the kids on this one and let them shoot their first-ever nature photos.

Location: On the shores of Olallie and Monon Lakes in Olallie Lake Scenic Area north of Mount Jefferson; see The Columbia River Gorge and Mount Hood Map 5, grid b2.

User Groups: Hikers, horses, dogs, and mountain bikes. No wheelchair facilities.

Permits: A federal Northwest Forest Pass, $5 per day or $30 annually, is required to park at the trailhead. Passes are available from ranger stations and many private vendors, online at website: www.wta.org, or by calling 800/270-7504.

Maps: For a map of Mount Hood National Forest and Olallie Lake Scenic Area, contact the Nature of the Northwest Information Center, 800 Northeast Oregon Street, Suite 177, Portland, OR 97232; 503/872-2750. Green Trails, Inc.'s excellent topographic maps of the region are available for $3.99 each at outdoor retail outlets. Ask for map number 525, Breitenbush. Ask the USGS for a topographic map of the Olallie Butte area.

Directions: From Estacada follow Highway 224 southeast 27 miles to Forest Service Road 46 just beyond Ripplebrook Campground. Continue straight on Forest Service Road 46, proceeding about 22 miles to Forest Service Road 4690. Turn left and drive eight miles to Forest Service Road 4220. Make a right and follow signs to Olallie Lake Resort. Turn right at the store at the head of Olallie Lake and find the trailhead in a short distance in Paul Dennis Campground.

Contact: Mount Hood National Forest, Clackamas River Ranger District, 595 Northwest Industrial Way, Estacada, OR 97023; 503/630-6861.

🔢 Ruddy Hill
5.6 mi/3.5 hrs

Ruddy Hill is on the edge of greatness. While the 5,943-foot peak probably doesn't qualify as "great" on its own, it's close enough to see greatness. From high on this route, Mount Jefferson and Pyramid Butte provide a stunning backdrop to Breitenbush Lake, which lies below to the southeast. From the parking lot start uphill on the Pacific Crest Trail and continue about 1.75 miles to a junction. Continue straight for less than a mile up the PCT to a side trail leading to the summit of Ruddy Hill. Or turn right on the Gibson Lake Trail and walk 1.5 miles along the ridge to Gibson Lake and Forest Service Road 4220, where it's about three-quarters of a mile back to the car. Along the way is a fine clifftop viewpoint of Olallie Butte and Horseshoe and Monon Lakes.

Location: In the Olallie Lake Scenic Area north of Mount Jefferson; see The Columbia River Gorge and Mount Hood Map 5, grid c2.

User Groups: Hikers, dogs, and mountain bikes. No horses are allowed. No wheelchair facilities.

Permits: A federal Northwest Forest Pass, $5 per day or $30 annually, is required to park at the trailhead. Passes are available from ranger stations and many private vendors, online at website: www.wta.org, or by calling 800/270-7504.

Maps: For a map of Mount Hood National Forest and Olallie Lake Scenic Area, contact the Nature of the Northwest Information Center, 800 Northeast Oregon Street, Suite 177, Portland, OR 97232; 503/872-2750. Green Trails, Inc.'s excellent topographic maps of the region are available for $3.99 each at outdoor retail outlets. Ask for map number 525, Breitenbush. Ask the USGS for a topographic map of the Olallie Butte area.

Directions: From Estacada follow Highway 224 southeast 27 miles to Forest Service Road 46 just beyond Ripplebrook Campground. Continue straight on Forest Service Road 46, proceeding about 22 miles to Forest Service Road 4690. Turn left and drive eight miles to Forest Service Road 4220. Turn right and continue through the Olallie Lakes area to the Pacific Crest Trailhead on the left, just beyond Breitenbush Lake Campground.

Contact: Mount Hood National Forest, Clackamas River Ranger District, 595 Northwest Industrial Way, Estacada, OR 97023; 503/630-6861.

69 Pyramid Butte/ Jefferson Park
11.5 mi/1.0 day

This is one of the premier day hikes in Oregon, and, not surprisingly, it draws premier summertime crowds. It's no longer a place for solitude, even off-season or on weekdays, but it is a place for some of the most stunning alpine scenery in the Northwest.

From the parking lot climb gradually up the Pacific Crest Trail, reaching an old PCT side trail to Pyramid Butte at about one-half mile. It's a mile and about 400 vertical feet up to good views on Pyramid Butte (elevation 6,095 feet). Moving on, the PCT leaves the forest and climbs into open alpine country, breaking out to amazing views of the entire Jefferson Park area on Park Ridge (elevation 7,018 feet) at 3.4 miles. The trail then drops two miles into Jefferson Park, with beautiful, wildflower-rich meadows and stunning views surrounding Russell, Park, Rock, Scout, and Bays Lakes. Tread lightly here; it's fragile, and you're only one of thousands to visit. Camping is not allowed on Scout or Bays Lake peninsulas, and all campsites should be well away from water sources. Campfires are very strongly discouraged and banned within 100 feet of water or trails. Keep in mind that this is a high-alpine area, where the weather can turn wintry alarmingly fast, even in summer. Bring plenty of bug juice. The swarming hordes are legendary here in midsummer. Continuing on the PCT, the trail joins with the South Fork Breitenbush River Trail (see hike in this chapter) 2.2 miles beyond Park Ridge near Russell Lake.

Location: In the northeast corner of the Mount Jefferson Wilderness; see The Columbia River Gorge and Mount Hood Map 5, grid c2.

User Groups: Hikers, dogs, and horses. No mountain bikes are allowed. No wheelchair facilities.

Permits: Free day-hiking and overnight wilderness permits, required for all hikers, can be obtained at trailheads or ranger stations. In addition, a federal Northwest Forest Pass, $5 per day or $30 annually, is required to park at the trailhead. Passes are available from ranger stations and many private vendors, online at website: www.wta.org, or by calling 800/270-7504.

Maps: For a map of the Mount Jefferson Wilderness, contact the Nature of the Northwest Information Center, 800 Northeast Oregon Street, Suite 177, Portland, OR 97232; 503/872-2750. Green Trails, Inc.'s excellent topographic maps of the region are available for $3.99 each at outdoor retail outlets. Ask for map numbers 525 and 557, Breitenbush and Mount Jefferson. Ask the USGS for a topographic map of the Mount Jefferson area.

Directions: From Estacada follow Highway 224 southeast 27 miles to Forest Service Road 46 just beyond Ripplebrook Campground. Continue straight on Forest Service Road 46, proceeding about 22 miles to Forest Service Road 4690. Turn left and drive eight miles to Forest Service Road 4220. Turn right and continue through the Olallie Lakes area to the Pacific Crest Trailhead on the left just beyond Breitenbush Lake Campground.

Contact: Mount Hood National Forest, Clackamas River Ranger District, 595 Northwest Industrial Way, Estacada, OR 97023; 503/630-6861.

🔟 South Fork Breitenbush River

12.4 mi/8.0 hrs

This trail is by no means the easiest access into the popular Jefferson Park area, which is a very good reason to use it. The South Fork Breitenbush Trail gains nearly 3,000 vertical feet in the first four miles. The grade is unrelenting, meaning you won't want to hit this one with a full pack. Backpackers would be better advised to use the Whitewater Trail (see hike in this chapter) instead. But for day hikers South Breitenbush can be a delight. The crowds are lighter, the route more challenging, and the sweet payoff (Jefferson Park) all the more rewarding.

In case you are considering an overnight stay, see Pyramid Butte hike in this chapter for Jefferson Park camping restrictions.

Location: A popular access route to the Jefferson Park area north of Mount Jefferson in Mount Jefferson Wilderness; see The Columbia River Gorge and Mount Hood Map 5, grid b1.

User Groups: Hikers, dogs, and horses. No mountain bikes are allowed. No wheelchair facilities.

Permits: Free day-hiking and overnight wilderness permits, required for all hikers, can be obtained at trailheads or ranger stations. In addition, a federal Northwest Forest Pass, $5 per day or $30 annually, is required to park at the trailhead. Passes are available from ranger stations and many private vendors, online at website: www.wta.org, or by calling 800/270-7504.

Maps: For a map of the Mount Jefferson Wilderness, contact the Nature of the Northwest Information Center, 800 Northeast Oregon Street, Suite 177, Portland, OR 97232; 503/872-2750. Green Trails, Inc.'s excellent topographic maps of the region are available for $3.99 each at outdoor retail outlets. Ask for map number 557, Mount Jefferson. Ask the USGS for topographic maps of the Mount Bruno and Mount Jefferson areas.

Directions: From Estacada follow Highway 224 southeast 27 miles to Forest Service Road 46 just beyond Ripplebrook Campground. Continue straight on Forest Service Road 46. Proceed 33 miles to Forest Service Road 4685. Turn left and drive about five miles to the trailhead on the right (east) side of the road on a major hairpin corner.

Contact: Willamette National Forest, Detroit Ranger District, HC 73, P.O. Box 320, Mill City, OR 97360; 503/854-3366.

71 Triangulation Peak
4.2 mi/2.5 hrs

Here's that easy, wildflower-meadow trail without a killer climb that you've been looking for. This path starts high (4,700 feet) and stays high, winding through wildflower meadows past Spire Rock, an impressive hunk of basalt if we've ever seen one. A side trail leads east to Boca Cave, a large cavern worth exploring if you're a cave person. It's not easy to access, however. The final stretch is a leg-sapper. Keep at it. At the top Triangulation Peak boosts you just high enough (5,400 feet) for outstanding views of the Jefferson Wilderness. You'll want to linger for a while at this former lookout site before the enjoyable walk back.

Location: East of Mount Jefferson in the Mount Jefferson Wilderness; see The Columbia River Gorge and Mount Hood Map 5, grid c1.

User Groups: Hikers, dogs, and horses. No mountain bikes are allowed. No wheelchair facilities.

Permits: Free day-hiking and overnight wilderness permits, required for all hikers, can be obtained at trailheads or ranger stations. In addition, a federal Northwest Forest Pass, $5 per day or $30 annually, is required to park at the trailhead. Passes are available from ranger stations and many private vendors, online at website: www.wta.org, or by calling 800/270-7504.

Maps: For a map of the Mount Jefferson Wilderness, contact the Nature of the Northwest Information Center, 800 Northeast Oregon Street, Suite 177, Portland, OR 97232; 503/872-2750. Green Trails, Inc.'s excellent topographic maps of the region are available

for $3.99 each at outdoor retail outlets. Ask for map number 557, Mount Jefferson. Ask the USGS for topographic maps of the Mount Bruno and Mount Jefferson areas.

Directions: From Salem drive about 52 miles east on Highway 22 to Detroit and continue six miles east to McCoy Creek Road/Forest Service Road 2233. Turn left (north) and follow the road nine miles. Veer right here, continuing on Forest Service Road 2233 to the junction with Forest Service Road 635. The trailhead is on the right at the junction.

Contact: Willamette National Forest, Detroit Ranger District, HC 73, P.O. Box 320, Mill City, OR 97360; 503/854-3366.

72 Whitewater to Jefferson Park
10.2 mi/7.0 hrs

You should know up front that this trail has nothing to do with Bill Clinton, failed savings and loan institutions, or any other part of that other Whitewater thing. In fact, the most scandalous thing to happen at this Whitewater likely involved people plopping a 12-person tent right on top of a meadow full of fragile wildflowers. The second most scandalous thing is the ease of entry this trail provides to Jefferson Park. It's the easiest way into the popular area—probably too easy for the taste of Jefferson Park lovers who cringe at the area's overuse. You follow Sentinel Creek northeast for 1.7 miles and then turn east along a ridgetop for two miles before dropping half a mile to the Pacific Crest Trail. The PCT leads north about a mile into wondrous Jefferson Park, where lakes, wildflowers, glacial mountain views, and flying insects dominate. See camping and fire restrictions in the Pyramid Butte/Jefferson Park hike, this chapter.

Location: The primary access route to Jefferson Park area north of Mount Jefferson in Mount Jefferson Wilderness; see The Columbia River Gorge and Mount Hood Map 5, grid c2.

User Groups: Hikers, horses, and dogs. No mountain bikes are allowed. No wheelchair facilities.

Permits: Free day-hiking and overnight wilderness permits, required for all hikers, can be obtained at trailheads or ranger stations. In addition, a federal Northwest Forest Pass, $5 per day or $30 annually, is required to park at the trailhead. Passes are available from ranger stations and many private vendors, online at website: www.wta.org, or by calling 800/270-7504.

Maps: For a map of the Mount Jefferson Wilderness, contact the Nature of the Northwest Information Center, 800 Northeast Oregon Street, Suite 177, Portland, OR 97232; 503/872-2750. Green Trails, Inc.'s excellent topographic maps of the region are available for $3.99 each at outdoor retail outlets. Ask for map number 557, Mount Jefferson. Ask the USGS for topographic maps of the Mount Bruno and Mount Jefferson area.

Directions: From Salem drive about 52 miles east on Highway 22 to Detroit and continue east to Forest Service Road 2243. Turn left (east) and drive to the trailhead at the end of the road.

Contact: Willamette National Forest, Detroit Ranger District, HC 73, P.O. Box 320, Mill City, OR 97360; 503/854-3366.

73 Independence Rock Loop
2.2 mi/1.0 hr

This lightly used loop trail is a bit of an oddity, one that's guaranteed to keep the kids jabbering all the way back to Portland. Begin at the west end and walk the two-mile, relatively easy clockwise loop, passing some unusually large anthills, unusually large old-growth trees, and an unusually large rock outcropping. You can even take a side trail up the rock to good local views of the region (not a place for children or novices). Hike back down the eastern leg and walk the road a short distance back to the car.

Location: East of Highway 22 near Marion Forks Campground; see The Columbia River Gorge and Mount Hood Map 5, grid d1.

User Groups: Hikers, horses, dogs, and mountain bikes. No wheelchair facilities.

Permits: A federal Northwest Forest Pass, $5 per day or $30 annually, is required to park at the trailhead. Passes are available from ranger stations and many private vendors, online at website: www.wta.org, or by calling 800/270-7504.

Maps: For a map of the Mount Jefferson Wilderness, contact the Nature of the Northwest Information Center, 800 Northeast Oregon Street, Suite 177, Portland, OR 97232; 503/872-2750. Green Trails, Inc.'s excellent topographic maps of the region are available for $3.99 each at outdoor retail outlets. Ask for map number 557, Mount Jefferson. Ask the USGS for a topographic map of the Marion Forks area.

Directions: From Salem drive 52 miles east on Highway 22 to Detroit and continue about 18 miles southeast to Marion Forks. Turn left (east) on Forest Service Road 2255 and proceed 0.8 mile. The western trailhead is on the left (north) side of the road.

Contact: Willamette National Forest, Detroit Ranger District, HC 73, P.O. Box 320, Mill City, OR 97360; 503/854-3366.

74 Marion Lake Loop
5.4 mi/3.0 hrs

Look up "overuse" in the hiker's encyclopedia and you might find a picture of the Marion lakeshore. Ropes are strung everywhere with signs reading "Please do not disturb." More than any other destination in the wildly popular Jefferson Wilderness, Marion has suffered from overuse and abuse. Strongly consider another wilderness day hike instead. You and the terrain will be better for it. If you do day hike here, follow the rules and stay on the trails to prevent more damage. From the trailhead the trail is broad and flat at first and then rises a bit beyond Lake Ann to a trail junction short of Marion Lake. Turn right (south) to find a side trail leading to picturesque Marion Falls and then continue down the trail to the lakeshore. Turn north here and walk back to another side trail, which leads left (west) back to the original junction on the main trail. Return the way you came.

To get away from at least part of the mob, leave the trail at the end of the lake loop and walk about 2.5 miles via the Blue Lake and Pine Ridge Trails to the 5,351-foot summit of Marion Mountain, where impressive views of Mount Jefferson draw your eyes to the northeast. For an even longer hike with a shuttle pickup, continue east on the Pine Ridge Trail 1.5 miles to Temple Lake and another 2.2 miles to the Pine Ridge Lake Trailhead at the end of Forest Service Road 2261.

Bring bug juice and leave behind the fishing gear. Marion Lake has a fish-choking algae problem, but the mosquito crop is quite healthy.

Location: In the central Mount Jefferson Wilderness; see The Columbia River Gorge and Mount Hood Map 5, grid d1.

User Groups: Hikers, horses, and dogs. No mountain bikes are allowed. No wheelchair facilities.

Permits: Free day-hiking and overnight wilderness permits, required for all hikers, can be obtained at trailheads or ranger stations. In addition, a federal Northwest Forest Pass, $5 per day or $30 annually, is required to park at the trailhead. Passes are available from ranger stations and many private vendors, online at website: www.wta.org, or by calling 800/270-7504.

Maps: For a map of the Mount Jefferson Wilderness, contact the Nature of the Northwest Information Center, 800 Northeast Oregon Street, Suite 177, Portland, OR 97232; 503/872-2750. Green Trails, Inc.'s excellent topographic maps of the region are available for $3.99 each at outdoor retail outlets. Ask for map number 557, Mount Jefferson. Ask the USGS for topographic maps of the Marion Forks and Marion Lake areas.

Directions: From Salem drive 52 miles east on Highway 22 to Detroit and continue southeast to Marion Forks. Turn left (east) on Marion Creek Road/Forest Service Road 2255 and follow it 4.4 miles to the trailhead at the road's end.

Contact: Willamette National Forest, Detroit Ranger District, HC 73, P.O. Box 320, Mill City, OR 97360; 503/854-3366.

75 Grizzly Peak/Pamelia Lake
10.4 mi/1.0–2.0 days

It's an easy day hike to a placid lake. It's also a grand overnight experience, with a possible climb to a stunning viewpoint in the morning. It's also a human superhighway in the summer, when sheer numbers of hikers are the only thing separating this route from being a perfect 10.

Start out through the deep, cool old-growth forest and walk along Pamelia Creek just over two miles to Pamelia Lake, whose level drops significantly late in the summer. No camping is allowed within 100 feet of the lake, but you can catch cutthroat trout here (state fishing license required). Ahead is the Pacific Crest Trail, with northern connections to Jefferson Park and southern connections to the Hunts Cove/Cathedral Rocks area.

To continue to Grizzly Peak, follow signs at the lake's outlet and start gently up the ridge-line. Good views begin about a mile up, as do beautiful meadows. Both get better the higher you climb. At 2.2 miles is a grand view-point, with sweeping views of Pamelia Lake and the southeast face of Mount Jefferson. At three miles the view from the 5,799-foot summit is similar, with the addition of other Cascade Peaks.

This is a grand one- or two-night back-packing trip, but it's likely to be filled to over-flowing in warm summer months. If you must spend the night, try it in late September or sometime in June. But be advised that snow is likely to linger on much of the Grizzly Peak Trail into early July. If you really want to do this area a favor, don't spend the night here. Do it as a day hike and camp elsewhere. Both you and the trail will be happier.

Location: Southwest of Mount Jefferson in the Mount Jefferson Wilderness; see The Columbia River Gorge and Mount Hood Map 5, grid c2.

User Groups: Hikers, dogs, and horses. No mountain bikes are allowed. No wheelchair facilities.

Permits: Free day-hiking permits, required for all hikers, can be obtained at trailheads or ranger stations. Overnight permits for Pamelia Lake are limited and should be ob-tained in advance from the Detroit Ranger District. In addition, a federal Northwest For-est Pass, $5 per day or $30 annually, is re-quired to park at the trailhead. Passes are available from ranger stations and many pri-vate vendors, online at website: www.wta.org, or by calling 800/270-7504.

Maps: For a map of the Mount Jefferson Wilderness, contact the Nature of the North-west Information Center, 800 Northeast Oregon Street, Suite 177, Portland, OR 97232; 503/872-2750. Green Trails, Inc.'s excellent topographic maps of the region are available for $3.99 each

at outdoor retail outlets. Ask for map number 557, Mount Jefferson. Ask the USGS for a topographic map of the Mount Jefferson area.

Directions: From Salem drive 52 miles east on Highway 22 to Detroit and continue south-east to Pamelia Road/Forest Service Road 2246, just after milepost 62. Turn left (east) and drive about four miles to the trailhead at the end of the road.

Contact: Willamette National Forest, Detroit Ranger District, HC 73, P.O. Box 320, Mill City, OR 97360; 503/854-3366.

76 Metolius River
12.0 mi/6.0 hrs

The Metolius River never ceases to amaze. Springing from an underground aquifer be-neath Black Butte, this is a river of mystery, and elements of natural magic are unveiled along the Metolius River Trail. You skirt the river in a steep canyon and watch remarkably clear, liquid-crystal water literally gush from the ground at many natural springs. Views of rapids and wildlife all along the route are spec-tacular. The Metolius is a noted fly fishing–only venue. Check with Oregon Fish and Game for licenses and restrictions. At about 2.75 miles the trail opens to the Wizard Falls Fish Hatch-ery, where staff members often arrange im-promptu tours. Turn around here for a 5.5-mile day hike, or continue north along either side of the river, crossing bridges at the fish hatch-ery and at Lower Bridge Campground to form an additional loop of about 6.5 miles. Return from the hatchery the way you came.

Location: North of Sisters in Deschutes Na-tional Forest; see The Columbia River Gorge and Mount Hood Map 5, grid d3.

User Groups: Hikers and dogs. No horses or mountain bikes are allowed. No wheel-chair facilities.

Permits: No permits are required. Parking and access are free.

Maps: For a map of the Deschutes National Forest, contact the Nature of the Northwest Information Center, 800 Northeast Oregon Street, Suite 177, Portland, OR 97232; 503/872-2750. Green Trails, Inc.'s excellent topographic maps of the region are available for $3.99 each at outdoor retail outlets. Ask for map number 558, Whitewater River. Ask the USGS for topographic maps of the Black Butte, Candle Creek, and Prairie Farm Spring areas.

Directions: From Sisters drive about eight miles west on U.S. 20 to Camp Sherman Road 14. Turn right (north) and drive five miles to Forest Service Road 1420. Continue straight for about three miles on Forest Service Road 1420 (follow signs for Canyon Creek Campground). Turn right on Forest Service Road 400 and continue less than a mile to the trailhead in the campground.

Contact: Deschutes National Forest, Sisters Ranger District, Highway 20, Pine Street, P.O. Box 249, Sisters, OR 97759; 541/549-7700.

PCT-8 Barlow Pass to Bridge of the Gods

54.5 mi/5.0 days

This scenic, though populated, section of the Pacific Crest Trail offers most of its best views in the first half, from Barlow Pass up to Timberline Lodge and then west around Mount Hood to Lolo Pass (23.5 miles). Be advised that stream crossings of the Zigzag, Sandy, and Muddy Fork Rivers can be hazardous, particularly late in the day. Strong hikers can jet from Timberline all the way around Mount Hood in one day via the Timberline Trail, but you might want to linger and enjoy the great local scenery at Ramona Falls, Paradise Park, Elk Cove, and other Mount Hood day-hiking destinations. From Lolo Pass the trail drops into the Columbia drainage between Bull Run and Lost Lakes and continues to Wahtum Lake in the Columbia Wilderness. From here to the gorge,

the trail is fairly nondescript, so many hikers prefer to detour west from Wahtum on the Eagle Creek Trail, a scenic, waterfall-lined path that connects with the Columbia Gorge Trail, which can be hiked north to the Columbia River Gorge crossing at Bridge of the Gods.

Location: From Barlow Pass on the south flank of Mount Hood to the Columbia River and the Oregon state line; see The Columbia River Gorge and Mount Hood Map 2, grid f3.

User Groups: Hikers, horses, and dogs. No mountain bikes. No wheelchair facilities.

Permits: A federal Northwest Forest Pass, $5 per day or $30 annually, is required to park at the trailhead. Passes are available from ranger stations and many private vendors, online at website: www.wta.org, or by calling 800/270-7504.

Maps: For a map of the Pacific Crest Trail, Oregon North, contact the Nature of the Northwest Information Center, 800 Northeast Oregon Street, Suite 177, Portland, OR 97232; 503/872-2750. Ask the USGS for topographic maps of the Mount Hood South, Mount Hood North, Bull Run Lake, Wahtum Lake, Carson, Tanner Butte, and Bonneville Dam areas.

Directions: To reach the Barlow Pass Trailhead, drive east from Portland on U.S. 26 beyond Government Camp to the junction with Highway 35. Follow Highway 35 several miles east to the Sno-Park turnout on the right (south) side of the road at Barlow Pass. (Many hikers begin this leg at Timberline Lodge.) To reach the Bridge of the Gods Trailhead, drive east on I-84 from Portland to the Cascade Locks/Exit 44. Follow the Bridge of the Gods road to the trailhead on the loop road leading to the tollbooth.

Contact: Mount Hood National Forest Information Center, 65000 East Highway 26, Welches, OR 97067; 503/622-7674; Columbia River Gorge National Scenic Area, 902 Wasco Avenue, Suite 200, Hood River, OR 97031; 541/386-2333 or 503/668-1440 (Portland number).

NORTHEAST OREGON

Northeast Oregon

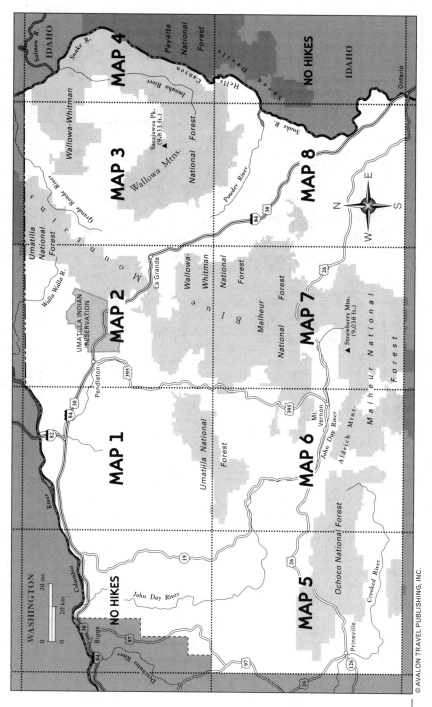

© AVALON TRAVEL PUBLISHING, INC.

Map 1

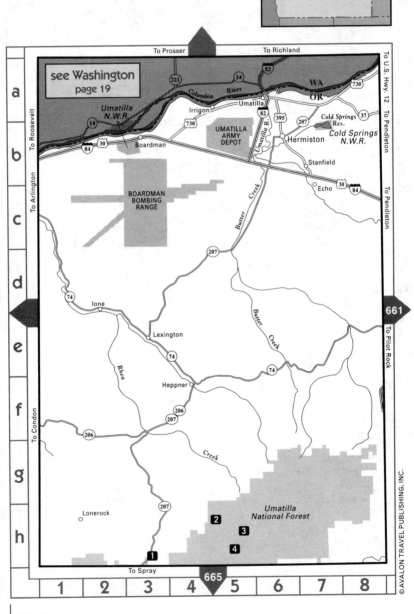

Map 2

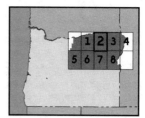

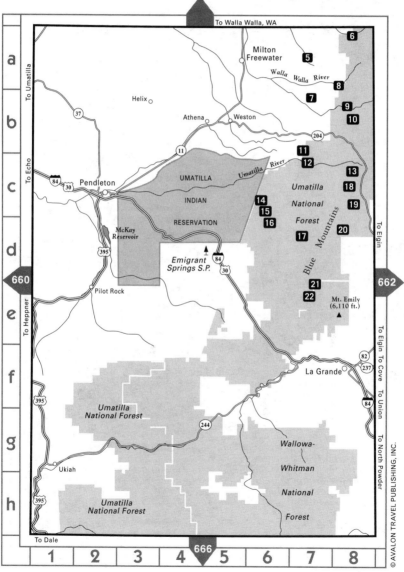

Map 3

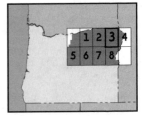

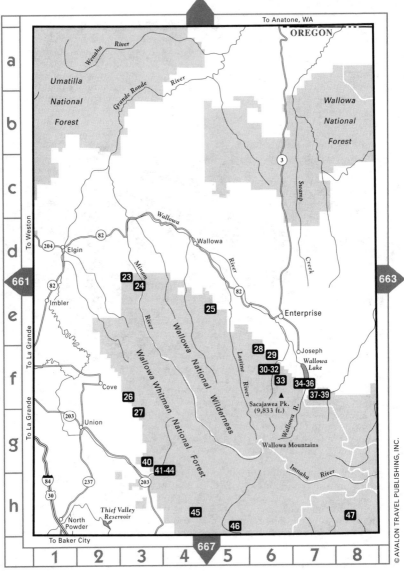

Map 4

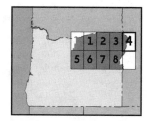

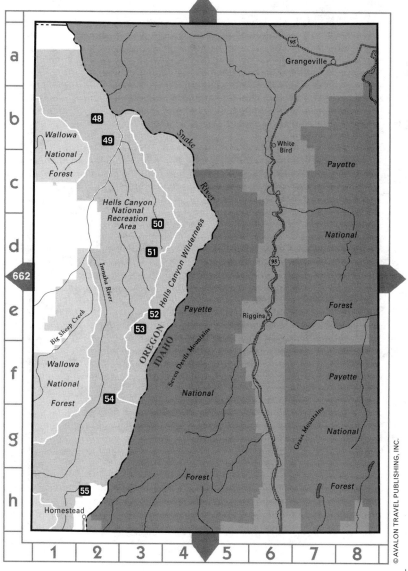

© AVALON TRAVEL PUBLISHING, INC.

Map 5

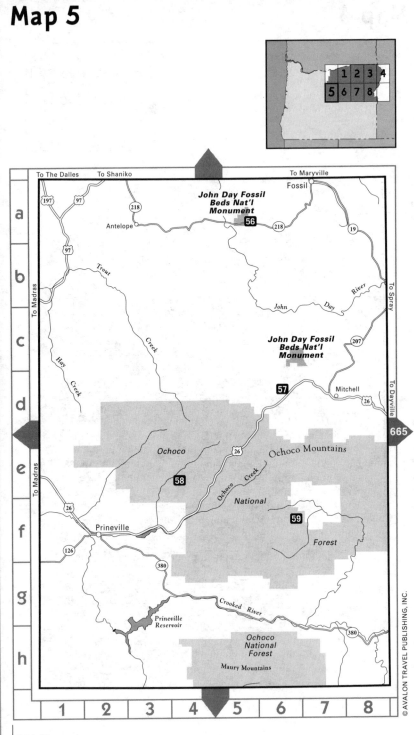

Map 5

To The Dalles   To Shaniko

To Maryville

Fossil

John Day Fossil Beds Nat'l Monument

197   97

218

56   218

19

Antelope

To Madras

Trout

Creek

John   Day   River

To Spray

John Day Fossil Beds Nat'l Monument

97

Hay

Creek

207

57   Mitchell

To Dayville

665

Ochoco

26   Ochoco Mountains

To Madras

58   Ochoco   Creek

26

National

59

Prineville

126   380   Forest

Crooked   River

Prineville Reservoir

380

Ochoco National Forest

Maury Mountains

© AVALON TRAVEL PUBLISHING, INC.

Map 6

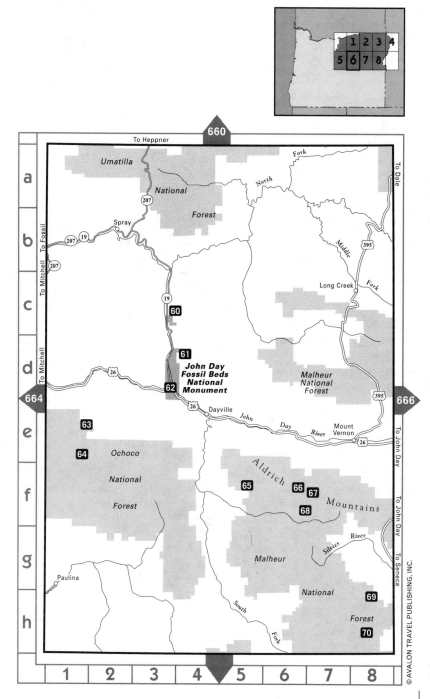

Map 7

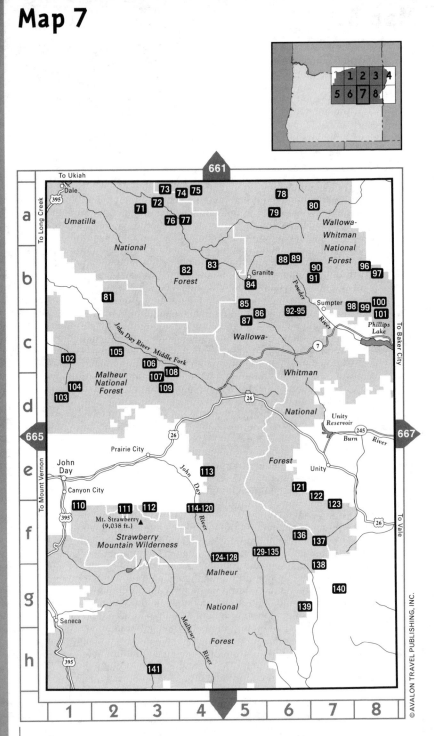

© AVALON TRAVEL PUBLISHING, INC.

Map 8

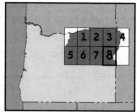

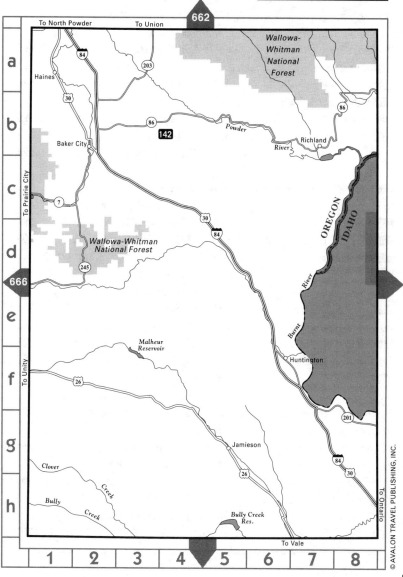

Northeast Oregon

(CONTINUED ON NEXT PAGE)

❶ Bull Prairie Lake
0.5 mi/0.5 hr

The gentle trail circles the wide blue Bull Prairie Lake, which is stocked annually with rainbow trout, making it a prime fishing spot. There are numerous points of access to the lakeshore, as well as to three floating fishing piers. Wildflowers brighten the lakeshore in the late spring; wild strawberries appear in the midsummer months.

Location: South of Heppner in Umatilla National Forest; see Northeast Oregon Map 1, grid h3.

User Groups: Hikers and dogs. No horses or mountain bikes are allowed. No wheelchair facilities.

Permits: A federal Northwest Forest Pass, $5 per day or $30 annually, is required to park at the trailhead. Passes are available from ranger stations and many private vendors, online at website: www.wta.org, or by calling 800/270-7504.

Maps: For a trail information report, contact the Heppner Ranger District at 541/676-9187. For a map of Umatilla National Forest, contact Nature of the Northwest Information Center, 800 Northeast Oregon Street, Suite 177, Portland, OR 97232; 503/872-2750. Ask the USGS for a topographic map of the Kimberly area.

Directions: From Heppner drive about 45 miles south on Highway 207 to Forest Service Road 2039. Turn left (east) onto this road and continue east to the Bull Prairie Recreation Area on the right side of the road.

Contact: Umatilla National Forest, Heppner Ranger District, 117 South Main Street, Heppner, OR 97836; 541/676-9187.

❷ Skookum Trail
5.0 mi/2.5 hrs

You start by climbing 1.5 miles through dry ponderosa and lodgepole pine forest, past Lucky Springs and a high promontory on the ridge. From here enjoy views of Copple Butte, Madison Butte, and the surrounding river canyons carved into the rough basalt rock. From this high point turn left at the fork in the trail and hike one mile west to the summit of Madison Butte (elevation 5,707 feet). There you find an old fire lookout station and even better views of the rugged terrain around you. Bring plenty of water as this dry, dusty trail can be very hot in midsummer.

This trail may be combined with the Alder Creek Trail (see hike below) to create a seven-mile loop. At the far end of this trail, turn east and hike one mile on the Madison Butte Trail to its junction with the Alder Creek Trail. Turn, hike south to the Alder Creek Trailhead, and then walk one mile up the road back to your vehicle.

Location: South of Heppner in Umatilla National Forest; see Northeast Oregon Map 1, grid h5.

User Groups: Hikers and dogs. No horses or mountain bikes are allowed. No wheelchair facilities.

Permits: A federal Northwest Forest Pass, $5 per day or $30 annually, is required to park at the trailhead. Passes are available from ranger stations and many private vendors, online at website: www.wta.org, or by calling 800/270-7504.

Maps: For a trail information report, contact the Heppner Ranger District at 541/676-9187. For a map of Umatilla National Forest, contact Nature of the Northwest Information Center, 800 Northeast Oregon Street, Suite 177, Portland, OR 97232; 503/872-2750. Ask the USGS for a topographic map of the Madison Butte area.

Directions: From Heppner drive 26 miles south on Highway 207 to Anson Wright County Park and County Road 670. Turn left (east) onto County Road 670, which becomes

Forest Service Road 22, and continue to a junction with Forest Service Road 2119. Turn left onto Forest Service Road 2119 and continue three miles before turning left onto Forest Service Road 21. Drive to the junction with Forest Service Road 21-140 and turn left, continuing north on this road for one-half mile. Turn left again onto Forest Service Road 21-146 and drive to the road's end and the trailhead.

Contact: Umatilla National Forest, Heppner Ranger District, 117 South Main Street, Heppner, OR 97836; 541/676-9187.

3 Alder Creek
6.0 mi/3.0 hrs

From the trailhead the route climbs gradually along Alder Creek and under the shading boughs of the creek's namesake trees. As the trail climbs, though, it leaves that cool, wet world behind and traverses a long, dry hillside before turning and climbing to a junction with the Skookum Trail. From the junction a three-mile hike east on the new trail takes you to the summit of 5,438-foot Copple Butte, while a two-mile hike west leads to the top of 5,707-foot Madison Butte. Visit either of these high points for great views of the surrounding mountains before returning the way you came. Or skip the side trips and just enjoy the view from the trail junction before heading back.

This trail may be combined with the Skookum Trail (see hike above) to create a seven-mile loop. At the far end of this trail, turn west and hike one mile on the Madison Butte Trail to its junction with the Skookum Trail. Turn, hike south on the Skookum Trail to its trailhead, and then one mile down the road back to your vehicle.

Location: South of Heppner in Umatilla National Forest; see Northeast Oregon Map 1, grid h5.

User Groups: Hikers, dogs, and horses. No mountain bikes are allowed. No wheelchair facilities.

Permits: A federal Northwest Forest Pass, $5 per day or $30 annually, is required to park at the trailhead. Passes are available from ranger stations and many private vendors, online at website: www.wta.org, or by calling 800/270-7504.

Maps: For a trail information report, contact the Heppner Ranger District at 541/676-9187. For a map of Umatilla National Forest, contact Nature of the Northwest Information Center, 800 Northeast Oregon Street, Suite 177, Portland, OR 97232; 503/872-2750. Ask the USGS for a topographic map of the Madison Butte area.

Directions: From Heppner drive 26 miles south on Highway 207 to Anson Wright County Park and County Road 670. Turn left (east) onto County Road 670, which becomes Forest Service Road 22, and continue to a junction with Forest Service Road 2119. Turn left onto Forest Service Road 2119 and continue three miles before turning left onto Forest Service Road 21. Drive to the junction with Forest Service Road 21-140 and then turn left, continuing north to the road's end and the trailhead.

Contact: Umatilla National Forest, Heppner Ranger District, 117 South Main Street, Heppner, OR 97836; 541/676-9187.

4 Nine Top
7.0 mi/3.5 hrs

Dry, dusty, and hot: combine those elements with a steep descent and a long ascent and you have the makings of a tough hike. Fortunately, this one is not long. The trail begins by dropping steeply through an open hillside of basalt and scrub brush. In places the trail is faint and hard to find; if you lose it, remember that the trail builder was apparently in a hurry to get to the creek and chose the fastest route possible: straight down. The rough descent ends at a river junction between Skookum and Swale Creeks. Cool off in the clear, clean waters as you ford the streams. Then begin the long, hot climb up the opposite wall of the valley. As you ascend, stop often, not only to rest, but also to admire the beautifully formed basaltic cliffs and rock formations that line the steep hillside. Both sides of the valley feature these geologic beauties, and it's interesting to admire them from a distance as well as up close. The trail ends at an old logging road on top of the second ridge. This road is difficult to access, so after a rest, turn and retrace your steps.

This is rattlesnake country, so be cautious.

Location: South of Heppner in Umatilla National Forest; see Northeast Oregon Map 1, grid h5.

User Groups: Hikers and dogs. No horses or mountain bikes are allowed. No wheelchair facilities.

Permits: A federal Northwest Forest Pass, $5 per day or $30 annually, is required to park at the trailhead. Passes are available from ranger stations and many private vendors, online at website: www.wta.org, or by calling 800/270-7504.

Maps: For a trail information report, contact the Heppner Ranger District at 541/676-9187. For a map of Umatilla National Forest, contact Nature of the Northwest Information Center, 800 Northeast Oregon Street, Suite 177, Portland, OR 97232; 503/872-2750. Ask the USGS for topographic maps of the Madison Butte, Monument, and Lake Penland areas.

Directions: From Heppner drive about 26 miles south on Highway 207 to Anson Wright County Park and County Road 670. Turn left (east) onto County Road 670, which becomes Forest Service Road 22, and continue to a junction with Forest Service Road 2119. Turn left onto this road and drive three miles to Forest Service Road 2120. Turn left onto Forest Service Road 2120 and drive to the road's end and the trailhead. Note that the last two or three miles are rough and could be impassable to passenger vehicles.

Contact: Umatilla National Forest, Heppner Ranger District, 117 South Main Street, Heppner, OR 97836; 541/676-9187.

5 The Horseshoe
18.2 mi/1.0–2.0 days

After climbing along the South Fork Walla Walla River for three miles, this long trail angles off to the left and climbs up a steep side canyon and along a narrow stream to Cub Springs. At the ridge saddle above the springs, you get moderate views of the South Fork and North Fork Walla Walla valleys. The route then drops down the north face of the ridge into the North Fork basin and the Horseshoe area, named for the horseshoe-shaped canyon that sits at the head of the North Fork River. Deer and elk thrive here, and both the North and South Fork Rivers are good trout streams. At the Horseshoe the trail ends at an intersection with the North Fork Walla Walla Trail (see hike below). Spend some time enjoying the sights here—good campsites are in the area—then return the way you came.

With a shuttle car you can make this into a one-way trip by hiking north along the North Fork Walla Walla Trail to its trailhead, just off Forest Service Road 65.

Location: Southeast of Milton-Freewater in Umatilla National Forest; see Northeast Oregon Map 2, grid a7.

User Groups: Hikers, dogs, and horses. No mountain bikes are allowed. No wheelchair facilities.

Permits: A federal Northwest Forest Pass, $5 per day or $30 annually, is required to park at the trailhead. Passes are available from ranger stations and many private vendors, online at website: www.wta.org, or by calling 800/270-7504.

Maps: For a trail information report, contact the Walla Walla Ranger District at 509/522-6290. For a map of Umatilla National Forest, contact Nature of the Northwest Information Center, 800 Northeast Oregon Street, Suite 177, Portland, OR 97232; 503/872-2750. Ask the USGS for topographic maps of the Tollgate and Big Meadow areas.

Directions: From Milton-Freewater drive about 12 miles east on Walla Walla River Road/County Road 600 to the River Forks junction. The trailhead is on the right at Elbow Creek Bridge, just past the county park.

Contact: Umatilla National Forest, Walla Walla Ranger District, 1415 West Rose Street, Walla Walla, WA 99362; 509/522-6290.

⑥ North Fork Walla Walla
13.0 mi/6.5 hrs

The upper sections of the Walla Walla River offer good trout fishing, wildlife-rich old-growth forest, and beautiful little campsites for backpackers. This trail follows the river downstream, paralleling the waterway for the entire length of the hike. The walking is easy, dropping just 1,400 feet over six miles, and leaves plenty of time for hikers to sit by the river and enjoy the rushing water. Take time to view the multitude of birds in the trees around the river and to hunt for fresh mushrooms or berries, both of which are plentiful here in the appropriate seasons.

Unless you are skilled in identifying mushrooms, don't eat any of those you find along the way. Some are delicious and harmless, but others are deadly.

Location: South of Walla Walla in Umatilla National Forest; see Northeast Oregon Map 2, grid a8.

User Groups: Hikers, dogs, horses, and mountain bikes. No wheelchair facilities.

Permits: A federal Northwest Forest Pass, $5 per day or $30 annually, is required to park at the trailhead. Passes are available from ranger stations and many private vendors, online at website: www.wta.org, or by calling 800/270-7504.

Maps: For a trail information report, contact the Walla Walla Ranger District at 509/522-6290. For a map of Umatilla National Forest, contact Nature of the Northwest Information Center, 800 Northeast Oregon Street, Suite 177, Portland, OR 97232; 503/872-2750. Ask for a topographic map of the Big Meadow area.

Directions: From Walla Walla drive 17 miles southeast on Mill Creek Road/County Road 582 to the junction with the Tiger Canyon Road/Forest Service Road 65. Turn right onto Tiger Canyon Road and continue about eight miles to the junction with Forest Service Road 6512. Turn right (south) and drive one mile to the trailhead, at the junction with Forest Service Road 651-020.

Contact: Umatilla National Forest, Walla Walla Ranger District, 1415 West Rose Street, Walla Walla, WA 99362; 509/522-6290.

⑦ South Fork Walla Walla
36.2 mi/3.0–4.0 days

This long, gentle trail follows the South Fork Walla Walla River closely, never straying more than a few dozen yards from its picturesque banks. The river is an angler's dream, with its big rainbow, brown, and brook trout. Non-anglers enjoy watching the rushing waters and the herds of elk, mule deer, and white-tailed deer that thrive in the valley. You may even see tracks of the elusive bobcats, cougars, and black bears that share the forest. Practice bear-safe camping techniques or you may see the bears themselves—up close. You can camp anywhere along the river.

Horses are common on this trail; motorcycle groups occasionally make excursions up the river, too.

Location: Southeast of Milton-Freewater in Umatilla National Forest; see Northeast Oregon Map 2, grid b7.

User Groups: Hikers, dogs, and horses. No mountain bikes are allowed. No wheelchair facilities.

Permits: A federal Northwest Forest Pass, $5 per day or $30 annually, is required to park at the trailhead. Passes are available from ranger stations and many private vendors, online at website: www.wta.org, or by calling 800/270-7504.

Maps: For a trail information report, contact the Walla Walla Ranger District at 509/522-6290. For a map of Umatilla National Forest, contact Nature of the Northwest Information Center, 800 Northeast Oregon Street, Suite 177, Portland, OR 97232; 503/872-2750. Ask the USGS for topographic maps of the Tollgate, Jubilee Lake, and Bone Springs areas.

Directions: From Milton-Freewater drive about 12 miles east on Walla Walla River Road/County Road 600 to the River Forks junction. The trailhead is on the right at Elbow Creek Bridge, just past the county park.

Contact: Umatilla National Forest, Walla Walla Ranger District, 1415 West Rose Street, Walla Walla, WA 99362; 509/522-6290.

8 Rough Fork
6.4 mi/3.2 hrs

An angler's trail, Rough Fork drops steeply into the valley of the South Fork Walla Walla River—a great trout stream—before ending at a junction with the South Fork Walla Walla Trail (see hike above). Getting down to the river, though, is no easy trick. The dry, dusty route drops nearly 1,800 feet, and rattlesnakes are common here, so you need alert ears and eyes. When you reach the bottom of the trail, explore either direction along the Walla Walla River before returning the way you came. Save plenty of time—the return trip takes twice as long as the trip down.

Location: North of Tollgate in Umatilla National Forest; see Northeast Oregon Map 2, grid a8.

User Groups: Hikers, dogs, horses, and mountain bikes. No wheelchair facilities.

Permits: A federal Northwest Forest Pass, $5 per day or $30 annually, is required to park at the trailhead. Passes are available from ranger stations and many private vendors, online at website: www.wta.org, or by calling 800/270-7504.

Maps: For a trail information report, contact the Walla Walla Ranger District at 509/522-6290. For a map of Umatilla National Forest, contact Nature of the Northwest Information Center, 800 Northeast Oregon Street, Suite 177, Portland, OR 97232; 503/872-2750. Ask the USGS for topographic maps of the Jubilee and Bone Springs areas.

Directions: From Tollgate drive 12 miles north on Forest Service Road 64, past Jubilee Lake, to the junction with Forest Service Road 6411. Turn left onto this road and continue two more miles to Forest Service Road 6403. Turn right and then drive past Mottet Campground to the trailhead on the left side of the road.

Contact: Umatilla National Forest, Walla Walla Ranger District, 1415 West Rose Street, Walla Walla, WA 99362; 509/522-6290.

9 Burnt Cabin
6.6 mi/3.3 hrs

Dropping into the Burnt Cabin Creek Valley, this trail follows the creek bottom to the South Fork Walla Walla River. The trout fishing is good in the Walla Walla, so bring a rod if you're interested. Or just bring a camera; both the Walla Walla and the Burnt Cabin are pretty forest streams with a large population of mule deer living nearby. You stand a good chance of seeing the deer in the early morning and late afternoon. The trail intercepts the South Fork Walla Walla Trail (see hike in this chapter) at the end of the route, so it is possible to create a loop trip or just extend your hike along that trail if you prefer.

Location: East of Pendleton in Umatilla National Forest; see Northeast Oregon Map 2, grid b8.

User Groups: Hikers, dogs, horses, and mountain bikes. No wheelchair facilities.

Permits: A federal Northwest Forest Pass, $5 per day or $30 annually, is required to park at the trailhead. Passes are available from ranger stations and many private vendors, online at website: www.wta.org, or by calling 800/270-7504.

Maps: For a trail information report, contact the Walla Walla Ranger District at 509/522-6290. For a map of Umatilla National Forest, contact Nature of the Northwest Information Center, 800 Northeast Oregon Street, Suite 177, Portland, OR 97232; 503/872-2750. Ask for a topographic map of Tollgate.

Directions: From Tollgate drive about one-quarter mile east on Forest Service Road 64 to the Forest Service guard station and a junction with Target Meadows Road/Forest Service Road 6401. Turn north on Target Meadows Road and continue 2.5 miles north to Forest Service Road 6401-050. Turn right and drive to the Target Meadows Campground. Stay left at the fork near the camp and continue to the trailhead on the right.

Contact: Umatilla National Forest, Walla Walla Ranger District, 1415 West Rose Street, Walla Walla, WA 99362; 509/522-6290.

🔟 Jubilee Lake National Recreation Trail Loop

2.6 mi/1.3 hrs

This gentle trail loops around the north and east shores of Jubilee Lake, offering an easy walk with pretty views of the large body of water and the surrounding hills. The steep (9 percent) grade just beyond the dam at the lake's outlet poses a bit of a challenge to wheelchair users, but the rest of the trail is level, wide, and hard-surfaced. Benches dot the route, offering irresistible opportunities to sit and contemplate the sparkling blue water. Looking for more than contemplation? The fishing is wonderful in Jubilee, and this trail passes several great casting locations where you can try to catch a big rainbow trout or two.

Location: East of Pendleton in Umatilla National Forest; see Northeast Oregon Map 2, grid b8.

User Groups: Hikers and dogs. Fully wheelchair accessible. No horses or mountain bikes are allowed.

Permits: A federal Northwest Forest Pass, $5 per day or $30 annually, is required to park at the trailhead. Passes are available from ranger stations and many private vendors, online at website: www.wta.org, or by calling 800/270-7504.

Maps: For a trail information report, contact the Walla Walla Ranger District at 509/522-6290. For a map of Umatilla National Forest, contact Nature of the Northwest Information Center, 800 Northeast Oregon Street, Suite 177, Portland, OR 97232; 503/872-2750. Ask for a topographic map of the Jubilee Lake area.

Directions: From Tollgate drive 12 miles north on Forest Service Road 64 to the Jubilee Lake Campground. The trailhead is located near the boat ramp.

Contact: Umatilla National Forest, Walla Walla Ranger District, 1415 West Rose Street, Walla Walla, WA 99362; 509/522-6290.

11 Beaver Marsh Nature Trail
0.5 mi/0.5 hr

Because this short nature trail is a favorite field-trip destination of science teachers throughout the area, you may find it somewhat crowded midweek, especially in late spring and early autumn. Don't let that stop you. Chances are you'll miss the school kids and find instead the varied hordes of wildlife that inhabit the area, including songbirds, migratory ducks and geese, cranes, herons, beavers, raccoons, muskrats, white-tailed deer, and mule deer. The beavers, by the way, have been especially busy here. They've established a small family colony and constructed dams that create the wetland marshes that attract many creatures. In fact, nature's engineers have been so active they've flooded the lower end of the trail, making it slightly shorter than it used to be.

Location: East of Pendleton in Umatilla National Forest; see Northeast Oregon Map 2, grid b7.

User Groups: Hikers only. No dogs, horses, or mountain bikes are allowed. No wheelchair facilities.

Permits: A federal Northwest Forest Pass, $5 per day or $30 annually, is required to park at the trailhead. Passes are available from ranger stations and many private vendors, online at website: www.wta.org, or by calling 800/270-7504.

Maps: For a trail information report, contact the Walla Walla Ranger District at 509/522-6290. For a map of Umatilla National Forest, contact Nature of the Northwest Information Center, 800 Northeast Oregon Street, Suite 177, Portland, OR 97232; 503/872-2750. Ask the USGS for a topographic map of the Bingham Springs area.

Directions: From Pendleton drive about 39 miles east on Umatilla River Road/County Road 900, which becomes Forest Service Road 32 at the forest boundary. Continue about 1.5 miles on Forest Service Road 32 to the Umatilla Forks Campground. Just past the campground turn left onto Forest Service Road 32-030 and drive to the road's end and the trailhead.

Contact: Umatilla National Forest, Walla Walla Ranger District, 1415 West Rose Street, Walla Walla, WA 99362; 509/522-6290.

12 Bobsled
10.0 mi/5.0 hrs

The fact that hunters love this trail hints at the plentiful wildlife in the area. Mule deer, white-tailed deer, and even elk roam this long ridgetop; red-tailed hawks and goshawks circle overhead. Climbing from the trailhead, the route gains more than 2,000 feet in elevation before leveling out on the ridge crest. The trail rides the top of the ridge south for several miles before petering out at an old jeep road. Here you have to turn around and retrace your steps, but you'll enjoy the dry pine forest and meadow views the second time around, too. If you hear a deep "whoomp, whoomp, whoomp" echoing through the pines, look closely through the lower branches for a big blue or spruce grouse. These birds seem fearless (some say stupid) and let people approach to within an arm's length at times.

Location: East of Pendleton in Umatilla National Forest; see Northeast Oregon Map 2, grid c7.

User Groups: Hikers, dogs, horses, and mountain bikes. No wheelchair facilities.

Permits: A federal Northwest Forest Pass, $5 per day or $30 annually, is required to park at the trailhead. Passes are available from ranger stations and many private vendors, online at website: www.wta.org, or by calling 800/270-7504.

Maps: For a trail information report, contact the Walla Walla Ranger District at 509/522-6290. For a map of Umatilla National Forest, contact Nature of the Northwest Information Center, 800 Northeast Oregon Street, Suite 177, Portland, OR 97232; 503/872-2750. Ask the USGS for a topographic map of the Bingham Springs area.

Directions: From Pendleton drive about 39 miles east on Umatilla River Road/County Road 900, which becomes Forest Service Road 32 at the forest boundary. Continue about 1.5 miles on Forest Service Road 32 to the Corporation Guard Station. The trailhead is on the right, opposite the old barn.

Contact: Umatilla National Forest, Walla Walla Ranger District, 1415 West Rose Street, Walla Walla, WA 99362; 509/522-6290.

⅓ Lick Creek
7.0 mi/3.5 hrs

It's possible to do this as a one-way hike, with a pickup vehicle shuttled to the opposite end. But the trail is short enough and pretty enough to make an out-and-back trip worthwhile. We recommend starting at the upper trailhead, with a walk through a pleasant second-growth forest before the trail turns and enters the wilderness area. At just under a mile you cross over Grouse Mountain Saddle and start down the Lick Creek Valley. Along the way you pass the cool waters of Zigzag Spring.

The old pine forest of the valley is broken periodically by large forest meadows full of lush grasses and wildflowers. Enter these quietly and slowly and you might catch sight of a mule deer grazing on the rich vegetation. If not, keep your ears alert for the deep "whoomp, whoomp, whoomp" calls of the spruce grouse that thrive here. These seemingly fearless birds often can be seen up close in the lower branches of trees and let humans approach to within 10 or 20 feet.

We've encountered a few individual birds that we literally had to kick (well, nudge with our feet) off the trail so we could pass.

Location: East of Pendleton in Umatilla National Forest within the North Fork Umatilla Wilderness; see Northeast Oregon Map 2, grid c8.

User Groups: Hikers, dogs, and horses. No mountain bikes are allowed. No wheelchair facilities.

Permits: A federal Northwest Forest Pass, $5 per day or $30 annually, is required to park at the trailhead. Passes are available from ranger stations and many private vendors, online at website: www.wta.org, or by calling 800/270-7504.

Maps: For a trail information report, contact the Walla Walla Ranger District at 509/522-6290. For a map of Umatilla National Forest, contact Nature of the Northwest Information Center, 800 Northeast Oregon Street, Suite 177, Portland, OR 97232; 503/872-2750. Ask the USGS for topographic maps of the Bingham Springs and Blalock Mountain areas.

Directions: From Weston drive 15.4 miles east on Highway 204 and turn right (south) onto McDougall Camp Road/Forest Service Road 3715. Continue south to the road's end and the trailhead. The lower trailhead is accessible from Pendleton. Drive east on Umatilla River Road/County Road 900, which becomes Forest Service Road 32 at the forest boundary. Continue on Forest Service Road 32 to the Corporation Guard Station. The trailhead is on the left.

Contact: Umatilla National Forest, Walla Walla Ranger District, 1415 West Rose Street, Walla Walla, WA 99362; 509/522-6290.

⅛ Nine Mile Ridge
13.6 mi/6.8 hrs

A long, tough ascent through the first two miles of trail—gaining more than 1,800 feet—

gets the hard work out of the way quickly. Then the trail levels off as it rolls along the crest of Nine Mile Ridge. Enjoy pretty views of the North Fork Umatilla Valley, Buck Mountain, and Grouse Mountain to the west. Equestrians often use this trail, and heavy use, combined with the general dry climate of the area, creates a trail that is often inches deep in fine dust. Bring plenty of water, and, on your return, take the time to dip at least your feet into the cool, refreshing waters of Buck Creek.

Location: East of Pendleton in Umatilla National Forest within the North Fork Umatilla Wilderness; see Northeast Oregon Map 2, grid c6.

User Groups: Hikers, dogs, and horses. No mountain bikes are allowed. No wheelchair facilities.

Permits: A federal Northwest Forest Pass, $5 per day or $30 annually, is required to park at the trailhead. Passes are available from ranger stations and many private vendors, online at website: www.wta.org, or by calling 800/270-7504. Party size is limited to 12 people.

Maps: For a trail information report, contact the Walla Walla Ranger District at 509/522-6290. For a map of Umatilla National Forest, contact Nature of the Northwest Information Center, 800 Northeast Oregon Street, Suite 177, Portland, OR 97232; 503/872-2750. Ask the USGS for topographic maps of the Bingham Springs and Andies Prairie areas.

Directions: From Pendleton drive about 39 miles east on Umatilla River Road/County Road 900, which becomes Forest Service Road 32 at the forest boundary. Continue about 1.5 miles on Forest Service Road 32 to the Umatilla Forks Campground. Just past the campground, turn left onto Forest Service Road 32-030 and drive to the road's end and the trailhead.

Contact: Umatilla National Forest, Walla Walla Ranger District, 1415 West Rose Street, Walla Walla, WA 99362; 509/522-6290.

15 Buck Mountain
7.2 mi/3.6 hrs

The incredibly steep first mile—an ascent of nearly 1,900 feet—discourages all but the hardiest hikers from exploring this long ridge trail. After that brutal opening, though, the trail rides the crest of Buck Ridge for a fairly level 2.6 miles to the end of the trail.

The meadows on the ridge and at the summit of Buck Mountain provide picturesque views of the surrounding wilderness area. Look for hawks, eagles, or falcons in the air overhead and everything from deer mice to mule deer on the ground around you. The old forest that covers the slopes of the ridge and mountain is made up of ponderosa and lodgepole pine, fir, and spruce.

Location: East of Pendleton in Umatilla National Forest within the North Fork Umatilla Wilderness; see Northeast Oregon Map 2, grid c6.

User Groups: Hikers, dogs, and horses. No mountain bikes are allowed. No wheelchair facilities.

Permits: A federal Northwest Forest Pass, $5 per day or $30 annually, is required to park at the trailhead. Passes are available from ranger stations and many private vendors, online at website: www.wta.org, or by calling 800/270-7504.

Maps: For a trail information report, contact the Walla Walla Ranger District at 509/522-6290. For a map of Umatilla National Forest, contact Nature of the Northwest Information Center, 800 Northeast Oregon Street, Suite 177, Portland, OR 97232; 503/872-2750. Ask the USGS for a topographic map of Bingham Springs.

Directions: From Pendleton drive about 39 miles east on Umatilla River Road/County Road 900, which becomes Forest Service Road 32 at the forest boundary. Continue about 1.5 miles on Forest Service Road 32 to the Umatilla Forks Campground. Just past the campground, turn left onto Forest Service Road 32-030 and drive to the road's end and the trailhead.

Contact: Umatilla National Forest, Walla Walla Ranger District, 1415 West Rose Street, Walla Walla, WA 99362; 509/522-6290.

16 Buck Creek
7.0 mi/3.5 hrs

Winding back and forth across pretty Buck Creek, this trail is a wonderful valley-bottom route that explores a deep forest of ponderosa pine, lodgepole pine, and spruce. Deer, black bears, coyotes, and a multitude of birds and small mammals inhabit this forest, and the trail gains just 800 feet in elevation over its length, so this is a good choice for anyone seeking a pleasant forest/creek hike without a strenuous workout. The hike ends at a junction with the Lake Creek Trail. Explore that trail before retracing your steps or simply return the way you came.

Location: East of Pendleton in Umatilla National Forest within the North Fork Umatilla Wilderness; see Northeast Oregon Map 2, grid d6.

User Groups: Hikers, dogs, and horses. No mountain bikes are allowed. No wheelchair facilities.

Permits: A federal Northwest Forest Pass, $5 per day or $30 annually, is required to park at the trailhead. Passes are available from ranger stations and many private vendors, online at website: www.wta.org, or by calling 800/270-7504. Party size is limited to 12 people.

Maps: For a trail information report, contact the Walla Walla Ranger District at 509/522-6290. For a map of Umatilla National Forest, contact Nature of the Northwest Information Center, 800 Northeast Oregon Street, Suite 177, Portland, OR 97232; 503/872-2750. Ask the USGS for a topographic map of the Bingham Springs area.

Directions: From Pendleton drive about 39 miles east on Umatilla River Road/County Road 900, which becomes Forest Service Road 32 at the forest boundary. Continue about 1.5 miles on Forest Service Road 32 to the Umatilla Forks Campground. Just past the campground, turn left onto Forest Service Road 32-030 and drive to the road's end and the trailhead.

Contact: Umatilla National Forest, Walla Walla Ranger District, 1415 West Rose Street, Walla Walla, WA 99362; 509/522-6290.

17 South Fork Umatilla
4.4 mi/2.2 hrs

This is a good trail for hikers who like water. The route crosses several small streams and creeks as it travels upstream along the main branch of the South Fork Umatilla River. You can't fish and you won't see wildlife, as the forest is thick second-growth, but hunters like the trail because of the big population of blue grouse.

Location: East of Pendleton in Umatilla National Forest; see Northeast Oregon Map 2, grid d7.

User Groups: Hikers, dogs, horses, and mountain bikes. No wheelchair facilities.

Permits: A federal Northwest Forest Pass, $5 per day or $30 annually, is required to park at the trailhead. Passes are available from ranger stations and many private vendors, online at website: www.wta.org, or by calling 800/270-7504.

Maps: For a trail information report, contact the Walla Walla Ranger District at 509/522-6290. For a map of Umatilla National Forest, contact Nature of the Northwest Information Center, 800 Northeast Oregon Street, Suite 177, Portland, OR 97232; 503/872-2750. Ask the USGS for a topographic map of the Bingham Springs area.

Directions: From Pendleton drive 39 miles east on Umatilla River Road/County Road 900, which becomes Forest Service Road 32 at the forest boundary. Continue on Forest Service Road 32 past the Umatilla Forks Campground to the South Fork Bridge and the trailhead on the right.

Contact: Umatilla National Forest, Walla Walla Ranger District, 1415 West Rose Street, Walla Walla, WA 99362; 509/522-6290.

18 Grouse Mountain
3.6 mi/1.8 hrs

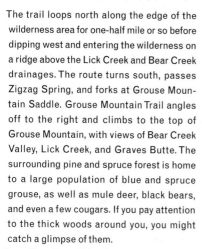

The trail loops north along the edge of the wilderness area for one-half mile or so before dipping west and entering the wilderness on a ridge above the Lick Creek and Bear Creek drainages. The route turns south, passes Zigzag Spring, and forks at Grouse Mountain Saddle. Grouse Mountain Trail angles off to the right and climbs to the top of Grouse Mountain, with views of Bear Creek Valley, Lick Creek, and Graves Butte. The surrounding pine and spruce forest is home to a large population of blue and spruce grouse, as well as mule deer, black bears, and even a few cougars. If you pay attention to the thick woods around you, you might catch a glimpse of them.

Location: East of Pendleton in Umatilla National Forest within the North Fork Umatilla Wilderness; see Northeast Oregon Map 2, grid c8.

User Groups: Hikers, dogs, and horses. No mountain bikes are allowed. No wheelchair facilities.

Permits: A federal Northwest Forest Pass, $5 per day or $30 annually, is required to park at the trailhead. Passes are available from ranger stations and many private vendors, online at website: www.wta.org, or by calling 800/270-7504.

Maps: For a trail information report, contact the Walla Walla Ranger District at 509/522-6290. For a map of Umatilla National Forest, contact Nature of the Northwest Information Center, 800 Northeast Oregon Street, Suite 177, Portland, OR 97232; 503/872-2750. Ask the USGS for topographic maps of the Bingham Springs and Blalock Mountain areas.

Directions: From Weston drive 15.4 miles east on Highway 204 and turn right (south) onto McDougall Camp Road/Forest Service Road 3715. Continue south to the road's end and the trailhead.

Contact: Umatilla National Forest, Walla Walla Ranger District, 1415 West Rose Street, Walla Walla, WA 99362; 509/522-6290.

19 North Fork Umatilla
19.6 mi/1.0–2.0 days

Day hikers frequently travel just the first 4.5 miles of the trail along the North Fork Umatilla River. The trail gains just 450 feet in elevation in that distance, which leaves plenty of time and energy to enjoy the startlingly beautiful forest and river environment. Beavers work along the river, building small dams and lodges in the cool water in the river's side channels. Just beyond the Coyote Creek Canyon (the last place to pitch a tent), the trail leaves the riverbank and begins a long, steep climb up the ridge north of the river. You get a mile-long break as the trail traverses the foot of the ridge. But the route turns straight up the hill and climbs 2,000 feet over the last four miles. The pine forest gradually thins, and from the ridgetop you get great views of the Umatilla Basin. Deer and elk are commonly seen in the broad meadows on the ridge.

Location: East of Pendleton in Umatilla National Forest within the North Fork Umatilla Wilderness; see Northeast Oregon Map 2, grid c8.

User Groups: Hikers, dogs, and horses. No mountain bikes are allowed. No wheelchair facilities.

Permits: A federal Northwest Forest Pass, $5 per day or $30 annually, is required to park at the trailhead. Passes are available from ranger stations and many private vendors, online at website: www.wta.org, or by calling 800/270-7504.

Maps: For a trail information report, contact the Walla Walla Ranger District at 509/522-6290. For a map of Umatilla National Forest, contact Nature of the Northwest Information Center, 800 Northeast Oregon Street, Suite 177, Portland, OR 97232; 503/872-2750. Ask the USGS for topographic maps of the Bingham Springs and Andies Prairie areas.

Directions: From Pendleton drive about 39 miles east on Umatilla River Road/County Road 900, which becomes Forest Service Road 32 at the forest boundary. Continue on Forest Service Road 32 past the Umatilla Forks Campground. Turn into the day-use area and drive to the trailhead at the end of the cul-de-sac.

Contact: Umatilla National Forest, Walla Walla Ranger District, 1415 West Rose Street, Walla Walla, WA 99362; 509/522-6290.

20 Lake Creek
8.0 mi/4.0 hrs

Beginning two miles outside the wilderness area, this trail offers a lesson in the differences in management of wilderness and non-wilderness lands. The first two miles lead through a collection of patchwork clear-cuts and second-growth forest. Resident deer herds frequent these sun-streaked open areas, so keep an eye out for browsing beasts. As the trail continues to drop along the Lake Creek Valley, it crosses the wilderness boundary and you enter a more open, older forest of ponderosa, lodgepole, white bark pine, blue spruce, and some Douglas fir. A number of faint side trails branch off the main route as you follow the creek. Some of these side trails peter out after a few hundred yards. Others lead up to West Buck Creek Rim, High Ridge, Nine Mile Ridge, and Horseshoe Prairie—and one climbs directly to the crash site of a World War II B-25 bomber. These side trips provide good views of the surrounding country.

The main trail itself pretty much sticks to the creek basin, which means the views are limited to close-ups of the forest ecosystem. But this is nothing to sneer at. The forest here is beautiful and offers a wonderful chance to find out what a true dry-side old-growth forest is like (it's very different from its counterpart on the wet west side of the state). The four-mile turnaround point is at the head of the Buck Creek Valley.

Location: East of Pendleton in Umatilla National Forest within the North Fork Umatilla Wilderness; see Northeast Oregon Map 2, grid d8.

User Groups: Hikers, dogs, horses, and mountain bikes. No wheelchair facilities.

Permits: A federal Northwest Forest Pass, $5 per day or $30 annually, is required to park at the trailhead. Passes are available from ranger stations and many private vendors, online at website: www.wta.org, or by calling 800/270-7504.

Maps: For a trail information report, contact the Walla Walla Ranger District at 509/522-

6290. For a map of Umatilla National Forest, contact Nature of the Northwest Information Center, 800 Northeast Oregon Street, Suite 177, Portland, OR 97232; 503/872-2750. Ask the USGS for topographic maps of the Andies Prairie and Bingham Springs areas.

Directions: From Tollgate drive about nine miles east on Highway 204 to the junction with Summit Road/Forest Service Road 31. Turn right (west) and continue 5.7 miles to Buck Mountain Road/Forest Service Road 3150. Turn right and drive 1.2 miles to the trailhead.

Contact: Umatilla National Forest, Walla Walla Ranger District, 1415 West Rose Street, Walla Walla, WA 99362; 509/522-6290.

21 North Fork Meacham
16.4 mi/2.0 days

Following the Bear Creek Trail (see hike below) for the first several miles, this route drops down into Bear Creek Valley and follows the small stream until it empties into North Fork Meacham Creek. Anglers might want to bring a pack rod, as smallish rainbow trout live in the waters of Meacham Creek. (Occasionally trout measuring up to 12 inches surface here, too.) The trail turns at the junction with the larger creek and follows it upstream to the junction of the North Fork Meacham and Pot Creek. You can camp here, or just hang out and watch for the deer, black bear, rabbits, and blue grouse that feed on the lush vegetation—including morel mushrooms and juicy huckleberries—in the two valleys. You might even see cougar tracks. The plentiful wildlife attracts a lot of hunters in the autumn, so if you visit then, wear bright clothing—preferably blaze orange—and stick to the trails. In the late-spring and summer months, especially, you need to watch out for rattlesnakes, too. They like to laze in the afternoon sunshine.

Location: East of Pendleton in Umatilla National Forest; see Northeast Oregon Map 2, grid e7.

User Groups: Hikers, dogs, horses, and mountain bikes. No wheelchair facilities.

Permits: A federal Northwest Forest Pass, $5 per day or $30 annually, is required to park at the trailhead. Passes are available from ranger stations and many private vendors, online at website: www.wta.org, or by calling 800/270-7504.

Maps: For a trail information report, contact the Walla Walla Ranger District at 509/522-6290. For a map of Umatilla National Forest, contact Nature of the Northwest Information Center, 800 Northeast Oregon Street, Suite 177, Portland, OR 97232; 503/872-2750. Ask the USGS for topographic maps of the Drumhill and Thimbleberry areas.

Directions: From Pendleton drive 33 miles east on I-84 to the Mount Emily exit. Turn left (north) at the bottom of the exit ramp and continue 12.5 miles north on Forest Service Road 31. At Forest Service Road 3113, turn left (west) and drive one mile to the trailhead on the right.

Contact: Umatilla National Forest, Walla Walla Ranger District, 1415 West Rose Street, Walla Walla, WA 99362; 509/522-6290.

22 Bear Creek
12.4 mi/6.2 hrs

From the trailhead the route drops down into Bear Creek Valley, a steep, dry descent through prime rattlesnake real estate. Don't expect to find fish in this narrow little brook, which feeds into North Fork Meacham Creek. Still, you should enjoy the cool, babbling waters—soaking your feet is a pleasure after the hot, dusty hike from the trailhead. The trail parallels the stream for several miles before you have to turn around and retrace your steps. Watch out for snoozing rattlesnakes on the way back, and keep an eye out for less threatening animals such as deer, rabbits, and big blue grouse.

Location: East of Pendleton in Umatilla National Forest; see Northeast Oregon Map 2, grid e7.

User Groups: Hikers, dogs, horses, and mountain bikes. No wheelchair facilities.

Permits: A federal Northwest Forest Pass, $5 per day or $30 annually, is required to park at the trailhead. Passes are available from ranger stations and many private vendors, online at website: www.wta.org, or by calling 800/270-7504.

Maps: For a trail information report, contact the Walla Walla Ranger District at 509/522-6290. For a map of Umatilla National Forest, contact Nature of the Northwest Information Center, 800 Northeast Oregon Street, Suite 177, Portland, OR 97232; 503/872-2750. Ask the USGS for topographic maps of the Drumhill and Thimbleberry areas.

Directions: From Pendleton drive 33 miles east on I-84 to the Mount Emily exit. Turn left (north) at the bottom of the exit ramp and continue 12.5 miles north on Forest Service Road 31. At Forest Service Road 3113, turn left (west) and drive one mile to the trailhead on the right.

Contact: Umatilla National Forest, Walla Walla Ranger District, 1415 West Rose Street, Walla Walla, WA 99362; 509/522-6290.

23 Minam River
88.8 mi/8.5 days

You don't get breathtaking panoramic vistas or endless horizons, but we doubt you'll be disappointed. This trail parallels the Wild and Scenic Minam River for its entire length, which provides all the spectacular scenery anyone could want. For more than 12 miles, the trail winds through pristine forest and riparian ecosystem with nary a sign of human presence. Then, roughly 12 miles from the trailhead, you pass an old lodge, airstrip, and a horse corral on the west bank of the river. This old outpost was used by a local rancher and hunting guide before the government designated the land as wilderness.

From the ranch the trail continues another 32 miles, along the same river and through the same ecosystem, to its end. It sounds long, but you won't be bored. Between exploring the deep, old-growth forest that lines the river and the lush meadows that dot the banks and stopping to fish for big, tough rainbow, cutthroat, and brook trout, you'll have all the adventure you can handle. If not, just keep hiking and you'll eventually reach the trail's end at Minam Lake, the source of the river. There you find views of the towering peaks of Brown Mountain, Matterhorn, and Eagle Cap.

Throughout the hike, be on the lookout for deer, elk, bighorn sheep, black bears, and cougars; they all roam this fertile valley. At the lake you have to turn around and retrace your steps along this long river trail, which brings your round-trip distance to nearly 90 miles.

There are many side trails and campsites along this long valley trail. If hiking the full length seems daunting, simply cut the hike to whatever length you want. For variation in terrain and scenery, use one of the many side trails to climb to the top of any of the surrounding valley walls.

Location: Southwest of Wallowa in Wallowa-Whitman National Forest within the Eagle Cap Wilderness; see Northeast Oregon Map 3, grid d3.

User Groups: Hikers, dogs, and horses. No mountain bikes are allowed. No wheelchair facilities.

Permits: A federal Northwest Forest Pass, $5 per day or $30 annually, is required to park

at the trailhead. Passes are available from ranger stations and many private vendors, online at website: www.wta.org, or by calling 800/270-7504.

Maps: For a trail information report, contact the Wallowa Ranger District at 541/426-4978. For a map of Wallowa-Whitman National Forest, contact Nature of the Northwest Information Center, 800 Northeast Oregon Street, Suite 177, Portland, OR 97232; 503/872-2750. Ask the USGS for topographic maps of the Jim White Ridge, China Cap, Steamboat Lake, and Eagle Cap areas.

Directions: From Wallowa drive about 19 miles west on Highway 82 toward the Minam Summit. Just one mile east of the summit, turn left (south) onto the Minam River Road, a narrow dirt road. Continue south to the road's end at Meads Flat. The trailhead is on the south side of the parking area.

Contact: Wallowa-Whitman National Forest, Wallowa Ranger District, Wallowa Mountains Visitor Center, 88401 Highway 82, Enterprise, OR 97828; 541/426-4978.

24 North Minam
70.0 mi/7.0 days

Following the main Minam River Trail for nearly 26 miles, this long route is gentle and easy to hike, despite its length. Along the way you find lots of campsites (picking the perfect spot from the many good choices is the hardest part of pitching your tent). At the junction with the river's north fork, though, the trail gets steep and stays that way for the final nine miles. Turn off the Minam River Trail and bear left straight up the rugged valley of the North Fork Minam River. This trail leads through a broad, marshy meadow full of beautiful wildflowers and biting flies—it's kind of a heaven and hell scenario—before climbing high into a long lake-filled basin. You sweep around

Steamboat Lake to the shores of Swamp Lake. Just south of Swamp Lake, a high U-shaped cliff hangs over the basin; Steamboat is bounded to the west by another cliff face. The views from here are great, and the best camping is near Steamboat. After you have your fill of the area, head back the way you came.

Location: South of Wallowa in Wallowa-Whitman National Forest within the Eagle Cap Wilderness; see Northeast Oregon Map 3, grid e3.

User Groups: Hikers, dogs, and horses. No mountain bikes are allowed. No wheelchair facilities.

Permits: A federal Northwest Forest Pass, $5 per day or $30 annually, is required to park at the trailhead. Passes are available from ranger stations and many private vendors, online at website: www.wta.org, or by calling 800/270-7504.

Maps: For a trail information report, contact the Wallowa Ranger District at 541/426-4978. For a map of Wallowa-Whitman National Forest, contact Nature of the Northwest Information Center, 800 Northeast Oregon Street, Suite 177, Portland, OR 97232; 503/872-2750. Ask the USGS for topographic maps of the Jim White Ridge, China Cap, Steamboat Lake, and Eagle Cap areas.

Directions: From Wallowa drive about 17 miles west on Highway 82 toward the Minam Summit. Just one mile east of the summit, turn left (south) onto Minam River Road, a narrow dirt road. Continue south to the road's end at Meads Flat. The trailhead is on the south side of the parking area.

Contact: Wallowa-Whitman National Forest, Wallowa Ranger District, Wallowa Mountains Visitor Center, 88401 Highway 82, Enterprise, OR 97828; 541/426-4978.

25 Middle Bear Valley
38.4 mi/3.5 days

A seemingly endless array of side trips, alternative routes, and loop possibilities are offered on this long, rambling trail as it meanders up the Bear Creek Valley. The basin is home to a fantastic variety of wildlife, including deer (white-tailed and mule), elk, mountain goats, bighorn sheep, black bears, cougars, bobcats, coyotes, beavers, badgers, eagles, hawks, falcons, and on and on. It's a good bet that you'll see representatives from one or more of these groups, so keep your eyes open and your camera ready. As you hike up the valley, the surrounding peaks tower overhead, including Goat Mountain, Sheep Ridge, Sturgill Saddle, and Lookout Mountain.

You'll find the first and best camping spot a little more than nine miles in, under the west face of Goat Mountain and opposite the mouth of Blowout Basin. Sheer rock walls form the face of many of the peaks; these are the best places for animal lovers to look for snowy-white mountain goats. Farther up the trail at nearly the 15-mile mark is Middle Bear Camp, a wide riverside camp that offers great views of the river as well as the towering Sturgill Buttes. This trail slices through a section of the Eagle Cap Wilderness that isn't heavily used, so you should find some real solitude and time for quiet exploration. The trail ends in Wilson Basin, another fine camping spot.

Location: South of Wallowa in Wallowa-Whitman National Forest within the Eagle Cap Wilderness; see Northeast Oregon Map 3, grid e5.

User Groups: Hikers, dogs, and horses. No mountain bikes are allowed. No wheelchair facilities.

Permits: A federal Northwest Forest Pass, $5 per day or $30 annually, is required to park at the trailhead. Passes are available from ranger stations and many private vendors, online at website: www.wta.org, or by calling 800/270-7504.

Maps: For a trail information report, contact the Wallowa Ranger District at 541/426-4978. For a map of Wallowa-Whitman National Forest, contact Nature of the Northwest Information Center, 800 Northeast Oregon Street, Suite 177, Portland, OR 97232; 503/872-2750. Ask the USGS for topographic maps of the Fox Point, Jim White Ridge, and North Minam Meadows areas.

Directions: From Wallowa drive approximately eight miles south on Bear Creek Road/Forest Service Road 8250 until you arrive at the junction with Forest Service Road 040. Turn right onto Forest Service Road 040 and continue to the Boundary Campground, where you'll find the trailhead.

Contact: Wallowa-Whitman National Forest, Wallowa Ranger District, Wallowa Mountains Visitor Center, 88401 Highway 82, Enterprise, OR 97828; 541/426-4978.

26 Traverse Lake
25.6 mi/2.0–3.0 days

High-lakes fishing, alpine meadows, old-growth forest, and picturesque vistas all embellish this long trail. The route climbs along East Fork Eagle Creek for about eight miles and then branches off into a side canyon in the shadow of a tall cliff. After traversing the cliff base, the trail climbs steeply around it, past Echo Lake, and tops out on the shore of Traverse Lake, the turnaround point at 12.8 miles. Camp at either Traverse Lake or Echo Lake. Broad, lush meadows link the two lakes, and you get great views as you climb around the cliffs and the old-growth forest that lines the valley bottom on the lower stretches of trail. Anglers enjoy the healthy populations of golden and brook trout in the lakes; wildlife lovers may very well see deer, mountain goats, hawks, eagles, and a variety of small mammals and birds. At Traverse Lake the trail fades away, so turn and retrace your steps to the trailhead.

Location: East of LaGrande in Wallowa-Whitman National Forest within the Eagle Cap Wilderness; see Northeast Oregon Map 3, grid f3.

User Groups: Hikers, dogs, and horses. No mountain bikes are allowed. No wheelchair facilities.

Permits: A federal Northwest Forest Pass, $5 per day or $30 annually, is required to park at the trailhead. Passes are available from ranger stations and many private vendors, online at website: www.wta.org, or by calling 800/270-7504.

Maps: For a trail information report, contact the Wallowa Ranger District at 541/426-4978. For a map of Wallowa-Whitman National Forest, contact Nature of the Northwest Information Center, 800 Northeast Oregon Street, Suite 177, Portland, OR 97232; 503/872-2750. Ask the USGS for topographic maps of the Bennet Peak and Steamboat Lake areas.

Directions: From Medical Springs drive two miles south on Forest Service Road 70. Turn left onto Forest Service Road 67. Continue about 15 miles to the junction with Forest Service Road 77. Bear left (north) onto Forest Service Road 77 and continue about five miles to Forest Service Road 77-500. Turn right and drive to the road's end and the trailhead.

Contact: Wallowa-Whitman National Forest, Wallowa Ranger District, Wallowa Mountains Visitor Center, 88401 Highway 82, Enterprise, OR 97828; 541/426-4978.

27 Diamond Lake
22.4 mi/2.0–3.0 days

This seldom-visited lake basin is well worth the considerable effort it takes to get here.

Leaving the trailhead and following the East Fork Eagle Creek Valley for the first 2.5 miles, the route is deceptively gentle. At the fork in the trail, though, you bear left and begin the grueling climb up the steep ridge—past vertical walls of rock—to a high point of 8,000 feet. Enjoy great views along the ridgetop while you catch your breath.

After you rest, drop down the trail into the basin, passing Tombstone Lake a quarter mile before reaching Diamond Lake. Both of these sparkling jewels are pristine mountain lakes full of fly-hungry brook trout. Anglers can savor tasty broiled brookies here, while non-anglers appreciate the graceful beauty of the evening trout rise, when the fish dimple the water to slurp insects off the surface. Keep an eye on the lakeshores, too: deer and mountain goats frequent this valley.

Location: East of LaGrande in Wallowa-Whitman National Forest within the Eagle Cap Wilderness; see Northeast Oregon Map 3, grid g3.

User Groups: Hikers, dogs, and horses. No mountain bikes are allowed. No wheelchair facilities.

Permits: A federal Northwest Forest Pass, $5 per day or $30 annually, is required to park at the trailhead. Passes are available from ranger stations and many private vendors, online at website: www.wta.org, or by calling 800/270-7504.

Maps: For a trail information report, contact the Wallowa Ranger District at 541/426-4978. For a map of Wallowa-Whitman National Forest, contact Nature of the Northwest Information Center, 800 Northeast Oregon Street, Suite 177, Portland, OR 97232; 503/872-2750. Ask the USGS for topographic maps of the Bennet Peak, Steamboat Lake, and China Cap areas.

Directions: From Medical Springs drive two miles south on Forest Service

Road 70. Turn left onto Forest Service Road 67. Continue driving about 15 miles on Forest Service Road 67 to the junction with Forest Service Road 77. Bear left (north) onto Forest Service Road 77 and continue about five miles to Forest Service Road 77-500. Turn right and drive to the road's end, where you find the trailhead.

Contact: Wallowa-Whitman National Forest, Wallowa Ranger District, Wallowa Mountains Visitor Center, 88401 Highway 82, Enterprise, OR 97828; 541/426-4978.

28 Chimney Lake

12.8 mi/6.4 hrs

After a three-mile climb through a steep series of switchbacks on the Bowman Trail (see hike below), the Chimney Lake route branches off to the right and continues the climb to the first of a series of beautiful mountain lakes. At 3.75 miles, you reach Chimney Lake, the first and by far the most popular, though certainly not the most picturesque. Farther up the trail is Wood Lake, a stunning forest pool that invites long, relaxing naps along its shores and peaceful nights contemplating the starry sky's reflection in the mirrored surface waters.

Location: South of Wallowa in Wallowa-Whitman National Forest within the Eagle Cap Wilderness; see Northeast Oregon Map 3, grid f6.

User Groups: Hikers, dogs, and horses. No mountain bikes are allowed. No wheelchair facilities.

Permits: U.S. Forest Service Region 6 Trail Park Passes are required to park at this trailhead. The window decal passes are available for $3 per day or $25 annually. The annual pass is valid at all Forest Service trailheads throughout Washington and Oregon.

Maps: For a trail information report, contact the Wallowa Ranger District at 541/426-4978.

For a map of Wallowa-Whitman National Forest, contact Nature of the Northwest Information Center, 800 Northeast Oregon Street, Suite 177, Portland, OR 97232; 503/872-2750. Ask for a topographic map of the North Minam Meadows area.

Directions: From Wallowa drive about nine miles south on Highway 82 to Lostine. Just inside town, turn right (south) onto Lostine River Road/Forest Service Road 8210. Continue about 13 miles south on Lostine River Road to the well-marked Lilyville Trailhead on the right.

Contact: Wallowa-Whitman National Forest, Wallowa Ranger District, Wallowa Mountains Visitor Center, 88401 Highway 82, Enterprise, OR 97828; 541/426-4978.

29 Bowman

18.8 mi/1.0–2.0 days

This long, rambling route takes you over hill, over dale, and through valley and forest. From the trailhead on the banks of the Lostine River, climb about four miles up the Bowman Creek Canyon to the saddle separating Wilson and Brownie Basins. Enjoy the stunning views here before traversing the head of Wilson Basin and dropping into the North Minam Valley via the Minam Meadows at mile five. These long, lush clearings are popular browsing grounds for the resident deer, elk, mountain goats, and bighorn sheep that roam here. Even if you don't see any of these creatures, you can still enjoy the brilliant displays of wildflowers that grace the meadows. Continue for another 4.8 miles down the trail from the meadows to the banks of the North Minam River and the North Minam Trail (see hike in this chapter). After relaxing a bit by this beautiful river (you'll find some wonderful campsites here), retrace your steps to the trailhead. You may appreciate the scenery even more on the return trip.

Location: South of Wallowa in Wallowa-Whitman National Forest within the Eagle Cap Wilderness; see Northeast Oregon Map 3, grid f6.

User Groups: Hikers, dogs, and horses. No mountain bikes are allowed. No wheelchair facilities.

Permits: A federal Northwest Forest Pass, $5 per day or $30 annually, is required to park at the trailhead. Passes are available from ranger stations and many private vendors, online at website: www.wta.org, or by calling 800/270-7504.

Maps: For a trail information report, contact the Wallowa Ranger District at 541/426-4978. For a map of Wallowa-Whitman National Forest, contact Nature of the Northwest Information Center, 800 Northeast Oregon Street, Suite 177, Portland, OR 97232; 503/872-2750. Ask for a topographic map of the North Minam Meadows area.

Directions: From Wallowa drive about nine miles south on Highway 82 to Lostine. Just inside town, turn right (south) onto Lostine River Road/Forest Service Road 8210. Continue about 13 miles south on Lostine River Road to the well-marked Lilyville Trailhead on the right.

Contact: Wallowa-Whitman National Forest, Wallowa Ranger District, Wallowa Mountains Visitor Center, 88401 Highway 82, Enterprise, OR 97828; 541/426-4978.

🔢 Frances Lake
16.2 mi/1.0–2.0 days

A long series of switchbacks through a thick pine forest offers few views and little of interest until near the end, when the trail finally seems worthwhile. Here the trail erupts from the forest onto the long shoreline of the big, blue, cold, and deep Frances Lake. This lake is home to a healthy population of lunker cutthroat, rainbow, and brook trout.

Anglers will love pulling the 12- to 14-inch torpedoes from the water; if they're lucky and skillful, they might even set a hook in an 18- or 20-incher. Of course, one of the reasons the fish are so big is the abundance of food, especially insects. That means plenty of attacking mosquitoes for most of us, so pack plenty of bug repellent. Several campsites line the lakeshore, making this a good backpacking destination.

Location: South of Wallowa in Wallowa-Whitman National Forest within the Eagle Cap Wilderness; see Northeast Oregon Map 3, grid f6.

User Groups: Hikers, dogs, and horses. No mountain bikes are allowed. No wheelchair facilities.

Permits: A federal Northwest Forest Pass, $5 per day or $30 annually, is required to park at the trailhead. Passes are available from ranger stations and many private vendors, online at website: www.wta.org, or by calling 800/270-7504.

Maps: For a trail information report, contact the Wallowa Ranger District at 541/426-4978. For a map of Wallowa-Whitman National Forest, contact Nature of the Northwest Information Center, 800 Northeast Oregon Street, Suite 177, Portland, OR 97232; 503/872-2750. Ask the USGS for topographic maps of the North Minam Meadows and Chief Joseph Mountain areas.

Directions: From Wallowa drive about nine miles south on Highway 82 to Lostine. Just inside town, turn right (south) onto Lostine River Road/Forest Service Road 8210. Continue about 13 miles south on Lostine River Road, just past the well-marked Lilyville Trailhead, to a small, poorly marked trailhead on the left.

Contact: Wallowa-Whitman National Forest, Wallowa Ranger District, Wallowa Mountains Visitor Center, 88401 Highway 82, Enterprise, OR 97828; 541/426-4978.

31 Maxwell Lake
8.0 mi/4.0 hrs

As the crow flies, the lake is less than two miles from the trailhead. But we all know crows get a straighter route than hikers usually do. In this case the steep ridge wall that must be climbed to get to Maxwell Lake necessitates a long, winding trail that more than doubles the distance to the lake. No need to worry, though. The climb is steady, but the switchbacks are gentle. Deep, thick, old-growth stands of pine, fir, and spruce make the surrounding forest strikingly beautiful. Big spruce grouse, great horned owls, and ravens share lodging in the tree branches; deer, elk, and a variety of small mammals roam the forest floor. At the pretty little forest lake at trail's end, enjoy a refreshing dip (at least your feet) and have a leisurely lunch before retracing your steps to the trailhead.

Location: South of Wallowa in Wallowa-Whitman National Forest within the Eagle Cap Wilderness; see Northeast Oregon Map 3, grid f6.

User Groups: Hikers, dogs, and horses. No mountain bikes are allowed. No wheelchair facilities.

Permits: A federal Northwest Forest Pass, $5 per day or $30 annually, is required to park at the trailhead. Passes are available from ranger stations and many private vendors, online at website: www.wta.org, or by calling 800/270-7504.

Maps: For a trail information report, contact the Wallowa Ranger District at 541/426-4978. To receive a map of Wallowa-Whitman National Forest, contact Nature of the Northwest Information Center, 800 Northeast Oregon Street, Suite 177, Portland, OR 97232; 503/872-2750. Ask the USGS for topographic maps of the North Minam Meadows and Steamboat Lake areas.

Directions: From Wallowa drive about nine miles south on Highway 82 to Lostine. Just inside town, turn right (south) onto Lostine River Road/Forest Service Road 8210. Continue about 16 miles south on Lostine River Road to Shady Campground, on the right side of the road. The trailhead is in the campground.

Contact: Wallowa-Whitman National Forest, Wallowa Ranger District, Wallowa Mountains Visitor Center, 88401 Highway 82, Enterprise, OR 97828; 541/426-4978.

32 East Lostine River
13.0 mi/6.6 hrs

As just one of many trails leading into the extremely popular Lakes Basin area, this route offers a good chance of solitude, at least until you get to the end. The route follows the East Fork Lostine all the way up the valley to its headwaters—a small alpine pond near Mirror Lake. The trail enters the northwest side of the Lakes Basin, and if you stay on that side you avoid most of the crowds, which tend to enter from the northeast side where the access trails are a bit shorter. Still, the Lakes Basin is one of the most beautiful areas in the state, and it attracts a lot of people. After exploring the area around Mirror Lake, return the way you came and enjoy the gentle down-valley hike through the quiet old-growth forest.

Location: South of Wallowa in Wallowa-Whitman National Forest within the Eagle Cap Wilderness; see Northeast Oregon Map 3, grid f6.

User Groups: Hikers, dogs, and horses. No mountain bikes are allowed. No wheelchair facilities.

Permits: A federal Northwest Forest Pass, $5 per day or $30 annually, is required to park at the trailhead. Passes are available from ranger stations and many private vendors,

online at website: www.wta.org, or by calling 800/270-7504.

Maps: For a trail information report, contact the Wallowa Ranger District at 541/426-4978. For a map of Wallowa-Whitman National Forest, contact Nature of the Northwest Information Center, 800 Northeast Oregon Street, Suite 177, Portland, OR 97232; 503/872-2750. Ask the USGS for topographic maps of the Steamboat Lake and Eagle Cap areas.

Directions: From Wallowa drive about nine miles south on Highway 82 to Lostine. Just inside town, turn right (south) onto Lostine River Road/Forest Service Road 8210. Continue about 18 miles south on Lostine River Road to the well-marked Two Pan Trailhead on the left.

Contact: Wallowa-Whitman National Forest, Wallowa Ranger District, Wallowa Mountains Visitor Center, 88401 Highway 82, Enterprise, OR 97828; 541/426-4978.

33 Blue Lake
13.2 mi/6.6 hrs

Following the West Fork Lostine all the way up the valley, nearly to its source at Minam Lake, this trail leads through some beautiful scenery and is very gentle. The valley is protected under the Wild and Scenic River designation, and the well-maintained trail climbs only 1,500 feet in the first five miles. At the junction with Blue Creek, the trail forks; the Blue Lake Trail leads off to the right, climbing the west wall of the valley. A short mile up the ridge, the route affords a spectacular view of Blue Lake, a sparkling little mountain pond on the western edge of the famous Lakes Basin, before dropping to the lakeshore. This little gem sits alone, far from the other, better-known basin lakes, so it often receives fewer visitors. Any hiker willing to settle for one beautiful, peaceful lake

instead of a whole basin full of crowded lakes has a good chance at finding solitude.

Location: South of Wallowa in Wallowa-Whitman National Forest within the Eagle Cap Wilderness; see Northeast Oregon Map 3, grid f6.

User Groups: Hikers, dogs, and horses. No mountain bikes are allowed. No wheelchair facilities.

Permits: A federal Northwest Forest Pass, $5 per day or $30 annually, is required to park at the trailhead. Passes are available from ranger stations and many private vendors, online at website: www.wta.org, or by calling 800/270-7504. Party size is limited to 12 people. Overnight-party size is limited to six people.

Maps: For a trail information report, contact the Wallowa Ranger District at 541/426-4978. For a map of Wallowa-Whitman National Forest, contact Nature of the Northwest Information Center, 800 Northeast Oregon Street, Suite 177, Portland, OR 97232; 503/872-2750. Ask the USGS for topographic maps of the Steamboat Lake and Eagle Cap areas.

Directions: From Wallowa drive about nine miles south on Highway 82 to Lostine. Just inside town, turn right (south) onto Lostine River Road/Forest Service Road 8210. Continue about 18 miles south on Lostine River Road to the well-marked Two Pan Trailhead on the left.

Contact: Wallowa-Whitman National Forest, Wallowa Ranger District, Wallowa Mountains Visitor Center, 88401 Highway 82, Enterprise, OR 97828; 541/426-4978.

34 Hurricane Creek
23.8 mi/2.0–3.0 days

Climbing along the pretty tumbling waters of Hurricane Creek, this valley-bottom trail provides a pleasant trip through a typical old-growth forest of this region. But it also provides plenty of mosquitoes, for the small creek repeatedly spreads and fills broad, marshy wetlands in which the biting pests breed and multiply. After a long (8.5-mile), gradual ascent through the valley, the trail suddenly turns straight up the ridge face and climbs to a high saddle above Crescent Lake and the heavily used Lakes Basin area for the final three miles. Visit Crescent Lake and explore the basin before returning the way you came. While you can find good camping spots all along the creek, Crescent Lake offers the best sites.

Location: South of Enterprise in Wallowa-Whitman National Forest within the Eagle Cap Wilderness; see Northeast Oregon Map 3, grid f7.

User Groups: Hikers, dogs, and horses. No mountain bikes are allowed. No wheelchair facilities.

Permits: A federal Northwest Forest Pass, $5 per day or $30 annually, is required to park at the trailhead. Passes are available from ranger stations and many private vendors, online at website: www.wta.org, or by calling 800/270-7504. Party size is limited to 12 people.

Maps: For a trail information report, contact the Wallowa Ranger District at 541/426-4978. For a map of Wallowa-Whitman National Forest, contact Nature of the Northwest Information Center, 800 Northeast Oregon Street, Suite 177, Portland, OR 97232; 503/872-2750. Ask the USGS for topographic maps of the Chief Joseph Mountain and Eagle Cap areas.

Directions: From Enterprise drive about nine miles south on Hurricane Creek Road/Forest Service Road 8205 to the road's end and the trailhead.

Contact: Wallowa-Whitman National Forest, Wallowa Ranger District, Wallowa Mountains Visitor Center, 88401 Highway 82, Enterprise, OR 97828; 541/426-4978.

35 Echo Lake
18.0 mi/2.0 days

Following the Hurricane Creek Trail (see hike in this chapter) for the first several miles, this trail begins as a gentle valley hike but changes quickly at the six-mile mark, where the trail forks. Our route leads up the steep, rough trail to the west and then climbs to beautiful Echo Lake. The beginning section of the trail is often crowded, as the Hurricane Creek Trail eventually leads into the popular Lakes Basin region of the wilderness. The crowds fall behind, though, when you turn and climb the three miles up the Granite Creek Valley toward Echo Lake. After a long series of switchbacks, you finally reach your destination, and the rewards are well worth the effort. The pretty little alpine lake nestled near the ridge crest provides a stunning foreground for the picturesque forest and peaks that surround it. Several campsites are available at the lake, but you'll most likely have the basin to yourself.

Location: South of Enterprise in Wallowa-Whitman National Forest within the Eagle Cap Wilderness; see Northeast Oregon Map 3, grid f7.

User Groups: Hikers, dogs, and horses. No mountain bikes are allowed. No wheelchair facilities.

Permits: A federal Northwest Forest Pass, $5 per day or $30 annually, is required to park at the trailhead. Passes are available from ranger stations and many private vendors, online at website: www.wta.org, or by calling 800/270-7504. Party size is limited to 12 people.

Maps: For a trail information report, contact the Wallowa Ranger District at 541/426-4978. For a map of Wallowa-Whitman National Forest, contact Nature of the Northwest Information Center, 800 Northeast Oregon Street, Suite 177, Portland, OR 97232; 503/872-2750.

Ask the USGS for topographic maps of the Chief Joseph Mountain and Eagle Cap areas.

Directions: From Enterprise drive about nine miles south on Hurricane Creek Road/Forest Service Road 8205 to the road's end and the trailhead.

Contact: Wallowa-Whitman National Forest, Wallowa Ranger District, Wallowa Mountains Visitor Center, 88401 Highway 82, Enterprise, OR 97828; 541/426-4978.

36 Lakes Basin
21.0 mi/2.0–3.0 days

The first few miles of trail climb through a lush valley forest alongside the West Fork Wallowa Creek, but those miles are very forgettable. It's not that they aren't pretty. On the contrary, this is a beautiful valley. But the scenery at the head of the valley, from mile five on, is so overwhelming that most hikers remember only the stunning beauty of the upper Lakes Basin area. This is the most visited part of the wilderness and one of the most popular wilderness areas in all of Oregon. The upper end of the route consists of an 11-mile loop around the basin, with potential side trips. The loop ends back at the main trail near the West Fork Wallowa Creek. From there, head back down the valley to the trailhead.

Location: South of Enterprise in Wallowa-Whitman National Forest within the Eagle Cap Wilderness; see Northeast Oregon Map 3, grid f7.

User Groups: Hikers, dogs, and horses. No mountain bikes are allowed. No wheelchair facilities.

Permits: A federal Northwest Forest Pass, $5 per day or $30 annually, is required to park at the trailhead. Passes are available from ranger stations and many private vendors, online at website: www.wta.org, or by calling 800/270-7504. Party size is limited to 12 people. Overnight party size is limited to six people.

Maps: For a trail information report, contact the Wallowa Ranger District at 541/426-4978. For a map of Wallowa-Whitman National Forest, contact Nature of the Northwest Information Center, 800 Northeast Oregon Street, Suite 177, Portland, OR 97232; 503/872-2750. Ask the USGS for topographic maps of the Aneroid Mountain and Eagle Cap areas.

Directions: From Enterprise drive about 12 miles south on Highway 82 to Wallowa Lake State Park and the trailhead at the end of the road (at the southern end of the lake).

Contact: Wallowa-Whitman National Forest, Wallowa Ranger District, Wallowa Mountains Visitor Center, 88401 Highway 82, Enterprise, OR 97828; 541/426-4978.

37 East Fork Wallowa
14.0 mi/7.0 hrs

You'll probably share the route with several others, as this is a very popular trail. But if you can bear with the crowds, you'll love the hike. A long, gentle ascent along the East Fork River offers plenty of opportunity to study and admire the deep, old-growth pine, spruce, and fir forest. Near the head of the valley, the trail passes Aneroid Lake, a large, beautiful forest pool that draws most visitors to its shores. For a bit of quiet solitude, try scrambling off-trail to the east of Aneroid, where you find Roger Lake, a much smaller, less spectacular pond that is nevertheless wonderful. Continuing on the trail beyond the lakes, the route ends at Tenderfoot Pass. Enjoy the great views and stunning panoramas before returning the way you came.

Location: South of Enterprise in Wallowa-Whitman National Forest within the Eagle Cap Wilderness; see Northeast Oregon Map 3, grid f7.

User Groups: Hikers, dogs, and horses. No mountain bikes. No wheelchair facilities.

Permits: A federal Northwest Forest Pass, $5 per day or $30 annually, is required to park at the trailhead. Passes are available from ranger stations and many private vendors, online at website: www.wta.org, or by calling 800/270-7504. Party size is limited to 12 people.

Maps: For a trail information report, contact the Wallowa Ranger District at 541/426-4978. For a map of Wallowa-Whitman National Forest, contact Nature of the Northwest Information Center, 800 Northeast Oregon Street, Suite 177, Portland, OR 97232; 503/872-2750. Ask for a topographic map of the North Minam Meadows area.

Directions: From Enterprise drive about 12 miles south on Highway 82 to Wallowa Lake State Park and the trailhead at the end of the road (at the southern end of the lake).

Contact: Wallowa-Whitman National Forest, Wallowa Ranger District, Wallowa Mountains Visitor Center, 88401 Highway 82, Enterprise, OR 97828; 541/426-4978.

38 Ice Lake
15.2 mi/1.0–2.0 days

The first few miles of trail climb through a lush valley forest along the West Fork Wallowa Creek. This is a good chance to stretch your legs and limber up before the trail forks at mile 2.5 and you start up the steeper, rougher Ice Lake Trail. This route leads to the west away from the West Fork Valley. A long series of mild switchbacks takes hikers to the top of the valley wall and to the shore of big, beautiful Ice Lake, a trout-filled pool of frigid water. You catch great views of the Matterhorn to the west and Sacajawea Peak to the north from the lakeshore. Spend a few hours, spend the night, or spend a long weekend at the peaceful campsites around the lake before returning the way you came.

Location: South of Enterprise in Wallowa-Whitman National Forest within the Eagle Cap Wilderness; see Northeast Oregon Map 3, grid f7.

User Groups: Hikers, dogs, and horses. No mountain bikes are allowed. No wheelchair facilities.

Permits: A federal Northwest Forest Pass, $5 per day or $30 annually, is required to park at the trailhead. Passes are available from ranger stations and many private vendors, online at website: www.wta.org, or by calling 800/270-7504. Party size is limited to 12 people.

Maps: For a trail information report, contact the Wallowa Ranger District at 541/426-4978. For a map of Wallowa-Whitman National Forest, contact Nature of the Northwest Information Center, 800 Northeast Oregon Street, Suite 177, Portland, OR 97232; 503/872-2750. Ask the USGS for topographic maps of the Aneroid Mountain and Eagle Cap areas.

Directions: From Enterprise drive about 12 miles south on Highway 82 to Wallowa Lake State Park and the trailhead at the end of the road (at the southern end of the lake).

Contact: Wallowa-Whitman National Forest, Wallowa Ranger District, Wallowa Mountains Visitor Center, 88401 Highway 82, Enterprise, OR 97828; 541/426-4978.

39 Hawkins Pass
24.0 mi/2.5 days

Following the West Fork Wallowa River from its mouth (in Wallowa Lake) to its source, this trail is a gentle river valley route until the final few miles, when it climbs the moderately steep pitch to the pass. Deer, elk, mountain goats, and bighorn sheep all populate this river valley; humans maintain a healthy population here, too.

This is one of the most popular access routes into the overused Lakes Basin region, and you are sure to have company on the trail on any summer weekend. Still, the trail is long enough to space out the hiking parties, and solitude can be found with a little patience and luck. The trail meanders through the deep old-growth pine, spruce, and larch forest of the valley and winds past more than a few forest meadows that are awash in wildflowers. Hugging the eastern edge of the Lakes Basin, the trail loops around Frazier Lake and climbs to Hawkins Pass for great views of the surrounding countryside.

Location: South of Enterprise in Wallowa-Whitman National Forest within the Eagle Cap Wilderness; see Northeast Oregon Map 3, grid f7.

User Groups: Hikers, dogs, and horses. No mountain bikes are allowed. No wheelchair facilities.

Permits: A federal Northwest Forest Pass, $5 per day or $30 annually, is required to park at the trailhead. Passes are available from ranger stations and many private vendors, online at website: www.wta.org, or by calling 800/270-7504. Party size is limited to 12 people.

Maps: For a trail information report, contact the Wallowa Ranger District at 541/426-4978. For a map of Wallowa-Whitman National Forest, contact Nature of the Northwest Information Center, 800 Northeast Oregon Street, Suite 177, Portland, OR 97232; 503/872-2750. Ask the USGS for topographic maps of the Joseph, Aneroid Mountain, and Eagle Cap areas.

Directions: From Enterprise drive about 12 miles south on Highway 82 to Wallowa Lake State Park and the trailhead at the end of the road (at the southern end of the lake).

Contact: Wallowa-Whitman National Forest, Wallowa Ranger District, Wallowa Mountains Visitor Center, 88401 Highway 82, Enterprise, OR 97828; 541/426-4978.

40 Eagle Lake
13.4 mi/6.7 hrs

Amble alongside a designated Wild and Scenic River, enjoying the tumbling rapids, tall pine forests, and diverse wildlife population. The trail parallels the Eagle River from the trailhead to the river's source: Eagle Lake. Along the way, numerous side trails lead up either of the valley walls to alpine lakes, scenic overlooks, and/or ridgetop meadows. The abundance of water all along the route makes this a strikingly beautiful hike but also one that is plagued with mosquitoes. Bring bug repellent anytime you visit before October.

Location: East of LaGrande in Wallowa-Whitman National Forest within the Eagle Cap Wilderness; see Northeast Oregon Map 3, grid g3.

User Groups: Hikers, dogs, and horses. No mountain bikes are allowed. No wheelchair facilities.

Permits: A federal Northwest Forest Pass, $5 per day or $30 annually, is required to park at the trailhead. Passes are available from ranger stations and many private vendors, online at website: www.wta.org, or by calling 800/270-7504. Party size is limited to 12 people.

Maps: For a trail information report, contact the Wallowa Ranger District at 541/426-4978. For a map of Wallowa-Whitman National Forest, contact Nature of the Northwest Information Center, 800 Northeast Oregon Street, Suite 177, Portland, OR 97232; 503/872-2750. Ask the USGS for topographic maps of the Bennet Peak, Krag Peak, and Steamboat Lake areas.

Directions: From Medical Springs drive two miles south on Forest Service Road 70. Turn left onto Forest Service Road 67. Continue about 15 miles to the junction with Forest Service Road 77. Bear left (north) onto this road and continue one mile to Forest Service Road 7755. Turn right and drive to the road's end, where you find the trailhead.

Contact: Wallowa-Whitman National Forest, Wallowa Ranger District, Wallowa Mountains Visitor Center, 88401 Highway 82, Enterprise, OR 97828; 541/426-4978.

41 Looking Glass
12.4 mi/6.2 hrs

Following Eagle Creek for the first few miles, this hike begins with a gentle ascent through the federally protected Wild and Scenic River valley. Enjoy the tumbling blue waters of the creek and the thick old-growth pine and spruce forest on the valley walls before you leave the creek basin. Then climb two miles to Looking Glass Lake, a clear, clean tarn nestled in a deep basin. When the wind isn't ruffling the water, the lake features a smooth, clear surface that reflects the surrounding peaks. Bring plenty of film, because the scenery is comprehensively picturesque. When the wind is stirring the surface is the best time to catch some of the big lunker cutthroat trout that thrive in these icy waters.

Location: East of LaGrande in Wallowa-Whitman National Forest within the Eagle Cap Wilderness; see Northeast Oregon Map 3, grid h3.

User Groups: Hikers, dogs, and horses. No mountain bikes are allowed. No wheelchair facilities.

Permits: A federal Northwest Forest Pass, $5 per day or $30 annually, is required to park at the trailhead. Passes are available from ranger stations and many private vendors, online at website: www.wta.org, or by calling 800/270-7504. Party size is limited to 12 people.

Maps: For a trail information report, contact the Wallowa Ranger District at 541/426-4978. For a map of Wallowa-Whitman National Forest, contact Nature of the Northwest Information Center, 800 Northeast Oregon Street, Suite 177, Portland, OR 97232; 503/872-2750. Ask for a topographic map of the Krag Peak area.

Directions: From Medical Springs drive two miles south on Forest Service Road 70. Turn left onto Forest Service Road 67. Continue about 15 miles to the junction with Forest Service Road 77. Bear left (north) onto this road and continue one mile to Forest Service Road 7755. Turn right and drive to the road's end, where you find the trailhead.

Contact: Wallowa-Whitman National Forest, Wallowa Ranger District, Wallowa Mountains Visitor Center, 88401 Highway 82, Enterprise, OR 97828; 541/426-4978.

42 Bench Canyon
10.2 mi/5.1 hrs

A steep, rough climb through a narrow canyon with few views may seem like a good trail to avoid, but think twice before ignoring this hike. Sure, it's strenuous (sometimes you have to scramble), but in the end you'll be glad you did it. The trail begins with a gentle riverside hike up Eagle Creek Valley to the junction with Bench Canyon. Our trail forks off to the left and immediately climbs up the canyon. After a long, sweaty ascent, you top out at Arrow Lake, a beautiful blue alpine lake under the flanks of a vertical rock wall. A short cross-country scramble leads to Heart Lake, another stunning mountain pool. Look for mountain goats around these ponds, as well as deer and elk.

Location: East of LaGrande in Wallowa-Whitman National Forest within the Eagle Cap Wilderness; see Northeast Oregon Map 3, grid h4.

User Groups: Hikers, dogs, and horses. No mountain bikes are allowed. No wheelchair facilities.

Permits: A federal Northwest Forest Pass, $5 per day or $30 annually, is required to park at the trailhead. Passes are available from ranger stations and many private vendors, online at website: www.wta.org, or by calling 800/270-7504. Party size is limited to 12 people.

Maps: For a trail information report, contact the Wallowa Ranger District at 541/426-4978. For a map of Wallowa-Whitman National Forest, contact Nature of the Northwest Information Center, 800 Northeast Oregon Street, Suite 177, Portland, OR 97232; 503/872-2750. Ask the USGS for topographic maps of the Bennet Peak, Krag Peak, and Steamboat Lake areas.

Directions: From Medical Springs drive two miles south on Forest Service Road 70. Turn left onto Forest Service Road 67. Continue about 15 miles to the junction with Forest Service Road 77. Bear left (north) onto this road and continue one mile to Forest Service Road 7755. Turn right and drive to the road's end, where you find the trailhead.

Contact: Wallowa-Whitman National Forest, Wallowa Ranger District, Wallowa Mountains Visitor Center, 88401 Highway 82, Enterprise, OR 97828; 541/426-4978.

🄳 Hidden Lake
15.6 mi/1.0–2.0 days

After more than six miles, your walk through a valley bottom ends abruptly when the trail forks at the junction with the Eagle Creek Trail and you angle off to the west toward Hidden Lake. From that junction the Hidden Lake Trail climbs nearly 1,000 feet in less than two miles as it ascends the valley wall and opens from the thick forest onto the lakeshore. On the way up the ridge, the trail passes Moon Lake, which is actually little more than a forest pond where frogs

and mosquitoes breed. At the trail's end you find some wonderful campsites scattered on all sides of Hidden Lake; each one offers great views of the surrounding forest and peaks.

Location: East of LaGrande in Wallowa-Whitman National Forest within the Eagle Cap Wilderness; see Northeast Oregon Map 3, grid h4.

User Groups: Hikers, dogs, and horses. No mountain bikes are allowed. No wheelchair facilities.

Permits: A federal Northwest Forest Pass, $5 per day or $30 annually, is required to park at the trailhead. Passes are available from ranger stations and many private vendors, online at website: www.wta.org, or by calling 800/270-7504. Party size is limited to 12 people.

Maps: For a trail information report, contact the Wallowa Ranger District at 541/426-4978. For a map of Wallowa-Whitman National Forest, contact Nature of the Northwest Information Center, 800 Northeast Oregon Street, Suite 177, Portland, OR 97232; 503/872-2750. Ask he USGS for topographic maps of the Krag Peak and Eagle Cap areas.

Directions: From Medical Springs drive two miles south on Forest Service Road 70. Turn left onto Forest Service Road 67. Continue about 15 miles to the junction with Forest Service Road 77. Bear right (south) onto this road and continue approximately seven miles to a junction with Forest Service Road 7745, and turn left (north) onto Forest Service Road 7745. Drive to the trailhead on the right, just one-half mile before the road ends.

Contact: Wallowa-Whitman National Forest, Wallowa Ranger District, Wallowa Mountains Visitor Center, 88401 Highway 82, Enterprise, OR 97828; 541/426-4978.

44 Horton Pass
29.0 mi/2.0–3.0 days

Yes, this hike through a river valley may be beautiful, but it's oh so long. After the first eight or nine miles, the scenery loses some of its charm. But just as your surroundings begin to get annoyingly familiar and common, you find yourself climbing through Horton Pass and looking down on the awe-inspiring Lakes Basin. This gorgeous, lake-speckled plateau is one of the most beautiful parts of Oregon and one of the most heavily visited wilderness areas in the Northwest. From Horton you survey Mirror Lake and the western edge of the basin. Drop down to the lakes and camp or explore the area before retracing your footsteps.

Location: East of LaGrande in Wallowa-Whitman National Forest within the Eagle Cap Wilderness; see Northeast Oregon Map 3, grid h4.

User Groups: Hikers, dogs, and horses. No mountain bikes are allowed. No wheelchair facilities.

Permits: A federal Northwest Forest Pass, $5 per day or $30 annually, is required to park at the trailhead. Passes are available from ranger stations and many private vendors, online at website: www.wta.org, or by calling 800/270-7504. Party size is limited to 12 people.

Maps: For a trail information report, contact the Wallowa Ranger District at 541/426-4978. For a map of Wallowa-Whitman National Forest, contact Nature of the Northwest Information Center, 800 Northeast Oregon Street, Suite 177, Portland, OR 97232; 503/872-2750. Ask the USGS for topographic maps of the Krag Peak and Eagle Cap areas.

Directions: From Medical Springs drive two miles south on Forest Service Road 70. Turn left onto Forest Service Road 67. Continue about 15 miles to the junction with Forest Service Road 77. Bear right (south) onto the road and continue about seven miles to the junction with Forest Service Road 7745. Turn left (north) onto this road and drive to the road's end and the trailhead.

Contact: Wallowa-Whitman National Forest, Wallowa Ranger District, Wallowa Mountains Visitor Center, 88401 Highway 82, Enterprise, OR 97828; 541/426-4978.

45 Little Kettle Creek
9.8 mi/6.8 hrs

A long, steady ascent along Little Kettle Creek leads almost three miles to the shores of Crater Lake. The valley walk is pleasant despite the constant climb. Old-growth pine, spruce, fir, and larch trees fill the valley, and elk and deer frequently browse here. Great horned owls perch in the deep forest near the trail, though they're much more elusive than the bigger beasts.

At Crater Lake the trail forks and sweeps around both sides in a loop. On the eastern shore the trail merges with the Cliff Creek Trail. Ignore that path and instead stay and relax at Crater Lake before retracing your steps. From the lake you enjoy great views of the high, craggy peaks that surround you: Krag Peak to the northwest, Truax Mountain to the southwest, Granite Mountain to the southeast, and Red Mountain to the northeast.

Location: East of LaGrande in Wallowa-Whitman National Forest within the Eagle Cap Wilderness; see Northeast Oregon Map 3, grid h4.

User Groups: Hikers, dogs, and horses. No mountain bikes. No wheelchair facilities.

Permits: A federal Northwest Forest Pass, $5 per day or $30 annually, is required to park at the trailhead. Passes are available

from ranger stations and many private vendors, online at website: www.wta.org, or by calling 800/270-7504. Party size is limited to 12 people.

Maps: For a trail information report, contact the Wallowa Ranger District at 541/426-4978. For a map of Wallowa-Whitman National Forest, contact Nature of the Northwest Information Center, 800 Northeast Oregon Street, Suite 177, Portland, OR 97232; 503/872-2750. Ask for a topogaphic map of the Krag Peak area.

Directions: From Medical Springs drive two miles south on Forest Service Road 70. Turn left onto Forest Service Road 67. Continue about 15 miles to the junction with Forest Service Road 77. Bear right (south) onto this road and continue approximately seven miles to the junction with Forest Service Road 7745. Turn left (north) onto Forest Service Road 7745 and drive to the trailhead on the right, just one-half mile before the road ends.

Contact: Wallowa-Whitman National Forest, Wallowa Ranger District, Wallowa Mountains Visitor Center, 88401 Highway 82, Enterprise, OR 97828; 541/426-4978.

46 Pine Lake
20.6 mi/2.0-3.0 days

Natural history merges with American history to make this a memorable hike for those interested in either or both pursuits. The deep old-growth pine, spruce, and larch forest of the West Fork Pine Creek Valley, through which this trail rambles, is strikingly beautiful. A broad variety of wildlife thrives in the lush forest, and the crashing white stream that pierces the center of the valley adds a wonderful backdrop of aquatic beauty and sounds. Near where the Middle Fork empties into the West Fork, the trail loops through the old site of the Queen Mine, the largest hard-rock mine in this old mining

district. From here the trail angles more steeply up the valley to Pine Lakes, and ultimately to a junction with the faint Granite Mountain Trail. Retrace your steps from here, or don't even bother to hike that final mile beyond Pine Lakes. Relax a spell at the sparkling lakes before returning to your car at the trailhead.

Location: North of Richland in Wallowa-Whitman National Forest; see Northeast Oregon Map 3, grid h5.

User Groups: Hikers, dogs, and horses. No mountain bikes are allowed. No wheelchair facilities.

Permits: A federal Northwest Forest Pass, $5 per day or $30 annually, is required to park at the trailhead. Passes are available from ranger stations and many private vendors, online at website: www.wta.org, or by calling 800/270-7504.

Maps: For a trail information report, contact the Wallowa Ranger District at 541/426-4978. For a map of Wallowa-Whitman National Forest, contact Nature of the Northwest Information Center, 800 Northeast Oregon Street, Suite 177, Portland, OR 97232; 503/872-2750. Ask the USGS for topographic maps of the Jim Town, Cornucopia, and Krag Peak areas.

Directions: From Richland drive about 12 miles east on Highway 86 to Pine and then turn left onto Halfway-Cornucopia Road/County Road 413. Continue about 13 miles north to the parking area at the road's end in Cornucopia. The trailhead is on the right side of the parking area.

Contact: Wallowa-Whitman National Forest, Wallowa Ranger District, Wallowa Mountains Visitor Center, 88401 Highway 82, Enterprise, OR 97828; 541/426-4978.

47 South Fork Imnaha
34.0 mi/3.0–4.0 days

This valley-bottom trail explores the beautiful Imnaha River, the fourth federally designated Wild and Scenic River in the Eagle Cap Wilderness. Though long, it is gentle, gaining just 4,000 feet over 17 miles. Those who don't want to hike the entire length can turn around at five miles. There the trail offers a fantastic view of Imnaha Falls, a thundering cascade that can be heard as you approach. Moving upstream from the falls, the trail hugs the north bank of the river, while providing access to an assortment of side trails. These wind their way up the valley walls and lead to tiny alpine lakes, deep canyons, and lush forest meadows. The main trail continues west along the river before ending at Hawkins Pass on the southern edge of the popular Lakes Basin region. Good camping spots are available all along the route.

Location: North of Richland in Wallowa-Whitman National Forest within the Eagle Cap Wilderness; see Northeast Oregon Map 3, grid h8.

User Groups: Hikers, dogs, and horses. No mountain bikes are allowed. No wheelchair facilities.

Permits: A federal Northwest Forest Pass, $5 per day or $30 annually, is required to park at the trailhead. Passes are available from ranger stations and many private vendors, online at website: www.wta.org, or by calling 800/270-7504. Party size is limited to 12 people.

Maps: For a trail information report, contact the Wallowa Ranger District at 541/426-4978. For a map of Wallowa-Whitman National Forest, contact Nature of the Northwest Information Center, 800 Northeast Oregon Street, Suite 177, Portland, OR 97232; 503/872-2750. Ask the USGS for topographic maps of the Deadman Point, Cornucopia, and Aneroid Mountain areas.

Directions: From Richland drive east on Highway 86 to the junction with Wallowa Mountain Loop Road/Forest Service Road 39. Turn left (north) onto Wallowa Mountain Loop Road and continue to the Imnaha River Road/Forest Service Road 3960. Turn left (west) and drive to the road's end and the trailhead.

Contact: Wallowa-Whitman National Forest, Wallowa Ranger District, Wallowa Mountains Visitor Center, 88401 Highway 82, Enterprise, OR 97828; 541/426-4978.

48 Nee-Mo-Poo
7.2 mi/3.7 hrs

Rich in natural and human history, this short, steep trail is a designated National Recreation Trail. This is the deepest canyon in all of North America—deeper and wider even than the Grand Canyon. (It's deeper, in fact, by more than 1,000 feet in some places. The notable difference here is that Hells Canyon lies between two mountain ranges, while the Grand Canyon is actually a gorge.) The human history of the area stretches back thousands of years, but the most renowned event is the war between the U.S. Army and members of the Nez Perce Indian Nation. The Nez Perce followed this trail after they refused to settle peacefully onto a U.S. government–established reservation. Led by Chief Joseph and Tu-Ekakas, the Nez Perce descended the trail from the high ridge crest to the banks of the Snake River. From there they crossed the river and continued a long, brilliant retreat through Idaho and Montana before being attacked one last time and captured within sight of the Canadian border and freedom.

Modern travelers still find the route steep and rough; at the riverside, they will find a sign describing the Nez Perce retreat and their treacherous river crossing. The name of the trail, by the way, is from the Nez Perce language and roughly translated means "The Real People."

This is rattlesnake country, so take care as you travel throughout the area.

Location: Northeast of Joseph in Wallowa-Whitman National Forest within Hells Canyon National Recreation Area; see Northeast Oregon Map 4, grid b2.

User Groups: Hikers, dogs, and horses. No mountain bikes are allowed. No wheelchair facilities.

Permits: A federal Northwest Forest Pass, $5 per day or $30 annually, is required to park at the trailhead. Passes are available from ranger stations and many private vendors, online at website: www.wta.org, or by calling 800/270-7504.

Maps: For a trail information report, contact the Hells Canyon National Recreation Area at 541/426-4978. For a map of Wallowa-Whitman National Forest, contact Nature of the Northwest Information Center, 800 Northeast Oregon Street, Suite 177, Portland, OR 97232; 503/872-2750. Ask the USGS for topographic maps of the Deadhorse Ridge and Cactus Mountain areas.

Directions: From Joseph drive east on Highway 350 to Imnaha and turn north onto County Road 735. Continue north on County Road 735 to Fence Creek, where the road becomes Forest Service Road 4260. Continue straight ahead on Forest Service Road 4260 to the road's end and the trailhead (in a cattle pasture).

Contact: Wallowa-Whitman National Forest, Hells Canyon National Recreation Area, Wallowa Mountains Visitor Center, 88401 Highway 82, Enterprise, OR 97828; 541/426-4978.

49 Snake River
**48.0 mi one way/
4.0–5.0 days**

Unlike the Colorado River's Grand Canyon, the grand canyon of the Snake River—Hells Canyon—can be hiked from north to south at river level. This is the trail on which to experience it. From the north end of Hells Canyon National Recreation Area, hike south (upstream) through the heart of North America's deepest canyon. The trail remains close to the water at all times.

When rocky outcroppings force the trail up the slope a bit, it still gives you great views of the beautiful wild river canyon. Several side trails lead up to the canyon rim, and periodic sandy beaches make for leisurely lunches or comfortable campsites. The trail ends near the Hells Canyon Dam on the south end of the canyon. A one-way trip can be accomplished by shuttling a car to the south end, thereby eliminating a very long return trip.

Location: Northeast of Joseph in Wallowa-Whitman National Forest within Hells Canyon National Recreation Area; see Northeast Oregon Map 4, grid b2.

User Groups: Hikers, dogs, and horses. No mountain bikes are allowed. No wheelchair facilities.

Permits: A federal Northwest Forest Pass, $5 per day or $30 annually, is required to park at the trailhead. Passes are available from ranger stations and many private vendors, online at website: www.wta.org, or by calling 800/270-7504.

Maps: For a trail information report, contact the Hells Canyon National Recreation Area at 541/426-4978. For a detailed map of Wallowa-Whitman National Forest, contact Nature of the Northwest Information Center, 800 Northeast Oregon Street, Suite 177, Portland, OR 97232; 503/872-2750. Ask the USGS for topographic maps of the Cactus Mountain, Wolf Creek, Lord Flat, Grave Point, Temperance Creek, and Old Timer Mountain areas.

Directions: From Joseph drive approximately 40 miles east on Highway 350 to Imnaha and then turn north onto County Road 735. Continue driving north on County Road 735 to Fence Creek, where the road becomes Forest Service Road 4260. Continue straight ahead on Forest Service Road 4260 to the road's end and the trailhead (located in a cattle pasture). To arrange a car shuttle, follow the directions to Hells Canyon Dam (see hike in this chapter).

Contact: Wallowa-Whitman National Forest, Hells Canyon National Recreation Area, Wallowa Mountains Visitor Center, 88401 Highway 82, Enterprise, OR 97828; 541/426-4978.

50 Temperance Creek
22.0 mi/1.0–2.0 days

A long, rambling descent along Temperance Creek leads through patches of wildflowers and soft grasses and alongside prime deer habitat (seldom do visitors not have the pleasure of spotting a few deer here). The trail drops more than 5,000 feet before ending at the Temperance Ranch on the bank of the Snake River in the center of Hells Canyon. On the way down you enjoy great views out over the Snake River Valley. On the way up you sweat profusely, so remember to carry plenty of water and sunscreen. You can camp anywhere you like along the creek, but the best camping spot is at Temperance Ranch, the turnaround point at mile 11.

Location: Northeast of the town of Joseph in the Wallowa-Whitman National Forest within Hells Canyon National Recreation Area; see Northeast Oregon Map 4, grid d3.

User Groups: Hikers, dogs, and horses. No mountain bikes are allowed. No wheelchair facilities.

Permits: A federal Northwest Forest Pass, $5 per day or $30 annually, is required to park at the trailhead. Passes are available from ranger stations and many private vendors, online at website: www.wta.org, or by calling 800/270-7504.

Maps: For a trail information report, contact the Hells Canyon National Recreation Area at 541/426-4978. To receive a detailed map of Wallowa-Whitman National Forest, contact Nature of the Northwest Information Center, 800 Northeast Oregon Street, Suite 177, Portland, OR 97232; 503/872-2750. Ask the USGS for topographic maps of the Hat Point, Old Timer Mountain, and Temperance Creek areas.

Directions: From Joseph drive about 40 miles east on Highway 350 to Imnaha and turn south onto County Road 727. Continue about one mile south on County Road 727 to Forest Service Road 4240. Turn east onto Forest Service Road 4240 and drive to the road's end and the trailhead.

Contact: Wallowa-Whitman National Forest, Hells Canyon National Recreation Area, Wallowa Mountains Visitor Center, 88401 Highway 82, Enterprise, OR 97828; 541/426-4978.

51 High
73.2 mi/7.0 days

After rising a brief mile up to Freezeout Saddle, the High Trail leads away to the north. Follow this route and you find nothing but stunning views, fascinating crevices and caves in the basalt cliffs, high desert wildflowers, lush grasses, and herds of mule deer and bighorn sheep. The trail weaves back and forth, always staying at the crest of the jagged canyon rim and always offering spectacular vistas that sweep across the length of Hells Canyon, taking in the Seven Devil's peaks of Idaho, Wallowa Mountains of Oregon, and deep, steep canyons on either side of the ridge. Watch your step, as the rocks roll and rattlesnakes sun themselves on the trail.

From Freezeout Saddle the trail rolls north for the next 19 miles, crossing several creek basins and the ridges that separate them. Spots to camp can be found along all of the seemingly countless creeks here and on the ridgetops above them. At 19 miles from Freezeout Saddle, the trail crosses Temperance Creek, one of the best campsites on this trail. From there it's another 16 miles of traversing steep, creek-lined ravines and basins before the route tapers down to the banks of the Snake River near Pleasant Valley. The trail ends at the Snake River, with great camping near the mouth of the Pleasant River.

Location: Northeast of Joseph in Wallowa-Whitman National Forest within Hells Canyon National Recreation Area; see Northeast Oregon Map 4, grid d3.

User Groups: Hikers, dogs, and horses. No mountain bikes are allowed. No wheelchair facilities.

Permits: A federal Northwest Forest Pass, $5 per day or $30 annually, is required to park at the trailhead. Passes are available from ranger stations and many private vendors, online at website: www.wta.org, or by calling 800/270-7504.

Maps: For a trail information report, contact the Hells Canyon National Recreation Area at 541/426-4978. For a map of Wallowa-Whitman National Forest, contact Nature of the Northwest Information Center, 800 Northeast Oregon Street, Suite 177, Portland, OR 97232; 503/872-2750. Ask the USGS for topographic maps of the Sheep Creek Divide, Hat Point, Old Timer Mountain, and Jaynes Ridge areas.

Directions: From Joseph drive about 40 miles east on Highway 350 to Imnaha and turn south on Imnaha River Road/County Road 727. Continue about 14 miles to the junction with Forest Service Road 4230. Turn left (east) onto Forest Service Road 4230 and drive to the road's end and the trailhead.

Contact: Wallowa-Whitman National Forest, Hells Canyon National Recreation Area, Wallowa Mountains Visitor Center, 88401 Highway 82, Enterprise, OR 97828; 541/426-4978.

52 Saddle Creek
21.4 mi/1.0–2.0 days

After your two-mile climb up Freezeout Creek, with a 1,500-foot elevation gain, your reward is fantastic views of the Hells Canyon Gorge and the Wallowa Mountains from Freezeout Saddle on the ridgetop. These views last for about one mile along the ridge; then the trail drops down the Saddle Creek draw into Hells Canyon and finally to the shore of the Snake River.

A variety of wildlife thrives here—mule deer, bighorn sheep, eagles, hawks, rattlesnakes, jackrabbits, and a huge array of bird species—so bring a camera and be prepared to see animals around every corner. Camping spots lie along Saddle Creek, but the best camping is at the Snake River.

Location: East of Joseph in Wallowa-Whitman National Forest within Hells Canyon National Recreation Area; see Northeast Oregon Map 4, grid e3.

User Groups: Hikers, dogs, and horses. No mountain bikes are allowed. No wheelchair facilities.

Permits: A federal Northwest Forest Pass, $5 per day or $30 annually, is required to park at the trailhead. Passes are available from ranger stations and many private vendors, online at website: www.wta.org, or by calling 800/270-7504.

Maps: For a trail information report, contact Hells Canyon National Recreation Area at 541/426-4978. To receive a detailed map of Wallowa-Whitman National Forest, contact Nature of the Northwest Information Center, 800 Northeast Oregon Street, Suite 177, Portland, OR 97232; 503/872-2750. Ask the USGS for topographic maps of the Sheep Creek Divide, Hat Point, Old Timer Mountain, and Jaynes Ridge areas.

Directions: From Joseph drive about 40 miles east on

Highway 350 to Imnaha, turn south on Imna-ha River Road/County Road 727, and con-tinue about 14 miles to the junction with Forest Service Road 4230. Turn left (east) and drive to the road's end, where you find the trailhead.

Contact: Wallowa-Whitman National Forest, Hells Canyon National Recreation Area, Wal-lowa Mountains Visitor Center, 88401 High-way 82, Enterprise, OR 97828; 541/426-4978.

53 Upper Snake
38.4 mi/2.0–3.0 days

In the first 11.2 miles, this trail leads up and over Freezeout Saddle and then drops down to the Snake River. There you turn south and hike upstream along the wide river to Stud Creek for the last eight miles. Bighorn sheep and mountain goats frequently dot the near-vertical canyon walls on your right and far across the river on your left. Golden and bald eagles often float overhead on the thermals that swirl around these jagged peaks. But don't get lost in the clouds; this is a rough, uneven trail that requires you to focus a lot of attention on your feet. Pause often to look around and enjoy the wild beauty of the area and then focus on the footing again. The best camps are at Battle Creek and the mouth of Saddle Creek.

You can avoid a long return trip by arrang-ing for a shuttle vehicle at the Stud Creek Trailhead, near the Hells Canyon Dam.

Location: East of Joseph in Wallowa-Whit-man National Forest within Hells Canyon Na-tional Recreation Area; see Northeast Oregon Map 4, grid e3.

User Groups: Hikers, dogs, and horses. No mountain bikes are allowed. No wheelchair facilities.

Permits: A federal Northwest Forest Pass, $5 per day or $30 annually, is required to park at the trailhead. Passes are available from

ranger stations and many private vendors, online at website: www.wta.org, or by call-ing 800/270-7504.

Maps: For a trail information report, contact the Hells Canyon National Recreation Area at 541/426-4978. For a map of Wallowa-Whit-man National Forest, contact Nature of the Northwest Information Center, 800 North-east Oregon Street, Suite 177, Portland, OR 97232; 503/872-2750. Ask the USGS for topo-graphic maps of the Sheep Creek Divide, Hat Point, Old Timer Mountain, and Jaynes Ridge areas.

Directions: From Joseph drive about 40 miles east on Highway 350 to Imnaha, turn south on Imnaha River Road/County Road 727, and continue about 14 miles to the junction with Forest Service Road 4230. Turn left (east) and drive to the road's end, where you find the trailhead.

Contact: Wallowa-Whitman National Forest, Hells Canyon National Recreation Area, Wal-lowa Mountains Visitor Center, 88401 High-way 82, Enterprise, OR 97828; 541/426-4978.

54 Stud Creek
2.0 mi/1.0 hr

This is an easy downstream jaunt along scenic Stud Creek to a steep side canyon. Camp-ground visitors are the most common users of the trail, but it is also a good place to hike if you want to spend time studying local flora and fauna. Though it's only one mile long, you may see rattlesnakes, mule deer, bighorn sheep, hawks, ravens, eagles (golden and bald), chukars, jackrabbits, and other wildlife.

Location: North of Richland in Wallowa-Whitman National Forest within Hells Canyon National Recreation Area; see Northeast Oregon Map 4, grid f2.

User Groups: Hikers, dogs, and horses. No mountain bikes are allowed. No wheelchair facilities.

Permits: A federal Northwest Forest Pass, $5 per day or $30 annually, is required to park at the trailhead. Passes are available from ranger stations and many private vendors, online at website: www.wta.org, or by calling 800/270-7504.

Maps: For a trail information report, contact the Hells Canyon National Recreation Area at 541/426-4978. For a map of Wallowa-Whitman National Forest, contact Nature of the Northwest Information Center, 800 Northeast Oregon Street, Suite 177, Portland, OR 97232; 503/872-2750. Ask the USGS for topographic maps of the White Monument and Squirrel Prairie areas.

Directions: From Richland drive about 30 miles east on Highway 86 to Copperfield. Drive across the Snake River Bridge into Idaho and turn north onto Forest Service Road 454. Continue about 23 miles north on Forest Service Road 454 to Hells Canyon Dam. Turn west, cross the dam back into Oregon, and head north (downstream) to the campground and the trailhead near the boat ramp.

Contact: Wallowa-Whitman National Forest, Hells Canyon National Recreation Area, Wallowa Mountains Visitor Center, 88401 Highway 82, Enterprise, OR 97828; 541/426-4978.

55 Hells Canyon Reservoir
9.6 mi/4.8 hrs

Following the western shore of the deep reservoir behind Hells Canyon Dam, the trail rolls along with little or no elevation gain. It passes through long, rolling sagebrush and wildflower pastures, both of which are havens for rattlesnakes. On either side of the river, the high canyon walls harbor eagles' nests as well as bighorn sheep herds. Look closely and you should see one or both of these big, beautiful creatures.

Location: North of Richland in Wallowa-Whitman National Forest within Hells Canyon National Recreation Area; see Northeast Oregon Map 4, grid h2.

User Groups: Hikers, dogs, and horses. No mountain bikes are allowed. No wheelchair facilities.

Permits: A federal Northwest Forest Pass, $5 per day or $30 annually, is required to park at the trailhead. Passes are available from ranger stations and many private vendors, online at website: www.wta.org, or by calling 800/270-7504.

Maps: For a trail information report, contact the Hells Canyon National Recreation Area at 541/426-4978. For a map of Wallowa-Whitman National Forest, contact Nature of the Northwest Information Center, 800 Northeast Oregon Street, Suite 177, Portland, OR 97232; 503/872-2750. Ask for a topographic map of the Homestead area.

Directions: From Richland drive about 30 miles east on Highway 86 to Copperfield. Turn north onto County Road 1039 and continue to the road's end and the trailhead.

Contact: Wallowa-Whitman National Forest, Hells Canyon National Recreation Area, Wallowa Mountains Visitor Center, 88401 Highway 82, Enterprise, OR 97828; 541/426-4978.

56 John Day Fossil Beds (Clarno) Interpretive Trails
1.0 mi/0.5 hr

Three short interpretive trails here (each about a half-mile round-trip hike) take you through the fascinating geological history of the Oregon high desert, where magnificent rock spires attract the interest of children and everyone else who passes by. Two are interpretive nature trail loops that describe separate geological eras. The third is an occasionally steep, rocky path to Clarno Arch, formed by a mud-flow deposit. On the way notice the fossilized logs and other records of the subtropical rainforest that once existed here. Watch out for rattlesnakes.

Other units of the John Day Fossil Beds are located on U.S. 26 near Ochoco Summit east of Prineville and farther east on U.S. 26 near the Highway 19 junction.

Location: Between Antelope and Fossil on Highway 218; see Northeast Oregon Map 5, grid a5.

User Groups: Hikers and dogs. No horses or mountain bikes are allowed. No wheelchair facilities.

Permits: No permits are required. Parking and access are free.

Maps: Ask the USGS for a topographic map of the Clarno area.

Directions: From Madras drive 45 miles north on U.S. 97 to Highway 218. Turn east and proceed about 24 miles to the Fossil Beds turnout, about one mile east of Clarno on the left (north) side of the road.

Contact: John Day Fossil Beds National Monument, 420 West Main Street, John Day, OR 97845; 541/575-0721 or 541/987-2333.

57 Twin Pillars
11.0 mi/7.0 hrs

This lightly used trail up the East Fork of Mill Creek leads into the heart of the quiet Mill Creek Wilderness to two awesome rock pillars, each 200 feet of sheer, vertical andesite. The creek leading through the dry pine forest is beautiful, with occasional meadows beckoning you to stop for lunch. Watch for traces of an old wagon road to Whistler Springs agate mines on the initial stretches. The grade is very level at first and then shoots uphill at about three miles, sending you on your way to the rock spires, which are first seen about half a mile later. You then drop to

a final creek crossing (last water stop) and continue another 1.2 miles uphill to a side trail that leads to the Pillars. The route up is steep and sandy, but great views at the Pillars' base make up for it. Watch for rock climbers. If this hike seems too long for a warm summer day, the Pillars can be reached by walking the same trail about 1.5 miles from the upper, Bingham Prairie Trailhead on Forest Service Road 27, but you miss the creek scenery unless you hike it all the way through downhill as a shuttle hike.

Creek crossings along the route can be difficult during the spring melt. Check trail conditions with rangers before departing. Other good hikes in this creek drainage include a 13-mile downhill shuttle hike from Whistler Point to Wildcat Campground and a 10-mile downhill shuttle hike from White Rock Campground on Wildcat Mountain to Wildcat Campground.

Location: Northeast of Prineville in the Mill Creek Wilderness; see Northeast Oregon Map 5, grid d6.

User Groups: Hikers, horses, and dogs. No mountain bikes are allowed. No wheelchair facilities.

Permits: A federal Northwest Forest Pass, $5 per day or $30 annually, is required to park at the trailhead. Passes are available from ranger stations and many private vendors, online at website: www.wta.org, or by calling 800/270-7504.

Maps: For a map of Ochoco National Forest, contact the Nature of the Northwest Information Center, 800 Northeast Oregon Street, Suite 177, Portland, OR 97232; 503/872-2750. Ask the USGS for a topographic map of the Wildcat Mountain area.

Directions: From Prineville drive nine miles east on U.S. 26 to Mill Creek Road/Forest Service Road 33. Turn north and proceed just over 10 miles to the trailhead in Wildcat Campground.

Contact: Ochoco National Forest, 3160 Northeast Third Street, P.O. Box 490, Prineville, OR 97754; 541/416-6500.

58 John Day Fossil Beds (Painted Hills)
0.3–1.6 mi/0.25–1.0 hr

Four easy trails within close proximity showcase the mysterious Painted Hills area, where multicolored rock and clay combine for a fantastic desert painting. The first trail, at the end of a short spur road, leads one-third mile to the Painted Hills Overlook, which offers a glimpse of the phenomenon. Grab an interpretive brochure that describes how these 30-million-year-old volcanic deposits got here and why they've taken on their colors. Prime viewing times are dawn and dusk, when colors are particularly vivid. Back down the spur road and across the access road to the north is the Carroll Rim Trail, which leads an eighth of a mile one-way to a fine viewpoint atop Carroll Rim. Bring your camera. A short distance farther west on the access road is a turnoff for the Painted Cove Trail. This is a 0.3-mile loop that introduces you to some of the fossilized remains found here. Interpretive pamphlets are available. Leaf Fossil Hills, the final trail, a bit farther down the access road, is another 0.3-mile nature loop, this one displaying fossilized remains of plants. Hiking them all is pleasant in the morning or evening, with some geology lessons thrown in free. Bring plenty of water in the summer and be aware of rattlesnakes.

Location: In the Painted Hills west of Mitchell; see Northeast Oregon Map 5, grid e4.

User Groups: Hikers and dogs. No horses or mountain bikes are allowed. No wheelchair facilities.

Permits: A federal Northwest Forest Pass, $5 per day or $30 annually, is required to park at the trailhead. Passes are available from ranger stations and many private vendors, online at website: www.wta.org, or by calling 800/270-7504.

Maps: Ask the USGS for a topographic map of the Painted Hills area.

Directions: From Prineville drive east on U.S. 26 to Bridge Creek Road, three miles west of Mitchell. Turn left (north) and follow signs about six miles to the John Day Fossil Beds National Monument. Turn left off Bridge Creek Road and find trailheads for the trails described all within a one-mile stretch.

Contact: John Day Fossil Beds National Monument, HCR 82, P.O. Box 126, Kimberly, OR 97848; 541/575-0721 or 541/987-2333.

59 Lookout Mountain
15.0 mi/1.0–2.0 days

This long, leg-sapping day hike takes you to new heights in wilderness adventure—literally and figuratively. At the flat, mesa-like top of 6,926-foot Lookout Mountain, wildflower meadows host deer, elk, and many other creatures, including you if you hoof it up the 3,000 vertical feet required to get here. The route passes through dry pine forests typical of this region but throws in some extras, such as a lovely field of iris blooms. The route steepens at two miles and maintains a steady uphill grade until the mountain mesa is reached at about 6.5 miles. Explore the site of a former lookout tower and some unusual fence-post formations used in a snow experiment. Return the way you came. Tighten those laces for the trip down. Be sure to pack plenty of water on this walk. You'll need it; water sources on the upper trail are iffy at best in the summer.

Location: East of Prineville in the Ochoco National Forest; see Northeast Oregon Map 5, grid f6.

User Groups: Hikers and dogs. No horses or mountain bikes are allowed. No wheelchair facilities.

Permits: A federal Northwest Forest Pass, $5 per day or $30 annually, is required to park at the trailhead. Passes are available from ranger stations and many private vendors, online at website: www.wta.org, or by calling 800/270-7504.

Maps: For a map of Ochoco National Forest, contact the Nature of the Northwest Information Center, 800 Northeast Oregon Street, Suite 177, Portland, OR 97232; 503/872-2750. Ask the USGS for topographic maps of the Lookout Mountain and Gerow Butte areas.

Directions: From Prineville drive about 16 miles east on U.S. 26 and veer right at signs for the Ochoco Creek Ranger Station. Continue about eight miles northeast on Forest Service Road 22 to Ochoco Creek Campground; the trailhead is in the day-use parking lot.

Contact: Ochoco National Forest, 3160 Northeast Third Street, P.O. Box 490, Prineville, OR 97754; 541/416-6500.

60 Foree Loop
0.5 mi/0.5 hr

Fossil and dinosaur enthusiasts will love this trail, as it loops through a small section of lava flows and provides great, up-close looks at the remains of creatures that died as long as 25 million years ago. The thick basalt lava covered this area following a score of massive volcanic eruptions. Most of the species trapped in the lava flows are long extinct or have changed dramatically in the intervening millennia. The route is flat, and the trail is well maintained.

The basaltic rock is very abrasive, so wear sturdy shoes while hiking. Also, please stay on the trail, because the fossils trapped in the rock are very delicate. It is illegal to remove any fossil remains.

Location: West of Dayville in John Day Fossil Beds National Monument; see Northeast Oregon Map 6, grid c3.

User Groups: Hikers and dogs. No horses or mountain bikes are allowed. No wheelchair facilities.

Permits: A federal Northwest Forest Pass, $5 per day or $30 annually, is required to park at the trailhead. Passes are available from ranger stations and many private vendors, online at website: www.wta.org, or by calling 800/270-7504.

Maps: For a trail information report, contact John Day Fossil Beds National Monument at 541/575-0721 or 541/987-2333. For a map of Umatilla National Forest, contact Nature of the Northwest Information Center, 800 Northeast Oregon Street, Suite 177, Portland, OR 97232; 503/872-2750. Ask the USGS for a topographic map of the Mount Misery area.

Directions: From Dayville drive five miles west on U.S. 26 and turn right (north) onto Highway 19. Drive a short distance to the scenic pullout signed for Foree Deposits. The trailhead is on the right.

Contact: John Day Fossil Beds National Monument, 420 West Main Street, John Day, OR 97845; 541/575-0721 or 541/987-2333.

61 Flood of Fire
0.5 mi/0.5 hr

A long, high bridge offers stunning views down into the John Day Valley and across the moonscape of the lava beds. More than 25 million years ago, basaltic lava boiled out of fissures in the earth and spread over miles. Countless animals of all sizes were trapped by the liquid rock and are preserved today as fossils in the abrasive rock. The John Day River cut a deep canyon through those layers of lava and exposed the various levels, as well as some of the fossilized remains that lie within. This short, flat trail offers spectacular views of all of this ancient destruction.

The basaltic rock is very abrasive, so wear sturdy shoes while hiking. Also, please stay on the trail, because the fossils trapped in the rock are very delicate. It is illegal to remove any fossil remains.

Location: West of Dayville in John Day Fossil Beds National Monument; see Northeast Oregon Map 6, grid d4.

User Groups: Hikers and dogs. No horses or mountain bikes. No wheelchair facilities.

Permits: A federal Northwest Forest Pass, $5 per day or $30 annually, is required to park at the trailhead. Passes are available from ranger stations and many private vendors, online at website: www.wta.org, or by calling 800/270-7504.

Maps: For a trail information report, contact John Day Fossil Beds National Monument at 541/575-0721 or 541/987-2333. For a map of Umatilla National Forest, contact Nature of the Northwest Information Center, 800 Northeast Oregon Street, Suite 177, Portland, OR 97232; 503/872-2750. Ask the USGS for a topographic map of the Mount Misery area.

Directions: From Dayville drive five miles west on U.S. 26 and turn right (north) onto Highway 19. Drive a short distance to the scenic pullout signed Foree Deposits. The trailhead is on the right.

Contact: John Day Fossil Beds National Monument, 420 West Main Street, John Day, OR 97845; 541/575-0721 or 541/987-2333.

62 Blue Basin Overlook
3.0 mi/3.0 hrs

Most of the trails in the lava beds are short and close to roads. But this longer, more primitive trail offers unbeatable views of the deep Blue Basin lava field and the blue-black valley of the John Day River. The route is hot and dry (don't expect to find much shade unless you bring your own), so carry plenty of water and sunscreen. The route also goes up and down a few rises, so you work a little harder than you would on other trails in the area, but again, it's worth it. This is one of the best places to see the 25-million-year-old fossil beds.

The basaltic rock is very abrasive, so wear sturdy shoes while hiking. Also, please stay on the trail, because the fossils trapped in the rock are very delicate. It is illegal to remove any fossil remains.

Location: West of Dayville in John Day Fossil Beds National Monument; see Northeast Oregon Map 6, grid d3.

User Groups: Hikers and dogs. No horses or mountain bikes are allowed. No wheelchair facilities.

Permits: A federal Northwest Forest Pass, $5 per day or $30 annually, is required to park at the trailhead. Passes are available from ranger stations and many private vendors, online at website: www.wta.org, or by calling 800/270-7504.

Maps: For a trail information report, contact John Day Fossil Beds National Monument at 541/575-0721 or 541/987-2333. For a map of Umatilla National Forest, contact Nature of the Northwest Information Center, 800 Northeast Oregon Street, Suite 177, Portland, OR 97232; 503/872-2750. Ask the USGS for a topographic map of the Mount Misery area.

Directions: From Dayville drive five miles west on U.S. 26 and turn right (north) onto Highway 19. Drive a short distance to the scenic pullout signed Foree Deposits. The trailhead is on the right.

Contact: John Day Fossil Beds National Monument,

420 West Main Street, John Day, OR 97845; 541/575-0721 or 541/987-2333.

63 South Prong
18.0 mi/1.0–2.0 days

This trail enters the north edge of the wilderness area and emerges from the south side, cutting through the eastern half in only nine miles. Climbing from the trailhead, the route parallels Payten Creek for several miles, offering bountiful views of the wild stream. After passing Pup Springs the trail climbs over the ridgetop, past Sundstrom Place, and descends into Black Canyon. The route then passes Black Creek, climbs the south wall, and provides stunning views of the whole Black Canyon. From the canyon rim the trail continues south, descending along Pronghorn Creek to the Mud Springs Campground.

If you have an extra vehicle, park one at Mud Springs and avoid the long backtracking hike.
Location: West of John Day in Ochoco National Forest within the Black Canyon Wilderness; see Northeast Oregon Map 6, grid e1.
User Groups: Hikers, dogs, horses, and mountain bikes. No wheelchair facilities.
Permits: A federal Northwest Forest Pass, $5 per day or $30 annually, is required to park at the trailhead. Passes are available from ranger stations and many private vendors, online at website: www.wta.org, or by calling 800/270-7504.
Maps: For a trail information report, contact the Paulina Ranger District at 541/477-6900. For a map of Ochoco National Forest, contact Nature of the Northwest Information Center, 800 Northeast Oregon Street, Suite 177, Portland, OR 97232; 503/872-2750. Ask the USGS for topographic maps of the Day Basin and Wolf Mountain areas.
Directions: From John Day drive about 45 miles west on U.S. 26 to Whiskey Creek and

the junction with Forest Service Road 12. Turn left (south) and continue about 18 miles to Forest Service Road 38. Turn left (east) and drive a few miles to the Cottonwood Trailhead, on the right. To reach the second trailhead at Mud Springs Campground, turn off Forest Service Road 38 about 10 miles before Cottonwood Campground and bear right onto Forest Service Road 5810. Continue four miles to the junction with Forest Service Road 5820. Turn right and drive about four miles south to Forest Service Road 200. Turn right and continue to Mud Springs Campground and the trailhead at the road's end.
Contact: Ochoco National Forest, Paulina Ranger District, 171500 Beaver Creek Road, Paulina, OR 97751-9706; 541/477-6900.

64 Black Canyon
24.0 mi/2.0 days

A stunning river hike, this trail bisects the wilderness area as it follows Black Creek downstream and through the heart of Black Canyon. Bighorn sheep and mountain goats roam this wild valley; eagles and hawks hunt from the sky above. The trail passes through Owl Creek Meadows, a broad field of wildflowers and wildlife. Deer and elk mingle in the meadows, browsing on the rich grasses and flowers. From the meadows the trail drops to the riverbank, where it stays for the rest of the journey. The creek is teeming with wild trout and is home to scores of birds and small mammals. Camp anywhere along the creek.
Location: West of John Day in Ochoco National Forest within the Black Canyon Wilderness; see Northeast Oregon Map 6, grid e1.
User Groups: Hikers, dogs, horses, and mountain bikes. No wheelchair facilities.
Permits: A federal Northwest Forest Pass, $5 per day or $30 annually, is required to park at the trailhead. Passes are available from

ranger stations and many private vendors, online at website: www.wta.org, or by calling 800/270-7504.

Maps: For a trail information report, contact the Paulina Ranger District at 541/477-6900. For a map of Ochoco National Forest, contact Nature of the Northwest Information Center, 800 Northeast Oregon Street, Suite 177, Portland, OR 97232; 503/872-2750. Ask the USGS for topographic maps of the Day Basin and Wolf Mountain areas.

Directions: From John Day drive about 45 miles west on U.S. 26 to Whiskey Creek and the junction with Forest Service Road 12. Turn left (south) and continue about 18 miles to Forest Service Road 38. Turn left, continue east on Forest Service Road 38 for about eight miles, and turn right onto Forest Service Road 5820. Drive south to the trailhead on the left.

Contact: Ochoco National Forest, Paulina Ranger District, 171500 Beaver Creek Road, Paulina, OR 97751-9706; 541/477-6900.

65 Cedar Grove
2.0 mi/1.0 hr

The Cedar Botanical Area is one of the only cedar groves within several hundred miles, and you can explore it on this trail. The rare (for eastern Oregon) grove is nestled in a steep, rocky canyon. Even if off-trail scrambling were allowed, it would be nearly impossible to maneuver in the thick trees and rocky slopes. It's better to stick to the well-made path and just enjoy the fragrant old trees as you hike along the easy grade.

Location: Southwest of John Day in Malheur National Forest; see Northeast Oregon Map 6, grid f5.

User Groups: Hikers and dogs. No horses or mountain bikes are allowed. No wheelchair facilities.

Permits: A federal Northwest Forest Pass, $5 per day or $30 annually, is required to park at the trailhead. Passes are available from ranger stations and many private vendors, online at website: www.wta.org, or by calling 800/270-7504.

Maps: For a trail information report, contact the Bear Valley Ranger District at 541/575-2110. For a map of Malheur National Forest, contact Nature of the Northwest Information Center, 800 Northeast Oregon Street, Suite 177, Portland, OR 97232; 503/872-2750. Ask the USGS for a topographic map of the Big Weasel Springs area.

Directions: From John Day drive 18 miles west on U.S. 26 and turn left (south) onto Fields Creek Road/Forest Service Road 21. Drive nine miles south on Fields Creek Road and turn right (west) onto Forest Service Road 2150. Follow this road for five miles to the trailhead.

Contact: Malheur National Forest, 431 Patterson Bridge Road, John Day, OR 97845; 541/575-3000.

66 McClellan Mountain
22.4 mi/2.0 days

A back route to the high, scenic McClellan Mountain (elevation 7,042 feet), this trail lacks wilderness designation, but it's so wild that the Oregon State Fish and Wildlife Commission has snatched it up to use as a bighorn sheep study area. You'll probably see the sheep if you look for them. Camping is good on the east flank of the mountain, near the headwaters of McClellan Creek.

Location: Southwest of John Day in Malheur National Forest; see Northeast Oregon Map 6, grid f6.

User Groups: Hikers and dogs. No horses or mountain bikes are allowed. No wheelchair facilities.

Permits: A federal Northwest Forest Pass, $5 per day or $30 annually, is required to park at the trailhead. Passes are available from ranger stations and many private vendors, online at website: www.wta.org, or by calling 800/270-7504.

Maps: For a trail information report, contact the Bear Valley Ranger District at 541/575-2110. For a map of Malheur National Forest, contact Nature of the Northwest Information Center, 800 Northeast Oregon Street, Suite 177, Portland, OR 97232; 503/872-2750. Ask the USGS for topographic maps of the Big Weasel Springs and McClellan Mountain areas.

Directions: From John Day drive 18 miles west on U.S. 26 and turn left (south) onto Fields Creek Road/Forest Service Road 21. Drive 4.5 miles south and then turn left (east) onto Forest Service Road 115. Drive 1.5 miles east on this road to the trailhead.

Contact: Malheur National Forest, 431 Patterson Bridge Road, John Day, OR 97845; 541/575-3000.

67 Field's Peak
8.0 mi/4.0 hrs

If high, lonely peaks are your idea of fun, look no farther than this trail. The route leads over Field's Peak, which at 7,400 feet is the highest point in Malheur National Forest. But since the trail starts at 6,600 feet, you don't need to climb much to get up high. The trail rises through a dry forest of spruce and pine to the summit, which offers fantastic views of the entire John Day Valley and McClellan Mountain.

Location: Southwest of John Day in Malheur National Forest; see Northeast Oregon Map 6, grid f7.

User Groups: Hikers and dogs. No horses or mountain bikes are allowed. No wheelchair facilities.

Permits: A federal Northwest Forest Pass, $5 per day or $30 annually, is required to park at the trailhead. Passes are available from ranger stations and many private vendors, online at website: www.wta.org, or by calling 800/270-7504.

Maps: For a trail information report, contact the Bear Valley Ranger District at 541/575-2110. For a map of Malheur National Forest, contact Nature of the Northwest Information Center, 800 Northeast Oregon Street, Suite 177, Portland, OR 97232; 503/872-2750. Ask the USGS for a topographic map of the Big Weasel Springs area.

Directions: From John Day drive 18 miles west on U.S. 26 and turn left (south) onto Fields Creek Road/Forest Service Road 21. Drive 4.5 miles south and then turn left (east) onto Forest Service Road 115. Drive 1.5 miles east on this road to the trailhead.

Contact: Malheur National Forest, 431 Patterson Bridge Road, John Day, OR 97845; 541/575-3000.

68 Riley Creek
4.4 mi/2.2 hrs

A thick forest of second-growth lodgepole pine and alder closes in around this trail, making a dark corridor along Riley Creek. The route is interesting but offers few scenic views. If you need a glimpse of wide-open spaces, this trail merges with the McClellan Mountain Trail (see hike in this chapter), but you have to climb 2,500 feet up, adding several more miles to the hike. It's better to turn around at the junction and return the way you came.

Location: Southwest of John Day in Malheur National Forest; see Northeast Oregon Map 6, grid f7.

User Groups: Hikers and dogs. No horses or mountain bikes are allowed. No wheelchair facilities.

Permits: A federal Northwest Forest Pass, $5 per day or $30 annually, is required to park at the trailhead. Passes are available from ranger stations and many private vendors, online at website: www.wta.org, or by calling 800/270-7504.

Maps: For a trail information report, contact the Bear Valley Ranger District at 541/575-2110. For a map of Malheur National Forest, contact Nature of the Northwest Information Center, 800 Northeast Oregon Street, Suite 177, Portland, OR 97232; 503/872-2750. Ask the USGS for a topographic map of the Mc-Clellan Mountain area.

Directions: From John Day drive about 15 miles south on U.S. 395 to the junction with County Road 63. Turn right (west) onto County Road 63 and drive six miles before turning right (north) onto Forest Service Road 21. Follow Forest Service Road 21 about seven miles to Forest Service Road 2190. Turn right and drive to the road's end and the trailhead.

Contact: Malheur National Forest, 431 Patterson Bridge Road, John Day, OR 97845; 541/575-3000.

69 Myrtle Creek
15.8 mi/1.0–2.0 days

Myrtle Creek is a lovely stream that yields strong, tough rainbow trout from deep, cold pools. The trail follows this river, explores various small side canyons—the first found within five miles of the trailhead—and offers great views of a high desert/forest ecosystem. The side trails up the adjoining canyons can add anywhere from a few hundred yards to several miles to your trip, so explorations are limited only by your endurance and available time. You really have to experience this rough, dusty landscape to appreciate it.

Location: North of Burns in Malheur National Forest; see Northeast Oregon Map 6, grid g8.

User Groups: Hikers, dogs, horses, and mountain bikes. No wheelchair facilities.

Permits: A federal Northwest Forest Pass, $5 per day or $30 annually, is required to park at the trailhead. Passes are available from ranger stations and many private vendors, online at website: www.wta.org, or by calling 800/270-7504.

Maps: For a trail information report, contact the Burns Ranger District at 541/573-7292. For a map of Malheur National Forest, contact Nature of the Northwest Information Center, 800 Northeast Oregon Street, Suite 177, Portland, OR 97232; 503/872-2750. Ask the USGS for a topographic map of the Myrtle Park Meadows area.

Directions: From Burns drive about 19 miles north on U.S. 395 to the junction with Forest Service Road 31. Turn left (west) and take Forest Service Road 31 for 15 miles to Forest Service Road 3100-226. Turn left and drive to the road's end and the trailhead.

Contact: Malheur National Forest, Burns Ranger District, HC-74, Box 12870, Hines, OR 97738; 541/573-4300.

70 West Myrtle Creek
3.8 mi/1.5 hrs

Dropping into the beautiful Myrtle Creek drainage, this busy route is shorter but steeper than the main Myrtle Creek Trail (see hike above) and accesses the river at the midpoint. The shorter route cuts your length of enjoyment but provides a little more diversity, as you're higher up. As the trail descends from the rim, you get fine views out over the river basin.

Location: North of Burns in Malheur National Forest; see Northeast Oregon Map 6, grid h8.

User Groups: Hikers, dogs, horses, and mountain bikes. No wheelchair facilities.

Permits: A federal Northwest Forest Pass, $5 per day or $30 annually, is required to park at the trailhead. Passes are available from ranger stations and many private vendors, online at website: www.wta.org, or by calling 800/270-7504.

Maps: For a trail information report, contact the Burns Ranger District at 541/573-7292. For a map of Malheur National Forest, contact Nature of the Northwest Information Center, 800 Northeast Oregon Street, Suite 177, Portland, OR 97232; 503/872-2750. Ask the USGS for a topographic map of the Myrtle Park Meadows area.

Directions: From Burns drive about 19 miles north on U.S. 395 to the junction with Forest Service Road 31. Turn left (west) onto Forest Service Road 31 and drive 19 miles to Forest Service Road 37. Turn left, drive four miles to Forest Service Road 440, and turn left. Continue to the road's end and the trailhead.

Contact: Malheur National Forest, Burns Ranger District, HC-74, Box 12870, Hines, OR 97738; 541/573-4300.

71 Battle Creek
7.8 mi/3.9 hrs

Following the course of Battle Creek, this heavily used trail is popular with equestrians and mountain bikers, as well as some trail motorcyclists. Still, on a midweek visit you could find yourself alone on the trail with a small herd of mule deer, a few elk, and maybe a pair of falcons flying overhead. The rough and rutted trail cuts through thick second-growth forest and crosses the creek several times.

Location: East of Dale in Umatilla National Forest; see Northeast Oregon Map 7, grid a3.

User Groups: Hikers, dogs, horses, and mountain bikes. No wheelchair facilities.

Permits: A federal Northwest Forest Pass, $5 per day or $30 annually, is required to park at the trailhead. Passes are available from ranger stations and many private vendors, online at website: www.wta.org, or by calling 800/270-7504.

Maps: For a trail information report, contact the North Fork John Day Ranger District at 541/427-3231. For a map of Umatilla National Forest, contact Nature of the Northwest Information Center, 800 Northeast Oregon Street, Suite 177, Portland, OR 97232; 503/872-2750. Ask the USGS for topographic maps of the Desolation Butte Northwest and Desolation Butte Southwest areas.

Directions: From Dale drive 10 miles east on Forest Service Road 10 to a junction with Forest Service Road 1010. Turn left onto Forest Service Road 1010 and continue to Forest Service Road 130. Turn right (south) and drive to the trailhead at the beginning of the first broad meadow.

Contact: Umatilla National Forest, North Fork John Day Ranger District, P.O. Box 158, Ukiah, OR 97880; 541/427-3231.

72 Big Creek Trail
12.6 mi/6.3 hrs

This gentle trail follows the cold, rushing waters of Big Creek as it drops just under 2,000 feet in elevation. The vibrant old pine and spruce forest in the valley and the turbulent blue waters of Big Creek make this a very enjoyable valley hike. You have to cross the creek twice and may have to ford those places if the footlogs are washed out.

Look for deer, elk, beaver, raccoons, and grouse along the way. You may also see scratch marks left high up on the big pines by the black bears that prowl this forest. Let those marks serve as a reminder to bear-bag your food and to practice other bear-smart camping techniques.

Location: Southeast of Ukiah in Umatilla National Forest within the North Fork John Day Wilderness; see Northeast Oregon Map 7, grid a3.

User Groups: Hikers, dogs, and horses. No mountain bikes are allowed. No wheelchair facilities.

Permits: A federal Northwest Forest Pass, $5 per day or $30 annually, is required to park at the trailhead. Passes are available from ranger stations and many private vendors, online at website: www.wta.org, or by calling 800/270-7504.

Maps: For a trail information report, contact the North Fork John Day Ranger District at 541/427-3231. For a map of Umatilla National Forest, contact Nature of the Northwest Information Center, 800 Northeast Oregon Street, Suite 177, Portland, OR 97232; 503/872-2750. Ask the USGS for a topographic map of the Desolation Butte Northwest area.

Directions: From Ukiah drive 24 miles southeast on Forest Service Road 52 to Big Creek Meadows and Forest Service Road 5225. Turn right and drive about 200 feet before turning right onto Forest Service Road 5225-020. Drive to the road's end and the trailhead.

Contact: Umatilla National Forest, North Fork John Day Ranger District, P.O. Box 158, Ukiah, OR 97880; 541/427-3231.

73 South Winom
6.6 mi/3.3 hrs

Looping around the southern edge of Winom Meadows, this trail skirts the wilderness boundary for nearly a mile before entering the protected area. The route leads gradually down the Winom Creek Valley, staying within a stone's throw of the water at all times. That makes for some pretty scenery and pleasant sound effects, but it also means the trail is prone to washing out. These washouts generally pose little problem for hikers, provided care is taken when crossing them. Look for elk and deer on the valley walls and in the small forest clearings along the route. The trail ends at a junction with the Big Creek Trail. At the junction turn around and retrace your steps upstream to the trailhead.

You can make a loop trip by combining this route with the Big Creek Trail (see hike above). To do so requires either a shuttle car or a 1.5-mile road walk between the two trailheads.

Location: Southeast of Ukiah in Umatilla National Forest within the North Fork John Day Wilderness; see Northeast Oregon Map 7, grid a3.

User Groups: Hikers, dogs, and horses. No mountain bikes are allowed. No wheelchair facilities.

Permits: A federal Northwest Forest Pass, $5 per day or $30 annually, is required to park at the trailhead. Passes are available from ranger stations and many private vendors, online at website: www.wta.org, or by calling 800/270-7504.

Maps: For a trail information report, contact the North Fork John Day Ranger District at 541/427-3231. For a map of Umatilla National Forest, contact Nature of the Northwest Information Center, 800 Northeast Oregon Street, Suite 177, Portland, OR 97232; 503/872-2750. Ask the USGS for a topographic map of the Desolation Butte Northwest areas.

Directions: From Ukiah drive 23 miles southeast on the Blue Mountain Scenic Byway/Forest Service Road 52 to the junction with Forest Service Road 52-440. Turn right (south) onto Forest Service Road 52-440 and continue one mile to the trailhead on the left side of the road, just past the Winom Creek Bridge.

Contact: Umatilla National Forest, North Fork John Day Ranger District, P.O. Box 158, Ukiah, OR 97880; 541/427-3231.

74 Forks
12.6 mi/6.3 hrs

Three rivers—the South Fork John Day, Meadow Creek, and White Creek—merge at the trailhead to give the area its name, but the trail soon leaves them all behind. The route climbs steeply to the ridge crest high above South Fork and rides that ridge south almost all the way to Silver Butte. The ridge turns before the butte is reached, however, and the trail ends at the junction with the rough jeep road that leads to the butte top. You don't really need to complete the road walk to the butte as the views from the trail are as good as any you find on Silver Butte. We recommend simply turning around and retracing your steps from the jeep track. That way you double your viewing pleasure because you are able to see all the vistas to the north that you missed as you hiked south.

Location: Southeast of Ukiah in Umatilla National Forest within the North Fork Day Wilderness; see Northeast Oregon Map 7, grid a4.

User Groups: Hikers, dogs, and horses. No mountain bikes are allowed. No wheelchair facilities.

Permits: A federal Northwest Forest Pass, $5 per day or $30 annually, is required to park at the trailhead. Passes are available from ranger stations and many private vendors, online at website: www.wta.org, or by calling 800/270-7504.

Maps: For a trail information report, contact the North Fork John Day Ranger District at 541/427-3231. For a map of Umatilla National Forest, contact Nature of the Northwest

Information Center, 800 Northeast Oregon Street, Suite 177, Portland, OR 97232; 503/872-2750. Ask the USGS for a topographic map of the Desolation Butte Southwest area.

Directions: From Ukiah drive 24 miles southeast on Forest Service Road 52 to Big Creek Meadows and Forest Service Road 5225. Turn right onto this road and drive two miles to the trailhead on the right.

Contact: Umatilla National Forest, North Fork John Day Ranger District, P.O. Box 158, Ukiah, OR 97880; 541/427-3231.

75 Silver Butte
9.0 mi/4.5 hrs

This route drops steeply for 4.5 miles from Silver Butte to the banks of the North Fork John Day River. The dry, hot trail cuts through the old pine and spruce forest as it angles down the long ridgeline and then plummets sharply through a series of switchbacks into the valley. The views are good from Silver Butte near the trailhead, but they quickly disappear as you enter the thick forest and work your way down the ridge.

Location: Southeast of Ukiah in Umatilla National Forest within the North Fork Day Wilderness; see Northeast Oregon Map 7, grid a4.

User Groups: Hikers, dogs, and horses. No mountain bikes are allowed. No wheelchair facilities.

Permits: A federal Northwest Forest Pass, $5 per day or $30 annually, is required to park at the trailhead. Passes are available from ranger stations and many private vendors, online at website: www.wta.org, or by calling 800/270-7504.

Maps: For a trail information report, contact the North Fork John Day Ranger District at 541/427-3231. For a map of Umatilla National Forest, contact Nature of the Northwest

Information Center, 800 Northeast Oregon Street, Suite 177, Portland, OR 97232; 503/872-2750. Ask the USGS for topographic maps of the Desolation Butte Southeast and Desolation Butte Northeast area.

Directions: From Ukiah drive 24 miles southeast on the Blue Mountain Scenic Byway/Forest Service Road 52 to Big Creek Meadows. Turn right at the meadows onto Forest Service Road 5225 and then drive to the road's end and the trailhead.

Contact: Umatilla National Forest, North Fork John Day Ranger District, P.O. Box 158, Ukiah, OR 97880; 541/427-3231.

76 Glade Creek
14.0 mi/7.0 hrs

This trail sticks to the thick pine and fir forest along the edge of the wilderness area, traversing a long ridge wall before dropping well into the wilderness area and slanting east toward the North Fork John Day River. The final leg of the journey down to the water is through a steep section of switchbacks that provide splendid views of the North Fork John Day Valley. The river, designated a Wild and Scenic River, is spectacular with its rough-and-tumble waters cascading both over dark basalt rock and under the shadowing branches of massive ponderosa pines, spruce, and the occasional fir. With a little patience, anglers should be able to catch a magnificent trout, and wildlife lovers stand a good chance of seeing deer, elk, beavers, and a variety of birds and small mammals.

Location: East of Dale in Umatilla National Forest within the North Fork John Day Wilderness; see Northeast Oregon Map 7, grid a3.

User Groups: Hikers, dogs, and horses. No mountain bikes are allowed. No wheelchair facilities.

Permits: A federal Northwest Forest Pass, $5 per day or $30 annually, is required to park at the trailhead. Passes are available from ranger stations and many private vendors, online at website: www.wta.org, or by calling 800/270-7504.

Maps: For a trail information report, contact the North Fork John Day Ranger District at 541/427-3231. For a map of Umatilla National Forest, contact Nature of the Northwest Information Center, 800 Northeast Oregon Street, Suite 177, Portland, OR 97232; 503/872-2750. Ask the USGS for a topographic map of the Desolation Butte Northwest area.

Directions: From Dale drive 10 miles east on Forest Service Road 10 to a junction with Forest Service Road 1010. Turn left onto Forest Service Road 1010 and continue 10 more miles to the trailhead on the left (north) side of the road.

Contact: Umatilla National Forest, North Fork John Day Ranger District, P.O. Box 158, Ukiah, OR 97880; 541/427-3231.

77 Lake Creek Ridge
9.8 mi/4.9 hrs

Following a rocky ridgeline, this route has a few steep pitches and is dry and dusty. It's also very enjoyable, as it is one of the few trails in this wilderness that stays high up on the ridges instead of following creeks through valley bottoms. Still, this wilderness is about wild water, and even this trail can't ignore that. As you near the east end, the trail drops quickly to a junction with the Granite Creek Trail (see hike in this chapter) near Snowshoe Springs. Enjoy the cool waters of the spring, and maybe take a quarter-mile side trip down the Granite Creek Trail to the North Fork River before retracing your steps up the steep, dry ridge.

This is rattlesnake country. Keep an eye and ear alert at

all times for the buzzing serpents; they frequently sun themselves on the rocky ridges.

Location: East of Dale in Umatilla National Forest within the North Fork John Day Wilderness; see Northeast Oregon Map 7, grid a4.

User Groups: Hikers, dogs, and horses. No mountain bikes are allowed. No wheelchair facilities.

Permits: A federal Northwest Forest Pass, $5 per day or $30 annually, is required to park at the trailhead. Passes are available from ranger stations and many private vendors, online at website: www.wta.org, or by calling 800/270-7504.

Maps: For a trail information report, contact the North Fork John Day Ranger District at 541/427-3231. For a map of Umatilla National Forest, contact Nature of the Northwest Information Center, 800 Northeast Oregon Street, Suite 177, Portland, OR 97232; 503/872-2750. Ask the USGS for a topographic map of Desolation Butte Lookout.

Directions: From Dale drive about 10 miles east on Forest Service Road 10 to a junction with Forest Service Road 1010. Turn left (north) onto this road and drive 14.7 miles to the trailhead on the left.

Contact: Umatilla National Forest, North Fork John Day Ranger District, P.O. Box 158, Ukiah, OR 97880; 541/427-3231.

78 Granite Creek
6.8 mi/3.4 hrs

Beautiful old pine forests, crystal-clear springwater, herds of deer and elk, trees full of grouse, huckleberries, mushrooms, and access to prime trout water are all bonuses of this trail. The route drops alongside the tumbling waters of Granite Creek as it rushes toward its junction with the North Fork John Day River. The trail down the valley is gentle, dropping just 400 feet in nearly four miles,

and affords plenty of opportunity to admire the stunning old forest as well as the cold water of the creek. The trail passes Snowshoe Springs before finally hitting the south bank of the North Fork John Day River. Anglers find plenty of big rainbow trout in the officially designated Wild and Scenic River, as well as a few German browns and maybe even some native cutthroat.

Location: North of Granite in Umatilla National Forest within the North Fork John Day Wilderness; see Northeast Oregon Map 7, grid a6.

User Groups: Hikers, dogs, and horses. No mountain bikes are allowed. No wheelchair facilities.

Permits: A federal Northwest Forest Pass, $5 per day or $30 annually, is required to park at the trailhead. Passes are available from ranger stations and many private vendors, online at website: www.wta.org, or by calling 800/270-7504.

Maps: For a trail information report, contact the North Fork John Day Ranger District at 541/427-3231. For a map of Umatilla National Forest, contact Nature of the Northwest Information Center, 800 Northeast Oregon Street, Suite 177, Portland, OR 97232; 503/872-2750. Ask the USGS for a topographic map of the Desolation Butte Southeast area.

Directions: From Granite drive 1.5 miles west on Forest Service Road 10 and turn right (north) onto Forest Service Road 1035. Continue three miles north to the road's end and the trailhead.

Contact: Umatilla National Forest, North Fork John Day Ranger District, P.O. Box 158, Ukiah, OR 97880; 541/427-3231.

79 North Fork John Day River
45.8 mi/3.0–4.0 days

Although long, this hike is spectacularly beautiful and very easy to walk. The route follows the shore of the North Fork John Day River across the breadth of the wilderness area, a stretch that was recently designated a Wild and Scenic River. This double layer of federal protection is fitting, as this is one of the wildest, most scenic, and most enjoyable rivers in the Pacific Northwest. Hikers, horseback riders, and trout anglers all swarm to this gentle trail for a variety of reasons. Anglers love the unlimited exposure to a top-notch trout stream. Hikers and equestrians enjoy the splendid scenery and gentle grade—the elevation drops just 1,900 feet over the route's 22-mile length. Pit toilets, numerous maintained campsites, and a well-kept trail all make backpackers comfortable and reduce their impact on this pristine river drainage. Look for elk, deer, black bears, and cougars (though you will probably only see the tracks of these elusive animals), as well as hawks, kingfishers, killdeer, eagles, ravens, Stellar's jays, whistle jacks, and other birds. The number of small mammal and bird species that thrive in this wilderness area is staggering, and they all contribute to the wonderful atmosphere.

With some planning and teamwork, it's possible—and recommended—to shuttle a vehicle to the end of the trail to avoid a long, backtracking trip out. Although the drive between trailheads is long, the roads are in good condition and a shuttle trip shouldn't take more than a couple of hours at most. That is probably worth the effort in order to save 12 or 14 hours of hiking back the way you came.

Location: Southeast of Ukiah in Umatilla National Forest within the North Fork John Day Wilderness; see Northeast Oregon Map 7, grid a6.

User Groups: Hikers, dogs, and horses. No mountain bikes are allowed. No wheelchair facilities.

Permits: A federal Northwest Forest Pass, $5 per day or $30 annually, is required to park at the trailhead. Passes are available from ranger stations and many private vendors, online at website: www.wta.org, or by calling 800/270-7504.

Maps: For a trail information report, contact the North Fork John Day Ranger District at 541/427-3231. For a map of Umatilla National Forest, contact Nature of the Northwest Information Center, 800 Northeast Oregon Street, Suite 177, Portland, OR 97232; 503/872-2750. Ask the USGS for a topographic map of Desolation Butte Lookout.

Directions: From Ukiah drive about 40 miles southeast on the Blue Mountain Scenic Byway/Forest Service Road 52 to the North Fork John Day Campground. A short access road at the northwest edge of the camp leads to the trailhead. Parking is available at the campground. The west end of the trail is accessible from Dale. Drive east on Forest Service Road 55 to a three-way fork. Follow the center route, Forest Service Road 5506, to the road's end and the trailhead.

Contact: Umatilla National Forest, North Fork John Day Ranger District, P.O. Box 158, Ukiah, OR 97880; 541/427-3231.

80 Crane Creek
10.2 mi/5.1 hrs

A large herd of elk winters in the valley and can be found browsing throughout the area all year long. The trail drops from the trailhead and follows the creek downstream to its junction with the North Fork John Day River— a designated Wild and Scenic River. Crane Creek is generally too small and shallow to support catchable trout, but the John Day is one of the great trout streams in this part of the state. Release what you don't plan to eat in a single meal in order to preserve a great fishery. Autumn is a pretty time to visit the area, but it can be crowded then. Elk hunters love this trail, so wear bright colors in the fall.

Location: North of Granite in Umatilla National Forest within the North Fork John Day Wilderness; see Northeast Oregon Map 7, grid a7.

User Groups: Hikers, dogs, and horses. No mountain bikes are allowed. No wheelchair facilities.

Permits: A federal Northwest Forest Pass, $5 per day or $30 annually, is required to park at the trailhead. Passes are available from ranger stations and many private vendors, online at website: www.wta.org, or by calling 800/270-7504.

Maps: For a trail information report, contact the North Fork John Day Ranger District at 541/427-3231. For a map of Umatilla National Forest, contact Nature of the Northwest Information Center, 800 Northeast Oregon Street, Suite 177, Portland, OR 97232; 503/872-2750. Ask the USGS for a topographic map of the Trout Meadows area.

Directions: From Granite drive five miles north on Forest Service Road 73. Find the trailhead on the left.

Contact: Umatilla National Forest, North Fork John Day Ranger District, P.O. Box 158, Ukiah, OR 97880; 541/427-3231.

81 Squaw Rock
18.6 mi/2.0 days

Rolling through the Vinegar Hill-Indian Rock Scenic Area, this trail offers spectacular scenery, as well as access to several other wonderful trails. From the ridge crest you can look out over the North Fork John Day Wilderness to the north and the Strawberry Mountain Wilderness to the south, not to mention all the beautiful summits, buttes, and valleys in between. The wildflower meadows that carpet the route are filled with a wide assortment of blooms—nearly every western mountain flower is represented—and the local wildlife populations include mule and white-tailed deer, elk, mountain goats, black bears, cougars, bobcats, grouse, hawks, eagles, ravens, and much more. The scenic views, flora, and fauna all combine to make this one of the best wilderness-style trails outside the officially designated wilderness area.

Location: North of John Day in Malheur National Forest; see Northeast Oregon Map 7, grid b2.

User Groups: Hikers, dogs, and horses. No mountain bikes are allowed. No wheelchair facilities.

Permits: A federal Northwest Forest Pass, $5 per day or $30 annually, is required to park at the trailhead. Passes are available from ranger stations and many private vendors, online at website: www.wta.org, or by calling 800/270-7504.

Maps: For a trail information report, contact the Long Creek Ranger District at 541/575-3000. For a map of Malheur National Forest, contact Nature of the Northwest Information Center, 800 Northeast Oregon Street, Suite 177, Portland, OR 97232; 503/872-2750. Ask the USGS for a topographic map of Desolation Butte Southwest area.

Directions: From John Day drive east on U.S. 26 to the junction with County Road 18. Turn north on County Road 18 and continue to the Four Corners. Turn right onto Forest Service Road 36 and continue north to the junction with Forest Service Road 45. Follow Forest Service Road 45 north to the trailhead at the forest boundary.

Contact: Malheur National Forest, Long Creek Ranger District, P.O. Box 849, John Day, OR 97845; 541/575-3000.

82 South Fork Desolation
16.2 mi/2.0 days

Climb alongside the Desolation River in a valley that is anything but desolate. The beautiful streamside meadows are dotted both with colorful wildflower blooms and deer and elk that browse lazily. The surrounding summits of Indian Rock, Squaw Rock, Boulder Butte, and Jumpoff Joe Peak loom above. The upper two miles of the route are seldom maintained and can be difficult to follow. Those who accept that challenge, though, find the markings of history on the land: the old hard-rock Portland Mine lies at the end of the trail.

Location: East of Dale in Umatilla National Forest; see Northeast Oregon Map 7, grid b4.

User Groups: Hikers, dogs, and horses. No mountain bikes are allowed. No wheelchair facilities.

Permits: A federal Northwest Forest Pass, $5 per day or $30 annually, is required to park at the trailhead. Passes are available from ranger stations and many private vendors, online at website: www.wta.org, or by calling 800/270-7504.

Maps: For a trail information report, contact the North Fork John Day Ranger District at 541/427-3231. For a map of Umatilla National Forest, contact Nature of the Northwest Information Center, 800 Northeast Oregon Street, Suite 177, Portland, OR 97232; 503/872-2750. Ask the USGS for a topographic map of the Desolation Butte Southwest area.

Directions: From Dale drive 22 miles east on Forest Service Road 10 to the junction with Forest Service Road 45. Turn right (south) onto this road and drive a quarter mile to the trailhead, on the left near the approach to the bridge.

Contact: Umatilla National Forest, North Fork John Day Ranger District, P.O. Box 158, Ukiah, OR 97880; 541/427-3231.

83 Saddle Camp
6.0 mi/3.0 hrs

Skirting the edge of the southern portion of the North Fork John Day Wilderness, this trail gets heavy use. Although not actually within the protected area, the trail does share many of the same characteristics. In fact with the old-growth pine, fir, and spruce forest, abundant wildlife, and pretty, wildflower-filled forest clearings, the only way to tell that this isn't a wilderness route is by looking at the people who use it: from time to time you see mountain bikers and motorcyclists on this trail.

Location: East of Dale in Umatilla National Forest; see Northeast Oregon Map 7, grid b4.

User Groups: Hikers, dogs, horses, and mountain bikes. No wheelchair facilities.

Permits: A federal Northwest Forest Pass, $5 per day or $30 annually, is required to park at the trailhead. Passes are available from ranger stations and many private vendors, online at website: www.wta.org, or by calling 800/270-7504.

Maps: For a trail information report, contact the North Fork John Day Ranger District at 541/427-3231. For a map of Umatilla National Forest, contact Nature of the Northwest Information Center, 800 Northeast Oregon Street, Suite 177, Portland, OR 97232; 503/872-2750. Ask the USGS for a topographic map of the Desolation Butte Southeast area.

Directions: From Dale drive 28 miles east on Forest Service Road 10 to the Olive Lake Campground. Follow Forest Service Road 10-481, a short spur road, past the campground to the trailhead on the east shore of Olive Lake.

Contact: Umatilla National Forest, North Fork John Day Ranger District, P.O. Box 158, Ukiah, OR 97880; 541/427-3231.

84 Crawfish Lake
4.0 mi/2.0 hrs

This trail follows Crawfish Creek as it winds along the northern edge of the wilderness boundary, but it doesn't actually dip into the designated area until it nears the lake at the trail's end. Still, this may as well be wilderness, because the land is wild, scenic, and beautiful. The only non-wilderness thing about this route is the fact that it crosses at least three old logging roads as it climbs into the Elkhorn Range. Old second-growth pine, spruce, and fir line the valley. Near the end of the trail, the path enters a ghostly gray forest of old snags and burned-out trees. In 1986 a fire roared through the area just north of Crawfish Lake, leaving behind a forest of silvery-gray tree trunks that have been stripped of their branches and leaves.

Location: West of Baker City in Wallowa-Whitman National Forest partially within the North Fork John Day Wilderness; see Northeast Oregon Map 7, grid b5.

User Groups: Hikers, dogs, and horses. No mountain bikes are allowed. No wheelchair facilities.

Permits: A federal Northwest Forest Pass, $5 per day or $30 annually, is required to park at the trailhead. Passes are available from ranger stations and many private vendors, online at website: www.wta.org, or by calling 800/270-7504.

Maps: For a trail information report, contact the Baker Ranger District at 541/523-4476. For a map of Wallowa-Whitman National Forest, contact Nature of the Northwest Information Center, 800 Northeast Oregon Street, Suite 177, Portland, OR 97232; 503/872-2750. Ask the USGS for topographic maps of the Crawfish Lake and Anthony Lakes areas.

Directions: From Baker City drive north on U.S. 30 to Haines and turn left (west) onto the Elkhorn Drive Scenic Byway/County Road 1146. Continue about 20 miles on this highway as it enters the national forest and becomes Forest Service Road 73. Drive past the Anthony Lake Campground, turn left onto Forest Service Road 320, and drive to the road's end and the trailhead.

Contact: Wallowa-Whitman National Forest, Baker Ranger District, 3165 10th Street, Baker City, OR 97814; 541/523-4476.

85 Baldy Creek
14.8 mi/1.0–2.0 days

Accessing a number of points, including the remote Baldy Creek drainage, Baldy Lake, several historical hard-rock mines, and an assortment of wildflower-filled meadows and clearings, this trail is a stairway to wilderness heaven. It climbs steeply through spruce, fir, and varied pine forest as it parallels Baldy Creek, crosses several small side streams, and cuts through a few small forest clearings. Look for deer, elk, and a variety of small mammals and birds in these areas. The trail ends near Baldy Lake, a beautiful alpine pool surrounded by towering ridges and peaks. Mount Ireland dominates the skyline. An old side trail leads to that summit, the site of an old forest fire lookout tower, from which the panoramic views are spectacular.

Location: West of Baker City in Wallowa-Whitman National Forest within the North Fork John Day Wilderness; see Northeast Oregon Map 7, grid c5.

User Groups: Hikers, dogs, and horses. No mountain bikes are allowed. No wheelchair facilities.

Permits: A federal Northwest Forest Pass, $5 per day or $30 annually, is required to park at the trailhead. Passes are available from ranger stations and many private vendors, online at website: www.wta.org, or by calling 800/270-7504.

Maps: For a trail information report, contact the Baker Ranger District at 541/523-4476. For a map of Wallowa-Whitman National Forest, contact Nature of the Northwest Information Center, 800 Northeast Oregon Street, Suite 177, Portland, OR 97232; 503/872-2750. Ask the USGS for topographic maps of the Crawfish Lake and Mount Ireland areas.

Directions: From Baker City drive north on U.S. 30 to Haines and turn left (west) onto the Elkhorn Drive Scenic Byway/County Road 1146. Continue about 20 miles on this highway as it enters the national forest and becomes Forest Service Road 73. The trailhead is on the left (south) side of the road, just past where the road nears the banks of the North Fork John Day River.

Contact: Wallowa-Whitman National Forest, Baker Ranger District, 3165 10th Street, Baker City, OR 97814; 541/523-4476.

86 Cunningham Cove
6.6 mi/3.3 hrs

Steep and rough, this trail climbs from the scenic beauty of the North Fork John Day River to Cunningham Saddle on the Elkhorn Crest. Along the way it repeatedly crosses Cunningham Creek and slices through several broad, wildflower-filled meadows. Campsites are available in virtually all of the meadows and clearings; any one of them makes a great place to spend a peaceful night. Still the best is yet to come. If you have the energy and inclination, press on to the trail's end at the saddle. From there you can enjoy the stunning vistas that sweep across the summits of Lee, Angel, and Van Patten Peaks. You also can look down on the beautiful Crawfish Meadows and the crystal-clear, ice-cold waters of Cunningham Creek.

Location: West of Baker City in Wallowa-Whitman National Forest within the North Fork John Day Wilderness; see Northeast Oregon Map 7, grid c5.

User Groups: Hikers, dogs, and horses. No mountain bikes are allowed. No wheelchair facilities.

Permits: A federal Northwest Forest Pass, $5 per day or $30 annually, is required to park at the trailhead. Passes are available from ranger stations and many private vendors, online at website: www.wta.org, or by calling 800/270-7504.

Maps: For a trail information report, contact the Baker Ranger District at 541/523-4476. For a map of Wallowa-Whitman National Forest, contact Nature of the Northwest Information Center, 800 Northeast Oregon Street, Suite 177, Portland, OR 97232; 503/872-2750. Ask the USGS for topographic maps of the Crawfish Lake and Anthony Lakes areas.

Directions: From Baker City drive north on U.S. 30 to Haines and turn left (west) onto the Elkhorn Drive Scenic Byway/County Road 1146. Continue about 20 miles on this highway as it enters the national forest and becomes Forest Service Road 73. Drive past the Anthony Lake Campground, turn left onto Forest Service Road 380, and drive three miles to the trailhead near Peavy Cabin.

Contact: Wallowa-Whitman National Forest, Baker Ranger District, 3165 10th Street, Baker City, OR 97814; 541/523-4476.

87 Peavy Trail
7.4 mi/3.7 hrs

Paralleling the upper reaches of the North Fork John Day River, this valley-bottom trail accesses several beautiful meadows and wildflower fields, as well as the dense valley forests of pine, larch, fir, and spruce. The trail meanders past an assortment of historic hard-rock and placer mines and eventually climbs to the Last Chance Mine below Columbia Hill. An abandoned shaft is all that remains of the mine; in this case getting there is all the fun.

Location: West of Baker City in Wallowa-Whitman National Forest within the North Fork John Day Wilderness; see Northeast Oregon Map 7, grid c5.

User Groups: Hikers, dogs, and horses. No mountain bikes. No wheelchair facilities.

Permits: A federal Northwest Forest Pass, $5 per day or $30 annually, is required to park at the trailhead. Passes are available from ranger stations and many private vendors, online at website: www.wta.org, or by calling 800/270-7504.

Maps: For a trail information report, contact the Baker Ranger District at 541/523-4476. For a map of Wallowa-Whitman National Forest, contact Nature of the Northwest Information Center, 800 Northeast Oregon Street, Suite 177, Portland, OR 97232; 503/872-2750. Ask the USGS for topographic maps of the Crawfish Lake and Anthony Lakes areas.

Directions: From Baker City drive north on U.S. 30 to Haines and turn left (west) onto the Elkhorn Drive Scenic Byway/County Road 1146. Continue about 20 miles on this highway as it enters the national forest and becomes Forest Service Road 73. Drive past the Anthony Lake Campground, turn left onto Forest Service Road 380, and drive to the road's end and the trailhead.

Contact: Wallowa-Whitman National Forest, Baker Ranger District, 3165 10th Street, Baker City, OR 97814; 541/523-4476.

88 Lakes Lookout
1.5 mi/1.0 hr

As it climbs to the former site of the old Lakes Lookout fire-watch tower, this steep, rough trail weaves through a maze of boulders and gnarled old trees. After the hard scramble to the summit, you'll want to sit back and

enjoy the incredible views of the peaks, ridges, and valleys in the distance.

Location: West of Baker City in Wallowa-Whitman National Forest partially within the North Fork John Day Wilderness; see Northeast Oregon Map 7, grid b6.

User Groups: Hikers, dogs, and horses. No mountain bikes are allowed. No wheelchair facilities.

Permits: A federal Northwest Forest Pass, $5 per day or $30 annually, is required to park at the trailhead. Passes are available from ranger stations and many private vendors, online at website: www.wta.org, or by calling 800/270-7504.

Maps: For a trail information report, contact the Baker Ranger District at 541/523-4476. For a map of Wallowa-Whitman National Forest, contact Nature of the Northwest Information Center, 800 Northeast Oregon Street, Suite 177, Portland, OR 97232; 503/872-2750. Ask the USGS for a topographic map of the Anthony Lakes area.

Directions: From Baker City drive north on U.S. 30 to Haines and turn left (west) onto the Elkhorn Drive Scenic Byway/County Road 1146. Continue about 20 miles on this highway as it enters the national forest and becomes Forest Service Road 73. Drive past the Anthony Lake Campground, turn left onto Forest Service Road 210, and drive to the junction with Forest Service Road 187. Turn right (south) to the trailhead at the road's end.

Contact: Wallowa-Whitman National Forest, Baker Ranger District, 3165 10th Street, Baker City, OR 97814; 541/523-4476.

89 Anthony Shoreline/ Hoffer Lakes
4.0 mi/2.0 hrs

The route begins on the broad, level, gravel trail that loops around Anthony Lake and offers good access to and views of the lake and surrounding peaks. Instead of completing the entire loop, though, you'll want to turn off midway and climb gradually through the surrounding pine forest to Hoffer Lakes. This steep, one-mile trail slices through the subalpine forest ecosystem before breaking out into a sun-dappled wildflower meadow on the banks of the twin lakes. This was once a single body of water, but sediment slowly piled up on the bottom of the old lake, forming a ridge right down the middle. Eventually plants colonized this mud bar, grabbing and holding even more sediment. Now the area between the lakes is high and dry. Eventually the lakes may disappear entirely as the process of sedimentation continues. Enjoy the warm sun and fragrant wildflowers of the lakeside environment while pondering the life cycle of the forest and its waters, then retrace your steps to Anthony Lake. There, continue around the lake to complete that loop trail.

Location: West of Baker City in Wallowa-Whitman National Forest; see Northeast Oregon Map 7, grid b6.

User Groups: Hikers, dogs, and horses. No mountain bikes. No wheelchair facilities.

Permits: A federal Northwest Forest Pass, $5 per day or $30 annually, is required to park at the trailhead. Passes are available from ranger stations and many private vendors, online at website: www.wta.org, or by calling 800/270-7504.

Maps: For a trail information report, contact the Baker Ranger District at 541/523-4476. For a map of Wallowa-Whitman National Forest, contact Nature of the Northwest Information Center, 800 Northeast Oregon Street, Suite 177, Portland, OR 97232; 503/872-2750. Ask the USGS for a topographic map of the Anthony Lakes area.

Directions: From Baker City drive north on U.S. 30 to Haines and turn left (west) onto

the Elkhorn Drive Scenic Byway/County Road 1146. Continue about 20 miles on this highway as it enters the national forest and becomes Forest Service Road 73. Drive to the Anthony Lake Campground. The trailhead is near the guard station.

Contact: Wallowa-Whitman National Forest, Baker Ranger District, 3165 10th Street, Baker City, OR 97814; 541/523-4476.

90 Lost Lake
17.0 mi/1.0–2.0 days

The first section of this hike follows the Elkhorn Crest Trail (see hike in this chapter) and affords stunning views of the surrounding peaks and valleys, including the upper reaches of the North Fork John Day River, a national Wild and Scenic River. At the junction with the Lost Lake side trail at mile five, turn east and gently descend through the subalpine forest and meadows on the flank of Mount Ruth. Lost Lake lies cradled in a small alpine basin above the North Fork Powder River. You can see Mount Ruth from the numerous lakeside campsites; the crest of the Elkhorn Range punctuates the rest of the horizon. For a little off-trail adventure, scramble up a faint side trail to Meadow Lake, an alpine tarn hidden just east of Lost Lake.

Location: West of Baker City in Wallowa-Whitman National Forest partially within the North Fork John Day Wilderness; see Northeast Oregon Map 7, grid b7.

User Groups: Hikers, dogs, and horses. No mountain bikes are allowed. No wheelchair facilities.

Permits: A federal Northwest Forest Pass, $5 per day or $30 annually, is required to park at the trailhead. Passes are available from ranger stations and many private vendors, online at website: www.wta.org, or by calling 800/270-7504.

Maps: For a trail information report, contact the Baker Ranger District at 541/523-4476. For a map of Wallowa-Whitman National Forest, contact Nature of the Northwest Information Center, 800 Northeast Oregon Street, Suite 177, Portland, OR 97232; 503/872-2750. Ask the USGS for a topographic map of the Anthony Lakes area.

Directions: From Baker City drive north on U.S. 30 to Haines and turn left (west) onto the Elkhorn Drive Scenic Byway/County Road 1146. Continue about 20 miles on this highway as it enters the national forest and becomes Forest Service Road 73. Drive to the Anthony Lake Campground. The trailhead is near the guard station.

Contact: Wallowa-Whitman National Forest, Baker Ranger District, 3165 10th Street, Baker City, OR 97814; 541/523-4476.

91 Summit Lake
22.6 mi/2.0 days

You get fantastic panoramic vistas on the final two miles of this newly constructed trail. Columbia Hill, Red Mountain, Mount Ruth, North Powder River, and Elkhorn Range are just a few of the spectacular geographic features that dominate the horizon here. The route begins with a long ridgetop hike south along the Elkhorn Crest Trail (see hike in this chapter). At the junction with the Summit Lake side trail at mile nine, turn east and begin the steep climb through two or three miles of rough trail. The final mile leaves the canopied pine and larch forest and enters a broad alpine meadow environment before reaching Summit Lake, also known as Elk Lake. Set deep in a mountainside perch and surrounded on three sides by sheer rock walls, this is an excellent spot to camp. This is the lair of eagles, too, so keep an eye on the sky and you might see a golden eagle soaring miles overhead on the thermal drafts.

Location: West of Baker City in Wallowa-Whitman National Forest partially within the North Fork John Day Wilderness; see Northeast Oregon Map 7, grid b7.

User Groups: Hikers, dogs, and horses. No mountain bikes are allowed. No wheelchair facilities.

Permits: A federal Northwest Forest Pass, $5 per day or $30 annually, is required to park at the trailhead. Passes are available from ranger stations and many private vendors, online at website: www.wta.org, or by calling 800/270-7504.

Maps: For a trail information report, contact the Baker Ranger District at 541/523-4476. For a map of Wallowa-Whitman National Forest, contact Nature of the Northwest Information Center, 800 Northeast Oregon Street, Suite 177, Portland, OR 97232; 503/872-2750. Ask the USGS for topographic maps of the Anthony Lakes and Bourne areas.

Directions: From Baker City drive about nine miles north on U.S. 30 to Haines and turn left (west) onto the Elkhorn Drive Scenic Byway/County Road 1146. Continue about 20 miles on this highway as it enters the national forest and becomes Forest Service Road 73. Drive to the Anthony Lake Campground. The trailhead is near the guard station.

Contact: Wallowa-Whitman National Forest, Baker Ranger District, 3165 10th Street, Baker City, OR 97814; 541/523-4476.

92 Crawfish Basin
4.0 mi/2.0 hrs

A 200-foot elevation gain along this two-mile trail gets you fantastic views of Lakes Lookout, Lee Peak, Angel Peak, and more. The route cuts across the northeasternmost section of the wilderness area and accesses Dutch Flat Saddle on the ridge above Crawfish Creek and Crawfish Lake. As you traverse the ridge, you can look down at the picturesque scenery of

Crawfish Meadows, several small unnamed alpine tarns and meadows, and the lush green spruce and pine forest that wraps itself around the jutting rock outcrops of the area. Turn around at Crawfish Lake.

Location: West of Baker City in Wallowa-Whitman National Forest partially within the North Fork John Day Wilderness; see Northeast Oregon Map 7, grid c6.

User Groups: Hikers, dogs, and horses. No mountain bikes are allowed. No wheelchair facilities.

Permits: A federal Northwest Forest Pass, $5 per day or $30 annually, is required to park at the trailhead. Passes are available from ranger stations and many private vendors, online at website: www.wta.org, or by calling 800/270-7504.

Maps: For a trail information report, contact the Baker Ranger District at 541/523-4476. For a map of Wallowa-Whitman National Forest, contact Nature of the Northwest Information Center, 800 Northeast Oregon Street, Suite 177, Portland, OR 97232; 503/872-2750. Ask the USGS for topographic maps of the Crawfish Lake and Anthony Lakes areas.

Directions: From Baker City drive about nine miles north on U.S. 30 to Haines and turn left (west) onto the Elkhorn Drive Scenic Byway/County Road 1146. Continue about 20 miles on this highway as it enters the national forest and becomes Forest Service Road 73. Drive a short distance past the Anthony Lake Campground, turn left onto Forest Service Road 210, and drive to the trailhead.

Contact: Wallowa-Whitman National Forest, Baker Ranger District, 3165 10th Street, Baker City, OR 97814; 541/523-4476.

93 Black Lake
2.0 mi/1.0 hr

Few trails twice this long touch half as many lakes, so this hike is truly special. The gentle trail, which gains just 250 feet in elevation, leaves from Anthony Lakes, climbs gradually away from the campground in the first half mile, and quickly reaches Lilypad Lake. Actually more of a broad wetland, the lake is shallow and covered with wide, green lily pads and, in midsummer, with brilliant yellow lily blooms. From that colorful marsh the trail continues its gentle ascent through thick forest to another broad meadow. At the upper end of the wildflower field, it reaches Black Lake, a deep, cool pond. Campsites line the shores of Black Lake and trout thrive in the chilly waters.

Location: West of Baker City in Wallowa-Whitman National Forest; see Northeast Oregon Map 7, grid c6.

User Groups: Hikers, dogs, and horses. No mountain bikes are allowed. No wheelchair facilities.

Permits: A federal Northwest Forest Pass, $5 per day or $30 annually, is required to park at the trailhead. Passes are available from ranger stations and many private vendors, online at website: www.wta.org, or by calling 800/270-7504.

Maps: For a trail information report, contact the Baker Ranger District at 541/523-4476. For a map of Wallowa-Whitman National Forest, contact Nature of the Northwest Information Center, 800 Northeast Oregon Street, Suite 177, Portland, OR 97232; 503/872-2750. Ask the USGS for a topographic map of the Anthony Lakes area.

Directions: From Baker City drive north on U.S. 30 to Haines and turn left (west) onto the Elkhorn Drive Scenic Byway/County Road 1146. Continue about 20 miles on this highway as it enters the national forest and becomes Forest Service Road 73. At the Anthony Lake Campground, turn left (south) onto the campground access road (Forest

Service Road 170). Drive to the road's end and the trailhead.

Contact: Wallowa-Whitman National Forest, Baker Ranger District, 3165 10th Street, Baker City, OR 97814; 541/523-4476.

94 Elkhorn Crest National Recreation Trail

45.2 mi/5.0 days

The highest trail in the Blue Mountains, this National Recreation Trail cuts through a wide variety of ecosystems and forest types, ranging from thick, young lodgepole pine to old-growth ponderosa pine, spruce, and larch. It also reaches above timberline and climbs through alpine and subalpine meadows along the ridgetop. Hiking south along the crest, you are awed by fantastic views that take in the Grande Ronde Valley and the Wallowa Mountains to the east, the shimmering Blue Mountains to the north and south, and the sprawling North Fork John Day Wilderness to the west.

Water is scarce on the high trail, but it can be found—six beautiful alpine lakes adjoin the trail, and you can reach at least five others via short side trails. The first and best camping sites lie just a few hundred yards off the main trail at Dutch Flat Lake, about five miles from the trailhead. Other camping is available at Lost Lake, about 10 miles in, and along the numerous springs and creek basins below Rock Creek Butte, about 20 miles in. Mule and white-tailed deer share the area with elk, black bears, mountain goats, marmots, badgers, hawks, eagles, ravens, and a host of other birds and small mammals.

Both ends of this trail are accessible by car, so if a shuttle vehicle can be dropped at one end—or if you can arrange a pickup—you can avoid a long backtrack hike.

Location: West of Baker City in Wallowa-Whitman National Forest; see Northeast Oregon Map 7, grid c6.

User Groups: Hikers, dogs, horses, and mountain bikes. No wheelchair facilities.

Permits: A federal Northwest Forest Pass, $5 per day or $30 annually, is required to park at the trailhead. Passes are available from ranger stations and many private vendors, online at website: www.wta.org, or by calling 800/270-7504.

Maps: For a trail information report, contact the Baker Ranger District at 541/523-4476. For a map of Wallowa-Whitman National Forest, contact Nature of the Northwest Information Center, 800 Northeast Oregon Street, Suite 177, Portland, OR 97232; 503/872-2750. Ask the USGS for topographic maps of the Anthony Lakes, Rock Creek, and Elkhorn Peak areas.

Directions: From Baker City drive north on U.S. 30 to Haines and turn left (west) onto the Elkhorn Drive Scenic Byway/County Road 1146. Continue about 20 miles on this highway as it enters the national forest and becomes Forest Service Road 73. Drive to the Anthony Lake Campground. The trailhead lies at the east end of the campground. The southern trailhead is reached from Baker City. Drive seven miles west on Pocahontas Road to Forest Service Road 6510. Turn left (south) and continue eight miles to the trailhead on the right, near Marble Pass.

Contact: Wallowa-Whitman National Forest, Baker Ranger District, 3165 10th Street, Baker City, OR 97814; 541/523-4476.

95 Van Patten Lake

1.0 mi/2.0 hrs

Though only a half-mile long (one way), this trail gains nearly 1,000 feet over that short distance. That makes for a real workout on any hike, regardless of the length. The trail climbs almost straight up the ridge to Van Patten Lake. From there you can take a well-deserved rest while admiring the wonderful scenery, which is dominated by Van Patten Peak to the west. To the east you see a panoramic display that features the North Powder Valley and the jagged Wallowa Mountains beyond.

Location: West of Baker City in Wallowa-Whitman National Forest; see Northeast Oregon Map 7, grid c6.

User Groups: Hikers, dogs, and horses. No mountain bikes are allowed. No wheelchair facilities.

Permits: A federal Northwest Forest Pass, $5 per day or $30 annually, is required to park at the trailhead. Passes are available from ranger stations and many private vendors, online at website: www.wta.org, or by calling 800/270-7504.

Maps: For a trail information report, contact the Baker Ranger District at 541/523-4476. For a map of Wallowa-Whitman National Forest, contact Nature of the Northwest Information Center, 800 Northeast Oregon Street, Suite 177, Portland, OR 97232; 503/872-2750. Ask the USGS for a topographic map of the Anthony Lakes area.

Directions: From Baker City drive north on U.S. 30 to Haines and turn left (west) onto the Elkhorn Drive Scenic Byway/County Road 1146. Continue about 20 miles on this highway as it enters the national forest and becomes Forest Service Road 73. Drive to the well-marked trailhead on the right.

Contact: Wallowa-Whitman National Forest, Baker Ranger District, 3165 10th Street, Baker City, OR 97814; 541/523-4476.

96 Dutch Flat
19.0 mi/1.0–2.0 days

Cutting through the valley between Van Patten Peak and Twin Mountain, this trail gradually climbs upstream along Dutch Flat Creek to prime vantage points of the surrounding forest and peaks. The first trail section passes through a lush old-growth forest of spruce, ponderosa and lodgepole pine, fir, and western larch. The abundance of larch trees makes this a great early autumn hike, as the tall, straight trees turn a brilliant shade of gold. Farther up the trail you encounter the rich grasses and wildflowers of Dutch Flat Meadow. The local population of red-tailed and rough-legged hawks likes to circle above this broad clearing in search of careless rodents and other small mammals that thrive here. Leaving the meadow, the trail climbs steeply toward Dutch Flat Lake. Enjoy a relaxing lunch at the lake, dip your feet in its icy waters, and then push on to Dutch Flat Saddle for great views before returning the way you came.

Location: West of Baker City in Wallowa-Whitman National Forest; see Northeast Oregon Map 7, grid b8.

User Groups: Hikers, dogs, and horses. No mountain bikes are allowed. No wheelchair facilities.

Permits: A federal Northwest Forest Pass, $5 per day or $30 annually, is required to park at the trailhead. Passes are available from ranger stations and many private vendors, online at website: www.wta.org, or by calling 800/270-7504.

Maps: For a trail information report, contact the Baker Ranger District at 541/523-4476. For a map of Wallowa-Whitman National Forest, contact Nature of the Northwest Information Center, 800 Northeast Oregon Street, Suite 177, Portland, OR 97232; 503/872-2750. Ask the USGS for topographic maps of the Anthony Lakes and Rock Creek areas.

Directions: From Baker City drive about 10 miles north on U.S. 30 to Haines and turn left (west) onto the Elkhorn Drive Scenic Byway/County Road 1146. Continue about 17 miles on this highway as it enters the national forest and becomes Forest Service Road 73. Drive about one mile west on Forest Service Road 73 to Forest Service Road 7307 and turn left. Continue one mile south to the road's end and the trailhead.

Contact: Wallowa-Whitman National Forest, Baker Ranger District, 3165 10th Street, Baker City, OR 97814; 541/523-4476.

97 Red Mountain Lake
2.6 mi/1.3 hrs

Thick stands of spruce, larch, and fir shade this route, making it a cool choice in the hot midsummer hiking season (and, thanks to the abundant larch, a colorful destination in late autumn). As the trail climbs the steep—indeed, sometimes very steep—ridge wall, views of the Powder Valley become increasingly plentiful. Near the end of the route, as you approach the lake basin, you encounter several broad wildflower meadows and cold-water springs. At the lake take in the panoramic views before tracing your steps back to the trailhead.

Location: West of Baker City in Wallowa-Whitman National Forest; see Northeast Oregon Map 7, grid b8.

User Groups: Hikers, dogs, horses, and mountain bikes. No wheelchair facilities.

Permits: A federal Northwest Forest Pass, $5 per day or $30 annually, is required to park at the trailhead. Passes are available from ranger stations and many private vendors, online at website: www.wta.org, or by calling 800/270-7504.

Maps: For a trail information report, contact the Baker Ranger District at 541/523-4476. For a map of Wallowa-Whitman National Forest, contact Nature of the Northwest Information Center, 800 Northeast Oregon Street, Suite 177, Portland, OR 97232; 503/872-2750. Ask the USGS for a topographic map of the Red Mountain area.

Directions: From Baker City drive about 10 miles north on U.S. 30 to Haines and turn left (west) onto the Elkhorn Drive Scenic Byway/County Road 1146. Continue about five miles on this highway to Muddy Creek and then turn left onto Muddy Fork Road. Continue about eight miles west to the junction with Forest Service Road 7301. Veer right on Forest Service Road 7301 and drive to the trailhead on the left.

Contact: Wallowa-Whitman National Forest, Baker Ranger District, 3165 10th Street, Baker City, OR 97814; 541/523-4476.

98 North Powder
5.2 mi/2.6 hrs

The trail begins with a mile-long traverse around the slope on the north shore of the Powder River. The broken forest and grassy clearings of this traverse later give way to a boulder field along the river bottom as you continue up-valley along its milky waters. Waterproof boots are essential here, as the trail slices through several marshy meadows. The route occasionally climbs the hillside into the pine forest, where you find wonderful campsites before the trail drops back to the river.

Location: West of Baker City in Wallowa-Whitman National Forest; see Northeast Oregon Map 7, grid c7.

User Groups: Hikers, dogs, horses, and mountain bikes. No wheelchair facilities.

Permits: A federal Northwest Forest Pass, $5 per day or $30 annually, is required to park at the trailhead. Passes are available from ranger stations and many private vendors, online at website: www.wta.org, or by calling 800/270-7504.

Maps: For a trail information report, contact the Baker Ranger District at 541/523-4476. For a map of Wallowa-Whitman National Forest, contact Nature of the Northwest Information Center, 800 Northeast Oregon Street, Suite 177, Portland, OR 97232; 503/872-2750. Ask the USGS for a topographic map of the Red Mountain area.

Directions: From Baker City drive 10 miles north on U.S. 30 to Haines and turn left (west) onto the Elkhorn Drive Scenic Byway/County Road 1146. Continue about five miles on this highway to Muddy Creek, turn left onto Muddy Fork Road, and continue about eight miles west to the junction with Forest Service Road 7301. Veer right on Forest Service Road 7301 and drive to the trailhead at the road's end.

Contact: Wallowa-Whitman National Forest, Baker Ranger District, 3165 10th Street, Baker City, OR 97814; 541/523-4476.

99 Killamacue Lake
6.4 mi/3.2 hrs

This trail climbs along the banks of Killamacue Creek to its source, Killamacue Lake. The little creek is a rough-and-tumble stream that bounds over boulders and countless small waterfalls as it drops nearly 2,000 feet in elevation in a little more than three miles. From the lake, you enjoy the clear, picturesque views of Chloride Ridge, Red Mountain, and Columbia Hill as you rest up after the strenuous climb up the trail.

Location: West of Baker City in Wallowa-Whitman National Forest; see Northeast Oregon Map 7, grid c8.

User Groups: Hikers, dogs, horses, and mountain bikes. No wheelchair facilities.

Permits: A federal Northwest Forest Pass, $5 per day or $30 annually, is required to park at the trailhead. Passes are available from ranger stations and many private vendors, online at website: www.wta.org, or by calling 800/270-7504.

Maps: For a trail information report, contact the Baker Ranger District at 541/523-4476. For a map of Wallowa-Whitman National Forest, contact Nature of the Northwest Information Center, 800 Northeast Oregon Street, Suite 177, Portland, OR 97232; 503/872-2750. Ask the USGS for topographic maps of the Rock Creek and Elkhorn Peak areas.

Directions: From Baker City drive about 10 miles north on U.S. 30 to Haines and turn left (west) onto the Elkhorn Drive Scenic Byway/County Road 1146. Continue about three miles on this highway to Rock Creek, then turn left onto Rock Creek Road, and continue about seven miles west to the junction with Forest Service Road 5520. Stay right on Forest Service Road 5520 and drive a short distance to the trailhead on the right.

Contact: Wallowa-Whitman National Forest, Baker Ranger District, 3165 10th Street, Baker City, OR 97814; 541/523-4476.

100 Pine Creek Reservoir
5.0 mi/2.5 hrs

The trail is actually just a continuation of the access road that brings hikers to the trailhead. It leads up Pine Creek Valley through—you guessed it—a thick ponderosa and lodgepole pine forest and on to the small lake at the valley's head. The reservoir lies in a deep basin, surrounded by steep rock walls and flanked by Rock Creek Butte and Elkhorn Peak. The lake mirrors these peaks, which makes for some lovely photographs.

Location: West of Baker City in Wallowa-Whitman National Forest; see Northeast Oregon Map 7, grid c8.

User Groups: Hikers, dogs, and horses. No mountain bikes are allowed. No wheelchair facilities.

Permits: A federal Northwest Forest Pass, $5 per day

or $30 annually, is required to park at the trailhead. Passes are available from ranger stations and many private vendors, online at website: www.wta.org, or by calling 800/270-7504.

Maps: For a trail information report, contact the Baker Ranger District at 541/523-4476. For a map of Wallowa-Whitman National Forest, contact Nature of the Northwest Information Center, 800 Northeast Oregon Street, Suite 177, Portland, OR 97232; 503/872-2750. Ask the USGS for topographic maps of the Rock Creek and Elkhorn Peak areas.

Directions: From Baker City drive about 12 miles west on Pocahontas Road to Forest Service Road 6460. Turn left and continue to the road's end and the trailhead.

Contact: Wallowa-Whitman National Forest, Baker Ranger District, 3165 10th Street, Baker City, OR 97814; 541/523-4476.

101 Twin Lakes
8.0 mi/4.0 hrs

Expect to find some great views, fragrant wildflowers, abundant wildlife, and a sublime wilderness experience when you hike this non-wilderness trail. The old-growth spruce, pine, and Douglas fir that line the trail provide a comfortable home to a large herd of white-tailed deer, as well as elk, black bears, and even a few cougars and bobcats. The trail climbs along (and sometimes crosses) Lake Creek, up the steep valley, to the overflowing waters of the Twin Lakes. Two miles into the hike, an old, abandoned trail leads away from the main trail (it climbs to Marble Pass eventually), while the main trail enters a long traverse through a wonderful wildflower meadow. Mountain goats are common both here and farther up the trail, where it accesses the rugged, rocky terrain around Twin Lakes.

Location: West of Baker City in Wallowa-Whitman National Forest; see Northeast Oregon Map 7, grid c8.

User Groups: Hikers, dogs, and horses. No mountain bikes are allowed. No wheelchair facilities.

Permits: A federal Northwest Forest Pass, $5 per day or $30 annually, is required to park at the trailhead. Passes are available from ranger stations and many private vendors, online at website: www.wta.org, or by calling 800/270-7504.

Maps: For a trail information report, contact the Baker Ranger District at 541/523-4476. For a map of Wallowa-Whitman National Forest, contact Nature of the Northwest Information Center, 800 Northeast Oregon Street, Suite 177, Portland, OR 97232; 503/872-2750. Ask the USGS for topographic maps of the Phillips Lake and Elkhorn Peak areas.

Directions: From Baker City drive 21.5 miles west on Highway 7 to the junction with Deer Creek Road/Forest Service Road 6550. Turn right (north) onto Deer Creek Road and continue four miles to Forest Service Road 6550-030. Turn north and drive three miles to the road's end and the trailhead. Note: Forest Service Road 6550-030 is very rough; high-clearance vehicles are recommended.

Contact: Wallowa-Whitman National Forest, Baker Ranger District, 3165 10th Street, Baker City, OR 97814; 541/523-4476.

102 Nipple Butte
6.0 mi/3.0 hrs

Craggy peaks, vertical cliffs falling away from the trail, and stunning views make this a gorgeous hike, despite its popularity with motorcyclists. The route gains just 500 feet in elevation, yet because it starts so high, the scenery is astounding. From the trail you catch panoramic views of the East Fork Beech and John Day Valleys, as well as down Nipple Creek

Canyon and across the entire Malheur National Forest. The views from the Nipple Butte summit are second only to what you'll find on Lake Butte. To get there, you have to scramble one-half mile cross-country shortly after you start up the trail. You'll be glad you did it though, not only for the great view but also for the solitude you'll find on the off-trail peak.

Location: North of John Day in Malheur National Forest; see Northeast Oregon Map 7, grid c1.

User Groups: Hikers, dogs, horses, and mountain bikes. No wheelchair facilities.

Permits: A federal Northwest Forest Pass, $5 per day or $30 annually, is required to park at the trailhead. Passes are available from ranger stations and many private vendors, online at website: www.wta.org, or by calling 800/270-7504.

Maps: For a trail information report, contact the Long Creek Ranger District at 541/575-3000. For a map of Malheur National Forest, contact Nature of the Northwest Information Center, 800 Northeast Oregon Street, Suite 177, Portland, OR 97232; 503/872-2750. Ask the USGS for a topographic map of the Magone Lake area.

Directions: From John Day drive about nine miles east on U.S. 26 to the junction with County Road 18. Turn left and drive about 14 miles north to Forest Service Road 279. Turn left (west) onto this road and continue three-quarters of a mile to the intersection with Forest Service Road 296. The main parking area is here; the trailhead is 400 yards west on Forest Service Road 296 at the fence line.

Contact: Malheur National Forest, Long Creek Ranger District, P.O. Box 849, John Day, OR 97845; 541/575-3000.

103 Magone Lake Loop
3.0 mi/1.5 hrs

The compact-dirt surface of this barrier-free trail makes the route difficult for wheelchair users in wet weather, but since dry, hot weather is the norm here, that isn't a frequent problem. Besides, the trail is so wonderful that even without a hard surface, it's a great place for all users. Wildflowers grow thickly in the lakeside meadows, and birds and animals abound, both in sheer numbers and the number of species represented. Look for at least three kinds of jays, two species of woodpeckers, an assortment of small songbirds, ravens, hawks, killdeer, and kingfishers, plus deer, elk, beavers, rabbits, muskrats, and porcupines. In Magone Lake itself you'll find frogs, water snakes, and—most important—big, hard-fighting rainbow and brook trout. The trail circles the lake and provides access for anglers of all abilities.

Location: North of John Day in Malheur National Forest; see Northeast Oregon Map 7, grid d1.

User Groups: Hikers and dogs. Wheelchair accessible. No horses or mountain bikes are allowed.

Permits: A federal Northwest Forest Pass, $5 per day or $30 annually, is required to park at the trailhead. Passes are available from ranger stations and many private vendors, online at website: www.wta.org, or by calling 800/270-7504.

Maps: For a trail information report, contact the Long Creek Ranger District at 541/575-3000. For a map of Malheur National Forest, contact Nature of the Northwest Information Center, 800 Northeast Oregon Street, Suite 177, Portland, OR 97232; 503/872-2750. Ask the USGS for a topographic map of the Magone Lake area.

Directions: From John Day drive about nine miles east on U.S. 26 to the junction with County Road 18. Turn left and drive about 12 miles north to Forest Service Road 3620. Turn left (south) onto this road and continue about 1.5 miles to the intersection with Forest Service Road 3618. Turn right and drive to the Magone Lake day-use area and the trailhead.

Contact: Malheur National Forest, Long Creek Ranger District, P.O. Box 849, John Day, OR 97845; 541/575-2110.

104 Magone Slide
1.5 mi/1.0 hr

The picnic area and fishing piers on Magone Lake are popular destinations for summer recreationists, but this trail is surprisingly free of crowds. The short trail leaves the day-use area at the lake and climbs just over 300 feet in elevation through a stand of vibrant ponderosa pines. (Their orange and brown bark is the primary source of color along this route.) The trail explores the area of the massive 1860s landslide, which scooped out the basin that later became Magone Lake. Evidence of the slide can be seen in the slope, where terraces formed as the hillside slumped. The trail leads to a viewpoint atop the largest of these terraces and offers a stunning view of the bar rock face from which the slide began.

The second viewpoint, Viewpoint A, is farther up the trail on another terrace. From this point you can enjoy outstanding vistas that sweep across Strawberry Mountain and take in the whole of the John Day Valley, as well as Magone Lake far below. During the spring and early summer, a few small meadows are awash with colorful wildflower blooms, and birds and animals frequently appear, especially pileated woodpeckers and white-tailed deer.

Location: North of John Day in Malheur National Forest; see Northeast Oregon Map 7, grid d1.

User Groups: Hikers and dogs. No horses or mountain bikes are allowed. No wheelchair facilities.

Permits: A federal Northwest Forest Pass, $5 per day or $30 annually, is required to park at the trailhead. Passes are available from ranger stations and many private vendors, online at website: www.wta.org, or by calling 800/270-7504.

Maps: For a trail information report, contact the Long Creek Ranger District at 541/575-3000. For a map of Malheur National Forest, contact Nature of the Northwest Information Center, 800 Northeast Oregon Street, Suite 177, Portland, OR 97232; 503/872-2750. Ask the USGS for a topographic map of the Magone Lake area.

Directions: From John Day drive about nine miles east on U.S. 26 to the junction with County Road 18. Turn left and drive about 12 miles north to Forest Service Road 3620. Turn left (south) onto Forest Service Road 3620 and continue about 1.5 miles to the intersection with Forest Service Road 3618. Turn right and drive to the Magone Lake day-use area and the trailhead.

Contact: Malheur National Forest, Long Creek Ranger District, P.O. Box 849, John Day, OR 97845; 541/575-3000.

105 Arch Rock
0.6 mi/0.5 hr

The claim to fame of this trail, which is listed on the National Trails Register, is that it provides access to Arch Rock. This unique geologic wonder is an ash flow tuff (a volcanic ash-rock formation), with a scenic arch and several small cavelike openings that the constantly blowing winds here carved into the rock.

Location: Northeast of John Day in Malheur National Forest; see Northeast Oregon Map 7, grid c2.

User Groups: Hikers and dogs. No horses or mountain bikes are allowed. No wheelchair facilities.

Permits: A federal Northwest Forest Pass, $5 per day or $30 annually, is required to park at the trailhead. Passes are available from ranger stations and many private vendors, online at website: www.wta.org, or by calling 800/270-7504.

Maps: For a trail information report, contact the Long Creek Ranger District at 541/575-3000. For a map of Malheur National Forest, contact Nature of the Northwest Information Center, 800 Northeast Oregon Street, Suite 177, Portland, OR 97232; 503/872-2750. Ask the USGS for a topographic map of the Susanville.

Directions: From John Day drive about nine miles east on U.S. 26 and turn north onto Bear Creek Road/County Road 18. Continue about 10 miles north to Four Corners. Turn right onto Forest Service Road 36 and drive about 10 miles northeast to the junction with Forest Service Road 3650. Turn right onto Forest Service Road 3650 and drive three-quarters of a mile to the trailhead on the right.

Contact: Malheur National Forest, Long Creek Ranger District, P.O. Box 849, John Day, OR 97845; 541/575-3000.

106 Sunrise Butte
7.2 mi/3.7 hrs

A moderately difficult hike, this trail pierces the Vinegar Hill-Indian Rock Scenic Area and offers stunning views into the Middle Fork Valley, over the surrounding peaks, and across the North Fork John Day and Strawberry Mountain Wildernesses. It cuts through a thin pine forest before climbing onto the sagebrush-covered ridge and then onto the Sunrise Butte summit, which was pockmarked by the ever-optimistic hard-rock miners of the last century. The hike is dry and hot in the summer months.

The final few miles of the access road are difficult to handle without a high-clearance four-wheel-drive vehicle. Those in low-clearance cars should park in the wide area at the end of the road's gravel section and walk the final mile.

Location: Northeast of John Day in Malheur National Forest; see Northeast Oregon Map 7, grid c3.

User Groups: Hikers, dogs, and horses. No mountain bikes are allowed. No wheelchair facilities.

Permits: A federal Northwest Forest Pass, $5 per day or $30 annually, is required to park at the trailhead. Passes are available from ranger stations and many private vendors, online at website: www.wta.org, or by calling 800/270-7504.

Maps: For a trail information report, contact the Long Creek Ranger District at 541/575-3000. For a map of Malheur National Forest, contact Nature of the Northwest Information Center, 800 Northeast Oregon Street, Suite 177, Portland, OR 97232; 503/872-2750. Ask the USGS for topographic maps of the Vinegar Hill and Boulder Butte areas.

Directions: From John Day drive 28 miles east on U.S. 26 to the junction with Highway 7. Turn left (north) and continue two miles before turning left onto County Road 20. Follow County Road 20 west about seven miles to Forest Service Road 4550. Turn right (north) and continue about four miles to Forest Service Road 4555. Turn right and drive to the road's end and the trailhead.

Contact: Malheur National Forest, Long Creek Ranger District, P.O. Box 849, John Day, OR 97845; 541/575-3000.

107 Tempest Mine
7.0 mi/3.5 hrs

This moderately rolling trail began as a wagon road for the hard-rock miners who prospected in the area. As such, it explores many of the old mining sites and pieces of equipment that miners used in their back-breaking work. Among the most unusual and interesting features are the long sections of corduroy road—roadbeds lined with logs to provide a hard, if somewhat rough, surface through muddy areas. The trail ends near the Tempest Mine. After exploring the area, return the way you came. Wildlife in the area includes deer and a variety of upland birds, such as pheasant and grouse.

Location: Northeast of John Day in Malheur National Forest; see Northeast Oregon Map 7, grid d3.

User Groups: Hikers, dogs, and horses. No mountain bikes are allowed. No wheelchair facilities.

Permits: A federal Northwest Forest Pass, $5 per day or $30 annually, is required to park at the trailhead. Passes are available from ranger stations and many private vendors, online at website: www.wta.org, or by calling 800/270-7504.

Maps: For a trail information report, contact the Long Creek Ranger District at 541/575-3000. For a map of Malheur National Forest, contact Nature of the Northwest Information Center, 800 Northeast Oregon Street, Suite 177, Portland, OR 97232; 503/872-2750. Ask the USGS for a topographic map of the Vinegar Hill area.

Directions: From John Day drive 28 miles east on U.S. 26 to the junction with Highway 7. Turn left (north) and continue two miles before turning left onto County Road 20. Follow County Road 20 about seven miles west to Forest Service Road 4550. Turn right (north) and continue about two miles to Forest Service Road 4559. Turn right and drive to the road's end and the trailhead.

Contact: Malheur National Forest, Long Creek Ranger District, P.O. Box 849, John Day, OR 97845; 541/575-3000.

108 Blackeye
4.8 mi/2.4 hrs

Following a ridge crest as it weaves west between several small creek valleys, this rough, steep trail provides moderate views. Deer prowl the area, as do some small herds of elk and colonies of big spruce grouse. The scenery is pretty, if a bit lackluster, as the second-growth forest is thick and all the same age, which offers little diversity. But rock hounds will enjoy the abundance of tiny quartz geodes. Expect to find a lot of hunters in this area in the autumn.

Location: Northeast of John Day in Malheur National Forest; see Northeast Oregon Map 7, grid d3.

User Groups: Hikers, dogs, and horses. No mountain bikes are allowed. No wheelchair facilities.

Permits: A federal Northwest Forest Pass, $5 per day or $30 annually, is required to park at the trailhead. Passes are available from ranger stations and many private vendors, online at website: www.wta.org, or by calling 800/270-7504.

Maps: For a trail information report, contact the Long Creek Ranger District at 541/575-3000. For a map of Malheur National Forest, contact Nature of the Northwest Information Center, 800 Northeast Oregon Street, Suite 177, Portland, OR 97232; 503/872-2750. Ask the USGS for a topographic map of the Vinegar Hill area.

Directions: From John Day drive 28 miles east on U.S. 26 to the junction with Highway 7. Turn left (north) and continue two miles before turning left onto County Road 20. Follow County Road 20 about seven miles west to Forest Service Road 4550. Turn right (north) and continue to Forest Service Road 4559. Turn right and drive to the road's end and the trailhead.

Contact: Malheur National Forest, Long Creek Ranger District, P.O. Box 849, John Day, OR 97845; 541/575-3000.

109 Davis Creek
9.1 mi one way/5.0 hrs

The trail ends are featureless and bland, for thick second-growth forest chokes off the views and hinders the movement of big animals. But as you near the route's center third, the thick single-aged forest gives way to a multiaged, old-growth pine and spruce forest that supports a large population of birds and animals, including pileated woodpeckers, great horned owls, white-tailed deer, black bears, and bobcats.

The route also climbs to the ridgetop, and the forest opens repeatedly to great views of the distant peaks and valleys, making up for the blocked views at the ends. Winding around several long-abandoned hard-rock mines of 19th century prospectors, the trail also provides nine wide bridges that span assorted creeks and ravines, which support bicycles and trail motorcycles. The best camps are at Little Butte Creek (mile six) and Deerhorn Creek (mile five).

Rather than do this as an out-and-back trip, arrange to have a second vehicle shuttled to the second trailhead, or arrange to be picked up when you get there.

Location: Northeast of John Day in Malheur National Forest; see Northeast Oregon Map 7, grid d3.

User Groups: Hikers, dogs, horses, and mountain bikes. No wheelchair facilities.

Permits: A federal Northwest Forest Pass, $5 per day or $30 annually, is required to park at the trailhead. Passes are available from ranger stations and many private vendors, online at website: www.wta.org, or by calling 800/270-7504.

Maps: For a trail information report, contact the Long Creek Ranger District at 541/575-3000. For a map of Malheur National Forest, contact Nature of the Northwest Information Center, 800 Northeast Oregon Street, Suite 177, Portland, OR 97232; 503/872-2750. Ask the USGS for topographic maps of the Dixie Meadows and Bates areas.

Directions: From John Day drive about 27 miles east on U.S. 26 to Austin Junction and turn north onto Forest Service Road 2614. Drive to a mining operation and turn left at the next intersection near the creek. The trailhead is on the north end of the parking area. The north trailhead is reached by continuing about one mile on U.S. 26 past Austin Junction to the junction with Highway 7. Turn north onto Highway 7 and drive two miles before turning left (west) onto County Road 20. Follow County Road 20 for about nine miles to Forest Service Road 2050. Turn left (south). At the next intersection turn left onto Forest Service Road 791. The trailhead is one-half mile farther at the next intersection.

Contact: Malheur National Forest, Long Creek Ranger District, P.O. Box 849, John Day, OR 97845; 541/575-3000.

110 Canyon Mountain Trail
31.0 mi/3.0 days

A high and dry route, the trail weaves north to south as it leads from the western edge of the wilderness to the center of the protected area near Indian Creek Butte. It stays along the ridgetop that makes up the spine of the Strawberry Range northwestern section. Spectacular views of the surrounding forest's blue-green valleys and craggy peaks emerge at almost every turn on the route. At about five miles the trail passes the first good camping spot as it crosses the small creek flowing from the flanks of the

8,007-foot Canyon Mountain. Near the trail's end at Indian Creek Butte, you cross Miner Creek, another fine place to camp. Mountain goats and deer roam this highland trail, as do a wide variety of other birds and animals. The trail stays on the ridge crest, seldom touching the creeks in the valleys below, so don't forget to carry a hearty supply of drinking water. Also bring lots of film—you'll find something worth photographing with almost every step you take.

Location: South of John Day in Malheur National Forest within the Strawberry Mountain Wilderness; see Northeast Oregon Map 7, grid f1.

User Groups: Hikers, dogs, and horses. No mountain bikes are allowed. No wheelchair facilities.

Permits: A federal Northwest Forest Pass, $5 per day or $30 annually, is required to park at the trailhead. Passes are available from ranger stations and many private vendors, online at website: www.wta.org, or by calling 800/270-7504. Party size is limited to 12 people.

Maps: For a trail information report, contact the Bear Valley Ranger District at 541/575-2110. For a map of Malheur National Forest, contact Nature of the Northwest Information Center, 800 Northeast Oregon Street, Suite 177, Portland, OR 97232; 503/872-2750. Ask the USGS for topographic maps of the Pine Creek Mountain and Canyon Mountain areas.

Directions: From John Day drive about two miles south on U.S. 395 to Canyon City and turn east onto Marysville Road/County Road 52. Continue about two miles east on Marysville Road to County Road 77. Turn right (south) and continue to the trailhead on the right.

Contact: Malheur National Forest, 431 Patterson Bridge Road, John Day, OR 97845; 541/575-3000.

111 Pine Creek
21.0 mi/1.0–2.0 days

Meandering south along a long ridgeline, the Pine Creek Trail is high, dry, and incredibly beautiful. The route leads from the northwest edge to the dead-center point of the wilderness area, utilizing the high spine of the Strawberry Range to get you south to the three-way trail junction located near Indian Creek Butte. A couple miles short of the trail's end, you'll find good camping opportunities at Miner Creek. Pitch a tent here for the night or retrace your steps from Indian Creek Butte to the trailhead and your vehicle.

Location: Southeast of John Day in Malheur National Forest within the Strawberry Mountain Wilderness; see Northeast Oregon Map 7, grid f2.

User Groups: Hikers, dogs, and horses. No mountain bikes are allowed. No wheelchair facilities.

Permits: A federal Northwest Forest Pass, $5 per day or $30 annually, is required to park at the trailhead. Passes are available from ranger stations and many private vendors, online at website: www.wta.org, or by calling 800/270-7504. Party size is limited to 12 people.

Maps: For a trail information report, contact the Bear Valley Ranger District at 541/575-2110. For a map of Malheur National Forest, contact Nature of the Northwest Information Center, 800 Northeast Oregon Street, Suite 177, Portland, OR 97232; 503/872-2750. Ask the USGS for a topographic map of the Pine Creek Mountain area.

Directions: From Prairie City drive six miles east on U.S. 26 and turn left (south) onto Pine Creek Road/County Road 54. Follow Pine Creek Road about five miles to Forest Service Road 811 and stay right. Drive south to the road's end and the trailhead.

Contact: Malheur National Forest, 431 Patterson Bridge Road, John Day, OR 97845; 541/575-3000.

112 Indian Creek
12.8 mi/6.4 hrs

The trail rolls over a low ridge and then begins a long climb up Indian Creek Valley. After passing under the east flank of Sheep Rock, hikers continue along the western foot of Strawberry Mountain, cutting through thick old-growth pine forest and wide meadows chock-full of wildflowers and delicious wild onions. From the trail's end at the Indian Creek headwaters, you can see the west face of Strawberry Mountain in all its splendor.

Location: South of Prairie City in Malheur National Forest within the Strawberry Mountain Wilderness; see Northeast Oregon Map 7, grid f3.

User Groups: Hikers, dogs, and horses. No mountain bikes are allowed. No wheelchair facilities.

Permits: A federal Northwest Forest Pass, $5 per day or $30 annually, is required to park at the trailhead. Passes are available from ranger stations and many private vendors, online at website: www.wta.org, or by calling 800/270-7504. Party size is limited to 12 people.

Maps: For a trail information report, contact the Prairie City Ranger District at 541/820-3311. For a map of Malheur National Forest, contact Nature of the Northwest Information Center, 800 Northeast Oregon Street, Suite 177, Portland, OR 97232; 503/872-2750. Ask the USGS for a topographic map of the Strawberry Mountain area.

Directions: From Prairie City drive about six miles west on U.S. 26 to Indian Creek Road/County Road 55 and turn left (south). Follow Indian Creek Road eight miles to the forest boundary. The trailhead is on the right, just as the road curves away to the left.

Contact: Malheur National Forest, Prairie City Ranger District, 327 Front Street, Prairie City, OR 97869; 541/820-3311.

113 Reynolds Creek
3.0 mi/1.5 hrs

This short river valley hike is the best early spring trail in the area, since it's usually the first to open up. Wildflowers bloom early, but by mid-June the color is gone, leaving just another little trail through a pleasant second-growth forest. The creek is pretty, though, and since most people avoid the area later in the year, this is a good trail for teaching kids about natural history without having to deal with crowds.

Location: South of Prairie City in Malheur National Forest; see Northeast Oregon Map 7, grid e4.

User Groups: Hikers, dogs, horses, and mountain bikes. No wheelchair facilities.

Permits: A federal Northwest Forest Pass, $5 per day or $30 annually, is required to park at the trailhead. Passes are available from ranger stations and many private vendors, online at website: www.wta.org, or by calling 800/270-7504.

Maps: For a trail information report, contact the Prairie City Ranger District at 541/820-3311. For a map of Malheur National Forest, contact Nature of the Northwest Information Center, 800 Northeast Oregon Street, Suite 177, Portland, OR 97232; 503/872-2750. Ask the USGS for topographic maps of the Isham Creek and Deardorff Mountain areas.

Directions: From Prairie City drive about six miles west on County Road 62/Forest Service Road 14 to the junction with Forest Service Road 2635. Turn left and continue four miles to the trailhead.

Contact: Malheur National Forest, Prairie City Ranger District, 327 Front Street, Prairie City, OR 97869; 541/820-3311.

⬛114 Little Strawberry Lake
3.5 mi/1.8 hrs

The trail begins with a gentle mile-long hike along Strawberry Creek before it turns west and climbs a narrow side valley to the shores of Little Strawberry Lake. There you find wide meadows that are lush with wildflowers and wild onions. This popular route gets a lot of visitors, especially on weekends and holidays. The campsites at the lake are hard to secure, but don't let that stop you. Just make a day hike of it.

Location: South of Prairie City in Malheur National Forest within the Strawberry Mountain Wilderness; see Northeast Oregon Map 7, grid f4.

User Groups: Hikers, dogs, and horses. No mountain bikes are allowed. No wheelchair facilities.

Permits: A federal Northwest Forest Pass, $5 per day or $30 annually, is required to park at the trailhead. Passes are available from ranger stations and many private vendors, online at website: www.wta.org, or by calling 800/270-7504. Party size is limited to 12 people.

Maps: For a trail information report, contact the Prairie City Ranger District at 541/820-3311. For a map of Malheur National Forest, contact Nature of the Northwest Information Center, 800 Northeast Oregon Street, Suite 177, Portland, OR 97232; 503/872-2750. Ask the USGS for a topographic map of the Strawberry Mountain area.

Directions: From Prairie City drive 12 miles south on County Road 60 to the road's end and the Strawberry Campground. The trailhead is near the day-use parking area.

Contact: Malheur National Forest, Prairie City Ranger District, 327 Front Street, Prairie City, OR 9869; 541/820-3311.

⬛115 Strawberry Basin
5.6 mi/2.8 hrs

Beautiful scenery and easy access bring the usual high number of users. Still, the majestic old-growth forest along the lower trail, which climbs beside Strawberry Creek, is a perfect example of a diverse, multiaged pine, spruce, and fir forest. Farther up the trail, the forest thins, and broad, sunny meadows open between the trees. Moving through the meadows, the trail climbs into the Strawberry Basin and accesses Strawberry Lake, Strawberry Falls, and Little Strawberry Lake.

Location: South of Prairie City in Malheur National Forest within the Strawberry Mountain Wilderness; see Northeast Oregon Map 7, grid f4.

User Groups: Hikers, dogs, and horses. No mountain bikes are allowed. No wheelchair facilities.

Permits: A federal Northwest Forest Pass, $5 per day or $30 annually, is required to park at the trailhead. Passes are available from ranger stations and many private vendors, online at website: www.wta.org, or by calling 800/270-7504. Party size is limited to 12 people.

Maps: For a trail information report, contact the Prairie City Ranger District at 541/820-3311. For a map of Malheur National Forest, contact Nature of the Northwest Information Center, 800 Northeast Oregon Street, Suite 177, Portland, OR 97232; 503/872-2750. Ask the USGS for a topographic map of the Strawberry Mountain area.

Directions: From Prairie City drive 12 miles south on County Road 60 to the road's end and the trailhead.

Contact: Malheur National Forest, Prairie City Ranger District, 327 Front Street, Prairie City, OR 97869; 541/820-3311.

⑯ Twin Springs
7.0 mi/3.5 hrs

A high promontory near the end of this route offers an outstanding look down onto Strawberry Lake. The trail hooks around the head of the Strawberry Creek drainage and leads to Red Basin, a wide, rolling meadow of wildflowers and small stands of trees. An old prospector's cabin is nestled along one edge of the meadows, and the creek weaves through the area. You find plenty of great campsites in the basin, which is so big you can easily get away from other campers.

Location: South of Prairie City in Malheur National Forest within the Strawberry Mountain Wilderness; see Northeast Oregon Map 7, grid f4.

User Groups: Hikers, dogs, and horses. No mountain bikes are allowed. No wheelchair facilities.

Permits: A federal Northwest Forest Pass, $5 per day or $30 annually, is required to park at the trailhead. Passes are available from ranger stations and many private vendors, online at website: www.wta.org, or by calling 800/270-7504. Party size is limited to 12 people.

Maps: For a trail information report, contact the Prairie City Ranger District at 541/820-3311. For a map of Malheur National Forest, contact Nature of the Northwest Information Center, 800 Northeast Oregon Street, Suite 177, Portland, OR 97232; 503/872-2750. Ask the USGS for a topographic map of the Strawberry Mountain area.

Directions: From Prairie City drive 12 miles south on County Road 60 to the road's end and the trailhead.

Contact: Malheur National Forest, Prairie City Ranger District, 327 Front Street, Prairie City, OR 97869; 541/820-3311.

⑰ Onion Creek
12.6 mi/6.3 hrs

The trail climbs alongside the creek, then erupts onto the ridgetop to views of the entire wilderness area, as well as north into John Day Valley and beyond. But dominating the views is Strawberry Mountain, which looms just to the south. As you continue along the trail, the peak gets closer and closer until you're standing just under the summit's east face. A short side trail leads up the rocky flank of the mountain to the true summit and even better views of the surrounding forest, peaks, and valleys. As the trail slices through the ridgetop meadows and clearings, the trail tread becomes faint and barely discernible. Rock cairns mark the route even when the trail seems to disappear. Avoid building new cairns, but feel free to add a stone to the existing piles; it is said to bring good luck.

Location: South of Prairie City in Malheur National Forest within the Strawberry Mountain Wilderness; see Northeast Oregon Map 7, grid f4.

User Groups: Hikers, dogs, and horses. No mountain bikes are allowed. No wheelchair facilities.

Permits: A federal Northwest Forest Pass, $5 per day or $30 annually, is required to park at the trailhead. Passes are available from ranger stations and many private vendors, online at website: www.wta.org, or by calling 800/270-7504. Party size is limited to 12 people.

Maps: For a trail information report, contact the Prairie City Ranger District at 541/820-3311. For a map of Malheur National Forest, contact Nature of the Northwest Information Center, 800 Northeast Oregon Street, Suite 177, Portland, OR 97232; 503/872-2750. Ask the USGS for a topographic map of the Strawberry Mountain area.

Directions: From Prairie City drive 12 miles south on County Road 60 to the trailhead on the left, just inside the forest boundary.

Contact: Malheur National Forest, Prairie City Ranger District, 327 Front Street, Prairie City, OR 97869; 541/820-3311.

118 Slide Basin
8.6 mi/4.3 hrs

This trail climbs along Strawberry Creek before cresting the ridge to head east on the Skyline Trail. You find a great array of ecosystem types and scenery along the way. The beautiful cool valley of Strawberry Creek is shaded by the thick old-growth pine forest, while the high ridge trail is open and airy with panoramic views of the surrounding peaks and valleys. On the Skyline Trail turn south just over two miles from the trailhead and climb the steep, rocky path into the Slide Basin, with intriguing rock outcroppings and more spectacular views. Near the end of the trail you'll find wonderful glimpses—and, finally, a full, awesome view—of Slide Falls. The path doesn't really end; it just fades away. When the trail is too faint to follow, return the way you came.

Location: South of Prairie City in Malheur National Forest within the Strawberry Mountain Wilderness; see Northeast Oregon Map 7, grid f4.

User Groups: Hikers, dogs, and horses. No mountain bikes are allowed. No wheelchair facilities.

Permits: A federal Northwest Forest Pass, $5 per day or $30 annually, is required to park at the trailhead. Passes are available from ranger stations and many private ven-

dors, online at website: www.wta.org, or by calling 800/270-7504. Party size is limited to 12 people.

Maps: For a trail information report, contact the Prairie City Ranger District at 541/820-3311. For a map of Malheur National Forest, contact Nature of the Northwest Information Center, 800 Northeast Oregon Street, Suite 177, Portland, OR 97232; 503/872-2750. Ask the USGS for a topographic map of the Strawberry Mountain area.

Directions: From Prairie City drive 12 miles south on County Road 60 to the road's end and the trailhead.

Contact: Malheur National Forest, Prairie City Ranger District, 327 Front Street, Prairie City, OR 97869; 541/820-3311.

119 Slide Lake
4.0 mi/2.0 hrs

This gentle trail leads upstream along Strawberry Creek. At the first trail junction at mile one, bear left on the Skyline Trail and follow that ridgetop trail east into the lower reaches of Slide Basin. As you near Slide Creek at mile 1.5, turn south and traverse the long hillside to the shores of the crystalline Slide Lake.

Location: South of Prairie City in Malheur National Forest within the Strawberry Mountain Wilderness; see Northeast Oregon Map 7, grid f4.

User Groups: Hikers, dogs, and horses. No mountain bikes are allowed. No wheelchair facilities.

Permits: A federal Northwest Forest Pass, $5 per day or $30 annually, is required to park at the trailhead. Passes are available from ranger stations and many private vendors, online at website: www.wta.org, or by calling 800/270-7504. Party size is limited to 12 people.

Maps: For a trail information report, contact the Prairie City Ranger District at 541/820-

3311. For a map of Malheur National Forest, contact Nature of the Northwest Information Center, 800 Northeast Oregon Street, Suite 177, Portland, OR 97232; 503/872-2750. Ask the USGS for a topographic map of the Strawberry Mountain area.

Directions: From Prairie City drive 12 miles south on County Road 60 to the road's end and the trailhead.

Contact: Malheur National Forest, Prairie City Ranger District, 327 Front Street, Prairie City, OR 97869; 541/820-3311.

120 The Strawberry Slide
4.0 mi/2.0 hrs

This route takes advantage of a short connector trail that links two of the prettiest areas in the wilderness. Climbing up the Strawberry Creek Valley to Strawberry Lake, you'll enjoy a valley dense with old-growth forest and high alpine country. When you've seen all there is to see and gotten your enjoyment of Strawberry Lake, slide on down the short side trail that leads to the east from the lake. A quarter mile down the path, enter the upper reaches of Slide Basin and Slide Lake. From here head north on the main Slide Lake Trail and loop back around to the trailhead.

Location: South of Prairie City in Malheur National Forest within the Strawberry Mountain Wilderness; see Northeast Oregon Map 7, grid f4.

User Groups: Hikers, dogs, and horses. No mountain bikes are allowed. No wheelchair facilities.

Permits: A federal Northwest Forest Pass, $5 per day or $30 annually, is required to park at the trailhead. Passes are available from ranger stations and many private vendors, online at website: www.wta.org, or by calling 800/270-7504. Party size is limited to 12 people.

Maps: For a trail information report, contact the Prairie City Ranger District at 541/820-3311. For a map of Malheur National Forest, contact Nature of the Northwest Information Center, 800 Northeast Oregon Street, Suite 177, Portland, OR 97232; 503/872-2750. Ask the USGS for a topographic map of the Strawberry Mountain area.

Directions: From Prairie City drive 12 miles south on County Road 60 to the road's end and the trailhead.

Contact: Malheur National Forest, Prairie City Ranger District, 327 Front Street, Prairie City, OR 97869; 541/820-3311.

121 Horseshoe
12.0 mi/8.0 hrs

Beginning as an old twin-track jeep trail, this route quickly narrows to a faint single-track path that climbs steeply through an area burned by a forest fire. It finally tops out on the ridge with views of the Monument Rock Wilderness and surrounding peaks. The route is hot, dry, and dusty, so bring plenty of water and sunscreen.

Location: South of Prairie City in Malheur National Forest; see Northeast Oregon Map 7, grid e6.

User Groups: Hikers, dogs, horses, and mountain bikes. No wheelchair facilities.

Permits: A federal Northwest Forest Pass, $5 per day or $30 annually, is required to park at the trailhead. Passes are available from ranger stations and many private vendors, online at website: www.wta.org, or by calling 800/270-7504.

Maps: For a trail information report, contact the Prairie City Ranger District at 541/820-3311. For a map of Malheur National Forest, contact Nature of the Northwest Information Center, 800 Northeast Oregon Street, Suite 177, Portland, OR 97232; 503/872-2750.

Ask the USGS for a topographic map of the Little Baldy Mountain area.

Directions: From Prairie City drive south on County Road 62/Forest Service Road 14 to Deardorff Creek. Turn left onto Forest Service Road 13 and continue 12 miles to the trailhead on the right side of the road.

Contact: Malheur National Forest, Prairie City Ranger District, 327 Front Street, Prairie City, OR 97869; 541/820-3311.

122 Elk Flat
5.0 mi/2.5 hrs

The gentle valley trail offers good access to and sights of the pretty creek, as well as the abundant wildlife that thrives in the area. Elk commonly graze the broad meadow (hence the name), and numerous campsites ring the flat. A cold, clear spring provides refreshing water on the edge of the meadow. At the far end of the trail, the route suddenly becomes steep and rocky, gaining more than 1,000 feet in elevation in the final few miles to the turnaround point, a ridge high above the Malheur River.

Location: South of Prairie City in Malheur National Forest; see Northeast Oregon Map 7, grid f7.

User Groups: Hikers, dogs, horses, and mountain bikes. No wheelchair facilities.

Permits: A federal Northwest Forest Pass, $5 per day or $30 annually, is required to park at the trailhead. Passes are available from ranger stations and many private vendors, online at website: www.wta.org, or by calling 800/270-7504.

Maps: For a trail information report, contact the Prairie City Ranger District at 541/820-3311. For a map of Malheur National Forest, contact Nature of the Northwest Information Center, 800 Northeast Oregon Street, Suite 177, Portland, OR 97232; 503/872-2750. Ask the USGS for a topographic map of the Little Baldy Mountain area.

Directions: From Prairie City drive about eight miles south on County Road 62/Forest Service Road 14 to Deardorff Creek. Turn left onto Forest Service Road 13 and continue about 10 miles to Forest Service Road 1370. Turn left and drive past the Little Malheur River Trailhead to the Elk Flat Trailhead on the left.

Contact: Malheur National Forest, Prairie City Ranger Distict, 327 Front Street, Prairie City, OR 97869; 541/820-3311.

123 Little Malheur River
14.6 mi/1.0–2.0 days

This trail bisects the lovely Monument Rock Wilderness. Its northern end begins in the Elk Flat area and gradually descends Elk Creek to its junction with the Little Malheur River. The trail continues down the valley along the river, and as more and more side creeks add their waters to the main stream, the Little Malheur becomes a top-notch trout fishery. Deer and elk move throughout the area, but so do cattle, so treat your drinking water meticulously. You'll find plenty of campsites along the stream.

Location: Southeast of Prairie City in Malheur National Forest within the Monument Rock Wilderness; see Northeast Oregon Map 7, grid f7.

User Groups: Hikers, dogs, and horses. No mountain bikes are allowed. No wheelchair facilities.

Permits: A federal Northwest Forest Pass, $5 per day or $30 annually, is required to park at the trailhead. Passes are available from ranger stations and many private vendors, online at website: www.wta.org, or by calling 800/270-7504. Party size is limited to 12 people.

Maps: For a trail information report, contact the Prairie City Ranger District at 541/820-3311. For a map of Malheur National Forest, contact Nature of the Northwest Information Center, 800 Northeast Oregon Street, Suite 177, Portland, OR 97232; 503/872-2750. Ask the USGS for a topographic map of the Bull-run Rock areas.

Directions: From Prairie City drive about eight miles south on County Road 62/Forest Service Road 14 to Deardorff Creek. Turn left onto Forest Service Road 13 and continue about 10 miles to Forest Service Road 1370. Turn left and drive to the trailhead on the left. To get to the southern end of the trail, continue south on Forest Service Road 13 past the Forest Service Road 1370 turnoff. Following the road to the Short Creek Guard Station, turn left (east) onto Forest Service Road 16, and drive 10 miles to Forest Service Road 1672. Take a left (north) turn onto Forest Service Road 1672 and drive to the road's end and the trailhead.

Contact: Malheur National Forest, Prairie City Ranger District, 327 Front Street, Prairie City, OR 97869; 541/820-3311.

124 Joaquin Miller
12.0 mi/6.0 hrs

Leading through the Canyon Creek Research Area, this trail offers a great chance to explore an old-growth ponderosa pine forest, which spreads along a long bench on the valley wall about two miles in from the trailhead. If trees don't excite you, maybe the herds of bighorn sheep and mountain goats that live around the head of Berry Creek (along the north side of this trail) will pique your interest. The brawny, head-banging sheep are a bit shyer than the mountain goats, so most of your sheep sightings are from a distance. Binoculars can be a real bonus, so pack 'em if you've got 'em.

Location: South of John Day in Malheur National Forest within the Strawberry Mountain Wilderness; see Northeast Oregon Map 7, grid f4.

User Groups: Hikers, dogs, and horses. No mountain bikes are allowed. No wheelchair facilities.

Permits: A federal Northwest Forest Pass, $5 per day or $30 annually, is required to park at the trailhead. Passes are available from ranger stations and many private vendors, online at website: www.wta.org, or by calling 800/270-7504. Party size is limited to 12 people.

Maps: For a trail information report, contact the Bear Valley Ranger District at 541/575-2110. For a map of Malheur National Forest, contact Nature of the Northwest Information Center, 800 Northeast Oregon Street, Suite 177, Portland, OR 97232; 503/872-2750. Ask the USGS for topographic maps of the Canyon Mountain and Pine Creek Mountain areas.

Directions: From John Day drive about nine miles south on U.S. 395 to County Road 65. Turn left onto County Road 65, continue four miles, and turn north onto Forest Service Road 6510. Drive north on Forest Service Road 6510 to the road's end and the trailhead.

Contact: Malheur National Forest, 431 Patterson Bridge Road, John Day, OR 97845; 541/575-3000.

125 Tamarack Creek
7.8 mi/3.9 hrs

In this part of Oregon, this trail is the best choice for those who want to see bighorn sheep. In fact, if you can't find them here, you'll be hard pressed to find them anywhere. The trail wraps around two sides of the Canyon Creek Research Area, beginning along the Pine Creek Ridge, turning, and then dropping down into the Tamarack Basin. By the way, tamarack is a regional name for the western larch. If possible, visit this area in the autumn when these trees turn gold and light up the dark green forest.

Location: South of John Day in Malheur National Forest within the Strawberry Mountain Wilderness; see Northeast Oregon Map 7, grid f5.

User Groups: Hikers, dogs, and horses. No mountain bikes are allowed. No wheelchair facilities.

Permits: A federal Northwest Forest Pass, $5 per day or $30 annually, is required to park at the trailhead. Passes are available from ranger stations and many private vendors, online at website: www.wta.org, or by calling 800/270-7504. Party size is limited to 12 people.

Maps: For a trail information report, contact the Bear Valley Ranger District at 541/575-2110. For a map of Malheur National Forest, contact Nature of the Northwest Information Center, 800 Northeast Oregon Street, Suite 177, Portland, OR 97232; 503/872-2750. Ask the USGS for topographic maps of the Canyon Mountain and Pine Creek Mountain areas.

Directions: From John Day drive about nine miles south on U.S. 395 to County Road 65. Turn left, continue four miles, and turn north onto Forest Service Road 6510. Drive north on Forest Service Road 6510 to the road's end and the trailhead.

Contact: Malheur National Forest, 431 Patterson Bridge Road, John Day, OR 97845; 541/575-3000.

126 East Fork Canyon Creek
19.8 mi/1.0–2.0 days 🥾 👟

Spectacular high-elevation views await at the end of this pretty but long valley-bottom hike. You pass through a beautiful old-growth forest that fills the valley of Canyon Creek as the trail follows it upstream for several miles. Then you pass Yokum Corrals Camp and the

Tamarack Creek Trail at mile three, before weaving up-slope just a bit. The trail leaves the creek near Miner Creek and cuts back and forth across the Canyon Creek Valley headwall. It passes in front of Hotel De Bum Camp at nine miles and finally reaches the ridgetop near Indian Creek Butte. The last stretch is fairly steep, but the views of the surrounding wilderness peaks and valleys are breathtaking.

Location: South of John Day in Malheur National Forest within the Strawberry Mountain Wilderness; see Northeast Oregon Map 7, grid f4.

User Groups: Hikers, dogs, and horses. No mountain bikes are allowed. No wheelchair facilities.

Permits: A federal Northwest Forest Pass, $5 per day or $30 annually, is required to park at the trailhead. Passes are available from ranger stations and many private vendors, online at website: www.wta.org, or by calling 800/270-7504. Party size is limited to 12 people.

Maps: For a trail information report, contact the Bear Valley Ranger District at 541/575-2110. For a map of Malheur National Forest, contact Nature of the Northwest Information Center, 800 Northeast Oregon Street, Suite 177, Portland, OR 97232; 503/872-2750. Ask the USGS for topographic maps of the Canyon Mountain and Pine Creek Mountain areas.

Directions: From John Day drive about nine miles south on U.S. 395 to County Road 65. Turn left, continue four miles, and turn north onto Forest Service Road 6510. Drive north on Forest Service Road 6510 to Forest Service Road 812. Turn right and drive to the road's end and the trailhead.

Contact: Malheur National Forest, 431 Patterson Bridge Road, John Day, OR 97845; 541/575-3000.

127 Table Mountain
12.4 mi/6.2 hrs

We confess that we don't quite understand why so few people use this trail, but we're not really complaining. The dearth of other hikers actually makes the trail even more special. On the long, lonesome hike along the ridgeline on the southern wilderness boundary, you find fantastic sweeping views of the whole wilderness area, as well as the southern half of Malheur National Forest. Deer, elk, mountain goats, and the occasional bighorn sheep roam this route; golden eagles and red-tailed hawks soar overhead. Although water is scarce, you can find it at Wall Creek, as well as Anchor Spring. Near the end of the trail you find Hotel De Bum Camp and a junction with the Canyon Creek Trail near Indian Creek Butte.

Location: South of John Day in Malheur National Forest within the Strawberry Mountain Wilderness; see Northeast Oregon Map 7, grid g4.

User Groups: Hikers, dogs, and horses. No mountain bikes. No wheelchair facilities.

Permits: A federal Northwest Forest Pass, $5 per day or $30 annually, is required to park at the trailhead. Passes are available from ranger stations and many private vendors, online at website: www.wta.org, or by calling 800/270-7504. Party size is limited to 12 people.

Maps: For a trail information report, contact the Bear Valley Ranger District at 541/575-2110. For a map of Malheur National Forest, contact Nature of the Northwest Information Center, 800 Northeast Oregon Street, Suite 177, Portland, OR 97232; 503/872-2750. Ask the USGS for topographic maps of the Big Canyon and Pine Creek Mountain areas.

Directions: From John Day drive about nine miles south on U.S. 395 to County Road 65. Turn left and drive about four miles to For-est Service Road 6510. Drive north on Forest Service Road 6510 to the road's end and the trailhead.

Contact: Malheur National Forest, 431 Patterson Bridge Road, John Day, OR 97845; 541/575-3000.

128 Buckhorn Meadows
5.4 mi/2.7 hrs

Beginning in Buckhorn Meadows, this trail provides the easiest and best access to Wildcat Basin, a gorgeous alpine bowl watered by a cool, clear spring. The route is a high traverse, for it gains just 1,000 feet in elevation yet ends 7,000 feet above sea level. Look for bighorn sheep, mountain goats, deer, and elk as you scan the backdrop of the high peaks and deep valleys laid out before you. In fact, the panoramic views are so pervasive they seem almost commonplace. There's nothing common about this place, though. Wildflower meadows speckle Wildcat Basin, and the cold, clear waters of Wildcat Spring are a welcome reprieve from the hot summer sun. Cougars and bobcats live in the wilderness, so you may see the namesakes of this place, too.

Location: South of Prairie City in Malheur National Forest within the Strawberry Mountain Wilderness; see Northeast Oregon Map 7, grid g5.

User Groups: Hikers, dogs, and horses. No mountain bikes are allowed. No wheelchair facilities.

Permits: A federal Northwest Forest Pass, $5 per day or $30 annually, is required to park at the trailhead. Passes are available from ranger stations and many private vendors, online at website: www.wta.org, or by calling 800/270-7504. Party size is limited to 12 people.

Maps: For a trail information report, contact the Bear Valley

Ranger District at 541/575-2110. For a map of Malheur National Forest, contact Nature of the Northwest Information Center, 800 Northeast Oregon Street, Suite 177, Portland, OR 97232; 503/872-2750 Ask the USGS for topographic maps of the Strawberry Mountain and Pine Creek Mountain areas.

Directions: From John Day drive about nine miles south on U.S. 395 to the junction with Forest Service Road 65. Turn left (east), continue about seven miles to Forest Service Road 15, and turn left. Drive one mile to the junction with Forest Service Road 1520. Turn left onto Forest Service Road 1520 and drive to the road's end and the trailhead.

Contact: Malheur National Forest, 431 Patterson Bridge Road, John Day, OR 97845; 541/575-3000.

129 Indian Creek Headwaters
2.2 mi/1.5 hrs

Short, steep, and rough, this trail is a quicker, though tougher, route into the headwater basin of Indian Creek than the main Indian Creek Trail (see hike in this chapter). Scenery is somewhat limited, but there are great views of the west and southwest faces of Strawberry Mountain. The trail gains nearly 1,000 feet in elevation in just over a mile, and most of the length is in open, dry terrain. Pack plenty of water and sunscreen and watch for rattlesnakes.

Location: South of Prairie City in Malheur National Forest within the Strawberry Mountain Wilderness; see Northeast Oregon Map 7, grid f5.

User Groups: Hikers, dogs, and horses. No mountain bikes are allowed. No wheelchair facilities.

Permits: A federal Northwest Forest Pass, $5 per day or $30 annually, is required to park at the trailhead. Passes are available from ranger stations and many private ven-

dors, online at website: www.wta.org, or by calling 800/270-7504. Party size is limited to 12 people.

Maps: For a trail information report, contact the Prairie City Ranger District at 541/820-3311. For a map of Malheur National Forest, contact Nature of the Northwest Information Center, 800 Northeast Oregon Street, Suite 177, Portland, OR 97232; 503/872-2750. Ask the USGS for a topographic map of the Strawberry Mountain area.

Directions: From Prairie City drive about 22 miles south on County Road 62/Forest Service Road 14 to Summit Prairie. Turn right (west) onto Forest Service Road 16 and continue about 12 miles to Forest Service Road 1640, just beyond Logan Valley. Turn right (north) onto Forest Service Road 1640 and drive to the road's end and the trailhead.

Contact: Malheur National Forest, Prairie City Ranger District, 327 Front Street, Prairie City, OR 97869; 541/820-3311.

130 Little Mud Lake
7.0 mi/3.5 hrs

Leading up around the western edge of the Little Riner Basin, this trail is a great seldom-used route into the picturesque Lakes Basin. The trail climbs along a small creek as it passes the Little Riner Basin, then turns steeply up the ridge face and climbs to the high Lakes Basin. You end up at the shores of Little Mud Lake, but side trails heading off toward other alpine lakes abound. This is a stunningly beautiful area and a truly wild wilderness. After exploring the Lakes Basin, return the way you came.

Location: South of Prairie City in Malheur National Forest within the Strawberry Mountain Wilderness; see Northeast Oregon Map 7, grid f5.

User Groups: Hikers, dogs, and horses. No mountain bikes are allowed. No wheelchair facilities.

Permits: A federal Northwest Forest Pass, $5 per day or $30 annually, is required to park at the trailhead. Passes are available from ranger stations and many private vendors, online at website: www.wta.org, or by calling 800/270-7504. Party size is limited to 12 people.

Maps: For a trail information report, contact the Prairie City Ranger District at 541/820-3311. For a map of Malheur National Forest, contact Nature of the Northwest Information Center, 800 Northeast Oregon Street, Suite 177, Portland, OR 97232; 503/872-2750. Ask the USGS for a topographic map of the Strawberry Mountain area.

Directions: From Prairie City drive about 22 miles south on County Road 62/Forest Service Road 14 to Summit Prairie. Turn right (west) onto Forest Service Road 16 and continue about 8.5 miles to Forest Service Road 924. Turn right (north) and drive 1.5 miles to Forest Service Road 039. Turn right and drive to the road's end and the trailhead.

Contact: Malheur National Forest, Prairie City Ranger District, 327 Front Street, Prairie City, OR 97869; 541/820-3311.

131 Mud Lake
3.0 mi/1.5 hrs

It's great for a day hike, but don't plan on making an overnight trip. The shores of Mud Lake really are muddy; the campsites are yucky, too. Still, the lake is pretty, as are the marshy areas around its perimeter, which are filled with wildflowers. But the best features of this trail are the lush old-growth forest and the solitude. It's almost a sure bet that hikers will have the trail to themselves. The trail climbs constantly but moderately, so it's fairly easy overall.

Location: South of Prairie City in Malheur National Forest within the Strawberry Mountain Wilderness; see Northeast Oregon Map 7, grid f5.

User Groups: Hikers, dogs, and horses. No mountain bikes are allowed. No wheelchair facilities.

Permits: A federal Northwest Forest Pass, $5 per day or $30 annually, is required to park at the trailhead. Passes are available from ranger stations and many private vendors, online at website: www.wta.org, or by calling 800/270-7504. Party size is limited to 12 people.

Maps: For a trail information report, contact the Prairie City Ranger District at 541/820-3311. For a map of Malheur National Forest, contact Nature of the Northwest Information Center, 800 Northeast Oregon Street, Suite 177, Portland, OR 97232; 503/872-2750. Ask the USGS for a topographic map of the Strawberry Mountain area.

Directions: From Prairie City drive about 22 miles south on County Road 62/Forest Service Road 14 to Summit Prairie. Turn right (west) onto Forest Service Road 16 and continue about 8.5 miles to Forest Service Road 924. Turn right (north) and drive 1.5 miles to Forest Service Road 039. Turn right and drive to the road's end and the trailhead.

Contact: Malheur National Forest, Prairie City Ranger District, 327 Front Street, Prairie City, OR 97869; 541/820-3311.

132 Lake Creek
8.0 mi/4.0 hrs

A long and beautiful river-valley hike ends at a sparkling little mountain lake under the flank of a steep butte. That's beautiful, but the route also climbs through prime elk territory, so you have a good chance of seeing these noble giants. The trail leaves the trailhead and climbs gradually but continually alongside the creek to the valley headwall. The trail then climbs at a steeper pitch up the headwall and finally ends near the shore of High Lake, which rests in the shadow of Indian Spring Butte. Other trails also lead past High Lake, so side trips can extend your hike. Or you may opt to spend the night at one of the beautiful little campsites around the lake before returning back down the valley.

Location: South of Prairie City in Malheur National Forest within the Strawberry Mountain Wilderness; see Northeast Oregon Map 7, grid f5.

User Groups: Hikers, dogs, and horses. No mountain bikes are allowed. No wheelchair facilities.

Permits: A federal Northwest Forest Pass, $5 per day or $30 annually, is required to park at the trailhead. Passes are available from ranger stations and many private vendors, online at website: www.wta.org, or by calling 800/270-7504. Party size is limited to 12 people.

Maps: For a trail information report, contact the Prairie City Ranger District at 541/820-3311. For a map of Malheur National Forest, contact Nature of the Northwest Information Center, 800 Northeast Oregon Street, Suite 177, Portland, OR 97232; 503/872-2750. Ask the USGS for a topographic map of the Strawberry Mountain area.

Directions: From Prairie City drive about 22 miles south on County Road 62/Forest Service Road 14 to Summit Prairie. Turn right (west) onto Forest Service Road 16 and continue about 8.5 miles to Forest Service Road 924. Turn right (north) and then drive to the road's end and the trailhead.

Contact: Malheur National Forest, Prairie City Ranger District, 327 Front Street, Prairie City, OR 97869; 541/820-3311.

133 Meadow Fork
9.2 mi/4.6 hrs

Old-growth pine, spruce, fir, and some larch fill the valley, and a sparkling river carves through its bottom. The trail parallels the water and climbs up the sometimes-steep valley to Little Riner Basin. There you find wildflower fields and views of the Kimport Ridge and the surrounding peaks. Continuing up the trail, you reenter the old-growth forest and climb steeply to Big Riner Basin and the trail's end. Enjoy the views of Slide Mountain and the long, green valleys that lead away to the south. Explore the area to your heart's content—there are plenty of local attractions—before retracing your steps down the valley to the trailhead.

Location: South of Prairie City in Malheur National Forest within the Strawberry Mountain Wilderness; see Northeast Oregon Map 7, grid f5.

User Groups: Hikers, dogs, and horses. No mountain bikes are allowed. No wheelchair facilities.

Permits: A federal Northwest Forest Pass, $5 per day or $30 annually, is required to park at the trailhead. Passes are available from ranger stations and many private vendors, online at website: www.wta.org, or by calling 800/270-7504. Party size is limited to 12 people.

Maps: For a trail information report, contact the Prairie City Ranger District at 541/820-3311. For a map of Malheur National Forest, contact Nature of the Northwest Information Center, 800 Northeast Oregon Street, Suite 177, Portland, OR 97232; 503/872-2750. Ask the USGS for topographic maps of the Strawberry Mountain and Logan Valley West areas.

Directions: From Prairie City drive about 22 miles south on County Road 62/Forest Service Road 14 to Summit Prairie. Turn right (west) onto Forest Service Road 16 and continue about 8.5 miles to Forest Service Road 924. Turn right (north) and drive 1.5 miles to Forest Service Road 039. Turn right and drive to the road's end and the trailhead.

Contact: Malheur National Forest, Prairie City Ranger District, 327 Front Street, Prairie City, OR 97869; 541/820-3311.

134 Snowshoe
5.8 mi/2.9 hrs

The offerings of this well-maintained trail are an old-growth forest environment and lots of solitude and serenity. The route drops down across the Big Creek Valley and climbs up the Snowshoe Valley alongside Snowshoe Creek. Elk often feed in the basin's grass and flower-filled meadows, and both deer and elk use the trail to get up and over Skyline Ridge. The trail terminates at a junction with the Skyline Trail. From here, retrace your steps to the trailhead.

Location: South of Prairie City in Malheur National Forest within the Strawberry Mountain Wilderness; see Northeast Oregon Map 7, grid f5.

User Groups: Hikers, dogs, and horses. No mountain bikes are allowed. No wheelchair facilities.

Permits: A federal Northwest Forest Pass, $5 per day or $30 annually, is required to park at the trailhead. Passes are available from ranger stations and many private vendors, online at website: www.wta.org, or by calling 800/270-7504. Party size is limited to 12 people.

Maps: For a trail information report, contact the Prairie City Ranger District at 541/820-3311. For a map of Malheur National Forest, contact Nature of the Northwest Information Center, 800 Northeast Oregon Street, Suite 177, Portland, OR 97232; 503/872-2750. Ask the USGS for topographic maps of the Strawberry Mountain and Roberts Creek areas.

Directions: From Prairie City drive about 22 miles south on County Road 62/Forest Service Road 14 to Summit Prairie. Turn right (west) onto Forest Service Road 16 and continue about 8.5 miles to Forest Service Road 924. Turn right (north) and drive 2.5 miles before turning right onto Forest Service Road 924-021. Follow the road 2.5 miles to the trailhead.

Contact: Malheur National Forest, Prairie City Ranger District, 327 Front Street, Prairie City, OR 97869; 541/820-3311.

135 Big Creek
10.6 mi/5.3 hrs

Making its way through a thick pine, spruce, and fir forest, this trail is a good choice on a hot summer day. While the surrounding ridgetop trails may provide more views, this trail offers a great combination of pretty scenery, refreshing water, and cool shade. The route parallels Big Creek for the first few miles and slices through some wonderful forest meadows, which offer great campsites and fragrant wildflowers. The trail's upper end climbs to Big Riner Basin and views of Slide Mountain and the jagged ridges around the area. The abundance of deer, elk, and black bears makes this a popular trail with hunters during the autumn hunting season. The trail ends in Big Riner Basin, so turn and retrace your steps to the trailhead from there.

Location: South of John Day in Malheur National Forest; see Northeast Oregon Map 7, grid f5.

User Groups: Hikers, dogs, and horses. No mountain bikes are allowed. No wheelchair facilities.

Permits: A federal Northwest Forest Pass, $5 per day or $30 annually, is required to park at the trailhead. Passes are available from ranger stations and many private vendors, online at website: www.wta.org, or by calling 800/270-7504.

Maps: For a trail information report, contact the Prairie

City Ranger District at 541/820-3311. For a map of Malheur National Forest, contact Nature of the Northwest Information Center, 800 Northeast Oregon Street, Suite 177, Portland, OR 97232; 503/872-2750. Ask the USGS for a topographic map of the Roberts Creek area.

Directions: From Prairie City drive about 22 miles south on County Road 62/Forest Service Road 14 to Summit Prairie. Turn right (west) onto Forest Service Road 16 and continue about 8.5 miles to Forest Service Road 924. Turn right (north) and drive 2.5 miles before turning right onto Forest Service Road 924-021. Follow the road to its end and the trailhead.

Contact: Malheur National Forest, Prairie City Ranger District, 327 Front Street, Prairie City, OR 97869; 541/820-3311.

136 Rail Creek
7.2 mi/3.7 hrs

Following a high ridgeline for much of the way, the trail offers fantastic views of the surrounding forest. Despite the trail's name, there is no source of water along the route, and the open, dusty ridge can get very hot in the summer, so bring plenty of water. Also keep a keen eye out for rattlesnakes. They like to stretch out and sun themselves along the ridge.

Location: South of Prairie City in Malheur National Forest; see Northeast Oregon Map 7, grid f6.

User Groups: Hikers, dogs, horses, and mountain bikes. No wheelchair facilities.

Permits: A federal Northwest Forest Pass, $5 per day or $30 annually, is required to park at the trailhead. Passes are available from ranger stations and many private vendors, online at website: www.wta.org, or by calling 800/270-7504.

Maps: For a trail information report, contact the Prairie City Ranger District at 541/820-3311. For a map of Malheur National Forest, contact Nature of the Northwest

Information Center, 800 Northeast Oregon Street, Suite 177, Portland, OR 97232; 503/872-2750. Ask the USGS for topographic maps of the Roberts Creek and Little Baldy Mountain areas.

Directions: From Prairie City drive about 20 miles west on County Road 62/Forest Service Road 14 until you reach the junction with Forest Service Road 1665. Turn left and continue to the road's end and the trailhead at the top of Lookout Mountain.

Contact: Malheur National Forest, Prairie City Ranger District, 327 Front Street, Prairie City, OR 97869; 541/820-3311.

137 Sheep Creek
10.8 mi/5.4 hrs

From the Lookout Mountain Trailhead, the trail begins with spectacular panoramic views before dropping steeply into the Sheep Creek Basin. At mile one the trail enters a thick second-growth forest of pine, larch, and spruce and then descends into the valley and along the noisy stream. Spruce grouse often call through the forest, and deer graze in the small streamside clearings. The turnaround point is at Sheep Creek and the trailhead there.

If a shuttle vehicle can be arranged, you can avoid a long backtrack. From the Lookout Mountain Trailhead, the route is downhill all the way. From the opposite end, it is all uphill. You decide how hard you work on this hike.

Location: South of Prairie City in Malheur National Forest; see Northeast Oregon Map 7, grid f7.

User Groups: Hikers, dogs, horses, and mountain bikes. No wheelchair facilities.

Permits: A federal Northwest Forest Pass, $5 per day or $30 annually, is required to park at the trailhead. Passes are available from ranger stations and many private vendors,

online at website: www.wta.org, or by calling 800/270-7504.

Maps: For a trail information report, contact the Prairie City Ranger District at 541/820-3311. For a map of Malheur National Forest, contact Nature of the Northwest Information Center, 800 Northeast Oregon Street, Suite 177, Portland, OR 97232; 503/872-2750. Ask the USGS for a topographic map of the Little Baldy Mountain area.

Directions: From Prairie City drive about 20 miles south on County Road 62/Forest Service Road 14 until you reach the junction with Forest Service Road 1665. Turn left and continue to the road's end and the western trailhead at the top of Lookout Mountain. To reach the eastern trailhead from Prairie City, drive about eight miles south on County Road 62/Forest Service Road 14 to Deardorff Creek and Forest Service Road 13. Turn left (east) onto Forest Service Road 13 and continue 15 miles to the trailhead on the right.

Contact: Malheur National Forest, Prairie City Ranger District, 327 Front Street, Prairie City, OR 97869; 541/820-3311.

🔢138 Skyline
35.6 mi/3.0 days

Cutting across the eastern portion of the wilderness, this trail provides access to some of the most beautiful backcountry in the state. The route follows the long, winding spine of the Strawberry Mountains, staying high on the ridge and affording stunning views of the surrounding wilderness. Good camping exists in the headwater basin of Snowshoe Creek (crossed at about five miles), as well as at Big Riner Basin at the trail's end. Climbing up the face of the ridge, the trail slashes through a long series of switchbacks before attaining the crest and entering the wilderness. From here the route rolls north under the flank of Dead Horse

Butte and on around to the west into Big Riner Basin. Look for deer, elk, and mountain goats along this route, and keep an eye on the sky, as you may see a soaring golden eagle. From Big Riner Basin the trail loops through the Lakes Basin. Side trails provide access to an assortment of alpine lakes, ponds, and puddles.

Since the trail is accessible on both ends, a shuttle car can eliminate the long backtrack, making this a good weekend trip or day trip.

Location: South of Prairie City in Malheur National Forest within the Strawberry Mountain Wilderness; see Northeast Oregon Map 7, grid g7.

User Groups: Hikers, dogs, and horses. No mountain bikes are allowed. No wheelchair facilities.

Permits: A federal Northwest Forest Pass, $5 per day or $30 annually, is required to park at the trailhead. Passes are available from ranger stations and many private vendors, online at website: www.wta.org, or by calling 800/270-7504. Party size is limited to 12 people.

Maps: For a trail information report, contact the Prairie City Ranger District at 541/820-3311. For a map of Malheur National Forest, contact Nature of the Northwest Information Center, 800 Northeast Oregon Street, Suite 177, Portland, OR 97232; 503/872-2750. Ask the USGS for a topographic map of the Strawberry Mountain area.

Directions: From Prairie City drive about 18 miles south on County Road 62/Forest Service Road 14 to Forest Service Road 101. Turn right (west) and drive two miles to the trailhead on the right. The western trailhead is accessible from John Day. Drive south on U.S. 395 to County Road 65/Forest Service Road 15. Turn left onto County Road 65 and continue to Forest Service Road 16. Turn left (east) and then turn north onto Forest

Service Road 1640. Drive to the end of the road and the trailhead.

Contact: Malheur National Forest, Prairie City Ranger District, 327 Front Street, Prairie City, OR 97869; 541/820-3311.

⓭⓷⓽ Crane Creek
13.0 mi/6.5 hrs

Take this historic trail and follow an old wagon/jeep route, the former Dalles Military Road. The trail traces the creek for its entire length and gains less than 500 feet in elevation, making this a very level and easy trail to hike or bike. The scenery is limited to the pretty little creek and the thick second-growth forest.

Location: South of Prairie City in Malheur National Forest; see Northeast Oregon Map 7, grid g6.

User Groups: Hikers, dogs, horses, and mountain bikes. No wheelchair facilities.

Permits: A federal Northwest Forest Pass, $5 per day or $30 annually, is required to park at the trailhead. Passes are available from ranger stations and many private vendors, online at website: www.wta.org, or by calling 800/270-7504.

Maps: For a trail information report, contact the Prairie City Ranger District at 541/820-3311. For a map of Malheur National Forest, contact Nature of the Northwest Information Center, 800 Northeast Oregon Street, Suite 177, Portland, OR 97232; 503/872-2750. Ask the USGS for a topographic map of the Crane Prairie area.

Directions: From Prairie City drive about 22 miles south on County Road 62/Forest Service Road 14 to Summit Prairie. Turn left onto Forest Service Road 16 and continue about four miles to Forest Service Road 1663. Turn right (south), drive one mile, and turn right onto Forest Service Road 809. Continue east a short distance to the trailhead on the left.

Contact: Malheur National Forest, Prairie City Ranger District, 327 Front Street, Prairie City, OR 97869; 541/820-3311.

⓭⓸⓿ North Fork Malheur
24.8 mi/2.0 days

After crossing the scenic North Fork Malheur River via a sweet footbridge, this trail rambles downstream along the west bank of the river, a cold, tumbling ribbon of water that harbors strong populations of rainbow and brook trout. The trail is well maintained and fairly level, dropping just 800 feet in about 12 miles. As you go you enjoy the old-growth forest and thick stands of alder and maple that line the riverbank. Camping is allowed anywhere along the river.

Location: Southeast of Prairie City in Malheur National Forest; see Northeast Oregon Map 7, grid g7.

User Groups: Hikers, dogs, and horses. No mountain bikes are allowed. No wheelchair facilities.

Permits: A federal Northwest Forest Pass, $5 per day or $30 annually, is required to park at the trailhead. Passes are available from ranger stations and many private vendors, online at website: www.wta.org, or by calling 800/270-7504.

Maps: For a trail information report, contact the Prairie City Ranger District at 541/820-3311. For a map of Malheur National Forest, contact Nature of the Northwest Information Center, 800 Northeast Oregon Street, Suite 177, Portland, OR 97232; 503/872-2750. Ask the USGS for a topographic map of the Flag Prairie Northeast and Northwest areas.

Directions: From Prairie City drive approximately eight miles south on County Road 62/Forest Service Road 14 to Deardorff Creek. Turn left onto Forest Service Road 13, continue about 14 miles to the Short Creek Guard Station, and then turn right onto Forest Service Road 16. Follow this road south

for about three more miles to Forest Service Road 1675 and turn left. Continue to the North Fork Campground and the trailhead.
Contact: Malheur National Forest, Prairie City Ranger District, 327 Front Street, Prairie City, OR 97869; 541/820-3311.

141 Malheur River National Recreation Trail
15.2 mi/7.6 hrs

The west bank of the picturesque Malheur River is the route followed by this National Recreation Trail. Big rainbow, brook, and golden trout thrive in the river, and assorted wildlife species travel along its shores. Deep forest surrounds this section of river and other roads are far away, so no sounds of human civilization intrude as you stroll.

Location: Southeast of Seneca in Malheur National Forest; see Northeast Oregon Map 7, grid h3.

User Groups: Hikers, dogs, horses, and mountain bikes. No wheelchair facilities.

Permits: A federal Northwest Forest Pass, $5 per day or $30 annually, is required to park at the trailhead. Passes are available from ranger stations and many private vendors, online at website: www.wta.org, or by calling 800/270-7504.

Maps: For a trail information report, contact the Burns Ranger District at 541/573-7292. For a map of Malheur National Forest, contact Nature of the Northwest Information Center, 800 Northeast Oregon Street, Suite 177, Portland, OR 97232; 503/872-2750. Ask the USGS for a topographic map of the Dollar Basin area.

Directions: From Seneca drive about 14 miles east on Forest Service Road 16 to Forest Service Road 1643. Turn right (south) on this road and continue 10 miles to Dollar Basin. Turn left (still on Forest Service Road 1643) and drive one more mile to the Malheur River. The trailhead is 200 feet downstream.

Contact: Malheur National Forest, Burns Ranger District, HC-74, Box 12870, Hines, OR 97738; 541/573-4300.

142 Historic Oregon Trail
4.2 mi/3.0 hrs

Throughout the 1800s, the Oregon Trail brought rugged settlers from Midwestern farming communities west to start new lives in the Oregon Territory. In 1993 the state of Oregon formally recognized the historic wagon-rutted route, thereby preserving many sections of it, including this bluff-top trail above the Powder River. A long, well-maintained interpretive trail system weaves through old homesteaders' encampments and passes deeply rutted wagon roads. (The magnitude of the westward migration is evident when you look at the two-foot-deep ruts and imagine the number of wagons that rolled over this land.) You also see an old lode mine, a mine that was cut deep into the earth to tap lodes, or veins, of gold ore. Take your time on this trail—the historic sites are worth enjoying, but so are the natural views of the Powder River Valley and the Elkhorn Mountains to the west.

Location: East of Baker City; see Northeast Oregon Map 8, grid b4.

User Groups: Hikers and dogs. Fully wheelchair accessible. No horses or mountain bikes are allowed.

Permits: No permits are needed.

Maps: Ask the USGS for a topographic map of the Flagstaff Hill area.

Directions: From Baker City drive six miles east on Highway 86 to the National Historic Oregon Trails Interpretive Center. The trail begins behind the center.

Contact: National Historic Oregon Trails Interpretive Center, Bureau of Land Management, P.O. Box 987, Baker City, OR 97814; 541/523-1843.

THE SOUTHERN CASCADES

The Southern Cascades

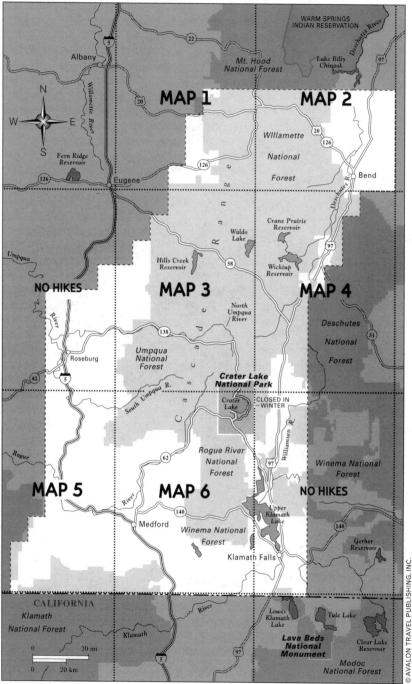

Map 1

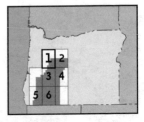

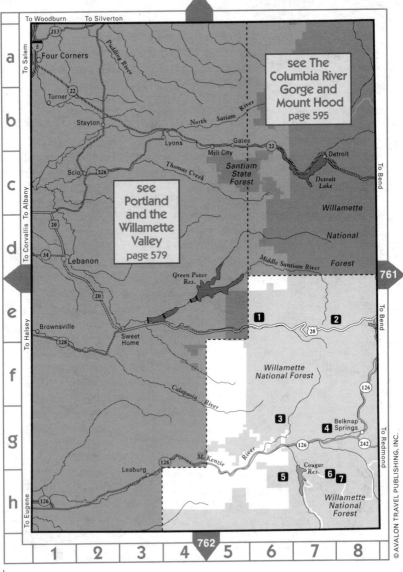

see The Columbia River Gorge and Mount Hood page 595

see Portland and the Willamette Valley page 579

To Woodburn   To Silverton

To Salem

To Corvallis

To Albany

To Halsey

To Eugene

To Bend

To Bend

To Redmond

Four Corners

Turner

Stayton

Lyons

Scio

Lebanon

Brownsville

Sweet Home

Leaburg

North Santiam River

Thomas Creek

Middle Santiam River

Pudding River

Calapooia River

McKenzie River

Gates

Mill City

Detroit

Detroit Lake

Santiam State Forest

Willamette National Forest

Green Peter Res.

Cougar Res.

Belknap Springs

Willamette National Forest

213

5

22

226

20

34

20

228

126

126

126

126

242

1 **2** **3** **4** **5** **6** **7**

761

762

© AVALON TRAVEL PUBLISHING, INC.

Map 2

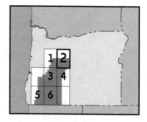

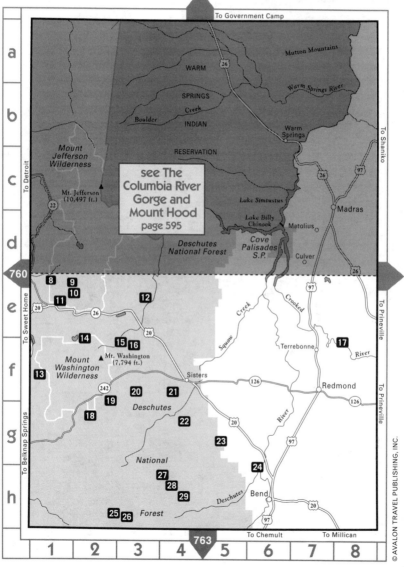

To Government Camp

a

b

c

d

760

e

f

g

h

1 2 3 4 5 6 7 8

To Detroit

To Sweet Home

To Belknap Springs

WARM

SPRINGS

Creek

Boulder

INDIAN

RESERVATION

Mutton Mountains

Warm Springs River

Warm Springs

To Shaniko

Mount Jefferson Wilderness

Mt. Jefferson (10,497 ft.)

see The Columbia River Gorge and Mount Hood page 595

Deschutes National Forest

Lake Simtustus

Lake Billy Chinook

Metolius

Cove Palisades S.P.

Culver

Madras

To Prineville

8

9

10

11

12

20

Squaw Creek

Crooked

To Prineville

14

15 16

Mount Washington Wilderness

Mt. Washington (7,794 ft.)

Terrebonne

River

17

13

Sisters

Redmond

To Prineville

242

20 21

Deschutes

19

18

22

River

23

24

National

27

28

29

Bend

25 26

Forest

Deschutes

To Chemult

To Millican

763

© AVALON TRAVEL PUBLISHING, INC.

Map 3

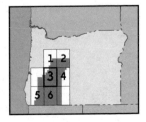

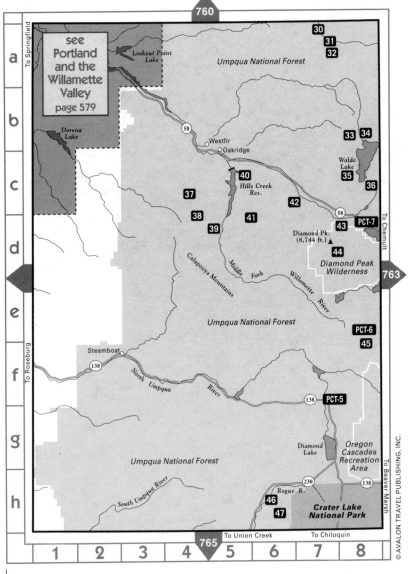

see Portland and the Willamette Valley page 579

760

To Springfield

Lookout Point Lake

Umpqua National Forest

30
31
32

Dorena Lake

58

Westfir
Oakridge

33 34

Waldo Lake

35

36

40
Hills Creek Res.

42

58

PCT-7

37

38

39

41

43

Diamond Pk. (8,744 ft.) ▲

44

Diamond Peak Wilderness

763

Calapooya Mountains

Middle Fork

Willamette River

Umpqua National Forest

PCT-6

45

To Roseburg

Steamboat

138

North Umpqua River

138 PCT-5

Umpqua National Forest

Diamond Lake

Oregon Cascades Recreation Area

To Beaver Marsh

South Umpqua River

230

Rogue R.

46

47

Crater Lake National Park

To Union Creek

To Chiloquin

765

1 2 3 4 5 6 7 8

To Chemult

© AVALON TRAVEL PUBLISHING, INC.

Map 4

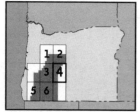

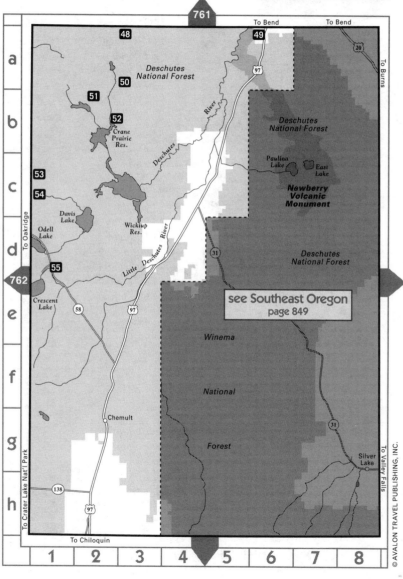

see Southeast Oregon
page 849

761

To Bend

49

To Bend

20

To Burns

48

Deschutes
National Forest

97

a

50

51

b

52

Crane
Prairie
Res.

Deschutes
National
Forest

Deschutes River

Paulina
Lake

East
Lake

Newberry
Volcanic
Monument

53

c

54

Davis
Lake

Wickiup
Res.

Odell
Lake

Little Deschutes River

31

d

Deschutes
National
Forest

To Oakridge

762

55

Crescent
Lake

58

97

e

Winema

f

National

g

Chemult

Forest

31

Silver
Lake

To Crater Lake Nat'l Park

138

97

h

To Valley Falls

To Chiloquin

1   2   3   4   5   6   7   8

© AVALON TRAVEL PUBLISHING, INC.

Map 5

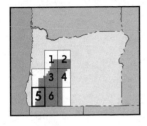

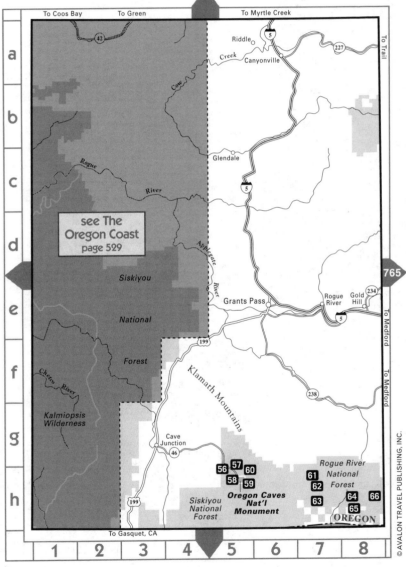

To Coos Bay   To Green   To Myrtle Creek

Riddle

Canyonville

Cow Creek

a

42

227

To Trail

b

Rogue

Glendale

c

River

5

5

see The
Oregon Coast
page 529

d

Applegate

Siskiyou

River

765

To Medford

e

National

199

Grants Pass

Rogue
River

Gold
Hill

234

5

Forest

Klamath Mountains

f

Chetco River

238

To Medford

g

Kalmiopsis
Wilderness

Cave
Junction

46

Rogue River
National
Forest

56 57 60

61

h

58 59

62

199

Siskiyou
National
Forest

**Oregon Caves
Nat'l
Monument**

63

64

66

65

To Gasquet, CA

OREGON

| 1 | 2 | 3 | 4 | 5 | 6 | 7 | 8 |

© AVALON TRAVEL PUBLISHING, INC.

Map 6

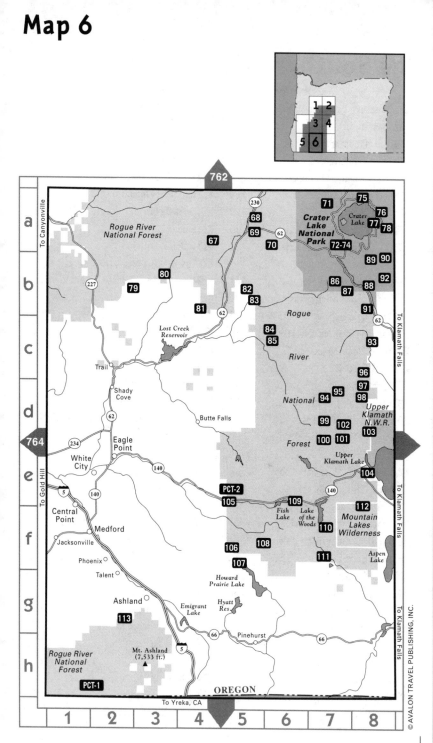

To Canyonville

To Klamath Falls

To Gold Hill

To Klamath Falls

To Klamath Falls

a

b

c

d

e

f

g

h

Rogue River
National Forest

Crater
Lake
National
Park

Crater
Lake

71   75
68   76
67 69   72-74 77 78
70   89 90
80   86   92
79   82   87 88
81 83   91
                 93
Lost Creek
Reservoir
84   96
85   97
Trail   94 95 98
Shady
Cove
Butte Falls   99 102   Upper
62   100 101   Klamath
Eagle   103 N.W.R.
Point
White
City   Upper
234   Klamath Lake
140   104
Central
Point   PCT-2
        105 109
Medford   Fish Lake
Jacksonville Lake of the   Mountain
              Woods 110   Lakes   112
Phoenix   106   108   Wilderness
Talent   107   111
Ashland   Emigrant Howard   Aspen
113   Lake   Prairie Lake   Lake
          Hyatt
Mt. Ashland Res.
(7,533 ft.) Pinehurst
Rogue River
National
Forest 66
PCT-1
        OREGON

227
230
62
62
62
62
140
140
5
66
66
5

Rogue

River

National

Forest

To Yreka, CA

© AVALON TRAVEL PUBLISHING, INC.

1   2   3   4   5   6   7   8

The Southern Cascades 765

The Southern Cascades

1 Rooster Rock

6.5 mi/4.0 hrs

You will swear you hear dinosaurs in the bushes. This portion of the Menagerie Wilderness is a menagerie, indeed, with many unusual rock formations that make it look more like a set from The Land That Time Forgot than a wilderness preserve. Getting there is half the, er, fun. This is a steep one. Follow the Trout Creek Trail up at a steady pace for about a mile and then proceed at a brutal pace for another two miles to a junction with the Rooster Rock Trail. The Rooster Rock Trail also begins on U.S. 20, just east of the Trout Creek Trail. It's about a mile shorter to the top via that route, but—get this—it's even steeper. Save it for the downhill plunge. From the junction the grade gets steeper than any grade should be allowed to get and then relents a bit as you drag the exhausted, quivering remnants of your body up to the top of Rooster Rock (elevation 3,567 feet). The total elevation gain is only about 2,300 feet, but it feels like twice that. We can only assume that the trail builders either hadn't been informed of that wondrous modern invention, the switchback, or sadistically chose to forget about them.

Location: In the Menagerie Wilderness north of U.S. 20; see The Southern Cascades Map 1, grid e6.

User Groups: Hikers, horses, and dogs. The trail is unsuitable for mountain bikes. No wheelchair facilities.

Permits: A federal Northwest Forest Pass, $5 per day or $30 annually, is required to park at the trailhead. Passes are available from ranger stations and many private vendors, online at website: www.wta.org, or by calling 800/270-7504.

Maps: For a map of the Menagerie Wilderness, contact the Nature of the Northwest Information Center, 800 Northeast Oregon Street, Suite 177, Portland, OR 97232; 503/872-2750. Ask the USGS for a topographic map of the Upper Soda area.

Directions: From Sweet Home drive 18.5 miles east on U.S. 20 to Trout Creek Campground. Just east of the entrance, the Trout Creek Trailhead is on the left (north) side of the highway.

Contact: Willamette National Forest, Sweet Home Ranger District, 3225 Highway 20, Sweet Home, OR 97386; 541/367-5168.

2 Iron Mountain

3.4 mi/2.0 hrs

Plant lovers come here for the five dozen rare plants and trees that thrive on Iron Mountain and nearby Cone Peak. View lovers come here for the vista from the Iron Mountain Fire Lookout. Which category you belong to might dictate how best to approach this extremely popular hike. View lovers should take the direct route, assaulting Iron Mountain straight up its face from the trailhead described above. It's a 3.4-mile round-trip with great views and a good sampling of the noted local plant life. Flower fans, however, might find an eastern route through meadows on the slopes of Cone Peak more rewarding. Ideally, you'll do both by hiking the whole works as a 5.7-mile shuttle walk. If so, start at the Sno-Park pullout on the left shoulder of U.S. 20, less than a mile beyond Tombstone Pass. On this ascent try to locate the three dozen tree varieties and more than 60 rare plant species. The trail climbs to a viewpoint at about two miles and then continues up to the ridgetop and southwest to the Iron Mountain Lookout. The direct route is very direct and nicely graded, the rock formations fascinating, the views absolutely to die for. Gaze as far north as Mount Adams in southern Washington. Count the volcanic peaks and quickly run out of fingers. Either way you walk this trail, it's a surefire hit.

Location: North of U.S. 20 near Tombstone Pass; see The Southern Cascades Map 1, grid e8.

User Groups: Hikers, horses, and dogs. No mountain bikes are allowed. No wheelchair facilities.

Permits: A federal Northwest Forest Pass, $5 per day or $30 annually, is required to park at the trailhead. Passes are available from ranger stations and many private vendors, online at website: www.wta.org, or by calling 800/270-7504.

Maps: For a map of the Willamette National Forest, contact the Nature of the Northwest Information Center, 800 Northeast Oregon Street, Suite 177, Portland, OR 97232; 503/872-2750. Ask the USGS for a topographic map of the Harter Mountain area.

Directions: From Sweet Home drive 35 miles east on U.S. 20 to Forest Service Road 15. Turn right at the Iron Mountain Trail sign and find the trailhead on the left side of the road.

Contact: Willamette National Forest, Sweet Home Ranger District, 3225 Highway 20, Sweet Home, OR 97386; 541/367-5168.

❸ Tidbits Mountain
4.0 mi/2.5 hrs

Here's a short, scenic day hike that gets you up high enough for some major views, yet is gentle enough to keep that spring in your step all the way back to the car. Shortly beyond the trailhead, you enter a majestic stand of old-growth forest, which stays with you until you leave the treeline about half a mile below the summit. The final stretch switchbacks through impressive rock fields, and the final 50 feet or so is a rough-rock scramble up the path of a stairway that once led to a summit fire lookout, which has since collapsed. Use care here. At the top enjoy the view of most of Oregon's volcanic peaks and the Calapooia River Valley. Retrace your footsteps to return to your car, plainly visible from the 5,184-foot summit perch. Your total elevation gain for the hike is about 1,100 feet.

Location: North of Blue River Reservoir in Willamette National Forest; see The Southern Cascades Map 1, grid g6.

User Groups: Hikers, dogs, and mountain bikes. No horses are allowed. No wheelchair facilities.

Permits: A federal Northwest Forest Pass, $5 per day or $30 annually, is required to park at the trailhead. Passes are available from ranger stations and many private vendors, online at website: www.wta.org, or by calling 800/270-7504.

Maps: For a map of Willamette National Forest, contact the Nature of the Northwest Information Center, 800 Northeast Oregon Street, Suite 177, Portland, OR 97232; 503/872-2750. Ask the USGS for a topographic map of the Tidbits Mountain area.

Directions: From Eugene drive 40 miles east on McKenzie Highway/Highway 126 to Blue River. Continue three miles east to Forest Service Road 15. Turn left (north) and proceed 4.7 miles to Forest Service Road 1509. Follow Forest Service Road 1509 just over eight miles to trailhead parking on the left. Walk one-quarter mile up Spur Road 877 to the trailhead.

Contact: Willamette National Forest, Blue River Ranger District, P.O. Box 199, Blue River, OR 97413; 541/822-3317.

❹ McKenzie River National Recreation Trail
27.0 mi one way/
2.0–3.0 days

Hiking doesn't have to stop when winter snows start. Quite the contrary, in fact.

Many lower-elevation trails are at their best in winter months, when wildlife is more frequently spotted and trails are relatively people-free. The McKenzie River Trail is a prime example. The lower portion is snow-free virtually all winter, and the upper stretches are snow-free much of the year. In autumn the colors are brilliant.

Whatever season you choose to come visit, you're not likely to leave disappointed. This is one of the better Wild and Scenic River hikes we've seen, with attractions too numerous to mention. They include 26.5 miles of mostly easy trail walking, three Forest Service campgrounds along the route for overnighters, numerous waterfalls and rapids, riverside hot springs facility, excellent fishing (state license required) and wildlife viewing, and many opportunities to get off the river trail and venture north or south to other scenic paths, such as a five-mile loop around lava-dammed Clear Lake. Hike the entire route or just small sections. Eleven trailhead parking areas along McKenzie Highway make it easy. And the lower 10 miles are usually snow-free all year. Many day hikers prefer this lower section, particularly the forested trail portion near the Lost Creek drainage. But a must-see portion is the Tamolitch Dry Falls area, where the river disappears underground at Carmen Reservoir Dam, but reappears (thanks to underground springs) in the pool below Tamolitch Dry Falls. The 3.5-mile stretch in between is a fascinating walk along a dry riverbed and a large lava flow that buried the river here well before the dam came along. The trailhead for this portion is off a side road at Trailbridge Reservoir's upper end, about 14 miles east of McKenzie Bridge.

Special note to mountain bikers: Some areas along the trail are quite congested with hikers during the summer. Ride slowly and in control around campgrounds and trailheads. Also, save the trail by staying off of it during very wet weather, when the grade is saturated.

Location: On the banks of the McKenzie River between McKenzie Bridge and Clear Lake; see The Southern Cascades Map 1, grid g7.

User Groups: Hikers, dogs, and mountain bikes. No horses are allowed. No wheelchair facilities.

Permits: No permits are required. Parking and access are free.

Maps: For a map of the Willamette National Forest, contact the Nature of the Northwest Information Center, 800 Northeast Oregon Street, Suite 177, Portland, OR 97232; 503/872-2750. Ask the USGS for topographic maps of the McKenzie Bridge, Belknap Springs, Tamolitch Falls, and Clear Lake areas.

Directions: Numerous trailheads are accessible along the route from McKenzie Highway/Highway 126. To reach the lower trailhead from Eugene drive about 50 miles east on McKenzie Highway. Proceed beyond McKenzie Bridge to the marked trailhead on the north side of the road near the McKenzie Bridge Ranger Station.

Contact: Willamette National Forest, McKenzie Ranger District, 57600 McKenzie Highway, McKenzie Bridge, OR 97413; 541/822-3381.

▣ Castle Rock
2.0 mi/1.0 hr

This is a good ego-builder for children. OK, and for you, too. It's a very easy mile from the trailhead, gaining about 600 barely noticeable vertical feet, to Castle Rock's 3,800-foot summit. The route is forested at first and then follows the ridgetop to the former lookout site. Great views await of the McKenzie River Valley, Cougar Reservoir, the Three Sisters, and Mount Washington. This is the easiest route to the top, but it's only one of many on the King Castle and Castle Rock Trail system in this area. Mountain bikers can combine the two trails, and area roads, for some challenging loop rides. Note that Forest Service Trail Park passes are required for all trailheads accessing this trail network.

Location: South of McKenzie Bridge in the McKenzie River drainage of Willamette National Forest; see The Southern Cascades Map 1, grid h6.

User Groups: Hikers, horses, dogs, and mountain bikes. No wheelchair facilities.

Permits: A federal Northwest Forest Pass, $5 per day or $30 annually, is required to park at the trailhead. Passes are available from ranger stations and many private vendors, online at website: www.wta.org, or by calling 800/270-7504.

Maps: For a map of the Willamette National Forest, contact the Nature of the Northwest Information Center, 800 Northeast Oregon Street, Suite 177, Portland, OR 97232; 503/872-2750. Ask the USGS for a topographic map of the McKenzie Bridge area.

Directions: From Eugene drive about 44 miles east on McKenzie Highway/Highway 126 to Forest Service Road 19, the Cougar Reservoir turnoff, about five miles west of McKenzie Bridge. Turn right (south) and proceed just under a mile on Forest Service Roads 19 and 410 to Forest Service Road 2639. Turn left (east) and drive half a mile to Forest Service Road 480. Turn right and proceed nearly six miles to the trailhead at the road's end. Note: The upper stretches of the road are very rough. A lower trailhead, located on the left on a major switchback corner about four miles down the road, adds about three-quarters of a mile and 500 vertical feet to the hike.

Contact: Willamette National Forest, McKenzie Ranger District, 57600 McKenzie Highway, McKenzie Bridge, OR 97413; 541/822-3381.

6 Olallie Ridge
6.0 mi one way/4.0 hrs

A cornucopia of day-hiking potential, this trail offers fine ridgetop views into nearby Three Sisters Wilderness. From the Horsepasture Saddle Trailhead, you can day hike 2.5 miles round-trip to views on Horsepasture Mountain, or continue south along the ridge to a grand Three Sisters viewpoint at Taylor Castle Peak (3.2 miles). Both are good round-trip day hikes, but longer-range hikers should consider hiking the entire six-mile ridgeline stretch between Horsepasture Saddle and the southern Pat Saddle Trailhead, about 11 miles farther south on Forest Service Road 1993. Good campsites are found at the Potholes, a meadow near Lamb Butte about 4.5 miles south of Horsepasture Saddle. After cresting a 5,200-foot high point near English Mountain, the trail drops 1.5 miles to the Pat Saddle Trailhead. From here the trail continues south past Olallie Mountain to Olallie Meadows, Bear Flat, and other destinations deep in the Three Sisters Wilderness (see hike in this chapter). Carry plenty of water on this route, especially if you're backpacking, as little water is available on the ridgetop.

Two other trails beckon from the Horsepasture Saddle Trailhead. One, the northern portion of the Olallie Trail, drops five miles down to the first trailhead on Forest Service Road 1993 (a Trail Park Pass is required to park at that trailhead; Willamette National Forest contact numbers are listed below if you need more information). The other, O'Leary Mountain Trail, drops 8.8 miles past its namesake and Macduff Peak to a trailhead just above Cougar Dam.

Location: East of Cougar Reservoir near the northwestern boundary of the

Three Sisters Wilderness; see The Southern Cascades Map 1, grid h7.

User Groups: Hikers, dogs, horses, and mountain bikes. No wheelchair facilities.

Permits: No permits are required. Parking and access are free.

Maps: For a map of Willamette National Forest and Three Sisters Wilderness, contact the Nature of the Northwest Information Center, 800 Northeast Oregon Street, Suite 177, Portland, OR 97232; 503/872-2750. Ask the USGS for topographic maps of the French Mountain and Chucksney Mountain areas.

Directions: From Eugene drive about 50 miles east on McKenzie Highway/Highway 126 to Horse Creek Road/Forest Service Road 2638 at McKenzie Bridge. Turn right (south) and drive two miles to Wapiti Road/Forest Service Road 1993. Turn right and proceed to the Horsepasture Saddle Trailhead, about 8.5 miles up Forest Service Road 1993 on the right side of the road.

Contact: Willamette National Forest, McKenzie Ranger District, 57600 McKenzie Highway, McKenzie Bridge, OR 97413; 541/822-3381.

🔟 Olallie Mountain/Olallie Meadows

7.0 mi/4.0 hrs

Mountain people and meadow people can go their separate ways here, and both come home satisfied. From the Pat Saddle Trailhead, head south on the Olallie Trail and hike through the peaceful but occasionally bug-filled Wolverine Meadow. The pace here is relaxed. At two miles is a junction: time to choose. For the mountain take a right turn and climb 750 feet in 1.5 miles to Olallie Mountain (elevation 5,700 feet). Views are grand all around, especially for fans of the Three Sisters and the French Pete Creek Valley. Look to the northeast and try to spot the

meadow people, who by now should be at lovely Olallie Meadows, lunching in wildflowers near the Olallie Guard Station. Backpackers can continue on from here for about 11 miles east through the heart of the Three Sisters Wilderness to Horse Lake (see hike this chapter). Yet another variation is the Pat Saddle Trail, a seven-mile loop around Olallie Mountain. The trail is mostly in meadows and can be difficult to find.

For another open-air viewpoint of the Three Sisters, consider the excellent 5.6-mile round-trip hike to Lowder Mountain. The trailhead is just over three miles back toward Cougar Dam on Forest Service Road 1993.

Location: South of McKenzie Bridge in the northwest corner of the Three Sisters Wilderness; see The Southern Cascades Map 1, grid h8.

User Groups: Hikers, dogs, and horses. No mountain bikes are allowed. No wheelchair facilities.

Permits: A federal Northwest Forest Pass, $5 per day or $30 annually, is required to park at the trailhead. Passes are available from ranger stations and many private vendors, online at website: www.wta.org, or by calling 800/270-7504.

Maps: For a map of the Three Sisters Wilderness, contact the Nature of the Northwest Information Center, 800 Northeast Oregon Street, Suite 177, Portland, OR 97232; 503/872-2750. Ask the USGS for topographic maps of the French Mountain and Chucksney Mountain areas.

Directions: From Eugene drive about 40 miles east on McKenzie Highway/Highway 126 to Blue River. Continue east, following Cougar Reservoir signs to Forest Service Road 19. Turn right (south) and drive to Cougar Dam. Turn left on Forest Service Road 1993 across Cougar Dam and drive about 15 miles to the Pat Saddle Trail on the right side of the road.

Contact: Willamette National Forest, Blue River Ranger District, 51668 Blue River Drive, Blue River, OR 97413; 541/822-3317.

8 Duffy and Mowich Lakes
9.0 mi/5.0 hrs

This popular Jefferson Wilderness trail serves double duty: it's an excellent day hike to two alpine lakes and, for the adventurous, a trek to a substantial peak. But it's also a primary access route to longer-distance backpacking trips into the Eight Lakes Basin area to the north and beyond. The route in follows the North Santiam River 3.5 easy miles to Duffy Lake and then a mile beyond to Mowich Lake, which has a broad, sandy beach perfect for lunching. If you're up for more, continue north about a mile to a side trail up Red Butte (elevation 5,848 feet) or another mile to the Eight Lakes Basin/Marion Mountain area (see hike in this chapter).

Location: Northeast of Three Fingered Jack in the Mount Jefferson Wilderness; see The Southern Cascades Map 2, grid e1.

User Groups: Hikers, dogs, and horses. No mountain bikes are allowed. No wheelchair facilities.

Permits: A federal Northwest Forest Pass, $5 per day or $30 annually, is required to park at the trailhead. Passes are available from ranger stations and many private vendors, online at website: www.wta.org, or by calling 800/270-7504.

Maps: For a map of the Mount Jefferson Wilderness, contact the Nature of the Northwest Information Center, 800 Northeast Oregon Street, Suite 177, Portland, OR 97232; 503/872-2750. Ask the USGS for topographic maps of the Marion Forks, Marion Lake, Three Fingered Jack, and Santiam Junction areas.

Directions: From Salem drive 52 miles east on Highway 22 to Detroit and continue 25 miles southeast to Big Meadows Road/Forest Service Road 2267. Turn left (east) and drive about three miles to the trailhead at the road's end.

Contact: Willamette National Forest, Detroit Ranger District, HC 73, P.O. Box 320, Mill City, OR 97360; 503/854-3366.

9 Rockpile Lake/ South Cinder Peak
13.5 mi/1.0–2.0 days

The trail that now runs between Rockpile Lake and South Cinder Peak provides a good backdoor entry into some of the more remote—and, thankfully, less-populated—regions of the Mount Jefferson Wilderness. The access route follows the Two Springs Trail through open countryside to a junction with the Pacific Crest Trail near small, clear Rockpile Lake (5.2 miles). A few campsites are found at this location. Turn north on the PCT and walk 1.3 miles to South Cinder Peak, where a side trail leads one-third mile to the 6,746-foot summit offering grand views of Mount Jefferson and Black Butte.

Longer-distance hikers can continue to trek west on the Swallow Lake Trail to access the Lake of the Woods Trail, Marion Lake, and the west side of the Jefferson Wilderness. Or the more ambitious can choose to continue north on the PCT to backpacking destinations at Carl Lake, North Cinder Peak, and the Cathedral Rocks/Hunts Cove area immediately south of Mount Jefferson.

Location: Northeast of Three Fingered Jack in the Mount Jefferson Wilderness; see The Southern Cascades Map 2, grid e1.

User Groups: Hikers, dogs, and horses. No mountain bikes are allowed. No wheelchair facilities.

Permits: A federal Northwest Forest Pass, $5 per day or $30 annually, is required to park at the trailhead. Passes are available

from ranger stations and many private vendors, online at website: www.wta.org, or by calling 800/270-7504.

Maps: For a map of the Mount Jefferson Wilderness, contact the Nature of the Northwest Information Center, 800 Northeast Oregon Street, Suite 177, Portland, OR 97232; 503/872-2750. Ask the USGS for a topographic map of the Marion Lake area.

Directions: From U.S. 20 at Santiam Pass, proceed for approximately eight miles east to Forest Service Road 12. Turn left (north) and then continue about four miles to Forest Service Road 1230. Proceed for about 1.4 miles straight on Forest Service Road 1230 to Forest Service Road 1234 and then veer left and drive just under one mile to Forest Service Road 1235. Take a right turn and then drive approximately four miles to the Bear Valley Trailhead, located at the road's end.

Contact: Deschutes National Forest, Sisters Ranger District, Highway 20, Pine Street, Sisters, OR 97759; 541/549-7700.

10 Canyon Creek Meadows Loop
7.0 mi/3.5 hrs

This loop into marvelous Cascade Meadows with the stunning Three Fingered Jack Peak as a backdrop is extremely heavily used, and it's easy to see why. It's an easy hike with an optional shorter, 4.3-mile loop that is easy enough for children, or a more challenging day hike if you walk the entire seven-mile route to the base of the mountain. And the scenery in midsummer is unparalleled.

The loop route is very heavily traveled—so much so that Forest Service managers request that everyone hike the loop clockwise, creating the illusion, at least, of fewer bodies. (There's no telling what would happen if you bucked the rules and went backwards. A counterclockwise citation?) With

that fact in mind, bear left at the first trail fork and hike 1.75 miles through a lodgepole forest to the lower Canyon Creek Meadow, with a stunning view of Three Fingered Jack. The wildflower meadows, rich with paintbrush and lupine, are magnificent in July. If you're looking for a closer mountain view (and the trail isn't still snow covered), turn left (south) and continue 1.5 miles through the upper meadow and up a tricky moraine path to a beautiful glacial cirque and an impressive view of the entire region. Back at the lower meadow, turn north and walk about a mile to a trail junction near Canyon Creek Falls. Turn right and walk about 1.5 miles back to the car. Or continue straight north up the creek about 0.7 mile to campsites at Wasco Lake, where the path joins the Pacific Crest Trail at Minto Pass.

Midsummer days in these meadows bring unrelenting hordes of mosquitoes. Bring bug juice or you shall surely perish.

Location: East of Three Fingered Jack in the Mount Jefferson Wilderness; see The Southern Cascades Map 2, grid e1.

User Groups: Hikers, dogs, and horses. No mountain bikes are allowed. No wheelchair facilities.

Permits: A federal Northwest Forest Pass, $5 per day or $30 annually, is required to park at the trailhead. Passes are available from ranger stations and many private vendors, online at website: www.wta.org, or by calling 800/270-7504.

Maps: For a map of the Mount Jefferson Wilderness, contact the Nature of the Northwest Information Center, 800 Northeast Oregon Street, Suite 177, Portland, OR 97232; 503/872-2750. Ask the USGS for a topographic map of the Three Fingered Jack area.

Directions: From Santiam Pass on U.S. 20, drive eight miles east to Forest Service Road 12. Turn left (north) and proceed about four miles to Forest Service Road 1230. Continue straight about 1.4 miles. Turn left onto Forest Service Road 1234 and follow it just under five miles to the trailhead at Jack Lake Campground.

Contact: Deschutes National Forest, Sisters Ranger District, Highway 20, Pine Street, Sisters, OR 97759; 541/549-7700.

🔟 Three Fingered Jack
10.5 mi/6.0 hrs

This is a challenging but highly rewarding walk up a portion of the Pacific Crest Trail to a viewpoint high on rugged, craggy Three Fingered Jack. Begin by following signs to the PCT and climbing 3.5 miles at a fairly strenuous pace to the ridgetop. From there continue north on the open ridge to steep switchbacks with excellent views of Black Butte, Three Sisters, and the western face of 7,841-foot Three Fingered Jack. The final 6,280-foot viewpoint of the mountain is spectacular, offering a close-up view of the layers and crevices of this ancient volcano. Watch for climbers high above. Carry plenty of water. You need to absorb it here before heading back down by the same route. You gain and lose about 1,400 vertical feet over the route. The trail receives fairly heavy use in the summertime; expect crowds on weekends.

Location: North of Santiam Pass on the southern slopes of Three Fingered Jack in the Mount Jefferson Wilderness; see The Southern Cascades Map 2, grid e1.

User Groups: Hikers, dogs, and horses. No mountain bikes are allowed. No wheelchair facilities.

Permits: A federal Northwest Forest Pass, $5 per day or $30 annually, is required to park at the trailhead. Passes are available from ranger stations and many private vendors, online at website: www.wta.org, or by calling 800/270-7504.

Maps: For a map of the Mount Jefferson Wilderness, contact the Nature of the Northwest Information Center, 800 Northeast Oregon Street, Suite 177, Portland, OR 97232; 503/872-2750. Ask the USGS for a topographic map of the Three Fingered Jack area.

Directions: From Salem drive 52 miles east on Highway 22 to Detroit and continue about 33 miles southeast to Santiam Pass. Follow signs to the Pacific Crest Trail parking lot on the left (north) side of the road.

Contact: Willamette National Forest, Detroit Ranger District, HC 73, P.O. Box 320, Mill City, OR 97360; 503/854-3366.

🔢 Black Butte
4.0 mi/3.0 hrs

If you were trying to make a platform for a perfect vista in the midst of Deschutes National Forest, you'd probably put together a cinder cone that looked a lot like 6,436-foot Black Butte. From the end of the road, the trail climbs steeply around the cone's perimeter to a lookout and lookout tower with magnificent views in every direction, taking in Mounts Jefferson, Hood, and Adams. Look down at the massive pile of rock beneath your feet, and you understand how the sheer bulk of this cinder cone forced the Metolius River (see hike in this chapter) underground when the cone was created by eruptions long, long ago. The peak itself has an interesting recent history as a Forest Service fire lookout site. In 1910, lookouts actually perched on a treehouse platform near the summit. More formal lookouts were built in 1922, and an 83-foot tower was constructed in 1934—thanks to an astonishing 1,000 stock pack trips to haul materials to the top. A lookout tower was built in 1995 off-site and then airlifted to the summit.

Note: this is a hot, dry trail in the summer. Carry plenty of water. The total elevation gain is 1,640 feet. The trail is usually snow-free June through November.

Location: North of Sisters in Deschutes National Forest; see The Southern Cascades Map 2, grid e3.

User Groups: Hikers, dogs, and mountain bikes. Horses by special permit only. No wheelchair facilities.

Permits: A federal Northwest Forest Pass, $5 per day or $30 annually, is required to park at the trailhead. Passes are available from ranger stations and many private vendors, online at website: www.wta.org, or by calling 800/270-7504.

Maps: For a map of the Deschutes National Forest, contact the Nature of the Northwest Information Center, 800 Northeast Oregon Street, Suite 177, Portland, OR 97232; 503/872-2750. Ask the USGS for a topographic map of the Black Butte area.

Directions: From Sisters drive 6.3 miles northwest on U.S. 20 to Green Ridge Road/Forest Service Road 11. Turn right (north) and proceed 3.9 miles to Forest Service Road 1110. Turn left (west) and drive 5.5 miles to the trailhead at the end of the road.

Contact: Deschutes National Forest, Sisters Ranger District, Highway 20, Pine Street, Sisters, OR 97759; 541/549-7700.

13 Sand Mountain
1.3 mi/1.0 hr

This is more a stroll than a hike, but the payoff is one of the more sterling mountain viewpoints in central Oregon, an area that is chock-full of them. Follow the road to a trail that switchbacks to Sand Mountain's lookout tower, restored to its original condition by volunteers. The tower is staffed by volunteers during summer months, and visitors are welcome. It's an impressive sight. Views extend in all directions, with Mount Washington seemingly close enough to touch and a dozen other Cascade volcanoes visible. Outside, a loop trail of just under a mile circles the crater of this old, 5,459-foot cinder cone. This is a grand experience for kids, who'll be talking about it long after you visit.

Location: South of Santiam Pass in the Mount Washington Wilderness; see The Southern Cascades Map 2, grid f1.

User Groups: Hikers, horses, and dogs. No mountain bikes are allowed. No wheelchair facilities.

Permits: Free day-hiking and overnight wilderness permits, required for all hikers, can be obtained at trailheads or ranger stations.

Maps: For a map of the Mount Washington Wilderness, contact Nature of the Northwest Information Center, 800 Northeast Oregon Street, Suite 177, Portland, OR 97232; 503/872-2750. Ask the USGS for topographic maps of the Clear Lake and Mount Washington areas.

Directions: From U.S. 20 at Santiam Pass, turn south on Big Lake Road (at the Hoodoo Ski Area sign) and proceed about three miles to a road fork. Stay right and take an immediate right on Forest Service Road 810. Drive three rough miles, staying straight at intersections, to a major left-hand turn leading to a gate near the top of Sand Mountain.

Contact: Willamette National Forest, McKenzie Ranger District, 57600 McKenzie Highway, McKenzie Bridge, OR 97413; 541/822-3381.

14 Patjens Lakes Loop
6.0 mi/3.0 hrs

You'll love it for the reflected views of Mount Washington. Your kids will love it for the easy grade and a chance to take a swim on a hot summer day, especially in Big Lake, which has the best swimming. Plenty of happy families walk the easy loop from Big Lake to much smaller Patjen Lakes and back. Don't forget the bug juice; mosquitoes enjoy this oasis of lakes in a dry, volcanic landscape as much as you do. Several good meadows are found along the loop, as well as occasional views of Mount Washington and the Three Sisters. Take your time and soak up some sun.

Location: At Big Lake, south of Santiam Pass in the northern Mount Washington Wilderness; see The Southern Cascades Map 2, grid f2.

User Groups: Hikers, dogs, and horses. No mountain bikes are allowed. No wheelchair facilities.

Permits: A federal Northwest Forest Pass, $5 per day or $30 annually, is required to park at the trailhead. Passes are available from ranger stations and many private vendors, online at website: www.wta.org, or by calling 800/270-7504.

Maps: For a map of the Mount Washington Wilderness, contact the Nature of the Northwest Information Center, 800 Northeast Oregon Street, Suite 177, Portland, OR 97232; 503/872-2750. Ask the USGS for a topographic map of the Clear Lake area.

Directions: From U.S. 20 at Santiam Pass, turn south on Big Lake Road/Forest Service Road 2690, signed for the Hoodoo Ski Area. Proceed to the trailhead on the right (north) side of the road, just a mile beyond Big Lake Campground.

Contact: Willamette National Forest, McKenzie Ranger District, 57600 McKenzie Highway, McKenzie Bridge, OR 97413; 541/822-3381.

15 Hand and Scott Lakes
3.7 mi/2.0 hrs

Hand and Scott Lakes, both conveniently located off Highway 242, can be hiked to individually or in a linked loop. Both offer excellent, quick exposure to the volcanic-wilderness traits that make this region unique. Scott Lake, the first trailhead for visitors driving from the west, has a dual trail-head, with paths departing west to deep-blue, beautiful, and worthwhile Benson Lake (three miles round-trip) and beyond to the airplane-view summit of 6,116-foot Scott Mountain (11 miles round-trip).

For a hike sampling Scott and Hand Lakes, head around the north shore of Scott Lake and proceed 1.5 miles to the old Hand Lake Shelter, which sits in a marvelous meadow of summer wildflowers. From here follow trail signs to Robinson Lake and walk around the northwest corner of Hand Lake to a massive lava flow. Turn around here and return the way you came, or cross the lava flow on an old wagon track. The trail ends here, but a side trail departs on the south side of the lava flow, leading to Hand Lake's southern beach, which can be walked back to the meadow and the Hand Lake Shelter trail junction. Combined, the two trails are likely the most heavily used day-hiking paths in this highway corridor.

Location: Northwest of McKenzie Pass in the southern Mount Washington Wilderness; see The Southern Cascades Map 2, grid f3.

User Groups: Hikers, dogs, and horses. No mountain bikes are allowed. No wheelchair facilities.

Permits: A federal Northwest Forest Pass, $5 per day or $30 annually, is required to park at the trailhead. Passes are available from ranger stations and many private vendors, online at website: www.wta.org, or by calling 800/270-7504.

Maps: For a map of the Three Sisters Wilderness, contact Nature of the Northwest Information Center, 800 Northeast Oregon Street, Suite 177, Portland, OR 97232; 503/872-2750. Ask the USGS for topographic maps of the North Sister, Mount Washington, Clear Lake, and Linton Lake areas.

Directions: From Eugene drive 50 miles east on McKenzie Highway/Highway

126 to the town of McKenzie Bridge. Continue about five miles east on McKenzie Highway to the Highway 242 junction. Head east on Highway 242 to the Scott Lake turnoff on the left (north) side of the road, about five miles west of McKenzie Pass. To begin at the Hand Lake Trailhead, continue east on Highway 242 a short distance to the trailhead marker on the left (north) side of the road. Note: Highway 242 is closed in the winter.

Contact: Willamette National Forest, McKenzie Ranger District, 57600 McKenzie Highway, McKenzie Bridge, OR 97413; 541/822-3381.

16 Pacific Crest Trail to Little Belknap Crater

5.0 mi/3.0 hrs

After you've stopped at the roadside Dee Wright Observatory, a stone lookout displaying all the major Central Oregon volcanic peaks, walk out on top of a lesser volcanic peak and see it up close and personal. Follow the Pacific Crest Trail north to the top of a massive (and sharp, so wear good boots) lava flow. The trail continues up at a steady pace, past several "islands" spared by the lava, with the crater visible ahead all the while and views of the Sisters to the rear. About 2.5 miles up the trail, a side trail leads right to the crater summit. It's about a quarter mile up the steep path, past several massive lava caves (actually open lava tubes) to impressive views at the top. If you're up for more, return to the main trail and climb larger, more imposing Belknap Crater to the west. Carry plenty of water on this hike; none is available, and you'll need it.

Location: North of McKenzie Pass in the Mount Washington Wilderness; see The Southern Cascades Map 2, grid f3.

User Groups: Hikers, dogs, and horses. No mountain bikes are allowed. No wheelchair facilities.

Permits: A federal Northwest Forest Pass, $5 per day or $30 annually, is required to park at the trailhead. Passes are available from ranger stations and many private vendors, online at website: www.wta.org, or by calling 800/270-7504.

Maps: For a map of the Mount Washington Wilderness, contact Nature of the Northwest Information Center, 800 Northeast Oregon Street, Suite 177, Portland, OR 97232; 503/872-2750. Ask the USGS for a topographic map of the Mount Washington area.

Directions: From Eugene drive 50 miles east on McKenzie Highway/Highway 126 to the town of McKenzie Bridge. Continue about five miles east on McKenzie Highway to the Highway 242 junction. Head east on Highway 242 to McKenzie Pass and the Pacific Crest Trail marker on the left (north) side of the road, half a mile west of the Dee Wright Observatory pullout.

Contact: Willamette National Forest, McKenzie Ranger District, 57600 McKenzie Highway, McKenzie Bridge, OR 97413; 541/822-3381.

17 Smith Rock State Park Loop

5.3 mi/3.0 hrs

You know Smith Rock is a special place even before you get close. Looming high above the dry plain like stone sentinels, Smith Rock's stone spires jut high into the sky, their sheer, smooth faces attracting top-notch rock climbers from around the globe. A day spent wandering the 5.3-mile loop trail here is always time well invested. You get close brushes with nature and human endeavor at their best.

From the parking lot walk to a cliff-top viewpoint and follow the trail down to the Crooked River. Cross the bridge and head either direction for the loop. Moving counterclockwise, you pass through sagebrush and pine below Red Wall, with many side trails leading left to climbing routes. Soon the trail becomes exposed and begins to climb up a steep ridge, with sweeping views of Smith Rock monoliths such as Monkey Face coming into view, as well as Black Butte, Mount Washington, Belknap Crater, Mount Bachelor, and the Sisters. You drop behind Monkey Face and return to the river, which is followed upstream below Asterisk Pass, where dozens of rock climbers will be clinging to the vertical rock walls above. Bring your binoculars to see both the climbers and the eagles that nest high on Smith Rock.

Location: Northeast of Redmond off U.S. 97 on the Crooked River; see The Southern Cascades Map 2, grid f8.

User Groups: Hikers, dogs, horses, and mountain bikes. No wheelchair facilities.

Permits: A federal Northwest Forest Pass, $5 per day or $30 annually, is required to park at the trailhead. Passes are available from ranger stations and many private vendors, online at website: www.wta.org, or by calling 800/270-7504.

Maps: For a free park brochure, contact the Nature of the Northwest Information Center, 800 Northeast Oregon Street, Suite 177, Portland, OR 97232; 503/872-2750. Ask the USGS for a topographic map of the Redmond area.

Directions: From U.S. 97 at Terrebonne, turn east on Smith Rock Way and follow signs about three miles to the park.

Contact: Oregon Parks and Recreation Department, 1115 Commercial Street Northeast, Salem, OR 97301; 800/551-6949.

18 Proxy Falls/Linton Lake
4.6 mi/3.0 hrs

These two McKenzie Pass trails are short and easy enough to combine into one longer day hike, with a short road trip in the middle. They're scenic, geologically fascinating, and very kid-proof, making them a hit with the whole family. The Proxy Falls Trail is a 1.4-mile round-trip walk over a lava flow to a pair of spectacular waterfalls that cascade down glacier-carved steps and seem to disappear into the earth. One-third mile down the trail is a junction; the left fork leads to the upper falls, the right fork leads to the lower. You'll want to visit both. Check out the splash pools, where the water fills to the edge but doesn't flow out. It's believed that the water exits through porous lava that filled the valley after glaciers receded, damming the stream that formed Linton Lake just up the valley. We prefer to chalk it up to plain old magic. To see Linton Lake, head 1.5 miles east on the highway to the trailhead and walk about 1.5 pleasant miles to the northwestern lakeshore. Like the falls below, Linton Lake is fascinating in that it has no outlet stream. Water from Obsidian Creek feeds the lake, which drains through seepage at the bottom. The trail leads another half a mile around the lake's left shoreline, for a total round-trip of about 3.2 miles.

Location: South of McKenzie Pass Highway in the Three Sisters Wilderness; see The Southern Cascades Map 2, grid g2.

User Groups: Hikers, horses, and dogs. No mountain bikes are allowed. No wheelchair facilities.

Permits: A federal Northwest Forest Pass, $5 per day or $30 annually, is required to park at the trailhead. Passes are available from ranger stations and many private vendors, online at website: www.wta.org, or by calling 800/270-7504.

Maps: For a map of the Three Sisters Wilderness, contact the Nature of the Northwest Information Center, 800 Northeast Oregon

Street, Suite 177, Portland, OR 97232; 503/872-2750. Ask the USGS for a topographic map of the Linton Lake area.

Directions: From Eugene drive 50 miles east on McKenzie Highway/Highway 126 to the town of McKenzie Bridge. Continue about five miles east on Highway 126 to the Highway 242 junction. Head about nine miles east on Highway 242 to the Proxy Falls Trail on the right (south) side of the road. To reach the Linton Lake Trail, proceed 1.5 miles south on Highway 242 to the trailhead on the right (south) side of the road. Note: McKenzie Pass Highway is closed in the winter.

Contact: Willamette National Forest, McKenzie Ranger District, 57600 McKenzie Highway, McKenzie Bridge, OR 97413; 541/822-3381.

19 Obsidian/ Sunshine Meadow Loop
12.0 mi/8.0 hrs

Sunshine Meadows near the Middle Sister is one of those special places that's so special it really isn't anymore. Crowds here have grown so large over the years that forest managers have tried everything short of outright permit limits to ease the burden on fragile meadows and campsites. Presently, backpacking into the area is strongly discouraged, and attempts are made to control numbers of day hikers by limiting parking spots at the trailhead. Make it a day hike and, if you can, make it off-season.

The trail itself is spectacular, starting in arid country, entering the woods, and traversing a wide lava flow to White Branch Creek just beyond four miles. Near here is a trail junction, the start of the meadow loop. Go right and hike through meadows filled with lupine to a large obsidian-flow crossing and, farther on, a junction with the Pacific Crest Trail. Turn left (north), pass Obsidian Falls, and enter the alpine heaven of Arrowhead Lakes Basin. Views of the Sisters are supreme. Ahead, the trail drops to Sunshine Meadows and Glacier Creek, where the side trail leads left back to the Obsidian Trail. It's a long-haul day hike, but absolutely worth every step, which we hope you make carefully. Backpackers use the Obsidian Trail as an excellent access route to longer hikes from Sunshine north to McKenzie Pass and south to Linton Meadows and a dozen other prime destinations. A climbing route to the Middle Sister summit also begins at Sunshine.

Location: Southwest of McKenzie Pass in the Three Sisters Wilderness; see The Southern Cascades Map 2, grid g2.

User Groups: Hikers, horses, and dogs. No mountain bikes are allowed. No wheelchair facilities.

Permits: A federal Northwest Forest Pass, $5 per day or $30 annually, is required to park at the trailhead. Passes are available from ranger stations and many private vendors, online at website: www.wta.org, or by calling 800/270-7504.

Maps: For a map of the Three Sisters Wilderness, contact the Nature of the Northwest Information Center, 800 Northeast Oregon Street, Suite 177, Portland, OR 97232; 503/872-2750. Ask the USGS for topographic maps of the North Sister and Linton Lake areas.

Directions: From Eugene drive 50 miles east on McKenzie Highway/Highway 126 to the town of McKenzie Bridge. Continue about five miles east on McKenzie Highway to the Highway 242 junction. Head east on Highway 242 about six miles to the Obsidian Trail sign on the right (south) side of the road. Note: Highway 242 is closed in the winter.

Contact: Willamette National Forest, McKenzie Ranger District, 57600 McKenzie Highway, McKenzie Bridge, OR 97413; 541/822-3381.

20 Scott Trail to Four-In-One Cone

10.0 mi/6.5 hrs

This direct-route access to the fabulous Three Sisters area would be a great day hike even if it didn't have the fascinating Four-In-One volcanic cone along the route. But it does, which means A) the hike is even greater, and B) so are the crowds. Nevertheless, a trek from Highway 242 to the cone and beyond to fantastic wildflower meadows surrounding the Pacific Crest Trail is a memorable experience. You cross solid rivers of lava on the four-mile, steadily uphill walk to a side trail leading a quarter of a mile up the Four-In-One Cone. The view from the top is worth the trek, and a lot more. Linger here between the four cinder cones, enjoy the spectacular view of the North Sister and other local peaks, and try to picture this area when all the volcanoes were still active. Below, the main trail leads another mile to a junction with the Pacific Crest Trail, where you can venture north to Matthieu Lakes and McKenzie Pass (see hike in this chapter). If you visit in July or August, the meadows of lupine here are as grand as any you'll ever see. The trail is named for Captain Felix Scott, who led the first wagon train across McKenzie Pass.

Location: West of McKenzie Pass in the Three Sisters Wilderness; see The Southern Cascades Map 2, grid f3.

User Groups: Hikers, dogs, and horses. No mountain bikes are allowed. No wheelchair facilities.

Permits: A federal Northwest Forest Pass, $5 per day or $30 annually, is required to park at the trailhead. Passes are available from ranger stations and many private vendors, online at website: www.wta.org, or by calling 800/270-7504.

Maps: For a map of the Three Sisters Wilderness, contact the Nature of the Northwest Information Center, 800 Northeast Oregon Street, Suite 177, Portland, OR 97232; 503/872-2750. Ask the USGS for a topographic map of the North Sister area.

Directions: From Eugene drive 50 miles east on McKenzie Highway/Highway 126 to the town of McKenzie Bridge. Continue about five miles east on McKenzie Highway to the Highway 242 junction. Head east on Highway 242 to the Scott Lake turnoff on the left (north) side of the road, about five miles west of McKenzie Pass. The trail starts on the south side of the highway. Note: Highway 242 is closed in the winter.

Contact: Willamette National Forest, McKenzie Ranger District, 57600 McKenzie Highway, McKenzie Bridge, OR 97413; 541/822-3381.

21 Pacific Crest Trail/ Matthieu Lakes Loop

5.75 mi/3.0 hrs

Bring your best horsey manners for this heavily traveled path. Equestrians flock here for the same reasons you will: good access, moderate grade, and outstanding scenery. The trail departs from an area near Lava Camp Lake and leads one-quarter mile to a junction with the Pacific Crest Trail. Turn left and head due south along an imposing wall of lava into the Three Sisters Wilderness. At just under one mile you hit a trail junction. Pick either route, because this is the start of the loop. The left fork climbs up a ridge with good volcanic-peak views and drops to South Matthieu Lake, a distance of about two miles from the junction. The right fork continues 1.4 miles up the lava flow to North Matthieu Lake and then another three-quarters of a mile to South Matthieu. The lake, a stunning body of crystal water at Scott Pass, has a few beautiful campsites, which are almost always occupied by PCT through hikers.

Location: South of McKenzie Pass in the Three Sisters Wilderness; see The Southern Cascades Map 2, grid f4.

User Groups: Horses, hikers, and dogs. No mountain bikes are allowed. No wheelchair facilities.

Permits: A federal Northwest Forest Pass, $5 per day or $30 annually, is required to park at the trailhead. Passes are available from ranger stations and many private vendors, online at website: www.wta.org, or by calling 800/270-7504.

Maps: For a map of the Three Sisters Wilderness, contact the Nature of the Northwest Information Center, 800 Northeast Oregon Street, Suite 177, Portland, OR 97232; 503/872-2750. Ask the USGS for topographic maps of the North Sister and Mount Washington areas.

Directions: From Eugene drive 50 miles east on McKenzie Highway/Highway 126 to the town of McKenzie Bridge. Continue about five miles east on McKenzie Highway to the Highway 242 junction. Head east on Highway 242 to McKenzie Pass and then continue one mile east to Forest Service Road 900, signed for Lava Camp Lake. Turn right (south) and drive one-third mile to the Pacific Crest Trail parking area on the right.

Contact: Deschutes National Forest, Sisters Ranger District, Highway 20, Pine Street, Sisters, OR 97759; 541/549-7700.

22 Black Crater
7.6 mi/6.5 hrs

This high, dry climb to the 7,251-foot summit of Black Crater is, as the name implies, a walk through the geologic present, past, and future of a rugged volcanic area. The trail wastes no time climbing up lightly forested slopes into the Three Sisters Wilderness. It rarely lets up in the first two miles, after which good views of surrounding peaks begin. About a mile from the top, you leave

the forest for good and enter an open, dry terrain that makes you expect a dinosaur to pop up from the nearest ravine. And one of the grandest ravines you could imagine is just ahead. It's actually a glacial valley with sheer cliff walls, just below the mountaintop. At the summit the sweeping, 360-degree view includes the North Sister, Mount Washington, the McKenzie Pass lava flows, and—on very clear days—Mount Adams to the north. It's perhaps the grandest all-around view of this fascinating volcanic plain, which never ceases to stir the imagination. Carry plenty of water and try to avoid this hike on an extremely hot day. The summit altitude is enough to make many a flatlander gasp for air on the final stretches. Bring plenty of film, but don't expect your photos to do this summit view justice. No lens can truly capture it. The elevation gain is 2,351 feet. The trail usually is snow-free June to November.

Location: Southwest of Sisters in the Three Sisters Wilderness; see The Southern Cascades Map 2, grid g4.

User Groups: Hikers, dogs, and horses. No mountain bikes are allowed. No wheelchair facilities.

Permits: A federal Northwest Forest Pass, $5 per day or $30 annually, is required to park at the trailhead. Passes are available from ranger stations and many private vendors, online at website: www.wta.org, or by calling 800/270-7504.

Maps: For a map of the Three Sisters Wilderness, contact Nature of the Northwest Information Center, 800 Northeast Oregon Street, Suite 177, Portland, OR 97232; 503/872-2750. Ask the USGS for topographic maps of the Mount Washington and Black Crater areas.

Directions: From Sisters drive west on Highway 242 for 11.5 miles to the trailhead parking lot on the left (south) side of the road. (If you're traveling from McKenzie Bridge, the trailhead is 3.5 miles east of McKenzie Pass.)

Contact: Deschutes National Forest, Sisters Ranger District, Highway 20, Pine Street, Sisters, OR 97759; 541/549-7700.

23 Camp Lake/Chambers Lakes
14.0 mi/1.0–2.0 days

Awesome, glaciated volcanic peak to the left; awesome, glaciated volcanic peak to the right—that's the scene at Camp Lake in the Chambers Lakes Basin, a crescent-shaped ring of lakes that sits smack dab in between the Middle Sister ("Hope") and the South Sister ("Charity"). Even though the area is very heavily visited in summer months, it's a grand spectacle, one made even grander by the sweat you shed getting here. From the Pole Creek Trailhead, start up the long grade, keeping left at the first junction (the right fork departs to Matthieu Lakes and Scott Pass) and right at the second junction (the left fork leaves for Green Lakes). Continue uphill, with good mountain views, to North Fork Squaw Creek and a side trail leading left just under a mile to Demaris Lake. Stay straight, climb to the ridgetop, and follow it to Camp Lake, the turnaround point, where camping is possible more than 100 feet from the lake. Other good (probably better) campsites can be found off-trail farther ahead in the Chambers chain.

Location: Between the South and Middle Sisters in the Three Sisters Wilderness; see The Southern Cascades Map 2, grid g5.

User Groups: Hikers, horses, and dogs. No mountain bikes are allowed. No wheelchair facilities.

Permits: A federal Northwest Forest Pass, $5 per day or $30 annually, is required to park at the trailhead. Passes are available from ranger stations and many private vendors, online at website: www.wta.org, or by calling 800/270-7504.

Maps: For a map of the Three Sisters Wilderness, contact the Nature of the Northwest Information Center, 800 Northeast Oregon Street, Suite 177, Portland, OR 97232; 503/872-2750. Ask the USGS for topographic maps of the North Sister, South Sister, Broken Top, and Trout Creek Butte areas.

Directions: From Sisters drive Highway 242 west for 1.5 miles and turn left (south) on Forest Service Road 15. Follow signs to Pole Creek Trail about 10.5 miles from the turnoff.

Contact: Deschutes National Forest, Sisters Ranger District, Highway 20, Pine Street, Sisters, OR 97759; 541/549-7700.

24 Shevlin Park Loop
5.0 mi/2.5 hrs

Dry pines, wet rocks, and lazy walks are in order at Shevlin Park, one of the city of Bend's many nearby getaways for hikers and mountain bikers. This five-mile loop trail, which begins just over a suspension bridge near the caretaker's house, weaves through the pines on either side of Tumalo Creek, taking you close to a large forest-fire burn and to some delightful creekside meadows in this scenic gorge. Quiet spots are easy to find, even with substantial mountain-bike traffic on the path. This is a good, year-round, low-elevation hike, suitable for the whole family. Mountain bikers love it because it's connected to downtown Bend (and its many cycle shops) by a bike-laned road.

Location: Northwest of Bend on Tumalo Creek; see The Southern Cascades Map 2, grid h6.

User Groups: Hikers, dogs, horses, and mountain bikes. No wheelchair facilities.

Permits: No permits are required. Parking and access are free.

Maps: Ask the USGS for a topographic map of the Shevlin Park area.

Directions: From downtown Bend follow Newport Avenue west (it becomes Shevlin Park Road) about four miles, cross Tumalo Creek, and look for the trailhead beyond a gate at the picnic area on the left side of the road.

Contact: Bend Metro Parks and Recreation Department, 200 Northwest Pacific Park Lane, Bend, OR 97701; 541/389-7275.

25 South Sister Summit/Moraine Lake

12.0 mi/9.0 hrs

They name the southernmost volcano of the Three Sisters chain "Charity," complementing "Faith" and "Hope," her two sisters to the north. You'll probably have a less charitable name for her about two-thirds of the way up the long, steep south shoulder, but not when you're standing on top. The South Sister, a stunningly beautiful dormant volcanic peak, is the most user-friendly peak in the Cascade chain. At 10,358 feet, Oregon's third-highest peak is taller than many mountains requiring technical climbing skills, conditioning, and gear. Unlike most peaks, it can be walked right to the summit by those with little or no mountaineering skill—just plenty of lung power and perseverance.

From Devils Lake Campground, climb up a deceptively easy trail to a junction with the Moraine Lake Trail. If you don't feel the South Sister summit in your soul today, veer right here, spend an enjoyable afternoon at a scenic lake, and cut your losses with a round-trip of about 4.5 miles. Otherwise trudge on and watch the trail progressively steepen. Above the treeline the route is obvious, skirting the west side of the Lewis Glacier to the summit, about four miles beyond the first Moraine Lake junction. The route is exposed, rough, and, for those not used to hiking at

high altitude, very strenuous. Take your time, take lots of water, and keep going. From the top you can see just about forever. Take photos all around and take note of the small lake in the crater. Your total elevation gain: 4,900 feet, just a throw from right field short of one mile. The route is usually accessible from June through October.

Location: From Cascade Lakes Highway 46 to the South Sister summit in the Three Sisters Wilderness; see The Southern Cascades Map 2, grid h2.

User Groups: Hikers, dogs, and horses. No mountain bikes are allowed. No wheelchair facilities.

Permits: A federal Northwest Forest Pass, $5 per day or $30 annually, is required to park at the trailhead. Passes are available from ranger stations and many private vendors, online at website: www.wta.org, or by calling 800/270-7504.

Maps: For a map of the Three Sisters Wilderness, contact the Nature of the Northwest Information Center, 800 Northeast Oregon Street, Suite 177, Portland, OR 97232; 503/872-2750. Ask the USGS for topographic maps of the Broken Top and South Sister areas.

Directions: From U.S. 97 in Bend, follow signs 27 miles to Mount Bachelor Ski Area. Continue 6.5 miles south on Cascade Lakes Highway/Highway 46 to the trailhead in Devils Lake Campground on the left (south) side of the highway.

Contact: Deschutes National Forest, Bend/Fort Rock Ranger District, 1230 Northeast Third Street, Suite A-262, Bend, OR 97701; 541/383-4000.

26 Green Lakes Loop

13.2 mi/1.0–2.0 days

You know you're in for a treat on the Green Lakes Loop even before you leave your car. As you pass Mount Bachelor Ski Area and begin the Century Drive Loop, you enter an almost unnatural world of natural beauty: stunning, crystal-clear lakes; broad, lodgepole pine forests; magnificent lava and obsidian rock formations; and broad alpine meadows. Wait until you get on the trail, where the real scenery begins. Green Lakes is a high alpine crossroads for nearly a dozen trails bisecting the Three Sisters Wilderness. As such it's a predictably overcrowded, overused destination. But this southern-loop access, entering via Fall Creek and exiting in the Soda Creek drainage, is the best and most scenic. And if you visit off-season, such as in September, you might find yourself in far less hiking company than you feared. In any case do yourself a favor and make this hike at least once in your lifetime. It's truly special.

From the trailhead follow Fall Creek steeply upstream and enter a wondrous display of rushing waterfalls, one after another for nearly two miles. Farther along, leave the creek, pass a junction with the Moraine Lake Trail, and walk along a spectacular wall of black, glassy obsidian. You'll soon arrive at a trail junction, where the main trail skirts to the right (east) side of the largest lake. By following side trails, you can make a full loop around all three lakes. The scenery is magnificent, the mountain views majestic, the route flat. Don't camp near the lake and stay out of restoration zones. Back at the trail junction, turn east on the Crater Ditch Trail, which leads 2.8 miles to the Soda Creek Trail and a speedy, 4.5-mile exit back to the car. The scenery on the way out seems less impressive than on the way in. But only slightly so. The route is usually accessible June through October.

For a less strenuous entry to the Green Lakes area, take the Broken Top Trail from the Crater Ditch Trailhead, reached via Forest Service Road 370 off Century Drive near Todd

Lake Campground. The road to the trailhead is rough, and the trail often is impassable until August.

Location: Between the South Sister and Broken Top in the Three Sisters Wilderness; see The Southern Cascades Map 2, grid h3.

User Groups: Hikers, dogs, and horses. No mountain bikes are allowed. No wheelchair facilities.

Permits: A federal Northwest Forest Pass, $5 per day or $30 annually, is required to park at the trailhead. Passes are available from ranger stations and many private vendors, online at website: www.wta.org, or by calling 800/270-7504.

Maps: For a map of the Three Sisters Wilderness, contact the Nature of the Northwest Information Center, 800 Northeast Oregon Street, Suite 177, Portland, OR 97232; 503/872-2750. Ask the USGS for topographic maps of the Broken Top and South Sister areas.

Directions: From U.S. 97 in Bend, follow signs 27 miles to Mount Bachelor Ski Area. Continue 4.5 miles south on Cascade Lakes Highway/Highway 46 to the Green Lakes Trailhead on the right (north) side of the highway.

Contact: Deschutes National Forest, Bend/Fort Rock Ranger District, 1230 Northeast Third Street, Suite A-262, Bend, OR 97701; 541/383-4000.

▨ Park Meadow
9.8 mi/6.0 hrs

This beautiful meadowland on the Broken Top's north flank is Oregon Cascade wilderness at its best. The trail, only moderately steep, winds up and down, through meadow and forest, to Park Meadow. The route, frankly, is relatively boring. But the meadows are magnificent, and the mountain views sublime. It's wild, quiet, and unforgettable. Don't camp in the meadows; some established sites are available in the woods nearby. Experienced route-finders seeking more solitude might consider continuing a mile west on the trail to a side trail leading south, up to hard-to-find Golden Lake and two more sterling tarns even higher on Broken Top's north face. The total elevation gain on the walk to Park Meadow is about 700 feet. Do yourself and this sterling spot a favor: make it a day hike and plan to spend a whole day.

Location: On the north side of Broken Top in the Three Sisters Wilderness; see The Southern Cascades Map 2, grid h3.

User Groups: Hikers, dogs, and horses. No mountain bikes are allowed. No wheelchair facilities.

Permits: A federal Northwest Forest Pass, $5 per day or $30 annually, is required to park at the trailhead. Passes are available from ranger stations and many private vendors, online at website: www.wta.org, or by calling 800/270-7504.

Maps: For a map of the Three Sisters Wilderness, contact the Nature of the Northwest Information Center, 800 Northeast Oregon Street, Suite 177, Portland, OR 97232; 503/872-2750. Ask the USGS for topographic maps of the Tumalo Falls, Broken Top, and Trout Creek Butte areas.

Directions: From downtown Sisters turn south on Elm Street, following signs for Three Creek Lake. Proceed approximately 14 miles on Three Creek Road/Forest Service Road 16 to the Park Meadow Trailhead. Hike 1.2 miles east on the old road to the main trailhead.

Contact: Deschutes National Forest, Sisters Ranger District, Highway 20, Pine Street, Sisters, OR 97759; 541/549-7700.

28 Tam McArthur Rim

5.2 mi/3.0 hrs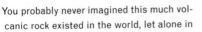

You probably never imagined this much volcanic rock existed in the world, let alone in one place. The Tam McArthur Rim Trail, a magnificent ridgetop walk overlooking Three Creek and Little Creek Lakes, puts you as close to Broken Top and the South Sister as you can get without making actual foot contact. It's almost like riding in an airplane as you scale the ridge, with 500-foot sheer rock cliffs dropping to your right. Views begin as you leave the forest at about three-quarters of a mile and don't stop until you're back in the car. Wildflowers proliferate on the tabletop plateau during summer months. At about 2.5 miles, look for a side trail leading one-quarter mile to the right to a viewpoint with a sky-high view of the whole volcanic Hee Haw Gang: the Sisters, Three Creek Lakes, Mount Bachelor, Black and Belknap Craters, Black Butte, Mount Washington, Three Fingered Jack, and Cascade peaks as far north as Mount Adams. Turn around here or continue along the rim another mile to the base of Broken Hand, where the trail ends and the rock climbing begins. This magnificent trail is fittingly named in honor of Lewis "Tam" McArthur, longtime head of the Oregon Geographic Board.

Snowfields linger on Tam McArthur Ridge well into summer, particularly beyond the viewpoint. While the elevation gain on the route is less than 1,000 feet, this trail earns a difficulty rating of 4 because of its altitude. The trailhead is higher than 6,500 feet, and the viewpoint more than 7,200. Hikers unaccustomed to hiking at altitude will find it challenging.

Location: East of Broken Top in the Three Sisters Wilderness; see The Southern Cascades Map 2, grid h4.

User Groups: Hikers, dogs, and horses. No mountain bikes are allowed. No wheelchair facilities.

Permits: A federal Northwest Forest Pass, $5 per day or $30 annually, is required to park at the trailhead. Passes are available from

ranger stations and many private vendors, online at website: www.wta.org, or by calling 800/270-7504.

Maps: For a map of the Three Sisters Wilderness, contact the Nature of the Northwest Information Center, 800 Northeast Oregon Street, Suite 177, Portland, OR 97232; 503/872-2750. Ask the USGS for topographic maps of the Tumalo Falls and Broken Top areas.

Directions: From downtown Sisters turn south on Elm Street, following signs for Three Creek Lake. Drive about 17 miles on Three Creek Road/Forest Service Road 16 to the trailhead parking area on the right, just off the road to Driftwood Campground at Three Creek Lake.

Contact: Deschutes National Forest, Sisters Ranger District, Highway 20, Pine Street, Sisters, OR 97759; 541/549-7700.

29 Tumalo Mountain
3.0 mi/2.0 hrs

This can be a quick sprint to a fine viewpoint for summertime visitors to the Mount Bachelor/Cascade Lakes Highway area south of the Three Sisters. Park in the Sno-Park parking lot and begin the steady climb (about 1,200 feet) to the top of Tumalo Mountain, a cindercone kid sister to nearby Mount Bachelor. You find good views of Mount Bachelor, Broken Top, and the South Sister from the top.

While the elevation gain on the route is only 1,500 feet, this trail earns a difficulty rating of 4 because of its altitude. The trailhead is at 6,200 feet, and the viewpoint more than 7,700. Hikers unaccustomed to hiking at altitude will find it challenging.

Location: North of Mount Bachelor in Deschutes National Forest; see The Southern Cascades Map 2, grid h4.

User Groups: Hikers and dogs. No horses or mountain bikes are allowed. No wheelchair facilities.

Permits: A federal Northwest Forest Pass, $5 per day or $30 annually, is required to park at the trailhead. Passes are available from ranger stations and many private vendors, online at website: www.wta.org, or by calling 800/270-7504.

Maps: For a map of the Three Sisters Wilderness, contact the Nature of the Northwest Information Center, 800 Northeast Oregon Street, Suite 177, Portland, OR 97232; 503/872-2750. Ask the USGS for topographic maps of the Tumalo Falls and Broken Top areas.

Directions: From U.S. 97 in Bend, follow signs 27 miles west to Mount Bachelor Ski Area. Proceed on Cascade Lakes Highway/Highway 46 to the trailhead in the parking area for Dutchman Flats Sno-Park on the right (north) side of the highway.

Contact: Deschutes National Forest, Sisters Ranger District, Highway 20, Pine Street, Sisters, OR 97759; 541/549-7700.

30 French Pete Creek
10.4 mi one way/6.5 hrs

Pack your low-stress attitude and high-speed film for this magical, forested walk along mossy French Pete Creek, where the water flows like liquid glass. The French Pete Valley, subject of a tireless preservation campaign that resulted in federal wilderness protection in 1978, is in a state of flux while mid-section stretches are reconstructed to bypass rotted log bridges. But even with a couple of bridgeless crossings, it remains a spectacular walk.

Most day hikers start at the lower trailhead described below and hike three miles in to the first frosty creek crossing, sans bridge, for a superb six-mile round-trip in this gardenlike setting. Even without better access to the trail's upper portions, you won't be disappointed by this day hike through glorious old-growth western cedar and Douglas fir. But if you're up to a longer march, consider hiking the entire route as a one-way shuttle hike, beginning at the Pat Saddle Trailhead described above. It's 10 miles of cool, shaded, spectacular downhill walking through a wondrous green valley.

Lug soles on wet logs are a recipe for broken bones. Carry a pair of tennis shoes or rubber sandals to make your stream crossings. Leave the log walking to loggers with cork boots.

Location: In the South Fork McKenzie River drainage of the Three Sisters Wilderness; see The Southern Cascades Map 3, grid a7.

User Groups: Hikers and dogs. Not recommended for horses. No mountain bikes are allowed. No wheelchair facilities.

Permits: A federal Northwest Forest Pass, $5 per day or $30 annually, is required to park at the trailhead. Passes are available from ranger stations and many private vendors, online at website: www.wta.org, or by calling 800/270-7504.

Maps: For a map of the Three Sisters Wilderness, contact the Nature of the Northwest Information Center, 800 Northeast Oregon Street, Suite 177, Portland, OR 97232; 503/872-2750. Ask the USGS for topographic maps of the Cougar Reservoir and French Mountain areas.

Directions: From Eugene drive 40 miles east on McKenzie Highway/Highway 126 to Blue River. Continue east to Forest Service Road 19. Turn right (south). To reach the upper trailhead, follow signs to Cougar Dam and turn left (east) across the dam on Forest Service Road 1993. Proceed about 15 miles to the Pat Saddle Trailhead on the right (south) side of the road. To reach the lower trailhead, continue south on Forest Service Road 19 a total of about 11 miles to the French Pete Creek Trailhead on the left (east) side of the road.

Contact: Willamette National Forest, Blue River Ranger District, P.O. Box 199, Blue River, OR 97413; 541/822-3317.

31 Rebel Creek/ Rebel Rock Loop
11.7 mi/8.0 hrs

If you liked the French Pete Creek Trail (see above), you'll love the challenging Rebel Rock Loop. This trail also has luscious old-growth passages but throws in smaller crowds, fascinating geological terrain, and an old lookout station with grand views. The trail starts gradually and then picks up serious steam after it crosses a creek chasm on a log bridge at about one mile. Continue up and east and then turn right (south) at the junction with the Rebel Rock Trail, which leads two miles to the old lookout and a great viewpoint just beyond it. It's just over four miles back to the car from here, mostly downhill. You'll be feeling this loop in your legs for several days. The total elevation change is more than 3,000 feet. Those looking for a short day hike might consider hoofing it to the creek bridge and back, a round-trip of about 2.2 miles.

Location: South of Blue River in the western Three Sisters Wilderness; see The Southern Cascades Map 3, grid a7.

User Groups: Horses, hikers, and dogs. No mountain bikes are allowed. No wheelchair facilities.

Permits: A federal Northwest Forest Pass, $5 per day or $30 annually, is required to park at the trailhead. Passes are available from ranger stations and many private vendors, online at website: www.wta.org, or by calling 800/270-7504.

Maps: For a map of the Three Sisters Wilderness, contact the Nature of the Northwest Information Center, 800 Northeast Oregon Street, Suite 177, Portland, OR 97232; 503/872-2750. Ask the USGS for topographic maps of the Cougar Reservoir, Chucksney Mountain, and French Mountain areas.

Directions: From Eugene drive 40 miles east on McKenzie Highway/Highway 126 to Blue River. Continue four miles east to Forest Service Road 19/Aufderheide Forest Drive. Turn right (south) and proceed 14.5 miles to the Rebel Rock Trailhead on the left (east) side of the road.

Contact: Willamette National Forest, Blue River Ranger District, P.O. Box 199, Blue River, OR 97413; 541/822-3317.

32 Chucksney Mountain Loop
11.0 mi/6.5 hrs

A pinch of old forest, a dash of high meadows, a smidgen of mountain views: it all mixes up well on the Chucksney Mountain Loop, which combines the Grasshopper and Box Canyon Trails for a high-variety, low-stress mountain hike. From the Box Canyon Visitor Center, elevation 3,728 feet, start on the Grasshopper Trail, which leads to Grasshopper Mountain. You are only with it for about a quarter mile, however. Turn right at the first two junctions and start switchbacking uphill on the Chucksney Mountain Loop. It's pretty in this mixed old-growth forest, especially in the spring when dogwoods and other low, bushy shrubs are in bloom. Trees thin and views thicken at about three miles, improving the higher you go. At four miles leave the forest altogether and enter a refreshing wildflower meadow, which continues for about a mile until the trail tops out at 5,760 feet. You find good views from here of the Three Sisters and the protective, pool-table-felt carpet of unspoiled wilderness surrounding them. After about a mile of level ridgetop walking, begin a quick descent down through alpine meadows back to the Grasshopper Trail. Take a hard left at the junction and walk 3.5 easy miles back to the car.

Location: Between Waldo Lake and Three Sisters Wildernesses; see The Southern Cascades Map 3, grid a7.

User Groups: Hikers, dogs, horses, and mountain bikes. No wheelchair facilities.

Permits: A federal Northwest Forest Pass, $5 per day or $30 annually, is required to park at the trailhead. Passes are available from ranger stations and many private vendors, online at website: www.wta.org, or by calling 800/270-7504.

Maps: For a map of the Three Sisters Wilderness, contact the Nature of the Northwest Information Center, 800 Northeast Oregon Street, Suite 177, Portland, OR 97232; 503/872-2750. Ask the USGS for a topographic map of the Chucksney Mountain area.

Directions: From Eugene drive 40 miles east on McKenzie Highway/Highway 126 to Blue River. Continue four miles east to Forest Service Road 19/Aufderheide Forest Drive. Turn right (south) and proceed 26 miles to Box Canyon Horse Camp on the right (west) side of the road.

Contact: Willamette National Forest, Blue River Ranger District, P.O. Box 199, Blue River, OR 97413; 541/822-3317.

33 Erma Bell Lakes
8.5 mi/4.5 hrs

Two scenic lakes, connected by a waterfall, only two miles down a flat path: sounds like a recipe for relaxation, right? Yep. To you and about a gazillion other people. The Erma Bell Lakes Trail is crowded. So much so, in fact, that solitude hounds might consider ambling off elsewhere in the Three Sisters or Waldo Lake Wildernesses. Still, it is awfully tempting to stroll the two miles to those two lakes, and if you're willing to hoof it a bit farther on a very nice loop hike, you leave a lot of people behind at that first waterfall junction.

To reach the lower and middle lake, hike to the first trail junction and then turn right. Beyond the waterfall side trail at 2.1 miles, the loop leads south about three-quarters of a mile to Upper Erma Bell Lake and then another 1.5 miles to a junction at a footbridge. Turn left and walk to Williams and Otter Lakes on the easy five-mile walk back north to the first junction and the car. Bring the bug juice to get through the mosquitoes. Bring the cattle prod to get through the gapers. Both can proliferate in midsummer.

Camping is prohibited at Otter Lake and Lower and Middle Erma Bell Lakes.

Location: North of Waldo Lake in the southeast corner of the Three Sisters Wilderness; see The Southern Cascades Map 3, grid b8.

User Groups: Hikers, dogs, and horses. No mountain bikes are allowed. No wheelchair facilities.

Permits: A federal Northwest Forest Pass, $5 per day or $30 annually, is required to park at the trailhead. Passes are available from ranger stations and many private vendors, online at website: www.wta.org, or by calling 800/270-7504.

Maps: For a map of the Three Sisters Wilderness, contact the Nature of the Northwest Information Center, 800 Northeast Oregon Street, Suite 177, Portland, OR 97232; 503/872-2750. Ask the USGS for topographic maps of the Chucksney Mountain and Waldo Mountain areas.

Directions: From McKenzie Highway/Highway 126 at Blue River, drive about 4.5 miles east to Forest Service Road 19. Turn right (south) and proceed 25.5 miles to Forest Service Road 1957. Turn left (east) and drive 3.5 miles to the trailhead in Skookum Campground. From Willamette Pass Highway/Highway 58, take the Westfir exit to Forest Service Road 19. Drive north about 31 miles to Forest Service Road 1957, turn right (east), and drive 3.5 miles to the trailhead in Skookum Campground.

Contact: Willamette National Forest, Middle Fork Ranger District, 49098 Salmon Creek Road, P.O. Box 1410, Oakridge, OR 97464; 541/782-2283.

34 Rigdon Lakes Loop
8.0 mi/4.0 hrs

Rigdon Lakes, an oft-visited destination from North Waldo Campground, forms the centerpiece for an easy half-day loop that's gentle enough for children or the aerobically challenged. From North Waldo Campground, head west on the Waldo Lake Trail (not the shoreline trail nearer the lake) for 1.7 miles to the Rigdon Lakes Trail, which forks to the right (north). Walk three-fourths of a mile to Upper Rigdon Lake and skirt the east shore, deciding whether to follow the side trail up to good Waldo Lake views on Rigdon Butte. From here drop about 1.25 miles to the lower lake and continue a short distance to Lake Kiwa and a junction with the Wahanna Trail. Turn south and walk 1.3 rhododendron-lined miles back to Waldo Lake, at the outflow of the North Fork of the Middle Fork Willamette River. It's a quick three-mile hop, skip, and jump back to the car. The total elevation gain for this pleasant loop is fewer than 300 feet. Be prepared for mosquito bombardment in summer months.

Location: North of Waldo Lake in the Waldo Lake Wilderness; see The Southern Cascades Map 3, grid b8.

User Groups: Hikers, dogs, and horses. No mountain bikes are allowed. No wheelchair facilities.

Permits: A federal Northwest Forest Pass, $5 per day or $30 annually, is required to park at the trailhead. Passes are available from ranger stations and many private vendors, online at website: www.wta.org, or by calling 800/270-7504.

Maps: For a map of the Waldo Lake Wilderness and Recreation Area, contact the

Nature of the Northwest Information Center, 800 Northeast Oregon Street, Suite 177, Portland, OR 97232; 503/872-2750. Ask the USGS for a topographic map of the Waldo Mountain area.

Directions: From Highway 58 three miles west of Willamette Pass, turn north on Waldo Lake Road/Forest Service Road 5897. Following signs to North Waldo Campground, proceed about 12.5 miles on Forest Service Roads 5897 and 5898 to the trailhead near the campground's boat launch parking area.

Contact: Willamette National Forest, Middle Fork Ranger District, 49098 Salmon Creek Road, P.O. Box 1410, Oakridge, OR 97464; 541/782-2283.

35 Waldo Mountain
6.0 mi/4.0 hrs

Here's that sky-high view of Waldo Lake and Diamond Peak you've been craving since the first time you visited crystal-clear Waldo Lake. If it's just the view you want, head straight up the Waldo Mountain Trail, about three miles and 2,000 vertical feet, to the manned lookout tower. Here you'll find the view you expected, and more. The Twins and Maiden Peak are nice backdrops to Waldo Lake, and Diamond Peak also shines nearby. Return by the same route, or if you're up for more, by all means continue east down Waldo Mountain's opposite shoulder to a junction with the Waldo Meadows Trail. Turn right (west) and walk through the thick meadow, eventually happening upon a side trail that leads half a mile south to Salmon Lakes and a nice waterfall near the lower lake. It's about 2.5 easy miles west back to the car from here.

Location: Northeast of Waldo Lake in the Waldo Lake Wilderness; see The Southern Cascades Map 3, grid c8.

User Groups: Hikers, horses, and dogs. No mountain bikes are allowed. No wheelchair facilities.

Permits: A federal Northwest Forest Pass, $5 per day or $30 annually, is required to park at the trailhead. Passes are available from ranger stations and many private vendors, online at website: www.wta.org, or by calling 800/270-7504.

Maps: For a map of the Waldo Lake Wilderness and Recreation Area, contact the Nature of the Northwest Information Center, 800 Northeast Oregon Street, Suite 177, Portland, OR 97232; 503/872-2750. Ask the USGS for topographic maps of the Blair Lake, Waldo Mountain, and Waldo Lake areas.

Directions: From Willamette Pass Highway/Highway 58 at Oakridge, turn east on Salmon Creek Road/Forest Service Road 24 and proceed 11 miles to a Y in the road. Veer left onto Forest Service Road 2417 and follow it six miles to Forest Service Road 2424. Turn right and follow the road to the trailhead on the right side of the road.

Contact: Willamette National Forest, Middle Fork Ranger District, 49098 Salmon Creek Road, P.O. Box 1410, Oakridge, OR 97464; 541/782-2283.

36 The Twins
6.6 mi/4.5 hrs

Another day, another cinder cone. This is a particularly worthwhile one, however, not only for its easy summit access (only a 1,600-foot vertical gain), but also for its relatively crowd-free path and awesome summit view. The viewpoint on top of the 7,360-foot peak provides a truly airplane-esque view of Waldo Lake, which can be seen directly to the northwest. You walk through dry forest and ashy soil for 1.5 miles and then cross the Pacific Crest Trail. The grade steepens a bit from here but is manageable all the way to the rim of the Twins' trough-shaped crater (creating "twin" peaks on a single mountaintop). From the north summit the view of Waldo Lake (all of it) and Diamond Peak is worth the climb up.

Location: East of Waldo Lake in the Waldo Lake Wilderness; see The Southern Cascades Map 3, grid c8.

User Groups: Hikers, horses, and dogs. No mountain bikes are allowed. No wheelchair facilities.

Permits: A federal Northwest Forest Pass, $5 per day or $30 annually, is required to park at the trailhead. Passes are available from ranger stations and many private vendors, online at website: www.wta.org, or by calling 800/270-7504.

Maps: For a map of the Waldo Lake Wilderness, contact the Nature of the Northwest Information Center, 800 Northeast Oregon Street, Suite 177, Portland, OR 97232; 503/872-2750. Ask the USGS for a topographic map of the Twins area.

Directions: From Highway 58 three miles west of Willamette Pass, turn north on Waldo Lake Road/Forest Service Road 5897. Following signs to North Waldo Campground, proceed approximately six miles to the trailhead on the right side of the road.

Contact: Willamette National Forest, Middle Fork Ranger District, 49098 Salmon Creek Road, P.O. Box 1410, Oakridge, OR 97464; 541/782-2283.

37 Mount June/ Hardesty Mountain
9.5 mi/5.5 hrs

It's a tradition: the Hardesty Mountain Trail, just off Highway 58, is one of this region's oldest, most time-honored day hikes. But it isn't what it used to be, quite literally. The viewpoint at the summit is largely obscured by trees, and many hikers who hoof it up the 4,000-foot, five-mile trail aren't convinced it was worth the effort.

In recent years more and more hikers have taken to hiking up Hardesty's taller cousin, 4,618-foot Mount June, which has a far shorter access trail and better views from its clifftop former lookout site. For the best of both worlds, hike the mere 1.1 miles to the top of June Mountain, 4,616 feet, and then continue east on the Sawtooth Trail 2.5 miles, passing Sawtooth Rock and winding up on the summit of Hardesty anyway. The Mount June/Sawtooth/Hardesty trip is about 9.5 miles round-trip, with a total elevation gain of only about 1,000 feet.

Location: South of Lookout Point Reservoir near the border between the Umpqua and Willamette National Forests; see The Southern Cascades Map 3, grid c4.

User Groups: Hikers and dogs. Horses and mountain bikes are not recommended. No wheelchair facilities.

Permits: No permits are required. Parking and access are free.

Maps: For a map of the Umpqua and Willamette National Forest, contact the Nature of the Northwest Information Center, 800 Northeast Oregon Street, Suite 177, Portland, OR 97232; 503/872-2750. Ask the USGS for a topographic map of the Mount June area.

Directions: From the Cottage Grove Ranger Station, follow Row River Road/Forest Service Road 2400 17 miles east to Layng Creek Road/Forest Service Road 17. Turn left on Road 17 and proceed five miles to Forest Service Road 1751. Turn left on Road 1751 and continue 6.4 miles to the junction with Forest Service Road 1721. Continue to the right on Road 1721 for two miles, to Forest Service Road 1721-941. Turn right and proceed one-third mile to the trailhead on the right (east) side of the road.

Contact: Umpqua National Forest, Cottage Grove Ranger Station, 78405 Cedar Park Road, Cottage Grove, OR 97424; 541/942-5591.

38 Brice Creek
5.5 mi one way/4.0 hrs

This scenic, all-season trail is an excellent, adjustable-length day hike for the whole family, with a beautiful stream beneath old-growth trees, good fishing, waterfalls, serene pools, and if you look closely, evidence of early mining activity in this valley. In fact, you might see some mining still going on. Brice Creek once was the Frank Bryce Trail, the primary access between Cottage Grove and the Bohemia Mining District in the early 1900s, and you still see amateur prospectors dipping a gold pan into its chilly waters on occasion, hoping for a gold surprise. Good campsites are found along the route.

Kids will love this trail for its easy grade, fascinating surroundings, and intriguing history. The easternmost 1.2 trail miles follow an abandoned flume that used to carry water for a power plant at Lund Park, an old mill site. Also look for remnants of an old dam just east of the East End Trailhead. The dam was removed to allow fish passage. Hiked as a 5.5-mile shuttle walk, starting at either the west trailhead or the Champion Lake Trailhead, or a shorter hike between any two trailheads, this is a great way to spend a day, any time of the year. If the weather cooperates and the track is dry, it can be an especially fun ride for mountain bikers.

Stay away from mining tunnels, new or old. They're dangerous.

Location: Southeast of Cottage Grove in northwestern Umpqua National Forest; see The Southern Cascades Map 3, grid d4.

User Groups: Hikers, dogs, horses, and mountain bikes. No wheelchair facilities.

Permits: No permits are required. Parking and access are free.

Maps: For a map of Umpqua National Forest, contact the Nature of the Northwest Information Center, 800 Northeast Oregon Street, Suite 177, Portland, OR 97232; 503/872-2750. Ask the USGS for a topographic map of the Rose Hill area.

Directions: From I-5 south of Eugene, take Exit 174 and follow signs east past either side of Dorena Reservoir until you come to the junction of Layng Creek Road/Forest Service Road 17 and Brice Creek Road/Forest Service Road 2470 at 19 miles. Bear right on this road and proceed 3.3 miles to the West Trailhead, 4.6 miles to Cedar Creek Campground Trailhead, 6.9 miles to Lund Park Trailhead, or 8.2 miles to the Champion Lake (East End) Trailhead.

Contact: Umpqua National Forest, Cottage Grove Ranger Station, 78405 Cedar Parks Road, Cottage Grove, OR 97424; 541/942-5591.

39 Bohemia Mountain
1.6 mi/2.0 hrs

Boom, you're there. Not without a lot of panting first, however. The Bohemia Mountain Trail gets serious in a hurry, climbing 687 feet in only 0.8 mile. But what a view from the top. The historic Bohemia mining district, including Musick Mine and the mining ghost town of Bohemia City, is laid out before you. And the mountain peaks—from Mount Shasta to Mount Hood—leave you even more breathless than did the trail. The summit, elevation 5,987 feet, is the highest point in the Cottage Grove Ranger District. Looking down from the peak's sheer-cliff summit area, you swear it's twice that high.

Bohemia was named after James "Bohemia" Johnson, an early immigrant who discovered gold here in 1863 and sparked a gold rush that would not end until the 1930s. Actually it still hasn't ended, judging by the amount of small-scale mining activity that continues in the region today. Visible below from the summit are Musick Mine and Bohemia City.

Location: Southeast of Cottage Grove in the Bohemia Saddle mining area of Umpqua National Forest; see The Southern Cascades Map 3, grid d5.

User Groups: Hikers and dogs. Horses are not recommended. No mountain bikes are allowed. No wheelchair facilities.

Permits: No permits are required. Parking and access are free.

Maps: For a map of Umpqua National Forest, contact the Nature of the Northwest Information Center, 800 Northeast Oregon Street, Suite 177, Portland, OR 97232; 503/872-2750. Ask the USGS for a topographic map of Fairview Peak.

Directions: From I-5 south of Eugene, take Exit 174 and follow signs east past either side of Dorena Reservoir until you come to the junction of Layng Creek Road/Forest Service Road 17 and Brice Creek Road/Forest Service Road 2470 at 19 miles. Bear right on this road and proceed 12 miles to Noonday Road/Forest Service Road 2212. Turn right and continue 8.8 miles to the junction with Sharps Creek Road/Forest Service Road 2460 and Champion Creek Road at Champion Saddle. Stay left on Forest Service Road 2460 and continue 1.1 miles to Bohemia Saddle. Turn left on the road to Bohemia Saddle County Park and find the trailhead on the right. Note: There are two routes to this trailhead. The one listed here follows the best roads.

Contact: Umpqua National Forest, Cottage Grove Ranger Station, 78405 Cedar Park Road, Cottage Grove, OR 97424; 541/942-5591.

40 Larison Creek
6.3 mi one way/3.0 hrs

Respect your elders. Especially if they're trees. The old-growth forest at the base of a narrow valley containing Larison Creek is the highlight of this excellent, family-style day hike. The trail starts along the waters of Larison Cove and heads up into the deep, green forest, maintaining a nearly level grade for the first three miles. After passing a deep pool, the trail climbs more steadily, leaving the creek for a clear-cut and dropping back down to more white-water highs in the creek canyon. After about 5.75 miles the path crosses the creek at its fork and continues uphill to the upper trailhead, reached by following Forest Service Roads 21, 2102, and 101. By shuttling to this spot, you can walk the pleasant, 6.3-mile stretch downhill one way.

For a higher-altitude hike in this area, gain a good view of the reservoir, Oakridge, the Sisters, and Diamond Peak by hiking eight miles round-trip to the top of Larison Rock. The trailhead is on Forest Service Road 5852.

Location: West of Hills Creek Reservoir in Willamette National Forest; see The Southern Cascades Map 3, grid c5.

User Groups: Hikers, dogs, horses, and mountain bikes. No wheelchair facilities.

Permits: A federal Northwest Forest Pass, $5 per day or $30 annually, is required to park at the trailhead. Passes are available from ranger stations and many private vendors, online at website: www.wta.org, or by calling 800/270-7504.

Maps: For a map of Willamette National Forest, contact the Nature of the Northwest Information Center, 800 Northeast Oregon Street, Suite 177, Portland, OR 97232; 503/872-2750. Ask the USGS for topographic maps of the Oakridge and Holland Point areas.

Directions: From Oakridge drive 1.25 miles east on Willamette Pass Highway/Highway

58 to Kitson Springs Road/Forest Service Road 23, where a sign indicates Hills Creek Reservoir. Turn right (south) and, in half a mile, fork right on Forest Service Road 21. The trailhead is at 3.3 miles on the right, near Larison Cove.

Contact: Willamette National Forest, Middle Fork Ranger District, 49098 Salmon Creek Road, P.O. Box 1410, Oakridge, OR 97463; 541/782-2283.

41 Middle Fork Willamette River
5.0 mi/2.5 hrs

This is the lower portion of a 40-mile trail that the Forest Service is building to extend from Hills Creek Reservoir all the way to the Middle Fork Willamette's headwaters at Lake Timpanogas (see hike in this chapter, Indigo Lake/Sawtooth Mountain). It's a pleasant walk (or ride) along the river upstream from Hills Creek Reservoir, especially if you have a shuttle to the far southern end at the junction of Roads 21 and 2127. The trail follows the east riverbank closely the entire way, at times even utilizing the river's upper bed as a pathway. Anglers love the trail for that very reason (a state fishing license is required). The river trail is also rich with wildlife, with creatures as small as a mallard and as large as a bull elk commonly spotted. This is another good year-round river trail for the whole family.

Location: South of Hills Creek Reservoir in Willamette National Forest; see The Southern Cascades Map 3, grid d6.

User Groups: Hikers, horses, dogs, and mountain bikes. No wheelchair facilities.

Permits: A federal Northwest Forest Pass, $5 per day or $30 annually, is required to park at the trailhead. Passes are available from ranger stations and many private vendors, online at website: www.wta.org, or by calling 800/270-7504.

Maps: For a map of Willamette National Forest, contact the Nature of the Northwest Information Center, 800 Northeast Oregon Street, Suite 177, Portland, OR 97232; 503/872-2750. Ask the USGS for a topographic map of the Warner Mountain area.

Directions: From Oakridge drive 1.25 miles east on Willamette Pass Highway/Highway 58 to Kitson Springs Road/Forest Service Road 23. Turn right (south) and proceed half a mile to Forest Service Road 21. Turn right and proceed 10 miles to Sand Prairie Campground. Turn right on Forest Service Road 134 and follow it through the campground to the parking lot at the group picnic site near the river.

Contact: Willamette National Forest, Middle Fork Ranger District, 49098 Salmon Creek Road, P.O. Box 1410, Oakridge, OR 97463; 541/782-2283.

42 Vivian Lake
8.0 mi/5.5 hrs

Vivian Lake is the goal on this highly popular day hike. But getting there is far more than half the fun. En route you pass by 286-foot Salt Creek Falls, Diamond Creek Falls, Fall Creek Falls, and other natural wonders, any one of which is worth the hike. Diamond Creek Falls, near the trailhead, will consume at least half a dozen frames of your film.

Find the trail leading across the creek, the beginning of a three-mile loop linking Salt Creek and Diamond Creek Falls. Go right and walk along the Salt Creek Canyon to a steep side trail that leads right to Diamond Creek Falls, a graceful cascade 100 feet high. Back on the main trail, continue a short distance to a junction. To return to the car, turn left and hike up and back. For Vivian Lake, go right over the railroad tracks, just over a mile to Fall Creek Falls (the smallest of the three), and another mile to scenic Vivian Lake, where photos of nearby Mount Yoran are in order. It's a grand lunch spot. For variety, return on whichever loop leg you skipped on the way in.

Location: Southwest of Willamette Pass in the Diamond Peak Wilderness; see The Southern Cascades Map 3, grid d7.

User Groups: Hikers, dogs, and horses. No mountain bikes are allowed. No wheelchair facilities.

Permits: A federal Northwest Forest Pass, $5 per day or $30 annually, is required to park at the trailhead. Passes are available from ranger stations and many private vendors, online at website: www.wta.org, or by calling 800/270-7504.

Maps: For a map of the Diamond Peak Wilderness, contact the Nature of the Northwest Information Center, 800 Northeast Oregon Street, Suite 177, Portland, OR 97232; 503/872-2750. Ask the USGS for a topographic map of the Diamond Peak area.

Directions: From Highway 58 five miles west of Willamette Pass, turn south into the parking lot and trailhead for Salt Creek Falls.

Contact: Willamette National Forest, Middle Fork Ranger District, 49098 Salmon Creek Road, P.O. Box 1410, Oakridge, OR 97464; 541/782-2283.

43 Yoran/Diamond View Lakes
8.5 mi/5.0 hrs

Diamond Peak is a true diamond in the rough among Central Oregon's Cascade jewels, and Yoran and Diamond View Lakes both rank as top-notch places to keep a watchful eye on it. Set in deep woods southwest of Odell Lake, Yoran Lake is a perfect day-hike destination with an elevation gain of only about 1,300 feet. It's the more popular walk of the two.

From the trailhead go straight at the junction and begin the moderate climb on an

alarmingly straight trail for four miles to the creek that flows from the lake. A side trail leads left to smaller Karen Lake. Stay straight for one-third mile and arrive at Yoran Lake, which has a pair of small, tree-covered islands at its north end. Avoid the side trail to the left. An unmaintained path leads to better lunch spots around the right shore, with prime views south to 8,750-foot Diamond Peak. Turn around here for the 8.5-mile round-trip or continue on the side trail, which links with the Pacific Crest Trail near Lils Lake. You can make a loop of about 11 miles total if you turn right (northeast) on the PCT, walk to Pengra Pass, and then back to the trailhead on an old road parallel to Odell Lake.

To reach the less-visited Diamond View Lake, turn left at the first trail junction on the Yoran Lake hike. From there it's 5.5 miles due south up Trapper Creek to the lake, with an elevation gain of about 1,000 feet. Diamond Peak looms to the west.

Location: Southwest of Willamette Pass in the Diamond Peak Wilderness; see The Southern Cascades Map 3, grid d8.

User Groups: Hikers, dogs, and horses. No mountain bikes are allowed. No wheelchair facilities.

Permits: A federal Northwest Forest Pass, $5 per day or $30 annually, is required to park at the trailhead. Passes are available from ranger stations and many private vendors, online at website: www.wta.org, or by calling 800/270-7504.

Maps: For a map of the Diamond Peak Wilderness, contact the Nature of the Northwest Information Center, 800 Northeast Oregon Street, Suite 177, Portland, OR 97232; 503/872-2750. Ask the USGS for a topographic map of the Willamette Pass area.

Directions: From the town of Oakridge, drive southeast on Willamette Pass Highway/Highway 58 to Willamette Pass. Proceed just beyond the summit to Forest Service Road 5810.

Turn right (south) and proceed around the northwest shore of Odell Lake to the trailhead parking lot on the right side of the road.

Contact: Deschutes National Forest, Crescent Ranger District, P.O. Box 208, Crescent, OR 97733; 541/433-3200.

44 Mount Yoran/Divide Lake
8.0 mi/5.0 hrs

Within spitting distance of Diamond Peak, the trail to Divide Lake, tucked up against the steep walls of Mount Yoran, is a photographers' delight. It's also one of the best day hikes in the Diamond Peak area. About half a mile from the trailhead, pass a junction with the Diamond Peak Trail and continue straight beyond Notch Lake to another junction. Go straight and you'd walk three miles downhill to Vivian Lake (see hike in this chapter) and a shuttle-hike exit near Willamette Pass. But for this hike veer right and climb to a ridge leading to Divide Lake at the southern base of 7,100-foot Mount Yoran. Mountain views from its shores consume many, many frames of film; sunset mountain-peak views from here in late summer are stunning. Good campsites can be found away from the shore. Continue around the right shore of the lake to a side trail that leads east and up about a mile to the Pacific Crest Trail and a grand vista of the wild territory to the east of the Cascade Divide.

For a quicker, more direct view of Diamond Peak from the trailhead above, walk the Hemlock Butte Trail a quick one-half mile from Road 23 to a fine summit viewpoint.

Location: North of Diamond Peak in the Diamond Peak Wilderness; see The Southern Cascades Map 3, grid d8.

User Groups: Hikers, dogs, and horses. No mountain bikes are allowed. No wheelchair facilities.

Permits: A federal Northwest Forest Pass, $5 per day or $30 annually, is required to park at the trailhead. Passes are available from ranger stations and many private vendors, online at website: www.wta.org, or by calling 800/270-7504.

Maps: For a map of the Diamond Peak Wilderness, contact the Nature of the Northwest Information Center, 800 Northeast Oregon Street, Suite 177, Portland, OR 97232; 503/872-2750. Ask the USGS for a topographic map of the Willamette Pass area.

Directions: From Willamette Pass Highway/Highway 58 at Oakridge, drive 1.25 miles east to Kitson Springs Road/Forest Service Road 23. Turn right (south) and follow signs to Hills Creek Reservoir. Proceed about 20 miles on Forest Service Road 23 to the Vivian Lake Trailhead, which is up a spur road on the left, just beyond the Hemlock Butte Trailhead.

Contact: Deschutes National Forest, Crescent Ranger District, P.O. Box 208, Crescent, OR 97733; 541/433-3200.

45 Indigo Lake/ Sawtooth Mountain
9.0 mi/6.5 hrs

The geographic-names people got it right when they named Indigo Lake, which is a pleasant, five-mile day hike for people staying at Timpanogas Campground. (The five miles include an optional one-mile loop around the lake once you arrive, having already climbed about 550 feet.) Indigo has a developed, walk-in campground that's perfectly suited to introducing young backpackers to the outdoors. In this magnificent setting they're liable to come back for much, much more in the years to come. Perched on the banks of the lake, they'll gaze south to the high, barren summit of Sawtooth Mountain and imagine climbing it someday.

Why not now? If you're up to it, follow a new trail from the lake's north shore up a steep 1.5 miles to a ridgetop junction with the Windy Pass Trail. Turn right and proceed another mile to the trail's high point. Look right for a side trail that leads about one-half mile straight up to the 7,300-foot summit, where the views are truly exceptional everywhere you look—especially down, into the deep blue waters of Indigo and Timpanogas Lakes, and perhaps at the rainfly of your tent. Continue west down the Sawtooth Trail about two miles to a trail junction. Turn right on the Sawtooth Trail, climb the very steep ridge and walk another two miles back to Lake Timpanogas. The loop, excluding the mile loop around Indigo Lake, is about nine miles. Carry plenty of film.

Location: South of Summit Lake and west of Cowhorn Mountain in the Oregon Cascades National Recreation Area; see The Southern Cascades Map 3, grid f8.

User Groups: Hikers, horses, dogs, and mountain bikes. No wheelchair facilities.

Permits: A federal Northwest Forest Pass, $5 per day or $30 annually, is required to park at the trailhead. Passes are available from ranger stations and many private vendors, online at website: www.wta.org, or by calling 800/270-7504.

Maps: For a map of Deschutes National Forest and Oregon Cascades National Recreation Area, contact the Nature of the Northwest Information Center, 800 Northeast Oregon Street, Suite 177, Portland, OR 97232; 503/872-2750. Ask the USGS for a topographic map of the Cowhorn Mountain area.

Directions: From Willamette Pass Highway/Highway 58 at Oakridge, drive 1.25 miles east to Kitson Springs Road/Forest Service Road 23. Turn right (south) and follow the signs to Hills Creek Reservoir. At one-half mile go right on Forest Service Road 21 and

proceed 32 miles to Forest Service Road 2154. Turn left and follow signs to Timpanogas Campground; the trailhead is in the day-use parking area.

Contact: Willamette National Forest, Middle Fork Ranger District, 49098 Salmon Creek Road, P.O. Box 1410, Oakridge, OR 97464; 541/782-2283.

46 Muir Creek
7.8 mi/3.9 hrs

Tracing the high west bank of Muir Creek, this trail offers fantastic views of the scenic river while cutting through majestic stands of old-growth Douglas fir, Pacific silver fir, white pine, western hemlock, and a few sugar pines. The multispecies forest attracts an equally diverse array of wildlife species, so as you hike this gentle, flat trail, look for deer, elk, bobcats, cougars, black bears, foxes, coyotes, porcupines, badgers, grouse, owls, hawks, eagles, and countless other birds and animals. If you don't see animals, you still enjoy the colorful display of wildflowers, including orange tiger lilies, scarlet gilia, columbine, and Indian paintbrush.

Location: North of Prospect in Rogue River National Forest; see The Southern Cascades Map 3, grid h6.

User Groups: Hikers, dogs, and horses. No mountain bikes. No wheelchair facilities.

Permits: A federal Northwest Forest Pass, $5 per day or $30 annually, is required to park at the trailhead. Passes are available from ranger stations and many private vendors, online at website: www.wta.org, or by calling 800/270-7504.

Maps: For a trail information report, contact the Prospect Ranger District at 541/560-3400. For a map of Rogue River National Forest, contact Nature of the Northwest Information Center, 800 Northeast Oregon Street, Suite 177, Portland, OR 97232; 503/872-2750. Ask the USGS for a topographic map of the Hamaker Butte area.

Directions: From Prospect drive about 12 miles north on Highway 62 to the junction with Highway 230. Stay left and continue 10.4 miles north on Highway 230. Turn left into the parking area, just before crossing the Muir Creek Bridge.

Contact: Rogue River National Forest, Prospect Ranger District, 47201 Highway 62, Prospect, OR 97536; 541/560-3400.

47 Minnehaha
6.2 mi/3.2 hrs

When this trail was built during the 1860s, prospectors, ranchers, and settlers used it to travel between the Rogue River Valley and the goldfields of the John Day Plateau. The modern route begins on an old two-track road and then gradually narrows to a path that weaves through the Minnehaha Basin. Spectacular views of pumice bluffs, picturesque waterfalls, and sprawling wildflower meadows emerge between the stands of Douglas fir, white pine, lodgepole pine, and old-growth hemlock forest. In autumn the forests blaze with color, as the leaves of the abundant vine maple and Oregon grape turn crimson and gold.

Location: North of Prospect in Rogue River National Forest; see The Southern Cascades Map 3, grid h6.

User Groups: Hikers, dogs, horses, and mountain bikes. No wheelchair facilities.

Permits: A federal Northwest Forest Pass, $5 per day or $30 annually, is required to park at the trailhead. Passes are available from ranger stations and many private vendors, online at website: www.wta.org, or by calling 800/270-7504.

Maps: For a trail information report, contact the Prospect Ranger District at 541/560-3400. For a map of Rogue River National Forest,

contact Nature of the Northwest Information Center, 800 Northeast Oregon Street, Suite 177, Portland, OR 97232; 503/872-2750. Ask the USGS for a topographic map of the Hamaker Butte area.

Directions: From Prospect drive about 12 miles north on Highway 62 to the junction with Highway 230. Stay left and continue 12 miles north on Highway 230. Turn right onto Forest Service Road 6530 and then continue one mile to Forest Service Road 6530-800. Turn right and go one-quarter mile to the trailhead.

Contact: Rogue River National Forest, Prospect Ranger District, 47201 Highway 62, Prospect, OR 97536; 541/560-3400.

48 Mirror Lake
7.0 mi/3.5 hrs

This is a very popular, easy day hike from the Cascade Lakes Loop to a pretty alpine lake, with further hiking options to Wickiup Plain and Le Conte Crater, as well as many interior Three Sisters Wilderness destinations beyond. Just before the lake, the trail merges with the Pacific Crest Trail. Turn left for your destination, a lake in a beautiful heather meadow with a view of the South Sister's top. No camping is allowed near the lake, but plenty of excellent off-trail campsites near small lakes and ponds can be found. Mirror Lake, 5,950 feet, also can be reached by hiking east from the Devil's Lake Trailhead (see directions in South Sister Summit/Moraine Lake hike). For a more solitary experience, turn off the PCT just short of Mirror Lake and hike four miles west to Nash Lake, a peaceful, relatively deserted destination. The elevation gain to Mirror Lake is 600 feet.

Location: West of Mount Bachelor in the Three Sisters Wilderness; see The Southern Cascades Map 4, grid a3.

User Groups: Hikers, dogs, and horses. No mountain bikes are allowed. No wheelchair facilities.

Permits: A federal Northwest Forest Pass, $5 per day or $30 annually, is required to park at the trailhead. Passes are available from ranger stations and many private vendors, online at website: www.wta.org, or by calling 800/270-7504.

Maps: For a map of the Three Sisters Wilderness, contact the Nature of the Northwest Information Center, 800 Northeast Oregon Street, Suite 177, Portland, OR 97232; 503/872-2750. Ask the USGS for topographic maps of the Elk Lake and South Sister areas.

Directions: From U.S. 97 in Bend, follow signs 27 miles west to Mount Bachelor Ski Area. Continue south on Cascade Lakes Highway/Highway 46 beyond Mount Bachelor to the Sisters Mirror trailhead on the right (west) side of the road, several miles past Devils Lake Campground.

Contact: Deschutes National Forest, Bend/Fort Rock Ranger District, 1230 Northeast Third Street, Suite A-262, Bend, OR 97701; 541/383-4000.

49 Deschutes River to Benham Falls

8.5 mi one way/4.5 hrs

This trail is becoming mountain bike central in Bend, one of the most mountain bike-crazed towns in the United States. But it's just as nice for hikers who enjoy walking through dry pine forest on the banks of the Deschutes River, which holds a special place in the nightly dreams of many rafters, anglers, and other nature lovers.

From the Meadow day-use area at the lower end of the trail, follow the path over an up-and-down grade all the way to Benham Falls. On the way, you pass several campgrounds, Lava Island Falls, Big Eddy Rapids, Dillon

Falls, and other natural sites. Notice how the lava flow across the river has pushed the water toward you, creating a swifter channel, and how collapsed lava domes contribute to some of the river's waterfalls. Taking note of all that, it's easy to be led astray by one of the myriad side trails, horse paths, and access routes to Forest Service Road 41, which parallels the river. But the river itself is a constant landmark: head upstream, and sooner or later the trail makes its way back to you.

The path is snow-free much of the year and is an especially good summer-heat retreat. We recommend riding or walking the route one way by leaving a shuttle car at one trailhead. To reach the northern trailhead at Benham Falls, drive south from Bend on U.S. 97. Turn right (west) at the Lava Butte exit, and then right into Lava Lands Visitor Center and follow Forest Service Road 9702 to Benham Falls.

Location: Southwest of Bend on the banks of the Deschutes River; see The Southern Cascades Map 4, grid a6.

User Groups: Mountain bikes, hikers, horses, and dogs. No wheelchair facilities.

Permits: A federal Northwest Forest Pass, $5 per day or $30 annually, is required to park at the trailhead. Passes are available from ranger stations and many private vendors, online at website: www.wta.org, or by calling 800/270-7504.

Maps: For a map of Deschutes National Forest, contact the Nature of the Northwest Information Center, 800 Northeast Oregon Street, Suite 177, Portland, OR 97232; 503/872-2750. Ask the USGS for a topographic map of the Benham Falls area.

Directions: From Bend follow signs west toward the Mount Bachelor Ski Area. About six miles from town, turn left before the golf course on a road signed Meadow Picnic Area. (If you arrive at the Inn of the Seventh

Mountain, you've gone too far.) The trailhead is along the river at the road's end.

Contact: Deschutes National Forest, Bend/Fort Rock Ranger District, 1230 Northeast Third Street, Suite A-262, Bend, OR 97701; 541/383-4000.

50 Horse Lake
8.0 mi/4.0 hrs

Let's put it this way: if you hoof it to Horse Lake in July or August, you're likely to be disappointed. Hordes of hikers are outnumbered only by mosquitoes then, and plenty of better day-hiking destinations await not far from this trailhead. But the Horse Lake Trail can be a pleasant walk off-season, or even in the dead of summer by combining it with other local trails, such as the Pacific Crest Trail, to form a longer loop hike. At the lake take the side trail around the north side for a view of Mount Bachelor. Return the way you came or add a little variety by walking a short distance down the Dumbell Lake Trail and then turning east on the Sunset Lake Trail, which skirts Colt and Sunset Lakes before connecting with the PCT and taking you back to the trailhead for an 8.8-mile loop. Long-distance shuttle hikers can continue west across the wilderness area from Horse Lake to Olallie Meadows (see hike in this chapter) and an exit near Cougar Reservoir. The elevation gain to Horse Lake is 650 feet. The route is usually accessible June through October.

Location: West of Cascade Lakes Highway and Elk Lake in the Three Sisters Wilderness; see The Southern Cascades Map 4, grid a3.

User Groups: Hikers, dogs, and horses. No mountain bikes are allowed. No wheelchair facilities.

Permits: A federal Northwest Forest Pass, $5 per day or $30 annually, is required to park at the trailhead. Passes are available from ranger stations and many private vendors,

online at website: www.wta.org, or by calling 800/270-7504.

Maps: For a map of the Three Sisters Wilderness, contact the Nature of the Northwest Information Center, 800 Northeast Oregon Street, Suite 177, Portland, OR 97232; 503/872-2750. Ask the USGS for a topographic map of the Elk Lake area.

Directions: From U.S. 97 in Bend, follow signs 27 miles west to Mount Bachelor Ski Area. Continue south on Cascade Lakes Highway/Highway 46 to the Elk Lake Trailhead on the left (west) side of the road, across from Elk Lake Resort.

Contact: Deschutes National Forest, Bend/Fort Rock Ranger District, 1230 Northeast Third Street, Suite A-262, Bend, OR 97701; 541/383-4000.

51 Six Lakes
5.0 mi/3.0 hrs

No matter how many people flock here, there's a lake for everybody. The wilderness area west of the Six Lakes Trailhead is dotted with literally hundreds of them, each awaiting discovery, and each working as a seasonal mosquito hatchery. Most people who walk this very heavily used trail wind up at one or both of the first two lakes, Blow or Doris. If you visit when the bugs aren't at full strength (definitely not July), the five-mile round-trip hikes to Blow Lake (one mile) and Doris Lake (2.5 miles) make nice half-day walks in the midst of a pleasant loop drive on the Cascade Lakes Highway. The forest is dry pine, and the grade even and mostly flat. Both lakes offer fine picnic spots. This is an exceptional area to hike on crisp, clear days in the fall. For longer hikes walk a total of six miles on the Six Lakes Trail to the Pacific Crest Trail and beyond to Cliff, Mink, Porky, or any of about a dozen small, scenic lakes in this region. Or continue west all the way across the Three Sisters Wilderness to the Roaring River/South Fork McKenzie River drainage and an exit to Blue River on McKenzie Highway.

Location: West of Cascade Lakes Highway in the Three Sisters Wilderness; see The Southern Cascades Map 4, grid b2.

User Groups: Hikers, dogs, and horses. No mountain bikes are allowed. No wheelchair facilities.

Permits: A federal Northwest Forest Pass, $5 per day or $30 annually, is required to park at the trailhead. Passes are available from ranger stations and many private vendors, online at website: www.wta.org, or by calling 800/270-7504.

Maps: For a map of the Three Sisters Wilderness, contact the Nature of the Northwest Information Center, 800 Northeast Oregon Street, Suite 177, Portland, OR 97232; 503/872-2750. Ask the USGS for a topographic map of the Elk Lake area.

Directions: From U.S. 97 in Bend, follow signs 27 miles west to Mount Bachelor Ski Area. Continue south on Cascade Lakes Highway/Highway 46 to the Six Lakes Trailhead, 2.5 miles south of Elk Lake Resort on the right (west) side of the highway.

Contact: Deschutes National Forest, Bend/Fort Rock Ranger District, 1230 Northeast Third Street, Suite A-262, Bend, OR 97701; 541/383-4000.

52 Cultus Lake
10.0 mi/6.0 hrs

If you're looking for a remote alpine-lake experience without a lot of visible distractions, go elsewhere. Cultus Lake has a resort on one side and plenty of motorboat traffic on its surface. But a trail around the lake's north shore leads through pine forest to quieter climes, whether you follow the trail's exten-

sion west of Little Cultus Lake or head uphill and north to the quaint Muskrat Shelter or Winopee Lake. To reach the former, turn left on the Cultus Lake Trail at the trail fork at 2.8 miles. To reach the latter, with an old trapper's cabin (a bare-bones structure that can still be used by visiting hikers) in a quiet meadow, veer right at the junction and walk 1.4 miles northwest on the continuation of the Winopee Lake Trail. The hike to Little Cultus is flat and makes a one-way shuttle hike of about 10 miles, running past West Cultus Lake Campground (boat and walk-in) and Deer Lake. The Muskrat Shelter hike is a round-trip of about 10 miles. Both trails are very buggy in the summer but make nice walks on clear late spring or autumn days. Another option is to hike the Winopee Trail to a side trail leading to the two Teddy Lakes.

Location: On the shore of Cultus Lake in the Three Sisters Wilderness; see The Southern Cascades Map 4, grid b2.

User Groups: Hikers, dogs, and horses. No mountain bikes are allowed. No wheelchair facilities.

Permits: A federal Northwest Forest Pass, $5 per day or $30 annually, is required to park at the trailhead. Passes are available from ranger stations and many private vendors, online at website: www.wta.org, or by calling 800/270-7504.

Maps: For a map of the Three Sisters Wilderness, contact the Nature of the Northwest Information Center, 800 Northeast Oregon Street, Suite 177, Portland, OR 97232; 503/872-2750. Ask the USGS for topographic maps of the Irish Mountain, Packsaddle Mountain, and Crane Prairie Reservoir areas.

Directions: From U.S. 97 in Bend, follow signs 27 miles west to Mount Bachelor Ski Area. Continue south on Cascade Lakes Highway/Highway 46, following signs to Cultus Lake Resort. Turn west on Forest Service Road 4630, right on Forest Service Road 4635, and go past the turnoff to Cultus Lake Campground to the trailhead on the left at a dead end.

Contact: Deschutes National Forest, Bend/Fort Rock Ranger District, 1230 Northeast Third Street, Suite A-262, Bend, OR 97701; 541/383-4000.

53 Waldo Lake Loop
22.0 mi/1.0–2.0 days

Waldo Lake is among the largest bodies of water in Oregon, and you can walk all the way around it in one day. We're not sure if that says more about the puniness of Oregon lakes or the buffed state of your legs. But it is possible, and more enjoyable than you might imagine for such a long haul. What makes it worth the work? The lake. It's probably more spectacular than any you've ever seen. The water redefines crystal clear, with absolutely no plant growth. Waldo Lake has been rated among the clearest in the entire world. Much of this route traverses lowland forest, with the lake always close at hand, but usually not within reach. Occasional side trails (closed to mountain bikes) take you to the lake's magnificent peninsulas, where you can watch for ospreys and other wildlife. Good campsites are in supply all the way around the lake.

The route, save for a couple steep pitches across rockslides and other obstacles, is gently rolling, with a total elevation gain of about 300 feet. Bring lots of moleskin and try it in one day, or consult a map and take one of the many shorter day hikes utilizing a portion of this trail. Backpackers also might consider using Waldo Lake's excellent campsites as stopovers in larger loop trips exploring the middle regions of the wilderness area. Side trails lead from the lake to Rigdon Lakes, the fish-rich Eddeeleo Lakes, Lake Chetlo and Waldo Meadows, Lithan Falls on Black Creek, Black Meadows on Fuji Mountain, and a half dozen other desirable destinations.

Like many trails in the greater Many Lakes region, mosquitoes are the lords of this realm in July and early August. Bug juice is the 11th essential here.

Location: All the way around Waldo Lake in the Waldo Lake Wilderness; see The Southern Cascades Map 4, grid c1.

User Groups: Hikers, dogs, horses, and mountain bikes. No wheelchair facilities.

Permits: A federal Northwest Forest Pass, $5 per day or $30 annually, is required to park at the trailhead. Passes are available from ranger stations and many private vendors, online at website: www.wta.org, or by calling 800/270-7504.

Maps: For a map of the Waldo Lake Wilderness and Recreation Area, contact the Nature of the Northwest Information Center, 800 Northeast Oregon Street, Suite 177, Portland, OR 97232; 503/872-2750. Ask the USGS for topographic maps of the Waldo Mountain and Waldo Lake areas.

Directions: From Highway 58 three miles west of Willamette Pass, turn north on Waldo Lake Road/Forest Service Road 5897. Following signs to North Waldo Campground, proceed about 12.5 miles on Forest Service Roads 5897 and 5898 to the trailhead near the campground's boat launch parking area.

Contact: Willamette National Forest, Middle Fork Ranger District, 49098 Salmon Creek Road, P.O. Box 1410, Oakridge, OR 97464; 541/782-2283.

54 Maiden Peak
11.5 mi/7.5 hrs

It's steep, it's crowded, it's dry. But year after year, the Maiden Peak Trail remains one of the most popular viewpoints in the Waldo Lake Wilderness. While similar views are available from other, less-crowded wilderness trails, this one is likely to remain a people-magnet thanks largely to its easy access just off Willamette Pass Highway. Most of the route is in forest, with the upper (steep) stretches exposed to the sun. The first views don't come until about five miles up the trail on this 3,000-foot ascent. Views at the summit, however, are superb. From the 7,818-foot former lookout site, gaze at Diamond Peak and literally every major local peak, as well as the Three Sisters and most of the Oregon Cascade volcano chain. Carry plenty of water.

Location: Southeast of Waldo Lake in the Waldo Lake Wilderness; see The Southern Cascades Map 4, grid c1.

User Groups: Hikers, dogs, mountain bikes, and horses. No wheelchair facilities.

Permits: A federal Northwest Forest Pass, $5 per day or $30 annually, is required to park at the trailhead. Passes are available from ranger stations and many private vendors, online at website: www.wta.org, or by calling 800/270-7504.

Maps: For a map of the Waldo Lake Wilderness, contact the Nature of the Northwest Information Center, 800 Northeast Oregon Street, Suite 177, Portland, OR 97232; 503/872-2750. Ask the USGS for topographic maps of the Odell Lake and the Twins areas.

Directions: From Highway 58 about a mile west of Willamette Pass, turn north on Forest Service Road 500, heading toward Gold Lake. Drive 1.5 miles to the parking area on the left side of the road. The trailhead is on the right.

Contact: Willamette National Forest, Middle Fork Ranger District, 49098 Salmon Creek Road, P.O. Box 1410, Oakridge, OR 97464; 541/782-2283.

55 Rosary Lakes
7.0 mi/3.5 hrs

These heavily visited Willamette Pass–area lakes are a popular overnight stop for through hikers on the Pacific Crest Trail, but they make a grand day hike from Willamette Pass as well. From the PCT Trailhead, elevation 5,100 feet, the trail makes a long traverse east through the dry forest before turning sharply uphill and north at just under two miles. Follow the west side of the Rosary Creek drainage upward to Lower Rosary, by far the largest of the three lakes.

Good lunch spots abound near the main trail and off a side trail that runs around the lake. Continuing on, walk past tall, columnar Pulpit Rock to the middle and upper lakes, which are relatively small lakes near the head of the valley, at about 6,400 feet. The Pacific Crest Trail continues north to Maiden Peak Saddle and, of course, far, far beyond.

Location: Northeast of Willamette Pass below Maiden Peak in the Waldo Lake Wilderness; see The Southern Cascades Map 4, grid d1.

User Groups: Hikers, dogs, and horses. No mountain bikes are allowed. No wheelchair facilities.

Permits: A federal Northwest Forest Pass, $5 per day or $30 annually, is required to park at the trailhead. Passes are available from ranger stations and many private vendors, online at website: www.wta.org, or by calling 800/270-7504.

Maps: For a map of the Waldo Lake Wilderness, contact the Nature of the Northwest Information Center, 800 Northeast Oregon Street, Suite 177, Portland, OR 97232; 503/872-2750. Ask the USGS for a topographic map of the Twins area.

Directions: From the town of Oakridge, drive southeast on Willamette Pass Highway/Highway 58 to Willamette Pass. Just beyond the Willamette Pass Ski Area, park in the Pacific Crest Trail parking lot, which is located on the north side of the road.

Contact: Deschutes National Forest, Crescent Ranger District, P.O. Box 208, Crescent, OR 97733; 541/433-3200.

56 No Name
1.1 mi/0.7 hr

Though short, this trail is long on scenery. It winds through a pretty forest of conifers and hardwoods, under moss- and lichen-covered cliffs, and along cold, rushing creeks. A large herd of black-tailed deer lives in these woods, and the gentle creatures typically don't mind being watched by respectful hikers. The black-tails are cousins of the mule deer, but they live in old-growth forests and are much smaller than the burly muleys, which thrive in the open country east of the Cascades. The trail loops through the deer's forest habitat before returning to the trailhead.

Location: East of Cave Junction in Siskiyou National Forest within Oregon Caves National Monument; see The Southern Cascades Map 5, grid h5.

User Groups: Hikers and dogs. No horses or mountain bikes are allowed. No wheelchair facilities.

Permits: A federal Northwest Forest Pass, $5 per day or $30 annually, is required to park at the trailhead. Passes are available from ranger stations and many private vendors, online at website: www.wta.org, or by calling 800/270-7504.

Maps: For a trail information report, contact Oregon Caves National Monument at 541/592-2100. For a map of Siskiyou National Forest, contact Nature of the Northwest Information Center, 800 Northeast Oregon Street, Suite 177, Portland, OR 97232; 503/872-2750. Ask the USGS for a topographic map of the Oregon Caves area.

Directions: From Cave Junction drive about 18 miles east on Highway 46 to the Oregon Caves National Monument Visitor Center. The trailhead is near the west end of the parking lot.

Contact: Siskiyou National Forest, Oregon Caves National Monument, 19000 Caves Highway, Cave Junction, OR 97523; 541/592-2100.

57 Cliff Nature Interpretive Trail
1.0 mi/0.5 hr

Interpretive signs describe the lush vegetation that carpets the floor of this old-growth forest and explain how the beautiful caves here were formed. The majestic mountains you see were once a seabed that was pushed skyward by the dynamics of plate tectonics, that is, when the continental plate collided with the Pacific plate. That collision forced the Siskiyous, including the local Red Buttes, upward. The limestone that had accumulated on the bottom of the sea was compressed into white marble; at the same time, water leached through the layers of limestone and marble, etching out the shiny white caves.

Today, water still drips from the roof, creating long, pointy stalactites and stalagmites. If you burn out on lessons in geology and biology, skip the signs and concentrate on the scenery. You won't be disappointed. In addition to the rich flora and fauna that thrive under the forest canopy, you find huge old Douglas firs that reach some 200 feet toward the sky, as well as panoramic views over the southern Siskiyous.

Location: East of Cave Junction in Siskiyou National Forest within Oregon Caves National Monument; see The Southern Cascades Map 5, grid h5.

User Groups: Hikers and dogs. No horses or mountain bikes are allowed. No wheelchair facilities.

Permits: A federal Northwest Forest Pass, $5 per day or $30 annually, is required to park at the trailhead. Passes are available from ranger stations and many private

vendors, online at website: www.wta.org, or by calling 800/270-7504.

Maps: For a trail information report, contact Oregon Caves National Monument at 541/592-2100. For a map of Siskiyou National Forest, contact Nature of the Northwest Information Center, 800 Northeast Oregon Street, Suite 177, Portland, OR 97232; 503/872-2750. Ask the USGS for a topographic map of the Oregon Caves area.

Directions: From Cave Junction drive about 18 miles east on Highway 46 to the Oregon Caves National Monument Visitor Center. The trailhead is near the visitor center and chalet.

Contact: Siskiyou National Forest, Oregon Caves National Monument, 19000 Caves Highway, Cave Junction, OR 97523; 541/592-2100.

58 Big Tree Loop
3.2 mi/2.0 hrs

The first half of this loop trail entails a long, steep climb, which means you face a long, steep descent over the second half. At just about the halfway point, you encounter the trail's namesake: the Big Tree. This Douglas fir has existed for at least one and a half millennia, or some 1,500 years. In other words, it was ancient when the Pilgrims established the first New World colonies, old when the Magna Carta was signed (1215), and a mere seedling when the Roman Empire fell (the last emperor was deposed in 476). Today, the tree is more than 12 feet in diameter (nearly 40 feet around) and hundreds of feet tall. The entire length of the trail loops through a beautiful old-growth forest; if you remember not to compare the rest of the forest to the magnificent Big Tree, you are awed by the number of truly big, old trees in the virgin landscape.

Location: East of Cave Junction in Siskiyou National Forest within Oregon Caves National Monument; see The Southern Cascades Map 5, grid h5.

User Groups: Hikers and dogs. No horses or mountain bikes are allowed. No wheelchair facilities.

Permits: A federal Northwest Forest Pass, $5 per day or $30 annually, is required to park at the trailhead. Passes are available from ranger stations and many private vendors, online at website: www.wta.org, or by calling 800/270-7504.

Maps: For a trail information report, contact Oregon Caves National Monument at 541/592-2100. For a map of Siskiyou National Forest, contact Nature of the Northwest Information Center, 800 Northeast Oregon Street, Suite 177, Portland, OR 97232; 503/872-2750. Ask the USGS for a topographic map of the Oregon Caves area.

Directions: From Cave Junction drive approximately 18 miles east on Highway 46 until you reach the Oregon Caves National Monument Visitor Center. The trailhead is located near the east side of the parking lot.

Contact: Siskiyou National Forest, Oregon Caves National Monument, 19000 Caves Highway, Cave Junction, OR 97523; 541/592-2100.

59 Lake Mountain (Meadow Mountain)
2.2 mi/1.1 hrs

Now follow closely. This trail passes a little alpine lake named Lake Mountain and ends on the flank of a peak. That peak, also called Lake Mountain, overlooks the lake. In other words this is a pretty, wetland hike to Lake Mountain where you can look up and see the summit of Lake Mountain. If that's all too cute and/or confusing for you, ignore the names and just enjoy drinking in the sights. The trail is pretty, and the abundance of water means there is an abundance of wildflowers (and, alas, mosquitoes). Early spring brings out the bright-yellow skunk cabbage blooms, early summer is brightened by trilliums, and midsummer boasts tiger lilies.

Location: East of Cave Junction in Siskiyou National Forest; see The Southern Cascades Map 5, grid h5.

User Groups: Hikers, dogs, and horses. No mountain bikes are allowed. No wheelchair facilities.

Permits: A federal Northwest Forest Pass, $5 per day or $30 annually, is required to park at the trailhead. Passes are available from ranger stations and many private vendors, online at website: www.wta.org, or by calling 800/270-7504.

Maps: For a trail information report, contact the Illinois Valley Ranger District at 541/433-4077. For a map of Siskiyou National Forest, contact Nature of the Northwest Information Center, 800 Northeast Oregon Street, Suite 177, Portland, OR 97232; 503/872-2750. Ask the USGS for a topographic map of the Grayback Mountain area.

Directions: From Cave Junction drive about 12 miles east on Highway 46 to Forest Service Road 4613. Turn right (south) and continue about five miles to the junction with Forest Service Road 070. Turn right and drive two miles to the trailhead on the left.

Contact: Siskiyou National Forest, Illinois Valley Ranger District, 26568 Redwood Highway 199, Cave Junction, OR 97523; 541/433-4077.

60 Elk Creek
4.0 mi/2.0 hrs

After threading through a valley, this pleasant hike takes you high on a ridge where you can survey the terrain you just covered. The creek basin is lined with a pretty stand of old second-growth forest. Deer and elk thrive in the forest environment, so you may be fortunate enough to see these gentle

creatures. The trail ends on a saddle near Grayback Mountain.

Location: East of Cave Junction in Siskiyou National Forest; see The Southern Cascades Map 5, grid h5.

User Groups: Hikers, dogs, and horses. No mountain bikes are allowed. No wheelchair facilities.

Permits: A federal Northwest Forest Pass, $5 per day or $30 annually, is required to park at the trailhead. Passes are available from ranger stations and many private vendors, online at website: www.wta.org, or by calling 800/270-7504.

Maps: For a trail information report, contact the Illinois Valley Ranger District at 541/433-4077. For a map of Siskiyou National Forest, contact Nature of the Northwest Information Center, 800 Northeast Oregon Street, Suite 177, Portland, OR 97232; 503/872-2750. Ask the USGS for a topographic map of the Grayback Mountain area.

Directions: From Cave Junction drive about 12 miles east on Highway 46 to Forest Service Road 4613. Turn right (south) and continue to the junction with Forest Service Road 070. Turn right, drive about one mile to Forest Service Road 079, and turn left. Follow this road to the trailhead on the right.

Contact: Siskiyou National Forest, Illinois Valley Ranger District, 26568 Redwood Highway 199, Cave Junction, OR 97523; 541/433-4077.

61 Collings Mountain
14.0 mi/1.0-2.0 days

Like Stein Butte, this area was named for an 1850s prospector—or rather, a pair of them—the Collings brothers, who established a number of placer mines in addition to dabbling in hard-rock mining.

The area is also known for other reasons: during the

1960s and 1970s, there was a concerted effort to find the elusive mythological beast of Pacific Northwest forests—Sasquatch (a.k.a. Bigfoot). Just under a mile into this hike, the trail loops past an old miner's cabin and a deactivated Bigfoot trap. Farther along, hikers will find a series of mineshaft openings; whether it is posted or not, it is extremely dangerous to enter these old holes, so shine a flashlight in, but stay out.

After the initial long, gradual climb along Grouse Creek Valley, the trail turns and climbs steeply to the long ridge crest that rolls south under the flank of Collings Mountain. You can scramble to the summit, but that really isn't necessary. From several points along the trail you enjoy views equal or superior to those afforded by the peak. As the trail moves south away from Collings Mountain, it drops gradually over the last three miles before ending at the Watkin Campground. Turn and retrace your steps, unless you have arranged for a shuttle vehicle to be left at this point.

Location: South of Applegate in Rogue River National Forest; see The Southern Cascades Map 5, grid h7.

User Groups: Hikers and dogs. No horses or mountain bikes are allowed. No wheelchair facilities.

Permits: A federal Northwest Forest Pass, $5 per day or $30 annually, is required to park at the trailhead. Passes are available from ranger stations and many private vendors, online at website: www.wta.org, or by calling 800/270-7504.

Maps: For a trail information report, contact the Applegate Ranger District at 541/899-1812. For a map of Rogue River National Forest, contact Nature of the Northwest Information Center, 800 Northeast Oregon Street, Suite 177, Portland, OR 97232; 503/872-2750. Ask the USGS for topographic maps of the Carberry Creek and Squaw Lakes areas.

Directions: From Applegate drive about seven miles east on Highway 238 to Applegate River Road/Forest Service Road 10. Turn right (south) and continue about six miles to the forest boundary and the Star Guard Station. Continue south another nine miles to Hart-Tish Park. The trailhead is in the upper end of the picnic area parking lot.

Contact: Rogue River National Forest, Applegate Ranger District/Star Ranger Station, 6941 Upper Applegate Road, Jacksonville, OR 97530; 541/899-1812.

62 Grouse Loop
2.8 mi/1.4 hrs

The best direction to hike this loop is clockwise. After crossing Forest Service Road 10, the trail climbs slightly as it parallels Grouse Creek for about one mile before turning north. During this ascent you trek through a timeless old stand of Douglas fir and sugar pine. The huge, old ponderosa pines that shoulder in alongside the other big trees add splashes of color and life to the dark forest. The gnarled orange and brown bark of these fragrant trees stands in welcome contrast to their brownish-gray brothers.

As the trail angles north, it tops out on a low ridge with views of Elliot Creek and Elliot Ridge, the peaks of the Red Butte Wilderness, and Applegate Lake. After a short traverse along the ridge, the trail drops gently through the forest in a long, looping route that ends back at Grouse Creek Valley, just across the road from the trailhead.

Location: South of Applegate in Rogue River National Forest; see The Southern Cascades Map 5, grid h7.

User Groups: Hikers, dogs, and mountain bikes. No horses are allowed. No wheelchair facilities.

Permits: A federal Northwest Forest Pass, $5 per day or $30 annually, is required to park

at the trailhead. Passes are available from ranger stations and many private vendors, online at website: www.wta.org, or by calling 800/270-7504.

Maps: For a trail information report, contact the Applegate Ranger District at 541/899-1812. For a map of Rogue River National Forest, contact Nature of the Northwest Information Center, 800 Northeast Oregon Street, Suite 177, Portland, OR 97232; 503/872-2750. Ask the USGS for topographic maps of the Carberry Creek and Squaw Lakes areas.

Directions: From Applegate drive about seven miles east on Highway 238 to Applegate River Road/Forest Service Road 10. Turn right (south) and continue about six miles to the forest boundary and the Star Guard Station. Continue south another nine miles to Hart-Tish Park. The trailhead is near the upper end of the picnic area parking lot.

Contact: Rogue River National Forest, Applegate Ranger District/Star Ranger Station, 6941 Upper Applegate Road, Jacksonville, OR 97530; 541/899-1812.

63 Da-Ku-Be-Te-De
9.6 mi/4.8 hrs

Named for a tiny tribe of Native Americans who called this area home for several centuries, this trail hugs the shore of the lake that was the center of their culture—also known as Applegate Lake. The trail is nestled between the shoreline and the road, so it lacks that true backcountry flavor. But it does provide great views of the lake and surrounding peaks, as well as access to some prime fishing spots. Rainbow and cutthroat trout swarm the lake's waters.

A good time to visit is autumn, when the crowds are gone and the atmosphere is more natural and serene. Then the autumnal colors

blazing in the surrounding forests reflect beautifully off the glassy lake surface. Hike to the trail's end and retrace your steps to your vehicle. To cut the distance in half by hiking just one way, you need to arrange a ride at the far end.

Location: South of Applegate in Rogue River National Forest; see The Southern Cascades Map 5, grid h7.

User Groups: Hikers and dogs. No horses or mountain bikes are allowed. No wheelchair facilities.

Permits: A federal Northwest Forest Pass, $5 per day or $30 annually, is required to park at the trailhead. Passes are available from ranger stations and many private vendors, online at website: www.wta.org, or by calling 800/270-7504.

Maps: For a trail information report, contact the Applegate Ranger District at 541/899-1812. For a map of Rogue River National Forest, contact Nature of the Northwest Information Center, 800 Northeast Oregon Street, Suite 177, Portland, OR 97232; 503/872-2750. Ask the USGS for topographic maps of the Carberry Creek and Squaw Lakes areas.

Directions: From Applegate drive about seven miles east on Highway 238 to Applegate River Road/Forest Service Road 10. Turn right (south) and continue about six miles to the forest boundary and the Star Guard Station. Continue another eight miles to the Swayne Viewpoint. The trailhead is at the south end of the parking area. To reach the southern trailhead, continue past Swayne Viewpoint to Watkin Campground.

Contact: Rogue River National Forest, Applegate Ranger District/Star Ranger Station, 6941 Upper Applegate Road, Jacksonville, OR 97530; 541/899-1812.

🗺64 Payette
18.4 mi/2.0 days

Hugging the shoreline of Applegate Lake, this scenic, flat trail loops around a broad, jutting headland, back around a narrow finger of water, and on down the shore of the picturesque lake, reaching nearly to the California border. The trail begins with a quick tour around French Arm before rolling west through thick maple, Douglas fir, alder, and pine forests on a mile-wide peninsula cutting into the big lake. Following the outer edge of the peninsula, the trail provides great fishing access, as well as stunning views across the blue water and beyond to Collings Mountain, Grouse Creek Basin, and several high ridges.

As the trail turns and moves back toward the mainland along the south side of the peninsula, it parallels a long, narrow finger of water that tapers up into Squaw Creek. The route crosses the creek at the end of the lake finger and continues rolling slowly south, sticking to the contours of the shoreline.

Location: South of Applegate in Rogue River National Forest; see The Southern Cascades Map 5, grid h8.

User Groups: Hikers, dogs, and mountain bikes. No horses are allowed. No wheelchair facilities.

Permits: A federal Northwest Forest Pass, $5 per day or $30 annually, is required to park at the trailhead. Passes are available from ranger stations and many private vendors, online at website: www.wta.org, or by calling 800/270-7504.

Maps: For a trail information report, contact the Applegate Ranger District at 541/899-1812. For a map of Rogue River National Forest, contact Nature of the Northwest Information Center, 800 Northeast Oregon Street, Suite 177, Portland, OR 97232; 503/872-2750. Ask the USGS for a topographic map of the Squaw Lakes area.

Directions: From Applegate drive about seven miles east on Highway 238 to Applegate River Road/Forest Service Road 10. Turn right (south) and continue about six miles to the forest boundary and the Star Guard Station. Continue another eight miles to the Applegate Dam. Turn left, crossing the dam, and drive one mile to French Gulch Campground.

Contact: Rogue River National Forest, Applegate Ranger District/Star Ranger Station, 6941 Upper Applegate Road, Jacksonville, OR 97530; 541/899-1812.

🗺65 Little Squaw Interpretive Trail
2.0 mi/1.0 hr

This short, gentle interpretive hike may seem too tame to offer a quality backcountry experience, but don't believe it. The flat trail loops around two large alpine lakes—both heavily visited by recreationists—and provides some top-notch fishing opportunities. Anglers can try for the large native rainbow and cutthroat trout that stalk the cold, clear waters. The trail begins by quickly crossing a narrow footbridge over the outlet of Little Squaw Lake and then works east along the shore of Big Squaw Lake. The route ends at Mulligan Bay on the big lake. Picnic areas are available at either end of the trail, as is potable water.

Location: South of Applegate in Rogue River National Forest; see The Southern Cascades Map 5, grid h8.

User Groups: Hikers and dogs. No horses or mountain bikes are allowed. No wheelchair facilities.

Permits: A federal Northwest Forest Pass, $5 per day or $30 annually, is required to park at the trailhead. Passes are available from ranger stations and many private vendors, online at website: www.wta.org, or by calling 800/270-7504.

Maps: For a trail information report, contact the Applegate Ranger District at 541/899-1812. For a map of Rogue River National Forest, contact Nature of the Northwest Information Center, 800 Northeast Oregon Street, Suite 177, Portland, OR 97232; 503/872-2750. Ask the USGS for a topographic map of the Squaw Lakes area.

Directions: From Applegate drive about seven miles east on Highway 238 to Applegate River Road/Forest Service Road 10. Turn right (south) and continue about 12 miles to the Applegate Dam. Turn left, cross the dam, and continue 8.5 miles east on Forest Service Road 1075 to the Squaw Lakes Trailhead on the left.

Contact: Rogue River National Forest, Applegate Ranger District/Star Ranger Station, 6941 Upper Applegate Road, Jacksonville, OR 97530; 541/899-1812.

66 Stein Butte
15.0 mi/1.0–2.0 days

The gold rush figures prominently in the history of this area. When the 49ers began to overrun the creeks around San Francisco, they pushed northward, and this land was hit hard in the 1850s and 1860s by gold-hungry prospectors. The Stein Butte Trail begins near the California border and after two miles dips briefly into that state before returning to Oregon. Over the next several miles, the route rides a high ridgeline parallel to the state line before topping out on Stein Butte; named for one of the original gold prospectors, this 4,400-foot-high peak offers stunning panoramic views of the Siskiyous, notably the peaks of the Red Butte Wilderness to the west. Just past Stein Butte, the trail turns sharply south and plunges down into California once again, ending at a junction with Forest Service Road 1050 at the Elliot Creek Trailhead.

You can hike this trail one way by arranging a shuttle car at the end. To reach the second trailhead, continue driving east on Carberry Creek Road/Forest Service Road 1040 to the junction with Forest Service Road 1050. Follow the road for three miles into California to the Elliot Creek Trailhead.

Location: South of Applegate in Rogue River National Forest; see The Southern Cascades Map 5, grid h8.

User Groups: Hikers and dogs. No horses or mountain bikes are allowed. No wheelchair facilities.

Permits: A federal Northwest Forest Pass, $5 per day or $30 annually, is required to park at the trailhead. Passes are available from ranger stations and many private vendors, online at website: www.wta.org, or by calling 800/270-7504.

Maps: For a trail information report, contact the Applegate Ranger District at 541/899-1812. For a map of Rogue River National Forest, contact Nature of the Northwest Information Center, 800 Northeast Oregon Street, Suite 177, Portland, OR 97232; 503/872-2750. Ask the USGS for topographic maps of the Carberry Creek and Squaw Lakes areas.

Directions: From Applegate drive about seven miles east on Highway 238 to Applegate River Road/Forest Service Road 10. Turn right (south) and continue about six miles to the forest boundary and the Star Guard Station. Continue another 13 miles to Carberry Creek Road/Forest Service Road 1040. Turn left (east) and drive one mile to the Seattle Bar Trailhead.

Contact: Rogue River National Forest, Applegate Ranger District/Star Ranger Station, 6941 Upper Applegate Road, Jacksonville, OR 97530; 541/899-1812.

67 Golden Stairs
8.6 mi/4.3 hrs

Following the eastern edge of the Abbott Creek Research Area, this trail leads, for the most part, through pristine, natural terrain. Humans made their primary impact a century ago, when the Abbott brothers prospected for and allegedly discovered gold here. The route is said to lead through the Abbott's strike, but forest has covered much of their work, and today the true value lies in the gold mine of natural treasures. Climbing through a thick old forest, the trail passes several distinct forest zones, beginning in a mixed conifer and hardwood stand and ending in a high alpine, true fir forest. The route also takes hikers through a number of small meadows and wetlands that attract herds of deer, elk, and mosquitoes. Be prepared with cameras and bug repellent.

Location: North of Prospect in Rogue River National Forest; see The Southern Cascades Map 6, grid a4.

User Groups: Hikers, dogs, and horses. No mountain bikes. No wheelchair facilities.

Permits: A federal Northwest Forest Pass, $5 per day or $30 annually, is required to park at the trailhead. Passes are available from ranger stations and many private vendors, online at website: www.wta.org, or by calling 800/270-7504.

Maps: For a trail information report, contact the Prospect Ranger District. For a map of Rogue River National Forest, contact Nature of the Northwest Information Center, 800 Northeast Oregon Street, Suite 177, Portland, OR 97232; 503/872-2750. Ask the USGS for a topographic map of the Abbott Butte area.

Directions: From Prospect drive six miles north on Highway 62 and turn left (west) onto Forest Service Road 68. Continue five miles west before turning right (north) onto Forest Service Road 6800-550. Follow the road for three miles to the trailhead on the left.

Contact: Rogue River National Forest, Prospect Ranger District, 47201 Highway 62, Prospect, OR 97536; 541/560-3400.

68 Anderson Camp
2.6 mi/1.3 hrs

Photographers dream of trails such as this, with its stunning views of the upper Rogue and Umpqua River Basins, as well as the jagged summits of Mount McLoughlin, Elephant Head, and the peaks around the Crater Lake rim. The route climbs steeply for nearly a mile, slicing through brilliantly colored wildflower meadows and thick old pine forests. Then it continues across a high divide and rolls west under the shadow of Anderson Mountain before ending at a junction with the Rogue-Umpqua Divide Trail. Anderson Camp is near the small pond just under the Anderson Mountain summit. Nineteenth-century shepherds drove their flocks through this area in search of the rich meadow grasses.

Location: North of Prospect in Rogue River National Forest; see The Southern Cascades Map 6, grid a5.

User Groups: Hikers, dogs, and horses. No mountain bikes are allowed. No wheelchair facilities.

Permits: A federal Northwest Forest Pass, $5 per day or $30 annually, is required to park at the trailhead. Passes are available from ranger stations and many private vendors, online at website: www.wta.org, or by calling 800/270-7504.

Maps: For a trail information report, contact the Prospect Ranger District at 541/560-3400. For a map of Rogue River National Forest, contact Nature of the Northwest Information Center, 800 Northeast Oregon Street, Suite 177, Portland, OR 97232; 503/872-2750. Ask the USGS for a topographic map of the Union Creek area.

Directions: From Prospect drive six miles north on Highway 62 and turn left (west) onto Forest Service Road 68. Continue three miles west before turning right (north) onto Forest Service Road 6510. Follow the road for 5.8 miles to Forest Service Road 6515. Turn right and drive 6.3 miles to the trailhead on the left.

Contact: Rogue River National Forest, Prospect Ranger District, 47201 Highway 62, Prospect, OR 97536; 541/560-3400.

69 Rogue Gorge
7.0 mi/3.5 hrs

Beginning from the viewing platform that overlooks the picturesque Natural Bridge, this level, gentle river trail is rich in views. The Rogue Gorge makes a particularly spectacular display of natural hydraulic power. The section of the river leading to the gorge is wonderful and scenic, rolling over boulders and through deep pools. Nearer to the gorge, the air reverberates with the thunderous roar of the churning, constricted water, as the river pounds through the narrow, constricting slot in the black basalt lava.

Location: North of Prospect in Rogue River National Forest; see The Southern Cascades Map 6, grid a5.

User Groups: Hikers and dogs. No horses or mountain bikes are allowed. No wheelchair facilities.

Permits: A federal Northwest Forest Pass, $5 per day or $30 annually, is required to park at the trailhead. Passes are available from ranger stations and many private vendors, online at website: www.wta.org, or by calling 800/270-7504.

Maps: For a trail information report, contact the Prospect Ranger District at 541/560-3400. For a map of Rogue River National Forest,

contact Nature of the Northwest Information Center, 800 Northeast Oregon Street, Suite 177, Portland, OR 97232; 503/872-2750. Ask the USGS for a topographic map of the Prospect North area.

Directions: From Prospect drive about eight miles north on Highway 62 to Natural Bridge Campground. Turn left onto the campground access road and continue west past the campground to the Natural Bridge Viewpoint at the end of the short road. The trailhead is on the north end of the viewpoint parking area.

Contact: Rogue River National Forest, Prospect Ranger District, 47201 Highway 62, Prospect, OR 97536; 541/560-3400.

70 Union Creek
8.8 mi/4.4 hrs

Union Creek is a multifaceted waterway, harboring old-growth forests of conifers as well as hardwood trees. It crashes through wild, white-water sections and babbles gently through gravel-lined pools. Beaver dams tame long sections of the creek, while kingfishers and herons hunt for trout in the wilder riffles. This trail parallels the creek upstream, sticking tightly to the north bank as it winds up the valley. The path is fairly level, with only a slight incline, and the tread is well maintained, making walking a simple pleasure.

Location: North of Prospect in Rogue River National Forest; see The Southern Cascades Map 6, grid a6.

User Groups: Hikers and dogs. No horses or mountain bikes are allowed. No wheelchair facilities.

Permits: A federal Northwest Forest Pass, $5 per day or $30 annually, is required to park at the trailhead. Passes are available from ranger stations and many private

vendors, online at website: www.wta.org, or by calling 800/270-7504.

Maps: For a trail information report, contact the Prospect Ranger District at 541/560-3400. For a map of Rogue River National Forest, contact Nature of the Northwest Information Center, 800 Northeast Oregon Street, Suite 177, Portland, OR 97232; 503/872-2750. Ask the USGS for a topographic map of the Union Creek area.

Directions: From Prospect drive about 10 miles north on Highway 62 to Union Creek Campground. Turn left into the campground. The trailhead is on the west side of the camping area.

Contact: Rogue River National Forest, Prospect Ranger District, 47201 Highway 62, Prospect, OR 97536; 541/560-3400.

71 Lightning Springs
8.0 mi/4.0 hrs

Dropping from the rim of the caldera west to the headwaters of Bybee Creek and down the creek valley, this steep trail slices through a thick forest of pine, spruce, and mountain hemlock. The creek is born out of the cold waters of Lightning Spring, which you pass in the first half mile. The route switchbacks down the widening valley, and the forest opens periodically onto broad wildflower meadows. Look for herds of deer and elk in these lush natural pastures. Also pause for a moment and scan the skies for hawks, eagles, or falcons that may be soaring overhead. The trail ends at a junction with the Pacific Crest Trail. Explore that route as much as you please before beginning the long, hard trek back up the trail.

Location: North of Fort Klamath in Crater Lake National Park; see The Southern Cascades Map 6, grid a7.

User Groups: Hikers only. No dogs, horses, or mountain bikes are allowed. No wheelchair facilities.

Permits: Permits are required for overnight stays and can be picked up at Crater Lake National Park.

Maps: For a trail information report, contact park headquarters at 541/594-2211. For a map of Crater Lake National Park, contact Nature of the Northwest Information Center, 800 Northeast Oregon Street, Suite 177, Portland, OR 97232; 503/872-2750. Ask the USGS for a topographic map of the Crater Lake West area.

Directions: From Fort Klamath drive about 16 miles north on Highway 62 to Mazama Village. Turn right (east) onto Munson Valley Road. Drive about six miles east to Rim Village. The trailhead is at the west end of the Rim Village parking lot.

Contact: Crater Lake National Park, P.O. Box 7, Crater Lake, OR 97604; 541/594-2211.

72 Discovery Point
2.6 mi/1.3 hrs

Climbing along the rim of the deep, water-filled caldera, this trail offers fantastic views of Crater Lake, Wizard Island, and the surrounding country. The route leads to a high overlook, from which explorer John Hillman first saw the glorious blue world of Crater Lake in 1853. The trail ends at Discovery Point. Enjoy the views from here and return the way you came.

Location: North of Fort Klamath in Crater Lake National Park; see The Southern Cascades Map 6, grid a7.

User Groups: Hikers only. No dogs, horses, or mountain bikes are allowed. No wheelchair facilities.

Permits: No permits are required.

Maps: To receive a trail information report, contact park headquarters at 541/594-2211.

For a map of Crater Lake National Park, contact Nature of the Northwest Information Center, 800 Northeast Oregon Street, Suite 177, Portland, OR 97232; 503/872-2750. Ask the USGS for a topographic map of the Crater Lake West area.

Directions: From Fort Klamath drive about 16 miles north on Highway 62 to Mazama Village. Turn right (east) onto Munson Valley Road. Drive about six miles east to Rim Village. The trailhead is at the west end of the Rim Village parking lot.

Contact: Crater Lake National Park, P.O. Box 7, Crater Lake, OR 97604; 541/594-2211.

73 Dutton Creek
4.8 mi/2.4 hrs

A steep, rocky climb straight down the Dutton Creek Valley offers hikers a good chance to explore a classic old-growth, high alpine forest of pine and hemlock trees. This thickly forested valley is narrow and steep, restricting views to the scenery close at hand. But you may still be fortunate enough to see deer, elk, grouse, foxes, porcupines, and other small birds and animals as you pass through. The trail ends at a junction with the Pacific Crest Trail, high above Castle Creek. Rest here before beginning the long, strenuous climb back up to the crater rim and the trailhead.

Location: North of Fort Klamath in Crater Lake National Park; see The Southern Cascades Map 6, grid a7.

User Groups: Hikers only. No dogs, horses, or mountain bikes are allowed. No wheelchair facilities.

Permits: Permits are required for overnight stays and can be picked up at Crater Lake National Park.

Maps: To receive a trail information report, contact park headquarters at 541/594-2211. For a map of Crater Lake National Park, con-

tact Nature of the Northwest Information Center, 800 Northeast Oregon Street, Suite 177, Portland, OR 97232; 503/872-2750. Ask the USGS for a topographic map of the Crater Lake West area.

Directions: From Fort Klamath drive about 16 miles north on Highway 62 to Mazama Village. Turn right (east) onto Munson Valley Road. Drive about six miles east to Rim Village. The trailhead is at the south end of Rim Village.

Contact: Crater Lake National Park, P.O. Box 7, Crater Lake, OR 97604; 541/594-2211.

74 Garfield Peak
3.4 mi/1.7 hrs

You won't find a better view of Crater Lake than the one offered here. The short trail climbs gradually up the west flank of Garfield Peak to the 8,054-foot summit. Situated on the very edge of the caldera, Garfield provides stunning views to the north, across the ink-blue waters of the lake and beyond to the jagged north rim. This high overlook also peers down on Phantom Ship, a rocky island on the south side of the lake, and Wizard Island, a relatively new cinder cone in this ancient volcano.

Location: North of Fort Klamath in Crater Lake National Park; see The Southern Cascades Map 6, grid a7.

User Groups: Hikers only. No dogs, horses, or mountain bikes are allowed. No wheelchair facilities.

Permits: No permits are required.

Maps: For a trail information report, contact park headquarters at 541/594-2211. For a map of Crater Lake National Park, contact Nature of the Northwest Information Center, 800 Northeast Oregon Street, Suite 177, Portland, OR 97232; 503/872-2750. Ask the USGS for topographic maps of the Crater Lake West and Crater Lake East areas.

Directions: From Fort Klamath drive about 16 miles north on Highway 62 to Mazama Village. Turn right (east) onto Munson Valley Road. Drive about six miles east to Rim Village. The trailhead is on the east side of Crater Lake Lodge.

Contact: Crater Lake National Park, P.O. Box 7, Crater Lake, OR 97604; 541/594-2211.

75 Bald Crater/ Boundary Springs
20.0 mi/2.0 days

The rough, gritty landscape bears testimony to this region's cataclysmic history. Volcanic activity created this land and has been reshaping it over the ensuing centuries. Starting up this trail, you follow the Pacific Crest Trail west for 3.2 miles over a high ridge between Red Cone and Desert Cone. These cinder-cone volcanoes are miniatures of what Mount Mazama may have looked like before it erupted and collapsed in on itself. Today all that's left is the mammoth gaping hole that slowly filled with water and became Crater Lake. The thick old forest and lush, colorful wildflowers that cover the landscape have turned the stark surroundings into a beautiful wilderness that harbors a great array of birds and animals.

At the junction at 3.2 miles, turn north onto the Bald Crater Trail. Hike along this long, level path as it passes under the flanks of Bald Crater Peak and to the side of Boundary Springs, the headwaters of the Rogue River. Enjoy the cool, peaceful campsites near the springs before retracing your steps to your car.

Location: North of Fort Klamath in Crater Lake National Park; see The Southern Cascades Map 6, grid a8.

User Groups: Hikers only. No dogs, horses, or mountain bikes are allowed. No wheelchair facilities.

Permits: No permits are required.

Maps: For a trail information report, contact Crater Lake National Park at 541/594-2211. For a map of Crater Lake National Park, contact Nature of the Northwest Information Center, 800 Northeast Oregon Street, Suite 177, Portland, OR 97232; 503/872-2750. Ask the USGS for topographic maps of the Pumice Desert West and Crater Lake West areas.

Directions: From Fort Klamath drive about 16 miles north on Highway 62 to Mazama Village. Turn right (east) onto Munson Valley Road. Drive about six miles east to Rim Village and the junction with Rim Drive. Turn left (north) onto Rim Drive and continue to North Entrance Road. Turn left and follow this road three miles north to the trailhead on the left.

Contact: Crater Lake National Park, P.O. Box 7, Crater Lake, OR 97604; 541/594-2211.

76 Cleetwood Cove
2.2 mi/1.5 hrs

Descending this steep, switchbacking trail is fairly easy, but the return hike to the trailhead can be a real sweat-producer. Despite the steepness, though, this trail isn't to be missed, as it's the only route to the shore of Crater Lake. At the bottom you find a wide, green picnic area and boat dock. A park concessionaire operates a motor launch that provides tours of the lake. If you dread the steep climb back to the trailhead, remember that several long benches have been built along the trail so weary hikers can rest and recuperate.

Location: North of Fort Klamath in Crater Lake National Park; see The Southern Cascades Map 6, grid a8.

User Groups: Hikers only. No dogs, horses, or mountain bikes are allowed. No wheelchair facilities.

Permits: No permits are required.

Maps: For a trail information report, contact Crater Lake National Park at 541/594-2211. For a map of Crater Lake National Park, contact Nature of the Northwest Information Center, 800 Northeast Oregon Street, Suite 177, Portland, OR 97232; 503/872-2750. Ask the USGS for a topographic map of the Crater Lake East area.

Directions: From Fort Klamath drive about 16 miles north on Highway 62 to Mazama Village. Turn right (east) onto Munson Valley Road. Drive about six miles east to Rim Village and the junction with Rim Drive. Turn left (north) onto Rim Drive and continue past North Entrance Road to the trailhead, about 4.5 miles ahead on the right.

Contact: Crater Lake National Park, P.O. Box 7, Crater Lake, OR 97604; 541/594-2211.

77 Wizard Island Summit
3.2 mi/3.0 hrs

These are actually two trails joined by a scenic boat ride. The first leg of the journey, the Cleetwood Cove Trail (see hike this chapter), brings you down a steep 1.1-mile route to the shores of Crater Lake, where you board a tour boat (for a fee) and ride to Wizard Island. From the island dock climb the long, switchbacking trail that weaves its way to the cinder cone summit of this mighty volcano. It's a great way to see Crater Lake from inside the caldera, and the summit offers unbeatable views of the entire lake. The boat also circles the caldera, offering close-up views of the lake and the caldera walls.

Boats run several times a day in the summer. At this writing, tickets are $12.50 for adults, $8 for children. Be sure to get a current schedule so you can catch the boat back to the Cleetwood Cove Trail before the end of the day.

Location: North of Fort Klamath in Crater Lake National Park; see The Southern Cascades Map 6, grid a8.

User Groups: Hikers only. No dogs, horses, or mountain bikes are allowed. No wheelchair facilities.

Permits: No permits are required.

Maps: For a trail information report, contact park headquarters at 541/594-2211. For a map of Crater Lake National Park, contact Nature of the Northwest Information Center, 800 Northeast Oregon Street, Suite 177, Portland, OR 97232; 503/872-2750. Ask the USGS for topographic maps of the Crater Lake East and Crater Lake West areas.

Directions: From Fort Klamath drive about 16 miles north on Highway 62 to Mazama Village. Turn right (east) onto Munson Valley Road. Drive about six miles east to Rim Village and the junction with Rim Drive. Turn left (north) onto Rim Drive and continue past North Entrance Road to the trailhead, about 4.5 miles ahead on the right.

Contact: Crater Lake National Park, P.O. Box 7, Crater Lake, OR 97604; 541/594-2211.

78 Mount Scott
5.0 mi/2.5 hrs

Climbing to the park's highest point, this is the trail of choice for hikers in search of picturesque views. The steep climb is well worth the effort: from the 8,920-foot summit and former lookout site, you can see Crater Lake, Scott Creek Canyon, Skell Head, Cloudcap Peak, Bear Butte, and countless other peaks and small cinder-cone volcanoes. There's no water along the rough trail, so carry plenty of your own. Bring lots of film, too, as better and better views await around every bend in the trail.

Location: North of Fort Klamath in Crater Lake National Park; see The Southern Cascades Map 6, grid a8.

User Groups: Hikers only. No dogs, horses, or mountain bikes are allowed. No wheelchair facilities.

Permits: No permits are required.

Maps: For a trail information report, contact park headquarters at 541/594-2211. For a map of Crater Lake National Park, contact Nature of the Northwest Information Center, 800 Northeast Oregon Street, Suite 177, Portland, OR 97232; 503/872-2750. Ask the USGS for a topographic map of the Crater Lake East area.

Directions: From Fort Klamath drive about 16 miles north on Highway 62 to Mazama Village. Turn right (east) onto Munson Valley Road. Drive about six miles east to Rim Village and turn right (east) onto Rim Drive. Continue east around the crater rim for 14 miles to the trailhead on the right side of the road.

Contact: Crater Lake National Park, P.O. Box 7, Crater Lake, OR 97604; 541/594-2211.

79 Sugar Pine
6.2 mi/3.1 hrs

It gains a mere 400 feet in elevation, but this trail does require hikers to ford the Rogue River in several places. That's great for summer hikers, but in spring and autumn the full waters may be inconvenient or troublesome. The trail stays under the dense forest canopy most of the time, so just enjoy the array of trees, including dogwoods, rhododendrons, Douglas fir, western hemlock, Pacific yew, vine maple, bigleaf maple, and sugar pine. Here and there the creek spreads out into wide, shallow, gravel-lined pools, which make great places to rest, relax, and gaze at the sun sparkling on the water.

Location: West of Prospect in Rogue River National Forest; see The Southern Cascades Map 6, grid b3.

User Groups: Hikers and dogs. No horses or mountain bikes are allowed. No wheelchair facilities.

Permits: A federal Northwest Forest Pass, $5 per day or $30 annually, is required to park at the trailhead. Passes are available from ranger stations and many private vendors, online at website: www.wta.org, or by calling 800/270-7504.

Maps: For a trail information report, contact the Prospect Ranger District at 541/560-3400. For a map of Rogue River National Forest, contact Nature of the Northwest Information Center, 800 Northeast Oregon Street, Suite 177, Portland, OR 97232; 503/872-2750. Ask the USGS for a topographic map of the Sugar Pine Creek area.

Directions: From Prospect drive 19 miles south on Highway 62 to Elk Creek Road and turn right (north). Continue 11.1 miles before turning left on Sugar Pine Road. Continue two miles to the junction with Forest Service Road 6610 and turn right. Follow the road for one mile before turning right onto Forest Service Road 6610-050. Passenger cars must park at this junction, but high-clearance vehicles may drive the final quarter mile to the trailhead.

Contact: Rogue River National Forest, Prospect Ranger District, 47201 Highway 62, Prospect, OR 97536; 541/560-3400.

80 Bitterlick
11.0 mi/5.5 hrs

Save this hike for a hot summer day. When the temperatures soar and higher trails are blistering nightmares, this cool forest route couldn't be better. Not only is it well shaded by the thick lodgepole and sugar pine forest, but you get to ford pretty little Bitterlick Creek no fewer than seven times. Ordinarily that could be a drawback, but when you're hiking in the 90-degree-plus dog days of August, those river fords are refreshing blessings. The route drops down the Bitterlick Valley alongside—and through—the creek for its entire length, with the exception of the first steep mile down the valley's headwall. The forest is a unique but lovely combination of lodgepole and sugar pine, Douglas fir, dogwood, hazel, bigleaf maple, vine maple, and incense cedar.

Location: West of Prospect in Rogue River National Forest; see The Southern Cascades Map 6, grid b3.

User Groups: Hikers, dogs, horses, and mountain bikes. No wheelchair facilities.

Permits: A federal Northwest Forest Pass, $5 per day or $30 annually, is required to park at the trailhead. Passes are available from ranger stations and many private vendors, online at website: www.wta.org, or by calling 800/270-7504.

Maps: For a trail information report, contact the Prospect Ranger District at 541/560-3400. For a map of Rogue River National Forest, contact Nature of the Northwest Information Center, 800 Northeast Oregon Street, Suite 177, Portland, OR 97232; 503/872-2750. Ask the USGS for topographic maps of the Sugar Pine Creek and Butler Butte areas.

Directions: From Prospect drive 19 miles south on Highway 62 to Elk Creek Road and turn right (north). Continue 14 miles before turning left onto Forest Service Road 66. Follow the road for four miles to the end of the pavement, where it becomes Forest Service Road 6640. Continue another four miles to the trailhead on the left.

Contact: Rogue River National Forest, Prospect Ranger District, 47201 Highway 62, Prospect, OR 97536; 541/560-3400.

81 Upper Rogue River
47.8 mi one way/5.0 days

The long, rambling trail parallels the wild, scenic Rogue River through a variety of forest types and ecosystems. You can split the trail into shorter, easier hikes, as it crosses several roads. From the southern trailhead the route leads upstream. The early portion is the least scenic, passing through young second-growth forest and straying from the banks of the river, which is tamed here by a dam downstream. As the trail moves beyond the first few miles, though, you enter an old stand of lodgepole and sugar pine trees adjoining a broad, sandy beach.

Continuing north, the route rolls up and down over a series of low ridges and rises as it plays touch-and-go with the riverbank. You find good fishing access along the way and good fishing, too, for big rainbow, brook, and cutthroat trout. North of Woodruff Bridge at mile eight, the trail winds past Natural Bridge, a rock arch spanning a small pool. Here the river fades to just a trickle as the bulk of the water is siphoned underground through a series of lava tubes.

As you near the Rogue Gorge area, a side trail at mile 13 leads into the narrow, deep gorge, while the main trail pushes on upstream to Big Bend and beyond. You pass several waterfalls before reaching the trail's end, in addition to a score or more of side creeks and feeder streams. Hemlock, fir, and Douglas fir forests shade the northern end of the trail. The views from this trail are dominated by the beautiful river, but you also get outstanding glimpses of the surrounding peaks and bluffs, all of which are the result of volcanic activity. Camping is good at many points along the river.

For the best experience, arrange for a shuttle car to be parked at the northern end of the trail or for someone to pick you up when you get there. You'll avoid the long backtrack.

Location: North of Prospect in Rogue River National Forest; see The Southern Cascades Map 6, grid b4.

User Groups: Hikers, dogs, and horses. No mountain bikes are allowed. No wheelchair facilities.

Permits: A federal Northwest Forest Pass, $5 per day or $30 annually, is required to park at the trailhead. Passes are available from ranger stations and many private vendors, online at website: www.wta.org, or by calling 800/270-7504.

Maps: For a trail information report, contact the Prospect Ranger District at 541/560-3400. For a map of Rogue River National Forest, contact Nature of the Northwest Information Center, 800 Northeast Oregon Street, Suite 177, Portland, OR 97232; 503/872-2750. Ask the USGS for topographic maps of the Pumice Desert West, Hamaker Butte, Thousand Springs, Union Creek, Prospect North, and Whetstone Point areas.

Directions: To reach the southern trailhead from Prospect, drive a short distance north on Highway 62 to the Prospect Ranger Station. Turn left (west) onto the access road just before the ranger station and drive across the river to the trailhead on the right. To reach the northern trailhead from Prospect, drive about 12 miles north on Highway 62 to Rogue Gorge and the junction with Highway 230. Stay left and continue about 19 miles north on Highway 230. Drive to the Crater Rim Viewpoint and the trailhead on the right. The trail can also be accessed at several points between the two ends of the trail.

Contact: Rogue River National Forest, Prospect Ranger District, 47201 Highway 62, Prospect, OR 97536; 541/560-3400.

82 Cold Springs
5.2 mi/2.6 hrs

The first mile leads through alternating sections of old timber cuts and young replanted forest. Just as the route enters a thick second-growth stand of forest, it passes a large pile of rocks, marked with a porcelain sign proclaiming this to be the grave site of the fabled giant logger Paul Bunyan. (Alas, the sign doesn't mention Babe, his great blue ox.) Continuing along the trail, the surroundings grow increasingly beautiful with each step. As you wind through a long series of forest and forest meadows, the trail alternates between the light, bright world of wildflowers and the dark, damp world of old-growth trees. The trail fades away and disappears near Cold Springs, a small seep that is often reduced to a mud hole by the trampling hooves of the domestic cattle that graze on this land.

Location: East of Prospect in Rogue River National Forest; see The Southern Cascades Map 6, grid b5.

User Groups: Hikers, dogs, horses, and mountain bikes. No wheelchair facilities.

Permits: A federal Northwest Forest Pass, $5 per day or $30 annually, is required to park at the trailhead. Passes are available from ranger stations and many private vendors, online at website: www.wta.org, or by calling 800/270-7504.

Maps: For a trail information report, contact the Prospect Ranger District at 541/560-3400. For a map of Rogue River National Forest, contact Nature of the Northwest Information Center, 800 Northeast Oregon Street, Suite 177, Portland, OR 97232; 503/872-2750. Ask the USGS for a topographic map of the Red Blanket Mountain area.

Directions: From Prospect drive one mile east on Prospect-Butte Falls Highway and turn left onto Red Blanket Road. Continue for a quarter mile and turn left onto Forest Service Road 6205. Follow this road for 4.5 miles before turning left onto Forest Service Road 6205-100. Drive 7.5 miles to the trailhead on the left.

Contact: Rogue River National Forest, Prospect Ranger District, 47201 Highway 62, Prospect, OR 97536; 541/560-3400.

83 Varmint Camp
6.2 mi/3.1 hrs

Winding through a thick mixed forest of hardwoods and conifers, this trail is a good destination on a hot summer day. The route stays close to Varmint Creek, with its temptingly refreshing water, and the cooling shade from the bigleaf maples and Shasta red firs keeps the temperature on the forest floor down, even when surrounding areas are heating up. The trail leaves the forest only occasionally to cross broad wildflower meadows and wild onion patches before ending at the turnaround point, Varmint Camp. One note: biting flies congregate in the sunny meadows, so wise hikers don't dawdle here.

Location: East of Prospect in Rogue River National Forest; see The Southern Cascades Map 6, grid b5.

User Groups: Hikers, dogs, horses, and mountain bikes. No wheelchair facilities.

Permits: A federal Northwest Forest Pass, $5 per day or $30 annually, is required to park at the trailhead. Passes are available from ranger stations and many private vendors, online at website: www.wta.org, or by calling 800/270-7504.

Maps: For a trail information report, contact the Prospect Ranger District at 541/560-3400. For a map of Rogue River National Forest, contact Nature of the Northwest Information Center, 800 Northeast Oregon Street, Suite 177, Portland, OR 97232; 503/872-2750. Ask

the USGS for a topographic map of the Red Blanket Mountain area.

Directions: From Prospect drive one mile east on Prospect-Butte Falls Highway and turn left onto Red Blanket Road. Continue one-quarter mile and turn left onto Forest Service Road 6205. Follow this road for 10.5 miles to the trailhead on the left.

Contact: Rogue River National Forest, Prospect Ranger District, 47201 Highway 62, Prospect, OR 97536; 541/560-3400.

84 Geyser Springs
2.2 mi/1.1 hrs

Look closely at the trees as you descend this steep trail and you may see a few of the porcelain insulators that once carried the telephone line down the Middle Fork Canyon from the Imnaha Guard Station to the Bessie Rock Guard Station. That phone line was used in the early decades of the 20th century to link the fire watch towers to the Forest Service ranger stations. This trail was part of a network of maintenance trails that served the phone line. The route drops sharply to the Middle Fork Rogue River, passing Geyser Springs about one-third mile down the slope. As the trail nears the river, you can see and hear several waterfalls. These cascades capture the attention of sightseers, while the torpedo-like rainbow, brown, and brook trout that slice through the Middle Fork grab the attention of anglers.

Location: East of Prospect in Rogue River National Forest; see The Southern Cascades Map 6, grid c6.

User Groups: Hikers and dogs. No horses or mountain bikes are allowed. No wheelchair facilities.

Permits: A federal Northwest Forest Pass, $5 per day or $30 annually, is required to park at the trailhead. Passes are available

from ranger stations and many private vendors, online at website: www.wta.org, or by calling 800/270-7504.

Maps: For a trail information report, contact the Prospect Ranger District at 541/560-3400. For a map of Rogue River National Forest, contact Nature of the Northwest Information Center, 800 Northeast Oregon Street, Suite 177, Portland, OR 97232; 503/872-2750. Ask the USGS for a topographic map of the Imnaha Creek area.

Directions: From Prospect drive 2.9 miles east on Prospect-Butte Falls Highway and turn left onto Forest Service Road 37. Continue another 3.1 miles to Forest Service Road 3795 and turn left. Follow this road for 2.7 miles and turn right onto Forest Service Road 300. Drive 1.2 miles to the trailhead.

Contact: Rogue River National Forest, Prospect Ranger District, 47201 Highway 62, Prospect, OR 97536; 541/560-3400.

85 Lower South Fork
10.6 mi/5.3 hrs

A scenic marvel, this trail ambles gently upstream alongside the South Fork Rogue River. The Rogue is the epitome of a wild mountain river, crashing over and around boulders, tumbling over gentle shelves, and glistening like crystal in the sunshine. Surrounding the picturesque river is a lush forest of mixed conifers and hardwoods. Douglas fir shares space with ponderosa, white, and sugar pines, and they all rub shoulders with alders and a few bigleaf maples. Wildlife also abounds here. In addition to healthy populations of big rainbow and cutthroat trout in the water, look for ouzels, herons, and kingfishers lurking around the water, as well as deer, beavers, raccoons, and other animals, large and small. The trail is relatively flat, and when you reach the end, it is a pleasure to return the way you came.

Location: Northeast of Butte Falls in Rogue River National Forest; see The Southern Cascades Map 6, grid c6.

User Groups: Hikers and dogs. No horses or mountain bikes are allowed. No wheelchair facilities.

Permits: A federal Northwest Forest Pass, $5 per day or $30 annually, is required to park at the trailhead. Passes are available from ranger stations and many private vendors, online at website: www.wta.org, or by calling 800/270-7504.

Maps: For a trail information report, contact the Butte Falls Ranger District at 541/865-2700. For a map of Rogue River National Forest, contact Nature of the Northwest Information Center, 800 Northeast Oregon Street, Suite 177, Portland, OR 97232; 503/872-2750. Ask the USGS for a topographic map of the Rustler Peak area.

Directions: From Butte Falls drive 8.5 miles north on Prospect-Butte Falls Highway and turn left onto Forest Service Road 34. Continue 8.1 miles to the trailhead parking area on the right side of the road, just one-quarter mile past the South Fork Bridge.

Contact: Rogue River National Forest, Butte Falls Ranger District, 800 Laurel Street, P.O. Box 227, Butte Falls, OR 97522; 541/865-2700.

86 Union Peak
10.8 mi/5.4 hrs

Rolling south along the Pacific Crest Trail for more than 2.5 miles, this trail cuts right through prime deer and elk country, so keep an eye out for the big animals. At the end of a long ridge that leads off to the west, you find a trail junction. Turn right and begin the long, steep climb to the 7,700-foot-high summit of Union Peak, which affords stunning panoramic views. The trail begins with a gentle ascent along the ridge but tilts upward as the summits nears; the final half mile is steep and requires some scrambling. It's a hard workout, but the views are worth the effort. Look out over Pumice Flat, Bald Top Mountain, Castle Point, and Rocktop Butte as you rest at the summit. After you have your fill of the vistas, return the way you came.

Location: North of Fort Klamath in Crater Lake National Park; see The Southern Cascades Map 6, grid b7.

User Groups: Hikers only. No dogs, horses, or mountain bikes are allowed. No wheelchair facilities.

Permits: Permits are required for overnight stays and can be picked up at Crater Lake National Park.

Maps: For a trail information report, contact park headquarters at 541/594-2211. For a map of Crater Lake National Park, contact Nature of the Northwest Information Center, 800 Northeast Oregon Street, Suite 177, Portland, OR 97232; 503/872-2750. Ask the USGS for topographic maps of the Crater Lake West and Union Peak areas.

Directions: From Fort Klamath drive about 16 miles north on Highway 62 to Mazama Village. Stay left and continue a few miles west on Highway 62 to the trailhead on the left.

Contact: Crater Lake National Park, P.O. Box 7, Crater Lake, OR 97604; 541/594-2211.

87 Annie Springs
1.2 mi/1.0 hr

Climbing past Annie Springs in the first half mile, this trail continues on to a junction with the Pacific Crest Trail, thus offering unlimited exploration and extended hiking. The trail traverses a ridge southwest of Munson Point and provides good views of that high peak. Other than that, though, the views are restricted to the beautiful forest and wildflowers that surround you.

Location: North of Fort Klamath in Crater Lake National Park; see The Southern Cascades Map 6, grid b7.

User Groups: Hikers only. No dogs, horses, or mountain bikes are allowed. No wheelchair facilities.

Permits: Permits are required for overnight stays and can be picked up at Crater Lake National Park.

Maps: For a trail information report, contact park headquarters at 541/594-2211. For a map of Crater Lake National Park, contact Nature of the Northwest Information Center, 800 Northeast Oregon Street, Suite 177, Portland, OR 97232; 503/872-2750. Ask the USGS for topographic maps of the Union Peak and Crater Lake West areas.

Directions: From Fort Klamath drive about 16 miles north on Highway 62 to Mazama Village and then turn right (east) onto Munson Valley Road. Continue a short distance east to the trailhead on the left, opposite the Mazama Campground.

Contact: Crater Lake National Park, P.O. Box 7, Crater Lake, OR 97604; 541/594-2211.

88 Godfrey Glen Loop
1.0 mi/0.5 hr

This gentle, flat trail loops through a deep old-growth forest, through fragrant wildflower meadows, and past beautiful Annie Creek Canyon and the tumbling Duwee Falls. Deer, grouse, and rabbits commonly appear here; elk, foxes, porcupines, badgers, and owls also inhabit this gorgeous forest, although they are seen less frequently. The trail does roll over a few low rises and ridgelines, but the well-maintained tread makes walking easy.

Location: North of Fort Klamath in Crater Lake National Park; see The Southern Cascades Map 6, grid b8.

User Groups: Hikers only. No dogs, horses, or mountain bikes are allowed. No wheelchair facilities.

Permits: No permits are required.

Maps: For a trail information report, contact park headquarters at 541/594-2211. For a map of Crater Lake National Park, contact Nature of the Northwest Information Center, 800 Northeast Oregon Street, Suite 177, Portland, OR 97232; 503/872-2750. Ask the USGS for a topographic map of the Union Peak area.

Directions: From Fort Klamath drive about 16 miles north on Highway 62 to Mazama Village and turn right (east) onto Munson Valley Road. Drive two miles to the trailhead on the right.

Contact: Crater Lake National Park, P.O. Box 7, Crater Lake, OR 97604; 541/594-2211.

89 Castle Crest Interpretive Wildflower Garden
1.0 mi/1.0 hr

Hike this interpretive trail for an unbeatable opportunity to study the region's beautiful native plants and flowers in an incredible setting. The route weaves along a wide, rocky path through a thin alpine forest and broad wildflower meadows, and alongside the remarkable Munson Creek. The best time to hike this short, exquisite trail is early summer and midsummer, when the vast array of wildflower species erupts in a rainbow of colors.

Location: North of Fort Klamath in Crater Lake National Park; see The Southern Cascades Map 6, grid b8.

User Groups: Hikers only. No dogs, horses, or mountain bikes are allowed. No wheelchair facilities.

Permits: No permits are required.

Maps: For a trail information report, contact park headquarters at 541/594-2211. For a map of Crater Lake National Park, contact Nature of the Northwest Information Center, 800 Northeast Oregon Street, Suite 177, Portland, OR 97232; 503/872-2750. Ask the USGS for topographic maps of the Crater Lake East and Crater Lake West areas.

Directions: From Fort Klamath drive about 16 miles north on Highway 62 to Mazama Village and turn right (east) onto Munson Valley Road. Drive about six miles east to Rim Village. The trailhead is opposite the park headquarters.

Contact: Crater Lake National Park, P.O. Box 7, Crater Lake, OR 97604; 541/594-2211.

90 Crater Peak
5.0 mi/2.5 hrs

It sounds like an oxymoron, but the natural phenomenon here really is both a crater and a peak. This trail meanders through a luxurious, old-growth alpine forest for two moderately steep miles. The route then slants uphill even more during the final half mile before reaching the summit of the 7,263-foot peak on a small crater's rim—evidence of this area's volcanic nature. From the top you enjoy 360-degree views that take in the awesome profiles of jagged mounts. To the south there's Sun Mountain, Scoria Cone, and Goose Nest; to the north lies the south rim of Crater Lake; to the east you see Dry Butte; and looming in the west is Union Peak. Make sure you bring plenty of water, as this is a dry trail. Bring plenty of film, too. The landscape isn't the only picturesque subject you find—look for deer, elk, hawks, eagles, and an assortment of small birds and animals.

Location: North of Fort Klamath in Crater Lake National Park; see The Southern Cascades Map 6, grid b8.

User Groups: Hikers only. No dogs, horses, or mountain bikes are allowed. No wheelchair facilities.

Permits: Permits are required for overnight stays and can picked up at Crater Lake National Park.

Maps: For a trail information report, contact park headquarters at 541/594-2211. For a map of Crater Lake National Park, contact Nature of the Northwest Information Center, 800 Northeast Oregon Street, Suite 177, Portland, OR 97232; 503/872-2750. Ask the USGS for topographic maps of the Crater Lake East and Maklaks Crater areas.

Directions: From Fort Klamath drive 16 miles north on Highway 62 to Mazama Village. Turn right (east) onto Munson Valley Road. Drive about six miles east to Rim Village and the junction with Rim Drive. Turn right (east) onto Rim Drive and go a few miles to the trailhead on the right.

Contact: Crater Lake National Park, P.O. Box 7, Crater Lake, OR 97604; 541/594-2211.

91 Pumice Flat
5.8 mi/2.9 hrs

Hikers get a lesson in the geologic past of the region when they set foot on this trail. Rolling along a gentle ridge slope, the trail enters a broad, dusty plain called Pumice Flat, which is composed of ash, abrasive basalt rock, and light, pocketed bits of pumice rock. The trail ends at a junction with the Pacific Crest Trail. Carry lots of water, as this route is dry. You'll undoubtedly need extra fluid to keep your throat cleared of the abrasive dust.

Location: North of Fort Klamath in Crater Lake National Park; see The Southern Cascades Map 6, grid b8.

User Groups: Hikers only. No dogs, horses, or mountain bikes are allowed. No wheelchair facilities.

Permits: Permits are required for overnight stays and can be picked up at Crater Lake National Park.

Maps: For a trail information report, contact park headquarters at 541/594-2211. For a map of Crater Lake National Park, contact Nature of the Northwest Information Center, 800 Northeast Oregon Street, Suite 177, Portland, OR 97232; 503/872-2750. Ask the USGS for topographic maps of the Maklaks Crater and Union Peak areas.

Directions: From Fort Klamath drive about 13 miles north on Highway 62 to the trailhead on the left, three miles south of Mazama Village.

Contact: Crater Lake National Park, P.O. Box 7, Crater Lake, OR 97604; 541/594-2211.

92 Stuart Falls
10.8 mi/5.4 hrs

After a long traverse on a gentle ridge slope, this trail enters the broad plain of Pumice Flat (see hike above). At the junction with the Pacific Crest Trail (around mile three), cross the PCT and continue west into the Red Blanket Basin. As you drop down the headwall of the Red Blanket Valley, you find yourself paralleling a tiny thread of water, which grows into a pretty little stream and continues to grow and widen as it drops through the steep valley. By the time the trail reaches the park boundary at the turnaround point, the stream is a wide, crashing creek; at the trail's end, the creek pounds over Stuart Falls, a beautiful white cascade that throws up a fine mist. Trail-weary hikers can cool down in the spray before returning along the steep trail they just descended.

Location: North of Fort Klamath in Crater Lake National Park; see The Southern Cascades Map 6, grid b8.

User Groups: Hikers only. No dogs, horses, or mountain bikes are allowed. No wheelchair facilities.

Permits: Permits are required for overnight stays and can be picked up at Crater Lake National Park.

Maps: For a trail information report, contact park headquarters at 541/594-2211. For a map of Crater Lake National Park, contact Nature of the Northwest Information Center, 800 Northeast Oregon Street, Suite 177, Portland, OR 97232; 503/872-2750. Ask the USGS for topographic maps of the Maklaks Crater and Union Peak areas.

Directions: From Fort Klamath drive about 13 miles north on Highway 62 to the trailhead on the left, three miles south of Mazama Village.

Contact: Crater Lake National Park, P.O. Box 7, Crater Lake, OR 97604; 541/594-2211.

93 Sevenmile
3.8 mi/2.0 hrs

The creek really is seven miles long, but the road knocks off the first five, making this hike about two miles one-way. From the trailhead, cross the turbulent waters of the creek and climb through the sunny hillside meadows above to the northern edge of Sevenmile Marsh. This wetland area is an ornithologist's dream come true. Birds of all feathers swarm through the food-rich marsh, devouring tender young plants and the armies of insects that thrive in this aquatic landscape. Above the marsh the trail enters a dry evergreen forest—primarily lodgepole pine and Douglas fir—and eventually ends at a junction with the Pacific Crest Trail near Ranger Springs.

Location: Northwest of Klamath Falls in Winema National Forest within the Sky Lakes Wilderness; see The Southern Cascades Map 6, grid c8.

User Groups: Hikers and dogs. No horses or mountain bikes are allowed. No wheelchair facilities.

Permits: A federal Northwest Forest Pass, $5 per day or $30 annually, is required to park at the trailhead. Passes are available from ranger stations and many private vendors, online at website: www.wta.org, or by calling 800/270-7504.

Maps: For a trail information report, contact the Klamath Ranger District at 541/885-3400. For a map of Winema National Forest, contact Nature of the Northwest Information Center, 800 Northeast Oregon Street, Suite 177, Portland, OR 97232; 503/872-2750. Ask the USGS for a topographic map of the Devils Peak area.

Directions: From Klamath Falls drive about 23 miles north on Highway 140 to Pelican and the intersection with County Road 53. Stay right and continue north on County Road 53. The road forks 34 miles north of Klamath Falls. Stay right (straight ahead), taking Forest Service Road 3300. Follow this road (which becomes Forest Service Road 3334 after 2.5 miles) to the trailhead at its end.

Contact: Winema National Forest, Klamath Ranger District, 1936 California Avenue, Klamath Falls, OR 97601; 541/885-3400.

94 Twin Ponds
5.0 mi/2.5 hrs

Thick stands of lodgepole pine provide welcome breaks from the countless ponds, puddles, and lakes that line this trail. Twin Ponds follows the Fort Klamath Military Road to Jacksonville (built in 1863), and although the path gains slightly fewer than 300 feet in total elevation, it gently rolls up and down smooth, low hills the entire way. The trail ends near Squaw Lake at a junction with the Pacific Crest Trail.

For a loop hike, combine this trail with a section of the PCT from Squaw Lake north to Center Lake and then follow the Badger Lake Trail back to the trailhead. The total distance is about 14 miles.

Location: Northwest of Klamath Falls in Winema National Forest within the Sky Lakes Wilderness; see The Southern Cascades Map 6, grid d7.

User Groups: Hikers, dogs, and horses. No mountain bikes are allowed. No wheelchair facilities.

Permits: A federal Northwest Forest Pass, $5 per day or $30 annually, is required to park at the trailhead. Passes are available from ranger stations and many private vendors, online at website: www.wta.org, or by calling 800/270-7504. Party size is limited to 12 people.

Maps: For a trail information report, contact the Klamath Ranger District at 541/885-3400. For a map of Winema National Forest, contact Nature of the Northwest Information Center, 800 Northeast Oregon Street, Suite 177, Portland, OR 97232; 503/872-2750. Ask the USGS for topographic maps of the Lake of the Woods North and Mount McLoughlin areas.

Directions: From Klamath Falls drive 32 miles northwest on Highway 140 to the junction with Forest Service Road 3661. Turn right (north) and continue 5.6 miles on Forest Service Road 3661 to the Fourmile Campground. The trailhead is on the east end of the camp.

Contact: Winema National Forest, Klamath Ranger District, 1936 California Avenue, Klamath Falls, OR 97601; 541/885-3400.

95 Badger Lake
10.4 mi/5.2 hrs

If you like water, you'll love this trail. It begins on the flat eastern shoreline of Fourmile Lake and then moves through a broad meadow and thick forest to Woodpecker Lake. From here it hopscotches north from Badger Lake to Lily Pond, several small unnamed tarns, Long Lake, and finally Center Lake. Hikers encounter several small rolling hills, but no real uphill sweats or downhill toe-breakers. The worst mountains involved

are those left on your arms by the swarming mosquitoes, which enjoy the water as much as we do.

Location: Northwest of Klamath Falls in Winema National Forest within the Sky Lakes Wilderness; see The Southern Cascades Map 6, grid d7.

User Groups: Hikers, dogs, and horses. No mountain bikes are allowed. No wheelchair facilities.

Permits: A federal Northwest Forest Pass, $5 per day or $30 annually, is required to park at the trailhead. Passes are available from ranger stations and many private vendors, online at website: www.wta.org, or by calling 800/270-7504. Party size is limited to 12 people.

Maps: For a trail information report, contact the Klamath Ranger District at 541/885-3400 For a map of Winema National Forest, contact Nature of the Northwest Information Center, 800 Northeast Oregon Street, Suite 177, Portland, OR 97232; 503/872-2750. Ask the USGS for topographic maps of the Lake of the Woods North and Pelican Butte areas.

Directions: From Klamath Falls drive 32 miles northwest on Highway 140 to the junction with Forest Service Road 3661. Turn right (north) and continue 5.6 miles on Forest Service Road 3661 to the Fourmile Campground. The trailhead is on the east end of the camp.

Contact: Winema National Forest, Klamath Ranger District, 1936 California Avenue, Klamath Falls, OR 97601; 541/885-3400.

96 Donna Lake
9.6 mi/5.0 hrs

Be prepared to work hard right off the bat here. The Donna Lake Trail begins with a steep series of switchbacks before tempering into a more moderate climb around the northern flank of Luther

Mountain. From this point the trail leads west through a long hillside traverse to the junction with the Sky Lakes Trail (see hike in this chapter), a long route that slices north to south through the wilderness area. Turn left and hike south for a little more than a mile to the next fork in the trail. The small path off to the left leads into the Donna Lake Basin, where thick, young stands of vibrant green forest offset the deep-blue lake waters in a picture-book setting. You encounter similar scenery at least three more times as you pass several other small lakes before reaching Donna Lake. Relax and enjoy the quiet camps and pleasing views around this lake before returning the way you came.

Location: Northwest of Klamath Falls in Winema National Forest within the Sky Lakes Wilderness; see The Southern Cascades Map 6, grid c8.

User Groups: Hikers and dogs. No horses or mountain bikes are allowed. No wheelchair facilities.

Permits: A federal Northwest Forest Pass, $5 per day or $30 annually, is required to park at the trailhead. Passes are available from ranger stations and many private vendors, online at website: www.wta.org, or by calling 800/270-7504. Party size is limited to 12 people.

Maps: For a trail information report, contact the Klamath Ranger District at 541/885-3400. For a map of Winema National Forest, contact Nature of the Northwest Information Center, 800 Northeast Oregon Street, Suite 177, Portland, OR 97232; 503/872-2750. Ask the USGS for topographic maps of the Pelican Butte and Devils Peak areas.

Directions: From Klamath Falls drive about 23 miles north on Highway 140 to Pelican and the intersection with County Road 53. Stay right and continue north on County Road 53. About 31 miles north of Klamath Falls, turn left (west) onto Forest Service Road 3484 and drive to the road's end and the trailhead.

Contact: Winema National Forest, Klamath Ranger District, 1936 California Avenue, Klamath Falls, OR 97601; 541/885-3400.

97 Snow Lakes
12.6 mi/6.3 hrs

Following the Nannie Creek Trail (see hike below), the first stretch of this trail entails a quick, steep series of switchbacks and a long uphill pull to the Sky Lakes Trail junction. At that junction, turn north onto the Snow Lakes Trail instead of heading south to Sky Lakes. Sweep uphill around the northernmost reaches of the Sky Lakes Basin. The forest and meadows here present an interesting mosaic of sun-brightened wildflower fields and cool, shady forest groves.

The route then loops around to the west to touch the shores of the Snow Lakes, a pair of pretty, cold ponds offering good views of the surrounding rimrock ledges. Backpackers should establish their camp at the lakes and then continue up the trail as it weaves through the rimrock bluffs and jagged ridge to stunning panoramic views of the lakes basin and the Wilderness.

Location: Northwest of Klamath Falls in Winema National Forest within the Sky Lakes Wilderness; see The Southern Cascades Map 6, grid d8.

User Groups: Hikers and dogs. No horses or mountain bikes are allowed. No wheelchair facilities.

Permits: A federal Northwest Forest Pass, $5 per day or $30 annually, is required to park at the trailhead. Passes are available from ranger stations and many private vendors, online at website: www.wta.org, or by calling 800/270-7504. Party size is limited to 12 people.

Maps: For a trail information report, contact the Klamath Ranger District at 541/885-3400. For a map of Winema National Forest, contact Nature of the Northwest Information Center, 800 Northeast Oregon Street, Suite 177, Portland, OR 97232; 503/872-2750. Ask the USGS for topographic maps of the Pelican Butte and Devils Peak areas.

Directions: From Klamath Falls drive about 23 miles north on Highway 140 to Pelican and the intersection with County Road 53. Stay right and continue north on County Road 53. About 31 miles north of Klamath Falls, turn left (west) onto Forest Service Road 3484 and drive to the road's end and the trailhead.

Contact: Winema National Forest, Klamath Ranger District, 1936 California Avenue, Klamath Falls, OR 97601; 541/885-3400.

98 Nannie Creek
4.6 mi/2.3 hrs

You would think that a trail that begins at 6,000 feet couldn't really go much higher. Think again. Almost immediately after leaving the trailhead, the trail leads into a long, steep series of switchbacks that weave up the rocky, pine-covered slopes of Luther Mountain. Fortunately, this run of switchbacks is the worst of the ascent.

As you leave the switchbacks, the trail angles through a long, level traverse as it crosses a broad, sloped meadow. From there the route climbs gently to Puck Lakes, through a thick stand of lodgepole pine, to the trail's end at a junction with the Sky Lakes and Snow Lakes Trails. Return from here, but explore at leisure before you do. It's worth it.

Location: Northwest of Klamath Falls in Winema National Forest within the Sky Lakes Wilderness; see The Southern Cascades Map 6, grid d8.

User Groups: Hikers and dogs. No horses or mountain bikes are allowed. No wheelchair facilities.

Permits: A federal Northwest Forest Pass, $5 per day or $30 annually, is required to park at the trailhead. Passes are available from ranger stations and many private vendors, online at website: www.wta.org, or by calling 800/270-7504. Party size is limited to 12 people.

Maps: To receive a trail information report, contact the Klamath Ranger District at 541/885-3400. For a map of Winema National Forest, contact Nature of the Northwest Information Center, 800 Northeast Oregon Street, Suite 177, Portland, OR 97232; 503/872-2750. Ask the USGS for topographic maps of the Crystal Springs, Pelican Butte, and Devils Peak area.

Directions: From Klamath Falls proceed approximately 23 miles north on Highway 140 to Pelican and the intersection with County Road 53. Veer to the right and continue north on County Road 53. About 31 miles north of Klamath Falls, take a left (west) onto Forest Service Road 3484 and continue driving to the road's end and the trailhead.

Contact: Winema National Forest, Klamath Ranger District, 1936 California Avenue, Klamath Falls, OR 97601; 541/885-3400.

99 Divide Trail
16.2 mi/2.0 days

A long, gradual ascent through the Cherry Creek Valley brings you to the high country of the Sky Lakes Basin. When you reach the first trail junction (at about four miles), continue straight on, crossing the Sky Lakes Trail and continuing west to the beautiful blue waters of Trapper Lake a short distance away. From here you're on the Divide Trail—a winding, high-elevation route that links the northern end of the Sky Lakes Trail to the Pacific Crest Trail. Shortly after rounding the northern end of Trapper Lake, you move through an alpine forest and meadow environment and come around the south shore of Marguerette Lake at mile 5.5. As you near the PCT, the route gets steeper and the terrain changes to open rock fields and heather meadows. Climb around the flanks of Luther Mountain and suddenly you are at the trail's end and on the PCT. From here you have a clear path south to Mexico or north to Canada. I'd recommend heading east, the way you came.

Location: Northwest of Klamath Falls in Winema National Forest within the Sky Lakes Wilderness; see The Southern Cascades Map 6, grid d7.

User Groups: Hikers and dogs. No horses or mountain bikes are allowed. No wheelchair facilities.

Permits: A federal Northwest Forest Pass, $5 per day or $30 annually, is required to park at the trailhead. Passes are available from ranger stations and many private vendors, online at website: www.wta.org, or by calling 800/270-7504. Party size is limited to 12 people.

Maps: For a trail information report, contact the Klamath Ranger District at 541/885-3400. For a map of Winema National Forest, contact Nature of the Northwest Information Center, 800 Northeast Oregon Street, Suite 177, Portland, OR 97232; 503/872-2750. Ask the USGS for topographic maps of the Pelican Butte and Crystal Springs areas.

Directions: From Klamath Falls drive about 23 miles north on Highway 140 to Pelican and the intersection with County Road 53. Stay right and continue north on County Road 53. About 29 miles north of Klamath Falls, turn left (west) onto Forest Service Road 3450 and drive to the road's end and the trailhead.

Contact: Winema National Forest, Klamath Ranger District, 1936 California Avenue, Klamath Falls, OR 97601; 541/885-3400.

100 Cherry Creek
10.6 mi/5.3 hrs

The Cherry Creek Valley is a long, glacier-carved basin filled with thick old-growth forests of pine and fir. This trail climbs the moderately steep valley, at first traveling high above the creek, but soon drops alongside the rushing water. The route leads through the heart of the Cherry Creek Natural Research Area, which is part of the wilderness area, and explores the basin's glacier-carved terrain. As you near the head of the valley, the trail leaves the creek once again and climbs steeply through a thick pine forest before erupting into an open meadow with spectacular views. The trail ends here at a junction with the Sky Lakes Trail (see hike below). Enjoy the meadow, the views, and the cool breeze that seems to always sweep through this basin.

Location: Northwest of Klamath Falls in Winema National Forest within the Sky Lakes Wilderness; see The Southern Cascades Map 6, grid d7.

User Groups: Hikers and dogs. No horses or mountain bikes are allowed. No wheelchair facilities.

Permits: A federal Northwest Forest Pass, $5 per day or $30 annually, is required to park at the trailhead. Passes are available from ranger stations and many private vendors, online at website: www.wta.org, or by calling 800/270-7504. Party size is limited to 12 people.

Maps: For a trail information report, contact the Klamath Ranger District at 541/885-3400. For a map of Winema National Forest, contact Nature of the Northwest Information

Center, 800 Northeast Oregon Street, Suite 177, Portland, OR 97232; 503/872-2750. Ask the USGS for topographic maps of the Pelican Butte and Crystal Springs areas.

Directions: From Klamath Falls drive about 23 miles north on Highway 140 to Pelican and the intersection with County Road 53. Stay right and continue north on County Road 53. About 29 miles north of Klamath Falls, turn left (west) onto Forest Service Road 3450 and drive to the road's end and the trailhead.

Contact: Winema National Forest, Klamath Ranger District, 1936 California Avenue, Klamath Falls, OR 97601; 541/885-3400.

101 Sky Lakes
15.4 mi/1.0–2.0 days

The centerpiece of the beautiful Sky Lakes Wilderness trail system, this route rolls north from the flanks of Imagination Peak to the sparkling shores of the Snow Lakes. The trail stays in the high country and weaves past countless lakes—each one a beautiful alpine pool—and dozens of jagged peaks and ridges. You pass through the cooling shade of alpine forests and fragrant heather meadows full of wildflowers and wildlife. From the trailhead climb west along the Cold Springs Trail to the junction with the Sky Lakes Trail at 2.7 miles. To hike the full length of the Sky Lakes route, you have to hike back one-half mile south to the Pacific Crest Trail, the trail's true southern end. From there hike north once again, taking in all the stunning scenery and sweeping vistas, to the northern terminus at the Snow Lakes Trail. There, turn and retrace your steps south to the trailhead.

Several trails climbing up from the east provide alternative access to this trail, most notably the Snow Lakes Trail at the northern end. With the aid of a shuttle car or by arranging to be picked up there, you can make this a one-way hike. We recommend, though, that you complete the round-trip. The scenery is worth seeing twice, and you can take advantage of a few short side trails that loop away from the main route for a mile or two before rejoining it. This allows you to see new country on the return leg, even though you are technically hiking the same route.

Location: Northwest of Klamath Falls in Winema National Forest within the Sky Lakes Wilderness; see The Southern Cascades Map 6, grid d7.

User Groups: Hikers, dogs, and horses. No mountain bikes are allowed. No wheelchair facilities.

Permits: A federal Northwest Forest Pass, $5 per day or $30 annually, is required to park at the trailhead. Passes are available from ranger stations and many private vendors, online at website: www.wta.org, or by calling 800/270-7504. Party size is limited to 12 people.

Maps: For a trail information report, contact the Klamath Ranger District at 541/885-3400. For a map of Winema National Forest, contact Nature of the Northwest Information Center, 800 Northeast Oregon Street, Suite 177, Portland, OR 97232; 503/872-2750. Ask the USGS for a topographic map of the Pelican Butte area.

Directions: From Klamath Falls drive about 22 miles northwest on Highway 140 to the junction with Forest Service Road 3651. Turn right (north) and continue eight miles on Forest Service Road 3651 before turning left (west) onto Forest Service Road 3659. Drive one mile to the trailhead on the left at the point of a hairpin turn.

Contact: Winema National Forest, Klamath Ranger District, 1936 California Avenue, Klamath Falls, OR 97601; 541/885-3400.

102 South Rock Creek
4.2 mi/2.1 hrs

An easy hike requiring a minimal time investment isn't supposed to be this pretty, but this one is simply beautiful. Hike three-quarters of a mile up the Cold Springs Trail, through thick old pine forests, and you'll arrive at a fork. Bear right and wander up the gently sloping trail that cuts cross-country to the headwaters of South Rock Creek. After crossing the small trickle of water, which eventually becomes the splashing, crashing Rock Creek, continue another quarter mile to the junction with the Sky Lakes Trail at Heavenly Twins Lakes. These sapphire blue pools *are* heavenly, as is the heather meadow that fills the broad lakes basin. After exploring the basin and the Sky Lakes Trail, return the way you came.

Location: Northwest of Klamath Falls in Winema National Forest within the Sky Lakes Wilderness; see The Southern Cascades Map 6, grid d7.

User Groups: Hikers, dogs, and horses. No mountain bikes are allowed. No wheelchair facilities.

Permits: A federal Northwest Forest Pass, $5 per day or $30 annually, is required to park at the trailhead. Passes are available from ranger stations and many private vendors, online at website: www.wta.org, or by calling 800/270-7504. Party size is limited to 12 people.

Maps: For a trail information report, contact the Klamath Ranger District at 541/885-3400. For a map of Winema National Forest, contact Nature of the Northwest Information Center, 800 Northeast Oregon Street, Suite 177, Portland, OR 97232; 503/872-2750. Ask the USGS for a topographic map of the Pelican Butte area.

Directions: From Klamath Falls drive about 22 miles northwest on Highway 140 to the junction with Forest Service Road 3651. Turn right (north) and continue eight miles on Forest Service Road 3651 before turning left (west) onto Forest Service Road 3659. Drive one mile to the trailhead on the left at the point of a hairpin turn.

Contact: Winema National Forest, Klamath Ranger District, 1936 California Avenue, Klamath Falls, OR 97601; 541/885-3400.

103 Cold Springs
5.4 mi/2.7 hrs

Watch for mule deer throughout the length of this hike, especially on the edges of small forest clearings and meadows. The trail climbs through thick, dusty stands of lodgepole pine and mountain hemlock, with big Douglas fir and spruce trees thrown in the mix. The trail ascends to a long ridgetop and rolls west with increasingly good views until ending at a junction with the Sky Lakes Trail. The end point is near the Punky Lakes, which is a good spot to rest before retracing your steps to the trailhead.

Location: Northwest of Klamath Falls in Winema National Forest within the Sky Lakes Wilderness; see The Southern Cascades Map 6, grid d8.

User Groups: Hikers, dogs, and horses. No mountain bikes are allowed. No wheelchair facilities.

Permits: A federal Northwest Forest Pass, $5 per day or $30 annually, is required to park at the trailhead. Passes are available from ranger stations and many private vendors, online at website: www.wta.org, or by calling 800/270-7504. Party size is limited to 12 people.

Maps: For a trail information report, contact the Klamath Ranger District at 541/885-3400. For a map of Winema National Forest, contact Nature of the Northwest Information Center, 800 Northeast Oregon Street, Suite

177, Portland, OR 97232; 503/872-2750. Ask the USGS for a topographic map of the Pelican Butte.

Directions: From Klamath Falls drive about 22 miles northwest on Highway 140 to the junction with Forest Service Road 3651. Turn right (north) and continue eight miles on Forest Service Road 3651 before turning left (west) onto Forest Service Road 3659. Drive one mile to the trailhead on the left at the point of a hairpin turn.

Contact: Winema National Forest, Klamath Ranger District, 1936 California Avenue, Klamath Falls, OR 97601; 541/885-3400.

104 Lost Creek
3.0 mi/1.5 hrs

It may be short, but the Lost Creek Trail packs in a good number of adventures and sights. Starting in a beautiful mixed forest of ponderosa pine, Douglas fir, alder, and spruce, the trail ascends gently up the Lost Creek Valley. This route then leaves the creek behind and cuts across a low ridge to ultimately reconnect with the creek at 1.2 miles. At this point you have to ford the cool, gurgling waters before pushing on up to the trail's end at a junction with the Pacific Crest Trail. Either turn and retrace your steps from this point or take a quick detour by walking either west on the PCT for one-half mile to Island Lake, or east for one-third mile to Bert Lake.

Location: Northwest of Klamath Falls in Winema National Forest within the Sky Lakes Wilderness; see The Southern Cascades Map 6, grid e8.

User Groups: Hikers, dogs, and horses. No mountain bikes are allowed. No wheelchair facilities.

Permits: A federal Northwest Forest Pass, $5 per day or $30 annually, is required to park at the trailhead. Passes are available

from ranger stations and many private vendors, online at website: www.wta.org, or by calling 800/270-7504. Party size is limited to 12 people.

Maps: For a trail information report, contact the Klamath Ranger District at 541/885-3400. For a map of Winema National Forest, contact Nature of the Northwest Information Center, 800 Northeast Oregon Street, Suite 177, Portland, OR 97232; 503/872-2750. Ask the USGS for a topographic map of the Pelican Butte area.

Directions: From Klamath Falls proceed approximately 22 miles northwest on Highway 140 to the junction with Forest Service Road 3651. Turn right (north) and continue driving for eight miles on Forest Service Road 3651 before turning left (west) onto Forest Service Road 3659. Drive one mile to the trailhead on the left at the point of a hairpin turn.

Contact: Winema National Forest, Klamath Ranger District, 1936 California Avenue, Klamath Falls, OR 97601; 541/885-3400.

105 Fish Lake
10.0 mi/5.0 hrs

Hugging the north shore of Fish Lake, this trail is wedged between the water and the road, so the best time to visit is midweek or in autumn, when the traffic is lighter. In addition to the pretty lake, enjoy the unusual geologic features of the area. Volcanic activity created this landscape—from the lake to the high peaks around it—and evidence of this tumultuous past is clear along the entire route. The most notable example of this region's volcanic nature is found a little less than 1.5 miles from the trailhead, where old lava tubes seem to swallow a river. The trail passes near Cascade Canal, a ditch dug in the early 1900s to provide water to Medford; as the trail nears the canal, the water drops out of the bottom of the ditch into the ancient lava tubes and then enters Fish Lake. The trail also passes through several small lava beds.

Location: Northeast of Ashland in Rogue River National Forest; see The Southern Cascades Map 6, grid e5.

User Groups: Hikers, dogs, horses, and mountain bikes. No wheelchair facilities.

Permits: A federal Northwest Forest Pass, $5 per day or $30 annually, is required to park at the trailhead. Passes are available from ranger stations and many private vendors, online at website: www.wta.org, or by calling 800/270-7504.

Maps: For a trail information report, contact the Ashland Ranger District at 541/482-3333. For a map of Rogue River National Forest, contact Nature of the Northwest Information Center, 800 Northeast Oregon Street, Suite 177, Portland, OR 97232; 503/872-2750. Ask the USGS for a topographic map of the Mount McLoughlin area.

Directions: From Ashland drive about one mile east on Highway 66 to Dead Indian Highway. Turn left (north) and continue 22 miles to Forest Service Road 37. Turn left and drive seven miles to North Fork Campground. The trailhead is on the right, opposite the camp.

Contact: Rogue River National Forest, Ashland Ranger District, 645 Washington Street, Ashland, OR 97520; 541/482-3333.

106 Soda Springs

5.0 mi/2.5 hrs

This steep trail drops through a small clearcut area, with views of Mount McLoughlin and Brown Mountain, before entering an old forest of mixed conifers and hardwoods. The main representative of the hardwood family is the thick, gnarled California black oak, whose meaty acorns were once sought by indigenous people. The trail drops steeply

through the forest past Soda Springs to the lower trailhead area. Retrace your steps from the springs to return to your vehicle.

Location: Northeast of Ashland in Rogue River National Forest; see The Southern Cascades Map 6, grid f5.

User Groups: Hikers and dogs. No horses or mountain bikes are allowed. No wheelchair facilities.

Permits: A federal Northwest Forest Pass, $5 per day or $30 annually, is required to park at the trailhead. Passes are available from ranger stations and many private vendors, online at website: www.wta.org, or by calling 800/270-7504.

Maps: For a trail information report, contact the Ashland Ranger District at 541/482-3333. For a map of Rogue River National Forest, contact Nature of the Northwest Information Center, 800 Northeast Oregon Street, Suite 177, Portland, OR 97232; 503/872-2750. Ask the USGS for topographic maps of the Brown Mountain and Robinson Butte areas.

Directions: From Ashland drive about one mile east on Highway 66 to Dead Indian Highway. Turn left (north) and continue 13.5 miles to Shell Peak Road. Turn left and follow Shell Peak Road, which becomes Forest Service Road 2500-100 at the forest boundary, to Forest Service Road 185. The trailhead is on the left, opposite Forest Service Road 185.

Contact: Rogue River National Forest, Ashland Ranger District, 645 Washington Street, Ashland, OR 97520; 541/482-3333.

107 Beaver Dam

4.2 mi/2.1 hrs

Explore a lovely, cool streamside forest as you hike upstream along Beaver Dam Creek. You sometimes see the stream's namesake residents, but you're more likely to find them up one of the many feeder creeks. The aquatic environment of the creek is captivating, but you should also try to enjoy the surrounding forest as you climb gently up the valley trail. The forest is full of big old-growth Douglas fir, white pine, true fir, and Pacific yew (whose bark yields the cancer-fighting drug Taxol). A sensitive tree, the yew thrives primarily in old-growth forest, and its presence proves how ancient this forest actually is.

The trail also accesses several splendid creekside meadows—gifts from previous generations of beavers whose reservoirs eventually filled with sediment and became meadows full of wildflowers. At times deer and elk can be found browsing in this lush vegetation.

Location: Northeast of Ashland in Rogue River National Forest; see The Southern Cascades Map 6, grid f5.

User Groups: Hikers and dogs. No horses or mountain bikes are allowed. No wheelchair facilities.

Permits: A federal Northwest Forest Pass, $5 per day or $30 annually, is required to park at the trailhead. Passes are available from ranger stations and many private vendors, online at website: www.wta.org, or by calling 800/270-7504.

Maps: For a trail information report, contact the Ashland Ranger District at 541/482-3333. For a map of Rogue River National Forest, contact Nature of the Northwest Information Center, 800 Northeast Oregon Street, Suite 177, Portland, OR 97232; 503/872-2750. Ask the USGS for topographic maps of the Brown Mountain and Robinson Butte areas.

Directions: From Ashland drive about one mile east on Highway 66 to Dead Indian Highway. Turn left (north) and continue 22 miles to Forest Service Road 37. Turn left and drive 1.5 miles to the trailhead near the Daley Creek Campground.

Contact: Rogue River National Forest, Ashland Ranger District, 645 Washington Street, Ashland, OR 97520; 541/482-3333.

108 Brown Mountain
10.6 mi/5.3 hrs

No matter when you visit, bring a plastic bag to carry your findings back home. In the spring and early summer, look for plentiful, delicious morel mushrooms (when rolled in a bit of melted butter and flour, then lightly browned, they make wonderful appetizers). Berry lovers are dazzled and delighted by the thick huckleberry patches that line the trail in autumn.

Following Little Butte Creek, the trail can be muddy and wet as it weaves through and around numerous swampy areas and thick stands of willow and alder. Eventually, though, the way steepens and you climb to a high ridge where the trail ends at a junction with the Pacific Crest Trail. Enjoy the views, explore the PCT briefly, and return the way you came.

Unless you are skilled in identifying mushrooms, don't eat any of those you find. Some are delicious and harmless; others are deadly.

Location: Northeast of Ashland in Rogue River National Forest; see The Southern Cascades Map 6, grid f6.

User Groups: Hikers, dogs, horses, and mountain bikes. No wheelchair facilities.

Permits: A federal Northwest Forest Pass, $5 per day or $30 annually, is required to park at the trailhead. Passes are available from ranger stations and many private vendors, online at website: www.wta.org, or by calling 800/270-7504.

Maps: For a trail information report, contact the Ashland Ranger District at 541/482-3333. For a map of Rogue River National Forest, contact Nature of the Northwest Information Center, 800 Northeast Oregon Street, Suite 177, Portland, OR 97232; 503/872-2750. Ask the USGS for topographic maps of the Brown Mountain,

Lake of the Woods South, and Lake of the Woods North areas.

Directions: From Ashland drive about one mile east on Highway 66 to Dead Indian Highway. Turn left (north) and continue 22 miles to Forest Service Road 37. Turn left and drive six miles before bearing right onto Forest Service Road 3705. Follow Forest Service Road 3705 for 3.5 miles to the trailhead.

Contact: Rogue River National Forest, Ashland Ranger District, 645 Washington Street, Ashland, OR 97520; 541/482-3333.

109 Rye Spur
12.2 mi/6.1 hrs

On this trail you explore a long canal that was dug in 1905 to divert water from Fourmile Lake to farms down the valley. Water still flows through the canal to Fish Lake, which dumps excess water into North Butte Creek. This trail parallels the old canal for nearly the entire length before angling away to end at the shores of Fourmile Lake. The route is relatively level, and the trail is wide and hard-packed.

Location: Northwest of Klamath Falls in Winema National Forest; see The Southern Cascades Map 6, grid e6.

User Groups: Hikers, dogs, horses, and mountain bikes. No wheelchair facilities.

Permits: A federal Northwest Forest Pass, $5 per day or $30 annually, is required to park at the trailhead. Passes are available from ranger stations and many private vendors, online at website: www.wta.org, or by calling 800/270-7504.

Maps: For a trail information report, contact the Klamath Ranger District at 541/482-3333. For a map of Winema National Forest, contact Nature of the Northwest Information Center, 800 Northeast Oregon Street, Suite 177, Portland, OR 97232; 503/872-2750. Ask the USGS for a topographic map of the Lake of the Woods North area.

Directions: From Klamath Falls drive 32 miles northwest on Highway 140 to the trailhead, which is on the right, just before the junction with Forest Service Road 3661.

Contact: Winema National Forest, Klamath Ranger District, 1936 California Avenue, Klamath Falls, OR 97601; 541/885-3400.

110 Mountain Lakes Loop
18.3 mi/2.0 days

Climbing the Clover Creek Trail to the Clover Lake Basin, you find a wonderful valley of old-growth lodgepole and sugar pine, Douglas fir, and spruce. The route leads through small, flower-filled meadows in the basin, and these are just a hint of grander meadows to come. At the lake take the trail leading off to the left (north) and begin the long clockwise circumnavigation of the Mountain Lakes Basin. Hundreds of pools—from puddles to actual lakes—dot the basin, and this long, winding trail passes most of them. Enjoy the sparkling waters, the colorful wildflower meadows on the shores of the lakes, and the multitudes of wildlife that thrive here. From elk and mountain goats to eagles and hawks, there are birds and animals galore in this mountaintop paradise. Unfortunately, you'll find mosquitoes galore, too, so bring your bug repellent.

Location: Northwest of Klamath Falls in Winema National Forest within the Mountain Lakes Wilderness; see The Southern Cascades Map 6, grid f7.

User Groups: Hikers, dogs, and horses. No mountain bikes are allowed. No wheelchair facilities.

Permits: A federal Northwest Forest Pass, $5 per day or $30 annually, is required to park at the trailhead. Passes are available from ranger stations and many private vendors, online at website: www.wta.org, or by calling 800/270-7504. Party size is limited to 12 people.

Maps: For a trail information report, contact the Klamath Ranger District at 541/885-3400. For a map of Winema National Forest, contact Nature of the Northwest Information Center, 800 Northeast Oregon Street, Suite 177, Portland, OR 97232; 503/872-2750. Ask the USGS for topographic maps of the Lake of the Woods South and Aspen Lake areas.

Directions: From Klamath Falls drive nine miles west on Highway 66 and turn right (north) onto Clover Creek Road. Continue 15.5 miles north to the junction with Forest Service Road 3852. Bear right onto Forest Service Road 3852 and drive to the road's end, where you find the trailhead.

Contact: Winema National Forest, Klamath Ranger District, 1936 California Avenue, Klamath Falls, OR 97601; 541/885-3400.

111 Clover Creek
8.0 mi/4.0 hrs

The first mile of the Clover Creek Trail drops gently through a lush, old-growth forest that is dominated by Douglas fir but also boasts huge specimens of hemlock, spruce, and pine trees. The initial short drop in elevation is quickly regained as the trail reaches Clover Creek and continues upstream through the steep creek valley. The forest frequently gives way to creekside meadows before the route climbs the final, steep pitch to Clover Lake, the largest of the cluster of ponds and tarns scattered about this meadow-filled basin. Some three dozen pools, ranging in size from tiny puddles to respectable alpine lakes, lie in the headwater basin of Clover Creek. That means this is an incredibly beautiful alpine environment. It also means acres of breeding ground for mosquitoes, so pack bug repellent along with your camera.

Location: Northwest of Klamath Falls in Winema National Forest within the Mountain Lakes Wilderness; see The Southern Cascades Map 6, grid f7.

User Groups: Hikers, dogs, and horses. No mountain bikes are allowed. No wheelchair facilities.

Permits: A federal Northwest Forest Pass, $5 per day or $30 annually, is required to park at the trailhead. Passes are available from ranger stations and many private vendors, online at website: www.wta.org, or by calling 800/270-7504. Party size is limited to 12 people.

Maps: For a trail information report, contact the Klamath Ranger District at 541/885-3400. For a map of Winema National Forest, contact Nature of the Northwest Information Center, 800 Northeast Oregon Street, Suite 177, Portland, OR 97232; 503/872-2750. Ask the USGS for topographic maps of the Lake of the Woods South and Aspen Lake area.

Directions: From Klamath Falls drive nine miles west on Highway 66 and turn right (north) onto Clover Creek Road. Continue 15.5 miles north on Clover Creek Road to the junction with Forest Service Road 3852. Bear right onto Forest Service Road 3852 and drive to the road's end and the trailhead.

Contact: Winema National Forest, Klamath Ranger District, 1936 California Avenue, Klamath Falls, OR 97601; 541/885-3400.

112 Varney Creek
8.8 mi/4.4 hrs

Working its way up the valley between Greylock Mountain and Mount Harriman, the Varney Creek Trail is overflowing with beautiful scenery. From the sun-dappled, old-growth forest to the sparkling creek that bounds through the valley, the sights close at hand are truly breathtaking. But when the forest ultimately opens onto one of the many small clearings in the area, the immediate surroundings fade in comparison to the beautiful high ridges that pop into view.

The route climbs alongside the creek, always moving up at a moderate pace, before crossing a broad scree slope and traversing the ridge wall to the trail's end at the junction of trails leading to Eb and Zeb Lakes. Retrace your steps from the junction or explore in either direction (and add to your total trail mileage) before returning down the valley.

Location: Northwest of Klamath Falls in Winema National Forest within the Mountain Lakes Wilderness; see The Southern Cascades Map 6, grid e8.

User Groups: Hikers, dogs, and horses. No mountain bikes are allowed. No wheelchair facilities.

Permits: A federal Northwest Forest Pass, $5 per day or $30 annually, is required to park at the trailhead. Passes are available from ranger stations and many private vendors, online at website: www.wta.org, or by calling 800/270-7504. Party size is limited to 12 people.

Maps: For a trail information report, contact the Klamath Ranger District at 541/885-3400. For a map of Winema National Forest, contact Nature of the Northwest Information Center, 800 Northeast Oregon Street, Suite 177, Portland, OR 97232; 503/872-2750. Ask the USGS for topographic maps of the Aspen Lake and Pelican Bay areas.

Directions: From Klamath Falls drive 20 miles north on Highway 140 and turn left (west) onto Forest Service Road 3637. Continue 1.8 miles before turning left (south) onto Forest Service Road 3664. Follow the road to its end and the trailhead.

Contact: Winema National Forest, Klamath Ranger District, 1936 California Avenue, Klamath Falls, OR 97601; 541/885-3400.

113 Wagner Butte
10.4 mi/8.0 hrs

A variety of Forest Service fire-watch stations, from simple cabins to cabins atop tall towers, used to stand on the Wagner Butte. The last was removed in the mid-1970s, when the Forest Service started using spotter planes instead of the remote lookouts. This trail explores the high, scenic route that early fire lookout guards followed to get to their posts. Because it was born out of utility rather than recreation, the trail is quite steep and gets you to the high ridgetop quickly. It's a bit of a workout, but the payoff is well worth it, as the views from the summit rank among the best in this part of the country.

Location: South of Ashland in Rogue River National Forest; see The Southern Cascades Map 6, grid g2.

User Groups: Hikers and dogs. No horses or mountain bikes are allowed. No wheelchair facilities.

Permits: A federal Northwest Forest Pass, $5 per day or $30 annually, is required to park at the trailhead. Passes are available from ranger stations and many private vendors, online at website: www.wta.org, or by calling 800/270-7504.

Maps: For a trail information report, contact the Ashland Ranger District at 541/482-3333. For a map of Rogue River National Forest, contact Nature of the Northwest Information Center, 800 Northeast Oregon Street, Suite 177, Portland, OR 97232; 503/872-2750. Ask the USGS for topographic maps of the Siskiyou Peak and Mount Ashland areas.

Directions: From Ashland drive about seven miles west on Highway 66 to Talent and turn left (south) onto Rapp Road. Drive one mile and veer right (west) on Wagner Creek Road and continue to Forest Service Road 22. Bear left (east) onto this road and drive to the trailhead parking area on the right (the trailhead itself is on the left side of the road).

Contact: Rogue River National Forest, Ashland Ranger District, 645 Washington Street, Ashland, OR 97520; 541/482-3333.

▬▬▬1 California Border to Highway 140
75.0 mi one way/8.0 days 🅰 🥾8

Breaking into Oregon, this part of the Pacific Crest Trail begins with a picturesque route around the southern boundary of Rogue River National Forest, passing Observation Peak and sliding through Jackson Pass before dipping down to a pleasant camp at Sheep Camp Springs, just 10 miles in. From here hook far to the north around Red Mountain and then drop back south through Siskiyou Gap, under Siskiyou Peak, and across Branch Creek on the 6,862-foot peak's eastern flank. Camping sites can be found at creekside.

From there the trail continues out around the lower section of the national forest. The scenery drops off for several miles, because the trail cuts through settled lands and crosses several roads and highways as it angles far to the east. After some 20 miles of rolling trail beyond Siskiyou Peak, the route turns north near Little Pilot Peak and passes several adequate, if unspectacular, campsites. The trail passes the dry, hot lava beds around Fish Lake and comes out at Highway 140 between that lake and Lake of the Woods. Both lakes boast great camping and are often used by long-distance through-hikers as layover camps, places to spend an extra day or two recuperating and resting.

Location: South of Ashland partially within Rogue River National Forest; see The Southern Cascades Map 6, grid h2.

User Groups: Hikers, dogs, and horses. No mountain bikes are allowed. No wheelchair facilities.

Permits: A federal Northwest Forest Pass, $5 per day or $30 annually, is required to park at the trailhead. Passes are available from ranger stations and many private vendors, online at website: www.wta.org, or by calling 800/270-7504.

Maps: For a trail information report, contact the Ashland Ranger District at 541/482-3333. For a map of Rogue River National Forest, contact Nature of the Northwest Information Center, 800 Northeast Oregon Street, Suite 177, Portland, OR 97232; 503/872-2750. Ask the USGS for topographic maps of the Dutchman Peak, Siskiyou Peak, Mount Ashland, Siskiyou Pass, Soda Mountain, Hyatt Reservoir, Little Chinquapin Mountain, Brown Mountain, and Mount McLoughlin areas.

Directions: From Ashland drive about eight miles south on I-5 to the Mount Ashland exit. Turn right (west) and drive a quarter mile to Mount Ashland Road. Bear right onto Mount Ashland Road, which becomes Forest Service Road 20 at the forest boundary, and continue 20 more miles to Forest Service Road 2025. Turn left (south) and drive to the trailhead on the right.

Contact: Rogue River National Forest, Ashland Ranger District, 645 Washington Street, Ashland, OR 97520; 541/482-3333.

▬▬▬2 Highway 140 to Crater Lake National Park
42.5 mi one way/4.0 days 🅱 🥾9

Just north of Highway 140, the trail jumps into the Sky Lakes Wilderness and weaves between the Rogue River and Winema National Forest for several miles. Trekkers won't even notice that, though, because this lake-filled alpine wilderness is so beautiful and great campsites are available along the first 20 or 25 miles. The trail sticks to the heart of the wilderness all the way north to Crater Lake National Park, making this a long, scenic section of trail with no immediate road access. Instead, you find countless wildflower meadows, hundreds of sparkling alpine lakes, and scores of jagged peaks and ridges, as well as deer and mountain goats. The trail traverses the west flank of Goose Egg—a high, round butte—and then makes a two-mile-long beeline straight into Crater Lake National Park.

Once you enter the park, the campsites begin to thin out, and over the last 10 miles, camping options are limited to park-designated sites only (check with the National Park Service for listings of acceptable camping areas). But as the campsites decrease in number, the scenic appeal of the trail grows. The volcanic nature of the area is immediately evident as you set foot inside park boundaries. The trail edges around Pumice Flat, a broad, abrasive rock and sand plateau, and angles to the west for views of Union Peak. It's a gentle, sloping hike from Union Peak to the Mazama Campground on Highway 62, the end of this section.

Location: Northwest of Klamath Falls within Rogue River National Forest, Winema National Forest, and Crater Lake National Park; see The Southern Cascades Map 6, grid e5.

User Groups: Hikers, dogs, and horses. No mountain bikes are allowed. No wheelchair facilities.

Permits: A federal Northwest Forest Pass, $5 per day or $30 annually, is required to park at the trailhead. Passes are available from ranger stations and many private vendors, online at website: www.wta.org, or by calling 800/270-7504.

Maps: For a trail information report, contact the Klamath Ranger District at 541/885-3400. For a map of Winema and Rogue River National Forests, contact Nature of the Northwest Information Center, 800 Northeast

Oregon Street, Suite 177, Portland, OR 97232; 503/872-2750. Ask the USGS for topographic maps of the Mount McLoughlin, Rustler Peak, Pelican Butte, Devils Peak, and Union Peak areas.

Directions: From Klamath Falls drive about 35 miles northwest on Highway 140 to the trailhead, just three-quarters of a mile beyond Lake of the Woods Campground.

Contact: Winema National Forest, Klamath Ranger District, 1936 California Avenue, Klamath Falls, OR 97601; 541/885-3400.

▮▮▮3 Crater Lake National Park
33.0 mi one way/3.0 days 🔼 👟9

The only disappointing thing about this section of trail is that even though it lies entirely within Crater Lake National Park, it doesn't provide a view of the sapphire-blue waters that fill the deep crater. (You can take a short hike up a side trail—Dutton Creek is the best—to get to the crater rim for views of the famous lake in the decimated hulk of what used to be Mount Mazama.) You will, however, find plenty of other fantastic sights to enjoy in this volcanic landscape.

From the trailhead the PCT winds north down to Castle Creek and the Dutton Creek Trail junction at mile four. From there it is a rolling, scenic traverse, with little elevation gain, around the decapitated mountain's west flank. After a long push due north, the trail banks east between two modest cinder-cone volcanoes, Desert Cone and Red Cone, and cuts along the southern edge of Pumice Desert. After crossing North Entrance Road, the trail veers north once more and climbs past the Pumice Desert, with great views of Timber Crater to the east. It's an easy, flat stroll to reach this section's northern end at the junction with Highway 138 just east of North Entrance Road, on the north edge of the park.

Location: North of Fort Klamath within Crater Lake National Park; see The Southern Cascades Map 6, grid b7.

User Groups: Hikers, dogs, and horses. No mountain bikes are allowed. No wheelchair facilities.

Permits: Permits are required for overnight stays and are obtainable from Crater Lake National Park.

Maps: For a trail information report, contact Crater Lake National Park at 541/594-2211. For a map of Crater Lake National Park, contact Nature of the Northwest Information Center, 800 Northeast Oregon Street, Suite 177, Portland, OR 97232; 503/872-2750. To obtain some USGS topographic maps of the area, ask for Pumice Desert East, Crater Lake East, Crater Lake West, and Union Peak.

Directions: From Fort Klamath drive approximately 23 miles north on Highway 62 to Mazama Village. Stay to the left and continue about one mile west on Highway 62 to the trailhead, which is on the right side of the road.

Contact: Crater Lake National Park, P.O. Box 7, Crater Lake, OR 97604; 541/594-2211.

◼◼◼◼ Crater Lake to Windigo Pass

30.0 mi one way/3.0 days 4 👟 🌲9

The Mount Thielsen Wilderness wraps around this section of the PCT, providing a pristine, heavily forested setting for a quiet, serene hike. Small alpine lakes and rocky peaks of modest height dot the wilderness. While these aren't high, jagged towers of granite and glaciers, the mountains here look friendly and wild at the same time. This wilderness offers a multitude of experiences. From high, open ridges with sweeping panoramic views, the trail drops into thick, shadow-streaked old-growth forests of Douglas fir, mountain hemlock, spruce, and lodgepole, sugar, and white pines. Watch for mule deer, elk, bighorn sheep, mountain goats, black bears, cougars, bobcats, and countless other small birds and animals. The trail rolls north past Mount Thielsen, along the high, open Sawtooth Ridge, under the west flank of Tipsoo Peak, to Mule Peak. You pass several small lakes—including the always-spectacular Maidu Lake—and cross the headwaters of dozens of creeks. The trail ends at Forest Service Road 60 in Windigo Pass.

Location: East of Diamond Lake within Umpqua National Forest; see The Southern Cascades Map 3, grid h8.

User Groups: Hikers, dogs, and horses. No mountain bikes are allowed. No wheelchair facilities.

Permits: A federal Northwest Forest Pass, $5 per day or $30 annually, is required to park at the trailhead. Passes are available from ranger stations and many private vendors, online at website: www.wta.org, or by calling 800/270-7504.

Maps: For a trail information report, contact the Diamond Lake Ranger District at 541/498-2531. For a map of Umpqua National Forest, contact Nature of the Northwest Information Center, 800 Northeast Oregon Street, Suite 177, Portland, OR 97232; 503/872-2750. Ask the USGS for topographic maps of the Pumice Desert East, Mount Thielsen, Miller Lake, Burn Butte, and Tolo Mountain areas.

Directions: From Diamond Lake drive about five miles east on Highway 138 to the trailhead on the left, just east of the junction with North Entrance Road.

Contact: Umpqua National Forest, Diamond Lake Ranger District, 2020 Toketee Ranger Station Road, Idleyld Park, OR 97447; 541/498-2531.

▆▆ 5 Windigo Pass to Willamette Pass

31.0 mi one way/3.0 days 🥾 ⛺

This portion of the Pacific Crest Trail really puts mosquito repellent to the test. They're insufferable here all summer long—thicker than lawyers at a multi-car pileup, and faster than a Portland meter maid. If you can stand that (and, believe us, you can't), the going is fairly pleasant here, thanks to the many lakes that give birth to the many mosquitoes. You travel over the southwest shoulder of Cowhorn Mountain (elevation 7,664 feet) and make good time through these plateau lakes to the largest one, Summit, where good campsites await at a public campground. Beyond, head past good views of Diamond Peak and Mount Bailey (elevation 8,363 feet) and Mount Thielsen (elevation 9,182 feet), cross Emigrant Pass, and enter the Diamond Peak Wilderness, which routes you around the eastern slopes of Diamond Peak and Mount Yoran into another lake-dotted glacial basin. Leaving the wilderness area, cross Pengra Pass and continue northeast to Odell Lake to an exit one-quarter mile southeast of Willamette Pass.

Location: From Windigo Pass in the Oregon Cascades National Recreation Area north through the Diamond Peak Wilderness to Willamette Pass; see The Southern Cascades Map 3, grid f7.

User Groups: Hikers, horses, and dogs. No mountain bikes are allowed. No wheelchair facilities.

Permits: A federal Northwest Forest Pass, $5 per day or $30 annually, is required to park at the trailhead. Passes are available from ranger stations and many private vendors, online at website: www.wta.org, or by calling 800/270-7504.

Maps: For a map of the Pacific Crest Trail, Oregon South, contact the Nature of the Northwest Information Center, 800 Northeast Oregon Street, Suite 177, Portland, OR 97232; 503/872-2750. Ask the USGS for topographic maps of the Tolo Mountain, Cowhorn Mountain, Emigrant Butte, Diamond Peak, and Willamette Pass areas.

Directions: To reach the Windigo Pass Trailhead, follow Highway 138 north from Diamond Lake to Windigo Pass Road/Forest Service Road 60. Turn north and go to the trailhead at Windigo Pass. To reach the Willamette Pass Trailhead, drive east on Highway 58 to a trailhead parking area near the Willamette Pass Ski Area.

Contact: Deschutes National Forest, Crescent Ranger District, P.O. Box 208, Crescent, OR 97733; 541/433-3200; Willamette National Forest, Middle Fork Ranger District, 49098 Salmon Creek Road, P.O. Box 1410, Oakridge, OR 97464; 541/782-2283.

▆▆ 6 Willamette Pass to McKenzie Pass

75.0 mi one way/ 7.0–8.0 days 🥾 ⛺

One of the more spectacular portions of the entire Pacific Crest Trail, this weeklong journey takes you through nearly all of the prime destinations in the magnificent Three Sisters Wilderness. The trail starts off with a bang, passing through Willamette Pass Ski Area and climbing gently to Rosary Lakes (see hike this chapter), which are beautiful but likely to be crowded with day hikers. On your right, Maiden Peak and then The Twins (see hikes this chapter) provide good side-trip opportunities for prime views of Waldo Lake, one of the clearest lakes in all the world. Continuing north, skirt the east side of the Waldo Lake Wilderness and enter yet another lake-dotted, mosquito-infested, glacier-scarred basin. Road access comes at Forest Service Road 600, 22 miles north of

Willamette Pass near Irish Lake. From here it's 13 miles to the next road access at the Cascade Lakes Highway after a short detour down the Elk Lake Trail (see hike in this chapter; Elk Lake Resort will hold PCT packages). From Elk Lake northward the trail passes through the heart of the wilderness, skirting the west sides of the Three Sisters, nicknamed Faith, Hope, and Charity. You also encounter large crowds at popular day-hiking destinations such as Sunshine Meadows (see hike this chapter), west of the North Sister. Leave the luscious parkland behind and enter high, dry volcanic plains on the remaining march to McKenzie Pass.

Location: From Willamette Pass north through the Three Sisters Wilderness to McKenzie Pass; see The Southern Cascades Map 3, grid f8.

User Groups: Hikers, horses, and dogs. No mountain bikes are allowed. No wheelchair facilities.

Permits: A federal Northwest Forest Pass, $5 per day or $30 annually, is required to park at the trailhead. Passes are available from ranger stations and many private vendors, online at website: www.wta.org, or by calling 800/270-7504.

Maps: For a map of the Pacific Crest Trail, Central Oregon, contact the Nature of the Northwest Information Center, 800 Northeast Oregon Street, Suite 177, Portland, OR 97232; 503/872-2750. Ask the USGS for topographic maps of the Willamette Pass, Odell Lake, The Twins, Irish Mountain, Packsaddle Mountain, Elk Lake, South Sister, North Sister, and Mount Washington areas.

Directions: To reach the Willamette Pass Trailhead, drive east on Highway 58 to a trailhead parking area near the Willamette Pass Ski Area. To reach the McKenzie Pass Trailhead, drive 55 miles east from Eugene on Highway 126, past McKenzie Bridge, to the Highway 242 junction. Head east on Highway 242 to McKenzie Pass and the Pacific Crest Trail marker on the left (north) side of the road, half a mile west of the Dee Wright Observatory pullout.

Contact: Willamette National Forest, Middle Fork Ranger District, 49098 Salmon Creek Road, P.O. Box 1410, Oakridge, OR 97464; 541/782-2283; McKenzie Ranger District, 57600 McKenzie Highway, McKenzie Bridge, OR 97413; 541/822-3381; Deschutes National Forest: Sisters Ranger District, Highway 20, Pine Street, Sisters, OR 97759; 541/549-7700.

■■■**7** McKenzie Pass to Barlow Pass

112.0 mi one way/
11.0 days

Like the section to the south described above, this portion of the Pacific Crest Trail is primarily in wilderness, passing through the Mount Jefferson and Mount Washington Wildernesses. Start by visiting the Dee Wright Observatory, a rock structure whose portals offer views of Cascade volcanoes and cinder cones. Cross the Belknap Lava Flow and pass Little Belknap Crater, and you're on your way to Mount Washington. The trail skirts the mountain's southern flank before turning west and then heading north out of the Washington Wilderness near Santiam Wagon Road. The next stop is Santiam Pass, where the trail crosses Highway 20 and enters the Jefferson Wilderness. Soon you pass Three Fingered Jack, Porcupine Peak, a chain of small ponds near Minto Pass, and crowded Wasco Lake on the way to Rockpile Mountain and stunning Rockpile Lake (see hikes in this chapter). For the next 10 miles, you're into thick day-hiking country, passing North Cinder Peak, Cathedral Rocks, Pamelia Lake (see hike this chapter), and the magnificent parkland setting of Jefferson Park (see hike this chapter). Climb up to Park Ridge and continue to the northern wilderness boundary and beyond to Breitenbush Lake, Olallie Lakes, Trooper Springs, Pinhead Buttes, Summit Butte, and Red Wolf Pass, and then back to civilization at Timothy Lake, south of Mount Hood. From here it's not far northeast to Wapinitia Pass and a crossing of Highway 26 at the Frog Lake Sno-Park. Continue north beyond Twin Lakes to the junction of Highway 35 at Barlow Pass, immediately south of Mount Hood. Parcels and supplies can be picked up at Timberline Lodge or at the Government Camp Post Office.

Location: From McKenzie Pass north through the Mount Washington and Mount Jefferson Wildernesses and the southern Mount Hood foothills to Barlow Pass; see The Southern Cascades Map 3, grid d8.

User Groups: Hikers, dogs, and horses. No mountain bikes are allowed. No wheelchair facilities.

Permits: A federal Northwest Forest Pass, $5 per day or $30 annually, is required to park at the trailhead. Passes are available from ranger stations and many private vendors, online at website: www.wta.org, or by calling 800/270-7504.

Maps: For maps of the Pacific Crest Trail, Central and Northern Oregon, contact the Nature of the Northwest Information Center, 800 Northeast Oregon Street, Suite 177, Portland, OR 97232; 503/872-2750. Ask the USGS for topographic maps of the Mount Washington, Clear Lake, Three Fingered Jack, Marion Lake, Mount Jefferson, Olallie Butte, Fort Butte, Boulder Lake, Pinhead Buttes, Mount Wilson, Timothy Lake, Wapinitia Pass, Wolf Peak, Mount Hood South, and Government Camp areas.

Directions: To reach the McKenzie Pass Trailhead, proceed 55 miles east from Eugene on Highway 126, past McKenzie Bridge, to the Highway 242 junction. Head east on Highway 242 to McKenzie Pass and the Pacific Crest Trail marker on the left (north) side of the road, half a mile west of the Dee Wright Observatory pullout. To reach the Barlow Pass Trailhead, drive 55 miles east from Portland on U.S. 26, just beyond Government Camp, to the junction with Highway 35. Follow Highway 35 several miles east to the Frog Lake Sno-Park turnout on the right (south) side of the road at Barlow Pass.

Contact: Willamette National Forest, McKenzie Ranger District, 57600 McKenzie Highway, McKenzie Bridge, OR 97413; 541/822-3381; Detroit Ranger District, HC 73, P.O. Box 320, Mill City, OR 97360; 503/854-3366; Mount Hood National Forest, Clackamas River Ranger District, 61431 East Highway 224, Estacada, OR 97023; 503/630-4256; Barlow Ranger District, Bear Springs Work Center, 73558 Highway 216, Maupin, OR 97037; 541/328-6211.

SOUTHEAST OREGON

Southeast Oregon

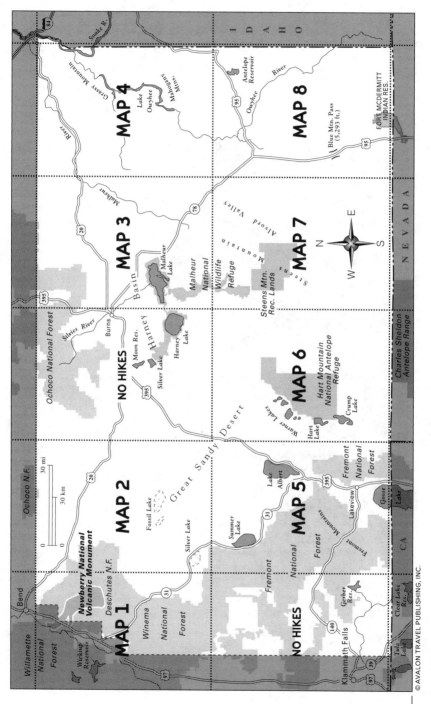

© AVALON TRAVEL PUBLISHING, INC.

Map 1

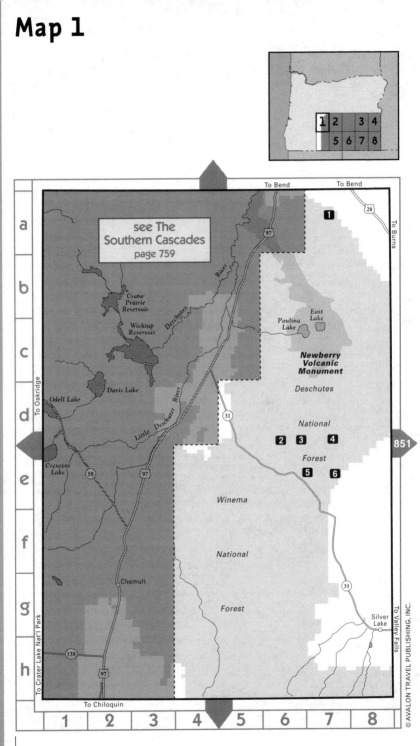

see The
Southern Cascades
page 759

To Bend
To Bend

1

20

To Burns

97

Crane Prairie Reservoir

Wickiup Reservoir

Deschutes River

Paulina Lake

East Lake

Newberry Volcanic Monument

Deschutes

Davis Lake

Odell Lake

Little Deschutes River

31

National

2 **3** **4**

Forest

5 **6**

Crescent Lake

58

97

Winema

National

Forest

Chemult

31

Forest

Silver Lake

To Oakridge

To Crater Lake Nat'l Park

138

97

To Chiloquin

To Valley Falls

© AVALON TRAVEL PUBLISHING, INC.

| | 1 | 2 | 3 | 4 |
| 851 | 5 | 6 | 7 | 8 |

Map 2

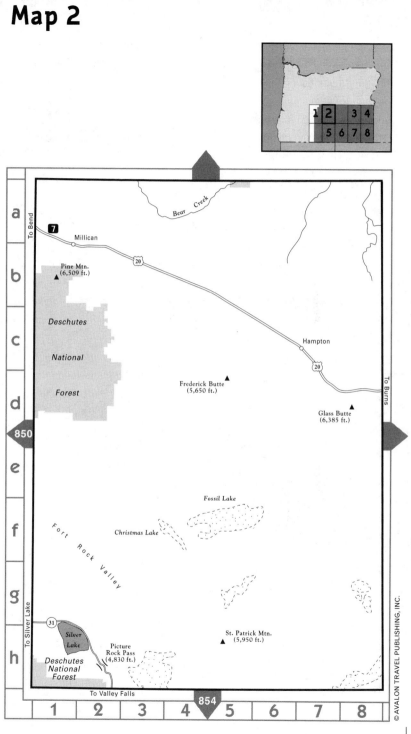

Map 3

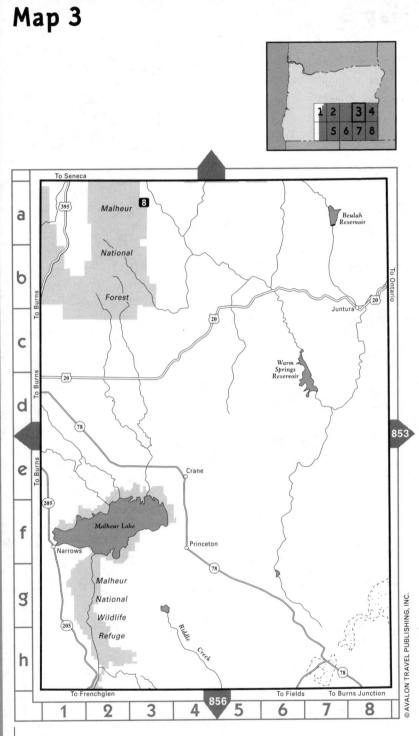

To Seneca

395

Malheur

8

Beulah
Reservoir

To Burns

a

National

b

Forest

20

To Ontario

20

Juntura

c

20

Warm
Springs
Reservoir

To Burns

d

78

853

Crane

To Burns

e

205

f

Malheur Lake

Narrows

Princeton

78

Malheur

g

National

Wildlife

205

Refuge

Riddle

Creek

h

78

To Frenchglen

856

To Fields

To Burns Junction

© AVALON TRAVEL PUBLISHING, INC.

| 1 | 2 | 3 | 4 | 5 | 6 | 7 | 8 |

1 2 3 4
5 6 7 8

Map 4

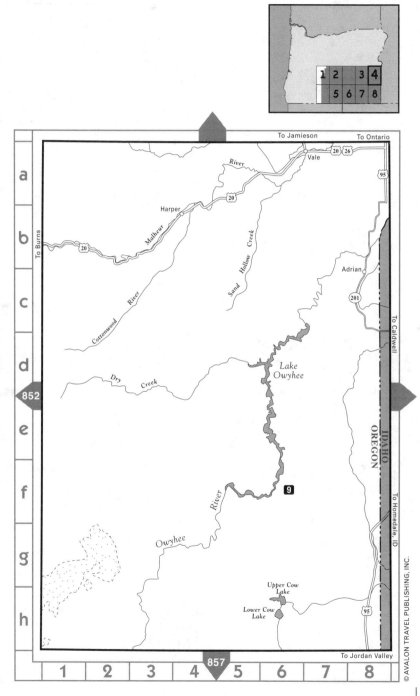

To Jamieson
To Ontario
River
Vale
20 26
95
Harper
To Burns
20
Malheur
Adrian
201
Sand Hollow Creek
Cottonwood
River
To Caldwell
Lake
Owyhee
Dry
Creek
OREGON
IDAHO
9
River
To Homedale, ID
Owyhee
Upper Cow
Lake
95
Lower Cow
Lake
To Jordan Valley

852

857

1 2 3 4 5 6 7 8

a b c d e f g h

© AVALON TRAVEL PUBLISHING, INC.

Map 5

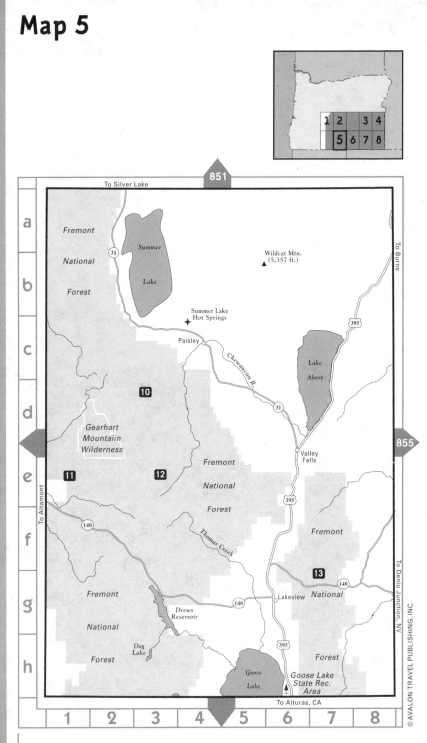

To Silver Lake

851

a

Fremont

National

Forest

Summer

Lake

Wildcat Mtn.
(5,357 ft.)

To Burns

b

Summer Lake
Hot Springs

Paisley

Chewaucan R.

Lake
Abert

c

10

31

d

395

Gearhart
Mountaiin
Wilderness

Valley
Falls

855

To Altamont

11

12

Fremont

National

Forest

e

140

395

Fremont

National

f

Thomas Creek

13

140

To Denio
Junction, NV

Lakeview

g

Fremont

National

Forest

Drews
Reservoir

140

395

Dog
Lake

Forest

h

Goose
Lake

Goose Lake
State Rec.
Area

To Alturas, CA

© AVALON TRAVEL PUBLISHING, INC.

1 2 3 4 5 6 7 8

Map 6

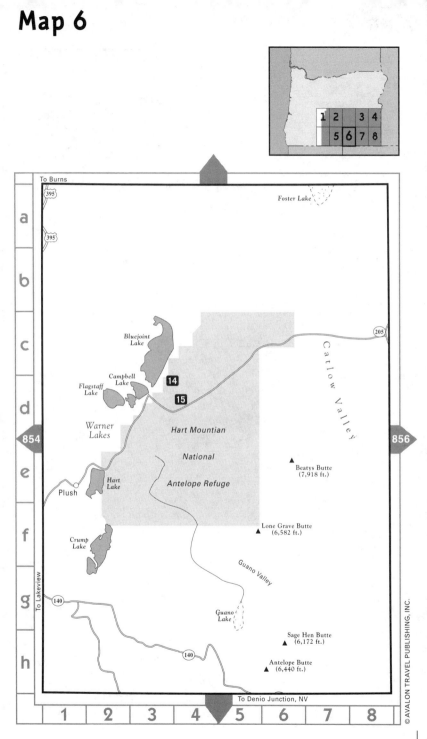

To Burns

(395)

Foster Lake

(205)

Bluejoint Lake

Campbell Lake

Flagstaff Lake

14

15

C a t l o w   V a l l e y

Warner Lakes

Hart Mountian

National

Antelope Refuge

Beatys Butte
(7,918 ft.)

Plush

Hart Lake

Lone Grave Butte
(6,582 ft.)

Crump Lake

Guano Valley

To Lakeview

(140)

Guano Lake

Sage Hen Butte
(6,172 ft.)

Antelope Butte
(6,440 ft.)

(140)

To Denio Junction, NV

854   856

Map 7

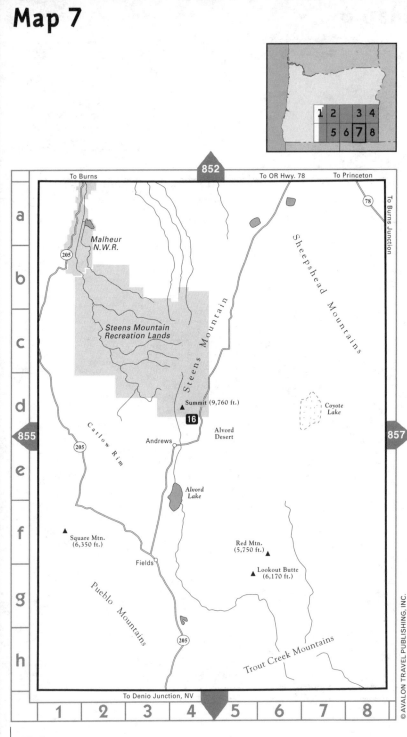

To Burns   To OR Hwy. 78   To Princeton

78

To Burns Junction

a

Malheur
N.W.R.

205

b

Steens Mountain
Recreation Lands

Sheepshead Mountains

c

Steens Mountain

d

▲ Summit (9,760 ft.)

16

Coyote
Lake

855

857

205

Catlow Rim

Andrews

Alvord
Desert

e

Alvord
Lake

f

▲ Square Mtn.
(6,350 ft.)

Red Mtn.
(5,750 ft.) ▲

Fields

▲ Lookout Butte
(6,170 ft.)

g

Pueblo Mountains

205

© AVALON TRAVEL PUBLISHING, INC.

h

Trout Creek Mountains

To Denio Junction, NV

1   2   3   4   5   6   7   8

Map 8

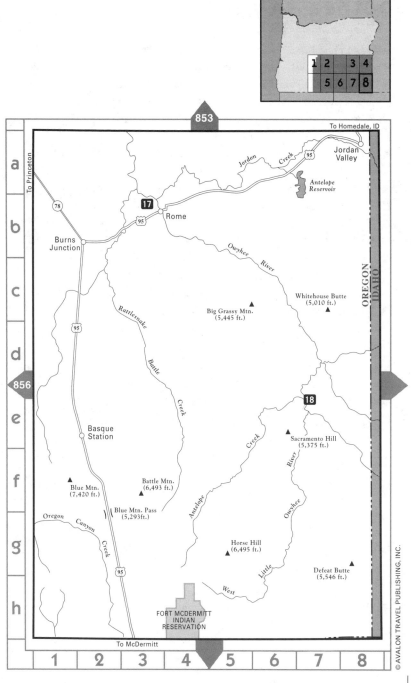

To Homedale, ID

a

To Princeton

Jordan Valley

Jordon Creek 95

Antelope Reservoir

78

b

17

Rome

95

Burns Junction

Owyhee River

c

Rattlesnake

Big Grassy Mtn. (5,445 ft.) ▲

Whitehouse Butte (5,010 ft.) ▲

OREGON IDAHO

d

95

Battle

Creek

18

e

Basque Station

Creek

Sacramento Hill (5,375 ft.) ▲

f

Blue Mtn. (7,420 ft.) ▲

Battle Mtn. (6,493 ft.) ▲

Antelope

River

Owyhee

Little

g

Oregon Canyon Creek

Blue Mtn. Pass (5,293ft.) ▲

95

Horse Hill (6,495 ft.) ▲

Defeat Butte (5,546 ft.) ▲

h

West

FORT McDERMITT INDIAN RESERVATION

To McDermitt

© AVALON TRAVEL PUBLISHING, INC.

1 2 3 4 5 6 7 8

Southeast Oregon

❶ Newberry Lava Caves
3.0 mi/1.5 hrs

On a hot August day in Bend, a lava tube is a pretty cool place to be. A set of short walks, bunched together off Forest Service Road 18 southeast of town, takes you there. The first walk, the Boyd Cave Trail, starts at the end of a short spur road and leads down a set of stairs into the cave, which extends 0.2 mile into the earth. Half a mile farther down the road is the turnoff for Skeleton Cave, which extends about half a mile in two lava tubes. Another two miles down the road is the 0.6-mile Wind Cave, which features a large cavern with a natural skylight. Maneuvering in this cave is difficult, and be advised that far, far more bats than you would ever like to encounter, particularly in the dark, spend winters in this cave and don't leave until April or May, depending on their mood. A short way farther down Forest Service Road 18 is Arnold's Ice Cave, which you can't enter because—true to its name—it's full of ice. Whichever cave you choose, come prepared. Bring flashlights and warm clothing. Even in summer the lava tubes can be cool.

If these caves whet your appetite for some major spelunking action, proceed about 12 miles south of Bend on U.S. 97 to the Lava River Cave (it's well signed, just east of the highway). This is the granddaddy of all Oregon lava tubes, stretching a mile west and getting progressively smaller with each step. If your flashlight goes out down here, the word "alone" takes on a whole new meaning.

Location: Southeast of Bend in Deschutes National Forest; see Southeast Oregon Map 1, grid a7.

User Groups: Hikers, horses, and dogs. No mountain bikes are allowed. No wheelchair facilities.

Permits: A federal Northwest Forest Pass, $5 per day or $30 annually, is required to park at the trailhead. Passes are available from ranger stations and many private vendors, online at website: www.wta.org, or by calling 800/270-7504.

Maps: For a map of Deschutes National Forest, contact the Nature of the Northwest Information Center, 800 Northeast Oregon Street, Suite 177, Portland, OR 97232; 503/872-2750. Ask the USGS for a topographic map of the Kelsey Butte area.

Directions: From Bend drive four miles south on U.S. 97 to China Hat Road. Turn left (east) and continue as the road becomes Forest Service Road 18. The Boyd Cave turnout is at about nine miles on the left.

Contact: Deschutes National Forest, Bend/Fort Rock Ranger District, 1230 Northeast Third Street, Suite A-262, Bend, OR 97701; 541/388-4000.

❷ Paulina Creek
9.5 mi one way/5.0 hrs

The Peter Skene Ogden Trail, named for an early pioneer/explorer, follows Paulina (Paul-EYE-na) Creek upstream to the beautiful Paulina Falls. Walking east along the banks from the trailhead, you'll notice that the water looks clean and pure, as if it has just sprung from the depths of the earth. It has. Paulina Creek is born just up the way in a spring on the Newberry Volcano, and it's just getting started on a long seaward journey when you stroll by. You find several other picturesque waterfalls along the way, and the hike can be shortened by placing a car at the McKay Crossing Trailhead about 2.8 miles up the trail (or, if you prefer, hike the nearly three miles from the lower trailhead to McKay Crossing as a day hike). If you lose the trail as it crosses a road, follow the yellow horseshoe markers. At trail's end you'll find a good vista of the twin 100-foot falls. No mountain bikes are allowed on the Paulina Falls Trail near the head of the creek. The trail gains 2,050 feet from bottom to top.

Location: North of La Pine in Newberry Crater National Volcanic Monument; see Southeast Oregon Map 1, grid d6.

User Groups: Hikers, dogs, horses, and mountain bikes. No wheelchair facilities.

Permits: A federal Northwest Forest Pass, $5 per day or $30 annually, is required to park at the trailhead. Passes are available from ranger stations and many private vendors, online at website: www.wta.org, or by calling 800/270-7504.

Maps: For a map of Deschutes National Forest, contact the Nature of the Northwest Information Center, 800 Northeast Oregon Street, Suite 177, Portland, OR 97232; 503/872-2750. Ask the USGS for a topographic map of the Finley Butte area.

Directions: From Bend drive 22 miles south on U.S. 97 to Forest Service Road 21, north of La Pine. Turn left at Ogden Group Camp and find the well-marked Peter Skene Ogden Trailhead in the parking lot.

Contact: Deschutes National Forest, Bend/Fort Rock Ranger District, 1230 Northeast Third Street, Suite A-262, Bend, OR 97701; 541/388-4000.

🛂 Paulina Lakeshore Loop
7.0 mi/3.5 hrs

Paulina Lake sits side by side with its sister, East Lake, in the ruined volcanic cone of Newberry Volcano. Both are filled with deep, cold, clear water, but Paulina is the larger, deeper lake, and a fine loop trail gives you a chance to sample its shore all the way around. You pass through developed campgrounds, meadows, forests, black-sand beaches, and summer homes, with 7,985-foot Paulina Peak standing as a backdrop.

Lava peninsulas that jut into the lake often attract anglers. For an added attraction scramble onto the lava flow that separated this once-huge caldera lake into two smaller ones. Some hikers might want to connect the Peter Skene Ogden (see hike this chapter) and Paulina Lakeshore Trails into a single hike of about 16 miles. If you're looking for a shorter hike, begin at the Little Crater Campground and arrange for a shuttle pickup at Paulina Lake Lodge. That shortens the seven-mile route by about 3.2 miles.

Location: In Newberry Crater National Volcanic Monument between Bend and La Pine; see Southeast Oregon Map 1, grid d6.

User Groups: Hikers only. No horses, mountain bikes, or dogs are allowed. No wheelchair facilities.

Permits: A federal Northwest Forest Pass, $5 per day or $30 annually, is required to park at the trailhead. Passes are available from ranger stations and many private vendors, online at website: www.wta.org, or by calling 800/270-7504.

Maps: For a map of Deschutes National Forest, contact the Nature of the Northwest Information Center, 800 Northeast Oregon Street, Suite 177, Portland, OR 97232; 503/872-2750. Ask the USGS for topographic maps of the Paulina Peak and East Lake areas.

Directions: From Bend drive 22 miles south on U.S. 97 to Forest Service Road 21, north of La Pine. Turn left, drive about 12 miles, and park near Paulina Lake Lodge, or continue around the south side of the lake and park at the Little Crater Campground.

Contact: Deschutes National Forest, Bend/Fort Rock Ranger District, 1230 Northeast Third Street, Suite A-262, Bend, OR 97701; 503/388-5674.

🛂 Newberry Crater Rim
21.0 mi one way/2.0 days

Somewhere along the line about 2,000 years ago, this grand old volcano caved in. Hopefully, on the march around its volcanic-caldera lip, you won't. The Newberry Crater Rim Trail samples the best scenery and geologic fascination the Newberry Crater National Volcanic Monument has to offer. Hiking counterclockwise, you climb steeply to grand views of the entire region on 7,984-foot Paulina Peak, which is snow-covered until late summer. Unfortunately, views around much of the rim are obscured by pine trees, but several outstanding viewpoints make the trip worthwhile. Several good campsites are found along the route, or you can drop from the rim on one of many trails that connect to other Deschutes National Forest destinations.

Backpackers must be prepared to carry plenty of water and make dry camps. No water is available on the rim.

Location: Around the rim of Newberry Crater in Newberry Crater National Volcanic Monument; see Southeast Oregon Map 1, grid d7.

User Groups: Hikers, dogs, horses, and mountain bikes. No wheelchair facilities.

Permits: A federal Northwest Forest Pass, $5 per day or $30 annually, is required to park at the trailhead. Passes are available from ranger stations and many private vendors, online at website: www.wta.org, or by calling 800/270-7504.

Maps: For a map of Deschutes National Forest, contact the Nature of the Northwest Information Center, 800 Northeast Oregon Street, Suite 177, Portland, OR 97232; 503/872-2750. Ask the USGS for topographic maps of the Paulina Peak, East Lake, Fuzztail Butte, and Lava Cast Forest areas.

Directions: From Bend drive 22 miles south on U.S. 97 to Forest Service Road 21, north of La Pine. Turn left and drive about 12 miles to the trailhead near Paulina Lake Lodge.

Contact: Deschutes National Forest, Bend/Fort Rock Ranger District, 1230 North-east Third Street, Suite A-262, Bend, OR 97701; 541/388-4000.

5 Obsidian Flow Interpretive Trail
1.0 mi/0.5 hr

Go ahead and try it: you can talk to the kids until you're blue in the face about plate tectonics, magma displacement, and ash fall, and they'll still show less interest in volcanism than, say, a shoe box. But put their noses up close to a glassy, black obsidian flow bigger than their neighborhood, and the light bulbs click on. The Obsidian Flow in Newberry Crater is the best place we've seen to do just that. It's a spectacular sight for kids of all ages, and it's all a short walk from the car. The trail follows the flow slightly uphill between the glass and the forest. Interpretive signs explain what it is, how it happened, and why it's here. Taking obsidian from the site is prohibited. If you're looking for a slightly longer hike, head east or west on the Newberry Crater Rim Trail (see hike above); a linking route crosses the Obsidian Trail not far from the trailhead.

Location: In Newberry Crater National Volcanic Monument between Bend and La Pine; see Southeast Oregon Map 1, grid e7.

User Groups: Hikers only. No horses, mountain bikes, or dogs are allowed. Not suitable for wheelchairs.

Permits: A federal Northwest Forest Pass, $5 per day or $30 annually, is required to park at the trailhead. Passes are available from ranger stations and many private vendors, online at website: www.wta.org, or by calling 800/270-7504.

Maps: For a map of Deschutes National Forest, contact the Nature of the Northwest Information Center, 800 Northeast Oregon Street, Suite 177, Portland, OR

97232; 503/872-2750. Ask the USGS for a topographic map of the East Lake area.

Directions: From Bend drive 22 miles south on U.S. 97 to Forest Service Road 21, north of La Pine. Turn left, drive about 12 miles, and proceed past Paulina Lake Lodge to the south side of the lake. The trailhead is on the right (south) side of the road between Paulina and East Lakes, 2.3 miles beyond the campground toll booth.

Contact: Deschutes National Forest, Bend/Fort Rock Ranger District, 1230 Northeast Third Street, Suite A-262, Bend, OR 97701; 541/388-4000.

6 The Dome
1.0 mi/0.75 hrs

This is one of the best, most easily accessed vista points from which to stare at the insides of Newberry, a collapsed old volcano. Follow the pumice-lined trail up at a gradual pace to the top of the Dome, elevation 7,200 feet. Views of the surrounding volcanic plain, including Fort Rock, are excellent. Look east to other, less-mature volcanoes in the Cascade chain and ponder how the scene will look if they, too, suffer the fate of Newberry. Stick to the trail on the way up and down since the pumice slopes are easily displaced and marred. Bring a jacket: it's usually windy at the top.

Location: In Newberry Crater National Volcanic Monument between Bend and La Pine; see Southeast Oregon Map 1, grid e7.

User Groups: Hikers and dogs. Mountain bikes are not recommended. No horses are allowed. No wheelchair facilities.

Permits: A federal Northwest Forest Pass, $5 per day or $30 annually, is required to park at the trailhead. Passes are available from ranger stations and many private vendors, online at website: www.wta.org, or by calling 800/270-7504.

Maps: For a map of Deschutes National Forest, contact the Nature of the Northwest Information Center, 800 Northeast Oregon Street, Suite 177, Portland, OR 97232; 503/872-2750. Ask the USGS for a topographic map of the East Lake area.

Directions: From Bend drive 22 miles south on U.S. 97 to Forest Service Road 21, north of La Pine. Turn left and follow Road 21 about 22 miles to the marked trailhead across from the southeast shore of East Lake.

Contact: Deschutes National Forest, Bend/Fort Rock Ranger District, 1230 Northeast Third Street, Suite A-262, Bend, OR 97701; 541/388-4000.

7 Dry River Canyon
4.0 mi/2.0 hrs

This is the place to go if you truly want to get away from it all—and from "them" all. Dry River Canyon, a silent, barren, geologically fascinating river valley, cuts through the center of an Oregon desert region commonly known as the Badlands. Not many hikers venture here, but those who do are blessed with that elusive natural gift: solitude. The narrow canyon is all that's left of a large river that cut through the ridge here during an ice-age flood. There's no trail per se—you just head off on your own, following the obvious river bed and a few game trails. The canyon roughly parallels U.S. 20, but you're low enough to avoid most of the noise. The hikable path peters out at about 1.5 miles, but you can scramble a short distance farther before hitting private property.

Always carry plenty of water when hiking here.

Location: East of Bend on U.S. 20; see Southeast Oregon Map 2, grid a1.

User Groups: Hikers, dogs, horses, and mountain bikes. No wheelchair facilities.

Permits: No permits are required. Parking and access are free.

Maps: Ask the USGS for a topographic map of the Millican area.

Directions: From Bend drive 20 miles east on U.S. 20 to an unmarked road leading to an old rock pit on the (right) north side of the highway. The road is about two miles west of the Dry River Canyon roadside viewpoint.

Contact: Bureau of Land Management, Prineville Office, P.O. Box 550, Prineville, OR 97754; 541/416-6700 or fax 541/416-6798.

8 Craft Cabin
16.0 mi/1.0–2.0 days

Winding through a steep series of canyons, this trail follows Pine Creek for nearly its entire length. You see mostly sagebrush and scrub pine in this dry country, with a few junipers thrown in. Still, the trail along the creek is pleasant and relatively cool, even during the heat of summer. Watch for rattlesnakes at your feet. Also watch for the snake's nemesis—the red-tailed hawk—overhead.

Location: Northeast of Burns in Malheur National Forest; see Southeast Oregon Map 3, grid a3.

User Groups: Hikers, dogs, horses, and mountain bikes. No wheelchair facilities.

Permits: A federal Northwest Forest Pass, $5 per day or $30 annually, is required to park at the trailhead. Passes are available from ranger stations and many private vendors, online at website: www.wta.org, or by calling 800/270-7504.

Maps: For a trail information report, contact the Burns Ranger District at 541/573-7292. For a map of Malheur National Forest, contact Nature of the Northwest Information Center, 800 Northeast Oregon Street, Suite 177, Portland, OR 97232; 503/872-2750. Ask the USGS for a topographic map of the Craft Point area.

Directions: From Burns drive 12 miles east on U.S. 20 and turn left (north) onto County Road 102. Continue north past the forest boundary, where the road becomes Forest Service Road 28. Continue north and turn right onto Forest Service Road 2850. Drive two miles east on Forest Service Road 2850 and then make a right turn onto Forest Service Road 2855. Drive three miles to the trailhead.

Contact: Malheur National Forest, Burns Ranger District, HC-74, Box 12870, Hines, OR 97738; 541/573-4300.

9 The Honeycombs
2.0–12.0 mi/1.0–8.0 hrs

The only trails that you find here are those created by the sharp hooves of mule deer, wild horses, and bighorn sheep. Make sure you have a map and compass; you are forced to navigate through a series of steep buttes and spires, many of which look very much alike. The Honeycombs are a network of deep gulches, tall pinnacles, and sagebrush steppes formed by tumultuous volcanic activity and several millennia of wind and water erosion.

The region's foundation is a quarter-mile-thick layer of basaltic rock that oozed out over the land during the massive lava flows tens of thousands of years ago. That volcanic birth has left a rough, jagged edge to the country. It has also left tokens of rare beauty: beautiful crystals and stones created by the hot lava. Rock hounds swarm this area in search of the thunder eggs (roundish rocks that, when cut open, reveal a beautiful interior of sparkling crystals in a variety of colors), agates, and petrified wood that litter the canyons. Watch for the deer, horses, and sheep that made the faint trails you see, as well as bald eagles, rabbits, rattlesnakes, coyotes, and many other small birds and animals.

The lack of designated trails through this desertlike environment makes the use of a compass and map essential. You must know your bearings and be able to find your way back to your car without the aid of a trail.

Location: Northwest of Jordan Valley near Owyhee River Reservoir; see Southeast Oregon Map 4, grid f6.

User Groups: Hikers and dogs. No horses or mountain bikes are allowed. No wheelchair facilities.

Permits: No permits are required.

Maps: For a map of the Owyhee River Reservoir region, contact Nature of the Northwest Information Center, 800 Northeast Oregon Street, Suite 177, Portland, OR 97232; 503/872-2750. Ask the USGS for topographic maps of the Owyhee Butte and Jordan Craters North areas.

Directions: From Jordan Valley drive about 17 miles north on U.S. 95 to Leslie Gulch/Succor Creek Road. Turn left and continue about 10 miles north on Succor Creek Road to the junction with Three Fingers Gulch Road. Turn left and then continue to Three Fingers Creek. There are no designated parking spaces and no official trails. Park in the wide turnouts along the dirt road and hike north cross-country at your leisure.

Contact: Bureau of Land Management, Vale District, 100 Oregon Street, Vale, OR 97918; 541/473-3144.

🔟 Blue Lake
8.0 mi/4.0 hrs

Climbing alongside a small creek, this trail makes for a long but moderate forest hike. The thick old-growth forest of white pine, Douglas fir, spruce, and lodgepole pine is the primary scenery for the first three-quarters of the route. Eventually, the trees give way to a few small clearings where wildflowers add a bit of color into the landscape.

The trail ends with a half-mile loop around the shores of sparkling Blue Lake. At the shoreline loop's western end, you find the terminus of the Gearhart Mountain Trail. If you camp at the lake, a short evening walk up this trail offers great views of the surrounding wilderness. From the lake return the way you came.

This hike can be combined with either the Boulder Springs or Gearhart Mountain hikes in this chapter to create simple one-way treks. You'll need to arrange a shuttle car to your chosen destination.

Location: North of Bly in Fremont National Forest within the Gearhart Mountain Wilderness; see Southeast Oregon Map 5, grid d3.

User Groups: Hikers, dogs, and horses. No mountain bikes are allowed. No wheelchair facilities.

Permits: A federal Northwest Forest Pass, $5 per day or $30 annually, is required to park at the trailhead. Passes are available from ranger stations and many private vendors, online at website: www.wta.org, or by calling 800/270-7504.

Maps: For a trail information report, contact the Bly Ranger District at 541/353-2700. For a map of Fremont National Forest, contact the Nature of the Northwest Information Center, 800 Northeast Oregon Street, Suite 177, Portland, OR 97232; 503/872-2750. Ask the USGS for topographic maps of the Gearhart Mountain, Campbell Reservoir, and Sandhill Crossing areas.

Directions: From Bly drive one-half mile east on Highway 140 and turn left (north) onto Campbell Road. Continue one-half mile north and then bear right onto Forest Service Road 34. Follow it for 19 miles before turning left (north) onto Forest Service Road 3372. Follow that road for eight miles and turn left (southwest) onto Forest Service Road 015. Continue to the road's end and the trailhead.

Contact: Fremont National Forest, Bly Ranger District, P.O. Box 25, Bly, OR 97622; 541/353-2700.

🔟 Boulder Springs
7.0 mi/3.5 hrs

You cover most of this hike's elevation gain in the first mile of trail, which runs alongside Deming Creek. After that, the route leaves the creek basin and starts a long traverse, climbing ever so gently to the north. As you leave the creek behind, the views grow in magnificence and magnitude. Around the flank of Gearhart Mountain, for example, you find stunning vistas of all the land between you and Crater Lake to the west. On a clear day, in fact, you can see the jagged rim of the crater. Shortly before the trail ends, the route drops through a pair of small draws. The first of these holds Boulder Creek, which begins just up the hill from here in Boulder Springs. Just beyond that you discover Boulder Meadow, a broad, sloping wildflower field where deer, elk, and mountain goats browse. The trail ends at a junction with the Gearhart Mountain Trail. Turn and retrace your steps from here.

This hike can be combined with either the Blue Lake or Gearhart Mountain hikes in this chapter to create a simple one-way trek. You'll need to arrange a shuttle car to your chosen destination.

Location: North of Bly in Fremont National Forest within the Gearhart Mountain Wilderness; see Southeast Oregon Map 5, grid e1.

User Groups: Hikers, dogs, and horses. No mountain bikes are allowed. No wheelchair facilities.

Permits: A federal Northwest Forest Pass, $5 per day or $30 annually, is required to park at the trailhead. Passes are available from ranger stations and many private vendors, online at website: www.wta.org, or by calling 800/270-7504. Party size is limited to 12 people.

Maps: For a trail information report, contact the Bly Ranger District at 541/353-2700. For a map of Fremont National Forest, contact the Nature of the Northwest Information Center, 800 Northeast Oregon Street, Suite 177, Portland, OR 97232; 503/872-2750. Ask the USGS for topographic maps of the Gearhart Mountain, Campbell Reservoir, and Sandhill Crossing areas.

Directions: From Bly drive one-half mile east on Highway 140 and turn left (north) onto Campbell Road. Continue one-half mile north and then bear right onto Forest Service Road 34. Follow it four miles before turning left (north) onto Forest Service Road 335. Follow this road for two miles and turn right onto Forest Service Road 018. Continue to the trailhead on the right, near the bridge over Deming Creek.

Contact: Fremont National Forest, Bly Ranger District, P.O. Box 25, Bly, OR 97622; 541/353-2700.

🔢 Gearhart Mountain
19.0 mi/2.0 days

Little Gearhart Wilderness is remarkably remote and wild, with only three trails cutting through it. The odds are good that you can hike as long as you wish here without seeing another human. From the trailhead start the long, steep climb through a dense old-growth forest of white, ponderosa, and sugar pine, blue spruce, and Douglas fir. In the first few miles, you pass under the jagged teeth of Palisade Rocks and the smooth crown of the Dome (elevation 7,380 feet). Then the climb tapers down to a gentle ridge walk along the summit ridge of Gearhart Mountain, a long, high peak that curves away to the north.

After traversing the 8,364-foot summit, the trail begins to

drop away to the north, eventually falling steeply down the snout of a long ridge to Gearhart Creek and, finally, Blue Lake. Camp at the small, scenic alpine pool. Enjoy the cool, refreshing waters and gorgeous reflected images before returning the way you came.

This hike can be combined with the Blue Lake or Boulder Springs hikes in this chapter to create simple one-way treks. You'll need to arrange a shuttle car to your chosen destination.

Location: North of Bly in Fremont National Forest within the Gearhart Mountain Wilderness; see Southeast Oregon Map 5, grid e3.

User Groups: Hikers, dogs, and horses. No mountain bikes are allowed. No wheelchair facilities.

Permits: A federal Northwest Forest Pass, $5 per day or $30 annually, is required to park at the trailhead. Passes are available from ranger stations and many private vendors, online at website: www.wta.org, or by calling 800/270-7504. Party size is limited to 12 people.

Maps: For a trail information report, contact the Bly Ranger District at 541/353-2700. For a map of Fremont National Forest, contact the Nature of the Northwest Information Center, 800 Northeast Oregon Street, Suite 177, Portland, OR 97232; 503/872-2750. Ask the USGS for topographic maps of the Gearhart Mountain, Campbell Reservoir, and Sandhill Crossing areas.

Directions: From Bly drive one-half mile east on Highway 140 and turn left (north) onto Campbell Road. Continue one-half mile north and then bear right onto Forest Service Road 34. Follow it 15 miles before turning left (north) onto Forest Service Road 34-012. Drive north to the road's end and the trailhead.

Contact: Fremont National Forest, Bly Ranger District, P.O. Box 25, Bly, OR 97622; 541/353-2700.

🔢 Crane Mountain
12.0 mi/5.0 hrs

Rather than climbing to the Crane Mountain summit as the eventual goal, the trail begins there and rolls up and down as it travels south along a ridge crest toward the California border. The climbs and descents are gradual and modest. But there's nothing modest about the views. From beginning to end, you'll find incredible views of southern Oregon and northern California. Look out over Steens Mountain, Mount Shasta, Red Mountain, and Sugar Peak. Closer at hand, admire the wildflower meadows and open forestlands.

Location: East of Lakeview in Fremont National Forest; see Southeast Oregon Map 5, grid g7.

User Groups: Hikers and dogs. No horses or mountain bikes are allowed. No wheelchair facilities.

Permits: A federal Northwest Forest Pass, $5 per day or $30 annually, is required to park at the trailhead. Passes are available from ranger stations and many private vendors, online at website: www.wta.org, or by calling 800/270-7504.

Maps: For a trail information report, contact the Lakeview Ranger District at 541/947-3334. For a map of Fremont National Forest, contact the Nature of the Northwest Information Center, 800 Northeast Oregon Street, Suite 177, Portland, OR 97232; 503/872-2750. Ask the USGS for topographic maps of the Crane Mountain and Crane Creek areas.

Directions: From Lakeview drive north on U.S. 392 to the junction with Highway 140 and turn east. Follow Highway 140 for about six miles before turning right (south) onto Forest Service Road 3915. Continue south for nearly 15 miles before turning right onto Forest Service Road 4011. Drive to the road's end. If driving a four-wheel-drive or high-clearance vehicle, you may continue on Forest Service

Road 015, but passenger cars should park at the end of the gravel road and hikers should walk the two miles of dirt road to the Crane Mountain summit and the actual trailhead.

Contact: Fremont National Forest, Lakeview Ranger District, HC-64, Box 60, Lakeview, OR 97630; 541/947-3334.

🎴 Poker Jim Ridge
24.0 mi/2.0 days

As in most wild lands of southeast Oregon, formal trails here are few and far between. But the steep drop on either side of this scenic ridge funnels visitors along the ridge crest already, so why go to the trouble of disturbing the sagebrush steppes with a broad, dusty trail? From the road the route follows a 12-mile panoramic excursion to the northeast shore of the shallow and warm Bluejoint Lake, which is perfect for overnight camping. The views from the ridge sweep across all of the refuge lands to the south, as well as the Green Lakes Basin to the north. Raptors, including red-tailed hawks, bald eagles, rough-legged hawks, and osprey, soar miles overhead. You can expect to share the ridge with mule deer, bighorn sheep, and maybe even some of the refuge's star residents, the pronghorn antelope (which actually aren't part of the antelope family, but are a distinct species). Carry plenty of water as this can be a hot, dry route in the summer and there is no water other than at Bluejoint Lake.

The mileage listed above is the round-trip distance to Bluejoint Lake. Unless you are backpacking, the route can be cut as short as you like.

Location: Southwest of Frenchglen in the Hart Mountain National Antelope Refuge; see Southeast Oregon Map 6, grid d3.

User Groups: Hikers and dogs. No horses or mountain bikes are allowed. No wheelchair facilities.

Permits: No permits are required.

Maps: To receive a map of the Hart Mountain National Antelope Refuge, contact the BLM Lakeview District at 541/947-2177, or the Nature of the Northwest Information Center, 800 Northeast Oregon Street, Suite 177, Portland, OR 97232; 503/872-2750. Ask the USGS for topographic maps of the Campbell Lake and Warner Peak areas.

Directions: From Frenchglen drive six miles south on Highway 205 and turn right (west) onto Rock Creek Road. Continue west to the Hart Mountain National Antelope Refuge headquarters and turn right (north) on Campbell Lake Road. At the ridge crest, park in the wide turnout on the right. There is no designated trail, but the route leads to the northeast along the ridge crest.

Contact: Bureau of Land Management, Lakeview District, HC-10, Box 337, Lakeview, OR 97630; 541/947-2177.

🎴 Willow Creek and Hot Springs
8.0 mi/5.0 hrs

Beginning with a mile of easy walking along Rock Creek, this non-designated trail offers good views of the local geology as well as abundant, beautiful desert flora. The fragrant sagebrush clumps are highlighted in the spring and early summer by colorful wildflower blooms scattered throughout the basin. At the junction of Rock and Willow Creeks, turn right and hike up the smaller Willow Creek Valley. Move quietly and keep an alert eye out for bighorn sheep, pronghorns, mule deer, and rattlesnakes. Up the rugged canyon, you pass a feeder stream on the north side of the valley. This comes from a small natural hot spring up on the slope. Unfortunately, it's not big enough to warm more than your toes. Moving beyond the spring, you eventually reach the headwaters of Willow Creek and find a rough-log corral that wildlife managers used to collect and study bighorn sheep. The corral is near the ridge rim at the canyon head. From that rim you can peer down to the north into the Flagstaff Lakes Basin, a green oasis in olive-drab surroundings.

Location: Southwest of Frenchglen in the Hart Mountain National Antelope Refuge; see Southeast Oregon Map 6, grid d4.

User Groups: Hikers and dogs. No horses or mountain bikes are allowed. No wheelchair facilities.

Permits: No permits are required.

Maps: To receive a map of the Hart Mountain National Antelope Refuge, contact the BLM Lakeview District at 541/947-2177, or the Nature of the Northwest Information Center, 800 Northeast Oregon Street, Suite 177, Portland, OR 97232; 503/872-2750. Ask the USGS for topographic maps of the Campbell Lake and Warner Peak areas.

Directions: From Frenchglen drive six miles south on Highway 205 and turn right (west) onto Rock Creek Road. Continue west to the Hart Mountain National Antelope Refuge headquarters and park in the visitor lot. There is no designated trail, but the route leads to the northwest along Rock Creek.

Contact: Bureau of Land Management, Lakeview District, HC-10, Box 337, Lakeview, OR 97630; 541/947-2177.

16 Alvord Desert
2.0–14.0 mi/1.5–10.0 hrs

During the Ice Age, this was a 200-foot-deep lake. But several millennia ago, those icy waters disappeared, leaving behind this broad, white alkali plain. The baked landscape is stark and remarkably lacking in variety—just mile after mile of dry, cracked mud. Early spring or mid-autumn is the best time for visiting. Even then, be aware that the blazing sun and reflective alkali plain can produce temperatures in the 90s or even low 100s. The desert is seven

miles across, and at the far side you find a refreshing stand of greasewood trees (bushes), but no available water. Enjoy the cooling shade before returning across the alkali plain.

This area should not be hiked in the midsummer months. At all times of the year, carry at least three times as much water as you would carry on a typical alpine hike (i.e., you need at least one gallon of water per person for a day hike here). Wear light-colored pants, a long-sleeved shirt, and a wide-brimmed hat to protect yourself from the sun.

Location: Southwest of Burns Junction in the Steens Mountain National Recreation Lands; see Southeast Oregon Map 7, grid d4.

User Groups: Hikers and dogs. No horses or mountain bikes are allowed. No wheelchair facilities.

Permits: No permits are required.

Maps: To receive a map of the Steens Mountain National Recreation Lands, contact the Burns District at 541/573-5241 or the Nature of the Northwest Information Center, 800 Northeast Oregon Street, Suite 177, Portland, OR 97232; 503/872-2750. Ask the USGS for a topographic map of the Alvord Desert area.

Directions: From Burns Junction drive south on U.S. 95 to the junction with Whitehorse Road. Turn right (west) and drive to the road's end at a junction with Fields-Denio Road. Turn right (north) onto Fields-Denio Road and drive to the trailhead on the right, just north of Frog Springs.

Contact: Bureau of Land Management, Burns District, HC 74-12533, Highway 20 West, Hines, OR 97738; 541/573-5241.

17 Wall of Rome
0.5 mi/1.0 hr

The route into the Wall of Rome isn't really an official trail—it's more like a boot-beaten path through the sagebrush and cheat grass. But this short trail is worth the time it takes to hike it simply because the towering basalt cliff is staggering in its stark beauty. The black rock soars hundreds of feet into the air and stretches for nearly a mile, reaching down into the Owyhee Valley. Along the foot of the wall are ancient, tiny petroglyphs. Finding one is truly a thrill; it lets you step 10,000 years into the past.

The lack of designated trails through this desertlike environment makes the use of a compass and map essential. You must know your bearings and be able to find your way back to your car without the aid of a trail, especially if you want to follow the wall down into the valley or explore the offshoot arroyos.

Location: North of Rome near the Owyhee River; see Southeast Oregon Map 8, grid b3.

User Groups: Hikers and dogs. No horses or mountain bikes are allowed. No wheelchair facilities.

Permits: No permits are required.

Maps: Ask the USGS for a topographic map of the Owyhee Bluff area.

Directions: From Burns Junction drive 12.5 miles to Rome on U.S. 95 and turn left (north) onto Rome Road. Continue three miles to the trailhead, found near the beginning of the rising cliff wall on the left.

Contact: National Historic Oregon Trails Interpretive Center, Bureau of Land Management, P.O. Box 987, Baker City, OR 97814; 514/523-1843.

18 Upper Owyhee River Valleys
8.0 mi/6.0 hrs

The key to enjoying this hike is to wear boots that can get wet and still be comfortable. The trail you follow is no trail at all—it's the riverbank. Hike up the Middle Fork Owyhee River Canyon (as the name implies, this is the river in the middle of the three that merge at Three Forks). The canyon is deep and narrow, so this is a wet, cool hike. In fact, you see sun-

shine only in the middle of the day when the sun is directly overhead. As you move upstream, the canyon narrows until it begins to resemble a slot canyon like those found in Southwest deserts. This is a rugged, difficult trail despite the lack of elevation gain. You have to cross and recross the river, sometimes walking directly up the cold waterway for several hundred yards at a time. Carry extra warm clothing even in the summer and use a stout hiking staff to increase your stability. With no trail to follow, you can walk as long as you like, or at least as long as the canyon will allow. It's very difficult to go more than four miles upstream, so turn around here or whenever you get tired and carefully make your way back downstream.

Location: Southeast of Burns Junction near the Owyhee River; see Southeast Oregon Map 8, grid e7.

User Groups: Hikers and dogs. No horses or mountain bikes are allowed. No wheelchair facilities.

Permits: No permits are required.

Maps: For a map of the Owyhee River region, contact Nature of the Northwest Information Center, 800 Northeast Oregon Street, Suite 177, Portland, OR 97232; 503/872-2750. Ask the USGS for a topographic map of the Three Forks area.

Directions: From Burns Junction drive about 18 miles east on U.S. 95 to Rome. Turn right (south) onto Skull Creek Road and continue about 14 miles southeast to the junction with Field Creek Road. Turn left (east) onto Field Creek Road and drive 2.5 miles before turning left (north) onto Fenwick Ranch Road. Continue to Three Forks. Park in the boat-ramp parking area.

Contact: Bureau of Land Management, Vale District, 100 Oregon Street, Vale, OR 97918; 541/473-3144.

Index

About the Authors

© DONNA MESHKE

Dan A. Nelson has been playing—hiking, biking, fly fishing, snowshoeing, and skiing—throughout the wild lands of Washington and Oregon since moving to the Blue Mountains of southeast Washington as a preschooler in 1970. During his adventures, whether reeling in cutthroat trout in the high Cascade Lakes or simply hiking through the open sand hills of the Juniper Dunes desert, he has gained a deep respect, admiration, and affinity for the diverse environments of the Pacific Northwest.

After earning a Bachelor of Arts degree in American History from Washington State University, Dan worked as a newspaper reporter, covering local government and environmental issues, before becoming a self-styled "professional backpacker."

For nearly a decade, he has been executive editor of *Washington Trails* magazine (previously known as *Signpost for NW Trails*), the monthly magazine of the nonprofit membership organization Washington Trails Association (www.wta.org). Dan also works as a columnist with the *Seattle Times*, specializing in gear reviews and weekend destinations. He is a regular contributor to *Backpacker* magazine and is editor of the book *Accessible Trails in Washington: A Guide to 85 Outings*, published in 1995 by The Mountaineers. He also authored *Best of the Pacific Crest Trail: Washington* (The Mountaineers, 2000), *Snowshoe Routes: Washington* (The Mountaineers, 1998), and *Predators at Risk in the Pacific Northwest* (The Mountaineers, 2000).

Ron C. Judd is an outdoor writer, photographer, and columnist at the *Seattle Times,* the Northwest's leading newspaper. A frequent contributor to *Outside* magazine, he also is the author of two other outdoor guides: *Inside Out Washington* and *Camping! Washington,* both published by Sasquatch Books.

A native of Duvall, Washington, and graduate of Western Washington University in Bellingham, Ron has traveled Northwest trails, roads, and waterways his entire life. After a career as a general news reporter around Puget Sound, he became a columnist specializing in the outdoors for the *Seattle Times,* where he also covers the Summer and Winter Olympic Games and other major sporting events.

When he's not rushing to meet a deadline for a column or guidebook, he can be found hiking, skiing, snowshoeing, camping, fishing, griping about traffic, or taping moleskin on his blistered heels at home in northwest Washington. His long-term career ambition continues to be staying out of the office as much as possible.

PACIFIC NORTHWEST REGIONS

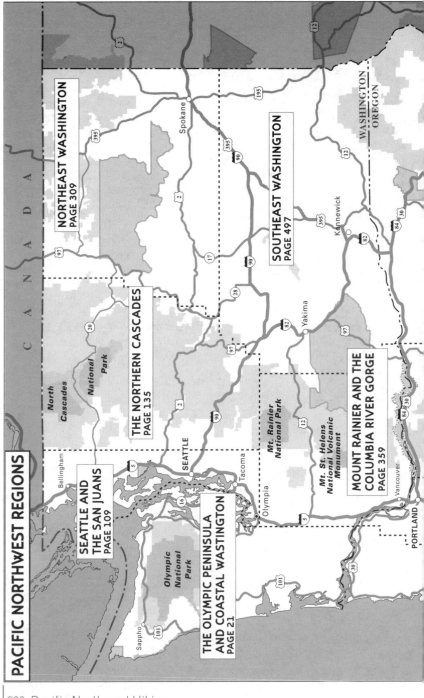

NORTHEAST WASHINGTON
PAGE 309

SOUTHEAST WASHINGTON
PAGE 497

THE NORTHERN CASCADES
PAGE 135

SEATTLE AND THE SAN JUANS
PAGE 109

MOUNT RAINIER AND THE COLUMBIA RIVER GORGE
PAGE 359

THE OLYMPIC PENINSULA AND COASTAL WASTINGTON
PAGE 21

CANADA

WASHINGTON
OREGON

North Cascades National Park

Mt. Rainier National Park

Mt. St. Helens National Volcanic Monument

Olympic National Park

Spokane

Kennewick

Yakima

Bellingham

SEATTLE

Tacoma

Olympia

Vancouver

PORTLAND

Sappho

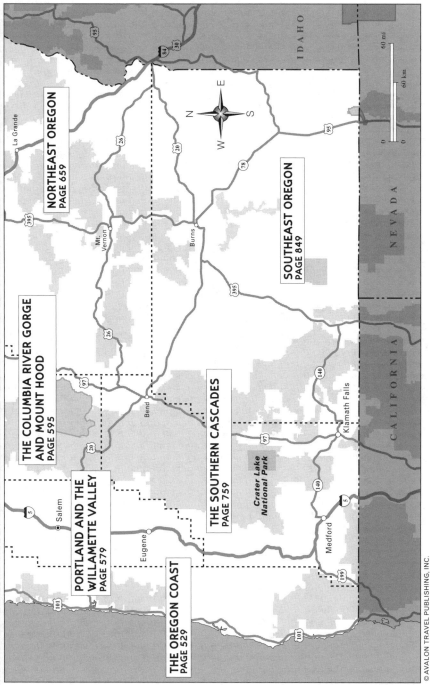

© AVALON TRAVEL PUBLISHING, INC.

THE OREGON COAST
PAGE 529

PORTLAND AND THE
WILLAMETTE VALLEY
PAGE 579

THE COLUMBIA RIVER GORGE
AND MOUNT HOOD
PAGE 595

THE SOUTHERN CASCADES
PAGE 759

Crater Lake
National Park

NORTHEAST OREGON
PAGE 659

SOUTHEAST OREGON
PAGE 849

La Grande

Mt.
Vernon

Burns

Bend

Salem

Eugene

Medford

Klamath Falls

IDAHO

NEVADA

CALIFORNIA

60 mi

60 km

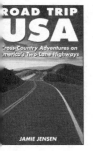